THE NEW INTERPRETER'S BIBLE
COMMENTARY

In Ten Volumes

Volume I	Introduction to the Pentateuch; Genesis; Exodus; Leviticus; Numbers; Deuteronomy
Volume II	Introduction to Narrative Literature; Joshua; Judges; Ruth; 1 & 2 Samuel; 1 & 2 Kings; 1 & 2 Chronicles
Volume III	Introduction to Hebrew Poetry; Job; Psalms; Introduction to Wisdom Literature; Proverbs; Ecclesiastes; Song of Songs
Volume IV	Ezra; Nehemiah; Introduction to Prophetic Literature; Isaiah; Jeremiah; Baruch; Letter of Jeremiah; Lamentations
Volume V	Ezekiel; Hosea; Joel; Amos; Obadiah; Jonah; Micah; Nahum; Habakkuk; Zephaniah; Haggai; Zechariah; Malachi
Volume VI	Esther; Additions to Esther; Tobit; Judith; 1 & 2 Maccabees; Book of Wisdom; Sirach; Introduction to Apocalyptic Literature; Daniel; Additions to Daniel
Volume VII	The Gospels and Narrative Literature; Jesus and the Gospels; Matthew; Mark
Volume VIII	Luke; John
Volume IX	Acts; Introduction to Epistolary Literature; Romans; 1 & 2 Corinthians; Galatians
Volume X	Ephesians; Philippians; Colossians; 1 & 2 Thessalonians; 1 & 2 Timothy; Titus; Philemon; Hebrews; James; 1 & 2 Peter; 1, 2 & 3 John; Jude; Revelation

EDITORIAL BOARD

LEANDER E. KECK
    Convener and Senior New Testament Editor
    Winkley Professor of Biblical Theology, Emeritus
    Yale University Divinity School

THOMAS G. LONG
    Senior Homiletics Editor
    Bandy Professor of Preaching
    Candler School of Theology
    Emory University

BRUCE C. BIRCH
    Old Testament Editor
    Dean and Woodrow W. and Mildred B. Miller
        Professor of Biblical Theology
    Wesley Theological Seminary

KATHERYN PFISTERER DARR
    Old Testament Editor
    Associate Professor of Hebrew Bible
    The School of Theology
    Boston University

WILLIAM L. LANE
    New Testament Editor
    Paul T. Walls Professor of Wesleyan and
        Biblical Studies, Emeritus
    Department of Religion
    Seattle Pacific University

GAIL R. O'DAY
    Homiletics Editor
    Almar H. Shatford Professor of Homiletics
    Candler School of Theology
    Emory University

DAVID L. PETERSEN
    Senior Old Testament Editor
    Professor of Old Testament
    Candler School of Theology
    Emory University

JOHN J. COLLINS
    Old Testament Editor
    Holmes Professor of Old Testament Criticism
        and Interpretation
    Yale University Divinity School

JAMES EARL MASSEY
    Homiletics Editor
    Dean Emeritus and Distinguished
        Professor-at-Large
    The School of Theology
    Anderson University

MARION L. SOARDS
    New Testament Editor
    Professor of New Testament
    Louisville Presbyterian Theological Seminary

* *The credentials listed here reflect the positions held at the time of the original publication.*

CHARLESTON COUNTY LIBRARY

WITHDRAWN

The New Interpreter's™ Bible Commentary

Volume Six

Esther
Additions to Esther
Tobit
Judith
1 & 2 Maccabees
Book of Wisdom
Sirach
Introduction to Apocalyptic Literature
Daniel
Additions to Daniel

ABINGDON PRESS
Nashville

THE NEW INTERPRETER'S BIBLE COMMMENTARY
VOLUME VI

Copyright © 2015 by Abingdon Press

This volume is a compilation of the following previously published material:
The New Interpreter's® Bible in Twelve Volumes, Volume III (Esther, Additions to Esther, Tobit, Judith), Copyright © 1999 by Abingdon Press.
The New Interpreter's® Bible in Twelve Volumes, Volume IV (1 & 2 Maccabees), Copyright © 1996 by Abingdon Press.
The New Interpreter's® Bible in Twelve Volumes, Volume V (Book of Wisdom, Sirach), Copyright © 1997 by Abingdon Press.
The New Interpreter's® Bible in Twelve Volumes, Volume VII (Introduction to Prophetic Literature, Daniel, Additions to Daniel), Copyright © 1996 by Abingdon Press.

All rights reserved.
No part of this work may be reproduced or transmitted in any form or by any means, electronic or mechanical, including photocopying and recording, or by any information storage or retrieval system, except as may be expressly permitted by the 1976 Copyright Act or in writing from the publisher. Requests for permission should be addressed to Permissions, Abingdon Press, 2222 Rosa L. Parks Boulevard, PO Box 280988, Nashville, TN 37228, or permissions@abingdonpress.org.

This book is printed on acid-free paper.

ISBN 978-1-4267-3583-7

Quotations from the HOLY BIBLE, NEW INTERNATIONAL VERSION. NIV. Copyright © 1973, 1978, 1984 by International Bible Society. Used by permission of Zondervan Publishing House. All rights reserved.

Quotations from the NEW REVISED STANDARD VERSION OF THE BIBLE. Copyright © 1989, Division of Christian Education of the National Council of the Churches of Christ in the United States of America. Used by permission. All rights reserved.

Quotations from the following are used by permission: *The Good News Bible*-Old Testament, copyright © American Bible Society 1976; New Testament, copyright © American Bible Society 1966, 1971, 1976. THE JERUSALEM BIBLE, copyright © 1966 by Darton, Longman & Todd, Ltd. and Doubleday, a division of Bantam Doubleday Dell Publishing Group, Inc. The New American Standard Bible, copyright © The Lockman Foundation 1960, 1962, 1968, 1971, 1972, 1973, 1975, 1977. *The New English Bible*, copyright © The Delegates of the Oxford University press and the Syndics of the Cambridge University Press 1961, 1970. *The Revised English Bible*, copyright © 1989 Oxford University Press and Cambridge University Press. *The Revised Standard Version of the Bible*, copyright © 1946, 1952, 1971 by the Division of Christian Education of the National Council of Churches in the USA. *The TANAKH: The New JPS Translation According to the Traditional Hebrew Text*, copyright © 1985 by Jewish Publication Society.

15 16 17 18 19 20 21 22 23 24—10 9 8 7 6 5 4 3 2 1

MANUFACTURED IN THE UNITED STATES OF AMERICA

Contributors

Sidnie White Crawford
  Associate Professor of Hebrew Bible and
    Chair of the Department of Classics
  University of Nebraska
  Lincoln, Nebraska
  (The Episcopal Church)
    Esther, Additions to Esther

Irene Nowell, O.S.B.
  Community Formation Director
  Mount St. Scholastica
  Atchison, Kansas
  (The Roman Catholic Church)
    Tobit

Lawrence M. Wills
  Associate Professor of Biblical Studies
  The Episcopal Divinity School
  Cambridge, Massachusetts
  (The Episcopal Church)
    Judith

Robert Doran
  Professor of Religion
  Ahmerst College
  Amherst, Massachusetts
    1 & 2 Maccabees

Michael Kolarcik, S.J.
  Assistant Professor
  Regis College
  Toronto, Ontario
  Canada
  (The Roman Catholic Church)
    Book of Wisdom

James L. Crenshaw
  Robert L. Flowers Professor of Old Testament
  The Divinity School
  Duke University
  Durham, North Carolina
  (Baptist)
    Sirach

Frederick J. Murphy
  Professor
  Department of Religious Studies
  College of the Holy Cross
  Worcester, Massachusetts
  (The Roman Catholic Church)
    Introduction to Apocalyptic Literature

Daniel L. Smith-Christopher
  Associate Professor of Theological Studies
  Department of Theology
  Loyola Marymount University
  Los Angeles, California
  (The Society of Friends [Quaker])
    Daniel, Additions to Daniel

---

* *The credentials listed here reflect the positions held at the time of the original publication.*

Contents

Volume VI

Esther
Sidnie White Crawford 1

Additions to Esther
Sidnie White Crawford 67

Tobit
Irene Nowell, O.S.B. 89

Judith
Lawrence M. Wills 159

1 Maccabees
Robert Doran 235

2 Maccabees
Robert Doran 347

Book of Wisdom
Michael Kolarcik, S.J. 425

Sirach
James L. Crenshaw 549

Introduction to Apocalyptic Literature
Frederick J. Murphy 695

Daniel
Daniel L. Smith-Christopher 713

Additions to Daniel
Daniel L. Smith-Christopher 817

Abbrevations 847

THE BOOK OF ESTHER
INTRODUCTION, COMMENTARY, AND REFLECTIONS
BY
SIDNIE WHITE CRAWFORD

For my mother—also a heroine.

THE BOOK OF ESTHER

INTRODUCTION

The Hebrew book of Esther is an exciting, fast-paced story that has captured the imagination of Jews over the centuries, although it has been less well-received by the Christian church. It contains all the elements of a popular romance novel: a young and beautiful heroine; a wicked, scheming villain; a wise older father figure; and an inept and laughable ruler. In the story good triumphs, evil is destroyed, and all ends happily. It is no surprise, then, that the book of Esther was so popular that, despite certain objections, including its failure to mention God even once (see below), it made its way into the Jewish canon by popular acclaim. Beneath its lighthearted surface, however, the book of Esther explores darker themes: racial hatred, the threat of genocide, and the evil of overweening pride and vanity. These layers of meaning make this book a worthwhile object of study.

DATE AND PROVENANCE

The book of Esther is set in the Jewish diaspora of the Persian Empire, during the reign of Ahasuerus, who is to be identified with Emperor Xerxes (486–465 BCE). Therefore, the book was written no earlier than the fifth century BCE. A later date is more probable, however, given the book's distance from the actual events of Xerxes' reign (see below). It is unlikely that Esther was written later than the third century BCE, since it lacks all Hellenistic coloring (including any evidence of Greek vocabulary) and displays a much more positive attitude toward Gentiles and Gentile rulers than do later works, such as Judith or 1 Maccabees. In addition, the author's familiarity with the Persian court setting and customs suggests a date within or close to the period of the Persian Empire. Therefore, a date in the late fourth or early third century BCE seems most likely.[1]

---

[1]. This is a revision of my previously stated position that Esther was written in the early fourth century BCE. While this date is still certainly possible, it is also possible to argue for the later date. See Sidnie A. White, "Esther," in *The Woman's Bible Commentary*, ed. Carol A. Newsom and Sharon H. Ringe (Louisville: Westminster/John Knox, 1992) 124.

It is probable that the book, set in the Persian diaspora, was written there as well. The characters evince no interest in the Judean homeland—not even, most strikingly, in the Jewish Temple in Jerusalem. Rather, the plot centers around the court in Susa, where Esther and Mordecai have made their lives. The author displays knowledge of the court of Susa and its immediate surroundings, as well as Persian court customs; but his knowledge about outlying provinces is quite hazy. Hence, Esther was most likely composed in the eastern diaspora of the Persian Empire for the Jews who resided there.

GENRE, STRUCTURE, AND STYLE

Any discussion of the genre of the book of Esther must begin with the acknowledgment that it is *written* literature, with no stylistic traits of oral literature. This work is meant to be read; in fact, the one rabbinic requirement concerning the Festival of Purim is the obligation to read the scroll publicly.[2] Further, although the author may have used sources in composing his work, the book is now a unified literary piece with a distinct and meaningful structure.

The genre of Esther is most easily described as an early Jewish novella (Wills) or short story (Fox).[3] Either term is acceptable if what is meant is a piece of literature with a single plot that has a clear beginning, middle, and end and whose action occurs within a specified length of time.[4] The Esther novella is related in type to the royal courtier tale, but it has a more complex plot and structure than a typical tale of that type (e.g., the stories in Daniel 2–6). As the book stands now, it is also a *Festlegende*, an explanation (or etiology) of the Festival of Purim, although the story's connection with that festival may be late and secondary. As either novella or *Festlegende*, the book is meant to be read as if it were history, even though it is clearly fictional. As Fox puts it, it is "a fictive text meant to be read by nonfictional conventions."[5]

Within the novella are several structuring elements that give the work a sense of symmetry and equilibrium. The most obvious structuring device is the use of banquets to form an elaborate envelope construction. Banquets occur in the book of Esther in pairs, with each one either opposing or complementing the other. A single banquet can belong to more than one pair, as shown in the following chart:

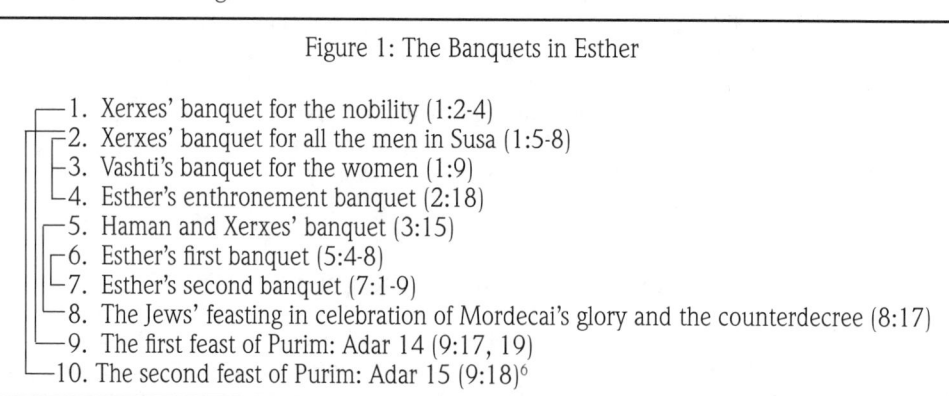

Figure 1: The Banquets in Esther

1. Xerxes' banquet for the nobility (1:2-4)
2. Xerxes' banquet for all the men in Susa (1:5-8)
3. Vashti's banquet for the women (1:9)
4. Esther's enthronement banquet (2:18)
5. Haman and Xerxes' banquet (3:15)
6. Esther's first banquet (5:4-8)
7. Esther's second banquet (7:1-9)
8. The Jews' feasting in celebration of Mordecai's glory and the counterdecree (8:17)
9. The first feast of Purim: Adar 14 (9:17, 19)
10. The second feast of Purim: Adar 15 (9:18)[6]

The first two and the last two banquets form a set: Numbers 1 and 9 are empire-wide, while numbers 2 and 10 are limited to the inhabitants of Susa. Banquet 2 for the men forms a pair with banquet 3, given for the women. Banquets 3 and 4 also form an oppositional pair, with banquet 3 given by Vashti and banquet 4 given for Esther. Banquets 5 and 8 oppose each other, while 6 and 7 complement each other. The resulting structure is a pleasing envelope construction.

---

2. *b. Meg.* 3.
3. Lawrence M. Wills, *The Jew in the Court of the Foreign King*, HDR 26 (Minneapolis: Fortress, 1990) 153-54; Michael V. Fox, *Character and Ideology in the Book of Esther* (Columbia: University of South Carolina Press, 1991) 146.
4. Wills, *The Jew in the Court of the Foreign King*, 153; Fox, *Character and Ideology in the Book of Esther*, 45.
5. Fox, *Character and Ideology in the Book of Esther*, 149 n. 22.
6. Fox, *Character and Ideology in the Book of Esther*, 157.

Banquets are not the only things in the book that occur in pairs. The main characters appear in three pairs of men and women: (1) Ahasuerus and Vashti, (2) Esther and Mordecai, and (3) Haman and Zeresh. Further, the protagonists, in groups of two, revolve around King Ahasuerus in a clear progression. The first pair is Esther-Mordecai; the second, Mordecai-Haman; the third, Haman-Esther; and the fourth, Esther-Mordecai. Note the progression through pairs and the symmetry of the envelope construction. The pairs motif recurs throughout the book: two groups of seven servants/noblemen (1:10, 14; the names of the two groups are suspiciously similar); two helpful eunuchs (2:8-9; 7:9), two meetings of Haman and Zeresh (5:10-14; 6:13); two decrees (3:12-14; 8:9-14), and a two-day celebration of Purim (9:21).

Finally, the motif of pairs lends itself to a major theme of the book: ironic reversal (peripety). Throughout the book of Esther, the expected outcome is reversed; people's status and character undergo sudden changes. Vashti is queen; then she is banished. Esther changes from humble orphan to powerful queen. Haman is forced to honor his enemy Mordecai. Haman is hanged on the gallows prepared for Mordecai. Mordecai becomes grand vizier in place of Haman. Most important, the Jews move from mourning to rejoicing. These reversals signal pivotal moments in the plot: Esther's character change in 4:15-17 enables her to save the Jews; Haman's honoring of Mordecai signals the beginning of his downfall, as recognized by Zeresh (6:13); and Mordecai's elevation (8:15-16) completes the salvation of the Jews. As Levenson nicely puts it, this theme is summarized by a single phrase in 9:1: "the reverse occurred" (נהפוך הוא *nahăpôk hû*).[7] The theme gives the book its movement: The plot is never in stasis; something is always changing. This is also a hopeful message to Jews living in diaspora; the status quo is never such, and things can always change.

The book of Esther has received rather low marks for its prose style. Carey A. Moore comments that "the author of Esther was no master of the Hebrew language, writing timeless prose."[8] Indeed, the prose of Esther sometimes seems to sink under its own weight. There are long lists of names (1:10, 14; 9:7-9) and endless descriptions of palace procedures, such as the banquet arrangements (1:5-9) and the Persian postal system (8:9-14). The language appears repetitious; there is an extraordinary number of verbal dyads in the text, such as "Ahasuerus, the same Ahasuerus" (1:1) and "to the governors over all the provinces and to the officials of all the peoples" (3:12).[9] The text also contains verbal and nominal chains, some of which occur several times, such as "to destroy, to slay, and to annihilate" (3:13; 7:4; 8:11). All of these features tend to weigh down the prose. However, as Levenson astutely points out, this is not a matter of bad writing, but the author's attempt to convey Persian "officialese," the style of writing common to bureaucracies both ancient and modern.[10] The story, after all, takes place in the Persian court, and if the events had actually happened, this is how they would have been reported.

The sometimes pompous language of the book is also part of a larger characteristic of this author: the use of humor to convey his message. The book, which was written for Jews living in exile, consistently lampoons their Gentile overlords. Ahasuerus is less an awe-inspiring ruler than an easily manipulated buffoon. Haman is an egomaniac whose vanity leads to his humiliation and downfall. The author also uses hyperbole to point to the surreality of the Persian Empire: Ahasuerus gives a banquet that lasts 180 days (six months! 1:4); the maidens are beautified for an entire year (2:12); and even at the denouement of the plot, when the Jews defend themselves against their enemies, the number of those slain (75,000) strains credibility (9:6, 15-16). Finally, the characters' reactions to events lead the reader to laugh. For example, Vashti's refusal to obey one order is thought to threaten the stability of the empire and leads to a decree declaring, of all things, that husbands should rule in their own houses and speak their own languages (1:21-22). The irony and humor found throughout the book mask, in a pleasant way, the author's very serious intent: to teach diaspora Jews that it is possible to lead a successful life in the sometimes inexplicable Gentile world in which they find themselves.[11]

---

7. Jon D. Levenson, *Esther*, OTL (Louisville: Westminster/John Knox, 1997) 8.
8. Carey A. Moore, *Esther*, AB 7B (Garden City, N.Y.: Doubleday, 1971) LIV.
9. Edward L. Greenstein, "A Jewish Reading of Esther," in *Judaic Perspectives on Ancient Israel*, ed. J. Neusner et al. (Philadelphia: Fortress, 1987) 238-39.
10. Levenson, *Esther*, 11.
11. Bruce W. Jones, "Two Misconceptions About the Book of Esther," *CBQ* 39 (1977) 171-81.

HISTORICITY

Although much ink has been spilled in attempting to show that Esther, or some parts of it, is historical, it is clear that the book is a work of fiction that happens to contain some historical elements. The historical elements may be summarized as follows: Xerxes, identified as Ahasuerus, was a "great king" whose empire extended from the borders of India to the borders of Ethiopia. One of the four Persian capitals was located at Susa (the other three being Babylon, Ecbatana, and Persepolis). Non-Persians could attain to high office in the Persian court (witness Nehemiah), and the Persian Empire consisted of a wide variety of peoples and ethnic groups. The author also displays a vague familiarity with the geography of Susa, knowing, for example, that the court was separate from the city itself.[12] Here, however, the author's historical veracity ends. Among the factual errors found in the book we may list these: Xerxes' queen was Amestris, to whom he was married throughout his reign; there is no record of a Haman or a Mordecai (or, indeed, of any non-Persian) as second to Xerxes at any time; there is no record of a great massacre in which thousands of people were killed at any point in Xerxes' reign. The book of Esther is not a historical record, even though its author may have wished to present it as history, since by doing so he could claim royal sanction for the purpose of his book: establishing Purim as an official Jewish festival.

The book of Esther, as stated above, is a *Festlegende*, an etiology for Purim, a festival probably originally celebrated in the eastern diaspora and slowly accepted in Judea (e.g., it is evidently not among the festivals celebrated among the Jews at Qumran). It is possible that Purim is a Jewish adaptation of a Persian festival, its connection with the story of Esther only secondary. However, the present book's intimate connection with the festival was probably the reason why it was ultimately allowed into the canon, unlike the very similar book of Judith. As Paton states, "It is connected in the closest way with the feast of Purim; and if the events here narrated did not create the feast, then the feast probably created the story."[13] Therefore, an investigation into the origins of Purim is warranted.[14]

Only two possibilities exist for the origins of Purim: the first that its origins lie in post-exilic Judaism, the second that it is an originally pagan festival adapted by the Jews. Those commentators who suspect a Jewish origin for Purim have searched through the known persecutions of Jews in the Hellenistic period to find a suitable antecedent. The most convincing argument, first put forth by Michaelis (1772),[15] holds that Purim was founded to commemorate the victory of Judas Maccabeus over Nicanor on 13 Adar 161 BCE. This argument, however, fails on several points. The book of Esther calls for the observance of Purim on the fourteenth and fifteenth of Adar, not on the thirteenth. Second Maccabees 15:36, which calls the fourteenth of Adar the "Day of Mordecai," carefully distinguishes it from the thirteenth, the "Day of Nicanor." The later rabbis (Jewish sages who, beginning in the second century, produced commentaries on the books of the HB) make the same distinction. Further, this identification, like all identifications with Jewish historical events, founders on the same rock: Purim is a feast whose character is essentially secular. Finally, the word "Purim" has no satisfactory Hebrew etymology; it appears to be a Hebrew corruption of either an original Aramaic form, פוריא (*pûrayyā*),[16] or the Babylonian *pūrū*, meaning "fate" or "lot." It seems best, therefore, to seek the origins of Purim in a Persian or Babylonian celebration. If Purim does have a foreign origin, then the Esther/Mordecai tale is easily explained as a justification for it. It is possible that the festival was originally a Persian feast, possibly the spring new year festival, adopted by the Jews of Susa that later spread to the rest of the Jewish community. Purim may also be connected to the Babylonian new year festival (which, however, was celebrated in Nisan, not Adar). All speculations on this subject run aground on the fact that we know very little about the eastern diaspora in the Persian period. Moore rightly declares, "Scholars have suggested much but proven very little about the probable origins of the festival of Purim."[17] In the end, a Persian origin for the festival seems most likely, with the tale of Esther and Mordecai added to bring it into the Jewish orbit.

---

12. Moore, *Esther*, 5.
13. Lewis B. Paton, *Esther*, ICC (Edinburgh: T. & T. Clark, 1908) 77.
14. The following remarks are dependent upon Paton, *Esther*, 77-94, and Moore, *Esther*, XLVI-XLIX.
15. Cited in Paton, *Esther*, 78.
16. C. C. Torrey, "The Older Book of Esther," *HTR* XXXVII (1944) 6.
17. Moore, *Esther*, XLIX.

ESTHER—INTRODUCTION

TEXTS AND VERSIONS

The book of Esther differs from other books of the Hebrew Bible in that it exists not just in its Masoretic form and more or less similar translations, but instead in three different versions, each with integrity as a separate literary piece. These versions are the Hebrew Masoretic Text (MT), the Septuagint (LXX), and the Alpha Text (AT).

The Masoretic Text, written in Hebrew in the late fourth–early third centuries BCE, used as its source a Hebrew story concerning Esther and Mordecai. The MT author added the etiology of Purim to the original story, and this version gained canonical status in Jewish Scriptures and later in Protestant Bibles.

The Alpha Text is a Greek translation of a Hebrew text similar to, but not identical with, the original Hebrew source of the MT (the AT is approximately 20 percent shorter than the MT). It contains several conspicuous differences from the MT, indicating a different author/redactor: The conspiracy of the two eunuchs (2:21-23) is missing; Persian law is not characterized as irrevocable, an important plot device in the MT; there is no mention of Purim; and, very important, the AT explicitly mentions God. The AT came into being at about the same time as the MT,[18] but never enjoyed canonical status, although it may have been popular in Egypt in the second century BCE (see Commentary on Addition F).

The Septuagint is a Greek translation of the Hebrew MT, made in the late second century BCE. It contains six long passages not found in the MT that were added to the LXX at the time of translation or later. These additions change the nature of the LXX, so that it is a distinctly different literary piece from the MT. The LXX has canonical status in the Eastern (Orthodox) churches and deuterocanonical status in the Roman Catholic Church (in the Vg, the Additions appear after the end of the Hebrew text). In modern translations, these Additions often appear in the apocrypha. In this commentary they appear at the end of the Hebrew book of Esther. The Additions were added to the Alpha Text of Esther sometime after the LXX came into being, evidently to bring the two Greek texts into conformity. The following diagram illustrates the relations of the various versions, in which proto-Esther stands for the hypothetical source(s) behind the MT and the AT.

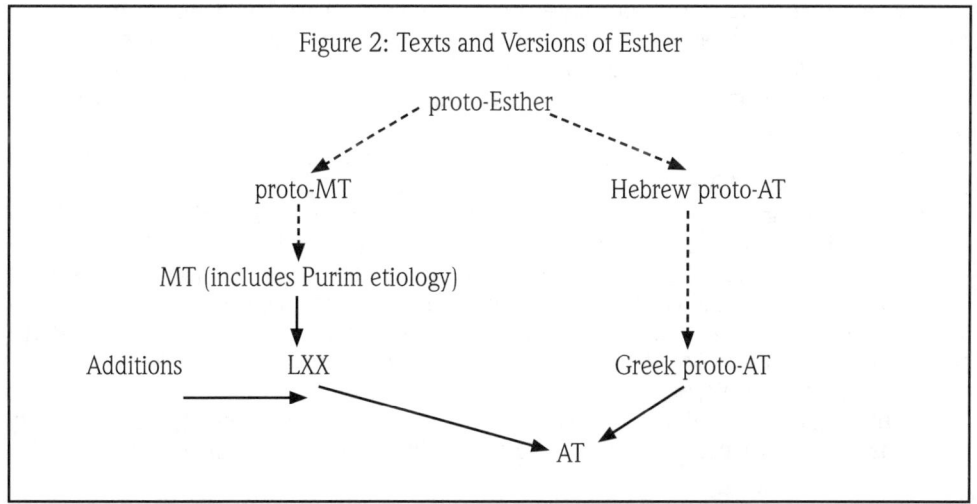

Figure 2: Texts and Versions of Esther

In addition, several other translations of both the MT and the LXX exist, including an Old Latin (OL) translation. The book of Esther also has two Targums (translations into Aramaic), which are more like midrashic free renderings than strict translations. Finally, the paraphrase

---

18. See David J. A. Clines, *The Esther Scroll: The Story of the Story*, JSOTSup 30 (Sheffield: JSOT, 1984); Michael V. Fox, *The Redaction of the Books of Esther*, SBLMS 40 (Atlanta: Scholars Press, 1991); Karen H. Jobes, *The Alpha-Text of Esther: Its Character and Relationship to the Masoretic Text*, SBLDS 153 (Atlanta: Scholars Press, 1996); Carey A. Moore, *Daniel, Esther and Jeremiah: The Additions*, AB 44 (Garden City, N.Y.: Doubleday, 1977).

of the first-century CE Jewish historian Josephus seems to show his familiarity with several of the versions, which he rendered freely. All of the versions will be taken into account at various points in the commentary.

THE ORIGINS OF ESTHER

It has long been suspected in the field of Esther studies that behind the three extant versions of the book of Esther (MT, LXX, and AT) lie sources that are no longer recoverable. Cazelles proposed a two-source theory for Esther. One source was liturgical, centered around Esther and the Jews in the provinces, and was concerned with the celebration of a festival. The second source was historical and centered around Mordecai and court intrigues leading to a persecution of the Jews in Susa. The two sources would have had much in common, including the two main characters and the basic plot structure, making them relatively easy to combine.[19] In a later analysis, Bardtke suggested that the author of Esther drew on a Jewish "midrashic" source, from which he reworked three tales: an apocryphal harem story about Vashti; the story of Mordecai, concerning court intrigue and the persecution of Jews in Susa; and the Esther story, about a young Jewish girl who becomes the king's favorite and saves her people from persecution.[20] Other scholars have preferred to talk about traditions lying behind the Esther story. The argument is complicated by the presence of the expanded version of the LXX, for which Semitic sources have been posited for Additions A, C, D, and F. Torrey suggested that the Greek versions of Esther are translations of Aramaic originals and that the Hebrew version is late and secondary, but his conclusions have not been widely accepted.[21] Rather, it seems most probable that the Hebrew MT, from which the LXX was translated, and the Hebrew proto-AT, from which the Greek AT was translated (this Greek text was later expanded using the LXX Additions), were constructed from a common story about Esther and Mordecai, two Jews living in the court of a foreign king who by their wits defeated the plot of Haman to destroy all the Jews of Persia. However, this story no longer exists; it may be hypothetically reconstructed from the three extant versions. A further question remains: Are there "sources" or "traditions" behind this tale and/or behind the Additions to the LXX?

Previous attempts to isolate sources, especially Cazelles's, have foundered on the attempt to assign blocks of material from the present form of MT Esther to specific sources. As shown above, the layers between MT Esther and its possible sources are too many, and the literary skill of the author too great, to allow for a convincing analysis. The search for plausible sources seemed to be stymied.

Some new light has been shed on the question. In 1992, Milik published fragments of an Aramaic manuscript(s) from Qumran Cave 4 that he entitled "4Qproto-Estheraramaic."[22] These fragments, Milik argued, contain the Aramaic source for the Greek source of the OL translation of Esther. Milik maintains that this Greek text was the original book of Esther. The LXX is, according to him, a revision of the OL's Greek source, while the Hebrew MT is a late (post–70 CE) and secondary translation. While Milik's arguments about the textual history of Esther are not at all convincing,[23] the fragments he presents may be an example of the type of source material the author of proto-Esther may have used when composing his story.

4Qproto-Estheraramaic, or as it is better named, *4QTales of the Persian Court*, consists of six manuscript fragments (4Q550), dating paleographically from the second half of the first century BCE.[24] The fragments appear to contain three distinct blocks of material, the first two of which

---

19. Henri Cazelles, "Note sur la composition du rouleau d'Esther," in *Lex tua veritas. Festschrift für Hubert Junker*, ed. H. Gross and F. Mussner (Trier: Paulinus Verlag, 1961) 17-29. Clines, *The Esther Scroll*, 115-26, does a masterful job of presenting both the strengths and the weaknesses of Cazelles's theory. Clines concludes that in modified form Cazelles's two-source theory is possible, but it is still not preferable to posit separate Esther and Mordecai sources.
20. Hans Bardtke, *Das Buch Esther*, KAT XVII/5 (Gütersloh: G. Mohn, 1963) 248-52.
21. Torrey, "The Older Book of Esther," 1-40.
22. J. T. Milik, "Les Modèles Araméens du Livre d'Esther dans la Grotte 4 de Qumrân," *RQ* 15 (1992) 321-99.
23. Sidnie White Crawford, "Has Esther Been Found at Qumran? 4QProto-Esther and the Esther Corpus," *RQ* 17 (1996) 307-25.
24. Milik, "Les Modèles Araméens du Livre d'Esther dans la Grotte 4 de Qumrân," 384. A paleographic date indicates only when the MS was copied. It is much more difficult to determine a date of composition; the terminus ad quem is the reign of Xerxes (486–465 BCE), in which the stories are set. The lack of animosity toward Gentiles (indeed, most of the characters may be Gentiles) may indicate a date of composition before the upheavals in the reign of Antiochus IV Epiphanes in the second century BCE.

contain clear parallels to the book of Esther. The first story, found in 4Q550[a-c], is set in the court of King Xerxes and appears to be addressed to a man whose father was named Patireza.[25] The text of frags. a-c is as follows:

Frag. a:
1. ... o]beyed Patireza your father [...
2. ... and [am]ong your servants of the royal wardrobe [...] to serve
3. the service of the king like all which [you have] receiv[ed ...] at the same hour
4. the temper of the king was stretched [... the bo]oks of his father should be read to him and among
5. the books was found a scroll [...] sealed with seven seals of Darius his father entitled:
6. .... Dar]ius the king to the servants of the empire which is the whol[e e]arth, Peace! On being opened and read, it was found written therein: Darius the king
7. ...]reign after me and to the servants of the empire, Pe[ac]e! Let it be known to him who violates or falsifies ...

Frag. b:
1. nobody but the king kn[ows] if there is [...
2. and his good name does not perish [and his] faithful[ness ...
3. the king come to Patireza son of ?[...
4. fear of the house of the scribe fell on him [...
5. the messenger of the king, Comm[and] and let it be given [...
6. my house and possessions to all who [...
7. being measured. And you will receive the office of your father. [...

Frag. c:
1. ...]the messenger of the king, Command the princess (?) [...]banish[ed ...
2. ... Patireza [your] father, from Ḥama' who arose concerning the service of [...] before the king [...
3. ...] and he was a faithful and tr[usty] servant before her [...
4. ... and the messenger said, [...
5. ... purp[le] ...

Interesting parallels to the book of Esther may be noted: The story is set in the Persian court, it takes place during the reign of Xerxes (note "Darius his father" in frag. a, line 5); and it resembles the royal courtier tale in genre. Some parallels are even more specific: In frag. a, the king has the royal annals read to him, as in Esther 6. Also, Patireza's son is rewarded by the king (frag. b), as is Mordecai in Esther 6. Finally, the name *Ḥama'* (חמא) in frag. c bears some resemblance to the name "Haman."

The differences between the two tales are also clear. First, the story in frags. a-c has no Jewish connection at all. Second, it is Patireza's son who is the object of the king's favor. If Patireza is to be equated with Mordecai, as Milik suggests (both being the son of Jair),[26] then 4Q550 mentions three generations: the father, Patireza, and his son, with the son being the protagonist of the story. Esther, of course, focuses on Mordecai. Third, a court conflict, which is at the heart of Esther, is not reflected in these fragments. And fourth, there are no direct linguistic connections between these fragments and any of the Esther versions.

---

25. "Patireza" is a Persian name. See Shaul Shaked, "Qumran: Some Iranian Connections," in *Solving Riddles and Untying Knots: Biblical, Epigraphic and Semitic Studies in Honor of Jonas C. Greenfield*, ed. Z. Zevit, S. Gitin, M. Sokoloff (Winona Lake: Eisenbrauns, 1995) 278.
26. Milik, "Les Modèles Araméens du Livre d'Esther dans la Grotte 4 de Qumrân," 332, restores the name of Patireza's father as Jair, thus making the connection to Esther even closer.

The situation with frag. d, consisting of three columns, is similar:

Column 1:
1. Behold, you know [. . .] and because of the errors of my fathers
2. who sinned before you and [. . .] I went out, a man of
3. Judah, one of the leaders of Benjam[in . . .] an exile is standing to be received [. . .] goo[d
4. a good man who serves [. . .] What may I do for you? You know [that it is not] possib[le
5. that a man like me is responsible [. . . your ki]ngdom, standing in front of you [. . .
6. . . .] that which you desire, entrust me with, and when [you d]ie, I will bury you in [
7. being the master of all. It is possible that my elevation in service bef[ore . . .

Column 2:
1. . . .] the decree [. . .] they left [. . .
2. . . .] plagues [. . .]he left [. . .] in the wardrobe [. . .
3. . . .] coronet of go[ld . . .] her [h]ead and five years passed [. . .
4. . . .] alone [. . . and the s]ixth passed [. . .
5. . . . si]lver and gold [. . . possess]ions which belong to Bagoshe, in double amount [. . .
6. and the sev[enth passed . . .] then in peace Bagasraw went up to the court of the king [. . .
7. Bagosh[e . . .] pronoun[ced . . . he was k]illed. Then Bagasraw went up to the co[ur]t of the king.
8. And he took his han[d . . .] on [his] head [. . .] kissed him, answered and said [. . .] Bagasraw, who [. . .

Column 3:
1. . . .] the Most High whom you revere and [wo]rship, it is He who rules over [all the ea]rth. Everything that he wishes is within his p[ow]er [. . .
2. . . .] any man who says anything bad against Bagasraw [. . . will] be killed, because there is nothing [. . .
3. . . .] ? for [e]ver [. . . th]at he saw [in the] two [. . .] And the king commanded that it be writt[en . . .
4. . . . em]pi[re . . .] in the court of the king's house [. . .
5. . . . a]rise after Bagasraw, those who read in this book [. . .
6. . . .] his wickedness will return on his own [head . . .
7. . . .] his des[cendants].[27]

Notice that the characters are different from those in frags. a-c: Bagasraw, Bagoshe, the king (unidentified), and an unidentified woman. It, too, has parallels to Esther: Frag. d opens with a prayer, which has certain similarities to the prayer of Esther in LXX Addition C. The description of "a man of Judah, one of the leaders of Benjamin, an exile" (col. 1, ll. 2-3) corresponds to the description of Mordecai in Esth 2:5-6. There is a dialogue between the king and a female protagonist, in which an adversary is criticized. The period of five years mentioned in column 2 is the same as the time lapse between Esther's ascension to the throne and her actions to save the Jews from Haman's plot. There is evidently a power struggle between Bagoshe, a non-Jew, and Bagasraw, a Jew, like the struggle between Haman and Mordecai. Bagasraw is received by the king in a manner similar to Esther's reception in LXX Addition D (taking into account the obvious difference that Bagasraw is a man and not the spouse of the king). The king makes a proclamation praising God, as in LXX Addition E.

However, the following caveats to the comparison should be noted: The parallels are not exact. The prayer in frag. d laments "the errors of my fathers," rather than present wrongdoing, as in LXX Addition C. Many of the parallels may plausibly be regarded simply as motifs of the

---

27. My translation has been greatly improved by study of the translation of John J. Collins and Deborah A. Green, "The Tales from the Persian Court (4Q550a-c)," in *Antikes Judentum und Frühes Christentum* (Berlin, New York: Walter de Gruyter, 1999) 39-50.

royal courtier tale genre; for example, the royal proclamation is equally reminiscent of those in Dan 2:46-47 and 6:25-27. Further, if Bagasraw is a seer, as suggested by col. 3, line 3, he more closely resembles Daniel than any character in the book of Esther.

Finally, frags. e-f of 4Q550:

Frag. e, frag. 1:1. . . .] before the king of Assy[ria? . . .
2. . . .] went at the summons [. . .
3. . . .] on yo[ur] faces [. . .
4. . . . Ba]gasraw [. . .

Frag. e, frag. 2:1. . . .] servant [. . .
2. . . .] remembrance [. . .

Frag. f:1. . . .] behold from the north comes evil [. . .
2. . . .] the building of Zion and in her shelter all the poor of [the] people [
3. . . .] space
4. . . .] come up upon it. They swell up between Medea and Persia and Assyria and the [Great] Sea
5. . . .] space

The only possible parallels to be noted between these fragments and the book of Esther are the phrase "on your faces" in frag. e, frag. 1, line 3, which may refer to prostrating oneself before royalty, and the mention of Medea and Persia in frag. f, line 4. On the other hand, in frag. f, lines 1-2 contain a paraphrase of Isa 14:31-32, while the book of Esther contains no allusions to any other biblical book.

In sum, *4QTales of the Persian Court* contains several intriguing parallels to the book of Esther in both its Hebrew and its Greek versions. These parallels permit us to posit some type of generic relationship between the two texts, but not enough to argue for any type of direct dependence. *4QTales of the Persian Court* may have been an example of a popular type of story— a royal courtier tale in which a Jew, against all odds, rises to success in the court of the Persian king. The author of Esther may have drawn from this type of tale when constructing his story.

THE IMPLIED THEOLOGICAL STANCE OF THE BOOK OF ESTHER

Although enjoying unwavering popularity among Jews throughout most of its existence, the book of Esther has come into its share of theological criticism. The reasons for this are the absence of religious elements in the book, and, among Christians, its perceived hostility toward Gentiles. The lack of religiosity in Esther is indeed striking. The book does not mention God even once. In addition, there is no prayer, no mention of the Temple, and no clear indication of religious activity on the part of Esther or Mordecai. The possible exception is the fast ordered by Esther in 4:16; however, that fast is not explicitly directed to God and seems to have no purpose beyond communal solidarity.[28] Furthermore, there is no indication that either Esther or Mordecai is obedient to the Torah; in fact, quite the opposite is true. Esther is married to a Gentile, eats non-kosher food, and appears to be so thoroughly assimilated that her husband and his court are unaware that she is a Jew. Jewishness, in fact, is a matter of ethnic identification rather than religious practice.

This lack of religion was noticed early on. The proto-AT, which stems from either the same or a very similar Semitic source as the MT, mentions God several times in natural places in the text (AT 5:9, 11; 7:17; 8:2, 34).[29] The LXX, which is a translation of the MT, deliberately adds

---

28. However, see Levenson, *Esther*, 19.
29. All verses of the AT are given according to the Cambridge Septuagint edition: *The Old Testament in Greek*, vol. 3, Part I: *Esther, Judith, Tobit*, ed. A. E. Brooke, N. McLean, H. S. J. Thackeray (London: Cambridge University Press, 1940).

long passages, as well as short references, that insert a distinct tone of religiosity and change the character of the book. Esther and Mordecai both pray (Add. C), and Esther declares that she has kept the commandments and lived as a good Jew (Add. D). Josephus and the Targums also add religious elements to the book of Esther, as do the rabbis. The rabbis speculate, for example, that Mordecai refuses to bow down to Haman because Haman wears an idol pinned to his chest.[30] These additions show that the mention of God or of religious practice would be natural in several places in the book; moreover, it is unlikely that an ancient Jewish reader, with even the vaguest familiarity with Israel's sacred history (e.g., the exodus) could have read a story of Jewish deliverance without understanding in it God's action.[31] Therefore, the lack of any theological statements in the book must be deliberate. What was the author's intention? The answer is not immediately apparent.

There are, however, two key passages in the book that contain theological implications. In the first, 4:13-14, Mordecai says to Esther:

> "Do not think that in the king's palace you will escape any more than all the other Jews. For if you keep silence at such a time as this, relief and deliverance will rise for the Jews from another quarter, but you and your father's family will perish. Who knows? Perhaps you have come to royal dignity for just such a time as this." (NRSV)

"Quarter" (מקום *māqôm*) is not a circumlocution for God, as is sometimes claimed, meaning that Mordecai is implying that if Esther does not act, God will (as God does in the book of Daniel). Rather, the passage indicates that Mordecai believes in a wider historical purpose, which includes the survival of the Jews; therefore, in this crisis, the deliverance of the Jews will occur somehow. Does this imply the hand of God in these events? It would seem so, for the only way the survival of the Jews as a historical issue makes any theological sense is for the Jews to be God's special chosen people. Therefore, for the author of Esther, there must be a God, and God must want the Jews to survive. How God will ensure their survival is unclear, however, especially to Mordecai. It is possible that Esther became queen just to fulfill God's purpose, but humans cannot know that. They must act, with profound hope that they are thereby participating in the divine scheme.

The second key passage would seem to support this interpretation. In 6:13*b*, Zeresh says to Haman: "If Mordecai, before whom your downfall has begun, is of the Jewish people, you will not prevail against him, but will surely fall before him." Why does Mordecai's Jewish identity guarantee his triumph and, consequently, Haman's downfall? It does so only if the Jews are somehow special; and in ancient Judaism their specialness is that of being God's people. Once again, belief in God and God's action in history is implied, but not directly stated. However, this implication, coupled with the Jewish context in which the book was read, probably smoothed Esther's entry into the canon.

Another feature of the book that commentators have argued may point to the author's theology is the series of remarkable coincidences moving the plot forward. These include Vashti's dethronement, Esther's enthronement, the king's insomnia (this coincidence is seemingly so obvious that both the LXX and Josephus attribute the king's sleeplessness to God), the reading of the passage concerning Mordecai in the royal annals, and Haman's early arrival in the court, just in time to honor Mordecai. According to Berg, these coincidences help to show that "the narrator believed in a hidden causality behind the surface of human history, both concealing and governing the order and significance of events."[32] However, what is equally important to note is that not one of these coincidences would mean anything without corresponding human action. Esther's enthronement means nothing if she does not choose to act for her people. The reading of the passage concerning Mordecai is meaningless unless Ahasuerus decides to reward him.

---

30. For references, see Louis Ginzberg, *The Legends of the Jews* (Philadelphia: Jewish Publication Society, 1946) 6:463.
31. Richard Bauckham, *The Bible in Politics: How to Read the Bible Politically* (London: SPCK, 1989) 123.
32. Sandra Beth Berg, *The Book of Esther: Motifs, Themes, and Structure*, SBLDS 44 (Missoula, Mont.: Scholars Press, 1979) 178.

Coincidences may reveal the hand of God, but, once again, humans cannot know that for sure. All they can do is act, in the hope that their action corresponds to the plan and purpose of God.

The theological implications teased out above may have more direct relevance in our secular culture than stories in which God intervenes directly and miraculously, such as that of Daniel. Along with the implicit belief that within the realm of human history God's plan includes the salvation of the Jews, the book of Esther also holds out the possibility that in the immediate circumstances things might not work out. Esther might not sway the king; Haman may succeed in his murderous scheme. However, for the author, the failure of Esther and Mordecai would not prove the absence of God (as it would by necessity in Daniel), since Esther and Mordecai can never be completely sure that they are acting in concord with God. This is certainly theologically ambiguous, but it corresponds with the modern believer's daily struggle to discern the will of God. The best anyone can do, the author of Esther implies, is to act within those circumstances in which one finds oneself and to take advantage of those opportunities with an attitude of hope, what Fox calls "an openness to the possibility of providence, even when history seems to weigh against its likelihood."[33] It is this openness that speaks to the skeptical end of the twentieth century and becomes a posture of profound faith.

The second charge, hostility toward Gentiles, is more easily disposed of. The book of Esther has never enjoyed great popularity in the Christian church, even to the present day. It had difficulty obtaining canonical status, particularly among the Eastern churches.[34] Esther is not quoted anywhere in the New Testament and is rarely mentioned by the church fathers. During the Reformation, Martin Luther was vehement in his dislike of the book. The attitude of many Christian commentators toward the book of Esther before the latter part of the twentieth century is nicely summarized by the remarks of L. B. Paton in 1908:

> There is not one noble character in this book. Xerxes is a sensual despot. Esther, for the chance of winning wealth and power, takes her place in the herd of maidens who become concubines of the King. She wins her victories not by skill or by character, but by her beauty. She conceals her origin, is relentless toward a fallen enemy, secures not merely that the Jews escape from danger, but that they fall upon their enemies, slay their wives and children, and plunder their property. Not satisfied with this slaughter, she asks that Haman's ten sons may be hanged, and that the Jews may be allowed another day for killing their enemies in Susa. The only redeeming traits in her character are her loyalty to her people and her bravery in trying to save them. Mordecai sacrifices his cousin to advance his interests, advises her to conceal her religion, displays wanton insolence in his refusal to bow to Haman, and helps Esther in carrying out her schemes of vengeance. All this the author narrates with interest and approval. He gloats over the wealth and the triumph of his heroes and is oblivious to their moral shortcomings. Morally Esther falls far below the general level of the Old Testament and even of the Apocrypha. The verdict of Luther is not too severe: "I am so hostile to this book that I wish it did not exist, for it Judaizes too much, and has too much heathen naughtiness."[35]

With the benefit of hindsight, it is clear that Paton fell victim to his own preconceptions of what a biblical book "should" be like, rather than reading the book for what it is: an entertaining story written for an oppressed minority that ties what was probably originally a pagan holiday into a Jewish context. The tone of the book is ironic and gives the audience a chance to chuckle at those who, in the reality of day-to-day life, rule over them. Ahasuerus is less a sensuous despot than a buffoon ruled by his emotions. Esther, who receives the bulk of Paton's criticisms, actually has no choice about entering the king's harem; once there, she makes the best of the situation and acts with courage and resourcefulness to save her people, who had been endangered by the bloated revenge fantasies of the Gentile Haman. Mordecai does not "sacrifice" his cousin but acts toward her with care and concern; when his personal quarrel with Haman threatens the whole Jewish people, he acts to save them in concert with Esther. The laconic reports in chapter 9

---

33. Fox, *Character and Ideology in the Book of Esther*, 242.
34. For a thorough discussion of Esther's canonical status in early Christianity, see Moore, *Esther*, xxi-xxx.
35. Paton, *Esther*, 96.

9 concerning the number of enemies killed may be disconcerting, particularly to Gentile readers, but it must be remembered that they are not real, that this is a work of fiction. What is more, it is reiterated that the Jewish people fight only in self-defense against their declared enemies. In this way, Esther is much less "anti-Gentile" than, for example, the book of Joshua, in which the Israelites fight aggressive wars leading to the wholesale slaughter of the Gentile inhabitants of Canaan. In fact, the book of Esther portrays a situation in which, under normal circumstances, Jews and Gentiles live harmoniously under Persian rule. Only the threat of annihilation causes the Jews to respond aggressively. Therefore, the objections of Paton (and others) to the book of Esther can be dismissed as, at best, misunderstanding, and, at worst, anti-Semitism.

S. Talmon has suggested a solution to the objections raised against Esther, especially its lack of religious elements, in his proposal to understand the book as a "historicized Wisdom tale."[36] Talmon sees the characters of the book as "types" of wisdom characters: Mordecai is the wise courtier; Haman is the foolish courtier; Esther is the adopted heir of the wise courtier; and Ahasuerus is the king manipulated by the court intrigues. While Esther should not be classified as wisdom literature,[37] it certainly falls within the parameters of the "royal courtier tale," in which a courtier rises to prominence, is endangered by the machinations of enemies, and is eventually vindicated. However, as Wills notes, Esther is more complex in its literary structure than a simple court legend (cf., e.g., Daniel 6).[38] There are two protagonists, Esther and Mordecai; there is a long subplot concerning Vashti; and the Jews act to secure their own rescue. Further, the book contains common folklore motifs—such as the stupid king, the clever court official, and the beautiful wise queen—so that the characters are not unique to wisdom literature.[39] Finally, as the book now stands, the establishment of the Festival of Purim is its *raison d'être*. Nevertheless, the book's emphasis on the ability to function well in a secular environment may point to an influence from wisdom literature (cf. Proverbs).

COMPARISON WITH JOSEPH, DANIEL, AND JUDITH

The book of Esther also lends itself to comparison with other stories of Jews in foreign courts, particularly those of Joseph (Genesis 37–50), Daniel, and Judith. The story of Joseph may have served as a model for the author of Esther.[40] Both are stories of Jews in a foreign court who overcome obstacles and achieve fabulous success. In both stories, the proximity of the protagonist to royal power results in the saving of his or her ethnic group, in Joseph's case his father's family, in Esther's the Jewish people. Both stories involve cases of concealed identity: Joseph is unrecognized by his brothers; Esther conceals her Jewishness. Most intriguing, several times the stories demonstrate almost exact linguistic correspondence, for example at Esth 6:11 and Gen 41:42-43:

Esther	Joseph
And he *clothed* Mordecai	And he *clothed* him . . .
and he caused him to ride	and he caused him to ride
in the square of the city	in his second chariot
and he cried out before him . . .	and they cried out before him . . .

However, the differences are also important, not the least of which is the fact that Joseph attributes the outcome of the story directly to God (Gen 45:5-8; 50:19), a declaration never found in Esther. Therefore, it seems best to presume that the author of Esther knew the Joseph story and used it when composing his story, but not in a relation of strict dependence.

---

40. For the following remarks I am dependent on the work of Berg, *The Book of Esther*, 124-42.
36. S. Talmon, " 'Wisdom' in the Book of Esther," *VT* 13 (1963) 419-55.
37. See the objections of James Crenshaw in "Method in Determining Wisdom Influence Upon 'Historical Literature,' " *JBL* 88 (1969) 129-42.
38. Wills, *The Jew in the Court of the Foreign King*, 151.
39. Susan Niditch, "Legends of Wise Heroes and Heroines," in *The Hebrew Bible and Its Modern Interpreters*, ed. Douglas Knight and Gene Tucker (Philadelphia: Fortress, 1985) 450.

Esther has also been compared to the book of Daniel, specifically to the cycle of royal courtier tales found in Daniel 2–6.[41] The correspondences are clear; both concern Jewish protagonists in foreign courts who, despite the machinations of enemies, rise to be trusted advisers to the king. Both stories display a tolerant attitude toward the Gentile ruler, and both assume that it is possible for Jews to lead comfortable, happy lives in the diaspora. These similarities, however, probably do not indicate dependence one way or the other, but rather adherence to the royal courtier tale genre, adapted for a Jewish audience.[42] The differences between the stories of Esther and Daniel and the conclusions their audiences are expected to reach are very striking. The character of Daniel is a pious Jew, keeping the dietary laws (Dan 1:8-16), praying several times a day facing Jerusalem (Dan 6:10), and, with his companions, bearing his identity as an observant religious Jew proudly and openly. Further, in every misadventure Daniel and his companions survive, God actively intervenes, causing them to interpret dreams (Dan 2:19-23; 4:19-27), providing mysterious signs (Dan 5:5, 24-28), and, in extreme cases, rescuing them from the fiery furnace and the lions' den (Dan 3:24-29; 6:20-23). The message of the Daniel cycle is clear: It is possible for Jews to achieve success under Gentile rule, but only if they are careful to live a pious and observant life, causing God to intervene directly on their behalf. This is radically different from Esther, in which Jewish observance is not an issue; God, if active at all, is only so in a veiled and indirect way, and human action is the primary tool of deliverance.

The third story with which Esther may be directly compared is that of Judith, found in the apocrypha. In fact, it may be argued that the author of the book of Judith, familiar with the story of Esther, set about to create a Jewish heroine more in keeping with the pious standards of his own time.[43] Both stories are supposedly historical tales (although Judith contains even wilder historic "bloopers" than does Esther; for example, Judith makes Nebuchadnezzar, the king of Babylon in the sixth century BCE, the king of Assyria with his capital at Nineveh!) about Jewish women who save their people from destruction at the hands of Gentiles. However, the character of Judith contrasts sharply with that of Esther. Judith is a pious widow who spends her time in constant prayer and fasting (Jdt 8:4-6). She is beautiful, as Esther is beautiful; but Judith's beauty is secondary to her piety. When the people of her town, Bethuliah, are endangered by the besieging army of Nebuchadnezzar's general Holofernes, she acts on their behalf, but only after beseeching God's aid in prayer (Jdt 9:1-14; this scene closely parallels Add. C in the LXX Esther, added to give Esther the appearance of piety). Judith then arrays herself beautifully and makes her way to the enemy camp (Jdt 10:1-13, parallel to Esth 5:1, also Add. D 1-6). However, once Judith is in the Gentile realm, she is careful to eat only kosher food (Jdt 12:1-2), and she prays and purifies herself daily (Jdt 12:5-9). This is in direct contrast to Esther, who does none of those things. Finally, when Judith is confronted by Holofernes' desire to sleep with her, she does not defile herself by having intercourse with a Gentile; rather, she waits until he is drunk, then cuts off his head and carries it back to Bethuliah in a sack (Jdt 13:1-10)! MT Esther marries the Gentile Ahasuerus without a qualm; the most the LXX author can do to repair the situation is to have Esther declare that she "abhors the bed of the uncircumcised" (Add. C 26). So, although Esther and Judith are often compared to each other,[44] it is their differences that are most striking. The pious Judith seems to be created as a foil for the perceived defects in the character of Esther.

How, then, can the book of Esther be understood by a contemporary audience? For the Jew, the function of the book of Esther as an etiology for the Festival of Purim takes priority. For the Christian, the question is harder to answer. I would suggest two related paths for entering the book of Esther. The first sees the character of Esther as a feminine model for the Jewish diaspora. The second sees the book of Esther as the story of an oppressed minority struggling

---

41. It is probable that these tales, which once circulated separately from the apocalyptic material in Daniel 7–12, were composed in the late Persian period diaspora. See John Collins, *The Apocalyptic Imagination* (New York: Crossroad, 1984) 70-72.

42. Many similar correspondences could be cited for the *Tale of Ahiqar*, a royal courtier tale set in the Assyrian Empire, in which the protagonist is not Jewish. However, the tale was evidently popular with Jewish audiences, since a copy of Ahiqar was found in the Jewish colony of Elephantine. See W. Lee Humphreys, "A Life-Style for Diaspora: A Study of the Tales of Esther and Daniel," *JBL* 92 (1973) 211-23.

43. It is probable that Judith was written during the period of the Hasmoneans. See Carey A. Moore, *Judith*, AB 40 (Garden City, N.Y.: Doubleday, 1985) 67-70.

44. Moore notes that the Church Fathers especially made this connection. See C. F. Moore, "Why Wasn't the Book of Judith Included in the Hebrew Bible?" in *No One Spoke Ill of Her: Essays on Judith*, ed. James C. VanderKam (Atlanta: Scholars Press, 1992) 66.

for recognition, and for life itself, in a majority culture that is indifferent, or even hostile, to its existence.

ESTHER AS HEROINE

Although the book of Esther takes its name from its chief female protagonist, the character of Esther has suffered much in the history of interpretation, especially Christian interpretation. Mainstream scholars have insisted on seeing Mordecai as the primary hero of the book, in spite of the fact that at the moment of crisis, Mordecai (who has brought the situation into being by his refusal to bow before Haman) can only go to Esther and ask her to intercede with the king.[45] Esther then devises a plan, carries it out with admirable skill, and, in the end, arranges for Mordecai to inherit Haman's position. Without Esther there would be no story.

Feminist scholars as well find little to admire in Esther, often preferring the deposed Vashti. Alice Laffey sums up the position: "In contrast to Vashti, who refused to be men's sexual object and her husband's toy, Esther is the stereotypical woman in a man's world."[46] Esther, it seems, is neither "woman" enough nor "man" enough to satisfy any of her critics.

Neither of these positions does justice to the character of Esther as she appears within the cultural confines of the book named after her.[47] As will be shown in the Reflections, Esther serves as a model of the successful Jew living in diaspora, and she is able to function as a model precisely because she is a woman. Within the culture we call "Western" or "Judeo-Christian," a culture that is admittedly male-dominated and patriarchal, women have been the constantly marginalized and oppressed gender. Lacking public power, women have historically been able to gain individual or private strength only by successfully exploiting the male power structure around them, as Esther does so well. Her actions are presented as a model to the Jews who, living in exile, are marginalized and powerless minority members of Persian society. Esther also attains her success without the element of the miraculous, which is so often a part of these royal courtier tales (e.g., Daniel). Rather, the oblique references to the providential action of God are so subtle that they might be missed by the casual reader. God is on the side of the oppressed, but works through human instruments to achieve the divine purpose. Esther is a human heroine for a human situation and, as such, speaks powerfully to all oppressed people through the centuries.

ANTI-SEMITISM, OPPRESSION, AND GENOCIDE

Although the book of Esther is entertaining and thought-provoking in many respects, its most salient theme for a modern theological understanding of the book is the fact that it is the story of an attempt by a Gentile to exterminate the Jewish people. Its importance to both Christians and Jews resides in the survival of the Jews in the face of the threats posed by the Gentile characters' active anti-Semitism or, at best, indifference. The relevance of this theme to a modern audience lies in a fact of history that responsible readers are compelled to acknowledge: the sorry history of Western Christianity's anti-Semitism, culminating in the murder of six million Jews in the Holocaust.[48] In the light of that history, arguments concerning Esther's "anti-Gentile" bias seem self-serving, to say the least. The book of Esther is about Jewish survival in the face of Gentile threat, and an enlightened interpretation in the post-Holocaust period must acknowledge the reality of that threat.

The book of Esther, with its theological underpinning of belief in the providence of God manifest in human events, also offers a message of hope to other minorities living in majority cultures, such as African Americans in the white-dominated United States. To those who are

---

45. See Moore, *Esther*, lii, who states, "Between Mordecai and Esther the greater hero in the Hebrew is Mordecai, who supplied the brains while Esther simply followed his directions."
46. Alice Laffey, *An Introduction to the Old Testament: A Feminist Perspective* (Philadelphia: Fortress, 1988) 216.
47. Sidnie White, "Esther: A Feminine Model for Jewish Diaspora," in *Gender and Difference in Ancient Israel*, ed. Peggy L. Day (Philadelphia: Fortress) 161-77; White, "Esther," in *The Women's Bible Commentary*. See also Fox, *Character and Ideology in the Book of Esther*.
48. Bauckham, *The Bible in Politics,* chap. 8.

oppressed the book gives a message of active faith and hope in the face of threat, and to those who rule that the rights of minorities are as important as the rulers' self-interest. For both groups, the greatest societal rewards come through tolerance and cooperation. Further, the book of Esther teaches that in every situation God is able to work through willing human agents (not by miraculous intervention) to ensure that justice is done. The message of the book of Esther is thus easily translatable to our contemporary situation.[49]

49. I would like to thank the following institutions and people: Albright College, especially the staff of the Gingrich Library; The W. F. Albright Institute of Archaeological Research, my scholarly home in Jerusalem; Katheryn Pfisterer Darr, Thomas G. Long, John R. Spencer, and Benjamin G. Wright III for their helpful comments on earlier drafts; and my husband, Dan D. Crawford, for his constant support.

BIBLIOGRAPHY

Berg, Sandra Beth. *The Book of Esther: Motifs, Themes, and Structure.* SBLDS 44. Missoula, Mont.: Scholars Press, 1979. A study of the literary structure of Esther.

Clines, David J. A. *The Esther Scroll: The Story of the Story.* JSOTSup 30. Sheffield: JSOT, 1984. Concerned mainly with a discussion of the sources of Esther.

Fox, Michael V. *Character and Ideology in the Book of Esther.* Studies in Biblical Personalities. Columbia: University of South Carolina Press, 1991. A commentary that focuses on Esther as a literary work.

Laniak, Timothy S. *Shame and Honor in the Book of Esther.* SBLDS 165. Atlanta: Scholars Press, 1998. A study of Esther using the anthropological categories of shame and honor.

Levenson, Jon D. *Esther: A Commentary.* OTL. Louisville: Westminster/John Knox, 1997. A commentary that makes extensive use of rabbinic material in addition to the standard historical-critical works.

Moore, Carey A. *Daniel, Esther, and Jeremiah: The Additions.* AB 44. Garden City, N.Y.: Doubleday, 1977. Focuses almost entirely on the LXX Additions to Esther.

———. *Esther.* AB 7B. Garden City, N.Y.: Doubleday, 1971. A standard historical-critical and linguistic commentary.

White, Sidnie A. "Esther." In *The Woman's Bible Commentary.* Edited by Carol A. Newsom and Sharon H. Ringe. Louisville: Westminster/John Knox, 1992, 124-29. A brief commentary from a feminist perspective.

OUTLINE OF ESTHER

I. Esther 1:1-22, The Deposition of Queen Vashti

    A. 1:1-9, Introduction to the Court of Susa
    B. 1:10-22, The Downfall of Vashti

II. Esther 2:1-23, Esther Becomes Queen

    A. 2:1-4, The Search for a New Queen
    B. 2:5-7, The Introduction of Esther and Mordecai
    C. 2:8-18, Esther Is Chosen Queen
    D. 2:19-23, Mordecai Discovers the Eunuchs' Plot

III. Esther 3:1-15, Haman's Plot to Destroy the Jews

    A. 3:1-6, Conflict Between Mordecai and Haman
    B. 3:7-11, Haman's Plot
    C. 3:12-15, Haman's Plot Is Carried Out

IV. Esther 4:1-17, Mordecai Turns to Esther

    A. 4:1-3, Mordecai's Reaction to Haman's Decree
    B. 4:4-17, Dialogue Between Esther and Mordecai

V. Esther 5:1–8:2, Haman's Plans Are Thwarted

    A. 5:1-8, Esther Acts: The First Banquet
    B. 5:9-14, Haman Builds a Gallows for Mordecai
    C. 6:1-11, Haman's Humiliation
    D. 6:12-13, Haman Is Warned by His Advisers
    E. 6:14–7:10, Esther's Second Banquet
    F. 8:1-2, Esther's Triumph

VI. Esther 8:3-17, The Undoing of Haman's Plot

    A. 8:3-8, Esther Petitions the King
    B. 8:9-14, Mordecai Writes an Edict
    C. 8:15-17, Mordecai's Appearance

VII. Esther 9:1–10:3, The Battles of Adar and the Festival of Purim

    A. 9:1-5, The First Battle
    B. 9:6-10, The Battle in Susa
    C. 9:11-15, The Fourteenth of Adar
    D. 9:16-19, The Jews Celebrate
    E. 9:20-32, The Letters of Purim
        9:20-28, Mordecai's Letter
        9:29-32, Esther's Letter
    F. 10:1-3, Appendix Concerning Mordecai

ESTHER 1:1-22

THE DEPOSITION OF QUEEN VASHTI

OVERVIEW

The function of this opening chapter is to set the story within the framework of the Persian Empire, to introduce several prominent themes, and to foreshadow important events in the main plot. The author also adopts an ironic and even satirical tone, which he will rarely relinquish. The careful reader will note that the only character from chapter 1 who appears in the rest of the story is King Ahasuerus, giving rise to the claim that the story of Vashti comes from a source separate from that of the following chapters, a source originally unrelated to the Esther story.[50] While this theory may be true (see Introduction), here the story of Vashti serves the important function of providing background and framework for the story of Esther.

50. See Bardtke, *Das Buch Esther*, 248-52.

ESTHER 1:1-9, INTRODUCTION TO THE COURT OF SUSA

COMMENTARY

1:1. The book of Esther, which purports to be a historical work (but see Introduction), begins by placing its story in a historical place and time, the court of an actual Persian king. The reader is introduced to King Ahasuerus, who ruled "from India to Ethiopia." "Ahasuerus" is not the name of a known Persian king; however, the author seems to assume that his audience will know which Persian king is meant. Many candidates have been proposed, from Cambyses, son of Cyrus, to Artaxerxes III Ochus, the last Persian emperor before the conquest of Alexander the Great. The LXX and Josephus understand Ahasuerus to be Artaxerxes, and Josephus specifically identifies the king in Esther as Artaxerxes I Longimanus (465–424 BCE). The AT at 10:3 identifies Ahasuerus as Xerxes as well. Linguistic and historical evidence indicate that Xerxes, the fourth Persian emperor (486–465 BCE), is meant. "Ahasuerus" is the Hebrew rendering of the Persian title *xšayâršā*, "mighty man," a title that Xerxes used on his monumental inscriptions. Further, Xerxes' kingdom extended from India to the borders of Egypt (inclusive) and from the Ionian coast to the Arabian desert, thus including most of the known world and agreeing with v. . Finally, one of Xerxes' four capitals was at Susa.[51] The number of provinces (127; Dan 6:2 mentions 120 satraps, while 1 Esdr 3:1-2 has 127 satraps) is not attested in Persian sources and seems to be an inflated number, perhaps in keeping with the author's hyperbolic tone.

1:2-4. Now that a historical time frame has been established, v. 2 introduces the actual story of the book. The phrase "sat on his royal throne" or "reigned from his royal throne" has the sense of "sat securely" and implies that Xerxes had established his rule securely enough by his third year to give a banquet to celebrate. The AT supplies the

51. For a good discussion of the evidence for the identification of Ahasuerus with Xerxes, see Paton, *Esther*, 51-54.

phrase "of his deliverance," and indeed the historical Xerxes did face rebellion in both Egypt and Babylon, which he swiftly quelled, at the beginning of his reign. However, the LXX states that the banquet is to celebrate his marriage to Vashti. The banquet takes place in Susa, the former capital of Elam and one of the four capitals of the Persian Empir. According to Herodotus, the Persian court wintered in Babylon and then, to escape the scorching heat, spent the spring in Susa and the summers in Ecbatana. The text differentiates between the city of Susa and its citadel (בירה *bîrâ*), the royal palace excavated by M. Dieulafoy in 1884–86, who discovered an acropolis containing the royal buildings.[52] This first banquet includes all the officials, both military and civic, of the entire Persian Empire, and lasts 180 days, or half a year. Xerxes must have indeed been secure on his throne to allow his government to grind to a halt while his officials banqueted for six months! A suspicion of hyperbole is raised.

1:5-9. This suspicion is confirmed by the description of the second banquet. This banquet is for the people of Susa, both the great, the palace officials, and the small, the regular people. The description of the garden of the king's palace, where the banquet is held, is meant to convey the opulence of the palace and the wealth of Xerxes. Several of the words occur only here in the Hebrew Bible, and they are piled up, one on top of the other, making an impression of luxury and richness but not creating a very coherent picture.[53] Verses 7-8 place a great deal of emphasis on the drink, in keeping with the Persian notoriety for heavy drinking bouts. In fact, v. 8 in the Hebrew informs us that the drinking was "according to the law" and that "there was no compelling," but "each man could do according to his will," a difficult verse to render into acceptable English. We know from Herodotus[54] that usually the king set the pace of drinking; when he drank, everybody drank. However, at this banquet "there was no compelling." Most commentators resolve the difficulty by taking the Hebrew word דת (*dāt*) to mean here "a special ruling"—that is, for this particular banquet the normal rule was suspended, and each man could drink as much or as little as he wanted.[55] The word *dāt* recurs throughout the book of Esther, always referring to a royal decision; the author is letting the reader know that everything in this court, including drinking, proceeds according to the whims of the king.

Finally, v. 9 introduces the second important character in the story, Queen Vashti. The name "Vashti," which comes from the Persian word *vahista* ("best"), is unattested in extra-biblical sources; Xerxes' queen was Amestris,[56] and she remained queen throughout his reign. The introduction of the unknown Vashti is the first clue to the vigilant reader that, despite its veneer of historicity, the book of Esther is a story. Vashti, like Ahasuerus, is giving a banquet—this one for the women—inside the palace. Historically, Persian men and women could eat together, but the women left when the drinking began.[57] It suits the purposes of the author to have the men and women separate as the story begins.

Berg has pointed out the importance of the banquet motif in the story of Esther.[58] Banquets signal important events (1:3-9; 3:15), indicate closure (2:18), and provide settings to move the action forward (5:5-8; 6:14–7:10). A banquet is a signal to the reader that something important has happened or is about to happen (see also Introduction).

---

52. M. A. Dieulafoy, *L'Acropole de Suse*, 4 vols. (Paris: Hatchetee, 1893).
53. Werner Dommershausen suggests that the author uses Persian loan words to create an exotic effect. See his *Die Estherrolle*, SBM 6 (Stuttgart: Katholisches Bibelwerk, 1968) 146. The use of Persian words here also reinforces the story's historical verisimilitude.
54. Herodotus 1.33.
55. See, e.g., Moore, *Esther*, 7-8.
56. Herodotus 7.61, 9.109-13.
57. Herodotus 5.18, 9.110.
58. Berg, *The Book of Esther*, 31-57.

REFLECTIONS

The extended description of the physical setting contrasts greatly with the usually scanty physical descriptions in the Hebrew Bible. Why, then, does the author give all this seemingly extraneous information? Through the description, we get a glimpse of the Persian character: ostentatious, showy, unbridled. This is in direct contrast to the usual

Jewish values of modesty and self-restraint (see Prov 11:2-4).[59] Although disapproval is never directly voiced, the message is clear: Such opulence, while immediately awe-inspiring, hides an empty and probably corrupt core. This will be proved as the events of the story unfold. Much the same sort of criticism can be leveled at contemporary society: The "consumerism" of the latter half of the twentieth century substitutes for deeper ethical and moral values. While the implied criticism found in Esther does not strike the radical note of the rejection of worldly goods found in the teaching of Jesus ("Sell all that you own and distribute the money to the poor, and you will have treasure in heaven; then come, follow me" [Luke 18:22 NRSV]), the author does wish us to recognize the ultimate unimportance of wealth.

59. See Levenson, *Esther*, 45.

ESTHER 1:10-22, THE DOWNFALL OF VASHTI

COMMENTARY

1:10-12. The satirical tone of the book of Esther comes to the forefront in this passage. It raises several questions: Why does the king summon Vashti? Why does she refuse to come? Why does the king need to consult his advisers? The Hebrew text quite clearly indicates that the king summons Vashti when he is drunk—that is, "when the heart of the king was good in wine"—thereby implying that his actions were not quite rational and that her refusal to obey was justified.[60] He sends seven eunuchs (eunuchs are important functionaries in the Persian hierarchy, as well as in harem life) to fetch her, all listed by name, which seems to be an attempt to give the text an air of historical verisimilitude. The figure seven, a number signifying a complete or finished group, recurs throughout the chapter; Vashti is summoned on the seventh day, the king sends seven eunuchs to fetch her, and, in v. 14, he consults with seven nobles.

The king sends the eunuchs to bring Vashti, wearing the royal crown, before the assembly in order to display her beauty before the assembled company. The king has already displayed his wealth and his generosity; what remains but his beautiful wife? However, Vashti refuses.

The Hebrew text gives no reason or justification for Vashti's refusal of a direct command from the king. Her refusal is shocking in its simplicity and directness; the all-powerful king who rules from India to Ethiopia, whose riches and power are immense, has been disobeyed—by his wife![61] However, her reason for refusing is still enigmatic. Is it because the king is drunk? Interpreters have offered several reasons. Josephus informs us that she refused to come because Persian law forbade wives to be seen by strangers, but his contention is historically inaccurate.[62] The rabbis infer, from the command that she wear the royal crown, that she was meant to wear *only* the royal crown—in other words, to appear naked, wearing only the crown.[63] However, in the Hebrew Vashti's refusal remains unexplained.

1:13-22. The king is enraged by her refusal; he has been publicly shamed in front of his court.[64] However, rather than confront

60. Josephus, in his attempt to improve the portrait of the king, leaves out any mention of drunkenness. See Louis Feldman, "Josephus' Portrait of Ahasuerus," *Australian Biblical Review* 42 (1994) 17-38.

61. The theme of obedience/disobedience, especially by a wife, runs throughout the book and features prominently in the turning point of the story. See Berg, *The Book of Esther*, 71-82.
62. See Herodotus 9.110 and Neh 2:6 for the presence of women, even royal wives, at banquets.
63. *Meg., Tg. Esth I, Tg. Esth II*. The rabbis are not sympathetic to Vashti, whom they identify as the granddaughter of Nebuchadnezzar, the Babylonian emperor who destroyed Jerusalem in 587 BCE. In fact, the Megilloth, not satisfied that the shameless Vashti would refuse to appear naked, adds that she had become leprous! None of this is implied in the Hebrew text.
64. The concept of honor/shame is important in ancient Mediterranean cultures and often informs the behavior of characters in ways our own culture does not expect. "Honor" and "shame" are attributes applied to the individual from the outside, by the society: A man gains honor by his behavior, while a woman avoids shame by hers. Ahasuerus has been shamed by Vashti's disobedience; on the other hand, the text may imply that Vashti would be shamed by appearing publicly at the banquet, a seemingly insoluble dilemma. For a further discussion of honor and shame in Esther, see Lillian R. Klein, "Honor and Shame in Esther," in *A Feminist Companion to Esther, Judith and Susanna*, ed. Athalya Brenner (Sheffield: Sheffield Academic, 1995) 149-75. See also Timothy S. Laniak, "From the Margin to the Middle: The Pattern of Shame and Honor in the Book of Esther" (unpublished Ph.D. diss., Harvard University, 1997).

Vashti directly, which we might expect, he turns to his advisers to determine what should be done "according to the law." The text's exaggerated emphasis on the law is apparent for the second time in the chapter: First, drinking is done according to law; now the king, in a dispute with his wife, must proceed according to law. This respect for the law will appear with more important consequences later in the story. The men the king consults are "wise men" who "know the times." The term "the times" (העתים *hā'ittîm*) may connote astrology (see Isa 47:12-13; Dan 2:27; 5:15; see also 1 Chr 12:32, with reference to the tribe of Issachar), but that phrase is in apposition to "all those who know law [דת *dāt*] and judgment [דין *dîn*]," so it probably simply refers to those who are knowledgeable about Persian customs, both legal and traditional. The author once more supplies us with a list of Persian names; some of these names occur extra-biblically, while others do not; none of them can be identified with any known historical figures (the AT omits them altogether). The use of the number seven here indicates that the author is familiar with the Persian court: Seven noblemen helped to defeat the false Smerdis in his conspiracy against Darius and thereafter enjoyed special privileges in the Persian court, such as unchecked access to the king.[65] They were the chief noblemen of the Persian court, so it is proper that the king should consult them.

The response of Memucan, one of the advisers, seems out of proportion to the crime. What has been a matter of personal disobedience suddenly becomes an affair of state, affecting all husbands and wives and threatening the stability of the kingdom. It is possible that Memucan is afraid Vashti is plotting a palace coup, but it is more likely that the author means for us to laugh; the pompous Persians turn a personal affront, which could be easily resolved, into a national crisis. The dignity of Persian men is so precarious that the actions of one woman threaten the whole house of cards. The king must take action not only within his own household, but throughout the entire kingdom as well; not only against Vashti, but also against all women; and not only for the sake of his own dignity, but for the peace and stability of all families. It is difficult to respect such silliness.

Memucan advises the king to make a law banishing Vashti and stripping her of her royal status (v. 19). The irony, of course, is that Vashti is forbidden to do precisely what she refused to do: appear before the king. The verse also introduces a concept that will prove important later in the story: the irrevocability of Persian law. According to Memucan, once a law has been promulgated by the king, it cannot be revoked. Such a rule goes against any principle of good government and common sense, and, indeed, does not seem historically to have been true of Persian law.[66] However, the concept appears elsewhere in Jewish literature (Dan 6:8-9, 12, 15), and the author of Esther will use it as an important plot device.

The king decides to implement this advice, and letters to that effect are sent throughout the kingdom (v. 22). The Persians maintained an excellent postal system, necessary in such a vast empire; various characters will utilize it throughout the story. What is interesting about the letters is that they do not mention Vashti at all; instead, they declare that every man should be master in his own house (a command from the king, who is not!) and should "speak according to the language of his people."[67] Note that the NRSV omits this final clause (presumably because of the difficulties of its interpretation) and that the NIV places it before the first clause. The decree itself is unenforceable and laughable; as Fox puts it, the Persian postal system "is put to service in the dissemination of inanity."[68]

Thus Vashti disappears from the scene, opening the door for the appearance of Esther and the main plot of the book.

65. Herodotus 3.84.

66. See Herodotus 9.109.

67. In the Persian Empire, many languages were spoken; in such a setting, language becomes an important indicator of ethnicity. Nehemiah forces Jews who had married non-Jewish women to repudiate their wives, one of the reasons being that their children spoke the language of their mothers and could not speak Hebrew (Neh 13:23-27).

68. Fox, *Character and Ideology in the Book of Esther*, 23.

REFLECTIONS

It seems difficult at first to pan any theological gold out of the first chapter of Esther. After all, the story is about Persian characters, set in a pagan court, with no glimmer of religion anywhere. However, the chapter does introduce two themes that this commentary will pursue: (1) the role and status of women and (2) power.

1. The character of Vashti the Queen serves as a foil to Esther the Queen, and very different fates await each. Vashti is queen and seems to function autonomously within the sphere of women; in 1:9 she gives a separate banquet for women. However, the extent of her power and autonomy swiftly becomes clear: The minute she opposes her husband the king, the entire machinery of the state descends on her head, and she loses all status and power. To many modern commentators, Vashti is a feminist hero, opposing the male power structure with what little independence she has.[69] It is easy to see why she is a more attractive character than is the pliant Esther. However, in the story Vashti fails, and Esther succeeds. What message is the author trying to convey? Can we reconcile that message to our differing ideas about the status and role of women in society? Further reflection is called for.

2. The theme of power—who has it, who receives it, who loses it—will recur throughout the story of Esther. In this section, the all-powerfulness of Ahasuerus is revealed as a sham; he does not even have power over his own domestic arrangements. First his wife successfully opposes him, and then he must turn to his advisers to tell him what to do about it. It is not enough to declare that one has power, the author is saying. To truly have power, one must have the accompanying wisdom and skill to exercise it.

---

69. Laffey, *An Introduction to the Old Testament*, 214-15; Timothy K. Beal, "Tracing Esther's Beginnings," and Bea Wyler, "Esther: The Incomplete Emancipation of a Queen," in Brenner, *A Feminist Companion to Esther, Judith and Susanna*, 87-110, 115-18.

ESTHER 2:1-23
ESTHER BECOMES QUEEN

OVERVIEW

This section introduces the main protagonists, Esther and Mordecai, and explains how the young Jewish girl Esther becomes the Persian queen. Esther is a beautiful, malleable young woman (the orphan who makes good); while her cousin Mordecai is presented as the model of the righteous and wise man.

ESTHER 2:1-4, THE SEARCH FOR A NEW QUEEN

COMMENTARY

"After these things" indicates an indeterminate length of time. It must be shortly after the events in chap. 1, for Ahasuerus's anger has passed; as we shall see, his emotions tend to change rapidly. Now he remembers Vashti. With love? Regret? Loneliness? The Hebrew text does not supply an answer, although Josephus supplies "with regret," because the king was fond of Vashti.[70] Interestingly, the LXX reads "the king remembered Vashti *no longer*"; thus he was ready to find another wife.

The Hebrew does not seem to carry this connotation, for the king also remembers what Vashti had done and "what had been decreed against her." The passive construction in the Hebrew (the NRSV correctly reflects this) deflects blame from the king onto his advisers, a pattern we shall see again.

Josephus's interpretation of the king's emotional state may well be correct, because the servants ("young men" [נערים *nĕʿārîm*], not the noble advisers of chap. 1) quickly propose a scheme to banish Vashti from the king's thoughts as well as from his courts. Young women are to be sought, and one of them will become the new queen. The only characteristics they must have are beauty and youth; the word translated as "virgins" is בתולות (*bĕtûlôt*), which actually means "young women of marriageable age," although most girls moved very quickly from the onset of puberty into marriage.[71] They are to come from all over the kingdom to be placed in the harem (or women's quarters) in the royal palace of Susa, under the care of Hegai, an official of the palace bearing the title "King's Eunuch." Each young woman is to be given "cosmetic treatments," an oblique hint at the sensuality of the Persian court. Finally, the girl who "pleases the king" the most, a deliberately vague phrase that echoes Memucan's advice in 1:19, will be queen instead of Vashti. Some translations render the Hebrew תמלך (*timlōk*) as "reign," but "reign" implies power; it is not clear whether the queen has power of her own or is simply the king's wife. Vashti attempted to exercise independent power and fell; there is no reason to assume that a young girl (13-14 years old), chosen for her ability to "please" the king, will wield any power of her own. Therefore, "be queen" seems the best translation in the present context; however, the author's irony may

---

70. Josephus *Antiquities of the Jews* XI.195.

71. For a discussion of the meaning of the term בתולה (*bĕtûlâ*), see Peggy L. Day, "From the Child Is Born the Woman: The Story of Jephthah's Daughter," in *Gender and Difference in Ancient Israel*, ed. P. L. Day (Minneapolis: Fortress, 1989) 58-74.

be at work here, since Esther eventually does "reign." Ahasuerus, once again relying on the advice of others, readily adopts the plan.

Two things should be noted. First, it is clear that in reality this story could not have taken place, since the Persian king was limited by law to marriage with a woman from one of the seven noble Persian families.[72] The author of Esther is clearly drawing on legendary motifs; the stories of King Shekriya and Scheherazade in *The Thousand and One Nights* and, from Jewish tradition, King David and Abishag the Shunammite (1 Kgs 1:1-4) immediately come to mind.[73] Second, there is no sense of coercion in the text; the young men (and the author) assume that the young women will wish to enter the king's harem; in any case, the women are not consulted. On this matter the king has power over his subjects, and he will exercise it. There is a contest for the girl who pleases the king the most (i.e., is best in bed; this is a sexual contest), and the winner will become queen.[74] (See Reflections at 2:5-7.)

72. Herodotus 3.84.

73. Michael V. Fox, *Character and Ideology in the Book of Esther*, 28, points out that Esth 2:2b is verbally dependent on 1 Kgs 1:2a.
74. Fox makes this point strongly in *Character and Ideology in the Book of Esther*, 28.

ESTHER 2:5-7, THE INTRODUCTION OF ESTHER AND MORDECAI

COMMENTARY

These three verses interrupt the flow of the narrative, yet they are necessary for the story because they introduce the two main characters, Esther and Mordecai. Their parenthetical character, similar to Ezra 2:2 and Neh 7:1, makes the introductions more conspicuous.

Mordecai, who bears a Babylonian name with the theophorous element Marduk,[75] is introduced first. He is identified first as a Jew, now in the post-exilic period of ethnic ("of the nation of Israel") rather than tribal ("of the tribe of Judah") designation, which will be Mordecai's primary epithet throughout the book. Next, the text states that he is in the citadel (not the city) of Susa, which implies that he is a court official (this is made plain in the LXX, Add. A 2). Finally, his genealogy is given: son of Jair, son of Shimei, son of Kish. The identity of these ancestors is open to question. Jair is probably Mordecai's father, but Shimei and Kish may be more remote ancestors. Shimei is known in the biblical tradition as a member of the house of Saul (thus a Benjaminite) who cursed David as he fled from Jerusalem (2 Sam 16:5-14), while Kish is the father of Saul, first king of Israel (1 Sam 9:1; 14:51). If these are the figures the author of Esther wishes to make the ancestors of Mordecai, then two connections with Saul have been established, connections that will be important later on. Finally, Mordecai's tribe, Benjamin, is given.

Verse 6 presents a problem. It begins with the relative pronoun (אשר *ʾăšer*), "who have been carried captive." The person referred to had been exiled with King Jeconiah (or Jehoiachin), the last king of Judah, in 597 BCE, which implies his nobility (2 Kgs 24:10-12). However, if the person referred to is Mordecai, at the time of this story he would be extremely old, at least 113![76] The NRSV solves the dilemma by identifying the "who" of v. 6 with Kish; but if Kish is the father of Saul, as seems likely for reasons to be made clear, this identification would be incorrect. The author seems to have made a blunder, perhaps thinking that Ahasuerus was the direct successor of Nebuchadnezzar, or at least he seems to have telescoped history; Mordecai's importance and royal connections are more important than the relatively minor matter of his age.

75. "Theophorous" means containing a reference to divinity, usually a divine name. For example, the name "Jonathan" in Hebrew (יהונתן *yĕhônātān*) contains the divine name "YHWH."

76. Paton, *Esther*, 168-69. The LXX omits the phrase concerning the exile; the AT does not contain the verse.

Esther is introduced in v. 7 as the ward of Mordecai. She has both a Hebrew name, "Hadassah" (הדסה *hădassâ*, meaning "myrtle"; this name appears only here in MT Esther and not in the Greek versions), and a Persian name, "Esther" (meaning "star," but some commentators also connect it with the Babylonian goddess Ishtar). "Esther" (אסתר *'str* in its consonantal form) also means "I will hide" in Hebrew, and the rabbis took this as a reference to Esther's concealment of her Jewish identity. The practice of having two names, a Jewish name and a name of one's place of exile, was common among Jews of the post-exilic period (see Dan 1:7).

Esther is an orphan, adopted "as a daughter" by Mordecai, whose relationship to her is not explained at this point. The LXX and *Meg.* 13*a* state that Mordecai took her "as a wife," which would make her entry into the king's harem heinous (and parallel with the kidnapping of Sarah, wife of Abraham, by Pharaoh in Gen 12:10-20; cf. *The Genesis Apocryphon*), but the Hebrew is perfectly clear and fits better with the pattern of the story, which accepts Esther's entry into the king's harem as a matter of course. Esther's status as an orphan mirrors the Jewish people's status as exiles: marginalized and powerless. This is the first clue that Esther is to be a role model. The only other thing we learn about Esther at this time is that she is beautiful (lit., "shapely of form and good of appearance"), thus meeting the one criterion for entrance into the king's harem.

Thus far the reader has been led to believe that Mordecai was the main protagonist of the story, with Esther playing a secondary role; his ethnicity, his public status, his genealogy, and his links with nobility are emphasized, while all that is revealed about Esther is that she is a beautiful orphan. However, it should be remembered that the book is named after Esther, not Mordecai.

REFLECTIONS

The theme of power appears again in these two sections with the juxtaposing of the power of the king and his court, who can disrupt the lives of every family in the empire at will by requiring their daughters to enter his harem, and the powerless status of Mordecai and Esther, an exile and an orphan respectively. The author passes by the dislocation of Esther's life without comment; the comfort of a young girl is nothing beside the desire of the king! We should pause, however, and reflect on the havoc that power can wreak on the lives of the powerless. The examples in our own time are legion: the forced exile of the Armenians by the Turks, which resulted in Armenian genocide; the removal to ghettos and concentration camps (followed by mass murder) of millions of Jews and others in the Holocaust; and the internment of Japanese Americans in prison camps by the American government during World War II. The author of Esther uses the juxtaposition of power and powerlessness as ironic foreshadowing; by the end of the story, the powerless exile and the orphan will control the Persian Empire. For modern readers, the picture of numerous girls being ripped away from their families and forced into the king's harem cannot be resolved so comfortably.

ESTHER 2:8-18, ESTHER IS CHOSEN QUEEN

COMMENTARY

2:8-11. Esther, along with all the other young women of Susa (according to Josephus, there were four hundred girls),[77] is taken into the harem and placed in the charge of Hegai. Notice that in the Hebrew text there is no hint of protest on the part of either Esther or Mordecai. The king's law is proclaimed, and

77. Josephus *Antiquities of the Jews* XI.201.

they obey it. This obedience to a seemingly immoral command troubled the rabbis, who claimed that Esther was taken by force or that Mordecai tried to hide her; however, these claims import moral standards into the text that do not apply in the situation the author is describing; it does not trouble the author (perhaps because his story is fictional) that a Jewish girl is about to become the concubine of the Gentile king. In v. 9, Esther's first action is recorded: She "wins" (נשׂא *nāśā*) the favor of Hegai. The active construction is important; she does not "find" (מצא *māṣā*) favor, but actively earns it. The result is positive: Hegai seems to treat her especially well; she receives her cosmetic treatments "quickly," as well as special food, seven maids from the palace, and the best place in the harem. This is Esther's first step on the road to political power, and she has negotiated it wisely and reaped the rewards. The mention of food is significant: Esther does not seem to eat kosher food, but just what is provided for her by Hegai. This is in contrast to Daniel, another Jew in a foreign court, who insists on obtaining kosher food (Dan 1:8-17). Both the LXX and the rabbis attempt to remedy this problem by having Esther demand, and get, kosher food (see Add. C).

It would have been difficult, within the confines of the Hebrew story, however, for Esther to demand kosher food, since v. 10 informs us that she did not reveal her ethnic background, "for Mordecai had commanded that she was not to tell." This implies that there is nothing in Esther's everyday behavior that would reveal that she was Jewish; in other words, she was not observant. No judgment of her is implied, either; the fact is simply passed over in silence. The reason for Mordecai's command is not given; this is the second unanswered question in the text (the reason for Vashti's refusal being the first). Some consider it a matter of political expediency,[78] but it may simply be a convenient plot device.[79] It may also imply that it was dangerous to be a Jew in the Persian court. In any case, Esther is triumphantly established in the harem, and every day Mordecai, who as a courtier would have access to the palace, checks on her welfare. How Mordecai could have inquired after her every day without revealing his identity as her foster father, and thus revealing her Jewishness, is not stated.

2:12-14. These verses outline the process by which all the girls were taken to the king. The process took twelve months, "according to the custom of women." Although דת (*dāt*) usually carries the force of law in our sense, here it seems to connote "custom" or perhaps "decree." This is the process that has been established, and no one can hasten it or bypass it.[80] Thus Esther will spend a full year in beauty treatments before being seen by the king, in spite of Hegai's favor. Six months are spent being massaged with oil of myrrh, and six months are given to perfumes and cosmetics. The details of this regimen are unclear to the modern reader, although some cosmetic burners and many perfume vials have been found in excavations in the Middle East.[81] It may be imagined as well that the women were instructed in court etiquette and possibly the sexual arts of pleasing the king. At the end of the year, each woman was brought to the king for one night. It is clear from the text, although not explicitly stated, that the purpose of this night was to have sexual intercourse, for in the morning the woman was returned to a different harem, the harem of concubines (פילגשים *pîlagšîm*; there is no mistaking the sexual connotation of the term). She would not see the king again unless summoned by name. The author here displays his knowledge of Near Eastern harem customs, well-known from the later Ottoman Empire. Although the women of the harem were sequestered and dependent upon male favor, a woman could wield enormous power from within the walls of the palace, especially if she were the queen and/or the mother of the heir. Persian history is speckled with tales of harem intrigue; Xerxes himself was killed in a harem coup. Therefore, although the women had no hand in selecting their lot, they did have the potential of acquiring power and influence.

---

78. See, e.g., Paton, *Esther*.
79. Moore, *Esther*, 28.
80. For a different view of the significance of the word *dāt*, see Kristin de Troyer, "An Oriental Beauty Parlour: An Analysis of Esther 2:8-18 in the Hebrew, the Septuagint and the Second Greek Text," in *A Feminist Companion to Esther, Judith and Susanna*, ed. Athalya Brenner (Sheffield: Sheffield Academic, 1995) 47-70.
81. See W. F. Albright, "The Lachish Cosmetic Burner and Esther 2:12," in Carey A. Moore, *Studies in the Book of Esther* (New York: Ktav, 1982) 361-68.

2:15-18. When Esther's turn comes (v. 15) for her night with the king, her importance is heightened by giving her a genealogy. She is the daughter of Abihail, the uncle of Mordecai. Abihail (אביחיל *'ăbîḥayil*, "my father is mighty") does not seem to be connected with any of the other Abihails in the biblical text (Num 3:25; 1 Chr 2:29; 5:14; 11:18), but his relationship to Mordecai assures the reader that Esther is of the same noble blood and, therefore, worthy to be queen. Her relationship to Mordecai is also clarified; she is his cousin as well as his adopted daughter. She continues her wise course of action; allowed to take whatever she wants with her to the king, she takes only what Hegai advises. Presumably Hegai, the "King's Eunuch," knows what the king prefers. Again, there is no negative judgment on the part of the author; both he and the reader are rooting for Esther to win the contest and become queen. It is clear that she should, since she "wins favor in the eyes of all who see her."

Esther is taken to the king in the seventh year of his reign. Four years have elapsed since the downfall of Vashti. Now events move quickly, and the parallelism of Esther's rise and Vashti's fall is obvious. The king "loves" (יאהב *ye'ĕhab*; the NRSV is correct; the NIV's "was attracted to" is too weak) Esther, whereas at Vashti his "anger burned"; Esther wins (active once again) his devotion, and he sets the royal crown on her head (the crown Vashti refused to wear) and makes her queen "instead of Vashti." Finally, he gives a banquet in honor of Esther, which contrasts with the second and third banquets in chap. 1. Vashti fell at a banquet; Esther completes her rise at a banquet. The banquet motif here signals the satisfactory closure of an episode.

In v. 18 the king shows his generosity to the entire empire by remitting their taxes (or possibly forced labor), as he did at the beginning of chap. 1 by entertaining them, once again forming an inclusio. The whole incident has been satisfactorily concluded; the vacancy created by the rebellious Vashti has been filled by the pliant and pleasing Esther, and the changeable Ahasuerus is once again content. However, two loose threads remain for the author to unravel: Esther's Jewishness remains undisclosed, and Mordecai's position at court, as well as the court's knowledge of his relationship to Esther, is indeterminate.

REFLECTIONS

1. This passage is troubling to the modern reader, and particularly troubling to women. Hundreds of young girls are rounded up, their wishes not consulted or even considered, placed in a strange locale away from their family and friends; subjected, willingly or unwillingly, to a series of "treatments"; and then given one night for the sexual performance of their life, all for the pleasure of one man! What makes it even worse is that the text, contrary to expectations, does not adopt a condemnatory attitude, but rather accepts the process as part of the status quo. In fact, the heroine (whose place in Scripture would seem to imply that she should be a role model) is applauded for her success in the process and her eventual triumph in the contest. It is difficult not to take the position of L. B. Paton, who remarked: "Esther, for the chance of winning wealth and power, takes her place in the herd of maidens who become concubines of the king. . . . Morally Esther falls far below the general level of the Old Testament."[82] However, such a dismissal of Esther's character would be doing the book a disservice. Even though we, as inheritors of Western culture, may decry the moral standards of an earlier era and, as inhabitants of the late twentieth century, deplore that era's treatment of women, it is unfair to judge the entire value of the biblical book by those standards. After all, the text of the Hebrew Bible is littered with stories most Christians and Jews consider of dubious morality (e.g., the story of Lot's daughters, Gen 19:30-38; the rape of the women of Jabesh-Gilead and Shiloh, Judges 21), and we do not discard them. Esther's actions must be judged within the social and cultural

---

82. Paton, *Esther*, 96.

parameters of her story, and within those parameters she acts prudently and wisely, thereby protecting herself, her kinsman, and, ultimately, her people.

2. Another theme that will be followed throughout this commentary is raised in this passage: Jewish identity, assimilation, and persecution. Esther's Jewish identity is clearly derived from her ethnicity, and not from her practice, since she appears to be fully assimilated to a Gentile life-style (in spite of the efforts of the Septuagint and the rabbis). Mordecai, while identified as a Jew, also betrays no hint of Jewish practice. His Jewish identity does not seem to have stood in the way of his court position or of Esther's becoming queen. Rather, each seems to have followed the advice of Jeremiah: "Thus says the LORD of hosts, the God of Israel, to all the exiles whom I have sent into exile from Jerusalem to Babylon: Build houses and live in them; plant gardens and eat what they produce. . . . Seek the welfare of the city where I have sent you into exile, and pray to the LORD on its behalf, for in its welfare you will find your welfare" (Jer 29:4-5, 7 NRSV). Jews have wrestled for centuries with the problem of assimilation vs. maintaining their Jewish identity, and Christians have leveled charges of exclusivism and pride against them. In the Holocaust, the most highly assimilated Jewish community in history, the German Jews, was destroyed, a victim of Christian anti-Semitism and indifference. The assimilation of the German Jews did not save them. The United States is home to the largest, and now most assimilated, community of Jews in the diaspora, yet troubling indications of anti-Semitism surface in America as well. Esther 2:10 may likewise indicate that, no matter how much one assimilates, it may be dangerous to be openly Jewish in the Persian court. Jewish experience has not changed significantly in 2,500 years.

ESTHER 2:19-23, MORDECAI DISCOVERS THE EUNUCHS' PLOT

COMMENTARY

Verse 19 opens with what Paton has termed a *crux interpretum*, a second gathering of the maidens.[83] The phrase is awkward in Hebrew, beginning with an infinitive construct after a series of converted imperfects. It makes no sense in the story line—since Esther has been made queen, there is no need for a second collection of young women. The LXX (and Josephus) solves the problem by omitting the phrase. The NRSV translation attempts to smooth over the difficulty by omitting the word שנית (*šēnît*, "a second time"), while the NIV includes it. Many explanations have been put forward to solve the problem, among them that the king, to arouse Esther's jealousy, demanded new concubines or that the courtiers, seeking to supplant Esther, introduced the king to new women. Fox opts for the explanation that the gathering refers to the second harem, the harem of the concubines mentioned in 2:14, and views the word בתולות (*bĕtûlôt*, "virgins" or "young maidens") as a slip of the authorial tongue. Moore emends "second" (*šēnît*) to "various" (שנות *šōnôt*) and claims it refers to the general time period, while Clines suggests that *šēnît* could mean "further" or "secondly," referring to a second event that occurred at the time of the gathering of the maidens—namely, the eunuchs' plot.[84] Cazelles, taking a literary-critical approach, views the phrase as a leftover fragment indicating two original sources.[85] Clines's explanation seems the most satisfactory, since it does not involve emendation, but the fact remains that in the present form of the book the phrase makes no sense.

The text passes on to Mordecai, described as "sitting in the king's gate"; in other words, he is a royal courtier (שער [*šaʿar*, "gate"]

---

83. Paton, *Esther*, 186.

84. Fox, *Character and Ideology in the Book of Esther*, 38; Moore, *Esther*, 29-30; and Clines, *The Esther Scroll*, 291. For a summary of the various views, see Paton, *Esther*, 186.

85. Cazelles, "Note sur la composition du rouleau d'Esther," 26.

refers to the royal court in its entirety; the LXX specifically states that Mordecai "served in the king's court").[86] However, rather than proceeding with the narrative, v. 20 inserts another parenthetical comment—that Esther had still not revealed her Jewishness or her kinsfolk, because she was obedient to Mordecai "as when he brought her up." Two things should be noticed. One, although the Targums and the LXX insist that Esther obeyed Jewish law while in the palace, this would have been impossible for her to do while continuing to conceal her ethnic identity. Second, she places her first loyalty with her adopted father rather than with her husband, thus disobeying the usual rules of patrilocal kinship, but obeying the demands of ethnic loyalty.[87] Therefore, Esther and Mordecai, rather than Esther and the king, continue to be the story's primary focus of partnership and loyalty.

Two eunuchs, Bigthan and Teresh, plot to overthrow the king (v. 21), with whom they are angry. The reason for their anger is not given and is not important for the story; but these types of court intrigues were not unusual in Achaemenid Persia. Xerxes and Artaxerxes II Ochus, for instance, were each killed in palace coups. This plot, however, is foiled by Mordecai, who reports it to Esther, who reports it to the king. This activity foreshadows their later partnership to foil Haman's genocidal scheme. The Hebrew text does not report how Mordecai learns of the plot; according to the LXX's treatment of the incident in Add. A, he overhears it (see the Commentary on Add. A). Mordecai seems to have easy access to Esther, who in turn, at the beginning of her marriage, has easy access to the king. Esther informs the king in Mordecai's name, but since her relationship to Mordecai is undisclosed, her action creates a minor anomaly. Finally, the matter is investigated (a sharp contrast to the king's usually impetuous procedure), punishments are meted out ("hanged on the gallows" may refer to impaling on a stake rather than hanging),[88] and Mordecai's name is duly recorded in the royal annals. It is very clear, however, that Mordecai is not rewarded for his good deed, a loose thread the author will exploit later. This is negligence on the king's part; Herodotus reports that the Persian monarchs were very diligent in handing out rewards, reporting the existence of a list of the "King's Benefactors" in the royal archives.[89] The entire incident is missing from the AT, probably to smooth out the previous reporting of the plot of the eunuchs in Addition A.[90]

Chapters 1–2 constitute a prelude to the main plot, about to begin in chapter 3. Chapter 1 safely removed the former queen Vashti from the scene and introduced the impetuous, mercurial character of Ahasuerus. Chapter 2 introduced the Jewish heroine and hero, Esther and Mordecai; made Esther queen; installed Esther in the palace and Mordecai in the court; and indebted the king to Mordecai. Now, with all the characters in place and the setting prepared, the main narrative is about to begin.

---

86. See Fox, *Character and Ideology in the Book of Esther*, 38-39, for further references.

87. This type of ethnic loyalty is usually rewarded in the biblical text. See the story of Jael, who is never explicitly identified as an Israelite, in Judges 4. A counterexample is Ruth, who is praised for abandoning her people, the Moabites, and throwing in her lot with Israel.

88. Herodotus 3.125, 159; 4.43.

89. Herodotus 3.139-41.

90. Fox, *Character and Ideology in the Book of Esther*, 40. Clines, *The Esther Scroll*, 105, points out that this incident establishes Mordecai's loyalty before his conflict with Haman. Jon D. Levenson, *Esther*, OTL (Louisville: Westminster/John Knox, 1997) 65, brings to light the connections between this incident and the Joseph story.

REFLECTIONS

Mordecai appears in this vignette as a righteous man performing a good deed without the thought of reward. Even after the rebels are executed, Mordecai does not seem to expect a reward, nor does Esther request one for him. They simply do what is right and then go on about their business. This behavior will prove a sharp contrast to the later actions of Haman, who wants the reward without having done the good deed (6:6-9). The author, without being explicit, presents Mordecai and Esther to the reader as models of wise and righteous conduct.

ESTHER 3:1-15

HAMAN'S PLOT TO DESTROY THE JEWS

OVERVIEW

This section introduces the main antagonist and the main conflict. Haman the Agagite is "the enemy of the Jews," and his scheme is no less than genocide. From here the plot moves quickly to its denouement.

ESTHER 3:1-6, CONFLICT BETWEEN MORDECAI AND HAMAN

COMMENTARY

Verse 1 introduces the fourth main character, Haman the Agagite. An uncertain amount of time has passed; but if the events in these verses are followed quickly by the action in vv. 7-11, then we are now in the twelfth year of Ahasuerus's reign, and five years have passed since Esther became queen. The king has a new favorite, whom he has promoted to the top of the palace hierarchy. Irony comes into play again: Mordecai, the king's benefactor, is unrewarded, while Haman, who has, as far as we know, done nothing, is rewarded with the highest office in the land. Haman, like Mordecai in 2:5, is given a genealogy; and that genealogy is an ominous one for the Jews. Haman is an Agagite, a descendant of Agag, king of the Amalekites, the hereditary enemies of the Jews (Exod 17:8-16; Num 24:20). Saul's encounter with Agag caused him to lose the kingship (1 Sam 15:8-33). Thus Haman, the descendant of Agag, and Mordecai, the kinsman of Saul, are natural enemies. In case the reader does not perceive the ominous implication of Haman's ancestry, the versions supply various substitutes for the term "Agagite," all pointing in the same dark direction. Josephus describes Haman as an Amalekite, and thus an enemy of the entire Jewish nation. And Deut 25:17-19 pronounces a curse on the Amalekites, demanding that they be totally destroyed by the Israelites. The LXX translates the term in two different ways, first by Βουγαῖον (*Bougaion*), probably a corruption of האגגי (*hāʾăgāgî*), but also possibly related to the Persian *Bagohi*, rendered by Josephus as *Bagoses*, a name or title of a notorious Persian general in Jerusalem who desecrated the Temple.[91] The second term, "Macedonian," is unrelated to Agagite, but refers to Alexander the Great and his successors, who at various times during the Hellenistic period (when the LXX was translated; see Commentary on Addition F 11) oppressed the Jews. The AT also uses "Macedonian," but MSS 93a corrupts "Agagite" to "Gogite," thereby creating an allusion to Israel's "enemy from the north" in Ezekiel 38–39. What all these names and titles indicate is that no good can come to the Jews from Haman's promotion.

In fact, trouble starts immediately. The king orders that all members of the court bow down before Haman—in other words,

---

91. Josephus *Antiquities of the Jews* 11.297. See Sidnie A. White, "Bagoas," in *Anchor Bible Dictionary*, 6 vols., ed. D. N. Freedman (New York: Doubleday, 1992) 1:567. Karen H. Jobes, *The Alpha-Text of Esther*, 125, suggests a "phonetic wordplay" between the terms *bougaios* and *bagoas*. See also the appearance of the name "Bagoshe" (Aramaic) in *4QTales of the Persian Court*. See Crawford, "Has Esther Been Found at Qumran?, 307-25.

perform the ritual of proskynesis. Mordecai refuses to obey this ruling.

Mordecai's refusal to bow to Haman, like Vashti's refusal to appear before the king, is mysterious. Is it because he is Jewish? Some commentators have taken the final clause of v. 4, "for he had told them that he was a Jew," as referring to Mordecai's refusal to bow.[92] However, that clause comes too late in the grammatical structure to refer to Mordecai's refusal, and it makes no sense historically. Jews in similar situations bowed to their superiors (see, e.g., the sons of Jacob to Joseph, Gen 42:6), and there is no (Jewish) law against it. Further, Mordecai could not have functioned as a royal courtier had he made a general refusal to bow. Therefore, he must be refusing to bow to Haman in particular. The versions supply various reasons for this refusal: The LXX (Add. C 7) claims that Haman demanded *divine* honors, which Mordecai would not render. The Targum states that Haman wore an idol pinned to his breast; if Mordecai bowed down to him, he would be guilty of idolatry.[93] Various commentators have also speculated concerning the reason: Paton puts it down to Mordecai's arrogance and petty self-seeking,[94] but Fox points out that this interpretation does not correspond to Mordecai's portrayal elsewhere as a wise courtier.[95] However, it should be noted that Mordecai's actions are not those of a wise courtier; rather, he and his people are put in grave danger, from which they must be extricated by Esther. Camp notes, "Mordecai himself is depicted as proud and somewhat fanatical, refusing to bow before Haman, the king's favorite."[96] Thus Mordecai's refusal to bow before Haman, which sets in motion the main plot of the story, is left unexplained.[97]

Mordecai's fellow servants question him concerning his refusal and, unable to receive a satisfactory answer, finally report to Haman, "because he [Mordecai] had informed them that he was a Jew." The author implies that the other servants see this as a contest of wills between Haman the Agagite and Mordecai the Jew, and they pit the two against each other to see who will prevail. Again, the motive for their behavior is not clear. Are they hostile to Mordecai for reporting the eunuchs' plot or because he is a Jew? The answer is not clear, but the conflict has suddenly become more than personal.

Haman evidently had not noticed Mordecai's insult until then, but now that it has been brought to his attention, he is furious. The last time the word for "anger" (חמה *ḥēmâ*) appeared in the text, it referred to the king, and the consequence was the banishment of Vashti (1:12). Haman's fury does not bode well for Mordecai. However, personal revenge is not enough for Haman. After finding out Mordecai's ethnicity (which is not a secret, unlike Esther's), Haman decides to destroy all the Jews in the entire empire (which, according to 1:1, encompasses the then-known world). This implied racial hostility is brought out by the versions; as Josephus states, "for he naturally hated the Jews, because his own race, the Amalekites, had been destroyed by them."[98] Dommershausen notes that Haman's desire to wipe out all the Jews is a reversal of the holy war command in 1 Sam 15:3, thereby strengthening the argument that Haman is motivated by racial hostility.[99]

92. E.g., Paton, *Esther*, 196.
93. *Tar.* 1.
94. Paton, *Esther*, 213.
95. Fox, *Character and Ideology in the Book of Esther*, 43.
96. Claudia Camp, "The Three Faces of Esther: Traditional Woman, Royal Diplomat, Authenticator of Tradition," *Academy* 38 (1982) 20.

97. See White, "Esther: A Feminine Model for Jewish Diaspora," 169.
98. Josephus *Antiquities of the Jews* 11.212.
99. Dommershausen, *Die Estherrolle*, 62.

REFLECTIONS

The theme of racial hostility is emphasized in this chapter, particularly by the epithets given to the main characters: Agagite and Jew. This racial hostility allows a personal quarrel to become a national crisis. Haman seems to feel that Mordecai's insult is motivated by his Jewishness. He resolves, therefore, to wipe out the entire Jewish people, evidently assuming that all Jews would behave in a similar fashion. Generalizations such as these have fueled fires of ethnic and racial conflict in many parts of the world throughout history. The conflict in South Africa in the twentieth century serves as a good example of such thinking. The system of apartheid introduced in South Africa beginning in 1913 was based solely on race; the governing assumption was that persons of darker complexions were inferior to those of lighter ones. Archbishop Desmond Tutu denounced the evil of apartheid with these words:

> The Bible declares right at the beginning that human beings are created in the image and likeness of God. I showed why this fact endows each person with a unique and infinite value, a person whose very hairs are numbered. And what makes any human being valuable therefore is not any biological characteristic. No, it is the fact that he or she is created in the image of and likeness of God. Apartheid exalts a biological quality, which is a total irrelevancy, to the status of what determines the value, the worth of a human being. Why should skin color or race be any more useful as a criterion than, say, the size of one's nose? What has the size of my nose to do with whether I am intelligent? It has no more to do with my worth as a human being than the color of my eyes.[100]

Tutu explicitly states what the author of Esther implies: The oppression of people based on race or ethnic group is evil. Races and ethnic groups exist. But there is no reason, as we will see by the end of the book of Esther, that they cannot coexist peacefully and equitably.

100. Desmond Tutu, *The Rainbow People of God* (New York: Doubleday, 1994) 64.

ESTHER 3:7-11, HAMAN'S PLOT

COMMENTARY

3:7. This verse presents an explanation for the origin of the Festival of Purim, the ostensible reason for the writing of the book of Esther and the reason for its inclusion in the canon. The scene takes place in the month of Nisan, an ironic gesture on the part of the author, for Nisan (a Babylonian month name; the old Hebrew equivalent is אביב [*'ābîb*]) is the month of the Passover and the exodus, the festival of salvation for the Jews (Deut 16:1-8). Here, however, it foreshadows not salvation but destruction, for Haman is having פור (*pûr*) cast for him, evidently by Persian diviners. Pûr is a borrowing from Old Babylonian *pūrū*, meaning "stone" or "lot," which appears to refer to the stones thrown to determine an auspicious day. These lots were used in the ancient world to determine the will of the gods; the high priest in Israel cast Urim and Thummim to determine God's will (e.g., Exod 28:30; Num 27:21; 1 Sam 14:41). Haman is trying to determine a day and a month—but for what? The Hebrew is almost untranslatable, but the LXX attempts to make sense of it by supplying "so as to destroy the race of Mordecai" (both the NRSV and the NIV are heavily reliant on the LXX). It is also possible that Haman is trying to ascertain a lucky day to go to the king with his request. However, the text in later chapters seems to assume that Haman is determining an auspicious day to slaughter the Jews, for the month of Adar, where the lot falls, is the date set to carry out the massacre (the LXX supplies "the thirteenth day"). This verse, as garbled as it is, appears intrusive in its context and may be a later addition, intended to tie the Festival of Purim more firmly to the story of Mordecai and Haman.[101]

3:8-10. Verse 8 finds Haman before the king. Haman lays out his charge, constructing

101. See Moore, *Esther*, 37; Fox, *Character and Ideology in the Book of Esther*, 47. However, Bardtke, *Das Buch Esther*, 243-44, disagrees.

a story made up of truths, half-truths, and outright lies.[102] He says that Jews are "scattered" and "separated" among all the peoples of the empire. That is true, according to contemporary sources. Jews lived throughout the Persian Empire, but the Persian Empire historically was extremely tolerant of multi-ethnic diversity.[103] It is a half-truth that their laws are different from those of every other people, for the Jews keep the Torah, their own special set of commandments—but they also obey the laws of whatever country they are in. Finally, it is a lie that they do not keep the king's law; this is witnessed by the behavior of Esther and Mordecai, who scrupulously obey the Persian law, while not paying particular attention, at least on Esther's part, to Jewish law. Haman offers no proof for his accusations, which, as Fox points out, are the epitome of what would later be recognized as anti-Semitic rhetoric.[104] Nor does Ahasuerus ask for any. The king colludes with Haman's policy of "don't ask, don't tell." If he knows it is the Jews whom Haman wishes to destroy, he may recoil from killing people he knows, such as Mordecai the Jew, "who sits in the king's gate."[105] It is easier not to know, especially when Haman follows up his request for a death warrant with a huge bribe. Ten thousand talents is an enormous sum, probably the equivalent of 375 tons of silver; the annual income of the Persian king was only 14,560 talents.[106] Notice Haman's rhetorical skill in v. 9 in employing a passive construction—"let a decree be used"—rather than an active one—"let the king issue." In this way, Ahasuerus does not have to take responsibility for a genocide in his empire, and he will become substantially richer. The king has so far not responded to Haman, no questions, no protest. In v. 10 he does respond, with an action: He gives his signet ring, the symbol of royal authority, to Haman. This act gives Haman the power to do whatever he wants (cf. Gen 41:42, where Pharaoh gives his signet ring to Joseph). Haman is identified here for the first time as "the enemy of the Jews." What was implied by his ancestry is made clear by his actions: He is the enemy who will actively work for Jewish destruction in the midst of Gentile indifference and passivity, symbolized by the king.

3:11. Ahasuerus speaks for the first time. The NRSV gives an exact translation of a cryptic phrase in Hebrew: "the money is given to you." Does the king give the money back to Haman, thereby exonerating himself from the guilt of accepting a bribe? The NIV (following the LXX) certainly accepts that understanding: "keep the money." Moore translates, "Well, it's your money"—in other words, do with it as you will.[107] It seems unlikely that the king turned down the money; in 4:7 Mordecai tells Esther how much Haman paid for the destruction of the Jews, implying that the king accepted it. In 7:4, Esther declares that the Jews have been "sold" into destruction. Ahasuerus certainly has no qualms about handing this unknown people over to Haman; once again he has not asked about their identity or proof of their crimes. The king, therefore, is not an anti-Semite, as is Haman, but is simply thoughtless and lazy, characteristics that are just as dangerous to the Jews as is Haman's evil. Clines has noted a parallel between this episode and the Vashti episode: Both are cases of disobedience against a royal edict, and the royal advisers, Memucan/Haman, respond in a way completely out of proportion to the offense, while the king unquestioningly acquiesces to their advice.[108]

---

102. Fox, *Character and Ideology in the Book of Esther*, 47-48.
103. See, e.g., the Murashu archives from the fifth century BCE, which indicate that Jews owned land in the neighborhood of Nippur, while a Jewish garrison existed on the Egyptian island of Elephantine, also in the fifth century. The term "Judean" seems to be an ethnic, rather than a religious, designation at Elephantine. See M. Dandamayev, "Babylonia in the Persian Age," and Morton Smith, "Jewish Life in the Persian Period," in *The Cambridge History of Judaism*, Introduction: *The Persian Period*, ed. W. D. Davies and L. Finkelstein (Cambridge: Cambridge University Press, 1984).
104. Fox, *Character and Ideology in the Book of Esther*, 47.
105. Fox, *Character and Ideology in the Book of Esther*, 48.
106. Moore, *Esther*, 38.
107. Moore, *Esther*, 40.
108. David J. A. Clines, *Ezra, Nehemiah, Esther*, NCBC (Grand Rapids: Eerdmans, 1984) 295.

REFLECTIONS

The charges that Haman levels against the Jews are the same type of charges leveled against the Jews from the beginning of the diaspora until today. Difference is seen as either mysterious and thus dangerous to the majority culture, or as hostile to the host culture. Josephus, in first-century Rome, had to defend the Jews against the charge of *amixia*, or "non-mingling," in his work *Against Apion*. As early as 38 CE, there were anti-Jewish riots in Alexandria, a center of Hellenistic learning and culture. The history of Christianity is stained with anti-Semitism. The expulsion of Jews from England in 1290 and from Spain in 1492 are only two examples. Because the Jews are perceived as different from the Gentile (whether Christian or not) culture in which they live, they often have become the target of bigotry from the majority population. This bigotry can take the form of active hostility, like that of Haman, or passive indifference, like that of Ahasuerus. Most people choose the path of indifference, but the result is the same: the destruction of innocent human beings.

ESTHER 3:12-15, HAMAN'S PLOT IS CARRIED OUT

COMMENTARY

In this section, Haman sets the official wheels of the Persian Empire in motion to carry out his plot. The scribes of the king, official court functionaries, are called together. Again, we glimpse the vast bureaucracy of the Persian Empire, which must be opposed by two small individuals. To emphasize the official nature of what is being done, the author gives the date, the thirteenth of the first month, Nisan. This date is not accidental: Thirteen is an unlucky number in both Babylonian and Persian lore, while in the Jewish calendar, the fourteenth day of Nisan begins the Passover. Salvation minus one day equals destruction.[109] The language of v. 12 emphasizes that this is an edict of the king; it is written in the name of Ahasuerus and sealed with his signet ring (which he has given to Haman). The edict is sent to the satraps (a Persian loan word; satrapies were the largest geographical entities within the Persian Empire, which never had more than thirty-one);[110] the governors, who ruled over provinces and cities (e.g., Tattenai, the governor of the province "Beyond the River" in Ezra 5:3, 6; 6:6, 13); and the princes, who are leaders of ethnic groups (e.g., Sheshbazzar, the "prince of Judah" in Ezra 1:8). It is sent to every province, every people in their own language. Historically, Persian officialdom functioned in several languages: Persian, Aramaic, and Akkadian.[111] However, they did not cater to every small language pocket in the empire (cf. Ezra 6:2-5, where the decree of Cyrus is written in Aramaic, not Hebrew). Haman appears to be saturating the empire with his decree, another case of the author's ironic hyperbole.

Verse 13 gives the content of the decree sent throughout the empire by the efficient Persian postal system. The Hebrew piles up words of destruction: "to destroy," "to slay," "to annihilate." All Jews are to be destroyed—men, women, children, young, old—no one is exempt. And then, the final indignity: Their goods are to be plundered. This is both a foreshadowing of events to come and a reminiscence of the paradigmatic salvific event, the exodus. At the time of the exodus, when the Jews were saved, they took the goods of the Egyptians, who gave them voluntarily in order to be saved from destruction (Exod 12:33-36). The destruction is to take place on one day, the thirteenth of Adar, which is almost a year away. It is puzzling within the story that Haman waits a whole year to destroy the Jews. However, if the date of Purim was fixed and originally separate from the Esther story (see Introduction), and if the author wished to retain the allusion to

---

109. The practice of using significant numbers was common in the ancient world; e.g., the famous number 666 in Rev 13:18 signifies, among other things, the threefold lack of perfection (seven being a perfect number).

110. A. T. Olmstead, *The History of the Persian Empire* (Chicago: University of Chicago Press, 1948) 59.

111. E.g., the Behistun Inscription, erected by Xerxes' father, Darius, which celebrates, in Perisan, Elamite, and Akkadian, Darius's victory over the magi at the beginning of his reign. This inscription was copied into Aramaic at Elephantine, for the use of the Jewish mercenaries there. See Olmstead, *The History of the Persian Empire*, 116-18.

the exodus by setting his story in the month of Nisan, then the somewhat artificial gap may be explained. Verse 14, which calls on everyone to be ready, presumes that people would be willing, even eager, to destroy the Jews. The riders of the postal system "hasten" out (cf. chap. 1, where the decree concerning Vashti is sent, but without the same urgency), and the decree is published in the citadel of Susa. The decree is called a דת (*dāt*) as in 1:15, which again emphasizes its royal, official character. This is not simply a desire of Haman's but the law of the land. Once again, as in chap. 1, a personal slight has been interpreted as a threat to the stability of the ruling regime and is turned into an empire-wide crisis. This time, however, it is not humorous, but deadly serious.[112]

112. See Fox, *Character and Ideology in the Book of Esther*, 56.

The reactions of three groups—the king, Haman, and the people of Susa—are contrasted at the end of v. 15: The king and Haman sit down to a feast (banquet #5, see Fig. 1: "The Banquets in Esther," p. 4), but the city (as opposed to the citadel) of Susa "was confused." Haman is triumphant, and the king is indifferent; so far the Gentiles present no hope for the Jews. However, the common inhabitants of Susa are confused; one can assume that they do not understand the reason for the decree and may be reluctant to carry it out. There is hope for the Jews here. This accords with the book of Esther's generally more positive portrayal of Gentiles than in later books, such as 3 Maccabees. Gentiles as a whole are not bent on destruction of the Jews, although individuals may be, and thus vigilance is always necessary.

REFLECTIONS

1. The responses of the three groups to the edict of destruction—triumph, indifference, and bewilderment—mirror the reactions of people today to acts of genocide throughout the world: triumph on the part of the perpetrators; indifference by most people not directly affected; and bewilderment from people sensitive enough to be appalled by the violence but powerless to do anything about it. In the book of Esther, all three reactions lead to the same result: destruction for the victims. Action is called for—action to save—but from whence the action will come is unclear.

2. The theme of power returns: Haman now has power. Unlike the foolish Ahasuerus, who is unable to wield the power he supposedly has, Haman proves quite competent in using it. Although power is now being used, it is not being used wisely. The biblical tradition approves of power only when it is used to govern well; such was Solomon's request in 1 Kings 29. Therefore, Haman's power, according to biblical norms, should not last long.

ESTHER 4:1-17

MORDECAI TURNS TO ESTHER

OVERVIEW

The focus of the story now turns to Esther and Mordecai. The fate of the Jews hangs on their courage and resourcefulness, especially that of Esther. It is striking that the author continues to avoid any mention of God, even in this moment of extreme danger for the Jewish people. It is righteous human action that must save the day.

ESTHER 4:1-3, MORDECAI'S REACTION TO HAMAN'S DECREE

COMMENTARY

The edict has been published in Susa, but Mordecai knows more; he knows *all* that Haman has done, as will be clear later in the chapter. How he knows this is not stated, any more than how he learned of the plot of the eunuchs in chap. 2. Mordecai's immediate response to the news of Haman's decree is shock and grief. He enacts the typical gestures of mourning: tearing his clothes (Gen 37:29, Reuben for Joseph); putting on sackcloth, a rough cloth made of some type of coarse material such as goat hair (Gen 37:34, Jacob for Joseph); putting ashes on his head (2 Sam 13:19, Tamar after her rape by Amnon); and weeping loudly and publicly (a function usually performed by women, but see 2 Sam 18:33, where David weeps over Absalom). The LXX adds the phrase "an innocent people is condemned to death!" All these gestures are usually reserved for mourning over the dead; it is as if Mordecai is mourning in advance over his own death and the deaths of his people. However, these gestures can also be efficacious in turning away divine wrath. For example, when the people of Nineveh hear God's pronouncement of doom from the mouth of Jonah, they tear their clothes and sit in sackcloth and ashes, for which gestures of repentance God forgives them (Jonah 3:6-9). However, the Ninevites also fast and pray, religious gestures that are not performed by Mordecai (although the Jews do fast in v. 3). This is in keeping with the rest of the book of Esther, from which obvious religious gestures are omitted (see Introduction). Therefore, Mordecai's actions seem more pessimistic, almost hopeless. One wonders whether Mordecai is simply grief-stricken or whether he might also be guilt-stricken, since it is his actions that have brought disaster upon the Jews. However, Mordecai nowhere in the Hebrew text expresses any guilt feelings (but see LXX Add. C, where he vigorously denies the unstated charge that his pride has caused destruction), nor does the author ever ascribe any guilt to him. Mordecai's gestures are mirrored by all the Jews throughout the empire when word of the decree reaches them. Again, the motivation for their actions is not stated. The obvious motive, petitioning God to act on their behalf, is glaringly absent.[113] In v. 2, Mordecai is unable to enter the palace dressed as a mourner, possibly because he is considered ritually unclean, although there is no extra-biblical evidence to support this custom in the Persian court. (See Reflections at 4:4-17.)

---

113. Several commentators have suggested that v. 3 should be placed immediately after 3:15 (see OL), but the verse serves a clear literary purpose here: By having the Jews echo the actions of Mordecai, the idea that Mordecai is the representative Jew in the story is emphasized.

ESTHER 4:4-17, DIALOGUE BETWEEN ESTHER AND MORDECAI

COMMENTARY

4:4-6. After a marked absence, Esther reappears in the narrative. For the first time, we have a scene in which she is the central character. Esther as queen has her own entourage of maids and eunuchs who keep her informed about the goings-on in the palace. They also know that Mordecai is her relative; therefore, they must know that she, like Mordecai, is a Jew, and yet her identity remains a secret from the king. The maids and eunuchs now tell her what Mordecai is doing. Her response comes in the form of an unusual Hebrew word, ותתחלחל (*wattithalhal*, "and she writhed"), which occurs in this conjugation only here in Esther. In the active conjugations it means "to dance," but in the reflexive sense it means "to writhe in anguish" and can be connected with the pain of childbirth. For example, the verb occurs in poetic texts, one concerning Sarah as the mother of Israel (Isa 51:2) and one portraying Yahweh as "bringing forth" Israel in travail (Deut 32:18). Mordecai's behavior seems to cause Esther intense distress, and she rushes to respond to news of her cousin's state, but not by inquiring the reason for his actions, as one might expect. Instead, she sends him clothes in place of his sackcloth, which he refuses. Her motivation is open to question. Does she wish to relieve his distress?[114] If so, fresh clothes will not help, since Mordecai's outward appearance is merely a reflection of his inner turmoil. Does she wish to enable him to enter the palace, since those dressed in sackcloth are not allowed in? Or does she simply want him to stop his embarrassing behavior? Only after he refuses her solution does she send Hathach the eunuch to find out why Mordecai is behaving this way. Hathach, a new character, appears to be one of the palace eunuchs assigned to Esther. She seems to rely on his discretion, for the ensuing dialogue is intimate, even confrontational, yet conducted entirely through a third party. No one, neither Esther nor her servants, seems yet to know about Haman's decree, even though it has been posted in the citadel of Susa (3:15). This indicates the kind of sheltered life Esther leads inside the harem and her dependence on the discretion and loyalty of her maids and eunuchs. The dialogue between Mordecai and Hathach takes place in the main city square (a place often associated with rites of mourning; see Jer 48:37-38), in full view of the public. Mordecai, it would seem, is not at this point concerned about discretion.

4:7-8. In these verses, Mordecai demonstrates that he knows the secrets of the palace. He knows the details of Haman's bargain with the king, including the bribe of ten thousand talents. He even has a copy of the decree, which he sends to Esther. Interestingly, the assumption is that both Esther and Mordecai are literate, a fact that might go unnoticed by the modern reader. Mordecai also has a plan of action, which he does not hesitate to communicate to Esther, since, as was stated in 2:20, "Esther obeyed Mordecai just as when she was brought up by him." He assumes that she will obey him now and repair promptly to the king to undo the threat Haman has posed to the Jews. In fact, in the LXX, Mordecai recalls Esther's obligation to him: "Remembering your humble station when you were supported by my hand. . . . Call upon the Lord, and speak to the king concerning us, and save us from death" (the LXX's mention of prayer is typical of that version's attempt to remedy the Hebrew's silence concerning God and religious practice).

4:9-17. The dialogue continues in this passage. Mordecai has assumed Esther's obedience to his command in v. 8, so her first response is something of a shock: She refuses to fall in with his plan. Esther has now been queen for five years and is steeped in palace etiquette (which she has already demonstrated by sending Mordecai clothes in v. 4), and her first response to Mordecai indicates that she cannot obey his command for

---

114. See White, "Esther: A Feminine Model for Jewish Diaspora," 169.

reasons of palace protocol. *Everyone* (including presumably Mordecai) knows that to appear before the king unsummoned is to court instant death, and she has not been summoned for thirty days. Therefore, she implies, it is obvious that she cannot carry out Mordecai's plan. It is unclear whether Esther's statement is historically accurate. Josephus accepts it as such, but claims that it applies only to the royal family (to avert the danger of a palace coup?) and supplies the colorful note that men with axes surround the king on his throne to prevent unauthorized access.[115] However, Herodotus is ambivalent on the subject. According to him, in the tradition of the Medes, unannounced entry before the king was unlawful,[116] but a petitioner might send in a message and request an audience. Esther does not even suggest doing this, leading to the conclusion that this may be a convenient plot device on the part of the author. It is part of the irony of the book that the first queen, Vashti, is banished for refusing to appear before the king when summoned, while the second queen, Esther, is asked to risk death by appearing before the king unsummoned. Also, the fact that Esther has not been summoned for thirty days indicates that her influence is at a low ebb, and she has no reason to believe that her intervention would be efficacious.

Many biblical leaders—for example Moses (Exod 4:10-13), Barak (Judg 4:8), and Jeremiah (Jer 1:6), all male—attempted to excuse themselves when called upon for drastic action on behalf of the Jews.[117] The author all but abandons the presence of the go-between to emphasize the importance and intensity of this dialogue. Mordecai is not prepared to excuse Esther so easily. He takes a severe tone, first reminding her that she is Jewish and that the decree applies to her as well. She is not safe in the palace, for it is from the palace that the danger emanates. Then, in v. 14, he threatens her: If she does not act, the Jews will receive succor elsewhere, but she and her family (which means Mordecai) will perish. The expression "relief and deliverance will rise for the Jews from another quarter" has excited much commentary, for it may contain an oblique reference to God. The AT, in fact, reads, "God will be their aid and their deliverance," while Josephus and the Targums have taken "quarter" in their MT source as a reference to God.[118] This is a plausible interpretation, but it may also simply refer to another human[119] who will help instead of the unwilling Esther. In any case, there seems to be an assumption that something, probably divine providence, is working to save the Jews, whether directly or through human action, and that Esther should choose to cooperate with it. This saves the book from the charge of irreligiosity; God works in the background, through human action. In fact, Mordecai implies ("who knows?") that Esther's ascent to the throne was providential, in order to save the Jews; so if she does not act, she will be disobeying God's unspoken plan.[120] Mordecai, even though he is usually obedient to Persian law, believes that in a conflict between Persian law and the Jewish people, Esther's loyalty must reside with her people.

Esther responds swiftly to Mordecai's pleas. Now that she has been persuaded to act on behalf of the Jews, she quickly comes up with her own plan and carries it out. She begins to give commands, not only to her servants but to Mordecai as well; and she expects to be obeyed. All the Jews in Susa are to gather and observe a three-day fast, while Esther and her maids (it is unlikely that Esther's maids are Jewish) also fast. Fasting, which is an act of petition (2 Sam 12:16-17; Jonah 3:7), is the only overtly religious act in the book of Esther. (Ironically, if the fast did take place, it would have coincided with the beginning of Passover, in direct violation of Jewish law, which forbids fasting on Passover [Exod 12:1-10].) However, since God is not mentioned (although the AT explicitly states that the fasting is directed toward God), its religious character is muted. Thematically, the fast stands in direct contrast to the banquets that occur throughout the book and, in

---

115. Josephus *Antiquities of the Jews* 11.204.
116. Herodotus 1.99; 3.72, 77, 84, 118, 140.
117. Fox suggests that these figures attempted to excuse themselves "out of feelings of personal unworthiness," rather than from Esther's concern for "personal safety." See Fox, *Character and Ideology in the Book of Esther*, 62. However, their protests contain a strong element of avoidance of danger, or at least personal discomfort.
118. Josephus *Antiquities of the Jews* XI.227; Tar. 1; Tar. 2.
119. So Fox, *Character and Ideology in the Book of Esther*, 63, and Clines, *Ezra, Nehemiah, Esther*, 302.
120. Levenson states that the phrase "who knows" "prefaces a guarded hope that penitential practice may induce God to relent from his harsh decree, granting deliverance where destruction had been expected (cf. 2 Sam 12:22, Joel 2:14, and Jonah 3:9)." See Levenson, *Esther*, 81.

particular, to Haman's feast with Ahasuerus before the fast and to Esther's banquets with the king and Haman after the fast. After the fast, Esther will go to the king, although she again reminds Mordecai that it is against the law for her to do so unbidden. However, she is reconciled to the danger and makes one of the most poignant statements in the book, "If I perish, I perish." Esther's status, even after having been queen for five years, remains precarious and her relationship with her husband is still uncertain. Esther's position as a woman in a male court is analogous to that of the Jews in the Gentile world, with the possibility of danger ever present under the surface. Esther has no guarantee that she will be successful. However, at this point she has taken responsibility for her own fate and has put the welfare of her people first, an action of which the author resoundingly approves. Mordecai is also satisfied; he leaves to carry out Esther's orders.

Mordecai's action in v. 17 signals the radical transformation the character of Esther has undergone in the last three chapters. When Esther was introduced in chap. 2, she was an orphan girl with nothing to recommend her but beauty of face and form. She was passive and obedient, obeying Mordecai, obeying Hegai, and "pleasing" everyone around her. She charmed the king, not least, one supposes, because she was pliant, unlike the spirited Vashti. Even after her marriage, she continued to obey Mordecai. She is not a character from whom we should expect great things. Now, however, she is transformed. She does not obey orders; she gives them. She is active, a risk-taker, not passively compliant. She is a queen, a figure of royal authority, such that even Mordecai hurries to obey her. Now she is a character in whom the reader can trust. Esther has taken charge, and we can rest assured that the danger to the Jews will be averted, no matter what pitfalls lie ahead.

REFLECTIONS

The actions of Esther in chapter 4 present us with an all-too-human portrait of a person's response when faced with a demand for action in a situation that she neither created nor asked for—a resounding "No!" Often life locates us in situations where we are capable of taking action on behalf of some oppressed person or people, but with possible negative consequences for ourselves. Esther's consequences are clear and absolute: She faces death. The consequences for us may be less absolute but nonetheless devastating—loss of job, family rupture, embarrassment, to name only a few. It is difficult at such times to overcome the self-centeredness of our everyday lives in order to discern God's call. In chapter 4, the writer acknowledges the difficulty of discerning that call. Mordecai does not know that Esther can or will be able to help—his use of "who knows?" and "perhaps" recognizes the uncertainty of the situation. But Mordecai is convinced of two things: Help will come for the Jews from somewhere, whether from God or from humans, and Esther, given her favorable circumstances, must act. If she does not, she (and her family) will be held responsible for her cowardice. This statement more than anything else in the book of Esther implies belief in the activity of divine providence, even though God remains unmentioned. The author of Esther has captured in a short two verses the dilemma of the average believer: How does one find the courage and faith to do what is right in the face of divine and human ambiguity? Esther's example may give us courage to reach beyond ourselves and act on behalf of others, placing our trust in God.

ESTHER 5:1–8:2

HAMAN'S PLANS ARE THWARTED

ESTHER 5:1-8, ESTHER ACTS: THE FIRST BANQUET

COMMENTARY

The language of this scene is laconic, almost anticlimactic (cf. the LXX's Add. D, which presents a much more dramatic and moving scenario). These eight verses are carefully structured, in a request/grant of request/offer form (ABCA´B´C´A) designed to create maximum suspense in the reader.[121]

5:1. After her three-day fast, Esther clothes herself in "royalty" (מלכות *malkût*). Although clothes are meant, the author's word choice conveys that her royal status is no longer bestowed on her from outside, but has become a personal quality. In contrast to Vashti, who refused to wear the royal crown before the king, Esther makes sure that she is adorned with all the proper paraphernalia before approaching Ahasuerus. One is reminded of her first night with the king, when she took only what Hegai advised her—advice that proved to be correct. We should admire Esther; if she is forced to play her hand within the male power structure of the palace, she is determined to play it well. After dressing appropriately, Esther sets out for the throne room, located in the inner palace, evidently some distance from her own apartments. The narrator, in marked contrast to Add. D and Josephus,[122] gives us no insight into Esther's inner state; she simply walks to the throne room.

5:2-5. Although in chap. 4 Esther had informed Mordecai that her life would be at risk if she approached the king, when the king sees her she immediately wins his approbation, and he extends the scepter to her. As in chap. 2, when she first meets Ahasuerus, Esther once more actively "gains" (נשאה *nāśě'â*) his favor (the NIV's "he was pleased" is misleading, for it takes away the active nature of Esther). Esther touches the head of the scepter, acknowledging the king's favor. She is given the title "queen" several times in this section, both by the narrator and by the king, emphasizing her elevated and favored position. However, if she loses that favor, her fate could be the same as Vashti's—and the Jews will be destroyed. She is playing a dangerous game.

Ahasuerus realizes that something urgent must have made Esther risk her life, for he immediately asks what her request is and promises to grant it. The phrase "up to half of the kingdom" is formulaic,[123] and both he and Esther know it is not to be taken literally; however, he certainly does mean to encourage her. We now expect Esther to fall on her knees and beg for the lives of her people, but instead she invites the king to a dinner party! Her request may seem anticlimactic, but in reality it is part of a clever stratagem. In the society of the ancient Near East, as indeed in Middle Eastern societies today, one never makes one's major request right away. Rather, through a series of minor requests that are granted, the road is paved for the major request. Therefore, as Clines points out, Esther's invitation is the first exchange in a play of courtesies.[124] By getting Ahasuerus to accept her hospitality, Esther obligates him to her and makes it more likely that he will grant her next, larger request. The inclusion of Haman is likewise strategic: She will have

---

121. Fox, *Character and Ideology in the Book of Esther*, 69-70.
122. Josephus *Antiquities of the Jews* XI.235.
123. See Herodotus 9.109; see also Mark 6:23.
124. Clines, *The Esther Scroll*, 304.

her enemy in her own territory and under obligation to her, rather than as a free agent in the court. The king, by granting her request (v. 5), thereby obligates himself to her and realizes that he is doing so.

5:6-8. The banquet scene, as a recurring motif, signals to the reader that something important is about to happen. The king and Haman are safely ensconced in Esther's apartments, and they have reached the drinking course, which we know from chap. 1 puts the king in an expansive mood. Ahasuerus once more asks Esther for her request, thereby indicating that he realizes the dinner invitation was not the real request. Now is surely the time for Esther to plead for the Jews, but instead she asks Ahasuerus to a second banquet! This second banquet is puzzling to readers and commentators alike. Verse 7, Esther's reply to Ahasuerus's questions, forms an ellipsis: "And Esther replied, and she said, 'My request and my petition. . . .'" Is she hesitating?[125] Perhaps weighing her chances for success? Her language in v. 8 is elaborate and courtly, implying a major request, but culminates only in an invitation to a second banquet. Cazelles sees this as evidence for two separate sources, but there is no second plot or telling of the story to support this.[126] Rather, by looking at the language of v. 8, it becomes clear that Esther is being very careful to make it impossible for the king not to grant her request. First, she flatters him ("if I have found favor"; notice that Esther gives the credit for her favor to Ahasuerus, although the narrator consistently gives it to her). Next she appeals to his judgment ("if it is good to the king"). Finally she delivers the closing punch, "to give my request and to carry out my petition." The king will prove his favor by coming to her banquet the next day, where she will finally "do as the king asks"—that is, make her petition. In other words, by coming to the second banquet, the king promises to do whatever she asks.[127] She has successfully backed him into a corner, and he has allowed it to happen.

The continued presence of Haman, whose voice is noticeably silent, is mysterious. The rabbis give various reasons for his attendance, such as that Esther was acting in accordance with Prov 25:21 ("If your enemies are hungry, give them bread to eat; and if they are thirsty, give them water to drink" [NRSV]), that she was still keeping her Jewishness secret, that she wished to make the king jealous, or that she was setting a trap for Haman and wanted him on hand.[128] Modern commentators, too, have tried to discern Esther's motive, theorizing that she wanted to lull Haman into a false sense of security, that she wanted to make the king jealous, or that she was trying to force the king to choose between her and Haman.[129] It seems most likely that Esther wishes to neutralize Haman and preclude counteraction on his part by having him present for her petition, which she now has gotten the king to promise to grant. So far, things seem to be going entirely Esther's way, but the narrator is about to remind us that the danger has not yet passed.

---

125. See P. Haupt, "Critical Notes on Esther," *AJSL* 24 (1907–8) 97-186, esp. 140.
126. Cazelles, "Note sur la composition du rouleau d'Esther," 27.
127. Clines, *The Esther Scroll*, 305.
128. For a good discussion of the rabbinic commentators, see Fox, *Character and Ideology in the Book of Esther*, 72.
129. See Moore, *Esther*, 56, for complete references.

REFLECTIONS

Here, for the first time, we see power exercised by a Jewish character. Esther, as was noted in chap. 2, has three disadvantages in the power game: She is a woman, she is Jewish, and she is an orphan. However, her exercise of power marks the first time in the book that power has been used wisely, for a legitimate end: the deliverance of the Jews. Although the author of Esther does not, as usual, mention God, the reader should recall that in biblical tradition God does use powerless women to carry out divine purposes. One thinks of Ruth the Moabite, who becomes the ancestor of the great King David (Ruth 4:13-22), and Mary of Nazareth, who, in Luke 1:46-48, states,

"My soul magnifies the Lord, and my spirit rejoices in God my Savior, for he has looked with favor on the lowliness of his servant" (NRSV).

ESTHER 5:9-14, HAMAN BUILDS A GALLOWS FOR MORDECAI

COMMENTARY

Although the narrator told us nothing about Esther's inner state when she appeared before the king, he fully reveals Haman's state of mind as he leaves Esther's first banquet. Verse 9a shows that Haman has reached the pinnacle of his glory, and he knows it. But his reaction to Mordecai's refusal to honor him is entirely out of proportion to the slight (note that Mordecai has returned to his customary station and mode of behavior). Haman, like Ahasuerus, the other Gentile male in the story, is ruled by his emotions; the phrase "good of heart" recalls Ahasuerus's emotional state in 1:10, which had disastrous consequences for Vashti. The female characters and the Jewish characters are more pragmatic and sensible (Mordecai allows his emotions to escape publicly only once (4:1), and Esther only after her personal danger is past (8:3); they are, therefore, ultimately successful.[130] However, in v. 10, Haman "restrains himself" and, once in his own house, gathers together his friends and family. This is the first mention of the Agagite's family, and it emphasizes the threat that Haman poses to the Jews: Not only is he himself a threat, but his heirs are as well, as all Amalekites are enemies to the Jews.

Mordecai's behavior in v. 9 is enigmatic. He has, presumably, carried out Esther's command concerning the fast and has once again taken up his court position. He continues his seemingly reckless behavior toward Haman; indeed, the narrator emphasizes this fact by using the words "rise" (קם *qām*) and "tremble" (זע *zāʿ*) to indicate Mordecai's continued defiance of Haman. Is Mordecai so convinced of Esther's success? As Moore points out, Mordecai is acting in a "needlessly rash" way.[131] It seems questionable whether Mordecai will even live until Esther's next banquet.

Indeed, that is Haman's purpose in calling his friends and family together. First, he indulges in some boasting, recalling his wealth (which must be vast, since in 3:9 he promised Ahasuerus 10,000 talents), his many sons,[132] and his honor from the king. Finally, he mentions the capstone: He alone dines privately with the king and queen. It is clear that Haman has no idea that Esther is Jewish or that she is related to Mordecai. Esther has successfully dissembled, and that will prove to be Haman's undoing.

Everything he recounts should make Haman ecstatic; however, he gets no pleasure from any of it ("all this does me no good") so long as Mordecai continues to function in the palace. The emphasis in v. 13 is placed on Mordecai the *Jew*, reminding the reader that this is not simply a personal quarrel, but an ethnic conflict with far greater consequences. What is Haman to do?

Zeresh, Haman's wife, comes up with a solution. Zeresh is a new character, another female playing a typical role: that of wife. Like the other females in the book, she thinks independently and leads the weaker Haman into action in response to her suggestions. She gives him the solution to his dilemma; his other (male) advisers, appearing as an afterthought in the sentence structure, merely acquiesce to her suggestion. This is exquisite irony on the part of the author, who began the tale with the unenforceable decree that "every man should be master in his own house" (1:22).

---

130. The "wrath of Haman" is a well-known negative example in later periods. For example, Dante, in *The Purgatorio*, uses Haman as an example of wrath in the Fourth Cornice, the "Reign of Wrath": "Next, down like rain, a figure crucified fell into my high fantasy, his face fierce and contemptuous even as he died. Nearby him great Ahasuerus stood, Esther his wife, and the just Mordecai whose word and deed were always one in good." Dante, *The Purgatorio*, trans. John Ciardi (London: New English Library, 1957) 179.

131. Moore, *Esther*, 60. Targum I makes it even more rash by having Mordecai taunt Haman.

132. According to Herodotus 1.136, the Persians valued having many sons, as did the Jews.

Zeresh's solution is a simple one—get rid of Mordecai! Haman was so busy plotting his grandiose revenge on all the Jews that he failed to find a solution to his immediate problem: continued disrespect by Mordecai. Again, a female character, even one on the enemy's side, proves the more astute and sensible thinker. Once Mordecai is out of the picture, Haman can freely enjoy all the rewards of his position, including the second banquet with the queen. The size of the gallows is part of the author's ironic hyperbole; "fifty cubits high" would be (as the NIV has it) approximately seventy-five feet. The language implies hanging, although Levenson, Clines, and others argue that this gallows is instead a pole for impaling the victim.[133] Haman finds the scheme good and arranges for the gallows to be made. In spite of Esther's recent success, things continue to look grim for Mordecai and the Jews. Haman still has the power to act against them.

133. Levenson, *Esther*, 93; Clines, *Ezra, Nehemiah, Esther*, 306.

Reflections

In this chapter in particular the influence from the wisdom tradition is strong, and the contrast between Esther and Haman is instructive. Esther has become the model of the wise courtier. From the beginning of the story, she has heeded the advice of others. She has acted as the Proverbs suggest: "Fools think their own way is right, but the wise listen to advice" (Prov 12:15 NRSV). She is careful in her speech: "Those who guard their mouths preserve their lives; those who open wide their lips come to ruin" (Prov 13:3 NRSV). And she does not antagonize those in power: "A king's wrath is a messenger of death, and whoever is wise will appease it" (Prov 16:14 NRSV). Rather, she manipulates the king into agreeing to her request in advance, much like the "wise woman of Tekoa" does to David in 2 Sam 14:4-17. She epitomizes the saying of Ecclesiastes: "Better is the end of a thing than its beginning; the patient in spirit are better than the proud in spirit" (7:8 NRSV). Haman, on the other hand, with his anger and pride, is the living example of the proverbial fool: "A fool gives full vent to anger, but the wise quietly holds it back," "A person's pride will bring humiliation, but one who is lowly in spirit will obtain honor," and "Better to be poor and walk in integrity, than to be crooked in one's ways even though rich" (Prov 29:11, 23; 28:6 NRSV). Finally, Haman should be reminded, "Do not boast about tomorrow, for you do not know what a day may bring" (Prov 27:1 NRSV).

To anyone familiar with the wisdom tradition, Haman's downfall seems more and more assured. It is not difficult to realize whom we are meant to emulate. Esther has, indeed, become a model through her wise conduct, not only for the diaspora Jews, but also for the contemporary reader who may have to work within a system that often rewards unethical behavior. The book of Esther reminds us that even when God appears to be absent (not even mentioned by name!), God can be most present, working through willing followers.

ESTHER 6:1-11, HAMAN'S HUMILIATION

Commentary

6:1-5. Esther's plan is proceeding, and Haman's plot against Mordecai is prepared when something happens that nobody could have predicted. The king is gripped by insomnia and orders that the royal records be read to him. Is it mere coincidence that the king cannot sleep, or is it divine providence? The Hebrew text leaves the question open, but the LXX, the AT, and Josephus make it very clear that God caused the king's sleeplessness.[134] This motif of royal sleeplessness, followed by some dramatic incident, also appears in Dan 6:18 and 3 Esdr 3:3. The "book of the remembrances of the things of the days" is the royal annals, mentioned also in 2:23. The Persian Empire, like most bureaucracies, kept vast archives that could be consulted as the need arose. For example, in Ezra 6:1-5 Darius searches the royal archives to discover the decree of Cyrus concerning the Temple in Jerusalem. So when the annals are read to him, Ahasuerus hears the passage concerning Mordecai's life-saving deed, recounted in 2:21-23. Is it coincidence that this particular passage is read? Once again, the MT does not say. Mordecai's lack of reward for his good deed, reported in v. 3, reflects badly on the king and must be remedied. The Persian emperors often bestowed the special title *orosangai*, "benefactor of the king," on someone as a reward for good deeds.[135] Mordecai, however, has received neither title nor reward. In fact, what should have been his has gone to Haman, who, as far as the text reveals, has done nothing to deserve his honors.

The king, who is incapable of doing anything without the advice of others, inquires concerning who is in the court. Presumably, it is very early, the end of the king's sleepless night. Again, is it coincidence or providence that Haman, overly eager to exact revenge on Mordecai, is in the courtyard? The text leaves it to the reader to decide. Haman, like Esther (5:1), is "standing" in the courtyard, waiting to be received by the king. The chapter will consistently draw attention to the contrast between Esther's audience with the king and that of Haman.

6:6. A series of what Dommershausen and Fox have termed "multiple silences" now begins:[136] The king does not say who is to be honored; Haman does not know it is Mordecai; the king does not know that Haman and Mordecai are enemies; and Haman does not tell the king the real situation. Add to this Esther's silence concerning her Jewishness and her relation to Mordecai, and Haman is caught in a trap of his own making. His ego will bring about his own humiliation. Indeed, the jaws of the trap are beginning to close now. The author takes great delight in Haman's egocentricity and subsequent humiliation; we are called upon to sit back and chuckle with him.

6:7-10. The king, in his question to Haman, uses the expression "the man whom the king delights to honor." This phrase, an ironic foreshadowing for both Haman and Mordecai, will be repeated by Haman four times in his reply. He presumes it is he, although he has done nothing to deserve praise. When he begins his reply in v. 7, he repeats the phrase, savoring it. This creates an anacoluthon, indicating a pause for thought, such as Esther used in 5:7.[137] The contrast is instructive, however; Esther uses the pause to create the illusion of humility ("if I have won the king's favor"), while Haman's pause is followed by his grandiloquent plan. Haman's eloquence in vv. 8-9 is extraordinary, for what he is requesting is no less than royal honors for himself. The honors he requests (cf. the LXX and Josephus)[138] are modeled on those given to Joseph in Gen 41:42-43, where Joseph receives linen garments, rides in the second royal chariot, and is hailed wherever he goes. However, again the contrast is significant: Joseph's honor is deserved, while Haman's imagined honor is not. The royal clothing reflects status and could be worn only by those entitled to it; Esther puts on "royalty" when she goes unsummoned to the king (5:1). The giving of royal clothes may reflect genuine Persian custom; Xerxes' daughter-in-law Artaynte requests, and gets, from the infatuated monarch a special robe made for him by Queen Amestris. This request later results in tragedy for Artaynte, much as it does for Haman.[139] The royal horse could be ridden only by the king. The crown on the horse has given trouble to commentators (some have assumed that a crown the king had worn must be meant), but seems to

---

134. Josephus, with his flair for the melodramatic, states: "But God mocked Haman's wicked hopes; and knowing what was to happen, he rejoiced at the event, for that night he deprived the king of sleep" (*Antiquities of the Jews* XI.247). *4QTales of the Persian Court* has a similar scene, but "the temper of the king was stretched."
135. Herodotus 8.85.
136. Dommershausen, *Die Estherrolle*, 86; Fox, *Character and Ideology in the Book of Esther*, 78.

137. An anacoluthon is a syntactical inconsistency or incoherence within a sentence. The deliberate use of the construction creates "space" in a sentence.
138. Josephus *Antiquities of the Jews* XI.254-255.
139. Herodotus 9.110-11.

be solved by Assyrian reliefs showing horses wearing tall pointed headdresses (assuming the custom remained the same in Persia).[140] The "man whom the king delights to honor" is to be robed and set on the horse by one of the "princes of the king, the nobles," probably a member of the seven noble Persian families referred to in chap. 1, whom the upstart Haman has displaced. Finally, this noble is to proclaim to the entire city the honor given to the man by the king. This is an unusually high honor Haman has concocted!

As he has done before, the king immediately and without reflection accepts the advice; the trap is sprung on Haman. This literary device of the author's resembles that of 2 Sam 12:1-7 and 14:1-17, where David equally quickly responds to advice; there, however, the trap is sprung on David himself, and he is caught in his own web. Here Haman, not the king, has woven the web of his own downfall. The author has turned what was probably a familiar type of tale on its head. It is Mordecai who is to be honored, not Haman. What is more, the king calls him Mordecai the *Jew*, heaping humiliation upon Haman. This also indicates that the king does not connect the edict of destruction he so blithely approved with the Jews, another example of the "multiple silences" of the text.

6:11. Haman obeys the king. The report of his action mirrors what Haman says in vv. 8-9, but very laconically; and we do not get any insight into Haman's emotions or Mordecai's reaction to this extraordinary event.[141] As before, the Greek tradition attempts to remedy this. The AT adds:

And Haman said to Mordecai, "Take off the sackcloth!" And Mordecai was troubled, like one who is dying; and in distress he took off the sackcloth. But then he put on the splendid garments, and he thought he beheld an omen, and his heart was to the Lord; and he was speechless.[142]

Josephus tells us that Haman was "confounded in his mind" and "in tears."[143] The rabbis add the interesting note that Haman's daughter, seeing Haman and Mordecai from her roof and supposing that Haman was riding and Mordecai leading him, emptied her chamber pot on Haman's head. When she discovered what she had done, she killed herself by jumping from the roof.[144] All these comments, however, are additions to the terse account of the Hebrew.

---

140. See Moore, *Esther*, 65.
141. Bernhard W. Anderson, "The Book of Esther," *IB*, 12 vols. (Nashville: Abingdon, 1954) 3:860, argues that the author omits any dialogue between Mordecai and Haman because he is more interested in plot than character. Fox, *Character and Ideology in the Book of Esther*, 78, however, claims that there is no dialogue because "Haman gritted his teeth and did what he had to do."
142. Translation according to Moore, *Esther*, 65.
143. Josephus *Antiquities of the Jews* XI.256.
144. *Meg.* 16a.

REFLECTIONS

Although this section, like the rest of Hebrew Esther, does not mention God, the author seems to assume the working of divine providence both in the "coincidences" of the plot and in the behavior of the characters. A well-timed sleepless night for the king, Mordecai's previously righteous behavior, and Haman's enormous ego all combine to bring about Mordecai's elevation and Haman's humiliation. Unfortunately, the narrative does not help us to distinguish between mere coincidence and the action of God. The characters certainly are not able to discern the difference: Haman is a fool; Esther is absent; and Mordecai registers no reaction to his fantastic rise in the king's favor. Only the reader might be able to see in these events more than just coincidence, but the narrator is silent on the point. The same dilemma arises when trying to discern true prophecy; according to Deuteronomy, "if a prophet speaks in the name of the LORD but the thing does not take place or prove true, it is a word that the LORD has not spoken" (18:22 NRSV). The hand of God in events is ambiguous; a person must act without sure knowledge.

The behavior of Haman in this passage functions as an object lesson in the perils of pride and self-seeking. One is reminded of the teaching of Jesus in Luke 14:7-11, where he instructs people not to elevate themselves, but to humble themselves, so that others may honor them. Haman is a negative example of this teaching, causing his own humiliation by reaching above himself, whereas Esther and Mordecai do not seek honor; rather, honor is given to them by others.

ESTHER 6:12-13, HAMAN IS WARNED BY HIS ADVISERS

COMMENTARY

After the extraordinary event that has just occurred, Mordecai simply returns to his customary station in the court. The narrator, as usual, gives no insight into his thoughts or emotions, for the focus is now on Haman. In one of the several reversals in the course of the story, Haman is now observing the rituals of mourning, as Mordecai did in 4:1-3. Mordecai was mourning for the anticipated death of the Jews; Haman is in mourning not only for his own humiliation, but also (although he does not yet know it) for his own death, an excellent example of the author's ironic foreshadowing. Haman turns again to his friends (also called "his wise men" [חכמיו *ḥăkāmāyw*]; however, unlike the "wise men" of 1:13, these advisers speak with wisdom) and his wife, Zeresh, but they do not give him sympathy as they did in 5:14; in fact, they counsel giving up. The expression "if Mordecai is of the Jewish people" is rhetorical; everyone knows Mordecai is a Jew, and the text constantly gives him that epithet. Zeresh (in the tradition of the wise woman; cf. 2 Sam 14:4-17; 20:14-22) is speaking here with the voice of the author. Haman cannot, according to them, defeat the Jewish Mordecai. Why? Because Haman is an Agagite—and thus cursed? Because the Jews are divinely protected? Once Haman's associates recognize that he has begun to fall, his doom in the story is sealed; we have reached the turning point of the book. Haman the Agagite cannot defeat Mordecai the Jew. As Levenson astutely observes, "Actions seem to come out of nowhere in this tale, but they gradually link together to form an immensely positive and meaningful pattern of Jewish deliverance: if the term 'theology' means anything in reference to the book of Esther, that is its theology."[145] However, we still await the action of the one appointed to bring about salvation: Queen Esther.

145. Levenson, *Esther*, 95.

REFLECTIONS

Haman is a sterling example of the foolish man warned against in the wisdom literature. Proverbs 26:27 warns, "Whoever digs a pit will fall into it, and a stone will come back on the one who starts it rolling" (NRSV). Haman brings about his own downfall by not obeying the precepts of wisdom. Wisdom assumes that God rewards those who act wisely and punishes those who do not. The focus is on human action, rather than divine intervention; God does not have to be mentioned, since the righteous moral program will work itself out without direct divine action. Who is the epitome of the wise courtier? Mordecai is one possible example, but he does not always act wisely (see Commentary on 3:1-6). Esther, however, from beginning to end of the story, is a model of wise counsel, patience, and modesty, using the circumstances at her disposal not to further herself but to aid her people. That she and her cousin Mordecai end up in the highest position in the empire (except for the king) is just reward for her righteous behavior, but she does not seek it. What she does seek, the salvation of the Jews, is the ethical centerpiece of the book. It is not right to murder an innocent people; it is right to seek to prevent that. This may seem to be stating the obvious, but self-interest often stands in the way of people's doing what is right. Esther overcame her self-interest in 4:16, and hers is a moral as well as a political victory.

ESTHER 6:14–7:10, ESTHER'S SECOND BANQUET

COMMENTARY

6:14–7:4. Esther 6:14 is a transitional verse carrying us from one scene to the next. The presence of the eunuchs reflects the royal convention of having guests escorted to the palace (recall that eunuchs are sent to escort Vashti to the king's banquet, 1:10-11). How different must Haman's emotional state be from that of the first banquet! He is losing control of events; the text conveys this by having him rush to Esther's banquet, subtly indicating that she is now in control. However, it is important to keep several things in mind. Although we the readers have been assured that Haman will ultimately fall, the outcome is still in doubt. Esther, as far as the text reveals, has no knowledge of Mordecai's honor and Haman's humiliation. As far as she (and the Jews) is concerned, the edict against the Jews still stands, Haman is still the vizier, and the danger is as acute as ever. Esther's actions must be viewed against that backdrop.

The scene of the second banquet opens in the same way as the first banquet. Esther is referred to as "queen," both by the narrator and by the king, emphasizing her status above Haman. When the guests reach the wine course, the king repeats his offer to Esther for the third time, in exactly the same language as before. Now is the moment for Esther to speak! The AT adds here, "Esther was uneasy about speaking because the enemy was right in front of her, but God gave her the courage for the challenge," supplying both Esther's emotional state and God's unseen action. However, the MT is ambiguous on both counts. Esther responds to the king, using the proper courtly phrases; notice that the phrase "found favor" (מצאתי חן *māṣā'tî ḥēn*) rather than "gained favor" (נשאה חן *nāśě'â ḥēn*) is used. Esther may, according to the narrator, actively gain favor, but when she speaks to the king she gives all the credit to him. She matches the words of the king's offer in her speech, "petition" and "request," but her request is a bombshell—her life and her people. The parallelism of the sentence ("petition" = "life"; "request" = "people") equates the two; Esther is now fully identified with the Jews. She indicates, however, by the order of her request that she realizes what will be more important to Ahasuerus— her own life. This king, ruled by his own selfish concerns, would be much more affected by the loss of his wife than by the slaughter of an entire group of his subjects. In v. 4, Esther gains steam; she declares that the Jews have been sold, a not-so-veiled allusion to the king's acceptance of Haman's bribe. She is careful, however, to make the verb impersonal ("we have been sold") so as not to make a direct accusation of the king. She goes on to repeat the verbs of the decree in 3:13: "to destroy, to slay, and to annihilate." The final clause of her accusation is a bit strange; the Hebrew is uncertain, and translations differ.[146] Is she really saying that slavery would be acceptable? Or is she just playing a rhetorical game? The last phrase in Hebrew, as it stands in the Masoretic Text, is almost untranslatable: "for there is not distress equivalent [שוה *šōweh*; the same word that Haman used in 3:8] in injury [*hapax legomenon*] to the king." Is she talking about financial loss or just unpleasantness? What Esther seems to be saying, and what the versions support, is, "If we had only been sold into slavery, I would keep silent,

---

146. For a complete discussion see Paton, *Esther*, 261-62.

for it would not be worth bothering the king about."¹⁴⁷ Note the parallel to Haman's "it is not worthwhile for the king to leave them alone" (3:8).¹⁴⁸ Everything in this court must be put in terms of what benefit it brings to the king.

7:5. Ahasuerus's reaction is astonishment. He appears to have no idea what she is talking about and obviously does not connect it with Haman's decree of destruction, which he approved in chap. 3. Why should he? He never inquired as to the identity of the people he was condemning to death, and by handing over his signet ring, he gave Haman the power to do as he pleased. Ahasuerus is now paying the penalty for his laziness and ignorance by facing the shame of his failure to protect his wife.¹⁴⁹ He demands to know the culprit.

7:6. The climax of the scene comes with Esther's ringing accusation: "A man, an adversary and an enemy! This wicked Haman!" At last the masks are off, the secrets revealed: Haman the Agagite is the blood enemy of Esther the Jew, and the king is forced to choose between the two. (It is still not clear what Ahasuerus himself realizes; Esther has not directly stated that she is Jewish, and Ahasuerus apparently did not know the identity of the people he had condemned to death.) In fact, the wording of the text allies the king and the queen against Haman; for the author, the choice has already been made. Haman, for his part, is dumbfounded (the NRSV's "terrified" better conveys the Hebrew [נבעת *nibʿat*] here). Esther has indeed successfully dissembled; until the moment of the accusation, neither the king nor Haman had an inkling of her purpose.

7:7. The king is once again "full of wrath." Why does he leave the room and go into the garden? Is it because he is presented with an unhappy choice, between Haman his favorite and Esther his queen? The AT, in which Esther notes that Haman is "your friend," certainly understands it this way. Or is he bewildered about what to do? This king, remember, never acts without advice (1:13-15; 2:2-4; 6:6), and now his advisers are pitted against each other. Haman, on the other hand, does the natural thing and begs for mercy from the queen by falling on her couch, where she is reclining while eating. Here is the supreme irony for Haman: He, who wished to slay all Jews because Mordecai refused to bow to him, must now bow to a Jew!

7:8. When Ahasuerus returns and sees Haman prostrate at Esther's feet, he accuses Haman of attempting to rape her. The accusation seems ridiculous under the circumstances. What could Haman possibly gain by ravishing the queen, who has just accused him of trying to kill her, with her husband nearby? The entire scene is farcical; after being accused of attempted murder, pompous Haman is forced to plead for mercy. The king's reaction is equally comic; he sees, not a plea for mercy, but an attempted rape! These characters continue to be self-centered in the extreme: Haman is (understandably) concerned for his own life, while the king sees only a threat to his honor. However unreal the accusation of rape may seem to the reader, it serves as a convenient excuse to prompt the king to do something. After all, it would be difficult for him to punish Haman for doing something that he had been given permission to do in the first place. What is more, the king had accepted a large bribe. However, if Haman is accused of raping the queen, then the king is free from all obligation to him. The minute the king makes the accusation, it is all over; the face of Haman is covered, a gesture of humiliation and mourning. Who the "they" are is unclear; it is probably the ever-present but silent servants.

7:9-10. In v. 9 a eunuch, the otherwise unidentified Harbonah, who must have been present throughout the scene, proves helpful again. He recalls the gallows Haman had erected for Mordecai, who, as Harbonah reminds the king, "spoke good concerning the king." This actually constitutes a second charge against Haman: plotting to kill the king's benefactor (Mordecai's relationship to Esther is still unrevealed). Ahasuerus needs no further prompting; he again makes a snap decision at the leading of others. Haman is hoisted on his own petard,¹⁵⁰ and, finally,

---

147. This agrees with Moore's understanding. See Moore, *Esther*, 70.
148. See Fox, *Character and Ideology in the Book of Esther*, 46.
149. See Klein's study of Ahasuerus's character in the context of honor and shame in "Honor and Shame in Esther," 153-56. See also Laniak, "From the Margin to the Middle, 130-41.

150. Josephus draws out the moral by adding a personal comment: "Wherefore I am moved to marvel at the Deity and to recognize his wisdom and justice, for not only did He punish Haman's wickedness, but also caused the penalty which had been contrived against another to fall upon Haman himself, and thus He has given others an opportunity to learn and know that whatever mischief a man prepares against another, he has, without knowing it, first stored up for himself" (*Antiquities of the Jews* XI.268).

"the wrath of the king subsided." This may be the greatest irony of the book. The last time that happened, a queen had been banished, and Ahasuerus had second thoughts, thus setting in motion the events of the book. Is there a possibility that he will again regret his hasty action?

REFLECTIONS

This passage raises the question of our culture's expectations for the appropriate behavior and role of women. Esther is usually applauded for her courage in accusing Haman to the king, but all too often she is condemned for not seeking mercy for him and remaining silent when he is condemned. As Paton says, "Her character would have been more attractive if she had shown pity toward a fallen foe."[151] But is Esther cruel or merely sensible? If Mordecai had behaved in such a way, would he have been condemned? Probably not. Esther is condemned for her behavior because she is a woman, and women "aren't supposed to behave like that." However, Esther is locked in a life-and-death struggle not of her own making—and the outcome seems to be the life of either the Jews or Haman. There are other examples of biblical women who themselves kill the enemy of the Israelites/Jews: Jael hammers a tent peg through the head of Sisera in Judg 4:17-22, and Judith cuts off the head of Holofernes (Jdt 13:6-10). These women are the subjects of universal praise. Esther's action is indirect: She does not kill Haman, but silently acquiesces to his death. Haman is not, it must be remembered, an innocent victim. He has already issued a decree of annihilation of the Jews and has built a gallows for Mordecai. Mercy, in those circumstances, would not be wise but foolhardy, leaving the fate of the Jews unresolved. Mercy, in any case, is not Esther's to grant, since Haman's crime is not just against her, but against all the Jews.

151. Paton, *Esther*, 264.

ESTHER 8:1-2, ESTHER'S TRIUMPH

COMMENTARY

These two verses finish the events of the very busy day, which began with the king's insomnia, and tie up a few loose ends. Esther and Mordecai's relationship is finally made public. Ahasuerus gives to Esther (again her royal title "queen" is emphasized) the "house" (בית [*bayit*] here in the sense of all belongings, as the NIV translates) of Haman. Evidently the property of criminals is confiscated by the state.[152] Also, women must have had certain rights of property ownership.[153] Ahasuerus, continuing on his impulsive course, takes his signet ring, which has evidently just been confiscated from Haman before his death, and gives it to Mordecai, thereby conferring royal power upon him. Esther also places Mordecai over her new possession, Haman's property. He becomes the overseer, but she still owns it (note that the AT has the king give Haman's property directly to Mordecai, which serves to denigrate Esther and elevate Mordecai in the story). Mordecai receives his position and wealth only because he is related to Esther, no matter what his personal merits—an important comment on the status of women in the MT text.

This scene is also, in effect, the pivotal point; the greatest reversal in the story has taken place. Esther/Mordecai and Haman have switched places. Haman is dead, and his wealth and position now belong to Esther and Mordecai respectively.

152. Herodotus 3.128-129.
153. See Herodotus 9.109, where Xerxes offers to give Artaynte cities, gold, and armies under her personal control.

REFLECTIONS

If the book of Esther were a movie, the screen would now fade to black and the credits would roll. The happy ending has been achieved; the villain is dead, the king and queen are reunited, and the hero has been rewarded. Now they can all live happily ever after. Life, however, is not a movie, and the author of Esther recognizes that. The king's character is unchanged; he has not admitted wrongdoing or responsibility. Esther and Mordecai are triumphant now, but their status is dependent on the whim of this mercurial king. The Jews, all but forgotten in this last section, are still under threat; the law of the Medes and the Persians cannot be changed. The sensitive reader will recognize that precariousness of the "happy ending." This recognition leads to a reflection on the changeable nature of human fortune. The author seems to be suggesting that ultimate security does not lie with human institutions. The natural (if unspoken) response to this human condition is that ultimate security rests with God.

ESTHER 8:3-17[154]

THE UNDOING OF HAMAN'S PLOT

OVERVIEW

Even though Haman's downfall has been achieved and Esther is triumphant, a major problem remains. Haman's edict remains in force, and, according to the conventions of the law of the Medes and the Persians, cannot be changed (see Commentary on 1:10-22); the genocide is still scheduled to take place on the thirteenth of Adar.

---

154. Note that the NIV verses correspond to those of the MT.

ESTHER 8:3-8, ESTHER PETITIONS THE KING

COMMENTARY

There is a paragraph marking in the Hebrew after the end of v. 2, signaling a major break in the action. Does this indicate that v. 3 begins a whole new scene? The verb (ותוסף *wattôsep*, "and she did again" or "and she added to do") probably indicates that this scene is happening on the same day as the events of the preceding scene. It does not seem to be, contra Paton,[155] a second unsummoned audience; why would Esther need to risk her life again? Further, Esther "speaks" (תדבר *tĕdabbēr*) rather than "comes" (באה *bāʾâ*) again. Although the king extends his scepter to Esther in v. 4, this should be taken as a sign of encouragement rather than clemency.

In this scene, Esther is again the principal actor; Mordecai, while evidently present (v. 7), says nothing the whole time. Esther begins by falling before the king's feet, as Haman fell at her feet to his undoing. Notice that she has no trouble bowing before the king, thereby indicating that Mordecai's refusal to bow before Haman was not unwillingness to bow generally, but to bow before Haman the Agagite in particular. She weeps, which is the first sign of emotion she has shown in the Hebrew text (cf. the Greek versions; one suspects a bit of playacting here, since Esther has been so cool and collected until now), and then she "implores" (ותתחנן *wattithannen*) him, a verb used of the entreaties of people in desperate straits (see Gen 42:21; 2 Kgs 1:13). All of the verbs indicate the severity of the situation; even with Haman gone, the Jews are in danger as long as the edict is still in force. This may imply that others besides Haman are eager to put his scheme into action. Esther is the only one who can make the king act to avert the danger.

Esther begins her speech with the longest preamble of any of her petitions, adding two new clauses, "if the thing seems right before the king" and "if I have his approval," to her previous formula; and she makes it intensely personal. "If I have found favor," and "if I am good in his eyes" suggest that the king would be carrying out her wishes as a personal favor to her, as a sign of his affection, not because it is morally right. This is exactly the right type of appeal to make to this emotional and mercurial monarch! The expression "let an order be written" is an impersonal construction, divesting the king of personal responsibility; Esther is doing precisely what Haman had done earlier. In v. 6, she does not claim to be in personal danger, as she did in 7:3, for that

---

155. Paton, *Esther*, 279.

would now be an insult to the king. But she does argue that it would cause her personal grief if the Jews were destroyed (the NRSV's "kindred" is a better translation of מולדתי [*môladtî*] than the NIV's "family," since it is more encompassing). Her argument is clear: The king should foil the plot of Haman (called by his full patronymic in v. 5) in order to avoid personal pain for his queen. This is not an ethical argument, but an emotional one; most important, it will work.

Ahasuerus responds in v. 7. He is given the title "king" (מלך *melek*), Esther is called "queen" (מלכה *malkâ*), and Mordecai is called "the Jew" (היהודי *hayyĕhûdî*). The last title has ceased to be a mere ethnic designation and has become an epithet of high dignity, equivalent to "king" and "queen." The king seems to take a defensive tone, pointing out that Haman has been hanged and his property handed over to Esther, "because he sent his hand against the Jews." This is not the reason given for Haman's execution in 7:8, where he is accused of assaulting Esther; however, it would appear that with Haman dead Ahasuerus would like to consider the whole problem solved. Unfortunately, since the original edict is irrevocable, the problem is not solved, as Ahasuerus acknowledges in the next verse. The king turns over complete responsibility to Esther and Mordecai; the "you" (plural) is in the emphatic position in the sentence, indicating that they, not him, are to remedy the situation. He gives them permission to write a new command in the king's name and seal it with his signet ring "as it is good in your eyes." He is again avoiding responsibility, even though, as he acknowledges at the end of v. 8, whatever is so written is irrevocable. Thus the game of the Persian court has not changed, although the players have; what Esther and Mordecai do will be for the benefit of the Jews, whereas what Haman did was against them. But the underlying problem that enabled these things to occur has not altered. The dilemma for Esther and Mordecai is now this: If Haman's decree, written in the king's name and sealed with the king's ring, is irrevocable, how can the Jews be saved?

REFLECTIONS

The still-precarious position of Esther and the Jews, hinted at in the last passage, is fully recognized here. Esther, weeping at the feet of the king, becomes a symbol for the Jews; she is a powerless woman dependent on a powerful man. The Jews are a powerless people in exile dependent on a powerful government. Esther uses the one weapon she can count on: her feminine charms. Modern women may cringe at the spectacle of Esther weeping at the king's feet. Esther, however, is a realist. If feminine charms work to avert the threatened massacre, she will use them. The moral underpinning of her action is sound. Modern Western women (and men) may eschew Esther's means, but she remains a powerful role model for the oppressed and downtrodden, whether because of gender or ethnicity.

ESTHER 8:9-14, MORDECAI WRITES AN EDICT

COMMENTARY

8:9-10. This section opens with a puzzling time delay.[156] The events of the last sections, beginning with 3:7, have taken place in the first month, Nisan, in the twelfth year of Ahasuerus's reign. Now, however, v. 9 tells us that we are in the third month,

156. Fox, *Character and Ideology in the Book of Esther*, 96-97.

Sivan, on the thirteenth day. Why the delay between the last scene and this one? The LXX has Nisan instead of Sivan, but this is clearly a harmonizing change, since there does not seem to be a scribal error in Hebrew. Paton supposes that the intervening time is filled with the events of 4:1–8:2; this is possible, but that would necessitate a wide gap between Haman's casting of the lot and his seeking an audience before the king or a gap between that audience and the writing of his edict, neither of which is mentioned in the text (although they are not precluded).[157] Clines notes that there is exactly a seventy-day difference between the date in 3:7 and this one (the first month; the third month, on the thirteenth day, allowing twenty-eight days per month), and sees this as a veiled allusion to the seventy years of exile.[158] This is possible, but more subtle than the author usually is. The delay remains inexplicable.

In this section Mordecai is the one giving instructions, in obvious contrast to Haman (Esther has momentarily disappeared, since the author wishes to emphasize the Haman/Mordecai contrast). The language of these verses reproduces that of both Haman's decree in 3:12-15 and the decree against Vashti in 1:22. Scribes are gathered together, and their writing is according to *Mordecai's* command (cf. 3:12). The edict is addressed to the satraps, the governors, and the princes (cf. 3:12) of the provinces from India to Ethiopia, 127 in total (see 1:1). However, there is a major difference: Mordecai's decree is also written to the *Jews*, and they are singled out and given pride of place. The decree is written in every group's own language (cf. 1:22; 3:12), and it is especially emphasized that, unlike before, it is specifically written to the Jews in their "script and their language" (i.e., Hebrew). The decree is signed in the name of Ahasuerus and sealed with his ring (cf. 3:12), and it is sent by the official Persian postal system (cf. 1:22; 3:13; the Hebrew is uncertain here, but has to do with the type of horses used). The narrator is emphasizing that this is an official decree, the same as Haman's; it becomes part of the law of the Medes and the Persians and, therefore, is irrevocable.

8:11-13. The content of the decree is given in these verses. The Jews receive permission to defend themselves, which they evidently were not allowed to do before. They may "destroy, kill, and annihilate" (cf. 3:13) any ethnic or provincial force, any adversaries, including women and children (cf. 3:13), and take their booty (cf. 3:13). This is to occur in one day, on the thirteenth of Adar (cf. 3:13), which is now nine months away. The edict assumes that there would be many people, enough to form "forces," willing to attack the Jews; thus the Jews must gather together to repel them. This decree effectively neutralizes Haman's decree without revoking it, which is not allowed; it will now be a fair fight between two opposing forces. The text emphasizes that a copy of the decree is made "law" (דת *dāt*, 3:14) in every province; this goes beyond Haman's actions in emphasizing the legality of the decree. Is there an assumption that some enemies might contest it (cf. Ezra 5:4–6:12, where the provincial governors attempt to contest, with Darius, a decree of Cyrus concerning the Jews)? The couriers go forth in haste (cf. 3:15) and quickly; the extra verb adds urgency to the narrative.

8:14. The chapter ends with the same phrase that 3:15 ended with and returns the action to Susa. The echoing that takes place throughout the decree emphasizes the wisdom doctrine of retributive justice, but the inclusion of women and children in the counterdecree has been criticized by some as "bloodthirstiness."[159] Gordis proposes an interesting solution to the moral dilemma: that the last phrase of Mordecai's decree is a "citation" of Haman's decree, so that "women and children" refer to Jewish women and children who might be attacked according to the terms of Haman's decree. Mordecai's decree thus simply allows the (male) Jews to defend themselves and their women and children.[160] The Hebrew, however, does not clearly identify to whom the women and children belong, so that Gordis's solution is not certain. It is also possible that the author viewed the enemies of the Jews as falling under the ban of holy war (Deut 20:16-17).[161]

---

157. Paton, *Esther*, 272.
158. Clines, *Ezra, Nehemiah, Esther*, 316.
159. E.g., Paton, *Esther*, 274; Moore, *Esther*, 80, 83.
160. R. Gordis, "Studies in the Esther Narrative," *JBL* 95 (1976) 49-53.
161. So Anderson, "The Book of Esther," *IB*, 3:886.

REFLECTIONS

It may seem strange that a law would have to be made allowing the Jews to defend themselves; indeed, the whole project of neutralizing Haman's decree, rather than revoking it, is almost comical. However, it is true that sometimes people get so caught up in legalism and seeking to be law-abiding that they lose sight of the moral ground on which the law should be based. If the law says to attack the Jews, then we should attack the Jews whether we want to or not. If the law does not say the Jews can defend themselves, then they cannot, no matter what the natural response would be. We saw examples of this type of behavior during the Holocaust. As the Nazis passed more and more stringent laws relegating the Jews to second-class citizenship and then to death, most Germans, even those who would later claim that they were not anti-Semites, continued to obey and even to cooperate with the authorities in their eagerness to be law-abiding. In the trial of Adolf Eichmann, for example, Eichmann claimed as his defense that he was simply "following orders"—that is, obeying the law of the land. He did not feel responsible for determining the morality of that law.[162] His behavior resulted in the deaths of millions of people. The attitude exemplified by Eichmann denies the principle that morality ultimately rests in God and that humans are called to be moral because they are created by God.

In Judaism, the law is not good in and of itself. Rather, it is good because it was given by God; its purpose is to make Israel "a holy nation" (Lev 19:2). Therefore, Mordecai and Esther are justified in their attempt to overturn a legal decree, for that decree violates the higher law of God, which views each human life as precious. Immanuel Kant agreed with this position when he claimed that any social law that denies the intrinsic moral worth of the individual violates the "categorical imperative" that we should always treat human beings as ends in themselves.[163] This principle, if applied, protects the minority within a majority culture. Or, as Jesus more simply and vividly put it, "In everything do to others as you would have them do to you; for this is the law and the prophets" (Matt 7:12 NRSV).

162. Hannah Arendt, *Eichmann in Jerusalem: A Report on the Banality of Evil*, rev. ed. (New York: Penguin, 1994) 135-50.
163. Immanuel Kant, *The Foundations of the Metaphysics of Morals*, trans. L. W. Beck (New York: Macmillan, 1990). Arendt, *Eichmann in Jerusalem*, 136, notes that Eichmann himself declared that he had ceased to live by Kant's moral principles.

ESTHER 8:15-17, MORDECAI'S APPEARANCE

COMMENTARY

The threat to the Jews now averted, Mordecai appears in his new role as second to the king. The author once again recalls, through similar wording, previous scenes. Mordecai, who was dressed in sackcloth in 4:1, now wears "royal robes" as Esther did and as Haman had wished to do (5:1; 6:8; cf. Joseph, who "went out from the presence of Pharaoh" [Gen 41:46]). The robes are made of the same type of cloth that decorated the royal pavilion in 1:6. Mordecai wears a "crown" (or "turban" [עטרה *ăṭārâ*]) of gold, as Vashti refused to do in 1:11. Mordecai thus combines in his person identifying markers associated with every main character except the king. Mordecai gains exactly what Haman wanted. (Esther's absence from the scene is notable. The text, slipping back into its androcentric world, is unable to give her the credit and recognition she deserves as the true heroine of the story.) The result is that the people of Susa, who in 3:15 were confused, now shout and rejoice. There is no hint of anti-Semitism here, or even expectation of it. Haman was the Jews' enemy because he was an Agagite, not because he was a Gentile. Verse 16 gives the joyous reaction of the Jews to the glory of Mordecai. The NIV translation of the Hebrew is paraphrastic: The term "light" (אורה *'ôrâ*) is parallel to other words of gladness and contrasts with the gloom of mourning in chap. 4 (see also Add. A; Job 12:25; Pss 97:11; 112:4).

Outside of the city of Susa, the Jews of the provinces rejoice over the decree with feasting and a holiday (this contrasts sharply with the king and Haman's feast after his decree in 3:15). Finally, the narrator states that "many from the people of the land became Jews (מתיהדים *mityahădîm*), for fear (פחד *paḥad*) of the Jews fell upon them." What is the significance of these words? The NRSV translates *mityahădîm* as "professed to be Jews," thereby skirting the question of whether those Gentiles actually converted. The LXX is blunt: "they were circumcised." However, in the relatively secular, or at least non-practicing, atmosphere of this book, what would it mean to "become a Jew"? It would have to be an ethnic rather than religious change, since religious practice seems to play no part in Jewish identity in the book of Esther. Also, what is the nature of the fear that falls upon them? Is it physical, the result of the superior forces of the Jews and a desire to be on the winning side? Or is it spiritual, a recognition that God is on the side of the Jews?[164] The sense is unclear, but the meaning comes through: The ultimate triumph for any minority people is to have the majority want to join them. However, as Clines notes, the phrase adds an "almost surrealist" end to the chapter.[165]

At the end of this chapter, with the plot of Haman averted and Mordecai firmly ensconced in power, we feel we have reached the end of the story. In fact, several scholars have raised the possibility that the original form of the story of Esther (proto-Esther) ended here. Indeed, the AT ends at v. 12 (AT 8:7). With the loose ends of the story tied up and the author recalling various earlier scenes in his grand climactic chapter, it is highly likely that proto-Esther ended here and that chaps. 9 and 10 were added by the author of the MT to tie the story in with the Festival of Purim.[166]

164. Fox, *Character and Ideology in the Book of Esther*, 104-6; Clines, *Ezra, Nehemiah, Esther*, 319.
165. Clines, *The Esther Scroll*, 318.
166. See Clines, *The Esther Scroll*, esp. chap. 5, and Michael V. Fox, *The Redaction of the Books of Esther*, 110-11.

REFLECTIONS

The parallelism between the appearance of Mordecai and the appearance of Joseph in Gen 41:42 is surely not accidental. The reader who recognizes the parallel knows that God enabled Joseph to reach the pinnacle of success; the suggestion is that God is also behind Mordecai's phenomenal success. The implication of God's guiding hand in the success of Mordecai must be teased out, but there is no other way for a faithful Jew to understand the text. God is, after all, the protector of Israel (e.g., Pss 44:1-8; 46:1-11; 68:1-10). So why should not God's unspoken protection be seen in the events of the book of Esther? Although it is unspoken, that theology of salvation permeates the book.

Mordecai's glorification may further be understood typologically by Christians. The New Testament emphasizes the glorification of Jesus (in human terms a humble peasant) by the hand of God, particularly in the scenes of the transfiguration (Matt 17:1-8; Mark 9:2-8; Luke 9:26-36) and the ascension (Luke 24:50-53). In Revelation, the lamb (symbolizing Christ) is glorified by God to reign in heaven (5:11-14). An important difference to bear in mind is that in the Christian tradition glorification takes place in anticipation of martyrdom (the transfiguration) or as a result of martyrdom (the ascension, Revelation). Mordecai's glorification takes place after he helps to *avert* martyrdom. There is no exaltation of the martyr's status in the story of Esther.

ESTHER 9:1–10:3

THE BATTLES OF ADAR AND THE FESTIVAL OF PURIM

OVERVIEW

Commentators debate whether chaps. 9–10 originally belonged to the book of Esther.[167] The AT, in particular, does not contain the following items found in the MT: an extended battle report, the second day of battle and celebration, the etiology of Purim, and the epilogue in 10:1-3. Instead, the AT contains a much shorter ending, which includes Esther asking the king's permission to put her enemies to death (including Haman's sons) and Mordecai issuing a decree annulling Haman's previous decree and commanding the Jews to celebrate. For these reasons, Torrey argued that 8:21 of the AT represented the original ending of his posited Aramaic original source of Esther.[168] Clines has suggested that the proposed Semitic source of the AT (the "proto-AT") ended at 8:17, when the king puts Mordecai in charge of the kingdom's affairs, and that the extant ending of the AT developed independently from that of the MT. Fox argues that the proto-AT actually concluded at 8:38 (excluding Add. E) with the decree of Mordecai. Jobes, on the other hand, argues that the present ending of the AT is a shortened version of the MT's ending, supplemented by material from the LXX.[169] In the MT itself, the various sections of chap. 9 often do not fit well together, and some of them may be secondary. The fact that the versions leave out various parts of chap. 9 (see pericope headings below) is a further argument for the secondary, redactional characte of chap. 9. However, it is difficult to determine the original or secondary character of any single component section. In this commentary the text is divided into units, some of which may have been interpolated into the present narrative. See textual studies of the versions for further information.

Regardless of the conclusion one reaches concerning the details of the redaction of the endings of the three extant versions, it seems clear that the original story of Esther (proto-Esther, no longer extant) did not contain either a battle report or an etiology of Purim, but rather ended with the triumph of Esther and Mordecai within the Persian court. This would give the original story more of the character of a royal courtier tale, as found in Daniel 2–6.[170] This understanding of the nature of proto-Esther may also be supported by *4QTales of the Persian Court*, a similar type of tale that apparently never departs from its court setting (see Introduction).

However, as the MT version of Esther now stands, it is a unified whole, as Berg has convincingly shown.[171] The various themes continue in chaps. 9–10, including the all-important theme of reversal; and the most important structural motif, that of banquets, would be incomplete without the inclusion of the Purim feasts in chap. 9 (see Fig. 1: "The Banquets in Esther," p. 4). Therefore, MT Esther must be treated as a unified literary work, with chaps. 9–10 as integral parts of the whole.

---

167. The following remarks are dependent upon Clines, *The Esther Scroll*, 74-92; Fox, *The Redaction of the Books of Esther*; Jobes, *The Alpha-Text of Esther*, 195-233.
168. Torrey, "The Older Book of Esther," 7, 14.
169. Jobes, *The Alpha-Text of Esther*, 203.
170. Wills, *The Jew in the Court of the Foreign King*, 153.
171. Berg, *The Book of Esther*, 31-47.

ESTHER 9:1-5, THE FIRST BATTLE

COMMENTARY

The action of this chapter is set on the thirteenth of Adar, the day appointed by Haman for the destruction of the Jews. Nine months have passed since Mordecai's edict was sent throughout the empire. As Paton exclaims, "Lively times are to be expected."[172] These verses bring to a climax two of the major themes of the book: ironic reversal and power. Verse 1 brings the theme of ironic reversal to its climax by putting emphasis on the fact that the tables have turned (נהפוך הוא *nahăpôk hû*') on the enemies of the Jews (the identity of these enemies is unclear, but they seem to be numerous). Anti-Semitism is accepted as a fact of life, unlike in earlier chapters, where anti-Semitism occurred because of a blood feud rather than natural antipathy between Jew and Gentile (although there have been hints of it along the way, such as the assumption of Haman's original decree that plenty of Gentiles would be willing to kill Jews). In 9:1, the enemies of the Jews "hope to dominate them," but that is changed so that the Jews will dominate the enemies (the NIV is paraphrastic but captures the sense). The Jews not only slay their enemies, but also become more powerful than they. In v. 2, the Jews gather together against those who would attack them, and "no one is able to withstand them [איש לא־עמד לפניהם *'îš lō' 'āmad lipnêhem*]." The LXX is again blunt in its translation, "no one resisted them," making it seem as if the Jews encountered no opposition. The NRSV's "no one could withstand them" (NIV, "no one could stand against them") probably better captures the sense of an inevitable, but not effortless,

victory. The action, in fact, seems more aggressive than defensive, since there is no clear mention of a Gentile attack, but that instead "fear" (פחד *paḥad*) falls upon them. The fear here is clearly physical, but it is also a more generalized fear of the new power that the formerly oppressed minority has. The action of the larger groups (v. 3) is reflected in the behavior of their leaders. The princes (NRSV, "officials"; NIV, "nobles") of the provinces, the satraps, the governors, and "the doers of the king's work" (a new phrase, possibly indicating a later redactor; this is a different order from earlier chapters, with the leaders of other ethnic groups, who might conceivably have opposed the Jews, placed first) help the Jews because of their fear of Mordecai. Here the fear is political, since Mordecai has now become second in the kingdom. The kind of aid given is not specified. Mordecai has certainly reached the epitome of greatness; the idiom "the man Mordecai" in v. 4 implies importance, since it is elsewhere applied to Moses, the leader of the Jews *par excellence* (e.g., in the story of the rebellion of Aaron and Miriam [Num 12:1-15] Moses is referred to as "the man Moses" [v. 3]; most significantly, Exod 11:3 reads "the man Moses was very great" in the sight of the Egyptian [Gentile] court). The Jews are victorious (v. 5), smiting their enemies with the "edge of the sword" (מכת־חרב *makkat ḥereb*; never used as an idiom for self-defense); this indicates again aggressive action on the part of the Jews against their enemies (the LXX omits this verse). This is the climax to the theme of power. Haman and his unnamed minions sought power over Mordecai and the Jews. Now the Jews and Mordecai have power over them.

172. Paton, *Esther*, 282.

REFLECTIONS

These verses, with their matter-of-fact recounting of wholesale slaughter, may be difficult for the reader to accept. They are certainly part of the reason why Martin Luther fulminated against the book of Esther: "I am so hostile to this book that I wish it did not exist, for it Judaizes too much, and has too much heathen naughtiness."[173] It is particularly difficult to reconcile the events of these verses with Christian notions of forgiveness and universalism. As Anderson says, "This is a case of do unto others as they would have done to you."[174] It is important, however, not to see these verses as a reflection of an actual historical event, but rather as the wishful thinking of an oppressed minority (cf. Psalm 137, a lament over the Babylonian exile, which ends with the children of the Babylonians being smashed against a rock). The focus is on the victory, not the slaughter. The Jews have not sought violence, but it has found them; and they must meet it or be destroyed (martyrdom is never considered by the author as an option, nor is it a desirable thing within the Jewish tradition). In the process, the Jews have moved from being a fearful and mourning people to a powerful and feared people (cf. similar sentiments in Psalms 124; 129). Those who wished to destroy the Jews are instead themselves destroyed. The Jews thus become the image of Esther, who changes from a silent, pliable girl into a strong and decisive woman.

173. Martin Luther, *Tischreden*, W. A. xxii, 2080, as quoted by Paton, *Esther*, 96.
174. Anderson, "The Book of Esther," 3:828.

ESTHER 9:6-10, THE BATTLE IN SUSA

COMMENTARY

9:6. The narrator now switches from the provinces to Susa. Even though we are told in 8:15 that the city of Susa rejoiced at Mordecai's ascendancy, the Jews still find 500 men to slaughter (there is no mention of women and children). This is a very large number for a city the size of Susa. Fox suggests, probably correctly, that it is hyperbolic.[175] Further, the verse does not say that the fighting took place in the city of Susa, but in the citadel of Susa. Does this mean that there was fighting within the palace, indicating hostility to the Jews within the Persian bureaucracy? Moore finds it unlikely that the king would tolerate fighting within the palace.[176] However, since in 3:15 the city of Susa was in consternation over Haman's decree, indicating sympathy for the Jews, it seems most likely that hostility to the Jews in Susa would have been found among Haman's cohorts in the bureaucracy. The scene as a whole is rather surrealistic: The enemies are evidently so hostile to the Jews that they act in spite of the fact that Mordecai the Jew is firmly in control in the palace.

9:7-10a. These verses announce the slaughter of the ten sons of Haman. The principle of retributive justice is strongly at work here; the children share in the punishment of the father. It is also possible that the author assumes that, in the nine months since Mordecai's decree, the sons of Haman have been attempting to carry out their father's program to overthrow Mordecai. Hence, they would be the leaders of the enemy forces. This completes Haman's downfall. He boasted of his position, his wealth, and his numerous sons in 5:11. First he lost his wealth to Esther and his position to Mordecai; now even his sons, his posterity, are lost. The names of Haman's sons are all Persian but otherwise unknown; they are probably included, like the other lists of names in 1:10, 14, to give the narrative an air of historical verisimilitude.[177] (The names in the MT are arranged in columns, for reasons that are not clear; cf. Josh 12:9-23.)

9:10b. Finally, the author reports that the Jews took no plunder, in spite of the fact that they had permission to do so (8:11), as did their Gentile counterparts in Haman's decree (3:13). This is a vivid contrast to Saul in his battle with Agag and the Amalekites (1 Samuel 15), where, in spite of the ban of holy war, he took booty and thus lost his throne.

175. Fox, *Character and Ideology in the Book of Esther*, 110.
176. Moore, *Esther*, 87.
177. Paton, *Esther*, 70-71.

The Jews do not make that mistake again! Rather, they place themselves in the camp of the righteous Abraham, who, in his victory over the kings of the plain, took no plunder (Gen 14:22-24).

The Jews' victory appears effortless (no Jewish losses are mentioned); yet, it is not attributed to God. No reason is given for the enemies' hostility—it just *is*, a natural fact of life.

REFLECTIONS

The notion that Gentiles are naturally hostile to Jews is a "fact" that Jews have seen borne out in their history over the centuries. Christian literature is rife with anti-Semitism, beginning with the Gospels' ill-starred attempts to shift the entire blame for Jesus' execution from the Romans onto the Jewish elders in Jerusalem. John Chrysostom's sermons against the Jews continued the tradition among the Church Fathers. Even today, the spurious *Protocols of the Elders of Zion* can be downloaded from the Internet. It is not surprising, therefore, that a "happy ending" to a Jewish story about an averted genocide should include the deaths of their enemies. The Christian, reading the book of Esther as Scripture, should resolve to build a world in which such a "happy ending" would not be necessary because the threat would not exist in the first place.

ESTHER 9:11-15, THE FOURTEENTH OF ADAR

COMMENTARY

Some scholars have found this a difficult set of verses to interpret because of their bloodthirsty tone; these objections are similar to those raised to the preceding section. Gerlemann claims that these verses owe their existence only to the need to explain the historical fact of a later two-day festival.[178] In fact, vv. 11-15 are not well integrated into the flow of the narrative, since the king's question and Esther's response are, as far as one can tell, completely unmotivated. In v. 11 the king, for the first time in the narrative, receives accurate information in a timely fashion. The report is of the 500 Gentiles who have been killed in the citadel (v. 6). There is no mention of any Jewish loss of life; the implication is that there was none. The king then does something he has never done before: He takes the initiative. He reports to Esther the 500 dead and the killing of the ten sons of Haman. Is his tone one of wonderment, amazement, horror, or ingratiation?[179]

He expresses no emotion concerning the battle losses. The king then asks Esther for her "petition and request" and promises that he will give it to her, using almost exactly the same vocabulary he used in chaps. 6–7. It is not clear why he does this; he has already given her a free hand, and her objective has been fulfilled. This whole exchange, like the second day of killing that follows it, seems redundant.[180]

Esther's response (v. 13) is also unexpected. Her opening phrase, "if it please the king," is almost abrupt compared to the long and elaborate formula she used in 8:5.[181] This may indicate that she is feeling more confident and secure in her position now that the king has effectually ceded control of events to her (it may also indicate the hand of a different author). She requests that the Jews of Susa be allowed to continue their slaughter a second day and that the corpses of the ten sons of Haman be defiled by public

---

178. Gilles Gerleman, "Studien zu Esther: Stoff—Struktur—Stil—Sinn," in Carey A. Moore, *Studies in the Book of Esther* (New York: Ktav, 1982) 308-49.
179. Fox, *Character and Ideology in the Book of Esther*, 112, believes that admiration is the only possible tone.
180. Paton, *Esther*, 287, sees it as not merely redundant, but reflecting "a malignant spirit of revenge."
181. D. N. Freedman, as reported by Moore, *Esther*, 88, noted that the use of the single phrase forms an inclusio with the same phrase in Esther's first request in 5:4, thus bringing her string of requests to a close.

exposure. Although the NRSV and the NIV have "hanged on the gallows," it is clear that a corpse's impalement on a stake is meant, since the ten sons of Haman are already dead, as reported in vv. 7-10. The use of the same phrase in 2:23; 5:14; and 6:9-10 may indicate that public impalement is meant there as well. Public exposure of a corpse is the ultimate degradation in the Hebrew tradition (Deut 21:22-23; 1 Sam 31:10-12). The principle of intergenerational retribution is at work in the treatment of the sons of Haman; their father's corpse was hanged and exposed, so theirs must be as well.

The king does exactly as Esther asks, and the Jews, in words parallel to v. 2, slay another 300 men. Again, emphasis is placed on the fact that they took no plunder. It is unclear why the Susan Jews need a second day, except to bring the story into line with the two-day festival. History here arises from custom, explaining why Susan Jews (or urban Jews?) celebrate the fifteenth rather than the fourteenth of Adar.

REFLECTIONS

It is unfortunate that Esther's reappearance in the narrative should be in such a bloodthirsty guise, but this is in keeping with the tone of the rest of the chapter, which is motivated by desire for revenge for past oppression. Since the book of Esther is a product of a society and a worldview that accepted violence motivated by ethnic or religious causes, it would be unlikely for Esther to deviate from this worldview. Fox terms Esther's action in this section as "punitive and precautionary"; the enemies of the Jews must be eliminated before they can act again.[182] Once more, the reader should not condone the violence, but deplore the necessity for it; according to the story, the Jews in Susa have no fewer than 810 enemies willing to murder them. This time, thanks to the skill and wit of Esther and Mordecai, the Jews are safe—but this will not always be the case. Self-preservation through violence is accepted as a necessity in the world in which the author lives (his matter-of-fact tone throughout this section so indicates), but that is not the ideal.

182. Fox, *Character and Ideology in the Book of Esther*, 112.

ESTHER 9:16-19, THE JEWS CELEBRATE

COMMENTARY

9:16.[183] According to this verse, the reason for the fighting on the thirteenth of Adar was self-defense ("the Jews gathered to stand for their lives"), harking back to Mordecai's decree in 8:11. Verse 16 follows very well after v. 10, omitting the section concerning the second day of fighting in Susa—a further indication that vv. 11-15 may be secondary. According to the text, the Jews in the provinces have slain 75,000 Gentiles, an enormous, hyperbolic number. The versions recognize the unreal quality of this number and reduce it, the LXX to 15,000 and the AT to 10,107 (a mysteriously exact figure). However, the huge number is also an indication of the widespread anti-Semitism that the author believed lurked in the provinces, and against which the Jews had to defend themselves. For the fourth time, the narrator emphasizes that the Jews took no spoils.

9:17-19. These verses give the historical basis for the celebration of the Festival of Purim. In v. 17, the theme of the feasts reappears; the Jews of the provinces fight on the thirteenth of Adar and rest on the fourteenth, celebrating with feasts. According to v. 18, the Jews in Susa (which becomes the representative for all walled cities) fight on

183. These verses are omitted by the AT.

the thirteenth and fourteenth, then celebrate on the fifteenth with a feast. Verse 19 makes it clear that this festival originated in the villages, in the countryside; it is a Jewish holiday belonging to the diaspora (the LXX glosses the verse by noting that urban Jews celebrate on the fifteenth). This must have been the situation that obtained in the author's (or perhaps a redactor's) time; originally Purim was a one-day festival, the day of celebration determined by one's place of residence. It is certainly a "good day," consisting of feasting, rejoicing, and sending gifts to others.[184] All of these actions recall motifs mentioned earlier in the story. These latter two feasts mirror the two feasts of Ahasuerus in 1:2, 4. The rejoicing that accompanies these feasts contrasts with the mourning that occurred following the decree of Haman (4:3). And finally, the "portions" (מנות *mānôt*) of food that the Jews send to one another recall the special "portion" that Hegai gives to Esther after she wins his favor (2:9), arguably the one incident (coincidence?) that set all the other events in the story in motion. There is no mention of prayers, sacrifices in the Temple, or any other ceremonial actions that ordinarily accompany festivals prescribed in the Torah (cf. Lev 23:4-44); it is, in keeping with the rest of the book, a seemingly secular festival. Respite from fighting is celebrated, not victory; it is safety, not slaughter, that is celebrated. This festival is the whole point of the book of Esther as it now stands, although its historical antecedents are very cloudy (see Introduction).[185]

184. See Berg, *The Book of Esther*, 45.

185. 2 Macc 15:13 mentions Adar 14 as "the Day of Mordecai," evidently a minor celebration. Is this the same as Purim? See Introduction.

ESTHER 9:20-32, THE LETTERS OF PURIM

OVERVIEW

The purpose for the letters written by Mordecai and Esther is to establish the Festival of Purim. The author is trying to account for the fact that Purim is not a festival decreed by Moses in the Torah. By whose authority does it exist? This is not a unique problem to the author of Esther; several festivals celebrated in contemporary Judaism are not legislated in the Torah. The most obvious comparison to Purim is Hanukkah, a festival commemorating the victory of Judas Maccabeus over the Seleucids in 164 BCE, as recounted in 1 Maccabees 4:1 and 2 Macc 10:1-8. However, Hanukkah commemorates an actual event in Jewish history; Purim, as has been demonstrated in this commentary, does not. The author solves this problem by artificially tying the Festival of Purim to the fictitious, but popular, story of Esther and Mordecai and by inserting the letters found here, giving the festival written sanction. A similar process is also found at Qumran, where the text 4QReworked Pentateuch interpolates legislation concerning the Wood Festival and the New Oil Festival, post-exilic, non-Mosaic festivals, into Leviticus 23.[186]

186. E. Tov and S. White, "4QReworked Pentateuch: 4Q364-367, with an appendix on 4Q365a," in *Discoveries in the Judaean Desert XIII* (Oxford: Oxford University Press, 1994) esp. 290-96.

Esther 9:20-28, Mordecai's Letter

COMMENTARY

9:20-22.[187] Mordecai writes in his own name, rather than in the name of the king, a report of the king's decree of the festival; but here the letter is addressed only to the Jews. He seems to be writing as a fellow Jew making a request, not as an official declaring the

187. The AT omits vv. 23-26, and the OL omits vv. 24-27.

ESTHER 9:20-28 COMMENTARY

law (דת *dāt*), in marked contrast to all other decrees issued in the book. As Fox points out, Mordecai is taking a bold step by inaugurating a new Jewish holiday.[188]

The section begins with Mordecai recording "these things" (הדברים האלה *haddĕbārîm hā'ēlleh*). To what does "these things" refer? The Jewish commentator Rashi believed that it referred to the events of the book of Esther. However, the phrase probably refers to the events just narrated, since elsewhere Mordecai makes no claim to authorship of the book. A summary of "these things" would appear to be found in vv. 24-26a. The locations to which Mordecai's letter is sent are described differently from previous chapters: "near and far" rather than "from India to Ethiopia," for example, possibly indicating the secondary character of this section.

Notice that Mordecai does not write to begin a yearly celebration, but to confirm one that is already taking place. The fourteenth and fifteenth of Adar now become the days of a yearly celebration. This differs from v. 19, where provincial Jews celebrated on the fourteenth and Susan Jews on the fifteenth. Mordecai seems to be requesting that all Jews everywhere celebrate both days. Verse 22 gives a clear reason for the celebration: the fact that the Jews had rest and reversal of fortune. Again the theme of reversal is highlighted. Their salvation through their own efforts is to be celebrated, not the slaughter of their enemies (if the victory was to be celebrated, the festival would fall on Adar 13 and 14). The manner of celebrating is an echo of v. 19, with the exception of the added injunction to give gifts to the poor. This may be a post-exilic emphasis; Neh 8:10-12, which contains directions for Rosh Hashanah, also emphasizes sending food to the poor, and Tobit invites the poor to his Pentecost feast (Tob 2:2). Yet, no mention is made of any overtly religious practice.

9:23-26. The Jews then confirm the holiday (v. 23) by accepting what they had already begun to do and what Mordecai had requested that they do.[189] This establishment of the holiday is evidently a three-part, reciprocal process: (1) The holiday is unofficially celebrated; (2) Mordecai writes a letter to make it official; and (3) the Jews affirm it. Verses 24-26a give a "precis" of events, slightly changed from the actual events of the book: Haman the Agagite, now the enemy of all the Jews, devises a plot to destroy them (Mordecai's role in this is not recounted; if Mordecai is the actual author of the letter, he may prefer to pass over his own, not very edifying, actions in silence) and casts "lots" (פור *pûr*) "to harass [המם *hummām*; note the assonance of *hummām* with Haman] and annihilate them." This is a different function for the *pûr* from that in chap. 3, probably indicating that the history of the name "Purim" and its connection to the festival were only imperfectly understood by this redactor. Haman's evil plot is turned back upon him. The king, rather than Esther, is given credit for foiling the scheme; Fox sees this heaping of credit on the king as further proof of Mordecai's skills as a courtier, but it is also proof of the androcentric bias of the text.[190] The Hebrew of v. 25 does not contain the name "Esther," but rather an unspecified feminine suffix, which may be the otherwise unmentioned Esther (so NRSV) or the plot itself (so NIV). The LXX makes the suffix masculine, thus referring to the plot. Finally, Haman and his sons are hanged (Moore points out that these events are telescoped, since the hanging of father and sons seems to take place at the same time),[191] with no mention of the tremendous slaughter recounted in earlier parts of the chapter. In spite of the valiant efforts of v. 26, it remains unclear why the days are called Purim. The verse does not clarify why the word is plural, since Haman only cast *pûr* (singular); nor does it explain why the holiday is named after an action of the enemy Haman. The holiday and its name existed before the book of Esther, and the author never manages successfully to tie the events of the book and the name together.

9:27-28. The Jews agree to celebrate Purim yearly, "in all their generations" (בכל־דור ודור *bĕkōl-dôr wādôr*) and by "family" (משפחה *mišpāḥâ*), the first time in Esther that these two terms appear.[192] The author is here (unintentionally?) revealing his distance

---

188. Fox, *Character and Ideology in the Book of Esther*, 117.
189. Levenson, *Esther*, 126, notes that this action on the part of the people is similar to that of the Israelites at Sinai when they affirmed the obligations of the covenant (Exod 24:3-8).
190. Fox, *Character and Ideology in the Book of Esther*, 120.
191. Moore, *Esther*, 120.
192. Lev 23:14, 21, 31, 41, 43 uses the term *dôr*, "generation," to emphasize that the Mosaic festivals are to be celebrated in perpetuity.

in time from the events narrated; Purim was already an established holiday at the time of writing. The purpose of this material is probably to convince those not already celebrating Purim of the historical validity of the festival. Notice the reference to "all who joined them"—that is, converts. This is an oblique reference to "those who became Jews" in 8:17. It is difficult to escape the sense that v. 28, which spells out the reason for the book of Esther, sounds like an ending: Purim will always be celebrated and will never be forgotten.

REFLECTIONS

Purim has proved to be a festival of enduring popularity, sometimes compared to the Christian celebration of Mardi Gras, which it resembled in its emphasis on feasting and hilarity (although the reasons for the two celebrations are very different). Purim begins on the fourteenth of Adar (usually sometime in March in the Western calendar), but is preceded by a minor fast, the Fast of Esther, on the thirteenth of Adar, during which observant Jews fast from sunup until sundown (this fast day came into existence c. 700–750 CE). On the fourteenth of Adar, the Scroll (*mĕgillat*) of Esther is read publicly in the congregation. In some traditions, this reading is accompanied by sound effects from the congregation. For example, there will be shouting and stamping of feet whenever Haman's name is mentioned. The fifteenth of Adar was originally celebrated as a feast day in towns walled in the time of Joshua. This was later extended to all cities, and now a two-day festival is generally kept by all. In Jerusalem there has also been a tradition of a three-day festival.

In every Jewish tradition, Purim is characterized by feasting at home and sending gifts of food to others. Charitable giving is also emphasized. It is now customary for Purim parties to be held, especially for children, for which the celebrants wear costumes, dressing up as Mordecai, Esther, Ahasuerus, and Vashti. This has led to some comparison with the American celebration of Halloween, but the comparison is superficial at best. Altogether, Purim is a delightful, well-beloved holiday.[193]

193. For further information, see Hayyim Schauss, *The Jewish Festivals: History and Observance* (New York: Schocken, 1938) 237-71.

Esther 9:29-32, Esther's Letter

COMMENTARY

These verses probably were originally separate and focused on Esther; the mention of Mordecai (always referred to as "the Jew Mordecai") should be viewed as an interpolation. If the name "Mordecai" is removed from v. 29, what is left is a separate letter from Queen Esther.[194] Esther is given her title and her patronymic; she is both queen and Jew, and she writes with full authority (more in keeping with the "law" [דת *dāt*] of the Persian chancellery) to establish what Mordecai could only request. "This second letter of Purim" must refer to Mordecai's letter, but the referent of "second" is unclear, since there has been, so far, only one letter. Therefore, "second" may be a later gloss, mistakenly referring to Esther's letter. The first words in v. 30 simply are "and he sent letters [וישלח ספרים *wayyišlaḥ sĕpārîm*]." The "he" may refer to Mordecai or may be a scribal or editorial change, with the original text reading "and *she* sent letters," referring to Esther.[195]

194. The remarks on this section are heavily dependent on Fox's emended text and his comments, arguing that this section can be viewed as a separate letter from Esther alone. See Fox, *Character and Ideology in the Book of Esther*, 123-27.

195. See Fox, *Character and Ideology in the Book of Esther*, 125, 286.

It is unlikely that Mordecai is also sending the letter, since he is referred to in the third person in v. 31. Verse 30 more clearly imitates the language of earlier passages in which letters were sent by repeating the phrase "one hundred and twenty-seven provinces" (1:1; 8:9). In v. 31, Esther "gives orders" that the days of Purim be observed, mandating a two-day festival. It is possible that "in their approved seasons" reflects some confusion about the time of the festival. Fox suggests removing "and Queen Esther" from v. 31 as a later gloss, because she is here confirming Mordecai's instructions. That this section is referring to Mordecai's letter is confirmed by the fact that Esther's letter seems to allude to the Jews' confirmation of the festival, explicitly requested in v. 21 (the same verb, "impose" [קים *qiyyam*, in the piel], is used).

The mention of fasts and lamentations in v. 31 is confusing in the context; the Hebrew is clearly not referring to fasts and lamentations associated with Purim,[196] but to other holy days.[197] The text simply seems to be saying: "Just as you take upon yourselves non-Mosaic fasts, so also you can take upon yourselves non-Mosaic festivals." This may be a hidden reference to one salient objection to the Festival of Purim: It was not legislated in the Torah. Verse 32 makes clear that the authority of Esther the Persian queen establishes Purim. This authorization of a festival by a woman who is the queen of a foreign empire and whose personal commitment to Judaism is, in the eyes of later readers, at least suspect may explain the confused state of the text. There may have been objection to this "foreign" feast in some circles (Judean?); thus an effort was made to show that Mordecai the *Jew*, and the Jews themselves, not the suspect Esther, established the Festival of Purim. Thus was Esther's hard-won authority partially removed.

---

196. Contra Paton, *Esther*, 301; Moore, *Esther*, 96-97.

197. In the present Jewish calendar the thirteenth of Adar is a minor fast known as Esther's Fast. But according to Ibn Ezra, "fasting and lamentations" refers to other holy days, like the Ninth of Ab, established (by prophetic word) in Zech 8:18-19.

REFLECTIONS

Esther has made her last appearance in her story. Her character has undergone rapid change and growth, from passive girl to powerful woman. She has been identified as a role model for Jews living in the diaspora, and it is time to ask whether she has been successful in that role. As a woman living in a patriarchal, androcentric culture, she has been completely successful, using the male power structure, beginning with Hegai and ending with Ahasuerus, to achieve her goals. As a Jew, a member of a minority community within a foreign empire, she has succeeded beyond all expectations, bringing her cousin Mordecai to power and achieving safety and security for the Jews. She has played her part with wisdom and skill throughout and has chosen to act according to what the author assumes, but does not state, is the will of God. As such, she is a role model for Jews living in dispersion and, indeed, for any oppressed minority. Some of the circumstances of her day are now in our day rightly condemned as wrong, such as the use of women as sexual objects and the use of violence to reach political ends. However, those were the realities that people in the author's time (and often in our own) had to face. Within those constraints, Esther is wholly admirable. She should be embraced as a heroine working to further God's will in the world.

ESTHER 10:1-3, APPENDIX CONCERNING MORDECAI

COMMENTARY

These verses may be a secondary addition (the AT does not contain them), written to give the book a more "fitting" conclusion. It can also be argued that they more convincingly tie chap. 9 to the rest of the book, since the glorification of Mordecai in these verses forms (with 8:1-2, the appearance of Mordecai in glory) an envelope for the fighting and letters in chap. 9.

10:1. Ahasuerus imposes a tax on his kingdom (this might be a corvée of labor, such as Solomon imposed in 1 Kgs 5:13). It is imposed on "the earth and the islands of the sea"—in other words, the known world, which is practically coextensive with the Persian Empire. The reason why the tax is imposed is not clear. When the king married Esther, he gave relief from taxes (2:18). Is he reimposing them here? This is possible, but not confirmed.[198]

10:2-3. The book's final verses are concerned with the greatness of Mordecai and the king (note the disappearance of Esther). Their greatness is recounted in formulaic language (cf. the descriptions of Azariah in 2 Kgs 15:1-6 and of Hezekiah in 2 Kgs 20:21-22) and is recorded in the royal chronicles, as is proper (cf. 2:23). Mordecai is not just generally great, however; he uses his greatness for the benefit of his fellow Jews, which, according to the message of the book, is how power is supposed to be used: for the benefit of others and not for self-aggrandizement. Although only the Jews are mentioned as beneficiaries of Mordecai's high office, the assumption of the text seems to be that his rule is beneficial to the entire empire and that no one suffers because he is Jewish. Here is another parallel to the Joseph story (Gen 47:13-26), where Joseph saves all of Egypt from famine. Again, that is the way government should act—for the benefit of all and the detriment of none. Mordecai is a living example of the wise ruler in action.

The major themes of the book—reversal, power, and escape from persecution—have been brought to closure. Although Ahasuerus is still on the throne, the pomposity and buffoonery of his court in chap. 1 have been replaced by the good and wise government of Mordecai in chap. 10. Mordecai's position has changed from threatened subordinate to all-powerful ruler, and the Jews have moved from the threat of annihilation to the beneficence of Mordecai's rule. Power, which was so important in chap. 1 that Ahasuerus had to banish Vashti to prove that he had it, has proved to be ephemeral in the hands of unworthy recipients. Only those worthy through strength of character (exemplified by the virtues of wisdom, modesty, and patience) have proved to be able to keep it (the exception to this is the king, who has hereditary power). Power, therefore, is not an end in itself but the reward of good character. Finally, the Jews have escaped from the sentence of genocide and achieved their goal, which was to live peacefully and securely within the Persian Empire. As Levenson states, "The scene with which the Masoretic Esther closes is one for which Jewish communities in the Diaspora have always longed: Jews living in harmony and mutual good will with the Gentile majority."[199]

---

198. D. Daube, "The Last Chapter of Esther," *JQR* 37 (1946—47) 139-47, has argued that the tax was a "peaceful substitute" for the plunder Ahasuerus would have received if Haman's plot had succeeded. However, there is no hint of this rather negative reason in the text.

199. Levenson, *Esther*, 133-34.

THE ADDITIONS TO ESTHER
INTRODUCTION, COMMENTARY, AND REFLECTIONS
BY
SIDNIE WHITE CRAWFORD

THE ADDITIONS TO ESTHER

INTRODUCTION

The so-called Additions to Esther, found in the Greek versions of Esther (LXX and AT), make the book of Esther a very different literary work from that in the Hebrew Bible (MT). The additions add drama, plumb the emotional depths of the characters, add information to fill in the gaps of the the MT, and, most important, supply an overt religious element that is lacking in the MT. To fully appreciate the LXX version of Esther, it is helpful to read it in its entirety, as it is found in the apocrypha of the NRSV. For the purposes of this commentary, however, each Addition will be treated separately. The Additions are not all from the same author, nor were they all composed in the same language. Josephus, who was certainly familiar with the LXX, does not use all the Additions (e.g., he does not include Add. A), perhaps indicating that he did not know them all or did not consider them original.[1]

The most striking change in the LXX version of Esther is the addition of religious elements. The additions continually mention God, and the LXX redactor introduces the name of God within the (translated) text of the MT:

"to fear God and obey his commandments" (2:20)
"call upon the Lord" (4:8)
"and the Lord drove sleep from the king that night" (6:1)
"for God is with him" (6:13).

Also, the Additions contain a dream sent by God (Addition A), prayers by Mordecai and Esther, fasting explicitly directed toward God, a manifest concern for keeping the purity laws, especially those concerning food and marriage, a mention of the Temple (all in Addition C), and a Gentile acknowledgment of the power of the God of Israel (Addition E).[2] The effect of all these changes is that God becomes the hero of the Greek story, and the importance of human action is greatly

---

1. Josephus *Antiquities of the Jews* Book XI.
2. Carey A. Moore, *Daniel, Esther and Jeremiah: The Additions*, AB 44 (Garden City, N.Y.: Doubleday, 1977) 158-59.

lessened; the LXX redactor makes clear to the reader that God acts to save the Jews and that, because of God's protective concern for the Jews, the outcome of the crisis is never in doubt.

This change in emphasis also leads to changes in the main human characters, Mordecai and Esther. Mordecai, as the recipient of the dream sent by God, becomes a typical biblical hero, like Joseph or Daniel, and is the chief human character in the drama. Esther, on the other hand, loses status from her portrayal in the MT: She becomes a romantic and emotional heroine, as in the Hellenistic romance novel, and, as such, is less attractive to modern readers.[3]

(See the annotated bibliography for the Hebrew book of Esther.)

---

3. For LXX Esther as a Hellenistic romance novel, see Lawrence M. Wills, *The Jew in the Court of the Foreign King*, HDR 26 (Minneapolis: Fortress, 1990) 197.

OUTLINE OF THE ADDITIONS TO ESTHER

I. Esther Addition A 1-17, Mordecai's Dream and the Eunuchs' Plot

    A. A 1-11, Mordecai's Dream
    B. A 12-17, The Plot of the Eunuchs

II. Esther Addition B 1-7, The Letter of Haman

III. Esther Addition C 1-30, The Prayers of Esther and Mordecai

    A. C 1-11, The Prayer of Mordecai
    B. C 12-30, The Prayer of Esther

IV. Esther Addition D 1-16, Esther Appears Before the King

V. Esther Addition E 1-24, Mordecai's Letter

VI. Esther Addition F 1-11, The End of the Greek Esther

    A. F 1-10, The Interpretation of Mordecai's Dream
    B. F 11, The Colophon of the Greek Esther

ESTHER ADDITION A 1-17 (AT 1:1-18; VG 11:2–12:16)[4]

MORDECAI'S DREAM AND THE EUNUCHS' PLOT

OVERVIEW

ddition A was composed in a Semitic language (Hebrew or Aramaic). This

---
4. The various numbering systems of the Greek texts are based on *The Old Testament in Greek*, vol. 3, Part I: *Esther, Judith, Tobit*, ed. A. E. Brooke, N. McLean, H. S. J. Thackeray (London: Cambridge University Press, 1940).

Addition probably dates to the late second century BCE, after the time of the Maccabean wars. Gentiles, according to Addition A, have become completely hostile to the Jews, such that their only hope of salvation lies with God.

ESTHER ADDITION A 1-11, MORDECAI'S DREAM

COMMENTARY

Addition A opens with a date formula. The story is set in the reign of Artaxerxes, probably Artaxerxes I, the son of Xerxes (465–424 BCE), and takes place in the second year of his reign, one year earlier than the opening scene of the MT (understanding the change of kings from Xerxes to Artaxerxes). It begins on the first day of Nisan, which, as we have seen in MT Esther (3:12; 8:9), strikes a note of salvation as it is the month of the exodus and Passover; this is also the time of the spring new year festival in Babylonian, Persian, and Second Temple Jewish calendars. Mordecai, who is clearly the central human character of Greek Esther, is introduced and his full genealogy given. It is appropriate to give his full genealogy when he is introduced, but if this were part of the original book of Esther, it would be unnecessary to repeat it in 2:5 (an indication of the secondary character of Add. A). The first thing Mordecai does in Greek Esther is to have a dream. This places him in the company of two other visionaries on whom he is modeled: Joseph and Daniel. Like theirs, Mordecai's visionary capacity is understood as a gift from God. He is then further identified as a palace functionary (something alluded to but never openly stated in the MT) and as one of the exiles brought to Babylon in 597 BCE (again, a point of unclarity in the MT). If Mordecai was brought to Babylon as a young man in 597, in the second year of Artaxerxes I he would have been approximately 175 years old—an incredibly venerable person!

Mordecai's dream is recounted in vv. 4-10. Chaos is consuming the earth. Two dragons appear, roaring and ready to fight. Both chaos and the dragon are major symbols found in apocalyptic imagery.[5] Chaos, the upheaval of the natural order, signals the absence of God

---
5. "Apocalyptic" is an adjective derived from the noun "apocalypse" (ἀποκάλυψις *apokalypsis*) and refers loosely to a group of themes, concepts, and motifs that frequently appear in works classified as apocalypses. These themes include divine intervention in human history, eschatological judgment by God, otherworldly conflicts, and visions. See Mitchell Reddish, *Apocalyptic Literature: A Reader* (Nashville: Abingdon, 1990) 28.

and the breakdown of the social order (cf. Isa 34:9-11; Joel 2:2-3). The word "dragon" (δράκων *drakōn*) encompasses a wide range of terrifying, yet real, beasts in the LXX, such as the jackal in Jer 9:11, and mythical animals such as Leviathan (Job 26:13; Ps 74:12-13 [LXX 73:12-13]), while in apocalyptic literature it becomes a major symbol of evil (Rev 12:3; 2 Bar 29:3-8). Thus it is clear that Mordecai's dream is a bad omen. A problem in the decoding of their appearance here in Esther, however, is that the dragons do not symbolize real beasts or nations (which are separately mentioned in v. 7), but humans. Further, there is not just one, but two, which is an anomaly; and the second is meant to symbolize Mordecai, one of the heroes of the book. The symbolism of "dragon" does not fit the (positive) character of Mordecai, so the author's choice of it is mysterious.

At the roaring of the dragons, the nations, as separate entities, prepare to fight. These nations will battle against the righteous nation, certainly to be identified with Israel (Wis 16:23; 18:7). This symbolism in Add. A turns the LXX version of Esther into an apocalyptic struggle between other nations and Israel (cf. Joel 2:2, 10-11; Zeph 1:15), not a conflict between individuals, as in Hebrew Esther. It should be noted that in the AT and the OL, the nations are ready to fight and are afraid, but their hostility is not directed toward Israel. Verses 8-9 sum up the vision in apocalyptic tones (cf. Joel 2:2; Matt 24:29). Israel is ready to perish from fear. There is no salvation on the human horizon. This dream sets the battle upon the cosmic stage, among the otherworldly powers, rather than on the human stage in a court conflict.[6]

The response, then, must come from the cosmic realm, from God, who responds to Israel's cry (see Exod 3:7-9, where God responds to Israel's cry by sending the human savior Moses). This first mention of God in LXX Esther signals the major difference between the Hebrew and the Greek versions: the presence of God as an active character in the drama. God's salvation, however, is enigmatic; a mighty river comes from a tiny spring, and light and sun follow. Water and light are symbols of salvation in Israelite literature (Zech 14:7-8; Wis 5:6). The referents of the symbols used here are not transparent; "spring" must symbolize Esther, but how the river achieves salvation is not explained, nor are the dragons ever destroyed. However, it is clear that God acts to save Israel, for it is stated that the lowly (exiled Israel) will "devour" the esteemed, a typical Jewish eschatological scenario (cf. Luke 1:52-53). Mordecai, like Joseph and Daniel, is puzzled as to the meaning of his dream. Mordecai may be troubled, but the reader is not meant to be; like Joseph's dream about his brothers (Gen 37:5-8), Mordecai's dream foreshadows the action to come. Therefore, the reader is reassured from the beginning of the book that everything will turn out well, for God's plan is at work. God becomes the main character in the LXX edition of Esther. God is the real hero; everything that happens is a result of the divine plan and maneuverings.

6. For a thorough discussion of the apocalyptic genre see John Collins, *The Apocalyptic Imagination* (New York: Crossroad, 1984) esp. chaps. 1 and 3. The transformation of the book of Esther from court tale (MT) to apocalyptic drama (LXX) is similar to the transformation that takes place in the book of Daniel, where the literary character of chapters 2–6 as royal courtier tales has been transformed by their inclusion in the apocalyptic book of Daniel.

REFLECTIONS

The absolute conflict between the nations and Israel in the LXX is far more severe than the sporadic and occasional hostility between Gentile and Jew, interspersed with episodes of goodwill, found in the MT. This is a product of the historical period of the LXX, during which the Hellenistic empires were, in their later period, far less tolerant of Jewish monotheism and ethnic solidarity than the Persians had been.[7] It is also,

7. See, e.g., V. Tcherikover, *Hellenistic Civilization and the Jews* (New York: Jewish Publication Society, 1959).

perhaps, far more typical of the Jewish experience in the diaspora than is the scenario of MT Esther. In later times, Western Christendom in particular has been radically intolerant of Jewish "otherness." Since the message of LXX Esther reassures the Jews that God will defend them, Christians are called to reexamine their past vis-à-vis the Jews and to consider a different, more tolerant path in the future.

God is vividly present from the very first verses of LXX Esther and is seen unabashedly as the deliverer of the Jews. This brings Esther into conformity with the general biblical theology in which God intervenes in the events of history for Israel's benefit. The LXX redactor had no doubts about the hints in MT Esther: It was God who delivered the Jews, with Mordecai and Esther acting as divine instruments.

ESTHER ADDITION A 12-17, THE PLOT OF THE EUNUCHS

COMMENTARY

These verses, more than any others in LXX Esther, are in conflict with MT Esther. They repeat, with variations, the episode found in Esth 2:21-23. If this material in Add. A were original, then Esth 2:21-23 would be redundant; however, it is more likely that A 12-17 comes from a later redactor. There is also a time conflict; this episode takes place before Esther becomes queen, while Esth 2:21-23 takes place after she has become queen. It is not possible that these are two separate episodes; the plot, the characters, and the result are the same. (Other conflicts will be pointed out as we move through the verses.) Finally, neither the OL nor Josephus contains these verses, indicating their lack of originality.

The names of the two eunuchs, Gabatha and Tharra, are probably corruptions of the Hebrew names Bigthan and Teresh and are otherwise unidentified. Mordecai overhears their plot (v. 12), thus clearing up an ambiguity in MT 2:21. He then informs the king himself, rather than going through Esther, as in Esth 2:22. Of course, since Esther is not yet the queen, it is impossible for her to inform the king, but this is a blatant contradiction of the MT. The king, as in the MT, takes direct action, and the eunuchs are executed.

As in the MT, the king makes a record of these events, although it is not titled "the book of the annals." The NRSV's 12:4*b*, where Mordecai also writes an account, is derived from the AT, but its purpose is not clear. Mordecai is ordered to serve in the court, but according to Add. A 2, Mordecai already serves in the court, an internal contradiction. Mordecai is also rewarded by the king, an appropriate action on the king's part; however, now MT 6:1-11 is entirely superfluous because Mordecai has already been rewarded.

The last verse of this section reveals its real purpose: to introduce Haman and to explain his enmity toward Mordecai. Haman is called the son of Hammadatha, as in the MT, but he is identified as a Bougaion. This may be a corruption of "Agagite," but it may also be a reference to the Aramaic בגהי (*bagōhî*), the name of a notorious eunuch under Artaxerxes I who desecrated the Temple. It is also possible that *bagōhî* is a eunuch's title, rather than a name;[8] the implication would then be that Haman was a eunuch, but this is contradicted by the fact that he had children. In any case, "Bougaion" (Βουγαῖον) is clearly a term of opprobrium. The AT has "Macedonian" rather than "Bougaion"; this refers to the successors of Alexander the Great, who conquered the Persian Empire in 332 BCE. The Persians and the Greeks were long-standing enemies; Xerxes had attempted to conquer the Greek mainland and was defeated at Salamis and Plateia, and Artaxerxes continued to

---

8. *4QTales of the Persian Court* contains the name "Bagoshe," belonging to an opponent of the protagonist, Bagasraw. "Bagoshe" resembles both "Bagohi" and Josephus's spelling of the name, "Bagoas." The proliferation of "bagohis," all in reference to Persian officials, gives support to the idea that the word is a title of an officer of the Persian Empire. See Josephus *Antiquities of the Jews* VII.1, and Papyrus #30 from the Jewish colony at Elephantine.

have trouble with the Athenians.⁹ Referring to Haman as a Macedonian thus makes him an enemy infiltrator of the Persian court. Further, in the Hellenistic period, the Macedonians, in the form of the Seleucid emperors beginning with Antiochus IV Epiphanes, became the major enemies of the Jews.[10] There can be no doubt that Haman is an enemy both to the Jews and to the Persians; indeed, the verse implies that, despite his "great honor" with the king, he was behind the plot of the eunuchs. Therefore, his enmity toward Mordecai stems from the fact that Mordecai foiled his plot to assassinate the king, rather than from Mordecai's failure to bow to him. This clears up the ambiguity of the conflict between Haman and Mordecai in the MT, since a reference to the conflict between Saul and Agag may not have been clear to a Greek-speaking Jewish audience. It also explains the inclusion of this episode at the beginning of the book.

Addition A consists of two separate episodes, neither of which is original to proto-Esther and may be the work of different authors.[11] The dream may have circulated separately before its inclusion in the Esther story; its imagery and symbols do not quite fit the events of the story, as its interpretation in Add. F reveals. The episode of the eunuchs' plot, however, is intrinsic to the story of Esther and Mordecai; its inclusion here, with its obvious reworkings, appears to be the work of a clumsy redactor.

---

9. A. T. Olmstead, *The History of the Persian Empire* (Chicago: University of Chicago Press, 1948) 250-59, 302-13.

10. Daniel 7–12, Jubilees, Judith, and the books of the Maccabees, all dating from the second and first centuries BCE, reflect this conflict. The fact that the AT also reflects it is a probable indication of the date of the AT.

11. Moore, *Daniel, Esther, and Jeremiah*, 180. Jon D. Levenson, *Esther*, OTL (Louisville: Westminster/John Knox, 1997) 41, suggests that Add. A may reflect a "variant telling" of the Esther story.

ESTHER ADDITION B 1-7 (AT 4:14-18; VG 13:1-7)
THE LETTER OF HAMAN

COMMENTARY

The inclusion of a copy of Haman's letter, which comes between 3:13 and 3:14 of the MT, stands in the tradition of including other copies of Persian decrees and letters in the Hebrew Bible (e.g., Ezra 1:2-4; 4:17-22; 6:3-12; 7:11-28).[12] The purpose of including it is to lend the narrative an air of historical veracity. The original language of this Addition is Greek; this is shown by its flowery rhetorical style and lack of the Semitic constructions usually found in Septuagintal Greek.[13] In content the letter is similar to another Greek composition, the letter of King Ptolemy Philopator, found in 3 Macc 3:12-29. The letter in 3 Maccabees reflects the anti-Semitism common throughout the Hellenistic Empire.

Verses 1-3. The extent of Artaxerxes' kingdom, described in v. 1, agrees with MT 1:1, as does the otherwise unknown 127 provinces. The word τοπάρχης (*toparchēs*, "governor") signifies the governor of a district. The preamble emphasizes the king's good intentions, but it is clearly disingenuous—what monarch has ever claimed not to want to bring peace and prosperity to his or her kingdom? The identity of the counselors is unknown, although the wise men of MT 1:13-14 may be meant. The grand rhetoric concerning Haman's goodness and wisdom is ironic—an unusual touch for the LXX redactor, who does not ordinarily imitate the ironic tone of the MT (recall that Haman is writing the decree!).

Verses 4-5. These verses contain the reasons for the decree. The anti-Semitism expressed is much more blunt than Haman's corresponding rhetoric in MT 3:8: The Jews are hostile; their laws (the Torah) are contrary to every other nation's; they do not obey the king's ordinances; and they follow a "perverse" law and are ill-disposed to the imperial government. This is typical of the heightened rhetoric of a Greek composition and may also reflect the Jews' experience of more extensive anti-Semitism during this period (cf. 3 Macc 3:13-29). Their destruction, according to Haman, is crucial to the stability of the kingdom.

Verses 6-7. The Jews are never identified by name, in keeping with MT Esther; however, one wonders how the identity of the intended victims is to be made known. The date, the fourteenth of Adar (v. 6), may be a copyist's error or may reflect confusion over the date or the reason for the celebration of Purim. If Purim is understood by the LXX redactor as a celebration of the defeat of the enemies, rather than as rest from the threat of destruction as in MT, then the original date of destruction must be the same as the date of the celebration. The writer of 2 Macc 15:36 refers to the fourteenth of Adar as the "Day of Mordecai," which may indicate some knowledge in the second century BCE of the festival that was later known as Purim. The mention of Hades in v. 7 indicates the letter's Greek origin.

---

12. See also Second Targum to Esther, which likewise includes a (different) copy of Haman's letter.

13. For a complete discussion of the rhetorical style, see C. A. Moore, "On the Origins of the LXX Additions to the Book of Esther," *JBL* 92 (1973) 382-93, and Moore, *Daniel, Esther, and Jeremiah*, 193.

REFLECTIONS

Unfortunately, between the time of the writing of MT Esther and the writing of LXX Esther, the nature of the charges leveled against the Jews had grown in strength and violence. That pattern has continued into the twentieth century: The Jews have been accused of forming a worldwide economic cabal, of drinking blood, of sacrificing Christian babies, and of corrupting Christian women.[14] None of these charges has been proved true, but that has not stopped some Christians (and some Muslims as well) from believing them. *The Protocols of the Elders of Zion*, a scurrilous diatribe against the Jews, first circulated in czarist Russia, is still available in the United States. Christians, as a group, have not had the will to condemn anti-Semitism as wrong and to fight against it. This would not surprise the redactor of LXX Esther, since he did not believe, as did the author of MT Esther, that it was possible for Jews and Gentiles to live together harmoniously. He believed, rather, that Jews will survive only with the active and overt intervention of God.

---

14. See Malcolm Hay, *Europe and the Jews: The Pressure of Christendom over 1900 Years* (Chicago: Academy Chicago Publishers, 1992), and Jacob Katz, *From Prejudice to Destruction: Anti-Semitism, 1700–1933* (Cambridge, Mass.: Harvard University Press, 1980).

ESTHER ADDITION C 1-30

THE PRAYERS OF ESTHER AND MORDECAI

OVERVIEW

This Addition, which follows MT 4:17, adds in the LXX tradition what was perceived as a lack in MT Esther: prayer and direct reference to God. The prayers are paraphrased by Josephus, indicating that they were present in his tradition.[15] This Addition, although now found only in Greek, was probably originally a Semitic composition. There exists in a late medieval manuscript an Aramaic version of Mordecai's prayer, containing similar passages in identical sequence. Moore suggests that the two compositions are related through the same original Hebrew text.[16] In addition, *4QTales of the Persian Court* contains a prayer by an unknown protagonist that contains similarities to Mordecai's prayer (see Introduction).

15. Josephus *Antiquities of the Jews* XI.239-253.

16. Moore, *Daniel, Esther, and Jeremiah*, 205-7.

ESTHER ADDITION C 1-11 (AT 5:12-17; VG 13:8-18), THE PRAYER OF MORDECAI

COMMENTARY

Mordecai begins his prayer by addressing God in the language of praise typical of other Hebrew Bible prayers: God is ruler of the cosmos, creator of all things, and protector of Israel (e.g., Psalms 8, 19, and 21). In vv. 5-7 the question of Mordecai's motive in refusing to bow to Haman, which was unclear in the Hebrew text (see Commentary on 3:1-6), is explained: Mordecai refused to bow to Haman, not because of his own pride, but because he will bow only to God. Therefore, according to his own explanation, Mordecai is acquitted of wrongdoing, a charge not so easily dismissed in the Hebrew text. Mordecai, in fact, claims that, left to himself, he would have been willing to kiss the soles of Haman's feet, the ultimate act of homage in the Persian court, but his sense of God's honor would not allow him to do so. His protestation does not reflect the actual practice of the Jews, who refused to worship other gods, but freely paid homage to human beings, including foreigners, and may be slightly self-defensive (see Commentary on 3:1-6).

Mordecai closes his prayer with references to God's historical acts in the life of Israel, references lacking in MT Esther. He refers to God as the God of Abraham, thereby invoking the covenant of Genesis 15 and 17; he reminds God that Israel is God's "inheritance," the chosen people (see, e.g., Deut 32:9). He mentions the exodus from Egypt, the paradigmatic salvific event in Israel's history, which is only obliquely alluded to in MT Esther by the mention of the month of Nisan (3:12; 8:9). Finally, Mordecai requests that his petition be granted so that Israel can escape death and continue to praise God, in keeping with the biblical notion that it is only the living who can praise God (see Ps

30:8-10 for similar language). The whole thrust of Mordecai's prayer is that God is the only one capable of saving Israel, and Israel trusts in God's protection as God's special possession—all sentiments missing in the MT. In fact, the word κύριος (*kyrios*, "Lord"), the Greek translation of יהוה (*Yahweh*), the proper name of God, is repeated eight times in the eight verses of the prayer, emphasizing God's special relationship with Israel. All Israel joins with Mordecai's prayer "as loudly as they could" in v. 11.

Mordecai's prayer counteracts the charge of the book of Esther's irreligiosity by placing LXX Esther squarely within the framework of Israel's covenant theology as expressed both in the historical and the prophetic traditions in the Hebrew Bible and in the psalms. The prayer, which is sincere and moving, expresses the faith that was implicit in MT Esther: It is God's plan that the Jews should survive, for they are God's chosen people. However, in the MT this is hardly hinted at, let alone made explicit; only in the actions of the characters, who act in the face of seemingly insurmountable odds, is the author's theology visible. The LXX makes this implied theology explicit, thereby making the book more palatable to a pious audience (but also removing the suspense in the process).

REFLECTIONS

Mordecai's prayer in Add. C is one of the first instances of "reflection" on MT Esther that we possess. Some readers might feel an emptiness at the heart of MT Esther as a biblical book: Where is the faith that should direct Mordecai's actions? The answer is given here: Mordecai's faith is based on the covenant between God and Israel, represented by Abraham and the exodus. Mordecai recalls the scriptural tradition of Israel and concludes that God will not abandon the Jews, even though the circumstances look very bleak. His prayer is mirrored by the prayers of Jews and Christians every day, when they turn to Scripture for comfort, hope, and reassurance.

ESTHER ADDITION C 12-30 (AT 5:18-29; VG 14:1-19), THE PRAYER OF ESTHER

COMMENTARY

Esther's prayer, like Mordecai's, serves to add a theological element to the narrative and also allows the reader to view Esther in a new light: as a pious Jewish female (the word "Lord" appears nine times in her prayer). As such, her character is more in keeping with the accepted Jewish norms of the Hellenistic period. Esther is completely reliant on others and, in this moment of extreme crisis, on God; she "flees to the Lord." All of the author's theological ideas are biblical; there are no new insights, as might be argued are present in MT Esther. The prayer itself is reminiscent of Dan 9:3-19, from approximately the same period in time. Daniel, like Esther, is fasting and wears sackcloth and ashes; he confesses Israel's sins and petitions for God's aid.[17]

The scene opens with Esther repeating all the gestures of mourning—sackcloth and ashes—in which Mordecai engaged (4:1). Esther goes even further, however; she puts dung on her head as well, a gesture testified to in the HB (Mal 2:3) only in cases of extremity. Thus disfigured, she begins her prayer.

Esther addresses God not only as the true king (as opposed to Artaxerxes), but also as the helper of the distressed. She will repeatedly stress two aspects of God's character: power

---

17. Moore, *Daniel, Esther, and Jeremiah*, 214-15. Moore notes that there are no linguistic similarities between Esther's prayer and the Greek version of Daniel's prayer.

and mercy. She also immediately makes her prayer personal; God must help her, for no one else can, and she is *in extremis* (reminiscent of Elijah's prayer during his struggle against Ahab and Jezebel, 1 Kgs 19:9-14). In v. 16, she reminds God of the covenant and of God's special relationship with Israel (the OL here contains a 134-word addition reciting the mighty acts of God). According to the LXX, Esther has received her knowledge from her family's tribe, but according to the AT she learned "from my father's book," thus implying the existence of the Torah. According to Esther, the Jews are in trouble because of idolatry (vv. 17-18); this is a typical deuteronomic formula and must refer to the Babylonian exile (2 Kgs 21:10-15; 23:26-27).[18] Such prayer is formulaic; there is no mention of idolatry in the book of Esther, in which the Jews are innocent victims of Haman's enmity. Verses 18-21 make the conflict into one not between humans but between Yahweh and the other gods, similar to the cosmic conflict in Add. A; the Jews exist as Yahweh's people and are threatened by the gods of other peoples, who are implacably hostile. The mention of "house and altar" is the only reference to the Temple in the book of Esther and may indicate a wider audience than the eastern diaspora, since MT Esther makes no mention of any of the cultic institutions of Israel. The expression "turn their plan against them" recalls the major theme of reversal in MT Esther.

In v. 23, Esther turns from the general situation to her own role in it. She needs courage and eloquent speech and, unlike MT Esther, is not reliant upon her own resources, but upon God. The "lion"—i.e., the king—is a symbol of anger, strength, ferocity, and judgment (cf. Prov 20:2). Lions appear constantly as a symbol of royalty in Assyrian and Persian reliefs, and in biblical thought the royal tribe of Judah is portrayed as a lion (Gen 49:9).

Esther, like Mordecai, claims her own innocence and answers the objections raised against her portrayal in the MT by protesting her piety (vv. 25-29). She hates intercourse with a non-Jew; there is a very strong strand in Jewish thought against intermarriage (see Deut 7:3-4; Ezra 10:2; Neh 13:23-27), although there is a counterstrand that does not condemn it (the book of Ruth). Esther keeps the dietary laws, and she has not "drunk the wine of libations"—i.e., wine poured out in offering to the gods. In other words, she has not participated in pagan worship practices. In fact, she keeps herself generally separate from the heathen. Although these claims are necessary in order for Esther to demonstrate her piety, obviously she would not be able to live in this fashion and keep her Jewish identity secret, a necessary plot device. The description of her crown as a "filthy rag" is particularly sharp; the Greek term ῥάκος καταμηνίων (*rhakos katamēniōn*) is better translated as "menstruous rag." In Jewish tradition, menstrual blood is ritually unclean and should not be touched (Lev 15:19-24). Esther's whole life as queen is, in fact, miserable to her. Josephus, since he is attempting to present a portrait of Esther that will be attractive to his Gentile audience, omits these verses (they are also lacking in OL).

Esther ends her prayer on a personal note, asking once again for courage, which is appropriate, for now she must act.

18. The prayer in *4QTales of the Persian Court* also refers to idolatry.

REFLECTIONS

Esther appears in these verses as a much more pious, and much more typical, biblical heroine. She more closely resembles the pious Judith, who likewise prays to God, covered in sackcloth and ashes, for aid during her crisis (Jdt 9:1-14) and keeps the dietary laws while in a heathen camp (Jdt 12:1-4). However, by her cleverness Judith avoids intercourse with a Gentile (Jdt 13:1-10); the redactor of LXX Esther, on the other hand, cannot avoid the fact that Esther is married to a Gentile king. The best he can do is to have her declare her hatred of the situation, but then it is unclear how she would have been able to fool the king so thoroughly.

The redactor's emphasis on Esther's separateness, for reasons of purity, from the Gentile court around her is exactly the kind of behavior that has made the Jews vulnerable to charges of hostility toward other cultures. However, this charge should be seen as insecurity on the part of the accusers, since the Jews do no harm to the greater community by keeping special dietary restrictions or practicing endogamy. Since God enjoins the Jews to keep the law, then any attempt to obstruct Jewish practice should be understood as a violation of God's will.

The author's theological understanding emerges in Esther's prayer, as it does in Mordecai's: God is ruler of all, righteous yet merciful. Israel is God's chosen people; yet they can be punished for sinning. However, when faced with true repentance, God is merciful and, further, always comes to the aid of the helpless in distress. Finally, the author of the prayer believes that nothing can be accomplished without God's help. These beliefs need no explanation, since they permeate the biblical text and are shared by the faithful in all times.

ESTHER ADDITION D 1-16 (AT 6:1-12; VG 5:4-19)

ESTHER APPEARS BEFORE THE KING

COMMENTARY

This Addition, which follows immediately after Add. C, replaces Esth 5:1-2 in the MT. It is a much better dramatic scene than that in the MT, which is rather anticlimactic. This Addition is the dramatic climax of the Greek Esther and has some of the elements of a Hellenistic romance.[19] In it God, the real hero of Greek Esther, gets full credit for the positive outcome. Addition D probably had a Semitic source text, possibly the same as Add. C.

Addition D begins on the third day, in accordance with the fast that Esther requested in 4:16. After putting aside the sackcloth she wore in Add. C, she dresses to exploit her best weapon: her beauty. Unlike the MT, where Esther relies on no one but herself, in this scene she again invokes God's help (placing emphasis once more on prayer) and takes with her two maids for support. Esther is evidently a great actress; she looks happy, even though she is petrified (recall that in Add. C she claimed to "loathe the bed of the uncircumcised"; that may be true, but the king is not aware of it!). In vv. 2-5, Esther is the epitome of royal feminine beauty, while in v. 6 the king is the epitome of royal masculine power.[20] The two forces stand juxtaposed.

While in the MT this scene was rather disappointing because Esther's acceptance by the king seemed so cut and dried, and she seemed not to be in danger, the LXX exploits the dramatic potential of the situation to the full. The king is fiercely angry; both the AT and the OL compare him to a bull, a metaphor for rage. As we saw in chap. 1, the rage of this king is cause for alarm. Esther is, in fact, so terrified that she faints. She has failed completely; she has been neither courageous nor eloquent of speech. This is in contrast to MT Esther, where she is completely successful. This major difference in the two Esthers makes the LXX character "a delicate Victorian," much less appealing to the female reader than MT Esther, who has the strength of character to act calmly in spite of tremendous danger. If the LXX emphasizes the danger, it also emphasizes Esther's feminine "weakness."[21]

Esther's failure enables the true hero to act. God gets the credit for making the king do a complete turnaround; the theme of reversal, now clearly the result of God's activity, reappears. Whereas earlier the king seemed about to kill Esther, now he comforts and reassures her. He reminds her that he is her husband (the Greek word is "brother" [ἄδελφος *adelphos*], meaning "close kinsman"; cf. Cant 4:9-10; 5:1-2) and informs her that the law does not apply to her. Does this mean that all the suspense has been for nothing? Evidently not, for he still touches her neck with the scepter.

Esther now seems to have the power of eloquent speech, for she compares the king to an angel of God and confesses her terror. Her use of the phrase "angel of God" is a little strange under the circumstances, since the king is not supposed to know that she is Jewish, but this may be asking for a little too much on the part of the redactor. Esther then faints again, leaving the reader a bit suspicious: Is her emotion

---

19. Elements of the Hellenistic romance include a beautiful heroine in danger, a fainting scene, and rescue by a powerful male. See Linda Day, *Three Faces of a Queen: Characterization in the Books of Esther*, JSOTSup 186 (Sheffield: Sheffield Academic, 1995) 214-21.

20. For a description of a Persian monarch enthroned in state, see Olmstead, *The History of the Persian Empire*, 282-83.

21. Michael V. Fox, *Character and Ideology in the Book of Esther: Studies in Biblical Personalities* (Columbia: University of South Carolina Press, 1991) 272. See also Day, *Three Faces of a Queen*, 170-77.

genuine or melodramatic? In any case, it has the desired effect upon the king.

Moore points out the similarities, mentioned above, of Adds. C and D to the book of Judith, an apocryphal work written in Palestine in the late second century BCE.[22] Both contain pious Jewish women who exploit their beauty to overcome, with God's help, Gentile enemies for the sake of their people. It is probable that the book of Judith (whose main character may have been created in reaction to the too-secular Esther) influenced the redactor of LXX Esther. Levenson suggests that "both heroines reflect an ideal of womanhood widespread in late Second Temple Judaism."[23]

---

22. Moore, *Daniel, Esther, and Jeremiah*, 220-22.

23. Levenson, *Esther*, 88.

REFLECTIONS

Again in Addition D the redactor of LXX Esther wants to ensure that the reader understands that God, only subtly alluded to in the MT, is present and orchestrating each event of the story. What was left to the perception of the faithful reader of the MT is spelled out by the LXX: God causes the king to accept Esther at the crucial moment. The two versions may be compared to the way in which a person might perceive the same event while it is happening and again at a later date: While the event is happening, things may appear to be coincidences, and events seem to happen at random. Someone might speak of having "good luck" or describe an event as "serendipitous." Later, the same event, viewed as part of a whole from the perspective of faith, may be seen as God's acting throughout to bring the event to its proper conclusion. Good luck becomes a blessing; serendipity becomes grace. The LXX Esther, which perceives the finger of God in the king's reaction, thus is a later retrospective on MT Esther.

ESTHER ADDITION E 1-24 (AT 8:22-32; VG 16:1-24)

MORDECAI'S LETTER

COMMENTARY

This Addition, which follows MT 8:12, serves the same function as does Addition B, giving the narrative an air of historical verisimilitude by rendering the actual text of the decree. Like Add. B, Add. E's original language was Greek; they are probably the products of the same author. Josephus paraphrases Add. E, while the Targums have their own versions of the king's letter.

Verse 1. Addition E's opening is similar, but not identical, to the opening of Add. B. The key difference is the expression "those loyal to our government," implying that there are those who are not loyal to the government. It is addressed to the 127 provinces from India to Ethiopia (1:10)—that is, the entire empire.

Verses 2-6. These verses contain a series of truisms concerning the corruption of power. Power without humility breeds arrogance and contempt (Prov 22:4); of course, the letter is referring to Haman. It is strange that Artaxerxes, by all historical accounts a faithful Zoroastrian, mentions the Jewish God; but recall that it is Mordecai who is writing. Like other Hellenistic stories (such as Daniel or Judith), it follows the conventional style in which the piety of the Jewish protagonist causes the conversion, or at least the acknowledgment of the power of the Jewish God, of the Gentile king or hero (Dan 2:47; 3:28-29; 4:1-3, 34-37; 6:26-27; Jdt 14:10). These verses also provide the king with an excuse: He was misled by one whom he considered a friend (this may be both a technical term and a sarcastic one), even though he himself was benevolent.

Verses 7-11. The letter now turns from general truths to the matter at hand. "More ancient records" probably refers to public monuments rather than to private records. Verse 8 recalls Add. B, in which the king desired to secure peace and quiet in the empire, indicating the same author. Verse 9, with its hint that the king did not do his job properly, is an indication that this is not a genuine royal edict—an ancient Near Eastern monarch would not have admitted weakness to his subjects! Haman is identified as a Macedonian (AT, "Bougaion"), and Macedonia is the subject of an overt racial slur (recall that the Persians and the Macedonians were enemies). Haman's honors are also recited (reminiscent of Add. B).

Verses 12-14. Haman's deception of the king in MT 3:8-11 is recalled, but it is not the destruction of the Jews per se that is condemned, but rather the destruction of Mordecai and Esther, which would cause direct injury to the king. The use of the term "savior" ($\sigma\omega\tau\acute{\eta}\rho$ *sōtēr*) in reference to Mordecai may be jarring in the light of its present christological overtones, but it was a common title for the Hellenistic emperors (e.g., Antiochus I Soter), and points to the Hellenistic date of this Addition. In v. 12, Haman is accused of seeking to destroy the king as well; this is not part of the plot of MT Esther, where Haman has no idea of the connection between Mordecai, Esther, and the king, but it is part of the LXX, where in Add. A Haman is behind the plot of the eunuchs. The ultimate end of Haman's scheme is revealed in v. 14: Haman would hand over the Persian Empire to the Macedonians! This makes no sense within the story world of Esther, but, in the wider historical context of the LXX, that is precisely what happened. The Macedonians, under Alexander the Great, conquered the Persian Empire, much to the detriment of both the Persians and the Jews.

Verses 15-16. God is given credit for Persian success; recall that under Persian rule the Jews were relatively unmolested. The description of Jewish law as "most righteous" reflects the sentiments of the author and should be contrasted with Haman's accusations in MT 3:8 and Add. B 4.

Verses 17-18. The point of the letter is reached in these verses, which essentially annul Haman's edict. This is contrary to what happens in MT Esther, where the Jews are given permission to defend themselves against the law of the Medes and the Persians, which cannot be revoked. The idea of annulment, however, agrees in substance with the AT at 8:16. The instruction not to execute Haman's decree should preclude the need for the slaughter in chap. 9, since that was supposed to be defensive in nature. However, it appears that by the time the LXX edition was redacted, chap. 9 was already part of Hebrew Esther. The author handles this contradiction by including the mention in v. 20 of the possibility that the Jews might still be attacked on the thirteenth of Adar.

Verse 18 also contains contradictions to MT chap. 9, which Add. E is supposedly anticipating. Haman is hanged at the gates of Susa, rather than at his own home. His whole family is hanged with him, contrary to the MT, which places the deaths of his sons months later. These differences might imply different sources or simply the work of a careless redactor.

Verses 19-20. These verses contain commands that would bring joy to the Jewish reader. The Jews are to be allowed to live under their own laws, a major issue in the Hellenistic period. Under the Persians, each ethnic group was allowed to be self-governing, provided they obeyed their Persian overlords. At the beginning of the Hellenistic period, under the Ptolemies until 198 BCE and then under the Seleucids until 175 BCE, the Jews were also allowed to govern themselves by the Torah. However, during the reign of Antiochus IV Epiphanes in 175, that privilege was revoked, and from then on the Jews were constantly engaged in a struggle to follow both the law of the land and their own law. The inclusion of this provision in v. 19 points to a date after 175 BCE.

Verses 21-22. Not only are the Gentiles to leave the Jews alone, but also they are to aid them (v. 20); according to v. 22, they are also to celebrate Purim (the celebration is enjoined for Adar 13, contra MT). This indicates a level of Jewish-Gentile cooperation not envisioned in other documents of the period (v. 22 is omitted by the AT and Josephus). This cooperation is in obedience to God, who made this day joyful for the "chosen people," a phrase not likely to be found in a genuine Persian edict.

Verses 23-24. The threats at the end are typical of royal edicts (e.g., the Behistun inscription), and the style is mimicked in Jewish literature that preserves royal decrees (e.g., 3 Macc 3:29). This language is also reminiscent of Isa 34:10, 13-15:

From generation to generation it shall lie waste;
  no one shall pass through it forever and ever.
. . . . . .
Thorns shall grow over its strongholds,
  nettles and thistles in its fortresses.
It shall be the haunt of jackals,
  an abode for ostriches.
Wildcats shall meet with hyenas,
  goat-demons shall call to each other;
there too Lilith shall repose,
  and find a place to rest.
There shall the owl nest and lay and hatch and
  brood in its shadow;
there too the buzzards shall gather,
  each one with its mate. (NRSV)

REFLECTIONS

We should be both heartened and distressed by Addition E—heartened, because the author envisions a level of Jewish and Gentile cooperation rarely seen. The Jews live by their own laws, as do the Gentiles; but the Gentiles help the Jews and even celebrate their holidays with them, all for the honor of God. However, the author indulges in a blatant racial slur against the Macedonians, indicating that the lessons of one situation do not necessarily carry over to the next one.

ESTHER ADDITION F 1-11 (AT 8:53-59; VG 10:4-13; 11:1)

THE END OF THE GREEK ESTHER

ADDITION F 1-10 (AT 8:53-58; VG 10:4-13), THE INTERPRETATION OF MORDECAI'S DREAM

COMMENTARY

This addition, which comes at the end of MT Esther, is a partner to Add. A, which introduced the Greek Esther. It contains the interpretation of the dream found in Add. A. Like Add. A, it was originally composed in Hebrew or Aramaic. Moore suggests that the dream was originally a separate entity that circulated independently and that when it was later adapted into the Esther story, its interpretation, based on the Esther story, was added.[24] Neither the dream nor its interpretation fits very well in the Esther story, and some of the elements of the interpretation vary among the versions. It is possible that Adds. A and F had a Palestinian provenance, given their strong anti-Gentile sentiment, characteristic of Jewish literature from Palestine in this period.

Verse 1 opens with Mordecai (again, not Esther, making Mordecai the main human character) giving his final valediction of the events that have just been narrated. God is given the credit for everything that has happened, which is the main point of the LXX version of Esther. Mordecai realizes, in retrospect, that his dream foreshadowed the events and proceeds to interpret them. Some of the elements of the interpretation are obvious: The two dragons are Mordecai and Haman; the nations are the hostile Gentiles; and the righteous nation is the Jews. Notice that the hostile Gentiles gather to destroy the "name" of the Jews—that is, to destroy them so thoroughly that even their name will be forgotten. This reflects the very human fear that somehow one's life will be blotted out, because there is no one to remember it. Here the fear is not individual, but that of an ethnic group. Ironically, this fear that Israel's name will be blotted out is the mirror image of Moses' command in Deut 25:17-19 that Amalek's (the tribe of Haman) name be utterly blotted out.

Other elements of the interpretation are not so obvious, however. According to the LXX, Esther is the river, while the tiny spring, the light (but cf. 8:16), and the sun are unaccounted for. It is not clear why Esther is the river and not the spring, or what the river has to do with resolving the conflict. In the AT, the tiny spring is Esther, the river is the enemies of the Jews, and the light and the sun are manifestations of God. This explanation for the spring and the river makes even less sense, for why would the enemies of the Jews come forth from Esther? Further, how is the conflict between the dragons resolved? What this shows is that the dream was not originally part of the story of Esther and only awkwardly relates to it.

The dream was selected, however, because it makes the main point of the Greek version very clearly. The Jews are saved because they cried out to God. The source of salvation is God, not human action, as could be argued in the MT. What is more, the story reflects

---

24. Moore, *Daniel, Esther, and Jeremiah*, 248-49.

the eternal, cosmic struggle between Jew and Gentile, in which God is on the side of the Jews. This is emphasized in v. 7, in which the nations are divided into lots, one lot for the Jews and one for everyone else. The lots are an obvious allusion to Purim (Esth 3:7; 9:24), but also are used a good deal in Jewish literature from Palestine during the Hellenistic period in a figurative sense to mean "portion" or "destiny." In the *Community Rule* from Qumran, one's "lot," or destiny, is either for good or for evil. In the *War Scroll*, the battles of the eschatological age are divided into "lots," belonging either to God or to Belial, with the final "lot" going to God.[25]

25. F. García Martínez, *The Dead Sea Scrolls Translated: The Qumran Texts in English* (Leiden: E. J. Brill, 1992) 3-32, 95-122.

Here "lots" seems to mean "portions," and Israel is God's portion (Deut 32:9). In ultimate conflicts, such as the one just recorded, God will vindicate Israel. This is comforting if you are on the right side. In the cosmic conflict between Jew and Gentile, of which the book of Esther is but one incident, the Jews, according to the redactor, will be vindicated.

As a result, the Festival of Purim should always be celebrated as a memorial to God's vindication, not as a celebration of human victory. It is here a two-day festival (although some Greek MSS omit "the fifteenth"). It is not just a diaspora festival, but a festival everywhere, as befits a commemoration of a cosmic victory.

REFLECTIONS

The "us" versus "them" mentality displayed in the book of Esther, particularly pointedly here and in Add. A, may make us uncomfortable, especially since the hostility seems aimed at some contemporary readers of the book. In fact, this mentality has left the book of Esther open to a lot of criticism over the centuries (see Introduction). It is important to remember the historical circumstances that led to that way of thinking, and the subsequent persecutions the Jews have had to endure throughout their history, as a tool to understanding the theology of the book of Esther. The important lesson for the contemporary reader to take away from this passage is that God is on the side of the oppressed. If we are in the position of oppressor, we can be sure that God will not vindicate us.

By sandwiching the story of Esther between the episodes of Mordecai's dream and its interpretation, the redactor makes clear that God is constantly and thoroughly in control of events. Thus when persecution occurs, even to those who, like Esther and Mordecai, are pious, the reader may find strength in the hope that God is working to carry out the divine purpose. MT Esther is, perhaps, more honest in alluding to the fact that not every evil situation is rectified (see Introduction, but LXX Esther makes the hope that motivates the characters in the MT a reality in Mordecai's statement, "These things have come from God").

ESTHER ADDITION F 11 (AT 8:59; VG 11:1), THE COLOPHON OF THE GREEK ESTHER

COMMENTARY

This colophon,[26] one of very few attested in Jewish literature of the Hellenistic period, purports to answer the questions of the date and provenance of the Greek version

26. Only one AT MSs contains this verse.

of Esther; in fact, however, it raises more questions than it answers. According to the colophon, which is a note appended to a manuscript in order to authenticate it, the "letter about Purim" was brought to Egypt in the fourth year of the reign of Ptolemy and Cleopatra. All the emperors of Ptolemaic Egypt were named Ptolemy, so the search must be narrowed to one who reigned at least four years and had a wife named Cleopatra. There are three possibilities:

Ptolemy VIII, Soter II, in 114 BCE
Ptolemy XII, in 77 BCE
Ptolemy XIV, in 48 BCE[27]

The most likely possibility seems to be Ptolemy XII, bringing the Greek Esther into Egypt in 77 BCE and putting its composition sometime in the late second century BCE, a date I have argued for on other grounds (see the Commentary on Add. A). Who brought it? A man named Dositheus and his son Ptolemy. Both are Greek names, indicating Greek-speaking Jews. The colophon states that Dositheus "said" that he was a priest and a Levite. Does this indicate suspicion of his veracity? The equivalence of priest and Levite, which are usually distinct categories, is ambiguous. Where did Dositheus and Ptolemy bring their book? The Greek simply says "brought in"; the NRSV supplies "to Egypt," implying that they brought it to Alexandria, which had one of the largest Jewish communities in the world at that time. What did they bring? The "preceding Letter about Purim," which must have included the whole of MT Esther plus Addition F, which includes this colophon, and Addition A, which goes with Add. F. It did not necessarily include the other Additions, although we cannot be certain. Note that by 77 BCE the festival was called Purim and was known in Judea. Why did they bring it? They claimed it was "authentic," which implies the existence of other, "inauthentic" versions. The AT existed in a previous form (see Introduction), the proto-AT, which ended before chap. 9 and did not contain the LXX Additions. Is this the "inauthentic" version that was circulating in Egypt and that Dositheus and Ptolemy wished to supplant?[28] If so, why did they wish to supplant it? It is also possible to understand "authentic" as referring to Purim itself. The letter would thus be an attempt to answer objections that Purim was an "inauthentic" holiday.

The colophon claims that this "letter of Purim" was translated by Lysimachus, son of Ptolemy. Is this the same Ptolemy mentioned earlier? Is Lysimachus the grandson of Dositheus, "the priest and Levite"? Is this version supposed to be official in some way? It may have been, but since we cannot identify Lysimachus, Ptolemy, or Dositheus, we do not know the source of their authority. Further, it is unclear what it means to be a "resident" of Jerusalem. It does not imply that Lysimachus was born there; rather, it connotes the presence of a community of Greek-speaking Jews, originally from Alexandria but now living in Jerusalem. It is possible that these Jews came in contact with a Hebrew book of Esther, certainly containing chaps. 1–10 and possibly containing Adds. A, C, D, and F, which had a Semitic source. Recognizing that this version differed from the one with which they were familiar in Alexandria, the proto-AT, they translated it into Greek and took it back to Alexandria to introduce it to the Jewish community there. Because it supposedly came from Jerusalem, it bore a certain authority; and its presence caused the proto-AT to go through a process of editing to conform to this Addition. It may have been in this period that Adds. B and E, more likely of Egyptian provenance, were added to both versions.[29] While this process is admittedly speculative, it does account for the differences that have been noted between the AT and the LXX, and between the Greek versions and the MT.

---

27. E. J. Bickerman, "The Colophon of the Greek Book of Esther," *JBL* 63 (1944) 339-62.

28. See also Day, *Three Faces of a Queen*, 231, who argues that "the A text is possibly the product of a Jewish community within the diaspora setting which is more integrated with non-Jews and more Hellenized in thought and behavior." I would argue that Alexandria fits this description nicely.

29. The good rhetorical Greek of Adds. B and E, which argues for their composition in a primarily Greek-speaking milieu, and their similarities to 3 Maccabees, which most commentators agree was composed in Egypt, make a strong case for Egyptian provenance. See George W. E. Nickelsburg, *Jewish Literature Between the Bible and the Mishnah* (Philadelphia: Fortress, 1981) 169-72.

REFLECTIONS

The colophon to Esther reflects in microcosm the problems of acceptance the book of Esther has had in various communities throughout the centuries. The missing theological obviousness in MT Esther had to be rectified by LXX Esther before it was accepted in Judea (although not everywhere in Judea, if its absence at Qumran is indicative). An "inauthentic" Greek version was supplanted by an "authentic" one. The book of Esther had trouble gaining canonical status in both Judaism and Christianity. Even after its place in the canon was secure, it was the object of vitriol, as evidenced by Martin Luther's comments about it.[30]

Today various groups again would like to reject Esther.[31] Why is this book so hard for the faithful to accept as part of the Bible? It may be because Esther offers no easy answers. The world according to Esther is not a comfortable and easy place: In MT Esther, God is hidden, and humans must live with theological ambiguity. In LXX Esther, hostility between peoples is an accepted fact, and life is a constant struggle. Just for these reasons, however, the book of Esther speaks most profoundly to the twenty-first century. Life is difficult; people are trapped in hostile situations; God often seems hidden. Faithful people are called to live in ambiguity, hoping, like Esther and Mordecai, that they have come to their situation "for such a time as this." Ultimately we must believe that "relief and deliverance . . . will arise" from God. That is the fundamental message of hope that the book of Esther contains.

30. Martin Luther, *Tischreden*, W. A. xxii, 2080, as quoted in Lewis B. Paton, *Esther*, ICC (Edinburgh: T. & T. Clark, 1908) 96.
31. See, e.g., Alice Laffey, *An Introduction to the Old Testament: A Feminist Perspective* (Philadelphia: Fortress, 1988).

THE BOOK OF TOBIT
INTRODUCTION, COMMENTARY, AND REFLECTIONS
BY
IRENE NOWELL, O.S.B.

THE BOOK OF TOBIT

INTRODUCTION

The book of Tobit tells the story of a good man named Tobit who seems to suffer without cause. In performing an act of charity, burying a dead man, he is struck with blindness and made dependent on his wife. He is so aggrieved by a quarrel with her that he prays to die. Meanwhile, in another city, a young woman named Sarah also prays to die because she has been married seven times, and each husband has died on the wedding night. God hears their prayers and sends the angel Raphael to heal them each of their distress.

Tobit remembers some money he has deposited in another city and sends his son Tobiah to get it. Tobiah and Tobit hire a guide, the angel Raphael in disguise, who not only leads Tobiah to the house of Raguel, Sarah's father, but also helps Tobiah catch a fish whose parts will be useful in healing both his father and Sarah. Raphael instructs Tobiah to ask for Sarah's hand in marriage. Tobiah burns the parts of the fish to drive away the demon who is killing Sarah's husbands; then he and Sarah pray and sleep happily through the night. Meanwhile Raguel, fearing the death of another son-in-law, has dug a grave. When he and his wife, Edna, discover that Tobiah and Sarah are well, they hold a fourteen-day wedding feast. Raphael, who has gone after Tobit's money, returns to the feast with Gabael, who has held the money in deposit.

Tobiah's parents are worried sick, however, because their son is late in returning. So Tobiah and his wife set out with Raphael on the return journey. As soon as Tobiah sees his father, he uses the remaining parts of the fish to heal his blindness. When the two men attempt to pay the guide, Raphael reveals his identity and instructs them to praise God. Tobit's song of praise is the last and longest prayer in this book, which contains prayers or blessings by every character except Anna, Tobit's wife, and Raphael. After a long and happy life, Tobit calls for Tobiah and Sarah, along with their children, to give them a final instruction. After their deaths, Tobiah gives both his parents and his parents-in-law honorable burials. Finally Tobiah himself dies at the age of 117.

TEXT AND LANGUAGE

The origins of the book of Tobit are somewhat murky. The book is available to us in three Greek recensions, several fragments of four Aramaic and one Hebrew manuscript, the Old Latin version, and the Latin Vulgate. The presence of Aramaic and Hebrew manuscripts at Qumran led to the conclusion that the original language was Semitic, although whether Hebrew or Aramaic is debatable. Most scholars lean toward Aramaic.[1]

The Qumran manuscripts are fragmentary, however. Thus for a primary text one of the Greek recensions is necessary. There are three Greek recensions: G^I, represented by two manuscripts, Vaticanus (B) and Alexandrinus (A); G^{II}, represented by the Sinaiticus MS, and G^{III}, preserved in MSS 44, 106, and 107. G^{II} has a strong Semitic flavor, many narrative details, and is substantially longer than the others. It has two major gaps, however—4:7-19 and 13:6-10. G^I is written in a more idiomatic Greek and is shorter and more concise than G^{II}. G^{III} is fragmentary, preserved only from 6:9 to 13:8.[2]

The Old Latin version (VL) represents G^{II} and is useful in correcting and reconstructing S. The Vulgate, Jerome says, was translated rapidly (in one day!) from an Aramaic version. Much of it is dependent on VL. Therefore, it is of less value textually than VL. However, it does provide some interesting interpretations of the story. The Qumran manuscripts support the priority of G^{II}, which will be used as the primary text for this commentary, corrected by the Qumran manuscripts and by the Old Latin, and supplemented by G^I where gaps are identified.

DATE

Speculation concerning the date of the book of Tobit has ranged from the seventh century BCE to the third century CE, with a definite preference for the third to second centuries BCE. There are several reasons to support this date with regard to *terminus a quo*. The confusion concerning historical and geographical data in seventh-century Assyria excludes an early date for the book. The title "law of Moses" or "book of Moses" (Tob 6:13; 7:11-13) became current after the writing of the books of Chronicles (4th cent. BCE; cf. 2 Chr 23:18; 25:4; 30:16). The author of Tobit presumes the authority of the prophets as proclaimers of God's Word (14:4). The prophets were canonized around 200 BCE. The fact that the Jews did not accept the book of Tobit in their canon also indicates a late date for the work.

The Maccabean revolt provides the *terminus ad quem*. There is no evidence in Tobit of the turmoil caused by the persecution begun by Antiochus IV Epiphanes (175–164). The emphasis on endogamy, a practice that died out in the first century BCE, the absence of comment on resurrection of the dead, whether belief or non-belief, and the discovery of copies of the book at Qumran support a *terminus ad quem* in the second century. Fitzmyer suggests that the Aramaic in the Qumran fragments represents the period between the end of the second century BCE and the beginning of the second century CE.[3] The most probable date for the writing of the book of Tobit, then, is between 200 and 180 BCE.

PLACE

The most difficult question concerning the origin of the book of Tobit concerns place. Palestine, Egypt, and Mesopotamia have been suggested as possibilities. Assyria and Persia are usually rejected because of the inaccurate geographical references. The eastern diaspora is a stronger possibility.

The other major area of the diaspora, Egypt, is also possible. Some connections exist between Tobit and the Elephantine papyri (5th cent. BCE). One source of Tobit is the story of Ahiqar (see

---

1. See, e.g., J. A. Fitzmyer, "The Aramaic and Hebrew Fragments of Tobit from Qumran Cave 4," *CBQ* 57 (1995) 671. See also C. A. Moore, *Tobit*, AB 40A (Garden City, N.Y.: Doubleday, 1996) 33-39, for further discussion.
2. See R. Hanhart, *Tobit*, Septuaginta; Vetus Testamentum Graecum 8/5 (Göttingen: Vandenhoeck & Ruprecht, 1983) 29-36.
3. Fitzmyer, "The Aramaic and Hebrew Fragments of Tobit from Qumran Cave 4," 667.

the section "The Story of Ahiqar," below), an Aramaic copy of which was found at Elephantine. The marriage contract discovered among the same papyri is very similar to the words of Raguel at the wedding of Sarah and Tobiah.[4] Yet there are also several arguments against Egypt. It seems unlikely that a story written in Aramaic would originate in second-century Egypt. Upper Egypt appears to be a faraway place when the demon is banished there (Tob 8:3).

The third possibility is Palestine. The chief objection to this locale is the setting of the story in the diaspora. Nonetheless, the interest in Jerusalem and its cult may indicate Palestinian provenance. The evidence does not allow a definite conclusion concerning the place of origin of our book.

CANONICAL STATUS

The book of Tobit is not included in the Hebrew Scriptures and thus is not a part of the Old Testament in the Protestant tradition. It is, however, contained in the Septuagint, the ancient Greek translation of Jewish holy books, and was translated by Jerome and included in the Latin Vulgate. Thus it remains part of the Old Testament canon for Roman Catholics and for the Orthodox churches.

GENRE

The book of Tobit is a work of narrative prose with several prayers in poetic form. The question of its historicity has been widely debated. There are several arguments against its literal historicity. First, inaccuracies appear in the report of Assyrian history. Sargon II (721–705) is missing from the recital of kings in chapter 1, perhaps echoing 2 Kgs 17:1-6 and 18:9-13, in which Sargon is not mentioned. The Assyrian king responsible for the deportation of Naphtali from Galilee, the deportation that presumably included Tobit, was Tiglath-pileser III (745–727), not Shalmaneser V as Tob 1:2 states. Second, the first-person narrative in the opening chapters may signal questionable historicity. Authors of antiquity sometimes used first-person narrative to make the teller of the tale, and not the author, responsible for its truth.[5] However, Miller argues that the redactors of texts such as Tobit, the Genesis Apocryphon, and Nehemiah preserved the first-person narrative whenever it was available precisely because it was valued as "original autobiography."[6] Third, the religious principles of the book are more consistent with the period of the author (2nd cent. BCE) than the period in which the story is set (8th–7th cents. BCE). Thus, while there may be a historical nucleus to the book, its primary function is not the telling of history. Rather, it has a didactic purpose: to teach and illustrate basic principles of religious faith.

The book of Tobit bears many characteristics of a "romance" that is cast as a successful quest.[7] The genre, however, is affected by the biblical context. The book also has many features of the Hebrew short story, as defined by Campbell.[8] Its characters are ordinary people whose everyday lives become signs of the working of God's providence. The religious purpose of the author is shown by the subject matter and by the use of biblical models and imagery. It is, however, a late example of the genre. A folktale element predominates, and the distinction between legend and Hebrew short story is blurred.

Hence, the book of Tobit belongs to a mixed genre, created to respond to the needs of the post-exilic community to which its author belonged, a genre shared with Esther, Judith, and Susanna.[9] Overall, the book of Tobit is best described as a Hebrew romance.

---

4. See "Contract of Mibtahiah's Third Marriage," *ANET* 222; see also R. Vattioni, "Studi e note sul libro di Tobia," *Aug* 10 (1940) 277.
5. B. E. Perry, *The Ancient Romances: A Literary-Historical Account of Their Origins* (Berkeley: University of California Press, 1967) Appendix 3, 325-26.
6. J. E. Miller, "The Redaction of Tobit and the Genesis Apocryphon," *JSP* 8 (1991) esp. 56-57.
7. See N. Frye, *Anatomy of Criticism* (Princeton, N.J.: Princeton University Press, 1957) 187-93; R. Scholes and R. Kellogg, *The Nature of Narrative* (New York: Oxford University Press, 1966) 228.
8. E. F. Campbell, Jr., "The Hebrew Short Story: A Study of Ruth," in *A Light unto My Path, Festschrift for J. M. Myers,* ed. H. N. Bream, R. D. Heim, and C. A. Moore (Philadelphia: Temple University Press, 1974) 91.
9. See O. Loretz, "Roman und Kurzgeschichte in Israel," *Wort und Botschaft des Alten Testaments,* ed. J. Schreiner (Würzburg: Echter, 1969) 325.

Other literary forms appear in the book, specifically poetic prayers (3:2-6, 11-15; 8:5-8, 15-17; 11:14-15; 13:1-18)[10] and wisdom speeches (4:3-21; 12:6-10; 14:3-11). The wisdom speeches, which contain several proverbs, may also be classified as farewell discourses.[11]

SOURCES FOR THE PLOT

The Grateful Dead. The plot of the center section of Tobit, the travelogue (chaps. 5–12), is derived from the folktale "The Grateful Dead."[12] The basic story of the Grateful Dead, as found in a widespread collection of folktales, concerns a man who impoverishes himself to ransom and bury a corpse that is being mistreated by the dead man's creditors. Shortly thereafter, when the poor man is on a journey, he is joined by a stranger who offers to be his servant in return for half of whatever the hero might acquire.

At this point the folktales diverge. The version best known in the Near East and in Eastern Europe is the form that is related to the book of Tobit. In this form the tale is combined with the tale of "The Monster in the Bridal Chamber." The hero in this combination of tales is advised by the stranger to marry a wealthy princess whose former bridegrooms have all perished in the bridal chamber. The stranger then keeps watch on the wedding night and slays the serpent that emerges from the mouth of the princess to kill the hero. Subsequently, the stranger demands half the bride as his payment, but as he threatens to divide the bride with his sword (or actually does), another serpent(s) comes out of the bride, and she is freed from enchantment. The stranger then reveals himself as the grateful dead man whom the hero had buried.[13]

Several similarities exist between this story and the plot of Tobit. Tobit is impoverished because of his practice of burying the dead. His son Tobiah (the hero has been divided into two characters of similar name) is accompanied on a journey by a mysterious stranger who advises him to marry a bride whose husbands have all died on the wedding night. Through the advice and service of the stranger, Tobiah survives the wedding night, and the bride is freed from enchantment. The stranger is offered payment of half the goods acquired on the journey (not, however, half the bride). He then reveals his identity and disappears.

The Story of Ahiqar. A second major source for the plot is the story of Ahiqar (NAB; NRSV, "Ahikar"), who appears in the book of Tobit in four passages (1:21-22; 2:10; 11:18; 14:10). The story seems to have been written originally in Aramaic sometime in the sixth century BCE.[14] Fragments of the story in Aramaic were found at Elephantine and have been dated to the fifth century BCE. The story of Ahiqar appears in several languages: Syriac, Arabic, Armenian, and Slavonic, and fragments in Ethiopic and Greek. These versions are much later than the Aramaic fragments.

The story of Ahiqar consists of a narrative portion and a set of proverbs. The narrative tells the story of the life of Ahiqar, a royal official at the courts of Sennacherib and Esarhaddon. Because he is childless, Ahiqar adopts Nadin,[15] his nephew, and trains him to succeed to his royal position. But Nadin, treacherous and ungrateful, accuses Ahiqar of disloyalty to the king. Ahiqar is condemned to death, but is secretly rescued by the executioner whose life Ahiqar had saved earlier. He remains hidden in a cave under his own house until the king, challenged to a contest of wisdom by the pharaoh of Egypt, expresses the wish that Ahiqar still lived. Thereupon Ahiqar emerges from hiding, answers the pharaoh's challenge, and is restored to his former honor. Meanwhile, Nadin is imprisoned and dies.[16] The proverbs of Ahiqar are probably older than

---

10. For an excellent analysis of the prayers found in the book, see P. J. Griffin, "The Theology and Function of Prayer in the Book of Tobit" (Ph.D. diss., The Catholic University of America, 1984).
11. A. A. Di Lella, "The Deuteronomic Background of the Farewell Discourse in Tob 14:3-11," *CBQ* 41 (1979) 380n. 1.
12. See K. Simrock, *Der Gute Gerhard und die dankbaren Todten* (Bonn: Marcus, 1856) 131-32; G. H. Gerould, *The Grateful Dead*, publications of the Folklore Society 60 (London: D. Nutt, 1980; reprinted, Folcroft, Pa.: Folcroft Library Editions, 1973) 7.
13. See S. Thompson, *The Folktale* (New York: Dryden, 1946) 50-53, for the basic synopsis. See Gerould, *The Grateful Dead*, 47-75, for a description of folktales from several places that demonstrate the combination he calls the Grateful Dead and the Poison Maiden.
14. J. M. Lindenberger, *The Aramaic Proverbs of Ahiqar* (Baltimore: Johns Hopkins University Press, 1983) 16-20.
15. This spelling of the name is found in the Qumran fragments 4QTob^d, 11:18.
16. See the synopsis of this story in Lindenberger, *The Aramaic Proverbs of Ahiqar*, 3-4. See also J. R. Harris in F. C. Conybeare, J. R. Harris, and A. S. Lewis, *The Story of Ahikar* (London: C. J. Clay & Sons, 1898) viii-x.

the narrative and were presumably added to the story to strengthen the impression of Ahiqar's wisdom.

Similarities between the story of Ahiqar and the book of Tobit can be seen both in content and in literary form. The life of Ahiqar resembles in broad strokes the life of Tobit. Both are faithful men who are unjustly plunged into darkness, but who, because of righteousness, are saved from death and restored to life. The story of Ahiqar is told in first-person narrative, similar to the beginning of the book of Tobit. The wisdom speech of Tobit to his son Tobiah (4:3-21) echoes proverbs in the story of Ahiqar.

General knowledge of the story of Ahiqar is presumed by the author of the book of Tobit. Ahiqar is made a relative of Tobit (1:21), ostensibly to enhance Tobit by connecting him with such a renowned sage. Ahiqar uses his position to help Tobit in his distress (1:21-22; 2:10). He and Nadin come to rejoice in Tobit's joy (11:18). In the final reference to Ahiqar, Tobit recounts a synopsis of Ahiqar's life (14:10-11).

Just as the journey of Tobiah (the central section) rests on the outline of the folktale combination of the "Grateful Dead"/"Monster in the Bridal Chamber," so also the life of Tobit (chaps. 1–4; 13–14; the frame) rests on the outline of the story of Ahiqar. The influence of these two sources clarifies the interweaving of first-person narrative, wisdom sections and prayers, and the theme of innocent suffering and vindication with the folktale quest for a bride.

These two sources, however, are insufficient to explain the motivations and the progress of the plot in the book of Tobit. The book is permeated with biblical themes and principles. Folktale elements from the "Grateful Dead"/"Monster in the Bridal Chamber" have been changed in conformity with the tenets of biblical faith. The grateful dead man has been replaced by an angel. The hero is now represented by two figures: the father-hero and the son-hero. The father-hero buries the dead out of respect for biblical injunctions (e.g., Deut 21:23) and is both tested and rewarded for his fidelity. The son-hero wins the bride, not because he buried the dead, but because he has a right to her by Mosaic law (Tob 6:12-13; 7:10; cf. Num 36:8-9). The marriage is planned in heaven (Tob 6:18; 7:11). The bride is delivered from the demon by God, who sends an angel to instruct the hero in exorcism and prayer (6:17-18; 8:2-9). The angel demands no payment but is offered half of the recovered money (12:15).

Modifications have also been made in the borrowing from Ahiqar. Ahiqar himself has been made a Jew. The figure of the son differs in the two stories. In Ahiqar, Nadin is an adopted son; in Tobit, Tobiah is a natural son. Nadin is a classic example of the ungrateful son; Tobiah is an example of the devoted, faithful son. The just man in the two stories is vindicated for different reasons. Tobit is vindicated simply because he is righteous; Ahiqar is vindicated because of a specific form of righteousness, almsgiving.

The Joseph Story. L. Ruppert proposes the Joseph story (Genesis 37; 39–50) as the link between extra-biblical sources and the biblical tradition that is fundamental to the book of Tobit.[17] The Joseph story, the basic biblical analogue to Tobit, is the third and most significant element that must be considered in outlining its plot. In the Joseph story, as in the book of Tobit, an elderly father sends a beloved son (Benjamin), whom he entrusts to a companion (Reuben or Judah; Gen 42:37; 43:8-9), on a dangerous journey to a distant land to obtain relief from a current need. The travelers recognize that the father's life is so bound up in that of the son that if the son should die, the father would go down to the nether world in grief (Gen 44:30-31; cf. Tob 6:15).

Upon his arrival the son meets a near relative (Joseph/Raguel) who inquires about his father's health (Gen 45:3; Tob 7:4-5). After the close kinship is revealed, the travelers are welcomed with tearful embraces (Gen 45:14-15; cf. Tob 7:6-8; Gen 43:27-30).[18] Meanwhile, although the father (or mother; note that in Tobit it is Edna who inquires concerning Tobit's health) fears the son's death (Gen 37:33-35; 43:14; cf. Tob 10:4, 7), the son escapes danger (Gen 39:1-6;

---

17. L. Ruppert, "Zur Function der Achikar-Notizen im Buch Tobias," *BZ* 20 (1976) 232-37. For the links between Ahiqar and the Joseph story, see also S. Niditch and R. Doran, "The Success Story of the Wise Courtier: A Formal Approach," *JBL* 96 (1977) 179-93.

18. G. Priero, *Tobia*, ed. S. Garofalo, 2nd ed., La Sacra Bibbia (Turin: Marietti, 1963) 37, comments on the frequency of tears in Tobit (e.g., 2:7; 3:1, 10; 5:18; 7:6-8, 16; 9:6; 10:4, 7; 11:9, 14). They are, perhaps, an echo of the frequent tears in the Joseph story (Gen 37:35; 42:30; 45:14-15; 47:29; 50:1, 17).

44:1–45:3; cf. Tob 6:3-4; 8:2-9) and is reunited with the father (Gen 46:30; cf. Tob 11:9-10).[19] With tearful embraces the father (or mother) proclaims readiness to die (Gen 46:30; Tob 11:9; cf. Tob 11:14). As the story draws to a close, the father summons his son(s) and grandchildren to his deathbed, asks for an honorable burial, and makes a statement about the future and about return to the homeland (Gen 47:27–48:2, 15-22; cf. Gen 50:24; Tob 14:3-8; 13:5). There is a final poetic speech by the father concerning the future (Genesis 49; Tobit 13).[20]

Biblical Type Scenes. In addition to the outline from part of the Joseph story, the central scene of the book of Tobit has another biblical analogue. Tobiah's betrothal (7:1-17), including the preceding departure from the father (5:17-22) and subsequent departure from the bride's home (10:7-13), is modeled on the biblical type scene of betrothal.[21] The two betrothal scenes closest in pattern to Tob 7:1-17 are Isaac's (Gen 34:1-67) and Jacob's (Gen 29:1-30). Genesis 29:4-6 appears almost verbatim in Tob 7:3-5 (see Commentary). In addition, each passage is linked to Tobit by a particular key word. The link to Isaac's betrothal scene is εὐοδόω (*euodoō*, "prosper," "make successful"). The link to Jacob's betrothal scene is ὑγιαίνω (*hygiainō*, "to be well"). The scenes are also similar in structure.

Two points of correspondence link Tobiah's betrothal scene with that of Moses (Exod 2:15-21): the number seven (a folktale element) and the name of the father-in-law. Seven daughters meet Moses at the well. The father of Moses' future bride is named Raguel (or Reuel). Moses' departure from his father-in-law (Exod 4:18*a*) also resembles the corresponding scenes in Tobit (10:11) and in Genesis (24:54-61).

The Book of Job. A final pattern influencing the book of Tobit appears in the book of Job. The structure of the two books is similar. Each book contains a "framing" section that sets the stage in the beginning and summarizes the situation at the end (Job 1:1–2:13; 42:7-17; Tob 1:1–3:17; 12:1–14:15). The central action is set into this frame (Job 3:1–42:6; Tob 4:1–11:18). The progress of Tobit's life is modeled on that of Job. Each man suffers bodily affliction, even though he is righteous (Job 2:7; 27:6; Tob 1:3; 2:10); each is grieved by the sharp words of a wife (Job 2:9-10; Tob 2:14–3:1) and prays for death (Job 7:15; Tob 3:2-6). After his testing, each man is vindicated and rewarded (Job 42:7-17; Tob 14:1-3). Imagery of light and darkness is prevalent in both books. More than a quarter of the occurrences of the words אוֹר (*'ôr*, "light") and חֹשֶׁךְ (*ḥōšek*, "darkness") in the Hebrew Bible are in the book of Job. The story of Tobit moves from light to darkness and back to light.

Conclusion. The outline of the plot of the book of Tobit is shaped by several sources. Extra-biblical literature has contributed the patterns of two folktales—the "Grateful Dead"/"Monster in the Bridal Chamber," and the story of Ahiqar—which form respectively a basis for the central travelogue and for the framing story of the just, guiltless man who suffers but is finally vindicated. Biblical literature has contributed four elements: The story of Joseph functions as a pattern for incorporating the story of Tobit into the flow of salvation history; the betrothal scene from the ancestor stories serves as a model for the central scene in Tobit; the book of Job provides a model for the structure of the book of Tobit, the life of its principal character, and its basic imagery; and finally, the story is set in, and permeated by, a context of faith. As Zimmermann says, "The woof comes from the folklore of mankind, and the warp and the pattern, the vitality and the color, come from the religious experience of the Jewish people."[22]

It is not similarities to a pattern, however, but the variations that are significant.[23] The differences between the book of Tobit and the folktales derive largely from the biblical context. The differences between the book of Tobit and its biblical models can be attributed to the influences of a different time and a different historical situation. The location differs from the ancestor stories. The need for burial of the dead, though a prominent theme in Genesis,[24] arises from a different cause. The essence of a just life—fear of God and charity toward others—remains

---

19. Note that in the Joseph story two beloved sons are separated from the father and are feared dead, Joseph and Benjamin. In the book of Tobit there is only one, Tobiah.
20. Ruppert, "Zur Function der Achikar-Notizen im Buch Tobias," 114-15.
21. R. Alter, *The Art of Biblical Narrative* (New York: Basic Books, 1981) 51.
22. F. Zimmermann, *The Book of Tobit: An English Translation with Introduction and Commentary*, Dropsie College Edition, JAL (New York: Harper and Bros., 1958) 12.
23. Alter, *The Art of Biblical Narrative*, 52.
24. I. Abrahams, "Tobit and Genesis," *JQR* 5 (1893) 348-50, was the first to point out the connection between Tobit and Genesis in the concentration on burial.

constant, but the ways in which justice is enacted differ for the characters in Tobit, who lived in exile, from the ancestors, who lived in Egypt and among the Canaanites. The outline of the plot of Tobit derives from several sources; however, the unique expression of this particular plot reflects the needs and preoccupations of the second-century diaspora.[25]

LITERARY ARTISTRY

The Narrator. There are two narrators in the book of Tobit: the first-person narrator of 1:3–3:1 and the third-person narrator of 3:17 through the end of the book. A bridge consisting of two prayers and the introduction of two new characters connects them, but it is unclear whether Tobit remains the narrator in the bridge.[26] The third-person narrator is unobtrusive, reliable, omniscient, and brief. The first-person narrator, by contrast, is more limited in perspective, less knowledgeable and less neutral.[27]

Dialogue and Reticence. The bulk of the story in the book of Tobit is carried by dialogue. Alter suggests the analysis of (1) the characters' own speech, particularly the first reported speech; (2) contrasting dialogue between characters; and (3) the discontinuity between speech and reticence.[28] The first reported speech of each character, with the exception of Raphael and Sarah, occurs in the first scene in which that character appears. The first speech is significant as a revelation of character (see Commentary on 2:13-14; 5:4-5). Comparing the speech of various characters is also instructive regarding character. For example, Tobit speaks with greater breadth than does Anna, who speaks in short questions. Also, Tobiah asks many questions and speaks with the haste of youth, whereas Raphael makes long speeches and is generally a vehicle of information (a fitting task for an angel).

The economy of the biblical author is most evident in the reticence of the characters. The most striking example is Sarah, whose only words are spoken in prayer (3:11-15; 8:8). Several times characters simply disappear from a scene (e.g., Tobiah in 2:3-8; 5:10–6:6; 7:11*b*–8:3; 8:20-21; Raphael in 7:9-17; 10:7-13; 11:9-15).

A frequent feature of dialogue shared in common by all speakers is inclusion—that is, beginning and ending a speech with the same word or phrase (e.g., "take courage" [θάρσει *tharsei*] in 5:10; "welcome" [ὑγιαίνων ἔλθοις *hygiainōn elthois*] in 5:14; "child" [παιδίον *paidion*] in 5:17; "will leave in good health/return in good health" [ὑγιαίνων πορεύσεται/ὑποστρέψει ὑγιαίνων *hygiainōn poreusetai/hypostrepsei hygiainōn*] in 5:21-22; "eat and drink" [φάγε καὶ πίε *phage kai pie*] in 7:10-11; "take courage, daughter" [θάρσει θύγατερ *tharsei thygater*] in 7:17; "take courage, child" [θάρσει παιδίον *tharsei paidion*] in 8:21; "my child has perished" [ἀπώλετο τὸ παιδίον μου *apōleto to paidion mou*] in 10:4, 7; "how much shall I pay him?" [πόσον αὐτῷ δώσω τόν μισθόν/πόσον αὐτῷ ἔτι δῶ μισθόν *poson autō dōsō ton misthon/poson autō eti dō misthon*] in 12:2-3).

Irony. There are two major and several minor types of irony in the book of Tobit. The basic conflict of the book—the problem that the apparent consequence of doing good is not prosperity but suffering—is an example of the "general irony of events."[29] The veiled identity of Raphael constitutes an example of the second major type of irony, "dramatic irony," in which the readers know what the characters do not.[30] Raguel's digging of the unnecessary grave (8:9-18) is also an example of dramatic irony. The "irony of self-betrayal" is evident in the contradiction between Anna's words and her actions, for she continues to watch the road even though she declares that Tobiah is dead. Irony carries the main theme of the book of Tobit: God blesses the righteous and punishes the wicked; yet God remains free. This final type of irony may be called "divine irony."

---

25. See Loretz, "Roman und Kurzgeschichte in Israel," 324-25.
26. Miller, "The Redaction of Tobit and the Genesis Apocryphon," 54-55.
27. See D. McCracken, "Narration and Comedy in the Book of Tobit," *JBL* 114 (1995) 403-9. I am grateful to McCracken for correcting my oversimplification regarding the differences between the two narrative voices.
28. Alter, *The Art of Biblical Narrative*, 182-83.
29. D. C. Muecke, *Irony* (London: Methuen & Co., 1970) 67.
30. Muecke, *Irony*, 64-66.

Imagery and Key Words. The book is built on a basic opposition between death and life. Only chap. 9 has no mention of death or burial. In addition to words referring specifically to death and life, the concept is imaged through the opposition between night and day, darkness and light, blindness and vision. Tobit's blindness is the physical symbol of the opposition between light and darkness, life and death. It ranks him with sinners as well as with the dead.

A group of abstract terms supports the basic opposition of death and life. Key words on the positive side of the opposition center around healing: health and wellness, safety and salvation, mercy and prosperity are frequently mentioned. With these gifts comes joy. The prayers are particularly filled with expressions of joy. The negative side of the opposition is represented by two clusters of words. The main characters experience and fear distress and reproach. Their distress has two consequences: grief and prayer for deliverance.

One of the major tenets of the book is that these contrasting realities of life and death, suffering and health, joy and sorrow, are in God's hands. The life-and-death opposition manifested in the characters' lives is reflected in the portrait of Jerusalem in the final chapters. For a time, Jerusalem will be desolate, but at the proper time it will be rebuilt.

Another set of key words serves to describe the characters in the book. Four adjectives are used consistently to describe Tobit: "noble/beautiful" (καλός *kalos*); "good" (ἀγαθός *agathos*); "righteous" (δίκαιος *dikaios*); and "charitable/merciful" (ἐλεήμων *eleēmōn*). The cognate nouns of two of these words, "charity" and "righteousness," along with "truth/fidelity" (ἀλήθεια *alētheia*), form an inclusio that frames the book (1:3; 14:9). Tobit exhorts Tobiah and his children, and also the whole people, to these virtues. These words appear also in descriptions of Raphael (5:14, 22) and in his exhortation to Tobit and Tobiah (12:6-8, 11). They describe not only the character of Tobit, but also the nature of God (3:2; 13:6). Thus the four key words characterize God, God's messenger, and the human characters in the book. God is noble and good, just and merciful. The messengers sent by God to assist human beings manifest the same qualities. Human beings, in response, are called to be noble and good, just and merciful.

Two further images in the book serve as symbols. The fish that attempts to swallow Tobiah's foot (6:3) is a symbol of death (see Commentary on 6:3-4). The number seven is a symbol of completion. Sarah loses seven bridegrooms.[31] Tobiah is the eighth husband; he ends the sorrow brought by the previous seven. He is adjured to bring joy to her heart, beginning with the fourteen-day (twice seven) wedding feast (8:20). Then the two return home to celebrate another seven happy days (11:18). Their children number seven sons (14:3). The messenger of God's providence, sent to bring God's healing and joy to this family, is Raphael, one of the seven angels who stand before God (12:15).

THEOLOGY

The Providence of God. A basic premise of the book is that God cares for human beings. God's plan shapes human history, affecting both individual lives and national destinies. Individual lives are woven together in a common journey. The circle of interwoven lives widens from the individual (Tobit) to the larger family, to the whole people, and finally to all nations who will come to Jerusalem.

The agents of God's providence are an angel, human beings, and natural objects and events. The developed figure of the angel (messenger) is one of the major contributions of the book of Tobit to Old Testament theology. The angel Raphael functions as guide and protector, conveyor of information, mediator of prayer, and one who tests. His words and identity, however, are veiled and ambiguous. God's work through him is not immediately obvious to the other characters in the story.

The primary agents of God's providence in this book are human persons. The clearest example is found in the actions of Tobiah. Through his obedience, God heals both Tobit and Sarah.

---

31. J. Craghan lists seven calamities for Tobit also. See Craghan, *Esther, Judith, Tobit, Jonah, Ruth*, OTM 16, ed. C. Stuhlmueller and M. McNamara (Wilmington, Del.: Michael Glazier, 1982) 138.

God's providence is also shown through natural materials, such as the medicinal properties of the fish organs.

The Justice of God. The book of Tobit also asserts that God is just. The understanding of God's justice is expressed in the theory of retribution: God rewards the just and punishes the wicked. The apparent contradiction of this theory, found in the suffering of the just man Tobit, generates the conflict of the plot. How can God be just if the apparent consequence of doing good is not prosperity but suffering? Only at the end is it clear that Tobit's unflinching faith is justified: The wicked are indeed punished (the destruction of Nineveh), and the just are rewarded (the prosperity of Tobit and his family).

The Freedom of God. Although Tobit ultimately receives reward, the story of his life demonstrates that the doctrine of retribution is not a simple equation. The concept of God in this book is not that of a deterministic fate, but of a personal God who is merciful and just, caring and provident, and who blesses the righteous out of the depths of divine freedom.

The Virtuous Life. The book of Tobit provides a guide and an example for human living. The virtuous life is demonstrated first of all in three sets of relationships in family life: the relationship between parents and children; the marriage relationship; and respect for women. The relationship between parents and children is characterized by instruction, obedience, respect, and love.

There are several examples of the faithful and supportive marriage relationship. The relationships between husband and wife for each of the three married couples differ, but love is expressed in each. The interaction between Tobit and Anna is the liveliest of the three and portrays both positive and negative sides of the relationship. The relationship between Raguel and Edna is less obvious, but there is evidence of mutual interdependence and support. The relationship between Tobiah and Sarah is set firmly upon trust in God's plan and obedience to God's law. It begins with prayer, in which marriage is seen as a gift from God. Raguel, Edna, and Tobit all express the hope that marriage will bring joy, and they regard children as a blessing. They recognize marriage not only as a bond between two people, but also as a bond between families.

The respect for women shown throughout the book is also an element of virtuous family life. The three female characters are carefully drawn and are given significant roles and distinct personalities. Sarah, although the most silent and passive character in the story, reveals in her prayer that she is strong in self-knowledge, capable of deliberation, and has been instructed in the law and in prayer. She is "sensible and beautiful" (6:12). Edna, who never appears without Raguel, has a more limited role and autonomy than Anna. Nonetheless both women are respected by their husbands and are contributing members of their families. Tobit's grandmother Deborah is honored for her instruction of the young Tobit. Women are regarded as competent persons, capable of relating to God through prayer and obedience to the law, capable of providing help and support to their husbands, capable of instructing and guiding their children. They do not, however, have public responsibilities in either the economic or the religious sphere. They are seen primarily in relationship to their families.[32]

Two virtues are expressed not only within the family, but also within the wider kinship group. The first is ἐλεημοσύνη (*eleēmosynē*), which is translated as "almsgiving," "charity," or "mercy." This virtue, mentioned in the inclusio that frames the book (1:3; 14:9), is linked to the major statement of the book that God rewards the just and punishes the wicked. What God rewards is almsgiving.[33] The second virtue exercised within the kinship group is hospitality. Raguel, whose character is modeled on that of Abraham, is the primary example of the hospitable person. The hospitality of Tobit can be seen in the alacrity with which he greets Raphael (5:10), his joyous welcome of his daughter-in-law Sarah (11:17), and the feasts he hosts (2:2; 11:17-18). Tobiah follows his father's example in inviting Gabael to join the wedding feast in Ecbatana (9:2, 5-6).

---

32. See B. Bow and G. W. E. Nickelsburg, "Patriarchy with a Twist: Men and Women in Tobit," in *Women Like This: New Perspectives on Jewish Women in the Greco-Roman World*, ed. Amy-Jill Levine (Atlanta: Scholars Press, 1991) 127-43.

33. See P. J. Griffin, "A Study of *Eleēmosynē* in the Bible with Emphasis upon Its Meaning and Usage in the Theology of Tobit and Ben Sira" (MA thesis, The Catholic University of America, 1982), for a thorough treatment of the structural and narrative significance of *eleēmosynē* in the book of Tobit. He notes that the word *eleēmosynē* appears more often in the book of Tobit than in any other OT book (22 times, compared to 13 times in Sirach; 7 times in Proverbs; 4 times in Isaiah; 3 times in Psalms; twice each in Deuteronomy, the Song of Songs, Baruch, and Daniel; and once in Genesis), and that its semantic development is one of the major contributions of the book of Tobit to OT theology. P. Deselaers defines *eleēmosynē* as "community building activity" (*solidarische handeln*). See Deselaers, *Das Buch Tobit: Studien zu seiner Entstehung, Komposition, und Theologie*, OBO 43 (Freiburg [Schwiez]/Göttingen: Universitätsverlag/Vandenhoeck und Ruprecht, 1982) 348-58.

Both *eleēmosyne* and hospitality are limited in the book of Tobit to one's own kindred and people (1:3, 8, 16-18; 2:2-3; 4:17). The diaspora setting of the story helps to explain the limitation to the covenant community. Survival as a people depended on mutual support. Fear of being led astray or contaminated by non-believers encouraged exclusivity. Yet the separation from non-Jews, though evident in matters of food (1:10-11) and marriage (1:9; 4:12-13), does not extend to contempt for other peoples, such as appears in Ezra–Nehemiah or the books of Maccabees.

The relationship of the righteous person to God is characterized by observance of the law and the practice of prayer. Tobit himself is the primary example of faithful observance (1:6-11). He exhorts his son to the same careful observance (chap. 4). Observance of the law is expected not only with regard to detailed external practices, but also through an inner spirit of piety toward God and charity toward neighbor. The relationship with God is to be characterized by fear (4:21; 14:6), love (14:7), and sincerity (4:6; 13:6; 14:7). The habit of prayer is the most pervasive expression of inner devotion to God.[34] The book has been called "a school of prayer";[35] the frequency of prayer and its incorporation at major turning points of the plot indicate its importance. The story is a graphic illustration that prayer is answered. The continual turning to God in prayer indicates that God is the real hero and principal actor of the book. The virtuous life, learned through prayer and the law, is modeled on God, who is righteous, merciful, and truthful.[36]

---

34. See Griffin, "The Theology and Function of Prayer in the Book of Tobit."
35. J. Goettmann, "Le livre des conseils ou le miroir du Juste engagé dans le monde," *BVC* 21 (1958) 36.
36. See Di Lella, "The Deuteronomic Background of the Farewell Discourse in Tob 14:3-11," 386-87.

BIBLIOGRAPHY

Craghan, John. *Esther, Judith, Tobit, Jonah, Ruth*. OTM 16. Edited by C. Stuhlmueller and M. McNamara. Wilmington, Del.: Michael Glazier, 1982. A theological commentary for a general audience, highlighting literary criticism.

Dancy, John C., W. J. Fuerst, and R. J. Hammer. *The Shorter Books of the Apocrypha*. Edited by P. R. Ackroyd et al. Cambridge: Cambridge University Press, 1972. Translation and brief commentary for the general reader.

Fitzmyer, J. A. *Tobit: Qumran Cave 4, xiv*. DJD 19. Edited by M. Broshi et al. Oxford: Clarendon, 1995. Critical edition of the Qumran fragments with a thorough analysis.

Hanhart, R. *Tobit*. Septuaginta, Vetus Testamentum Graecum 8/5. Göttingen: Vandenhoeck & Ruprecht, 1983. The critical edition of the Greek recensions.

Moore, Carey A. *Tobit*. AB 40A. Garden City, N.Y.: Doubleday, 1996. A new translation and comprehensive commentary, based on both the Greek recensions and the Qumran fragments.

Nickelsburg, G. W. E. "Tobit." In *Harper's Bible Commentary*. Edited by J. L. Mays. New York: Harper & Row, 1988. Analysis of literary, religious, and social aspects of the book, plus commentary.

OUTLINE OF TOBIT

I. Tobit 1:1–3:17, Distress in Ecbatana and Nineveh

    A. 1:1-22, Tobit's Virtuous Life
    B. 2:1–3:6, Tobit's Distress and Prayer
    C. 3:7-15, Sarah's Distress and Prayer
    D. 3:16-17, God's Answer to Both: Raphael

II. Tobit 4:1–6:1, Preparation for the Journey to Media

    A. 4:1-21, Tobit's Instructions to His Son
    B. 5:1–6:1, The Hiring of a Guide

III. Tobit 6:2-18, The Journey to Media

    A. 6:2-9, Catching the Fish
    B. 6:10-18, Raphael's Instructions

IV. Tobit 7:1–11:18, Resolution and Recovery

    A. 7:1–8:21, Sarah's Healing
    B. 9:1-6, Recovery of the Money
    C. 10:1–11:18, Tobit's Healing

V. Tobit 12:1–14:15, All's Well That Ends Well

    A. 12:1-22, Revelation of Raphael's Identity
    B. 13:1-17, Tobit's Prayer
    C. 14:1-15, Epilogue

TOBIT 1:1–3:17

DISTRESS IN ECBATANA AND NINEVEH

OVERVIEW

The first section of the book of Tobit introduces readers to the main characters and to the conflict that drives the plot. This is a story of two families: Tobit's family in Nineveh, and Raguel's family in Ecbatana. The title character, Tobit, is described as a scrupulously virtuous man who is struck with blindness while performing a virtuous act, burying the dead. His wife, Anna, is an industrious woman with a sharp tongue. They have one child, their son, Tobiah. The first member of Raguel's family to be introduced is Sarah, the daughter of Raguel and Edna. She is in great distress because a demon, Asmodeus, keeps killing her bridegrooms. The prayers of Sarah and Tobit bring another major character into the story, the angel Raphael. Raphael is commissioned by God to bring healing to both. Finally, God is an actor behind the scenes throughout the book.

Two plots are introduced in this opening section. The first plot develops in three sequences. The first sequence begins with the statement of Tobit's character: "he has walked on the paths of truth and righteousness." This statement gives rise to questions: How is his righteousness manifested? What will be his reward? These two questions are answered almost immediately. Tobit performs acts of charity, especially burying the dead. His reward seems to be blindness. The second sequence begins with the announcement that Tobit has married Anna, a woman of his own kindred. Anna and their son, Tobiah, will be major actors in the following story. The third sequence begins with the news that Tobit has gone to Media and deposited money there. The question raised by this sequence is, What will happen to the money? The second main plot begins with the introduction of Sarah. Her distress gives rise to the question, How will she be delivered? The plots join in 3:16-17 with the answer to the prayers of Tobit and Sarah. Raphael has been sent, but now the question remains: How will he function? Two new questions are also posed: How will Tobit be healed? How will Tobiah meet and marry Sarah?

The conflict of the story arises from the suffering of Sarah and Tobit. Each character seems to be afflicted unjustly. The theory of retribution, which is described most fully in Deuteronomy 28, holds that righteous people will be blessed by God, while wicked people will be punished. Both Sarah and Tobit seem to be righteous. Why, then, are they afflicted? Does their suffering suggest that God is not just, and the theory does not hold? How can this conflict be resolved?

The resolution to the conflict is suggested already at the end of this first section. In answer to the prayers of Tobit and Sarah, God sends the angel Raphael to heal them both. Thus the suspense of the story resides not in whether they will be healed, but in how they will be healed.

Other major elements of the book are mentioned in the first section:

(1) Prayer is a major theme throughout the book. Six substantial prayers are woven into the plot. Five of the characters turn to God in prayer.

(2) Acts of charity (almsgiving) are presented as the chief element of Tobit's righteousness. These acts also are the primary support of Tobit's hope for a happy life. Anna challenges Tobit precisely on this point when she asks what good his righteous deeds have done him (2:14). God's apparent disregard

of Tobit's faithfulness in charitable acts is the reason for the despair in his prayer.

(3) An angel is commissioned as a minister of God's providence.

(4) The inclusion not only of individual characters, but also of two families, suggests the importance of marriage and family life.

TOBIT 1:1-22, TOBIT'S VIRTUOUS LIFE

COMMENTARY

1:1-2. The first two verses of the book begin with the title character and give the setting of the story. The name of the main character in the Qumran fragments is "Tobi" (טובי *ṭwby*), which is probably a shortened form of "Tobiah," the name of his son.[37] Tobit is introduced with a five-member genealogy. The names are all theophoric—that is, they contain the name of God, אל (*'ēl*). For example, Tobi-el means "God is my good"; Hanani-el, "God has shown mercy": Rapha-el, "God heals." These names in Tobit's genealogy suggest the piety of his family.

Tobit's tribe is also identified. Naphtali is a northern tribe; its territory runs from the south end of the Sea of Galilee northward to the Huleh basin. In the eighth century BCE the Assyrians took over Galilee, including the territory of Naphtali. Many of the leading citizens were taken captive into Assyria. The sorrow of this captivity is described by the eighth-century prophet Isaiah (Isa 9:1[8:23]). But Isaiah also holds out hope for the people: "The people who walked in darkness have seen a great light" (Isa 9:2[9:1]).

The book begins as historical annals do, with "the book of the deeds" (βίβλος λόγων *biblos logōn*; cf. LXX 3 Kgdms 14:29; 15:7, 23, 31; 16:5, 14, 20, 27). Some of the historical information in the title, however, is incorrect. The author has confused Tiglath-pileser III (745–727 BCE), the Assyrian ruler who deported the citizens of Galilee, with his successor, Shalmaneser V (727–722 BCE), who began the siege of Samaria, the capital city of the northern kingdom. Shalmaneser's successor, Sargon II (722–705 BCE), defeated the northern kingdom, destroyed the capital city, and took captive the ten tribes of Israel.

1:3. The story of Tobit begins with a first-person narrative that continues until the scene changes to the house of Raguel in Ecbatana (3:6). Tobit describes himself with three words that will characterize him throughout the book: truth (ἀλήθεια *alētheia*), righteousness (δικαιοσύνη *dikaiosynē*), and charity (ἐλεημοσύνη *eleēmosynē*). These character traits are illustrated by the practices of his youth (vv. 4-9), his continued fidelity when he was taken into captivity (vv. 10-15), and the specific charitable act of burying the dead (vv. 16-22).

1:4-5. Tobit is a living example of fidelity to the law of God as it is laid out in Deuteronomy. The book of Deuteronomy requires that worship be centralized in the Jerusalem Temple and that all sacrifices be offered there (Deut 12:11-14). When the ten northern tribes separated from Judah in the tenth century BCE, their king, Jeroboam, did not want his people to continue worshiping in Jerusalem. The Temple was a strong reminder of the power of David and Solomon; the temple liturgy encouraged support of the Davidic monarchy, which continued to rule in Judah. So Jeroboam built two alternate shrines for the people of his kingdom—one in Bethel and one in Dan. Since he had no ark of the covenant, he installed golden bulls (or calves) in each of the shrines, presumably as pedestals for the God of Israel. These bulls are always judged to be idolatrous by the authors of the books of Kings, who are from the southern kingdom, Judah (see 1 Kgs 12:27-31). In fact, they may well have been occasions for idol worship by the Israelites in the north. Tobit claims that, even though he lived in the north and was a citizen of the northern kingdom of Israel, he never participated in the worship at Dan. He even claims that he went alone to Jerusalem to worship.

---

37. The name has been given a Greek ending in both major recensions (Τωβιθ in G^II; Τωβιτ in G^I). See J. A. Fitzmyer, *Tobit: Qumran Cave 4, XIV: Parabiblical Texts*, Part 2, DJD 19, ed. Magen Broshi et al. (Oxford: Clarendon, 1995) 51-52. The name is found in Tob 7:2, 4.

Another historical incongruity appears in Tobit's statement that he had been living at the time of the division of Israel into two kingdoms (922 BCE). Since Tiglath-pileser's deportation of the Israelites to Assyria took place at the end of the eighth century, that would make Tobit a very old man, indeed!

1:6-7. Deuteronomy also prescribes certain festivals that must be celebrated in Jerusalem: Passover, Weeks, and Booths (Deut 16:1-17). Tobit claims that he went faithfully to Jerusalem for the festivals and offered the required tithes (vv. 6-7).

❖ ❖ ❖ ❖

EXCURSUS: TITHES

Tithes (the contribution of a tenth of one's income) are prescribed in several places in the law. In Leviticus a tithe of crops and animals is required in order to support the priesthood and maintain the Jerusalem Temple (Lev 27:30-33). In the legislation in Numbers (Num 18:21-24, 30-32), which precedes the centralization of worship prescribed in Deuteronomy, the tithe is intended to support local worship—the Levites and the local sanctuaries—and possibly also for upkeep of the levitical cities (Joshua 21) in the time of David. A tenth of this tithe was to be given to the Jerusalem sanctuary (Num 18:25-29). When Deuteronomy abolished the local sanctuaries and minimized the service of the Levites, the tithe was to be used for a sacrifice and festal banquet at the Temple in Jerusalem (Deut 14:22-26). Every third year, however, the same tithe was to be used for the relief of the poor in the home area of the giver (Deut 14:18-29; cf. Deut 26:12). Thus on years one, two, four, and five of the seven-year sabbatical cycle, the pilgrim brought the tithe in kind or in money to Jerusalem; in years three and six, the tithe was stored for the needy—strangers, orphans, widows, and landless Levites.

In the post-exilic period, however, when the entire Pentateuch became normative, the three passages were interpreted as referring to three different tithes. Thus the first fruits of crops and the firstborn of animals were to go to the priests in the Temple (Lev 27:26-27, 30-33), and the first tithe of crops and animals to the Levites (Num 18:21-24). The "second tithe" was intepreted in two ways. Either the tithe for the banquet (Deut 14:22-26) was replaced by the "poor tithe" (Deut 14:28-29) in the third and sixth years, or the "poor tithe" was levied over and above the banquet tithe in those years, thus becoming a "third tithe." Josephus, a first-century CE Jewish historian, regarded the "poor tithe" as a "third tithe."[38]

The situation in the book of Tobit is complicated further by a discrepancy between the two major recensions of the book. G^I mentions a "third" (τὴν τρίτην *tēn tritēn*) which is specified in the Old Latin as a "third tithe" (*et tertii ad decimationem*). G^{II} describes the tithe of "the third year" (ἐν τῷ τρίτῳ ἔτει *en tō tritō etei*). Whether Tobit is giving two tithes or three, he is scrupulously careful to follow the law concerning tithes.

38. Josephus *Antiquities of the Jews* 4.8.22.

❖ ❖ ❖ ❖

1:8. Tobit credits his grandmother Deborah with teaching him the law to which he is so faithful. She is the first of several strong women to appear in this book. Tobit's respect for her authority mirrors the advice of Ben Sira, whose book was written about the same time as the book of Tobit: "The Lord . . . confirms a mother's right over her children" (Sir

3:2 NRSV; cf. Sir 3:4, 6, 10). Tobit will follow her example in instructing his own son and grandchildren (4:3-21; 14:3-11).

1:9. Tobit also follows the custom of endogamy, marriage within the tribe and clan. The custom seems to be based on the laws concerning the daughters of Zelophehad, in whose case there was no male heir to guarantee the retention of the ancestral property within the tribe and clan (Num 27:5-11; 36:2-12). In order to keep the heritage within the ancestral tribe, these women were required to marry within the clan: "Every daughter who possesses an inheritance in any tribe of the Israelites shall marry one from the clan of her father's tribe, so that all Israelites may continue to possess their ancestral inheritance" (Num 36:8). The custom is also based on the example of the ancestors. Abraham sends a servant back to his kindred in Mesopotamia to find a wife for his son Isaac (Gen 24:3-4). Rebekah and Isaac give similar instructions to their son Jacob (Gen 27:46–28:5). In the post-exilic period interpretation of the law, marriage within Judaism is encouraged as a protection against the false worship of the Gentiles. The custom is carried to the extreme by Ezra and Nehemiah, who force the returning exiles to divorce their non-Jewish wives (Ezra 10; Neh 13:23-30; cf. Neh 10:31). Tobit is very careful in his observance of this custom. He marries not only within Judaism, not only within his tribe and clan, but also within his "ancestral family" (πατριά *patria*). Deselaers considers *patria* to represent the "ancestral house," a unit even smaller than the clan.[39]

1:10-11. Tobit's fidelity to the law, practiced so earnestly in his homeland, continues after he is deported to Assyria. The example he gives concerns the dietary laws, an observance that gained significance during the exilic period. Tobit implies that he has kept the dietary laws found in the Pentateuch concerning clean and unclean food (see Lev 11:1-47; Deut 14:3-21), the prohibition against eating blood (Lev 7:26-27; 17:10-14; Deut 12:23-25; 15:23), and the avoidance of food sacrificed to idols (Exod 34:15). Again Tobit describes himself as the only one who remains faithful to the law.

1:12-13. Now Tobit asserts his belief in the theory of retribution. Because he is faithful, God rewards him. Tobit's good fortune consists in obtaining a position of responsibility in the Assyrian court as the procurator for King Shalmaneser. This is a position of great trust for a man who is a deportee from a defeated country. He travels from Nineveh, in modern Iraq, to Media (the land of the Medes), in modern Iran, to buy for him.

---

39. Deselaers, *Das Buch Tobit, Studien zu seiner Entstehung, Komposition, und Theologie*, 309-15.

❖   ❖   ❖   ❖

EXCURSUS: THEORY OF RETRIBUTION

The theory of retribution is expressed most clearly in Deuteronomy 28. A series of blessings that apply to every situation in life is listed as a reward for obedience to God's commandments (Deut 28:1-14). A series of curses that correspond exactly to the blessings and expand upon them is listed as a consequence of disobedience (Deut 28:15-68). The theory is illustrated throughout the historical books of Joshua–2 Kings. When the people are faithful, they are successful; when they sin, they are defeated (e.g., Josh 7:1–8:29; Judg 3:7-11). The theory holds for individuals also: David's sin leads to his punishment (2 Sam 11:1–12:15).

Neither in Deuteronomy nor in the book of Tobit, however, is retribution an automatic or impersonal equation. Blessing comes when it is undeserved (see Deut 7:7-8). The author of Deuteronomy continually emphasizes the dangers to Israel of attributing blessing and prosperity to their own power or merits (see Deut 8:17-18; 9:4-6). The election of Israel is the free choice of a loving God who chooses them as a special people for no reason other than love of their ancestors (see, e.g., Deut 4:32-40; 7:6-11; 10:15; 23:6). A corollary to God's undeserved blessing is that no punishment is without hope. If the people return to the Lord and obey, God will have mercy on them (Deut 30:1-10).

In addition to undeserved blessing, however, Israel also experiences what seems to be undeserved suffering (Deut 8:2, 5). This "testing," according to Deuteronomy, is for the purposes of discovering the people's fidelity (8:3) and of showing them that the blessings are gifts from God and are not earned by their own power (Deut 8:16-17). Tobit believes in the theory of retribution, but he seems dangerously close to attributing his good fortune to his own merits.

1:14. Another historical incongruity appears here. Tobit lives in Nineveh and works for the king. This is not implausible, since there were four great cities in the heartland of Assyria: Nineveh, Asshur, Calah, and Arbela. But Nineveh was not established as the capital city until the reign of Sennacherib, twenty or more years after the reign of Shalmaneser V.

Tobit also gains prosperity in his new position. He is able to deposit in savings ten talents worth of silver. The exact value of this deposit is impossible to calculate, but a talent is usually considered the equivalent of three thousand shekels. Thus ten talents is a large sum of money.

1:15. Shalmaneser V (726–722) was in fact succeeded, not by Sennacherib, but by Sargon II (721–705), who was not in the direct line of succession. The book of Tobit seems to be dependent on 2 Kings, which mentions Shalmaneser (18:9) and Sennacherib (18:13), but not Sargon. Only Isaiah (Isa 20:1) mentions Sargon.

Sargon II began a dynasty that lasted until the end of the Assyrian Empire in 612 BCE. He was succeeded by his son Sennacherib in 705. A change in political power always stirred up hope in occupied countries, and widescale revolt often followed the death of a powerful ruler. Sargon spent most of his reign reconquering the territory won by his father, Tiglath-pileser III, and adding new territory to the empire. The Medes were involved in the struggle against Urartu. It is possible that this unrest made the roads to Media unsafe, as Tobit reports.

1:16-17. At this point in the narrative Tobit begins to recount his acts of charity (*eleēmosynē*). After listing two common works of mercy, feeding the hungry and clothing the naked, he describes in detail his primary work of burying the dead. His account indicates that life for the Israelite exiles in Assyria was already precarious under Shalmaneser, even though Tobit himself holds a position of trust. Bodies of the exiles were simply thrown out and left unburied. To be left unburied was an abomination for Jews.

Burial of the dead as a practice of charity is a theme found also in Genesis. Jacob makes his proper burial a sign of Joseph's charity and fidelity toward him (Gen 47:29).[40] Burial is the specific practice of charity that receives the most attention lin the book of Tobit (e.g., 1:18-20; 2:3-8; 4:3-4, 17; 6:15; 14:1-13). In the Greco-Roman period, burial, rather than cremation, was the customary practice among thel Jews. They considered it a work of mercy to bury not only family members but also strangers, even non-Jews.[41]

1:18-20. Shalmaneser's successor, Sennacherib, ruled Assyria for twenty-four years (705–681). During the reign of Hezekiah, king of Judah, Sennacherib laid siege to Jerusalem at least once and perhaps twice. Although he defeated and sacked several other Judean cities, notably Lachish, he did not destroy Jerusalem. According to 2 Kgs 18:14-16, Hezekiah paid him a large tribute. It is possible that this payment relates to a first invasion in 701, which Sennacherib himself reports, claiming that he "shut up Hezekiah like a bird in a cage." In 2 Kgs 19:35-36, the story is told that, when Sennacherib was encamped opposite the Ethiopian troops under King Tirhakah (2 Kgs 19:9), who had

---

40. This is one of three occurrences of ἐλεημοσύνη (*eleēmosyne*) in the Pentateuch. The other two occurrences (Deut 6:25; 24:13) are renderings of צדקה (*ṣĕdāqâ*). All three connote a characteristic of a person. See Griffin, "The Theology and Function of Prayer in the Book of Tobit," 8-10.

41. See *t. Meg.* 3:16; *t. Git. 3:14*. See also Zeev Weiss, "Social Aspects of Burial in beth She'arim: Archaeological Finds and Talmudic Sources," in *The Galilee in Late Antiquity*, ed. Lee I. Levine (Cambridge, Mass.: Harvard University Press, 1992) 365.

come to help Hezekiah, a disaster struck the Assyrian army and Sennacherib returned home in disgrace. Is this the same invasion or a later one? The presence of Tirhakah, whose reign did not begin until 690, the occurrence of two differing reasons for Sennacherib's departure, and the announcement of his death (681 BCE) immediately following (2 Kgs 19:37) argue for two invasions—one in 701 and the other at a later date, but before 687, when Hezekiah died.[42]

Josephus also reports the incident.[43] He tells three stories of Sennacherib's disgrace from different sources. Two concern Sennacherib's siege of Pelusium; the third concerns Jerusalem. In the first instance, Sennacherib departs because of fear of Tirhakah. In the second, he leaves because mice have chewed up the bows and armor of his soldiers. In the third, he retreats because God has sent a pestilence into the camp (cf. the angel of the Lord in 2 Kgs 19:35). Josephus reports Sennacherib's death immediately following the third story.

Tobit relates that Sennacherib's anger against the Israelites was great because of his forced retreat from Jerusalem. For this reason he executed many of them and left them unburied. Thus the need for Tobit's charitable act of burying the dead increases. This action puts Tobit himself in danger of death. He saves his life by fleeing but loses all his property except the money that has been deposited with Gabael in Media. He and his family are reduced to temporary poverty.

1:21-22. Sennacherib was assassinated, apparently, by two of his sons. A third son, Esarhaddon, who claimed to be in hiding at the time of the assassination, took the Assyrian throne (680–669 BCE) and established peace at home and in the territories. The book of Tobit, which is apparently dependent upon 2 Kings for its historical information, has telescoped the events even further than has 2 Kings. Tobit reports that Sennacherib was killed less than forty days after his return from Jerusalem.

The succession of Esarhaddon is good news for Tobit. Through the good word of his nephew Ahiqar, Tobit is allowed to return to Nineveh. Ahiqar is modeled on the wise man of the same name who was active at court during the reigns of Sennacherib and Esarhaddon (see Introduction).

42. "Mesopotamia," *ABD* 4:743-47.
43. Josephus *Antiquities of the Jews* 10.1.4-5.

REFLECTIONS

1. The overwhelming impression conveyed by Tobit's report of his youth is that of a man scrupulously faithful to the law. Even when observance becomes difficult because of the division of the kingdom, Tobit remains faithful. Even when his neighbors and family transfer their allegiance and change their practices, Tobit perseveres. The plurality of modern society presents constant challenges to believers who strive to remain faithful to their religious belief and practices. It is sometimes difficult to find a supportive community to encourage one in worshiping regularly and helping the poor. Tobit suffers from the lack of such a community.

2. A gnawing suspicion arises that Tobit is overly careful. His interpretation of the law seems too literal. "He alone" is better than all his kindred. If there is a suggestion that perhaps two or even three tithes are called for, Tobit is there with his offering. He marries not just within Judaism, but within his ancestral family.

Tobit's letter-of-the-law fidelity prepares the reader for the challenge that will come to his faith. Is he relying on external practices to earn a reward from God? Or is a loving relationship with God the source of his fidelity and reward enough? Is he capable of enduring ambiguity, the test of suffering and the uncertainty that comes in its wake? Or will he crumble in despair?

These questions confront everyone who strives to lead a holy life. Is security or love the motive for faithful observance? Only love is strong enough to sustain us to the end.

3. The theory of retribution is alive and well in the twenty-first century. How often does one hear (or think), "Why me? What did I do to deserve this?" It comes to mind when good things happen. In *The Sound of Music*, Maria sings "Somewhere in my youth or childhood, I must have done something good!" She is expressing the theory of retribution, that good things happen to us because we have been good. It does not seem to occur to her that something good could happen simply as a free gift of God. More often, however, the question "Why me?" is provoked, not by blessing, but by suffering. "When bad things happen to good people," to cite Kushner's title, we want a reason, an explanation.[44]

The assumption that retribution—good or bad—is an automatic equation (good behavior = blessing; bad behavior = suffering) is both immature and a denial of basic tenets of the Christian faith. It is left over from our childhood, when our parents disciplined us with reminders of this theory. It also regards suffering simply as punishment for sin. It is undoubtedly true that there is a connection between sin and suffering. But the connection is not simple. It is not always the sinner who suffers; sometimes innocent people suffer for the sins of others. Sometimes suffering is not caused by sin at all, but is simply a part of human life. No human being, no matter how holy, lives a life free of suffering.

There is a further danger in Christianity: identifying suffering as a badge of true holiness. The center of Christian faith is the death and resurrection of Jesus Christ. We believe that the sinless one took on the sins of all humanity. "God made him to be sin who knew no sin, so that in him we might become the righteousness of God" (2 Cor 5:21). We also believe that we are called to complete in our bodies what is lacking in the sufferings of Christ (see Col 1:24). This is the great reversal, the redemption of human suffering that gives it meaning. But this is not an automatic equation. Just as it is not possible to say that anyone who suffers must be a sinner, neither is it possible to say that anyone who suffers must be holy.

So it is perilous to see the theory of retribution as automatic. Doing so causes us to make false judgments: Sufferers are sinners; the prosperous are holy (or the reverse). It also causes us to deny God's freedom. God is free to give good gifts to us whether we deserve them or not. God is free to forgive our sins without charge. God is also free to allow us to suffer, to allow human life to take its course, whether we deserve it or not. Human beings are also free to accept blessings with thanksgiving, free to accept suffering in patience and hope (and the reverse). Tobit is about to learn both aspects of this freedom.

4. Tobit is described as a righteous man because he does merciful works. The seven corporal works of mercy in Christian tradition are these: Feed the hungry, give drink to the thirsty, clothe the naked, shelter the stranger, visit the sick, minister to prisoners, and bury the dead (see Matt 25:35-36). These works are expressions of a living faith in action. Too often we take the easy route, exercising compassion at a distance by writing a check or dropping off a bag of clothes. Tobit's example shows us that sometimes it is necessary to experience other people's misery firsthand. What people need is not only financial help but also a human touch. There are countless opportunities to serve in food kitchens or to work in homeless shelters. Prisoners are in need of visitors, as well as education and religious services. These "hands-on" works of mercy are not easy. We may experience scorn and rejection. We may be repulsed by dirt and disease. Perseverance in the works of mercy, however, has a surprising reward. Those whom we serve begin in turn to teach us the amazing compassion of God.

5. Burying the dead remains one of the corporal works of mercy. In normal situations most people are not compelled actually to dig graves for abandoned corpses

---

44. Harold S. Kushner, *When Bad Things Happen to Good People* (New York: Schocken, 1981).

(although this may be necessary in war-torn areas). However, it is certainly a duty of families to arrange for the proper burial of their dead, and a responsibility of the state when the deceased has no family.

What is "proper burial" of the dead? In North American culture much money is spent in the denial of death. The body is made to look as lifelike as possible. Elaborately decorated caskets are sometimes purchased. The casket is lowered into the grave only after the family has left. Huge memorial markers may be installed. The question is not whether the body of a human being should be honored. It certainly should. All human beings are created in the image of God and destined for resurrection, body and soul. The question is one of emphasis. How can we as a culture learn to face and ritualize the reality of death? Only an honest recognition of that reality allows us to believe with grateful awe in the reality of resurrection.

TOBIT 2:1–3:6, TOBIT'S DISTRESS AND PRAYER

COMMENTARY

Tobit's first-person narrative now moves from the general summary of his good life to a specific story of his burying the dead. This specific act of charity results, even if indirectly, in the suffering that will afflict him throughout most of the book. This suffering constitutes the conflict of the book: Why is this good man afflicted? This question is asked by Anna, Tobit's wife (2:14), and by Tobit himself in his lament (3:6).

The Vulgate adds a comparison between Tobit and Job:

Now this trial the Lord therefore permitted to happen to him, that an example might be given to posterity of his patience, as also of holy Job. . . . For as the kings insulted holy Job, so his relatives and kindred mocked him, saying, "Where is your hope, for which you gave alms and buried the dead?" (2:12, 15-16)

By implication, Anna is compared to Job's wife. Moore notes, however, that this is a false comparison, since Job's wife was angry with God, whereas Anna is angry with Tobit.[45]

2:1-2. The family of Tobit prepares to celebrate one of the three great pilgrimage festivals of Judaism, the Feast of Weeks. This feast, like the other two (Passover/Unleavened Bread and Booths), is a celebration of harvest. The Feast of Weeks is observed at the beginning of the wheat harvest (May/June). Its date is set by Deuteronomy as seven weeks (or fifty days) after the offering of the first fruits of the barley harvest—that is, after the Feast of Unleavened Bread (Lev 23:15-16; Deut 16:9-10). The fifty-day count gives the Greek name to the feast, πεντηκοστή (*pentēkostē*, "Pentecost," "fiftieth").

Because Passover is connected to the historical event of the exodus from Egypt, the Feast of Weeks became associated with the historical context of the covenant-making on Mt. Sinai (see Exod 19:1).

Because Tobit is in exile, he cannot make the pilgrimage to Jerusalem as Deuteronomy required (Deut 16:16). But he is careful to observe the other prescription for the celebration: "All shall give as they are able, according to the blessing of the LORD your God that he has given you" (Deut 16:17 NRSV; see also Deut 16:11, 14). He decides to share his festival meal with a poor Israelite as his offering to the Lord.

Tobiah is sent to find a poor person. Tobit teaches his son the law of God by example. Tobit's practice of charitable acts agrees with the advice of his contemporary, Ben Sira.[46]

---

45. Moore, *Tobit*, 135.

46. See Griffin, "A Study of *Eleēmosynē* in the Bible with Emphasis upon Its Meaning and Usage in the Theology of Tobit and Ben Sira," for a thorough analysis of the concept in both books.

His sharing of the festival meal replaces his offering of the customary sacrifice. Ben Sira says that "one who gives alms sacrifices a thank offering" (Sir 35:4 NRSV). The recipient of Tobit's alms will be a faithful Israelite. Ben Sira advises one to give to "a brother or a friend" (Sir 29:10 NRSV), to a person who is devout rather than to a sinner (Sir 12:1-7).

2:3-6. Instead of finding a poor Israelite to share the meal, Tobiah finds the body of an Israelite in need of burial. The man seems to have been executed, killed in the marketplace. Moore points out that ἐστραγγάληται (*estrangalētai*) should be rendered as "exposed" instead of "strangled."[47] The corpse has not been buried but instead has been put on public display (cf. Esth 9:13).

Tobit's action is predictable. The burial becomes the focus of his entire effort. His festival dinner is sandwiched between preparations for the burial and the burial itself. The occasion reminds him of a saying of the prophet Amos (Amos 8:10) concerning the approaching day of judgment against Israel. The citation points up the irony of the situation. Amos's oracle decries wealthy Israelites who are exploiting the poor. Tobit, on the other hand, seems to have had his feast turned to mourning precisely because he is helping the poor.

2:7-8. The burial becomes the occasion for further mockery by his neighbors. No one else seems to care that fellow Israelites are lying unburied. Rather, the one man who is tending to this duty is scorned for his actions. His characteristic act of charity seems to result in curse, not in blessing.

2:9. After the burial Tobit washes himself and sleeps outside, perhaps because of ritual uncleanness from contact with a corpse. According to pentateuchal legislation, Tobit will remain unclean for seven days as a consequence of burying the dead. Ritual washing is called for on the third and seventh days, but only on the seventh day is the uncleanness removed. Anything Tobit touches will also become unclean and have the power to communicate uncleanness. It would seem that Tobit's house, though not the place of the man's death, could well be considered unclean also, since the corpse was probably kept there until evening. Josephus reports the Jewish custom that "after the funeral the house and its inhabitants must be purified."[48] Tobit's attempts to comply with the ritual even in exile constitute a further example of his rigorous observance of the spirit of the law as well as of the letter.

---

47. Moore, *Tobit*, 128.

48. Josephus *Against Apion* 2.27.

❖ ❖ ❖ ❖

EXCURSUS: UNCLEANNESS AND PURIFICATION

According to Num 19:11-22 there are several consequences of contact with a dead body. They include the following: (1) A person who touches a human corpse is unclean for seven days. The ritual for purification calls for washing on the third and seventh days with lustral water—i.e., water in which the ashes of the red heifer have been mixed. (2) The tent in which a person dies is unclean for seven days. The tent as well as all the vessels and persons in it must be sprinkled with lustral water on the third and seventh days. (3) Anything touched by an unclean person also becomes unclean and renders unclean anyone else who then touches it. (4) The person who remains unclean defiles the sanctuary of the Lord and shall be cut off from the community.

Further questions are raised by the circumstances: Was lustral water for purification available to the Israelites in Nineveh? Apparently ashes of the red heifer were saved after the destruction of the Temple in 70 CE and until the Amoraic period (3rd–4th cents. CE),[49] but their availability in Nineveh is questionable. Was this legal purification necessary chiefly for entrance into the Temple or for participation in the temple liturgy? If so, the exiles had no immediate legal need for purification.

49. See "Purity and Impurity, Ritual," *EncJud* 13. 1406.

2:10. The attitude toward Tobit's medical condition reflects a traditional belief. Although it is unknown whether scales on the cornea are ever caused by hot bird droppings, Tobit's blindness is attributed to natural causes. Nonetheless, medical assistance is useless to him. Every attempt to heal him drives him further into darkness (cf. the woman with a hemorrhage in Mark 5:26; Luke 8:43). Only God has the power to heal.[50] Ben Sira advises that one honor physicians because their services are needed, but also remember that "their gift of healing comes from the Most High" (Sir 38:1-15).

2:11. Anna goes to work outside the home in order to earn money the family needs for sustenance and survival. It appears that the work she did was weaving, an assumption that is made specific in the Old Latin version. In ancient Mesopotamia, women of the lower classes were employed by the temples and the palace in various occupations—cooking, baking, cleaning, spinning, and weaving.[51] Woven cloth was made from both goat hair and sheep's wool; it was dyed and fashioned into various items of clothing. Because of her family's need, Anna becomes the Bible's first working mother.

2:12. Anna is a capable and independent woman. There is indication that she is good at her job. Her employers not only pay her full wages, but also give her a bonus. The bonus, a young goat, becomes the occasion for the first dialogue between Tobit and his wife.

2:13-14. This dialogue is revealing of the characters of both Anna and Tobit. Dependent on her wage-earning ability, the blind Tobit strikes out at his wife with the suspicion that her bonus is stolen goods. His suspicion reveals both the pain of the helpless man and his extreme concern for obedience to the law.

This scene is still part of the first-person narrative. As narrator, Tobit reports his anger and disbelief, but he gives no indication that his suspicion against Anna is justified.

Initially Anna answers Tobit's suspicion with a simple explanation (2:14*a*). In the face of his persistent disbelief and anger, however, she turns the conversation to her own advantage by attacking him on a vulnerable point. His trust in the justice of God to reward good deeds seems to have been in vain. Either his apparent good works are false, or he has been betrayed by God (2:14*b*). In either case, he is now forced to depend on her. The economy of speech by the narrator in this scene is noteworthy. There is no comment about Anna's emotional state. It is revealed entirely by her words.

Anna has now raised the critical question concerning the theory of retribution and Tobit's trust in it. If virtue is truly rewarded with blessing and, conversely, if suffering is a sign of wickedness, then how can the suffering Tobit claim to be a virtuous man? If the blessings are not there, perhaps the righteousness does not exist either.

3:1-2. Prayer is one of the strongest and most pervasive elements in the book of Tobit.[52] The title character Tobit prays at three significant points in his life: (1) when he has reached a point of despair because of his blindness and his dependence on his wife; (2) when he is healed; and (3) when he realizes that God has sent an angel to help him. He also exhorts his son to pray (4:5, 19), and later also his grandchildren (14:9). The immediate cause of this first prayer is Tobit's argument with Anna. Her attack on his virtue and his motivation is the final blow, leading him to pray for death.

Tobit begins in traditional fashion by focusing first on God. His concept of God

50. See Bernd Kollmann, "Göttliche Offenbarung magisch-parmakologischer Heilkunst im Buch Tobit" *ZAW* 106 (1994) 291.
51. Rikvah Harris, "Women," *ABD* 6:949.

52. For my analysis of the prayers in the book I am greatly dependent on Griffin, "The Theology and Function of Prayer in the Book of Tobit."

emphasizes the same virtues that are predicated of himself in the introduction (1:3): righteousness (δικαιοσύνη *dikaiosynē*), charity/mercy (ἐλεημοσύνη *eleēmosynē*), and truth (ἀλήθεια *alētheia*). Just as these virtues are demonstrated through Tobit's actions, so also Tobit asserts that they are demonstrated through God's actions. God's deeds are righteous; God's ways are mercy and truth. These three virtues characterize God's judgment of the whole world. Whatever Tobit's own distress may be, he acknowledges that it is not a reflection of malice or capriciousness in God.

3:3-4. Tobit then turns to the possible causes of his suffering. Although he has earlier asserted that he is also righteous, charitable, and true, he is aware of his sinfulness and the sinfulness of his people. His sins may be unwitting, but they offend the justice of God. He regards himself not as an individual before God, but as a member of God's people. Since the people have been sinful, he shares in their guilt and in their punishment.

Tobit recognizes that only God can remedy his situation. He begs God to remember him and to look upon him. God's remembering is not simply recollection. It brings divine mercy into one's life (see Noah in Gen 8:1; the Israelites in Exod 2:24; Hannah in 1 Sam 1:19). For God to look upon a person also implies divine mercy. Tobit asks God to look upon him with favor.

3:5-6. In keeping with his belief in the theory of retribution (God punishes the wicked and rewards the just), Tobit acknowledges God's right to exercise strict justice. But Tobit is deeply wounded by grief. His long-term grief over his illness has been brought to a crisis by the argument with his wife, Anna. He suffers crushing anguish. He can think of only one way that God's mercy might be exercised for him. So, even as he prays that God might act according to the divine will, he asks to be allowed to die. It has not occurred to him that God might mercifully give him a happy life. There is no indication that death is the only response Tobit will accept, but it is the only one that he can imagine.

❖ ❖ ❖ ❖

EXCURSUS: BELIEFS ABOUT DEATH

In his prayer for death, Tobit follows the example of some of Israel's ancestors. When Moses is overwhelmed by the people's murmuring in the desert, he prays: "If this is the way you are going to treat me, put me to death at once—if I have found favor in your sight—and do not let me see my misery" (Num 11:15 NRSV). When Elijah is fleeing from the wrath of Jezebel, he prays: "It is enough; now, O LORD, take away my life, for I am no better than my ancestors" (1 Kgs 19:4 NRSV). In his anger over God's mercy toward Nineveh, Jonah says, "It is better for me to die than to live" (Jonah 4:8 NRSV).

None of these people pray for death in the hope of eternal life. Their prayers are simply pleas to be released from present suffering. Tobit's prayer makes clear that he has no hope for life after death. Once God takes his life breath, he expects simply to return to dust. His "eternal home" will be the grave.

Belief in resurrection and in meaningful life after death began to emerge only with the latest OT texts. Israel had encountered the cult of the dead in Egypt, and perhaps also in Mesopotamia, and had rejected the tendency to idolatry that sprang from it. Only in the middle of the second century BCE did a concept of resurrection develop. Even so, both concept and details were hotly contested. Did resurrection apply only to the righteous (2 Macc 7:14), or would there be a general resurrection of righteous and wicked alike (Dan 12:2)? Did resurrection include the body (2 Macc 7:11, 22-23), or did it apply only to an immortal soul (Wis 3:1-4; 9:15)? The controversy over resurrection of the dead also is evident in the NT. The Sadducees attempt to show the foolishness of such a belief when they challenge Jesus with the story of the woman with seven husbands (Mark 12:18-27). Paul escapes his enemies when he turns a trial against him into an argument over belief in resurrection (Acts 23:6-10).

The author of the book of Tobit does not believe in resurrection. Rather, he believes in Sheol (Greek, Hades), a shadowy existence that can best be described as suspended animation (3:10; 4:19; 13:2). In Sheol there is neither pain nor pleasure, neither joy nor sorrow. There is no ranking of persons by power or wealth—only the radical equality brought about by death (Job 3:11-19). One joins one's ancestors in the family grave and persists there (e.g., Gen 15:15; 1 Kgs 11:21; 1 Chr 17:11; Ps 49:19). There is no agreement on whether God can or cannot be found in Sheol (see Pss 6:5; 139:8).

REFLECTIONS

1. Tobit will not eat his festival dinner until he can share it with a poor person. Some churches take up collections for the poor during penitential seasons, such as Lent, and at festival times, both religious and secular, such as Thanksgiving and Christmas. Are there other celebrations that might remind us to share the gifts we have been given with those who have less? What a response to consumerism it would be if each of us celebrated our birthdays by giving a gift to the poor.

2. Tobit not only teaches his son the observance of the law, but also shows it to him in practice. Thus his son has a living example to follow. Moreover, Tobit involves him in the charitable act. My father used to say that there are three ways to teach someone how to tie a knot: (1) Tell her how; (2) take a string and show her how; (3) give her a string and let her do it as you describe and demonstrate. Only the third way is effective for long-term learning. Tobit shows himself to be a good teacher as he involves Tobiah in his charitable act.

3. Tobit does everything he can to be cured. Sickness and suffering are not simply to be endured; every reasonable effort must be made to relieve the situation. The skill of physicians and the knowledge of pharmacists are gifts from God to be used in the improvement of human life. However, no human being can cure every illness; no human being can forever escape death. In the end, life and death, sickness and health, are in the hand of God.

Great suffering may also lead to prayer for death. There comes a time when death, even if it means oblivion, is preferred to a life of agony. Tobit, however, does not take matters into his own hands. Instead, he asks God for death. He does not attempt suicide, but it is clear that if death comes to him he will not resist it. Our society struggles with the arrival of death. Physician-assisted suicide, which is often a response to extreme suffering, is an attempt to hasten the arrival of death. Advance directives, on the other hand, are instructions not to resist death by extraordinary means when there is no hope for a reasonable quality of life in the future. For Christians, this decision to allow death to arrive is shaped by respect for God's gift of life in the present, courage to share in the sufferings of Christ (Phil 3:10), and faith that, having died with him, we will also share in Christ's resurrection (Rom 6:10).

4. Women have been severely criticized for working outside the home and not staying home to care for house and children. Paradoxically, women on welfare have been criticized for not having outside jobs. It is a no-win situation in our society. The story of Anna illustrates that such mistrust and criticism are millennia old. However, in this book, which is so concerned with family values, Anna also demonstrates that a working mother is not necessarily destructive of the family. In fact, her employment sustains the family.

5. Tobit suspects his wife of stealing, or at least of accepting stolen goods. The virtue of kindness that he exercises in public seems to falter at home. His distress at his own situation leads him to lash out at the one person who is his primary support. This is an all-too-common response to frustration and stress. Because we cannot or will not deal with the primary cause of our stress, we take it out on those who have little or nothing to do with it. Often the victims of our reaction are those closest to us, those whom we assume will not abandon us. In the worst case, this projection of anger onto an innocent victim explodes into domestic violence, either verbal or physical.

TOBIT 3:7-15, SARAH'S DISTRESS AND PRAYER

COMMENTARY

In the next section the scene shifts from Tobit's house in Nineveh to Raguel's house in Ecbatana. The two scenes are parallel: Each consists of (1) hard words and grief (2:13–3:1, 7-9); (2) prayer for death (3:2-6, 12-15); (3) God's acceptance of the prayer (3:16); and (4) the consequence of the prayer (3:17). The events in Ecbatana not only parallel those in Nineveh, but also are simultaneous ("on the same day" [ἐν τῇ ἡμέρᾳ ταύτῃ *en tē hēmera tautē*, 3:7], "on that day" [ἐν τῇ ἡμέρᾳ ἐκείνῃ *en tē hēmera ekeinē*, 3:10], "at that very time" [ἐν αὐτῷ τῷ καιρῷ *en autō tō kairō*, 3:11, 16-17]).

In v. 17 it becomes evident that the narrative voice has changed. From 1:3 to 3:1 the narrator is Tobit himself; from 3:17 to the end of the book, the story is told by a third-person narrator. Between 3:1 and 3:17 appears a bridge containing the prayer of Tobit (Tobit speaking in the first-person) and the introduction of Sarah and her prayer (possibly still Tobit telling the story from hindsight). But in 3:17, Tobit is spoken of in the third-person.[53]

There are significant differences between the two narrative voices. The third-person narrator has greater freedom of movement than the first-person narrator, can report thoughts and feelings of other characters, and observes actions even when characters seem to be alone. Tobit the narrator reveals no other character's thoughts and feelings—only his own. He tells the story of the conflict between Tobit (the character) and Anna with objectivity and realizes the truth that Anna was indeed given the goat that the character Tobit suspected had been stolen. But Tobit the narrator is not always reliable. In emphasizing his own fidelity to God's law, he announces that he alone went to Jerusalem to worship (1:6), a fact that Tobit the character later contradicts (5:14). Thus the third-person narrator is omniscient and reliable. The first-person narrator is neither.[54]

3:7. Another main character is introduced in this section: Sarah, daughter of Raguel. Her name, which means "lady" or "gentlewoman," links her to the ancestral story of Sarah, wife of Abraham. Like Abraham's wife, the Sarah of this story is kept from those for whom she is not destined (3:8; 6:18; cf. Gen 12:10-20; 20:1-18). Through Tobiah, she will become the mother of sons who are the hope of the future people of God (Tob 14:3; cf. Gen 17:19, 21).

Ecbatana, the home of Raguel's family, is the ancient capital of Media. The site of modern Hamadan is Iran; it is located in the Zagros mountains about 325 miles southeast of Nineveh.

3:8-9. Echoing the final word of Tobit's prayer (ὀνειδισμός *oneidismos*, "reproach"),

---

53. See Miller, "The Redaction of Tobit and the Genesis Apocryphon," 54-55. He compares this narrative shift with the Genesis Apocryphon and concludes that in both works the first-person narrative was highly valued but fragmentary.

54. McCracken, "Narration and Comedy in the Book of Tobit," 403-9.

the narrator reports the distress of Sarah, who is "reproached" by her father's maids. The same word will recur as the reason for her prayer for death (v. 10) and twice in the prayer itself (vv. 13, 15).[55]

Sarah is afflicted by the demon Asmodeus, who keeps killing her bridegrooms. The story of her affliction is repeated five times in the course of the narrative. In each telling, the emphasis shifts and the suspense heightens. In this section, the narrator (v. 8) presents the basic facts in a simple and straightforward fashion: (1) Sarah has been married to seven men (2) whom the demon Asmodeus has killed (3) before the marriages could be consummated. The taunts of the maids (vv. 8-9) repeat the first and last points—seven husbands, dead before the consummation of the marriages. But the maids twist the facts of the second point in order to deepen Sarah's grief. They accuse her of murdering the men and seem to know nothing of the demon Asmodeus. They point out Sarah's childless state and the likelihood that she will remain so. Sarah will repeat the story in her prayer (v. 15); Tobiah (6:14-15) and Raguel (7:11) will recount the same events with additional details.

The name of the demon is perhaps derived from the Persian *aeshma daeva*, "demon of wrath."[56] The role of the demon in the story is related to the folktale "The Monster in the Bridal Chamber" (see Introduction). The hero in this tale is advised by a stranger to marry a wealthy princess whose former bridegrooms have all perished in the bridal chamber. On the wedding night, a serpent emerges from the mouth of the bride-princess to kill the hero. The stranger kills the serpent and frees the bride from her affliction. In the book of Tobit, Sarah will be freed from her affliction through the assistance of the angel Raphael (8:3).

Seven, the number of Sarah's dead husbands, is significant throughout the book. In the Bible it signifies completion or fullness. Sarah has already had a complete number of chances at marriage; she should expect no more. Tobiah will be outside the number, one more than can be expected. Her marriage to him will be sheer gift.

3:10. Sarah is the most silent character in the book of Tobit. After listening to the cutting abuse of the maids, to which she makes no reply, she retires to an upstairs room with the intention of hanging herself. As she deliberates over her decision, we are allowed to overhear her interior monologue.

Sarah contemplates suicide as a solution to her distress. Suicide is not directly prohibited in the OT. Those who commit suicide when faced with military defeat, imminent capture, or disgrace are not condemned for their actions: e.g., Saul and his armor bearer (1 Sam 31:4-5); Ahithophel (2 Sam 17:23); Zimri (1 Kgs 16:18); Razis (2 Macc 14:41-46). The prohibition of suicide, however, is implied in the prohibition concerning bloodshed (Gen 9:4-6) and the command not to kill (Exod 20:13). Sarah ultimately rejects suicide out of love for her father, who would suffer for her action. Instead, she pleads with God either to take her life or to end her suffering.

3:11-13. Sarah, like Tobit, is sorely aggrieved by abuse, enough so to consider death. But she is capable of deliberation and strong enough to abandon her life to God rather than to cause grief for others. She understands the proper formula for prayer. She faces the window, no doubt toward Jerusalem (see Dan 6:11), spreads out her hands in the traditional gesture, and begins with the formula, "Blessed are you" (v. 11; cf. Dan 3:26, 52; Jdt 13:17). She blesses God and calls upon all creation to help her give praise. She puts her trust in the mercy and holiness of God.[57] She moves almost immediately from the invocation to the heart of her plea. Her whole body is involved in the prayer—hands, face, eyes. Having rejected suicide, she asks God for death in order to be delivered from her distress.

3:14-15. Sarah calls upon God again, this time with the title "Master" (δέσποτα *despota*), connoting subservience before the all-powerful God. Sarah recognizes God's holiness; she also knows her own: She is "innocent of any defilement with a man"; she has never disgraced either her own name

---

55. G. W. E. Nickelsburg, "Tobit," in *Harper's Bible Commentary*, ed. James L. Mays (New York: Harper & Row, 1988) 794.

56. For more on Asmodeus, see Moore, *Tobit*, 154. Moore also points to the ongoing debate about the origin of the name "Asmodeus" (147). It is possible that the name derives from Hebrew שמד (*šmd*), "to destroy."

57. 4QTob[a] confirms the reading of "your holy name" in 3:11 (שמך קדישא *šmk qdyšʾ*), which also appears in G[I], in the Old Latin, and in the Syriac.

or that of her father. In accordance with the theory of retribution, she should be able to expect reward from God. But now she has no hope. There is no one else with whom to make a proper marriage; she cannot perform the daughterly duty of providing Raguel with an heir. All she wants is deliverance from her misery. She prays for death, but she also allows for the fact that God might "look favorably" upon her, "have mercy" on her, and silence the reproaches she has endured. She is willing to accept any response from God that relieves her of her anguish.[58]

It is instructive to compare her prayer with that of Tobit. The author has skillfully contrasted the prayer of an older man with that of a young woman. Tobit recalls the historical situation of exile and the sins of his ancestors before asking God to take his life. Sarah, although she begins her prayer with a traditional formula of blessing, moves almost immediately to her own situation. Tobit asks God not to turn away from him (v. 6); Sarah turns toward God. She also gives God greater freedom in dealing with her. Tobit says to God, "Deal with me as you will," but then presents only one alternative: "Command my spirit to be taken from me" (v. 6). Sarah presents the same solution, "Command that I be released from the earth" (v. 13), but also allows for another possibility (v. 15).

Interior monologue and prayer are the two most reliable witnesses to the inner life. Thus this scene reveals several things about Sarah's character. She has a clear understanding of who she is. She knows that her father loves her (vv. 10, 15). She also knows her own integrity and innocence (vv. 14-15). She expects to abide by the custom of marriage within the kinship group; however, she is well aware of the empty future ahead for her if there is no eligible man to marry. There are no other possibilities for her life. "Why should I still live?" she cries (v. 15).

[58]. The end of 3:15 in G^{II} is corrupt. G^{I} and VL, representing the recension G^{II}, indicate that she asks God to "look favorably" upon her and "have mercy" on her so that she might "never again listen to such reproaches."

REFLECTIONS

Belief in demons does not play a major role in modern religious consciousness. We are, however, very aware of evil in the world and in our own lives. The demon in this story has left Sarah hopeless. She has lost seven husbands and can expect no more. Evil still has power to render people hopeless. Some men and women feel trapped in abusive marriages. Parents who are unemployed despair of being able to feed themselves and their children. Floods or tornadoes, as they destroy a lifetime of work and precious keepsakes, crush a family's hopes. People caught in an oppressive political system fear for their lives if they attempt reform.

In the fight against evil, we are challenged to act even when the situation seems hopeless. We are called to help others—to staff shelters, to work in relief programs, to join the struggle for justice and peace. We also recognize, however, that in the end evil can be overcome only with God's help. We are also called to pray.

Sarah's prayer is a courageous cry in the face of despair. Her belief that God cares, that God is both powerful and merciful, keeps her from committing suicide. Our own daily prayer, "Deliver us from evil," gives us courage to do what we can against evil and strengthens our faith that in all things we conquer because of him who has loved us (Rom 8:37).

TOBIT 3:16-17, GOD'S ANSWER TO BOTH: RAPHAEL

COMMENTARY

The prayers of Tobit (vv. 2-6) and Sarah (vv. 11-15), which occur simultaneously, are also answered simultaneously. The answer to both prayers joins the two main plots, the sequence dependent on Tobit's charitable deeds, leading to his blindness, and the sequence culminating in Sarah's affliction by the demon Asmodeus. Each sequence has ended with a prayer. Both prayers are heard, and Raphael is sent in answer to heal Tobit's blindness, to free Sarah from Asmodeus, and to marry her to Tobiah.

Scholars often point out that these verses destroy the suspense by telling the reader the outcome of the plot in advance. However, creating suspense is not the main purpose of this story. Its main purpose is to show God's action in the lives of ordinary believers. These verses serve that purpose well.

First, God's action is revealed by the fact that God hears. The confidence of Tobit and Sarah that God will pay attention to their cries is well founded. Second, God acts indirectly through a mediator, sending an angel to answer both prayers. Third, God intends a surprise. Sarah fears that there are no other potential husbands. Tobiah has not so much as thought of marriage. No one has prayed for the angel's third task. It is simply a gift from God.

REFLECTIONS

It is often difficult to believe that God hears and answers prayer. We pray intensely, and nothing seems to happen. Tobit and Sarah do not know that their prayers have been answered. Tobit is still blind, still smarting from Anna's sharp words. Sarah is still unmarried, still bruised by the maid's words. Many events will happen before their suffering is relieved. But both prayers have been answered: The angel is already on the way.

TOBIT 4:1–6:1

PREPARATION FOR THE JOURNEY TO MEDIA

OVERVIEW

What will happen to the money Tobit deposited with Gabael? This question, generated by the exposition of the plot (1:14-15), now introduces the sequence concerning a journey into Media. Tobit begins the sequence by remembering the money (4:1). He decides to send Tobiah to Media for it (4:2) and informs him of his decision (4:3, 20). The decision to send Tobiah to Media hints at the answer to another question raised in the exposition: How will Tobiah (NRSV, Tobias) meet and marry Sarah?

Tobiah's response to information concerning the money is twofold. He agrees to go to Media (5:1), but he poses two complications: First, how will he identify himself to Gabael (5:2)? Tobit solves this problem by telling him about the signatures (5:3). The second complication will bring Raphael into the picture. Responding to Tobiah's objection that he does not know the way to Media, Tobit instructs him to find a trustworthy guide (5:2-3). The guide Tobiah finds is Raphael (5:4). This fact forms the initial answer to the question of how Raphael will function.

Several facts about Raphael move the sequence forward. He knows the way to Rages and is acquainted with Gabael (5:6). Raphael's expertise, coupled with the uprightness of his supposed family (5:13-14), convinces Tobit to approve him as a guide. Tobit's approval leads immediately to the departure of Tobiah and his guide (5:15-17). But in spite of the guide's good qualifications, Tobiah's parents worry (5:18–6:1): Will he return safely? Meanwhile the reader learns two other facts about Raphael that contribute to the plot. Tobit has asked about Raphael's family and character and been satisfied with the answers. The reader also learns that Raphael's origins are upright and that he is trustworthy, but for another reason: He is an angel of God (5:4). Thus the reader has a better grasp of the truth of Tobit's reassurance to Anna than does Tobit himself. It is true, as he says, that an angel accompanies Tobiah (5:17, 22). The other piece of information, which at this point is more significant to the reader than to the characters, is that Raphael knows the way to Ecbatana (5:6). This fact also contributes a partial answer to the question of how Tobiah will meet and marry Sarah.

Three remaining questions have been generated by this sequence (4:1–6:1): Will Tobiah get the money? Will he meet and marry Sarah? Will he return safely? Two questions untouched by the sequence remain from the exposition: How will Sarah be delivered from Asmodeus? How will Tobit be healed?

TOBIT 4:1-21, TOBIT'S INSTRUCTIONS TO HIS SON

COMMENTARY

Chapter 4 is Tobit's farewell discourse to Tobiah.[59] The farewell discourse is a speech usually given when a person is about to die, addressed to that person's descendants or followers as a kind of legacy or inheritance. The farewell discourse may include the announcement of the speaker's departure; a reminder of the past; an exhortation to be faithful to God's commandments and to one another; a prediction of the future; a blessing of peace and joy; and a promise that God will remain with the hearers. Several of the major figures in Israel's history are reported to have given farewell discourses: Jacob (Gen 47:29–49:33); Moses (the whole book of Deuteronomy); Joshua (Joshua 22–24); David (1 Chronicles 28–29). There are three farewell discourses in the book of Tobit: two by Tobit (4:3-21; 14:3-11) and one from Raphael (12:6-10).[60]

4:1-2. Tobit assumes that, since he has asked God for death, death is imminent. There are two important matters to attend to before he dies: the money deposited with Gabael (cf. 1:14) and the instruction to be given to his son, Tobiah. Tobit takes care of these things in reverse order.

4:3-4. Tobit has instructed Tobiah by example; now he instructs him also by word. In teaching his son, Tobit is following the example of his grandmother Deborah (1:8). His instruction begins with an exhortation to care for Tobit and Anna, Tobiah's parents. Tobit, who is so attuned to death and burial, wants to be sure that the proper rituals are performed for him. Tobiah is also instructed to honor his mother.

This section resembles the biblical wisdom literature, especially the Wisdom of Ben Sira, a book written about the same time as the book of Tobit. The responsibility of parents to instruct their children and of children to heed that instruction is a frequent wisdom theme. Ben Sira says, "He who teaches his son will make his enemies envious,/ and will glory in him among his friends./ When the father dies he will not seem to be dead,/ for he has left behind him one like himself" (Sir 30:3-4 NRSV; see also Prov 13:24; 19:18; 22:15; 23:13-14; 29:15, 17; Sir 7:23-24; 30:1-13). Proverbs advises the child to heed the instruction: "My child, do not forget my teaching,/ but let your heart keep my commandments;/ for length of days and years of life/ and abundant welfare they will give you" (Prov 3:1-2 NRSV; see also Prov 1:8-9; 2:1-5; 4:1-13, 20-22; 5:1-2; 7:1-4; 13:1; 19:27; 23:22-25).

The instruction to honor one's mother is especially significant: "With all your heart honor your father,/ and do not forget the birth pangs of your mother./ Remember that it was of your parents you were born;/ how can you repay what they have given to you?" (Sir 7:27-28 NRSV; cf. Prov 6:20; 10:1; 15:20; 19:26; 20:20; 30:17; Sir 3:1-16). Children are to be particularly solicitous when the parents are old: "My child, help your father in his old age,/ and do not grieve him as long as he lives;/ even if his mind fails, be patient with him;/ because you have all your faculties do not despise him" (Sir 3:12-13 NRSV).

Echoes of the Pentateuch also appear in this section. In Jacob's farewell discourse, he requests proper burial from his sons (Gen 47:29-31). The command in the decalogue to honor parents is singled out for emphasis by a motive clause, "that you may have a long life in the land" (Exod 20:12; Deut 5:16). The primary pentateuchal influence, however, is Deuteronomy, in which the duty of parents to instruct their children is emphasized. Israel is exhorted to teach the children the saving deeds of God (Deut 4:9; see also Deut 4:10;

---

59. Verses 7-19b are missing from the Sinaiticus MS, the primary representative of the Greek recension G[II]. They appear in the other major Greek recension (G[I]), which is based on the MS Vaticanus and Alexandrinus (B, A). Translations are usually supplemented from the Old Latin version (VL) and an eleventh-century CE manuscript, MS 319, which represent the recension G[I]. Fragments of two Qumran manuscripts contain a few verses of this section (4QTob[a] has v. 7, and 4QTob[e] has vv. 7-9). See Fitzmyer, *Tobit: Qumran Cave 4*, 1-2.
60. See Di Lella, "The Deuteronomic Background of the Farewell Discourse in Tob 14:3-11," 380-89. For a thorough and careful analysis of this chapter, see M. Rabenau, *Studien zum Buch Tobit*, BZAW (Berlin: Walter de Gruyter, 1994) 27-66.

6:1-2). The great commandment to love God is to be drilled into the children (Deut 6:7; see also Deut 11:19-20). Much important instruction is to be given as a response to the question of children: "When your son asks you . . ." (Deut 6:20-21; see also Deut 32:7). In the closing chapters of Deuteronomy, the injunction to educate the children regarding God's law appears twice (Deut 31:12-13; 32:46).

4:5-6. Tobit gives Tobiah a general rule for life: Remember God and keep the law; do good and avoid evil. To remember God is to seek God's presence actively in one's life. Awareness of God's presence then forms the foundation for discerning and doing what is good. Faithfulness to this way of life, according to the theory of retribution, results in reward.

4:7. Tobit tells Tobiah of a way in which the practice of righteousness is to be enfleshed—giving alms. He returns to the image he used in his prayer (3:6) of God's face being turned away. Tobit links the relationship with God to one's relationship to the poor. God's response to Tobiah will mirror Tobiah's response to the poor.

4:8. Tobit enunciates a principle of moderation. Alms are to be given in proportion to the resources of the giver.

4:9-11. Tobit lists the benefits of giving alms. Alms, rather than impoverishing the giver, actually are a way of storing treasure against the day of need. When Tobit says that alms are a way of escaping death, he is not declaring a belief in life after death. There is no evidence of this belief in the book. Rather, he is asserting the conviction that alms will protect the giver from premature death, a strong statement in the mouth of one who expects to die soon! Alms also are equivalent to offering sacrifice, a practice unavailable to the Israelites in exile.

❖   ❖   ❖   ❖

EXCURSUS: ALMSGIVING

Almsgiving (ἐλεημοσύνη *eleēmosynē*) is perhaps the most significant virtue in the book of Tobit (see Introduction).[61] The development of the concept conveyed by this word is one of the major contributions of this book to OT theology. Griffin describes four categories of meaning for *eleēmosynē* in this book: (1) "as charitable deed" (e.g., 1:16; 14:10; cf. 1:3; 2:14); (2) "as monetary alms and almsgiving" (e.g., 4:8*b*, 16-17; 12:8); (3) "as characteristic of a person," specifically Tobit (7:7; cf. 9:6; 14:11); (4) "as characteristic of God" (3:2; 13:6).[62] The third and fourth categories represent most of the usage in the OT, with the exception of the later books Ben Sira and Daniel. The first two categories represent NT usage. The book of Tobit (along with Ben Sira), in which all four meanings are represented, stands at the midpoint of the development of the word. The active expression of *eleēmosynē* in charitable deeds and monetary alms predominates in this book. Tobit specifies his charitable deeds as feeding the hungry, clothing the naked, and burying the dead (1:1-17). He enjoins the same acts of *eleēmosynē* on his son (4:3-4, 16-17).[63]

The basic principles regulating almsgiving are the same in Tobit and Deuteronomy, although the concept is not as fully developed in the latter. Alms are to be given willingly (Deut 15:10; see Tob 4:8, 16) and in proportion to one's income (Deut 16:17; see also Deut 15:14; Tob 4:8, 16). Charity to the needy is restricted to those within the community (4:17; see Deut 14:29; 16:14).

Ben Sira, however, is most similar to the book of Tobit in the theology regarding almsgiving. According to Ben Sira, giving alms delivers the giver from sin (Sir 3:30-31;

---

61. For a full treatment of the structural and narrative significance of *eleēmosynē* in the book of Tobit, see Griffin, "A Study of *Eleēmosynē* in the Bible with Emphasis upon Its Meaning and Usage in the Theology of Tobit and Ben Sira," 61-62.
62. Griffin, "A Study of *Eleēmosynē*," 2-5.
63. Griffin, "A Study of *Eleēmosynē*," 19, 60.

see Tob 12:9-10) and is a worthy offering before God (Sir 34:18–35:4; see Tob 4:11). The almsgiver is saved from premature death and destruction (Sir 29:10-13; 40:17, 24; see Tob 4:10; 12:9; 14:10). The giving of alms is limited, however, to the righteous (Sir 12:1-7; see Tob 4:17). The amount to be given is to be decided according to the means of the giver, but without fear or hesitation (Sir 18:15-18; 35:9-10; see Tob 4:8, 16).[64]

64. Griffin, "A Study of *Eleēmosynē*," 67-76.

4:12-13. Marriage is an important theme in the book of Tobit, both the blessing of it and the necessity for a proper attitude toward it. In his catalog of virtues, Tobit includes respect for marriage. First, he instructs his son to be faithful to the sexual demands of marriage and to avoid fornication. Then he teaches his son the proper way to find a wife.

Endogamy, marriage within the kinship group, is understood by Tobit as a requirement, taught both by the law (Exod 34:15-6) and by the examples of the ancestors. Abraham, whose wife may have been related to him (Gen 20:12), insists that his servant "not get a wife for [his] son from the daughters of the Canaanites" but go to Abraham's own homeland to find a wife for Isaac (Gen 24:3-4). Rebekah and Isaac give similar instructions to their son Jacob (Gen 27:46–28:5). Nothing is said in the Pentateuch concerning kinship between Noah and his wife. For this information, the book of Tobit depends on a tradition found in the book of *Jubilees* (4.33).[65] Tobit himself married within his own family (ἐκ τοῦ σπέρματος τῆς πατριᾶς ἡμων *ek tou spermatos tēs patrias hēmōn*, 1:9). According to Tobit, refusal to follow the example of the ancestors in this very important matter will result in disaster for young Tobiah. Tobit ignores the fact, however, that both Joseph (Gen 41:45) and Moses (Exod 2:21; see Num 12:1) married foreign wives.

The way to find a proper wife was hotly debated in the centuries following the Babylonian exile. The strongest condemnation of marriage to foreigners appears in the books of Ezra and Nehemiah (Ezra 9:1-4; Neh 13:23-27). Ezra demands that men divorce their foreign wives (Ezra 10:1-44). By contrast, the book of Ruth, which may have been written in the post-exilic period, tells the story of a foreign wife who becomes the great-grandmother of King David.

4:14. As he approaches the end of his discourse, Tobit presents a collection of maxims to guide his son in his relationship toward others, toward himself, and toward God. He is to be honest in his dealings with others, especially those who work for him (Ben Sira also advises justice toward laborers [Sir 7:20], asserting that withholding wages is equivalent to murder [Sir 34:26-27]). Again, Tobit equates one's relationship to God with that to one's neighbor; to act justly toward the laborer is to serve God. Tobiah must also be just toward himself. His life is to be based on wisdom and discipline.[66] His actions will bring reward, according to the theory of retribution.

4:15. The Golden Rule, "what you hate, do not do to anyone," is to guide Tobiah's actions. He is to avoid drunkenness, the enemy of discipline and wisdom. Ben Sira similarly advises against excessive drinking: "Let not winedrinking be the proof of your strength" (Sir 31:25; see also Sir 31:26-31).

4:16-17. The principles regarding almsgiving reappear: giving according to one's means; giving to the just but not to sinners. Even the dead and those who mourn them are to be cared for. The command to "place bread on the grave of the righteous" seems to speak of offering food to the dead.[67] Because this practice is expressly forbidden by Deuteronomy (Deut 26:14; see Ps 106:28)—one of the main sources for the theology of the book of Tobit—

65. See J. Gamberoni, "Das 'Gesetz des Mose' im Buch Tobias," in *Studien zum Pentateuch: Festschrift for W. Kornfield*, ed. G. Braulik (Wien/Freiburg: Herder, 1977) 230; R. H. Pfeiffer, *History of New Testament Times* (New York: Harper and Bros., 1949) 267.

66. Verse 14 of the Old Latin (VL) has a phrase that is missing in Greek (BA): "be wise in all that you say [*esto sapiens in omnibus sermonibus tuis*]."

67. The Greco-Roman practice was to eat a feast at the grave in honor of the dead on the day of burial, on the ninth day after the funeral, and then at the end of the period of mourning to pour out a libation on the grave. See Tacitus *Annals* 6.5; Petronius *Satyricon* 65. See also J. M. C. Toynbee, *Death and Burial in the Roman World* (Ithaca: Cornell University Press, 1971) 50-51.

it probably refers to gifts of food for the mourners (see Jer 16:7; Ezek 24:17, 22).[68]

4:18. Tobiah must recognize that he is not self-sufficient. He is to seek out the wise and accept any useful advice. Again Tobit reflects the same principles as does Ben Sira, who counsels the young to wear away the doorstep of the wise (Sir 6:36; cf. Sir 6:32-35).

4:19. With regard to God, Tobiah is to be generous in praise. He is to expect help and reward from God; on the other hand, he is to accept whatever God sends. Thus the theory of retribution is both affirmed (v. 14) and questioned (v. 19). Tobiah's faith is to be founded on the memory of God's goodness to the chosen people and on the commandments of his father.

Tobit's instruction in vv. 14-19 echoes the proverbs that are part of the story of Ahiqar (see Introduction). Tobit exhorts Tobiah, "Do not drink wine to the point of drunkenness or let drunkenness go with you on your way. . . . Pour out your bread on the grave of the righteous but do not give to sinners" (vv. 15, 17).[69] Ahiqar says, "My son, it is better to remove stones with a wise man than to drink wine with a fool. My son, pour out thy wine on the graves of the righteous rather than drink it with evil men."[70] One of the Aramaic

---

68. See Moore, *Tobit*, 173, for a full discussion of this issue.
69. Translation mine, more literal to show the relationship to Ahiqar. The Old Latin (OL) and the Vulgate read, "Pour out your wine [*vinum tuum*] and your bread."
70. Syr 2:9-10ᴬ. See F. C. Conybeare, J. R. Harris, and A. S. Lewis, "The Story of Ahikar," *APOT* 2.730. Much discussion has centered on this verse as a means to explain the incomplete reading in Tobit 4:17ᴮ: "pour out your bread." See, e.g., D. C. Simpson, "The Book of Tobit," *APOT* 1.191. This parallel only appears in versions of Ahiqar that are later than Tobit. See, e.g., Sefire 5,7, in J. A. Fitzmyer, *The Aramaic Inscriptions of Sefire*, BibOr 193 (Rome: Pontifical Biblical Institute, 1967) 96-97: "you must not gi[ve th]em food." Fitzmyer goes on to say: "The verb must come from the root נסך (*nsk*) which normally means to 'pour a libation.' But it is used here in a generic sense with לחם (*leḥem*, "bread") and means 'to provide food.' F. Rosenthal (*BASOR* 158 [1960] 29, n. 3), compares Akkad. *nasaku*, 'throw down food, meals.' Cf. Dn 2:46" (Fitzmyer, *The Aramaic Inscriptions of Sefire*, 108).

God], who casts down the exalted person and e[xalts the humble person]."[71] This proverb can be compared to v. 19: "If [the Lord] chooses otherwise, he casts down to deepest Hades."[72]

4:20-21. Finally Tobit comes to the practical point of his speech to Tobiah, the recovery of the money that has been deposited with Gabael. He informs his son of the amount and location of the money and adds a moral instruction to the practical information. The theory of retribution, which is the reward in this present life, is again affirmed: Faithfulness to God will bring Tobiah great wealth. Faithfulness to God is defined by three elements. First, Tobiah is to fear God, to maintain loving reverence in his relationship to God. The second and third elements are the negative and positive consequences of fear of the Lord: avoiding sin and doing good. Tobit's sentiment is a common wisdom theme. It appears in Psalm 34:

Come, O children, listen to me;
  I will teach you the fear of the LORD.
Which of you desires life,
  and covets many days to enjoy good?

. . . .

Depart from evil, and do good;
  seek peace and pursue it."

(Ps 34:11-12, 14 NRSV; see also Ps 37:27; Prov 3:7; 14:16; Sir 21:2)

---

71. *Story of Ahiqar*, col. x, ll. 149-50; Sachau, pl. 47ᴮ: text in A. Cowley, *Aramaic Papyri of the Fifth Century B.C.* (Oxford: Clarendon, 1923) 217; translation mine. References to the Aramaic text of the story of Ahiqar are traditionally numbered according to the system of E. Sachau, *Aramäische Papyri und Ostraka aus einer jüdischen Militär-Kolonie zu Elephantine* (Leipzig: J. C. Hinrichs, 1911).
72. The Old Latin (VL) has the additional phrase, "whomever he wishes, he raises [*quem ergo voluerit ipse allevat*]."

REFLECTIONS

1. Caring for elderly parents is a great concern in our society. People are living longer today than at any time in history. Adults do not ordinarily continue to live with parents in the family home, especially after marriage. The elderly often are left alone after the death of a spouse, and they frequently face economic anxiety and frail health. Their sons and daughters, the "sandwich generation," are burdened with their own children, homes, jobs, and economic needs. Tobit instructs his son never to abandon his mother. Presumably he would include himself if he were not so certain of his imminent death. How can we be faithful to Tobit's instruction? How can society help?

How can the church help? The growing trend toward complexes for assisted living, where older people have both privacy and the opportunity for convenient health care, communal meals, recreation, and sometimes also religious services, is a partial solution. Home health care and Meals on Wheels serve some of the needs of the elderly. Situations where nursing home care is a necessity place a strong obligation on family members to visit frequently. Are there other solutions?

2. The instruction of children is perhaps more vital now than at any time in history. Children are more mobile, have more money, and develop a social life outside the family at a very early age. The crucial responsibility of parents to instill values and to provide support is difficult. Tobit teaches Tobiah both by example and by word. His teaching did not begin only when he believed his death to be imminent, however. This responsibility for children's instruction from infanthood on is another area in which parents need the help of society and the church.

3. The word *almsgiving* is rarely used in modern American English. Hopefully the concept is not so rare. When my mother went into a nursing home, her mail began to come to me. Hardly a day passes that I do not receive at least one or two appeals for charitable contributions. The frequency of the appeals indicates to me that someone must be answering them. Other ways of giving alms are also available. People who have more energy than money help with projects such as Habitat for Humanity, which provides low-cost housing for the needy. Soup kitchens and shelters are staffed by volunteers and are supported by contributions of food and bedding as well as money. Major fund drives, such as United Way, organize our charitable contributions. The Salvation Army and the St. Vincent de Paul Society help us turn our crowded closets into "clothing the naked."

The list of possibilities is long. Tobit's exhortation gives us the guidelines: Give willingly; give according to what you have—little or much; and rejoice that your gift has become a treasure, an excellent offering in the presence of God. Christians believe that almsgiving does not merely save them from premature death, but leads to eternal life. In the Gospel of Luke, Jesus says that the treasure is not for this life only: "Sell your belongings and give alms. Provide money bags for yourselves that do not wear out, an inexhaustible treasure in heaven that no thief can reach nor moth destroy" (see Luke 12:33).

4. The Golden Rule is stated here in the negative, rather than in the positive as in the Gospels ("Do to others as you would have them do to you" [Matt 7:12; Luke 6:31]). This saying has long been the "rule" for believers. It is based on the commandment "you shall love your neighbor as yourself" (Lev 19:18). Leviticus adds: "You shall love the alien as yourself, for you were aliens in the land of Egypt" (Lev 19:34 NRSV). The sabbath commandment in Deuteronomy prescribes rest even for slaves, because the Israelites are to remember that they were once slaves in Egypt (Deut 5:15).

Robert Fulghum says that everything he needed to know he learned in kindergarten.[73] Most of us learned the Golden Rule at least that early. It really is everything we need to know. Tobit's whole instruction can be summarized with this simple sentence. Paul tells us that it is, in fact, the whole law: "Owe no one anything, except to love one another; for the one who loves another has fulfilled the law" (Rom 13:8).

5. Just and prompt payment of laborers is an issue of social justice that has intensified in the modern world. In *Rerum Novarum* (1891), Pope Leo XIII promoted the recognition of workers as partners with management in the production of goods.[74]

---

73. Robert Fulghum, *All I Really Need to Know I Learned in Kindergarten: Uncommon Thoughts on Common Things* (New York: Villard, 1988).
74. *Rerum Novarum* 1, 6, 26, 28. See *Contemporary Catholic Social Teaching* (Washington, D.C.: VSCC, 1991) for a modern reprint of the encyclical.

The Vatican II document *Gaudium et Spes* states that "remuneration for work should guarantee one the opportunity to provide a dignified livelihood for oneself and one's family on the material, social, cultural, and spiritual level."[75]

Capitalism is not a good in itself; profit cannot be the only or even the primary goal. Justice toward all, especially toward the more vulnerable members of society, is both Tobit's demand of Tobiah and the demand placed on all who would be faithful to God's teaching.

6. Tobit does not forbid his son to drink wine; rather, he advises his son to avoid drunkenness. There are two issues here: moderation and addiction. Moderation is the exercise of discipline recommended by Tobit. I have heard asceticism defined as "taking only what one needs." Saint Benedict advised his followers to practice moderation in all things.[76] The other issue is addiction, the enslavement to something. Addiction is an illness that can only be healed with help. For example, Alcoholics Anonymous provides lifelong support to those who suffer from alcohol addiction.

7. Tobit advises Tobiah to "seek advice from every wise person." The practice of spiritual direction has a long history among believers. It is rooted in the wisdom tradition of the instruction of a "son" (disciple) by an elder. In the Christian tradition it flowered among the desert fathers and mothers and continued especially in monasticism. Today many people seek out a "wise person" who will help them look at their lives honestly in order to see both the direction in which God is leading them and the pitfalls that lie in the way. Tobit's advice is an affirmation of the communal nature of faith. We do not go to God alone, but as a community, each helping the other.

75. *Gaudium et Spes* 67.2. See *The Documents of Vatican II*, ed. Walter M. Abbott, S. J. (New York: Herder & Herder, 1966), for an English translation.
76. RB 48.9; cf. 40.6. See *RB 1980: The Rule of St. Benedict*, ed. Timothy Fry et al. (Collegeville, Minn.: Liturgical Press, 1981).

TOBIT 5:1–6:1, THE HIRING OF A GUIDE

COMMENTARY

Following the long speech of chap. 4 the action resumes. The primary purpose of chap. 5 is to introduce the angel Raphael, who will act as a guide for the young Tobiah. The reader is already prepared for Raphael's appearance. He has been sent in answer to the prayers of Tobit and Sarah to heal them both (3:17). Now the reader discovers how Raphael will function: as a guide on the journey.

Raphael is a main character in the scenes of preparation, journeying (chap. 6), and conclusion (chap. 12). In these scenes, his identity as an angel is kept clearly before us. The narrator introduces him as the angel Raphael (5:4). After the lengthy negotiation over identity and trustworthiness, we are reminded (ironically) by the unsuspecting Tobit that an angel travels with Tobiah (5:17, 22). The narrator continues to refer to Raphael as "the angel" throughout the journey (6:2, 4, 7). But as soon as the travelers approach Ecbatana, Raphael's angelic character fades from sight. We are not reminded of it again until the revelation speech in chap. 12.

5:1-2. In his response to his father's long speech, Tobiah presents several anticipated difficulties. He seems somewhat helpless. He does not know how to get the money; he does not know how he will be recognized by Gabael. He does not even know how to get to Media. This uncertainty contributes to the impression of Tobiah as an inexperienced young man. He is not unwilling, however, to go on the journey. His questions show that he has already taken the task upon himself, and he accepts and acts upon the answers his father gives him.

5:3. The experienced father reassures his worried son. First he tells Tobiah what he must present to Gabael in order to get the money. The matter of the signed bond is somewhat confusing in the text. Apparently, according to a practice known in the ancient world, the document was written in duplicate on the same parchment or papyrus. Then the document was torn or cut in half. Tobit took his half home and put Gabael's half with the money. Tobit will now give Tobiah the half in his possession, so that he can claim the money (see 9:2).

Tobit deals with Tobiah's other difficulty by instructing him to find a trustworthy guide who will travel with him and show him the way to Media. Although this difficulty seems secondary to the task of regaining the money, the money will become secondary as the plot progresses and the instructions of the guide will become primary.

5:4. The appearance of Raphael in this scene gives several clues to his angelic status. First, Tobiah simply finds Raphael standing in front of him. The immediacy suggests an angelic appearance. Raphael is an ironic character, one "who poses as less than he is" and "who understates things."[77] As a character, he is an example of dramatic irony, in which the readers know what the characters do not.[78] The narrator sets up the ironic situation by informing the reader that Tobiah "did not perceive that he was an angel of God."

5:5. Raphael claims to be an Israelite; the reader knows that he is an angel. His subsequent announcement of his purpose, "I have come here to work," is also ironic. The reader knows what his task is (3:17), but Tobiah does not.

5:6. Raphael knows exactly what Tobiah needs, and he claims extraordinary knowledge. He knows Media well. He knows all the routes, all its plains, all its roads, and he knows that the way is safe (5:6, 10, 16). Raphael knows the very kinsman Tobiah intends to visit, and he knows the distance to Ecbatana, which Tobiah does not intend to visit but will. In fact, however, Raphael's knowledge of geography is not very good. Rages is approximately 185 miles from Ecbatana. The distance took Alexander's army eleven days to cover.[79] Perhaps an angel moves more swiftly! Also, Ecbatana is not situated on a plain, but has a higher altitude than Rages.

5:7-8. Tobiah politely begins to negotiate with the potential guide, but the young man still needs the approval of his father. In fact, his father will pay the wages. The aura of haste that surrounds Raphael is another characteristic that hints at his angelic status. He agrees to wait, but insists that Tobiah not be long (see also 8:3; 9:1-6; 11:3).

5:9. When Tobiah informs Tobit that he has found a possible guide, Tobit's response reveals his love for his son. He wants to know Raphael's lineage and his trustworthiness. His concern for strict religious observance, which he will deduce from Raphael's supposed family, is emphasized again. Only a man who can be trusted both to know and to observe the law of God is worthy to be his son's companion.

The irony continues in this section. Raphael's name, like Tobit's, is ironic in the context of the story. He plays upon the meaning of his name, "God heals," saying to Tobit, "Take courage! God's healing is near."

5:10. Tobit's grief and constant awareness of his blindness spill out in his very first words to Raphael: "What joy is left for me?" His treatment of the unknown Raphael is notable for its reverence. Tobit greets Raphael first, although the latter appears to be the younger, since Tobiah addresses Raphael as "young man" (vv. 5, 7, 9).

5:11-12. Raphael seems reluctant to reveal his identity to Tobit. This is a common theme in angelic appearances. Both the angel who wrestles with Jacob (Gen 32:30) and the angel who announces Samson's impending birth (Judg 13:18) refuse to reveal their names. Tobit's characteristic gentleness is again revealed as he turns aside a sharp remark (v. 12) by repeating without rancor his question concerning Raphael's family and by asking pardon for his persistence.

5:13. The pseudonym Raphael uses to mask his identity is also an ironic revelation of his function. He tells Tobit, "I am Azariah [YHWH has helped], son of Hananiah [YHWH is merciful]." The statement is true, but not in the sense that Tobit understands it.

5:14. Tobit's own words are also ironic. Twice he has expressed his desire for a true answer concerning Raphael's identity (vv. 12,

---

77. Edwin Good, *Irony in the Old Testament* (Sheffield: Almond, 1981), 14. See also Aristotle *Ethics* 4.7.14 1127b; Frye, *Anatomy of Criticism*, 40.
78. D. C. Muecke, *The Compass of Irony* (London: Methuen, 1969), 104-5; see also Muecke, *Irony*, 64-66.
79. See Arrian, *Anabasis Alexandri*, trans. P. A. Brunt, LCL (Cambridge, Mass.: Harvard University Press, 1976) 3:20.

14). When Raphael does answer him, Tobit exclaims, "Welcome!" (lit., "May you come in wellness!"). The word ὑγιαίνω (*hygiainō*, "to be well") is subsequently picked up by Raphael (v. 16) and becomes an ironic echo of the angel's name and function. Tobit concludes that Azariah (Raphael) is of good lineage. Indeed!

5:15-16. Tobit's business arrangements with Raphael demonstrate Tobit's justness and his generosity. He states clearly what the salary will be, and he promises a bonus if the travelers return safely. Raphael answers Tobit with a typical angelic answer, "Fear not" (cf. Gen 21:17; Dan 10:12; Luke 1:13, 30; 2:10; Acts 27:24). Then he repeats the key word *hygiainō* ("to be well"). This word, which occurs only forty times in the whole Septuagint, appears twenty-five times in the book of Tobit. Eight of the occurrences are in vv. 16-22 (translated "good health" or "safe"). A key theme of the book is healing, "to be well."

5:17. Tobit, the man of prayer, pronounces a blessing upon Raphael and upon his son, Tobiah. His prayer for Tobiah is another example of irony. Tobit's prayer for a good angel to accompany his son has already been answered. The readers know this, but he does not.

5:18-20. The final character to appear in this section is Anna, the mother. Again she reveals the immediacy of her emotions. She has been described as a woman inclined to passion and despair.[80] As her son, Tobiah, leaves, she makes a scene, weeping and complaining that Tobit is sending him away.

Anna follows the pattern set in the dialogue of chap. 2. As soon as the immediate subject of her worry is stated, she turns the conversation to an attack on Tobit, accusing him of preferring money to the life of their son. She strikes again at Tobit's trust in God's providence, implying that she is content with what God sends, but that he apparently is not.

The personal pronouns are significant in this and subsequent scenes. Anna, identified by the narrator as "his [Tobiah's] mother," says to Tobit, "Why is it that *you* have sent *my* child away?" (v. 18, italics added). After a single mention of "our child" (v. 19), she continues to refer to Tobiah as "my child" (10:4, 7) until he returns from the journey that has worried her so much.

5:21–6:1. Tobit responds to his wife's worry with assurance. His words are deeply ironic. He repeats the religious cliché with which he bade farewell to Tobiah, "a good angel will go with him." He does not know how true his statement is. The scene closes with an incredible economy of detail. After Tobit's comforting words, the narrator tells us, Anna stops weeping.

[80]. W. Dommershausen, *Der Engel, die Frauen, das Heil: Tobias, Ester, Judit*, SKK 17 (Stuttgart: Katholische Bibelwerk, 1970) 9.

REFLECTIONS

1. The Letter to the Hebrews warns us not to neglect hospitality, because through it some have entertained angels unawares (Heb 13:2). Tobit welcomes Raphael with respect even though he sees him simply as a man in search of a job. There is a fascination with "angels in disguise" in popular culture. Stories abound in which an ordinary person—night nurse, postal worker, tow-truck driver, cleaning woman—is recognized later as an angel. The angel is known because he or she brings a message (*angel* means "messenger"). The message may give encouragement to do the right thing even though it is hard. It may provide comfort in the face of sickness or death. It may be a warning that one's life has taken a wrong turn. In the last analysis, the message is always, "God loves you."

2. Wellness is a popular theme in our society. There are wellness workshops and wellness retreats. Books promise to teach us wellness. Exercise machines and health clubs promise to lead us there.

What is wellness? What does it mean to be a truly healthy human being? The word *health* has to do with wholeness. A healthy person is a "whole" person. Our experience teaches us that wholeness does not, however, always mean the absence of disease or injury. Wholeness has far more to do with the integrity of a person's spirit. The Special Olympics give us a glimpse of those who may not be physically sound but whose courage and joy testify to their health and wholeness.

The challenge of wellness comes in the recognition that we do not have absolute control over our lives. We do what we can to maintain physical health—eating wisely, exercising, resting—and spiritual health—prayer, companionship, the practice of virtue. But we only do this well if we accept our own situation honestly—our strengths, our weaknesses, the accidents or diseases that may afflict us. True wellness is a consequence of humility, the recognition that life and health are gifts from God.

3. The book of Tobit portrays God's providence working subtly in the midst of ordinary life. The angel sent to help Tobit and Sarah seems to be an ordinary human being. A common fish is the means of healing. Even the ordinary speech of the characters reveals the hidden work of God. Both Tobit and Raphael use the customary greeting: "Well-come." Tobit assures Anna of Tobiah's safety with the pious wish, "An angel goes with him." Part of the irony in this story comes from the characters' unconscious use of these terms and phrases.

Many of our common English words also conceal religious concepts. "Good-bye" is a contraction of "God be with you." "Holiday" comes from "holy day." We use phrases out of habit: "God bless you," "God keep you." We wish each other well without knowing it with "farewell" and "welcome." A brief moment of attention to our language may also reveal to us the hidden work of God.

TOBIT 6:2-18

THE JOURNEY TO MEDIA

OVERVIEW

The book of Tobit bears some characteristics of the romance. A common form of the romance is the successful quest, which falls into three main stages: the dangerous journey, the mortal struggle, and the exaltation of the hero. The hero may embark on the journey for several reasons—e.g., to rescue a bride from a perilous situation or to obtain hidden treasure. Frequently the struggle involves a dragon-killing theme—e.g., victory over a serpent or water monster, such as Leviathan. After the hero passes through the symbolic death of the struggle, the conquered sea monster may become the source of life for him or for others. Throughout the quest, the romantic hero moves in a double world. He is human, not divine, but extraordinary events happen in his favor. The ordinary laws of nature yield to his marvelous actions. At the successful completion of the quest, a "new society" may form around the hero and heroine. This new society is often inaugurated by a festive ritual, such as a wedding or a banquet.[81]

In the book of Tobit the central movement of the plot is a quest for money (4:1-2, 20–5:3), which becomes a quest for a bride (6:10-18; cf. 4:12-13). The hero, Tobiah, embarks on a dangerous journey. He conquers a water animal (6:3-6), which becomes a means of life and healing (8:2-3; 11:10-14). With the help of an angel, he survives a mortal struggle with a demon (8:2-3; cf. 6:17-18). During the quest the angel's assistance puts the hero in touch with a world beyond ordinary human experience. The story ends with a description of the happy and prosperous life of the hero and his bride after the successful completion of the quest (14:1-2, 11-15). The wedding signals the hope for the "new society," the new Jerusalem whose future citizens are symbolized in their seven sons (13:9-18; 14:3).

The journey falls into two segments, each dealing with one of the questions generated by preparation for the journey. It begins with the last question from the previous sequence: Will Tobiah return safely? On the first night of the journey he is attacked by a fish, which attempts to swallow his foot (6:3). By heeding Raphael's encouragement and advice, he conquers the fish (6:4); in obedience to Raphael's instructions, he sets aside its gall, heart, and liver for future use (6:5-6). Raphael's response to Tobiah's inquiry concerning these strange instructions suggests an answer to the two questions that have been ignored since the exposition: How will Tobit be healed? The fish's gall can restore sight (6:9). How will Sarah be delivered from Asmodeus? The burning of the fish's heart and liver will drive away demons (6:8).

The second segment of the journey begins as the travelers approach Ecbatana (6:10). The repetition of this place-name, which occurs in 3:7 (see also 5:6) hints that this section will deal with the question of whether Tobiah will meet and marry Sarah. Raphael introduces the subject immediately and advises Tobiah of his right to marry Sarah (6:11-13). In response, Tobiah objects. He has heard of Sarah's affliction and of the deaths of the previous bridegrooms (6:14-15). Again he raises the question that concluded the previous sequence: Will I return safely? Raphael urges him to twofold obedience: First, he should obey his father's will and marry a woman from his own family (6:16), and, second, he should obey Raphael's instructions and, with prayer and the burning of the fish's liver and heart, deliver Sarah from Asmodeus (6:17-18). Thus the fish, which represents the first threat to his safe return, becomes the first assurance of his safety. Tobiah's response is

---
81. Frye, *Anatomy of Criticism*, 187-93.

assent and intense love for Sarah. The question is answered: How will Sarah be delivered from Asmodeus?

The four major questions treated by this sequence have collapsed into two: Will Tobiah marry Sarah, escape death, and deliver her? Will Tobiah return safely and heal Tobit? The only question left untreated in this sequence is whether Tobiah will get the money. That question is intensified, since the action seems to be shifting toward Ecbatana and away from Rages.

TOBIT 6:2-9, CATCHING THE FISH

COMMENTARY

6:2. A trio departs from Nineveh on the journey: the angel, the boy, and a dog. The narrator continues to remind us that the guide is really an angel in disguise. The dog (which reappears in 11:4) is probably a feature of underlying folktale.

They camp the first night along the Tigris River. In the story this marks the end of a long day, which began with the payment of Anna's wages (2:12). The geography is confused. Nineveh lies on the eastern side of the Tigris River; the travelers intend to travel farther east to Ecbatana (and Rages). There is no need for them to backtrack to the river.

❖ ❖ ❖ ❖

EXCURSUS: DAY AND NIGHT

The terms "day" (ἡμέρα *hēmera*) and "night" (νύξ *nyx*) are significant in this story of blindness and sight. The distribution of the terms signals the flow of the plot. The word "day" occurs primarily at the beginning and end of the book (14 times in the first five chaps., 14 times in chaps. 8–11, and 4 more times in chaps. 12–14, but not at all in 6:1–8:18. The word "night" occurs almost exclusively in this central section (10 times in chaps. 6–8, and once in 10:7 [Anna weeps all night]; it occurs only one other time, when Tobit is afflicted with blindness in 2:9). Of the ten occurrences between chapters 6 and 8, seven refer to the wedding night of Tobiah and Sarah. Of the three remaining uses, two refer to the wedding nights of the previous bridegrooms (6:14; 7:11) and one to the travelers' first night on the journey. Thus the following pattern emerges:

	1:1–6:1	6:2–8:18	8:19–11:18	12:1–14:15
day	14x	—	14x	4x
night (wedding)	—	7x	—	—
night (other)	1x	3x	1x	—

The story begins with Tobit walking "all the *days* of his life" in truth and righteousness (1:3). He buries a man on Pentecost after *sunset* (2:4, 7) and is then plunged into *night* (2:9). Tobiah joins him in a journey into night—a night that begins with the journey into Media (6:2) and ends in Ecbatana as the servants fill in a grave before dawn (8:18). "Night," which had begun as a word of sorrow (2:9; 6:14; 7:11), gradually becomes a word of joy (6:11, 13, 16; 7:10-11): "They slept the whole night"

(8:9). Anna, however, does not yet know of the transition from night to day. She still keeps watch by *day*, goes home at *sunset*, and weeps all *night* (10:7). But her sunset has already been conquered by the dawn in Ecbatana. Tobiah's journey into night (6:1–8:18) has resulted in a return to daylight both for Sarah, whose previous wedding *nights* ended in disaster (6:14; 7:11), but who now celebrates a fourteen-*day* wedding feast (8:20; 10:7), and for Tobit, who celebrates his return to light by another seven-*day* feast with the newlyweds (11:18). The final chapters of the book tell of the happy length of *days* of them all.

❖   ❖   ❖   ❖

6:3-4. A very large fish leaps out of the water and attempts to swallow Tobiah's foot. In G^I the fish attempts to swallow Tobiah whole! The fish serves as a symbol of the power of death. The struggle with the fish occurs at night, a traditional time for the dominance of evil. This night is the first on the journey that will lead Tobiah to risk death in order to deliver Sarah from Asmodeus. The fish symbolizes not only the beginning of this struggle with death, but also the means to life. Once it is conquered, its vital parts become for Tobiah the means to heal both his bride and his father. Thus the fish recalls the traditional association of water and water monsters with chaos, which, once conquered, become the means for creation (e.g., Gen 1:2; Job 38:8-11; 40:25–41:26; Pss 74:13-15; 89:10-11; 104:25-26; 107:23-30; Isa 27:1-3; 51:9-11).[82]

6:5. The procedure described here concerning the parts of the fish to be used for each healing is repeated twice more for each healing, suggesting the folktale "law of three" and increasing anticipation of the actual events. In answer to Tobiah's question, Raphael tells him what will happen when the fish's heart and liver are burned (v. 8). In response to Tobiah's fear, Raphael makes the instruction specific to him: "When you go into the bridal chamber . . ." (vv. 17-18). The final repetition describes Tobiah's actions on the wedding night (8:2-3). Each repetition grows more specific in detail until Sarah's deliverance is accomplished. The initial instructions for Tobit's healing also are given by Raphael in response to Tobiah's question (v. 9). The two repetitions in chap. 11 (11:7-8, 11-13) increase in specific detail. When each healing finally occurs, the reader knows exactly what to expect.

6:6. Tobiah follows Raphael's instructions precisely, a continuing sign of his trusting obedience. He then eats part of the fish. It will become important to note that there is no mention that Raphael also ate (cf. 12:19). Finally, Tobiah salts the fish. This may simply be a reference to a common means of preserving food, but it may also reflect the belief that salt is a purifying agent that can drive away evil influences, thus removing the deathly quality of the fish and enhancing its life-giving properties.[83]

6:7-9. Raphael now assumes his role as messenger. In answer to Tobiah's question, he tells him how to use the parts of the fish for healing. His reply indicates that he knows who has which affliction. In the instruction regarding evil spirits he mentions "a man or a woman"; in the instruction regarding eye ailments he simply mentions "a man" or "a person" (ἄνθρωπος *anthrōpos*). The reader knows that it is a woman who is afflicted by a demon and a man who is blind. (See Reflections at 6:10-18.)

---

82. See also *Enûma elish* 4.31-146, in *ANET*, 66-67.

83. See Zimmermann, *The Book of Tobit*, 80-81.

TOBIT 6:10-18, RAPHAEL'S INSTRUCTIONS

COMMENTARY

6:10-11. Raphael announces that they are staying in Ecbatana at the house of Raguel. This has been the real goal of the journey all along (cf. 3:17; 5:6), though Tobiah has thought that they were heading for Rages.

The second long day of this story (6:10–8:18) is hastened on its way by the constant repetition of "night," ("this very night," vv. 11, 13, 16; 7:10-11). Suspense builds as attention is continually drawn to Sarah's eighth wedding night: "Tonight we must stay with Raguel" (v. 11); "Tonight I will ask the girl's father" (v. 13); "Tonight we must speak for the girl" (v. 13; see also 7:10-11).

6:12-13. Raphael continues to supply information as he exhorts Tobiah to marry Sarah. The exchange between Tobiah and Raphael is a virtual monologue by Raphael, punctuated by only a single objection from Tobiah. The marriage of Tobiah and Sarah will be founded on Tobiah's obedience to the message the angel brings. Raphael tells Tobiah that he, as the closest relative, has the right to marry her. He even states that Raguel would incur the death penalty for refusing the marriage, a penalty mentioned nowhere else with regard to endogamy.

6:14-15. Tobiah's speech manifests the qualities characteristic of him in the first section of the book. He speaks with the haste of youth; short clauses often linked by "and" come tumbling out without apparent order. But his speech makes up in passion what it lacks in organization. He musters all the arguments he knows to avoid what he fears is a life-threatening marriage.

Tobiah's speech contains the fourth repetition of the story of Sarah's seven previous husbands (see 3:8-9, 15). It contains all three of the basic facts told by the narrator (3:8): (1) Sarah has been married to seven husbands; (2) the wicked demon Asmodeus has killed them; (3) they have died before the marriage could be consummated. But Tobiah's own preoccupation is evident in his fourfold repetition that the bridegrooms have died: "her husbands died in the bridal chambers . . . they died . . . it was a demon who killed them . . . it kills any man who desires to approach her" (vv. 14-15). Finally Tobiah expresses his real fear: "If *I* should die" (v. 15, italics added). The demon's motive for killing Sarah's bridegrooms appears in the Qumran manuscript 4QTob[a], Greek MS 319, and the Old Latin: It is in love with her.

6:16-18. Raphael instructs Tobiah in the means to free Sarah from the demon Asmodeus—means that include not only the use of the fish entrails but also prayer. (It seems that Tobiah has already forgotten what he learned about the fish at the Tigris.) Raphael also declares that Sarah was set apart for Tobiah before the world existed. They are to be gifts to each other. Tobiah will save her from her affliction, and she will be his companion and the mother of his children.

Throughout the journey Tobiah obeys Raphael. He follows Raphael's curious instructions concerning the fish (vv. 3-6), and he allows Raphael to persuade him concerning marriage to Sarah. The willingness to marry a kinswoman also accords with his father's command (4:12-13). Having heard all of the angel's words, Tobiah immediately falls in love with Sarah—a strange comment to our modern ears. Tobiah loves her because she has been designated by God for him and because she is the means for his obedience to his father. Tobiah's love is an act of the will, not a movement of the emotions.

REFLECTIONS

1. Guided by an angel of God, Tobiah journeys into night and is threatened by a monster of chaos. Obedient to the angel's instructions, he conquers the watery monster and saves its life-giving parts. Through his obedience, not only he but also his father and his future wife will be brought from night into day. Christian life is often called the Way (see Acts 9:2; 18:25-26; 19:9, 23; 24:4, 14, 22). Living a Christian life can be described as a successful quest. We, too, go into night and are threatened by death and evil. But, like Tobiah, we are not alone. In various ways God leads us on the journey. Through obedience we and those whose lives we touch will be brought from night into eternal day. Our obedience is modeled on Christ, who is himself the Way (John 14:6).

2. The fish, symbol of chaos, becomes a means to life. The sage in the Wisdom of Solomon says that "God did not make death," there is "no destructive poison" in the creatures of the earth (Wis 1:13-14 NRSV). The poison results from being swallowed by created things, enslaved by them. How many healing drugs are death-dealing when used in excess! Tamed and applied wisely, however, they can restore life.

TOBIT 7:1–11:18

RESOLUTION AND RECOVERY

OVERVIEW

The three questions remaining at the end of the journey will be answered in the three-part resolution. Resolution 1 focuses on the question with which the journey ended: Will Tobiah meet Sarah, escape death, and deliver her from Asmodeus?

The arrival of Tobiah and Raphael at Ecbatana and at Raguel's house (7:1-2) commences the sequence of resolution 1. Tobiah's revelation of his kinship with Raguel (7:5), implying his right to Sarah (see 7:10), leads to his request that Raphael ask Raguel for Sarah as Tobiah's bride (7:9). Raguel overhears and objects in words similar to Tobiah's earlier words (7:11; cf. 6:14). Tobiah's insistence and his refusal to eat lead Raguel to agree to the betrothal (7:11). The betrothal itself has several consequences. First, the banquet continues, and Sarah and the bridal chamber are prepared (7:14-17). Subsequently, Tobiah is led to Sarah (8:1). He remembers Raphael's dual instructions (8:2). He burns the heart and liver of the fish, which results in the expulsion of the demon and his binding by Raphael (8:2-3). He prays with Sarah (8:4-8), and both survive the night and sleep peacefully (8:9). Thus the first major question (Will Tobiah marry Sarah, escape death, and deliver her from the demon?) is answered positively.

Between resolutions 1 and 2 appears a transitional sequence. Raguel, anticipating a negative answer to the question of Tobiah's survival, digs a grave for him (8:9-10). His discovery that Tobiah is still alive (8:14) has a threefold result: Raguel prays in thanksgiving (8:15-17); he has his servants fill in the grave (8:18), thus ending all reference to the death of Sarah's husbands; and he joyfully prepares a wedding feast (8:19).

The enforced delay caused by the wedding feast (8:19) leads directly into the two final sequences of the resolution. Because he cannot leave Ecbatana, Tobiah sends Raphael to collect the money (9:1-3). Here is the first mention of the money since the departure (5:19). The question of the money is resolved with dispatch. Raphael goes to Rages (9:5), obtains the money with the aid of the signed bond (cf. 5:3), and brings Gabael to the wedding feast, along with the money (9:6). The second major question of the resolution (Will Tobiah get the money?) has also been answered positively.

One question remains: Will Tobiah return safely and heal Tobit? The question is intensified because the enforced delay in Ecbatana has caused his parents to worry (10:1-7). At last Tobiah, Raphael, and Sarah depart for Nineveh (10:7–11:1). Armed with the gall of the fish and Raphael's repeated instruction (11:4, 7), Tobiah arrives, is announced by his mother (11:5-6), and heals his father (11:10-14). As a consequence of his healing, Tobit prays in thanksgiving (11:14-15) and in his joy becomes the cause of joy for the city (11:16-18). Sarah's arrival increases the joy (11:17), and the wedding feast is celebrated again (11:18). The final question is answered. Tobiah has returned safely with both money and bride and has healed his father. The grief of the exposition (3:1, 10) has been turned to the joy of the resolution. The challenge concerning Tobit's reward for charitable deeds (2:14) has also been answered.

TOBIT 7:1–8:21, SARAH'S HEALING

COMMENTARY

The events ending this second long day of the story (6:10–8:18) concern not only the deliverance of Sarah from the demon that has been afflicting her, but also the joining of two families. The significance of family is evident, first, in the scene in which the travelers arrive. The recognition of Tobiah as Tobit's son is a cause of great joy. Second, the close family relationship gives reason both for the marriage to happen and for Raguel's hesitation out of fear for Tobiah's life. Finally, the marriage itself is the joining not only of Tobiah and Sarah, but also of their families.

Tobiah's betrothal to Sarah (7:1-17), including the preceding departure from his father (5:17-22) and subsequent departure from the bride's home (10:7-13), is modeled on the biblical type scene of betrothal. Elements that recur in the betrothal type scene (e.g., Gen 24:1-61; 29:1-14; Exod 2:15-22) are a traveler, one or more young women, a well, the drawing of water, a sense of haste, and a meal.[84] Not all of these elements appear in this scene.

7:1-2. When the travelers arrive in Ecbatana, Tobiah puts his newfound love for Sarah into action. He orders his guide, Raphael, to bring him immediately to the house of Raguel. Raphael complies with dispatch.

Raguel, whose name means "friend of God," shows in this scene the characteristic virtues of another friend of God, Abraham. Abraham is noted for his hospitality, entertaining angels unawares (Gen 18:1-15; cf. Gen 19:1), and for his fatherhood, both of a beloved child and of a host of nations (Gen 17:4-5). Raguel is also generous in hospitality. As soon as he has greeted Tobiah and Raphael, he brings them into his home and introduces them to his family.

"Raguel" is also the name of Moses' father-in-law (spelled "Reuel" in most translations; Exod 2:18; Num 10:29) and of an archangel in *1 Enoch* 20:4; see also *1 Enoch* 23:4).[85] Tobiah has been instructed by his father to follow the example of the ancestors in finding a wife from his own kindred. He has not only done that, but has also found a father-in-law worthy of his ancestors.

7:3-5. The scene of welcome is based primarily on Jacob's betrothal (Gen 29:1-30). In Genesis, Jacob, the son sent by his father to find a proper bride (Gen 28:1-5), arrives in Haran and greets a group of shepherds. When Tobiah and Raphael arrive at the house of Raguel, they have the following conversation with Edna:

Gen 29:4-6	Tob 7:3-5
Jacob said to them, "Brothers, where do you come from?" They said, "We are from Haran."	Edna asked them and said to them, "Where are you from, brothers?" And they said to her, "We are descendants of Naphtali exiled to Nineveh."
He said to them, "Do you know Laban son of Nahor?" They said, "We know him."	And she said to them, "Do you know Tobit our brother?" And they said to her, "We know him."
He said to them, "Is he well?" "He is well," they replied.	And she said to them, "Is he well?" And they said to her, "He is alive and well."

The two betrothal scenes are linked by the key word ὑγιαίνω (*hygiainō*, "to be well"). This concept is highly significant for the book of Tobit. About two-thirds of the occurrences of the word in the Septuagint are found in the book of Tobit.[86] The two passages also fall into a similar pattern. The traveler is greeted with embraces when he makes himself known as a relative (Gen 29:12-13; see Tob 7:6). He loves his prospective bride (Gen 29:18; see Tob 6:18), who is beautiful (Gen 29:17; see Tob 6:12). The father of the bride is reluctant to agree to the marriage (Gen 29:23-27;

---

84. See Alter, *The Art of Biblical Narrative*, 51-61.
85. *APOT* 2.210, 204.
86. There are 48 occurrences of ὑγιαίνω (*hygiainō*) in the Septuagint; of these, 25 are in the Sinaiticus recension of Tobit and 8 in the recension represented by Vaticanus and Alexandrinus. There are only 15 additional occurrences in the Septuagint.

see Tob 7:10-11), and in both cases seven is a significant number. Laban requires Jacob to serve seven years for Leah and seven more for Rachel (Gen 29:20, 27); Raguel is reluctant to agree to Tobiah's marriage to Sarah because of the deaths of seven previous husbands (Tob 7:11). Jacob serves a total of fourteen years; Tobiah and Sarah have a fourteen-day wedding feast (Tob 8:20).

The betrothal scene of Tobiah also resembles the betrothal scene of Isaac (Gen 24:1-67). The two scenes are linked by structure and vocabulary. In both scenes, the father sends someone (servant or son) to find a bride from his own kindred (Gen 24:3-4; see Tob 4:12-13), although Tobit is unaware that this is the purpose of his son's journey. The man in whose care the future bride is found prepares a meal for the traveler (Gen 24:33; see Tob 7:9), but the traveler refuses to eat until the betrothal has been arranged (Gen 24:33; see Tob 7:11). The host yields, recognizing that the marriage has been decided by the Lord (Gen 24:50; see Tob 7:11). He gives the woman to the traveler, saying, "Take her with you" (Gen 24:51; see Tob 7:12). When the host wants to delay the travelers, the servant/son asks, "Let me go back to my master/father" (Gen 24:56; see Tob 10:7); the return journey follows immediately.

The key word εὐοδόω (*euodoō*, "to prosper, make successful") also links the two scenes. The word occurs seven times in the Septuagint of Genesis 24 (LXX Gen 24:12, 21, 27, 40, 42, 48, 56). It appears in the words of Abraham, who sends his servant (Isaac's surrogate) to find a bride for his son from his kindred. It occurs in the prayers and hopes of the servant and in the servant's account of his mission. In the book of Tobit, *euodoō* is found in Tobit's hope for his son's journey. In the wedding ceremony, Raguel prays for Tobiah and Sarah: "May the Lord of heaven prosper you both" (v. 11; see also v. 12). At their departure, Raguel repeats his prayer (10:11), and Edna extends the hope for prosperity to them all (10:12). Finally, the word occurs in Tobiah's own account of his journey (10:13; 11:15).

7:6-8. The theory of retribution surfaces again in Raguel's exclamation concerning Tobit. He repeats the adjectives used throughout the work to describe Tobit, "good and noble, upright and charitable" (cf. 1:3; 9:6; 14:2). He bewails the disaster that has befallen Tobit in his blindness. How is it that such a good person could be overtaken by suffering rather than prosperity (cf. 2:14)?

The scene is filled with tears. Raguel weeps; Edna weeps; Sarah weeps. They weep for joy at recognizing a relative. They weep in sorrow over Tobit's misfortune.

7:9. From this point on Raguel, the host, seems continually occupied with banquets. The first of these feasts is spread in welcome of the two travelers. The scene echoes Genesis 18, where Abraham and Sarah prepare a feast for God in the person of three strangers.

The marriage scene presents the crisis in Tobiah's development into a mature person. He has already begun to take control of the action by his command that Raphael bring him to the house of Raguel (v. 1). As they recline to eat, Tobiah gives Raphael another command: "Ask Raguel to let me marry my kinswoman Sarah" (v. 9). This statement reveals several things about Tobiah at this crucial moment. He is not yet ready to take his life in his own hands and ask in his own name; he is still dependent on Raphael, the guardian appointed by his father. But that relationship is changing. Although he asks Raphael to make the request, he has made his own decision and is beginning to act on it with dispatch.

7:10-14. Raguel is caught in a dilemma regarding his daughter. He knows that he must obey the Mosaic law (as interpreted in his time) and marry her to a near kinsman (see 6:12-13). According to the decision rendered regarding the daughters of Zelophehad (Num 36:5-12), the daughters of a man who has no sons must marry into a clan of their own ancestral tribe, lest their heritage pass from one tribe to another.

But, according to the Qumran text 4QTob[b], Raguel loves Sarah dearly. He is aggrieved over the misfortune of the seven previous bridegrooms, and he repeats the story for the fifth and final time. Like the maids (3:8-9), he knows nothing of Asmodeus. But he adds yet another note to increase the suspense: All of the other bridegrooms, like Tobiah, were kinsmen. Raguel also knows nothing of Raphael's angelic status and his advice. And he is concerned for good reason. Perhaps even the keenness of his hearing can be attributed to his fearful anticipation of Tobiah's question.

The next statement Tobiah makes signals the turning point in the depiction of his character. At this moment he takes responsibility for his own life and decisions: "I will neither eat nor drink anything until you settle what belongs to me" (v. 11). From here on Tobiah is in charge of his own actions. He is ready to become the instrument of healing. In spite of his reluctance, Raguel is persuaded by Tobiah's persistence to agree to an immediate marriage.

The terms "brother" (ἀδελφός *adelphos*) and "sister" (ἀδελφή *adelphē*) are terms of endearment, expressing the intimate relationship between husband and wife or between lovers (see Cant 4:9-10, 12; 5:1-2; 8:1). Tobit uses the term "sister" for Anna (5:22; 10:6), as do Raguel for Edna (7:15) and Tobit for Sarah (8:4, 7). Both of Sarah's parents call her Tobiah's "sister" (8:21; 10:12). The term contributes to the idea that marriage joins not only two individuals, but also two families.

The marriage ceremony itself consists of several elements: First, the father gives the bride to her prospective husband, joining their hands (i.e., giving her hand in marriage). Second, there is an oral statement of the marriage, in which the father proclaims the marriage and declares it to be in accordance with the law of Moses; the father also blesses the couple. Third, a written contract is completed. Finally, a meal is eaten. All members of the family are involved in the ceremony. The father and the bride have major roles; the bride's mother brings the material for the written contract.

The formula pronounced by Raguel, "Take your sister; from now on you are her brother and she is your sister, given to you from this day and forever" (v. 11), echoes the ancient marriage formula found at Elephantine. It is unusual, however, that the father rather than the bridegroom makes the statement. In the "Contract of Mibtahiah's Third Marriage" (5th cent. BCE), the formula reads: "She is my wife and I am her husband from this day forever."[87]

The ceremony is permeated with references to the law and customs concerning marriage. Raphael has already exhorted Tobiah to marry Sarah in accord with his father's command (6:16). He states that Raguel must give Sarah to Tobiah under pain of death, "according to the decree in the Book of Moses" (6:13). Raguel reiterates this obligation (v. 10) and refers to "the decree of the book of Moses" twice in the marriage ceremony (vv. 11-12). The written contract also states that "he gave Sarah to Tobiah as his wife according to the decree of the Mosiac law" (v. 13).

The marriage ceremony is reminiscent of Israel's covenant theology, for the relationship between husband and wife is one image used by the prophets to describe the covenant (see, e.g., Hosea 2; Jer 2:2). The marriage formula is echoed by the covenant formula: "I will be your God; you will be my people" (see Jer 30:22; Ezek 36:28). The Sinai covenant is also sealed by a meal (Exod 24:1-2, 9-11). Eating together, sharing the same food, is a sign of sharing the same life.

7:15-17. Edna prepares her daughter for her eighth wedding night. She is a strong mother. She exhorts her daughter to courage in what seems to be an impossible situation. Twice she uses a word that appeared in connection with both healings, θάρσει (*tharsei*, "take courage"). The word occurs six times—first in Raphael's encouragement of Tobit (5:10), twice in this scene at the beginning of the wedding night (v. 17), twice at the conclusion of the wedding night (8:21), and once as Tobiah prepares to heal his father (11:11). Edna also pronounces a blessing over her daughter.

8:1. When the meal is finished, Tobiah is led to the bedroom, the site of his impending confrontation with Asmodeus. Apparently Sarah is already there (7:15-17).

8:2. Tobiah's chief action in the remainder of the book is healing. He follows Raphael's instructions regarding the fish's liver and heart. The notion that foul odors would drive away demons was common in the ancient world. Josephus reports that a certain Jewish exorcist named Eleazar drove demons out of people by holding a ring in which an aromatic herb was embedded to the nose of the one afflicted.[88] The practice, which comes from

---

87. *ANET*, 222. See Moore, *Tobit*, 225-33, for an analysis of ancient marriage practices.

88. Josephus *Antiquities of the Jews* 8.2.5. For a fuller treatment, see B. Kollmann, "Heilkunst im Buch Tobit," *ZAW* 106 (1994) 292-93. See also R. Pautrel and M. Lefebvre, "Trois textes de Tobie sur Raphaël," *RSR* 39 (1951) 120; G. J. Botterweck, "גד," *TDOT* 3:135.

the tradition of folk medicine, is magical. In the book of Tobit, however, the magical nature is muted; it is recommended by an angel along with prayer as only one part of a complicated remedy.

8:3. The second part of the remedy requires the assistance of the angel. As soon as the demon is repelled by the foul odor, Raphael follows him to Egypt and binds him there. Upper Egypt is the southern part of that country. Except for the Nile Valley and the Mediterranean coastal fringe, Egypt is primarily desert, and demons were believed to live in desert places. The angel protects the human beings by taking the demon back where he belongs and preventing any further access to them. Raphael returns immediately, another indication of the haste that characterizes the angel.

8:4. The third part of the remedy is also given to Tobiah through Raphael's instruction. Tobiah and Sarah are to pray together. The prayer indicates that the banishing of the demon is not due to magic, but to the power of God.

8:5. Tobiah's prayer reveals that he is a worthy son of his father. He begins by blessing God with a threefold invocation.[89] The invocation is similar to Sarah's prayer (3:11), moving from God, to God's name, and then to God's works. But like his father, Tobiah will connect his story to that of his people, so he invokes God as the "God of the ancestors." He recognizes God as the God of both the past and the future, faithful to the ancestors and blessed forever.

8:6. Tobiah then recalls an example from the Word of God that is appropriate to his situation (Gen 2:18-24; see also Gen 2:6). He acknowledges God as the creator, especially of human beings, and as the originator of marriage. From the mention of creation in v. 5, he moves to the creation story and aligns himself with the very beginning of the history of his people (see 3:3-5). In recalling the story of Adam and Eve, he cites three elements: God recognized that human beings should not be alone; the woman was created as help and support for the man; and the man and the woman are the parents of all the living. These elements he regards as the foundation of his own marriage. It is not good for him or for Sarah to be alone; they need each other. God has given them to each other. He hopes that Sarah will be his help—a help like himself. They are each the only child of faithful parents in exile. They are both obedient and honor God's law. They are even related. Suitable partners for each other, they hope also to follow the example of Adam and Eve and have children.

It is instructive to note what part of the story Tobiah leaves out. There is no mention of the tree of the knowledge of good and evil or of the strain in the relationship between Adam and Eve after they eat the fruit of that tree. His recalling of the creation story shows his hope for a positive marriage experience.

8:7. Tobiah's prayer reveals his respect for his new wife and his hopes for a long and happy marriage. He also believes in his own goodness. He knows that his marriage is based on obedience and faith, and not on lust. Obedience is the foundation of his love for Sarah (see 6:18). He asks for a blessing on the marriage bond sworn between them. He prays that God will be merciful to them and that they may grow old together. This is also a prayer for protection from the demon that has so recently been banished. Both he and Sarah have faced death and are now willing to pray for life. The Old Latin (VL) adds the request: "Bless us with children."

8:8. Sarah proclaims her agreement by saying, "Amen, Amen." These are the only words she speaks in the presence of another human being.

8:9a. A reasonable assumption in this verse is that Tobit and Sarah consummate their marriage. Jerome's Latin translation of the book of Tobit, however, adds a comment that Tobiah and Sarah did not consummate the marriage for three nights.[90] Tobiah says to her: "Sarah, get up and let us pray to God today and tomorrow and the next day. For these three nights we are joined to God; when the third night is over, we will be joined to each other. For we are the children of saints, and we must not be joined together like pagans who do not know God" (vv. 4-5). This interpretation is found nowhere else in

---

89. See Griffin, "The Theology and Function of Prayer in the Book of Tobit," esp. 174-85.

90. *Sarra exsurge deprecemur Deum hodie et cras et secundum cras quia istis tribus noctibus Deo vingimur terteia autem transacta nocte in nostro erimus coniugio filii quippe sanctorum sumus et non possumus ita coniungi sicut et gentes quae ignorant Deum.* Vg 8:4-5.

the textual tradition. The Vulgate text, however, inspired the medieval Christian practice of the "Tobias-nights," three days of continence after the wedding before the marriage was consummated.

8:9b-10. Raguel's fear that Sarah's eighth bridegroom will meet the same fate as the previous seven is not allayed by the prayers and blessings of the marriage ceremony. While Tobiah and Sarah are sleeping peacefully, he gets up to dig the eighth grave. His fear is inspired not only by love for his daughter, but also by sensitivity about his own honor. Sarah has already recognized the importance of honor to her father (3:10). We glimpse it in the motive he gives for his secret grave-digging: If necessary, Tobiah might be buried "without anyone knowing about it." Otherwise, he says, "we would become an object of ridicule and derision."

Raguel's digging of the unnecessary grave for Tobiah is an example of dramatic irony. There is a disparity of understanding between readers and characters. We know the grave is unnecessary, but Raguel does not. A further ironic touch appears in Raguel's presumption that he can bury Tobiah without anyone's knowing about it. Will the guide ask no questions? Will his parents never miss him? Have the neighbors not noticed the arrival of the strangers?

8:11-14. In this scene Raguel and Edna appear together. The tenderness of Raguel's feeling is suggested by the fact that he cannot bring himself to check the situation. Instead, he asks his wife to send a maid to report on Tobiah's condition. The request indicates Edna's authority over the maids.

8:15. Upon hearing the good news that their son-in-law is alive and sleeping peacefully, Raguel and Edna turn to prayer.[91] This prayer is usually attributed to Raguel alone (as the Greek in G^I suggests and the Old Latin states directly), and it seems to be the prayer of an individual. But G^{II} clearly says, "They blessed . . . they said."

This prayer, like those of Sarah and Tobiah, contains a threefold blessing. In contrast to the previous prayers, however, the invocation comes, not in the first strophe, but at the beginning of each strophe. Also in contrast to the previous prayers, God is addressed directly, "Blessed are you." The first strophe also calls God's people to bless the Lord.

8:16. After the blessing, the second strophe reports the current situation. Raguel (and Edna) had feared that this eighth bridegroom would die, but God has prevented that tragedy. They recognize that their good fortune is due to the mercy and compassion of God and that God has power to protect people. They acknowledge that God's ways are surprising.

8:17. The third strophe turns to thanksgiving and petition. God is addressed as "Master" (δέσποτα *despota*). Raguel and Edna ask God to care for their daughter and son-in-law, to be merciful to them, to keep them safe, and to give them full lives. God has already acted in compassion and mercy; to be consistent, God should continue to do so. They also seem to play on God's compassion by referring to Tobiah and Sarah as "two only children." Just as the prayer of Tobiah flowed from the context of marriage, so also the prayer of Raguel and Edna represents the petition of parents for their offspring.

8:18-20. Raguel orders the grave to be filled in and plans a second banquet more generous than the first. He prepares a fourteen-day wedding feast, twice as long as the ordinary celebration. His primary motivation is love for his daughter. He instructs his new son-in-law to bring joy to her spirit. The introduction to this banquet suggests even more strongly the parallel between Raguel and Abraham (cf. v. 19 with Gen 18:6-7).

8:21. Raguel tells Tobiah of his right to inherit Raguel's estate, a point Raphael had made on the journey (6:12). The inheritance will be received in two portions: half now, half when Raguel and Edna die. The right to inherit is set within the context of family. The marriage of Tobiah and Sarah has joined the families of Tobit and Raguel, the effect of which is that their property also becomes common. The property of both families will now come to the children of both families, and since they are the only children, Tobiah and Sarah will inherit all of the property.

The word that introduces both healings (θάρσει *tharsei*, "take courage") is repeated by Raguel at the end of his talk with Tobiah.

---

91. See Griffin, "The Theology and Function of Prayer in the Book of Tobit," esp. 186-204.

REFLECTIONS

1. Blessing is a sharing of God's life and power. In Gen 1:28, God blesses human beings with the power to participate in creation and the responsibility of caring for it. The genealogy in Genesis 5 is evidence of the effectiveness of God's blessing. God also blessed the ancestors—Abraham, Isaac, and Jacob—with children (Gen 17:15-17; 26:3; 28:13-15). Human beings are also empowered to bestow God's blessing. Isaac blessed Jacob (Gen 28:1-4). Rebekah's family blessed her (Gen 24:60). Jacob blessed his sons and through them the whole people (Gen 49:1-28).

The blessing of children by their parents has been a custom in many homes. But it is not just solemn occasions that call for blessing. Blessings are appropriate when one leaves the house, at bedtime, before an important event, at celebrations. Blessing is a sharing of God's life and power. It symbolizes the gift of life that parents have given their children; it symbolizes the gift of life that comes from God. Blessing renews the family's bond with one another and with God.

2. Tobiah is the chief minister of healing in the book. He prepares himself for this task by prayer, obedience, and love. All three of these preparations are other-centered. Through prayer, he recognizes that the power to heal belongs to God and that he is only the minister of that power. His obedience puts into action the recognition that the wisdom to heal belongs to God. This wisdom may be passed from one human being to another (or be communicated by an angel!), but its origin is in God. Tobiah's love for Sarah and for his father turns his focus totally toward them, and not to his own aggrandizement.

Power, love, and wisdom are demanded of those who exercise ministry in the Christian community today. The Holy Spirit bestows these gifts (see 2 Tim 1:7) so that the ministry of Christ may continue in the world. The person called to ministry must always remember that these gifts come from God. In a spirit of humility and obedience, faithful ministers will listen to God's Word in Scripture and in the voices of the needy as well. They will act, trusting in God's strength rather than in their own. They will lead others to grateful praise of God.

3. Marriage is a solemn undertaking. The marriage of Tobiah and Sarah begins in a ceremony of blessing. Both parents speak a blessing over the couple. The various forms for blessing a bride and groom in a modern wedding echo the prayer of Tobiah in recalling God's plan of mutual support in the creation of Adam and Eve and in praying for children and a happy old age.

The marriage of Tobiah and Sarah is founded on prayer and community. In their prayer (8:5-8), marriage is construed as a gift from God, dependent upon God for success and perseverance. It is seen as part of God's plan, reaching back to Adam and Eve, and as a participation in God's creation. Their marriage contributes to the ongoing life of God's people. It symbolizes the relationship between God and the people and the love of Christ for the church (Eph 5:31). When the broader focus is lost and a wedding is seen as a private event involving only two people, the creative, world-building power of marriage also is lost. Married people are a living symbol of the church and thus are cocreators with God.

4. God surprises us all with great generosity. In the Gospel of Luke, when the angel tells Zechariah, the father of John the Baptist, that he will have a son (Luke 1:13), Zechariah doubts the angel's word. Vincent McCorry, in *More Blessed Than Kings*,[92] has observed that this was not because Zechariah did not believe that God could give him a son, but because he doubted that God *would!* Raguel does not doubt the power

---

92. Vincent P. McCorry, *More Blessed Than Kings* (Westminster, Md.: Newman, 1954) 14-15.

of God to care for his family. His prayer is evidence of that. But he does not believe that God *will* care for his daughter and her eighth bridegroom. When Raguel realizes his mistake, his response is noteworthy. He is not embarrassed; he does not offer excuses. In genuine humility, he turns to God in surprised thanksgiving. Raguel is a worthy model to teach us how to respond to God's generous gifts.

TOBIT 9:1-6, RECOVERY OF THE MONEY

COMMENTARY

9:1-2. The original purpose of the journey, at least in the minds of Tobit and Tobiah, was to recover the money Tobit had deposited with Gabael (1:14; 4:1-2, 20). Now Tobiah is prevented from accomplishing that goal by his marriage, which in fact was God's purpose for the journey. So Tobiah sends his faithful guide to recover the money and to bring Gabael to the wedding.

9:3-4. Tobiah knows that his journey will already be longer than he anticipated, and he does not want to lengthen the delay. He knows well that his father will be expecting him on a certain day and will grieve when he does not arrive. His concern is well founded (cf. 10:1-7).

The fourteen-day wedding feast is the longest stretch of time in the story. The progress of the feast is not recounted, but the sense of its length is indicated by the repeated reference to counting the days. Tobiah tells Raphael that Tobit is counting the days (9:4). The narrator tells the reader that Tobit is, indeed, counting the days (10:1). Thus, although the length of telling time for the fourteen-day wedding feast is short (8:19–10:7, only 16 verses), the sense of its length is conveyed psychologically by the notion of counting days and the sevenfold repetition of the word "day" between the two ends of the fourteen-day feast (8:19; 10:7*b*).

9:5. The pace of the interlude, Raphael's journey to get the money, is extremely rapid. There is no indication of the length of the two-way journey. An uninformed reader might assume that Raphael traveled to Rages one day and returned with Gabael the next. The distance to Rages, however, is approximately 185 miles. An angel might be able to cover the distance in a day, but what of the servants and camels and Gabael on the return journey? It is virtually impossible for the travelers to have reached Ecbatana before the wedding feast ended.

Gabael acknowledges the signed bond with no comment and immediately presents the money in sealed bags. Thus Tobiah's concern about how to demonstrate his right to the money is unfounded (5:2). The signed agreement between Tobit and Gabael is recognized as valid.

Raphael's other purpose in making the journey is to convey information. He informs Gabael of Tobiah's marriage and invites him to the wedding feast.

9:6. When the travelers return to Raguel's house, Gabael greets Tobiah with the key words that describe Tobit's character: "good and noble, righteous and charitable" (καλοῦ καὶ ἀγαθοῦ, δικαίου καὶ ἐλεημοποιοῦ *kalou kai agathou, dikaiou kai eleēmopoiou*). He proclaims Tobiah to be "the very image" of his father; he is also "good and noble" (see 1:3; 7:7; 14:2). Gabael adds another blessing to the many already showered on this marriage. He, too, recognizes the familial implications of the union and extends the blessing to Sarah's parents. This is clear in the Old Latin text: "the father and mother of your wife [*patri et matri uxoris tuae*]." Sinaiticus reads: "your father and your wife's mother." (See Reflections at 10:1–11:18.)

TOBIT 10:1–11:18, TOBIT'S HEALING

COMMENTARY

The final question posed by the exposition—Will Tobiah return safely and heal Tobit?—is answered in the affirmative in this section. The distress of Tobit and Anna keeps the tension alive. However, the reader is now assured by Tobiah's success in delivering Sarah from the demon that he can also use Raphael's advice to heal his father. The departure from Ecbatana is a long Near Eastern farewell. It serves to reiterate the emphasis on family and to continue the spirit of grateful joy that surrounds the wedding feast.

The last major scene of the resolution is told slowly, with careful detail and repetition, pointing to the careful construction of the scene. The procedure to be followed with the parts of the fish is given twice more (11:6-8, 11-13; see 6:9). Each telling provides a fuller account. The description of the healing process alternates with the parents' welcome and gradually takes precedence.

Detail and repetition slow the climax of the scene, and the alternation in perspective presents it in a style suggestive of cinematic technique (in which the action is seen first from the angle of one camera, and then from another).[93] In what follows, note that the perspective of Tobiah and Raphael appears in the passages on the left, the perspective of Anna and Tobit in the passages on the right. The passages on the left emphasize the healing process; the passages on the right emphasize the welcoming. Tobit's eyes are the major focus of the passages on the left, and the act of seeing is the major motif of those on the right. Both perspectives merge at the end of the passage:

Raphael said to [Tobiah],
"Have the *gall* in your hand!" (11:4).

> Meanwhile *Anna* sat watching the road . . .
> When she saw him coming,
> she exclaimed to his father,
> "*Tobit*, your son is coming" (11:5-6).

Raphael said to Tobiah,
"I am certain that his eyes will be opened.
Smear the fish *gall* on them.
This *medicine* will make the cataracts
shrink and peel off from his eyes;
then your father will again be able
to see the light of day" (11:7-8).

> Then *Anna* ran up to her son,
> *threw her arms around him*, and said to him,
> "Now that I have seen you again, son,
> I am ready to die!" And *she sobbed* aloud.
> *Tobit* got up and stumbled out
> through the courtyard gate (11:9-10).

Tobiah went up to him
with the fish *gall* in his hand,
and holding him firmly,
blew into his eyes.
"Courage, father," he said.
Next he smeared the *medicine* on his eyes,
and it made them smart.
Then, beginning at the corners of Tobit's eyes,
Tobiah used both hands to peel off the cataracts.

> When Tobit saw his son,
> he *threw his arms around him* and *wept*,
> he exclaimed, "I can see you, son,
> the light of my eyes!" (11:10-14)

The return journey gives Raphael one more chance to instruct Tobiah. The arrival in Nineveh reveals the great love uniting all the members of Tobit's family. Their joy increases even more with Tobit's healing and his welcome of Sarah. The moment is punctuated by yet another prayer.

10:1-3. The relationship between Tobit and Anna is artfully portrayed in this scene as both worry about the delay of their son. Tobit's interior monologue reveals his own concern. He rehearses all the things that might have gone wrong. He wonders whether Gabael is dead, when his real fear is that Tobiah is dead.

10:4-5. Anna is the more vocal of the two parents. As Tobit's worry mounts over Tobiah's delay, hers does as well. In contrast to Tobit's silence, she begins to weep and wail.

---

93. B. F. Kawin, *Telling It Again and Again: Repetition in Literature and Film* (Ithaca: Cornell University Press, 1972), discusses several examples of this cinematic technique.

Now not only does she refer to Tobiah as "my child," but she also takes the responsibility for his absence, a responsibility she had previously laid at Tobit's feet (5:18): "Woe to me, my child, the light of my eyes, that *I* let you make this journey" (italics added). Tobit's reassurance is not as effective in silencing her as it was when the journey began. She continues to wail and cry the whole night. The Old Latin (VL) and one of the Greek manuscripts (LXX^d, recension G^{III}) indicate that she also stopped eating.

10:6. Anna expresses Tobit's real worry. He, however, does not confess his concern to her. Rather, he replies to her gently and with reassurance. Ironically, he mentions that something unexpected may have happened. It is certainly true that none of the characters except Raphael expected the marriage that is causing Tobiah's delay.

10:7-9. Anna's worry over Tobiah has the peculiar mix of despair and hope so often characteristic of mothers. Even as she repeats "my child has perished," she stations herself near the road to watch for his return. This juxtaposition of maternal hope and despair is reminiscent of Rebekah, who sends one son away to keep the other from killing him (Gen 27:42-45); of Hannah as she grieves over her barrenness, yet has the courage to pray (1 Sam 1:7-11); and of the Shunammite woman as she doubts and hopes in Elisha's promise of a son and as she prays for the life of that son (1 Kgs 4:16-17, 28-30).

Anna's sharp tongue is again in evidence, and, as before, the target of her words is her husband, Tobit. She turns his reassurance into a retort and insists that his hope (which her actions reveal that she also holds) is in vain. Tobit suffers not only from her cutting words, but also from her sleeplessness and loss of appetite.

The departure scene reveals both Tobiah's care for his parents and Raguel's characteristic hospitality. Tobiah insists on leaving, in spite of Raguel's urging that he remain. Tobiah has already recognized that his parents are worried (9:4). He knows that Tobit is counting the days, as indeed he is (9:4; 10:1). Tobiah knows also that Anna (along with Tobit) does not believe that he will return alive (v. 7; cf. v. 3).

10:10. The warmth of Raguel's nature is demonstrated by his tender farewells to his daughter and new son-in-law. He is a rich man, with servants, slaves, flocks, and herds. He is also a generous man. He gives lavish and frequent feasts, and he does not hesitate to give Tobiah half of everything he owns when the newlyweds depart. He has kept his promise with regard to the inheritance (8:21).

10:11-13. This is the most extended and affectionate of the departure/arrival scenes and the only one in which there is genuine interaction between Tobiah and the other characters (cf. 5:17-22; 7:1-8). Raguel bids him a fatherly farewell with a prayer for his safety and prosperity. Edna entrusts her beloved daughter, Sarah, to him. Both Raguel and Edna address him as their own son.

Raguel is a concerned father. He exhorts Sarah to honor Tobiah's parents as her own and to live a life worthy of a good reputation. Edna, too, is concerned for her daughter. She exhorts her new son-in-law concerning responsibility for his wife and her happiness.

Edna hopes to see her motherhood extended in grandchildren. The expectations of the older generation concerning the marriage of Tobiah and Sarah are instructive. In addition to the expectation of marriage within law and custom (see 1:9; 4:12-13; 7:10-11) is the hope that their marriage will bring joy (v. 12; see 8:20; 11:17). Children are seen as a blessing in marriage. Everyone concerned with the wedding of Tobiah and Sarah hopes to see their children (vv. 11-12; see 6:18; 13:16; 14:3, 9, 11).

Tobiah responds to these blessings with a pledge of honor and a feeling of happiness and joy, which overflows in thanksgiving to God.[94]

11:1-4. The return journey is summarized in one verse (v. 1). Raphael, who seems always to be in a hurry (cf. 5:8), hastens Tobiah on the last stage of the journey by preparing him for his second act of healing. Raphael was sent to heal both Tobit and

---

94. The textual situation of the final sentence is complex. The Old Latin is the clearest: "I have been commanded by the Lord to honor you all the days of my life" (*Iniunctum est mihi a Domino honorari uos omnibus diebus uitae uestrae*). G^I reads, "He blessed Raguel and Edna his wife" (κατευλόγει Ραγουὴλ καὶ Ἔδναν τὴν γυναῖκα αὐτοῦ *kateulogei Ragouēl kai Ednan tēn gynaika autou*). But G^{II} (Sinaiticus) omits this sentence. G^I lacks the following sentence, but G^{II} is corrupt. It reads, "May it be successful for you to honor them all the days of your life" (Εὐοδώθη σοι τιμᾶν αὐτοὺς πάσας τὰς ἡμέρας τῆς ζωῆς αὐτῶν *Euodōthē soi timan autous pasas tas hēmeras tēs zōēs autōn*).

Sarah (3:17). However, God's providence is manifested chiefly through human agents. Through his obedience to Raphael's instructions, Tobiah is enabled to be the instrument of God's healing. The dog, a remainder of the story's folktale origin, appears only at the beginning and end of the journey (see 6:2).

11:5-6. The two great loves of Anna's life are her husband and her son. Since Tobiah's departure, Anna has been referring to him as "my child" (5:18; 10:4, 7). Now she watches the road by which "her son" is to come. The welcome scene reveals Anna's tenderness toward her husband. Aware of his worry and inability to see, she turns to Tobit (who is with her as she watches the road) and says "Tobit, *your* son is coming."

11:7-8. God's providence in the healing of Tobit is manifested through natural materials. (The heart, liver, and gall of the fish are medicines that correspond to ancient healing lore.) Fish gall was used in Assyria as a medicine for eye ailments.[95] The use of gall from other animals, especially pigs and turtles, is also known from Egypt. The medicinal use and preparation of gall is also discussed by Pedanius Dioskurides, Pliny, and Galen.[96]

11:9-10. When her son finally comes, Anna embraces him and declares with tears that her life has reached its fulfillment. He is alive; now she is ready to die. The scene is reminiscent of Jacob's greeting to Joseph, whom he had supposed was dead (Gen 46:29-30). Tobit also loves his son. As soon as he hears the news of Tobiah's arrival, the blind man gets up and stumbles out through the gate.[97]

11:11-12. Tobit is afflicted with blindness due to a thickening or whitening of the cornea, a condition often treated with gall. Tobit reports that his eyes sting or smart.[98] The effectiveness of the gall in healing is directly related to its caustic, heat-producing properties. The medical knowledge of eye diseases and their remedies is amazingly accurate in the book of Tobit.[99]

11:13-15a. Tobit's response to the healing is first an expression of delight in the son who is truly the "light of his eyes."[100] Then this man of prayer turns immediately to God. His prayer is an ecstatic outburst of joy.[101] He begins with a triple blessing: He blesses God, God's name, and God's angels. Four times he uses the word εὐλογέω (*eulogeō*, "to bless"). Twice he mentions God's angels, even as he unknowingly stands in the presence of the angel sent by God to help him. Despite its brevity, the prayer contains the basic principle of Tobit's life and of the book: God afflicts, and God has mercy.[102] Blessed be God! His exclamation closes as it opened, with delight in seeing his son Tobiah.

11:15b. The scene ends with a summary that echoes Raphael's commission in 3:17. In one sentence Tobiah relates the successful resolution to two of the three questions left at the end of the journey: Will Tobiah meet Sarah, marry her, and deliver her from Asmodeus? Will Tobiah recover the money? The scene itself has answered the third question: Will Tobiah return safely and heal Tobit? Meanwhile Tobit[103] continues blessing God and rejoicing.

11:16-18. Tobit's welcome of Sarah and the simple reference to another seven-day feast end this scene speedily. His welcoming of Sarah reveals his joy and his concept of marriage. He continues to shower blessings everywhere. The root word "bless" (*eulogeō*) appears six times during his welcome. He blesses Sarah, her parents,[104] his son, and God. He also recognizes Sarah as his daughter, thus emphasizing the family connections brought about by marriage. He calls her "daughter" four times in this short speech. Tobit also repeats the key word ὑγιαίνω (*hygiainō*, "be well," "well-come") twice in his greeting of Sarah.

From here to the end, the characteristic tone of the book is joyful. Tobit cannot stop rejoicing and praising God (11:15-16). When he announces God's gift to him, all the Jews

---

95. W. von Soden, "Fischgalle als Heilmittel für die Augen," *AfO* 21 (1966) 81-82.
96. See Kollmann, "Göttliche Offenbarung magisch-parmakologischer Heilkunst im Buch Tobit," 293-97, for a detailed treatment of ancient medical use of gall.
97. The Qumran fragment 4QTob[e] specifies that he went "to meet his son."
98. This is clear in the Old Latin *momordit;* the Greek text is corrupt.
99. Kollmann, "Göttliche Offenbarung magisch-parmakologischer Heilkunst im Buch Tobit," 297.
100. The Hebrew fragment 4QTob[e] supports the reading of VL and G[I] in 11:13 that, when the films were removed from his eyes, "and he saw his son" ([בנו] וירא את *wyr' 't* [*bnw*]).
101. See Griffin, "The Theology and Function of Prayer in the Book of Tobit," esp. 206-23.
102. "He has had mercy on me" appears in G[I] (ἠλέησάς με *eleēsas me*) and VL (*ipse misertus est mei*), but not in G[II].
103. It is clear in VL that Tobit, not Tobiah (as G[II]), rejoices.
104. G[II] mentions only Sarah's father, but G[I] and VL include her mother.

in Nineveh also rejoice. At the wedding feast, Ahiqar and his nephew Nadin[105] join in the general rejoicing. According to all of the reliable textual witnesses except G^{II} (G^{I}, VL, Syriac, Vulgate), everyone celebrates with joy for seven more days.

---

105. "Nadin" is the correct spelling of the name of Ahiqar's nephew, as testified by 4QTob^d frg. 2. The Greek and Latin MSS have a variety of spellings.

REFLECTIONS

1. The older generation looks forward to the children of Tobiah and Sarah with delight. The love that holds their marriage together must bear fruit in some way. The joy that surrounds their marriage will be redoubled by the gift of life to others. Children are a gift in marriage; the outward turning of the energy that comes from mutual support is a necessity. This truth is not simple. Some couples are unable to have children. Their struggle to conceive and the sometimes interminable wait to adopt can cause great suffering. Some couples decide for good reason not to have children. There may be other concerns: health; economic distress; other family pressures. Some, on the other hand, remain childless out of selfishness. They are truly barren. Some who have children abuse or neglect them. The trust placed in them by God and society is betrayed; the gift is destroyed.

2. A painting by the nineteenth-century artist Jean-François Millet is titled *Waiting*. It portrays an old woman, her back to the observer, leaning forward into the road, down which she looks intently. To her right an old man, apparently blind, hesitates in a doorway. The painting is an interpretation of Anna and Tobit waiting for Tobiah. The painter was scorned for portraying biblical characters as nineteenth-century French peasants, but his message is very clear: The parents are still waiting for their beloved child.

All parents worry about their children, some more than others. Raising children is an awesome responsibility. The challenge of balancing the need to protect them with the need to give them freedom is ever present. In the end, parents must recognize that they exercise this responsibility in the name of God, who gave their children life. God alone can care for them in every situation.

3. Our mobile society causes us to say good-bye to loved ones with increasing frequency. The farewell at Ecbatana is permeated with blessings and expressions of love. Those kissed with tenderness at the beginning of the journey are instructed to stretch out their love toward those who wait for them at its end. God is entrusted with the responsibility of caring for the departing ones, for those left behind, and for those who await their arrival. Here is a model for our frequent good-byes.

4. In the story the angel instructs Tobiah to use methods of healing known to the medical community of his time. Ben Sira exhorts us to "honor physicians for their services" (Sir 38:1 NRSV; see also Sir 38:2-8). God works through natural means, through the power of created elements and the knowledge and skill of human beings. There are two ways we can strive to be healed of our ills, and both are necessary: Pray to God and seek the services of competent medical personnel (see Sir 38:9-15).

Tobit's immediate response to his healing is grateful prayer. Jesus praises the leper who returns to give thanks for his cure and grieves over the nine who do not (Luke 17:17-18). It is easy to turn to God in prayer when we are in need and to forget to return in praise when God answers our prayer. Tobit is an example for us of genuine gratitude.

5. Dom Columba Marmion, a nineteenth-century Belgian Benedictine, said that joy is a sign and a consequence of the presence of God.[106] The irrepressible joy of the last chapters of the book of Tobit is certainly a sign of God's presence and power. The characters in this story allow God to work in them and through them. They do not hinder God's action by resistance. Therefore, God's blessing and love can flow into them and through them to others. The only possible response is genuine joy.

106. Columba Marmion, *Christ the Ideal of the Monk: Spiritual Conferences on the Monastic and Religious Life*, trans. by a nun of Tyburn convent (St. Louis: B. Herder, 1926) 104-5, 130.

TOBIT 12:1–14:15
ALL'S WELL THAT ENDS WELL

OVERVIEW

A few loose ends remain to be tied up in the final chapters. The reader knows that Raphael is an angel, but the characters do not. The offer of wages for him (12:1-5), far exceeding the promise in 5:15-16, leads to Raphael's refusal of payment and the revelation of his identity (12:15). The main themes of the plot are reiterated in his exhortation (12:6-10): God, who rewards charitable deeds, is just and deserving of praise. Raphael then summarizes the plot and his function in it (12:12-14), exhorting Tobit and Tobiah to pray in thanksgiving (12:17-20). Raphael's exhortation is followed by Tobit's song of praise (13:1-18).

The story has returned to its original calm. The epilogue (14:1-15) reports the permanent state of prosperity of the characters and their final end, thus reinforcing the claim of the plot that God rewards charitable deeds.

TOBIT 12:1-22, REVELATION OF RAPHAEL'S IDENTITY

COMMENTARY

Chapter 12 consists primarily of Raphael's farewell discourse. (See the Commentary on 4:1-21 for a description of the farewell discourse form.) Raphael's farewell discourse includes the following elements of the form: the announcement of his departure (v. 20); a reminder of the past (esp. vv. 12-14); and an exhortation to be faithful to God's commandments and to one another (esp. vv. 6-10). The only prediction is the promise that "those who give alms will enjoy a full life" (v. 9). Two other elements that are ordinarily found in the form are a blessing of peace and joy and a promise that God will abide with the hearers. Raphael's presence has itself been a blessing and a sign that God remains with Tobit and Tobiah. The idea of blessing is reversed as Raphael reminds them repeatedly to bless God (vv. 6, 17-18, 20), which they promptly do (v. 22).

In the book of Tobit, Raphael's role as a symbol of the providence of God is threefold: He has prepared Tobiah for the two healings; he has guided Tobiah on the way; and he continues to inspire and encourage the spirit of prayer. But because God heals (the meaning of Raphael's name) and because the providence of God leaves room for human freedom, Raphael leaves the main action to the human characters throughout the book. He continually fades from sight as they make use of his instructions and preparations. Thus it is no surprise that when his mission is over, he ascends to God; and Tobit and Tobiah can no longer see him (v. 21). Raphael's mission has been successful. They are healed; they have found the way; and they turn in thanksgiving to God (v. 18).

12:1. Tobit had promised Raphael a drachma a day for guiding Tobiah to Media and had also suggested the possibility of a bonus if they returned safely (5:10, 15-16). Tobit also exhorted Tobiah to pay promptly the wages of those who worked for him (4:14). Consistently he has practiced what he preaches, and this scene is no exception. As soon as the wedding feast is over, he summons Tobiah to pay Raphael both wages and bonus.

12:2-3. Tobiah's response reveals his gratitude, his humility, and his generosity. In a string of short clauses he lists the gifts of Raphael: guidance, the two healings, the return of the money. Humbly he gives credit to Raphael for the two healings, although the angel had only given the instructions. Tobiah does not mention his own part in carrying out Raphael's instructions.

12:4-5. Tobiah has suggested that he might give Raphael half of the riches they have brought back, and Tobit agrees to the suggestion. When Raphael is summoned, Tobiah makes the offer (the Greek texts omit the name, but the Old Latin identifies Tobiah as the one who makes the offer). The concept of giving half the wealth is a remnant of the story's folktale background. In the tale of "The Grateful Dead," a stranger (the ghost of the grateful dead man) offers to serve and guide the traveler for half of whatever he may acquire. In the book of Tobit, half the wealth signifies Tobit's and Tobiah's generosity.

Tobiah ends his offer to Raphael with the customary blessing, "Go in health." Thus in this story of healing the key word, ὑγιαίνω (*hygiainō*, "to be well"), appears for the last time in the farewell to the angel whose name is "God heals."

12:6-7a. Raphael does not directly refuse payment. Rather, he delivers a wisdom speech, instructing the two men in the basic principles of a good life: prayer, almsgiving, and the theory of retribution. These themes constitute the theological pillars of the book. Raphael begins with an instruction concerning prayer. He reminds the men that prayers of praise and thanksgiving can never be offered in isolation. None of us alone can muster enough strength to give God fitting praise. Thus, in the tradition of the psalms, hymns are ordinarily addressed to others who might join in praising God. Twice Raphael tells them to proclaim to "all the living" what God has done for them. Then, to help them remember, he gives them a little proverb contrasting God's work and a king's secret. Wisdom entails knowing which to hide and which to proclaim.

12:7b-10. Raphael's final statement about prayer ("prayer with fasting is good")[107] is embedded in the beginning of an exhortation concerning almsgiving ("better than both is almsgiving"). His words about almsgiving are based on the theory of retribution. Thus all three themes are linked together.

First, Raphael states the positive principle of retribution: "Do good and evil will not overtake you." Then he illustrates what "doing good" means through the primary example of almsgiving. The benefits of almsgiving are many: It is truly life-giving; it sustains life better than wealth does; it preserves life by cleansing one from sin; and it saves one from death and ensures a full life. Raphael closes this part of his speech with the negative side of retribution: "Those who sin and do evil are their own worst enemies."

The book of Sirach, written in the same century as the book of Tobit, also emphasizes the benefits of almsgiving. Giving alms delivers one from sin (Sir 3:30-31) and saves one from death (Sir 29:10-13; 40:17, 24).[108]

12:11-14. In the second part of his farewell, Raphael finally reveals to Tobit and Tobiah his angelic identity. He sets his revelation under the rubric of the proverb he had given the two men earlier concerning the proclamation of the works of God. Raphael also practices what he preaches.

Raphael eases into the revelation of his identity first by describing his mission. He identifies three of his functions: mediating prayer, testing, and healing. He tells Tobit and Tobiah what the reader has known since 3:17: He was sent, specifically in answer to their prayer, to heal Tobit and Sarah.

Raphael does not perform the healings himself. Rather, his name declares that it is God who heals. In fact, Tobiah performed the actions that led to both healings. The angel has only been the messenger between God and human agents.

Raphael's role as one who tests is not developed in the book. Several possibilities of testing suggest themselves: (1) He is somehow implicated in Tobit's having become blind (2:3-10); (2) he tests Tobit by not revealing his identity (5:11-14); (3) he tests the obedience and trust of Tobiah in the incidents with the fish, the marriage, and the healings. These possibilities, however, remain

---

107. G[II] reads "prayer with truth" (προσευχὴ μετὰ ἀληθείας *proseuchē meta alētheias*), but G[I] reads "with fasting" (μετὰ νηστείας *meta nēsteias*) and is supported by the Old Latin (*cum ieiunio*).

108. See Griffin, "A Study of *Eleēmosynē* in the Bible with Emphasis upon Its Meaning and Usage in the Theology of Tobit and Ben Sira," 68-76.

in the realm of speculation. Since so much of the book echoes Genesis, the suggestion of "angel as one who tests" may be based on the model of the angel with whom Jacob wrestled (Gen 33:24-25).

Raphael's statements concerning healing and testing provide a necessary caution concerning the theory of retribution. In this theory, the good are rewarded, and the wicked are punished. But Raphael says that he was sent to put Tobit to the test precisely because of his good deed of burying the dead. It seems that doing good results in suffering rather than in blessing. But "at the same time" (ἅμα *hama*; a word suggesting the introduction of Raphael in chap. 3), he is also sent to heal Tobit and Sarah. Suffering and healing come simultaneously from God. This ambiguity is a major part of the book's message. Only from God's perspective can blessing and suffering be understood.

Raphael functions as a mediator of prayer throughout the book. He is sent in answer to prayer (3:16-17). He instructs Tobiah to pray on the wedding night (6:18). He urges Tobit and Tobiah to pray in thanksgiving (12:6-7, 17-20). Now he reveals that he presents prayers before the glory of the Lord (v. 12).

12:15. Finally, Raphael proclaims his true name and identity. He is one of the seven "angels of the presence." In the OT, angels (or heavenly beings) surround the throne of God (see 1 Kgs 22:19; Job 1:6; 2:1; Ps 89:5-7). The book of Revelation describes seven angels (or spirits) standing before the throne of God (Rev 1:4; 4:5; 8:2).

The names of three of these angels are known to us from the Bible: Gabriel (Dan 8:16; 9:21; Luke 1:19, 26); Michael (Dan 10:13, 21; 12:1; Jude 9; Rev 12:7); and Raphael (only in the book of Tobit). The apocryphal book *1 Enoch* (dating back to at least the 3rd cent. BCE) lists the following six names: Uriel, Raphael, Raguel, Michael, Saraqael, and Gabriel (*1 Enoch* 20:1-8). One of the Greek fragments of Enoch, discovered at Akhmim at the end of the nineteenth century, adds the name of Remiel. Both Akhmim fragments add a final phrase: "Seven names of archangels."[109]

12:16-17. The response of Tobit and Tobiah to Raphael's revelation of his angelic identity is typical of the OT: They fall on their faces (see Gen 18:2; 19:1; Num 22:31; Judg 13:20; Dan 8:17). Raphael's encouragement is also a typical angelic response, "Do not fear" (see Gen 21:17; Luke 1:13, 30).

12:18-20. A theology of angels is further developed in Raphael's final words. He insists that he is only a messenger; thanks and praise are due to God, not to him. Worship of angels is forbidden by the NT (Col 2:18; Rev 22:8-9), just as worship of the "host of heaven" was forbidden by the OT (see Deut 4:19; 17:3; Jer 8:1-2). He also describes himself as a spirit. What seemed to them to be evidence of a body—eating and drinking—was only illusion.[110] The spiritual nature of angels is suggested also in the NT (see Matt 22:30 and par.; Heb 1:14).

12:21-22. Once they have recovered from their fear, Tobit and Tobiah cannot stop praising and thanking God. Like the disciples after Jesus' ascension, they continually bless God in joy (see Luke 24:52-53). God's care of them has been revealed through God's messenger, an angel.

---

109. See *The Apocryphal Old Testament*, ed. H. F. D. Sparks (Oxford: Clarendon, 1984) 174, 208; G. W. E. Nickelsburg, "Tobit and Enoch: Distant Cousins with a Recognizable Resemblance," ed. D. J. Lull, SBLSP 27 (Atlanta: Scholars Press, 1988) 54-68.

110. The statement that he ate nothing appears in G^II (οὐκ ἔφαγον οὐθέν *ouk ephagon outhen*). The Qumran text 4QTob^a says that he drank nothing (אשתי א[ל] [*l' štyt*]). G^I contains both (οὐκ ἔφαγον οὐδὲ ἔπιον *ouk ephagon oude epion*).

REFLECTIONS

1. Generosity to those who work for us is made difficult by the impersonalization of much of today's labor. When the worker is a housekeeper, a cook, a gardener, or someone else with whom we interact personally, it is much easier to give an appropriate bonus, gift, or helping hand. How can we discover ways (other than the ubiquitous Christmas bonus) to be generous to other workers in our technological society?

Tobiah lists all the good things brought to him by Raphael. The acknowledgment of a worker's value and achievement is often worth more than monetary reward. Tobit and Tobiah also meet with Raphael in person. What has largely contributed to the success of many companies is the personal attention paid to the workers and their needs. Perhaps there is a way, within the structure of modern business, for supervisors on each level to be empowered to share a worker's evaluation and to give a bonus.

2. Raphael instructs Tobit and Tobiah to praise God with thanksgiving. A habit of prayer that begins with thanksgiving is not just a good idea—it is a recipe for happiness. But this habit must be learned; it is not our natural inclination. There are about twice as many laments as there are hymns in the book of Psalms. Almost all the requests for prayer that come to the minister have to do with trouble: Someone is sick or has lost a job. It seems we are eager to pray when we are in need, but forget to praise God when good things happen to us.

The habit of giving thanks to God leads to the awareness that alone we can never muster enough strength to give God fitting praise. We need others to help us. The psalms teach us how to ask: We call faithful people (Ps 149:1), all nations and peoples (Ps 117:1), everything that has breath (Ps 150:6). Psalm 148 provides the longest list: "fire and hail, snow and mist, storms, winds, mountains, hills, fruit trees and cedars, wild beasts and tame, snakes and birds, princes, judges, rulers, subjects, men, women, old and young" (see Ps 148:8-12).

"It is good to conceal the secret of a king, but to acknowledge and reveal the works of God" (Tob 12:7). Raphael calls us also to proclaim to all the world the good things God has done for us.

3. Prayer, fasting, and almsgiving are three pillars of righteous living in Jewish tradition. Christians, too, declare days of fasting and prayer. Many churches keep the tradition of almsgiving, providing places for food, clothing, and money to be collected for the poor. Lent is a special time for these practices.

Raphael's words teach us that the three practices cannot be separated: "Prayer with fasting is good, but better than both is almsgiving with righteousness" (12:8). Prayer without action is empty, a soul without a body. Fasting by itself is a work of pride, proving one's self-discipline. Charitable giving without the other two is cold; the gift has never touched the giver's life. Raphael shows us that genuine prayer will lead us to share God's concern for the poor. That concern will urge us to fast, to take only what we need so that we will have something to share with the poor.

TOBIT 13:1-17, TOBIT'S PRAYER

COMMENTARY

Chapter 13 is the last and longest prayer in this book of prayer.[111] It can be considered in two parts: (1) Tobit's praise of God's justice and mercy and gratitude for his healing (vv. 1-8) and (2) Tobit's meditation on the new Jerusalem (vv. 9-18).[112]

13:1-8. These verses comprise the prayer of an individual who has been delivered from the deepest distress and affliction (see 3:2-6). The prayer is couched, however, in general terms and phrases that draw from the wealth of biblical prayers. Thus, like the prayers of Hannah (1 Sam 2:1-10) and Jonah (Jonah 2:30-10), it becomes a prayer of thanksgiving for all who are delivered from distress.

In this way Tobit himself becomes a model for his people Israel. He can bear witness that the God who chastises also shows mercy, that the One who leads down to the darkness of Sheol also leads out into the light. He can also assert that the God who has scattered

---

111. For a thorough analysis, see Griffin, "The Theology and Function of Prayer in the Book of Tobit," 224-348. His strophic structure differs from mine.
112. The text of G^{II} is incomplete. It is supplemented by G^{I} from v. 6*i* ("I give praise in the land of my captivity") through v. 10*b* ("and bless the king of the ages").

the people will again gather them. For this reason, Tobit calls his kindred to turn to God and join in his praise.

This prayer has elements of both the songs of thanksgiving and the hymns. As in songs of thanksgiving, the memory of Tobit's own affliction and deliverance is very near. He expresses his intention to give thanks and praise to God. However, no detailed description of his distress appears. The general phrases concerning God's deliverance resemble the hymn, as do the repeated calls to give praise and the list of reasons for praise.

Just as the story of Tobit's life exhibits the basic principles of deuteronomic theology in narrative form, so also this prayer exemplifies much of deuteronomic theology in the language of prayer. The concept of joy permeates Deuteronomy (e.g., Deut 12:7; 14:26; 16:11; see Tob 13:1, 7). The theory of retribution is a deuteronomic concept (Deuteronomy 28). If the people obey God, they will have long life in the land; if they disobey, they choose death and doom (Deut 30:17-20; see Tob 13:5). The living God gives people a choice between life and death (v. 1). Deuteronomy exhorts the people to turn back to God with their whole heart and soul (Deut 30:2, 10; see Tob 13:6). In Deuteronomy, Israel is required to worship God in the place the Lord chooses—that is, Jerusalem (e.g., Deut 12:5, 11, 14). In his youth, Tobit was faithful to the cult in Jerusalem (1:6-8). Now confident of a return from exile, he exhorts his people to praise God again in Jerusalem (v. 8).

Weitzman uses the allusion in Tobit 13 to Deuteronomy 32 (cf. Tob 13:2 with Deut 32:39; Tob 13:6 with Deut 32:20) to link Tobit 12–13 with Deuteronomy 31–32, the farewell speech and song of Moses. He concludes that the biblical allusions in the book of Tobit move from the beginning of the Pentateuch (the betrothal scenes from Genesis, the similarity between Raguel and Abraham, the Joseph story) to its end (Deuteronomy). He also notes that the allusions all come from scenes that take place outside the land of Israel. The farewell speech and the Song of Moses occur just before the people's entrance into the land. Thus the biblical allusion to the whole Pentateuch reinforces the content of Tobit's life story and his song. Tobit's life is lived according to the Torah from beginning to end. His song promises that the banishment from the land of Israel will soon end.[113]

After the title, the first section can be divided into four strophes: (1) invocation and call to prayer (vv. 1b-2); (2) reasons for praise (vv. 3-5); (3) call to conversion (v. 6a-h); (4) Tobit as example of one who praises God (vv. 6i-8). Strophe 1 is a general, third-person statement concerning God. Strophes 2 and 3 are in the second person, directed to the hearers. Strophe 2 begins and ends with a statement about being scattered among the nations. Strophe 3 has an inner unity owing to the repetition of "whole heart," "whole soul," "whole voice." It ends with an echo of strophe 1 ("bless," "king of the ages"). Strophe 4 is Tobit's own, first-person declaration of praise. He repeats the notion of God's kingship from strophes 1 and 3. The whole poem is bound together by the repetition of the key words of blessing and praise: εὐλογητός/εὐλογέω (eulogētos/eulogeō, "bless") in vv. 1 and 6; ἐξομολογέω (exomologeō, "give thanks/acknowledge") in vv. 3, 6, 8; ὑψόω (hypsoō, "exalt") in vv. 4, 6-7.

The second section of Tobit's prayer (vv. 9-17) can be considered in four units: (1) the call to Jerusalem, vv. 9-11; (2) curses and blessings, vv. 12-14; (3) Tobit's own prayer, vv. 15-16d; (4) the new Jerusalem, vv. 16e-18. The division is based on content. The poetic structure is not clear, and the lengths of the units vary. Each unit contains a call to praise God (vv. 10, 13, 15, 18).

The key word "bless/blessed" recurs frequently in this second part of Tobit's prayer (eulogeō in vv. 10, 13, 15, 18; eulogētos in vv. 12, 18). Two repeated terms connoting the breadth of the prayer are "all" (πᾶς pas; see also vv. 4-5) and "forever/ages" (αἰών aiōn; see also vv. 1, 4, 6). All who are captives, all who are distressed for all generations will be comforted (v. 10). All who despise, hate, revile, destroy, overthrow Jerusalem will be cursed (v. 12). All the children of the righteous will be gathered together (v. 13). All who grieve over all Jerusalem's afflictions will behold all its joy (v. 14). All of Jerusalem's walls will be built of precious stones; it will stand as God's house for all ages (v. 16). Its light will shine to all the ends of the earth,

---

113. S. Weitzman, "Allusion, Artifice, and Exile in the Hymn of Tobit," *JBL* 115 (1996) 49-61.

and people from all the ends of the earth will come to give praise (v. 11). All its houses will sing, "Hallelujah," as God is praised for all the ages (v. 18).

The hope for the new Jerusalem is everlasting. God will cherish the distressed within it for all generations forever (*aiōn*). Those who stand in awe of Jerusalem will be blessed forever (v. 12), and those who rejoice over it will see its joy forever (v. 14). Jerusalem will be rebuilt as God's house forever (v. 16), for God is King and Lord of "forever" (vv. 10, 13), whose name will be blessed forever and ever (vv. 11, 18).

Tobit's description of Jerusalem as the hope of the future reflects the vision of Israel's prophets. Jerusalem will be rebuilt with precious stones (Isa 54:11-12) and will be the source of great light (Isa 60:1-3), which many nations will come to see (Isa 60:1-14; see also Mic 4:2; Zech 8:22). Those who love Jerusalem will rejoice (Isa 66:10, 14), while those who do not serve Jerusalem will be destroyed (Isa 60:12). In the prophets' glorious vision of the future, the scattered will be gathered again (Isa 35:1-10; 52:1-12; Jer 31:7-14), and the blind will be restored to sight (Isa 35:5; 42:16; 58:8, 10). The new Jerusalem upon which Tobit builds his hope is the one the prophets have described.

In Tobit's final prayer, his personal character traits are raised to a public and national level. He, an ordinary man, a model of the true Israelite, is willing to present himself as an example for his people. His trust in God's justice and mercy is strong enough not only to support his own life, but also to demand an equal trust from his nation. His love of Jerusalem flows through his whole life, allowing him to identify with it to such an extent that he can recognize its sorrow as his sorrow, and hope for its joy as he has known joy. His awareness of his responsibility to make public proclamation in thanksgiving for God's gifts to him (see 12:6-7, 18-20) leads him to call all his people to join in his hymn of grateful praise. Even as he recognizes that his life is dependent on the pleasure of God (see 3:6), he knows that his life makes a difference. He is set up as an example, and he is called to exhort and instruct not only his son and his grandchildren, but all the kindred of his nation and finally all humanity (vv. 8, 11).

13:1a. Tobit wrote his prayer with joy. The concept of joy occurs frequently in the book of Tobit: He complains that because of his affliction he has no joy (5:10); God brings joy to Raguel and Sarah by means of Tobiah (8:16, 20); joy returns to Tobit (11:15-16) and to all the Jews of Nineveh through God's mercy (11:17-18). The prayers are particularly filled with expressions of joy: Raguel's (8:16-17) and Tobit's (13:1, 7, 10-11, 13-14).

13:1b-2. Tobit begins his prayer with *eulogētos* ("blessed"). This word begins four other major prayers in the book: Sarah's (3:11); Tobiah's (8:5); Raguel's (8:15); and Tobit's (11:14). Tobit praises the living God and, as Raphael had exhorted him, calls his people to praise God before all other living beings (see 12:6). He proclaims that God and God's kingdom are eternal (see 3:11; 8:5, 15; 11:14).

In the second verse of his prayer, Tobit announces the theme of the whole prayer: God is just in everything, both in chastisement and in mercy. This theme appears throughout the book. The earlier prayers ask God for mercy (3:15; 8:7, 17); the later prayers praise God for righteousness in both punishment and mercy (11:15; 13:2, 5, 9; cf. 14:5).

God's power and presence extend to all places. Nothing can escape the One who leads down to Sheol/Hades and back again. In his counsel to Tobiah (4:19), Tobit reminded his son of the power of God. Tobit knows of it from his own experience. He considered himself as good as dead (5:10), but God's mercy restored him to the light (11:14-15). These ideas appear frequently in other biblical prayers as well—for example, the Song of Hannah (1 Sam 2:6), the prayer of Jonah (Jonah 2:3, 7), and some psalms (e.g., Pss 30:4; 86:13). The idea is echoed also in the book of Wisdom (Wis 16:13, 15).

13:3-5. Each strophe of this poem builds on the preceding one. In the second strophe, the general statements of strophe 1 concerning God's righteousness and power are applied specifically to exiled Israel. Tobit is an example for the exiled nation, which also seems as good as dead (see Ezek 37:1-14). Thus the second strophe begins with a summons to the dispersed Israelites to praise God among the nations where they have been scattered.

Even there they remain in God's hand, and they must proclaim God's greatness before all the living (12:6; see Deut 32:3; Sir 39:15). Proclaiming God's deeds among the nations also is a frequent theme in the psalms (see Pss 9:12; 96:3; 105:1).

Who do they proclaim? Their God is the Lord, the eternal God (see Pss 18:32; 40:6; 71:19; 77:14). This God is "our Father." The concept of God as the father of the people Israel begins with Exod 4:22: "Israel is my son, my firstborn" (see Hos 11:1; Jer 31:9). The title "my father" appears in Jer 3:4 and Sir 51:10. However, most references to God as "our Father" appear in prayers of the post-exilic period (Isa 63:16; 64:7; see also Sir 23:1, 4; Wis 14:3).[114]

Israel, however, has not been exiled simply for the purpose of proclaiming God before the nations. The people must recognize God's righteousness in their chastisement (see 3:2-5). God as father disciplines disobedient children (see Prov 13:24; Sir 30:1), but will again have mercy and gather them together (see Ps 104:46; Jer 23:3; Ezek 36:24).

13:6a-h. The third strophe builds on the second. Since it is God who chastises and has mercy, exiles and gathers, Israel can hope for mercy only by turning to God. This is the great prophetic cry of שׁוּב (*šûb*, "turn"; e.g., Isa 31:6; Jer 3:12, 14, 22; Hos 14:2-3). When Israel turns, God, too, will turn (Zech 1:3; Mal 3:7); never again will God's face be hidden (see Ps 30:8).

Israel, however, must act in wholeness and in truth (see 4:6; 14:9). With open eyes, Israel must see God's action, bless God's righteousness, and exalt the One who rules over all times and places (Pss 145:13; 146:10). Again Tobit is the example. He walks in truth and righteousness (1:3). Both his eyes and his heart have been opened to God's light (11:13-15, 17). He praises God's righteousness (3:2).

13:6i-8. In the final strophe of the first section, Tobit declares his own praise of God. He, the true Israelite, gives himself as an example to the nation. He has called Israel to praise with four imperatives: "acknowledge/give thanks" (*exomologeō*) in vv. 3 and 6; "recount/show" (ὑποδείκνυμι *hypodeiknymi*) in v. 4;[115] "bless" (*eulogeō*) in v. 6; and "exalt" (*hypsoō*) in vv. 4 and 6. He repeats two of these verbs and a related verb in his own recital of praise: "acknowledge/give thanks" (*exomologeō*) in v. 6; "declare/show"(δείκνυμι *deiknymi*) in v. 6; "exalt" (*hypsoō*) in v. 7. He who has suffered adversity praises God and proclaims God's greatness. He who has called Israel to declare God's majesty before the nations himself declares God's strength and majesty before his own sinful nation, Israel.

Tobit repeats the call to turn and act in righteousness. In words echoing the "perhaps" of Joel 2:14, he declares his confidence in God's mercy (see also Amos 5:15; Jonah 3:9). Perhaps God will relent and act mercifully (lit., "do alms" [ποιήσει ἐλεημοσύνην *poiēsei eleēmosynēn*]).

Three linked words of the book appear in these last two strophes. If Israel acts in "truth" (ἀλήθεια *alētheia*, v. 6) and "righteousness" (δικαιοσύνη *dikaiosynē*, v. 6), the Lord of righteousness (*dikaiosynē*, v. 6) will show "mercy" (ἐλεημοσύνη *eleēmosynē*, v. 6) to them. The book itself is framed by an inclusio of these three words (1:3; 14:9; see also 3:2).

Tobit ends the first section in the same spirit of joy with which he began. He concludes this prayer made "in the land of his exile" by calling for prayer "in Jerusalem" to the God who rules all space, "the king of heaven."

13:9-11. In the first unit of the second section, Tobit suggests that the pattern of his own story offers hope to Jerusalem, destroyed and depopulated. He repeats the terms "afflict" (μαστιγόω *mastigoō*) and "have mercy" (ἐλεέω *eleeō*) from his general description of God and from his call to the exiled Israelites (see vv. 2, 5). He refers to God as "King of the ages" and "King of heaven," echoing his initial statement about God and his final petition (see vv. 2, 7). He emphasizes again the need for righteousness (see v. 6), and just as he called the exiled Israelites to give thanks

---

114. See Angelika Strotmann, *"Mein Vater Bist Du!" (Sir 51, 10): Zur Bedeutung der Vaterschaft Gottes in kanonischen und nicht kanonischen frühjüdischen Schriften*, FTS 39 (Frankfurt am Main: Josef Knecht, 1991).

115. The Qumran text 4QTob[e] and G[I] have an imperative at the beginning of 13:4. G[II], however, has the third-person verb, "He has shown."

and bless God, so, too, now he calls the city to do the same.[116]

The theme of retribution undergirds the unit. The powerful God, King of the ages, who punished Jerusalem for wickedness, will restore the city and its righteous citizens. Restoration comes, however, not only because of the renewed righteousness of the people, but also because of the mercy of God. The central concern of the section is introduced: Jerusalem, God's holy city, must be restored and the Temple rebuilt. Then the Israelites will be comforted, and all nations will be drawn to the city to worship God. The theme of joy continues to permeate the prayer.

13:12-14. The second unit begins with curses and ends with beatitudes. The list of curses varies in the textual witnesses. The Qumran text 4QTob[a] and the Old Latin offer the fullest text:

Cursed be all who despise you and revile you;
cursed be all who hate you
and speak a harsh word against you;
cursed be all who destroy you
and pull down your walls.[117]

Anyone who has destroyed Jerusalem in the past or who does so in the future comes under this curse.

Cursing does not dominate the unit, however—blessing does. The beatitudes that end the unit are anticipated in v. 12 with a blessing on those who stand in awe of Jerusalem. In G[II], the same term used for "fear" of the Lord (οἱ φοβούμενοί σε *hoi phoboumenoi se*) is here applied to God's city. (In G[I], the blessing is for those who "love" the city [οἱ ἀγαπῶντές σε *hoi agapōntes se*].) The city is then called to rejoice over the people who will be gathered again within it to bless God (see vv. 3-5, 10, 18). God is named "Lord of the ages" (see "King of the ages" in v. 10).

The beatitudes balance the curses, and the theme of joy recurs. Along with a threefold exclamation, "Happy are (μακάριοι *makarioi*)," is a threefold statement of joy: Those who rejoice (χαρήσονται *charēsontai*) in Jerusalem's peace and those who once grieved over its afflictions now will rejoice (*charēsontai*) and behold Jerusalem's joy (χαράν *charan*) forever.[118]

13:15-16d. In the third unit Tobit breaks in as the singer of the prayer. Here the call to praise is to himself ("my soul" [ἡ ψυχή μου *hē psychē mou*]). He calls himself to bless the Lord, "the great King" (see "king" in vv. 6-7, 10 and "kingdom" in v. 1). His reason for praise echoes the reason he has given to Jerusalem: The city will be rebuilt as the house of God (see v. 10). He speaks a beatitude over himself, a prayer that his descendants will see the restored city and themselves give thanks to "the King of heaven" (see v. 7).

13:16e-17. The fourth unit is a description of the new Jerusalem. The name of the city is repeated four times, as if Tobit cannot let go of the delight of its name (see "name" in v. 11). The promise of rebuilding from vv. 10 and 16 is fulfilled in Tobit's vision. Gates, walls, towers, and streets will be made of gold and precious stones. As if answering the call to prayer, even the gates and the houses will sing hymns and cry out, "Hallelujah" (see Ps 24:7, 9).

Tobit ends his prayer just as he began it, with a call to praise: "Blessed be God . . . for all ages!"[119] This call is addressed to the new Jerusalem, wherein God's name will be blessed forever.[120] Jerusalem remains the place where God has chosen to set the divine name (see Deut 12:5, 11).

---

116. There are a couple of textual problems: In 13:9, G[I] (G[II] is not available) reads, "works of your children [τὰ ἔργα τῶν υἱῶν *ta erga tōn huiōn*]," whereas the Old Latin reads "works of your hands [*in operibus manuum tuarum*]." In 13:10, G[I] reads, "Give thanks to the Lord worthily [ἀγαθός *agathos*]," where 4QTob[a] reads, "with righteousness [בקושטא הודי *bqwšṭʾ hwdy*]." In 13:11, where G[II] reads "your holy name [τὸ ὄνομα το ἅγιον σου *to onoma to hagion sou*; i.e., Jerusalem's]," G[I] and the Old Latin have the name of God (G[I]: τὸ ὄνομα κυρίου τοῦ θεοῦ [*to onoma kyriou tou theou*]; VL: *ad nomen Dei mei*).

117. The first line of the curses is found only in the Qumran text 4QTob[a] ([כי] די עלי די [די] כל ביזין [די] כל ארי[רין *ʾyryn kl dy byzyn wl dy ʿly ky*) and the Old Latin (*Maledicti omnes qui spernunt te, et omnes qui blasphemant te*). G[II] has only lines 3-5 (ἐπικατάρατοι πάντες οἵ ἐροῦσιν λόγον σκληρόν ἐπικατάρατοι ἔσονται πάντες οἱ καθαιροῦντες σε καὶ κατασπῶντες τὰ τείχη σου *epikataratoi pantes, hoi erousin logon sklēron, epikataratoi esontai pantes hoi kathairountes se kai kataspōntes ta teichē sou*). G[I] has only line 2 (ἐπικατάρατοι πάντες οἱ μισοῦντές σε *epikataratoi pantes hoi misountes se*).

118. G[I] reads Jerusalem's "glory" (δόξαν *doxan*). See G[II] 13:16, where Tobit's descendants see Jerusalem's "glory."

119. "For all ages" appears in 4QTob[a] (עלמיא [ʿlm] *ʿlmy*) and the Old Latin (*im omnia saecula saeculorum*).

120. 4QTob[a] and VL begin the last line with "for in you" (דביכי *dbyky*; *quoniam in te*).

Reflections

1. Tobit believes that, just as his suffering mirrors that of his community, so also his healing is a sign of hope for it. Christians have been taught that together we are the body of Christ, that "if one member suffers, all suffer together with it; if one member is honored, all rejoice together with it" (1 Cor 12:26 NRSV). It is impossible for Christians to celebrate eucharist without being joined to one another. In the Liturgy of the Word we tell the story that gives us a common identity. We recite the creed that expresses our common belief. As we pray in petition for those in need and in thanksgiving for those who have been blessed, we acknowledge that their pain and joy are also ours. We share the meal that expresses the sharing of our lives. If we eat and drink without discerning the body (i.e., Christ in one another), we eat and drink judgment on ourselves (see 1 Chr 11:29). Finally, we are set forth to live the mystery we have celebrated: our oneness in Christ Jesus.

2. In Christian theology the new Jerusalem is also the hope of the future. The book of Revelation describes a glorious city in which "there shall be no more death or mourning, wailing or pain" (see Rev 21:4). The glory of God will be its light (Rev 21:23); the river of life-giving water will flow from God's throne (Rev 22:1). God will be so present there that a temple will no longer be needed (Rev 21:22). There all the faithful will see God's face and praise God's name forever (Rev 22:3-4).

The new Jerusalem is an image of the life that awaits God's faithful people. The reality of this new life is impossible to describe. "Eye has not seen, and ear has not heard" what God has prepared (see 1 Cor 2:9). We know two things: This new life has been won for us by Christ, and our delight will be the sharing of God's presence with one another.

TOBIT 14:1-15, EPILOGUE

COMMENTARY

At its end, the story returns to its original calm. The epilogue (14:1-15) reports the permanent state of prosperity of the characters and their final end, thus reinforcing the claim of the plot (and the theory of retribution) that God rewards charitable deeds.

Tobit's final instruction to Tobiah (vv. 3-11) is the third and final farewell discourse of the book (see chaps. 4 and 12).[121] It has several of the elements of the farewell discourse: Tobit announces his imminent death (v. 11); he recalls the past and predicts the future; he recalls the words of the prophets concerning the exile and predicts that they will indeed be fulfilled (vv. 4-7); he also recalls the story of Ahiqar (v. 10). He exhorts his children and grandchildren to keep God's commandments and to be virtuous and honest (v. 9). He wants to protect his children and grandchildren from the destruction he is sure will overwhelm Nineveh (vv. 9-10).

14:1-2. The end of Tobit's life is a confirmation of the truth of the theory of retribution. He, a just man, is richly blessed. He enjoys a full old age[122] with prosperity, and he lives to see his grandchildren, seven in number,[123] signifying a perfect fullness. Deuteronomy promises these rewards to the just (e.g., Deut 4:40; 5:29; 6:1-2; 11:21; 30:19-20). Tobit is

---

121. See Di Lella, "The Deuteronomic Background of the Farewell Discourse in Tob 14:3-11," 380-89.

122. There is a textual problem concerning Tobit's age when he lost his eyesight (14:2). The Qumran texts (4QTob[a] and 4QTob[e]), along with the Old Latin and G[I], indicate that he was fifty-eight years old when he lost his eyesight. G[II] alone says that he was sixty-two.

123. The number "seven" for Tobiah's sons comes from the Old Latin (*septem filios eius*). Fitzmyer also restores 4QTob[a] and 4QTob[c] to read "seven," although he acknowledges they could also read "six," which is what G[I] reads (τοὺς ἓξ υἱούς *tous hex huious*). G[II] does not mention Tobit's grandchildren. See Fitzmyer, "The Aramaic and Hebrew Fragments of Tobit from Qumran Cave 4," 663; Fitzmyer, *Tobit: Qumran Cave 4*, 29-31, 57-59.

like Job, who, although he suffered for a time, "lived one hundred and forty years, and saw his children, and his children's children, four generations . . . and Job died, old and full of days" (Job 42:16-17 NRSV). The description of the righteous person in Psalm 112 promises powerful and blessed descendants, wealth, and riches (Ps 112:1-3). Wisdom herself gives long life, riches, and honor (Prov 3:16; 8:18): "The reward for humility and fear of the LORD is riches and honor and life" (Prov 22:4 NRSV).

14:3-8. Tobit exhorts his son to trust the Word of God, spoken through the prophets (vv. 3-4, 8). He has already demonstrated his familiarity with the Word of God and his habit of looking to that Word to shed light on his own life. When the joy of his Pentecost feast turned to mourning, he recalled the appropriate words of the prophet Amos (Tob 2:6; cf. Amos 8:10). Now he exhorts his son to believe God's Word and to act on it. Tobiah will live to see his father's faith justified (v. 15). (The author, writing in the 2nd cent. BCE, already knows that Assyria was defeated and Nineveh destroyed.)

Tobit cites Nahum, a seventh-century prophet whose whole work consists of rejoicing over the fall of Nineveh in 612 BCE. The Greek recension G¹ reads "Jonah" instead of Nahum. Jonah is a fictional work about a prophet who is sent by God to Nineveh. When, after some resistance to God's call, he finally goes to Nineveh, his words are instrumental in converting the whole city. God, who had intended to punish the Ninevites, instead forgives them, much to Jonah's chagrin. Tobit's whole message is changed if one reads "Jonah" instead of "Nahum." Tobiah would have no need to leave Nineveh. All its citizens would turn to God, and God would turn to them in blessing instead of destruction.

Tobit's vision of the restoration of Israel echoes the prophets and the books of Ezra–Nehemiah. Jeremiah describes a vision of the restored Jerusalem and its faithful population (Jer 31:7-14; 33:6-22). Ezekiel envisions the Lord's return to a glorious new temple, built according to the pattern of the old one (Ezek 43:1-5; see also Ezek 40:1–42:20). The prophet Haggai had the singular commission to tell the returned exiles to rebuild the destroyed Temple, and within a few months the work began. However, Haggai remarks that to those who "saw this house in its former glory" the new Temple seemed like nothing (Hag 2:3). Ezra also reports the weeping of the old men who had seen the former Temple (Ezra 3:12-13).

14:9. After his discourse on the prophetic word, Tobit instructs his son and grandchildren in righteous living as he had earlier instructed his son (4:3-21) and as his grandmother had instructed him (1:8). His exhortation includes those virtues of which his own life has been an example: truth, righteousness, almsgiving (1:3), and mindfulness of God and prayer (see 3:2-6; 5:17; 11:14-15; 13:1-18). Not only are his son and his grandchildren to live such lives, but they also are to exhort their children as he has done for Tobiah and for them.

14:10-11a. Tobit concludes by telling a little story to illustrate his belief that "almsgiving frees one from death, and keeps one from going into the dark abode" (4:10; see also 14:11), just as he, the almsgiver, has been freed from darkness (11:14). (For a synopsis of the story of Ahiqar, see the Introduction.) This incident is itself an example of theology of narrative—that is, telling a story in order to inculcate virtue in the midst of a book that is doing the same thing. Throughout the book, the instructions of the father to the son are embodied for the son in the actions of the father. For Tobiah, Tobit's actions speak as loudly as his words.

14:11b-14. Tobit, who had risked everything to give honorable burial to others (1:17-20; 2:7-10), is himself buried with honor. After Anna's death, she is buried next to Tobit. Raguel and Edna are buried in Ecbatana. Finally, the death of Tobiah is reported. Thus this book, which is preoccupied with death and the ceremonies surrounding it,[124] closes with the deaths of all the main characters except Sarah and Raphael.

Tobiah assumes the responsibility for the care of his parents and his wife's parents in their old age and for their honorable burial. He is again obedient to his father, but now it is the obedience of the grown man, responsible

---

124. In this book of 244 verses, 53 verses, or almost 22 percent, contain one or more words referring to death or burial. (This count applies to G^II. Where there are lacunae in G^II in chaps. 4 and 13, this count applies to G^I.) Chapter 9 is the only chapter that does not mention death.

for his own actions. He heeds his father's instruction in carrying out the proper burial of Tobit and in burying his mother next to his father (see 4:3-4). He also obeys his father by leaving Nineveh immediately after the death of Anna (see v. 10). He is an example of filial love.

Tobiah's life also testifies to the validity of the theory of retribution. Like his father, he is a just man. He lives a long life, dying at the age of 117. He is also prosperous, having inherited the estates of both Tobit and Raguel, and he has a full number of descendants: seven sons.

In his prayer on their wedding night, Tobiah had asked that he and Sarah might grow old together. There is a hint of the patriarchal background of the book in the fact that the death of Sarah, the most silent character, is not even reported. This gap, however, also allows the reader to assume that she did not die young. Surely an early death would have been mentioned. It would seem that Tobiah's prayer was answered.

14:15. The final verse of the book announces the destruction of Nineveh. Alter describes one of the functions of narration as providing a "chronicle of public events and context of meaning."[125] The chronicle of public events is minimal in Tobit, occurring only in chaps. 1 and 14. The title of the book situates the beginning of the story in the reign of Shalmaneser. The succession of Assyrian kings is briefly (and incorrectly) noted, and a few pertinent events during each reign are mentioned (1:15, 18, 21). The story of Tobit's early days is woven into this brief chronicle.

From the last mention of the reign of Esarhaddon in 2:1 until this final chapter, the book is silent concerning public events in Assyria. In chap. 14, the fall of Nineveh to Cyaxares,[126] king of Media, is reported. This public event is also woven into the lives of Tobit and Tobiah. Tobit predicts Nineveh's fall, relying on the prophet's word. Tobiah, having heeded the warning and left Nineveh, rejoices over its fall.

The chronicle of events does not simply provide a historical backdrop for the story of Tobit. It also provides a subtle context for interpretation. Assyria, personified in its kings, was wicked. These kings were responsible for the exile, suffering, and death of many of God's people. Tobit is an example of those who suffered under their rule. His virtue grew under the distress they caused. But, as his life witnesses to the truth that God rewards the righteous, the fate of Nineveh testifies that God punishes the wicked. For this reason, Tobiah rejoices (v. 15). The narrative economy is striking. Nineveh and its rulers appear only at the beginning and end of the story. But even this subtle reference to the wicked city and its fall provides an effective contrast to the story of the just man set in its midst.

---

125. Alter, *The Art of Biblical Narrative*, 75-81.

126. The name of the conqueror of Nineveh is confused in the various translations: G^{II} and the Old Latin seem to be reading the name "Ahiqar." G^{I} reads: "Nebuchadnezzar and Ahasuerus." In fact, Nineveh fell to Nabopolasar of Babylon and Cyaxares of Media in 612 BCE.

REFLECTIONS

1. A certain psychological exercise recommends that a person write his or her own epitaph. What do you want to be remembered for? It might be equally revealing to consider what you would want to say in your farewell discourse. What would you want to remember? What would you want to recommend to your survivors? For what would you give thanks to God? Tobit had two chances to give a farewell discourse. Some of us might not have a chance to give even one!

2. The commandment to honor one's parents is not so much a command for children to obey parents as it is a command for adults to care for their aged parents. Tobiah and Sarah give a worthy example to follow of caring for parents in their old age. Ben Sira promises a reward for this solicitude:

Help your father in his old age,
    and do not grieve him as long as he lives;

even if his mind fails, be patient with him;
    because you have all your faculties do not despise him.
  For kindness to a father will not be forgotten,
    and will be credited to you against your sins;
  in the day of your distress it will be remembered in your favor;
    like frost in fair weather, your sins will melt away.
  Whoever forsakes a father is like a blasphemer,
    and whoever angers a mother is cursed by the Lord. (Sir 3:12-16 NRSV)

Care for aged parents is of increasing concern in modern society. As Social Security and Medicare falter, the burden on the family increases. The community, the church, and the extended family share responsibility as we strive to honor this commandment.

3. In the book of Tobit, the chronicle of public events provides a contrast to the lives of faithful people. Nineveh falls in disgrace; Tobit lives a long and virtuous life. The man who was once punished for having buried outcasts is now buried with honor. The story of Tobit is told to illustrate the theory of retribution: The good are blessed, and the wicked are punished. But the story also teaches that retribution is not always obvious: The good may suffer for a while, and the wicked may prosper. People who strive to be faithful to God's way continue to be challenged by this apparent injustice. Christian faith in the resurrection postpones the day of reckoning and puts retribution out of sight. Nonetheless, innocent suffering continues to be a stumbling block. The book of Tobit teaches a hard truth: Reward and punishment are in the hands of God. Eternal life is not won by the righteous; it is God's gift.

THE BOOK OF JUDITH
INTRODUCTION, COMMENTARY, AND REFLECTIONS
BY
LAWRENCE M. WILLS

THE BOOK OF JUDITH

INTRODUCTION

The book of Judith is a Jewish novel, likely written in about 100 BCE, that celebrates the victory over a foreign power by the hand of a woman. Although never part of Jewish Scriptures, it did become part of the Christian Bible, now consigned to the apocrypha. The anonymous author probably wrote in Hebrew, although there is no copy of a Hebrew original still in existence, and no fragments or quotations of it were discovered among the Dead Sea Scrolls.

It falls naturally into two parts. In the first part (chaps. 1–7), Nebuchadnezzar, king of the Assyrians, is engaged in a major campaign against Arphaxad, king of the Medes. Many of the nations to the west refuse to ally with Nebuchadnezzar, but he proceeds against Arphaxad nevertheless and defeats him easily. He then turns against the nations who spurned him, which include Judea and Samaria, and commissions his general Holofernes to mobilize vast numbers of troops to invade these nations, moving inexorably toward Judea. His forces pause below the mountain village of Bethulia, which must be taken in order for him to move through its pass and proceed on to take Jersualem; and he commences a siege that cuts off the water to the village. The first part thus ends with a pause in the action, as the Israelites contemplate the disaster that is about to befall them.

In the second part (chaps. 8–16), Judith is introduced as a beautiful, wealthy, and pious Jewish widow who has lived a life of prayer and fasting in a special tent or booth on the roof of her estate. She emerges from this relative seclusion to put into motion a plan to thwart the enemy advance. She leaves Bethulia with her favorite maid and goes to the enemy camp. There she captivates Holofernes and his soldiers and lies to manipulate Holofernes to her ends. Hoping to seduce Judith, Holofernes drinks wine until he is quite drunk and passes out, whereupon Judith takes this opportunity to slice off his head with his own sword. Carrying the head with them, she and her maid return to their village, display the head on the wall, and instruct the villagers to attack the Assyrians the next day. When the Assyrians see that their general has been beheaded, they flee and are decisively beaten by the Israelites.

Popular among both Jews and Christians over the centuries, the story of Judith has nevertheless suffered from strongly ambivalent reactions in the modern period. The interest in biblical history and "higher criticism" that developed in the nineteenth century left Judith out of the picture. By genre, it seemed like a romance or fiction; as history, it was—and is—suspect; in its theology, it was unremarkable; in its depiction of moral character, it presented a heroine who was often considered either morally tainted or decidedly dangerous. As a result, the book of Judith has been viewed as offensive, ludicrous, or—worst of all—irrelevant for biblical theology. Only with the rise of feminist studies of the Bible and an interest in the female characters has a new appreciation for the book developed. This interest has remained strong and has produced a wealth of new studies and a much more positive appreciation for Judith.

HISTORICAL SITUATION AND DATE

Judith begins with a dating formula (using the year of the reign of a major king) that is like the accounts in the biblical history books (1 Kgs 15:1; 16:15, 29; 2 Kgs 12:1; 13:1); yet, the first personage encountered, Nebuchadnezzar, king of the Assyrians, is clearly implausible. Nebuchadnezzar was king of the Babylonian Empire, not the Assyrian, and since both Nebuchadnezzar and the Assyrian Empire were well known to Jews, an accidental error is inconceivable. This one historical impossibility is followed by a number of other difficulties. In the first two chapters alone, we meet the presumably important King Arphaxad of the Medes, who is unknown to history, and geographical problems of all sorts arise with the place-names: Some are unknown; some are in the wrong place. Perhaps most serious of all, however, is what we find at 5:18-19. Achior has faithfully recounted Israelite and Jewish history, but then proceeds to describe events that occurred *after* both Nebuchadnezzar and the Assyrians had long since disappeared. The audience would clearly have been aware of the historical and geographical inaccuracies and would likely have understood the book accordingly as a work of fiction. Some scholars have sought to solve this problem by arguing that the two parts of the book (the military campaigns of chaps. 1–7 and the response of Judith in chaps. 8–16) are of unequal value historically and that there is still a historical kernel to the book, or that to avoid persecution the book makes use of fictitious personages to refer to contemporary leaders, much as the members of the Qumran sect referred to Romans as Kittim. This is not likely, however, because the entire work bespeaks a period of triumph and freedom from external oppression, not a secret text of hope in a time of adversity.

The earliest known references to the story of Judith come in the first century CE. The book probably influenced the description of Deborah in the *Biblical Antiquities* of the author known as Pseudo-Philo,[1] and the first reference by name to the story of Judith is by Clement of Rome, a Christian author who wrote near the end of the first century. He incorporates the story positively, with no hint of a concern about the historical problem, and when Judith is quoted by the later Christian fathers, there is likewise no question as to the historicity of the text. Judith is not quoted as scripture by Jews, but is the subject of legendary treatment, and no one among Jewish authors objects or comments on the reliability of the text. Through the medieval period Judith is treated as a revered figure, but rarely does anyone raise any historical questions. When we come to Martin Luther, however, we encounter a very modern-sounding criticism. In his preface to the book of Judith, he writes, "It hardly squares with the historical accounts of the Holy Scriptures, especially Jeremiah and Ezra."[2] His solution to this problem is also very modern and has in fact become the accepted scholarly consensus: "Some people think this is not an account of historical events but rather a beautiful religious fiction. . . . Such an interpretation strikes my fancy, and I think that the poet deliberately and painstakingly inserted the errors of time and name in order to remind the reader that the book should be taken and understood as that kind of a sacred, religious composition."

---

1. Richard I. Pervo, "Aseneth and Her Sisters: Women in Jewish Narrative and in the Greek Novels," in *"Women Like This": New Perspectives on Jewish Women in the Greco-Roman World*, ed. Amy-Jill Levine (Atlanta: Scholars Press, 1991) 159 n. 71.
2. Martin Luther, *Luther's Works*, 55 vols. (Philadelphia: Muhlenberg, 1960) 35:337-38.

Although the stated historical setting in the era of the Assyrian Empire still pushed some scholars to argue for an early dating—that is, before the exile in 587 BCE—most now focus on evidence that it was written at a much later period. There are terms and personages that correspond to the period of the Persian rule of Judea (539–332 BCE) and other terms and ideas that correspond to the period of Greek rule (332–165 BCE) or to the period of the independent Judea under the Maccabees (or Hasmoneans; 165–63 BCE), when Greek customs were still influential in Jewish life. Moore has conveniently listed the terms and names in each category, the most important of which are given here.[3] For dating in the Persian period, we note especially that in 350 and 343 BCE there were invasions of the west by Artaxerxes III Ochus of Persia that were similar in scope to the fictitious invasion by Nebuchadnezzar and Holofernes. He came as far as Egypt (see Jdt 1:10). More important, he had a general named Holofernes and a counselor, probably a eunuch, named Bagoas (cf. Jdt 12:11). Thus the connections to Judith are very strong and suggest at least that the memory of this invasion fired the imagination of the author of Judith. In addition, there are a number of terms that are associated with the Persian era, even though they might also have lingered in the popular consciousness long afterward.

There are no precisely datable Greek terms or ideas, but several motifs—the wearing of garlands and olive wreaths, the worship of a king as a god, and people reclining instead of sitting at table—could have entered in any time after 332 BCE. Some of the most convincing datable motifs arise in connection with the Hasmoneans (the dynastic name of the Maccabees), who achieved independence from the Greeks (Seleucids) in 165 BCE. The high priest as a political and military leader, the ascendancy of the Jerusalem council, and the close similarity between the exhibiting of Holofernes' head and the exhibiting of the head of Nicanor after he had been defeated by Judah the Maccabee (1 Macc 7:43-50; 2 Macc 15:30-32) all speak for a date after the Maccabean revolt.

Even more important for consideration, the *ideals* expressed in Judith correspond closely to the ideals of the later Hasmonean rulers, especially John Hyrcanus I (135–104 BCE) and Alexander Janneus (103–78 BCE). Hyrcanus in 107 BCE annexed Samaria, the provincial designation of the northern half of the old kingdom of Israel. He thus realized a Hasmonean dream of reestablishing the approximate borders of David's and Solomon's united Israel.[4] A dating of the book in this period would even provide a possible origin of "Nebuchadnezzar, king of the Assyrians." Assyria in biblical prophecies was often read as Syria in the literature of this period; thus "Nebuchadnezzar king of the Assyrians" could have been read as a satirical reference to "Antiochus, king of the Syrians," from whom the Maccabees had gained their independence.[5] In the process of annexing Samaria, John Hyrcanus also destroyed the Samaritan temple on Mt. Gerizim, and so rid the land of cult practices not strictly based on the hegemony of Jerusalem. This illuminates Judith's otherwise very odd statement in 8:18-20 that the Jews had successfully rooted out the worship of "gods made with hands." Further, the conversion of Achior, though it would find some precedents in ancient Jewish tradition, would be more comprehensible in the light of John Hyrcanus's move to convert the Idumaeans to Judaism by force. One could argue that the forced annexation of Samaria and the forced conversion of Idumaeans would not lead to such warm relations as are depicted in Judith, but to the Hasmoneans the annexation and conversion would be seen as liberation, and this is precisely why Judith is at such pains to *idealize* them. The boldness of Judith's affirmations make most sense in a situation where unity is imposed. The book of Judith thus idealizes Samaria and Judea together as "Israel" and does not have, as some scholars have suggested, a hidden Samaritan identity. To be sure, other scholars argue that the author of Judith is secretly opposed to the rule of the Hasmoneans, but the agreements with the Hasmonean rulers far outweigh the possible challenges within the text.[6] Even if

---

3. Carey A. Moore, *Judith*, AB 40 (Garden City, N.Y.: Doubleday, 1985) 50-55, 67-70.
4. Lee I. A. Levine, "The Age of Hellenism: Alexander the Great and the Rise and Fall of the Hasmonean Kingdom," in *Ancient Israel: A Short History from Abraham to the Roman Destruction of the Temple*, ed. Hershel Shanks (Englewood Cliffs, N.J.: Prentice Hall, 1988) 186-89.
5. George W. E. Nickelsburg, *Jewish Literature Between the Bible and the Mishnah* (Philadelphia: Fortress, 1981) 109.
6. Arguing for the subversive position of Judith over against the Hasmonean rulers are André Lacocque, *The Feminine Unconventional: Four Subversive Figures in Israel's Tradition* (Minneapolis: Fortress, 1990) 41, and Jan Willem van Henten, "Judith as Alternative Leader: A Rereading of Judith 7–13," in *A Feminist Companion to Esther, Judith and Susanna*, ed. Athalya Brenner (Sheffield: Sheffield Academic, 1995) 243-44. Moore, *Judith*, 67-70, is in agreement with the position adopted here.

Judith were a subversive text within the Hasmonean kingdom, that would still at least date the text in the period that is here proposed.

It has also been suggested that the author was a Samaritan because of the importance of the regions of Samaria, a Sadducee because of the coordination of Judith's practices with the temple administration, or a Pharisee because of the practices of fasting and prayer.[7] Arguing against the first two possibilities are the idealized union of Judea and Samaria into "Israel" (noted above) and the Hasmonean idealization of the high priesthood as a governing office. Whether the author was a Pharisee is impossible to determine, but it should be noted that the practices of the protagonist provide a parallel to the development of fasting, penitence, and prayer of the Pharisees and others in the Judaism of this period. It is likely, then, that the anonymous author lived in Palestine and wrote in Hebrew near the end of the second century BCE. A narrative tradition that may have arisen in the Persian period was possibly utilized, which would explain the Persian parallels;[8] but the concerns of the author clearly point to a composition in the later historical context.

GENRE

Although Judith was included as part of the canon of the Christian Bible as a historical text and was so understood by many, in the modern world a number of scholars have considered it a novel or a romance (the terms are essentially interchangeable) on the analogy of Greek novels. The classicist Ulrich von Wilamowitz judged it a novel, as did Ruth Stiehl, Franz Altheim, and Moses Hadas.[9] Although the Jewish texts are shorter than their Greco-Roman counterparts, they are earlier and should perhaps be considered important parts of a broad international literary development that includes, in addition to the main Greek and Roman novels, smaller novels that arise from various indigenous ethnic groups of the Hellenistic world.[10]

Some scholars have emphasized the similarity of Judith to oral folk narratives and have pressed this category as a genre designation.[11] While this similarity is very important (see below), the present shape of Judith is like the other written novels of the period. To be sure, Jewish novels sometimes developed out of pre-existing narratives, which may in turn have been derived from oral legends. The development from oral legend to novel can be seen in the combination of originally independent stories in Daniel 1–6 with the visions of Daniel 7–12 to form a larger whole, and then later in the addition of the Prayer of Azariah and the Song of the Three Jews and Susanna to form the apocryphal version of Daniel. The development toward the novel can also be discerned in certain other contemporary Jewish works, such as *Testament of Joseph* from the *Testaments of the Twelve Patriarchs, Testament of Job,* and *Testament of Abraham*, which begin to take on a novelistic coloring as a keener interest in description and character development gives rise to an expansion of the narrative. Other contemporary texts seem to be like histories in that they do not appear to be intended as fictions, and yet they also tend toward an exciting narration of the protagonists' personal situations: 2 Maccabees, 3 Maccabees, Artapanus, and the *Tobiad* Romance, and *Royal Family of Adiabene* from Josephus's *Antiquities of the Jews* 12.154-236, 20.17-96.[12] The novelistic developments should be seen as experiments that push toward the creation of a new art form. In addition to the more obvious elements of the novel, such as rousing action, international sweep, wealth, danger, sex, violence, and

---

7. See Moore, *Judith*, 70-71; Toni Craven, *Artistry and Faith in the Book of Judith* (Chico, Calif.: Scholars Press, 1983) 118-20.

8. Nickelsburg, *Jewish Literature Between the Bible and the Mishnah*, 108-9.

9. Ulrich von Wilamowitz et al., *Die griechische und lateinische Literatur und Sprache*, 3rd ed. (Leipzig: Teubner, 1912) 189; Ruth Stiehl and Franz Altheim, *Die aramäische Sprache unter den Achaimeniden* (Frankfurt am Main: Vittorio Klostermann, 1963) 200; Moses Hadas, *Hellenistic Culture: Fusion and Diffusion* (New York: Norton, 1959) 165-66.

10. J. R. Morgan and Richard Stoneman, *Greek Fiction: The Greek Novel in Context* (London: Routledge, 1994); Lawrence M. Wills, *The Jewish Novel in the Ancient World* (Ithaca: Cornell University Press, 1995). Greek novels can be found in B. P. Reardon, *Collected Ancient Greek Novels* (Berkeley: University of California Press, 1989), and William F. Hansen, *Anthology of Ancient Greek Popular Literature* (Bloomington: Indiana University Press, 1998).

11. Mary P. Coote, "Response," in Luis Alonso-Schökel, *Narrative Structures in the Book of Judith* (Berkeley, Calif.: Center for Hermeneutical Studies in Hellenistic and Modern Culture, 1974) 21-26; Pamela Milne, "What Shall We Do with Judith? A Feminist Reassessment of a Biblical Heroine," *Semeia* 62 (1993) 37-58.

12. Wills, *The Jewish Novel in the Ancient World*, 16-30, 185-211. A good English translation of some of the non-canonical Jewish texts listed here, with scholarly introductions, can be found in James H. Charlesworth, *The Old Testament Pseudepigrapha*, 2 vols. (Garden City, N.Y.: Doubleday, 1985).

use of dialogue, more subtle themes are woven into the text that include the use of everyday characters, domestic settings, and the exploration of the interior life of psychology and emotion. In addition, in both the Greek and the Jewish novels, there is a strong focus on the female protagonist. But while the Greek novels of antiquity portray a young couple in love, separated by challenging circumstances, in the Jewish novels a vulnerable woman is often more alone at the center. She is often directly involved with her extended family, but she faces the trials of life and death alone.

The character of Judith has similarities to two types of characters in Greek novels. In some ways, such as in respect to her beauty, wealth, and piety, she is like the young heroines; in terms of being a self-directed and commanding figure and a widow, she is also like some of the Greek widows.[13] The widows, however, are not generally depicted positively, but are sexually driven, powerful, and sinister, controlling the protagonists' lives. Jerome makes a comparison between Gentile widows and Christian widows that is illuminating: "Gentile widows are wont to paint their faces with rouge and white lead, to flaunt in silk dresses, to deck themselves in gleaming jewels, to wear gold necklaces, to hang from their pierced ears the costliest Red Sea pearls, and to reek of musk."[14] Jerome's stereotype is thus similar to that of the Greek novels; it is all the more striking, then, that Judith does all these things as well, albeit in the service of God, and is seen positively throughout. Another similarity to the Greek novels is the fact that the female protagonist is so much more engaging and active than the male protagonists. This aspect is also found as a genre trait in the Greek novels,[15] but is emphasized even more in Judith. Still, there is one important way in which Judith differs from the Greek and the Jewish novels: the invulnerability of the heroine. The Greek and Jewish novels all feature a vulnerable heroine, and usually a vulnerable hero as well, but Judith is not buffeted by events. She is more like the male hero of epic.

The classical historian Moses Hadas was so convinced that Judith is related to the Greek novels that he objected to just those aspects of the text that are dissimilar to the other novels. A story of a Greek widow in Plutarch, *Amatorius* 2, for example, is very similar to Judith. She remains chaste and curries the favor of a powerful man who she secretly knows killed her husband. Finally she poisons both the suitor and herself and dies triumphantly. In the Greek novel *An Ephesian Tale* by Xenophon of Ephesus, the beautiful young Anthia must also kill a suitor who is trying to rape her. The tragic ending in Plutarch seems appropriate in Greek narrative, and the innocent and threatened heroine in Xenophon seems appropriate as well, but the author of Judith is judged by Hadas to have missed the point of the genre. "What makes the Judith story awkward is the mixed atmosphere of piety and license; the erotic has come in [as in the Greek novels], and shows its leering face despite the author's efforts to smother it in piety. If the constraints of the religious motivation (in itself admirable) are removed, the story would spring back into the pattern of Greek romance."[16] We will turn again below to the heroic Judith, and can perhaps explain the source of the problem as Hadas sees it.

A remaining issue concerning the Jewish novels is whether they were considered historically true or were treated in the ancient world as fictitious, as scholars now often consider them to be. Although many of the known novelistic works were eventually canonized as part of the Christian Bible, it is not clear that these writings were all considered historical at the time of their writing. Several of them contain an obvious historical error that would likely have been easily recognized as such by the audience: Esther becomes a Jewish queen of Persia; in Dan 5:31 Babylon falls to "Darius the Mede" (Darius was a famous Persian king); Tob 14:15 refers to Xerxes king of Media (Xerxes was also a famous Persian king); and in *Joseph and Aseneth*, Joseph rises to become pharaoh until a young prince reaches maturity. Judith's Nebuchadnezzar, king of the Assyrians, is simply another example of this phenomenon, even though it may be the most outrageous historical mistake of all. The audience would have understood why these two evil empires were combined in Judith, and would have applauded it, but they would never

---

13. Achilles Tatius *Leucippe and Clitophon* 5-8; Heliodorus *An Ephesian Story* 7-8.
14. Jerome *Epistle* 127.3, quoted in Pervo, "Aseneth and Her Sisters," 156-57.
15. David Konstan, *Sexual Symmetry: Love in the Ancient Novel and Related Genres* (Princeton: Princeton University Press, 1994).
16. Hadas, *Hellenist Culture*, 169.

have been fooled into thinking this was a retelling of actual historical events. It is this aspect of these novels that helps to define their genre and distinguish them from other prose narratives, like the Gospels.

LITERARY ASPECTS OF JUDITH

The literary qualities of Judith are significant, but it is often a challenge to describe the attractions of a work of "popular," as opposed to "classical," literature.[17] Popular novels have a function to entertain, perhaps to instruct, but are often perceived as falling short of the higher criteria of excellence that have been arrived at in the study of "classical" literature. Still, it is unfair, and ultimately inaccurate, to apply the standards of classical literature rigidly to popular literature. The latter will come up short, and the essential nature of such literature, and its positive qualities and social function, may be missed. Just as the moral ideals in Judith were questioned by commentators in the modern period, so also the literary qualities of the book have often been dismissed by those who misperceived its literary genre and function. These criticisms fall into two categories: the disproportionate length of the first part concerning the rise of the military threat to Bethulia and the rhetorical excesses of the whole.

Cowley, who appreciated other literary qualities about the book, took the author to task for creating a first half that takes too long to come to the introduction of the heroine.[18] Dancy was less kind: "Dramatically [the first half] is spoiled by tedious descriptions and confusions, stylistically by exaggerations and empty rhetoric."[19] Even Alonso-Schökel, who set the tone for the literary-critical approaches, denigrated the first part in favor of the second.[20] It seems that most critics were unappreciative of the first part and failed to recognize its contribution to the narrative as a whole. The first part, which is not quite half of the book (even if the Song of Judith at the end is omitted), does *seem* to be longer; actually, the greater share of attention is devoted to the events in the second part. The reader's impression is that the first part is taken up with military movements and engagements, but it is really mostly talk. The talk is, first of all, a way of revealing the characters of Nebuchadnezzar and Holofernes and how they will try to attain world domination, but it is also a means to introduce Achior into the story, his view of the role of Israel in history, the reactions of the Israelites to the crisis, and what is religiously at stake. But these are far from plodding; they develop all the issues of the context of Judith's decisive act. And since Judith was probably read as entertainment, it simply would not do to have the climactic scene arrive too soon.

On the question of the rhetorical excesses, in general, these were perhaps noted most emphatically by Pfeiffer: "The turgid style, the patent exaggerations, the stately pomp and ceremony throughout, unrelieved by a sense of humor, give to the book a baroque rather than a classic appearance."[21] It is quite revealing of his lack of sympathy for the genre that he says that the book of Judith does not have a sense of humor. Quite the opposite is the case.

In response to these criticisms, it is important to see popular literature in its proper context. It is precisely the goal of the author of Judith to impress the reader with an unrestrained exuberance and to have an immediate impact. The author of Judith makes an art of excess: the descriptions of the troops, the artificial geographical sweep, the pillage and destruction, the gory central scene—all of these serve to keep the reader riveted. This is the same approach that is found in other novelistic works, both Jewish and Greek. It should also be noted that the author of Judith did not work with established models of what the novel genre should look like; the novel was a bold experiment, only in the first stages of development. Nonetheless, the author had introduced innovative improvements over the other novels. Whereas some of the more primitive novels of this period were characterized by duplicated scenes (the Additions to Esther)

---

17. Wills, *The Jewish Novel in the Ancient World* 1-39, 212-45; Hansen, *Anthology of Ancient Greek Popular Literature*, 3-13.
18. Arthur E. Cowley, "The Book of Judith," in *APOT* 1:242-43.
19. J. C. Dancy, *The Shorter Books of the Apocrypha*, CBC (Cambridge: Cambridge University Press, 1972) 68.
20. Luis Alonso-Schökel, *Narrative Structures in the Book of Judith* (Berkeley, Calif.: Center for Hermeneutical Studies in Hellenistic and Modern Culture, 1974) 5.
21. Robert H. Pfeiffer, *History of New Testament Times* (New York: Harper and Bros., 1949) 299.

or separate small narratives strung together (the Additions to Daniel), Judith attains a length that is larger than the other novels of the apocrypha, and yet maintains a smooth, taut narrative. To be sure, there are two different movements to the story, but there is a logical relationship between them, and the author exercises many literary gifts. In many ways, Judith is the best constructed of the Jewish novels.

Toni Craven made a major breakthrough in the literary appreciation of the whole of the book when she identified certain aspects of the function of the first part.[22] There are many parallels and contrasts between the first part of the book and the second and, in addition, parallels and contrasts within each part. This results in a complex and intentional structuring of the two parts that greatly enriches the reading experience, *once one is prepared for such a reading*. Some of the most important correspondences can be represented thus:

First half
   A Campaign against disobedient nations; the people surrender (1:1–3:10)
      B Israel is "greatly terrified"; Joakim prepares for war (4:1-15)
         C Holofernes talks with Achior; Achior is expelled (5:1–6:13)
         C´ Achior is received in Bethulia; Achior talks with the people (6:14-21)
      B´ Holofernes prepares for war; Israel is "greatly terrified" (7:1-5)
   A´ Campaign against Bethulia; the people want to surrender (7:6-32)

Second half
   A Introduction of Judith (8:1-8)
      B Judith plans to save Israel (8:9–10:9a)
         C Judith and her maid leave Bethulia (10:9b-10)
            D Judith overcomes Holofernes (10:11–13:10a)
         C´ Judith and her maid return to Bethulia (13:10b-11)
      B´ Judith plans to destroy Israel's enemy (13:12–16:20)
   A´ Conclusion about Judith (16:21-25)

Craven's discernment of the pattern of parallels and contrasts allows a much more sympathetic—and ultimately enjoyable—reading of the first half of the book. Each half is in the form of a chiasm—that is, a structure that resembles the Greek letter *chi*, or χ, and in which motifs in the first half are repeated in the second, except reversed.[23] This allows each part to have an effective center, yet move to a culmination. The first part ends with a calm that is not a resolution; it is the dread of Holofernes' attack. The question hanging over the Jews is, "Who is lord, Nebuchadnezzar or God?" The second part removes the Israelites' fear of Holofernes and answers that question resoundingly, "God is Lord and works even through the hand of a woman." The structuring of the narrative is simple and complex at the same time. There are numerous structural relationships, yet they point to a single overall arc: rising action, denouement, falling action. Although Craven's findings have strongly influenced the present commentary on Judith, the outline followed in this commentary has been altered slightly from hers. The text has been broken up into more equal sizes that reflect content more than literary structure.

In addition to the pattern of balanced parallels and oppositions of motifs that Craven analyzed, we can detect several other important narrative operations as well. First, there is a typical hero pattern in the novel. This common cross-cultural narrative structure usually portrays a male hero, sometimes withdrawn from society, who comes forward when the community is threatened by a larger-than-life monster and slays it. At this point, there are essentially two resolutions of the story: either a comic one or a tragic one. In the comic resolution (usually associated with myths and fairy tales), the hero returns to a celebration with the community, and

---

22. Craven, *Artistry and Faith in the Book of Judith*, 60-62.
23. On chiasm see also Adele Berlin, "Introduction to Hebrew Poetry," *The New Interpreter's Bible Commentary*, 10 vols. (Nashville: Abingdon, 2015) 3:10-11, and using the language of "concentric construction," Michael Kolarcik, S.J., "The Book of Wisdom," *NIBC*, 6:432-34.

peace and fertility are restored to the land. In the tragic ending (usually associated with epic poetry and tragedy), the hero either dies in the process or returns to a community in which he cannot really participate. Judith can easily be seen as an adaptation of the hero pattern: In the beginning, she is outside of society in the tent on her roof. She comes out of seclusion to "arm" herself in beautiful garments, moves forward to engage the monster, slays the monster, and returns to a celebration of the community. The ending is closer to the comic resolution, although this question will be taken up again in regard to the ending of the work (see Commentary on 16:21-25). The similarity of Judith to heroic narratives has been noted by various scholars. Coote has suggested the cross-cultural tale pattern more typical of the heroine called "wife disguised as a man frees her husband," which depicts a faithful wife (here, Judith is a "wife" of Israel) who disguises herself as a man to rescue her husband.[24] However, it seems more likely that what we see in Judith is not a female pattern such as this, but a more radical adaptation of a male warrior-hero pattern. The role reversal in Judith and the flouting of normal sexual taboos is much stronger than in most heroine tales of disguise.[25]

The hero pattern is a broad and varied phenomenon, occurring in all parts of the world, and it has attracted the attention of scholars who see the possibility of isolating a "monomyth," a single narrative structure that is the model of all hero tales worldwide. While this goal may never be attained in detail, it is clear that there are common patterns of the hero narrative and that comparing Judith with some of the reconstructions of cross-cultural patterns could be instructive. The best-known attempt to isolate a single pattern with variations is that of Joseph Campbell.[26] His summary of the typical hero story pattern—and the vast majority of the narratives he cites concern male heroes—is as follows (slightly simplified): The mythological hero, setting forth from his hut or castle, proceeds to the threshold of adventure. There he encounters a shadow presence that guards the passage. The hero may defeat or conciliate this power and go alive into the kingdom of the dark. Beyond the threshold the hero journeys through a world of unfamiliar, yet strangely intimate, forces, some of which severely threaten him. When he arrives at the nadir of the mythological world, he undergoes a supreme ordeal and gains his reward. The triumph may be represented as the hero's theft of the boon he came to gain. The final work is that of return; the hero reemerges from the kingdom of dread. The boon that he brings restores the world.

The elements of the narrative are very similar to the book of Judith: the departure of the hero, the crossing of the threshold into a dark region of danger (see below on the gates of Bethulia as a threshold), the trials of the hero and the slaying of a monster (in this case, Holofernes), the stealing of a great boon to humanity (the head of Holofernes), the return of the hero, the reentry into society by crossing the threshold again, and the restoration of peace. What we have in the case of Judith is a hero narrative cast in a more realistic setting that brings down to earth many of the elements of the story pattern. Further, Campbell's analysis helps us to understand why some of the characters of Judith are so one-dimensional. The literary or theological value of the book of Judith is not contained in the development of Judith's character or in an analysis of evil as embodied in Holofernes. The complexity that usually makes characters interesting is not present. Judith does not grow as a character and is not mixed of good and evil qualities. It is emphasized that she is wise, virtuous, and capable; but she does not discover anything about herself (cf. in this regard Esther 4). She is like the figures of myth, who are likewise often one-dimensional. The hero of myth is born fully formed in his heroic traits. The remarkable virtues of this person, according to Campbell, are more predestined than achieved in the course of life. Thus both the hero and the monster reach their end by destiny. There is very little need to create multidimensional characters.

The hero pattern is thus the overarching structure for the book of Judith, but contained within it are interesting smaller structures as well that serve to illuminate important segments of

---

24. Coote, "Response," 21-26.
25. Milne, "What Shall We Do with Judith?" 37-58, also looks to the male hero narrative pattern isolated by Heda Jason, "Ilja of Murom and Tzar Kalin: A Proposal for a Model for the Narrative Structure of an Epic Struggle," *Slavica Hierosylimitana* 5-6 (1981) 47-55. An interesting study of the "female hero" in modern literature also explores the adaptation of the male hero pattern in modern novels about women. See Carol Pearson and Katherine Pope, *The Female Hero in American and British Literature* (New York: Bowker, 1981).
26. Joseph Campbell, *The Hero with a Thousand Faces* (New York: Pantheon, 1949) esp. 245-46. On Judith as a heroic quest, see Mary Garrard, "Judith," in *Artemisia Gentileschi: The Image of the Female Hero in Italian Baroque Art* (Princeton, N.J.: Princeton University Press, 1989) 281.

the departure and return of the hero. One of these is the preparation of Judith, or her transition out of her life of quietism in chap. 8 (see the Overview of chaps. 8–16). It is best described as what anthropologists would call a "rite of passage," a ritually marked transition that involves separation from society, a liminal period in which normal markers of social order, such as age, class, gender, or status, are obliterated and sacred information is imparted, and incorporation or aggregation back into the social order with a new status.[27] At 8:11-27, Judith has scolded the rulers of Bethulia for being weak willed and has told them that she has a plan to deliver them. She then must prepare herself, and enters into a state of ritual cleansing and self-abnegation in which she uncovers her mourning garments, prays, bathes, and then reclothes herself in rich apparel and cosmetics. The scene is remarkably similar to the central prayer scenes of the female protagonists in the Additions to Esther and *Joseph and Aseneth*.[28] At a turning point near the middle of the narrative, the female protagonist turns to prayer and begins a process of penitence and self-abasement. She condemns her beauty, puts on sackcloth as a garment of mourning, prays, and afterward reclothes herself in beautiful garments and emerges to perform her mission (see also the much less stylized scenes in Tob 3:10-15 and Sus 22-23).

This scene is related to Jewish penitential theology that developed in the post-exilic period, already found, for instance, in Nehemiah 9, Daniel 9, some of the psalms, and Baruch and the Prayer of Manasseh in the apocrypha, and emerging later in Jas 4:8-10. The themes emphasized in these texts differ, as do the content of their prayers. Still, in all the Jewish novels except Judith, the introspective female protagonist is buffeted and psychologically tested.[29] The amount of space devoted to this issue and the depth of the psychological interest vary from Susanna (the least attention) to *Joseph and Aseneth* (the most), but it is interesting that Judith is not psychologically buffeted despite her situation. Moore compares the prayer in Judith with that of Add. Esth 14:1-19,[30] but misses this crucial difference. Neither does Judith show any penitence. Esther, and even more so Aseneth, purifies herself by a penitence that involves an abject self-abasement. The rituals of mourning are incorporated, which would be typical in the Bible in a moment of crisis, but Esther goes beyond this; it has become a quasi-ascetic repudiation of those aspects of her body associated with her beauty: "Instead of costly perfumes she covered her head with ashes and dung, and she utterly humbled her body; every part that she loved to adorn she covered with her tangled hair" (Add. Esth 14:2). The heroines' awareness of sin, associated with their bodies, is overwhelming in Esther and *Joseph and Aseneth*. Yet Judith knows nothing of this. Even her fasts do not appear to have an explicit penitential aspect. Judith undergoes an experience of transformation without being transformed. The author takes up the paradigm and the literary pattern of the buffeted Jewish heroine who is penitent and prayerful, but gives her no recognition of sin. She is simply perfect as she is.

In addition, another important segment of the hero's quest, crossing the threshold into the sphere of darkness and danger and returning again,[31] is marked very clearly in the narrative as an important passage as well. Craven notes in her structural arrangement of Judith a correspondence between the departure of Judith and her maid through the gates of Bethulia at 10:9b-10 and their return at 13:10b-11. These corresponding scenes contain a number of important, ritualized elements. When Judith, with the help of her maid, has prepared for her quest by means of the dressing scene, she commands the town elder Uzziah, "Order the gate of the town to be opened." Accompanying her departure is a series of gestures of Uzziah and the townspeople that are typical of the departure scenes in heroic poetry (see Commentary on 10:6-10). When the two return again she also says, "Open, open the gate!" which marks clearly the return of the hero and her incorporation back into the safety of the known village. Although there is still a battle to be fought when she returns, the immediate danger to her—and especially to her honor as a pious Jewish woman—is while she is in the liminal period between her going and coming.

---

27. Arnold van Gennep, *The Rites of Passage* (Chicago: University of Chicago Press, 1960); Victor Turner, "Betwixt and Between: The Liminal Period in Rites de Passage," in *The Forest of Symbols: Aspects of Ndembu Ritual* (Ithaca: Cornell University Press) 93-111.
28. Wills, *The Jewish Novel in the Ancient World*, 224-32; Alice Bach, *Women, Seduction and Betrayal in Biblical Narrative* (New York: Cambridge University Press, 1997) 202-3.
29. Wills, *The Jewish Novel in the Ancient World*, 147-48.
30. Moore, *Judith*, 195-97.
31. Campbell, *Hero with a Thousand Faces*, 90-91.

This is also the period in which she flaunts her sexuality, engages in deceit and manipulation, and murders Holofernes. It is also the dramatic center of the book.

Aside from these structural elements of the novel, there are also certain aspects of the literary style that deserve attention. Judith utilizes a number of techniques that enliven the narrative: anticipation of future events; retardation and acceleration of plot; vivid visual description; and irony and humor. Concerning the anticipation of events that appear later in the text, we must assume that the story of Judith was well known, whether from oral tradition or from written narratives, such as the present text. This would be quite likely if, as discussed above, an older narrative tradition from the Persian period was at the core of the present Hasmonean-era text. Anticipation is a way of building suspense about future events, but it also introduces a kind of irony—that is, a perception on the part of the audience about what they think will happen that is different from the perspective of the characters. The anticipation in Judith is sometimes suspenseful, sometimes ironic and humorous. It is suspenseful when Achior's exile to the village of Bethulia anticipates his witness there to the events that are about to unfold. It is ironic and humorous when statements that are made take on a different meaning in the light of anticipated events, such as Holofernes' blustery statement to Achior: "You shall not see my face again until I take revenge on this race!" (6:5). Anticipation can often be seen in the irony of many of the statements in Judith's and Holofernes' dialogue (e.g., 11:6; 12:4).

The retardation and acceleration of the plot are among the most effective techniques of the author, creating excellent pacing of the narrative. This is often accomplished by the alternation of narrative and dialogue, action and rest, and alternation of location, but most often by the use of vivid description.[32] The audience fully anticipates the beheading of Holofernes—they know that is what the story is about—to such an extent that the amount of text that goes before it has surprised many critics. Just as the Gospel of Mark has been characterized as a passion story with a long introduction,[33] so also Judith is a beheading with a long introduction. With this in mind, one can see chaps. 1–7 as a series of episodes that use retardation and acceleration, in addition to alternation of types of discourse, to set the stage for the climactic decapitation. Chapter 1 launches immediately into a military drama between two great world powers, followed by a rest (1:16). The narrative moves again into a brisk description of military events and another rest (3:10). Israel's response to war follows, which is described almost like military preparations (4:1-15). There are several extended dialogues following (5:1–6:9), after which there are intrigues that involve a combination of vivid description with some retardation of the plot and dialogue, as Achior is expelled from Holofernes' camp and welcomed into Bethulia (6:10–7:18). In 10:11-23 we find a similar combination of vivid description, plot retardation, and dialogue as Judith reverses the direction of Achior's movement and goes from Bethulia to Holofernes' camp.[34] From 11:1 to 12:18 there is dialogue, and then at the climactic scene in Holofernes' tent, we find slight retardation of the plot as Judith approaches Holofernes (12:19–13:7), and then acceleration of the plot as Judith beheads Holofernes, collects the head and the tent canopy, moves through the camp, climbs up the mountain and back to Bethulia, all in three verses (13:8-10)! The military campaign at the end of Judith (15:1-7) is also told in the same quick, bold strokes as the military campaigns at the beginning of Judith.

If there is one literary device that most characterizes the book of Judith, however, it would be irony.[35] In this respect Judith is in good company; irony is at the center of the Gospel of John, the book of Jonah, and Plato's portrait of Socrates.[36] The irony is ubiquitous in Judith and plays on several levels. On the broadest level, it is found in the unexpected development that the great Assyrian general Holofernes is felled by the hand of a woman. This is the central irony that underlies the structure of the book as a whole, and it is referred to often, both in Judith's prayer in chap. 9, and in the Song of Judith in chap. 16. The irony spills over into the dialogue,

---

32. On alternation of location, see Craven, *Artistry and Faith in the Book of Judith*, 61; on description, see Alonso-Schökel, *Narrative Structures in the Book of Judith*, 7.

33. Martin Kähler, *The So-Called Historical Jesus and the Historic, Biblical Christ* (Philadelphia: Fortress, 1964) 80.

34. On the "exchange" of Achior and Judith, see Adolfo Roitman, "Achior in the Book of Judith: His Role and Significance," in *"No One Spoke Ill of Her": Essays on Judith*, ed. James C. VanderKam (Atlanta: Scholars Press, 1992) 31-45.

35. Moore, *Judith*, 78-85.

36. See Gail R. O'Day, "The Gospel of John," *NIBC*, 8:481, 695-96.

creating an extended train of ironic utterances, as characters time and again speak words that have one meaning for them and another for the audience. Judith, who is very clever, seems to be uttering double entendres intentionally, playing with Holofernes as a cat plays with a mouse. But Holofernes is also prone to making pronouncements that will come back to haunt him; he is too obtuse to realize what is going on around him. The two strands of ironic statements—Judith's and Holofernes'—thus proceed simultaneously through much of the novel. Related to this is the discrepancy between Holofernes' self-understanding and the pitiable end for which he is destined. His bloated self-image clouds his judgment, so that he not only sees in himself what he wants to see, but also he sees in Judith only what he chooses. If Holofernes had been clever enough to catch Judith's irony, he would have been clever enough to avoid her trap, even get the best of her. But he was not. Surrounding these larger ironies are smaller examples that are still significant. Nebuchadnezzar claims to be "lord of the whole world" (2:5); yet the narrative confirms that God is lord, and this will be proved, not on the great battlefields or in the famous cities of the ancient Near East, but outside the tiny mountain village of Bethulia. Also Achior, though an Ammonite, is more stalwart in his defense of Israel than is Uzziah, one of the rulers of Bethulia. We may note one last example of irony that also relates to the moral evaluation of Judith: She is fastidious about the observance of kosher laws, and yet she violates Jewish views of the permissible actions of a pious widow. This irony lies at the center of Judith's liminal actions.

BIBLICAL PARALLELS

The reader familiar with the Bible will immediately recognize in Judith parallels to many biblical stories. The text is indeed a rich tapestry of biblical allusions. The most important of these are listed and analyzed by Dubarle,[37] and here the most important ones will be mentioned. In addition to the explicit references to Abraham, Isaac, and Jacob (Jdt 8:25-27) and to Simeon (Jdt 9:2-4), there are evident influences of narrative motifs from many biblical texts.

The fact that the main character is a woman naturally attracts our attention to biblical stories that focus on female characters. The general theme of the ruse of a woman recurs in biblical literature, from Rebekah's manipulation to secure the birthright for her son Jacob in Genesis 27, to Tamar's ruse to have sex with her father-in-law in order to raise up a child in the name of her dead husband in Genesis 38.[38] Rahab the prostitute's aid to the two spies sent into Jericho (Joshua 2; 6:22-25) bears more than a passing resemblance to parts of Judith. It is not simply that Judith also "plays the harlot" with Holofernes; Rahab, like Achior, is also a non-Israelite who joins Israel, and her speech (Josh 2:9-14) is very similar to Achior's speech in Judith 5. At several points in the HB there is an execution of a warrior by a woman, which was considered a shameful form of death. In Judg 9:50-55, Abimelech is killed by a woman who drops a millstone upon him. Emphasized here is that Abimelech does not want to die at the hand of a woman, a mark of shame that is found also in Jdt 16:5 (see also 2 Sam 4:5-12; 20:14-22).

The most important of the parallels to women in active roles, however, is the story of Deborah the prophet in Judges 4–5, and especially the role of Jael in murdering the general Sisera. In Judges 4, the prose version of the story, King Jabin of Canaan has sent his general Sisera to attack the Israelites. Deborah the prophet instructs Barak to lead the Israelites out to fight Sisera. She promises Barak that the Lord will defeat Sisera and adds, "The LORD will sell Sisera into the hand of a woman." Barak routs the forces of Sisera, but Sisera himself takes refuge in the tent of Jael. He lies down, and while he is sleeping, Jael takes a tent peg and drives it through his head. Judges 5 is then a victory song of Deborah in celebration. The most obvious similarities to Judith are the heroism of a woman who gives courage to her people in a time of oppression by a foreign power, her call to arms to the men to defend themselves, and also the murder scene in which a woman—now not Deborah but Jael—kills the general of the foreign king. More specifically we may note that both women are very strong, patriotic people and that the execution scenes both

---

37. A. M. Dubarle, *Judith: Formes et sens des diverses traditions*, 2 vols. (Rome: Pontifical Biblical Institute, 1966) 1:137-64.
38. Esther Fuchs, "Who Is Hiding the Truth? Deceptive Women and Biblical Androcentrism," in *Feminist Perspectives on Biblical Scholarship*, ed. Adela Yarbro Collins (Chico, Calif.: Scholars Press, 1985) 137-44.

take place in a tent while the general is incapacitated and lying down.[39] The victory song of Judith is partly modeled on the Song of Deborah and also on Moses' Song of the Sea in Exodus 15. In a fascinating development, we also see that a first-century CE retelling of Bible history, Pseudo-Philo's *Biblical Antiquities* 30-31, modifies the story of Deborah by adding elements evidently drawn from Judith.[40] The influence of the stories has now moved in the opposite direction!

There are similarities as well to male warriors and leaders in the Bible. Judith is not only like Deborah, but she is also like the other judges and prophets who arise when God hears the prayers of the people (Jdt 4:13; cf. Judg 2:11-23), to give the land rest from oppression for a number of years afterward (Jdt 16:25; cf. Judg 3:11, 30; 5:31).[41] We note, for example, Ehud's killing of Eglon, king of Moab (Judg 3:12-30). Once Ehud has assassinated the king in his inner chamber, Ehud leaves the doors closed so that the servants are pacing without, wondering what is taking the king so long. This is played to comic effect, just as is the analogous scene in Jdt 14:14-18.

Other texts have left their mark on Judith, not just in the similarity of the motifs, but in the use of words as well: Abram's (Abraham's) pursuit of the captors of Lot in Genesis 14 (cf. Judith 15), the motif of the complaining of the people in Exodus 17 (cf. Judith 7), the story of David and Goliath in 1 Samuel 17 (cf. Judith 13), the bluster of Nebuchadnezzar in Daniel 2–4 and the insistence that the king be worshiped as a god in Daniel 6 (cf. Judith 2), and the repentance in sackcloth, even for the cattle, in Jonah 3:5-8 (cf. Jdt 4:10). Some of these parallels may result from the oral circulation of good story motifs, but others are either much too close to be independent or use similar words. Thus the essence of Judith is not a literary rendition of an originally oral story, as may be the case for Tobit, Esther, or Daniel 1–6. Judith uses broad folklore themes, to be sure, but the parallels reveal an author at work who is borrowing heavily from a number of biblical texts and weaving them together into a unified story. Dubarle likens this process to the "anthological style" of other post-exilic Jewish works and of such Christian texts as Luke 1–2.[42] It would be wrong, however, to say that Judith is an imaginative interpretation that simply mines and develops a number of biblical passages. For one thing, non-Jewish traditions can also be postulated that are in many cases just as close as the biblical: the Ugaritic epic of Aqhat, for example, tells the story of the woman Paghat, who, enraged over the death of her brother Aqhat, avenges him by inebriating his murderer and slaying him while he is on his bed.[43] The use of written texts in the composition of another written text does not preclude the use also of motifs and themes from oral tradition,[44] but what is important here is that Judith is not just the sum total of the myriad motifs that it appears to borrow, now strung together. It uses these many building blocks, and yet still reflects the single vision of a talented author who communicates the exuberance of Judith's freedom in a new genre, the novel.

---

39. Sidnie Ann White, "In the Steps of Jael and Deborah: Judith as Heroine," in *"No One Spoke Ill of Her": Essays on Judith*, ed. James C. VanderKam (Atlanta: Scholars Press, 1992) 5-16.
40. Pervo, "Aseneth and Her Sisters," 159n. 71.
41. White, "In the Steps of Jael and Deborah," 12; van Henten, "Judith as Alternative Leader," 243-44.
42. Dubarle, *Judith*, 1:137-64.
43. *ANET*, 155.
44. Susan Niditch, *Oral World and Written Word: Ancient Israelite Literature* (Louisville: Westminster/John Knox, 1996) 8-24.

BIBLIOGRAPHY

Commentaries:

Cowley, Arthur E. "The Book of Judith." In *APOT* 1:242-67. An older translation with introduction and notes, it is still valuable.

Dancy, J. C. *The Shorter Books of the Apocrypha*. CBC. Cambridge: Cambridge University Press, 1972. Includes an excellent, but somewhat dated, short commentary on Judith.

Enslin, Morton S., and Solomon Zeitlin. *The Book of Judith*. JAL VIII. Leiden: Brill, 1972. Greek text and English translation with notes. Formerly a standard treatment, it was written before the important contributions of literary and feminist studies. It is still quite valuable.

Moore, Carey A. *Judith.* AB 40. Garden City, N.Y.: Doubleday, 1985. The major commentary in English. Clearly written, with a wealth of historical and geographical information, it incorporated the literary and feminist scholarship that was available at the time of its publication.

Studies on Judith:

Alonso-Schökel, Luis. *Narrative Structures in the Book of Judith.* Berkeley, Calif.: Center for Hermeneutical Studies in Hellenistic and Modern Culture, 1974. A pioneering literary study of Judith, important both for its focus on the literary structures of the text and for the responses included in it by Mary P. Coote and Alan Dundes that pressed folklore parallels to Judith.

Bal, Mieke. "Head Hunting: 'Judith' on the Cutting Edge of Knowledge." *JSOT* 63 (1994) 3-34. Reprinted in Brenner, *A Feminist Companion.* A provocative and insightful feminist interpretation of artistic depictions of Judith that illuminates the biblical text as well.

Brenner, Athalya, ed. *A Feminist Companion to Esther, Judith and Susanna.* Sheffield: Sheffield Academic, 1995. Part of a series of volumes of previously published feminist analyses of biblical texts.

Craven, Toni. *Artistry and Faith in the Book of Judith.* Chico, Calif.: Scholars Press, 1983. With Alonso-Schökel, Craven launched the recent wave of literary-critical studies.

Elder, Linda Bennett. "Judith." In Elisabeth Schüssler Fiorenza, ed., *Searching the Scriptures.* Vol. 2. New York: Crossroad, 1993–94. Focuses on the many sides of Judith's role as a woman in the story.

Garrard, Mary. "Judith." In *Artemisia Gentileschi: The Image of the Female Hero in Italian Baroque Art.* Princeton: Princeton University Press, 1989. This brilliant analysis connects the various Renaissance and Baroque paintings of Judith to the psychological and interpretive issues that are present in the ancient text as well.

Jacobus, Mary. "Judith, Holofernes, and the Phallic Woman." In *Reading Women: Essays in Feminist Criticism.* New York: Columbia University Press, 1986. One of the best essays on the psychological and sexual issues in Judith. Like Garrard, Jacobus incorporates an analysis of visual images as a means of sensitizing the reader to the issues in the biblical text as well.

Lacocque, André. *The Feminine Unconventional: Four Subversive Figures in Israel's Tradition.* Minneapolis: Fortress, 1990. A theologically engaging consideration of the "subversive" side of seemingly domesticated biblical narratives about women.

Levine, Amy-Jill. "Sacrifice and Salvation: Otherness and Domestication in the Book of Judith." In *"No One Spoke Ill of Her": Essays on Judith.* Edited by James C. VanderKam. Atlanta: Scholars Press, 1992. One of the most provocative and thoughtful readings on the symbolism of Judith's reversal of typical male/female gender codes.

McNeil, Brian. "Reflections on the Book of Judith." *The Downside Review* 96 (1978) 199-207. A Roman Catholic reflection on the place of Judith in the church's teachings.

Milne, Pamela. "What Shall We Do with Judith? A Feminist Assessment of a Biblical 'Heroine.' " *Semeia* 62 (1993) 37-58. An excellent and balanced reflection on whether Judith should be considered a feminist work.

Pervo, Richard I. "Aseneth and Her Sisters: Women in Jewish Narrative and in the Greek Novels." In *"Women Like This": New Perspectives on Jewish Women in the Greco-Roman World.* Edited by Amy-Jill Levine. Atlanta: Scholars Press, 1991. Draws many parallels between the Jewish novels and the Greek and includes interesting insights on Judith.

Skehan, Patrick. "The Hand of Judith." *CBQ* 25 (1963) 94-110. Argues strongly that the Song of Judith was modeled on the Song of the Sea in Exodus 15 and that both were used in celebrations of Passover.

Stocker, Margarita. *Judith, Sexual Warrior: Women and Power in Western Culture.* New Haven: Yale University Press, 1998. Excellent on the appropriation of Judith in the Reformation-era debates and in art.

VanderKam, James C., ed. *"No One Spoke Ill of Her": Essays on Judith.* Atlanta: Scholars Press, 1992. Excellent essays by Amy-Jill Levine, Sidnie White Crawford, Nira Stone, Adolfo Roitman, Carey Moore, and Patrick Skehan.

Wills, Lawrence M. *The Jewish Novel in the Ancient World.* Ithaca: Cornell University Press, 1995. The first book-length study to bring all the Jewish novels and related literature together into one genre analysis.

OUTLINE OF JUDITH

I. Judith 1:1–7:32, Nebuchadnezzar Threatens the West and Israel

    A. 1:1–2:13, The Rising Threat of Nebuchadnezzar Against the West
        1:1-16, Nebuchadnezzar's Campaign Against Arphaxad
        2:1-13, Nebuchadnezzar Commissions Holofernes to Destroy the Nations Who Did Not Ally with Him
    B. 2:14–7:32, Holofernes' Campaign Narrows to a Siege of Bethulia
        2:14-28, Campaign Initiated Against Disobedient Nations
        3:1-10, The People of the Seacoast Surrender
        4:1-15, Israel Prays and Prepares for War
        5:1-21, Achior Tells Holofernes of Israel's History
        5:22–6:21, Holofernes Responds by Expelling Achior, Who Is Received in Bethulia
        7:1-18, Holofernes Prepares for War and Places Bethulia Under Siege
        7:19-32, The People Despair and Want to Surrender

II. Judith 8:1–16:25, Judith Arises to Rescue Her People

    A. 8:1-8, Introduction of Judith
    B. 8:9–10:10, Judith Resolves to Save Israel
        8:9-36, Judith Addresses the Citizens of Bethulia
        9:1-14, Judith Purifies Herself and Prays
        10:1-10, Judith Emerges from Prayer to Go Forth
    C. 10:11–13:10*a*, Judith Overcomes Holofernes
        10:11-23, Judith Enters the Enemy Camp and Is Taken to Holofernes
        11:1-23, Judith's Dialogue with Holofernes
        12:1-20, For Three Days Judith Lives in Holofernes' Camp
        13:1-10*a*, Judith Beheads Holofernes
    D. 13:10*b*–15:7, Judith Returns to Bethulia and Initiates Counterattack
        13:10*b*-20, Judith and Her Maid Return to Bethulia
        14:1-10, Judith Issues Orders and Achior Converts
        14:11–15:7, The Assyrians Discover Holofernes' Headless Body and Are Put to Flight
    E. 15:8–16:25, Celebration and Conclusion
        15:8-13, All of Israel Celebrates
        15:14–16:17, Judith's Victory Song
        16:18-20, Thanksgiving Offerings
        16:21-25, Memorial of Judith

JUDITH 1:1–7:32

NEBUCHADNEZZAR THREATENS THE WEST AND ISRAEL

OVERVIEW

The book of Judith can be divided into two parts, the first of which (1:1–7:32) describes a threat to the Israelites that arises from Nebuchadnezzar, king of the Assyrians, and his general Holofernes. Nebuchadnezzar had demanded that all the nations of the west ally with him to defeat Arphaxad, king of the Medes. Although many of the nations refuse to join him, he defeats Arphaxad nevertheless. The first chapter thus begins with a description of battles on the eastern horizon between two great nations, the Assyrians and the Medes. Once the Medes have been conquered, Nebuchadnezzar turns to conquer the nations who spurned his request. This group of nations, those to the west of Assyria, includes Judea and Samaria. He commissions his general Holofernes to muster an army of huge proportions and to attack each nation in turn, accepting as allies those who choose to surrender and laying waste those who do not. Israel will not capitulate, and begs God for help as they await the assault of Holofernes from the north. Standing between Jerusalem and the path of the Assyrians is a series of mountain villages, which are quickly fortified as the first line of defense.

The first half of Judith thus presents a tremendous sweep of nations and battles, military threats, the intrigue of stratagems, abject demonstrations of humility on the part of Israel, and the delivery of Israel's newfound ally, Achior, to Judith's village. All of the issues of the first half come to bear on a single village in the mountains forty miles north of Jerusalem. It ends on a note of calm before the storm, with the Israelite people in despair.

JUDITH 1:1–2:13, THE RISING THREAT OF NEBUCHADNEZZAR AGAINST THE WEST

OVERVIEW

Like modern action movies, Judith leaps immediately into a rousing action scene that is only preparatory to the longer military campaigns to follow. The presence of a "chapter 1," set chronologically well before the main action of the story, is not unusual in the literature of this period (see, e.g., Esther 1, Tobit 1, Matthew 1–2, and Luke 1–2). The function of this introduction is not simply to engage the reader with exciting action—although that is an important element of popular literature; the carefully orchestrated rising action serves to dramatize, first, that Nebuchadnezzar is apparently invincible, since even the great king Arphaxad is defeated by him, and second, that Nebuchadnezzar is bent on world domination and will not stop his expansion until the entire subcontinent is under his control.

Judith 1:1-16, Nebuchadnezzar's Campaign Against Arphaxad

COMMENTARY

1:1-4. The book of Judith opens in a way that is typical of the history books of the Bible, by dating the events described to the year in the reign of the major king (see 1 Kgs 15:1; 16:15, 29; 2 Kgs 12:1; 13:1). However, although the reader is perhaps meant to think of the genre of history writing, it is mock history that is likely intended, for Nebuchadnezzar is identified as the king "who ruled over the Assyrians in the great city of Nineveh." The historical Nebuchadnezzar ruled, not the Assyrians, whose capital was indeed in Nineveh, but the Babylonians. Both empires were remembered as being oppressive to the Israelite and Jewish people: The Assyrians had destroyed the northern kingdom of Israel and deported the leading citizens in 721 BCE, and Nebuchadnezzar and his Babylonian army had defeated Jerusalem and the southern kingdom of Judah (later called Judea) in 586 BCE, when he also destroyed the Temple and deported many citizens to Babylon (see esp. 2 Kings 24–25; Jer 39–40:6). Because Assyria and Babylon were considered the two "evil empires" of Israelite and Jewish history, there is no question that both the author and the audience would have been aware of the error of combining them; this was doubtless a signal within the writing that the novel that followed, though as rousing as military history, was meant ironically and even humorously. It would be all the more satisfying if the two evil empires could be merged into one figurehead that would march forward only to be defeated by the stratagems of an Israelite woman.

No sooner has an impossible combination of empires appeared on the stage of "history" than it is met by another fictitious king created for this role: "Arphaxad who ruled over the Medes in Ecbatana." There is no known king of the Medes by that name, but neither would the reader expect such a figure to exist based on the playful combination of Nebuchadnezzar and the Assyrians just encountered. The irony of this fictitious king would have been surprising for another reason as well: The mighty Assyrians, who in this book will crush Arphaxad and the Medes in 1:13-15, were actually defeated by the Medes in 612 BCE.

The might of Arphaxad's kingdom is quickly communicated by means of a description of Ecbatana's city walls; the dimensions of the walls and towers go far beyond any fortifications that were likely built for that city. The size of the gates is emphasized to provide an opportunity for the author to conjure for the audience the awesome image of Arphaxad's troops passing through. This is just the first of many examples of how the author uses description to bring forth an exciting narrative that is almost "cinematic" in what it evokes. Ecbatana figures historically and accurately in Ezra 6:2 and appears in Tob 3:7 as the home of Sarah, the woman who will marry Tobit's son. Thus the city is part of the eastern home of diaspora Jews and would have been a known entity to the audience. Perhaps more important for the literary technique here is the historian Polybius's remark[45] that exaggerated descriptions of the palace, as here in Judith, were common in sensationalist histories. The author has in just a few lines plunged us into a dramatic world of the clash of great nations. At this point we might compare a similar effect achieved in a very different way in the Additions to Esther. Whereas MT Esther began as a court narrative with a description of the pomp and splendor of the great Persian palace, the Additions begin by recounting a dream that came to Mordecai:

Noises and confusion, thunders and earthquake, tumult on the earth! Then two great dragons came forward, both ready to fight, and they roared terribly. At their roaring every nation prepared for war, to fight against the righteous nation. (Add. Esth A 5-7 NRSV)

---

45. Polybius *History* 10.27.7-8.

We later learn that the two dragons are Mordecai and Haman and that the nations are those arrayed against Israel. Thus in this Addition the scope of the worldwide danger is communicated in a portentous dream that borrows from apocalyptic imagery.

The book of Judith, which reflects in general an excellent and exciting plot development, opens in a way that seems quite awkward. The long opening sentence (broken up by most translations into several sentences) sets the scene by drawing the reader immediately into the high drama of the narrative. A long run-on sentence is used to describe two great nations pitted against each other, but what do they have to do with Israel? We are not told until the next chapter. The book of Esther employs a similar technique of beginning with a long description and a run-on sentence, but there the drama is more court intrigue, here it is the threat of external military campaigns (see also the Commentary on Jdt 8:1-3).

1:5-6. The lists of peoples and lands serves to communicate the worldwide extent of the war that is threatened. They sometimes seem repetitive to the modern reader, or at least unknown and confusing, but this should not detract from our ability to appreciate the literary effects of the treatment of nations and places. Here the great plain on the border of Ragau is in Persia; Ragau (Rages), like Ecbatana, is an important city in Tobit. The famous regions of Persia, near the Tigris and Euphrates rivers, are a stirring setting for the action about to take place. The fortunes of the Jews are thus seen in an international context, and in the company of the major nations of the world. This "global" focus was also known to the prophets (e.g., Amos and Isaiah), but here the nations are not simply condemned from afar; rather, they become characters in a drama, much as Nineveh and Assyria do in Jonah. Throughout Judith, some of the geographical sites are unknown, some anachronistic (such as Persia, which only arose as a world power a century after the Assyrians had been defeated), some simply located incorrectly. The technique of piling up the list of nations is similar to the description of the court festivities in Esther 1; so also is the sweep of lands, seemingly from one end of the world to the other, which Esth 1:1 accomplishes in one short clause.

1:7-10. Nebuchadnezzar's power and reach are awe inspiring; the progress of his messengers moves methodically from east to west, ultimately passing through the region of Judea to Egypt, as far as Ethiopia. Most of the geographical entities are well-known, well-established areas of the major nations. The author is clearly trying to convey the sense of doom as the shadow of Nebuchadnezzar's might moves over the land (cf. the image of Assyria as a great world tree in Ezek 31:2-9 and the use of the tree or vine overshadowing the earth in Herodotus).[46] Since in the reader's mind Nebuchadnezzar would be associated with Babylon, it is also relevant to note a Babylonian inscription that may have influenced Daniel 4: "Under Babylon's everlasting shadow, I have gathered all the peoples in peace." Judith does not use a tree metaphor here, but the sense of a shadow across the land, whether understood negatively or positively, is similar in the different passages, and the idea of eastern empires would have conjured such notions.

Samaria and Jerusalem are mentioned only in passing here, a small part of the blur of nations that are being encompassed. This is quite deliberate, as the "real" geographical focus of the narrative, Jerusalem, is intentionally submerged in the list of nations, creating the illusion that *world* history is at stake, which will, as the story proceeds, become more narrowly focused on the area of Syria-Palestine, then on Judea and Samaria, then on Bethulia as the gateway to Judea, then on one woman from the village of Bethulia. "Samaria" was the name given to Israel, the northern half of Israel/Judah, when it became a province under the Assyrians, Babylonians, Persians, and Greeks. The names of the regions of Samaria and Judea reflect the political realities of the post-exilic period, when the former was the name of the province occupying the land that was once northern Israel, and the latter the area of the older southern kingdom of Judah, the temple-state governed from Jerusalem. It will be quite revealing to follow the disappearance of these two real-world terms and their replacement by the more idealized "Israel" for both

---

46. Herodotus *Histories* 1.108; 7.19.

of these areas, implying a united Israel (see Commentary on 4:1-15). The use of "Israel" as the ideal term for the region is not unusual, but it is carried through more systematically and creatively in Judith than is usually the case elsewhere.

1:11-12. The nations, like Arphaxad, have underestimated Nebuchadnezzar. He was, of course, considered by the author of Judith to be a mere mortal, but still no ordinary man—he is the arch adversary and should be neither underestimated nor overestimated. The nations shame him by snubbing his messengers. Nebuchadnezzar's rage is based not only on a desire for world domination, but also on a desire for revenge. The dramatic tension is thus also increased, as negotiation or coexistence—short of complete capitulation—is becoming less likely.

Part of the important cultural background of the book of Judith is the ancient Mediterranean concept of honor and shame. In ancient cultures, honor and shame were important and very public aspects of a person's or a nation's standing, quite different from our modern, more internalized values of self-esteem (positive) and guilt (negative). Symbols of honor and shame and ritual ways of honoring or shaming another person are interwoven into the biblical texts, but modern readers are apt to disregard these elements as mere externals.[47] Honor and shame are certainly at issue here and will be a constant in this book (2:14; 4:12; 5:21; 8:22-23; 9:2). Judith, for example, will not just kill Holofernes, but will reverse his threat of shame upon him and the Assyrians. Interestingly, the list of nations whose lot has been combined with Judea's includes the Ammonites and the Moabites, nations with a very checkered history of involvement with Israel and Judah, raising the question for the next segment of the story: Will these peoples remain practical allies, or will some reveal their past nature and go over to the side of the enemy? They reappear in the narrative at 5:2.

1:13-16. The "seventeenth year" probably evokes the career of the historical Nebuchadnezzar of Babylon, who was known to have captured Jerusalem in the eighteenth year of his reign (Jer 32:1). The reader would thus imagine that this Nebuchadnezzar had cleared the way to move toward Jerusalem in the following year. Nebuchadnezzar runs Arphaxad through in the mountains of Rages, much as Alexander the Great had forced Darius of Persia to retreat from Ecbatana and flee into the mountains. The great city of Ecbatana is destroyed, but as noted above, it is also shamed. The greatness of Arphaxad and Ecbatana were described above, but Nebuchadnezzar has here easily defeated him without the help of those nations he invited to ally with him. The might of Nebuchadnezzar is thus even more dramatically demonstrated.

The feasting is an appropriate way to bring chap. 1 to a close. The action has moved very swiftly and with much slaughter; the feasting allows a temporary lull as the reader makes a transition to the next major movement of the story. There will be other such rests to allow for transitions to new movements in the story (see Commentary on 2:28).

---

47. D. D. Gilmore, ed., *Honor and Shame and the Unity of the Mediterranean* (Washington, D.C.: American Anthropological Association, 1987); Timothy S. Laniak, *Shame and Honor in the Book of Esther* (Atlanta: Scholars Press, 1998).

Judith 2:1-13, Nebuchadnezzar Commissions Holofernes to Destroy the Nations Who Did Not Ally with Him

COMMENTARY

The menace that is threatening in chap. 1 is made explicit here: Nebuchadnezzar announces his designs on "the whole region," a phrase used eight times in the first two chapters.[48] The summoning of all of Nebuchadnezzar's ministers and nobles, and the decision that everyone who had not obeyed his command should be destroyed are similar to certain parts of Daniel 1–6 (cf. esp. Dan 2:2-5; 3:2-9; 6:6-8). In the case of Daniel 1–4, it is also Nebuchadnezzar who is

---

48. Moore, *Judith*, 127.

the offending king. Daniel was evidently one of the influences on the book of Judith (see Introduction). Regarding Nebuchadnezzar's second-in-command, Holofernes, there is also a likely historical origin for the name that is here used in a very unhistorical way. When Artaxerxes III Ochus of Persia invaded Asia Minor and Egypt, including Judea, in 350 and 343 BCE, his general was named Holofernes, who in turn had an officer named Bagoas, which is the name of Holofernes' officer in Jdt 12:11. These names, probably known from this campaign of Artaxerxes III, were used for the officers of this invading army.

Another indication that we are not in the realm of history but in that of imaginative literature is the repeated characterization of Nebuchadnezzar as "lord." This motif is introduced here for the first time, but will be built on later in the narrative until it takes on ironic and even comic dimensions in chaps. 11–13. The word "lord" in Greek, κύριος (*kyrios*), would have multiple uses, always denoting the clear superior in a hierarchical relation—for example, ruler as opposed to subject, master as opposed to slave, husband as opposed to wife, or in the case of gods, "lord of heaven," and so on. As such, it was adopted by Greek-speaking Jews as the standard word to translate the divine name YHWH. Thus in Judith we find the intentional double meaning of "lord" as God and "lord" as earthly superior. Only the arrogant and deluded Holofernes will mistake Judith's references to the divine Lord for references to himself and Nebuchadnezzar as earthly lords. Whenever the word appears, there is usually an ironic wink to the audience concerning this double meaning. Other language associated with God is then also used to extend this characterization of Nebuchadnezzar's divine self-concept. With this in mind, we can detect a string of Jewish divine terms applied by Nebuchadnezzar to himself: "Thus says the Great King, the lord of the whole earth. . . . For as I live, and by the power of my kingdom. . . . Take care not to transgress any of your lord's commands." The divine pretensions of Nebuchadnezzar are here not stated explicitly—he does not require worship as a god, even though Holofernes will require this for him at 3:8. However, to the Jewish audience his words here will reverberate as sentences associated with God. Further, Nebuchadnezzar's statement (v. 12) that he will accomplish this by his own hand sets up a contrast with Judith's later statement that God will deliver the Jews through her hand (8:33; 12:4). Although, strictly speaking, it is Holofernes who takes on the traits of the blustery tyrant, demanding worship for Nebuchadnezzar as a god, the tradition of Nebuchadnezzar in Daniel would probably have made this association automatic.

Dialogues such as this also point to one of the important patterns of the work: the structural opposition between the protagonists and the antagonists (see the Introduction). Just as Holofernes is a servant of Nebuchadnezzar, and will demand worship of him as a god, so also Judith is a servant of God, and demands proper worship of God by the Bethulians.[49] This set of contrasting correspondences will be extended further when we see that Holofernes has a faithful attendant in Bagoas, and Judith in her unnamed maid.

A number of images of Nebuchadnezzar's threatened campaign would have resonances for the audience. According to Herodotus,[50] earth and water were Persian symbols of surrender and humility.[51] The hyperbole of the rhetoric concerning the number of troops is typical of the Assyrians' boasting in Judith; but interestingly, according to the author the reality is said to match their rhetoric, for the images of how many troops they marshal into the field is often enormous. In 2:19-20, it is said that even those who accompanied the troops were like a "swarm of locusts, like the dust of the earth—a multitude that could not be counted." The threatened deportation would remind the readers of both the Assyrian deportation when the north was defeated by Sargon II in 721 BCE and the deportations by Nebuchadnezzar of Babylon in 597 and 587 BCE that gave rise to the exile. The divine language associated with Nebuchadnezzar and his harsh rhetoric here would also call to mind for the reader the language of God's covenant in Deuteronomy. In chaps. 5, 8, and 9, Achior and Judith articulate the basic

---

49. Craven, *Artistry and Faith in the Book of Judith*, 53-59. According to W. D. Davies and Dale Allison, *The Gospel According to Saint Matthew*, ICC, 3 vols. (Edinburgh: T. & T. Clark, 1988–97) 1:193, Matthew 1–2 poses an analogous question, "Who is king, Herod or Jesus?"
50. Herodotus *Histories* 6.48.2.
51. Moore, *Judith*, 133.

premises of deuteronomic theology, which holds that if Israel obeys God's commands, it will prosper; if it disobeys God's commands, it will suffer. Here Nebuchadnezzar presents a worldly version of that theology, in which he arrogates to himself the prerogatives of God. The message that Nebuchadnezzar had sent ahead was accepted by some, rejected by most. Now he has a new message for those who rejected an alliance with him; in vv. 10-11 those who yield will be held "until the day of their punishment"—an almost eschatological sense of his judgment on the nations. Those who resist will be slaughtered and plundered. Nebuchadnezzar's final words to Holofernes that he should obey his lord's commands also sound somewhat like God's words to Moses in Deut 6:1-3.

REFLECTIONS

The book of Judith challenges the modern reader's notion of what constitutes "biblical literature." Concerning its genre, Morton S. Enslin said, "The story of Judith is an example of Jewish fiction at its best."[52] But even those people who grant that not every part of the Bible is historically accurate may have difficulty allowing for deliberate *fiction* in the Bible. The book of Judith is written in the style of history—its opening mimics the introduction of historical epochs in the biblical history books—and yet it immediately turns history on its head by introducing the chief antagonist as "Nebuchadnezzar who ruled over the Assyrians."

Are there other fictions in the Bible? Is Tobit or Esther a fiction? Do even the Gospels and the book of Acts bear a distant relationship to the Jewish novels and the Greek and Roman novels? We are left to our own inferences about how the different texts might have been read, but whereas the Gospels and Acts were never seen as fictions, some of the texts that share similar literary techniques probably were: for example, Susanna, Esther, Judith, and Tobit. They were probably written and read as edifying entertainments and only later included as part of the canonical literature of Jews (in the case of Esther) and Christians (in regard to all four texts), and accepted as sacred history. The significance of the texts must be judged from a number of different perspectives, including that of the imaginative symbolism that underlies such writings as Job, Jonah, Esther, the parables of Jesus, and Judith.

There seems to have been in the ancient world a less clear, or at least a less explicit, distinction between history and fiction. In the Hebrew Bible the journalistic notion of objectivity was not the criterion for judging truthfulness, but rather, the overall claim of the text on one's belief system. Plato has been credited with introducing the idea into Western thought that true statements are ones that correspond to the world.[53] But with this notion in Jewish, Greek, and Latin literature came the idea that seemingly realistic narrative could be written—what looked like a history or a biography—that was yet intentionally an invented world, a story of "what if."

Connected with the category of fiction, both in the ancient world and in our own, is the category of entertainment, and here, too, Judith may challenge typical ideas of what is appropriate to a "biblical" text. The description of events in Judith, as noted in the Introduction, is often almost cinematic and is paced so as to create tension and excitement. The pleasure in reading is not unique to Judith; it is a part of the appreciation of most of the books of the Bible. Yet Judith seems to accentuate the entertaining aspects of storytelling and to deemphasize the larger theological themes.

The modern reader's reactions to this emphasis on entertainment over theology might run along two lines. First, is this sort of literature appropriate for inclusion in

---

52. Morton S. Enslin and Solomon Zeitlin, *The Book of Judith*, JAL VIII (Leiden: Brill, 1972) 38.
53. Northrop Frye, *The Secular Scripture* (Cambridge, Mass.: Harvard University Press, 1976) 17-20.

the Bible? Second, even if it is appropriate, does it communicate a theological message that can speak to readers and worshipers in the twenty-first century? The answer to the first question might simply be that the wide variety of literary genres in the Bible, most of which are imaginative and not strictly historical, argues for a broad view of what is "appropriate." Paradox, irony, satire, sarcasm, parable, humor, myth—these types of discourse are also in the Bible, and they often create unreal worlds as a means of communicating unusual experiences. The answer to the second question is perhaps more difficult. Does Judith retain any theological significance for modern readers if it is understood as a fictitious work of literature? At the time of its composition, as well as today, the application of Judith does not lie in its journalistic account of a military campaign, but in the values it communicates to its readers. Truth for this text, as in Esther and Tobit, lies not in the facts of history, but in the creation of community and the inculcation of values. What is clearest in this invented world is ethnic and religious identity and—more explicitly than in Esther—reverence and trust in God and a model for the penitential theology and spirituality of the community.

JUDITH 2:14–7:32, HOLOFERNES' CAMPAIGN NARROWS TO A SIEGE OF BETHULIA

OVERVIEW

Although the first chapter demonstrated the power of these two great nations, it is only in the chapters that follow that it becomes clear what the threat is for Judea and Israel. Holofernes' campaign will take up the next six chapters. It is an account that includes military campaigns, theological discussions, and intrigues of shifting loyalties. Although often deprecated in relation to chaps. 8–16, many significant themes are raised and important plot developments introduced. The narrative moves methodically from the broadest possible perspective to a focus on the nations to the west (including Judea and Samaria). Then, as the vast armies move inexorably toward the Mediterranean, the focus narrows once again to the area north of Jerusalem, and then to the tiny mountain village of Bethulia, which overlooks a pass through the mountains that the Assyrians will have to take to reach Jerusalem and beyond. The first part of the book of Judith will conclude with the Bethulians' being besieged and in despair, fainting from thirst.

As noted in the Introduction, there are structural parallels and oppositions in the first part of Judith that can be summarized thus:

A Campaign against disobedient nations; the people surrender (2:14–3:10)
  B Israel is "greatly terrified"; Joakim prepares for war (4:1-15)
    C Holofernes talks with Achior; Achior is expelled (5:1–6:13)
    C´ Achior is received in Bethulia; Achior talks with the people (6:14-21)
  B´ Holofernes prepares for war; Israel is "greatly terrified" (7:1-5)
A´ Campaign against Bethulia; the people want to surrender (7:6-32)[54]

This chiastic pattern (i.e., like a Greek *chi*, or X, which crosses and reverses itself; the last items are like the first, but in the opposite order) gives a satisfying structure to the first part that ties together the worldwide military drama and the tribulation of the people of tiny Bethulia. (Since some of these passages are only a few verses, they are subsumed under larger sections in the commentary that follows.) At the center of this chiasm is the long dialogue between Holofernes and Achior, in

54. Craven, *Artistry and Faith in the Book of Judith*, 60-63.

which Achior reveals himself to be an eloquent spokesman for Judaism and the most heroic figure of this half of the book. Achior is literally and figuratively at the center of the first part of Judith. Craven also points out that at the center of this chiasm, in the dialogue between Holofernes and Achior, lies the central question of the narrative, "What god is there except Nebuchadnezzar?"[55] It is not until the center of the chiasm in the second part, when Judith overcomes Holofernes (10:11–13:10a), that this question is given a resounding answer.

55. Craven, *Artistry and Faith in the Book of Judith*, 60-63.

Judith 2:14-28, Campaign Initiated Against Disobedient Nations

COMMENTARY

2:14-20. Holofernes' campaign is not told with a historian's eye for strategy and detail, but with a storyteller's ear for image and emotion. The lists of officers, soldiers, and livestock are intended to convey the enormousness of the armies, culminating in images that seem almost cinematic ("like a swarm of locusts, like the dust of the earth"). Alonso-Schökel notes this aspect of the author's descriptive ability, and Hägg sees this same quality in the Greek novel.[56] Further, when the author says that Holofernes' army was organized "as a great army is marshaled for a campaign," he seems to signal a humorous and ironic tone, as if to say, "this fiction is just like the real thing." The suspicion that there is a humorous tone here is partially confirmed in the next verse, where we learn of the auxiliary animals and provisions. Whenever the troops are described, there is always a barely restrained excess or comic hyperbole of the auxiliary peoples, animals, or baggage (2:20; 7:2, 18). The Assyrian auxiliary crowds are also referred to as a "mixed crowd," a sarcastic epithet that may reflect the policy of the Hasmoneans to purify the religion, and therefore the peoples, of the land of Israel (see Introduction), which Judith herself seems to echo in 8:18. It is possible that the descriptions are also modeled on the stories of Israel's deliverers in the book of Judges. In the cycle of stories about Gideon (Judges 6–8), the Midianites and the Amalekites are mighty nations oppressing Israel from the east: "For they and their livestock would come up, and they would even bring their tents, as thick as locusts; neither they nor their camels could be counted; so they wasted the land as they came in" (Judg 6:5 NRSV). However, this description of the livestock and tents has a definite role in Judges 6, and the devastation of the livestock is like that of locusts; in Judith the role of these images does not make as much sense on the realistic level but is exaggerated and repeated, probably for comic effect. Aside from this literary effect, one may wonder if the size of the Assyrian army is to be contrasted to what in the author's time was the proud tradition of the Maccabees, who had fought a guerrilla campaign using small bands of troops against the vast armies of the Seleucid kings. The Maccabees, it is also to be noted, between sorties hid in the mountains like those near Judith's village.

2:21-27. The hyperbolic description of troops, auxiliary personnel, and provisions just mentioned is also matched by the excessive detail of the geographical movements. The campaign that has been promised is now realized with destructive force. Many nations and peoples are defeated, and the cruelty of Holofernes is depicted as well. The description of the campaign builds in intensity from v. 14 to v. 27, as it moves from the gathering of officials and soldiers, animals and equipment, to the movements of the campaign and a first mention of plundering (v. 23), to wholesale slaughter and destruction (v. 27). Every conceivable kind of destruction is listed as a drumbeat to increase the sense of a plague of locusts upon the land, as v. 20

56. Alonso-Schökel, *Narrative Structures in the Book of Judith*, 7; Tomas Hägg, *The Novel in Antiquity* (Berkeley: University of California Press, 1983) 55-56.

suggested. The slaughter and plundering carried out by Nebuchadnezzar is in itself not out of line with the policy of holy war in the ancient Near East, which was adapted in some traditions in Israel (especially in Deut 7:1-2; 20:1-20, although it is not clear that this command was ever carried out as such). It is not even clear that Judith is opposed to this principle (see Commentary on 5:14-16 for Achior's account of the destruction caused by Israel's conquest). Here, however, the specter of the ancient Near Eastern holy war is bearing down upon the land of Judea.

The author uses good storytelling technique in describing the campaigns, providing details and magnifying the size of the armies gathered. In terms of the author's perspective, it is "from the bottom looking up"—that is, the proud but small kingdom of Judea looking up at the magnitude of the great worldwide empires. If one compares the fifth-century BCE Greek historian Herodotus on the military movements of the Eastern empires, one finds a much more equal perspective, even though the Persian armies were much larger than the Greek. Herodotus communicates the perspective of one who fundamentally believes that the Greeks were a world-class empire; the book of Judith is written from the perspective that the Jews were in danger of being swept under a rug. Perhaps midway between the "bottom-up" perspective of Judith and the "equal perspective" of Herodotus is the adventurous tone of the *Alexander Romance*, a historical novel written in Egypt in about 200 BCE that gives a similar list of known and unknown nations allied against Egypt and communicates a similar sense of foreboding: "It is not just one nation that is advancing upon us but millions of people. Advancing on us are Indians, Nokimaians, Oxydrakai, Iberians, Kauchones, Lelapes, Bosporoi, Bastranoi, Azanoi, Chalybes, and all the other great nations of the East, armies of innumerable warriors advancing against Egypt."[57] In addition to the obvious similarity with Judith, this passage is interesting because it also depicts the same invasion of the west that likely influenced Judith's account, that of the Persian king Artaxerxes III Ochus, whose general and eunuch were named Holofernes and Bagoas respectively (see Introduction and Commentary on 2:1-13).

2:28. While "fear and dread" fall on the people here, in 15:2 Judith will cause "dread and fear" to fall on the Assyrians.[58] In the tradition of the exodus (Exod 15:15-16) and in Rahab's recounting of it (Josh 2:9), the nations tremble in fear at God's mighty acts. After the pounding crescendo of the previous verses, the author astutely inserts a pause, comparable to the pauses at 1:16; 3:10; 6:21; and 7:32. The effect of the description, whether intended or not, is to make the situation of these non-Israelite cities as sympathetic as those of Israel. We almost forget as the story progresses—or the author would like us to forget—that not only is Judith saving her village or Israel as a whole, but also she is saving that part of the world that has not already been destroyed by Holofernes. Holofernes' campaign is truly a scourge upon the land, and it has the potential to create a sort of kinship of oppressed peoples. However, whatever kinship is created seems to evaporate when some of the peoples of the region quickly surrender and become allies of Holofernes. The list of seven cities is intriguing. Moore notes that seven is a number signifying completeness in biblical literature, and perhaps the number is more significant than the names of the cities.[59] Five of the cities were famous and known well to Judeans: Sidon and Tyre (Matt 15:31; Acts 21:3-4; 27:3), Jamnia (1 Macc 4:15; 5:58), Azotus or Ashdod (Josh 13:3; 1 Macc 4:15), and Ascalon or Ashkelon (1 Macc 10:86); Sur and Ocina are unknown. The known cities would have been important centers of competition with Judea. When John Hyrcanus I (134–104 BCE) expanded his kingdom, Azotus and Jamnia came under Hasmonean control, while Sidon, Tyre, and Ascalon remained independent. Moore also raises, but wisely dismisses, the theory that since Gaza is missing from the list, Judith must have been written after Alexander Janneus destroyed the city in 96 BCE. The evidence of the text simply cannot be pressed to such a specific conclusion. (See Reflections at 3:1-10.)

---

57. *Alexander Romance* 1:2.
58. Craven, *Artistry and Faith in the Book of Judith*, 54.
59. Moore, *Judith*, 139-41.

Judith 3:1-10, The People of the Seacoast Surrender

COMMENTARY

3:1-4. There is a stark contrast between the former haughtiness and smugness of the peoples of the seacoast toward Nebuchadnezzar's messengers in 1:11 and their abject and total surrender here. There they underestimated him as "only one man"; here they overestimate him and prostrate themselves before his power, almost as if he were a god (v. 8). There is clearly a fearful and emotional response to the destruction they have witnessed; all of the categories of property that the peoples of the coast are willing to surrender to Nebuchadnezzar in v. 3 were mentioned in 2:24-27 as part of Nebuchadnezzar's path of destruction. (It is a part of this storyteller's technique to describe events by listing categories.) There is also a contrast between their immediate capitulation and the reaction of the Israelites in chaps. 4 and 7. Although the latter do not stand up to Judith's tough standards (8:9-27), they are still a good deal more resilient than the peoples of the coast. It was the common practice in the ancient Near East to deport and relocate conquered peoples and in the Greco-Roman world to enslave them (although neither practice would rule out the other). Much of Greek language of resistance to foreign monarchs was based on the notion of freedom versus slavery; nations should fight to the death to avoid enslavement to foreign nations just as individual citizens should do as well.[60] One of the accompanying elements of the war between Greece and Persia was the desire to liberate Greek colonies in Asia Minor from enslavement to Persian rule. Aesop presents a fable of the two roads presented to people: the rough, thorny, and dangerous path that leads to freedom and the smooth, level, pleasant path that leads to slavery.[61] Thus the book of Judith dramatizes the Greco-Roman notion of freedom in addition to the biblical tradition of national independence through loyalty to God as found in Isa 10:24-27; 30:1-7.

3:5-8. Surprisingly, when Holofernes does arrive in the seacoast towns, his is a bloodless takeover. He garrisons troops in the cities, and the inhabitants welcome him enthusiastically with the same festivities—garlands and dances with tambourines—that will be used in the Bethulians' victory celebration in 15:12-13. Some invading armies in the ancient world were greeted as liberators, as was Cyrus of Persia (see Isa 45:1-8); but after chap. 2, the mild actions of Holofernes and the positive reactions of the cities are most unexpected. Holofernes' only destruction mentioned for these cities is in regard to religious institutions: He destroys the shrines and sacred groves. Ironically, according to Judith herself (8:18-20), this is precisely what the Israelites have done in their own nation, and this is what the later Hasmonean kings also do in converting people by force and destroying the Samaritan temple on Mt. Gerizim. For the coastal cities, however, it appears to be a sort of deal with the devil: the loss of their religious freedom in exchange for peace with Holofernes. These were the terms that the early Maccabees faced when they chose to fight. Presumably, we are to see a lack of moral fiber in these people of the coast, neighbors of Israel. They have taken the easy road to slavery rather than the challenging road to freedom.

Holofernes institutes a policy of destroying the shrines and sacred groves of the conquered peoples, presumably to show that the Jerusalem Temple will be destroyed as well. "Sacred groves" probably refers to the somewhat vague references in the HB to the wooden poles used in the worship of the goddess Asherah. They were destroyed in various reforms in an attempt to centralize worship in Jerusalem (1 Kgs 14:15; 2 Kgs 18:4). Greek sacred groves are probably not intended. Daniel 3 also presents an imaginative story in which Nebuchadnezzar requires worship of a golden statue, and in Daniel 6 an edict is passed that no one may pray to anyone, human or divine, except King Darius. Language used in the Daniel stories, especially Daniel 3, has evidently influenced the author here, for not only is there a requirement of

---
60. Orlando Patterson, *Freedom* (New York: Basic Books, 1992).
61. *Life of Aesop* 94.

exclusive veneration involving Nebuchadnezzar, but also in both texts the various peoples and languages of the land are emphasized (see Dan 4:1). However, whereas Daniel dramatizes the requirement—or at least the attraction—of worshiping foreign gods in foreign lands, it says nothing of the destruction by Nebuchadnezzar of other cult centers on principle.

3:9-10. When Holofernes finally reaches Judea—once again, the name of Judea is submerged in the list until the very end, and mentioned as if an afterthought—there is another pause in the action for rest and to collect bounty. This prepares the audience for the next transition in the narrative. Although many geographical names in Judith are unknown or appear to be mentioned incorrectly, many others, especially as we move closer to Jerusalem, are known and descriptive for the account. The plain of Esdraelon (the Greek form of "Jezreel") lies between the hills of Galilee to the north and those of Samaria and Judea to the south. It is thus a good resting place for the expeditionary forces. Gaba lay on the western end of the plain near the Mediterranean, and Scythopolis on the eastern, near the Jordan River. Dothan was near the plain to the south. Holofernes would thus have been poised about forty miles north of Jerusalem, awaiting the proper moment to take the mountain passes and proceed on his course. This would also place Holofernes very near the spot where Jael had slain Sisera, the closest biblical model for the actions of Judith.[62]

62. Enslin and Zeitlin, *The Book of Judith*, 77.

REFLECTIONS

Ernst Haag argued that Judith is a parabolic narrative, that it is not intended to be a real history, but a story that stands for another truth: the workings of God and Israel.[63] In his view, Nebuchadnezzar becomes a transhistorical figure who stands for those who would oppose Israel. But there is more to this symbol as well. In Judith, and to a lesser extent in Daniel, Nebuchadnezzar represents worldly power run amok. Worldly power, whether in Judith's day or our own, becomes reduced to the ego of the tyrant if it is unchecked by broader religious or ethical concerns. And at a time when the dominant nations were coming from the west and not the east, Nebuchadnezzar could also stand for the power and attraction of the Hellenistic culture that threatened to transform the texture of religious life. After all, the peoples of the seacoast had capitulated willingly and welcomed the Assyrians with dance. Although Nebuchadnezzar may appear one-dimensional, he is all-encompassing enough to allow us to see in him all the forces that oppose a faith in God, whether religious, worldly, or emanating from within the concerns and desires of our everyday life. Nebuchadnezzar is not Satan—for that one would have to look elsewhere in the Bible and not in Judith. But Nebuchadnezzar is the titanic force of the world that can overwhelm those who are unprepared.

Craven shows that in this text Nebuchadnezzar is also characterized through his relationship with Holofernes; they are in a lord/servant relationship that mirrors that of God and Judith.[64] In Nebuchadnezzar and Holofernes, we find a pair of personalities who model worldly power for the reader. Nebuchadnezzar is, first of all, a powerful king who is victorious in great battles, but he is also a vengeful despot who tries to destroy every country that spurned his invitation to an alliance. This can be seen as the outward manifestation of a powerful world leader. But it is in Holofernes' treatment of his king that we begin to see the psychological seductions of power as well. Holofernes not only vanquishes nations and secures their loyalty for his king, but he also violently removes all their forms of worship and requires them to worship his lord, Nebuchadnezzar (3:8).

63. Ernst Haag, *Studien zum Buch Judith: Seine theologische Bedeutung und literarisches Eigenart* (Trier: Paulinus, 1963).
64. Craven, *Artistry and Faith in the Book of Judith*, 109.

The story suggests that such monstrous egos as that of Nebuchadnezzar seem to find their Holoferneses, people who will crush others to enlarge the stature of those whom they admire. Nebuchadnezzar only gave orders to defeat the rebellious nations (2:4-13), but Holofernes finds it necessary to demand that Nebuchadnezzar alone be worshiped as a god. He seems to need it more than Nebuchadnezzar does. Thus Nebuchadnezzar becomes a distant tyrant, but Holofernes is the willing mouthpiece of the king's interests. In this we find a fascinating insight into the pyramid of power relationships and perceive that unhealthy, unbalanced, ungrounded leaders will readily find servants who have no identity without them. "What god is there except Nebuchadnezzar?" asks Holofernes (6:2). Nebuchadnezzar is "lord of the whole earth." As Craven notes, the book of Judith counters this claim with the argument that God is the lord of the whole earth, and God can prove it by the hand of a single woman.[65]

Further, in contrast to the Assyrian pyramid of power relationships, the model of balanced, functional relationships—relationships that are grounded in the worship of God—is found among the Israelites. The community's coming together in prayer at a time of crisis is what is portrayed in 4:6-15, and it is this demonstration that receives God's response. This community will endure and not capitulate as the peoples of the seacoast did. The parable, then, that Haag sees in Judith is a parable for our day as well. It is a parable about power, about the contrasting models of worldly power and divine power, and about the psychological relationships that follow from each model: a dysfunctional model of the veneration of false gods and the functional model of a community turning to God in a period of crisis.

65. Craven, *Artistry and Faith in the Book of Judith*, 109.

Judith 4:1-15, Israel Prays and Prepares for War

COMMENTARY

4:1-5. Now the "Israelites," or more specifically the "Israelites living in Judea," are mentioned for the first time. However, the word of Holofernes' conquests also goes out to "every district of Samaria" (v. 4). The term "Israelites" in the narrow sense applied to inhabitants of the north who were conquered by the Assyrians in 721 BCE, although the term also communicates the ideal self-image of both Jews and Samarians (see Matt 10:6; John 1:31, 47; 2 Cor 11:22; Phil 3:5). Samaria was the resettled capital and the province of the old northern kingdom; the mixed ethnic and religious makeup of that region was a source of friction with the Jews of Jerusalem, and this friction had boiled over into conflicts on a number of occasions (see Ezra 4; Nehemiah 4; and Commentary on 1:7-10). John Hyrcanus I, who ruled Jerusalem from 135 to 104 BCE, finally subdued Samaria and destroyed the Samaritan temple on Mt. Gerizim. This did not end hostilities between Jews and Samaritans, as the NT indicates (Luke 10:29-37; 17:11-19; John 4:9), but it did place control of Samaria in Jewish hands. Unlike the other cities of the region, the Samaritan cities and Judea do not seek terms of peace, but brace for war. It is, indeed, surprising that Samaria is portrayed so positively, essentially in alliance with Judea. It is possible, as Moore suggests, that the positive view of Samaria indicates that Judith was written after Samaria was annexed, rather than before when tensions might have been high.[66] Other scholars have argued that the annexation would hardly improve relations, but only pacify the resistance; but the author probably romanticized the notion of a united "Israel," as David and Solomon had constituted it, and this common cause of Samaria and Judea reflects that. The book of Judith may represent a fictionalized and romanticized vision of what John Hyrcanus enforced

66. Moore, *Judith*, 67-70.

by the sword. Despite the ambiguity of the geographical term "Israel," from this point on it will dominate as the common designation for the defenders of Bethulia and Jerusalem.

In the parenthesis of v. 3 it is explained that the people of Judea "had only recently returned from the exile" and rededicated their Temple with the returned vessels, an event that occurred two hundred years after the fall of the north to Assyria. We have seen such inaccuracies before, and once again it appears to be a deliberate merging of two separate historical epochs. One may wonder why v. 3 was added, since it calls attention to the historical problems and hardly adds information necessary for the reader's understanding of the narrative. Regardless of how clumsy it seems, it has been taken as evidence for a Persian-era dating for Judith, since it states that the Israelites had only *recently* returned. However, it is probably not a direct reference to the return from the Babylonian exile, but reverberates with the experience of the audience, who, after the Maccabean revolt, had also only recently rededicated the Temple. (Note especially the reference to "the sacred vessels and the altar and the temple which had been consecrated after their profanation"; see also 1 Macc 4:36-61; 2 Macc 10:1-8.)

Judith, as the widow who is an unexpected heroine of faith, is often compared to the widow and her seven sons who are martyred in 2 Maccabees 7, but there is a further important parallel with 2 Maccabees that comes out at this point: the connection to "temple propaganda."[67] In different ways, the novel Judith and the novelistic history 2 Maccabees keep the Temple and its sanctity in sight in the narrative at all times. Although the action for most of the remainder of the book will take place near Judith's village of Bethulia, Jerusalem is constantly in mind; in fact, the author and the original audience may have been in that city. (This argues against the hidden Samaritan origin of Judith that some scholars have suggested, despite the references that might point in that direction.) Both Judith and 2 Maccabees dramatize a struggle over the Temple that God watches over, even though God intervenes directly only in 2 Maccabees. In the Introduction it was noted that there is irony concerning miracles in such texts: The novels generally lack the miraculous intervention of God or depict only minor miracles, as at Add. Esth 15:8, while the novelistic histories often contain quite dramatic miracles.

4:6. Once again, a historical name, "Joakim," is probably pressed into service inaccurately. A high priest named Joakim is mentioned in Neh 12:26, but he would not have had the broad powers over political and military affairs that this Joakim possesses.[68] In the days of the Davidic monarchy, the king and the high priest had always coexisted. After the exile, Judah/Judea was officially a province of the Persian and then successively of two of the Greek empires, the Ptolemaic and the Seleucid. Once again, a governor and a high priest coexisted in the administration of the Temple and the province. When the Maccabees achieved a victory in dealing with the Seleucid rulers in 165 BCE, they did not immediately establish a separate kingdom, but rather an independently governed province of the Seleucid Empire. One of the Maccabee brothers, Jonathan, took on the office of high priest in 152, and this became the basis of Hasmonean politics thereafter.[69] Simon, his brother and successor, finally declared full independence from the Seleucids in 141 BCE and took on two other titles, *ethnarchēs* (ἐθνάρχης, "leader of the people") and *stratēgos* (στρατήγος, "general of the army"). His impressive coronation as high priest is recounted in 1 Maccabees 14, along with a hymn praising his accomplishments. Like Judith, he is described as a deliverer of Israel on the model of the judges (see the Introduction on parallels between Judith and Deborah). Following Simon, John Hyrcanus I was also named high priest, leader of the people, and general. The broad powers of Joakim thus match those of the Hasmonean high priests from Jonathan to John Hyrcanus (152–104 BCE).

Judith's village, Bethulia, is named for the first time in this verse. The site is unknown and probably fictitious, but it is clearly in Samaritan territory.[70] Lest it be inferred,

---

67. Robert Doran, *Temple Propaganda: The Purpose and Character of 2 Maccabees* (Washington, D.C.: Catholic Biblical Association, 1981).
68. Moore, *Judith*, 150.
69. Levine, "The Age of Hellenism," 185-87.
70. Moore, *Judith*, 69.

however, that this text retains a hidden allegiance to Samaritans, the Jerusalem Temple and the high priest are strongly emphasized at vv. 3-8. It is more likely that the desire to re-create a romanticized vision of the united Israel of David and Solomon motivates the author.

4:7. As noted regarding 3:9-10, Holofernes' army is resting in the plain of Esdraelon, facing the mountains of Samaria as the only obstacle to their southern advance. Joakim's orders to fortify the passes are thus good strategy, although it may seem a hopeless gesture. The narrowness of the passes, only wide enough for two to pass at a time, does not imply that Holofernes' invading armies can be held back, but that Holofernes has no choice but to take the passes first to ensure that his vast armies can be moved through the mountains.

4:8-11. Joakim wrote letters to all "Israelites" to pray and fast, much as Esther in time of danger gives a directive to all the Jews living in Susa to pray and fast as well (Esth 4:16). Interestingly, in Esther, Jerusalem and Judea are never mentioned. In Judith, Jerusalem is the center for the community, and diaspora Jews are never mentioned. Sackcloth and ashes were ritual signs of mourning in ancient Israel, but they were also signs of penitence or protest (Esth 4:1-2; 2 Macc 3:19).[71] The penitential theology assumed in v. 9 reflects an important development in post-exilic Judaism that culminates in early Christian asceticism. The pattern of sin/punishment/repentance/salvation found in Deuteronomy 28–32 gives rise to the inclusion of penitential prayers in post-exilic texts (Nehemiah 9; Dan 9:4-19; Bar 1:1-3).[72] Although the only fast required by Jewish law in the HB is the one-day fast on the Day of Atonement (Lev 16:29-30), fasting was evidently an integral part of the post-exilic penitential theology, where it is also sometimes associated with sackcloth and ashes (Neh 1:4; 9:1; Dan 9:3). It may have arisen originally as a response to the destruction and the exile (Zech 7:3-5).

The public scene of wailing and tribulation is very similar to other passages from this period, such as 2 Macc 3:14-21 and 3 Macc 1:16-21. These scenes are almost interchangeable, but Judith does emphasize the sackcloth and ashes more (cf. 2 Macc 3:19 and 3 Macc 1:18 in this regard), while 2 and 3 Maccabees emphasize more the public consternation. That they "humbled themselves" is also part of the religious experience of the penitential theology. Humility is not considered a positive virtue in Greek thought; it is understood as a negative idea of humiliation or shame in the continuum of honor and shame. In Hebrew thought, there is a positive tradition of God watching over the humble: "For you deliver a humble people, but the haughty eyes you bring down" (Ps 18:27 NRSV); "Toward the scorners he is scornful, but to the humble he shows favor" (Prov 3:34 NRSV). There is also a tradition connecting humility with true wisdom: "The wisdom of the humble lifts their heads high, and seats them among the great" (Sir 11:1 NRSV). The NT also picks up the Hebrew tradition: "Humble yourselves before the Lord, and he will exalt you" (Jas 4:10). This remains a virtue in the Christian as well as the Jewish religion,[73] and Judith is in fact known later in Christian tradition as a symbol of humility who vanquishes arrogance.

The meaning of "senate [γερουσία *gerousia*] of the whole people [δῆμος *dēmos*] of Israel" has caused some problems for scholars. It is a common expression in the Greek world for the city council that represented the free citizens, or *dēmos*, of a city. For Jews, however, was it the same as the Sanhedrin, mentioned in the NT, in Josephus, and in rabbinic literature? These sources do not agree on the role of the Sanhedrin; the NT and Josephus see it as a council headed by the high priest or ruler that oversaw political and administrative matters of Jerusalem, while the rabbinic sources limit its oversight to religious questions. The former was probably the case in the period of Judith, and the *gerousia* here probably refers to such an administrative Sanhedrin. The Greek word συνέδριον (*synedrion*) that is the basis of the Hebrew term סנהדרין (*Sanhedrîn*) is used in its feminine form at 6:1 for Holofernes' war council. Here it is significant that the *gerousia* of the high

---

71. See Harvey Guthrie, "Fast, Fasting," *IDB* 2:241; Gary A. Anderson, *A Time to Mourn, a Time to Dance: The Expression of Grief and Joy in Israelite Religion* (University Park: Pennsylvania State University Press, 1991).
72. Rodney Alan Werline, *Penitential Prayer in Second Temple Judaism: The Development of a Religious Institution* (Atlanta: Scholars Press, 1998).
73. See *1 Clement* 13:3, 56:1.

priest and the senate of the "whole people of Israel" is followed to the letter. The perspective of the author is that the high priest sits as head of the government of the Temple, of Jerusalem, and of the Israelite people—a likely perspective of someone who was a full supporter of the Hasmonean rulers (see 1 Macc 12:6).

There is, perhaps, another message in this passage, however: The actions carried out by the high priest in the Jerusalem Temple and by the mass of Israelites in the outlying regions are not simply a coordinated response; they are essentially liturgical. That is, the timing and orchestration of the fasting, praying, and wearing of sackcloth appear to be a coordinated practice that may reflect religious observances at the time of the author. We will see that Judith times her prayer to coincide with the incense offering in the Temple in Jerusalem (9:1), and here as well we may detect signs that it is not simply a coordinated vigil, but more of a liturgical act: Every man in Israel, it is stated, prayed to God and humbled himself with fasting, and they all, including slaves and cattle, put sackcloth around their waists, and those living in Jerusalem knelt before the Temple, put ashes on their heads, and spread their sackcloth out before the Lord (cf. Judith's practice in 9:1). Finally, they draped the altar with sackcloth and prayed. It is not clear that any of this represents an actual liturgical practice as much as it does a liturgical ideal, or sense of Israel's engaging in penitential prayer *together*.

Two things are unusual about the penitential theology, however. First, Judith will later pray without so much as a hint of her own penitence (chap. 9). Unlike Esther in Additions to Esther or Aseneth in *Joseph and Aseneth*, Judith does not repent of her sins; nor does she repent on behalf of Israel. Second, it is not only the men and women who are draped in sackcloth, but also the children, resident aliens, slaves, and cattle! Is this a symbol of the completeness of Israel's penitence, or is it intended to be as humorous to the ancient reader as it is to the modern? Craven, probably correctly, takes it to be the latter, as we find the same motif used at Jonah 3:8, most likely also in a humorous way.[74] Still, is it meant to be satirical as well as humorous? Is the practice of the excessive use of sackcloth meant to be satirized? At Matt 6:16-18, Jesus condemns the outward show of the fasting of the "hypocrites," a term Matthew usually applies to the Pharisees. Zechariah 7:3-5 may have been critical of the show of fasting as well. In Judith, however, the prayers of the Israelites are answered, and it is because they have fasted (v. 13). Further, Judith will be described as a devout woman who regularly fasts and wears sackcloth. True, this is precisely the ritual asceticism that she stops performing to take up her task of defeating Holofernes, and it is not explicitly stated that she goes back to these practices at the end (16:21-25); but there is no indication that there is anything wrong with these practices or that she has somehow transcended them. It is more likely that in the high spirits of the book, the excesses are intended to be humorous, but there does not seem to be a clear satire of the acts themselves.

4:12-15. The inheritance in v. 12 is the land of Israel as a promise from God, which resulted from the conquest of Canaan (Deut 26:1; Josh 11:23; cf. Jdt 8:22; 9:12; 13:5; 16:21). This is, perhaps, more evidence that the author affirms a notion of an ideal Israel.

It is surprising that the readers are told in v. 13 that "the Lord heard their prayers," since this is precisely the question that the residents of Bethulia must grapple with in 7:23-31. The dramatic tension, therefore, would seem to be lessened by this intimation that all will be well. The tension about *whether* the Jews will be saved does not seem to be a strong factor in the reader's interest, however; the tension appears to build around *how* Judith will risk her dignity and keep it at the same time in order to save her people. The book of Judges also states that God heard the cries of the Israelites and sent them deliverers (e.g., Judg 3:9, 15); in the Introduction it is noted that Judith is like one of the judges—sent by God to deliver the people in distress. It should be noted, however, that the text does not explicitly say that God sent Judith or raised her up as a deliverer. God hears the prayers of the Israelites, but Judith appears to act more independently than the judges. It is also interesting that other novels of this period anticipate a happy ending in the narrative by informing the reader that God has heard the prayers of

---

74. Craven, *Artistry and Faith in the Book of Judith*, 115.

the pious and has foreordained a happy ending (see Tob 3:16-17 and the Greek novel by Xenophon of Ephesus, *Ephesian Tale* 1.6, where an oracle predicts that the young protagonists will be separated but reunited). (See Reflections at 5:1-21.)

Judith 5:1-21, Achior Tells Holofernes of Israel's History

COMMENTARY

5:1-4. The Moabites and the Ammonites are now on Holofernes' side, although at 1:12 they were listed as nations under the threat of the Assyrian advance. Presumably, just as other nations succumbed to the fear of the Assyrians (3:1-8), so also did the Moabites and the Ammonites. They had a very mixed history of relations with Israel (Gen 19:30-38) and fought on the side of the historical Nebuchadnezzar against Jerusalem (2 Kgs 24:2); more recently, the Maccabees had fought against the Ammonites (1 Macc 5:6). One tradition (Deut 23:3-6) had emphasized the distinction between Israel and these neighbors and excludes them and their descendants from entry into the assembly of the Lord. Holofernes in v. 3 addresses them with the ethnic term "Canaanites," which was ordinarily used at a much earlier period. However, it still occurs in the postexilic period as a designation for the neighboring peoples, probably (though not necessarily) in a pejorative way (Zech 14:41). The negative attitude had worked its way into the vocabulary of Judaism; one title for Satan, Beelzebul, "Lord of the Flies," was derived from the Canaanite deity Baal-zebul, or "Baal the Prince." At any rate, the negative tradition regarding the Moabites and the Ammonites seems to be reflected here, subsumed under the umbrella category "Canaanites." If the book of Judith idealizes the golden age of united Israel, it also taps into the ancient notion of the surrounding peoples as Canaanites, whom the Israelites are to conquer to acquire a new inheritance. The same anachronism is taken up by Matt 15:21-28 when Jesus heals a Canaanite woman, but there it may be utilized to undercut an ancient antagonism rather than accentuate it. Still, note that Achior, an Ammonite, will arise as a friend of Israel and a convert to Judaism.

As the expedition has come closer and closer to Jerusalem, the list of nations involved has shrunk; only names such as Assyrians, Moabites, Ammonites, and Canaanites are mentioned now in the list of nations, and the list of allies—or at any rate, fellow victims—has disappeared. Even Samaria as a separate entity (see Commentary on 4:1-15) is no longer mentioned. The world has been reduced to Israel and the ancient mortal enemies. The "governors of the coastland" would also include the cities mentioned in 2:28 who surrendered in 3:1-8. The ethnic origins of some of these cities would be directly or indirectly related to the Canaanites, but the generalization that Holofernes makes in v. 3 is more a catchall for the author's perspective than an attempt to designate the cities correctly.

The variety of nations has subtly changed over the course of the novel. Samaria and Judea, the usual names for their regions at the time of the composition of the book, have gradually disappeared as designations of geographical areas and have been replaced by Israel. Samaria is not used after chap. 2, and Judea is rarely used after chap. 4 (once in 8:21 and once in 11:19 in conversation with Holofernes). Israel is the ancient and traditional name of David's kingdom, and it was still used as a proud affirmation by Jews; but its use in Judith appears to be an invocation of the golden age, a designation that has intentionally swallowed up both halves of the old kingdom and negated the historical tensions. Another older term, "Hebrew," is used at 10:12 and 14:15, and the older term "Judah," rather than "Judea," is used at 14:7. When Holofernes looks for a term with which to insult Achior by associating him with the Israelites, he calls him an Ephraimite, using another ancient term for Israel. At the same time, the enemies of Israel are becoming somewhat more clearly drawn, with designations that also come from the golden age of Israelite history. The Moabites and the Ammonites begin as victim-nations along with Judea, on the direct path of Holofernes' campaign; later they will ally with Holofernes and will be called Canaanites. Thus old terms for Israel's neighbors, Moabites and Ammonites, are replaced by an even more archaic term from the early history of Israel that is more negative (Deut 7:1). Joining this group later are the sons of Esau, or Edomites (7:8, 18), yet another ancient enemy of the Israelites. Out of a plethora of national names, the essence of the conflict has now been distilled into its ancient opponents: Israel on one side and the Canaanites, Moabites, Ammonites, and Edomites on the other. The process is not unlike that at Esth 3:1, where the audience learns that Haman is an Agagite, an Amalekite and an ancient enemy of the Israelites (1 Samuel 15); however, this tension is only alluded to in Esther, while it is played upon constantly in Judith.

The series of questions Holofernes asks does not convey a realistic picture of what a military strategist might ask, and the Jewish audience would already know the answers. However, they serve a dramatic function in pointing to the larger themes that will dominate the book. The questions move in a progression from those that are immediate, concrete, and realistic (e.g., "How large is their army?") to broader issues that are also capable of double meanings (e.g., "In what does their power and strength consist?"). The final questions point to a reflection on the ultimate theological and ethical affirmations of Israel: "Who rules over them as king?" "Why have they alone refused to come out and meet me?" The reader would naturally see these as theological questions, with an answer that sets Israel apart from the other nations: God is king, and this allegiance precludes the reverence of any other king (cf. 3:8). Holofernes asks about worldly kings and powers, while the audience understands that the true king and commander is God. Here we find another example of the irony mentioned above at 2:1-4, which comes to dominate much of the dialogue here and later in the book. The opponents understand terms on a mundane level, while the audience perceives that they refer to God. (See the Introduction for a discussion and comparison of this kind of irony; see also chaps. 11–13.)

Does the irony in Holofernes' question—that is, the implication for the reader that no one was king of Israel except God—imply that Judith was written at a time when the leader did not claim this title? Before the foundation of David's dynasty, the Israelite league of tribes held that God's kingship should suffice for Israel; there should be no permanent king or dynasty (1 Samuel 8; 12). This view was supplanted by, or coexisted with, a belief in the Davidic monarchy. It is clear that the Maccabees did not begin by designating themselves king, but perhaps revivified the old league belief in the ideal—if not the reality—of the charismatic prophet (1 Macc 14:41-42) and the Maccabees as successors to the judges as deliverers. At some point, however, they took on the title of king as well, in addition to the titles of high priest, ethnarch (leader of the people), and strategos (general of the army; see Commentary on 4:6). It is certain that Judas Aristobulus I (104–103 BCE) and the leaders after him called themselves king, but it is unlikely that John Hyrcanus I (135–104 BCE) did. Although it would be a weak argument to assert that the irony in Holofernes' question implies that Judith was written at a time in which there was no king, it is true that Judith affirms the religious and political power of the high priest and may undercut the role of an earthly king, a theory of government compatible with that of the Hasmoneans between 152 BCE (the assumption of the title of high priest) and 104 BCE (the assumption of the title of king).

5:5-21. Although various derivations and meanings for Achior's name have been suggested, such as the Hebrew "light is my brother," it is almost certainly the case that it is a slightly altered form of "Ahikar."[75] In the ancient Near Eastern *Story of Ahikar*, Ahikar is an Assyrian court adviser who is falsely accused, imprisoned, and marked for execution, but who is later vindicated to save the kingdom through his wise counsel. A version of the story dating from about 400 BCE was found among the texts of a Jewish military colony at Elephantine in Egypt, and we find that Ahikar was easily adapted to new ethnic roles: He is a Jewish courtier in Tob 1:21-22; 2:10; 14:10, and his story is assimilated to

---

75. Henri A. Cazelles, "Le personnage d'Achior dans le livre de Judith," *RSR* 39 (1951) 125-37.

Aesop in Greek tradition. Although in Judith he has become an Ammonite general and is not described as the wise man of tradition, it would be wrong to conclude that he cannot be modeled on "Ahikar the wise." Just as Judith is a woman of action, so also Achior, to be treated heroically, must be depicted as a man of action. Achior's conversion is also prompted by the needs of the story. As a wise and brave man, he must naturally in this novel come to see the truth about God that is revealed in Israelite history. He embodies the type of the "righteous Gentile," such as Balaam (Numbers 22–24), Rahab (Joshua 2–6), and Naaman (2 Kings 5),[76] and like the first of these, places himself in danger by uttering true words—one might almost say prophecies (cf. 6:2)—about the Israelites.

Achior, a non-Jew, thus becomes a very important character in this overwhelmingly Jewish book. As an "objective" observer, he can recite Israelite history and the mighty acts of God in a way that sounds even more impressive. He also puts it in terms of "deuteronomic theology," the view of God associated with Deuteronomy and the deuteronomistic history, which holds that if Israel abides in God's laws, God will bless them, and if Israel disobeys God's laws, God will punish them. Achior's explanation of Israelite history makes it much easier for Judith to explain to Holofernes at 11:9-15 that she has betrayed her people because they have abandoned God and as a result are doomed. In addition, Achior, who has met Holofernes, will later be in a position to identify the severed head in Judith's possession as that of Holofernes. The form of Achior's speech is the recitation of the mighty acts of God in bringing the Israelites to the promised land (Deuteronomy 1–3; 26:5-10); yet, while it is positive in regard to Israelite history, it still retains the appearance of objectivity. It is ironic, for instance, that he mentions the abandonment of the Chaldean gods, which might have been seen by the Jewish audience as part of the same ancient Near Eastern polytheism as the Ammonite gods. Thus the "creedal" aspect of Abraham's separation from Chaldean polytheism would have been recognized by Judith's audience. Likewise, the violent conquest of Canaan (Josh 11:16-23) is not described from the Ammonite point of view (although in the tradition the Hebrews did not displace the Ammonites and the Moabites; Deut 2:9-19).

Despite the fact that the Jewish audience would have heard the creedal aspects of Achior's speech, there is still an attempt to represent his speech at times from an outsider's perspective. Abraham was supposedly expelled from his homeland, instead of separating himself by choice. The story of Exodus is told in vv. 10-12, but rather than having Moses *lead* the Hebrews out of slavery, the Egyptians *expel* them. This is in agreement with the view often expressed in the contemporary Greek historians on Jewish history. The technique of putting into the mouths of Gentiles some of the anti-Jewish prejudices of the time is also utilized in the Additions to Esther 13, where the content of Haman's anti-Jewish decree, lacking in MT Esther, is given in a very plausible way. There is a further dramatic function of Achior's speech here, found in his introduction. He tells Holofernes, "I will tell you the truth about this people. . . . No falsehood shall come from your servant's mouth." Since Achior and Judith will become partnered in the narrative as the only two people brave enough to stand up to Holofernes, Achior's words here evoke a comparison with Judith's words at 11:5. There she will offer the same assurances, but she will be lying.

The list of five nations in v. 16 is an abbreviation of the usual list of six nations (Exod 3:8; Josh 9:1; Judg 3:5) or seven nations that are to be conquered, even wiped out, in the conquest of Canaan (Deut 7:1-2; Josh 3:10). "Shechemites" does not appear in the older lists; Shechem was a Samaritan city captured by John Hyrcanus I. Shechemites may be included here to show that they were a people conquered as part of the conquest, or because Judith (in 9:2) will invoke the revenge of Simeon and Levi on Shechem for the rape of Dinah (Genesis 34).

The deuteronomic theology is stated clearly in vv. 17-19; with the perspective of hindsight, the fall of Israel and Judah is directly laid to the sins of the people (although the entire focus is on the fall of Judah only). Jeremiah reflects this theology as well (Jeremiah 26–35), but he lived at the center of the crisis and counseled an adjustment on the part of

76. Moore, *Judith*, 158.

the defeated people to the effects of their sins. Texts such as Daniel 1–6 likewise indicate an attempt to understand life in exile. But v. 19 indicates a different period in Jewish religious life, a realized goal of life in God's temple-city. It likely represents the heady, aggressive policy of the Hasmonean rulers some years after the Maccabean revolt and the rededication of the Temple. The historical impossibility of Nebuchadnezzar king of the Assyrians is made glaringly obvious here: The events described, deportation and destruction of the Temple, were accomplished by Nebuchadnezzar, king of Babylon.

Achior concludes in vv. 20-21 by giving the counsel that in his mind is inescapable: If the people of Judea can be found to be sinning, then attack; they will surely fall. If they have not sinned, they will be invincible; the Assyrians will be routed and shamed. At this point Achior can be seen to be the mouthpiece of unconscious prophecy, similar to the role of Balaam in Numbers 22–24 or of the high priest Caiaphas in John 11:47-53. Holofernes will also sarcastically refer to this speech (6:2) as prophecy, although the audience knows that is precisely what it is. Phrases in the conclusion of Achior's speech ("let my lord pass by them," "their lord and god") set up the comparison between Nebuchadnezzar as lord and God as Lord that will later be used by Judith to create a series of ironic statements that are understood in one way by Holofernes and in another way by the audience. In both cases Achior plays this part unknowingly, addressing Holofernes with a clear meaning, while Judith will later be deliberately deceptive.

REFLECTIONS

1. Achior here provides a marvelous opportunity for the reader to hear the essence of Israelite history as told from an outsider's perspective. His account is positive and affirming of Israelite tradition, and it inevitably makes the modern reader wonder how his or her religious community would be described by an outsider. The book of Judith in general is about the military defense of the community; this scene is about the theological defense of the community as well.

Here the perspective of the author is that the values of Israel, which are grounded in the actions of Israel's God, shine out beyond its borders and are recognized by anyone who has eyes to see this. In other words, the grounding in God is what sets Israel on a firmer basis, and it is not up to Israelites to trumpet its cause; it is self-evident. This, according to the author, is in sharp contrast to the other peoples round about, who have embraced Nebuchadnezzar as a god. The author seems to suggest, across the centuries, that if you want your own religious community to be thought of well, it is not a matter of public relations or bragging; it is a matter of grounding your faith in God in such a way that its integrity is self-evident. A religious faith that affects the lives of its adherents is bound to be noticed.

2. The essence of Israelite theology was wrapped up in history, and Achior's recounting of Israelite history also focuses on the important principle of deuteronomic theology. The peace and prosperity of Israel before the exile, the destruction of Jerusalem by the Babylonians during the exile, and the restoration of Israel after the exile could all be explained by this theory of history. Further, the author of Judith could also explain the peace and independence of Judea after the Maccabean revolt by recourse to this theology. The victories of the Hasmonean rulers confirmed the author's view that Israel's successes were a reward from God.

In our time, however, this kind of thinking comes under closer scrutiny. Does God choose one nation over another? Will God always reward the righteous nation with peace and prosperity? Does deuteronomic theology have a danger of becoming the self-fulfilling prophecy of the "winners"? With a more complex view of history, most religious people today would see peace and prosperity as both blessing from God and awesome responsibility. Most would recognize that the moral standing of modern nations is shot through with contradictions, blind spots, unrealized dreams of freedom, dignity, and equality. The deuteronomic theology of more than two millennia ago seems far too simplistic. And yet it still challenges us, as Achior's speech implies, to ground the community of faith in a relationship with God regardless of the consequences and to hope for God's blessings as a result.

Judith 5:22–6:21, Holofernes Responds by Expelling Achior, Who Is Received in Bethulia

COMMENTARY

5:22–6:1. Although Achior's words will seem eminently sensible to the audience, the hubris of Holofernes and his allies blinds them from turning away. The question of Holofernes in 5:4, "In what does their power and strength consist?" was ironic, because the audience knew that the answer was "in God." The peoples of the seacoast and the Moabites are oblivious to this truth, and as a result they have accepted the worship of Nebuchadnezzar as god. Nebuchadnezzar's power consists in his armies, in which they have placed their hopes.

Holofernes' tent is mentioned for the first time, but it will be the dramatic setting for many of the dialogues to come, and especially for the meeting of Holofernes and Judith. The meeting here is called a "council" (συνέδριον *synedrion*), a term used elsewhere for Holofernes' meetings, unlike the γερουσία (*gerousia*), used for the city council meeting of the high priest in Jerusalem (4:8). The term *synedrion* is the Greek word from which the Hebrew סנהדרין (*Sanhedrîn*) is derived, but in Greek usage it usually means "meeting," and especially "war council," as it does here (cf. 2 Macc 14:5).

6:2-4. "Mercenaries of Ephraim" is an odd expression. Ephraim appears in some of the lists of the northern tribes of Israel, but the term also came to be used to represent the northern tribes as a whole. In Holofernes' mouth, it is likely a sarcastic attempt to associate Achior the Ammonite with the people he appears to be championing. As noted above, it is another use of an archaic term to re-create the golden age of heroes and villains of Israelite history. The term "mercenaries" (μισθωτοί *misthōtoi*) might also be better translated more contemptuously as "hirelings" or "hired workers," representing the class hierarchy of honor and shame that would have prevailed at this time.

"Who is god but Nebuchadnezzar?" makes explicit the contrast that underlies the entire book. Further, Holofernes' identification of himself as one of "Nebuchadnezzar's servants" should be compared with Judith's reference to herself as Holofernes' servant a number of times (11:5, 10, 16-17; 12:4), although her words often allow for the possibility that she is referring to herself as a servant of God. Holofernes—perhaps appropriately from his point of view—talks about this "god" Nebuchadnezzar in a strangely detached way when he says, "He will send his forces." Holofernes is actually the bearer of the full might of Nebuchadnezzar's army; it is he who is sending his forces. Holofernes seems to understand his role as an agent of his god's will, much as Judith understands her own role. Holofernes also makes his pronouncement using biblical idioms for prophecy: "he has spoken" and "none of his words shall be in vain." Holofernes is precisely a false prophet; he believes truly in his god and the words of his god, and he delivers his prophetic oracle as a biblical prophet would. He is not a false mouthpiece for a true god (cf. 1 Kgs 22:13-28; Jeremiah 28), but a true mouthpiece for a false god (cf. Isa 44:9-20; Wis 13:1–15:17; Letter of Jeremiah; Bel and the Dragon). It is again troubling for the modern reader, however, to find that the closest parallels to Nebuchadnezzar's policy of destruction should be found in the "holy war" passages of the HB.

6:5-13. Holofernes' sarcasm is evident here as he speaks of "this race that came out of Egypt." As noted in the Commentary on

5:5, this was what pagan historians knew of Israelite history, and so the author's depiction of Holofernes' words would have the ring of verisimilitude. Holofernes quite humorously tells Achior, "You shall not see my face" until he exacts his revenge on Bethulia, but the audience knows that the next time Achior sees Holofernes' head it will be severed from the rest of his body. Although Achior speaks in a truthful manner without any ironic double meanings, Holofernes will often accidentally make statements that are susceptible to two layers of meaning, and Judith will intentionally use language in this way. Holofernes' words have a way of coming true that he does not intend, precisely because he is speaking unwisely. In Esther 6, Haman unwisely and unintentionally suggests to the king a reward that will fall to his nemesis, Mordecai. The wisdom tradition counseled against rash proclamations: "The wise of heart will heed commandments, but a babbling fool will come to ruin" (Prov 10:8 NRSV) and "The talk of fools is a rod for their backs, but the lips of the wise preserve them" (Prov 14:3 NRSV). This is a tradition from which Holofernes and Haman could have profited.

Holofernes emphasizes that his servants will kill Achior and that his slaves will exile him to one of the villages. Since Achior was the leader of the Ammonites, this is intentionally an attempt to shame him. With his parting words, Holofernes cannot help giving another unconscious prophecy: "If you really hope they will not be taken, do not look downcast!" Things look bleak for Achior, but the audience knows that he will be deposited in safe hands and that Holofernes is giving Achior good advice: Achior does hope they will not be taken, and he has reason to be happy. Holofernes closes with another formula of prophecy, "I have spoken, and none of my words shall fail to come true."

6:14-21. The description of the servants depositing Achior at the foot of the hill on which Bethulia sat and the Bethulians admitting him to their town takes up a considerable number of verses, more verses, in fact, than some of the military campaigns of the first two chapters. This section is very important in the structure of the work; as noted in the Overview at 2:14, this passage is at the center of the chiasm of the first part of Judith, and it corresponds to and is a reversal of the dialogue between Holofernes and Achior and the rejection of the latter's advice. It is also a narrative break from the talk of the last two chapters and shows the shift of focus from the campaigns of nations to the experiences of a few individuals, who are now seen to be very important. Achior's movement—unintentional as it is—is very significant, and in addition to being coordinated with previous passages (5:1–6:13), it is balanced and contrasted with passages to come concerning Judith: He moves from Holofernes' camp to Bethulia, she from Bethulia to Holofernes' camp. He presented the deuteronomic theology in truth; she will present it as part of a lie. He will convert from paganism to follow the God of Israel; she will feign an abandonment of God to join Holofernes' god.[77] Furthermore, Achior's movement allows the reader an effective transition from Holofernes' camp to the interior of Bethulia. Uzziah's banquet (a festive occasion?) may seem out of place, but it is a sign of hospitality that Achior has now been ritually welcomed, and it balances the banquet that Judith will receive when she changes places with Achior and is accepted into Holofernes' tent (12:10-20). Further, it provides another rest in the story before the next narrative movement (see Commentary on 2:28).

---

77. Adolfo Roitman, "Achior in the Book of Judith: His Role and Significance," in *"No One Spoke Ill of Her": Essays on Judith*, ed. James C. VanderKam (Atlanta: Scholars Press, 1992) 31-45.

REFLECTIONS

That pagan kings demanded worship as gods is today a stereotype of ancient polytheism, but this practice was not common in the ancient world. It was the practice in Egypt, but not in Assyria, Babylon, or Persia. Greek kings and Roman emperors often received divine honors in Egypt or in the east, but seldom in Greece and Rome. Even where reverence of the king was practiced, political and military domination in the ancient world almost never entailed the outlawing of the conquered people's religion; religious persecution was not considered an expedient of military strategy. Polytheism allowed for a pluralism of religious observances, and so requiring the religious reverence of the king, or of any other cult (such as Isis and Serapis in Egypt), did not entail the elimination of the conquered people's own religious traditions. Only in the Maccabean revolt and its aftermath do we find religious persecution and the outlawing of a local religious tradition as a means of political control. In this text we have another case of a later historical development read back into the earlier period. (Esther 8:17 likewise reflects a form of forcible conversion that was not known in earlier centuries.)

This introduces us to the irony that we have lived with in the West for so many centuries, and still do: The idea of a monotheistic God often gives rise to the notion that only one concept of God can be permitted. If there is one God, there can be only one religion. Conflict and persecution then follow in the interest of realizing the vision of one community under one God. Polytheistic cultures, on the other hand, have generally felt free to recognize gods of other cultures, even to embrace them or harmonize them—"My god X must be the same as your god Y." To blame monotheism for religious persecution would be simplistic, however. Polytheistic cultures engage in conflict and persecution as well; they simply do not use "one community under one God" as their rallying cry and are not as likely to oppose local religious institutions as a means of political domination.

In the heat of this novel the reader almost forgets that the violent suppression of local religious worship had its closest parallel not only in what the Jews had actually experienced a few decades earlier under the Greek Seleucids, a religious persecution that had provoked the Maccabean revolt, but also in what the successors of the Maccabees had done to the various ethnic groups that lived within the borders of a renewed Israel. The description here is unsettlingly close to the program of the Jewish ruler John Hyrcanus, almost as if it were based upon it. Hyrcanus destroyed the Samaritan temple on Mt. Gerizim, rid the land of other competing cults, and forcibly converted many people to Judaism. The parallel to the administration of Judea may have been intended; the religious persecution by Holofernes culminates in the declaration, "What god is there except Nebuchadnezzar?" (6:2). That of Hyrcanus would have been similar, except that it culminated in "What God is there except the Lord?"

For us, the lessons of history must be faced, and we need look no further each day than the headlines concerning conflicts on different continents. The persecuted often become the persecutors, seething with the need to reverse the memory of persecution, inflicting a just destruction on the former perpetrators. And this, of course, is the theme of Judith. The way out is not easy, but it is clear that the chain of memory and reversal is a powerful motive for violence, and it is the responsibility of communities of faith to examine closely the power of justification, the religious rallying cries that will be given for the next reversal.

Judith 7:1-18, Holofernes Prepares for War and Places Bethulia Under Siege

COMMENTARY

7:1-5. It is not until chap. 7 that the climactic battle is ready to be joined. The enormousness of Holofernes' army is impressed upon the reader, with a description that is very visual. It is what the citizens of Bethulia see that strikes fear in their hearts. The author again notes the auxiliary soldiers and supplies as a way of indicating not only the size of the army, but also its unwieldiness. Although it is a fearsome sight to the Israelites, to the audience it is also a bloated giant, waiting to be slaughtered. Once again, despite the fact that the Bethulians will lack the resolve that Judith demands, they are still far braver than the nations of the coastlands mentioned in 2:18–3:8, who not only surrender at the sight of the Assyrians, but abandon their religious traditions as well.

7:6-18. Holofernes has arrayed his troops for the most visual effect to terrify the Israelites, and he is preparing for battle. Joining the neighboring groups with whom Israel had had dicey relations in the past are the chieftains of the Edomites. This was another group who would have had ancient bad associations for the Israelites. The progenitor of the Edomites was Esau (Genesis 25–33), whose animosity toward Jacob was considered to be indicative of the relations between their progeny. There was a more recent association, however, in that in the author's day the Edomites were known as Idumeans, and John Hyrcanus had forcibly converted many of this group to Judaism. One of those converted was the grandfather of Herod the Great, so their status was not marginal; still, at the end of the second century BCE, when the conversion was probably a recent event, this reference would have appeared divisive.

It is significant that the neighboring nations are not just allied with Holofernes; they lead the attack. Their suggestion is a clever stratagem, and it is they who take the initiative in securing the mountaintops around Bethulia, ensuring that their stratagem will work (7:13, 17-18). Unlike Achior's advice, the advice from these neighboring peoples is malicious in intent and, though clever in the short term, from the audience's point of view lacks the insight that Achior possessed about the bigger picture of Israel's fortunes. An artful and novelistic use of description is in evidence here as the Assyrians move to engage and outsmart the Israelites.

Judith 7:19-32, The People Despair and Want to Surrender

COMMENTARY

7:19-22. Cutting off the water supply has had its effect: The Israelites cry out to God, but now their courage has failed, and they begin to despair. Although it was stated in the Introduction that the depiction of emotion was common in both Jewish and Greek novelistic literature, this description of the sufferings of the Jews in Bethulia is actually very restrained when compared to other texts (e.g., 2 Macc 3:14-21 and the even more extreme account in 3 Maccabees 4).

7:23-28. The Bethulians complain to Uzziah much as the Israelites complained to Moses during the exodus. In Exodus 15–17 there are three episodes in which the Israelites seem to have quickly forgotten God's former miracles and complain about their new trials (see also Deut 6:16). One of these episodes, Exod 17:1-7, contains several parallels to the book of Judith, if we also look ahead to Judith's reaction to this scene. The texts tell a similar story: There is a lack of water; the Israelites complain to their leader and say that it would have been better to be a slave; there is a critique of their testing of God; the leader calls on God; the leader delivers the people; and there is an issue over the acclamation, "the Lord is with us."[78] A crucial difference is that the function of the leader in Judith is divided between Uzziah and Judith; she steps up here to take the role of leader from the recognized male authority in the community.

7:29-31. Uzziah, whose name means "the Lord is my power," is much more resolute than the townspeople, but he fashions a compromise that Judith will later find unacceptable: If God has not sent rain within five days, they will surrender.

7:32. A calm pervades the town of Bethulia, but it is the calm of despair. Nevertheless, it is an effective narrative transition much like the pauses that have come before at junctures in the story (see Commentary on 2:28).

---

78. van Henten, "Judith as Alternative Leader," 235.

JUDITH 8:1–16:25

JUDITH ARISES TO RESCUE HER PEOPLE

OVERVIEW

A bit less than halfway through the novel, Judith is finally introduced. She will now dominate the second half of the book, not just in the sense that she is the principal character, center stage most of the time—although indeed she is—but also in the sense that she is the deliverer of Israel when none of the men will step forward. We will meet her in her estate, where she spends most of her days in seclusion, but she will come forward to address the elders of Bethulia. She will pray and prepare herself to do battle with Holofernes with the best weapons at her disposal: her beauty, her courage, and her ability to manipulate through deceit.

The structural outline of the whole of Judith given in the Introduction attempts to divide the content of the narrative at important transition points, but within that overall outline there are other structural patterns at work that will be pointed out in the Commentary. These include the overall pattern of the heroic quest, within which we find two specially noted rites of passage, one involving the special preparation of the heroine in prayer, fasting, and clothing, and one involving the departure across the threshold of the city from known and safe space to unknown and unsafe space, the slaying of Holofernes, and the return across the threshold back to the city. Toni Craven's discovery of clearly marked structural patterns of parallels and contrasts in the first part and in the second part allows us to discern these and other important dynamics of the narrative as part of a chiastic structure. For the second part, her outline can be summarized thus:

A Introduction of Judith (8:1-8)
  B Judith plans to save Israel (8:9–10:8)
    C Judith and her maid leave Bethulia (10:9-10)
      D Judith overcomes Holofernes (10:11–13:10a)
    C´ Judith and her maid return to Bethulia (13:10b-11)
  B´ Judith plans to destroy Israel's enemy (13:12–16:20)
A´ Conclusion about Judith (16:21-25)

In the second part there is a center that is more discretely set off from the rest of the chiastic structure than was the case in the first part: the heroine's slaying of the "monster" who threatens Israel.

JUDITH 8:1-8, INTRODUCTION OF JUDITH

COMMENTARY

The second part of Judith begins stylistically in a way very similar to the first. In both halves a principal character is named, after which there is a long and seemingly awkward digression to describe a second, weaker character, before the main narrative resumes, recounting the deeds of the principal character.[79] In chap. 1 Nebuchadnezzar is introduced by a long sentence that is largely taken up with a parenthesis on Arphaxad, before

---
79. Enslin and Zeitlin, *The Book of Judith*, 58, 112.

Nebuchadnezzar's exploits are resumed in 1:5. In chap. 8, Judith is introduced by a long sentence that is given over to a parenthesis on her genealogy, and only after a description of her husband's death is her background taken up again.

Judith hears about the events and comes to the fore in response to a crisis, like a hero or heroine of folklore or like one of the deliverers of Israel in the book of Judges. The name "Judith" is the feminine equivalent of "Judah" or "Judas," from which the province name "Judea" is derived ("Judah" [יהודה *yĕhûdâ*] in Hebrew became "Judea" [Ἰουδαία *Ioudaia*] in Greek). It is from the word "Judean" that the English word "Jew" ultimately derives; her name thus means "Jewess." Assuming that the name was invented for the character, it could have been chosen to be emblematic of the ideal herione—that is, it communicates the fact that the Jews would be saved by a heroic "Jewess." It is also possible that it evokes the name of one of the heroes of the Maccabean revolt, Judah the Maccabee. This seems even more likely when we consider the close parallels between Judah the Maccabee's defeat of Nicanor (1 Macc 7:47; 2 Macc 15:35; see Commentary on 14:1-4). The name of Judith certainly argues against the possibility of a Samaritan origin for the book, unless the protagonist's name has been changed.

Judith's genealogy is given in some detail— the only extended genealogy for a woman in the Bible (though Matthew 1 includes women in the genealogy of Jesus). Genealogies are common in the Bible, both in early texts and in late ones (*Jub* 4:1-33; Tob 1:1-2; Matt 1:1-17; Luke 3:23-38), and they may serve a different function in the two cases.[80] In early texts they are used to tie together a larger patriarchal history, or what has been called the "primal history." Israelite history is, in effect, the history of one long genealogy; Abraham's family and their genealogies anchor the parts of that history to one idealized lineage. The late genealogies function to tie individuals back in to the primal history as a means of authenticating their identity. The hero or heroine must have proper credentials, but may be a "loner" all the same.

This is found in hero legends cross-culturally. The names in Judith's genealogy are unremarkable in general, but two things are significant. First, the genealogy is traced back to Israel. This is another indication that the author intends to idealize the reconstitution of a united Israel and not just Judea as a Hellenistic temple-state, even if the actual achievement of the Hasmoneans was closer to the latter. Second, there are connections in the genealogy to Simeon (Salamiel and Sarasadai are his grandson and son, Num 1:6), which would be relevant for Judith's later affirmation of the role of Simeon in avenging the rape of Dinah (Jdt 9:2).

It is also significant that while Judith is identified by her genealogy, her husband, Manasseh, is not; in fact, he is identified in relation to Judith. This is very unusual and points to an important aspect of the second half of the book: the reversal of expected gender roles. Manasseh, through his loss of genealogy, is already depicted in a passive way, but there may be more. Are we to infer from the description of his death that he died most unheroically—that is, in bed, brought low by a sunstroke? Holofernes will also die in his bed in a most undignified way.[81] Judith is characterized in opposition to the men around her, first her husband, and later, the town leaders of Bethulia and Achior. She is aggressive and active, like a male warrior, while they are weak willed, passive, "feminine" by most cultures' standards. As noted in the Introduction, the male protagonists of the Greek novels are also generally passive compared to the female, but this is carried much further in the book of Judith.

Judith's character is demonstrated by the heroic vigilance she brings to everyday piety. After the death of her husband, Judith observes the ritual mourning of the widow for three years and four months, much longer than was required by Jewish law.[82] In addition, she fasts each day except for the holidays on which fasting is not allowed, and sets up a tent on her roof for her prayer and fasts. In Jewish practice it was forbidden to visit graves on sabbaths and festivals, and

---

80. Robert R. Wilson, "Old Testament Genealogies in Recent Research," *JBL* 94 (1975) 169-89.

81. Amy-Jill Levine, "Sacrifice and Salvation: Otherness and Domestication in the Book of Judith," in *"No One Spoke Ill of Her": Essays on Judith*, ed. James C. VanderKam (Atlanta: Scholars Press, 1992) 105-17.
82. Roland de Vaux, *Ancient Israel*, 2 vols. (New York: McGraw-Hill, 1965) 1:40.

her mourning practices are likewise not performed on these days; she comes down from her tent into her quarters (10:2). Her piety is thus prodigious and will sound similar to later Christian asceticism.[83]

She was also a beautiful woman, very wealthy and secure in her social position. These two traits, great beauty and wealth, are always the characteristics of the heroine in the Greek novels, and for the Jewish novels as well: Judith, Susanna, Esther, and Aseneth are all described in this way. The author of Judith makes good use of detail, and we note here that the wealth of Manasseh, and now of Judith, is spelled out in categories. They are the same that were used to emphasize the size and extent of Holofernes' army: gold and silver (2:18), slaves (2:20), livestock (2:17), and fields (3:3). Is the author trying to suggest that just as Holofernes controls a vast army and its auxiliaries, so also, in an analogous way, Judith administers her own empire? It certainly does help to characterize our protagonist as a woman with a commanding presence and a will to succeed, and the analogy to Holofernes' vast power is probably intended. Further, Judith maintains the estate after Manasseh's death, like the "capable wife" of Prov 31:10-31, who excels not only in domestic crafts and running a household, but in buying fields and planting vineyards as well. Although one may wonder how Judith can administer a large estate while praying and fasting in her tent, the person responsible on a daily basis may be her servant, "who was in charge of all she possessed" (v. 10). Still, we need hardly look for a realistic answer; the capable wife of Proverbs 31 also does seemingly impossible things. But although Judith is described so positively, it is interesting that she does not seek a new husband or enter into a levirate marriage to raise up a son for her dead husband, as Jewish law would require (Deut 25:5-10). Judith is simply not a typical model of Jewish womanhood. To be sure, there are other traces in this period of a Jewish piety that allows for celibacy and voluntary childlessness. The Qumran sectarians and the Therapeutae (fem., Therapeutrides) described by Philo in *On the Contemplative Life* encouraged celibacy, and Wis 3:13–4:6 seems to encourage a celibate spirituality. In early Christianity as well, celibacy for some is presumed in 1 Corinthians 7; 1 Tim 5:14; and perhaps Matt 19:12.

Moore also raises another question: Why is the character Judith a widow and not a virgin or a married woman?[84] Here we probably have to concede that even Judith could not rise above all social conventions of ancient Judaism. The risk to her dignity in approaching Holofernes was great, and perhaps titillating to the audience; but for a virgin or a married woman to place herself in that kind of jeopardy would be quite another matter. A young unmarried woman was under the strict control and protection of her father and his family until she married, and then that control was passed over to her husband. An attack on a young woman in ancient society was an affront to the man who had charge of her and was a shame to him as much as it was to her. A widow, on the other hand, was no longer under the control and protection of a man. Widows and orphans were among the most vulnerable social categories in ancient Israel because they were not under the protection of any male relative; as a result, the prophets often felt compelled to take up the cause of the unattached widows and orphans. Judith herself retained a wealthy estate, but if a widow was not wealthy, she might find herself without protection. Even the levirate law, which might have the effect of allowing a widow at least temporary support from her dead husband's brother, is not intended for *her* welfare, but to raise a son for the deceased husband. As a result of these structural aspects of Jewish culture, the fact that Judith is a widow becomes almost a necessity. A young virgin or a married woman could never be depicted in such an unprotected position without causing severe discomfort in the audience; only a widow could be depicted in so flagrant a violation of decorum. The unprotected nature of even a wealthy widow's situation may still be in evidence, however, in the fact that the author must emphasize that even though she was unattached, "no one spoke ill of her." The quotation in the introduction from Jerome on Gentile widows indicates the social reproach that might attach to an unprotected widow.

---

83. The connection to asceticism has been probed by scholars. See Wills, *The Jewish Novel in the Ancient World*, 15, 123, 139, 228-44.

84. Moore, *Judith*, 180.

Judith, because "she feared God with great devotion," maintained an impeccable reputation even though she will later flout many commandments and conventions associated with Jewish piety.

Judith spends most of her days fasting in seclusion in a tent or booth on the roof of her house. Is her tent intended to call to mind Sukkot (the Jewish Festival of Booths), the tabernacle in the wilderness wanderings (also a σκηνή *skēnē* in Greek), a synagogue, or none of these? There are important parallels with each. The restoration of observances during Sukkot in Ezra 3:4-5 includes the same offerings mentioned at Jdt 4:14: daily burnt offerings, regular burnt offerings, new moon and festival offerings, freewill offerings (see also Lev 23:33-38), and the booths of the Festival of Sukkot could be constructed on roofs (Neh 8:13-18). The tabernacle, or tent of meeting (Exodus 25–26), in addition to being the locus for the worship of the Israelites during their wanderings, was also a paradigm for the Temple. Since Judith's prayer is timed to correspond to the temple sacrifices (9:1), this parallel is suggestive. Her prayer in the tent is also similar to the prayers in synagogues, but the synagogue as a place for prayer and study, rather than for a public meeting, may not have come into being until after the writing of Judith. Although there are similarities to each of these forms of sacred space and worship, none of them appears to be clearly in mind to the exclusion of the others.

There is one other possibility that should be considered. Lying behind Judith's practice of fasting and praying at the same time that the priests in the Jerusalem Temple were offering sacrifices is likely a development of ancient Jewish worship that occurred away from the Temple. The huge provisions for the temple sacrifices in Jerusalem were presented each month by one of the twelve tribes on a rotating basis. In addition, a form of local worship was instituted in the land of each tribe during the period of their responsibility. A pillar was erected by each tribe, and for four days during that month people from the tribe came together at the pillar to fast and pray. The prayers and readings of the temple service were also read in the local communities. The similarity to Judith's practice is obvious: A local worship experience that involves fasting and mourning rites takes place at a time that coincides with the priestly rituals in Jerusalem. To be sure, Judith's practice is not limited to the period of her tribe's provision of animals and crops. However, pious Jews evidently began to pray and fast in the public square on a regular basis year-round, a practice that may have been the actual forerunner of the synagogue. This evolved further into a twice-weekly prayer and fast among the Pharisees, although it is not clear whether they alone performed it in this way. The Mishnah, a collection of Jewish laws compiled in about 200 CE, limits the practice to prayer only,[85] but that implies that other aspects had also been involved. Tertullian, a Christian theologian writing at the end of the second century CE, describes—albeit critically—the practice of public prayer, fasting, and wearing of sackcloth: "A Jewish fast is universally celebrated; while neglecting the temples [meaning synagogues?], in every open place they continue to send prayer up to heaven. And though by dress and ornamentation of mourning they disgrace the duty, still they do affect a faith in abstinence."[86] Judith's prayer and fasting, not tied to an annual rotation, represent a continuous practice that is more like this latter development. It is still timed to coincide with a Jerusalem temple observance, but like the personal piety of the Pharisees, it is carried out continuously. Her activities are by no means identical to these practices, but this fictitious representation of her extreme piety is probably influenced by actual local practices.

---

85. Sidney B. Hoenig, "The Ancient City-Square: The Forerunner of the Synagogue," *ANRW* 2.19.1 (1979) 448-76.

86. Tertullian *On Fasting* 16.

JUDITH 8:9–10:10, JUDITH RESOLVES TO SAVE ISRAEL

Judith 8:9-36, Judith Addresses the Citizens of Bethulia

COMMENTARY

8:9-20. The news of the town meeting comes to Judith while she is in seclusion. Judith does not simply appear or emerge from her tent ready to do battle. Presumably, out of modesty she does not come out of her home to meet the magistrates, even though it is a time of crisis. Soon her actions will be quite different, but at this point she sends her favorite slave. This woman will figure prominently in the unfolding narrative (see 10:2). Judith immediately proceeds to upbraid the magistrates. Just as Holofernes had addressed his war councils in the first part of the story, so also she addresses the elders of Bethulia. This underscores the fact that a significant amount of the second part will be taken up with dialogue as well. She makes several points in addressing them. Her first charge is that it was wrong to test God by imposing a time limit within which to act. If the human realm is impossible to comprehend, she reasons, how can people fathom God's actions? God is free to come to their aid at any point—if God so chooses. There is a close Greek parallel to this motif, the Lindus chronicle, in which the Greek city of Lindus, besieged by Darius of Persia, prays to Athena to bring rain within five days. Rain does come, and Darius realizes that Lindus enjoys divine protection and passes it by. This is clearly intended to be a positive assessment of the city's prayer. The author of Judith has taken this tradition and challenged it: Fervent prayer is not sufficient before God, but a strict humility before God's decrees is called for. It is often thought that this is one of the key theological ideas in Judith, but it is not clear whether the author is really concerned about this theologically or whether it is more of a narrative device. It characterizes Judith as a more valiant soldier of virtue than the other citizens of Bethulia. The testing of God here is not as serious a case as the creation of a golden calf while Moses was on Mt. Sinai (Exodus 32) or the complaints of the people in the wilderness during the exodus (Exodus 15–17; Numbers 11; see Commentary on 7:23-28). It could also be said to have been caused by more extreme conditions. Still, Judith does not entertain any pleas of mitigating circumstances (v. 30).

Her next point is sometimes missed in a quick reading of her speech. Having noted that God is free to choose, Judith asserts that the residents of Bethulia can yet be confident that God will come to their aid because there is no longer anyone among them who worships idols. For Judith this is the criterion of the deuteronomic theology by which God grants either favor or punishment. How is she so sure that the worship of idols has been removed from the land? At the time of the composition of Judith the Hasmonean kings had succeeded in pacifying the land and, more important, had destroyed the Samaritan temple on Mt. Gerizim, expanded the borders to approximately the size of the united Israel under David and Solomon, and converted by force peoples such as the Idumeans. The author must have seen the Hasmonean settlement of the country as the successful expulsion of idol worship.

8:21-23. If God chooses not to help, the stakes are very high: Bethulia is the only fortified town standing between the Assyrians and their entry into Judea. If idol worship has been eradicated from the land, Judith reasons, it is difficult to imagine God allowing the devastation of Judea—and the devastation and servitude will this time be permanent, not as before in Egypt or in the exile. Presumably, two related views are being emphasized simultaneously: Although God operates with a free will that cannot be tested or limited, God shows favor to those who remain faithful. The devastation that would result from an Assyrian invasion is not described in terms of human suffering as it is elsewhere, but in terms of the resulting shame: The Temple will be desecrated, and the Israelites will become an offense and a disgrace serving as slaves among the Gentiles. This time the slavery will have no salvific resolution as it did in Egypt, followed by the exodus, or in the exile, followed by the restoration. This time it will be permanent and will result in utter dishonor and shame (see Commentary on 1:11-12).

8:24-27. Judith turns from indicative to imperative. God's rescue of the people Israel does not come about on its own; the citizens of Bethulia must act. Judith provides a compelling theological understanding of the Bethulians' situation: They should not put God to the test; rather, God is "testing" them (the same Greek word [πειράζω *peirazō*] is used in both cases), just as God tested Abraham, Isaac, and Jacob, the three patriarchs. There are many tests that could be associated with Abraham, Isaac, and Jacob, the greatest of which would be God's demand that Abraham sacrifice Isaac (Genesis 22), but the reference may be to the collective endurance of the three major patriarchs (cf. Heb 11:8-21). In this text, a specific example is given regarding only Jacob—that is, his sojourn to Paddan-aram ("Syrian Mesopotamia") to find a wife from among the daughters of Laban (Genesis 28–31). Whereas the people had decided that God was punishing them for their sins (7:28), or simply abandoning them (7:30), Judith insists that God is testing their mettle. These views are found in other texts that the Bethulians might have drawn on. That God punishes the Jews for their sins was the basis of the deuteronomic theology, even if, as Second Isaiah and Jeremiah insisted, the punishment was only temporary. A similar view was expressed in Judith's day in 2 Macc 5:17-20. However, God's teaching and discipline are also found in early biblical traditions (Deut 8:5; Ps 94:12; Prov 3:11-12), but became much more strongly emphasized after the exile, and especially in the period contemporary with Judith (Sir 6:18-22; 1 Cor 11:32; 2 Cor 6:9; Heb 12:5-11; Jas 1:2-4; *1 Clement* 56). God's testing is often compared to teaching and discipline: "God is found by those who do not put him to the test, and manifests himself to those who do not distrust him.... When his power is tested, it exposes the foolish" (Wis 1:2-3). And "Having been disciplined a little, the righteous will receive great good, because God tested them and found them worthy of himself" (3:5; see also Sir 2:1-6). Thus the patriarchs are like the righteous: tested and found worthy of God.

8:28-29. The wisdom of Judith and the approval of her character by everyone are emphasized. Still, there are questions about the precise nature of her wisdom. On the one hand, while she is on her estate she is like the capable wife of Proverbs 31, but on the other hand, when she proceeds out to engage Holofernes, she is not. One must, therefore, distinguish clearly between "wisdom" and "cleverness."[87] Jacob, for example, was clever, even a "trickster," in his dealings with others, but never is he described as wise. Joseph, on the other hand, is described as "discreet and wise" (Gen 41:39); he can interpret dreams and knows enough to retreat from the advances of Potiphar's wife (Genesis 39–41). Other figures in the HB tend to fall into one paradigm or the other—that is, wisdom as piety or wisdom as cleverness. There are wise women in the HB who are clever, such as the wise woman of Tekoa (2 Sam 14:1-7) and the wise woman of Abel (2 Sam 20:14-22). On the other hand, Daniel is wise and pious (Dan 1:20; 4:15; 5:11-16). Judith seems to combine the two paradigms; she is wise and righteous, like Joseph, but she is very clever in dealing with evil and uses deceit as one of her best weapons, like Jacob. She is a trickster, but not for her own ends; unlike Jacob, she is a trickster in the service of others.

8:30-36. Uzziah wants Judith to pray for the people because she is a redeemer for them, a mediator between the people and God. Moses was earlier considered a mediator figure, as were the prophets at times; this was probably the original meaning of Deut 18:15-18. Even a woman could be so depicted: Deborah and Jael team up to deliver Israel in a narrative that has greatly influenced the author of Judith (see Introduction). Uzziah wants Judith to pray for rain to relieve their thirst and allow them to hold out longer; it does not occur to him at this point that Judith is capable of removing the threat of Holofernes altogether (but note

---

87. Susan Niditch, *Underdogs and Tricksters: A Prologue to Biblical Folklore* (San Francisco: Harper & Row, 1987) 93-125; Lawrence M. Wills, *The Jew in the Court of the Foreign King: Ancient Jewish Court Legends* (Minneapolis: Fortress, 1990) 23-38.

v. 35). Judith, however, has bigger plans than bringing rain. She instructs Uzziah to stand by, but informs him that she means to deliver Israel by her hand. Judith will not divulge her plan, but she does prepare the reader for the heroic importance of her deed "for endless generations" and that it will be a memorial to her, as the conclusion implies (16:21-25). She speaks with a conviction and authority that does not allow for second-guessing. Uzziah responds accordingly by endorsing her command, but he is taking his strength from her, more so than was the case of Barak and Deborah (Judges 4–5). Uzziah is pliant with Judith as he was with the people of Bethulia. He admits that the people forced him to make an oath that will test God. His excuse is similar to that of Aaron after the making of the golden calf (Exod 32:22). The oath is presumably inviolable because it was a solemn vow to God (7:28), but in folktales and traditional literature the inviolability of an oath is often also an important narrative device that forces the actions of the protagonists (see Josh 9:19-20; Judges 11; Esth 1:19; 8:8; Dan 6:8, 12). Here, rather than demanding that the magistrates rescind the oath, Judith presumes its inviolability and must work quickly to save the Bethulians before the five days are up. The tension of the story is thus maintained, as she must operate with a ticking clock in the background.

REFLECTIONS

The Bethulians, including their leader Uzziah, are prepared to capitulate if God does not intervene within a set time. The urgent petitions of the Israelites in Jerusalem were earlier said to be heard by God (4:13), but the Bethulians remain in doubt. Although Judith rebukes them for testing God, is she being too demanding? Are we to experience the outrage that Judith feels toward the weakness of the Bethulians, or should we be sympathetic toward these decent and ordinarily pious people who have been placed in an extreme situation? The catastrophe that apparently awaited them would probably give pause to most people and likewise force them to consider surrendering as the other nations had done. Judith is not gentle in response to their actions, however, since to her mind they tested God much as the Israelites had murmured against Moses in the wilderness wanderings.

Perhaps both here and in the exodus narrative the modern reader experiences some of the doubt that is in the hearts of the Israelites. The reader knows how the two stories will end, but can also imagine not having the courage of Moses or Judith. Real human beings rarely exhibit perfect courage or certainty. These writings seem to recognize that, for at the same time that such scenes exhort the readers to greater courage, they also allow us to experience doubt in a situation where we know all will end well. Although some of Judith's cocksureness may seem less than humble to modern readers, the book of Judith explores the issue of courage and trust from three different perspectives. First, Judith expresses absolute trust. In upbraiding the Bethulians, she argues that they should leave their fate in God's hands: "Let us call upon him to help us, and he will hear our voice, if it pleases him" (8:17). The Israelites in Jerusalem also turn to the Lord in prayer and fasting, and their plea is so urgent that they even put sackcloth on their cattle—a comic touch, but surely one that reflects their sincerity. Where there are heartfelt pleas among the Israelites, God responds (4:13). Even the Ammonite Achior seems to get it when it comes to Israelite history: "As long as they did not sin against their god they prospered. . . . Their Lord and God will defend them" (5:17, 21).

Trust in God is the operative mode for Judith, for the Israelites in Jerusalem, and even for Achior, but not for the Bethulians, whose perspective exhibits the second kind of trust, which is imperfect. Their resilience had a limit, and they transfer their anxieties onto God by setting a time limit within which to act.

And if the Bethulians are to be the "sympathetic sinners" in the text—those whom we cannot really condemn just for being human—there is another group whose capitulation is not sympathetic and who display a third level of trust. The "people who lived along the seacoast" (2:28) not only succumb to their fears, with none of the tension or soul-searching that the Bethulians exhibit, but also demonstrate that they have readily abandoned their gods and dance before Holofernes with garlands and tambourines (3:1-8). Surely this is the opposite of trust in their gods; their allegiance was so ephemeral that they could watch their gods be destroyed, accept Nebuchadnezzar as their new "deity," and celebrate the transformation.

It is not necessary, then, to say that we should be like Judith. We are probably more like the Bethulians, and will remain so. But the text invites us to see three levels of trust and to embrace a life that is oriented toward a sincere trust in God. While Judith's position in regard to the Bethulians may seem overly strict, it is the larger theme of trust in God to which the book ultimately points.

Modern North American readers will probably never be trapped under siege in a mountain village as a general and his mighty army choke off all hope, but the text serves to affirm the need of trust in God in seemingly impossible situations. And those will occur. Whether someone tests God or offers a prayer that imposes a time limit on God is not important; that is probably not as serious as Judith makes it out to be. But in the text her strong reaction serves to put the theme of trust—sincere trust—into sharper relief.

Judith 9:1-14, Judith Purifies Herself and Prays

COMMENTARY

The Jewish novels of this period each have scenes that focus on the prayers and interior thoughts of a significant female character. Susanna has a moment of decision in which she must choose whether to capitulate to the demands of the wicked elders to lie with them or to preserve her virtue, even at the risk of being wrongly convicted and put to death for adultery. The young Sarah in the book of Tobit laments her continuing ill fortune that seven of her fiancés have died on their wedding night, and prays for death. Esther in the Additions confesses to God her repugnance at the situation she finds herself in, and Aseneth in *Joseph and Aseneth* enters into a state of penitence and prayer that lasts for seven days. Similarly Judith has her scene of ritual preparation and prayer. All of these novels have in common the focus on the woman's experience of reflection and decision, but three of them, Additions to Esther, *Joseph and Aseneth*, and Judith, have developed a type scene that is much more dramatic and formulaic.[88] It is presented as a marked transition that is similar to what anthropologists call a "rite of passage" (see Introduction). Arnold van Gennep and Victor Turner divide rituals that mark important human transitions into three distinct stages: separation, liminal period, and incorporation or aggregation. The separation is the marked movement from normal or mundane time and space to the liminal period, a special status that is more in touch with the divine. It is sacred time and space, not marked by the usual everyday indications of time, space, social order, gender, and so on. Last comes incorporation, in which the person moves back into mundane time and space, often with a new status or changed disposition. In Judith each part is marked by clear outward indicators of role or status: The woman begins in the clothing of wealth and position; takes off these clothes (separation); clothes herself in the garments of mourning, which eliminate the indicators of social or gender roles; and begins to pray; then she bathes and reclothes herself in new garments similar to the old, but even more splendid (incorporation).[89] When Judith emerges from

88. Wills, *The Jewish Novel in the Ancient World*, 224-32; Bach, *Women, Seduction, and Betrayal in Biblical Narrative*, 201-3.

89. van Gennep, *The Rites of Passage*; Turner, "Betwixt and Between," 93-111.

her ritualized prayer and reclothes herself, her actions are also very similar to those of Esther and Aseneth. At Add. Esth 15:1 we read, "On the third day, when she had ended her prayer, she took off the garments in which she had worshiped, and arrayed herself in splendid attire." This same scene is found in other Jewish novels and is sometimes greatly expanded, as in *Joseph and Aseneth*, where the heroine repents of her idolatry by covering herself in ashes mixed with her tears for seven days. Men are sometimes also depicted engaging in the rituals of mourning or protest, as Mordecai does in Esther 4, but the woman's scene of grief and self-abasement is more heartrending and penitential. This rite works perfectly to demarcate in narrative form the process of penitence, and it was likely well established in the literary tradition of Judaism (Neh 9:1). Even if the other known Jewish novels were composed later than Judith, there was still a developing penitential novelistic tradition of which Judith was one part, evidenced also by the insertion of the Prayer of Azariah and Susanna into the book of Daniel.

9:1. Judith begins here by prostrating herself, putting ashes on her head, and uncovering the sackcloth that she is presumably wearing under her widow's garments (see 8:5). This seems strange as a mourning custom, but she is presumably exposing her true state of pious self-abnegation—that is, the customs of mourning have become a form of ascetic spirituality. Sackcloth was a coarse, dark cloth woven from the hair of goats and camels. Turner notes that in the liminal state the person undergoing a rite of passage is often colored dark in some way, which is identified with the earth, and is allowed to become filthy.[90] We are reminded that the mourning ritual, which was a marked rite of passage in Israel, included, in addition to the wearing of sackcloth, the covering of the head in ashes, and in Add. Esth 14:2 with dung. Thus the usual ritual of mourning in Israel seemed to include that aspect of liminal symbolism that Turner suggests represents a dissolution of normal distinctions and an identification with undifferentiated earth.

Sackcloth and ashes are symbols of the grief of mourning, which Judith is exhibiting here to enter into a state of purification and prayer. Compare the parallel moment in Additions to Esther:

Then Queen Esther, seized with deadly anxiety, fled to the Lord. She took off her splendid apparel and put on the garments of distress and mourning, and instead of costly perfumes she covered her head with ashes and dung, and she utterly humbled her body; every part that she loved to adorn she covered with her tangled hair. (Add. Esth 14:1-2 NRSV)

Esther then proceeds to a deeply felt prayer and is penitent over her sin and the sin of her people. Judith, however, is not penitent. She never mentions her own sin, nor in her prayer does she mention the sin of her fellow Israelites—that comes up only in her upbraiding of the elders and in her lie to Holofernes. Judith does not have a rending self-examination as Esther and Aseneth do, but like them she has crossed the threshold into the liminal state of a profound ritual, where she can meet God more directly. Her ritual has prepared her for a relationship with God that is more direct than is the case for the other Bethulians. As a result, what we seem to have in Judith is a merging of two quite different narrative paradigms: the male hero pattern and the pattern of the penitential Jewish woman. The latter is drained of its original content and pressed into the service of a new theme where it works quite well: The beautiful woman of Israel, like a warrior, readies herself for the quest by stripping away her old garments, praying, bathing, and reclothing herself in the special armor that she is called upon to wear: beguiling clothes, jewelry, and cosmetics.

The timing of her prayer is quite significant, coinciding as it does with the evening incense offering in the Temple in Jerusalem (Exod 30:7-8). We may note by comparison that in John 19:14 it is stated that Jesus' crucifixion occurred at the same moment that the Passover lambs were slaughtered in the Temple. This aligns Judith's practices with those in the Temple, although her actions, even those up to this point, have not been strictly orthodox (her lack of a levirate marriage, her mourning beyond the period required by law). This seems to point to a contradiction in her observance of Jewish law, but this was probably not a difficulty for

---

90. Turner, "Betwixt and Between," 96, 107.

the ancient reader of the book of Judith. It is not presumed by the audience that this is a normal practice for Jews; rather, in the narrative world of this book the protagonist follows the dictates of her heartfelt piety and is not bound by the ordinary codes of conduct. It is actually in the nature of the Jewish and Christian novels for the protagonists to engage the spirit of the law without always conforming to the letter. Thecla, for instance, in the early Christian *Acts of Paul and Thecla* (34), actually baptizes herself because she thinks she is about to die.

9:2-10. Although Judith's genealogy at 8:1 did not explicitly mention Simeon (except in some ancient MSS), here she makes explicit what was implied there (see Commentary on 8:1): She is descended from Simeon, one of the twelve sons of Jacob and ancestor of the tribe of Simeon. She takes up the most important story associated with Simeon, his revenge on Shechem for the rape of his sister Dinah (Genesis 34). Just as Mattathias, the father of the Maccabee brothers, is likened to Phineas because of the latter's zeal for executing idolaters (Num 25:6-15), so also Judith takes up the cause of a patriarchal avenger. Simeon and his brothers, outraged after Shechem raped their sister Dinah, deceitfully agreed that he could marry her on condition that all the males of Shechem's clan be circumcised. They consented, but while they were still sore, Simeon and Levi came upon them unawares, killed all the males, and took Dinah back with them. The other sons of Jacob then plundered the city, took women and children and livestock, and returned to Jacob. In Gen 34:30 and 49:5-7 Jacob condemns the violent spirit of Simeon and Levi because it will create trouble with the peoples of the land. Judith, however, adopts Simeon as a positive model. She takes up the same cause as Simeon's (v. 4) and sets out a plan of revenge that will be modeled on his. In Judith's view, God orchestrated Simeon's revenge out of a shared sense of outrage. The description of the revenge is gruesome: the slaughter of the males, the taking of the women and enslavement of the daughters, the plundering of the spoils—all this in Judith's view is a justified response for the rape of Dinah.

The violence is not really different from the Genesis account of the slaughter by the sons of Jacob, but here it is all God's doing (v. 5). To be sure, Judith was not the only ancient source to take a positive view of the revenge on Shechem. *Jubilees* 30 and *Testament of Levi* affirm the role of Simeon and Levi, and *Joseph and Aseneth* 23 notes Simeon's violent spirit without condemning it. God's action against the Shechemites thus is not considered by the author of Judith to be a brazen and reckless act on the part of Simeon as it is in Genesis, but part of God's judgment on Shechem for the rape of Dinah. God was acting as "redeemer" (גאל *gōʾēl*) through Simeon; God struck down "slaves along with princes," which, along with v. 10, seems to be an echo of God's judgment in Isa 24:2. Judith's belief that it is God's doing appears to be based on the assumption that God wills all actions and events. The very fact that it happened indicates that God orchestrated it; wisdom texts sometimes express a similar opinion concerning natural phenomena (Job 38:35; Bar 3:34) and, in a general way, historical events (Wisdom 10–19).

Judith emphasizes that unlike the warriors Simeon and Levi, revenge in this case is left in the hands of a widow (v. 4). She returns to this theme in v. 9, and in v. 10 entreats God to destroy Holofernes and his army by the hand of a female. Judith here picks up another motif from the book of Judges, for at Judg 9:53 Abimelech is shamed because he is mortally wounded by a woman and is later known for this (2 Sam 11:21). In a world conscious of honor and shame, for a warrior to be killed by a woman was a great shame.

According to Judith, the rape of Dinah was a pollution of "their blood" (vv. 2, 4), and the point of this emphasis is well taken: The Assyrians intend to defile and pollute the sanctuary in Jerusalem. There is a clear parallelism and contrast, with the implication that Assyria is "raping" Jerusalem. This is perhaps not an unusual metaphor for conquest, but the book of Judith draws it out in specific ways. Looking back, the Assyrian rape of Jerusalem is like Shechem's rape of Dinah; and looking forward, the Assyrians will knock the horns off the altar with their swords (v. 8), just as Judith will decapitate Holofernes. By the parallel Judith draws, she is developing the notion that she will be the *gōʾēl* of Jerusalem, the raped woman. In ancient Israel, the *gō'ēl* was the male family member whose responsibility it was to avenge an attack on any other family member. In the patriarchal period of clans, tribes, and extended families, it was accepted that the "avenger of blood" (גאל הדם *gō'ēl haddām*) would achieve justice for wronged parties; but this function was also regulated and contained by the safeguard of "cities of refuge," into which the avenger of blood could not go to attack the perpetrator of the offense (Num 35:19; Deut 19:6). The concept of *gō'ēl* stands behind the revenge on Shechem, and it stands behind Judith as well as does a concept of extended-family solidarity: "Not only members of a clan, but also their possessions, form an organic unity, and every disruption of this unity is regarded as intolerable and as something which must be restored or repaired."[91] The king can be a *gō'ēl* of the poor who are oppressed (Ps 72:14), and God can act as a *gō'ēl* as well (Jer 50:34). Judith here presents herself to God as the only available *gō'ēl* (although this word or its equivalent is not used), all the men having fallen away.

Judith, in vv. 6b-8a, quotes a line that is evidently from the Greek translation of Exod 15:3, part of Moses' Song of the Sea, which he sang after the death of Pharaoh and his armies. She takes up this line again in her victory song at 16:2. Several terms in v. 11 ("helper," "protector," "savior") are also influenced by the Song of the Sea (Exod 15:2), where they occur in the same order.[92]

Judith intimates to God—and to the audience—what her weapon of choice will be: "the deceit of my lips." Deceit is not an expedient that she falls back on as a last resort when she is in Holofernes' presence, but the very basis of her plan from the beginning. It is a weapon of power that will allow God, through her, to strike down "slaves along with princes, and princes on their thrones" (v. 3). The power of deceit was recognized in wisdom teachings roughly contemporary with Judith (see Jas 3:5-12; cf. Wis 1:8; Matt 12:36-37), but it is usually viewed by the pious as unequivocally negative. Judith clearly intends to use the weapon for good, but in the liminal state of this novel, she is clearly reversing the accepted standards of Jewish ethics.

9:11-14. Judith here takes up the language of humility. The positive valuation of the humble is unusual, though not unknown, in Greek and Roman culture. The *Life of Aesop*, a Greek novel roughly contemporary with Judith, champions Aesop as a humble satirist of the wealthy, a role for him that was generally recognized in Greek culture. Aesop was one of the seven sages, but he had to sit on a footstool. Diogenes Laertius notes that when Chilo asked Aesop what Zeus was doing, Aesop answered, "He is lowering what is high, and exalting what is low."[93] Still, humility in Greek and Roman culture remained more of a novelty than a central theological value. In Jewish culture, it is a common theme in the psalms: "For you deliver a humble people, but the haughty eyes you bring down" (Ps 18:27 NRSV; see also Pss 10:18; 138:6; 146:7-9). It is also present in the Magnificat of Mary in Luke 1:46-55 and its model, the Song of Hannah in 1 Sam 2:1-10. It is from v. 11, and from her remark on her low status as a woman and a widow, that some have found a theology of humility in the book of Judith.[94] There are, however, problems with this judgment. This prayer shows proper piety on Judith's part, but if the book was written during the expansion of the Hasmonean rulers, the humility may ring somewhat hollow. Granted, this may be confusing the author's situation and that of the fictional character Judith, who lived, after all, in a situation of persecution; but the piety of humility does not seem as genuine in one so triumphalistic. The talented author of Judith is probably not attempting to create a humble heroine or articulate a theology of humility. Judith is merely being characterized as the perfect heroine; the humble Jewish widow is capable of decapitating the mighty Assyrian general. As Moore says in regard to this question, "If most, or at least many, of the important ideas of Judaism exist in Judith, that is all they really do, that is, they do not seem alive and vibrant."[95]

---

91. Helmer Ringgren, *TDOT*, 2:351.
92. Moore, *Judith*, 192.
93. *Lives*, Chilo 2.
94. Brian McNeil, "Reflections on the Book of Judith," *Downside Review* 96 (1978) 200.
95. Moore, *Judith*, 195.

REFLECTIONS

The book of Judith has remained popular over the centuries, perhaps more popular in the pre-modern period than in the modern. For Jews, Judith was a military heroine associated with Hanukkah, but for Christians she often represented virtues, especially penitence. Chartres Cathedral depicts her as she was often known, as putting ashes on her head. Although Judith's penitential actions are dramatically displayed, she seems unaware of any sins she might have commited. She could be characterized as what Stendahl has called a "robust conscience."[96]

The tendency in Judaism of this period and in early Christianity was to "raise the stakes" of sin. Sin was a more pressing part of religious life; it could keep one from approaching God with a pure heart, and it could separate one group or "sect" of Jews or Christians from another. The washings that Judith practices are not unrelated to the baptism Christians have instituted "for the forgiveness of sins" (Mark 1:4). But is Judith being hypocritical in taking up the practices of penitence without the self-examination? People sometimes conceive of their sin as the individual transgressions of daily life, or in terms of the larger picture of a doctrine of sin that defines the individual in relation to God. It is often difficult to reconcile the consciousness of everyday sins with theological beliefs about the origin and nature of sin. The book of Judith at first seems not to be much help here, because it shows Judith as far removed from her fellow citizens, who display human weakness and sin before God. But the book of Judith portrays a kind of spirituality, arising just before the beginnings of Christianity, that emphasized the cleansing from sin as a prelude to turning to God in prayer. This "penitential theology" has been a form of spirituality for those who might themselves be considered far from sin, the penitence of the righteous. The practices Judith undertakes are thus not intended simply to cleanse her from sinful acts; they are a form of worship in which one can approach God. Perhaps she is not being hypocritical, but is simply "at home" in this form of prayer. Sin, and the response to sin, becomes a way of defining the relationship of the human to God.

A central pastoral concern today, however, is to address the problem of sin in such a way as to recognize the different reactions of parishioners. Some feel comfortable with a doctrine of sin that defines the person as sinful before God or with a penitential spirituality that is conducive to this worship experience, while a fascination or obsession with sin can for others mask psychological problems of guilt, shame, and even unresolved conflicts from the past. The book of Judith presents the "comfortable" model of penitential spirituality of her period, but it does not address this second problem, which is for the modern reader often the harder question.

96. Krister Stendahl, "The Apostle Paul and the Introspective Conscience of the West," *HTR* 56 (1963) 199-215, reprinted in his *Paul Among Jews and Gentiles* (Philadelphia: Fortress, 1976) 78-96.

Judith 10:1-10, Judith Emerges from Prayer to Go Forth

COMMENTARY

10:1-5. Once Judith's prayer is finished, she rises to move forward with her plan. She is moving from the liminal period into the third phase of this rite of passage, incorporation. Judith's bathing can be compared to the similar scenes in the other Jewish novels, where the heroines emerge from the liminal state, bathe, and redress themselves for their new mission in life. In other cultures, traditions of the hero often include special scenes in which the hero dresses for battle or dons special armor before proceeding to the greatest test of valor. The hero usually has at his side a faithful servant who is instrumental in outfitting him.[97] Here also Judith, with the help of her maid, puts on the special armor that will be necessary for her great conflict. Her new identity is as a rich and beautiful seductress—one might even say a courtesan. She takes off her sackcloth and mourning garments, bathes, anoints herself with perfume, beautifies her hair, and puts on a full assortment of jewelry. Her beautification here includes the very items that Esther in the Additions condemned in herself. In fact, the listing of the items of beautification is very complete—ointment, combing, tiara, festive attire, sandals, anklets, bracelets, rings, earrings, and "all her other jewelry." Judith uses every means at her disposal to entice men, and Esther is not the only person to speak negatively of such cosmetics. At Isa 3:16-24, the wealthy daughters of Zion are condemned for wearing just such makeup, and the listing of items is very similar to Judith's. Judith clearly is threatening to violate the normal standards of clothing for pious Jewish women. She emerges from this a changed woman—or to be more exact, her true nature is now revealed. Now her beauty is so great that each man she meets is awestruck. This is very similar to the way Esther and Aseneth are described after they emerge from their prayer scenes.

Judith's vegetarian diet ensures a strict conformity with kosher food laws, just as Daniel and his three friends remained kosher by eating only vegetables in the court of Nebuchadnezzar (Dan 1:8). Like the beautiful clothes, the food also signifies that Judith has ritually left the confines of her tent and given up her fasts. The food may also have another role. If the book of Judith really is like the hero's quest, then her kosher food becomes almost like a magical charm or protective substance that, along with her bathing, keeps her from becoming polluted by contact with Holofernes.

The maid may seem at first to be an incidental character in the book, but she is actually quite integral. She functions as Judith's lieutenant in much the same way that Bagoas will for Holofernes. But there is something more subtle at play here as well. She is a loyal servant who does Judith's every bidding, and she will be freed by Judith at the end; yet she is never named and never speaks. She takes her identity entirely from Judith and joins in Judith's great service for others, but in a very subordinate way. She never establishes a personality of her own. The maid represents, from the point of view of the slave owner, the ideal slave, a motif also encountered in the Greek novels and in Esth 15:2-3.[98] Yet, on the other hand, as the counterpart to Holofernes' servant Bagoas, she is seen to be characterized quite positively in contrast to him; whereas Bagoas is talkative, gullible, and subservient, the maid is calm, deliberate, and loyal. One is the contrasting image of the other. In addition, since the maid is an effective assistant at just the moment Judith needs her (13:9-10), she becomes forever identified with her mistress's brave act and is often depicted in paintings alongside Judith. As Bal points out, Judith and the maid are both focused in the paintings; they *know* what Holofernes, Bagoas, and the Assyrian soldiers do not know.[99] In some paintings, such as those by Michelangelo and Artemisia Gentileschi, Judith and her maid are depicted as partners, while in others, there is an unmistakable suggestion that the maid represents the darker side of Judith: The maid is ugly and forbidding, sometimes more closely identified with the deed, while Judith can stand tall, beautiful, and pure (see the paintings by Sandro Botticelli, Michelangelo Caravaggio, and Antiveduto Grammatica).[100] Stocker also notes that the maid is sometimes depicted as the older version of Judith herself, a *memento mori*, or reminder of mortality and death, which also serves to underscore the fleeting nature of the power Judith derives from her beauty.[101]

---

97. Albert B. Lord, *The Singer of Tales* (New York: Atheneum, 1976) 86-91; C. M. Bowra, *Heroic Poetry* (London: Macmillan, 1952) 188-97.

98. Jennifer A. Glancy, "The Mistress-Slave Dialectic: Paradoxes of Slavery in Three LXX Narratives," *JSOT* 72 (1996) 71-87.

99. Mieke Bal, "Head Hunting: 'Judith' on the Cutting Edge of Knowledge," *JSOT* 63 (1994) 27.

100. For photographs of paintings depicting Judith, see Nira Stone, "Judith and Holofernes: Some Observations on the Development of the Scene in Art," in James C. VanderKam, ed., *"No One Spoke Ill of Her": Essays on Judith* (Atlanta: Scholars Press, 1992) 73-93; Moore, *Judith*; Garrard, "Judith"; Mary Jacobus, "Judith, Holofernes, and the Phallic Woman," in *Reading Women: Essays in Feminist Criticism* (New York: Columbia University Press, 1986); and Bal, "Head Hunting."

101. Margarita Stocker, *Judith, Sexual Warrior: Women and Power in Western Culture* (New Haven: Yale University Press, 1998) 33. It should be noted, however, that since in the ancient text the maid is not in the inner chamber with Judith at the moment of the decapitation, any inclusion of the maid in that scene in later paintings is an editorial change.

10:6-10. The development of novelistic description in Judith is remarkable, especially as it is sometimes done with considerable subtlety. In this passage, we find, first of all, retardation of plot—that is, a simple act, Judith and her maid leaving Bethulia, is drawn out by the addition of a number of small details to add texture and to increase the narrative tension the audience is feeling. The interchanges between Judith and her maid, on the one hand, and the elders and the young men at the gate, on the other hand, are played out in a series of verbal and physical exchanges. The scene becomes almost ceremonial as Judith and her maid find the elders, receive Uzziah's blessing, bow down, ask the elders to open the gate, wait for them to have the order executed, and exit as the men watch her trail off into the valley. Alonso-Schökel has rightly called this last effect "cinematographic";[102] the ritualism and detail make the entire scene come to life before the eyes much like an American western film.

According to Bowra, a standard feature of heroic quest traditions is that upon departure a blessing of the gods is invoked for the hero's safe travel, often by an elderly figure.[103] Such an episode is probably what we see here in Uzziah's blessing of Judith at the gates. This is part of the large structural pattern of the quest of the hero, but at this point there is also introduced a second rite of passage. It follows the preceding one and encompasses the period between the time when Judith moves out of Bethulia toward Holofernes' camp and when she returns. Campbell talks of the hero's passing over the threshold between the known world and the unknown into the region where the monster resides.[104] It is significant that Judith walks out at night, which connotes here the unknown place of danger. We should also recall that the word "liminal" comes from the Latin word *limen*, or "threshold," which is both literally and figuratively what is here being marked. In Craven's structural division of Judith, she also notes the importance of these two gate scenes. They hold corresponding places in the chiasm, both before and after the longer section of Judith's vanquishing of Holofernes.[105] After praying and preparing herself through the rite of passage above, she has one last dialogue with Uzziah and, as she is ready to proceed to the next passage, gives a command to "order the gate of the town to be opened." Upon her return in 13:11 she again says, "Open, open the gate!" The gates are a marked portal through which she enters into a new zone. It is not simply the zone of the warrior, since she will continue to act as a warrior, a general, and a strategist on the model of Deborah when she returns in chaps. 14–15. The zone she is in while she is between the gates—a liminal period between the thresholds—is one of being sexually provocative, treacherous, deceitful, and murderous. She meets her nemesis and greatest challenge, Holofernes, while in this zone, and Judith's violations of Jewish taboos for female behavior occur during this period; her challenge to gender roles is located in this zone. It is important to note that although Judith is beautiful both inside and outside this zone, she lies only while she is inside it. Within this zone, nearly every word out of her mouth is deceptive, provocative, flattering, and deceitful.

That people are struck by Judith's beauty is constantly emphasized (10:7, 14, 19, 23), which is also a standard, even required motif of the Greek novels. In the Greek novels this usually places the heroine in jeopardy as one man after another tries to press his attentions upon her, but in Judith it is the means she will use to gain the upper hand.

The text in v. 8 says, "She bowed down to God," even though it is not clear why she does so at this point. It could be taken as another pious gesture, but Moore accepts an emendation of the text that would read, "She bowed down to them"—i.e., the men—as she took her departure.[106] This is less abrupt, and she makes a similar bow upon being admitted to the presence of Holofernes (10:23). The two bows are somewhat at odds with her commanding personality, but that might be just the point. They are balanced actions that show her social graces as she moves to take control of the situation. (See Reflections at 11:1-23.)

---

102. Alonso-Schökel, *Narrative Structures in the Book of Judith*, 7.
103. Bowra, *Heroic Poetry*, 184-86.
104. Campbell, *The Hero with a Thousand Faces*, 90-91.
105. Craven, *Artistry and Faith in the Book of Judith*, 62-63.
106. Moore, *Judith*, 201-2.

JUDITH 10:11–13:10a, JUDITH OVERCOMES HOLOFERNES

Judith 10:11-23, Judith Enters the Enemy Camp and Is Taken to Holofernes

COMMENTARY

10:11-16. Interestingly, the retardation of plot in the preceding scene is followed by the sudden jolt of the present one. There is finally a meeting of Israelites and Assyrians, which has been threatened for most of the book, and the Assyrians appear to be in the commanding position. Judith's plan, which up to now has only been hinted at, is beginning to be realized. The reader sees Judith at work on the enemy, and in her first words she is already lying. The Assyrian soldiers, also struck by her beauty, usher her along with a comical show of respect. The Assyrians begin to speak in an extended irony in which almost every line can be understood in two ways, depending upon whether the "lord" referred to is Holofernes or God: "You have saved your life by hurrying down to see our lord . . . some of us . . . will hand you over to him [lit., deliver you into his hands]." The audience at this point would have been aware of each reference and would not have missed the ironic distance between the show of the troops and their apparent obtuseness about the meaning of their own words. The obtuseness of the characters is an important part of the comic irony in the Gospel of John as well (see John 3:4; 4:11; 9:25).

10:17-23. Here also a vivid description enlivens the narrative. One can almost see the hubbub and excitement spread through the camp as men not only are struck by her beauty, but also marvel at what it indicates about Israelites in general. The soldiers draw the conclusion that the audience would want them to draw: that Israelite women—and therefore men as well—are superior to any on earth. This means of affirming ethnic superiority is typical of much of the writing of this period, both in the dominant Greek and Roman culture, and of the various indigenous peoples. It is found in a very similar way in *Joseph and Aseneth* 1:4-5, where it is said that Aseneth was "tall and comely, and more beautiful than any young woman on earth. Indeed, she bore little resemblance at all to Egyptian women, but was in every way more like the women of the Hebrews: as tall as Sarah, as comely as Rebecca, as beautiful as Rachel." The *Genesis Apocryphon* (20:2-6) from Qumran is equally complimentary in regard to Sarah.

We first encounter Holofernes in a tent that is parallel to Judith's tent, but rather than a retreat for righteous fasting and praying, it is a palace in miniature, sumptuously decorated with precious stones. It is probably not meant to be effeminate, as its appearance may strike the modern reader, although this is not implausible considering the way Holofernes will later be "unmanned." Enslin suggests that there may be evident here contempt for the luxury of the Eastern despot and his finery.[107] One similarity to Judith's tent that does remain is that Holofernes is generally secluded in it. He meets with his officers in the tent, and while alive always appears in it. This tent has two chambers, and his bedchamber, covered with a canopy, is where he hopes to take Judith to bed and where he will later die. The canopy that covers the bed and separates the chambers will also be of great importance later.

One might wonder whether the structure of the tent is significant. It has at least two chambers, the inner sleeping chamber, separated from the outer chamber by the specially decorated canopy. Is this structure intended to call to mind the Temple in Jerusalem, albeit as a sort of mirror image? The Second Temple consisted of a series of concentric courts, with the Temple itself standing

---

107. Enslin and Zeitlin, *The Book of Judith*, 133-34. See also Horace *Epodes* 9.16 concerning the bed canopy of Marc Antony.

at the center and the altar just outside facing it. Within the Temple was the holy of holies, or inner sanctum, and like the bedchamber of Holofernes' tent, it was separated by a curtain from the rest of the Temple. The curtain was richly decorated, with some of the same colors as those of Holofernes' curtain (Exod 26:31). The curtained area of the Temple was entered only once a year on the Day of Atonement, and then only by the high priest. Judith will enter Holofernes' inner sanctum to kill him, just as the high priest enters the holy of holies, and one might say that she will "sacrifice" him. At this last point the parallel breaks down, however, because the sacrifice on the Day of Atonement is carried out on the alter in front of the Temple, and only some of the blood is carried into the holy of holies. Still, the parallel is suggestive, for the curtain of the Temple was quite symbolic of its integrity and sanctity; in early Christianity, it became a powerful symbol of the access Christ had created to the realm of God (Matt 27:51; Hebrews 9–10). (See Reflections at 11:1-23.)

Judith 11:1-23, Judith's Dialogue with Holofernes

COMMENTARY

11:1-8. Holofernes is as gracious to Judith as she is to him. He does not treat her as a member of a conquered people, but immediately presses her to find out why she has abandoned her village. Judith begins her speech by asking him to "accept the words of your slave," as if it were a humble petition addressed to God. In a way, it is, as the next sentence continues the double-layered reference to "my lord": "I will say nothing false *to my lord* this night." Judith is equivocating with the truth; she will lie to one lord while being truthful with the other. She must use her two cultivated weapons, her beauty and her deceptive tongue (9:10), to distract and manipulate her oppressor: "If you follow out the words of your servant, God will accomplish something through you, and my lord will not fail to achieve his purposes." One might argue that here the double entendre gets Judith into a moral gray area when she says, "I will say nothing false to my lord this night." However, we must understand her intention: Her lies to Holofernes are a form of "truth" to God, since they serve God. This skates very close to lying to God, but that is precisely the point. For the audience, the exhilaration in reading Judith consists in skating close to the edge of moral violations. It is a release of moral tensions. Moore points out that to gain Holofernes' trust, Judith swears by what is holy to him—that is, the name of Nebuchadnezzar—and broadly praises Nebuchadnezzar.[108] Her flattery of Holofernes is shameless and almost as much a violation of the truth as is her lying: "Not only do human beings serve Nebuchadnezzar because of you, but also the animals of the field and the cattle and the birds of the air will live." In the book of Daniel, the king's protection of the animal kingdom is associated with Nebuchadnezzar both in the words of Daniel himself (Dan 2:37-38) and in Nebuchadnezzar's own grandiose self-image (Dan 4:12). The power of Nebuchadnezzar is elsewhere understood to be a gift of God, and strictly temporary (Jer 27:4-7).

11:9-15. Other than her maid, Judith has only one ally in her stratagem, and that is Achior. Without realizing it—although one might suspect the workings of God—Achior has helped to set up the situation that will lead to the Assyrians' downfall. In chap. 5 he presented the deuteronomic principle that could establish the vulnerability of the Israelites: If they have sinned, then their God will not protect them. Judith reiterates this principle and draws a firm conclusion: Now they have sinned and are about to fall to Holofernes. Judith spins a complicated scenario of the practices of the Bethulians that will violate God's laws. The content of her words is clearly directed to the reading audience; it refers to practices that can only really be understood within the context of Jewish laws concerning temple practices. That God could not countenance a violation in the light of the desperation of the Bethulians' situation is part of Judith's deception. The accommodation of God's law to times of crisis was

---

108. Moore, *Judith*, 209.

certainly an accepted view in the Hasmonean state (1 Macc 2:32-41). Also, the violation at hand is carefully chosen to show a deference to the priesthood in Jerusalem. This is the real focus of the religious world of the author and audience of Judith. On the assumption that the author is not trying to present a list of violations of Jewish law that Holofernes would understand, but rather a list that the audience would understand, it appears that killing their livestock might have meant slaughtering the animals without draining the blood thoroughly as Lev 17:10-14 required (see also Acts 15:20). This, at any rate, is what the Latin versions understood by it. Since this is a part of the priestly office in Jerusalem, it matches the other violations. In their desperation, the Bethulians are eating the firstfruits and tithes of wine and oil that should have been reserved for the priests. These are precisely the same offerings that are mentioned at 1 Macc 3:49 when the Maccabee rebels hold an alternative temple service at Mizpeh before the capture and rededication of the Jerusalem Temple. The strictness of observance is emphasized by saying that the people could not so much as touch the offerings once they had been consecrated. Tobit 1:6-8 also presents an idealized view of a pious diaspora Jew bringing his offerings to Jerusalem.

The Bethulians are not acting alone, however. Judith's lie incriminates Jerusalem as well, because even there the council has allowed the citizens to do these things; more to the point, the Jerusalem council is prepared to give its permission to Bethulia as well. Bethulia is waiting for messengers to return from Jerusalem, which provides a specific point in time for their transgression to be complete in God's eyes. The precise time line imposed on the action is parallel to the time line that the Bethulians had imposed upon themselves by making a vow to surrender if God had not brought rain within five days. Although Judith says she must pray to learn when the Israelites have violated God's laws, the audience would recognize that the time line for this made-up offense is the same as that for the Bethulians' actual offense.

11:16-18. Judith states her conclusion about these violations of law with a sentence that is a marvelous double entendre: "God has sent me to accomplish with you things that will astonish the world." The polytheistic religion of the ancient Near East would have held that a people's strength in war was related to the strength of their gods; but monotheism in Israel, and especially the deuteronomic theology, held that Israel's setbacks were not because God was weak, but because God was stronger than all nations and had willed for Israel to be overrun. Thus Judith says that God will inform her when the violation has occurred and will collude with the foreign nations to punish Israel. This theology would be laughable to a real adherent of the Assyrian gods, and in fact Holofernes had rejected it when it was spoken by Achior (5:20–6:4). However, Holofernes readily accepts it from Judith. Sensing an easy victory over her sexually and over her people as well, he need not quibble over theology.

11:19-23. Judith's language in v. 19 is laden with images from the prophets. Just as Achior spoke like a prophet, and as Nebuchadnezzar had as well, so also does Judith speak. In form her words are like an "oracle of salvation" from Second Isaiah (the section of Isaiah written during the exile, Isaiah 40–55. Isaiah 40:3-4, for example, familiar to Christians from its use in the Gospels (Matt 3:3; Mark 1:2; Luke 3:4-6; John 1:23), prophesies that a way will be made for the Lord through the desert to Jerusalem (see also Isa 35:8-10; 42:16; 51:11). Likewise, Judith, in an audacious affirmation of her own role, says, "There I will set your throne," which is similar to what God promises to David in 2 Sam 7:13 and Ps 89:4. "You will lead them like sheep without a shepherd" picks up a common motif in the HB that is found also in the NT (Ezek 34:8; Zech 10:2; 13:7; Matt 9:36; 26:31). Shepherds are also likened to watchdogs that do not bark in Isa 56:10-11, an image that Judith uses here as well. When Achior had said these same things by "prophecy" (5:21; 6:2), Holofernes condemned him. Here, however, Holofernes and his retinue marvel at Judith's wisdom (vv. 20-21). This, too, is ironic, because her wisdom consists in cleverness, the cleverness required to lie to them successfully and convince them that she is giving them wise advice.

Holofernes once again unknowingly speaks words that condemn his own cause, "God has done well to send you . . . to bring destruction on those who have despised my lord." His statement that "your god shall be my god" has caused trouble for scholars. It is the same statement that Ruth makes to Naomi in Ruth 1:16 when Ruth becomes an Israelite. But does Holofernes mean this? In the narratives of this period pagan kings, even oppressive ones, sometimes come to confess the God of Israel (Dan 2:47; 3:28-29; 4:34-37; 2 Maccabees 3; see also 2 Kgs 5:17). Still, Holofernes is being effusive and overly solicitous, but he is hardly converting to a worship of Israel's God. Perhaps he means that Judith will adopt his god, especially if, as he assumes, she will become a wife or courtesan of Nebuchadnezzar. Alternatively, perhaps Holofernes is again unknowingly accurate in his statement. If Judith does as she has promised, her God will be his God—in judgment. At any rate, the passage is probably intentionally ambiguous to show that Holofernes is swept up in the commonality of their purpose. It is, after all, only the audience who understands the meaning of Holofernes' words, and not he himself. Holofernes sums up his list of unintentional prophecies by affirming that Judith will be "renowned throughout the whole world," which the audience knows to be most decidedly true.

REFLECTIONS

From the time Judith leaves the gates of Bethulia until the time she returns, there are two constant motifs: (1) the Assyrians, struck by her beauty, will stumble over themselves in trying to cater to her requests, and (2) Judith all the while will be speaking in comic and ironic utterances. Although there have been comic elements before, they dominate the text for nearly three chapters. All good comedy works with tensions within the audience and effects a release of tensions, and Judith is no exception. It is effective partly because it creates and sustains a comic situation of the pious heroine taking a sojourn outside of her seclusion and respectability to flout social conventions, entice the lustful Holofernes, walk through the menacing enemy troops, and return to the safety of her village. What is interesting about Judith is that it represents the most extended use of comedy in the Bible and combines both the "low" and "high" comedy of burlesque and satire.

This is one of the aspects of Judith that make it very "modern." We can also sense the tensions in our society over sexual taboos that give rise to a comedy of release, and we are aware in our own time of the political implications of comedy in constructing a world (or a new world) with certain values "tested" and then reinstated. By discerning the relation of Judith's comedy to its political affirmation, we are reminded of this process in our day. Comedy draws us in and entertains us, testing our community values and rebuilding community at the same time. In Judith we can see this in the portrayal of a woman who flouts the prevailing codes of conduct and is ultimately returned to her modest and pious life.

When we talk of examining public values, groping for direction in the new day of the twenty-first century, making intelligent choices in the face of daunting new ethical dilemmas, we rarely think of that kind of discourse that is all around us and that comments on our perplexity the most directly—comedy. The positive and negative effects of comedy are felt by all members of our community alike, and in forms that are constant influences on our lives—television, film, literature, theater. The bold example of Judith reminds us that just as comedy represented a commentary on the political and religious situation of its day, so also the comedy of our own day is the most ubiquitous means of commenting on our disjointed world. And it is not just a "secular" commentary; included in its subject matter are the values of our society and the religious beliefs as well. Just as it is incumbent upon us to ask who the prophets are of our day, we must also address the question of who the Judiths are, for that is where we will find a mirror of the tensions and changes within our society.

Judith 12:1-20, For Three Days Judith Lives in Holofernes' Camp

COMMENTARY

12:1-9. Although Holofernes has intentions to wine and dine Judith, she resists and, in complete control of the situation, imposes on him her own requirements. She will eat the food she has brought with her so as not to break any kosher laws. Holofernes has no objection; he is even solicitous of her needs throughout. The supplies she and her maid have brought are sufficient for the period up until the time "the Lord carries out by my hand what he has determined." The careful adherence to kosher dietary laws, so careful that in some cases it becomes a strict vegetarianism, is found in the novelistic literature of this period (Dan 1:8-16; Add. Esth 14:17; Tob 1:10-11; 2 Macc 5:27).

Judith is remarkably free to move about as she pleases, which once again demonstrates her control of those who have been struck by her beauty. She arranges for an opportunity to go outside the camp to pray, which also establishes a pattern of her leaving very early each morning so that she will ultimately be able to escape.[109] Judith's departure each day also allows her to bathe. This is probably not principally meant for erotic effect, although Susanna's bathing or Bathsheba's bathing (2 Sam 11:2) might suggest that. Verse 9, however, emphasizes that Judith returned purified, so ritual observance must be the purpose of her bath. In the ritual of the Day of Atonement, the high priest bathes before he puts on the special linen garments in which he will perform the sacrifice and the scapegoat ritual. Judith also puts on special garments after bathing, but they are hardly the special linen garments of the high priest. Other forms of bathing in Judaism are perhaps more relevant. Baptism was practiced in a number of contexts at the turn of the first century BCE. For John the Baptist, baptism was described as being for repentance, and for Christians in general it was a ceremony for converts. In both of these cases, baptism was evidently a single ceremony and was not repeated. Jews may have practiced baptism for converts at this time, but the evidence for this practice does not go back any earlier than the first century CE. The Qumran sect provides a much closer parallel to Judith's bathing. The *Manual of Discipline* connects bathing with repentance, but unlike the baptism of John the Baptist, the number of cisterns at Qumran indicate that bathing was a more common, if not a constant, practice. Ritual bathing had evidently become a part of the increased notion of purity at Qumran, and was also part of the Pharisaic ideas of keeping food pure when coming in contact with Gentiles.[110] At the end of the menstrual period a Jewish woman would bathe, but presumably only once (Lev 15:19-24), and that does not appear to be the point of this motif. It is more likely that it is an idealized notion of purification derived from the requirement that a woman and a man must bathe after having sexual intercourse (Lev 15:18). Although Judith has not had sexual intercourse with Holofernes, her presence in his sleeping quarters and in his thoughts renders her symbolically unclean (cf. Matt 5:27-28). In this fictional world, she bathes in order to cleanse herself from even the insinuation of sexual intercourse. Perhaps her bathing is now simply a regular part of her personal devotion, paralleling the bathing that she performed at the end of her prayer in 10:3.

12:10-20. Holofernes' banquet includes servants only and not soldiers, a fortunate or providential detail if Judith is to be able to accomplish her plan. That Judith remains in control of Holofernes and the other persons around her is seen in the odd combination of phrases used by Holofernes: "Go and persuade her," "it would be a disgrace," "if we do not seduce her, she will laugh at us." On one hand, Holofernes displays the bravado of one who thinks he will soon have sex with Judith,

---

109. Moore, *Judith*, 219.

110. James VanderKam, *The Dead Sea Scrolls Today* (Grand Rapids: Eerdmans, 1994) 170; Louis Finkelstein, *The Pharisees: The Sociological Background of Their Faith*, 2 vols. (New York: Jewish Publication Society, 1966) 1:121-28.

whether she is agreeable or not; on the other hand, he awaits her word and has yet to say no to a single one of her unusual requests. Judith's personal power over Holofernes is only magnified by her insinuations that he will have his way with her. His excitement is growing at the same time that he treats her with more deferential respect, making the scene even more humorous and ironic, and ultimately making Holofernes appear weaker. Bagoas is also little more than a comic character. Despite the fact that the name "Bagoas" was associated with a powerful counselor in the invasion army of Antiochus III Ochus (see Commentary on 2:1-13), he functions only as an attendant to Holofernes, lacking even the quiet resolve of Judith's maid.

The ambiguity of the word "eunuch" (εὐνοῦχος *eunouchos*) may also be played upon here. The primary meaning, a castrated official who oversees the king's harem, was broadened to include any counselor in the royal court (for both meanings, cf. Esth 2:3; Isa 56:3-4; and Matt 19:12 with 2 Chr 18:8). Bagoas is called a eunuch in Judith, and this name was a common one for eunuchs in the Persian courts.[111] As Holofernes' attendant and go-between with Judith, which aspect of Bagoas are we seeing, a powerful counselor or a keeper of the harem, a harem that will now include Judith? Perhaps both are intended in a humorous way: Bagoas sees himself as a powerful counselor, but he is really a keeper of the harem who fetches women for the general's pleasure. As a eunuch, he seems to have desires for Judith, but only because he identifies so completely with Holofernes.

His words to Judith are suggestive without being crude, reflecting his and Holofernes' view of Judith's status—that is, as an ornament in Holofernes' harem, and soon to be an ornament in Nebuchadnezzar's, but one who deserves the respect befitting her beauty and status. Bagoas invites her to become like the Assyrian courtesans, a compliment in his eyes compared with her provincial origins as a "Hebrew woman." But for Judith to become an Assyrian courtesan is for the readers another threat to her purity. In the later Greek novels the hero and heroine are forced by circumstances to become "other" to their aristocratic Greek status. They are abducted and dragged across the eastern Mediterranean, lose their identity and status, are almost forced into prostitution, are forced to become slaves or enter marriages with wealthy men or women who lust after them, and so on. The descent into becoming "other" has been noted as a principal threat by which the protagonists are buffeted, and this is a theme of the other Jewish novels, Susanna, Additions to Esther, Tobit, and *Joseph and Aseneth* as well. But even though Judith is faced with the prospect of descending into the "other," she is never buffeted. Here the threat is stated as clearly as anywhere: A pious Jewish widow may be forced into having sexual relations with an Assyrian general and taken to a palace of Nebuchadnezzar to become like one of the Assyrian courtesans. Yet Judith is in absolute control of the situation. The tension is humorous and not really felt; as a result, Judith can even stoke the fires of Holofernes' desire by answering in an extremely suggestive way herself: "Whatever pleases Nebuchadnezzar I will do at once, and it will be a joy to me until the day of my death." Her words here are yet another example of double entendre, which by now seems to be her only mode of discourse in the Assyrian camp. This gives credence to the view that a rite of passage is initiated in her passing out of the gates of Bethulia, and ending when she reenters the gates at 13:11 (see Introduction and Commentary on 10:6-10). Between these points Judith is almost always lying or equivocating with the truth, and she is almost always speaking in her own special form of discourse, which consists of references on two levels at once. This is the gift of the "deceitful tongue" that she prayed for in 9:10.

Since all of Judith's violations of taboos of female behavior occur at the center of this novel, in a zone where the most important action occurs, one might assume that the novel encourages this illicit behavior, or at least decreases the distinction between acceptable and unacceptable behavior in a pious Jewish woman. If it is true, however, that Judith enters into a sort of liminal state, then Turner's theories about the liminal period suggest just the opposite. He notes the monstrous and animalistic features of

---

111. Pliny *Natural History* 13.41.

masks worn by various peoples during the liminal state in their initiation ceremonies.[112] Another anthropologist has concluded that "primitive" people made little distinction between human and animal, and therefore in the liminal state the human could slide over into the animal. Turner disagrees, and holds the opposite view: The animal forms humans take on in the liminal state serve precisely to impose clear distinctions between the different orders of reality as encountered in everyday life. In the same way, by allowing the pious behavior of a woman to pass over into the liminal state to impious behavior, the book of Judith effectively teaches a rigid distinction between the two, a distinction that would be maintained in the non-liminal state.

The puzzling detail of the lambskins (v. 15) may be simply an element added for atmosphere, an indication of Holofernes' generous hospitality, or it may suggest a special precaution to avoid ritual contamination. Menstrual impurity can be communicated by a woman to beds and mats (Lev 15:20-23); perhaps these special lambskins are held to protect Judith from impure contact, moving, as it were, in the opposite direction—that is, from her environment onto her.

Now Judith is reclining with Holofernes at dinner, and on this night he expects to ravish her. Judith seems to be cooperative, even excited herself, but for an entirely different reason. Her apparent cooperation could only excite Holofernes all the more, for although Judith eats and drinks what her maid has prepared, Holofernes now commences drinking wine in a celebratory mood—in fact, more than he has ever drunk in a day. He is indeed out of his mind with desire, which has clearly clouded his thinking. He believes himself to be in control and intends to seduce her with wine, but it is he who is under her control and who is becoming drunk instead.[113] The description of the mythical opponent as given by Campbell could be used to describe Holofernes or Nebuchadnezzar: "The tyrant is proud, and therein lies his doom. He is proud because he thinks of his strength as his own; thus he is in the clown role, as a mistaker of shadow for substance; it is his destiny to be tricked."[114]

112. Turner, "Betwixt and Between," 96, 107.
113. Alonso-Schökel, *Narrative Structures in the Book of Judith*, 12.
114. Campbell, *The Hero with a Thousand Faces*, 337.

Judith 13:1-10a, Judith Beheads Holofernes

COMMENTARY

The climactic scene is prepared for in some detail: Bagoas dismisses the servants and closes the tent from the outside. Judith's maid will stand outside the bedchamber—that is, the inner chamber of the tent, which was covered with the rich canopy (10:21). Judith alone remains in the inner chamber with Holofernes, who is now passed out drunk on his bed. The beheading scene, however, is told quickly, having been anticipated for twelve chapters. Her prayer invokes the power of God to come to the aid of Jerusalem, another indication that this book does not have a hidden Samaritan orientation.

Judith's actions are charged with sexual imagery, as many scholars have noted.[115]

First, the vertical bedpost is a phallic symbol upon which Holofernes has hung his sword, another phallic symbol. Holofernes' head is now beside the post, but because he is drunk, he has lost his virility and potency, just at the time when he expected to demonstrate them. Judith grasps him by the hair of his head, and praying again for strength, with two strokes severs his head from his body, an act that many commentators have viewed as a symbolic castration; at first impotent, he is now unmanned. She dethrones him by rolling him off the bed, and she takes the canopy from the posts. If the name "Bethulia" means virgin and Holofernes intended to rape the virgin, then the process has now been reversed and Judith has "raped" Holofernes by penetrating his inner chamber, "deflowering" him, and breaking his canopy. A confirmation of

115. Alan Dundes, "Response," in Alonso-Schökel, *Narrative Structures*, 28-29; Levine, "Sacrifice and Salvation"; Jacobus, "Judith, Holofernes, and the Phallic Woman," 110-36; Stocker, *Judith, Sexual Warrior*, 3-23.

the importance of the canopy, if not its sexual meaning as Holofernes' "hymen," is the fact that Judith will present it as a votive offering in the Temple in Jerusalem (16:19). If this reading of sexual symbolism seems more than what was intended by the author, it should be noted that sexual symbolism such as this is not unusual in popular tales,[116] although it may have been more unconscious than deliberate. Some scholars, to be sure, do not find sexual images present in the narrative,[117] but this text, perhaps more than any other in the OT, is capable of being interpreted in these terms.

Among the biblical passages that have likely influenced the author of Judith is the struggle between David and Goliath (1 Samuel 17). In preparation for his encounters with Goliath, David takes off the armor of Saul, which is a symbol of strength, and chooses the weapons of the weak: five smooth stones taken from a riverbed. Thus he affirms the power of the weak just as Judith does. He places the stones in his pouch as he marches out, just as Judith has placed in her pouch her kosher food, a necessary "weapon" for her stay in Holofernes' camp. Finally, David's utterance to Goliath is similar to Judith's language, although David has no need for double entendre: "This very day the LORD will deliver you into my hand, and I will strike you down and cut off your head" (1 Sam 17:46 NRSV). David first strikes Goliath in the head with a stone to subdue him, then, lacking a sword of his own, David, like Judith, stands over his adversary, takes his sword, and cuts off his head. When the enemy forces saw that their leader had been beheaded, they fled.

The food pouch, which had before represented Judith's special care in remaining kosher, now becomes the trophy pouch containing Holofernes' head and canopy. The grisly irony of this fact has attracted much attention, because in many of the paintings of Judith decapitating Holofernes, she appears with her maid, and it is their secret pact to carry home his head in a pouch that seems to connect them in the reader's memory, even though the maid is not present in the story when Judith actually beheads Holofernes. The meticulous practices of the two women have bound them together until today. The act is quickly concluded in the text in just a few verses, and their escape from the Assyrian camp and their retracing of the steps back up the mountainside to Bethulia is almost instantaneous. Everything in the book has prepared for this moment, and so it was not necessary to dwell on it. The quick release of tension flows as a result of Judith's act, and it is a credit to the pacing of the narrative that the author seems to speed up or slow down the action in just the right places.

---

116. Bruno Bettelheim, *The Uses of Enchantment: The Meaning and Importance of Fairy Tales* (New York: Vintage, 1977) 232-33, 268-73, 289-92; Erich Fromm, *Forgotten Language: An Introduction to the Understanding of Dreams, Fairy Tales and Myths* (New York: Grove, 1957) 240-41.

117. Moore, *Judith*, 72-73, 240.

REFLECTIONS

The book of Judith has provoked very different moral valuations in artists, theologians, and commentators over the centuries. Many Victorian-era writers and some later writers have strongly questioned the morality of Judith's position. What is more surprising are the authors who are far from being Victorian prudes who nonetheless find Judith threatening. Sigmund Freud was quite interested in Judith, but he participated in the typical evaluation of his day and demoted her from a brilliant and strong-willed heroine to a petulant woman who, like a moth to light, was brought within Holofernes' bedchamber and was actually raped by Holofernes as a result. She takes up his own sword and beheads him only in revenge for his violation of her.[118]

Yet, interestingly, commentators in the ancient world reveal no defensiveness about Judith whatsoever. *First Clement*, the earliest known Jewish or Christian work to mention Judith, saw her unequivocally as a heroine of the faith. It is perhaps by finding in Judith a symbol of something else that Christians and Jews could accommodate her

---

118. See Jacobus, "Judith, Holofernes, and the Phallic Woman."

with so little reservation. Other Christian authors have championed her cause, praising her virtues of celibacy and fasting. She has consistently appeared in Christian reflection as a military heroine, as a symbol of virtue (usually chastity or humility), or as a symbol of the virgin Mary victorious over Satan. Reading of part of the Song of Judith (chap. 16) occurs in the lectionary passages associated with Mary and with Joan of Arc.[119] Jews likewise elevate her as a heroine associated with the values of the Maccabean revolt. She has continually been depicted with Hanukkah menorahs, a holiday associated with a miracle at the time of the Maccabean revolt. In art as well, Judith was early on consistently depicted as positive, whether as a military heroine or as a saintly, pious heroine of virtue.[120]

How do we account for this difference between the positive early attitudes toward Judith's actions and the often unsettled or even negative views in the modern period? The key seems to be in locating precisely when the change occurred, and it illuminates the ambivalent modern reactions to her character. The Christian artistic representations of Judith began to change unmistakably around 1600.[121] The Renaissance artists around 1500 still portrayed Judith positively, but by 1600, a certain ambivalence entered into the depictions, as can be seen in Cristofaro Allori's painting of 1607: a calm and beautiful Judith with a face as smooth as an egg holds Holofernes' head by the hair at her side, her fingers clenched into a tight fist. It is like a trophy that she has effortlessly yanked out by the roots. By this time, a number of other Renaissance painters began to portray Judith sadistically or Holofernes sympathetically, as if to suggest now that their identification with Holofernes as a man was stronger than their hatred of him as an enemy of God. Particularly to be noted in this category are Michelangelo Caravaggio and Bernardo Cavallino. Not surprisingly, Christian theologians also by this time, but evidently not before, began to condemn the book more forthrightly. Capellus (Louis Cappel), a French Huguenot Protestant, writing in 1689, called it "a most silly fable invented by a most inept, injudicious, impudent and clownish Hellenist."[122]

Two factors probably entered in at this period to change drastically the common perception of Judith. First is the introduction of a kind of realism. While Judith was a sort of Joan of Arc figure, no matter how outrageous, she was heroic and a defender of the faith. But Luther's historical observations (see Introduction), still quite positive, signal the beginnings of a realistic concern to bring Judith into the known world, where she simply became too dangerous and unsettling for many people's sensibilities. When the unreal, liminal state of Judith's actions were seen as occurring in the real world in real time, the crucial distinction was lost and a threat to good order was perceived in her actions. Second, as Stocker shows, Judith became a common biblical figure in arguments on both sides of the Reformation debates.[123] The many ruling queens in the monarchies of Europe at this time gave rise to a so-called gynecocratic (rule by women) controversy, and in that context Judith could easily be taken up as a heroine or a villain, depending on one's loyalties for or against a queen.

Because Judith is such a strong female character, the question of the moral evaluation of her actions is intimately bound up with the question of whether the work should be considered feminist. Recent commentators have disagreed on this, and feminist scholars have disagreed as well.[124] The answer to this question may depend on what century one is referring to. From the time of its composition to the sixteenth century, Judith's act was portrayed warmly and positively by male religious leaders. She

---

119. McNeil, "Reflections on the Book of Judith."
120. Some of the important examples of artistic depictions can be seen in Stone, "Judith and Holofernes," 73-93; Moore, *Judith*; Garrard, "Judith"; Jacobus, "Judith, Holofernes, and the Phallic Woman"; and Bal, "Head Hunting."
121. Jacobus, "Judith, Holofernes, and the Phallic Woman."
122. Quoted in Moore, *Judith*, 46.
123. Stocker, *Judith, Sexual Warrior*, 67-119.
124. Pamela Milne is a good example of a scholar who is not comfortable with the designation of Judith as feminist. See Milne, "What Shall We Do with Judith?" 37-58. Stocker, *Judith, Sexual Warrior*, argues forcefully that the character represents an uncontainable burst of freedom. It should be noted, however, that Stocker's book is much stronger on the art and literature of the early modern period, when Judith becomes more charged, and less successful in addressing the ancient Jewish text.

was a heroine of the church and the synagogue. It does not seem appropriate to call this Judith a feminist creation. When society changed, however, and Judith came to be viewed as a more flesh-and-blood figure, she was perceived as threatening to good order and her achievement was called into question by male commentators. By the simple criterion of the challenge to male order, this Judith can be considered feminist.

JUDITH 13:10b–15:7, JUDITH RETURNS TO BETHULIA AND INITIATES COUNTERATTACK

Judith 13:10b-20, Judith and Her Maid Return to Bethulia

COMMENTARY

13:10b-17. Judith's call to open the gates corresponds to her request to open the gates at 10:9 and marks an important point in Judith's heroic quest: She has moved out of her tent of isolation, traveled forth to meet the dragon, slayed it, and now returns. Her words also serve multiple functions; in addition to marking her return across the threshold of the gates, they also take up the language of an enthronement psalm or a victory ode (see Commentary on 16:1-17).[125] Compare Ps 24:7: "Lift up your heads, O gates! and be lifted up, O ancient doors! that the King of glory may come in" (NRSV). Her call as she returns, "God our God is with us," is similar to the psalm, and the continuation of her words in v. 14, "Praise God, who has not withdrawn his mercy from the house of Israel" also resounds like a victory ode. The literal gates of Bethulia, then, become like the figurative gates of the psalms (which are themselves based on the actual gates of the Temple). A longer victory song is to come in chap. 16.

In the meantime, she must demonstrate to her fellow citizens her first victory over the Assyrians. Producing the head of Holofernes is certainly dramatic, and the canopy represents another important trophy of her conquest. She further emphasizes the reversal and shame for Holofernes by stating, "The Lord has struck him down by the hand of a woman." This statement is also made in Judith's prayer at 9:10, and it echoes the tradition of another woman deliverer, the unnamed wise woman of Abel (2 Sam 20:14-22). It is also difficult not to connect her words "my *face* that seduced him to his destruction" with the fact that his face is in her hand. One is left with the image of her face and his, with the beauty of Judith's face vanquishing the power of Holofernes. Like Hamlet holding up the skull of Yorick, Judith in a more macabre situation can sum up this relationship between Holofernes and herself; the image of Judith's face juxtaposed with Holofernes' is certainly the one that many artists have chosen to depict. Judith is also quick to assure the Bethulians that Holofernes had not defiled her. It would have been hard for them to believe that she could have gotten close enough to Holofernes to chop off his head and still escape his advances. Although they have not seen what the audience has seen, they still believe her word.

13:18-20. Uzziah's blessing on Judith is very similar to the blessing of Jael for having killed Sisera in the Song of Deborah (Judg 5:24), and also the blessing of Mary at Luke 1:42. In each case the woman blessed is the "most blessed of women." The blessings of Judith and Jael come after a great victory, and in this they are also like Melchizedek's blessing of Abram (Abraham) at Gen 14:19-20.

125. Alonso-Schökel, *Narrative Structures in the Book of Judith*, 12.

The latter contains several parallels to Uzziah's blessing: "Blessed be Abram by God Most High, maker of heaven and earth; and blessed be God Most High, who has delivered your enemies into your hand!" As in Judith, we find here a double blessing—of the individual and of God—and they both bring in the themes of creation and deliverance from enemies. Uzziah continues with an assurance that the memory of Judith's deed will live on forever, a theme that will close the book as a whole (see Commentary on 16:21-25).

Judith's act is acclaimed by Uzziah and the people of Bethulia, and like Judith herself, they balance the credit for the deed between Judith and God. Still, her heroism is being praised, and memory of it will last forever. This last point is crucial for the heroic paradigm, as every culture must sing the praises of its heroes long after they are gone; the end of the book of Judith will be taken up with this theme. The people then authenticate Uzziah's words with "Amen! Amen!" (See Reflections at 14:1-10.)

Judith 14:1-10, Judith Issues Orders and Achior Converts

COMMENTARY

14:1-4. Judith's cleverness does not end with the decapitation of Holofernes, or with her quick escape, but extends to the stratagem by which she will use Holofernes' head to defeat his entire army. Judith orchestrates some clever stagecraft to manipulate the Assyrian soldiers into discovering the headless corpse of Holofernes at the most effective moment possible. She again demonstrates complete authority over the Bethulians, and also complete control over the enemy. Hanging the head of the leader of the enemy is encountered elsewhere in the Bible (1 Sam 17:54; 31:9-10; 2 Kgs 10:7-8; Matt 14:8). It perhaps originated in the procession of trophies; a famous bas-relief in the Arch of Titus in Rome depicts the procession through Rome of the trophies taken from Jerusalem after the destruction of the city and the Temple. Prominent among them is a menorah, the symbol of the Jewish religion. Aside from the close parallels to David's decapitation and exhibition of Goliath's head, there are even closer and more contemporary parallels in Judas Maccabeus's defeat of the Seleucid general Nicanor in 1 Macc 7:47 and 2 Macc 15:35: "Judas hung Nicanor's head from the citadel, a clear and conspicuous sign to everyone of the help of the Lord." This example is especially significant since the name of Judith may be inspired by the name of Judas Maccabeus (see Commentary on 8:1-8), and also because this treatment of Nicanor's head was part of the introduction of an annual festival celebrating his defeat, called Nicanor's Day.

In other words, the memory of this deed is celebrated continually just as the memory of Judith's is said to be (13:19-20; 16:23).

14:5-10. Judith's language in summoning Achior indicates that she is not simply interested in authenticating the identity of Holofernes' head. As already noted, the issues of honor and shame are prominent in Judith, as they are in Esther and other texts in the Bible. Holofernes had shamed Israel because he "despised" it and also because he sent Achior to Bethulia "as if to his death." By bringing Achior in to identify the head of Holofernes, Judith begins the process of reversing the balance of honor and shame, which must be done publicly. Achior's reaction is dramatic, even more dramatic than that of the Bethulians in 13:17. However, he escaped from close contact with Holofernes and had known the man face-to-face. Further, his stronger reaction—he actually collapses—convincingly confirms beyond doubt that the head is indeed that of Holofernes. In addition, it dramatizes the fulfillment of Holofernes' foolhardy prediction that "you shall not see my face again from this day until I take revenge on this race" (6:5). It is very ironic that Achior immediately faints at the sight of Holofernes' head, since Judith had been so bold and nerveless both in taking it and in handling it.[126] Thus their expected gender roles have been reversed; and this is unusual in Jewish novels (cf., e.g., Esther fainting as she comes before the king, Add. Esth 15:7).

---

126. Moore, *Judith*, 235.

Achior blesses Judith, as did Uzziah and the people in chap. 13. One is reminded of the many blessings that occur in the final chapters of Tobit, but there the number of blessings is perhaps exaggerated for comic effect. In Judith the blessings match the drama and heroism of the moment. Achior's blessing is interesting in that it is not what we would expect from an Ammonite: "Blessed are you in every tent of Judah." This signals Achior's perception of the power and benevolence of Israel's God, which he had interpreted for Holofernes in chap. 5. Achior also characterizes Judith as a heroic *warrior:* "those who hear your name will be alarmed." It is not simply that Judith has found an opportunity at this juncture in history to save her people; she is a heroine for the ages, capable of striking fear in the hearts of other enemies as well. But it is significant that Achior as well recognizes that the deliverance comes from both Judith and God: "When Achior saw all that the God of Israel had done, he believed firmly in God." Although Judith credits God alone, neither Judith nor God is forgotten in any of the blessings by the others. It is sufficient evidence of God's power and protection that Achior believes in God and is circumcised and joins Israel. Since Achior (or Ahikar) is a Jewish courtier in Tobit, it may be that these two novels share a tradition of the appropriation of the famous Assyrian courtier Ahikar (see Commentary on 5:5-21).

That Achior, an Ammonite, was circumcised appears to violate Jewish law, which forbids the admission of an Ammonite or a Moabite to the tenth generation (Deut 23:3). Was Achior past the tenth generation?[127] Like Ruth, a Moabite, was Achior granted a special dispensation? It is probably simply the case that this Jewish novel allows for a romanticized, but fictionalized, entry of the famous Achior into the Israelite fold, as in Tobit. The same novel that could demonize "Nebuchadnezzar the king of the Assyrians" could idealize "Achior the Ammonite."

127. So Craven, *Artistry and Faith in the Book of Judith,* 103n. 68.

REFLECTIONS

Achior's conversion is one of the warmer moments in a book marked by satire and humor. It is briefly but provocatively told. The reason for his conversion is stated simply: "Achior saw all that the God of Israel had done." We are prepared for this conversion, however, by the relatively long speech of Achior in chap. 5.

Any scene of conversion brings to the fore issues of the meaning of religion for the audience, whether ancient or modern. It may be helpful to pause and consider other biblical accounts of conversion, for they reflect some significant differences from each other, and yet all contribute to a picture of conversion that is very modern. First of all, there is the moving depiction of Ruth's conversion, which is addressed to her mother-in-law, Naomi, as Ruth's representative of the Israelite faith: "Where you go, I will go. . . . Your people shall be my people, and your God my God" (Ruth 1:16 NRSV). Ruth, like Achior, is from an excluded ethnic group that had been an enemy of Israel. Both of their descriptions are short but somehow profound. And neither convert chooses at this time to state abstract articles of faith—they are entering a community that comes under the protection of a different understanding of God from the one they have known. Other conversion scenes include Abraham, who is the first to become a worshiper of God (Genesis 12); this becomes the coming-to-faith paradigm for Jews and Christians. The personal encounter with God marks it as different from Achior's and Ruth's, but it is in this respect similar to the description of Paul's experience of the risen Lord in Acts 9. One other example may be helpful. The Ethiopian eunuch in Acts 8:26-40 is reading Isaiah, but is instructed by Philip concerning "the good news about Jesus." This is the only one of these scenes in which someone is catechized or instructed as preparation to conversion.

The various scenes focus on different aspects of conversion: direct encounter with God, joining a new community, catechesis. Which of these is the most important? Like all good literature, the various examples are more suggestive than descriptive in a journalistic way. By combining them, one would begin to get a fuller notion of the nature of what the new faith meant to those in the story, and what a new faith may mean for us today.

Before we turn from this scene of conversion, however, we should remember that different aspects of conversion are not just relevant for those who have converted; they also express the core beliefs of a religion and provide the psychological and reflective experience of coming to a new understanding of faith, even for those who have lived within a particular religion all their lives. In this core one usually sees the whole represented: The God of history is also the God of mercy, of life, of community, of creation. Coming to a new faith and renewing an old faith may be similar processes, and most people's religious lives involve a number of "conversions" in the form of changes and renewals.

Achior's own conversion scene, though quite simple, also implies more than meets the eye. He has already shown that he knows Israel's history, and he is finally convinced to convert by the dramatic rescue of Israel through the hand of Judith. The brevity of the scene challenges the modern reader to ask, What is the core that would define *my* faith? What would make me convert? What would be the cinching evidence before our eyes that what God did in the past God is also doing today? Being manifest in nature? Transforming the world? Creating community? Bringing about justice? Entering into people's lives? The story of the conversion of Achior can raise questions that address the very definition of the core of the religious life of people in the present world, both those who have converted and those who have not.

Judith 14:11–15:7, The Assyrians Discover Holofernes' Headless Body and Are Put to Flight

COMMENTARY

14:11-18. The Bethulians follow Judith's orders to the letter, and the Assyrians respond exactly as she predicted. The Assyrians at first are rousing their troops with the full expectation that they will destroy "these slaves." The story is told with some retardation of the plot, as the reader is treated to a full description of the Assyrian camp in preparation, knowing that they are about to discover what has happened. The message that the Israelites have appeared to challenge the mighty Assyrians is sent up the chain of command to a character we have come to know very well, Bagoas. He is hesitant to disturb Holofernes from what he assumes will be his satisfied repose with Judith. Bagoas's reaction to seeing Holofernes' headless body is not very different from Achior's reaction to seeing Holofernes' head, although it has the opposite import for their lives. The author of Judith does not dwell on Bagoas's reaction, but shows its consequences. The reversal of honor and shame is spelled out: "The slaves have tricked us! One Hebrew woman has brought disgrace on the house of King Nebuchadnezzar." But the reversal is more dramatically—and humorously—brought home by Bagoas's concluding remarks, the last we shall hear from him: "Holofernes is lying on the ground, and his head is missing!"

14:19–15:7. The Assyrians somewhat surprisingly believe Bagoas when he tells them that their leader has lost his head, and they immediately fly into a panic. The description of panic and consternation is similar to others in contemporary literature, such as 2 Macc 3:14-21 and 3 Macc 1:16-29, but the present text is less wordy, depicting in just a few verses the scattering of the Assyrian troops. The key to the routing of the

Assyrians is seen in one sentence, "Overcome with fear and trembling, they did not wait for one another"—that is, because of their stark fear there was no unit of soldiers left to turn against the vastly outnumbered Bethulians; rather, all fled separately. The panic and routing of the Assyrians is not based on the appearance of an angel or any other kind of apparition, as it is, for example, in 2 Maccabees 3–4. The Vulgate does mention the appearance of an angel, as does Judas Maccabeus concerning the routing of Nicanor's troops (1 Macc 7:40-42).[128] Word was quickly sent to the nearby Israelite villages, who attacked the flanks of the retreating Assyrians. The villages mentioned are unknown, perhaps fictitious, introduced to give the local color of the area around the fictitious town of Bethulia. Well-known regions are then brought into the picture, Gilead and Galilee, as they join in inflicting heavy casualties until the Assyrians had gotten beyond the borders of Israel. The author has probably been influenced by the story of Abram (Abraham) pursuing the captors of Lot in Genesis 14, for in the LXX version Choba and Damascus appear, and the clause "they fell upon" them is rendered in the same way. This is another indication that the present author is working with the biblical text and not just oral-traditional models.

The revenge of the Israelites on the retreating Assyrians is noted, although figures are not given as they are in Esth 9:16. The plundering of the Assyrian camp is also emphasized, in contrast to Esth 9:10, 15-16, where it is stated that the Jews did not touch the plunder. Judith turns over to the Temple all the items that she has received from the spoils (16:19; cf. Josh 6:19, 24), but the other Israelites keep their plunder for themselves. First Maccabees 7:44-47 may have provided a model for this description, as it describes the enemy troops fleeing while being attacked on both flanks by Jews from the surrounding villages, followed by the plundering of the soldiers. The triumph and reversal in Esther are also very similar, in that in both texts, there is first the removal of the immediate danger (execution of Holofernes, execution of Haman), then a broader revenge on the multitude of followers.

128. Moore, *Judith*, 234.

REFLECTIONS

It is generally a problem for the modern reader that a large part of the idea of deliverance in the Hebrew Bible involves taking vengeance on the enemies. One need only compare the beautiful first words of Ps 137:1, 4-5:

By the rivers of Babylon—
   there we sat down and there we wept
   when we remembered Zion.

. . . . .

How could we sing the Lord's song
   in a foreign land?
If I forget you, O Jerusalem,
   let my right hand wither! (NRSV)

with the same psalm's conclusion:

O daughter Babylon, you devastator!
   Happy shall they be who pay you back
   what you have done to us!
Happy shall they be who take your little ones
   and dash them against the rock! (Ps 137:8-9 NRSV)

The expression of this kind of revenge seems horrifying. We have difficulty endorsing this kind of revenge, even though it has been in the twentieth century that the worst forms of violence have been unleashed by the nations that have laid claim to being the most "advanced." We rightly have reservations about the expression of vengeance, and must reflect on the use of power in order to balance it wisely against past wrongs.

The total destruction of a city, including the killing of all its inhabitants and the taking of all its property, was condoned in the ancient Near East and also in the Hebrew Bible. The "holy war" idea, or total ban, was part of the conquest theme; when the Israelites took possession of the promised land they were to destroy the cities totally, killing all the inhabitants and destroying the property and livestock (Deut 7:1-2; 20:16-18; Josh 6:19, 24). A partial ban was in effect against cities outside the promised land. According to this less stringent policy, all males in the city would be killed, but the women and children would be taken as slaves and the spoils collected and kept (Deut 20:10-15). Although these brutal policies were considered acceptable in the ancient Near East, it is disturbing to encounter them in our own Holy Scriptures. However, it is not clear that they were ever enforced as such. Some of the nations that God instructed the Israelites to annihilate in the programmatic statements about the conquest (e.g., Deut 7:1-2) were archaic names at the time of writing and not real nations that the Israelites would have known; others were still in existence, and so therefore had clearly not been destroyed. One of the messages of the text may be that because they were not annihilated, the peoples remained in the land to cause problems for the centralization of Israelite worship thereafter. As destructive as the Israelite wars were, the language of holy war is a language of hyperbole, often told looking back at an idealized time. It is also sometimes suggested that the conquest of Canaan took place at a "primitive" time in Israel's history and was a necessary part of God's ordained plan to provide a land of inheritance for the descendants of Abraham. As a result, the violence of the settlement is partially mitigated.

What may be more important, however, for interpreting this aspect of Judith is its genre. The book of Judith is an entertaining, high-spirited, and perhaps fictitious novel. The level of violence is not really the difference between the early and late texts; the difference is the "seriousness" of the early texts and the belief that the violence was divinely authorized. The modern reader often feels unsure whether the comic nature of Judith (and also of Esther) excuses the violence as an extended happy ending or merely makes such violent notions of revenge more palatable. The effect of a text like Judith is to create one-dimensional characters representing good and evil, which then permits a one-dimensional solution to the problem of revenge: It is justified in an absolute way because the enemy is so deserving of such a punishment. It is this aspect that should give us pause as we consider the effects of perceiving our enemies to be one-dimensional figures. It is only a short step from perceiving a one-dimensional enemy to justifying a one-dimensional—that is, total—notion of revenge. As the technological means of exercising a total ban on a city or a nation have been brought into existence, the imperative falls upon us all the more urgently to discern the multidimensionality of those who might oppose us.

JUDITH 15:8–16:25, CELEBRATION AND CONCLUSION

Judith 15:8-13, All of Israel Celebrates

COMMENTARY

That Bethulia has been tied by strong bonds to Jerusalem and the temple officials there has been emphasized often in Judith, and here the bonds are especially tight. The high priest Joakim and "the elders of the Israelites who lived in Jerusalem" come to Bethulia to witness and acclaim the actions of the local citizens. They give Judith her second blessing, which is also confirmed with the "Amen!" of the people. Verse 9 has been used in the Roman Catholic liturgy regarding the virgin Mary and Joan of Arc. The Israelites celebrate by plundering the enemy camp for thirty days. This will resonate in the reader's mind with the thirty-day rest that Holofernes enjoyed while he collected supplies before turning toward the Israelites (3:10). Holofernes' last rest before setting his face against the Israelites is thus balanced by the celebration of the plundering of his camp, in which his supplies are dispossessed. All of the riches of Holofernes' own tent are given to Judith, which she loads onto her carts and mules to take, as we learn in 16:19, to the Temple in Jerusalem.

The women of Israel bless Judith and dance a special dance in her honor. There is a strong tradition in Israel of women dancing and singing victory songs and dances. The Song of Miriam at Exod 15:21 is sung after the pharaoh and his troops are drowned in the Red Sea. It follows immediately upon the Song of the Sea, which is quoted in Judith's song in chap. 16. More typical of the victory songs is probably the song sung by the women after David slew Goliath (1 Sam 18:6): "The women came out of all the towns of Israel, singing and dancing . . . with tambourines, with songs of joy, and with musical instruments" (NRSV). The tambourine is also known from ancient depictions found in archaeological excavations; it was a small hand drum without the metal rattles found on modern tambourines. The dance of Jephthah's daughter and her companions is an interesting parallel because it also comes after a victory; yet, in this case it is also a lament because Jephthah has vowed to sacrifice as a thank offering the first person who comes out to meet him, who, unfortunately, is his daughter (Judg 11:29-40). Since the daughter's virginity is emphasized, and since the dance is said to become an annual dance for the daughters of Israel, the sacrifice of the daughter seems to have become a special part of women's spirituality. These passages provide some of the cultural background of victory songs and dances. In most cases, they are sung by women; and Cross and Freedman argue that Moses' Song of the Sea was originally attributed to Miriam as well (as it is now at Exod 15:21).[129] What is unusual is the use of wands and olive wreaths, which was originally a Greek practice. However, 2 Macc 10:7 and 3 Macc 7:16 indicate that during the Hasmonean period they had been adapted to Jewish practice as well.

---
129. F. M. Cross and D. N. Freedman, "The Song of Miriam," *JNES* 14 (1955) 237-50.

Judith 15:14–16:17, Judith's Victory Song

COMMENTARY

The book of Judith concludes with a hymn of thanksgiving, just as does Tobit. The interrelation of prose narrative and hymnic praise is common in the HB and the apocryphal books, but it is practically unknown in Greek literature.[130] Important examples include Moses' Song of the Sea in Exodus 15, the juxtaposition of Judges 4 and 5, Deuteronomy 32–33, 2 Samuel 22, Jonah 2, and the insertion of the Prayer of Azariah and the Song of the Three Jews in the Additions to Daniel. The structure of the hymn has been debated, as has its authorship. Is the song made of disparate parts? If so, were they composed by different authors and inserted at this point in the narrative? Was the story of Judith told in song before the prose narrative was written, as was likely the case with the Song of Deborah in Judges 5? We shall consider these questions as we analyze each of the parts in turn.

Two theories have been suggested for the structure of the Song of Judith. Jansen proposed that the song is composed of three separate hymnic fragments: (1) vv. 1-4, introduction to a thanksgiving psalm; (2) vv. 5-12, account of the story of Judith; and (3) vv. 13-17, enthronement hymn.[131] Jansen asserts that parts of the Song of Judith may pre-date the book of Judith, but it is now a purely literary composition—that is, it may have arisen from hymnic traditions, but it is now a written piece that functions within the book of Judith. Particularly suggestive about this theory is the observation that not only are there differences between the three sections in terms of theme, but also vv. 5-12 contain unmistakable references to the story of Judith. Craven argues instead that this arrangement imposes artificial breaks in the text and that there are motifs that join these sections together. A better analysis, in her mind, would be the following: (1) vv. 1-2, hymnic introduction; (2) vv. 3-12, narration of the epic event; (3) vv. 13-17, hymnic response. This structure has similarities to Moses' Song of the Sea in Exodus 15.[132] Here it will be argued that Craven's structure is ultimately more helpful, although the structure of the song is still somewhat irregular, and some of Jansen's observations should not be overlooked. Skehan also argues that there is a general patterning of the Song of Judith on Moses' Song of the Sea in Exodus 15.[133] There is, first of all, an important parallel between Jdt 16:2 and Exod 15:3 in the LXX version: "For the Lord is a God who crushes wars." In Judith's prayer at 9:2, she quoted a bit more of this passage, so the allusion to Exodus 15 is virtually certain. Further, in Exodus the hand of God finds expression in the hand of Moses, and this is similar to the emphasis on the hand of Judith in this book. The association of the Song of the Sea with Miriam also introduces a women's festival.

However, it is possible that Skehan (and Craven following him) have overemphasized the relationship with the Song of the Sea. Even if Exodus 15 was alluded to in the Song of Judith, many other parallels in HB psalms can be detected, especially in vv. 13-17. Further, concerning the parallel between Miriam and Judith, as we have seen it was typical for women to be involved in the victory song. To be sure, there is one clear allusion to Exod 15:3 in the Song of Judith, but the author of Judith constantly includes words and phrases from biblical passages without the parallel necessarily carrying over to the entire chapter. There is really very little verbal or thematic agreement between the Song of Judith and the Song of the Sea that is not also present in the so-called enthronement psalms. These hymns sing the worship of God, who is victorious in a cosmic battle, and, as a result, rules or is enthroned in heaven. God is praised by those who have been saved and metes out punishment upon those who opposed God. The parallel to Moses' Song of the Sea will thus be noted without an assumption that Judith's song is modeled on it.

15:14. Judith is at the center of the book and of the song, and her position here as deliverer of "all Israel" is emphasized. Here we may compare the gathering and confession of the people in Ezra 10 and Nehemiah 8–9. In both cases it is a ceremonial gathering that is understood to represent all the people.

16:1-9. The song begins in a way typical of the victory songs in the HB, with a reference to tambourines and cymbals (see Commentary on 15:12). There is typical parallelism of lines—that is, in each of the pairs of lines, the second line repeats or parallels some of the motifs of the first:

---

130. Lacocque, *The Feminine Unconventional*; see also Steven Weitzman, *Song and Story in Biblical Narrative: The History of a Literary Convention in Ancient Israel* (Bloomington: Indiana University Press, 1997).
131. H. Ludin Jansen, "La composition du chant de Judith," *AcOr* 15 (1936) 63-71; see also Moore, *Judith*, 252-57.
132. Craven, *Artistry and Faith in the Book of Judith*, 105-12.
133. Patrick Skehan, "The Hand of Judith," *CBQ* 25 (1963) 94-110.

Begin a *song* to my God with *tambourines,*
   sing to my Lord with *cymbals.*
Raise to him a new *psalm;*
   exalt him, and *call* upon his name.

"Song" and "tambourines" in the first line correspond to "sing" and "cymbals" in the second, while "raise" and "psalm" in the third line correspond in idea to "exalt" and "call" in the fourth line. This can be schematized as an AABB pattern, in which the first two lines have parallel terms or motifs, and the last two lines have different parallel terms or motifs.[134] Consider also the AABB pattern in v. 3, with the following parallel motifs: the Assyrian came down/came down with myriads; their numbers blocked/their cavalry covered. As is often the case with Hebrew poetry, however, such neat parallelism is not maintained throughout the poetic composition. We find three roughly parallel lines in v. 2 and five in v. 4. Contrast this with the Song of the Sea, in which parallelism is used in a fairly consistent way. One rhetorical effect in the Song of Judith that does come through strongly, however, is the parallel use of a motif over a number of lines that is resolved with a strong exclamation. Note the AAAAA pattern in v. 4, which culminates in "But the Lord Almighty has foiled them by the hand of a woman" in v. 5; the AAA pattern in v. 6, which is followed by "but Judith . . . with the beauty of her countenance undid him"; and an even stronger crescendo, the AAAAAA pattern in vv. 7-9*a*, which climaxes in v. 9*b:* "and the sword severed his neck!" The loosely constructed stanzas utilize a series of parallel motifs, leading to a climactic affirmation of Judith's heroic act.

We also detect in this section a number of motifs that were found in Judith's prayer in chap. 9: the God who crushes wars, v. 2, and the myriad warriors and cavalry in v. 3 occur also at 9:7; the threat to the women and children in v. 4 occurs in 9:2 (but also, ironically, in Judith's boast of what Simeon had done to the Shechemites in 9:4); and the reprise that God delivered the Israelites by the hand of a woman in v. 5 occurs at 9:10. One subtle difference, however, is that the theme of chap. 9 is that Judith will act by deceit, while in chap.

---

134. See Berlin, "Introduction to Hebrew Poetry," 3:4-8.

16 she has overcome Holofernes through her beauty.

16:10. There is no ready explanation for the reference to the Persians and the Medes. The Medes were destroyed in chap. 1 by Nebuchadnezzar, and so would presumably be viewed more sympathetically; and the Persians were mentioned earlier as one of the nations addressed by Nebuchadnezzar. The Persians and the Medes are often referred to together in texts of this period (e.g., Ezra 6:2; Esth 1:19; 10:2; Dan 5:28; 6:7), and so a conventional combining of their names would not be too surprising. But it is also quite likely that, since the core of the book of Judith may have arisen in the Persian period and referred to a Persian invasion (see Introduction), that background of the book has remained here in the song. That the Persians "trembled" and the Medes "were daunted" are motifs from the divine warrior hymns (see Commentary on 16:13-17).

16:11-12. In these two verses the author emphasizes the victory of the oppressed or the humble (ταπεινός [*tapeinos*] can be translated either way) over the haughty. This was a theme of Judith's prayer in chap. 9 (esp. 9:11; see Commentary there). In the psalms and elsewhere there is often a reversal of the oppressed and haughty in the eyes of God, but in Judith it is a military victory as well. Judith has reversed the shame that Holofernes intended to inflict upon Israel and has inflicted it upon him: "Sons of slave-girls pierced them through." This hyperbole emphasizes that a woman has killed Holofernes and that tiny Bethulia has routed the mighty Assyrian army, but the image that it was accomplished by the sons of slave girls is intended to be one of shame.

16:13-17. This last section of the Song of Judith has a fairly consistent structure. After the introductory call to worship, each verse is a stanza composed of two central parallel lines. The parallel motifs are as follows: v. 13, "great"/"wonderful"; v. 14, "spoke and made"/"sent forth spirit and formed"; v. 15, "mountains shaken"/"rocks melt"; v. 16, "sacrifice is a small thing"/"fat of offerings is a little thing"; v. 17, "Lord will take vengeance"/"he will send fire and worms." In each verse there is a summary line after the two parallel lines (taking the first line of v. 14

as the summary line of v. 13). The only exception to this pattern is the transitional line at the beginning of v. 17, "Woe to the nations. . . ." Each stanza has parallels in hymnic traditions, many found together in one psalm or another.

Reference to the "new song" in v. 13 is a common call to worship in the book of Psalms (e.g., Pss 13:3; 40:4; 96:1; 149:1; cf. Isa 42:10).[135] In regard to the connection between prose narrative and song in the biblical tradition, Weitzman notes a connection between the songs embedded in narrative, such as the Song of Judith, and the psalms: "Just as the Psalms were thought of as the prayers and songs of biblical heroes uttered at significant moments in their lives, so too the songs in biblical narrative were reread and rewritten in light of biblical psalmody." Thus, although the influence of Exodus 15 and Judges 5 on Judith 16 can be assumed, these are by no means the only influences, or even the main influences.

The creation by God's Word (v. 14) is a common motif, found in Genesis 1 ("And God said, let there be . . ."), and in the enthronement psalms as well. Psalm 33:6 states: "By the word of the LORD the heavens were made, and all their host by the breath of his mouth" (NRSV).

The shaking of the mountains and the melting of the rocks (v. 15), or expressions like these, are often present in enthronement psalms as well (see Psalm 99:1: "The LORD is king; let the people tremble! He sits enthroned upon the cherubim; let the earth quake!" [NRSV]). These motifs are sometimes part of that adaptation of the enthronement psalm called the divine warrior hymn, in which God must defeat enemies in heaven in order to be enthroned.[136] Psalm 18:7 is particularly dramatic in this regard: "Then the earth reeled and rocked; the foundations also of the mountains trembled and quaked, because he was angry" (NRSV). We find the motif of the earth quaking even when a human king is enthroned (1 Kgs 1:38-40).

The apparent critique of sacrifice in v. 16 has raised questions for some scholars, who wonder how such a devoted observer of Jewish cultic practices as Judith could question the value of sacrifice. One need only look down two verses to v. 18, the prolific sacrifices of the people, to find a striking contradiction to this verse. However, although sharp language about an overreliance on sacrifice is present in the HB (e.g., Ps 50:8-15; Hos 6:6, quoted in Matt 9:13; 12:7), the closest parallel to this passage is in Ps 40:6: "Sacrifice and offering you do not desire, but you have given me an open ear. Burnt offering and sin offering you have not required" (NRSV). It is, perhaps, the remnants of an older psalm, or at least the effect of the psalm genre, that provokes this sentiment here, not a sudden and quite isolated desire by the author of the book of Judith to caution the readers about insincere sacrifice.

Ideas similar to this summary line ("whoever fears the Lord is great forever") are also found in one of the psalms mentioned above, Ps 33:18-19:

Truly the eye of the LORD is on those who fear
  him,
 on those who hope in his steadfast love,
to deliver their soul from death,
 and to keep them alive in famine. (NRSV)

This particular example is interesting because it includes not only the motif of the protection of those who fear God, but also the protection from death that could give rise to the hyperbole in Judith of being "great forever."

The motif of judgment (v. 17) also finds a parallel in enthronement psalms. The positive praise of God in some of the psalms turns to announcement of God's terrible presence for those in heaven or on earth who oppose God (cf. Ps 96:13: "He is coming to judge the earth. He will judge the world with righteousness" [NRSV]). The day of judgment in Judith might seem too eschatological for the hymns of praise, but the harsh judgment of the wicked can sometimes be found where God's victory is seen eschatologically as the victory over the enemies in heaven and on earth, as in Isa 24:21, 23:

On that day the LORD will punish
  the host of heaven in heaven,
 and on earth the kings of the earth.

. . . .

---

135. Weitzman, *Song and Story in Biblical Narrative,* 73.
136. Paul D. Hanson, *The Dawn of Apocalyptic* (Philadelphia: Fortress, 1975) 300-316; Niditch, *Oral World and Written Word,* 21-24.

> The LORD of hosts will reign
> on Mt. Zion and in Jerusalem. (NRSV)

Isaiah 66:24 contains this as well as other important parallels to v. 17 in Judith:

> And they shall go out and look at the dead bodies of the people who have rebelled against me; for their worm shall not die, their fire shall not be quenched, and they shall be an abhorrence to all flesh. (NRSV)

These examples push us to consider whether the book of Judith at this point is also expressing an eschatological, even apocalyptic, notion of the day of judgment. This idea has been argued by some scholars, but opposed by Enslin,[137] who suggests that the author is simply reusing common traditions. This is probably the case, if only because there is nothing in the Song of Judith, or in the book as a whole, to match this notion; only 9:4-5 even approaches it. Verse 17 may use the same terms as in Isaiah 66, and may even capture the sense of apocalyptic judgment, but it stands alone in the book of Judith in this regard. It is likely used in its present position as a final warning of extreme judgment to come upon those, like Nebuchadnezzar, who rise up "against my people."[138] Worms as a punishment is found elsewhere in this period (Isa 14:11; Sir 7:17; Acts 12:23; *Testament of Job* 20), but there may be a particular allusion here to the death of Antiochus IV Epiphanes, the tyrant opposed in the Maccabean revolt, as recounted in 2 Macc 9:9.

Several aspects of vv. 13-17 indicate that this section may have been an independent enthronement psalm that was appropriated by the author of Judith to be used at this point in the novel: It contains many parallels to other enthronement psalms, the structure is different from vv. 1-12, and there is no reference to the narrative about Judith. Craven argues that two references to the fear of God in vv. 15-16 represent the culmination of the song and of the book as a whole.[139] Although Nebuchadnezzar had laid claim in 2:5 to being the "lord of all the earth," the author affirms here that the lordship of God is the true religion. To be sure, within the present structure of the song, these lines function in this way; but the fear of God is also a common motif in the enthronement psalms, and so it is quite possible that we have here a fragment of a pre-existing psalm. (See Reflections at 16:21-25.)

---

137. Enslin and Zeitlin, *The Book of Judith*, 175n. 17.
138. Craven, *Artistry and Faith in the Book of Judith*, 110.
139. Craven, *Artistry and Faith in the Book of Judith*, 109.

Judith 16:18-20, Thanksgiving Offerings

COMMENTARY

The entourage of people from Bethulia makes a pilgrimage to Jerusalem to bring offerings; it appears that both the women and the men in 15:12-13 have made the journey. They purify themselves to make the offerings—but is it because they have touched dead bodies (Num 19:11-22), or is it another example of the special piety reflected in Judith's earlier asceticism? The answer is not clear. The offerings they bring are nearly identical to those offered by the high priest Joakim in 4:14 at the height of the crisis. A requirement of the ban, or חרם (*ḥērem*; mentioned in the Reflections at 14:19–15:7), is that the property of a defeated city is to be offered to God (see Josh 6:19, 24). Judith presents the inner canopy that she took from Holofernes' tent as a special votive offering. The offering of significant items of defeated warriors is known from elsewhere (for example, David's offering of the sword of Goliath, 1 Sam 21:9), but Judith offers, not Holofernes' sword of power, but the canopy of his inner sanctum, which she penetrated to slay him. Even in death Holofernes is unmanned and shamed. The three-month celebration is exaggerated, but should be seen as a literary motif, and not intended as realistic. One should note, however, that it is still festive—that is, sacred time—and it is emphasized that Judith remains with them during this period. (See Reflections at 16:21-25.)

Judith 16:21-25, Memorial of Judith

COMMENTARY

Judith returns to her wealthy estate, but it is not clear that she returns to the same conditions of her ascetic discipline as described in 8:2-4. Levine points out the differences in the description here: Judith returns to her estate, but not necessarily to her tent; she no longer communes directly with God, but rather returns to contact with the society of Bethulia, even though she does not accept any of the many marriage proposals.[140] She has evidently given up her special life of spirituality, but does not totally integrate into society. As can be seen in other cultures, it is common for the hero not to be able to integrate into society. The lack of integration, therefore, should not surprise us; but the lack of isolation, the lack of a special spiritual life does. Perhaps the author intentionally is choosing to be ambiguous about Judith's precise relations to society, as she becomes memorialized. A similar technique can be detected at two important memorializing scenes in the NT. At Mark 16:8, the resurrection of Jesus is prepared for but never confirmed; the original text of Mark ends on a searching but ambiguous note: "They said nothing to anyone, for they were afraid" (NRSV). Similarly, but less often noted, the memorializing of Paul at the end of Acts is ambiguous. Paul expounds to the Jewish leaders of Rome his message about Jesus, and some are convinced, while others are not. Paul condemned "this people's" unbelief, but we are not told what became of those who believed, or whether there was any change of heart; rather, it is simply said that he continued preaching for two years "with all boldness and without hindrance." Thus the open-ended conclusion about the person being memorialized is more a norm than an exception in these texts.

What is emphasized is that she was greatly honored as a heroine both in life (v. 21) and in death (vv. 23-25). Her beauty is still irresistible, and her fame only increases. She gives away her wealth and frees her maid as benevolent gestures that, like the ancient code of honor, would establish her role as patroness. Thus she dies with an enormous store of honor and patronage, befitting the death and memorializing of the heroine.[141] Her strength and independence as a woman—to the extent that in her genealogy she even takes precedence over her husband, Manasseh (8:1)—is now subtly brought back under control by the placing of her body in her husband's burial cave. The Pandora's box that was opened is now safely closed.

The last line, "No one ever again spread terror among the Israelites," is probably modeled on Judg 5:31: "The land had rest forty years" (see also Judg 3:11, 30). Within the book of Judith, however, it concludes the structural outline of the second half of the book by mirroring a line from the introduction of Judith: "No one spoke ill of her, for she feared God with great devotion" (8:8).

---

140. Levine, "Sacrifice and Salvation," 27.

141. Lawrence M. Wills, *The Quest of the Historical Gospel: Mark, John, and the Origin of the Gospel Genre* (London: Routledge, 1997) 40-41.

REFLECTIONS

The ending of the book of Judith is so positive concerning the memory of her that it raises the question of the position of Judith among the heroes of Judaism. Was she an intermediator figure, like Moses? Was she like one of the prophets or judges? Was she described in a way parallel to the Maccabean warriors and martyrs? In the Greek and Roman world, the heroes of the culture were honored in death and were thought to have lasting positive effects long afterward. Temples and monuments can still be found that attest to the strength of this tradition, and it likely influenced the later Christian devotion to saints' tombs and the Jewish reverence for the graves of the rabbis.

Reverence for the dead and the cult of dead ancestors may have also existed in ancient Israel, although evidence for this in some cases arises from the fact that it was vigorously condemned. Some special reverence for the revered dead must have remained, however, for even in the New Testament we see at issue the reverence for the tombs of the prophets (Matt 23:27).

Today as well it is partly through such memorializing experiences that a community—whether a local community or a whole nation—comes together and its values are reaffirmed. A memorial ceremony is a liturgy that enacts the community's response to the death of a hero and the community's creation of a memory of that person. The collective memory becomes more "real" in some cases than the actual person's life, and it is reaffirmed in further memorials over the years. The somber reverence that today attaches to national cemeteries, monuments, and statues is vivid proof that we are addressing here a powerful part of a society's consciousness of its past.

What, then, is the nature of the remembrance of Judith? Judith is honored during her lifetime, and she is buried in the cave of her husband, Manasseh, which may evoke for the readers Abraham's purchase of the cave of Machpelah for Sarah's burial. Throughout we have noted how Judith is depicted like one of the judges, who were raised up by God when the people cried out for help. In the book of Judith, God also hears the prayers of the Israelites (4:13), and, like the judges, Judith brings peace to the land for many years (16:25). Judith is clearly described as having an elevated place in the memory of Israel, stated as positively, for example, as that of Mordecai in Esth 10:3. But whereas Mordecai is described as a benefactor of Jews, he is not memorialized as directly, expecially not in terms of his death and burial. There was no cult described at the tomb of Judith as there was for Greek and Roman heroes, but her memory is kept and her tomb marked, as with the judges.

What kinds of values are memorialized in Judith? She is a more complex hero than is usually the case. She explicitly says that she uses deceit and beauty, but she is also a military heroine who coolly decapitates an enemy general and directs a major military attack. Her piety and her relation to God are the first priority in her life, and yet are the first things she risks losing—in appearance at any rate—in the interest of saving her people. In Judith, however, it is not just the individual heroine who is being memorialized, but the collective heroism of Israel and the collective religious values as well. Heroes are seen as partially responsible for our present well-being, and yet we do not just receive them as they are; we often ignore their inconsistencies and project onto them a loftier vision of what we think people are capable of. Abraham Lincoln, for example, possessed many fine qualities as a leader, but his memory in popular culture also became shaped by the values society projected onto him. And like the judges or Judith, Lincoln's memory in popular culture takes on quasi-religious overtones, as his tomb is venerated as an American icon. In the collective memory, then, Judith becomes larger than life, even if she is a fictional character, and reminds us of the ways that our own heroes have been idealized as well.

THE FIRST BOOK OF MACCABEES
INTRODUCTION, COMMENTARY, AND REFLECTIONS
BY
ROBERT DORAN

THE FIRST BOOK OF MACCABEES

INTRODUCTION

The first and second books of the Maccabees describe the revolt of the Jews in Judea against the Seleucid Empire in the second century BCE. They are two separate works, as 2 Maccabees is not the sequel to 1 Maccabees but an independent telling of the same events. Both works, in different ways, deal with the problem of how Jews were to maintain their own cultural and religious identity within the larger empire of the Seleucids. Both works show how friction grew between the inhabitants of Judea and the Seleucid monarch Antiochus IV Epiphanes, until he decided to outlaw the practice of Judaism within Judea, leading to the profanation of the Temple in Jerusalem. In response to this attack on their culture and religion, various groups of Jews rose up in revolt, spearheaded by the Maccabean family. First Maccabees begins with the actions of Antiochus IV against the Jews and the profanation of the Temple, and it focuses on the first generation of the Maccabees, sometimes called the Hasmoneans, from the father Mattathias through his sons Judas, Jonathan, and Simon. During this time, the Temple was retaken and purified, and the independence of Judea was proclaimed in 142/41 BCE. The narrative ends with the death of Simon in 135/34 BCE. The narrative of 2 Maccabees is preceded by two letters addressed by the Jews in Judea to the Jews in Egypt, requesting that the Egyptian Jews celebrate the Feast of the Purification of the Temple—i.e., the Feast of Hanukkah. The first letter is dated to 124 BCE, while the second purports to be written in the time of Judas Maccabeus. The narrative portion of 2 Maccabees begins in the reign of Antiochus IV's predecessor, Seleucus IV. It provides more details about events leading up to the oppression of Judea in Jerusalem, highlights the martyrdom of Jewish resisters, and concentrates on the figure of Judas Maccabeus. The account ends while Judas is still alive after the defeat of the Seleucid commander Nicanor in 161 or 160 BCE.

HISTORICAL BACKGROUND

The Ancient Near Eastern Setting. Once the dust had settled from the battles over who would inherit Alexander the Great's conquests, three major powers had emerged in the eastern

Mediterranean: the Macedonian Empire, the Ptolemaic Empire based in Egypt, and the Seleucid Empire. The Seleucid Empire was the true heir to the Achaemenid, or Persian, Empire. It stretched from the western coast of Asia Minor to present-day Afghanistan and was the largest of the Hellenistic kingdoms. The Seleucid Empire also lay claim to Coelesyria, which the Ptolemaic Empire had controlled since 301 BCE. Size brought its own problems, and the Seleucid kings would see their territory whittled away during the third century BCE. In the west, partly as a result of the Celtic invasions in Asia Minor in 278–277 BCE, various states in Asia Minor arose—Bithynia, Pontus, Cappadocia, and the Attalids at Pergamum. In the east, Bactria and Parthia seceded. Although the Seleucid kings kept an interest in their Iranian possessions, no doubt for reasons of military defense, they did not maintain as strong an influence as in Syria and Mesopotamia. Antiochus III reasserted Seleucid authority in Iran during his expedition there (212–205/4 BCE), for which he assumed the title "Great King," but Parthia and Bactria remained unconquered, and Seleucid control of eastern Iran remained rather superficial. Antiochus III also sought to restore Seleucid control over western Asia Minor and marched into Coelesyria in 202 BCE. He seized control of Coelesyria, Phoenicia, and Palestine with a decisive victory over the Ptolemaic forces at Panium in 200 BCE.

Antiochus's attempt to restore the Seleucid kingdom to its former glory failed, however, for a new player had entered the power game in the eastern Mediterranean. Rome, however hesitatingly and clumsily, was emerging as the dominant force. By its victories over Philip V of Macedonia at Cynoscephalae in 197 BCE, over Philip's son Perseus at Pydna in 168 BCE, and finally over the Achaean League in 146 BCE, Rome gained complete control of Macedonia and Greece. Antiochus III also fell before the Romans at Magnesia in 190 BCE, and the subsequent Treaty of Apamea in 188 BCE took away most of his possessions in Asia Minor and saddled him with a heavy indemnity. When Antiochus IV attempted to extend Seleucid influence into Egypt, the Roman envoy C. Popillius Laenas delivered to him the senate's order that he leave Egypt, and he did so in humiliation. Rome was the dominant power in the East from the second century on. The weaker party in any dispute would appeal to Rome, and Rome's representatives were frequently in the East investigating conflicts and advising the senate on solutions.

The Ptolemaic and Seleucid empires would continue, however, although wracked by dynastic struggles between rival claimants to the throne. The Seleucid Empire ended when Pompey the Great annexed Syria in 64 BCE; the Ptolemaic Empire formally lasted longer, ending when Cleopatra VII committed suicide in 30 BCE. While weak, these empires could still muster impressive forces. Antiochus VII Sidetes invaded Judea in 135/34 BCE, besieging Jerusalem and reinstating Seleucid rule, if only for a brief time. Later, about 112 BCE, John Hyrcanus could not resist the incursions of Antiochus IX Cyzicenus. When Alexander Jannaeus, king of Judea 103–76 BCE, tried to extend his territory west to the port of Ptolemais (Akko) early in his reign, he was decisively defeated by Ptolemy IX Soter II (Lathyrus); later, about 88 BCE, he was defeated by the Seleucid monarch Demetrius III Eucaerus.

Judea. When Antiochus III defeated the Ptolemaic forces at Panium in 200 BCE, he forthwith gained control of the small city-state of Judea. Judea had been ruled by the Ptolemies for over a century, but the details of its administration remain very hazy, since the sources at our disposal are not concerned with these sociopolitical questions.[1] Following is a discussion of the main narrative sources used to search out life in pre-Maccabean Jerusalem.

(1) First Maccabees provides almost no details of Judean life before the revolt. It does mention that there were some anonymous "renegades" who wanted Jews to conform to the way of life of the nations round about and so had a gymnasium built in Jerusalem (1 Macc 1:11-15).

(2) Second Maccabees provides more details about the high priests in Jerusalem and their role in the building of a gymnasium. It gives names and events not otherwise recorded.

(3) The Jewish historian Josephus, writing at the end of the first century CE, provides information about Jerusalem in the pre-Maccabean period in his works *The Jewish War* and

---

1. A full listing of these sources can be found in the work by Lester L. Grabbe, *Judaism from Cyrus to Hadrian*, 2 vols. (Minneapolis: Fortress, 1992), and in the revised edition of Emil Schürer, *The History of the Jewish People in the Age of Jesus Christ*, 4 vols. (Edinburgh: T. & T. Clark, 1973–87). The interested reader may consult the full discussion in those works.

Antiquities of the Jews. The latter work in particular includes citations of official letters by Seleucid rulers about the Jews. It also contains a narrative about one Jewish family, the Tobiads, which is usually called the Tobiad romance.[2] This story tells of the rise to prominence of Joseph the Tobiad, who took over the role of tax collector for the Egyptian Ptolemies from his uncle, the miserly high priest Onias. Josephus tells the story in a most confusing way, but some scholars believe that they can glean some historical data from this fanciful account and date the events to the rule of Ptolemy III Euergetes (246–221 BCE). According to this story, the seven oldest sons of Joseph fought against their younger half brother, Hyrcanus, and this rivalry was in part responsible for the Seleucids' intervening in Judah to offset the Ptolemaic connections of Hyrcanus.

(4) The last part of the canonical book of Daniel also recounts the events preceding and during the reign of Antiochus IV in the visions of Daniel 7–12. The events are cast in the form of a symbolic vision, with the kings of the south, the Ptolemies, waging war against the kings of the north, the Seleucids. The exact significance of some of the references is unclear.

(5) The first book of *Enoch,* a pseudepigraphic work (portions of which have been found among the Dead Sea Scrolls), also recounts in symbolic form the history of Israel up to the time of the Maccabees (*1 Enoch* 83–90). Here the symbols are of animals fighting against one another.

(6) The work of Jesus ben Sira, a teacher in Jerusalem around 190–170 BCE, evidences a deep concern for the role of wisdom in creation. True wisdom comes from God, and Ben Sira identifies divine wisdom with the Torah, or Law of Moses (Sir 24:8-29). He places great emphasis on proper worship in the Temple.

From these various sources, then, scholars attempt to piece together a sense of what life was like in Judea in the third century BCE, and what happened there.

From a decree found in Josephus, we know that Antiochus III affirmed the right of the Jews to live according to their ancestral religion.[3] He also mentioned that the Jews had a "council" (γερουσία *gerousia*), but we do not know precisely who its members were (probably wealthy aristocracy) or how they were chosen. Although Antiochus does not mention the high priest in his letter, the Greek historian Hecataeus of Abdera, who wrote around 300 BCE, stated that the high priest was a leading figure in civil as well as religious matters. Hecataeus's work is reported by a later Greek writer of the first century BCE, Diodorus Siculus.[4] In his idealized picture of the Jews, Hecataeus wrote that Moses appointed priests to be "judges in all major disputes, and entrusted to them the guardianship of the laws and customs. For this reason the Jews never have a king, and authority over the people is regularly vested in whichever priest is regarded as superior to his colleagues in wisdom and virtue. They call this man the high priest, and believe he acts as a messenger to them of God's commandments."[5]

Ben Sira (50:1-21) also lavishes praise on the high priest of his own day, Simon son of Onias, and notes how Simon built the walls of the temple enclosure and fortified the city against siege. The Tobiad romance has the high priest in charge of paying tribute to the Ptolemies, although the point of the story is the transfer of this power to a non-priest, Joseph the Tobiad. Scholars have deduced from this that the high priest was the only authority in Judea, but we do not know whether the Ptolemies or the Seleucids installed another imperial functionary alongside the high priest.

Nothing much changed through the transfer of power from the Ptolemies to the Seleucids. However, the defeat of Antiochus III by the Romans in 190 BCE put the Seleucid Empire under a heavy indemnity. The description of the attempt by Seleucus IV, Antiochus's successor, to obtain money from the Jerusalem Temple as told in 2 Maccabees 3 should be seen in the light of the Seleucid emperor's need for money to keep up payment of that indemnity. More important, the author of 2 Maccabees recounts how Jason, the brother of the high priest Onias III, outbid his brother to take from him the office of high priest (2 Macc 4:7-10). We do not know if previously every high priest had to pay for reinstatement at the advent of a new ruler, but the accession

---

2. Josephus *Antiquities of the Jews* 12.157-236.
3. Josephus *Antiquities of the Jews* 12.138-146.
4. Diodorus Siculus 40.3.1-8.
5. Diodorus Siculus 40.3.5.

of Antiochus IV saw the bestowal of the high priesthood on the highest bidder. The narrative of 2 Maccabees in particular forces us to consider the competition and rivalries among various groups in pre-Hasmonean Jerusalem. Following is a highlight of important areas for the reader to keep in mind while working through 1 and 2 Maccabees.

Factions in Jerusalem. In any discussion of the causes of the rebellion in Judea, one has to remember that the small state of Judea (traveling about twenty miles in any direction from Jerusalem would take one outside its territory) was ruled by wealthy priestly and lay families. At times, this situation is described as an ideal one: "the holy city was inhabited in unbroken peace and the laws were strictly observed" (2 Macc 3:1 NRSV). The high priest is described by Sirach as being surrounded by the whole congregation, lifting up their hands and voices in unison and harmony as they worshiped God (Sir 50:1-21). Such an idyllic picture is, however, rudely countered by the descriptions of factional fighting and murder committed by one group against another (see, e.g., 2 Macc 4:3).

Several influential families can be identified from the sources: the Oniad family of Zadokite high priests, Onias III and Jason (2 Macc 3:1; 4:7); the Bilgah family, Simon, Menelaus, and Lysimachus (2 Macc 3:4; 4:23-29); the Hakkoz family, John and Eupolemus (1 Macc 8:17; 2 Macc 4:11); the Jehoiaribs, i.e., the Hasmonean family; the family of Jakim, Alcimus (1 Macc 7:5); and the Tobiads.[6] Although the Tobiads, who were lay leaders and not priests, do not appear at all in 1 and 2 Maccabees, Josephus in one account describes how the sons of Tobias urged Antiochus IV to invade Jerusalem.[7] It is also important to keep in mind that other wealthy lay families vied for power and prestige in Judea. As for the priestly families, it seems significant that the chronicler, in the lists of ancestral houses of the priests apart from the high priest Zadok, mentions the other four families (1 Chr 24:7, 10, 12, 14). Hakkoz's descendants were barred from the priesthood after the return from exile because their family name could not be found in the genealogical entries (Ezra 2:61-63), but their presence in the list in Chronicles as well as their diplomatic activity in the second century BCE (2 Macc 4:11; 1 Macc 8:17) attests to their continued prominence. From the narrative in 2 Maccabees, one can see how the Bilgah family seized the opportunity offered by the split in the Zadokite family between Onias and his brother Jason and how the Hakkoz family sided with the Hasmoneans, while Alcimus of the family of Jakim pursued his own quest for power. Thus the causes of the Maccabean revolt must be seen as having arisen from the competition between ambitious families in the small city-state of Judea.

There are other signs that all was not well in Judea. The discoveries at Qumran have shown that discontent was present in the third century BCE. In *1 Enoch* 1–16, part of a pseudepigraphic work dated to the third century BCE, a story similar to that of Gen 6:1-8 is told of how angels from heaven brought sin and pollution upon the earth. The story is paradigmatic for the way the author of *1 Enoch* and his community viewed their world as one of disorder and confusion. Later, in the second century BCE, the author of the book of Daniel depicted the history of the world from the Babylonians to the Greeks as chaotic and bestial (Daniel 7). Within Judaism itself there was dissension over the cultic calendar as seen in the book of *Jubilees,* which favors a solar instead of a lunar-solar calendar. There was debate over other legal questions as well, if 4QMMT found at Qumran is to be dated early. Even the traditionalist Ben Sira includes in his work a prayer for the deliverance of Jerusalem and the Jewish nation from foreign oppression (Sir 36:1-22). Within both 1 and 2 Maccabees we also meet a group called the Hasideans (1 Macc 2:42; 7:13; 2 Macc 14:6). We do not know who they were, but their choice of name—"pious," "loyal ones"—suggests that they thought others were not so pious and loyal as they. The *Damascus Document* also hints that members of its exclusivist group were found throughout Judea.[8] Clearly, not everyone thought that all was well in Judea.

Persecution by Antiochus IV. The accounts of the persecution enforced by Antiochus IV Epiphanes differ in 1 and 2 Maccabees. Here is a schematic outline of the events:

---

6. Josephus *Antiquities of the Jews* 12.158-236.
7. Josephus *The Jewish War* 1.31-32.
8. CD 12:19.

1 Maccabees—Introduction

> Figure 1: A Synoptic Chart of Antiochus's Persecution
>
> | 1 Maccabees | 2 Maccabees |
> |---|---|
> | 1. "Renegades" ask to be like other nations; they build a gymnasium. | The high priest Jason asks to build a gymnasium as a way to adopt the Greek way of life. The high priest Menelaus commits acts of sacrilege, which lead to an uprising of the people. |
> | 2. An arrogant Antiochus IV invades Egypt, plunders it, and then plunders Jerusalem and the Temple. | After Antiochus IV's second invasion of Egypt, a civil war breaks out between Jason and Menelaus. In response to this, a bestial Antiochus plunders the Temple. |
> | 3. Two years later, a military garrison is set up in Jerusalem. | Antiochus installs governors in Judea and in Samaria. He then commands another attack on Jerusalem. |
> | 4. Sometime later, Antiochus IV imposes a cult on Judea, profanes the Temple, and prohibits the Mosaic Law. | Finally, Antiochus IV outlaws Judaism in Judea, profanes the Temple, and installs another cult. |
> | 5. When news reaches Antiochus that the Temple has been recaptured and purified by the Jews, he dies. | Antiochus IV dies before the Temple is purified. |

The two accounts are basically the same, but with important differences that will be discussed in the commentary. Both accounts agree that some Jews built a gymnasium and that Antiochus IV imposed a cult on Jerusalem. The characterization of Antiochus IV differs in both. In 1 Maccabees, Antiochus IV is arrogant from the start and seeks to impose a unified worship and behavior throughout his empire. In 2 Maccabees, he is at first portrayed neutrally, then as sympathetic, but finally as enraged against the Jews. Second Maccabees shows that the cult was imposed after a series of disturbances and uprisings in Jerusalem, and it places much of the blame on the unruly passions of the emperor. On the other hand, 1 Maccabees states that the cult was imposed because the emperor wished all nations to be the same and to give up their particular customs (1 Macc 1:41-42). Antiochus is thus portrayed in 1 Maccabees as zealous in the spread of Hellenization, of striving to conform everyone to Greek customs, while in 2 Maccabees he is shown initially as encouraging the adoption of Greek customs by some Jews.

It must be said that Antiochus IV was not a Hellenizing zealot. He certainly wanted to keep the Seleucid Empire together, but all evidence suggests that he encouraged the maintenance of local customs and traditions and did not seek to suppress them. We should see as rhetorical polemic, therefore, the statement in 1 Macc 1:41 concerning a decree to force all peoples to abandon their customs. However, we should also be sensitive to the pressure there must have been to learn the ways of the Seleucids. The Seleucid monarch was extremely powerful, and it would have been in the best interests of rulers within his empire to be on good terms with him. What we find is that during the reigns of Antiochus III and Antiochus IV a number of older cities were recognized as *poleis* (πόλεις), i.e., Greek cities, and were renamed. Obviously this was thought to be a beneficial step for the cities concerned—indeed, a goal to strive for.

The high priest Jason must have thought so, because he had Jerusalem renamed as Antioch-at-Jerusalem (2 Macc 4:9, 19) and built a gymnasium, an exercise and educational establishment that every "decent" Greek city was supposed to have. One must also recognize, however, that we know almost nothing about what this process of renaming entailed. Did the renaming of an ancient city like Jerusalem as Antioch-at-Jerusalem necessarily signify the adoption of a new constitution? Was the *gerousia* under Antiochus III different from that under Antiochus IV and his successors? Earlier scholars argued that, theoretically, if not in practice, a new constitution was adopted, but the minimal evidence seems to support the continuance of older customs. In addition, nothing indicates that citizenship in Antioch-at-Jerusalem was limited to wealthy friends of Jason. As for the gymnasium, we simply do not know what its curriculum was; evidence from what took place in Athens should be applied cautiously to Jerusalem, since each city controlled its own educational process. What we do know is that the people in the gymnasium would have been taught to speak Greek, as well as to carry out the exercises and sports that any well-reared Greek citizen would have learned. The emperor would certainly have had interpreters available, but the ability to become a member of the club by partaking in gymnastic exercises and by conversing in Greek would no doubt have made for a more amicable relationship with the powerful monarch. Moreover, the renaming of Jerusalem around 175 BCE and the building of a gymnasium brought about no local upheaval, even though the author of 2 Maccabees sees it as the start of the Hellenization and the religious factionalism it produced (2 Macc 4:11-17).

The trouble developed following a series of events. Factional war broke out between the high priest Menelaus and the former high priest Jason while Antiochus IV was campaigning in Egypt. Antiochus's reaction to this revolt was to enter Jerusalem by force, massacre the population, and pillage the Temple (2 Macc 5:1-21). Antiochus appointed overseers in Jerusalem and over the Samaritans (2 Macc 5:22-23). Later, there were two more missions against Jerusalem, one by Apollonius, captain of the Mysians (1 Macc 1:29-35; 2 Macc 5:24-26), and one by Geron the Athenian, to compel the Jews to abandon their laws (1 Macc 1:44-51; 2 Macc 6:1-2). Since these missions were probably not mere whims, it seems safe to conclude that the populace of Jerusalem and Judea was considered by the Seleucid authorities to be restless and that the decision to stamp out forcibly the practice of Judaism was the final step in a series of unsuccessful attempts to settle affairs in Jerusalem. Indeed, the persecution was limited to Judea, Samaria (2 Macc 6:2), and neighboring Greek cities (2 Macc 6:8-9). Jews in other major cities of the Seleucid Empire, such as Antioch, were not, so far as we know, affected.

The persecution aimed at every aspect of Jewish observance. Torah scrolls were burned, circumcision was forbidden, and the sabbath was not to be observed. Jews were forced to participate at pagan festivals and compelled to eat pork. Observance of Torah was outlawed under threat of death. The Temple was profaned and turned into a temple for pagan festivals.

A great deal of energy has been spent trying to pinpoint exactly which cult was imposed upon Jerusalem by Antiochus IV. The sources tell us that the temple was dedicated to Zeus Olympios (2 Macc 6:2), that a desolating sacrilege and an altar were placed on top of the altar of burnt offering in the temple courtyard (1 Macc 1:54, 59; 4:43-44), and that both the king's birthday and the feast day of the god Dionysos were celebrated monthly (2 Macc 6:7). There may also have been temple prostitutes (2 Macc 6:4). The term "desolating sacrilege" (βδέλυγμα ἐρημώσεως *bdelygma erēmōseōs*, 1 Macc 1:54) is the same as that found in Dan 9:27; 11:31, where the Hebrew (שקוצים משמם *šiqqûṣîm mĕšōmēm*) is a play on the name "Ba'al Shamen," or "Lord of Heaven," the Syrian counterpart of Zeus Olympios. Based on this, some scholars have argued that the cult was Syro-Canaanite, assuming that one cult substituted for another. However, 1 Macc 1:47 speaks of many altars, sacred precincts, and shrines for idols, and 2 Macc 10:2 details that altars had been built in the public square of Jerusalem and also that there were sacred precincts. Rather than the imposition of the worship of one god in place of Yahweh, it seems that the worship of many gods, including Dionysus and Zeus Olympios, took place. Thus regular paganism, characterized by the worship of many gods and goddesses, was introduced.

Antiochus IV would later change his mind and revoke the persecution (2 Macc 11:27-33), but the enigma still remains as to why he started a policy so at variance with the usual workings of the Hellenistic world, wherein states normally respected the existing gods and cultic practices of the various cities. Antiochus III and Seleucus IV had supported the cult in Jerusalem. Scholars have attempted to find a specific answer to the problem. Suggestions that Antiochus was either crazy or a zealous Hellenizer do not explain why only this small area of his kingdom was affected.

Goldstein has suggested that Antiochus IV, a former hostage in Rome, was attempting to set up an empirewide Antiochian citizenship similar to Roman civic and religious programs, but his ingenious theory lacks supporting data.[9] Other scholars have sought an explanation from within the factions in Jerusalem. E. Bickermann argued brilliantly that the initiative for the persecution came from the "Hellenizers" in Jerusalem, who wanted to reform Judaism and remove the barriers that separated Jews from Gentiles;[10] the persecution of opponents would have followed Jewish models of persecution such as that carried out by Jehu (2 Kings 9–10). V. Tcherikover did not follow the notion of a Reform Judaism, but stressed that the Hellenizers were an upper-class elite, whereas the common people were staunchly anti-Hellenistic.[11] He speculated that the people, led by the legal and spiritual leaders, the scribes, attempted to throw out both Jason and Menelaus; it was their pious revolt that led to Antiochus's persecution and the installation of a Syrian military colony, which set up its own worship in the Jerusalem Temple. Goldstein agreed with both Bickermann, in holding that the religion imposed was a kind of polytheistic Judaism, and Tcherikover, in that the religion was brought in by Antiochus's military colony in Jerusalem, a colony made up of Jewish soldiers who followed that kind of practice.[12] K. Bringmann stressed that, while Menelaus created the new religion in line with the Syrian military colony, Antiochus issued the orders primarily to consolidate his own power and to provide a stable source of revenue.[13]

I have emphasized that Antiochus IV, when he gained the Seleucid throne in 175 BCE, quickly knew that the Ptolemies were eager to renew hostilities to regain Coelesyria. The Ptolemies would have invaded in 180 BCE if Ptolemy V Epiphanes had not been assassinated. Once his widow had died in 176 BCE, the new government did little to conceal its hostile intentions and, in fact, finally attacked in late 170 or early 169 BCE. In this atmosphere of hostility on his southern border, Antiochus IV would have wished to have a region favorable to him and so acceded to Jason's request to rename Jerusalem. The gymnasium with its attached *ephebium* would have trained young men in military exercises for possible use as auxiliary forces. When Antiochus IV was rebuffed from Egypt by the Romans in 168 BCE, he may have felt even more strongly the need for a secure southern border and hence the imposition of paganism in Judea. However, I would not wish to hold that Antiochus was guided only by political concerns, as one cannot easily separate religion and politics in the ancient world. Rather, Antiochus IV may have heard stories that the Jews had a misanthropic attitude toward other nations, as stated even in the positive account of Hecataeus of Abdera, who wrote that "as a result of their expulsion from Egypt, [Moses] introduced an unsocial and intolerant mode of life."[14] Antiochus may have decided that this aspect of religious polity had to be suppressed. Why this institution of paganism required the burning of the books of the Law, the prohibition of circumcision, and the end of the daily offering in the Temple remains an enigma. Given the meager quality of our sources and their highly polemical stance, scholars will continue to debate and put forward explanations.

The Sequel to the Revolt. The last event recorded in 1 and 2 Maccabees is the death of Simon Maccabeus in 135/34 BCE. It is hinted that he was succeeded by his son John Hyrcanus, who would rule from 135/34 to 104 BCE. After repulsing the attempted coup of his brother-in-law Ptolemy, John was forced to submit to Seleucid forces under Antiochus VII Sidetes and to pay tribute. After Antiochus died in 129 BCE while campaigning against Parthia, the Seleucid throne remained weak, and John Hyrcanus seized the opportunities offered by this Syrian weakness. During the course of his thirty-year reign, the territory of Judea expanded enormously to the east, north, and south. Early in his career, John captured two fortified towns in Transjordan: Medeba and Samoga. Then he turned north and captured Shechem and Mount Gerizim;

---

9. Jonathan A. Goldstein, *I Maccabees*, AB 41 (Garden City, N.Y.: Doubleday, 1976) 104-21.
10. Elias Bickermann, *The God of the Maccabees: Studies on the Meaning and Origin of the Maccabean Revolt*, SJLA 32 (Leiden: Brill, 1979).
11. V. Tcherikover, *Hellenistic Civilization and the Jews* (Philadelphia: Jewish Publication Society, 1961).
12. Jonathan A. Goldstein, *2 Maccabees*, AB 41A (Garden City, N.Y.: Doubleday, 1983) 98-112.
13. K. Bringmann, *Hellenistische Reform und Religionsverfolgung in Judäa: Eine Untersuchung zur jüdisch-hellenistische Geschichte (175–163 v. Chr)* (Göttingen: Vandenhoeck and Ruprecht, 1983).
14. Diodorus Siculus 40.3.4.

Figure 2: Chronology of 1 and 2 Maccabees

Dates: BCE	Seleucid[1] Calendar	Events:	References: 1 Maccabees	2 Maccabees	Daniel
333–323		Conquests of Alexander the Great	1:1-9		7:7; 11:3-4
202		Antiochus III invades Coelesyria, begins Fifth Syrian War			
200		Antiochus III defeats Ptolemy V at Paneas			11:5
198		Antiochus III controls Coelesyria, including Judea; Jews allowed to live by their own law			
196		Onias III becomes high priest			
190		Roman army defeats Antiochus III at Magnesia			11:18
		Treaty of Apamea; Antiochus V taken as hostage to Rome			
187		Death of Antiochus III, succeeded by Seleucus IV			11:19
180		Ben Sira finishes his writings			
		Heliodorus's attempt to loot the Temple		3:1-40	11:20
		Simon schemes against Onias		4:1-6	
175	137	Death of Seleucus IV, accession of Antiochus IV	1:10-15	4:7	7:8, 23-25; 11:21
		Jason appointed high priest (Onias deposed)		4:7	9:2a; 11:22?
		Hellenization of Jerusalem begins		4:7-17	
172		Menelaus appointed high priest (Jason deposed)		4:23-50	
171/170		Sixth Syrian War between Antiochus IV and Ptolemy VI			
170/169		Antiochus IV invades Egypt	1:16-19		
169	143	Syrian attack on Jerusalem	1:20-28[2]	5:11-14	11:28
168		Antiochus IV's second invasion of Egypt;		5:1	11:29
		Roman ultimatum to withdraw obeyed;			11:30a
		Jason's coup attempt		5:5-10	
167	145	Second Syrian attack on Jerusalem:			9:26b; 11:30b
		Massacre by Apollonius	1:29-32	5:21-26	9:12-14?
		Construction of the citadel (Akra)	1:33-40		
		Enforced Hellenization by Antiochus IV	1:41-50		
		Judaism outlawed, Temple defiled	1:51-64	6:1-10	9:27; 11:31-35; 12:11
		Maccabean revolt in Modein	2:1-28		
		Slaughter of innocents on sabbath	2:29-38	6:11	
		Guerilla attacks led by Mattathias	2:39-48		
166	146	Death of Mattathias	2:49-70		
		Martyrdoms of Eleazar, seven brothers, and mother		6:12–7:42	
		Judas becomes leader of the revolt	3:1-9	8:1-8	
		Judas's early victories:	3:10-26	8:5	
		Apollonius defeated at Lebonah	3:10-12		
		Seron defeated at Beth-horon	3:13-26		

Dates: BCE	Seleucid[1] Calendar	Events:	References: 1 Maccabees	2 Maccabees	Daniel
165	147	Antiochus IV's campaign to Persia	3:27-37		
		Victory over Seleucid armies led by Ptolemy, Nicanor, and Gorgias	3:38–4:25	8:8-29; 11:1-15	
164	148	Amnesty offer gained by Menelaus First expedition of Lysias	4:28-35	11:1-15	
	148	Peace negotiations of Lysias and the role of the Romans		11:16-21, 34-38	
	149	Death of Antiochus IV, accession of Antiochus V Eupator (Lysias regent)[3]	6:1-17	9:1-29; 10:10-11	11:40-45
		Cleansing and rededication of the Temple	4:36-61	10:1-9	
		Restoration of ancestral customs by Antiochus V		11:22-26	
		Jewish defensive campaigns:			
		Idumea	5:3-5, 65a	10:14-23	
		Ammon	5:6-8		
		Gilead	5:9-13, 24-51	8:30-33; 10:24-38; 12:17-31	
		Galilee	5:14-23		
		Philistia	5:65b-68		
		Siege of the citadel by Judas	6:18-27		
162	150	Seleucid invasion led by Lysias:	6:28-63	13:1-26[4]	
		Execution of Menelaus		13:3-8	
		Battle near Modein		13:9-17	
		Siege of Beth-zur	6:28-31, 49-50	13:18-22	
		Battle at Beth-zechariah	6:32-47		
		Siege of Jerusalem	6:48-54		
		Peace made with Lysias	6:55-63	13:23-26	
161	151	Demetrius I ascends:	7:1-7	14:1-2	
		Lysias and Antiochus IV executed			
		First Seleucid campaign led by Bacchides:	7:8-25		
		Alcimus appointed high priest	7:9-18	14:3-10	
		Seleucid invasion led by Nicanor:	7:26-50	14:11–15:37	
		Defeated by Judas at Caphar-salama		End of 2 Maccabees	
		Defeated by Judas at Adasa			
		Judas's Treaty with Rome	8:1-32		
160	152	Second Seleucid campaign by Bacchides:	9:1-53		
		Death of Judas Maccabeus at Elasa	9:18		
		Jonathan appointed "ruler and leader"	9:28-31		
159	153	Death of Alcimus; no high priest appointed	9:54-57		
157		Third Seleucid campaign by Bacchides:	9:58-73		
		Siege of Bethbasi	9:62-69		
		Peace made with Jonathan	9:70-73		
152	160	Revolt of Alexander Balas (Epiphanes)	10:1-14		
		Jonathan appointed high priest	10:15-21		
		Demetrius makes overtures to Jonathan	10:22-47		
151		Alexander defeats Demetrius (who is slain)	10:48-50		
150	162	Alexander weds Cleopatra	10:51-66		
147	165	Demetrius II invades Seleucia	10:67-68		
		Jonathan defeats Apollonius at Jamnia	10:69-89		

Dates: BCE	Seleucid[1] Calendar	Events:	References: 1 Maccabees	2 Maccabees	Daniel
145	167	Ptolemy VI of Egypt defeats Alexander Balas; Demetrius II made king	11:1-19		
		Jonathan's alliance with Demetrius II	11:20-38, 41-53		
		Trypho sets up Antiochus VI as king	11:39-40, 54-56		
		Jonathan's alliance with Antiochus VI	11:57–12:38		
		Trypho usurps the throne	12:39		
143		Jonathan slain by Trypho	12:40-53; 13:23-30		
		Simon becomes leader	13:1-22		
142	170	Simon's alliance with Demetrius II; Judean independence	13:31-42		
		Simon conquers Gazara	13:43-48		
141	171	Citadel in Jerusalem captured	13:49-53		
140	172	Demetrius II captured and imprisoned	14:1-3		
		Diplomacy with Rome and Sparta	14:16-24		
		Simon appointed high priest	14:25-49		
138	174	Antiochus VII grants rights to Simon	15:1-9		
		Antiochus VII defeats Trypho	15:10-14		
		Renewed ties with Rome	15:15-24		
		Campaign led by Cendebeus against Jews	15:37–16:10		
135/34	177	Simon and sons murdered by Ptolemy	16:11-17		
		John Hyrcanus becomes high priest	16:18-24		

1. Dates given in 1 or 2 Maccabees.
2. 1 Maccabees records this attack following Antiochus's first invasion of Egypt, 2 Maccabees following his second invasion.
3. 1 Maccabees places the death of Antiochus IV after the cleansing of the Temple.
4. Dated 149 (163 BCE) in 2 Maccabees.

he also subdued the Samaritans and destroyed their temple. Then he marched south to Idumea and captured its two main cities, Adora and Marisa. Late in his reign, he conquered the Macedonian colony at Samaria and also captured Scythopolis. The details of how John accomplished this expansion are debated, in part because the dating of a document preserved by Josephus is disputed.[15] Does it belong early in John's reign at the time of Antiochus VII or later, during the reign of Antiochus IX? If later, then John Hyrcanus's forces are seen to be weak and unable to resist Seleucid attacks. We know that John Hyrcanus hired mercenaries, but how many and how effective a fighting force are unknown.[16] Could he have successfully controlled the area he is said to have conquered without some support from the native populations? Hyrcanus was certainly the strong man of the area, but how were the forcibly circumcised Idumeans so compliantly integrated into the Jewish way of life?[17] Although facing some internal opposition in his thirty-year reign,[18] Hyrcanus succeeded in forging a Jewish state such as had not existed from pre-exilic times. Josephus lavishly praises him and states that he was the only person to unite in himself the roles of ruler, priest, and prophet.

Hyrcanus's son, Aristobulus I, ruled for one year (104–103 BCE). He continued the policy of expansion and appropriated Galilee.[19] Aristobulus is said by Josephus to have transformed the

15. Josephus *Antiquities of the Jews* 14.249-250.
16. See Josephus *Antiquities of the Jews* 13.249.
17. See Josephus *Antiquities of the Jews* 13.257-258; 15.253-256.
18. Josephus *The Jewish War* 1.67-68.
19. See Josephus *Antiquities of the Jews* 13.318-319.

government into a kingdom and to have put the diadem on his own head.[20] His successor, his brother Alexander Jannaeus (103–76 BCE), was continually embroiled in foreign and domestic wars. Josephus gives a list of the territory conquered by Alexander: northern Transjordan; most of the coastal cities as far north as Caesarea, Idumea, Samaria, and Galilee—a kingdom almost as large as Solomon's.[21] Such a major territorial expansion raises questions about the identity of those persons introduced into the new realm. Aristobulus is said to have forced inhabitant of Galilee who wished to remain in the country to be circumcised and to live according to the laws of the Jews.[22] During the expansion under Alexander Jannaeus, the city of Pella is said to have been razed because its inhabitants would not promise to accept and practice the ancestral customs of the Jews.[23] These statements raise the question of what being a "Jew" meant. Did it mean merely that the conquered cities were to be under the control of the king of Judea? Or did it mean, as the requirement of circumcision suggests, that the conquered population was to be treated as resident aliens in the land, following the commands of Exod 12:48; 22:20; and throughout Deuteronomy? What was their status vis-à-vis the citizens of Judea? Who would determine that all the male inhabitants of every village were circumcised? The incorporation of so many towns with different cultural traditions would have sparked a debate over what it meant to be a Jew—a native-born citizen of Judea, or one who was circumcised and followed the requirements of the resident alien, or someone who was circumcised and followed all the Torah?

THE ETHICS OF VIOLENCE

War dominates these books. They include stories of incredible courage under torture, as in the stories of Eleazar and the mother who encouraged her seven sons to die rather than transgress the Mosaic Law (2 Macc 6:18–7:42). There are stories of great daring, as in the story of another Eleazar who attempted to attack and kill the king and so end the battle. Eleazar fought through the ranks of the opposing army and killed an elephant on which he thought the king was riding, even though he knew that it would mean his own death, sacrificing his own life for those of his comrades and his nation (1 Macc 6:43-46). The story of Razis (2 Macc 14:37-46) shows a man ready to die rather than be captured, a mentality that was much admired in the ancient world. As Euripides the Greek playwright said, "Not death is evil, but a shameful death."[24] There are stories of night raids and tactical maneuvers, the stuff of which thrilling movies are made.

But woven into these accounts is a much more disquieting thread, for we find stories in which whole towns are razed. Throughout the accounts of the battles against neighboring cities in Gilead runs the refrain "and killed every male by the edge of the sword" (1 Macc 5:28 NRSV; see also 1 Macc 5:35, 51). Cities are burned to the ground. In one grisly scene, the army of Judas as well as the men, women, and children they are bringing back to Judea walk over the bodies of their slain enemies (1 Macc 5:51). In another scene, a lake near a town seems to be running over with the blood of those slain by the Maccabean forces (2 Macc 12:13-16). The delight in the destruction of human life seems almost palpable.

These stories imitate those found in the book of Judges. In trying to understand the ethics of violence in the books of the Maccabees, the analysis that Susan Niditch has made of the war accounts in the Hebrew Scriptures is very informative.[25] Niditch categorizes some of the narratives of the destruction of whole cities, in particular the killing of human beings, as narratives that portray the Israelites as instruments of God's justice, requiting the sins and misdeeds of their opponents. We see just such an attitude in the books of the Maccabees, as the Gentiles are consistently depicted as attempting to destroy the Maccabean forces without provocation

---

20. Josephus *Antiquities of the Jews* 13.301.
21. Josephus *Antiquities of the Jews* 13.395-397.
22. Josephus *Antiquities of the Jews* 13.318-319.
23. Josephus *Antiquities of the Jews* 13.397.
24. Euripides *Fragments*, as quoted by Epictetus *Discourses* 2.1.
25. S. Niditch, *War in the Hebrew Bible: A Study of the Ethics of Violence* (New York: Oxford, 1993).

(1 Macc 5:1; 2 Macc 12:2). Such an attitude also lies behind the ethnic cleansing that Simon pursues as he forces the inhabitants of Gazara and Beth-zur to leave; in the case of Gazara, he purifies the city (1 Macc 13:43-47; 11:65-66). The campaigns are also seen as purifying God's land of idol worship.

There are other instances in the books of Maccabees that fit Niditch's category of the ideology of expediency, an ideology in which force is used to instill terror. When the citizens of Antioch rebel against King Demetrius, Jonathan brutally suppresses the uprising as his troops fan out through the city and kill about one hundred thousand persons (1 Macc 11:41-51). Here Jonathan is portrayed as using brutal tactics to stop the revolt quickly. His tactics succeed, and he wins great renown.

For those who have been reared in the just-war tradition, which justifies waging war only as a last resort and prohibits attacking innocent civilians and annihilating defeated enemies, these stories do not provide an example that we would wish to follow. The books of the Maccabees are replete with judgments on their opponents as barbarous, godless, and sinful. There is no attempt to see the opponents as fellow human beings. War and the defeat of the enemy are glorified. In reading these stories, then, we have to realize that they tell us a great deal, not about how we ought to behave, but about what kind of group produced them. As Niditch states, "the more stable a group or person is, the surer they are of their identity, the less likely they are to be warlike, and the less rigid and totalistic their war ideologies are likely to be."[26] We can begin to understand that the communities out of which these books came felt themselves to be under attack and knew that their existence depended on building up their own self-esteem by denigrating their opponents. When we read these books, then, we can empathize with the protagonists in their struggles and seek to understand their point of view, but without sympathizing with their war practices and their demonization of their enemies. What reading these books should do is strengthen our commitment to explore ways to implement policies that embody the perspective of just-war theory. We should not be anesthetized by these stories of slaughter, but resolve that war and violence should be the last resort to settle conflicts, and that conflict will never make us forget that our enemies are human. If wars and conflicts result from insecurity and a sense of injustice, we must work to bring social justice and fair treatment to all nations and peoples. We must strive to bolster the self-image of all.

The books of 1 and 2 Maccabees also force readers to confront the problem of self-defense versus pacifism, particularly in the narrative of Jews who, despite attempting to live their lives in solitude, are hunted down and killed (1 Macc 2:29-41). Within this narrative, the right to defend oneself and one's country is strikingly affirmed. What we have to remember in reading these books is that there were no constraints on the emperor's will. If he wanted to, he could order the execution of all who opposed his will. The non-violent techniques used by Gandhi in India and by Martin Luther King, Jr., in the United States worked to a certain extent because both India under British rule and the United States are societies in which the rule of law constrains what leaders and police can do. Such techniques would have been of no avail in the Seleucid regime. To preserve one's own heritage and culture when threatened, one had to defend oneself. There was no escape. These books on war, therefore, while they affirm the right of a society to defend itself by recourse to war, do not address the question of the right of an individual in today's society to object conscientiously to serving in the military. That is another issue.

Finally, these books about war and events of the public arena reflect a male perspective. Women appear even less than in works like the *Iliad*. We learn that Jonathan and Simon had sons, but no mention is made of their wives. When women do appear in the stories, it is in the role of mother, as in the martyrdom stories (1 Macc 1:60; 2 Macc 6:10; 7), or as an image to describe social upheaval with the women leaving their houses and being seen in the streets (2 Macc 3:19-21). These are very male-dominated works.

26. Niditch, *War in the Hebrew Bible*, 21.

1 MACCABEES—INTRODUCTION

THE DATING OF EVENTS

How to harmonize the dates given in the books of Maccabees has long puzzled commentators. Chronology in the study of Judaism is always complicated by the fact that the lunar-solar calendar was never perfect, being off by about ten days. Moreover, when trying to chart the events recounted in 1 and 2 Maccabees, scholars have been faced with inconsistencies between the two books (e.g., while 1 Macc 6:20 dates Lysias's second expedition to 150 of the Seleucid era, 2 Macc 13:1 dates it to 149 of the Seleucid era). Further confusion sets in when we realize that there were two systems for calculating the dates of the Seleucid era, which was held to begin from the conquest of Babylonia by Seleucus I. One system started the year following the Macedonian calendar, which began in the autumn, and so year 1 of the Seleucid Macedonian system would correspond to the time of autumn 312 to autumn 311 BCE. The second system, following the Babylonian calendar, started the year in spring, and so year 1 of the Seleucid Babylonian system would be from spring 311 to spring 310 BCE. The author of 1 Maccabees uses the Jewish names of the months (1:54; 4:52; 7:43, 49; 14:27; 16:14) and places the Festival of Booths in the seventh month (10:21), presuming a system beginning in spring. However, he dates the death of Antiochus IV to the year 149 of the Seleucid era (6:16), whereas the Babylonian cuneiform tablets, which also use a calendar that begins in spring, date Antiochus's death in 148 of the Seleucid era. Scholars have outlined three solutions to keep all the dates in balance and maintain the basic reliability of the sources:

(1) There is one system of dating in 1 Maccabees that begins in autumn 312.[27] According to this chronology, the suppression of Jewish worship would have begun in 168 BCE, and the Temple would have been purified in December 165 BCE. One problem for this solution is found at 10:21, where the Feast of Booths is said to occur in Tishri, the seventh month, presupposing a calendar beginning in spring.

(2) There are two systems of dating in 1 Maccabees, one for internal Jewish events, like festivals, that begins, like the Seleucid Babylonian system, in spring 311 BCE, and one for external events, such as the dates for Seleucid expeditions, that is based on the Seleucid Macedonian system, which began in autumn 312 BCE.[28] According to this chronology, Antiochus's persecution would have begun in 167 BCE, and the Temple would have been purified in December 164 BCE.

(3) There are two systems of dating in 1 Maccabees, as in theory 2, except that the calendar for dating internal Jewish events would have begun in spring 312 BCE.[29] According to this system, the suppression of Jewish worship would be dated to 168 BCE and the purification of the Temple to 165 BCE.

Deciding upon one from among these theories is exceedingly complex. Bickermann's theory, theory 2, is the one most widely accepted and the one followed in this commentary. Most scholars hold that the author of the epitome in 2 Maccabees followed the Seleucid Macedonian system.

STYLE, WORLDVIEW, AND DATE

First Maccabees opens with a prologue that speaks of Alexander the Great and his exploits (1 Macc 1:1-10), but the narrative covers events from sometime after the accession of Antiochus IV Epiphanes in 175 BCE until the death of Simon Maccabeus in 135/34 BCE. Furthermore, the book is structured around the Hasmonean family. After a description of the apostasy of some from Judaism and the subsequent persecution when Antiochus tries to force all peoples to abandon their native customs (1:41), the narrative focuses on the patriarch Mattathias and his three sons—Judas, Jonathan, and Simon—as they lead the fight against those who wish to do away with their ancestral religion.

---

27. Bringmann, *Hellenistische Reform und Religionsverfolgung in Judäa,* 15-40; J. VanderKam, "Hanukkah: Its Timing and Significance According to 1 and 2 Maccabees," *JSP* (1987) 23-40.
28. Bickermann, *The God of the Maccabees,* 155-58.
29. Grabbe, "Maccabean Chronology: 167–164 or 168–165 BCE?" *JBL* 110 (1991) 59-74.

Style. Although 1 Maccabees gives the appearance of a straightforward narrative, it is not so straightforward as it seems. The author intersperses various documents into the narrative to provide the proper aura of documentation required to foster belief in the historical correctness of the account. (The authenticity of some of these documents has been disputed. See the Overview of 1 Macc 8:1-32 and Commentary on 1 Macc 10:22-45; 12:1-23 for details.) Yet this is a narrative interspersed with traditional poetic passages and whose syntax imitates that of narrative sections of the Hebrew Scriptures. It is, then, a narrative that consciously aims at incorporating its story into the tradition of the Hebrew Scriptures. It is not a retelling of Hebrew Scriptures as, for example, the pseudepigraphic book of *Jubilees,* which recounts the primeval history of humanity and the history of God's chosen people up to the time of Moses, or as the *Temple Scroll* from Qumran,[30] which restates much of the legislation from Exodus, Leviticus, and Deuteronomy. Rather, 1 Maccabees perceives the events it tells as another reenactment of the events of the Hebrew Scriptures. This is seen in the way the author views the execution of the Hasideans in 7:16 as being in accordance with the words of Ps 79:2-3—that is, the author sees the words of the psalm actualized in the events of his own day. This view of present-day events reflecting the Scriptures can be compared to the way the Qumran covenanters and the authors of the Gospels interpret the psalms and the prophets as talking about events in their own history. The author has not written a simple presentation of facts, but has woven a highly textured narrative.

That the syntax of 1 Maccabees reflects the narrative sections of the Hebrew Scriptures can be seen in the opening sentence, which begins as so many Hebrew narratives (e.g., Joshua, Judges, Ruth, 2 Samuel) begin and is then followed by a string of clauses all connected by "and." In addition, the Greek of 1 Maccabees is filled with Semitisms much like those in the LXX. There are also places in the text where one can understand what is going on if one presupposes that an original Hebrew text has been misunderstood or mistranslated (e.g., 9:2; possibly 3:37; and the enigmatic transliteration at 14:27). All this has led scholars to posit that 1 Maccabees was originally written in Hebrew and that our present text is a translation, while the original Hebrew text is missing. The Greek translator follows closely the translation style of other portions of the Hebrew Scriptures, so that one can often reconstruct what the original Hebrew text would have looked like. As the discoveries at Qumran have shown, writings in Hebrew were plentiful at this time, and so a writing in Hebrew should not surprise us.

The author also at times shows the inner connections of incidents by inserting literary linkages. For example, at 1 Macc 3:37, the author states that Antiochus IV was going through the upper provinces and then repeats the phrase at 6:1, thus binding Antiochus into the whole first series of actions and successes of the Hasmoneans. The same technique of intercalation is used to set the alliance of Jonathan with Rome between two attacks by commanders of Demetrius (11:63; 12:24). The author also carefully places in the narrative the documents that show the growing prestige and power of the Hasmoneans.

Even though the original text of 1 Maccabees was probably written in Hebrew, one should be aware of what a careful job the Greek translator has done. He shows considerable awareness of the Greek translation of the Hebrew Scriptures, but also is able to show connections in his choice of Greek phrasing and sections. For example, the use of the same root for the verb and the noun at 2:42 and 7:12 ("there united [συνήχθησαν *synēchthēsan*] . . . a company [συναγωγή *synagōgē*]"; "there appeared [ἐπισυνήχθησαν *episynēchthēsan*] . . . a group [*synagōgē*]") and the repetition of the same phrases throughout 7:1-25 bind the section together (see also 9:58-73). It is, for the most part, a thoughtful translation.

Worldview. That the author of the books of Maccabees wrote in Hebrew in imitation of the style of the Hebrew Scriptures was no accident. The author consciously set out to show how the Maccabean revolt closely followed ancestral traditions. Particularly noteworthy is the way the author has spliced the narrative with poetic compositions that echo traditional psalms of lament and rejoicing. Just as the author of the Gospel of Luke used hymns in the opening chapters

---

30. 11QTemple.

of his work to give his Gospel a traditional flavoring, so too did this earlier author. The author also models his heroes on biblical antecedents. Mattathias's opening act of rebellion explicitly echoes that of Phinehas in Num 25:6-13. Mattathias, as he lies dying, gives his testament, as Jacob had done (Genesis 49), and commissions his sons just as Moses had commissioned Joshua (Deut 31:7-23; Josh 1:6-9) and David had commissioned Solomon (1 Chr 22:13; 28:20). The Maccabeans are also related to the former judges of Israel. The most explicit reference to these judges is at 9:73, where Jonathan is said to "judge" Israel; Jonathan's election to succeed Judas also shows the influence of Jephthah's election (Judg 10:18; 11:6-11). The structural principle of the book of Judges is that when the Israelites do what is wrong in the eyes of the Lord, they are punished, but when they cry out, the Lord raises up someone to deliver them, and the land is at peace while that judge lives (Judg 2:16-18; 3:7-11). That same principle is operative in 1 Maccabees. Judas turns away God's anger (3:8) as he becomes the savior of Israel (9:21), under whom the land is at peace—if only for a while (7:50). When the land is in great distress after Judas's death, Jonathan is chosen to lead the people, and he succeeds so well that the sword no longer hangs over Israel (9:73). When destruction again threatens after Jonathan's capture, Simon takes command, and soon the country is at peace again (14:4). The ideology of the Judges also appears in the way towns are put under the ban and whole towns and their inhabitants are destroyed (5:28, 35, 44). Judas acts toward Ephron in accordance with the regulations of Deut 20:10-15 (1 Macc 5:45-51), and Simon's ethnic cleansing of Gazara/Gezer (1 Macc 13:47-48) attempts to follow the command not to have any covenant with the inhabitants of the land and to tear down their altars (Deut 7:1-6; Judg 2:1-2). The author of 1 Maccabees also frequently uses the term "foreigners" (ἀλλόφυλοι *allophyloi*) to describe the Gentiles (3:41; 4:12, 22, 26, 30; 5:15, 66, 68; 11:68, 74), a term often found in Judges and 1 Samuel.

It is also important to note how the Jewish enemies of the Hasmoneans are characterized: They are the lawless (1 Macc 2:44; 3:5-6; 7:5; 9:23, 58, 69), the workers of lawlessness (1 Macc 3:6; 9:23), sinners (1 Macc 2:44, 48, 62), and impious persons (1 Macc 3:8; 6:21; 7:5-9; 9:73). More significantly, they are "renegades" (παράνομοι *paranomoi*; see 1 Macc 1:11; 10:61; 11:21), a term used to describe those who would lead Israel astray (Deut 13:12-15), to characterize those who attacked and raped the Levite's concubine and so started a civil war (Judg 19:22), and to describe the followers of Jeroboam, who brought on the split of David's kingdom (2 Chr 13:7). The author of 1 Maccabees uses only these labels to describe the Jewish opponents of the Hasmoneans—with one exception, Alcimus. Except for the high priest Alcimus, the enemies' names would be forever forgotten if not for 2 Maccabees. The author thus uses labels effectively to emphasize that the Hasmonean party is right and its enemies wrong, to set up a strong us/them dichotomy.

The author of 1 Maccabees thus frames his narrative in biblical imagery. His heroes have been raised up by God to defend the people, just like the judges before them. The Hasmoneans are skillfully portrayed as upholding the traditional ancestral faith while their enemies are destroyers of the social fabric, those who bring in foreign ways. The opposition to foreigners extends to the Seleucids and to the Ptolemies, but not to the Romans. The Romans are portrayed as trustworthy and loyal, whereas the Ptolemies and the Seleucids are consistently untrustworthy. This may evidence a proper lack of knowledge of the Roman way of handling affairs, but it also shows how the author is willing to view in a favorable light anyone who does not attempt to wrest away Israel's independence, for this is the aim of the author—to celebrate the gaining of independence—and this is what he means by proclaiming the Hasmoneans the family through whom deliverance was given to Israel (5:62; cf. 13:41-42).

Date. It is not known who wrote 1 Maccabees, when or where it was written, or when it was translated into Greek. Since Josephus seems to base his account on the Greek version, it must have been translated sometime before the end of the first century CE. The fact that it was written in Hebrew, as well as the accuracy of some of its geographical data, suggests that it was composed in Israel. Its style of writing suggests someone well-versed in the traditional Scriptures of Israel. The erudite echoing of the Hebrew Scriptures suggests someone from the scribal class, or someone educated by a teacher like Sirach.

Scholars have consistently used two factors in determining a date for 1 Maccabees: its pro-Hasmonean stance and its concluding sentence, which refers to the annals of the high priesthood of John Hyrcanus (who ruled until 104 BCE). Bar-Kochva has suggested that the author, by the vividness and accuracy of his descriptions of the battles of Judas, must have been an eyewitness to the events and was, therefore, writing early in the reign of John Hyrancus.[31] However, a vivacious writing style and accurate geography can be achieved by others besides eyewitnesses. Most scholars have combined the above two factors to suggest a date late in Hyrcanus's reign or just after his death. S. Schwartz has argued, however, that the pro-Hasmonean stance of the author and his keeping of foreigners at arm's length are in conflict with what we know happened during the lengthy reign of Hyrcanus and his successors, when whole groups were incorporated into the area controlled by Hyrcanus. (For details on the reign of John Hyrcanus, see the section "Historical Background," above.) Schwartz therefore proposed a date early in Hyrcanus's reign, before such assimilation began. Schwartz's point is well taken, but the conclusion to the book still sounds as it if were written after the death of John Hyrcanus; thus Schwartz proposes that it was added later.[32] I would suggest that one should look more carefully at the assumption that the work is pro-Hasmonean. It clearly approves the gaining of independence, describes the Hasmonean founders as biblical heroes, and claims that they were the family through whom deliverance came to Israel. It is striking, however, that the author portrays Simon as having died while drunk at a banquet, which need not have been mentioned. There is also contrast between the utopian picture of Roman government in chapter 8 and the one-man rule imposed by Simon (14:41-45). Therefore, 1 Maccabees may be seen as a critique of the developments that had taken place under Hyrcanus and his successors, opposing the assimilation of non-Jews (which Schwartz points to), and the increasingly regal life-style of the Hasmoneans. Thus it is plausible to date 1 Maccabees to shortly after the death of John Hyrcanus.

FIRST AND SECOND MACCABEES IN JEWISH AND CHRISTIAN TRADITION

The events recounted in 1 and 2 Maccabees were, and are, celebrated in the Jewish community with the Feast of Hanukkah. In that festival, God's miraculous deliverance of the covenant people from their oppressors is remembered. The message of Hanukkah has been meaningful to a community that has sought to preserve its traditional beliefs and customs in an often hostile environment. Such a community could always look back and recall how the Seleucid kings had tried to stamp out Judaism, but were prevented from doing so by God's working through the Maccabees. In this way, the community could be reassured that it would never be deserted by God. Particularly symbolic of that deliverance is a story found not in 1 and 2 Maccabees, but in the later rabbinic tradition. This story recounts how the Jews, when they retook the city of Jerusalem and were preparing to reinstate proper worship in the Temple, found only one jar of oil for the temple lamps, which would have lasted but a single day. Miraculously, that one jar kept the lamps lighted for eight days. Enemies had tried to snuff out Judaism, but it had survived. This tradition also extolled the martyrdom accounts, particularly that of the mother and her seven sons (2 Maccabees 7), which was expanded by naming the mother Hannah and by the addition of more grisly torments for the martyrs. Much later, the heroism of the Maccabees in resisting oppression and defending their own culture and religion was especially meaningful in the nineteenth-century Zionist movement.

---

31. Bezalel Bar-Kochva, *Judas Maccabeus* (Cambridge: Cambridge University Press, 1988).
32. S. Schwartz, "Israel and the Nations Roundabout: 1 Maccabees and the Hasmonean Expansion," *Journal of Jewish Studies* 42 (1991) 16-30.

Early Christian communities also found the message of 1 and 2 Maccabees congenial. Not only could this record of events be used to validate the book of Daniel as prophetic and true, but also the story of a community faithful to God's commandments in the face of an idolatrous oppressor resonated with the life situation of many Christians in the Roman Empire. The books were particularly recommended for their martyrdom accounts. The feast of the Maccabean martyrs was celebrated at Antioch in Syria; at Carthage in North Africa, center of a Christian community determined not to be polluted by the contagion of the outside world, the martyrs were extolled. The great Christian thinker of the third century CE, Origen of Alexandria, wrote to exhort Christians to undergo martyrdom: "What dead person could be more deserving of praise than he who of his own choice elected to die for his religion? This is what Eleazar did, who welcoming death with honor rather than life with ignominy, went up to the rack to die of his free choice" (see 2 Macc 6:19).[33] The characters in 1 and 2 Maccabees still provide examples of endurance for what one believes in, even if that endurance means death.

33. Origen *To the Martyrs* 22.

BIBLIOGRAPHY

Bar-Kochva, Bezalel. *Judas Maccabeus.* Cambridge: Cambridge University Press, 1988. A fascinating analysis of the battles in 1 Maccabees by a military historian of the Hellenistic period. Essential reading for these battle scenes.

Bickerman, Elias. *The God of the Maccabees: Studies on the Meaning and Origin of the Maccabean Revolt.* SJLA 32. Leiden: Brill, 1979. A ground-breaking work, first published in German in 1937, on the background of the persecution.

Bringmann, Klaus. *Hellenistische Reform und Religionsverfolgung in Judäa: Eine Untersuchung zur jüdisch-hellenistische Geshichte (175–163 v. Chr).* Göttingen: Vandenhoeck and Ruprecht, 1983. Bringmann stresses the political and economic factors at play in the intervention by Antiochus IV.

Doran, Robert. *Temple Propaganda: The Purpose and Character of 2 Maccabees.* Washington, D.C.: Catholic Biblical Association, 1981. This work places 2 Maccabees in its literary and historiographical setting.

Geller, M. J. "New Information on Antiochus IV from Babylonian Astronomical Diaries," *BSO(A)S* 54 (1991) 1-4. Provides in handy format the diary entries pertinent to the Maccabean revolt.

Goldstein, Jonathan A. *1 Maccabees.* AB 41. Garden City, N.Y.: Doubleday, 1976.

———. *2 Maccabees.* AB 41A. Garden City, N.Y.: Doubleday, 1983. An erudite commentary whose comments on particular verses are worth consulting, but which is marred at times by overarching theories.

Grabbe, Lester L. *Judaism from Cyrus to Hadrian.* 2 vols. Minneapolis: Fortress, 1992. A survey of all the relevant materials; includes a bibliography.

Harrington, Daniel J. *The Maccabean Revolt: Anatomy of a Biblical Revolution.* Wilmington, Del.: Michael Glazier, 1988.

Momigliani, Arnaldo. "The Second Book of Maccabees," *CP* 70 (1975) 81-88. Makes the festivals in 2 Maccabees central to its explanation.

Mørkholm, Otto. *Antiochus IV of Syria.* Copenhagen: Gyldendalske Boghandel, 1966. Important for reconstructing a more balanced view of Antiochus IV.

Schürer, Emil. *The History of the Jewish People in the Age of Jesus Christ (175 BC–AD 135).* 3 vols. Revised by G. Vermes, F. Millar, M. Goodman. Edinburgh: Clark, 1973–87. An excellent reference book.

Sievers, Joseph. *The Hasmoneans and Their Supporters: From Mattathias to the Death of John Hyrcanus.* Atlanta: Scholars Press, 1991. A sensible attempt to reconstruct the history of this turbulent period.

Tcherikover, Victor. *Hellenistic Civilization and the Jews.* Philadelphia: Jewish Publication Society, 1961. First published in Hebrew in 1931 and later revised, this book contains a wealth of information. It and Bickerman's book still guide most scholarly treatments.

OUTLINE OF 1 MACCABEES

I. 1 Maccabees 1:1–2:70, Mattathias

    A. 1:1-64, The Persecution
        1:1-10, Introductory Scene
        1:11-15, The Apostasy
        1:16-28, The Visitation of Antiochus IV
        1:29-40, The Occupation of Jerusalem
        1:41-64, The Imposition of Paganism
    B. 2:1-70, The Career of Mattathias
        2:1-14, The Family of Mattathias
        2:15-28, The Actions at Modein
        2:29-48, The Exploits of Mattathias
        2:49-70, The Death of Mattathias

II. 1 Maccabees 3:1–9:22, Judas Maccabeus

    A. 3:1-9, Hero of His People
    B. 3:10-26, Judas's First Victories
        3:10-12, Victory Against Apollonius
        3:13-26, Victory Against Seron
    C. 3:27–4:35, Major Seleucid Counterattacks
        3:27-37, The King's Decision
        3:38–4:25, The Battle Against Nicanor and Gorgias
            3:38-60, Preparations for Battle
            4:1-25, The Battle at Emmaus
        4:26-35, The Campaign of Lysias
    D. 4:36-61, The Cleansing of the Temple
    E. 5:1-68, Wars with Neighbors
        5:1-8, Battles in Idumea and Ammon
        5:9-54, Battles in Galilee and Gilead
        5:55-62, The Failure of Joseph and Azariah
        5:63-68, Further Successes
    F. 6:1-17, The Death of Antiochus IV
    G. 6:18-63, Attacks Under Antiochus V Eupator
        6:18-31, The Pre-Invasion Events
        6:32-47, The Battle at Beth-zechariah
        6:48-54, The Siege of Jerusalem
        6:55-63, The End of the Assault by Antiochus V Eupator
    H. 7:1-25, The Expedition of Bacchides and Alcimus

1 MACCABEES—INTRODUCTION

   7:1-7, The New King, Demetrius
   7:8-20, The Incursion of Bacchides
   7:21-25, The Inability of Alcimus to Rule
 I. 7:26-50, The Rule of Nicanor
   7:26-32, The Treachery of Nicanor
   7:33-38, Nicanor Threatens the Temple
   7:39-50, The Death of Nicanor
 J. 8:1-32, The Relationship with Rome
   8:1-16, An Idealized Description of the Romans
   8:17-32, The Exchange of Letters
 K. 9:1-22, The Death of Judas

III. 1 Maccabees 9:23–12:53, Jonathan

 A. 9:23-73, Jonathan's Rise to Power
   9:23-31, The Succession of Jonathan
   9:32-49, Early Campaigns of Jonathan
   9:50-53, The Strategy of Bacchides
   9:54-57, The Death of Alcimus
   9:58-73, The Last Expedition of Bacchides
 B. 10:1–12:53, Jonathan's Rule
   10:1-14, Jonathan and Demetrius I
   10:15-21, Jonathan and Alexander Epiphanes
   10:22-45, The Reaction of Demetrius I
   10:46-66, Jonathan and Alexander
   10:67-89, The Uprising of Demetrius II
   11:1-19, The Coming of Ptolemy VI
   11:20-53, Demetrius II
     11:20-37, Demetrius's Rise to Power
     11:38-53, The Rule of Demetrius II
   11:54-74, Jonathan and Antiochus VI
   12:1-23, The Relationship with Rome
   12:24-38, Further Campaigns for Antiochus VI
   12:39-53, The Capture of Jonathan

IV. 1 Maccabees 13:1–16:24, Simon

 A. 13:1-30, Simon Replaces Jonathan
   13:1-11, Simon Takes Command
   13:12-24, Trypho's Invasion
   13:25-30, Jonathan's Tomb
 B. 13:31–14:3, Judea Gains Independence
   13:31-42, The Removal of Tribute
   13:43-53, Further Acquisitions by Simon
   14:1-3, The Capture of Demetrius
 C. 14:4-49, The Praise of Simon
   14:4-15, Hymn of Praise
   14:16-24, Diplomacy with Rome and Sparta
   14:25-49, "The Great Assembly"
 D. 15:1–16:10, Further Seleucid Threats
   15:1-14, The Rise of Antiochus VII Sidetes

15:15-24, Continued Roman Support
15:25-36, Antiochus's Change of Heart
15:37–16:10, The Expedition of Cendebeus
E. 16:11-22, The Death of Simon
F. 16:23-24, Conclusion

1 MACCABEES 1:1–2:70

MATTATHIAS

1 MACCABEES 1:1-64, THE PERSECUTION

1 Maccabees 1:1-10, Introductory Scene

COMMENTARY

The opening verses of 1 Maccabees locate the events the author is going to narrate within the larger framework of history. The passage is in some sense one long sentence, since the ten verses are a series of main clauses all connected by the particle "and" (καί *kai*). The end of the passage is indicated by the repetition of the phrase "came out of "; just as Alexander came out, so also Antiochus came out. This grammatical style reflects Hebrew syntax, and the opening words of 1 Maccabees ("and [he] came out" [καὶ ἐγένετο *kai egeneto*]) are the same as those found at the beginning of Joshua, Judges, Ruth, and 2 Samuel in the LXX. The work is thus squarely placed in the Jewish historiographical tradition.

1:1. Alexander began his journey of conquest from Pella, the capital of Macedonia, in the spring of 334 BCE. The author has Alexander leave the land of the Kittim, a word used variously in the Old Testament. At Gen 10:4 and 1 Chr 1:7, the Kittim are the descendants of Yavan and thus Japheth. Jeremiah 2:10 locates the sites of the Kittim as one extreme of the world, while Ezek 27:6 has them as trading partners of Tyre. In these two passages the Kittim are often identified with Cyprus; Josephus similarly identifies the Kittim as being from Kition, a Phoenician city on the island of Cyprus.[34] Balaam predicts in his fourth oracle that ships shall come from Kittim and oppress Asshur and Eber (Num 24:24). Here again the Kittim are a maritime force, and Eber might be interpreted as the Hebrews (see Gen 10:21-24). Perhaps deriving from this use, Kittim became a term in later apocalyptic texts to designate a far-off people who will wage war. At Dan 11:30, the Kittim are the Romans, who shame Antiochus IV, and in *Jub.* 24:28-29 they are an ultimate enemy who will confront the accursed Philistines. In the *Pesher on Habakkuk* from Qumran,[35] the Kittim have dominion over Israel and appear to be the Romans; in the *War Scroll* from Qumran, they are the last world power to oppress God's people.[36] Elsewhere in 1 Maccabees, Perseus, king of Macedonia, is described as being the king of the Kittim (1 Macc 8:5). Thus, although the author of 1 Maccabees calls the Macedonians "Kittim," one may suggest that this term is no neutral geographical indicator but that even in 1 Maccabees the term carries the overtones of an oppressive world power.

Alexander's success was enormous. He first defeated a Persian army led by satraps at Granicus in northwest Asia Minor (in spring 334 BCE), then one led by King Darius himself at Issus in southeast Asia Minor in autumn 333. From there he moved to conquer the Syrian coast (332) and occupy Egypt in the winter of 332/331 BCE, before returning to defeat decisively King Darius at Gaugmela in northern Iraq in late 331. Darius fled to the Median capital of Ecbatana while Alexander occupied Babylon and Persia. Darius hastily retreated further, but was finally arrested and killed by his own satraps. The last Achaemenid was dead, and Alexander was master of Asia. But he was still not content; he pushed

---

34. Josephus *Antiquities of the Jews* 1.28.
35. See 1QpHab 2:12–6:12.
36. See 1QM 1:2; 15:2A.

on through present-day northern Iran and Afghanistan to Pakistan and the Punjab valley before turning back; he died at Babylon on June 10, 323 BCE. While he may not have conquered the ends of the earth—his western ambitions remained unfulfilled—Alexander had united a formidable empire, inaugurating the Hellenistic world.

1:2-4. At v. 2, Alexander is said to have slain "the kings of the earth." In fact, Alexander was usually not cruel to those he defeated, except in the case of the usurper Bessus. The author of Maccabees describes the normal behavior of victors (cf. 2 Kgs 25:6-7). After Alexander's conquests, the land is said to be at peace, a phrase found frequently in 1 Maccabees (7:50; 9:57; 11:38, 52; 14:4). It is used here to describe the absence of war. The phrase is used in the Hebrew Scriptures as well, particularly in the book of Judges. After the Israelites had repented of worshiping other gods, the Lord sent them deliverers in the persons of Othniel and Ehud, who defeated the enemies and left the land at "rest" (see Judg 3:11, 30), and under the good king Asa, the land was said to have been "at rest" (2 Chr 14:1). The phrase as used here, however, seems to fit better the context of its use at Zech 1:11, where the angels of the Lord who have patrolled the earth report that the whole earth is at peace, a peace that is oppressive to Israel.

The greatness of Alexander's success is said to have "lifted up" his heart. In the Hebrew Bible, this phrase symbolizes arrogance, as when King Jehoash of Judah, who became too cocksure, went to battle against the king of Israel and was defeated (2 Kgs 14:10; 2 Chr 25:19). Obadiah predicts doom to Edom, whose proud heart has "lifted it up" (Obad 3). Daniel so characterizes the king of the south, Ptolemy IV, after his early victory over Antiochus III, whereas Antiochus ultimately prevails over Egypt (Dan 11:12). Thus the phrase "his heart was lifted up" is a hint that something bad is going to happen to Alexander.

All the countries must pay tribute. The phrase again echoes the LXX (Josh 19:48*a*; Judg 1:28-31, 33, 35) and encapsulates the loss of independence of all the various conquered peoples.

1:5-9. At the height of his power, Alexander is suddenly struck down. Many stories circulated as to the cause of Alexander's death. Some claim that Alexander was poisoned.[37] Others relate that he died after drinking too strong unmixed wine.[38] Plutarch and Arrian report that his death came after a feverish sickness and discount other suggestions.[39] The author of 1 Maccabees does not detail how Alexander died, but the suddenness of the event at the height of his power suggests divine judgment (cf. the oracle of Isaiah against Babylon [Isa 14:5-21] or that of Obadiah against Edom [Obad 1-4]). The death of Antiochus IV was also seen as divine punishment. The same language ("to fall sick" [ἔπεσεν ἐπὶ τὴν κοίτην καὶ ἔγνω ὅτι ἀποθνήσκει *epesen epi tēn koitēn kai egnō hoti apothnēskei*] lit., "to fall on his bed," "perceive/realize that he was dying") is used to describe Antiochus IV when he hears the news of the victorious Judas Maccabeus (1 Macc 6:8-9).

First Maccabees depicts Alexander as dividing his kingdom among his followers. This is similar to what is found in the late work of Pseudo-Callisthenes, who portrays Alexander, on his deathbed, writing a will.[40] Diodorus reports that when asked to whom he left the kingdom, Alexander said, "To the strongest."[41] By contrast, the author of 1 Maccabees links the rulers of his own day with that proud ruler. He describes an orderly transition of power, whereas, in fact, there were many long, hard-fought campaigns among rival leaders. Only in 306 BCE did Antigonus and his son Demetrius, who then ruled jointly over much of Greece, Asia Minor, and Syria, assume the diadem, and they were followed in this a year later by Ptolemy and Seleucus.

1:10. "A sinful root" comes forth from these kings. By using the term "root" (ῥίζα *rhiza*), the author intimates the beginning of future troubles. (The same image is used at Isa 14:29, when King Ahaz of Judea dies.) Antiochus IV Epiphanes was the youngest son of Antiochus III, "the Great." After the Romans decisively defeated Antiochus III at

---
37. Arrian *Anabasis* 7.27.
38. Diodorus Siculus 17.117.
39. Plutarch *Alexander* 75-77; Arrian *Anabasis* 7.25-26.
40. Pseudo-Callisthenes *Life of Alexander* 3:33. This account of the life of Alexander was written in part to glorify the foresight of Alexander and to promote the city of Alexandria.
41. Diodorus Siculus 17.117.

the battle of Magnesia (190 BCE), this youngest son was handed over to the Romans as a hostage. Antiochus III was succeeded in 187 BCE by his older son, Seleucus IV. Around 176, the Romans exchanged Antiochus for Seleucus IV's son Demetrius. On Seleucus IV's death in 175 BCE, Antiochus seized the opportunity to gain control of the kingdom in place of his brother's son. "The one hundred thirty-seventh year" of the Seleucid kingdom would be 176–175 BCE; a cuneiform king-list from Babylon presents Antiochus IV as the immediate successor of Seleucus IV in September 175. The reference to Antiochus as a hostage in Rome intimates that there are other powers in the world besides the successors of Alexander and looks forward to the favorable description of the Romans in chapter 8.

1 Maccabees 1:11-15, The Apostasy

COMMENTARY

1:11-13. After the prologue, with its emphasis on the arrogance and sudden death of Alexander the Great, the detailed narrative opens with an account of apostasy. These verses again are filled with biblical allusions. "Certain renegades" echoes Deut 13:12-15, which describes certain renegades who lead astray the inhabitants of a town by saying, "Let us go and worship other gods" (Deut 13:13 NRSV). The civil war against the Benjaminites started when "certain renegades" attacked and raped the concubine of a Levite (Judg 19:22). The division between the northern kingdom of Israel and the southern kingdom of Judah started because "certain renegades" encouraged Jeroboam to defy Solomon's son Rehoboam (2 Chr 13:7). The theme of being like the nations is also linked to wrongdoing in the Bible (Exod 34:15; Deut 7:2-4; 1 Sam 8:4-8). Second Kings 17:7-18 gives a long reflection on why the northern kingdom was captured by Assyria, the primary reason being that the Israelites followed the ways of the nations round about them. At 1 Macc 1:15, the Judeans "abandoned the holy covenant" (ἀπέστησαν ἀπὸ διαθήκης ἁγίας *apestēsan apo diathēkēs hagias*; a verb found with this meaning at Deut 13:10, 13; 32:15; Josh 22:18-19, 23, 29) and join with the Gentiles (lit., "yoke themselves" [ἐζευγίσθησαν *ezeugisthēsan*]; see Num 25:3; Ps 106:28, where Israel yoked itself to Baal of Peor). They "sold themselves to do evil" (ἐπράθησαν τοῦ ποιῆσαι τὸ πονηρόν *eprathēsan tou poiēsai to ponēron*) as the Israelites of the northern kingdom had done before them (2 Kgs 17:17) and also the wicked King Ahab (1 Kgs 21:20, 25).

1:14-15. The renegades built a gymnasium. Second Maccabees 4:7-17 fills out the details of this undertaking. The educational, social, and physical exercise complex that composed the gymnasium was the hallmark of a Greek city, and so building one in Jerusalem signaled a rejection of traditional Jewish customs. They "removed the marks of circumcision," an operation first described at some length by a Latin author, Celsus.[42] The apostle Paul also suggests that such an operation was possible: "Was anyone at the time of his call already circumcised? Let him not seek to remove the marks of circumcision" (1 Cor 7:18 NRSV). Since the Greek ideal of beauty viewed circumcision as a mutilation, and since the custom was for athletes in Greek games to compete in the nude, some strove to remove the marks of circumcision. It is unlikely, however, that all the Jews, including priests, who exercised in the Jerusalem gymnasium underwent this operation. Other contemporary descriptions of the apostasy (Dan 11:32; 2 Macc 4:7-17; *Jub.* 30; *1 Enoch* 90:6-9) make no mention of it. The literal translation, "made foreskins for themselves," shows that the author of 1 Maccabees has wrought a trenchant metaphor to describe his opponents as complete apostates, acting against the covenantal regulation: "This is my covenant, which you shall keep, between me and you and your offspring after you: Every male among you shall be circumcised. . . . Any uncircumcised male who is not circumcised in the flesh of his foreskin shall be cut off from his people; he has broken my covenant" (Gen 17:10, 14 NRSV).

42. Celsus *On Medicine* 7.25.

1 Maccabees 1:16-28, The Visitation of Antiochus IV

COMMENTARY

1:16-19. The war between the Seleucid and the Ptolemaic empires began when the guardians of Ptolemy VI Philometor moved to invade Seleucid territory and recapture Syria and Palestine (late 170 or early 169 BCE). Antiochus IV reacted swiftly and won a decisive victory near Pelusium, on the Mediterranean coast near the border of Egypt. Antiochus seems to have tried to install his sister's son, Ptolemy VI, in power, with himself as Ptolemy's regent. The author of 1 Maccabees describes Antiochus IV, however, as being as ambitious as Alexander the Great to extend his empire and to gain plunder.

1:20-24a. No reason is given by the author for this sudden violent attack on Jerusalem in the autumn of 169 BCE. No doubt the author wishes it to be seen as the result of the Judeans' forsaking of the covenant, although he also accuses Antiochus IV of arrogance. In 2 Macc 5:1-26, the attack of Antiochus is placed after his second invasion of Egypt and is seen as being caused by factional fighting within Jerusalem, which Antiochus understands as a rebellion against his authority. The Babylonian astronomical diaries recount that in November/December 169 Antiochus IV confiscated funds from the Esagil (temple) in Babylon. Polybius also writes that Antiochus sacrilegiously pillaged the temples.[43] The desecration of the Jerusalem Temple must be seen, therefore, as part of a policy of Antiochus IV to gain additional monies. The actions as described in 1 Maccabees, however, do seem to go beyond simply taking funds from a temple.

Antiochus IV "entered the sanctuary"—i.e., the inner courts of the Temple, not the holy of holies. According to 3 Macc 1:9-12, a king was allowed to enter the sanctuary, but not the holy of holies. Antiochus took away the altar of incense (see Exod 30:1-10), the lamp stand (see Exod 25:31-40), the table of showbread (see Exod 25:23-30), the incense dishes, and the libation bowls (see Exod 25:29). The curtain referred to seems to be the curtain before the holy of holies, where the ark of the covenant had stood (Exod 26:31-35). Thus, while Antiochus IV is not said to have himself entered the holy of holies,[44] taking the curtain would have been seen as an act of desecration (cf. Mark 15:38, where, at the death of Jesus, the curtain is torn from top to bottom). "The crowns" refers to decorations on the Temple, as at 4:57, and perhaps to the clasps of gold on the curtains, as at Exod 36:13. "The hidden treasures" perhaps was money left in the Temple on deposit. Antiochus IV, known to Greek historians such as Polybius as having sought to restore his fortunes through robbing various temples, did a thorough job at Jerusalem.

1:24b-28. The narrator here breaks into poetic format, with parallelism between the constituent parts—for example, "shed much blood"/"spoke with arrogance"; "land"/"house of Jacob." Just as traditional imagery was often used in the narrative, so also this poem, in traditional lament format, draws on traditional style. One might compare it with the way the author of the Gospel of Luke uses hymns in the opening chapters to create an atmosphere of traditional piety. The author of 1 Maccabees, by the use of such a traditional format, thus shows respect for tradition and arouses sympathy for the presentation among hearers or readers.

---

43. Polybius 30.26.9.

44. Josephus insists that Pompey the Great was the first foreigner to enter the holy of holies. See *Antiquities of the Jews* 14.71-72; *The Jewish War* 1.152.

1 Maccabees 1:29-40, The Occupation of Jerusalem

COMMENTARY

Antiochus IV had been able to conquer Egypt so successfully in his first campaign in part because Rome was engaged in fighting Perseus, king of Macedon, who was defeated on June 22, 168 BCE. When the opposition to Antiochus IV in Egypt proclaimed Ptolemy VIII Euergetes II and Cleopatra to be joint rulers, Antiochus's protégé joined with them. So Antiochus once again laid siege to Alexandria. But this time the Romans intervened, and the Roman ambassador C. Popillius Laenas came before Antiochus to deliver an ultimatum for him to withdraw all his forces from Egypt and Cyprus. Antiochus had to submit to the superior power of Rome and ignominiously return to Syria. An Egyptian priest, Hor, had recorded a dream he had that Antiochus and his army would leave Egypt by July 30, 168 BCE, and his dream was confirmed by events.

1:29-31. The expression "a chief collector of tribute" is usually interpreted in the light of 2 Macc 5:24, where this figure is identified as Apollonius, captain of the Mysians. The Greek translator might easily have misread the Hebrew "chief collector of tribute" (שר המוסים *śar hammûsîm*) as "captain of the Mysians" (שר המיסים *śar hammîssîm*).

The sending of a force to strengthen the city of Jerusalem would seem to fit in with the strategic necessity of defending Antiochus's southern border with Egypt. This strengthening of Jerusalem, however, is described as oppression by the author of 1 Maccabees. As the text now stands, Antiochus's intent is to collect tribute, just as Alexander had taken tribute (1:4), and an official comes with a large force, just as Antiochus IV had invaded Egypt before plundering it (1:17, 19). The enemies of the Jews are described as using peaceable words to work deceit (this negative description of enemies is found elsewhere in 1 Maccabees; e.g., 7:10, 15, 27-30; 10:46; 11:2-3). The author of 2 Maccabees intensifies the heinousness of the deed by having the invasion take place on a sabbath. Many inhabitants are slaughtered, and the city is looted, burned, and left defenseless by the destruction of its walls (cf. Jer 51:58).

1:32. There is a sudden change from the third-person singular to the third-person plural. The third-person plural can be used in place of the passive tense, or it may be that the large force mentioned in v. 29 is considered not collectively now but as being made up of individuals. (This latter phenomenon is seen in 2 Kgs 25:5 LXX: "the army [sing.] of the Chaldeans pursued the king, and they overtook him.")

The women, children, and livestock are groups distinct from the fighting males. When the tribes of Reuben and Gad wished to stay in the land of Jazer and Gilead and not cross over the Jordan, Moses allowed them to leave their little ones, their wives, their flocks, and all their livestock behind, but all men armed for war had to cross over to help conquer the promised land (Num 32:25-27; cf. Deut 3:19). Exodus 20:17 and Deut 5:21 classify women and livestock as possessions. Taking away the women and children ensures that the city will not reproduce itself and survive; taking the livestock removes the means of sustenance. The combination of women, children, and livestock, therefore, represents the life of a town.

1:33. According to 2 Macc 5:5, this whole operation was motivated by an attempt by the former high priest Jason to gain control of Jerusalem after hearing a false rumor that Antiochus IV had died. Although the destruction of its walls would strip the city of its defenses, in order to provide some security "the city of David" was fortified and became the occupying force's citadel. There was a citadel in Jerusalem in Persian times, which seems to have been located north of the temple area (Neh 7:2), and this citadel had apparently been destroyed prior to the time of Antiochus IV. According to 2 Macc 4:12, there was, indeed, a citadel in Jerusalem before the persecution of Antiochus IV. This citadel seems to have been within the city of David (2 Macc 5:5), since Jonathan later built a barrier between the citadel and the city (1 Macc 12:36). In 1 Macc 1:33, "citadel" parallels the fortified "city of David," and so it should perhaps be taken in the more general sense of "stronghold," rather than referring to the citadel within the city.

1:34-35. In the citadel was stationed "a sinful race, perverse men." The two phrases are in apposition. "Perverse men" refers to 1:11, with the biblical resonance of renegades and apostates from Judaism. "A sinful nation" is found at Isa 1:4 in a bitter reproach against a rebellious Israel:

> Ah, sinful nation,
>   people laden with iniquity,
> offspring who do evil,
>   children who deal corruptly,
> who have forsaken the LORD,
>   who have despised the Holy One of Israel,
>   who are utterly estranged! (NRSV)

Those living in the citadel, therefore, would seem to be Jews who did not rebel against Antiochus IV. They are characterized as a "snare," using a term by which Joshua had described the nations left in the land (Josh 23:13), and with which Hosea (5:1) and Jeremiah (5:26; cf. Ps 119:110) had described sinners within Israel.

1:36-40. The author again breaks into a poetic lament, wherein the verses evidence strong parallelism. The language echoes Lam 5:2: "Our inheritance has been turned over to strangers, our homes to aliens," as well as the oracle against Jerusalem uttered by Amos: "I will turn your feasts into mourning,/ and all your songs into lamentation" (Amos 8:10 NRSV; cf. Lam 5:15-18). It stresses the gap between those who now dwell in Jerusalem and true Israelites, connects these events with the destruction of Jerusalem in 587 BCE, and depicts the author as the true upholder of Israelite tradition.

1 Maccabees 1:41-64, The Imposition of Paganism

COMMENTARY

The author now describes the measures undertaken by Antiochus IV to impose control over Judea, measures that meant the abolition of the observance of the law in Judea. The author of 1 Maccabees states that these measures were part of a general plan to homogenize all the peoples (v. 41). Antiochus's effort may be seen as hubris against God, with perhaps an allusion to Gen 11:6, where God sees that humans are one people and one language and are conspiring to act against heaven, and so scatters them. The same kind of homogenizing effort is also found in Daniel 3, where Nebuchadnezzar is said to have set up a golden statue and to have commanded all "peoples, nations, and languages" to worship it. Antiochus IV was the first Seleucid king to use the title "god manifest" (Ἐπιφανής θεός *Epiphanēs theos*); from his depictions on coins, he appears to have had a particular devotion to Olympian Zeus, rather than to Apollo, as had been customary among the Seleucids. Daniel 11:37-38 speaks of Antiochus's honoring the god of fortresses (Zeus Olympios) rather than "the gods of his ancestors, or to the one beloved by women" (NRSV; Tammuz); it is also suggested that Antiochus considered himself greater than these other gods. However, there is no evidence that Antiochus IV attempted to stamp out the customs and traditional religious observances of other nations; in fact, he seems to have promoted local customs. Such a move by Antiochus IV to abolish the religious practice of a people would have been deeply at odds with the usual practice of the time, whereby ancient states respected the existing gods and cultic practices of differing localities.

Nevertheless, Antiochus is consistently portrayed as instigating the abolition of Jewish observances. Both biblical and extra-biblical sources indicate that the attack on Jewish observances emanated from Antiochus himself. At Dan 11:30-31, he is said to "take action against the holy covenant" (NRSV) and to send forces to profane the Temple. The first-century BCE historian Diodorus Siculus relates how Antiochus VII Sidetes was told by his friends:

> Antiochus, called Epiphanes, on defeating the Jews had entered the innermost

sanctuary of the god's temple, where it was lawful for the priest alone to enter. He found there a marble statue of a heavily bearded man seated on an ass, with a book in his hands. He supposed it to be an image of Moses, the founder of Jerusalem and organizer of the nation. Moses was the person who had ordained for the Jews their misanthropic and lawless customs. Since Epiphanes was shocked by such hatred directed against all mankind, he had set himself to break down their traditional practices.[45]

This incredibly untrue depiction evidences some of the anti-Jewish nonsense circulating about the Jews. Later, in a letter to Lysias, his guardian, Antiochus V reversed this prohibition against Judaism (see 2 Macc 11:23-25), which he attributes to his father.

The letters of the king (v. 44) complete the agenda of the renegades mentioned in v. 11—to follow after other customs (1:11; cf. Deut 13:2). The text makes clear that this meant the abandonment of all that was distinctive of Judaism—Jewish festivals, daily offerings, sabbaths, circumcision, kosher laws—but it is not clear exactly what replaced them. Elias Bickermann suggests that the religion was a Hellenistic reform of Judaism, whereby the worship of the God of the Jews was replaced by the cult of Ba'al Shamen ("Lord of the Heavens"); the desolating sacrilege in 1 Macc 1:54 is a translation of the term at Dan 11:31 (השקוץ משומם *haššiqqûṣ měšômēm*), which is a pun on the word *Shamen*.[46] Jonathan Goldstein suggests that the divine triad of Zeus, Athena, and Dionysus was worshiped.[47] However, these suggestions remain highly speculative. What we do know is that (1) the Temple was dedicated to Zeus Olympios (2 Macc 6:2); (2) unlawful sacrifices were made on the altar of burnt offering (1 Macc 1:59; 2 Macc 6:5); (3) other altars were placed in the cities of Judea (1 Macc 1:54) and in the agora of Jerusalem (2 Macc 10:2); (4) feasts of Dionysus were celebrated, as was the king's birthday (2 Macc 6:7); (5) pigs were sacrificed, as was frequently done in Greek religious practices. We do not know whether cultic statues were set up, although later writers make this claim.[48] The proliferation of altars and the various festivals suggest that, rather than the cult of one particular deity or trio of deities, what was established was the worship of various gods and goddesses.[49]

1:45. "Burnt offerings and sacrifices and drink offerings" refer to the burnt offerings, grain offerings, and drink offerings that were to be offered daily, on sabbaths, and on feast days (see Numbers 28–29). "To profane sabbaths" was to become guilty of death (Exod 31:12-17; cf. Neh 13:17-18; Ezek 20:13, 16).

1:46-49. The term "priests" (ἅγιοι *hagioi*) literally means "holy ones" (Latin manuscripts read "holy things"). What is being described is the elimination of the distinction between clean and unclean, which is so much a part of the Torah. The sanctuary is no longer the only holy place (Lev 17:1-9; Deut 12:2-14), the most holy place in Israel (Ezek 45:3), but there are to be other altars and other offering places, and the offering of swine and other unclean animals signifies the end of the kosher laws of Leviticus 11. The prohibition of circumcision made a Jewish male's body uncovenanted (Gen 17:11). Thus the distinguishing marks of the religious culture of Judea—sacred time, sacred space, sacred food, and sacred body—were eliminated (the language "to make themselves abominable" reflects the language of Lev 11:43-44; 20:25-26).

1:50. The change from indirect speech to direct speech heightens the sense of immediacy and impending threat. The Greek word for "command" (ῥῆμα *rhēma*) is frequently found in the Greek translation of the Bible for what God says in the Torah (e.g., Lev 17:2; Num 30:1 [LXX 30:2]; Deut 12:32 [LXX 13:1]; 25:58; 31:9).

1:51. The opening words of v. 41 are repeated. This verse further describes the way in which Antiochus's decree was to be implemented.

1:52-53. Many of the people are said to follow the king's order (v. 42) to forsake their ancestral tradition. At Dan 11:30, Antiochus is said to "pay heed to those who forsake the holy covenant" (NRSV; cf. Prov. 28:4: "Those who forsake the law praise the wicked, but

---

45. Diodorus Siculus 34/35.1,3-4.
46. Bickermann, *The God of the Maccabees*, 61-75.
47. Goldstein, *1 Maccabees*, 148-58.
48. See Jerome *Commentary on Daniel* 8:14-15; 11:31, citing Porphyry, a pagan philosopher and historian of the late third century CE.
49. F. Miller, "The Background to the Maccabean Revolution: Reflections on Martin Hengel's 'Judaism and Hellenism,'" *JJS* 29 (1978) 1-21.

those who keep the law struggle against them" [NRSV]). Just as the successors of Alexander caused many evils on the land (1:9), so also did those who now forsake the law.

Only those who resist the king's command deserve the name of "Israel." Where they fled is not specified, but more than 150 cave complexes have been discovered in the Judean foothills, southwest of Jerusalem. Hewn into the chalk rock, parts of these cave complexes are connected by low and narrow passages. The entrances to the various segments of the complex could be blocked and defended from the inside; there were water installations, areas for storage rooms, and means of providing ventilation. These complexes would have been fully operational at the time of the Jewish revolts against Rome in 66–70 and 132–135 CE, but they were also in use, if not quite so elaborately, during the Hellenistic period. As Amos Kloner states, "The warrens appear to have been of local design and execution, and their integration within and around settlements points to their extensive use during the Hellenistic and Roman periods."[50] (The hiding places are also mentioned at 1 Macc 2:29-31.)

1:54-59. The fifteenth day of Chislev, the ninth month in the Jewish calendar, would be about the middle of December. The author of 2 Maccabees as well as the author of 1 Maccabees would date the removal of this sacrilege on the 25th day of Chislev (1 Macc 4:52, 54; 2 Macc 10:5). The author of 2 Maccabees follows the schema whereby punishment and reward fall on the same day, and so connects the profanation of the Temple with the feast of Antiochus's birthday (25 Chislev), rather than with the actual erection of the abomination of desolation. The book of Daniel speaks of the removal of the daily burnt offering (Dan 8:11) and the setting up of the desolating abomination (Dan 9:27; 11:31). The erection of altars throughout the towns of Judea and the burning of incense in the streets signify the ways in which all the community of Judea was to be involved in this transformation. Demosthenes says that one should fill the streets with the savor of sacrifice,[51] and a decree from Asia Minor in the late second century BCE speaks of both the official sacrifice and the household sacrifice to honor the goddess Artemis on her feast day.[52] One might compare the action of King Josiah against such practices (2 Kgs 23:4-20).

The word for "books" (βιβλία *biblia*) in v. 56 is the same word used for "letters" in v. 44. Perhaps the author suggests that the "books"—that is, letters—of the king replace the "books" of the law. The burning of the book of the law might be compared to the cutting and burning of Jeremiah's scroll by King Jehoiakim (Jeremiah 36).

1:60-63. The author has chosen to highlight the execution of women here not only to show the cruelty of the persecutors, but also to symbolize the attempt to destroy the traditions of the Jews (cf. 2 Macc 6:10). Since it is through women that a people continues, the gruesome sight of babies and mothers executed together strongly signifies the stamping out of a people.

In v. 62, the language is that of war and siegecraft. Interestingly, the resistance of those who do not obey the king's command is signified by their not eating unclean food. The same concern occurs in the book of Daniel, where Daniel and his companions, captives in the service of Nebuchadnezzar, king of Babylon, refuse to eat the royal rations of food and wine so as not to defile themselves (Dan 1:8-16). When Antiochus IV defiles sacred spaces and sacred times, some Jews do not allow their "covenanted" bodies to be breached by ingesting unclean food. The result of both actions—the womens' actions to covenant their sons and the men's to not eat unclean food—is the same: death.

1:64. The time of wrath upon Israel is recognized by Mattathias (1 Macc 2:49) and is taken away by the actions of Judas Maccabeus (1 Macc 3:8). The author here follows a pattern whereby the sins of Israel bring on the wrath of God, but their repentance prompts God to send a deliverer. The pattern of sin/repentance/deliverance is strongly expressed in Judg 2:11-14; 3:7-10. The "wrath of the Lord" is also prominent in the accounts of the reasons for God's punishment and exile of Israel (2 Kgs 17:7-18) and Judah (2 Kgs 21:14-15; 22:16-17; 23:26-27).

---

50. Amos Kloner, "Underground Hiding Complexes from the Bar Kokhba War in the Judean Shephelah," *BA* 46 (1983) 219.
51. Demosthenes *Oration* 21.51; cf. Aristophanes *Birds* 1233.

52. *Sylloge Inscriptionum Graecarum*, ed. W. Dittenberger, 4 vols. (Leipzig: Hirzel, 1915–24) 2:695.

REFLECTIONS

Wars, with their attendant violence and oppression, are not merely about geographical boundaries. Perhaps even more, wars concern questions of cultural identity. We may never know exactly what prompted Antiochus IV to attempt to stamp out the ancestral religious traditions of Judea in 167 BCE. He may have wanted to eliminate any opposition in an area near the border with Egypt, or he may have been venting his anger at being humiliated by the Romans on an available target. Why these motives entailed systematic destruction of the religion of Judea is unclear. The author of 1 Maccabees has presented the conflict as a question of self-determination and does not mention the Roman setback to Antiochus IV in Egypt. Rather, Antiochus is portrayed as a powerful monarch who tries to impose his will on a much smaller nation. The Jews, who stood firm, are depicted as wishing to maintain their cultural traditions. Several issues arise as one ponders this narrative.

1. The question of minority rights immediately comes to mind as one reads the account of the oppression of the Jews under Antiochus. Within a large, multi-cultural nation, how are the rights and ethnicity of the minority to be respected and protected? The issue is exemplified particularly when one discusses religion in the public schools. If the holy days of the majority group are discussed in school by a teacher (e.g., Christian feasts, like Christmas), should the teacher not also discuss the holy days of other religions, like Judaism, Islam, and Hinduism? If prayer were to be allowed in public schools, should the prayers of all religious groups be said along with those of the religion of the majority? The issue becomes particularly acute when an element of a minority's religious practice seems to run counter to the majority culture. If peyote, a hallucinogenic drug, is sacred to Native American worship, can the majority culture decide the use of this substance should be prohibited because it is a drug? What if a religious group practices animal sacrifice? Should they be allowed to perform a sacrifice in public? How far does the majority need to go to respect minority rights?

2. The author of 1 Maccabees paints Antiochus IV as a hubristic propagandist for his own gods and so demonizes him. All war propaganda does the same. The Germans during World War I were called "pillaging, raping Huns." All communists became tarred with the slogan "Better dead than Red." Politicians regularly accuse their opponents of being "socialist" or, inversely, "fascist." Such a temptation to demonize and to ostracize opponents as "the other" is always present when conflict or disagreement arises, but it is a tendency that should be resisted. The rhetoric of violence, of estrangement, must be eschewed if common ground is to be found among all peoples. Successful diplomatic negotiations may, in fact, hinge on treating one's opponent with respect.

3. The author of 1 Maccabees skillfully uses language to portray the Maccabees as righteous upholders of traditional Jewish religion and contrasts their opponents as evil to draw boundaries around who is a "real" Jew. The members of any group will not always agree with each other on everything, but the rhetoric can quickly escalate into polarized language whereby one group hurls anathemas at the other. Are Sunni Muslims true Muslims, or are only Shiites true Muslims? Does one group have a monopoly on salvation? Can one Christian group agree to disagree with another without setting up barriers between them? When discussing such questions, we must not neglect to determine what are the social causes of division. Ecumenical dialogue almost requires as a prerequisite a social stability that brings with it the confidence to allow others to be different.

1 MACCABEES 2:1-70, THE CAREER OF MATTATHIAS

1 Maccabees 2:1-14, The Family of Mattathias

COMMENTARY

2:1-5. The vague time reference "in those days" does not allow one to specify when Mattathias decided enough was enough—before the plundering of Jerusalem by Apollonius (1 Macc 1:29) or after? Before the decrees of the king (1:41) or after? Before the erection of the abomination of desolation (1 Macc 1:54) or after? Modein, seven miles east of Lydda and seventeen miles northwest of Jerusalem, lay in the mountains. It is described later as the ancestral home of Mattathias and his family (1 Macc 2:70; 9:19). This makes all the more intriguing the notice that Mattathias resided in Jerusalem and that he was not there only on priestly duty for an appointed cycle (cf. Zechariah, the father of John the Baptist, in Luke 1:8). What does such information tell us about Mattathias's social status, wealth, and relationship to those other priests, who participated in the gymnasium at Jerusalem (2 Macc 4:14-15)? No data are available to answer these questions, but one can safely assume that Mattathias was not an ignorant country priest. According to 1 Chr 24:7, the house of Jehoiarib, whom the writer of 1 Maccabees names Joarib (v. 1), had the first of the twenty-four priestly courses in the temple service. The surnames of the five sons of Jehoiarib/Joarib remain enigmatic; "Maccabeus" most likely means "Hammerer."

2:6-13. Mattathias breaks into a lament similar to the laments found in Mic 7:1 and Jer 4:31. The language also echoes that of Lam 2:11; 3:48; 4:10, as well as that of the personal lament of Jer 15:10-21. In place of the phrase "to live there," many Greek manuscripts read "and they sat there," where the sense would be of someone sitting among ruins (cf. Lam 1:1; Hag 1:4).

Since it is unusual to compare a building to a man, some manuscripts read "people" instead of "temple." Cities are frequently personified and said to be ashamed (e.g., Nah 3:1-17; Jer 50:11-12). The language of honor and shame was also used in connection with the destruction of Jerusalem in 587 BCE (Jer 51:51). The parallel line in v. 9a speaks of the taking away of the Temple's glorious accoutrements. One might see the image of a properly outfitted man versus a man in hand-me-down clothing (cf. Lam 4:1-2, 7-8).

The poetic parallelism of 9bc is clear: infants//youths; killed//by the sword. The pride of a city is its children. A city renews itself through the children of its citizens; without them a city dies. The image of fainting children and slain youth is poignantly expressed in the laments over the destruction of Jerusalem in 587 BCE:

> The young and the old are lying
>   on the ground in the streets;
> my young women and my young men
>   have fallen by the sword;
> in the day of your anger you have killed them,
>   slaughtering without mercy.
> (Lam 2:21 NRSV; cf. 2:11)

The author continues using traditional images of war, looting, and slavery in vv. 9-11.

Like earlier writers, the author of this lament mourns over the wasted beauty of the city (v. 12). "Our holy and beautiful house,/ where our ancestors praised you,/ has been burned by fire,/ and all our pleasant places have become ruins" (Isa 64:11 NRSV; cf. Lam 1:10; Dan 11:31-32). From the first-person singular of v. 7, the lament moves to the first-person plural as Mattathias's lament becomes that of the faithful Israelite.

2:14. The donning of sackcloth is another traditional ritual act of mourning. Jacob put on sackcloth when he thought that his son Joseph had been killed by wild animals (Gen 37:34), and David ordered his men to put on sackcloth when he heard of Abner's death

(2 Sam 3:31). The author of 1 Maccabees, by this concatenation of traditional images, metaphors, and ritual action, paints Mattathias as a staunch upholder of ancestral custom.

1 Maccabees 2:15-28, The Actions at Modein

COMMENTARY

2:15-18. Although Mattathias and his sons left Jerusalem, they could not escape the decrees of the king (1:51). The scene stresses the separation of Mattathias and his sons from those who actively support the king's program. Nevertheless, the king's officers address Mattathias respectfully as a powerful clan leader and suggest that others follow his lead. In return, Mattathias and his family will obtain the privilege of membership in the royal court (1 Macc 10:65; 11:27) and wealth.

2:19-22. Mattathias answers by contrasting his kinsfolk's unswerving devotion to the covenant with the apostasy of all others. The author uses traditional language, not "turning aside . . . to the right hand or to the left," the language Moses had used when he instructed the Israelites to follow the path of God's commandments (Deut 5:32-33). Those who have "chosen to obey [the king's] commandments" have forgotten what Moses said and brought on the curses written in the book of Deuteronomy (Deut 29:25-28).

2:23-26. Mattathias's attachment to his ancestral traditions is further demonstrated by his action toward an apostate Jew, recalling how Phinehas, the grandson of Aaron, acted during the wandering of the Israelites in the desert (Num 25:6-15). The Israelite males had been led astray by their non-Israelite wives to worship other gods, and one Israelite male defiantly brought a Midianite woman to his tent in the sight of Moses. In retribution, Phinehas speared both the man and the woman (Num 25:1-8). Through his zeal, Phinehas averted a plague on Israel, and a perpetual priesthood was granted to him and his descendants (Num 25:8-9, 12-13; Ps 106:28-31; Sir 45:23-25). By using this model, the author of Maccabees suggests not only that Mattathias is the real priestly descendant of Phinehas, but also that the action of Mattathias will avert the persecution of the Jews and that his descendants will be duly rewarded.

2:27-28. The hills to which Mattathias and his sons flee are probably those to the northeast of Modein, near Gophna and bordering on Samaria. Second Maccabees 5:27, with no mention of Mattathias or Modein, portrays Judas Maccabeus as fleeing to the wilderness. He and his sons leave everything they own (v. 28) rather than "leave" the law and the ordinances (v. 21).

1 Maccabees 2:29-48, The Exploits of Mattathias

COMMENTARY

After Mattathias's dramatic revolt comes a discussion of what he achieved. First, however, is told the story of another group who wished to have no part in the changes to their ancestral traditions. Will Mattathias behave like them?

2:29-38, The Seekers After Righteousness and Justice. The Judean wilderness was a traditional hiding place (see 1 Sam 23:14, where David hides from Saul). It also came to symbolize the place where Israel had covenanted with God (see Jer 2:2-3; Hos 2:14-15). First Maccabees describes the group that flees there in traditional terms, usually given in the order "justice and righteousness" (see, e.g., Jer 22:15; 23:5; Ezek 18:27; 33:14, 19; 45:9). Zephaniah 2:3 exhorts the people to do justice and seek righteousness and humility so that they might perhaps be hidden on the day of the Lord's wrath. Qumran covenanters were exhorted in their *Community Rule* to do truth and righteousness and justice.[53] In a description of God's renewing the land, the Isaianic tradition foretells that justice will dwell in the wilderness and righteousness in the fruitful field (Isa 32:16).

In contrast to Mattathias and his followers, who left everything behind in the city, this group takes all the elements of social living with them—sons, wives, and livestock (note how for this patriarchal author wives came after sons, but at least before livestock). "Troubles" here refers to the evil being done in the land by those who have forsaken the law (1 Macc 1:52-53). This effort to set up an alternate social existence is opposed by the people in Jerusalem, the city of David, which has now become the center of apostasy (1:33-40; 2:18; for more on the hiding places, see Commentary on 1:53).

The seekers after righteousness choose to die "in their innocence" (ἐν τῇ ἁπλότητι ἡμῶν *en tē haplotēti hēmōn*). The same word is found concerning Daniel (1 Macc 2:60) and has the overtones of integrity and sincerity (1 Chr 29:17; Wis 1:1). Those who sought justice (v. 29) are destroyed unjustly. "Heaven and earth" are frequently invoked to witness covenant violations (Deut 4:26; 30:19; 31:28; 32:1; Isa 1:2). The total annihilation of humans and livestock recalls the tradition of the ban (Josh 6:21; 1 Sam 15:3; 22:19); it is also similar to the victory stele of Mesha, the ninth-century BCE king of Moab.[54] A variation on this story is told in 2 Macc 6:11. There the group assembles for sabbath worship and is not said to have left on a permanent basis; this account states that all were burnt to death. Another similar story is found in the *Testament of Moses* 9. There Taxo, from the tribe of Levi, upon witnessing the evils that have come upon the nation, exhorts his seven sons never to transgress God's commandments and advises them to fast for three days and then to go into a cave in the open country and wait to die rather than submit to apostasy. The mind-set is that one should flee from all contact with contagion and sin, and the only way to avoid them completely is to commit suicide.

2:39-41, The Response of Mattathias and His Friends. The language of v. 39 reflects the ritual mourning for the dead (as in 1:25-27), establishing a rhetorical bond between Mattathias and his group and those seekers of righteousness who had died. Mattathias is consciously depicted as surrounded by his friends, in contrast to the king and his closest companions, called the king's friends (see, e.g., 1 Macc 2:8; 3:38; 6:10). The language of v. 40 catches the sense of a group caught in a quandary and coming to a decision in a time of crisis ("each said to his neighbor" as at Judg 6:29; 10:18; 2 Kgs 7:3, 9; Jdt 7:4; 1 Macc 3:43). The community aspect of the decision is further enhanced by the reference to "brothers," by the use of the first-person plural, and by the repetition of "our." One might also note how the singular for "life" is used—not "for our lives," but "for our life," as though the community has one life. The result is a community-based decision that, in these particular circumstances and in order to maintain the community's existence, defensive warfare on the sabbath will be allowed. Bar-Kochva has cogently pointed out that previously there had not been any ban against warfare on the sabbath, otherwise Jews could not have served in Hellenistic armies (as they certainly did).[55] Nonetheless, the emphasis in both this and the previous passage is on defense on the sabbath in particular (2:32, 34, 38, 41), not just on any day; there were many who opposed any kind of warfare on the sabbath. The pseudepigraphic book of *Jubilees* states that anyone who made war on the sabbath should die,[56] a position maintained by some into the first century CE. Allowing oneself to be killed by refusing to fight on the sabbath was considered a pious act.[57] Both the emphasis on this being a community-based decision and its rhetorical placement (between the preceding pious opponents of Antiochus and the succeeding attachment of the Hasideans to Mattathias) illustrate the author's attempts to link the Hasmoneans to the most Torah-observant traditions.

---

53. CD 1:5; 8:2.
54. James B. Pritchard, ed., *Ancient Near Eastern Texts Relating to the Old Testament (ANET)*, 3rd ed. with supplement (Princeton: Princeton University Press, 1969) 321.
55. Bar-Kochva, *Judas Maccabeus*, 474-81.
56. *Jub.* 50:12-13.
57. M. D. Goodman and A. J. Holladay, "Religious Scruples in Ancient Warfare," *Classical Quarterly* 36 (1986) 151-71. See also Josephus *Against Apion* 1, 212.

2:42-48, The Deeds of Mattathias. These verses describe the consequences of Mattathias's action in killing the king's officer and fleeing to the hills (cf. 1 Macc 2:24-28). The connecting particle "then" (τότε *tote*; the same word is used to start v. 29) suggests that the decision to resist even on the sabbath brought in these supporters—i.e., the decision to defend oneself on the sabbath is ratified by important members of the community.

2:42-43. A group called the Hasideans now join Mattathias and his followers. Some manuscripts read "Judeans," but "Hasideans" appears the preferable reading (Ἀσιδαῖοι [*Asidaioi*] reflects the Aramaic חסידיא [*ḥăsîdayyā*] and the Hebrew חסידים [*ḥăsîdîm*], "pious," "loyal ones"). The author of 1 Maccabees, in discussing the execution of some Hasideans (7:12-17), quotes Ps 79:2 (where the Hebrew term [*ḥăsîdîm*] is found) to describe their fate. The transliteration suggests that the Hasideans were a well-known group, but their exact identity has evoked much scholarly discussion. Are they to be connected with "the wise ones" of Dan 11:33 or with those described allegorically in *1 Enoch* 90:6-9? Are they to be linked to the Essenes or to the Pharisees? The term "Hasidean" itself draws upon traditional terminology, where those loyal to God are referred to as *ḥăsîdîm*. In 2 Macc 14:6, Judas Maccabeus is said to be the leader of the Hasideans, whereas here and at 1 Maccabees 7:13 the Maccabees are distinguished from them. The phrase translated "mighty warriors" (ἰσχυροὶ δυνάμει *ischyroi dynamei*) is also used to describe Judas Maccabeus in his fitness to lead the army after Mattathias's death (2:66). The word has overtones of leadership when it is used in 1 Chronicles to describe the heads of ancestral houses (1 Chr 5:24; 7:2, 5, 7, 9, 11). This quality of leadership is also evident in 1 Macc 7:13, where the Hasideans are said to be first among the sons of Israel. The Hasideans are thus a distinguished people, and their willingness to offer their own lives for the sake of the law responds to Mattathias's call to all who are zealous for the law to follow him (2:27). In 1 Maccabees, then, the Hasideans are neither pacifist nor apocalyptic, but important folk devoted to the law. Besides them come others. The translation "to escape their troubles" (cf. 2:29) must be seen in the light of 1:52-53: the group is fleeing from the evil in the land.

2:44-48. Describing the rebels as an army may be a trifle grandiose, but they were an effective fighting force that set out to redress what had taken place. The phrase "sinners and renegades" echoes the terms used of the group stationed in the Akra (1:34). The survivors of this counterattack now fully join the Gentiles, as they had sought to do early (see 1:11-15). Mattathias destroys the pagan altars built in the towns around Judea. Mattathias also undoes the king's ban of circumcision (1:48). The pursuit of the "sons of arrogance" (author's trans.) recalls the arrogance of Antiochus IV (1:21, 24). Just as the king tried to make Israel forget the law (1:49) and destroyed the books of the law (1:56-57), so also Mattathias now rescues the law. Mattathias's actions recall those of Judith, who, before cutting off the head of the Assyrian commander Holofernes, prayed, "Now indeed is the time for aiding your heritage" (Jdt 13:5 NAB). "Gain the upper hand" is literally "did not give horn to the sinner." The horn is a traditional symbol of strength (cf. 1 Kgs 22:11; Ps 148:14). Sirach complains that the kings of Judah abandoned the law and gave their horn to others and their glory to a foreign nation (49:4-5).

REFLECTIONS

This account of the exploits of Mattathias emphasizes how he and his friends overturn the damage done to ancestral traditions by the arrogant decrees of Antiochus IV. The narrative evinces solidarity with those who went down into the wilderness and were executed, but has Mattathias and his group choose another course in order to prevent complete annihilation of their cause. As such, the narrative forces us to ask questions about the proper use of violence. The rebels who went down to the desert certainly had not planned a guerrilla campaign, or they would not have taken along their families and livestock. They simply wanted to be left alone. Would they have defended themselves if attacked on a day other than the sabbath? Although the narrative does not give us the answer, wanting instead to emphasize the heinous nature of the crime, it nonetheless raises the issue of pacifism. (For further reflections, see the section "The Ethics of Violence" in the Introduction.)

1 Maccabees 2:49-70, The Death of Mattathias

COMMENTARY

As did other great leaders in giving farewell addresses, Mattathias gathers his sons to deliver his last will and testament (cf. Jacob, Genesis 49; Moses, Deuteronomy 33; Joshua, Joshua 23; Samuel, 1 Samuel 12; and David, 1 Kings 2). The death of Mattathias contrasts with that of Alexander the Great (1:6-9). Whereas Alexander's successors brought evil upon the land, however, Mattathias's sons will bring a renewal of ancestral traditions.

2:49-50. The same formula used of Jacob (Gen 47:29) and David (1 Kgs 2:1) is used here: "When the days drew near for x to die. . . ." The arrogance of Antiochus has been mentioned before (1:21, 24), as has the "anger" toward Israel (1:64). Mattathias entreats his sons that just as he had burned with zeal (2:24-26), so also must they act.

2:51-60. In Mattathias's exhortation of his sons to give their lives for the covenant, the author of 1 Maccabees provides a list of the great actions of the past. Covenants or treaties made between two parties usually followed a standard structure: a list of the stipulations of the treaty, requirements for the deposit and public reading of the covenant, and the list of witnesses to the covenant. The covenant would usually begin with a historical prologue, which would describe the previous relationships between the two parties, particularly the benevolent acts of a suzerain toward his vassals or the rebellion of a vassal or his ancestors against the suzerain. This historical element is well represented in the covenant scene of Joshua 24, and it provides the opening framework for the book of Deuteronomy, a work steeped in covenantal concerns that is, on some level, a testament of Moses before his death. At Deut 32:7-14, Moses appeals to the people to remember how God had acted properly toward them, and that they had been unmindful of the rock that bore them, forgetful of the God who had birthed them (Deut 32:18). Joshua also recounts to the people all that they have seen God do and encourages them to observe the commandments (Josh 23:2-6). The list in 1 Maccabees urges the sons to remember how God had acted faithfully toward covenant partners in the past, when those partners had acted faithfully in return. Mattathias's list of those persons worthy of imitation is interesting both for who is included and who is not. Contrasted with the list of famous men in Sirach 44–50, Mattathias omits, among others, Enoch, Noah, Isaac, Jacob, Moses, Aaron, Solomon, Elisha, Isaiah, Hezekiah, and Josiah. The author of 1 Maccabees thus lists a select group of heroes—and no heroines.

2:52. The author links the testing of Abraham, when he is commanded to slay his son Isaac (Genesis 22), with the present situation, drawing especially on the phrase from Gen 15:6, where Abraham's faith in God is credited to him as righteousness. Because of this verse, Abraham became a paradigm of faithfulness (cf. Rom 4:3). The book of *Jubilees* lists many tests in which Abraham was found faithful (*Jub.* 17:17-18), beginning with a famine in the land of Chaldea and his rejection of idol worship. Pseudo-Philo also has a story in which Abraham in Chaldea is thrown into a fiery furnace because he rejects idols.[58] The testing of Abraham parallels the situation the Maccabees now find themselves in.

2:53. Joseph's rejection of the attempted seduction by Potiphar's wife (Genesis 39) is retold in *Jub* 39:1-10. There Joseph resists because "he remembered the Lord and the words which Jacob, his father, used to read" (*Jub* 39:6). Joseph, through his gift of dream interpretation, becomes lord of Egypt in

---
58. Pseudo-Philo *Biblical Antiquities* 6.

Gen 41:40-45. With this example, the author of 1 Maccabees suggests that faithfulness leads to exaltation and rule.

2:54. Phinehas has already been cited as the model for Mattathias's zeal (1 Macc 2:26). Here Mattathias claims to be a descendant of Phinehas and thereby sets the stage for later Hasmonean claims to high priestly station (see also Sir 45:23-26).

2:55. "Because he fulfilled the command" might also be translated "when he had completed the task." Joshua was commissioned by Moses (Num 27:18-23) and by God (Josh 1:2-9), and his role is glorified in Sir 46:1-7. After Joshua conquered the promised land and divided it among the Israelite tribes, he gathered all the tribes at Shechem and made a covenant with the people to turn away from other gods and to serve Yahweh alone. Although Joshua is not explicitly called a "judge" (κριτής *kritēs*) in 1 Maccabees, elsewhere he is reported to have made "statutes and ordinances" (חק ומשפט *ḥōq ûmišpāṭ*; LXX νόμον καὶ κρίσιν *nomon kai krisin*; see Josh 24:25), and he is the first leader mentioned in the book of Judges (1:1–2:10). He is put on the list because he conquered the land, and, as mentioned in the Introduction, the author of 1 Maccabees draws heavily on the language and ideology of the book of Judges.

2:56. Caleb, along with Joshua, reported positively about the land he and others were sent to spy out (Numbers 14). Caleb and Joshua were the only representatives allowed to enter the promised land. Caleb settled around Hebron (Josh 14:6-15). The author of 1 Maccabees again ties reward to the land to faithful discharge of duty. (Sirach speaks of Caleb and Joshua opposing the assembly to prevent them from sinning [Sir 46:7-10]).

2:57. That David was rewarded because he was "merciful" (ἔλεος *eleos*) seems out of place in this list. Perhaps one should see behind *eleos* the Hebrew word denoting acts of covenant faithfulness (חסד *ḥesed*). As such, *eleos* would reflect what David said in his song of thanksgiving (2 Sam 22:21-25). David's trust in God is clearly stated in his fight against Goliath (1 Sam 17:45-47). That David's dynasty would last forever is promised in 2 Sam 7:13-16 (see also Psalm 89; Sir 47:2-11). Although John Hyrcanus would later lay claim to the title of king, the author of 1 Maccabees does not bestow such a title on any of the Hasmoneans, but gives them only the title "leader" (ἡγούμενος *hēgoumenos*, 14:35).

2:58. Elijah, the great miracle-working prophet of the ninth century BCE, appeared when King Ahab of Israel began to worship the Canaanite storm god Baal. Baal was believed to bring life-giving rain to restore fertility to the land. Elijah showed the futility of worshiping Baal by proclaiming that Yahweh would bring a drought on the land; in a dramatic contest with the priests of Baal, Elijah proved that Yahweh is the real bestower of health and fertility (1 Kgs 17:1–18:46). Elijah proclaimed his zeal for God at Mount Horeb (1 Kgs 19:1-14) where Yahweh appeared to him not in a mighty wind or an earthquake or fire, but in a whisper, assuring Elijah that there were others in Israel who had not worshiped Baal (1 Kgs 19:11-18). In keeping with Elijah's fiery confrontation with the storm god Baal, Elijah was taken up to heaven in a chariot of fire during a whirlwind (2 Kings 2).

2:59-60. In Daniel 3, when King Nebuchadnezzar has made a huge golden statue that he commands all peoples and nations to serve, Shadrach, Meshach, and Abednego, Jewish captives of the Babylonians (Dan 1:6-7), refuse to worship the idol. They are denounced to the king and thrown into a fiery furnace, in which they are miraculously preserved. This miracle prompts Nebuchadnezzar to honor the God of the Jews and to promote them in Nebuchadnezzar's service.

In Daniel 6, envious opponents plot to destroy the innocent and praiseworthy Daniel through his obedience to his God. Accordingly, they require that everyone in the whole kingdom worship only the king, Darius, for thirty days. When Daniel ostentatiously disobeys the command, he is thrown into a den of lions, but is saved by an angel of God. Daniel's accusers are forthwith gobbled up by the lions, the king himself honors Daniel's God, and Daniel prospers.

One might suggest reasons why these models were chosen. Abraham is the father of the Jews. Joseph and Joshua rose to important positions, whereas Caleb received an inheritance in the land. Phinehas and David represent the two major institutions in Israel: priesthood and monarchy. Elijah was victorious against idol worship, and Daniel and his three companions overcame the commands to worship idols of Persian kings, the forerunners of the Seleucid rulers.

2:61-64. The author uses traditional sentiments to draw a conclusion from the historical examples: "Do not put your trust in princes,/ in mortals, in whom there is no help./ When their breath departs, they return to the earth;/ on that very day their plans perish" (Ps 146:3-4 NRSV; cf. 1 Sam 2:4-5; Ps 26:1; Isa 14:14-21). An exhortation to abide by the covenant follows on this conclusion. When Moses was about to die, he summoned Joshua and used the same exhortation, so that Joshua would lead the people into the promised land (Deut 31:7, 23; Josh 1:5-9, 18).

2:65-68. Mattathias now plans for the future, and the author shows in some sense the organization of the rest of the book, in inverse order, around Judas and Simon. Interestingly, Jonathan is not mentioned, nor is he given a hymn in the narrative, as are Judas (3:3-9) and Simon (14:4-15).

2:65. The most praise is given to Simon, here called Simeon. He replaced Mattathias as leader of the family and is described with the attributes of a leader ("wise in counsel"), somewhat like the ideal leader described in Isa 9:6. This Simeon contrasts with Simeon, the son of Jacob, into whose council Jacob hopes never to come (Gen 49:6), whereas Simon is lauded as a wise leader (14:4-15).

2:66. Judas is to be the commander in chief. Instead of "battle against the peoples," one might translate "battle for the tribes," on the analogy with 1 Macc 3:2, where the same syntax is used in "fight for Israel." Judas is to be the standard bearer in fighting on Israel's behalf.

2:67-68. The final injunctions of Mattathias, in a chiastic pattern, are intended to unite the Torah observers and to urge them to take vengeance on their enemies, the Gentiles. The language resonates with that of Moses' final injunctions (Deut 32:43-47), as well as with the words of the divine warrior at Isa 59:18: "According to their deeds, so will he repay;/ wrath to his adversaries, requital to his enemies" (NRSV). The conflict is set up between the Jewish people and the Gentiles, and it brings to a fitting close this introduction to the body of the work; the first chapter was concerned to point out the attempt to eradicate Jewish ancestral traditions by the Gentiles, and the second the response to that attempt.

2:69-70. Again using traditional language, the death of Mattathias is described in a way similar to the description of Jacob's death (Gen 49:28-29, 33; 50:10). Mattathias is "gathered to his ancestors," as were Moses (Deut 32:50), the generation of Joshua (Judg 2:11), and the husband of Judith (Jdt 16:22); the phrase also occurs in the prediction of the death of the good king Josiah (2 Kgs 22:20) and in the story of Bel and the Dragon (Bel and the Dragon 1). The mourning of all Israel, here for Mattathias, is recorded also when all Israel mourns over the defiled sanctuary (1 Macc 4:39) and at the deaths of Judas (1 Macc 9:20) and Jonathan (1 Macc 13:26).

REFLECTIONS

As we read of the determination of Mattathias to resist with force the attack on Judaism by Antiochus IV, we might pause to consider the long tradition in the West concerning "just" warfare. Under what conditions should one go to war, and how should one conduct oneself in war? Moral and legal standards have been set up as to whether force should be used in a given instance. In considering what these standards may be, one might ponder these questions:

(1) Who has the authority to declare war? One answer might be only the legally constituted ruling authority, such as the United States Congress or the United Nations.

(2) What circumstances lead to the outbreak of war? The presumption should be that a nation will not go to war. We should in no way seek to harm our neighbor. A nation should not embark on war for any reasons of revenge or self-aggrandizement, but to right some injustice, to defend itself, and to restrain wrongdoing. War is permissible to protect innocent life, to secure basic human rights, and to ensure that one can

lead a decent existence. Those who go to war should have as their aim the restoration of peace. Thus nations should choose war only as a last resort after every other avenue to ensure peace or to right the wrong has been exhausted. Whoever goes to war should have a reasonable hope of success, for otherwise lives will be endangered and lost for no purpose.

(3) What is acceptable conduct toward armed belligerents and toward unarmed civilians? Under no circumstances, according to just-war theory, can unarmed civilians be targeted. If attacked, one should attempt to restrain but not to annihilate the enemy. This criterion becomes increasingly difficult to observe once the possibility of nuclear warfare appears.

When we look at the actions of Mattathias and his sons in the light of these criteria, we see that they were undergoing a massive attack on their standard of living and on their cultural existence. The author has gone out of his way to exaggerate the evil intention of Antiochus IV to eradicate Judaism. By describing the massacre of the seekers after righteousness, the author shows that there was no alternative; one could not even opt out of society. The high priest, not Mattathias, was the leader of Judah, but the high priest is not shown as being directly opposed to the actions of Antiochus IV (see 2 Maccabees 4). The author of 1 Maccabees thus grants Mattathias a different kind of leadership from that of the high priest. Major members of society, the Hasideans, rally behind Mattathias's leadership. More important, Mattathias is cloaked in the mantle of divine authority, since his actions are so closely linked to those of the divinely inspired Phinehas. While this obviates the problem of Mattathias's not being a duly appointed leader, the narrative also poses other problems. Many persons may lay claim to divinely inspired leadership, but how is one to judge the validity of their claim?

The narrative also raises questions about how a war should be conducted. When Mattathias is depicted as forcing all citizens of Judea to be circumcised (1 Macc 2:46), this action could be interpreted as going beyond the limits set by the requirements for just conduct in war. Within our own day, the development of weapons of mass destruction, of missiles that can be sent long distances and not always with pinpoint accuracy, forces us to wonder whether any war can ever be just according to the traditional criteria of just war. Will not such weapons of mass destruction inevitably cause the deaths of civilians?

1 MACCABEES 3:1–9:22

JUDAS MACCABEUS

1 MACCABEES 3:1-9, HERO OF HIS PEOPLE

COMMENTARY

3:1-2. The author stresses that Judas is the son of Mattathias. Following the death of his father, Judas assumes the role of leader of the resistance to Antiochus's policy. He is joined by all who had rallied to his father.

3:3-9. Whereas in the first two chapters the author used poetry to describe the distress of Israel, he now uses poetry to laud Judas.

3:3-6. The text first emphasizes that Judas fights for his people, not for himself. Judas is described in bigger-than-life terms, as he singlehandedly defends the camp. The traditional image of the warrior is that of a lion, used of Judah (Gen 49:9), God (Isa 31:4; cf. Hos 5:14; 11:10; Amos 3:4-8), and the enemies of Israel (Jer 4:7; 5:6). Given the references in the poem to Jacob/Israel (3:7-8), as well as the previous resonances between Jacob and Mattathias in giving their last will and testament, the linkage with Judah seems strong. The image of "burning" the troublers of Israel reflects also the wrath of divine judgment (Isa 66:15; Obadiah 18). "Those who troubled his people" are probably Jews (see 7:22). The phrase recalls Elijah, who, when King Ahab called him the troubler of Israel, responded that it was not he but Ahab who troubled Israel (1 Kgs 18:18). Achar (i.e., Achan), who violated the holy war conditions by taking booty from what had been consecrated to God at the capture of Jericho (Joshua 7), is also called the troubler of Israel (1 Chr 2:7). Judas's actions here resemble those of Mattathias (2:47).

3:7-8. Verse 7 has a play on words between "embittered" (ἐπίκρανεν *epikranen*) and "made glad" (εὔφρανεν *euphranen*). Judas embittered (*epikranen*) many kings, but he made glad (*euphranen*) Jacob. Judas's destruction of the ungodly from the land of Judah recalls the campaigns of Joshua when he conquered the promised land (Joshua 10–11). Just as the description of the renegades at 1 Macc 1:11 recalls Deuteronomy 13, so also Judas's destruction of the ungodly (v. 8) alludes to Deuteronomy 13, which commands Israel to destroy anyone advocating idol worship. The anger of the Lord, which had fallen on Israel (1:64; 2:49), is "turned away," as the author again relies on traditional language (see Num 25:4; 2 Chr 12:12; 29:10; 30:8; Ps 106:23; Ezek 10:14; Dan 9:16; Hos 14:4; Zech 1:2).

3:9. Judas's renown stretches to the ends of the earth, as will Simon's (14:10). Israel, which had been driven into hiding (1:53), is now brought back. The gathering-in of those who had been dispersed is a theme found earlier (e.g., Isa 11:12; 27:13, where God is going to bring back the people who have been dispersed to other lands).

1 MACCABEES 3:10-26, JUDAS'S FIRST VICTORIES

1 Maccabees 3:10-12, Victory Against Apollonius

COMMENTARY

Apollonius, who has not been mentioned before, appears abruptly without introduction. At 10:69, the governor of Coelesyria is called Apollonius. In 2 Maccabees, three people are named Apollonius: Apollonius of Tarsus, son of Menestheus, who was the governor of Coelesyria and Phoenicia (2 Macc 3:5; 4:4); Apollonius, the captain of the Mysians (5:24); and Apollonius, son of Gennaeus, a local governor (12:2). Josephus identifies the Apollonius of 1 Macc 3:10 as the governor of Samaria.[59] The author of 1 Maccabees makes no effort to identify Apollonius further, which might suggest that he was well-known or that "Apollonius" is recognized as a Greek name.

This Apollonius was able to muster a fighting force from the district of Samaria, most probably from people of Gentile origin who had settled there (cf. 2 Kgs 17:24-41). Here is a clear instance in which "Israel," for the author of 1 Maccabees, refers not to the geographical northern kingdom, but to those persons whom he considers to be the followers of ancestral tradition—specifically, those who have joined with the Maccabees.

No details of where the encounter took place are given; most likely it was an ambush as against Seron, somewhere between Shechem and the Gophna Hills. (Cf. the summary account of Judas's exploits at the start of his career in 2 Macc 8:5-7.) The author describes the event like a single combat between Judas and Apollonius, much like the fight between David and Goliath (1 Sam 17:40-54), when David took the sword of Goliath (1 Sam 17:51) and the Philistines were routed.

59. Josephus *Antiquities of the Jews* 12.287; see also 12.261.

1 Maccabees 3:13-26, Victory Against Seron

COMMENTARY

3:13-14. Seron, although described as the commander of the Syrian army, was most likely one of the commanders of the mercenary garrisons in the region. He commanded a more formidable fighting force than Apollonius had. Seron decides, on his own initiative, to put down Judas's uprising and so gain a reputation.

3:15. Seron's army comprises "godless men." In 1 Maccabees, "godless" (ἀσεβής *asebēs*) usually refers to those Jews whom the author considers apostates (3:8; 6:21; 7:5, 9; 9:25, 73). They have joined Seron's force, and their aim is the opposite of Mattathias's exhortation to his sons (2:67).

3:16. The public road Seron takes up the steep ascent to the mountain plateau—about twelve miles northwest of Jerusalem, between the villages of Lower and Upper Beth-horon—is extremely treacherous because of its winding narrowness, and yet not as bad as other possible routes from the west to Jerusalem. It lies near the Gophna Hills, where Judas and his forces were concentrated.

3:17-22. The objection of Judas's troops to fighting against this large army may result from their long wait in ambush, but the author of 1 Maccabees phrases the whole exchange in traditional language. The stipulations for waging war in Deuteronomy 20 emphasize that Israel should not fear enemies with larger forces, for God is with Israel (Deut 20:1-4). This theme is dear to the author of Deuteronomy, as seen at Deut 7:7-8, where

God states that Israel was chosen not because it was more numerous than any other people, but because God loved Israel, and at Deut 9:1-3, where God promised that the Israelites would defeat the more powerful nations in the promised land because God would be with them. This remains an important theme throughout the deuteronomic history. The phrase "to save by many or by few" echoes the words of Jonathan, the son of Saul, as he initiates the first victory of the Israelites over the Philistines (1 Sam 14:6). It is also reminiscent of the story of Gideon in Judges 7, where with a drastically reduced number of troops so that Israel would not claim credit for the victory, Gideon prevails because God fights with him. (See also the prayer of Judith before she sets out to confront Holofernes [Jdt 9:7-11], and her song of victory after killing him [Jdt 16:11].) Unlike the OT examples, however, the author of 1 Maccabees avoids using the terms "Lord" and "God" and uses "heaven" as a substitute.

The author contrasts the aggression of the enemy against the whole community with the defensive nature of Judas's own stance to preserve the ancestral traditions (vv. 20-21). The author thus has Judas claim that he fights in a just cause. God is portrayed as the divine warrior, as in the Song of Moses (Exod 15:3, 7).

3:23-24. The surprise attack brings the desired result. The estimate of 800 slain is modest compared to other battles. "The land of the Philistines" refers to the Hellenized cities on the southern coastal plain, although they were no longer so called. Sirach uses the term "Philistine" to refer to a nation his soul detests (Sir 50:26), so the phrase probably carried pejorative connotations as a non-Israelite area.

3:25-26. The fame of Judas expands, just as God promised to the Israelites in the desert that the nations would tremble at the report of Israel's deeds (Deut 2:25), and as the fame of David spread to all lands after his defeat of the Philistines (1 Chr 14:17).

REFLECTIONS

1. The author, using traditional language, themes, and poetry, continues to portray the Maccabees as being steeped in, and upholders of, their traditional religion. He also seeks to show that they are not terrorists, but freedom fighters. As such, they claim that God is on their side, working through them to restore rightful worship. The symbiosis of divine and human action is particularly clear where the verb "crush" (συντρίβω *syntribō*) is used to describe God's action in v. 22 and to describe the act committed upon Seron, following Judas's attack, in v. 23. Judas is portrayed as a hero for his nation to emulate. One can only admire the courage of Judas and his small band as they fight to maintain their right to worship their God. Such constancy in the face of attack is admirable. However, we must also learn to be cautious when confronted with such a heroic figure. The inherent glorification of warfare, of the warrior as the hero to be emulated and imitated, rather than uplifting those who seek to redress a situation through mediation and arbitration, can lead to a glorification of violence in society. We must constantly remind ourselves that the presumption should always be against warfare, against the taking of life. So, although Judas and his followers fought against extermination of their culture, their actions must be seen as a last resort when all other efforts for peace had failed, and must not lead to a glorification of violence. One should hope that a well-trained army would never need to be so used.

2. The claim "God is with us" brings its own problems. German soldiers in Hitler's army went into battle with "God is with us" inscribed on their belt buckles. Such an attitude raises the stakes, since it polarizes a situation into us versus them, where only one side can be right and no room is left for mediation and arbitration. Religious and political leaders need to be extremely cautious in so invoking the deity as to demonize their adversaries. One can see the problem in the way Judas is portrayed as searching out lawbreakers, burning those who troubled his people, and destroying the ungodly out of the land (1 Macc 3:5, 8). Who determines what is ungodly? The zeal of Judas here prefigures that of the Inquisition in tracking down heretics, or of those who sought out "witches" in Puritan Massachusetts. Judas has gone over from defensive action, from acting so as to be able to serve God in his own way, to offensive action, destroying anyone who does not agree with his interpretation of how the law should be obeyed. Even though we may be inspired by Judas's constancy in faith, nevertheless we must be wary of adopting all the attitudes encapsulated in the narrative.

1 MACCABEES 3:27–4:35, MAJOR SELEUCID COUNTERATTACKS

1 Maccabees 3:27-37, The King's Decision

COMMENTARY

According to the author of 1 Maccabees, the Jewish uprising is the determining factor of all the policies of the Seleucid king. In reality, the small Jewish revolutionary force was no match for the Seleucid army. Even the author of 1 Maccabees must admit that, whenever the Seleucid army is fully directed against Judea, it is victorious (1 Macc 6:33-54; 9:1-17). In fact, Antiochus IV mustered his forces to take effective control of the eastern satrapies, and not because of the revolt led by Judas, which was dealt with by Lysias, a subordinate. The Parthian kingdom began to expand gradually under Mithridates I of Parthia (175–138 BCE), so that at the death of Antiochus IV (164 BCE), it covered the whole of Iran and subsequently Mesopotamia. Antiochus's expedition, if not directly against the Parthians, was designed to hold together the Seleucid kingdom.

3:27-28. Antiochus's reaction is typical of Seleucid kings and their allies, who are frequently described as becoming angry (5:1; 6:28; 9:69; 11:22; 15:36). They are not as in control of their emotions as a wise leader should be. Often pay was given in advance to encourage and boost the soldiers' morale, but a year's pay would be very unusual. By connecting it to the expedition against Judea, the author heightens the importance of Judas's uprising.

3:29. The Seleucid Empire, through the Treaty of Apamea in 188 BCE, had lost its provinces in western Asia Minor and was forced to pay a heavy indemnity. The final payment of the indemnity had been made in 173 BCE and was no longer a consideration by the time of the events of this chapter, which occurred after 166 (2:70). Nevertheless the empire was still without funds and sorely needed to shore up its treasury in whatever way it could. The Seleucids, starting with Antiochus III, had tended to use temple funds to replenish their own depleted resources.[60] Antiochus IV was lavish in his expenditures, and no doubt he found temple treasuries a convenient target from which to refill his coffers. In fact, Antiochus IV died shortly after attempting to despoil the sanctuary of Artemis in Elam.[61] The author of 1 Maccabees associates the depletion of funds with the interference of Antiochus IV in changing the laws of all the nations (1:41), although, as mentioned previously, there is no evidence that Antiochus made any such change outside of Judea.

3:30. Antiochus IV was munificent toward the Greek temples in Delos, Athens, and elsewhere. Polybius tells us that "in the sacrifices he furnished to cities and in the honors he paid to the gods he surpassed all those who had been kings before him. This is shown by the temple to Olympian Zeus at Athens and the statues around the altar at Delos."[62] Polybius in particular stresses Antiochus IV's extravagance, saying that he would

---

60. Polybius 10:27; Diodorus Siculus 28:3; 29:15; Strabo 16.1.18; Justin *Epitome* 32.2.1-2.
61. Polybius 31.9.1-4.
62. Polybius 26.1.10-11; cf. 29.24.13.

suddenly give unexpected presents to people he had never met before.[63]

3:31. "Persia" refers to the entire territory of historical Persia. The author of 1 Maccabees thus connects the king's decision to go to Persia with the expense needed to outlay an expedition against the Jewish uprising, and so enhances the latter's importance.

3:32-33. The "royal lineage" is not necessarily a blood relationship, as "kinsman of the king" was a title given to a high-ranking courtier (see 2 Macc 11:1). Lysias was appointed regent and deputy to the king in the western districts. Antiochus V Eupator, who at this time was about seven or eight years old, was co-regent with his father in case anything happened on the eastern expedition (see 2 Macc 9:23-25).

3:34. Antiochus IV would almost certainly have taken elephants, an important part of his army, on the eastern expedition. Theoretically, the Treaty of Apamea forbade the Seleucids to possess war elephants. The Greek text, in giving the impression that all the elephants remained with Lysias, underscores the importance of the confrontation with Judas. Presumably, Lysias would have much to worry about in administering the Seleucid Empire, but the author highlights the events in Judea.

3:35-36. The author dramatizes Antiochus's command about Judea with the blanket order to destroy all the residents of Judea and Jerusalem. Earlier the author had stressed that Antiochus had strong support from many in Judea (1:52) and that a Seleucid garrison had been established in Jerusalem (1:33-35). Antiochus clearly did not want to destroy those supporters. Rather, the author reflects the perception of Judas's band that this was a life-and-death struggle for the survival of their culture, a perception that builds on the fate of the seekers after righteousness (2:38). The irony is that Lysias is sent to stamp out the strength of Israel, while the reader knows that this strength is from heaven (3:19) and thus cannot be stamped out.

Antiochus IV is said to intend to set up military settlements in Judea, thus abolishing the *polis* of Antioch-in-Jerusalem (2 Macc 4:9, 19), as well as revoking any privileges that had previously been bestowed on the citizens of Judea. The author of 1 Maccabees makes no mention of such a *polis* or of such privileges. Either he did not know of them, or he wanted to erase them completely from memory. The author once again emphasizes only the dire straits that Judea was placed in, as well as the tyrannous character of Antiochus IV.

3:37. Antiochus IV left on his eastward march in 165 BCE. Opinions differ as to whether it was in early or late summer; the answer depends on whether the co-regency of his son Antiochus V, which lasted eighteen months, began when Antiochus IV left for Persia or a little earlier. Also, the exact date of Antiochus IV's death is unknown; his death became known in Babylon sometime between November 20 and December 18, 164 BCE.

---

63. Polybius 26.1.9.

1 Maccabees 3:38–4:25, The Battle Against Nicanor and Gorgias

1 Maccabees 3:38-60, Preparations for Battle

COMMENTARY

3:38-41, On the Seleucid Side. 3:38. To emphasize the importance of this battle, the author of 1 Maccabees reports that Lysias, the deputy king, oversaw the arrangements appointing a triumvirate to lead the Seleucid forces against Judas. The author of 2 Maccabees, on the other hand, states that Philip, the Seleucid official in charge of Jerusalem (2 Macc 5:22), appealed for help from Ptolemy, the governor of Coelesyria and Phoenicia, who appointed Nicanor, leader of a large army, with Gorgias as his deputy

(2 Macc 8:8-9). The more circumstantial account in 2 Macc 8:9-36, with its well-defined chain of command (rather than a triumvirate), is more likely. Nicanor, as one of the king's first friends (2 Macc 8:9), may have governed one of the important coastal regions. Gorgias later became governor of Idumea after the purification of the Temple (2 Macc 12:32).

3:39. The figures seem exaggerated. Second Maccabees reports that the army comprised only 20,000 soldiers (2 Macc 8:9), a number that may reflect the battles of David against the Arameans (2 Sam 10:6, 18). Such a large cavalry force would not have been of much use in the hills of Judea.

3:40. Emmaus, literally "Ammaus," is about 20 miles west-northwest of Jerusalem. According to 1 Macc 9:50, Emmaus lay within the province of Judea. At the eastern edge of the Aijalon Valley, this position controlled the western entrances to Jerusalem and provided easy access to the rear. It was a fertile land with good water supply, and so it was an excellent choice for a camp for a long period.

3:41. Merchants were used as contractors in Hellenistic army camps, but the authors of 1 and 2 Maccabees (2 Macc 8:11) stress the enemy's evil intentions by relating that they were slave traders. Also, since Nicanor's force came from Syria, it has been suggested that they were joined by forces from Idumea, not Syria. The original Hebrew may have read "Idumea" (אדם *'ĕdôm*) rather than "Syria" (ארם *'arām*). This is bolstered by the fact that the defeated enemy will flee to Idumea (1 Macc 4:15).

3:42-60, On the Jewish Side. 3:42. Judas and his brothers learn of the large force massed to attack. The phrase "misfortunes had increased" (ἐπληθύνθη τὰ κακά *eplēthynthē ta kaka*) recalls the era of chaos immediately following Alexander's death (1:9). The term "final destruction" (ἀπώλειαν καὶ συντέλειαν *apōleian kai synteleian*) refers to Antiochus's commands to dismantle Judea and turn it into a military colony (vv. 35-36). Although the Israelites had frequently sinned against God in previous times, God had not made an end of them (Jer 4:27; 5:10, 18; Ezek 11:13-21). Hope thus remains for the beleaguered forces of Judas.

3:43-44. The same emphasis on community, signified by each speaking to the other, is also found at 2:40. The members of each group exhort those of the other to fight, just as Joab had exhorted his brother Abishai when they were surrounded by their enemies (2 Sam 10:11-12; 1 Chr 19:12-13). The exhortation also echoes the promise of Amos that the fallen booth of David will be raised up (Amos 9:11), as well as the hope expressed in Jeremiah that God will build up the people and not tear them down, plant them and not pluck them up (Jer 24:6; 42:10). Preparations for war must be paralleled by prayer and petition.

3:45. The author breaks into a lament over Jerusalem, perhaps as an explanation for why the troops assembled at Mizpah (v. 46). Note the parallel style, typical of the poetry of the Hebrew Bible.

3:46. Mizpah has been identified with a site eight miles north of Jerusalem. It was here that the Israelites assembled to punish the tribe of Benjamin for the rape of the Levite's concubine (Judges 20–21). Here, also, Samuel assembled all the people to repent and fast, and God aided the Israelites in winning a great victory over the Philistines (1 Sam 7:5-11). Since Jerusalem cannot be seen from Mizpah, the term "opposite" may be used loosely as, for example, at 1 Macc 6:32, where Beth-zechariah is said to be "opposite" Beth-zur, even though the two sites are ten kilometers apart. Or "opposite" could translate the Hebrew word נגד (*neged*), which can mean "like," "comparable to" (cf. Gen 2:18, 20). Mizpah is not far from the Beth-horon ascent, and so an army could easily retreat into the Gophna Hills from this site.

3:47. Fasting, putting on sackcloth, sprinkling ashes on the head, and tearing clothes are all traditional mourning customs. Although often elements of mourning past events or catastrophes, such deeds also were signs of repentance intended to avert divine punishment for past misdeeds—see, for example, the reactions of Ahab, when he heard Elijah's prediction of how his dynasty would fall (1 Kgs 21:27); the whole community of Israel, before confessing their sins and those of their ancestors (Neh 9:1); and the king of Nineveh, when he heard Jonah's prophecy (Jonah 3:5).

3:48. This verse is extremely difficult to translate. The NRSV translation, "to inquire into those matters about which the Gentiles consulted the likenesses of their gods," not only is difficult to justify grammatically, but also suggests an analogy between the Torah and idol worship that the author of 1 Maccabees would have been unlikely to make. Some Greek manuscripts read, "about which the Gentiles sought to write/paint on them the images of their idols," indicating that books of the law that had been defiled were unrolled to remind God of the iniquities that had been performed (1:56-57). This variant reading, although attempting to make sense of the text, is not easy to justify. Public mourning is often accompanied by public reading of the Torah in adherence to the covenant (Neh 9:1-3). But no mention is made of such painting in 1 Macc 1:56-57. Neither does this reading do justice to the Greek preposition περί (*peri*), which means "concerning." Moreover, a book or scroll is unrolled so that it can be read. A better translation of this verse would be: "They unrolled the book of the Torah concerning those things about which they were inquiring, namely, the Gentiles and the likenesses of their idols." This would mean that the assembled congregation read those sections of the Torah that told how the Gentiles and their idols were to be dealt with (e.g., Deuteronomy 4; 7). The reading of the law may also be compared with the consultation of the Lord before battle (Judg 20:18; 1 Sam 23:2; 2 Sam 5:19, 23).

3:49. The priestly vestments mentioned here are those used for service in the Temple (Exod 28:40-43; 39:1). The *War Scroll* from Qumran suggests that the vestments the priests wore for battle could not be brought into the Temple,[64] and so distinguishes between two sets of vestments. First fruits, which may have included the firstborn of clean animals (see Exod 13:12-15; 34:22-26; Lev 23:17-20; Deut 12:6-18), were obligatory offerings brought during the Second Temple period around the Feast of Weeks or the Feast of Tabernacles. First fruits and tithes were the portion of the priests and Levites (Exod 23:19*a* ; Num 18:13; Deut 18:4) and, by the second century BCE, normally would have been offered only at the Temple in Jerusalem. Mizpah is thus depicted here as an alternate Jerusalem, since Jerusalem was defiled and under the control of the Seleucids and their followers.

There were different kinds of tithes: some were allotted to the sanctuary (Lev 27:30-33), some to the Levites (Num 18:21-24), and some to the offerers themselves to eat in the presence of the Lord (Deut 14:22-28). God had promised through the prophet Malachi that if the people gave tithes to the sanctuary, God would bless them with fruitfulness (Mal 3:10), and Tobit is described as diligently obeying the law about tithing and even surpassing it to the extent of giving a second and a third tithe (Tob 1:6-8; see also the mention of tithes and first fruits in 2 Chr 31:5-12; Neh 12:44; 13:5, 10; Jdt 11:13).

The mention of the Nazirites is another indication that Mizpah is considered a substitute for Jerusalem. At the end of their vows, Nazirites had to present themselves at the Temple in order to show that their obligations had been discharged by cutting their hair and offering a sacrifice (Num 6:13-20).

3:50-53. Once again, the author of 1 Maccabees breaks into poetry, here a community lament and prayer for help, echoing the language of 1:39-40; 2:12; 3:35; and 3:45. The appeal for help is found frequently in the psalms (e.g., Pss 20:2; 35:2; 38:22; 62:7; 94:17; 108:12; 121:1-2).

3:54. Trumpets were to be sounded before going to war "so that you may be remembered before the LORD your God and saved from your enemies" (Num 10:9 NRSV).[65]

3:55-57. The division of the army (v. 55) follows the example of Jethro's advice to Moses (Exod 18:21, 25) and Moses' actual division of the people (Deut 1:15), but it differs from the account of Judas's division of the troops in 2 Macc 8:22. Since the division is not used in describing the strategy of the battle, the author is portraying Judas as a traditionalist, a portrayal that continues with the description of his actions in v. 56, which are based in the regulations of Deuteronomy (Deut 20:5-8). The movement of the camp should be seen as in tandem with the action of Gorgias (1 Macc 4:1-5), not as preceding

---

64. See 1QM 7:11-12.

65. Cf. 1QM 10:7.

it. Judas left Mizpah, and Gorgias set out for Mizpah independently of each other. By leaving Mizpah, Judas resolved to use the element of surprise, even without the advantage of Gorgias's leaving the camp.

3:58-60. Judas's speech reflects the one that the priest is assigned to give to the Israelites before going to war (Deut 20:2-4). The Qumran *War Scroll* also recounts a speech by the priest, wherein the phrase "be courageous" (lit., "be powerful sons") is found (see also 2 Sam 2:7; 13:28).[66] Judas encourages his soldiers with the same sentiments found at 1 Macc 2:7. The description of the strength of the Seleucid forces, followed by the move from a defensive posture at Mizpah to a more offensive move toward the enemy's camp, leads to this rather despairing assessment of the outcome: Better to die fighting (v. 59). Nevertheless, Judas ends with a strong conditional statement: "One never knows, God might help us and we could win" (see v. 60). The author thus keeps the reader in suspense as to what will happen.

66. See 1QM 15:7.

1 Maccabees 4:1-25, The Battle at Emmaus

COMMENTARY

4:1-5. The Seleucids decide to try a surprise night assault against the assembly at Mizpah, about which the Syrians have been informed. The Syrians were guided through the Judean hills by scouts from the Jerusalem citadel, probably Jews who were not of Judas's persuasion. In his hubris, Gorgias thinks the Jews are fleeing, but to the contrary, Judas is preparing to attack.

4:6-18. Judas's forces, which number 3,000 men (cf. 7:40; 9:5), are outmatched more than thirteen to one. Judas's forces are not fully equipped, in contrast to the heavily armed Seleucid forces. Judas's rallying cry, using the language of Deut 1:21, again recalls that of the priest before battle (Deut 20:3-5; the prayer of the priest before battle in the Qumran *War Scroll* also alludes to the defeat of Pharaoh [1QM 11:9-10]). Judas prays that their cry will be heard, just as the prayer of the suffering Israelites in Egypt was heard by God, who remembered the covenant with Abraham, Isaac, and Jacob (Exod 2:23-24). Further, when David defeated Goliath, it was known in all the earth that "there is a God in Israel" (1 Sam 17:46 NRSV). Thus with his appeal to the faith of his troops and the tactical advantage of attacking from the hills, Judas wins a convincing victory and puts the enemy to flight.

4:15. Gazara, about four and one-half miles northwest of Emmaus, was the closest Seleucid fort (1 Macc 7:45). If Gorgias's forces included Idumeans (see Commentary on 1 Macc 3:42), some of the force retreated homeward. Azotus is biblical Ashdod, whose territory extended to near Gazara (1 Macc 14:34). The flight, therefore, was to the north, the south, and the east.

4:16-18. Having won the battle, Judas and his troops regroup. Second Maccabees 8:26, however, gives an alternate reason for their stopping the pursuit: The next day was the sabbath (probably due to that author's desire to emphasize Judas's Torah observance).

4:19-22. Returning from the plateau around Mizpah, Gorgias and his expeditionary force see from the burning camp that the battle is over. Judas had exhorted his soldiers not to be frightened (4:8), but that is now the reaction of the enemy. The author also suggests that Judas's army was as ready for battle as ever, and this fierceness results in the enemy's flight.

4:23-25. Once all danger is past, the Israelites are free to plunder the enemy camp. The riches have been brought in part by slave traders (3:41). Blue and purple are the famous "Tyrian" dyes. The pair "blue and purple," like "silver and gold," is found frequently in the Hebrew Scriptures to describe the rich furnishings of the Temple (e.g., Exod 25:4; 35:23, 25, 35). In this case, these colors probably refer to the outer clothing of the infantry and the cavalry. Polybius described the cavalry of Antiochus IV, as they paraded in the festival of Daphnae, as wearing purple outer garments, some of which were golden and adorned with figures.[67] The Israelites celebrate their victory by marching home (presumably to Mizpah) to the sound of hymns (Pss 106:1; 107:1; 136:1; cf. 2 Chr 20:21). The battle account is thus framed liturgically by the penitential service (3:47) and this chant of victory. The author's closing comment draws once more on traditional language (Exod 14:13; 1 Sam 11:13; 19:5; 2 Kgs 13:5).

67. Polybius 30.25.10.

REFLECTIONS

1. The author has emphasized through his liturgical frame for the whole battle around Emmaus the importance of prayer and repentance if one is to succeed. The forces of Judas are seen as totally devoted to God's law, and this inner conviction drives them to victory. In contrast, the Seleucid forces are given no inner resolve; they are simply obeying the vengeful orders of the king and, with their slave traders, are hoping to gain wealth. In our own time we have seen how hard it is even for the most advanced military power to defeat an army that is driven to defend its own homeland. The narrative here in 1 Maccabees makes us reflect on how a major military power should use its power in the world. Antiochus IV's pique at being rebuffed is clearly not a model for any commander in chief to follow. Nor is the decision to utterly annihilate one's opponent, no matter how great the provocation may be. Rather, greatness is shown not by excessive use of force, but by benevolent treatment. Only the really strong can afford to be gracious. The message of this narrative should be that one should not try to impose solutions, but should try to gather all parties together to see if, by patient diplomacy, disagreements can be resolved.

2. The Seleucid Empire encompassed a great deal of territory and many different cultures and races, and it finally broke apart as different regions sought independence. How can one nation allow its diverse cultural groups the freedom to express their own individual spirit, to maintain their own cultural identities, and yet not cause the nation to so split apart that it cannot hang together? How can the diverse groups learn to respect each other's traditions and cultures? This problem has been present since the growth of nationalism in the nineteenth century. If one tries to suppress cultural differences and create a homogeneous society, eventually the dam holding back these repressed feelings will break. One solution for such divisions might be for us all to try to learn more about one another's traditions and cultures. We need to seize every opportunity to teach children, youth, and adults about the many religious traditions that make up the fabric of society, and so to bring them to understand other perspectives and not ignorantly reject them as "other."

1 Maccabees 4:26-35, The Campaign of Lysias

COMMENTARY

4:26-27. The plans of Antiochus (3:34-36) and his deputy Lysias are frustrated, as Lysias admits here; Antiochus makes the same admission at 6:8. This theme of "man proposes but God disposes" runs throughout the book.

4:28-29. The phrase "the next year" raises questions. If one dates Antiochus's march to the eastern satrapies in late 165 BCE, then this decision would have occurred in late 164 BCE. This length of time is surprising, and the author of 1 Maccabees makes no attempt to fill in the gap. From letters preserved in 2 Maccabees 11, however, we learn that Antiochus IV, at the prompting of the high priest Menelaus, offered amnesty to the Jews in March 164 BCE, by which they could enjoy their own laws as formerly (2 Macc 11:27-33). Lysias and Ptolemy Macron seem to have been brokers to the peace terms (2 Macc 11:16-21; 2 Macc 10:12). These peace negotiations would have taken place during this time covered by the phrase "the next year." The author of 1 Maccabees makes no mention of these negotiations because he insists on painting his Jewish enemies, as well as Lysias and Antiochus, as implacably opposed to Judas and true Judaism. Why the negotiations failed is not known. The increase in Judas's forces from 3,000 in 4:6 to 10,000 in 4:29, even allowing for inflated figures, suggests that Judas had used the time to recruit.

According to the author, Lysias assembles an even larger force of infantry than does Ptolemy, but with fewer cavalry (3:38), no doubt anticipating a battle in the Judean hills. Lysias also chooses a new route. Instead of the approach from the west, he moves into the Judean hills from the southeast, through Idumea and Mt. Hebron. Beth-zur, where they encamped, was on Judea's southern border with Idumea (1 Macc 4:61; 14:33) and has been identified with Khirbet el Tabeiqa. (According to 2 Macc 11:5-6, Lysias besieges Beth-zur.)

4:30-33. Judas's prayer first remembers and thanks God for past victories before asking for help in the present situation. The word for "Philistines" (ἀλλόφυλοι *allophyloi*, v. 30) is the same as the word for "foreigners" in v. 26, so the examples of David (1 Samuel 17) and Jonathan (1 Sam 14:1-15) are appropriate in a battle against armies invading the land. In the requests for help (vv. 31-33), Judas calls his group "your people Israel," "those who love you," and "all who know your name," whereas his opponents remain unnamed, a generic enemy. Judas calls on the divine warrior to instill fear into their enemy, and they will praise God as did Moses and the Israelites (Exodus 15).

4:34-35. "Rout" (τροπή *tropē*) should be translated "reversal." If 5,000 soldiers had fallen, presumably there would have been a panicked retreat, but Lysias is here described as withdrawing in an organized way (2 Macc 11:16 describes a panicked flight). In reality, Lysias, as vice regent, may have received news of Antiochus IV's death and decided to return to Antioch to act as regent for Antiochus V. This is not suggested by the author of 1 Maccabees, who records the king's death after the purification of the Temple.

The Maccabees are shown to be ready (cf. 4:21), cast in a heroic mode as prepared to die with honor. They stand in marked contrast to the shameful behavior of their enemy, who turn and run (4:35). Their action corresponds to the prayer of Judas that the enemy be ashamed of their troops and cavalry (4:31-32). A further contrast is made between Judas and his men, who fight for their country, and those who fight for money with no inner conviction (4:35). The very brevity of the battle scene, as compared to the lengthy prayer of Judas, suggests that the author is hazy about the details.

1 MACCABEES 4:36-61, THE CLEANSING OF THE TEMPLE

COMMENTARY

After his victories, Judas goes up to Mt. Zion. The victory march to God's holy mountain is part of an ancient mythic pattern describing the battles of the divine warrior, as exemplified in the great hymn of victory at Exodus 15. The Temple is where God dwells, the connecting point where heaven and earth meet, a stabilizing force for the maintenance of the proper order of creation. With the Temple desecrated, the world of the Jews was askew; therefore, it was essential that the Temple be reconsecrated and the world put right.

4:36-37. The enemies have been crushed by the divine warrior (v. 30; cf. Exod 15:3).

The term "dedicate" or "renew" (ἐγκαινίζω *egkainizō*) is used to describe Solomon's dedication of the Temple (1 Kgs 8:63; 2 Chr 7:5 LXX), the dedication of the Temple under Ezra (Ezra 6:16-17), Asa's repair of the altar (2 Chr 15:8), and Nehemiah's dedication of the walls of Jerusalem (Neh 12:27). The expression "go up" (ἀναβαίνω *anabainō*) is the language of the psalms (Pss 24:3; 121:4). The wholeness of the community is emphasized as all the army goes up. So, too, when Solomon dedicated the Temple, all the people of Israel assembled (1 Kgs 8:1-5).

4:38. The author refers to the desecration described earlier (1:31; 2:12). He draws on descriptions of a defeated city to heighten the emotional effect: Micah had foretold how the temple mount would become a wooded height (Mic 3:12), and Isaiah graphically depicted the desolate state of a destroyed land (Isa 34:13-15). The author moves from the outer court, with its altar, to the inside of the Temple, with its courts and chambers (1 Chr 9:23-24; 28:11-18).

4:39-40. The mourning ritual is described as it was at 1 Macc 2:70; 3:47. The trumpets are to be blown to serve as a reminder before God (Num 10:1-10). The scene is reminiscent of the restoration of temple worship under Asa (2 Chr 15:8-15), when trumpets and horns were blown as the people renewed their covenant.

4:41. The citadel, called the Akra, overlooked the sanctuary from the south (see 1:33). It was still under the enemy's control, and thus troops were required to protect the priests purifying the Temple.

4:42-43. The purity required of priests is described in Leviticus 21. Priests are to delight in the law, as God delights in covenant faithfulness (Mic 7:18; for a statement of such delight, see Psalm 118). The defiled stones were part of the desolating sacrilege (1:54; cf. Jer 32:34), like the stones in a leper's house (Lev 14:40); thus they had to be put in a place that must be avoided if one is to remain ritually pure.

4:44-46. The altar of burnt offering could not be treated like the altars of idols (Deut 12:2-3). It was sacred and yet desecrated. So, just as the remaining parts of the bull used for a purification offering are still sacred, even though they have absorbed the sanctuary's impurities and must be put in a clean place (Lev 4:11-12), so also the altar can be kept on the temple hill—a clean place—until a prophet determines what should be done (see 14:41; Deut 18:15, 18-19).

The phrase "until a prophet arises" has sometimes been given an eschatological interpretation because of phrases found in the Qumran literature: "[the men of holiness] should not depart from any council of the law . . . but shall be ruled by the first directives which the men of the Community began to be taught until the prophet comes and the Messiahs of Aaron and Israel."[68] In the *Damascus Document* from Qumran, there seem to be two moments, for God raised up "the Teacher of Righteousness," but one still had to wait until there arose "he who teaches justice at the end of days."[69] This last figure may be identified with the eschatological high priest, the Messiah of Aaron,[70] since part of the role of priests was the teaching of the law (Deut 33:10). Since the phrase at 1 Macc 4:46 (and 14:41) echoes the language of Deut 18:15, there is no need to read it as eschatological. It is also similar to the phrase found at Ezra 2:63 (= Neh 7:65), "until there should be a priest to consult Urim and Thummim" (NRSV), which has no eschatological meaning. Thus the author of 1 Maccabees expects the proper restoration of a normal functioning community, and such communities have a prophet. The phrase at 1 Maccabees envisions that when God sends a prophet, as God had promised for every generation (Deut 18:15-19), the prophet will solve all the knotty problems. The author longs for the restoration of the time when the full functioning community of Judah had priests, kings, and prophets, with the prophet functioning as a counterweight to the power of the king (see 1 and 2 Kings). It is interesting that the author of 1 Maccabees speaks of a prophetic figure rather than a priest or a teacher; perhaps it may hint at the author's view of his own role.

4:47-51. The altar is rebuilt according to the regulations found in Exodus and Deuteronomy (Exod 20:25; Deut 27:5-6). The temple furnishings, stripped away by Antiochus

---

68. 1QS 9:10-11. See also the Messianic Anthology, 4Q175, where Deut 18:18-19 is quoted.
69. CD 1.1; 6.11.
70. See 4Q 541.

IV (1 Macc 1:21-24), are restored according to the stipulations of Exodus 25–27.

4:52-55. On December 14, 164 BCE, the birthday of Antiochus IV (see 1:59; 2 Macc 6:7), the daily offering was resumed (Exod 29:38-42). When Daniel had asked how long the prohibition on the regular burnt offering would last, the angel had responded, "For two thousand three hundred evenings and mornings" (Dan 8:14 NRSV), or 1,150 days, about three and a half years, which corresponds roughly to the extent of the desecration of the sanctuary, according to 1 Macc 1:54–4:55. The correspondence of time was taken as an indication that God was behind the action. The rejoicing is similar to that at the dedication of Solomon's Temple (2 Chr 5:11-14) and at the dedication of the city wall by Nehemiah (Neh 12:27). Under Judas, deliverance prospered (3:60) and is confirmed in the restoration of the temple worship.

4:56-59. The Feast of Dedication is patterned after the Feast of Tabernacles (Lev 23:33-36) and the dedication of the Temple by Solomon (1 Kings 8) and Hezekiah (2 Chronicles 29). Mention of burnt offerings (Lev 6:8-13), sacrifices of well-being (Leviticus 3), and thanksgiving offerings (Lev 7:11-15) is also made at Hezekiah's restoration of worship (2 Chr 29:31-35). The Temple is restored to its former glory, and the disgrace is removed (cf. 1:39-40). Judas, his brothers, and "all the assembly of Israel" (all true believers) determine that this feast should be an annual celebration.

4:60-61. The author concludes this section by describing the defensive measures taken to ensure that the Gentiles would not repeat what they had done at Jerusalem (1:31; 3:45, 51), or attack from the south (4:29). The refortified walls are not those of the whole of Jerusalem, but of the temple mount itself. The Akra remained in enemy hands.

REFLECTIONS

Solomon's prayer at the dedication of the first Temple in Jerusalem shows an awareness that if heaven and earth cannot contain God, still less could the Temple that Solomon had built (1 Kgs 8:27). Yet a community requires a place to gather in order to worship together. When a church building or other place of worship is destroyed by a hurricane or by a fire, the community rallies around the congregation and starts to find ways to rebuild. We all need a familiar place, familiar songs and practices. Whenever there is a change in liturgy, opposition arises, as in the sixteenth-century Year of Grace rebellion in England and the opposition to the Second Vatican Council decision to replace Latin with the vernacular in Roman Catholic worship. Some worshiping communities still prefer the resonances of the King James Version of the Bible to more accurate contemporary translations. People like what is familiar, what is traditional. That is how the community is accustomed to meeting God. The reintroduction of purified worship in the Temple reflects that same human tendency, for religion is not just intellectual—the whole person is involved. That means that we are moved by the hymns and the familiar gestures and words of prayer, by the familiar sights and sounds, the traditional stories. Through such human interaction, the religious culture is transmitted from one generation to another.

1 MACCABEES 5:1-68, WARS WITH NEIGHBORS

OVERVIEW

This section deals with raids across the Jordan, into Galilee, to the south, and in the coastal plain. The attacks are said to be in response to the hostile posture of neighboring peoples, a hostility that parallels that encountered by the Israelites when they entered the land (Josh 9:1-2; 11:1-5), as well as the resistance to rebuilding the Temple after the exile (Ezra 4–5). Psalm 48:4-7 speaks of the panic of kings gathered together against Zion when they behold the Temple as a symbol and focus of the people's commitment to the covenant worship.

1 Maccabees 5:1-8, Battles in Idumea and Ammon

COMMENTARY

5:1-2. The neighboring Gentiles become angry, as Antiochus IV had been angered (3:27), and their plan, like his (3:35), is to destroy the Jews. This time, however, the efforts are directed not at the strong Judas, but at the weaker Jews living in foreign domains.

5:3-5. First, Judas moves against the Idumeans. The "descendants of Esau" are described in the book of *Jubilees* as being angry with Esau for reconciling with Jacob (Genesis 35), and they attack Jacob and his sons (*Jubilees* 37–38). The reference to the descendants of Jacob (v. 2) conjures up this ancient rivalry with Esau. Akrabattene may refer to the area southwest of the Dead Sea, the ascent of Akrabbin (Num 34:4). Josephus, however, mentions an area called Akrabattene in Samaria, near the region of Gophna.[71] It is unknown exactly who the sons of Baean are. Baean is the name given in the LXX to one of the towns of Moab (Num 32:3). Could it, therefore, refer to the Moabites? One might recall how Joshua warned the Israelites about not joining to the nations round about, for they would then be a snare and a trap (Josh 23:11-13), and that the daughters of Moab had led Israel astray (Num 25:1-3; Ps 106:28-39). Whatever group is meant, one should note how the language here is that of the ban, the vow to complete destruction, which one finds in Numbers and Joshua.

5:6-8. In 1 Maccabees, Timothy seems to be a local ruler of the Ammonites, whereas in 2 Maccabees (8:30-33; 9:3; 10:24) a Timothy is said to be a high Seleucid official (2 Maccabees seems to have exaggerated the importance of Timothy). Jazer (Num 21:32) was near Heshbon in the Transjordan. If Akrabattene is situated in Idumea, then Judas is pictured as making a counterclockwise movement from Idumea through Moab to Ammon, following the course laid out in the book of Numbers. Such a parallel may explain the use of the ancient names. (See Reflections at 5:63-68.)

---

71. Josephus *The Jewish War* 2.234-235, 568.

1 Maccabees 5:9-54, Battles in Galilee and Gilead

COMMENTARY

The action now moves to the north, with Judas and his brothers rescuing Jews from their Gentile neighbors and bringing them back to Judah.

5:9-20, The Attack of the Gentiles and Judas's Response. 5:9-13. Gilead is the region east of the Jordan. The location of Dathema is uncertain (4:29 places it a night's journey from Bozrah). The language of destruction is the same as that used by Antiochus IV (3:35). The situation of the Jews in Gilead is depicted in terms similar to that of the Gibeonites in Josh 10:1-11. The land of Tob was southeast of the sea of Galilee, in northern Gilead, from whence Jephthah the judge came (Judg 11:3; cf. 2 Sam 10:6, 8). However, the text literally reads "in the lands of Toubias," which refers to southern Gilead.

5:14-15. The messengers come "with their garments torn," a sign of having traveled a long distance (cf. Josh 9:3-15, where the Gibeonites tricked Joshua into thinking that they had traveled a long distance by wearing such clothing). Torn clothes could also be the sign of messengers bringing bad news, as when the news of the capture of the ark by the Philistines was brought to Eli (1 Sam 4:12), or when Saul's death was reported to David by a man "with his clothes torn and dirt on his head" (2 Sam 1:2 NRSV).

"Galilee of the Gentiles" (Isa 9:1; 8:23 MT) refers to the seacoast towns of Ptolemais, Tyre, and Sidon. The term used for "Gentiles" (ἀλλόφυλος *allophylos*) often signifies "Philistines" in the LXX.

5:16-20. The Maccabees are constantly portrayed as consulting the people (2:41; 4:44). The great assembly resonates with the crowd that gathered at the dedications of the Temple under Solomon (1 Kgs 8:65; 2 Chr 7:8), Hezekiah (2 Chr 30:13), and Ezra (Ezra 10:1), as well as Nehemiah's assembly to stop the oppression of the Jewish poor (Neh 5:7). The term "assembly" (ἐκκλησία *ekklēsia*) translates a basic Hebrew term (קהל *qāhāl*) that signifies the community of Israel. At this assembly, Judas divides his forces to deal with the emergencies facing the people. Presumably Azariah is one of those "leaders of the people" whom Judas had appointed (3:55).

When a prohibition like the one Judas makes in v. 19 is given, the reader knows that eventually it will be broken. It is broken at 5:55-62.

5:21-23, The Conflict in Galilee. Simon's activity is quickly summarized but glorified highly. The number of dead corresponds to the force under Simon's control (v. 22). Ptolemais is also known as Acco or Acre. Arbatta is otherwise unknown; a Narbatta lay south of Mt. Carmel in the neighborhood of Caesarea, and perhaps this is meant here.[72] The return (v. 23) is almost liturgical in character, as the men, women, and children all return to Judea with merriment and festivity. In the book of Isaiah, the ransomed of the Lord are described as returning to Zion in the same way (Isa 51:11).

5:24-44, Judas in Gilead. In contrast to Simon's activity, which is described in a very summary fashion, Judas and Jonathan are given much more attention.

5:24-27. The Nabateans at this time were nomadic traders based in southern Transjordan. While the author suggests that Judas was on friendly terms with them, 2 Maccabees records a battle before peace is reached (2 Macc 12:11-12). The cities (v. 26) are located east and north of the River Yarmuke in Transjordan. They are described in terms reminiscent of the description of the towns of the promised land (Num 13:28). The Jews are to be destroyed, as had been threatened earlier by Antiochus IV (3:35) and the Gentiles in Gilead (5:9).

5:28-44. The author now proceeds to list victories of Judas against the Gentiles of Gilead. All the towns listed in v. 26, except for Alema, are dealt with. The string of victories here recalls those of Joshua (Josh 10:28-43). Judas burns towns with fire as Joshua burned Jericho (Josh 6:24) and Ai (Josh 8:28), and takes their spoils. Note the repetition at vv. 28, 35, and 51, where the destruction of three different centers is told in basically the same terms.

5:31. The townspeople of Dathema, under threat of annihilation, cry out to God. A similar phrase is used of the people of the Philistine city Ekron when the ark of the covenant is put in its midst and causes death and pestilence among the inhabitants (1 Sam 5:12). The trumpets sound the alarm as directed (Num 10:6), and the great shout adds to the din of warfare, as one side tries to intimidate the other. (See 1 Sam 4:5-6, where the great shout that goes up from the Israelites' camp when the ark of the Lord is brought to it frightens the Philistines.)

---

72. See Josephus *The Jewish War* 2.291, 509.

5:33-34. The division of the army into three companies occurs frequently in the OT: Gideon divided his forces into three (Judg 7:16), as did Abimelech (Judg 9:43), Saul (1 Sam 11:11), and David (2 Sam 18:2). The *War Scroll* from Qumran also divides the Sons of Light into three arrays against the Sons of Darkness.[73] Battle and prayer are combined as before when the Israelites had assembled at Mizpah against the invasion of Ptolemy, Nicanor, and Gorgias (3:43-54). In Solomon's prayer at the dedication of the Temple in Jerusalem, he asked that when the Israelites went out to battle and prayed facing Jerusalem and the Temple, God would hear them (1 Kgs 8:44-45; 2 Chr 6:34-35). Thus "to cry out in prayer" may refer to a battle cry like the one in Judg 7:18, " 'For the LORD and for Gideon!' " (NRSV), or to a watchword like that at 2 Macc 13:15, "God's Victory" (NAB). Once again, the number of dead corresponds to the number of Judas's men.

5:35-36. These verses describe a series of victories told in shorthand as Judas deals with the besieged towns of Gilead. The location of Maapha is unknown; it may refer to Mizpah of Gilead.

5:37-44. The battle against the last city, Carnaim, is described here. Timothy is introduced as someone whom the reader has already encountered, suggesting that he is the Timothy of 5:6. His force is described as numerous, with Arabs as mercenaries. The enemy looks for a sign to see whether Judas and his forces are eager to fight. A similar tactic is used by Jonathan, the son of King Saul, when he sees God's hand behind the answer that the Philistine guards give to him. He knows that God has given them into his hand when they tell him to come up to them, rather than come down to Jonathan themselves (1 Sam 14:6-15). As in Jonathan's case, fear comes upon the enemy of Judah, a fear sent by God as requested in the earlier prayer at Mizpah (4:32). Judas stations "officers" (γραμματεῖς *grammateis*), the same term used in Deut 20:5-9; Josh 1:10; 3:2 LXX. The enemy "were defeated" (συντρίβω *syntribō*), literally "were crushed" (3:22-23; 4:10, 14, 30, 36), one of the author's favorite words (cf. its use at Exod 15:3 LXX).

"Carnaim" literally means "horns," a symbol of strength. Karnaim is mentioned by Amos (6:13) and has been identified with the town Ashteroth-karnaim, mentioned in Gen 14:5. According to 2 Macc 12:26, there was a temple of Atargatis/Astarte at Carnaim.

The term "could stand before" (ὑποστῆναι *hypostēnai*) is the same verb used earlier to mean "to resist" (5:40). Thus Timothy's prediction at that point proves true.

5:45-54, The Return to Jerusalem.
5:45-51. Ephron was nine miles east of the Jordan River, opposite Beth-shan. The scene described in these verses recalls two events from the Israelites' march through this region. Judas's request for his people to peacefully pass through the land is similar to Moses' petitions to the king of Edom (Num 20:14-17) and to the king of the Amorites (Num 21:21-22). However, since Judas cannot bypass Ephron, as Moses had the kingdom of Edom, Judas destroys it, as Moses conquered the Amorites (cf. Deut 20:10-15). Ephron is "razed" (ἐκριζόω *ekrizoō*; lit., "uprooted"), the same verb used by Zephaniah to declare that Ekron would be uprooted (Zeph 2:4 LXX). The final image of the whole group of men, women, and children marching over the corpses is particularly grisly and triumphalistic.

5:52. Beth-shan (Scythopolis) was west of the Jordan. Note how 2 Macc 12:29-31 stresses the goodwill of the citizens of Scythopolis toward the Jews.

5:53-54. The triumphal return to Zion again parallels the victory march of the Divine Warrior (Exod 15:1-17), as at 5:23. The return is the in-gathering of the people prayed for at Ps 106:47. The language parallels that of Isaiah 35; 51:9-11. The fact that no one had died was seen as a sign of God's care and of the sinlessness and purity of the troops, as compared with the exodus generation, whose warriors had all perished because of their lack of trust in God's power to defeat their enemy (Numbers 13–14; Deut 1:34-36; 2:16). (See Reflections at 5:63-68.)

---

73. See 1QM 8.

1 Maccabees 5:55-62, The Failure of Joseph and Azariah

COMMENTARY

The reversal suffered by Joseph and Azariah is in stark contrast to the success of Judas and Simon. They rashly seek to make a name for themselves as Seron (3:14) and David had (2 Sam 8:13; 1 Chr 17:8). Jamnia was also a center of opposition to the Jews (2 Macc 12:8-9).

The same word (ἐτροπώθη *etropōthē*, "reversal") used to describe the conquest of Carnaim is used here to tell of the reversal of Joseph and Azariah (v. 61). Just as the Israelites did not listen to Moses, but went up to fight against the inhabitants of the promised land (Num 14:40-45; Deut 1:41-44), so also Joseph and Azariah do not listen to Judas and his brothers. And just as God raised up judges to deliver Israel (Judg 2:16-18), so also Judas and his brothers are to bring deliverance (v. 62). The contrast between the two groups recalls the revolt of Korah against the authority of Moses and Aaron in the wilderness (Numbers 16). The phrase "not belong to the family" (οὐκ ἦσαν ἐκ τοῦ σπέρματος *ouk ēsan ek tou spermatos*; lit., "not of the seed of") is found at Num 16:40 to state that only direct descendants of Aaron shall approach to offer incense before the Lord. Here, it indicates that the Maccabees have been divinely appointed to bring deliverance to Israel. (See Reflections at 5:63-68.)

1 Maccabees 5:63-68, Further Successes

COMMENTARY

5:63-64. Just as David's fame increased (1 Sam 18:30), so also does that of Judas and his brothers, as foretold in the hymn to Judas (3:9).

5:65-66. Judas had previously fought against the sons of Esau (5:3) and then traveled counterclockwise northward on the eastern side of the Jordan. Now he fights against them in the south and travels clockwise to the coastal plain. Marisa lies to the west of Hebron.

5:67-68. These priests, like Joseph and Azariah (v. 61), seek to do brave deeds as had Judas and Simon (5:56). They act "unwisely" by not heeding the determination of the assembly (v. 16). Judas, on the contrary, is completely successful (3:6). He follows the commands of Deuteronomy (Deut 7:5, 25; 12:3) in dealing with idols, just as Hezekiah (2 Chr 31:1) and Josiah (2 Chr 34:3-7) had done.

REFLECTIONS

This chapter with its stories of the battles against neighboring peoples is chilling. As well as being intended to destroy idols, justification for the war is provided in that the Gentiles started the persecution of the Israelites. The actions of Judas and his followers, however, go far beyond any criteria for just conduct of war. In their first engagement, they put their enemies under the ban (5:5), the vow to total destruction. This language is kept up through the repetition of "killed every male by the edge of the sword; then he seized all its spoils and burned it with fire" (5:28 NRSV; cf. vv. 35, 51), as well as the burning of idols (5:44, 68). The tradition of putting one's enemies under the ban is one of the most troubling ethical issues in the OT.

The Hebrew Scriptures have been the inspiration for concern for the weaker members of a society—for widows, orphans, and children (Exod 22:21-24)—and passages from the Bible have inspired those who seek social justice for the oppressed. Passages such as Amos 5:24 have become slogans for advancement: "Let justice roll down like waters,/ and righteousness like an ever-flowing stream" (NRSV). The exodus story of liberation from slavery has been used by African American slaves and by liberation theologians as a model for the plight and the hope of the oppressed.

Yet there is a tradition of violence within the Bible, a tradition used by the Puritans in the American colonies to inspire the colonists to extirpate the Native Americans. How is one to reconcile the respect for life shown in the Bible with the command by God to annihilate every living thing, both humans and animals (1 Sam 15:3)?

Susan Niditch, in exploring these issues, describes two uses of the ban.[74] The most difficult instances to understand are those when the Israelites pledge their enemies as a sacrifice to God in exchange for God's leading them to victory (see, e.g., Num 21:2-3). Niditch suggests that such passages must be put within a sacrificial context, in which human beings are the most precious offering to God. This practice of human sacrifice is condemned by the dominant threads of the OT (Deut 12:31; Lev 18:21), but not by threads within Israelite culture itself. A number of scholars have suggested that child sacrifice was part of a state-sponsored cult within ancient Israel until the reforms of the Judean king Josiah in the seventh century BCE.

The second group of traditions about the ban are those that treat the ban as evidence of God's justice, a way of uprooting the sources of impurity and idolatry that might infect Israel. When Achan transgresses God's covenantal demands and takes some of the things devoted to the Lord, he and his family are put under the ban and destroyed, in order to eradicate that sin from Israel's midst (Joshua 7). In 1 Maccabees, the destruction of the Gentiles is seen as punishment for their determination to wipe out Israel (1 Macc 5:1-2, 9, 27). Although Judas does not kill every breathing thing (cf. Josh 10:28, 30, 32, 35-37, 39, 40; 11:11, 14) but only every male, one must still note what this implies. In that culture, the father was believed to provide the seed, whereas the mother provided the matter. By killing every male, Judas was destroying that city's race. In addition, no mention is made of the women and girls, although Num 31:15-18 provides that young girls who had not yet slept with a man be kept alive and assimilated into the Israelite camp. What will happen to these defenseless women in the towns of Gilead after the Maccabees leave? Although the author of 1 Maccabees insists that Judas and Simon bring back not only the Jewish men but also their wives and children (5:23, 45), the enemies' wives and female children are not worth discussing. The most horrifying image is that of 5:51, where the returning men, women, and children are depicted as walking over the corpses of their enemies.

Whether or not the actions in 1 Maccabees happened in precisely the way described, what is important to note is the way language is being used to engender an implacable hostility toward one's enemy—they are to be exterminated. This is how one is to deal with neighbors.

What steps can one take to break down such prejudicial attitudes? One must first teach against the dehumanizing of one's enemy, and decry those elements of one's tradition that do so. Rather than seeing one's own racial, religious, or sexual group as having the right to impose its views and behaviors on all others, one must seek out those elements of commonality that unite diverse groups. We must not resort to ethnic cleansing or social ostracism, wherein certain groups are excluded from entering "our" domain. Rather than accepting the position that "whoever is not with me is against me" (Matt 12:30 NRSV; cf. Luke 11:23), we might take the position that "whoever is not against us is for us" (Mark 9:40 NRSV; cf. Luke 9:50). Rather than restricting the command to love one another (cf. John 13:34), one might extend the notion of neighbor to include the hated "Samaritan" (see Luke 10:25-37).

---

74. Niditch, *War in the Hebrew Bible*.

1 MACCABEES 6:1-17, THE DEATH OF ANTIOCHUS IV

COMMENTARY

The news of the death of Antiochus IV was announced in Babylon in November–December 164 BCE, before the cleansing of the Temple. The author of 1 Maccabees, however, places Antiochus's death after the Temple has been purified and after Judas and Simon have defeated neighboring peoples and brought back threatened Jews to Judah and Mt. Zion. By modeling the narrative on Joshua's conquest of the land, the author suggests that Judas and his group have cleansed the land along with the Temple. Thus Antiochus defiled both the Temple and the land, whereas Judas restored both. Then, appropriately, the persecutor dies while repenting of what he had done. Such a reward for dastardly deeds fits well with the scheme of Deuteronomy, which presumes that the good flourish but the wicked suffer (Deut 7:11). (For other accounts of Antiochus's death, see Dan 11:40-45; 2 Macc 1:13-17; 9:1-29; Polybius 31.9; Appian *Syriaca* 66.)

6:1-4. The author uses exactly the same language as at 3:37 to describe Antiochus's journey to the eastern satrapies, and so he sees this section as a fitting conclusion to the events narrated in between. Elymais (Elam) was properly the mountainous country west of Persia. The temple attacked by Antiochus was that of Artemis/Aphrodite/Nanaia. Strabo narrates how Mithradates I of Parthia (175–138 BCE) later attacked this same temple.[75] Nowhere else is it mentioned that Alexander visited this temple of Artemis. He would not simply have left weapons behind, but would have dedicated them to the goddess. Whereas Alexander is shown to be respectful of this temple and Artemis worship, Antiochus is disdainful. A battle need not have taken place, since the citizens' readiness to fight may have caused a retreat, just as Gorgias retreated (4:21-22).

6:5-7. Before reaching Babylon, Antiochus receives reports that Judas has undone his design. The message is a summary of 1 Maccabees 3–4. The phrase "been routed" recalls the defeat of the army led by Ptolemy, Nicanor, and Gorgias (4:1-25). Lysias's campaign (3:28-35) is mentioned; the "plunder" that Judas captured is recalled (3:12; 4:23). The strength of the Jewish army reminds the reader that Judas's forces had grown from 3,000 (4:6) to more than 11,000 (5:20). The phrase "torn down the abomination" recalls the purification of the Temple (4:43-47; the rebuilding of the fortification was described at 4:60-61). In effect, all of Antiochus's plans have been thwarted.

6:8-13. Antiochus's reaction to news from Judea has changed from anger (3:27) to perplexity and discouragement (4:27) and now to astonishment and fear (6:8). The author of 1 Maccabees, since his map of the world centers on Judea, views Antiochus IV's death as caused by his failure in Judea. While the Jews rejoice (4:58; 5:54), Antiochus lies in distress, finally realizing that he is dying (v. 9).

Unlike Mattathias's last words, which looked to the future (2:49-68), Antiochus's last words are repentance of past deeds. Antiochus's reflections on the complete reversal of his fortunes use images like those in Psalm 42 (1 Macc 6:11), a prayer for help. Antiochus was in fact a benefactor through his building projects and support of traditional customs in other parts of his empire and the Mediterranean world. His policy toward Judea was an aberration of his normal behavior.

The repentance ascribed to Antiochus IV (vv. 12-13) is similar to that ascribed to the wicked Judean king Manasseh in the Prayer of Manasseh, an apocryphal composition from around the first century BCE. Manasseh, portrayed in the Bible as the most wicked king of Judah (2 Kgs 21:1-18), is said to have repented of his sins while in exile and to have composed a prayer of entreaty (see 2 Chr 33:18-19, even though 2 Chronicles does not provide the prayer). The present apocryphal prayer fills that gap. Antiochus is seen to repent of his misdeeds (1:20-28; 3:35).

---
75. Strabo 16.1.18.

He is said to die in a "strange land." Persia did lie in his own kingdom, but the author stresses the pathos of his death: To die away from one's homeland and one's ancestors was to be cut off from a proper resting place. (A similar fate befalls the high priest Jason in 2 Macc 5:9-10.)

6:14-17. In contrast to the description of Alexander's properly providing for his succession by dividing his kingdom (1:6), Antiochus is described as leaving behind a mess. He names Philip as ruler of the kingdom and guardian of his son without any mention that he had appointed Lysias over half his kingdom and as guardian (3:32-33) and had left him half the forces. The following division within the kingdom is therefore placed at Antiochus's feet. The author seems unaware that Antiochus's son was already co-regent and suggests rather that Lysias's action in elevating him to rule is improper.

The date given for Antiochus's death, the 149th year (163 BCE), is wrong according to the Babylonian reckoning of the Seleucid era, which counted from March–April 311 BCE and according to which Antiochus IV died in the year 148. If the Seleucid era is reckoned according to a Macedonian form that began in September–October 312 BCE, Antiochus would have died in the year 149. Scholars have suggested, therefore, that dates for events of royal Seleucid history are given in 1 Maccabees according to the Macedonian form of the Seleucid era.

REFLECTIONS

Antiochus IV is described as having died bitter and disappointed. The author of 1 Maccabees states that Antiochus had thought on a grand scale of uniting all his kingdom as one people, all having the same customs (1 Macc 1:41-42). It was a plan on the magnitude of Napoleon's or Hitler's or of the uniting of European nations under one command. But such a vision of unity was ultimately a vision of uniformity, achieved at the expense of diversity and freedom. Yet one must also recognize the value of striving for unity, of seeking to avoid the conflicts and tensions that arise out of difference. Diversity also carries responsibility, the need to respect the values and traditions of others, the need not to strive to homogenize everything or to maintain that everything and everybody who does not agree with you is wrong. Unity that respects diversity is a worthwhile goal, but one hard to keep in sight. A start can be made by fighting not to be led, or rather misled, by stereotypes.

1 MACCABEES 6:18-63, ATTACKS UNDER ANTIOCHUS V EUPATOR

OVERVIEW

The death of Antiochus IV did not bring any respite, according to the author of 1 Maccabees, from attacks from the Seleucids. The letter preserved at 2 Macc 11:22-26, if written at the accession of Antiochus V, would suggest that amnesty was granted at the death of Antiochus IV. The author of 1 Maccabees allows for no such respite, however. The Hasmoneans are depicted as pursuing their goal of winning independence from the Seleucid monarch.

1 Maccabees 6:18-31, The Pre-Invasion Events

COMMENTARY

6:18. The citadel remains under enemy control, manned primarily by the Seleucid garrison. They continue to harass the Jews in the temple area (cf. 4:60-61) and are involved in other actions aimed at defeating the Hasmoneans.

6:19-20. The Gentiles round about had determined to destroy the race of Jacob in their midst (5:1-2), and likewise Judas resolves to destroy the Gentile group within Judea. The author emphasizes the community aspect of the assembly—all the people (i.e., the true Israelites) are gathered to participate in the siege. The siege probably began in spring 162 BCE, "in the one hundred fiftieth year," according to the Babylonian reckoning of the Seleucid era, which the Jews used to date their annual events; this year spanned April 162 BCE to March 161 BCE. The "siege towers," possibly a stage for artillery machines, may have been spoils from earlier victories.

6:21-27. The siege prompts a delegation to the new king. The "ungodly Israelites" are the opposite of those who had joined Mattathias (3:2) and like those who accompanied Seron. Note that no names are given; they are simply categorized as the godless. The author of 1 Maccabees opens the speech of the ungodly like a complaint found often in the psalms: "How long will you fail to do justice and to avenge our kindred?" (v. 22; cf. Pss 13:1-2; 74:10; 94:3). The speech contains phrases used earlier to describe this group (1:43-44). The godless are said to follow "strange" (ἀλλότριος *allotrios*) customs (1:44); those who were "found" (εὑρίσκω *heuriskō*) not doing so were "put to death" (ἀποθνήσκω *apothnēskō*; 1:50, 57). Now they complain that their countrymen "have become hostile" (lit., "were estranged" from us), that they "have put to death" as many as they "have caught" (lit., "found"). In this context, these Jews complain that they, who followed strange customs, have been turned into strangers and what they had done to Jews who kept the tradition is now being done to them. They have lost their inheritance because they have become strangers/foreigners/aliens.

Verses 25-26 provide a summary of the events described in chapter 5, wherein the forces under Judas are seen as moving outside the territorial limits of Judea and attacking forces in Idumea, Galilee, and Gilead. What is justified in 1 Maccabees 5 as a defensive measure to protect oppressed Jews is described by their enemies as offensive warfare; the fortifying of Beth-zur and Mt. Zion (4:60-61) is seen as preparation for battle. The difference in perception shows how actions can be misinterpreted, particularly when there is suspicion, and lead to the breakdown of any negotiations. Verse 27 is a prophecy of what will happen under Simon, who will establish control over Joppa, extend the borders of his nation, and gain control of the citadel and evict those who dwell within it (13:11, 43-50; 14:5-6).

6:28-31. Antiochus V Eupator was actually only about eleven years old at this time, and Lysias remained in control. The author repeats the language describing Antiochus IV (3:27) to hint at the troubles to come. The size of the army assembled is enormous—larger than was possible for the Seleucid army. The exaggerated size of this army highlights the seriousness with which Judas is now being taken and the increased danger to Judas's army. The army takes the same southern route that Lysias had taken previously (4:29). The "engines of war" (see 6:20) are siege devices. According to this account, Beth-zur will not be captured until after the battle of Beth-zechariah (vv. 49-50). It is unlikely, however, that the Seleucids would have marched toward Jerusalem and left a fortified city at their rear to harass them. (Indeed, 2 Macc 13:18-25 describes a series of battles at Beth-zur, but no attack on Jerusalem.)

1 Maccabees 6:32-47, The Battle at Beth-zechariah

COMMENTARY

6:32-39. Judas encamps his troops at Beth-zechariah, about six miles north of Beth-zur. Lysias thus marches his army out to meet them (vv. 33); the author provides a vivid description of their march (vv. 35-39). The war elephant was the centerpoint for each formation, its flanks defended by one thousand infantry, with five hundred cavalry protecting the infantry. Each formation/phalanx thus operated independently (v. 36); the role of the cavalry was to protect the phalanxes (v. 38). The infantries' armor and shields provide a blazing sight (v. 39).[76]

6:40-42. As the valley narrowed, troops had to be assigned to secure the ridges. The orderly advance ensures that no gaps would appear in the phalanx that could be exploited. In spite of the impressive appearance of Lysias's army, Judas and his army attack (v. 42), killing six hundred Seleucid soldiers. Those who fall are probably the advance group whose role would be to locate ambushes.[77]

6:43-46. Judas's brother Eleazar (see 2:5), in an act of bravery, kills the royal elephant; it is highly unlikely that a Seleucid king would be riding on the elephant. Eleazar, like Judas himself (3:6; 9:21), dies to save his people and wins proper fame, as contrasted to Joseph and Azariah (5:57). Eleazar's action reflects the ideal warrior, the virtue of self-sacrifice for the cause.[78]

6:47. The author does not state outright that Judas was defeated, but only that the Jews "turned away" (ἐκκλίνω *ekklinō*) in flight. The same Greek verb is used in Num 20:21 LXX to describe how Israel turned away from Edom when the Edomites, refusing to give the Israelites passage through the land, confront them heavily armed. The same verb is found also at Deut 20:3, where the Israelites are exhorted not to turn away from their enemies. This strategic withdrawal, where discretion is the better part of valor, perhaps intimates that the main body of the Seleucid army was not engaged. (In 2 Macc 13:22, Judas wins a victory over Lysias.)

---

76. Polybius notes that armies used to polish their arms to cause apprehension. See Polybius 11.9.1-2.
77. See Josephus *Antiquities of the Jews* 12.372.
78. Such heroism is exemplified in the classics by the stand of Leonidas and the Spartans at Marathon to hold back the Persian forces. See Herodotus 7.207-228.

1 Maccabees 6:48-54, The Siege of Jerusalem

COMMENTARY

The king now starts to undo what Judas had accomplished (see 4:60-61): He captures Beth-zur and besieges Jerusalem; the terms used for the siege devices are the same as for those Judas had used against the citadel (6:20).

Because of the "sabbatical year," when the land was not worked (Exod 23:11; Lev 25:3-7), the Jews had not been able to set aside enough provisions and thus are unable to withstand the siege (vv. 49, 53). Such food shortages most likely occurred in the year following the sabbatical year. Moreover, the refugees brought from Galilee and Gilead (5:23, 54) had helped to deplete the supplies before the new harvest after the sabbatical year could be gathered in. This section ends with a traditional way of breaking off after a battle (cf. Judg 9:55; 1 Sam 26:25).

1 Maccabees 6:55-63, The End of the Assault by Antiochus V Eupator

COMMENTARY

6:55-57. The confusion that the author had seen as being brought on by the death of Antiochus IV (1 Macc 6:14-17) now begins to manifest itself as a power struggle between Antiochus IV's generals. Whereas the author has been emphasizing that the Jews had no provisions (6:49-53), suddenly Lysias claims that the reason for pulling out is that the Seleucid army is low on food. Perhaps the sabbatical year had affected the besiegers' ability to find provisions for the large army locally. Lysias does not explicitly refer to the advance of Philip, but his listeners must have known even from the vague phrasing that something important was afoot. Josephus specifies that Lysias's speech, given by order of the king, intentionally misrepresents the true reason for their withdrawal.[79]

6:58-59. The expression "let us come to terms" (δῶμεν δεξιάς *dōmen dexias*) is literally, "give the right [i.e., good] hand." This is the first mention of peace negotiations in 1 Maccabees. From the correspondence collected in 2 Macc 11:16-38 (particularly vv. 27-32), one can deduce that peace negotiations had already been initiated during the reign of Antiochus IV. No mention is made of these overtures in 1 Maccabees, however, possibly because they involved Jewish groups other than the Maccabees. For the author of 1 Maccabees, only the Maccabees count as Jews; other groups are either naive (1 Macc 7:12-18) or part of the "godless." Lysias seeks to reverse the decrees of Antiochus IV (1:41, 44).

6:60-63. Lysias's proposal pleases the king, who guarantees it with an oath (cf. 8:21), but who then proceeds to break this sacred promise once the Jews have evacuated the temple mount. The Seleucids have already been depicted as deceitful (1:30), and the narrative will continue to show them to be untrustworthy (7:10-18, 27; 11:2). The wall Judas Maccabeus had built around the sanctuary (4:60) was destroyed, but there is no mention that the temple service restored by Judas was interfered with. Lysias returns home and defeats Philip.[80]

---

79. Josephus *Antiquities of the Jews* 12.379-381.

80. 2 Macc 9:29 states that Philip fled to Egypt, but Josephus (*Antiquities of the Jews* 12.386) holds that Philip was captured and put to death by Eupator.

REFLECTIONS

The Seleucids are shown as finally being forced to negotiate with the Hasmoneans when news reached them that they were under threat from another quarter. The advice of Lysias to come to terms and let the Jews live under their own laws is good advice. However, the Seleucids feel that they are in a position of strength and so are not bound by the negotiated terms. We must reflect on how each of us is bound by contracts made, and how we too should feel bound to honor such contracts, which have been negotiated in good faith, even if later conditions change. Should not a company honor the retirement benefits it has promised to its employees? Are not employees required to give an honest day's work for an honest day's pay? Negotiations have to be entered into in good faith, and once completed must be respected.

1 MACCABEES 7:1-25, THE EXPEDITION OF BACCHIDES AND ALCIMUS

OVERVIEW

This section is held together by certain repetitions of phrases and plays on words that are important to note. Alcimus and others bring charges against the people (v. 6), and Alcimus returns to the king and brings charges against Judas and his followers (v. 25). When Alcimus is commanded to take "vengeance" (ἐκδίκησις *ekdikēsis*) on the sons of Israel (v. 9), the group of scribes "seek just peace terms" (v. 12; ἐκζητῆσαι δίκαια *ekzētēsai dikaia*), and the Hasideans, first among the sons of Israel, say that Alcimus "will not harm" (οὐκ ἀδικήσει *ouk adikēsei*) the people (v. 14). Alcimus swears that he "will not seek evil" (οὐκ ἐκζητήσομεν κακόν *ouk ekzētēsomen kakon*, v. 15). The execution of the Hasideans is thus the first step in the fulfillment of the king's command and is followed by other damage on the sons of Israel (v. 23). In response, Judas takes vengeance on those who had deserted him (v. 24). This section is thus a unity.

1 Maccabees 7:1-7, The New King, Demetrius

COMMENTARY

7:1. Demetrius I Soter, the son of Seleucus IV and nephew of Antiochus IV Epiphanes, had been a hostage at Rome under the terms of the Treaty of Apamea. When he perceived the crisis in leadership after the death of Antiochus IV, he asked permission of the Roman senate to return. When permission was not granted, he slipped out of Rome with the help of the historian Polybius.[81] He landed at Tripolis in 162 BCE (2 Macc 14:1-2). In Syria, he apparently won the support of the army and settlers as a legitimate member of the Seleucid family over Lysias, regent to the young Antiochus V. The Roman senate did not at first recognize Demetrius, and it kept up contact with rebellious elements in the Seleucid Empire. Timarchus, the satrap of Babylonia, and his brother Heraclides, satrap of Media, did not recognize Demetrius; Ptolemaus, satrap of Commegene, also led a revolt. Timarchus was not defeated until late 161 or early 160 BCE. It is within this context of Demetrius's attempt to gain control over a fragmenting Seleucid Empire that one must place the events of chapter 7.

7:2-4. Having taken control of the country, Demetrius marches on the royal palace at Antioch, 170 miles north of Tripolis. By executing Antiochus and Lysias, Demetrius consolidated his position, as Solomon had done when he came to power and had a rival son of David executed (1 Kgs 2:12-46).

7:5. As frequently in 1 Maccabees, trouble comes to the Jews from within their own ranks (1:1; 6:21; 9:23, 38), although later on these groups have no effect on the king (10:61; 11:21-25). So far in the narrative, the role of the high priest has not been an issue (as it will be in 2 Maccabees 4–5), although we have learned that Mattathias and his family are priests (2:1), that some priests fought unwisely (5:67), and that Judas chose blameless priests who cleansed the sanctuary and restored sacrifice (4:42-53). According to the narrative, proper temple worship had been in place since then; therefore, there must have been a high priest in place to celebrate the annual feast of Yom Kippur, although that high priest is not named. According to 1 Maccabees, Alcimus is appointed high priest by Demetrius I; at his death in 159 BCE, no mention is made of his replacement until the appointment of Jonathan in 152 BCE. Many more high priests are named

---

81. Polybius 31.11-15.

in 2 Maccabees: Jason, 175–172 BCE; Menelaus, 172–163 BCE; Alcimus, possibly from 163 BCE. The writer of 2 Maccabees also reports that Alcimus was already high priest before the time of Demetrius I Soter (2 Macc 14:3), whereas the writer of 1 Maccabees claims that Alcimus went to Demetrius requesting to be high priest (1 Macc 7:5). As the high priest seems to have been appointed by the king and required reappointment by a new king (2 Macc 4:7-10, 24), the contradiction may be more apparent than real. However, the question remains as to who carried out the duties of high priest in the Temple restored by Judas.

7:6-7. The delegation's complaint is similar to the one voiced to Antiochus earlier (6:22-27). The word used here for "ruin" (ἐξολεθρεύω *exolethreuō*) is from the same root used at 3:8 to describe how Judas had "destroyed" the ungodly out of the land.

1 Maccabees 7:8-20, The Incursion of Bacchides

COMMENTARY

7:8-11. Just as Lysias chose Ptolemy to lead an expedition against Judas (3:38), so also Demetrius chooses Bacchides, governor of the Trans-Euphrates province, between the Euphrates and Egypt. It is not clear whether this expedition was prior to or concomitant with Demetrius's move against Timarchus, who invaded Mesopotamia and planned to cross the Euphrates and invade Syria. The text as it stands suggests that Alcimus is commanded to take vengeance. The primary purpose of the expedition, however, seems to be to establish Alcimus's religious and political authority as high priest (v. 20). The action seems to take place in Jerusalem (see 7:19).

Like the chief of the Mysians (1:29-30), Bacchides speaks deceitfully, but Judas is wary of capture (7:10-11).

7:12-18, The Hasideans. 7:12. Unlike Judas, some Israelites are convinced by Bacchides's overtures. The term translated "scribe" (γραμματεῖς *grammateis*) is found only once elsewhere in 1 Maccabees (5:42) and is there translated "officers," following the usage of the Pentateuch when referring to commanders of the army and public officials (see Num 11:16; Deut 20:5, 8-9; Josh 1:2; 8:33; 23:2; 24:1). In this context of negotiations for just terms, this is probably the proper nuance here as well. As opposed to its English denotation of a scribe's being a writer or intellectual, the term "scribe" used in this context should be seen as connoting a leader of the community, a role that would not exclude fighting.

7:13-14. The translation of v. 13 should read: "The Hasideans were the first [or leaders] among the sons of Israel, and they were seeking peace from them." The Hasideans are described in 2:42 as mighty warriors and a group who gathered with Judas, using language similar to that describing the group of scribes/officers who gathered with Alcimus and Bacchides. The Hasideans are leading members of the Israelite community who trust the words of Alcimus. There is thus presented a difference of opinion between Judas and the Hasideans over what strategy to employ. Judas's stance, for the author of 1 Maccabees, is one of uncompromising hostility toward the Seleucids, whereas the Hasideans believe that accommodation can be made. What exactly were the terms the Hasideans were proposing? Given that Judas does not trust Bacchides and Alcimus because they have come with a large force (7:11), perhaps Judas and the Hasideans differed over whether an occupation army should be in the land. The Hasideans feel they can trust the peaceful words this time (in contrast to what happened in 1:30), because an Aaronide priest is negotiating with them. The author of 1 Maccabees suggests that not everyone who says he or she is a Jew, even if a priest, is to be believed, but only those who adhere to the party of Judas and his followers. The thrust of the passage, then, is less against the Hasideans than it is against Jews like Alcimus.

7:15. Alcimus speaks "peaceable words" and promises no harm to the Hasideans. Peaceable words and oaths, however, have led to trouble before. The chief of the Mysians had spoken peaceable words to the residents of Jerusalem and had then attacked them (1:30). Antiochus V had negotiated a peace treaty with the Judeans, but had then broken his oath (6:61-62).

7:16. As the reader might expect from earlier examples, Alcimus goes back on his oath, seizing and killing sixty of the Hasideans. A similar execution of Jewish leaders was carried out by the Babylonians at the fall of Jerusalem in 586 BCE (2 Kgs 25:18-21; Jer 52:24-27).

7:17. The fate of the Hasideans is said to fulfill Ps 79:2-3. Note that "faithful ones" (חסידים *ḥăsîdîm*) is the same word that the NRSV translates as "your faithful" in Ps 79:2, and so a linguistic connection is being made between the people who have been killed and the words of the psalm. The author of 1 Maccabees has therefore related the text of the Hebrew Scriptures to a contemporary event. He saw his own times as being under the guidance of God, and in this his reading of the Hebrew Scriptures is formally similar to that of the Qumran covenanters, but without a sense that he is living in the end times. Note also the similarity to the lament sung after the citadel was built in Jerusalem (1:37).

7:18. The people "fear and dread." In the book of Judith, fear and dread of Holofernes fall upon the people of the cities on the coastlands when they hear how he has destroyed the cities of Syria (Jdt 2:28). In contradistinction to God, who does all things in faithfulness and justice (Ps 111:7; Prayer of Azariah 5 [Dan 3:28 LXX]), Alcimus acts wrongly and breaks the ordinance and the oath (6:62).

7:19-20. Beth-zaith lay south between Jerusalem and Beth-zur. What Bacchides did at Beth-zaith is told very cryptically. Instead of "deserted," the Greek used here (αὐτομολέω *automoleō*; see also v. 24) should be translated, "those who made peace with him" (cf. Josh 10:1-4; 2 Sam 3:8 LXX; 2 Sam 10:19). The action of Bacchides thus duplicates that of Alcimus in breaking agreements made, as Bacchides kills those who had made peace with him. Bacchides no doubt thought that he was executing justice on war criminals, whereas the author of 1 Maccabees stresses the act's perfidy. The expression "he slaughtered them into a great pit" pre-supposes some action of throwing the corpses into a pit (cf. Jer 41:7). His job of pacification done and Alcimus installed as high priest and dependent on the king's support, Bacchides returned to the king.

REFLECTIONS

The narrative here centers on the question of trust. Whom can one trust? When does trust move over into gullibility? The Hasideans trusted the Aaronide high priest Alcimus to their doom. But their trust was misplaced; they should have learned to be more suspicious as we readers have learned to be from the author's depictions of the actions of the chief of the Mysians (1:30) and Antiochus V (6:61-62). In the United States, for instance, people have become increasingly suspicious and cynical toward their leaders, both religious and political. The exposés of the excesses of televangelists and the prosecution of some pastors and priests for sexual abuse have forced us to be more concerned and alert to signs of abuse of power. Within the political realm, the ramifications of Watergate still linger. Yet the paranoia of paramilitary groups who see their government as evil reminds us that a society cannot survive without some degree of trust among its citizens. We must be "wise as serpents and innocent as doves" (Matt 10:16 NRSV), trusting yet wary.

1 Maccabees 7:21-25, The Inability of Alcimus to Rule

COMMENTARY

7:21-23. To say that Alcimus "struggled" (ἀγωνίζομαι *agōnizomai*) to hold the high priesthood conveys the wrong nuance. It might be better to say that Alcimus fought or strove for the high priesthood. Here one begins to sense that the struggle has now become over who will have the political authority of the high priest as chief of state. The breakthrough will come when Jonathan achieves a modicum of independence (10:15-21). Alcimus is joined by "troublers of the people." In the opening hymn of praise to Judas, he is said to have burned those who troubled the people (3:5). Exactly what they did to the people is unspecified. Earlier, apostates had done evil in the land (1:52) in the context of religious persecution, but that is not mentioned here. The author tells us only that the damage done was great, using language previously applied to the captain of the Mysians (1:30), and that it exceeded the damage done by the Gentiles. The hatred characteristic of civil war can be seen here, as parties engaged in a civil war often resort to dehumanizing their opponents more than they would strangers.

7:24. The destructiveness of civil war continues as Judas now attacks those who had made peace with Bacchides and Alcimus. This group has been caught in the middle; some of its members were seen by Bacchides as war criminals, while Judas sees them as traitors to "the cause." One can perhaps sense that this group who had accepted Alcimus and submitted to the Seleucids was quite large, as Judas is reduced to guerrilla tactics and acts as Mattathias had done by going around within the borders of Judea (2:45), avoiding the cities.

7:25. As a wrestler tests the opponent's strength, so Alcimus and Judas strive with each other. The author suggests that Alcimus was losing. Although Alcimus is said to bring "malicious charges" against Judas and his followers, it is more likely that Alcimus called for reinforcements to stamp out harassment from Judas's band.

1 MACCABEES 7:26-50, THE RULE OF NICANOR

1 Maccabees 7:26-32, The Treachery of Nicanor

COMMENTARY

"Nicanor" was a fairly common name, and so this is unlikely to be the same Nicanor mentioned in 3:38, or the Nicanor who helped Demetrius flee from Rome.[82] The author of 2 Maccabees states that this Nicanor had been in charge of the Seleucid elephant force (2 Macc 14:12) and repeats the charge that Nicanor hated the Jews (14:39; however, the account in 2 Macc 14:11-36 is quite different). Nicanor's mission, "to destroy the people," is the same command given to Lysias (3:35, 39). Like Bacchides and Alcimus (7:10), Nicanor is described as having a larger force and yet first trying deceit (v. 27-28). The attempt to capture Judas is described very sensationally; Judas almost succumbs to Nicanor's treachery, but somehow learns of his plan (vv. 29-31). When the ruse fails, Nicanor tries an open assault (v. 31). The exact location of Caphar-salama is unknown, but it probably lies between Jerusalem and the Gophna Hills. Nicanor suffers a minor setback and retires to the citadel in Jerusalem (v. 32). No description of the battle is given, nor is there any indication of losses on Judas's side.

---

82. See Polybius 31.114.4; Josephus *Antiquities of the Jews* 12.402.

1 Maccabees 7:33-38, Nicanor Threatens the Temple

COMMENTARY

7:33. Nicanor now devises a new strategy and goes up to the Temple. The priests and elders come out from the temple court (which Nicanor could not enter) to greet the Seleucid commander peaceably (cf. v. 29), with no deceit in mind. Alcimus presumably was still with the king. The temple worship had included sacrifices on behalf of the ruling king from early Second Temple times (Ezra 6:10).

7:34-35. Nicanor openly shows his hostility by acting arrogantly as Antiochus IV had done on entering the sanctuary (1:21-24). The author uses the language of the psalms (Ps 44:13; 80:6) to describe how Nicanor mocks the priests, and he also notes that Nicanor defiles the priests, as Antiochus IV had ordered the sanctuary to be defiled (1:46). Nicanor's threat to destroy the Temple echoes the destruction of the First Temple (2 Kgs 25:9; 2 Chr 36:19; 1 Esdr 1:55; 4:45; 6:16).

7:36-38. The undefiled priests go into the inner court of the priests and pray. Their prayer recalls those of earlier times. When he dedicated the First Temple, Solomon had prayed that God would listen to the people whenever they turned to God (1 Kgs 8:22-53). When Jerusalem and its God were mocked by the Assyrian commander, King Hezekiah of Judea rent his clothes and sent his priests to Isaiah the prophet to ask him to pray for the people (2 Kgs 19:1-7; see also Isa 10:7-19). The author of 1 Maccabees has placed this assault of Nicanor in the context of an attack against God's Temple. As such, one knows the outcome: He will be destroyed.

1 Maccabees 7:39-50, The Death of Nicanor

COMMENTARY

7:39-40. Nicanor seems to have requested reinforcements, possibly from some troops on the coastal plain, like those of Seron (3:13). Nicanor went to meet them at the ascent of Beth-horon, the route Seron had taken to Jerusalem (3:16). Judas has 3,000 men, the same number who fought with him at the battle of Emmaus (4:6), which also took place near the Beth-horon ascent; however, this number was considerably fewer than the forces he had mustered in other campaigns (see 5:20). The exact location of Adasa is unknown, but it seems to lie near the top of the Beth-horon ascent.

7:41-42. The prayer before battle, which is ascribed to Judas, picks up on the reference in the priests' prayer to the blasphemies of Nicanor by remembering how Sennacherib's army had uttered similar blasphemies when the Assyrians besieged Jerusalem in 701 BCE (2 Kgs 18:14-35). In that encounter, the angel of the Lord is said to have struck down the Assyrians, and the king of the Assyrians, Sennacherib, is said to have died soon after (2 Kgs 19:35-37). Judas asks for the same result to be meted out to Nicanor. The author of 2 Maccabees refers to the same biblical precedent when recounting the two battles against the two Nicanors (2 Macc 8:19; 15:22).

7:43-46. The battle is not described in great detail, specifying only the date, the defeat of Nicanor's army, and the fact that the divine vengeance falls first on the blasphemer. The Seleucid soldiers fled to Gazara (cf. 4:15), the closest Seleucid fort to the west. The trumpets alerted the men in the nearby villages to block the paths of the retreating army down the steep Beth-horon descent (cf. Num 10:6; Judg 3:27). Just as the entire army of Sennacherib had been destroyed (2 Kgs 19:35; Isa 37:36), so also all of Nicanor's army is killed.

7:47. Nicanor's body is dismembered in retaliation for this blasphemy (note the more colorful description at 2 Macc 15:30-35). One might compare the treatment of the bodies of the Athenian commanders Nicias and Demosthenes. The general assembly of the Syracusans condemned them to death, and their bodies were thrown out before the gates of the city and offered for a public spectacle.[83] The treatment of this slain king recalls such incidents from Israel's past: King Saul's body was fastened to the wall of Bethshan (1 Sam 31:10); David brought Goliath's head to Jerusalem (1 Sam 17:54); Holofernes' head was hung from the parapet of Bethulia (Jdt 14:1, 11); and seven descendants of Saul were impaled at Gibeon on the mountain before the Lord (2 Sam 21:6, 9). The author of 1 Maccabees specifies that Nicanor's body is kept outside Jerusalem, so as not to defile the city.

7:48-50. The joy and festivity following the victory are similar to those at the dedication of the Temple (4:58-59). Surprisingly, the author does not mention that the Feast of Purim falls on 14 Adar. Since Adar falls around March, the battle took place either in March 161 or March 160. The account concludes with a formula known well from Judges (3:11, 30; 5:31; 8:28), which will be used again (9:57; 11:38, 52; 14:4). Although in Judges the formula speaks of the rest having lasted for many years, here it is only for a few days, because the Seleucid threat remained.

83. See Plutarch *Nicias* 27-28.

REFLECTIONS

This narrative shows how the Seleucids with their underling Alcimus tried to impose their rule by using scare tactics in killing former opponents and by threatening to wipe out the most sacred Jewish institution: the Temple in Jerusalem. Yet the narrative also shows how such methods were ineffective. When given the chance, the people rose up from their villages and pursued the enemy (7:46). When a people are determined to resist, no amount of coercion can overcome them. They may be cowed for a while, but eventually they will rise up. The collapse of the Soviet Union is a contemporary illustration of this fact. For so long, it appeared that the peoples of the Soviet Union would always be under the thumb of the Soviets. Yet, given the chance for freedom, the people took it. Times of transition are also times of uncertainty, and there have been excesses in the attempts of the former Soviet states to forge independent nations, just as one might deplore the vengeance wreaked on Nicanor by dismembering him. But this narrative reminds us that might does not make right, and until a group can be led to see that what is being proposed for them is for the good of them all there will be resistance. A minority, no matter how well-intentioned and how confirmed in their own belief that what they are doing is God's will, should not attempt to force through legislation with which the majority is not in agreement. Rather, they must debate their ideas in the open forum, in order to explain and attempt to persuade others to their views. Coercion never pays in the end.

1 MACCABEES 8:1-32, THE RELATIONSHIP WITH ROME

OVERVIEW

The formulaic phrase at the end of chapter 7 allows the author space before discussing the reaction of Demetrius to the news of Nicanor's defeat; note how 8:1 and 9:1 both begin with "And Judas/Demetrius heard. . . ." The author describes here the delegation

Judas sent to the Romans and draws a utopian picture of the Roman state. Josephus preserves the text of a letter of the consul Gaius Fannius (Roman consul in 161 BCE) on behalf of the Jewish envoys to the officials of the island of Cos.[84] Whatever the questions surrounding the exact tenor, language, and status of the letter preserved at 1 Macc 8:23-32 (Was it a treaty between equal nations, or was it diplomatic recognition by Rome of Judas and his supporters?), the author of 1 Maccabees sees it as a significant document to which he constantly refers (12:1-4; 14:16-19, 24; 15:15-24). Judea is seen as an independent nation among other nations. In this connection, it is interesting to note how the Jewish historian Eupolemus, who may be identical with the ambassador Judas sent to Rome (8:15), records letters of friendship from King Solomon to Vaphres, to the kings of Egypt, and to Souron, king of Tyre and Sidon and Phoenicia.[85] In this way, Solomon's status as equal to that of the Tyrians and the Egyptians is proclaimed. Here in 1 Maccabees, the independent status of Judea is evidenced by its ability to interact on an equal plane with other nations; one can see how the goal of the author of 1 Maccabees is the independence of Judea.

What is also striking about this discussion of the Romans is its utopian picture of them; they are generous to their friends, devastating to their foes. The Romans have been exalted, yet they are not proud (8:13-14). Their constitution is a mixture of egalitarian, aristocratic, and monarchic features. While the description of the Roman constitution in 1 Maccabees is not as detailed as that of Polybius,[86] it does contain a hint of a suggestion as to what is the best kind of government. A utopian description is, of course, also a critique of other systems. First of all, it is a critique of a monarchic form of government, such as that of the Seleucids, the inherent instability of which is shown in the dynastic infighting after the death of Antiochus IV. The description of the Romans, victorious in all their battles as was Alexander the Great, also contrasts with the puffed-up arrogance of Alexander (1:3) and Antiochus IV (1:22-24). But does this utopian description also critique the later Hasmonean rulers? Jonathan and Simon both wear purple and crowns (10:20; 14:43) and Simon is to be leader and priest forever, until a trustworthy prophet should arise (14:41), not a ruler for one year only. Simon appoints all the officials (14:42); there appears to be no group, like the Roman senate, to balance his power.

84. Josephus *Antiquities of the Jews* 14.233.
85. See Alexander Polyhistor "On the Jews," in Eusebius of Caesarea *Preparation for the Gospel* 9:31–34.1.

86. Polybius 6.11-18.

1 Maccabees 8:1-16, An Idealized Description of the Romans

COMMENTARY

8:1-2a. Timarchus, the rebel satrap of Media, had obtained a decree from the senate, recognizing him as king, by which the Romans sought to undermine the position of Demetrius I.[87] Judas is thus acting very shrewdly. One would like to know exactly how Judas came to know about the Romans—through Jews who had visited them? Through mercenaries? The book of Daniel (11:18, 29-30) shows knowledge of Roman intervention in Seleucid affairs, but

87. Diodorus Siculus 31.27a.

1 Maccabees mentions nothing of Antiochus IV's humiliation in 168 BCE at the hands of the Roman legate C. Popillius Laenas, who forced Antiochus to leave Egypt.

The Romans are described in terms of their integrity, strength, and "brave deeds." The same phrase is used to describe the actions of Judas, Jonathan, and Simon (5:56), forging a link between the Hasmoneans and the Romans.

8:2b-4a. The author puts forward first a list of the victories of the Romans, starting from the far west to the east. "The Gauls" is most probably a reference to the tribes of Cisalpine Gaul who lived in what is today northern Italy and who were subdued by Rome over a period from 200 to 180 or possibly 175 BCE. These wars against the Gauls and the Ligurians were the first major step toward the Romanization of a sizeable piece of the Italian peninsula. The Carthaginian general Hamilcar Barca had conquered much of southern and southeastern Spain in 237–229 BCE, and so Spain was to become the scene for battles between Carthage and Rome in the Punic Wars. The victory under Scipio Africanus in 206 led to the annexation of two provinces soon after. These provinces proved turbulent, but Rome continually expanded its position. War erupted again in the 150s, and resistance finally was quelled in 133 BCE. It is noteworthy that the author of 1 Maccabees says that the Romans' goal in subduing Spain was to get control of the gold and silver (v. 3); the silver mines in Spain, particularly those near Cartagena and in the Sierra Morena, made possession of this territory extremely profitable.

8:4b. The reference to kings who came against the Romans may be an imprecise description of the great Carthaginian generals Hamilcar, Hasdrubal, and Hannibal, or it may introduce the following list of rulers to the east of Rome. The Romans had imposed indemnity payments (yearly tribute) on Philip V of Macedonia, one thousand talents to be paid over ten years and of fifteen thousand talents on Antiochus III.

8:5. The Romans are said to have been attacked by aggressive kings, a statement that does not adequately account for Roman ambition and expansion.

King Philip V of Macedon (238–179 BCE) was defeated after the Second Macedonian War (200–197 BCE) by the Roman consul Flaminius at Cynoscephalae in Thessaly. Perseus, son of Philip and king of Macedonia (179–168 BCE), fought the Third Macedonian War (171–168 BCE) but was defeated by the Roman consul Aemilius Paullus at Pydna in 168 BCE. The author of 1 Maccabees magnifies the exploits of the Romans by suggesting that other rulers on the same scale as Philip and Perseus had come against Rome in the past and had been defeated as well.

8:6-8. The author next moves closer to home by recounting the Romans' victory over Antiochus III, father of Antiochus IV, whose Seleucid kingdom was called Asia. Named "the Great" because, like Alexander, he had made incursions into India and Arabia, Antiochus III recovered the coastal territories of Asia Minor in 197/96 BCE. In 196 BCE, he crossed over to Thrace, bringing him into conflict with the Romans. In the ensuing war, he was defeated in 190 BCE at Magnesia ad Sipylum, just north of Smyrna in Asia Minor. The Romans did not take Antiochus III prisoner; instead by the Treaty of Apamea in 188 BCE he had to pay a high indemnity and evacuate all territory north and west of the Taurus Mountains. Much of this territory was incorporated into the kingdom of Eumenes II of Pergamum. The treaty required twenty hostages between the ages of eighteen and forty-five, and the future Antiochus IV was one of them. After the peace of Apamea, the Seleucids no longer had the possibility of acquiring major influence in western Asia Minor or in Europe. Their empire still stretched from the Taurus Mountains to eastern Iran, but they no longer had control in India or in the Greek state of Bactria. In his expedition to the east (212–208 BCE), Antiochus III regained the formal recognition of Seleucid supremacy by the Parthian ruler Arsaces II,[88] but Parthia remained fairly independent. Antiochus III also seems to have restored Seleucid administration in Media. The author of 1 Maccabees is, therefore, incorrect in speaking of Antiochus III's giving up of India, Media, and Lydia; in fact, he gave up all pretensions to Lydia. India was not his to give, and he maintained control of Media. Perhaps the author is referring to the general fact that the enormous Seleucid Empire was difficult to control and frequently on the verge of losing territory.

8:9-10. The war of the Achaean league with Sparta in 146 led to war with Rome; the Achaeans were defeated by the Roman consul Lucius Mummius that same year, and democracy ceased to be the accepted form of government. In particular, Corinth was completely destroyed, and Mummius auctioned the women and children into slavery, broke down the walls, and confiscated the armaments of any city that had fought against

---

88. See Polybius 10.27-31.

Rome. Pausanias, writing in the second century CE, mentions that even in his day the Romans still sent out a governor of Achaia.[89] Thus the description by the author of 1 Maccabees is generally correct, but quite anachronistic for the time of Judas.

8:11-13. The author here gives a summary statement concerning the Romans: Those who oppose them are defeated; those who are friends are protected. As such, the reference could be to Carthage and the islands taken from it as well as to the Greek islands. The universal scope of Rome's domination is emphasized.

8:14-15. In Rome during this period, only victorious generals were allowed to wear a diadem and purple-colored clothing, which were royal prerogatives, during triumphal celebrations. Senators wore a broad purple upright stripe stitched to or woven into the fabric of their tunics.

The number of senators was about 300 until Sulla in 81 BCE doubled the number. It is not known where the author got the number 320—by adding the magistrates to the 300 senators, or possibly an analogy to the Jewish Sanhedrin.[90] The senate did not meet daily but only when summoned by the magistrates.

8:16. Usually, there were two consuls, and only in an emergency would a single dictator be appointed. It has been suggested that the author of 1 Maccabees concluded that there was only one consul because sometimes only one magistrate's name was mentioned in documents (see, e.g., 1 Macc 15:16). The author has put forward an idealized mixed blend of aristocracy and monarchy. The claim that there was no envy or jealousy among the Romans neglects the competition among leading families, the legislation passed in 181 BCE against bribery in elections, and the numerous prosecutions of leading figures.

89. Pausanias 7.16.5-6.

90. See *t. Sanh.* 7:1; *Sanh.* 88b. Little is known about the second-century BCE Sanhedrin, except that it existed. See 2 Macc 1:10; 4:44; 11:27. See also Josephus *Antiquities of the Jews* 12.138.

1 Maccabees 8:17-32, The Exchange of Letters

COMMENTARY

8:17-20. As he had done before (4:42), Judas takes the initiative. Eupolemus, from the priestly clan of Hakkoz (1 Chr 24:10), was the son of the man who had won concessions from Antiochus III (2 Macc 4:10); it is possible to identify him with the Eupolemus who wrote in Greek "On the Kings of Judea," fragments of which survive. Nothing is known about Jason, son of Eleazar. It is noteworthy that both have Greek names.

"The yoke" (ζυγός *zygos*) was a frequent metaphor for servitude and slavery (see Gen 27:40; Lev 26:13; Isa 9:4; 10:27; 14:5, 25, 29; Ezek 34:27). In the ceremony of the red heifer, the heifer must never have been used for profane work—i.e., have been under a master—before being used in the ritual (Num 19:2). Thus Judas asks not to be enslaved but to be a friend of the Romans (8:11-12). The Roman historian Livy recounts that at the end of Rome's war with Perseus "the Macedonians and Illyrians were to be free, so that it might appear to all peoples that the arms of the Roman people do not bring servitude to freemen but rather freedom to slaves."[91]

The ambassadors open their address by referring to the "people" (πλῆθος *plēthos*) of the Jews, rather than to the "nation" (ἔθνος *ethnos*; cf. 8:23; 12:3) or "people" (δῆμος *dēmos*; see 1 Macc 8:29). *Plēthos* sometimes translates the Hebrew "congregation" (קהל *qāhāl*; see Exod 12:6; 2 Chr 31:18), but one should note how it had just been used in 8:15 to refer to the Roman people.

8:21-22. The Romans had not yet recognized Demetrius I as king and may have been glad to further embarrass him. Only a very general statement of Roman agreement is made. There is no mention of an execration or oath, which would have been a necessary part of a formal treaty. No doubt the original document was inscribed on bronze tablets and kept at Rome. Verses 31-32 suggest that this is a letter that is being copied, although

91. Livy 45.18.1.

the full form of a letter is not present. The copy was presumably written in Latin or Greek, translated into Hebrew in the first edition of 1 Maccabees, and then translated into Greek for the extant text of 1 Maccabees. One should not expect to be able to reconstruct the exact wording of the document.

8:23-30. After the introductory wish for well-being come parallel clauses requiring that each come to the aid of the other, although the clause "as the occasion may indicate" (vv. 25, 27) allows for a wide range of interpretation. The phrase "without receiving any return" (v. 26; lit., "taking nothing") parallels "without deceit" (v. 28) and probably should be understood to mean "not accepting any bribes." Any changes had to have the consent of both parties.

8:31-32. The letter concludes by quoting another letter of the Romans to Demetrius I; the imagery is similar to that of 2 Chr 10:10-14. The Romans never followed up on the threat. Did events move too rapidly for them? Or did they use the loophole provided by the condition "as the occasion may indicate"? Whenever the senate decided that Rome could exploit a situation to its own advantage, the senate would act. Roman policy was guided by political considerations, rather than by questions of law and morality, as, for example, the Seleucids found out when the Romans unilaterally added to the Treaty of Apamea that the Seleucids could not make war on Egypt. Finally, whatever the Maccabees might have thought, the relationship they had forged with the Romans was most probably not a treaty between equals.[92] After defeating the king of Macedonia and the Seleucid king, the Romans became the dominant power in the world. Rome most likely granted the Maccabees a friendship pact, which gave Judah the appearance of being protected by Rome but did not necessarily mean that the Romans would indeed intervene to protect nations subject to other kings—although such a pact could provide the pretext for going to war with those kings. In fact, such a friendship pact was *de facto* an acknowledgment of Roman suzerainty.

Nevertheless, the author of 1 Maccabees sees this document as a major step toward independence from the Seleucids and keeps referring to it (12:1, 3-4; 14:18, 24).

---

92. S. Mandell, "Did the Maccabees Believe That They Had a Valid Treaty with Rome?" *CBQ* 53 (1991) 202-20.

REFLECTIONS

To someone who knows the future relations between Rome and Judea, this chapter is particularly poignant and ironic. That reader knows that the Romans took control of Judea under Pompey the Great in 63 BCE and—after the failure of Herod the Great's son Archelaus in 6 CE—ruled Judea as a province. The Jews revolted against the Romans twice, first in the great revolt of 66–73 CE and then in the revolt of Bar Kochba in 132–135 CE. Both times they were defeated and crushed. In the first revolt, the Temple in Jerusalem was burned and destroyed and not rebuilt. This destruction of the Temple led to a major restructuring of Jewish life and traditions, for the Temple had been where God had met the people and where the sacrifices commanded in Leviticus had been performed. No longer would those sacrifices be offered to God.

No doubt the Roman juggernaut would eventually have taken control of the Near East. One can see in the subsequent history of the Seleucid monarchs how Rome meddled in order to gain advantage. This early attempt by the Jews to gain the support of this powerful backer was advantageous in the short term, but disastrous for the long haul. If one allies oneself with a stronger partner, will such a move eventually lead to some loss of one's own independence? What compromises and concessions might one have to make in order to stay in union with such a partner? But if one does not have powerful allies, will one's independence be lost anyway? These questions beset the countries of Europe as they inched their way toward the creation of the European Economic Community, but they are also part and parcel of ordinary federal and local economic issues. Will a merger of school districts mean the loss of control over curricular issues? Will a business merger take someone out of the decision-making process? Yet, if one does not merge, can one have a viable school offering a sophisticated curriculum, or a business that can really compete? The old adage that there is unity in diversity should be kept in mind. Strength comes through acknowledging the diverse talents that each person, each community, and each nation brings. It is when unity means conformity that strength fails.

1 MACCABEES 9:1-22, THE DEATH OF JUDAS

COMMENTARY

Chapter 9 centers on the second expedition of Bacchides to Judea. It opens with Demetrius sending Bacchides and Alcimus a second time, and ends with Bacchides deciding not to come again (v. 72). In between come the deaths of Judas and Alcimus and the rise of Jonathan, who will combine in himself their positions as leader and high priest. At the beginning of the chapter, Judas and his followers are in control of Jerusalem, except for the citadel; at the end, Jonathan is in Michmash.

9:1. Bacchides and Alcimus were first sent to Judah shortly after Demetrius had come to power (1 Macc 7:5-25). Alcimus must have remained at the court of Demetrius during the governorship of Nicanor.

"The right wing" (δεξιὸν κέρας *dexion keras*; lit., "the right horn") in battle formation refers to the right flank of the army (9:12). We cannot be exactly sure what it refers to here. Metaphorically, it could mean the strongest part of the army. In 161 or 160 BCE, Demetrius had defeated Timarchus, the rebellious satrap of Media, and so was free to move against Judas.

9:2. The geography of this verse is difficult to reconstruct. As written, the Seleucid army is encamped at a town called Mesaloth in Arbela, but scholars have suggested that "Mesaloth" is a misunderstanding of the Hebrew word for "public roads" (מסלות *měsillôt*). Bacchides would thus have camped at a crossroad. Arbela was identified by Josephus with Arbela in Galilee, and some scholars have followed him and consequently emended "Gilgal" to "Galilee."[93]

Other scholars have wondered why Bacchides would carry out a campaign in Galilee, from which the Jews had been evacuated (5:23), when his object was Judas and his force in the Judean hills. Thus Bar-Kochva has suggested that "Arbela" should be corrected to "Mount Beth El" (הר בית־אל *har bêt-'ēl*), the high plateau north of Ramallah, and the "Gilgal" refers to the road that ran from the ancient Gilgal near Jericho to a small village, Beth ha-Gilgal, on the mountain plateau.[94] Bacchides would thus have tried a new tactical approach, coming neither from the west as Seron (3:16), Ptolemy, Nicanor, and Gorgias had done (3:40), nor from the south like Lysias (4:29; 6:31), but from the east.

9:3-4. On the Seleucid Babylonian calendar, the date of this campaign would be April/May 160 BCE. Bacchides is advancing from the north toward Jerusalem. Berea is most likely to be identified with a small town about ten miles north of Jerusalem, near Ramallah.

9:5-6. Elasa most probably should be identified with Il'asa, southwest of Al Bira and about half a mile distant from it. Three thousand is the number of men Judas had against Gorgias (4:6) and Nicanor (7:40). Those who were too frightened to go into battle were supposed to have left the army already, according to regulations (see Deut 20:8), but these soldiers are terrified by the "huge number of the enemy forces," and they desert the camp, dropping off like leaves. The same verb, "drop," is used at Isa 64:5 in a confession of sin: "We have all withered like leaves,/ and our guilt carries us away like the wind" (NAB). It is also used at Deut 28:40 as

---

93. Josephus *Antiquities of the Jews* 12.421.

94. Bar-Kochva, *Judas Maccabeus*, 382-84. His suggestion seems more likely than others.

an image of what will happen to an unfaithful people: "You shall have olive trees throughout all your territory, but you shall not anoint yourself with the oil, for your olives shall drop off" (NRSV). Judas's army was reduced to the number of men that he had had in the battle against Seron (3:24): eight hundred men.

9:7-10. The author of 1 Maccabees begins to forecast the outcome of the battle. The word so often used in 1 Maccabees to depict the defeat of enemies (3:23; 4:14, 36; 5:7, 21, 43; 7:43) is now used to say that Judas is "crushed" (συντρίβω *syntribō*) in his heart, and the language of exhortation, "Do not lose heart" (Deut 20:3 NRSV), is reversed here as Judas is feeling shaken (v. 8). It is interesting to compare the confident tone of Judas's earlier speeches. In earlier battles, his supporters had also complained of the scarcity of soldiers, but Judas had stressed that size had nothing to do with victory (3:17-22). Judas also had insisted it was better to die than to see misfortune, but that everything depended on God's will (3:59-60). Even though he had retreated before, as after the battle of Bethzechariah (6:47, 54), now Judas follows the heroic ideal: death with glory rather than life without it. The phrase "if our time has come" resonates with the lament of someone feeling without hope: "Our time has come, our days are filled up, our time is at hand" (Lam 4:18 LXX). It also is attuned with Gen 6:13 LXX: "The time of every human has come before me, for the earth is filled with injustice by them, and behold, I will destroy them and the earth." Thus the phrase foretells the end; no mention of help from heaven is made, for the author knows none will come.

9:11-13. The cavalry takes position on the two wings, while the "slingers and archers" skirmish ahead of the phalanx formation in two parts. The author mentions the length of the battle to stress the bravery of the doomed Israelites.

9:14-18. The Seleucid phalanx had moved forward first to engage the Jewish infantry and would have carried the day, so Judas was forced to attempt an assault on the position where he assumed Bacchides would be and perhaps win the day by killing the enemy commander. The author of 1 Maccabees states that the right wing of the Seleucid army is crushed, but Bacchides seems to have strategically withdrawn so that Judas and his cavalry could be caught in the pincer movement. They retreat as far as "Mount Azotus." Mount Azotus is unknown, and the city of Azotos/Ashdod is in the coastal plain. Scholars have suggested that the Greek translator read אשדוד (*'ašdôd*) rather than אשדות (*'ăšēdôt*), meaning "slopes." The slopes of the mountain could then refer to the area around Beth El. The Seleucid left wing follows after Judas. No explicit mention is made of Bacchides and the right wing's turning about, but Judas now seems to be caught in between. The author notes how, after desperate fighting, Judas himself falls, as befits a warrior. At the loss of their commander, the rest of the Jewish army flee.

9:19-22. Since the Jews had dismembered Nicanor's body (7:47), it is unlikely the Seleucid forces would have magnanimously allowed Judas's brothers to collect his body. However, the author provides no details of a fight over his body. Josephus speaks of a truce, but this does not seem based on reliable information.[95] It is also unclear how Jonathan and Simon would have been able to provide a proper burial without any interference from the now victorious Seleucid forces. The author, however, stresses the continuity of generations: Jonathan and Simon, Judas's successors, are described burying him using a phrase similar to that which was used when Mattathias was buried (2:70) and which will be used of Jonathan (13:25-27). "Buried in the tomb of one's ancestors" is a phrase similar to ones used of Jacob (Gen 47:30), of Gideon (Judg 8:32), and of Samson (Judg 16:31). Judas is shown not to have been dishonored, as Saul had been (1 Sam 31:8-10), for to be buried away from one's ancestral land was a cause for shame (1 Kgs 13:22). Just as Mattathias had been mourned (2:70), so also is his son. The dirge to Judas resembles the one intoned over Saul and his son Jonathan (2 Sam 1:19, 25, 27), and resonates with the paean to Judas at the beginning of his career, where it is said that deliverance prospered through him (3:6). All Israel is said to grieve, emphasizing the significance of Judas's role for the nation, although not all Jews mourned his passing. On v. 22, scholars have pointed to the formula found often

---

95. Josephus *Antiquities of the Jews* 12.432.

in the books of Kings: "Now the rest of the acts of Solomon, all that he did as well as his wisdom, are they not written in the Book of the Acts of Solomon?" (1 Kgs 11:41 NRSV). Scholars have debated whether the author implies that he based his work on written or oral sources. One should note a significant difference, however, between this verse and the formula in the books of Kings: The acts of the various kings have been written down. This confession of being unable to record all the deeds of heroes at their death was a common classical literary device. The author of 1 Maccabees thus does not seem to refer to ancient records, as in the books of Kings, but rather glorifies the magnitude of Judas's exploits.

REFLECTIONS

What had Judas actually accomplished? At his death, he was not in control of Jerusalem, his forces had been drastically reduced, and the early story of Jonathan (9:33-49) shows him, despite the author's best efforts, to be nothing but a guerrilla on the run, desperately seeking to avoid capture. Yet Judas's fame lives on despite his failures. One might compare the end of his life to that of King Saul in 1 Samuel 31. Saul, too, saw his bid for independence from the Philistines end in disaster. Saul, too, is lamented by David in "The Song of the Bow" (2 Sam 1:19-27), which is cited by the author of 1 Maccabees with reference to Judas. Yet Saul's failures are emphasized, while Judas's victories are stressed. History, of course, is written by the victors. The dynasty of David continued, while Saul's line failed. Judas's brothers continued after him and founded the Hasmonean dynasty. Their struggle for independence against all odds was rewarded, and it is perhaps the hope of ultimate victory that is so important a part of the story of Judas: He began something that did not die with him. The early Zionists would look back to Judas and the Hasmoneans as their heroes, for they had fought on, and when one died, another was there to take his or her place. Judas's was a movement that could not fail, for it depended not on him alone but on the vision that his father had sparked in many minds.

1 MACCABEES 9:23–12:53

JONATHAN

OVERVIEW

Jonathan is an enigmatic yet crucial figure in the Maccabean revolt. Leader of the rebel groups for seventeen or eighteen years, twice as long as Judas, he became high priest and a figure to be reckoned with in Seleucid dynastic politics. Yet, unlike Judas and Simon, he is not mentioned in Mattathias's last will (2:65-66), nor does he receive a poem to laud or lament him.

1 MACCABEES 9:23-73, JONATHAN'S RISE TO POWER

1 Maccabees 9:23-31, The Succession of Jonathan

COMMENTARY

9:23. As in Judges, 1 Maccabees envisions a pattern whereby once a judge dies, Israel sins, is punished, and then another judge is raised up (Judg 2:11-23). In 1 Maccabees, whenever there is a break in the action, the lawless and renegades stir things up again (7:5; 9:58; the language here resembles that of Ps 92:7). When Mattathias first rose up, the surviving renegades had fled to the Gentiles, and Mattathias had free rein within the borders of Israel (2:44-46). Judas is praised for confounding lawless evildoers and destroying the ungodly out of the land (3:6-8). Now, at the death of Judas, the sinners come forward again in the borders of Israel.

9:24. This verse is frequently used as an argument that most Jews deserted Jonathan's cause, because the government controlled the food supply and thus could entice people to its side. Given, however, the unusual meaning this would give to "country" (χώρα *chōra*) as well as the penalty of sterility of the land as punishment for sin in the OT (Deut 11:16-17; 1 Kgs 8:35-40; Jer 12:4; Sir 39:29), one should not exclude the possibility of the author's suggesting that the famine symbolizes the rule of the godless over the land.

9:25-27. Bacchides keeps up the pressure against Judas's followers. Note how the author maintains the anonymity of Bacchides' lieutenants and simply classifies them as godless. There is a connection between Bacchides' making sport of/scoffing at the friends of Judas and the treatment of the prophets, who were scoffed at by the unfaithful "until the wrath of the LORD against his people became so great that there was no remedy" (2 Chr 36:16 NRSV). The author of 1 Maccabees sees his time as an era without prophets (4:46; 14:41). Did he envision his era as extending from the time of Haggai and Zechariah or Malachi? "Prophet," of course, encompasses much more than foretelling the future. A prophet is the interpreter of God's law (4:46), but Moses, Joshua, and the judges were also called prophets (Sir 46:1; Prologue to Sirach). The trouble is not as magnified as at Dan 12:1 or Mark 13:19 in speaking of the tribulation before the end of the world.

9:28-31. Unlike Judas, who was appointed by his father (2:66), Jonathan is elected to the post of ruler (cf. Judg 10:18; 11:6-11). But the same formula of succession that was used for Judas (3:1) is used for Jonathan.

1 Maccabees 9:32-49, Early Campaigns of Jonathan

COMMENTARY

This period, from the death of Judas to the death of Alcimus, which is said to be thirteen months long (9:3, 54), is one of acute distress for Jonathan and his small band. They are forced to hide near a waterhole in the wilderness of Tekoa, about fifteen miles southeast of Jerusalem. The chronology of the following events is not very exact. The attack on the Jambrites is framed by two references to Bacchides (vv. 34, 43) that are very similar. The first serves to locate Bacchides on the east bank of the Jordan, where he and his army can entrap Jonathan in Transjordan on his way back from Medeba to Judea (vv. 43-49).

9:35-42. The situation had become so desperate that Jonathan sent away his brother and, presumably under the heading "the multitude," all those not able to fight, like women, children, and the elderly (v. 35). They were to travel with all their baggage (cf. 1 Macc 5:13, 45) across the Jordan to their friends, the Nabateans (1 Macc 5:25). The wagon train was intercepted and Jonathan's brother John was killed (v. 38) by a tribal group, the Jambrites, from the area around Medeba, a town near the northeastern tip of the Dead Sea (v. 36). We do not know whether this action was in concert with Bacchides, or just another tribal raid. No connection is made between this group and the Nabateans. When a wedding is arranged between the Jambrites and some other tribal group (v. 37)—exactly what "Canaan" and "Nadabath" refer to is uncertain—Jonathan and his group ambush the wedding party and kill many of the Jambrites to avenge the death of John; they also regain much baggage (vv. 38-40) the Jambrites had taken from them. Jonathan and his group then slink back to the safety of the marshes of the Jordan valley (v. 42). The reader gains a sense from this narrative of the shrinking size of the followers of Jonathan. Even toward the end, Judas had been followed by three thousand men (9:5), but Jonathan's group can win a victory only by ambushing a wedding party, not a terribly noble feat.

9:43-49. Moving on the sabbath, either to catch the Jews off guard or to take advantage of their piety (cf. 2:29-41), Bacchides sets out to trap Jonathan's guerrilla band on the banks of the Jordan, between the river and the marshes of the Dead Sea (v. 45). The author tries to make the most of this sorry engagement by giving Jonathan a pre-battle speech (vv. 44-46) similar to that of Judas at 3:18-22. Jonathan tries to embolden his men by stating that Bacchides acted in a cowardly way and by exaggerating the number of Seleucid dead (vv. 47, 49). Jonathan, in fact, was lucky to escape alive.

1 Maccabees 9:50-53, The Strategy of Bacchides

COMMENTARY

After his return to Jerusalem, Bacchides strengthens key areas. Jericho would control the Jordan valley and Emmaus the way to the plain. Beth-zur, Gazara, and the citadel (v. 52) were already fortified. The other cities lay north of Jerusalem in northern Judea and southern Samaria, as if to deny the rebels access to those parts of Judea where Judas had been so successful. Bacchides' strategy seems to have been to control those areas with several garrisons and to force the cooperation of leading citizens through taking their sons as hostages. Since Bacchides' attempt is to harass "Israel" (the author's term for true believers), these leading citizens were no doubt different from the "godless" who had been put in charge of the country (9:25), and the fortifications would have been used to strengthen the latter's position.

1 Maccabees 9:54-57, The Death of Alcimus

COMMENTARY

9:54-56. In 159 BCE, Alcimus, the high priest appointed by Demetrius, died. The Temple area had been rebuilt quickly under Judas (4:43-49), and Alcimus was probably doing some renovations and upscaling the repairs begun by Judas. Such building activity suggests that the activity of Jonathan had been severely curtailed and that the decline in warfare had led to an economic upswing. During this work, Alcimus died. The author of 1 Maccabees attributes the cause of his death to the action of God, as the passive verb "was stricken" implies. The sense of just deserts is shown as Alcimus, who had given orders that something be done to God's house, now cannot set his own house in order. The author gives the worst spin on what Alcimus was intending: Instead of renovation, Alcimus was breaking down the wall that separated the court of the priests from the rest of the Israelites, breaking laws of separation between the sacred and the profane (Ezek 42:13-14; 44:4-27). By mentioning the work of the prophets, the author may be referring to the work of the prophets Haggai and Zechariah in rebuilding the Temple (Ezra 5:1; 6:14). It is also noteworthy that the Jewish writer Eupolemus has Solomon build the Temple according to the command of Nathan the prophet.[96]

9:57. This verse shows how little we know of what was going on in Judea. On Alcimus's death, Bacchides went back to the king. Surely Bacchides would have left someone in charge of the now fairly pacified country. But no mention is made of any such ruler, nor are we told who became high priest until Jonathan's appointment in 152 BCE (1 Macc 10:21). Josephus holds that no one was high priest after Alcimus.[97] Such a length of time with no high priest to officiate Yom Kippur seems quite unusual, even if, for example, the high priest Menelaus was probably unable to perform the ritual while Judas controlled the Temple in 163 BCE (1 Macc 4:42). The author of 1 Maccabees gives us no information about the high priestly office before Alcimus (a proper anti-hero for him) or until Jonathan's appointment, so there likely may have been a high priest about whom we know nothing.

The reason why Bacchides left the country may have had nothing to do with the death of Alcimus. Demetrius I was involved in 159/58 in an attempt to oust Ariarathes IV from Cappadocia and support his rival, Orophernes. So Bacchides' main force may have been needed back in Antioch. After his departure from Judea, the pressure against Jonathan eased (cf. 7:50). Even with the garrisons still in place (vv. 25, 50), the author sees the absence of the Seleucid forces under Bacchides as bringing rest to the land (v. 57). This period must have been extremely important for Jonathan and his followers, for this respite of two years seems to have allowed them to regroup.

---

96. See Eusebius *Preparation for the Gospel* 9.34.2.

97. See Josephus *Antiquities of the Jews* 20.237, a lapse of seven years; *Antiquities of the Jews* 12.414, 419, 434; 13.46, a lapse of four years.

1 Maccabees 9:58-73, The Last Expedition of Bacchides

COMMENTARY

As earlier (7:5-7), the peace is disrupted by the lawless, who conspire to bring Bacchides back to capture Jonathan and his followers. The Greek has a play on words in vv. 57-58: The land was "quiet" (ἡσύχασεν *hēsychasen*), and Jonathan was living in "quiet" (ἡσυχία *hēsychia*). Throughout this section, in fact, the author repeats similar words: "plan" (βουλή *boulē*, vv. 60, 68); "plotted," "counseled" (βουλεύομαι *bouleuomai*, vv. 58, 69); "consulted," "counseled" (συμβουλεύομαι *symbouleuomai*, vv. 59, 69); "capture," "seize" (συλλαμβάνω *syllambanō*, vv. 58, 60-61).

9:60-61. Although Bacchides is said to have come with a large force, it is clear from his later failure to capture Bethbasi that it was not the force with which he first came to Judea (7:10). This is also evident from the way he tries to get Jonathan first through allies who were already in place in Judea. The sequence of events is difficult to reconstruct. The NRSV has Jonathan's men kill fifty leaders of this "treachery" (lit., "evil"). This translation presumably understands the last phrase as referring to those who had tried to capture Jonathan. But the Greek has no change in subject from v. 60, where Bacchides' allies are told to seize Jonathan, and v. 61, where the same verb is used to describe the seizure of the fifty leaders; Jonathan is not mentioned until v. 62. Therefore, the reader may presume that Bacchides' allies tried to seize Jonathan, but when they couldn't, they seized instead fifty men from the countryside whom they credited with being associated in some way with the damage Jonathan was doing (cf. 7:6-7). These fifty might then be compared to the sixty Hasideans who had sought to make peace with Bacchides and Alcimus (7:12-18).

9:62-64. Bacchides had made the country north of Jerusalem too difficult for Jonathan to pass through because of the garrisons stationed there, so Jonathan retreated south as he had done before (9:33), although not as far. Bethbasi lay about a mile and a quarter southeast of Bethlehem, on the way to Tekoa and the Jordan valley. The author tries to magnify the strength of Bacchides' forces, but Bacchides needed to supplement his detachment with his allies in Judea.

9:65-68. The course of the siege is confused. The NRSV suggests that Jonathan leaves Bethbasi with a small force, fights against some otherwise unknown nomadic tribes, and then turns back to attack Bacchides—a rather circuitous route to raise the siege. The text is difficult to reconstruct; one is not sure whether to read singular or plural verbs. The main problem lies in the verb "struck down" (ἐπάταξεν *epataxen*, v. 66). The sense of the passage would seem to be that Jonathan slipped away from the siege to gain allies, as those in the citadel had done against Judas's siege (6:18-27). Jonathan had friends among the Nabateans, if not among the Jambrites (9:35), as had Judas before him (5:25), and so he may have gone for reinforcements to Odomera and the people of Phasiron, and "placed" them beside him (ἐπέταξεν *epetaxen*), a verb attested by some Greek manuscripts. At v. 67, then, Jonathan's small group, plus his reinforcements (not "he" as in the NRSV), begins to attack Bacchides' forces from the rear while Simon sallies out from the town and crushes Bacchides' group. Bacchides had relied on his allies in Judea, but they had been no help. The ability of Jonathan and Simon to mount such a counteroffensive shows their use of the two years to increase in numbers and their fighting ability; it also brings into view Jonathan's diplomatic skills.

9:69-72. Bacchides' reaction to defeat is anger. Is it a blind rage? Or has Bacchides become aware that it is not Jonathan who is disturbing the peace in Judea, but these "lawless" ones? Is it, in fact, a signal of peace toward Jonathan? That is how Jonathan understands it, and his penchant for making agreements is made apparent. Whereas Judas had refused the offers of peace made by Bacchides (7:10-11) and Nicanor (7:27-30), Jonathan now takes the initiative. The returned captives are not the hostages in the citadel (9:53; 10:6) but others possibly taken during this last campaign. The words of Bacchides in v. 71 echo the words of Alcimus to the Hasideans (7:15).

9:73. In almost idyllic terms, the author depicts the period after Bacchides' departure. It recalls Isa 2:4: "He shall judge between the nations,/ and shall arbitrate for many peoples;/ they shall beat their swords into plowshares,/ and their spears into pruning hooks" (NRSV). Jonathan returns to settle at Michmash in the rugged hills about seven miles north of Jerusalem, where King Saul had settled (1 Sam 13:2) and that was settled at the time of Ezra and Nehemiah (see Ezra 2:27; Neh 7:31; 11:31). Like the judges and the kings, Jonathan governs the people ideally by rooting out the godless. Of course, the citadel and the other garrisons were still in power and Jonathan probably did not undertake any more military activity lest the Seleucid forces return. What one would like to know is what Jonathan was doing from 157 BCE to 152 BCE, when 1 Maccabees resumes the narrative.

When Jonathan is next heard of, Demetrius wishes him to become his ally—that is, he considers Jonathan able to supply him with auxiliary forces. When Bacchides had used his allies in Judea (9:60, 63), they had been bested by Jonathan's forces, and the reader should not forget that Judas's forces had faced a Seleucid phalanx and fought them all day long (9:12-13). Jonathan probably kept this reserve of battle-hardened troops battle trim, ready for any developments. Neither are we told anything about how Jonathan actually lived. We do not know whether he or his men took part in the temple liturgy, although when Jonathan becomes high priest no mention is made of sweeping changes in the way the ritual was carried out. How would one have distinguished between followers of Jonathan and other Jews? Was the distinction based more on allegiance to certain patrons, but raised to the level of theological absolutes to maintain loyalty and the ability to fight a civil war?

REFLECTIONS

The narrative reinforces the sense that the only factor capable of holding the country together was the movement under Jonathan. No matter how hard the Seleucid forces pressed Jonathan, no matter what harassment Bacchides inflicted on the people, no matter how many fortresses were erected to control the people, Jonathan's opponents had no effective leadership. Alcimus could have been a rallying point for the opposition; he clearly was energetic and pushed a program of restoration after the devastations of the war. Yet he died too early to be of any real use to them. His death is seen by the author of 1 Maccabees as divine retribution, as evidence once again that God was on the side of the Maccabees. When Bacchides tried to raise a force from those opposed to Jonathan, he found they were ineffective. Here again one sees the importance of dedicated single-mindedness on behalf of one's cause. Jonathan won out because he was willing to stay longer, endure longer, and put his life on the line. When a local population stiffly resists foreign oppression and seeks to maintain its own way and culture, its stubborn resistance will win out and it likely will not be defeated in the end.

1 MACCABEES 10:1–12:53, JONATHAN'S RULE

1 Maccabees 10:1-14, Jonathan and Demetrius I

COMMENTARY

10:1-2. After five years of relative stability, external factors once again threaten the land. Demetrius I had not made many friends; his failure in Cappadocia (157–154 BCE) had won him enemies in Asia Minor, his harsh treatment of his subjects led Antioch to revolt (which he suppressed with even harsher measures), and he had made an enemy of Ptolemy Philometor by trying to gain control of Cyprus in 155/54 BCE. A pretender to the Seleucid throne, Alexander Balas, who claimed to be the son of Antiochus IV, went to Rome and in 152 BCE gained permission from the senate to claim the throne of his ancestors.[98] Before October 152 BCE, Alexander arrived in Ptolemais, where the garrison went over to his side. One is not sure whether there were several battles between the two or only one before Demetrius's defeat and death in the summer of 150 BCE. In 1 Maccabees the contest between the two kings is taken up again at 10:48, and only one battle is described. In between is collected a series of documents from Demetrius and Alexander Balas, bidding for the services of Jonathan. Questions have been raised about the authenticity of these documents, particularly whether they are exact reproductions of the contents. One can wonder where the letters would have been kept, and how the author of 1 Maccabees could retrieve them from archives, which most likely did not have the same degree of organization as today's libraries. On the other hand, we do have from the ancient world collections of documents, such as the Zenon papyri, that have been preserved and have come down to us.

10:3-6. As Ptolemais lay south of Antioch but north of Jerusalem, Demetrius may have hoped to harass Alexander from the rear. The author of 1 Maccabees portrays Demetrius as conscious of the wrongs he has done against the Jews, just as Antiochus IV had been (6:12), and willing to do anything to save his throne. Jonathan's military accomplishments are well-known, even after a lapse of five years. Jonathan is here raised to the position of leader of a vassal state, ally of the Seleucid throne and with the authority to raise and equip an army. It is a remarkable achievement to rise from a rebel in hiding to head of the nation in seven years. The hostages had been taken to keep the countryside from helping Jonathan (9:53). Now that Jonathan is to be an ally of the Seleucids, there is no need to keep them.

10:7-9. Jonathan makes the most of the occasion by having Demetrius's letter (which is not extant) read aloud publicly in Jerusalem; one wonders how the listeners knew the letter was genuine. Jonathan's authority to muster troops would have affected the citadel, as Judas had already shown a desire to attack it (6:19-20). Nevertheless, in spite of their misgivings, the troops in the citadel respect the king's wishes, even though Jonathan has shrewdly not yet formally responded to Demetrius's offer.

10:10-14. Like Judas, who had restored the Temple (4:47-51), Jonathan sets out to restore and refortify Jerusalem, which had been decimated by Lysias. He uses the kind of stone King Josiah is said to have used to rebuild the Temple (2 Chr 34:11). Jonathan is now so powerful that the Gentile garrisons Bacchides had established (9:50-52) flee, except for some apostates left in Beth-zur. Their plight, however—holed up in Beth-zur—is the reverse of what they had done to the Israelites when they were in power (1:52-53). In fact, the citadel remained intact, and the garrisons seem to have remained (11:41; 12:45). Perhaps some deserted or were recalled to help Demetrius against Alexander Balas.

---

98. Polybius 33.18.12.

1 Maccabees 10:15-21, Jonathan and Alexander Epiphanes

COMMENTARY

10:15-16. The bidding war for Jonathan's services begins. As a new player on the block, Alexander has to learn about Jonathan; one wonders from whom he had heard that Jonathan was such a valiant warrior in such glowing terms. "Friend of the king" was not the highest-ranking title in the Seleucid hierarchy. Mattathias had been asked to be one (2:18), and the author of 1 Maccabees seems to feel that it is an important title (3:3; 6:14, 28; 7:8).

10:17-20. The flattering letter that Alexander writes Jonathan, calling him "brother" (ἀδελφός *adelphos*), a title reserved for the highest dignitaries, is not written in good Greek. The phrase "man of valor" (ἀνὴρ δυνατός *anēr dynatos*, v. 19) is used frequently in the LXX (see Ruth 2:1; 2 Kgs 5:1; 15:20; 24:14; 1 Chr 5:2; 12:21). The letter does contain evidence that the Seleucid ruler, even if at that point a pretender to the throne, appointed Jonathan to the high priesthood. Jonathan's appointment is thus legitimate, and he becomes the official political and religious leader of Judea. Along with the letter, Alexander sends Jonathan "a purple robe and a golden crown." Friends of the king customarily wore a purple robe, and priests in the Hellenistic period wore purple robes and gold crowns.

10:21. Jonathan dons the sacred vestments (Exod 28:1-5) on the fifteenth day of the seventh month (October), 152 BCE, during the Festival of Booths (Lev 23:33-36, 39-42; Deut 16:13-15). It is interesting that this occurs just five days after the celebration of Yom Kippur, when the high priest's presence was most required for the ritual atonement of the people (Leviticus 16). However, Jonathan may be playing on the symbolism of the festival whereby the people of Israel are reminded how God brought them out of the land of Egypt (Lev 23:43), and during which the law is to be read aloud every seventh year (Deut 31:10-13). The Festival of Booths was the first festival celebrated on the return from exile (Ezra 3:1-5), and it was the festival celebrated by Ezra (Neh 8:13-18). According to 2 Maccabees, the festival of Hanukkah at Judas's purification of the Temple was associated with the Festival of Booths (2 Macc 1:9; 10:6).

What is perhaps most striking is the very brevity with which this important event is recounted; the narrator immediately proceeds to describe the recruiting of troops and the securing of arms. The only religious act attributed to Jonathan is a prayer in battle (11:71), not a specifically high-priestly deed. Could this lack of emphasis be due to opposition to Jonathan's being high priest? Some scholars have suggested that the wicked priest of the Qumran documents is Jonathan, but such specificity is hard to obtain from these texts. What v. 21 does suggest is that Jonathan has taken the proposals from both Demetrius and Alexander without allying himself with either.

1 Maccabees 10:22-45, The Reaction of Demetrius I

COMMENTARY

10:22-24. Demetrius acts as if he has not already written to Jonathan (10:3-6). Demetrius's style reflects Hebrew syntax: "they may be with me to a help" (v. 24 author's trans.).

10:25-45. In contrast to the previous two letters (10:3, 18), Demetrius now addresses one "to the nation of the Jews." While it does mention the high priesthood (v. 32), it does not name Jonathan at all. This had led some scholars to hold either that the letter does not belong in its present context, or that in fact Demetrius thought that he could gain the allegiance of Jews who may have been opposed to Jonathan and his supporters.

10:26-28. Demetrius claims that the Jews have remained loyal to their treaty with him. Is this a rhetorical ploy, or does the letter belong in another context? Does the treaty refer to Bacchides' agreement (9:71) or to the general framework of a suzerain-vassal treaty? A treaty bound both parties. In its present context, the term "enemies" (ἐχθροί *echthroi*) refers to Alexander, but one should recall that there were frequent uprisings against Demetrius. Does this offer of immunities and gifts betray a note of desperation?

10:29-33. Comparison with a similar letter of Antiochus III indicates that the phrase "payment of tribute" probably should be understood as a head tax or a poll tax.[99] The mention of a "salt tax" (v. 29) may indicate that the Jews originally delivered to the king a quantity of salt, for which later a payment in cash was substituted. Note, however, that Demetrius II later relinquishes claims to the salt pits (1 Macc 11:35). "Crown levies" were at first presents to the king from his subjects, but later became compulsory upon his accession—and whenever he required them. A tax rate of one-third to one-half of a crop was extremely high and would have been very oppressive to the local economy. Would the Seleucids have so punished their supporters among the Jews? The three districts (v. 30) are named in the letter of Demetrius II (11:34). Verse 31 is difficult, but probably should read that Jerusalem was to be exempted from tithes and revenues, rather than that Jerusalem's tithes and revenues were to be free from taxation. Relinquishing control of the citadel (v. 32) was a major concession by Demetrius. No wonder the inhabitants of the citadel had earlier been afraid, as Jonathan now has a legitimate claim on the citadel. The release of all Jewish slaves throughout the entire Seleucid kingdom without compensation (v. 33) and cancellation of all customs and tolls on their way back to Judea are highly magnanimous and highly improbable.[100]

10:34-35. Demetrius further proclaims that, before and after holy days, Jews are to be exempted from customs and tolls and that they are not to be involved in legal affairs, in order to enable them to go to Jerusalem to celebrate their festivals (cf. v. 63). The list of festivals is similar to that at Ezek 45:17; thus it suggests Jewish input into the content of the letter. The limit of three days refers to a journey of three days, and thus may specify the distance within which one was required to bring the actual tithes in the form of crops or animals, and not to turn it into money. It would thus be interpreting Deut 14:24, a specification also found at Qumran in the *Temple Scroll*.[101]

10:36-37. Jews served under both the Ptolemies (e.g., the Jewish generals Onias and Dositheus)[102] and the Seleucids.[103] The Jews in the army are presumably to be kept in special detachments in which they could follow Torah regulations. Would this include keeping the sabbath? The end of v. 37 suggests that Jews had been able to follow their ancestral traditions in Judea since the beginning of the reign of Demetrius I.

10:38-43. The three nomes lay near the area that had been the stronghold of Maccabean opposition. The high priest is recognized, as in v. 32, as the political leader of the Jewish nation. According to v. 1, Ptolemais was currently under the control of Alexander Balas. What exactly is being referred to in vv. 41-42 is difficult to reconstruct. One cannot be sure whether government officials have been withholding payments (so NRSV), or whether the priests have been using money given for sacrifices to fund other activities. What is clear is that Demetrius is being quite generous to the Temple. Again, in v. 43, what the king is actually allowing is hard to piece together. He seems to be granting to the Jerusalem Temple and its precincts the right of asylum for debtors, although the term for "asylum" is not used. The NRSV translation suggests that such refugees are to be forgiven their debts and get off scot-free. The Greek text is difficult, and perhaps what is being allowed is that the property of the refugees is not to be confiscated, rather than that their debts are forgiven.

10:44-45. The king further promises to pay out of his own budget the cost of rebuilding the Temple, the walls around Jerusalem, and all the walls of towns in Judea. Darius had agreed to shoulder the cost of rebuilding the Temple (Ezra 8), but Demetrius goes beyond that. The usual conclusion to a letter is missing.

---

99. See Josephus *Antiquities of the Jews* 12.142.
100. Cf. *Letter of Aristeas* 12-27; Josephus *Antiquities of the Jews* 12.144.
101. See 11QTemple 43.12-13; 52.13-14.
102. Josephus *Against Apion* 2.49-52.
103. Josephus *Antiquities of the Jews* 12.147-153.

1 Maccabees 10:46-66, Jonathan and Alexander

COMMENTARY

10:46-47. As Demetrius had worried, the Jews remember the wrongs done by him (v. 5) and do not trust his words; they are unlike the Hasideans, who had trusted Alcimus, sent by Demetrius (7:16). Again, the first offer of Demetrius (10:3-9) is ignored.

10:48-50. The sequence of events here is difficult to reconstruct. The NRSV follows one group of manuscripts that suggest that there was one decisive battle in which Alexander's army prevails and Demetrius dies. In another group of manuscripts, Alexander's army is routed, and Demetrius pursues and prevails, only to fall in battle.[104] This final battle took place sometime in the summer of 150 BCE.

10:51-58. The author of 1 Maccabees seems not to know that Ptolemy had helped Alexander in his bid for power in order to avenge himself on Demetrius for attacking Cyprus (see Commentary on 10:1-14). The syntax of Alexander's letter (vv. 52-54) follows Hebrew structure; it contains no flowery phrases and gets right to the heart of the matter. Ptolemy's daughter, Cleopatra Thea, is presented as the medium through which relations between two males take place when Ptolemy offers her in marriage to Alexander (v. 54). Ptolemy's response uses basically the same words (vv. 55-56). Neither letter has the opening greeting formula or the closing date. Ptolemais, on the seacoast, was easily reached from Egypt. The wedding took place in late summer 150 BCE.

10:59-60. Jonathan is invited to Ptolemais to meet Alexander. One can perhaps see why the author of 1 Maccabees gives the correspondence between Alexander and Ptolemy such prominence, for now the author, by having Alexander write to Jonathan to meet him, as Ptolemy had written to Alexander to meet him, puts Jonathan on the same playing ground as the Ptolemaic and Seleucid monarchs. Jonathan is also equated with the two kings as he travels "with pomp" (v. 60; cf. v. 58). One wonders how they communicated. Did Jonathan know some Greek, or did they use interpreters?

10:61-66. This time the scoundrels from Israel do not succeed in turning the king against Jonathan, as they had in the past (6:21-27; 7:5-7). Jonathan is granted immunity and is raised from the rank of friend to that of a "first friend." He becomes the military and political ruler in Judea.

104. See Justin *Epitome* 35.1.10-11.

1 Maccabees 10:67-89, The Uprising of Demetrius II

COMMENTARY

10:67-68. Demetrius I, before he finally engaged Alexander in battle, had sent his two sons, Demetrius and Antiochus, to Asia Minor. Alexander, after some initial popularity, had proved to be an inept ruler with little control over his empire. Around 148/47 BCE, he lost the two important satrapies of Media and Susiane. In 147 BCE, Demetrius, little more than thirteen years old, landed in Phoenicia with an army of mercenaries. Alexander, who had resided at Ptolemais, moved to Antioch, perhaps to check any attempt by Demetrius II to gain the capital.

10:69-73. Not much is known of what exactly transpired after Demetrius's arrival in "the land of his ancestors" (v. 67) except what is told here. The governor of Coelesyria, Apollonius, goes over to Demetrius's side and is confirmed in his position. Jonathan, however, remains loyal to Alexander (see v. 47). Apollonius takes up position on the coastal plain at Jamnia. Technically Apollonius is Jonathan's superior, and the reference to Jonathan as high priest (v. 69) underlies this difference in status. The Hebrew syntax of the message he sends to Jonathan (vv. 70-73) and the way it is tied in to the battle description suggest that the author of 1 Maccabees wrote what he thought Apollonius should have said. Apollonius sends a warrior's taunt and boast to Jonathan, emphasizing that it would be a disgrace for him to fight such a puny adversary, recalling how Goliath had mocked David (1 Sam 17:42-44) and how the experienced fighter Abner does not wish to fight his less experienced foe Asahel, but when forced to kills him (2 Sam 2:18-23). Apollonius contrasts Jonathan, a hill-person, with his own city forces on the plain. It is a taunt that was made earlier by the Arameans against Israel (1 Kgs 20:23-30). The statement that there would be "no stone or pebble" (v. 73) recalls the David and Goliath episode as well (1 Sam 17:40-49). The reference to ancestral defeats may allude to Judas's defeats at Beth-zechariah (6:47) and Elasa (9:18), but the use of "ancestral" (πατήρ *patēr*) suggests rather the Philistine defeat of the Israelites (1 Sam 4:1-11) and the defeat of Saul (1 Sam 31:1-7). One should also note the contrast between Apollonius's cavalry and Jonathan's forces, which are predicted to be unable to withstand such a mobile force. The battle description will maintain this contrast between cavalry and infantry.

10:74-76. Upon receiving this message, Jonathan first moves to secure Joppa, on the edge of his territory. It was strategically important to secure as a buffer to prevent attack from the rear on his way toward Apollonius.

10:77-85. Apollonius, knowing that Jonathan has responded to his taunt and that Apollonius is cut off from Demetrius's forces by Jonathan's capture of Joppa, seeks out the more advantageous position around Azotus than the rougher country of Jamnia (v. 77). He sets a trap so that Jonathan's flanks and rear will be vulnerable (v. 79), but Jonathan's skirmishers uncover them (v. 80). The battle is described: Jonathan's infantry are encircled and Apollonius's cavalry shoot arrows at them. In this description, Jonathan's infantry stands fast (v. 81) while the cavalry grows tired, the exact opposite of Apollonius's taunt. Note that the word translated "his men" is literally "people" (λαός *laos*, vv. 80-81), perhaps to emphasize the national quality of Jonathan's group.

Several details are missing from this picture. Where is Jonathan's cavalry (cf. Judas in 9:11-17)? It would be very foolish for a commander not to have cavalry to protect the flanks and rear of his infantry. Nor are we told what kind of cavalry Apollonius had. Did he deploy super-heavy cavalry, the cataphracts, which were heavily armed, as well as skirmishing mounted archers? The archers would try to make breaks in the infantry formation; the cataphracts would attack infantry but were not too effective against a fully defensive phalanx and because of their heavy armor would tire easily. It appears that Jonathan and Simon kept up a circular defensive posture with their shields up and their long pikes extended, so that the heavy cavalry troops could not penetrate and the arrows could be deflected. By afternoon the cavalry, both heavy and light, were tired (v. 81). Simon then drew out his infantry from the defensive into an offensive line (v. 82). They attacked Apollonius's phalanx and crushed it (v. 83). The cavalry could not stand in the plain and scattered and fled to Azotus (Ashdod). But Jonathan and his forces followed and plundered and burned Azotus and the surrounding towns; he also burned the temple of Dagon "and those who had taken refuge in it" (this temple is known from 1 Sam 5:1-5).

10:86. No mention is made of Apollonius's fate, but with his support for Demetrius II gone, the town of Askalon supports Alexander's cause and welcomes Jonathan with great pomp (cf. vv. 58-60).

10:87-89. Alexander had now been relieved of a threat to his south and, realizing the importance of Jonathan's support, raises his status still higher; "King's Kinsman" is a higher rank than first friend (v. 65). Jonathan can now fasten his purple cloak with a golden buckle. Ekron lay on the road from Jerusalem to the coast and was a clear extension of Jonathan's sphere of influence.

REFLECTIONS

The dynastic rivalry between different claimants to the Seleucid throne gave Jonathan the opportunity he needed. Only when the Seleucids were weak could the small state of Judea hope to gain its independence. Jonathan, with a battle-hardened following, was a strong man whom neither side could ignore. He was able to play hard-nosed politics as he strove to gain every advantage from his position. Playing both ends against the middle is a dangerous game, however. One has to make sure that one knows with whom one is dealing and not rely on anyone too much.

Jonathan's wheelings and dealings in international politics raise the issue of what role moral issues should play in such affairs. Jonathan was out for all he could get, although he did harbor resentment against Demetrius I for his early treatment of Jonathan (10:46). But is this a model for the way individuals or states should behave? Should one be concerned only for what one can get? Should one not be concerned also for what is happening to others or to other states? Is national interest to be defined only in terms of what is good for one's own nation? Are there not some issues that transcend narrow boundaries? Certainly we should be concerned about human rights, about genocide, about the starvation of millions. Yet implementing such policies is extremely difficult and must be carefully considered. Issues of morality should be aired and raised in policy discussions, not treated as naive and out of place.

Thinking only of one's own national gain in such circumstances as Jonathan found himself in can bring short-term benefits, but long-term loss. When one of the parties wins control, then the victor may not look so kindly on promises extracted under duress.

1 Maccabees 11:1-19, The Coming of Ptolemy VI

COMMENTARY

Chapter 11 continues the account of Jonathan's exploits outside the borders of Judea, as well as his attempts to oust the final Seleucid garrisons from within Judea. Jonathan's prominent position among the various Seleucid claimants to the throne is again emphasized, as is his trustworthiness compared to that of both the Ptolemies and the Seleucids.

11:1-3. Ptolemy VI Philometer, father-in-law of Alexander Epiphanes, intervened in the dynastic struggle, probably early in 145 BCE, since the final decisive battle and Ptolemy's subsequent death occurred in midsummer 145 BCE. The image of his troops being as numerous as sand on the seashore is a familiar one (Gen 22:17; Josh 11:4; Dan 3:36 LXX). The author of 1 Maccabees, who favors Alexander Epiphanes because of Jonathan's alliance with him, portrays Ptolemy as a treacherous land-grabber. Other historians state that Ptolemy really came to help Alexander, but turned against him either because he saw Alexander's incompetence or because of an attempt on Ptolemy's life by Alexander's minister Ammonius (see v. 10).[105] The author describes Ptolemy as being deceitful, like the Seleucids before him (see 1:30; 7:10). Some of the southern coastal towns may have been friendly toward Demetrius II, as Jamnia, Joppa, and Azotus had been (10:69, 75, 83), and so Ptolemy's garrisoning of them may have been a prudent action. The author of 1 Maccabees interprets the action as a sinister move against the trusting Alexander.

11:4-7. Earlier, people had tried unsuccessfully to persuade a king to turn against Jonathan (10:61), and the same happens here. Despite the people's attempt to disparage Jonathan for the damage he had wrought in Azotus, Ptolemy greets Jonathan "with

---
[105]. See Diodorus Siculus 32.9c; Josephus *Antiquities of the Jews* 13.106-107.

pomp." Since the destruction of Azotus had been the result of a battle with the forces of Demetrius II (10:83-85), Ptolemy could not openly break with Jonathan without seeming to side against Alexander. The river Eleutherus lay two hundred miles north of Joppa, far north from Judea.

11:8-12. Seleucia by the sea was the port of Antioch. Here Ptolemy's break with Alexander is made clear. The author of 1 Maccabees puts all the blame on Ptolemy VI for now, using his daughter as barter with Demetrius II, just as he had offered her to Alexander (10:54-56). We are not sure where Demetrius and Alexander were. Josephus records that Demetrius landed in Cilicia,[106] and 1 Maccabees places Alexander there also (11:14), whereas Diodorus Siculus locates Alexander in Antioch at the time of Ptolemy's about-face.[107]

11:13. After he had made an alliance with Demetrius II, which promised him the rule of his father's kingdom (11:9), it seems unlikely that Ptolemy would actually seize control. According to Diodorus Siculus, Antioch was in an uproar at Ptolemy's turnaround.[108] The people revolted against Alexander's supporters, but did not want Demetrius II, and so they offered the crown to Ptolemy, which he declined. Rome had rejected Antiochus IV's attempt in 168 BCE to unite the Seleucid Empire and Egypt, and the author of 1 Maccabees had earlier stated that Antiochus IV wished to be king of Egypt (1:16). Now that the Achaean League had been defeated in 146 BCE, Rome was dominant in the region, and so Ptolemy may have been satisfied with the ceding of Coelesyria and Palestine by Demetrius.[109]

11:14-19. Ptolemy and Alexander join in battle near Antioch at the river Oenoparas. Alexander is defeated and forced to flee; Arabia here would refer to the northern desert, east of Damascus. Ptolemy is severely wounded in the battle, and dies soon after, leaving Demetrius the sole victor. Yet he cannot stop Ptolemy's army from returning to Egypt, so he seizes Ptolemy's war elephants, orders the garrisons in the coastal cities exterminated, and refuses to cede Coelesyria and Palestine. He became king in 145 BCE.

---

106. Josephus *Antiquities of the Jews* 13.86.
107. Diodorus Siculus 32.9c.
108. Diodorus Siculus 32.9c.
109. Diodorus Siculus 32.9c.

1 Maccabees 11:20-53, Demetrius II

1 Maccabees 11:20-37, Demetrius's Rise to Power

COMMENTARY

11:20-22. Jonathan takes advantage of the struggles in Syria to mount an attack on the citadel, as Judas had done at the death of Antiochus IV Epiphanes (6:18-20). Once again, as always at the beginning of each new king's reign (1:11; 10:61; see also 6:21-27; 7:5-7), opponents, labeled as lawless renegades, rise up to cause trouble. Demetrius II's response is the same as that of earlier monarchs (3:27; 6:38). He moves south to Ptolemais, the former stronghold of Alexander, where Jonathan had met Alexander (10:60). Whereas previous monarchs had straightaway sent an army to enforce their will, Demetrius II's insecure hold of the throne is shown by his writing a letter to request that Jonathan stop the siege and to ask for a meeting. The word for "meeting" (ἀπάντησις *apantēsis*) can have both a positive and a negative (i.e., "battle") connotation, so Jonathan's decision to go is risky.

11:23-24. Wisely, Jonathan keeps in play the bargaining chip of the siege of the citadel and goes to meet the king, surrounded by leaders of the nation, to show that he has strong national support. He is armed with gifts, which the king could well use. Jonathan's tactics prevail.

Figure 3: Seleucid and Jewish Leaders in 1 and 2 Maccabees		
Seleucid Rulers	Maccabean Leaders	Jewish High Priests
Antiochus III (223–187)		**Onias III** (196?–175)
Seleucus IV Philopator (187–175) (son of Antiochus III)		
Antiochus IV Epiphanes (175–164) (brother of Seleucus; originally regent for Seleucus's son)		**Jason** (175–172) **Menelaus** (172–162)
Antiochus V Eupator (164–162) (son of Antiochus IV; regent Lysias)	**Mattathias** (began revolt, 167) **Judas Maccabeus** (166–160)	
Demetrius I Soter (161–150) (son of Seleucus IV)		**Alcimus** (161–159) **no high priest** (159–152)
	Jonathan (160–143) (high priest 152–143)	
Alexander [Balas] V Epiphanes (150–145) (claimed to be son of Antiochus IV)		
Demetrius II Nicator (145–138; 129–125) (son of Demetrius I) **Antiochus VI Epiphanes** (145–142) (son of Alexander Balas)		**Simon** (143–134) (high priest 140–134)
Antiochus VII Sidetes (138–129) (younger brother of Demetrius II)		**John Hyrcanus** (134–104)

11:25-27. Just as Alexander had not listened to complaints against Jonathan (10:61-65), so too neither does Demetrius II. He confirms Jonathan in the high priesthood (cf. 10:20) as one of the king's chief friends (cf. 10:65), and possibly with the privilege of levying troops (10:6) and the offices of general and governor of the province (10:65).

11:28-29. Jonathan and Demetrius work out a deal. No mention is made of lifting the siege of the citadel, but this too must have been part of the bargain (see 11:41). Judea will not be completely free from paying tribute (cf. 13:39), but only from the levies specified in the appended letter.

11:30-32. The opening greeting of Demetrius's letter to Lasthenes links Jonathan with the nation of the Jews (cf. 10:18, 25). According to Josephus, Lasthenes, from Crete, was the leader of a mercenary army that Demetrius had engaged in his attempt to take the throne.[110] The honorific title "Father" may signify that Lasthenes was a high-ranking minister in the royal court.

11:33-36. Demetrius's relationship with the nation of the Jews is depicted in terms of treaty obligations. The Jews have kept their obligations, and now Demetrius is conferring his benefits. Jonathan keeps control of "the three districts," an area outside the borders of Judea (see 10:38). The exemptions Demetrius II allows are similar to those that Demetrius I is said to have allowed (10:30-32).

---

110. Josephus *Antiquities of the Jews* 13.86.

What is interesting is the way recipients of the exemptions are described: "all those who offer sacrifice in Jerusalem" (v. 34). Is this similar to the release from tolls (10:34-35) and to the tax-free status of Jerusalem (10:31)? Or is the nation of the Jews now being defined as those who sacrifice in Jerusalem? Demetrius promises that these grants shall last forever (v. 36), a promise he will soon revoke.

11:37. This verse seems to return from the letter to Lasthenes to the one to Jonathan and the nation of the Jews. The grant is to be set up in a conspicuous place as a memorial. (Cf. the setting up of the stone of witness by Joshua after the people complete their covenant with God [Josh 24:24-27].) Demetrius I had already been said to have declared Jerusalem holy (10:31).

1 Maccabees 11:38-53, The Rule of Demetrius II

COMMENTARY

11:38. This section is framed by the refrain "the land was quiet before him" (11:38, 52), but the appearance of that phrase almost guarantees something is going to disturb the peace. Historians report that Demetrius or his chancellor was cruel to the citizens of Antioch.[111] When Demetrius dismisses the regular troops, but keeps the mercenaries, he finds himself embattled on two fronts—from the unemployed soldiers and the harassed citizens of Antioch, and from supporters of another pretender to the throne, the son of Alexander.

11:39-40. Originally, Trypho's name was "Diodotus." "Trypho" means "magnificent," "luxurious." He is probably to be identified with the Diodotus who was a former general of Alexander and who, together with Hierax, attempted to crown Ptolemy VI as king (cf. 1 Macc 11:13) rather than have Demetrius II rule.[112] Since coins with the image of Antiochus VI date from the year 167 of the Seleucid era (or 145 BCE), these events must have taken place soon after Alexander's death in midsummer of that year. As reported in 11:16, Alexander had fled after his defeat to the desert east of Damascus. Although he was killed, his young son Antiochus was not; he is in the guardianship of Imalkue the Arab (v. 39).[113] Trypho reports "what Demetrius had done" and urges Imalkue to relinquish Antiochus to him so that he might be set up as king in his father's place.

11:41-51. Jonathan, always the opportunist, saw in Demetrius's difficulties a chance to gain back what he had just bargained away: control of the citadel, as well as the removal of all Syrian garrisons (v. 41). Demetrius, in no position to haggle, yields, promising greater blessings. In return, Demetrius requests Jewish troops, which Jonathan quickly sends (vv. 43-44), to help counteract the unrest in Antioch. These troops prove invaluable to Demetrius. In vicious street fighting, the Jewish soldiers pacify the city of Antioch (vv. 45-48). While 1 Maccabees does not mention the action of the king's mercenaries in these events, the Greco-Roman historian Diodorus Siculus does not mention the Jews, and so one can sense the nationalistic flavor of the accounts.[114] The author of 1 Maccabees extols the glory of the victory—the Jews have won wealth and a name for themselves by defeating civilians (v. 51).

11:52-53. The Jews had saved Demetrius II from one threat, but another, in the form of an army led by Trypho, is about to appear. This time, the Jews will not help. While Jonathan and the Jews have kept their goodwill toward Demetrius, he has not kept his word to them. Demetrius follows in the tradition of the Seleucids (6:62; 7:27-29) and the Ptolemies (11:1, 12), who could not be trusted. We cannot be sure of exactly what way Demetrius treated Jonathan harshly. Josephus states that Demetrius demanded taxes from Judeans going back to the time of the "first

---

111. See Diodorus Siculus 33.4; Livy Summary of Book 52.
112. See Diodorus Siculus 32.9c; 33.3; Josephus *Antiquities of the Jews* 13.131.
113. Diodorus Siculus gives this Arab chieftain the name "Iamblichos," which is found in Emesa and in inscriptions from Palmyra. See Diodorus Siculus 33.4a.
114. Diodorus Siculus 33.4.2-3.

kings,"[115] but the phrase in 1 Maccabees usually refers to hardships in battle (9:7, 68; 10:46; 15:14). Given the short time frame in which these events happened, the phrase may signal that Demetrius II is acting like his father, Demetrius I (10:46).

115. Josephus *Antiquities of the Jews* 13.143.

REFLECTIONS

The people of Antioch had genuine grievances against Demetrius II—he had treated them very harshly—but the author of 1 Maccabees makes no mention of it and rather has Jonathan act as Demetrius's enforcer to crush any resistance to his rule. The author is only too eager to tell of the Jewish people's misfortunes, but those of other nations do not concern him. Rather, he glories in the triumph of Jonathan's army over civilian fighters.

While it is important to be proud of one's religious and ancestral traditions, one must never lost sight of the basic humanity that unites us all. Does the advancement of one's own national interests above all other concerns ultimately benefit one's own nation? Moral factors must also be brought into play. In fact, one can see how none of Jonathan's manipulations won him respect. As soon as Demetrius had no use for Jonathan, Demetrius rejected him. A policy based solely on what is good for you, and not on what is best for others as well, is bound to fail.

These same concerns apply in the area of social policy. One should seek social justice, not simply what is best for oneself. We must not forget that tax codes, with their economic implications, also make moral statements about the kind of people we want to be thought of as. Our education and health policies reflect how we treat people, how we would want to be treated if we were they. As the great Rabbi Hillel said, "If I am not for myself, who am I? But if I am only for myself, what am I? And if not now, when?"[116] Thus individualism, who am I, must be balanced by concern for others; we must not be only for ourselves. And we should start behaving that way now, not at some distant time.

116. *Pirke Aboth* 1.14.

1 Maccabees 11:54-74, Jonathan and Antiochus VI

COMMENTARY

11:54-56. The first army Demetrius sends against Trypho is defeated. Gaining strength, Trypho wins control of Chalcis and then, in 145/44, forces Demetrius to leave Antioch and move to Seleucia or Cilicia.[117] The author of 1 Maccabees reports a single battle in which Demetrius is defeated and forced to flee, making no mention of his destination (v. 55).

11:57-59. Antiochus VI, son of Alexander Balas and Cleopatra Thea, is only two years old, but official letters must be sent in his name. As at the accession of a new king, Jonathan's position as high priest needs to be reconfirmed, as does his control over the four districts that Alexander had given to him (the three of 11:34 plus possibly Akrabattene on the eastern boundary of Judea and Samaria or maybe Ekron [10:89]). Jonathan is enrolled as a Friend of the new king with the prerogatives of a Kinsman (10:89). Jonathan's brother Simon is made a Seleucid appointee, as governor of the coastal area from Syria to Egypt. The Hasmoneans thus become integrated

117. For Seleucia, see Livy Summary of Book 52; for Cilicia, see Josephus *Antiquities of the Jews* 13.145.

into the Seleucid administration, ironically fulfilling what the "renegades" had sought to do. One wonders if the author of 1 Maccabees was aware of the irony.

11:60-62. Jonathan loses no time in using his position and Simon's position to traverse the province of Trans-Euphrates—the province west of the Euphrates—both gaining the allegiance of the cities to Antiochus VI and consolidating his own power. Askalon had received him beforehand (10:86), but Gaza has to be subdued (v. 61). Jonathan acts in a way similar to the way Bacchides, the earlier Seleucid general, had acted in Judea (9:53); he takes hostages to ensure the people's compliance. He ranges from Gaza in the southern coastal area to Damascus, well north and to the east of the Ladder of Tyre.

11:63. Demetrius II still controls the coastal region north of Tyre, and some of his forces come into Galilee while Jonathan is north in Damascus. Their mission was probably not, as the NRSV translates the end of v. 63, "to remove him from office," but to turn him away from his mission of consolidating the hold of Antiochus VI in the area from Gaza to Damascus.

11:64-66. Jonathan, last mentioned as being in Damascus (v. 62), marches south to meet Demetrius's army (v. 64). The easiest way to Kadesh was to travel south to Lake Gennesaret and then north through the plain of Hazor to Kadesh (see v. 67). Either Simon had been left behind in Judea, or he was now left behind while Jonathan marched north from the lake. Bacchides, deputy of Demetrius I, had fortified Beth-zur with troops and stores of food (9:52). Simon's successful siege of Beth-zur anticipates his siege of the citadel (13:49-50). Capture of the town prevents it from becoming a base of attack from the rear.

11:67-74. The enemy forces have time to prepare for the battle, and so they choose a site that allows them to set an ambush. As Jonathan's troops march out, they are caught in the trap, which, except for the bravery of a few, would have succeeded (v. 71). Nothing more is known about the family of Chalphi than that Judas son of Chalphi was one of the two men who did not desert Jonathan. Mattathias son of Absalom was the other; this may be the Absalom who was one of the ambassadors sent to Lysias (2 Macc 11:17). Jonathan, in the midst of the battle, performs the ritual of mourning (cf. Josh 7:6-9)—tearing his clothes, putting dust on his head, and praying—before returning to the fray. This time, he is successful and overruns the enemy's camp. Jonathan has fulfilled his mission of securing the area for Antiochus VI, and so he returns to Jerusalem.

REFLECTIONS

The price for advancement in the Seleucid power structure now appears. Jonathan has to behave as Bacchides had done by taking hostages to maintain order. He has to continue fighting so as to maintain his position and Simon's status as governor. In some ways, we become what we do. Jonathan had set out to gain respect within the Seleucid power structure, and in so doing he became a Seleucid functionary. When planning what we are to do, we should, like chess players, look ahead to see the consequences of our choices.

1 Maccabees 12:1-23, The Relationship with Rome

COMMENTARY

Just as Judas is said to have used the respite after his victory over Nicanor to contact the Romans (1 Maccabees 8), so also Jonathan, now that the southern coastal area has been subdued, renews diplomatic relationships with Rome and initiates contacts with other nations. Serious questions have been raised about the authenticity of the Spartan correspondence, though some scholars maintain that it is genuine. What is interesting to note is the very different circumstances under which Judas and Jonathan wrote. In Judas's time, the Seleucid kingdom was united under Demetrius I, while during Jonathan's career Demetrius II and Antiochus VI were fighting for the throne. Judas operated within Judea, while Jonathan had a well-equipped army traversing the province of Trans-Euphrates. Judas was a rebel from the Seleucid king; Jonathan was his Kinsman and Simon one of his governors. Jonathan is depicted as a respected member of the club, meeting with kings (10:60; 11:6) and forming alliances with them. The author of 1 Maccabees wants to put Jonathan on the world stage, and thus heighten the importance of Jonathan and the Jewish nation.

12:1-4. This section is enclosed between two encounters with commanders of Demetrius (11:63; 12:24). The friendship with Rome is a reference to Judas's earlier agreement (see 8:17-32). As noted in the Commentary on 8:17-32, such a friendship pact did not oblige the Romans to intervene but did give them an excuse to do so and might make a Seleucid king hesitate before acting, although Demetrius I had not done so. The brevity of the description of the Roman mission has led some scholars to suggest that it is simply a doublet of Simon's later embassy (15:15-24).

One wonders what "other places" the author of 1 Maccabees had in mind in v. 2. The very vagueness suggests that he had no information but the letter to Sparta to go on, but that he wishes to place Judea on a level with other nations. The Spartans had left the Achaean League and so had not been party to its defeat but had remained on good terms with Rome. Perhaps Sparta's relationship with Rome is the reason behind the attempt of the Jews to forge a kinship relationship with the Spartans, who would then speak to Rome on their behalf. However, the text of 1 Maccabees says nothing of this and simply speaks of Jonathan's wishing to become an ally and friend with other nations. Such a move seems to imply more than a hope for deterrence against any future Seleucid monarch; rather, it seems to be part of a strategy for complete independence. It should also be considered in the light of the "creative" history whereby many nations sought to enhance their prestige by connecting their heroes to the mythical heroes of Greece. Within the Jewish tradition, for example, Cleodemus Malchus has the sons of Abraham accompany Heracles to Africa,[118] and Tacitus reports that the name "Jew" derives from Mt. Ida in Crete, thus forging a Cretan origin for the Jews.[119]

12:5-6. Jonathan's letter to the Spartans follows. The Jewish senate was mentioned in a letter of Antiochus III,[120] but precisely what its membership was is unknown. Most probably it was composed of priests and leading members of the local aristocracy.

12:7-8. Jonathan reminds the Spartans of a letter that was sent from Onias to Arius. The Greek manuscripts give the name of the Spartan king as "Darius," while v. 20 names him Arius. The king referred to is probably Areus I (c. 312–265 BCE), rather than Areus II (262–254 BCE), who died as a child. Onias is probably the Jewish high priest Onias I (c. 320–290 BCE). Areus I had his hands full in combatting the encroachments of Macedonia, and the reader may wonder why he would seek an alliance with Judea. The letter quoted in vv. 20-23 does not explicitly speak of the formation of such an alliance. It is concerned, rather, with kinship and so with hospitality and diplomatic support. Such concerns could be the basis for forging an alliance.

12:9-10. Without the usual epistolary well-wishing, Jonathan gets to the reason for sending the letter: "to renew our family ties and friendship with you" (v. 10). The phrasing of these verses seems to present a backhanded compliment—i.e., "We don't really need you, but let's not become estranged." This may be an apologia against those who do not think Judea should become entangled in foreign alliances.

12:11-12. The wording of these verses is what is normally found at the beginning of letters, as the letter writer expresses care and concern for the addressees. The phrasing is similar, for example, to the opening well wishes of letters of Paul: "I thank my God every time I remember you, constantly

---

118. Josephus *Antiquities of the Jews* 1.239-241.
119. Tacitus *Histories* 5.2.
120. Josephus *Antiquities of the Jews* 12.142.

praying with joy in every one of my prayers for all of you" (Phil 1:3-4 NRSV; cf. Rom 1:9).

12:13-15. Jonathan alludes to the "many trials and many wars" the Jews have faced. It is unclear who the "other allies and friends" he refers to were (v. 14). Again, these verses seem like a backhanded compliment—i.e., "We don't really need allies." As such, it seems directed more at a Jewish than a Spartan audience. The role of prayer recalls 3:18-23, 53; 9:46.

12:16-18. These verses introduce the two ambassadors who deliver the letter to the Spartans: Numenius and Antipater. Their trip to Sparta is described later (14:22); in addition, Numenius will be sent to Rome by Simon (14:24). Jonathan requests a reply to his letter.

12:19-23. Jonathan includes here a copy of the letter that was sent to Onias. In the letter, Arius alludes to a writing that suggests that the Spartans and the Jews "are brothers and are of the family of Abraham" (v. 21). Scholars would dearly love to have the writing to which Arius refers. It is interesting that the Greek historian Herodotus states that the progenitors of the Spartan royal house came from Egypt,[121] and Hecataeus of Abdera holds that the Greek hero Danaos, whose descendants populated the Peloponnese, and Kadmos, the founder of Thebes, left Egypt when Moses led the Israelites out.[122] As mentioned earlier, Cleodemus Malchus had linked the descendants of Abraham with Heracles, and the Spartan kings were said to be descendants of Heracles. However the connection was made, it most probably would have been through figures of primeval history. The reference to livestock and property (v. 23) seems more appropriate to groups living alongside one another (cf. Gen 34:23). It may be a concretely phrased formula to express kinship and friendship through the fact that both parties hold something in common, even though neither would use the other's possessions without consent.

---

121. Herodotus 6.53.
122. See Diodorus Siculus 40.3.2.

1 Maccabees 12:24-38, Further Campaigns for Antiochus VI

COMMENTARY

12:24-25. The commanders of Demetrius's armies return, a "larger force than before," to launch a second campaign. Their first campaign against Jonathan had ended in defeat (11:63-74). Previously the commanders had advanced south as far as Kadesh in Galilee. This time, Jonathan marches north before they can enter Judean territory (v. 25). Hamath was in the Orontes valley, well north of Jerusalem. This would seem a long way for Jonathan to go to make sure that his opponents did not enter Judea. Since he had not gone beyond the Eleutherus River earlier (11:7), since Simon's rule was over the Ladder of Tyre (also south of the Eleutherus), and since the enemy is said to flee across the Eleutherus River (v. 30), the reader should therefore see the confrontation as having taken place at the southern border of the region of Hamath, near the traditional northern limit of Israel's territory (see Num 34:8; Josh 13:5; 1 Kgs 8:65; 2 Kgs 14:25; Ezek 47:15).

12:26-32. Just as Gorgias had prepared a night assault on Judas (4:1), so also the commanders of Demetrius plan a night raid on Jonathan's army. Their planned surprise attack, as well as their tricky retreat with no fighting, reinforces the sense that Jonathan's force is invincible.

Jonathan pursues them, but they elude him and cross the Eleutherus. So Jonathan turns "aside against the Arabs who are called Zabadeans" and conquers and plunders them (v. 31). The Zabadeans lived about thirty miles northwest of Damascus. Perhaps there is a connection between these people and the Zabdiel who murdered Alexander Balas (11:17). Jonathan is once again in control of the whole region of Coelesyria.

12:33-38. While Jonathan controls the north, Simon makes sure the southern coastal area remains quiet. Jonathan assembles the elders as Judas had assembled the people (6:19). Jonathan's military preparations, therefore, are seen as not arbitrary but the result of common consent. Jonathan's fortification of strategic areas in Judea, as well as Simon's installation of garrisons at Beth-zur (11:65-66), at Joppa, and at Adida, near Lydda between the coastal plain and the hill country of Judea, seems to be part of a well-orchestrated plan to secure, perhaps to enlarge, the territory of Judea against all comers. Secure in his control of the area of Coelesyria, Jonathan once again tackles the problem of the citadel in Jerusalem, the remaining vestige of Seleucid authority over Judea (11:20-21, 41). He strengthens Jerusalem's walls and repairs "the section called Chaphenatha" (v. 37) and seeks to starve out the inhabitants of the citadel, as Bacchides had successfully done to the sanctuary (6:51-54).[123] The eastern valley referred to is the Kidron Valley.

123. "Chaphenatha," an Aramaic word, is unknown outside of 1 Macc 12:37. Some scholars identify it with the "Second Quarter" (2 Kgs 22:14) at the northwest of the temple area.

1 Maccabees 12:39-53, The Capture of Jonathan

COMMENTARY

12:39-40. Jonathan has aimed at securing Jerusalem and Judea from all attack, and a further goal seemed the complete independence of Judea from Seleucid control. While Jonathan is carrying out these operations, Trypho has been busy in northern Syria. He controls Antioch and most of its hinterlands, and the coastal cities of Aradus, Orthosia, Byblus, Berytus, Ptolemais, and Dora. Demetrius II retained Seleucia, Sidon, and Tyre. With Demetrius so contained, Trypho feels he needs to curtail Jonathan's power. The author of 1 Maccabees, however, implies that the reason for Trypho's treacherous attack is his ambition to be king in Antiochus's place and that Jonathan, as a loyal subject of Antiochus VI, would not allow this (v. 39). Beth-shan (i.e., Scythopolis) is strategically placed in the Jordan valley. It appears as if Trypho was coming through the Plain of Esdraelon from Ptolemais, as that is where Trypho takes Jonathan (12:45, 48). Trypho may have known that the western and southern approaches—Joppa, Adida, Beth-zur—were well fortified.

12:41-48. The author plays on the double meaning of "to meet" (ἀπαντάω *apantaō*), which can imply a meeting either in war or in friendship. When Jonathan comes to meet Trypho with a large, experienced force (v. 41), Trypho is forced to meet him in feigned friendship (vv. 42-45). Jonathan is used to being courted with gifts and promises (see chap. 10), so Trypho's actions would seem legitimate. Jonathan is already a Friend and Kinsman of Antiochus VI (11:57-58), and Trypho cunningly lets him think he is on the same level as Trypho. Jonathan should have been suspicious of Trypho's offer to hand Ptolemais over to him, since the people of that city had been hostile to the Jews (5:15, 22). But Jonathan had once before been honorably received in Ptolemais by Alexander Balas, father of Antiochus VI (10:59-65), and even when threatened by Demetrius II there Jonathan had been able to emerge unscathed (11:22-28). One is not sure what the other strongholds mentioned were, but Trypho's offer of these cities and troops proved too tempting. When he enters the town, the people close the gates, seize him, and kill all the men with him. The reader of 1 Maccabees knows by now that one should never trust a Seleucid official (1:30; 7:16).

12:49-52. The two thousand troops left in Galilee, presumably in the Plain of Esdraelon through which one would travel from Ptolemais to Beth-shan and which separated Galilee from Samaria, successfully deter the forces Trypho has sent to capture them, and they return to Judea. Realizing that Jonathan has been captured, they conclude that he is dead along with his companions; they do not know that Trypho has captured him alive. As all Israel mourned at the deaths of Mattathias (2:70) and Judas (9:20), so now Jonathan is mourned. Great distress came upon Israel after Judas's death (9:27); now fear comes to Israel at what might happen.

12:53. The nations surrounding Judea react to news that the Jews' leader and helper (cf. 9:30) is gone by trying to "destroy them." The message once again is driven home that one should be suspicious of one's neighbors and of the Seleucid Empire.

REFLECTIONS

Jonathan is a fascinating character. He was much more successful than Judas in gaining effective control of Judea and in widening its borders. He rose from being a rebel on the run to a high-ranking official in the Seleucid bureaucracy, and his army was feared by his enemies. Yet for some reason he got no respect. His name is omitted when Mattathias entrusts the fight to his sons (2:65-66), and he is not given a hymn of praise as Judas and Simon are (3:3-9; 14:4-15). Much of his activity in rallying and organizing the people is passed over, and yet the years he spent judging the people (9:73) must have been crucial for the success of the revolt. Jonathan remains a shadowy figure, even though he brings Israel into the arena of international politics. Perhaps there is too much of the diplomat about Jonathan and not enough of the dashing warrior for the author. Yet it is precisely that ability to negotiate a settlement that brings such success and prosperity to Israel. One of our great temptations is to romanticize war. But war destroys and maims and kills and embitters lives. War must be the last resort after all attempts to arrive at a peaceful solution have failed. Jonathan, in this light, might be someone to emulate.

Yet he also is a figure to warn us how not to behave. When he does use force, he uses it to compel submission (11:61), as an instrument of repression. Jonathan's ambition, his desire to wear purple and the gold buckle, to be on speaking terms with Rome and Sparta, to extend the territory of Judea beyond its borders, is what we must be wary of. That ambition is what brought Jonathan down. Trypho saw that Jonathan was greedy for power, and so he tempted him with the offer of more to make Jonathan let down his guard. Then he pounced and caught Jonathan in his trap. That longing for more has started so many wars and led to the downfall of so many people. "For the love of money is a root of all kinds of evil" (1 Tim 6:10 NRSV). To resist seeking more at the expense of others is a hard lesson to learn.

1 MACCABEES 13:1–16:24

SIMON

1 MACCABEES 13:1-30, SIMON REPLACES JONATHAN

OVERVIEW

This section deals with the replacement of Jonathan by the last surviving Maccabean brother, Simon. Simon has been associated with Jonathan since the death of Judas (9:19, 32, 37, 62-67; 10:82; 11:59, 64-66; 12:33, 38), sharing in his exploits. Now he is to fulfill the prophecy of his father Mattathias (2:65) and become a father to Israel. But first Jonathan has to die, and so this section describes the treachery of Trypho, his murder of Jonathan, and Jonathan's burial.

1 Maccabees 13:1-11, Simon Takes Command

COMMENTARY

13:1-3a. Ever since Bacchides had gone back to his own land (9:69), Jonathan had been able to secure Judea and fight outside the land. Now, as before (3:10, 13, 35-36; 5:1-2; 6:27; 7:8, 26; 9:1), forces are massed to invade Judea. As before, the people are afraid as they see all the promises of Seleucid kings broken. It is not clear whether Simon had been at Adida (12:38) all this time, or with the troops that Jonathan had sent back (12:46). Frequently Jonathan and Simon had divided the operations between them (11:65; 12:32-33), and this had strategically been an important division of labor. The author emphasizes, as earlier with Judas (3:3) and Jonathan (9:73), that the people are with Simon.

13:3b-6. Simon exhorts the people by recalling the past and making that the basis for his future actions, as Mattathias had recalled the deeds of the ancestors in times of distress (2:51-64; cf. the speeches of Mattathias [2:19-22] and Judas [3:58-60]). Simon at this point thinks his brother Jonathan is dead. The reasoning behind v. 5 seems to assume the deuteronomic theory that death is punishment for sin. But if such good men as his father and brother died, then it must not have been because of their sin; times of distress had come upon Israel, and no one could be good enough to escape death.

13:7-11. Simon's speech is effective, and he is unanimously chosen leader in place of Jonathan. Simon knows that Trypho will attack, and so he completes the fortification of Jerusalem that Jonathan had begun (12:35-37). He already has a garrison in Joppa (12:33-34) but now decides to make sure that no uprising against it will take place, and the inhabitants are summarily thrown out of their city. As Joppa lay on the coast to the west of Adida (12:38) and the Beth-horon ascent (3:16), Simon was strengthening the western approach to Judea. Jonathan son of Absalom, who leads the troops to Joppa, is the brother of Mattathias, who stood by Jonathan when he was caught by an ambush (11:70). This may be the same Absalom who served as one of the ambassadors sent earlier to negotiate peaceful terms with Lysias (2 Macc 11:17).

1 Maccabees 13:12-24, Trypho's Invasion

COMMENTARY

This section is bounded by Trypho's entering (v. 12) and leaving the land (v. 24). For the first time we learn that Jonathan is still alive, and the drama arises as to what his fate will be.

13:12-13. Rather than approach Judea from the north through the Plain of Esdraelon, Trypho chooses to take the coastal route but does not first attempt to take Joppa. Jonathan is not dead but is being held prisoner by Trypho. Simon's army encamps at Adida.

13:14-16. With that force at Joppa behind him and Simon's army in front, Trypho decides to try deceit, a typical Seleucid trick, according to the author (e.g., 1:30; 7:10, 27). Trypho claims that Jonathan owes money, perhaps taxes that the high priest should have collected or a fee for being granted the high priesthood (cf. 2 Macc 4:7, 24). Trypho also asks for two of Jonathan's sons as hostages. Hostage taking was a typical tactic: Antiochus IV (1:10; 8:7) had been a hostage in Rome, and Bacchides (9:53) and Jonathan (11:62) had taken hostages also. This is the first time we know that Jonathan was married.

13:17-19. The author of 1 Maccabees states that Simon recognizes that Trypho's request is a ploy. Yet he consents to pay lest, according to the author, he be seen as conniving at Jonathan's death and so gaining the leadership of Israel. The author does not mention that the sons of Jonathan might have been a potential source of opposition to Simon as leader and that, in agreeing to Trypho's demands, Simon might not have been too unhappy to have them out of the way. We do not know how old the two boys were, nor are we told what subsequently happened to them. Perhaps Trypho killed them when he killed Jonathan (v. 23). As expected, Trypho breaks his word (v. 19), just as Bacchides (7:18) and Demetrius II (11:53) had done before him.

13:20-24. Trypho now attempts to invade the land. Simon keeps his army between the coastal plain and the hill country, and so forces Trypho to go south through Idumea to try a southern assault, as Lysias had done (4:29; 6:31). Adora was about five miles southwest of Hebron. Since to get to Jerusalem from there Trypho would have had to pass Beth-zur (where Simon had stationed a garrison [11:65-66]), the men of the citadel, isolated and in need of provisions (12:36), may have offered to act as guides for Trypho, as they had for Gorgias and his cavalry (4:2). The wilderness referred to may be the wilderness of Tekoa (9:32). When the weather prevents Trypho's surprise attack, he moves across the Jordan to Gilead, thus making a circular tour of the land of Judea. The snowfall suggests winter, so, given the date in 13:41, this must have taken place during the winter of 143/42 BCE. The location of Baskama (v. 23) is unknown. Trypho's invasion has been frustrated, and he, like Bacchides (9:69), leaves Judea, which would now be at peace under Simon as it had been previously under Jonathan (9:73).

1 Maccabees 13:25-30, Jonathan's Tomb

COMMENTARY

Simon buries Jonathan, and "all Israel" mourned his death (v. 26). The monument Simon erected over the family tomb was large, showy, and presumably quite expensive. Eusebius of Caesarea, in his *Onomasticon* (under the entry for Modein) of the early fourth century CE, wrote that it was still standing in his time. It has not survived, and its description in 1 Maccabees is not detailed enough so that one can reconstruct it. On a platform of hewn stones, Simon placed a row of seven pyramids ("alongside" [κατέναντι *katenanti*], rather than "opposite" one another as in the NRSV, v. 28)—one each for his parents and four brothers and possibly one for himself; or perhaps seven is seen as a particularly potent number. Surrounding the pyramids were huge columns bearing trophies of arms and carved ships. Pyramids are usually associated with Egypt, but they were found in Italy and later in Jerusalem. Trophies of suits of armor were common among the Greeks, and the Romans adopted the custom by the mid-second century BCE. In Jerusalem, the so-called tomb of Jason has graffiti seemingly representing a naval battle. No one is sure why the non-seafaring Jews would put carved ships on a monument for the Maccabees. Was it part of regular decorative practice? Or does it suggest that the control of the seaport Joppa now gave the Jews access to the sea? What the monument clearly attests is the pretension of the Hasmoneans to display their wealth and power.

1 MACCABEES 13:31–14:3, JUDEA GAINS INDEPENDENCE

1 Maccabees 13:31-42, The Removal of Tribute

COMMENTARY

13:31-32. Exactly when Trypho came to the throne and had Antiochus VI murdered is a vexed question. The last coins of Antiochus are dated 142/41, which seems to be closest to the time line of 1 Maccabees (13:41 refers to 170 Sel Bab, or 142–141 BCE). Other ancient authorities, however, date Antiochus's murder to 139 BCE.[124] Trypho assumed the title Autokrator, and dated his coins not by the Seleucid era but by his own regnal years. Since Trypho was not descended from the Seleucids, he wanted to show his break with Seleucid tradition. His accession to the throne increased the chaos in the Seleucid realm.[125] "Asia" refers to the Seleucid Empire (8:6; 12:39).

13:33-38. Simon kept increasing the defenses of Judea begun under Jonathan and decided to reconcile with Demetrius II. However, there is no explicit request for reconciliation, and the wording of these verses implies that Simon has been on Demetrius's side all along and is asking for relief (cf. 7:6-7). The term for "relief" (ἄφεμα *aphema*) covers both tax relief (v. 37) and pardon (v. 39). The appended letter from Demetrius, however, speaks of Simon's having sent a gold crown and a palm branch to Demetrius (vv. 36-37), a clear recognition of kingship (cf. 2 Macc 14:4), as well as a peace offering, but the author of 1 Maccabees does not portray Simon as asking for peace with Demetrius II.

As before (11:23-37), Demetrius II shows a willingness to use tax concessions to win friends. He was, in fact, not in control of the southern part of his empire, and so could afford to be generous.

The greeting (v. 36) is different from that of Demetrius's previous letter (11:30), mentioning "the priests" and ranking Simon as a "friend of kings" (cf. 11:20; 11:27, 54).

Simon had formally recognized Demetrius II as king, as Jonathan had done (11:24). This is the first indication that Simon had also succeeded Jonathan as high priest. There is no mention here of Demetrius's confirming Simon as high priest, except in the greeting of the letter. Demetrius's previous concessions (11:34-36) had been canceled (11:53). Although Demetrius II in fact would not have been able to destroy the strongholds Simon had built (v. 38), given that he was still at war with Trypho, this concession is a legal victory for Simon.

13:39. The verb translated "pardon" (ἀφίημι *aphiēmi*) is the same root as the words "release from tribute" in v. 37. Demetrius neatly glosses over Simon's and Jonathan's support of Antiochus VI. One is not

---

124. Livy says that Antiochus VI was murdered by surgeons in league with Trypho (Summary of Book 54).
125. See Diodorus Siculus 33:28.

sure whether the taxes mentioned here are more general than the ones remitted earlier (10:34; 11:35) or whether Jerusalem served as the place where all the taxes in Judea were collected.

13:40. Demetrius's request for Jews to join his bodyguard is not surprising. Jews are well-known for their military prowess, and Demetrius I had recruited Jewish soldiers for his army and allowed them to follow their own laws (10:36-37). In addition, troops sent by Jonathan had been instrumental in saving Demetrius II earlier (11:45-51).

13:41-42. Scholars debate exactly when the events in these verses took place, some placing them before 170 Sel Bab (i.e., before June 142), while others place it later. Clearly, the people (and the author) view Demetrius's concessions as the equivalent of granting them independence. The phrase "the yoke of the Gentiles" is a familiar image of the punishment that Israel would suffer if it disobeyed God's laws (Deut 28:48; Lam 1:14). The prophets had foretold that God would remove the yoke of their oppressors (Isa 9:4; 10:27; 14:25; Jer 30:8; Ezek 34:27). Within 1 Maccabees, the yoke is the oppression of the Greeks (i.e., the Seleucids [8:18]), begun when the renegades yoked themselves to the Gentiles (1:15). Simon, who had already been named a commander by Antiochus VI (11:59) and leader by the people (13:7), is now officially recognized as high priest. Although the narrative refers to "the first year of Simon," the Seleucid dating system continues to be used (13:51; 14:1, 27; 16:14).

1 Maccabees 13:43-53, Further Acquisitions by Simon

COMMENTARY

Simon continues the policy of extending his control. Bacchides had fortified Beth-zur, Gazara, and the citadel (9:52). With Beth-zur already taken (11:65-66), Simon now turns his attention to the two others.

13:43-48. Gazara (Gezer), an important site on the road from Jerusalem to Joppa, had a Seleucid garrison (4:15; 9:52) and was strategically situated on a hill surveying the coastal plain. Although Judas had already constructed "siege engines" (μηχανή *mēchanē*, 6:20), the weapon now used by Simon is an advanced Hellenistic siege device (ἑλεόπολις *heleopolis*). As earlier at Beth-zur (11:65-66), Simon allows the inhabitants to live while turning them into war refugees (v. 47). Simon does not engage in the practice of the ban as Judas had done (e.g., 5:28, 35) but contents himself with cleansing the city and repopulating it with devout Jews (v. 47), just as Josiah had cleansed the land and the Temple (2 Chr 34:3-8). Gazara had a good water supply and fertile land, so Simon was able to reward his supporters, as well as gain a base for operations in the coastal plain. Archaeologists have uncovered an elaborate system of cisterns in Gazara, suggested to be Jewish ritual bathing "pools" (מקואות *miqwāʾôt*), but the suggestion is far from certain. A Greek inscription found at Gazara reads: "Says Pampras: may fire pursue Simon's palace." Although the date and exact reference of the inscription are unsure, if dated to Simon's time, this curse may have been written by one of Simon's prisoners of war (cf. 14:7).

13:49-53. The citadel at Jerusalem, originally built by Antiochus VI in 169/68 (1:33), had housed a Seleucid garrison and served as a haven for Jews opposed to the Maccabees. Those trapped there, who had been under siege since Jonathan's time (almost two years, 143 to 141 BCE; see 12:36), now sue for peace. Almost exactly the same words are used to describe the outcome of this siege as the one at Gazara (cf. vv. 45-48 with v. 50), but the celebration is described more fully (v. 51). The author also parallels the capture of the citadel by Simon to the capture of the sanctuary by Judas (cf. 4:41-61; cf. also 4:36 with 13:51), and both events are to be celebrated yearly (v. 52). With the threat of foreign troops gone, the southern fortifications of the Temple can be repaired, and Jewish troops can occupy the citadel. We learn that Simon has a son who (literally) was a man (v. 53), i.e., not simply come of age, but someone who had reached warrior status (cf. 5:63). While Simon lives in Jerusalem, his son, commander of the army, lives at Gazara (Gezer), watching the coastal plain and guarding the western entrance to Judea.

REFLECTIONS

The author captures the mood of the followers of Simon at the recapture of the citadel. Here is proof positive that the yoke of the Gentiles had been removed, that Israel had gained its independence. This was a time to remember and to celebrate, just as the Fourth of July is a day for all U.S. citizens to rejoice in the gaining of their independence. Yet independence brings with it consequences for others. The joy of the Israelites contrasts starkly with what must have been the despair of those evicted from their homes in Gazara and their forced relocation. The cleansing of Beth-zur, Gazara, and the citadel and their repopulation by those who observed the law echo the injunctions to Joshua to clear the promised land of its former inhabitants and the call of Ezekiel to cleanse the land of uncleanness.

Should injunctions for ethnic cleansing be followed? Humans in conflict situations feel a need to draw sharp boundaries between themselves and other groups. We are the pure ones; we must have no part with you. In times of insecurity, communities pull the wagons into a circle to defend their own group, however defined, against all others. The only way to stop this only too human reaction is to somehow build each group's sense of security and well-being so that no one will react defensively but all will realize that problems can be worked out through mediation rather than by recourse to violence. Humans must learn to cooperate and respect each other's cultural and religious differences. Otherwise, there will be no end to conflict. Such attempts at reconciliation will be extremely difficult, as often atrocities are committed by both sides. To forgive is hard to accomplish when one cannot forget the past. Perhaps one way to do so is to think of the future, of the children who will come after us. Do we want them to continue the feuding? Or do we want them to learn to live in peace?

1 Maccabees 14:1-3, The Capture of Demetrius

COMMENTARY

The situation in the Seleucid Empire was at a stalemate, with Demetrius II, Trypho, and Simon each controlling his own area. Trypho had sought Roman support, but the Romans, while accepting his gifts, had them inscribed with the name of Antiochus VI, whom Trypho had murdered.[126] According to the author of 1 Maccabees, Demetrius tries to break the deadlock by going to Mesopotamia, which had remained loyal, to secure help. Demetrius's action was more likely an attempt to push back the Parthian forces that had invaded Seleucid territory (according to cuneiform tablets, Mithradates I [Arsaces] ruled in Babylon and Seleucia on the Tigris in July 141 and in Uruk by October 141). Demetrius left in autumn 141/40 BCE (172, according to the Seleucid Macedonian calendar), and was at first successful, since Persis, Elymais, and Bactria helped his effort. However, in Media he was defeated and captured in 140/39 BCE. His bold hope not only to help the eastern provinces but also to create an army strong enough to come back and defeat Trypho failed. Mithradates treated Demetrius honorably, settling him in Hyrcania and marrying him to one of his daughters.[127]

126. Diodorus Siculus 33:28a.

127. See Diodorus Siculus 33.28; 34.15; Appian *Syriaca* 67-68; Justin *Epitome* 36.1.2-6; 38.9.2-3.

1 MACCABEES 14:4-49, THE PRAISE OF SIMON

OVERVIEW

The rest of chapter 14 is given over to the praise of Simon. First comes a eulogy (vv. 4-15), comparable to that at the beginning of Judas's rule (3:3-9), followed by praise of Simon by Rome and the Spartans (vv. 16-24), and finally the decree of the people in honor of Simon (vv. 25-49).

1 Maccabees 14:4-15, Hymn of Praise

COMMENTARY

The rule of Simon is idealized and abounds in allusions to Hebrew Scriptures.

14:4. Like Judas (7:50) and Jonathan (9:57), Simon provides rest to the land, just as the judges had (Judg 3:11, 30; 5:31). Whereas those in the citadel had sought evil against the people (6:18), Simon seeks the good of the nation.

14:5-7. Simon's wartime exploits are celebrated, starting with his capture of Joppa during Jonathan's reign (12:33). The phrase "to crown all his honors he took Joppa for a harbor," literally "with all his glory," should be understood from the context as referring to Simon's troops (cf. Isa. 8:7, where the king of Assyria and all his glory are to come against Israel). Promises of enlarged territory in response to Torah obedience (v. 6) are found in Exodus (34:24) and Deuteronomy (19:8-9). Verse 7 highlights Simon's victories over the three main fortresses (11:65-66; 13:43-50) as well as the campaigns in which he must have gathered many captives. His Torah faithfulness is again stressed (v. 7*b*; cf. 11:66; 13:48, 50), and so he finds that no one resists him (cf. Deut 7:17-26; 11:25; Josh 1:5).

14:8-15. Once Simon's exploits in war have been praised, affairs in Judea are described in idyllic terms; these verses echo other descriptions of peace in the OT. The elderly can sit in the streets, reminiscing (v. 9; cf. Zech 8:4-5). The people are free to farm their land without fear of enemy attack or looting, and without having to pay oppressive taxes to outsiders (v. 8; 13:41-42), and the land's productivity flourishes (vv. 8, 10; Lev 26:3-5; Zech 8:12-13; cf. Ezek 34:25-31). The mourning and lamentation, such as followed Antiochus IV's sacking of Jerusalem (1:25-28), where the elders groaned and the young men became faint, are reversed. Just as Judas's renown went to the ends of the earth (3:9), so too does Simon's as his actions of defense and provisioning (13:33) are recalled. Just as Solomon brought safety to the land (1 Kgs 4:25), so too does Simon (v. 11). As the prophets Micah (4:4) and Zechariah (3:10) had foreseen, people sit under their own vines and fig trees (v. 12). Simon is the perfect picture of a just ruler (v. 14*a*), as envisioned by Ps 72:4 and Isa 11:3-4. Simon's destruction of the ungodly (v. 14*b*) again mirrors Judas (3:8). In particular, Simon adds to the work of Judas by restoring the sanctuary (4:49), as he wipes out the wrongs done against it under Antiochus IV, who had dishonored the Temple and taken away its glorious vessels (2:8-13).

1 Maccabees 14:16-24, Diplomacy with Rome and Sparta

COMMENTARY

14:16-19. The authenticity, chronology, and meaning of the events in these verses pose great difficulty. The author's Judeocentrism is evident in his claim that Rome and Sparta were deeply grieved at Jonathan's death. It is unlikely, however, that the Romans would take the initiative to write to a client state, such as Judea, without the formality of an embassy; the text of a letter from the Romans is not given, although they are said to have renewed their alliance with Judea (14:18). The reference to bronze tablets recalls those sent in Judas's time (8:22). As a result, Simon sends an ambassador to Rome with a gift to confirm the alliance (14:24), a Roman answer is received (15:15-21), and Demetrius II is said to confirm Simon in the high priesthood, because the Romans had received the envoys of Simon with honor (14:38-40). It seems more likely that Simon did follow in the steps of Judas and Jonathan in seeking an alliance with Rome; the letter of 15:15-21 is probably the result of that embassy. Demetrius has already recognized Simon as high priest in an earlier letter written sometime in 142 BCE (13:36-40). Simon would not have had time to send an embassy to Rome after Jonathan's death (probably in the winter of 143/142 BCE, when no sailing could take place) and receive a reply before Demetrius wrote that letter preserved in 13:36-40. Perhaps Demetrius only needed to know that Simon had sent ambassadors to Rome.

14:20-23. As at 12:5, 16-17, the Spartan correspondence is linked with an embassy to Rome. "Rulers" (ἄρχοντες *archontes*) is a very generic title and does not suggest which specific officials are in view. Jonathan's letter to the Spartans had mentioned a council of the Jews in its address (12:6), but it is not mentioned here. The ambassadors (v. 22) are the same as those sent by Jonathan (12:16). Verses 22-23 seem to indicate that this letter was in response to an embassy sent by Simon.

14:24. As noted above, this embassy of Numenius was probably prior to the renewal of friendship by both Romans and Spartans. A mina weighs 431 grams, so the shield would have weighed 431 kilograms, approximately 862 pounds, a significant gift.

1 Maccabees 14:25-49, "The Great Assembly"

COMMENTARY

The decree to memorialize the Maccabees by recording their deeds on bronze tablets to be put on "pillars on Mount Zion" (v. 27) is depicted as a spontaneous outpouring of thanks by the people. Its preface (vv. 27-28) and its concluding arrangements concerning publication follow the basic usage in contemporary honorific inscriptions. After the preface comes a historical rundown of the achievements of the Hasmoneans (vv. 29-30)—particularly Simon (vv. 31-40)—and this is followed by the resolution of the people (vv. 41-43), which was binding on them all (vv. 44-45).

14:25-26. The people's response seems to refer to v. 19, or may simply be a response to all that Simon achieved in chapter 13. The word used for "people" here (δῆμος *dēmos*) reflects official inscriptional usage (cf. its usage in the correspondence with Rome and Sparta [8:29; 12:6; 14:20-23; 15:18]). Throughout the decree, the usual term for "people" (λαός *laos*) is used. In his lament over what was happening to Israel, Mattathias had said that Jerusalem was "no longer free, she has become a slave" (1 Macc 2:11 NRSV). The people now recognize that Mattathias's descendants have redressed that lament and that they have given back to Israel its freedom.

14:27-28, The Preface. The date is September 140 BCE. The first year of Simon's high priesthood was 170 Sel Bab (142/41), so the third would be 172 Sel Bab (140/39 BCE).

Why the translator did not translate *Saramel* or *Asaramel* is unknown. The text has been interpreted both as a place name, "the court of the people of God" (reflecting Hebrew חצר עם־אל [*ḥăṣar ʿam-ʾēl*]), or as a title for Simon, "prince of the people of God" (שר עם־אל *śar ʿam-ʾēl*). Both have difficulties; the place name is not usually given after the date in such documents; one does not know how the preposition "in" (ἐν *en*) could be placed before a title.

The opening words of the decree (v. 28) make a distinction between various groups. Throughout the decree itself the basic grouping is "the Jews and their priests" (v. 41) or "the people and priests" (v. 44). The opening words mention also "the rulers of the nation and the elders of the country" (v. 28). The book of Ezra distinguishes between rulers and elders, reflecting a distinction between Jerusalem and the rest of the country (Ezra 10:8, 14). The wording of the decree, then, emphasizes that all important groups were included (as at Ezra 10:1). The decree was probably drafted by the nation's leaders and then read aloud to the people.

14:29-40, The Exploits of the Hasmoneans. 14:29-30. The author gives a very bland description of the tumultuous events under Antiochus IV with no specific mention of the actions of Mattathias or Judas; recall Judas's speeches (3:20-21, 58-59) as well as Mattathias's last will (2:49-50). Verse 29 recalls that Judas and his brothers were honored in Israel and among the Gentiles (5:63). Jonathan (v. 30) is mentioned as immediate predecessor of Simon in the high priesthood (10:20). His murder by Trypho is glossed over by the biblical expression "[he] was gathered to his people" (v. 30; cf. Gen 25:8, 17; 49:33; 2 Kgs 22:20).

14:31-34. Recorded on the bronze tablets is the invasion of Trypho (13:1-20). No mention had previously been made of Simon's using his own money either as ransom for Jonathan (13:15-19) or for the gold shield sent to Rome (14:24), but no doubt the booty taken in various campaigns had increased his wealth. Certainly the monument to his family at Modein (13:25-30) attests to his fortune. It is almost *de rigueur* in honorific texts to tell of personal wealth spent on public benefactions. Verses 33-34 provide a summary of Simon's build-up of Judea's defenses and fortification of towns of Judea (13:33), and of Beth-zur (11:65-66), Joppa (12:33-34; 13:11), and Gazara (13:43-48).

14:35. The people's response to Simon's actions is recorded. In the narrative of 1 Maccabees, the people had made Simon their leader (13:7-9) before Jonathan's death and before the events listed above, except for capturing Beth-zur and Joppa. The decree may suggest that there was another public assembly after Jonathan's death at which Simon was appointed high priest as well. Normally, as with Jonathan (10:20-21), the high priest was appointed by the Seleucid king. Simon is praised for his righteousness and faithfulness (cf. 1 Sam 26:23; 1 Macc 2:52).

14:36-37. The author concludes this list of Simon's achievements by mentioning, in the place of emphasis, the capture of the citadel (13:49-52). The descriptions of the actions of those in the citadel reflect 1:34-37; 6:18.

14:38-40. In the narrative of 1 Maccabees, Demetrius II writes to Simon as high priest (13:36) and is portrayed as being only too happy to have an ally against Rome, with no mention of a threat from the Romans. Had Simon sent an embassy to Rome after Jonathan's death in the winter of 143 BCE and before Demetrius's letter in 142 BCE? The Jews were called friends and allies by the Romans (8:31), but not brothers, as they had been by the Spartans (12:7; 14:20).

14:41-49, The Offices of Simon. This section is framed by two occurrences of the verb "to be pleased," "to agree," "to resolve" (εὐδοκέω *eudokeō*): (1) at v. 41, the Jews and the priests "agreed"/"resolved" and (2) at v. 46, all the people "agreed"/"resolved." The verb is also found at v. 47, where Simon agrees to be high priest, commander, ethnarch, and protector. Some scholars think that the decree ends in v. 45, while others see the provisions for publication in v. 48 as showing that the decree runs through v. 49. It has even been suggested that v. 41 refers to a different, more restricted group of leaders than all the people of v. 46; if that is the case, one would then have an approval of Simon by influential leaders distinct from his final approval by the people. What one has in vv. 42*b*-43 is a specification of what it means for Simon to be leader, high priest, and commander, and v. 46 resumes what was said in vv. 41-45. At v. 42*b* begins a string of five clauses all beginning with "in order that," "for the purpose that" (ὅπως *hopōs*).

14:41-42a. "High priest" and "leader" are the same titles given to Simon in 13:42. The grouping "the Jews and their priests" reflects the use of "Jews" in v. 40 and the fact that the following offices Simon holds are related to the sanctuary and so affect the priests in a particular way. The twofold grouping reflects the dual role of Simon as high priest and commander. "Forever" (αἰών *aiōn*) certainly means that Simon will be high priest for his lifetime (the same expression is used in Exod 21:6 to describe how a slave who prefers to stay with his slave wife rather than go free will have his ear pierced and then serve his master "for ever," i.e., for life). The expression may suggest hereditary holding of the position, but not necessarily. Simon's descendants are not mentioned, whereas Aaron's are when the priesthood is given to them as a perpetual ordinance (Exod 29:9). The promise of the land made to Abraham, Isaac, and Israel was explicitly enjoined to their descendants forever (Exod 32:13), and God promised David that his dynasty would rule forever (2 Sam 7:12-13). The condition "until a trustworthy prophet should arise" was mentioned earlier in connection with what to do with the polluted stones of the altar (4:47). The author is aware that the events recounted occurred after the prophets ceased to appear (9:27), and so may reflect less an opposition to Simon than a hope for further restoration. The role of the "trustworthy prophet" has been variously interpreted: (1) The prophet is to replace Simon. (2) The prophet is to decide whether Simon is fit to be ruler. (3) Only a prophet, not an assembly of people and priests, has the right to appoint a ruler, as the trustworthy prophet Samuel (1 Sam 3:20) had anointed Saul and David (1 Sam 10:1; 16:13). Most scholars seem to agree that the prophet will decide whether Simon is fit to be a ruler, but the recognition by the priests and the people of their own limitations may be more likely. (See Commentary on 4:46.)

14:42b-43. The specification of what the titles "leader" and "high priest" entail is given in a string of purpose clauses that outline Simon's rights; as high priest and governor, he is the one in charge of the sanctuary and the one who controls appointments. He has the power to break any opposition to him by appointing his own men to important positions. What goes for the sanctuary applies also to Simon's power to have his own appointees in defense and administration. After this first clause comes a repetition of the opening words of the clause, which probably should be omitted as a simple reduplication. Second, Simon is to be obeyed by everyone, so that any opposition to his will would be seen as illegal. Third, Simon's authority extends to all aspects of civil and criminal law, since his name is required on every contract. Fourth, purple dress and a gold buckle were noble prerogatives (10:89; 11:58).

14:44-45. These verses spell out Simon's powers in negative terms. Not only can no one oppose Simon's decrees, but also the right of assembly is taken away. The word for "convene" (ἐπισυστρέψαι *episystrepsai*) here has a pejorative connotation at Num 16:42 (17:7 LXX), where it refers to the rebellious assembly of the congregation against Moses and Aaron; at 2 Kgs 15:15, the noun form is used to describe the conspiracy of Shallum against King Zechariah; at Ps 64:2 (Ps 63:2 LXX), the noun form is used to describe the plots of the wicked against the pious. The phrase "liable to punishment" means the death penalty at Lev 20:9, 11-13, 16, 27.

14:46-49. Just as the people had made Simon leader and high priest (v. 35), so also now they agree to hand over to Simon the just-mentioned rights (v. 46). Simon agrees to the job under the conditions outlined (v. 47). Jonathan had been "ruler" (ἄρχων *archōn*) of the people (9:30; 12:53), but now Simon is "ruler" (ἐθνάρχης *ethnarchēs*) of the nation (cf. Esth 3:12), which comprises all Jews, people and priests (cf. v. 41). No mention is made of putting the bronze tablets on pillars (vv. 48-49). They are simply to be made conspicuous. The treasury here refers to the temple treasury (see 2 Macc 3:6). God thus becomes a witness to this bargain between the people and Simon. Similar provisions are found in inscriptions for copies of the document to be displayed publicly and for a copy to be sent to the honoree.

Some scholars have suggested that the public statement of the unlimited powers given to Simon suggests that in fact Simon did not really have such unopposed power and that he had to face opposition in trying to place his own followers in power in the sanctuary and throughout the country from those already entrenched in those positions. No doubt there was opposition to Simon's rise to such heights of power. However, to see hints of opposition in this document requires that one assume that the condition of waiting for a trustworthy prophet is a limitation of Simon's power, not that of the Jews and their priests, and also that one argue from the document's silence whereby Simon is not declared king and no reference is given to his freeing Judea from taxation. Arguments from silence are not particularly convincing, however, especially since there is no hint in 1 Maccabees that Simon wants to be king. Some scholars have also worried as to why Simon waited until his third year before having such a decree drawn up. The author of 1 Maccabees, however, places the decree after the removal of Demetrius II from power (14:1-3) and suggests by this arrangement that it was only then that Simon could so publicly proclaim his quasi-independent position of ethnarch.

With this decree in honor of Simon, the book of 1 Maccabees seems to reach a climax. The wrongs of chapters 1 and 2 have been righted, and Judea is free from the yoke of the Gentiles and under its own ethnarch. The paeans to Judas (3:3-9) and Simon (14:4-15) round out the grand exploits of the Hasmoneans. Antiochus IV had polluted the Temple, outlawed Jewish religion, and installed a citadel in Jerusalem. In contrast, Judas had cleansed the Temple and restored ancestral religion, and Simon had rid Jerusalem of the citadel. Both of these deeds were celebrated with songs and music (4:52-59; 13:51-52). The testamentary hymn of Mattathias (2:49-68) had foretold the pre-eminence of these two men.

REFLECTIONS

1. The description of life under Simon is utopian and idyllic, fulfilling the prophets' promises of the good life to come. The land is at peace, each person under his or her own vines and fig trees. The law is observed. But this harmonious picture in the hymn of praise hides some problems. Those who disagree with Simon's notion of what Torah observance means are characterized as renegades and outlaws. The extension of the borders of Judea brings with it the expulsion of non-Jews from their homes and property. Success in war means the capture and enslavement of enemies. Thus success for some means loss for others. Behind the glory of empire lies the misery of slaves. The division of society into the haves and the have-nots is a critical issue.

When we read this picture of an ideal society, we must look at our own societies and ask whether each citizen has what he or she needs to live a full and prosperous life. Our concern must be that each citizen be given the opportunity to use the talents given to him or her to the best advantage. We must not rest until the inadequacies due to poor housing, insufficient health care, and lack of proper educational opportunities are done away with. We must strive to see that all people can have productive, fulfilling jobs that provide a decent wage to support their families. Our societies must not consist of two tiers of citizens, with the poor and unfortunate neglected. The ideal society must be one in which social justice reigns, in which we shall all be brothers and sisters, no matter what our racial or ethnic heritage or income level.

2. The second reflection that this chapter awakens is the contrast between the utopian picture of the hymn and the political structure envisioned by the decree. The decree makes clear the authoritarian nature of Simon's rule. He accumulates all positions of power to himself, and his edicts are to be obeyed. If it is true that he supplied the towns with food (14:10), it was at the cost of the people's independence.

He controlled the legal apparatus as well as the police force (14:42-43). The reader may be reminded of some contemporary governments that promise food and jobs for everyone—but the promise carries also the heavy hand of the authoritarian police that go with it. What must be sought is a way to keep such promises without imposing a stifling governmental structure. What is first needed, of course, is a division of powers. The separation of the legislative from the executive and the judiciary branches of government is crucial. But one must also be concerned about the freedom of the press, a freedom to investigate unhindered. Such a freedom must not be compromised by the organs of the press being under the control of a few wealthy people who might wish to propagate a particular point of view. So, as always, we must be vigilant to see that our freedoms are preserved. But freedom brings a responsibility to work to make a better, more just society.

1 MACCABEES 15:1–16:10, FURTHER SELEUCID THREATS

1 Maccabees 15:1-14, The Rise of Antiochus VII Sidetes

COMMENTARY

As the narrative is framed in 1 Maccabees, the reader might think that Antiochus VII was the son of Demetrius II, who was defeated and captured by Trypho (14:3). Rather, he is the son of Demetrius I and the brother of Demetrius II. Antiochus, surnamed Sidetes because he had been raised in Side in Pamphylia, determines again to take up the fight against Trypho. At the time Antiochus had been living in Rhodes. His letter to Simon (15:2-9) is probably one of many such letters sent to local leaders for support of his cause against Trypho.

15:1-2. The term "priest" could mean priest *par excellence,* i.e., high priest as in the following verse. The title "ethnarch" picks up on the title used at 14:47 and recognizes the quasiindependent status of Judea. Antiochus already claims the title "king" in his greeting.

15:3-5. The term "scoundrels" (λοιμοί *loimoi,* v. 3) literally means "plague" but is applied in Greek literature to subversive persons (it is used earlier at 10:61 and also at 15:21). Does it refer only to Trypho or also to Antiochus VI and Alexander Epiphanes? Antiochus blames all the troubles of the Seleucid Empire on Trypho (cf. the complaint against Judas at 7:7). It is not known from where he got the money to recruit "a host of mercenary troops" and to equip warships. To encourage Simon's help, Antiochus confirms the tax exemptions and gifts (v. 5) granted by Demetrius I (10:38-43) and by Demetrius II (13:37-40).

15:6. Antiochus grants Simon the right to mint his own coinage in Judea. Other cities in the Seleucid Empire could issue coinage, but being granted the privilege evidenced the increased status of Judea. No coins from Simon's time are extant, so we do not know whether he actually exercised this privilege.

15:7. Exactly what "freedom" Antiochus means to grant Jerusalem is vague. At 10:31, Demetrius I had made Jerusalem holy and free from taxation. Perhaps the same is meant here. Demetrius I had given Jonathan the right to prepare weapons (10:6), and Demetrius II had granted permission to gain control of the strongholds (11:42).

15:8-9. Demetrius II had also promised that the grants would not be cancelled from this time on (11:36), and he promised glory (11:42), but then had reneged (11:53).

15:10-14. Since Trypho controlled much of the coastline, Antiochus found it difficult to enter the kingdom. However, Demetrius II's wife, Cleopatra Thea, who was besieged by Trypho at Seleucia, let Antiochus land. She also married him, since Demetrius II had since married a Parthian princess. The year 174 (v. 10) in the Seleucid Macedonian calendar system was 139/38 BCE. Antiochus was proclaimed king and defeated Trypho in northern Syria. Trypho withdrew to Dor, a powerful fortress on the Phoenician coast, where Antiochus besieged him (vv. 11-13). The phrase "not to go out or go in" (v. 14) is repeated at 15:25, when the siege of Dor is picked up again.

1 Maccabees 15:15-24, Continued Roman Support

COMMENTARY

The author of 1 Maccabees tends to interpolate some events within others, often using frame language to connect the narrative; e.g., Antiochus's actions (3:37) are recounted (6:1); the defeat of Nicanor (7:43-49) is repeated (9:1) and frames Judas's embassy to Rome; Jonathan's battles against the commanders of Demetrius II (11:63-74; 12:24-32) frame Jonathan's embassy to Rome. So here Antiochus's siege of Dor (15:14, 25) frames the Romans' letter of alliance to Simon. The people's decree stated that Demetrius II had heard that the envoys of the Jews had been accepted with honor (14:40), so Simon's delegation probably was sent soon after Jonathan's death. In fact, Lucius, the consul, wrote the same letters to King Demetrius, which must have been before the failure of Demetrius II's campaign against Parthia became known. The only consul named Lucius between 142 and 137 BCE was Lucius Caecilius Metellus Calvus, consul of 142 BCE. It seems, then, as if this letter should be dated earlier than the time of Antiochus VII Sidetes. However, the author of 1 Maccabees, by positioning the response of the Romans here, concludes the list of honors accorded to Simon that began with a letter from Rome (14:16-18). The author also provides a break between the positive attitude of Antiochus VII toward the Jews and the negative one he adopts from v. 27 on.

15:15. Numenius was last mentioned at 14:24 as being on his way to Rome. It was common practice to send a copy of a letter to a person mentioned in the letter.

15:16. The common Roman practice for letter writing was for the writer to fully identify himself or herself, using not only the family name but also any official title he or she held. The addressee is Ptolemy VIII Euergetes (146–116 BCE), whom a Roman commission headed by Scipio Aemilianus had visited in 140/39 BCE.[128] Polybius, the Greek historian who probably accompanied Scipio, found the Greek and Jewish population of Alexandria virtually wiped out by Ptolemy's purges after his return to power.[129]

15:17-21. "Friends and allies" was the same phrase used when Judas set up an alliance with Rome (8:20); Jonathan is said to have renewed these ties (12:3). Verse 19 repeats much of what had been set out in the letter the Romans had sent in reply to the embassy that Judas had sent to them (8:24-28). The gold shield mentioned (v. 18) is the one described earlier (14:24). By accepting the shield (v. 20), the Romans signify the renewal of the relationship. Note that the Jews present a gift to the Romans but that none is given in return, so the relationship is not that of equals. The request that Rome's allies hand over "fugitives" (λοιμοί *loimoi*, v. 21; see "scoundrels," 10:61) is similar to the requirement of Antiochus III by the Treaty of Apamea to deliver up to Rome's allies any of their deserters.[130] Augustus later gave the same privilege to Herod.[131]

15:22-24. The list of recipients first names kings (v. 22) and then countries (v. 23; cf. 15:15). The mention of Demetrius II indicates that the letter must have been written before news of his capture by the Parthians; Attalus II was king of Pergamum (159–138 BCE); Ariarathes V, king of Cappadocia (163–130 BCE); Arsaces (i.e., Mithradates I), king of Parthia (c. 171–138/37 BCE). "The Sampsames," most probably to be identified with Samsun on the Black Sea, was called "Amisos" by the Greeks. Myndos was near Halicarnassus on the southwest coast of Asia Minor. Sicyon

---
128. Diodorus Siculus 33.28b.1-3.
129. Polybius 34.14.1-7.
130. Polybius 21.42.10; Livy 38.38.7.
131. Josephus *The Jewish War* 1.474.

was a city near Corinth. Caria and Lycia lay in the mountainous region of southwest Asia Minor, and Pamphylia lay in the middle of the southern coast of Asia Minor. Samos, Rhodes, and Cos are islands off the southwest coast of Asia Minor. Halicarnassus was a city lying within Caria; Phaselis, a city within Lycia; Side, a city within Pampylia. Aradus, the main city of north Phoenicia, was situated on an island off the coast. Gortyna was an important city in southern Crete. Cnidus, a city, lay on a long peninsula at the southwest corner of Asia Minor. The island Cyprus at this time was under Ptolemaic control, as was the great North African city of Cyrene, to the west of the Egyptian delta.

1 Maccabees 15:25-36, Antiochus's Change of Heart

COMMENTARY

15:25-27. The narrative picks up where it ended before the report of the embassy to Rome (v. 14). But whereas before Antiochus VII had been so friendly to Simon, now his attitude has changed. Simon sent reinforcements as well as money to help the king defray his expenses (v. 26), but such gifts also signified the recognition of Antiochus VII as king. However, Antiochus insults Simon by not accepting (v. 27) his gifts, in contrast to Rome's acceptance of the golden shield (15:20). Since the troops of the Seleucid Empire had rallied to Antiochus (15:10) and his main enemy Trypho was trapped, Antiochus no longer had need of Simon's friendship. Just as Demetrius II had changed his attitude when his troubles disappeared (11:52-53), so also now Antiochus changes his, continuing the Seleucids' record of deception.

15:28-31. Athenobius, "the king's Friend" (v. 28), is unknown outside of 1 Maccabees. Simon is not invited to talk with Antiochus, but to a lower level delegation. The message contains no courteous address, but starts right away with claims. Two main points of honor for Simon had been his control over Joppa as an opening to the sea (14:5, 34) and his cleansing of Gazara (13:43-48; 14:7, 34) and of the citadel (13:49-52; 14:7, 36-37). It is interesting that the citadel is here called a "city"; at 1:33 it encompassed the city of David, distinct from Jerusalem. In addition to the three cities mentioned, Simon also held Ekron (10:89), Adida (12:38; 13:13), and four other districts (11:34, 57). Whereas earlier the author of 1 Maccabees states that the citadel (14:36), Seleucid forces (1:30), and Jewish renegades (7:22) did great damage in Jerusalem and Israel, he now reports that Antiochus claims that Simon has done so to Seleucid territory (v. 29). Simon thus is classified with those forces against whom Antiochus VII intended to fight (15:4). A single indemnity of one thousand talents (v. 31) was high, but not beyond the reach of the Hasmoneans. Jonathan had promised three hundred for the districts of Samaria (11:28), and the golden shield sent to Rome would have cost a small fortune.

15:32a. Antiochus VII had promised to increase Simon's glory (15:9), but when Athenobius saw Simon's present glory, he was amazed. One might compare his reaction to that of the Queen of Sheba to Solomon's magnificence (1 Kgs 10:4-5), or to the incident in which King Hezekiah displayed Jerusalem's wealth to Babylonian envoys (2 Kgs 20:12-19).

15:32b-35. Antiochus VII had claimed that he was acting to regain control of the kingdom of his ancestors (15:3-4), and likewise now Simon reacts to Antiochus by claiming that he also only took back control of the inheritance of his ancestors (v. 33). He replies only to the charge about the citadel, and not to Antiochus's vague mention of many places (v. 29). Simon does not attempt to argue that Joppa and Gazara lie within the ancestral inheritance, but reports that they cause great damage to Judea, not Judea to them (15:29), and offers a tenth of the king's demand.

15:36. Athenobius returned "in wrath" to Antiochus to report Simon's reply. The anger of the king usually means trouble (3:27; 6:28)—and an expedition against Judea.

REFLECTIONS

What is interesting in this narrative is how Simon seems to go against basic rules of behavior of a subordinate to a superior. The wisdom teacher Sirach admonished his pupils, "Among the great do not act as their equal" (Sir 32:9 NRSV; cf. 13:11). The book of Proverbs recommends: "Do not put yourself forward in the king's presence/ or stand in the place of the great;/ for it is better to be told, 'Come up here,'/ than to be put lower in the presence of a noble" (Prov 25:6-7 NRSV). Simon's action in voluntarily sending men and abundant supplies to Antiochus VII in his siege of Dor could be taken as his acting as an equal to the king. Yet Simon's ostentatious display of wealth to the king's representative and then his refusal to pay what the king demanded only served to infuriate his superior. Simon acted unwisely and seems to have had the same weakness for gaining respect that Jonathan had had. The same ostentation had led Simon earlier to erect an enormous monument to his family. Simon had "made it"; he had risen from being the third son in a family from the outskirts of Judea to being the ruler of Judea, and he wanted everyone to acknowledge his success. He wanted respect. The lesson we have to learn from his actions is that we need to instill such self-confidence in all of our children that they will not need the outward trappings of success, but will be happy and content in being who they are. On the level of foreign affairs, strong nations must learn to be indulgent to smaller nations who are so concerned about their status and honor. The stronger nation must shows its strength, not by saber rattling, but by granting the proper respect that all nations should expect from one another.

1 Maccabees 15:37–16:10, The Expedition of Cendebeus

COMMENTARY

15:37. Trypho managed to escape the noose around Dor and flee to Apamea, his hometown, by way of Ptolemais and Orthosia, a port north of Tripolis. There, besieged once more, he took his life. It is to be noted that 1 Maccabees leaves Trypho at Orthosia and does not record his death.

15:38-41. While Antiochus VII goes north in pursuit of Trypho, he arranges to gain control of the southern coast. He, like Demetrius I (7:8-9), Demetrius II (10:69; 11:63; 12:24), and Trypho (12:40), knows that the power of the Jews must be curtailed. Cendebeus is given the office that Simon had held (11:59). Cendebeus was to fortify Kedron (v. 39), about four miles southeast of Jamnia and about eight or nine miles southwest of Gazara; it has also been identified by some scholars with Nihson, just over two miles southeast of Gezer, but such a base would be close to the mountains and almost twelve miles from Jamnia. With this fortified base, Cendebeus could sally out to attack the western routes to Jerusalem.

Cendebeus first invades Jamnia (v. 40), as Apollonius had done (10:69). From there he provokes Israel by raiding the land, taking captives, and murdering. His forces must not have been large enough to mount a full-scale assault in the now well-fortified Judea, but he concentrated on drawing the Jewish forces into the plain, as Apollonius had done (10:71-73). Kedron provided a base closer to the areas occupied by the Jews for quick, harassing incursions (v. 41). The continuing raids produce their desired effect and provoke the Hasmoneans to venture onto the plain.

16:1. John is in command of Gazara, which overlooks the plain. His garrison may not have been strong enough on its own to take on Cendebeus's forces, but he was aware of what Cendebeus "kept doing" (συνετέλεσεν *synetelesen*), not "had done," as in the NRSV, because the verb is in the imperfect. (The same verb is used elsewhere in 1 Maccabees to describe complaints; e.g., 8:31; 10:5; 11:40.)

16:2-3. Here the reader learns that Simon had another son besides John: Judas.[132] Nothing is known of the mother as, in this warrior book, family life is not considered. Simon's opening words recall earlier statements about him and Judas (3:6; 13:3; 14:26, 36), as well as the claim that deliverance was given to Israel exclusively through this family (5:62). The statement "I have grown old" (v. 3) usually comes before the last testament and blessing (Isaac, Gen 27:1-2; Joshua, Josh 23:2; Samuel, 1 Sam 12:2; Tobit, Tob 14:3). The Greek "Heaven's mercy" (ἔλεος *eleos,* lit., "the mercy") is a substitute for naming God (3:44; 4:24), just as "heaven" is substituted for God (3:19, 50; 4:24). Just as Jonathan had replaced Judas (9:30) and Simon had replaced Jonathan (13:8), so also Simon's sons will replace him. The text has the singular "my brother," which seems to be a translation mistake; the Hebrew word אחי (*'ḥy*) without vowels can be read either "my brother" or "my brothers" (the same mistake seems to be present at 13:8). However, the reader might recall how Mattathias, in his dying speech, mentioned only Judas and Simon (2:65-66) and that now two young men, Judas and John, replace the two old men, Judas and Simon. Help from heaven has been a constant theme in 1 Maccabees (see 3:19, 50, 53, 60; 4:24; 12:15).

16:4. The Greek reads "he picked" (ἐπέλεξεν *epelexen*), but the subject here is most likely John, as in v. 1. Jonathan had also had 40,000 hand-picked warriors (12:41) when he went to meet Trypho. Cendebeus's strategy suggests that his was not a force of the full strength of the Seleucid army. Cavalry is mentioned for the first time on the Jewish side, perhaps in response to the description of Cendebeus's force, but earlier battles such as that at Elasa presuppose the use of cavalry (9:11-17). John and Judas do not take the direct route back to Gazara, but first go north to Modein. We are not told why. Perhaps he wished to avoid Seleucid raiding parties or to have Adida and Modein behind him and Gazara to his left as he went down the plain. To start marching from so far to the north seems to preclude choosing the route as a surprise tactic. The appearance of Modein here makes a nice reprise to the opening days of the Maccabean revolt (2:1).

16:5-8a. The description of the battle leaves much to be desired. As written, it seems as if the Seleucid forces were apprised of their movements and that the two forces met in the plain not far from Modein. In that case, the stream would most likely by the Wadi Aijalon, rather than the Sorek near Kedron, which would have required the Israelites to have marched about fourteen miles before arriving at the battle scene. John, as Judas had done before him (5:41-43), fearlessly leads his soldiers across a stream. The Greek literally says "he divided the people" (διεῖλεν τὸν λαόν *dieilen ton laon,* v. 7), so that the sense of the engagement of the whole community is conveyed. John's tactics are determined by the size of the enemy's cavalry. Usually the cavalry units were on the wings of the infantry, but John must have realized that his cavalry was no match for cavalry that was either too numerous or too well armed. He decides to place his cavalry among, not "in the center of," the infantry. Perhaps his plan was to divide his forces into several mobile units to attack the more massed phalanx of the Seleucids; perhaps he had noted that the enemy's phalanx was stretched wide because of the plain, and he used the cavalry within the infantry to force gaps in the enemy's phalanx. One does not know what the enemy's cavalry was doing. The author says only that the trumpets were sounded (1 Macc 5:33 [Num 10:8]) and that the enemy was routed, almost as though the trumpets decided the battle, as at Jericho (Joshua 6).

16:8b-10. The grammar of these verses is a little confused, as subjects of verbs are left out. It seems as if the Seleucid forces fled to the fortress, i.e., Kedron, which Cendebeus had been ordered to fortify (15:39). But during the pursuit Judas is wounded, and so John pursues alone until Cendebeus reaches Kedron. Others keep going until they reach the watchtowers positioned within the limits of Azotus (Ashdod). In the mosaic map of Judea found at Madeba, towers are depicted in the open country between Azotus and Jamnia. What John burned is unclear: Was it Azotus, the last-mentioned city, which previously Jonathan

---

132. At 16:14, another son is named, Mattathias, and Josephus mentions another. See Josephus *Antiquities of the Jews* 13.228.

had burned (10:84)? Or does "it" really refer to "the towers"? Or does "it" refer to Kedron? The author does not say that John pursued to Azotus or that the escapees fled to Azotus, but only to the towers within the limits of Azotus, whose borders reached to Gazara (14:34). As for "it" being a mistake for an original "them," one can more easily explain why a later copyist would have corrected the text from an unusual "it" to "them" rather than the other way around. One would then need to suppose that a translator mistook the original ישׂרפה (*yiśrĕpehā*, "he burned it") and read ישׂרפם (*yiśrĕpēm*, "he burned them"). If "it" does refer to Kedron, it is likely that the author meant that John destroyed Cendebeus and those who took refuge in the fortress. Whatever the case, John followed the usual Maccabean practice of burning the town before returning to Judea. Later, John is said to be in Gazara (v. 19), so it is not clear whether he went back to Jerusalem before disbanding the army.

1 MACCABEES 16:11-22, THE DEATH OF SIMON

COMMENTARY

After an interval of three years, in the winter of 134 BCE, Simon's son-in-law, Ptolemy, son of Abubus, attempted a coup. He knew that Antiochus VII was opposed to Simon (15:27, 36, 38-39) and perhaps that Antiochus was preparing to invade Judea, which he did a few months later, when he ultimately captured Jerusalem. This victory of Antiochus VII is not mentioned in 1 Maccabees, a loose end left untied.

16:11-12. The fertile plain of Jericho is now securely in Hasmonean hands. One should note how Simon had kept powerful positions within the family. We learn here that Simon had at least one daughter besides his four sons; the author also indicates that Ptolemy was related by marriage to the family through whom deliverance was given to Israel (5:62). The wealth of Simon has already been indicated (15:32).

16:13. As Alexander's heart had been lifted up (1:3), so now is Ptolemy's. He wishes to control the country, as Simon had done. And like Nicanor, who had sought to take Judas and his brothers deceitfully and so destroy the people (7:26-27), and typical of the Seleucids, Ptolemy uses deceit "against Simon and his sons, to do away with them." In particular, note how Ptolemy VI sought to get control of the Seleucid kingdom by treachery (11:1).

16:14. On a tour of inspection to determine how the country was being administered, Simon visits Jericho. The eleventh month of the Sel Bab year 177 would have fallen in January/February of 134 BCE. Winter would have been a good time to visit the warm area of Jericho, as summer is much too hot there.

16:15-17. Dok was a small fortress near Jericho that some scholars have identified with the top of the Mount of Temptation. Ptolemy commits one of the cardinal sins in the GrecoRoman world by breaking the law of hospitality. Once one had eaten or drunk with a guest, one was bound to treat that guest properly. On the contrary, Ptolemy prepares an ambush and kills the drunken Simon and his sons, repaying good with evil (cf. Ps 7:4). According to Josephus, Ptolemy did not immediately kill Simon's sons and wife but waited until later, when besieged by John.[133] We cannot be sure which version is true, although Josephus's account is highly emotional and sensational. This discrepancy alerts us to the fact that ancient historians differed in their accounts of how leaders died—Alexander the Great was variously depicted as killed by poisoning, by carousing, or by a fever (see Commentary on 1:5-9). Given this tendency of ancient historians to create a death that they thought was appropriate, it is interesting that the author of 1 Maccabees reports that Simon and his sons get drunk at a great carousal and then are killed. Josephus, more discreetly, writes that Simon dies at a banquet, which a discerning reader would know included heavy drinking.[134] Did the

---

133. Josephus *Antiquities of the Jews* 13.228-235.
134. Josephus *Antiquities of the Jews* 13.228-235.

author of 1 Maccabees feel obliged to tell the truth no matter what? He did not feel so obliged in describing the death of Antiochus IV because of disappointment and regret over what Antiochus had done in Judea (6:8-13). How would the author of 1 Maccabees have come by his knowledge of Simon's death?

The motif of being killed by one's enemies while one is drunk is found elsewhere in the Hebrew Scriptures. In 1 Kgs 16:8-10 it is used to describe the death of Elah, king of Israel. In Judith (12:10–13:10), Holofernes gets drunk at his own banquet, with dire results. The wisdom tradition in Judaism is against drunkenness:

> It is not for kings, O Lemuel,
>   it is not for kings to drink wine,
>   or for rulers to desire strong drink;
> or else they will drink and forget
>   what has been decreed,
> and will pervert the rights of all
>   the afflicted.
> (Prov 31:4-5; cf. 23:29-35 NRSV)

Why would the author of 1 Maccabees insist, then, that Simon was drunk? Does he feel that this is the only way Simon could be overcome? But even this answer gives the picture of an old man taking part in the all-male ritual of drinking to excess, possibly with courtesans available. Such a picture of excess reinforces the image of magnificent extravagance conveyed in the "splendor of Simon" (15:32). The family of Mattathias is shown as indulging in the luxuries and extravagances of the wealthy.

16:18-22. Just as Alcimus had needed help from the Seleucids to control the country (7:20), so also Ptolemy now seeks help. "To turn over to him the towns and the country" resonates with what Antiochus VII had demanded (15:28-31). However, "country" in this context would refer to the territory of Judea (7:7, 20; 11:64; 12:25; 13:34; 14:6), just as the phrase "the country and the towns in it" (14:17) clearly refers to Judea. So Ptolemy had more in mind than placating Antiochus's demands; he intended to submit Judea again to Seleucid control. With such a goal, Ptolemy seems to bring the reader back to the beginning of the narrative, when renegades from Israel wanted to make a covenant with the Gentiles (1:11).

Ptolemy acts quickly to control the land. He needs to control Jerusalem and the temple mount, which Simon had fortified and where he had lived (13:52). Ptolemy also needs to win over the army leaders by bribes (16:11); most important, he needs to do away with John to complete his plan (16:13). The author emphasizes that John acts in self-defense, as opposed to Ptolemy's treachery.

1 MACCABEES 16:23-24, CONCLUSION

COMMENTARY

The ending tells us that John ruled successfully, so Ptolemy's rebellion did not last long. According to Josephus, John reached Jerusalem ahead of Ptolemy's men and gained control of the city. At that, Ptolemy retreated to Dok, where John besieged him. John is said to have abandoned the siege because a sabbatical year was coming on. Ptolemy fled to Zenon, the ruler of Philadelphia (Amman) in Transjordan.[135] That same year, Antiochus VII invaded Judea and besieged John in Jerusalem. After a lengthy siege marked by surprisingly indulgent behavior from Antiochus, who allowed a truce so that the Feast of Tabernacles could be celebrated, John and Antiochus VII reached a settlement in Jerusalem. The walls of Jerusalem were demolished and coins of Antiochus were minted. Later John accompanied Antiochus on his expedition against the Parthians (130/29 BCE).[136] Only after Antiochus's death on this campaign could John exert his own power. The independence of Judea depended on Seleucid weakness. None of this, however, is reported by the author of 1 Maccabees. He leaves Jerusalem free and independent.

---

135. Josephus *Antiquities of the Jews* 13.230-235.

136. Josephus *Antiquities of the Jews* 13.249-251.

Many questions remain unanswered in this narrative: How will Antiochus VII react to the death of his general Cendebeus? What will happen to the treacherous son-in-law? Does the author presuppose that the reader knows what happens? Why does he end at this point and choose this ending? No mention is made, as had been for Mattathias (2:70), Judas (9:20-21), and Jonathan (12:52; 13:26), that all Israel bewailed Simon's death. Rather, the author ends with a formula, so different from that at Judas's death (9:22) but so similar to that found throughout the books of Kings (e.g., 1 Kgs 14:29; 16:27; 2 Kgs 14:15, 18, 28; 20:20) and used of all rulers, both good and bad. One suspects that the author is hinting that the Hasmoneans have become a ruling family with all that it entails—wealth, a bureaucracy (responsible for writing the high priest's annals), and family intrigue. The heady days of the opening revolt against the Seleucids have been replaced by Hasmonean institutionalization.

REFLECTIONS

The narrative of 1 Maccabees seems to end where it had begun. As the "lawless renegades" had sought Seleucid intervention at the beginning of the story to bring about their control of Judea, so now within the Hasmonean family there are strife and fighting for control of Judea, and one side seeks the support of the Seleucids to gain control. Is the teaching of Ecclesiastes right? Is all vanity? And is there nothing new under the sun (Eccl 1:2, 10)? Perhaps. The author certainly reminds us that nations rise and fall, that rulers come and go, that "uneasy lies the head that wears a crown."

But that is not the total message of the book, for the author also acknowledges that the Maccabees had been the family through whom God had wrought deliverance in Israel. He emphasizes that God does act faithfully to the people if they attempt to follow God's commandments. Torah faithfulness, a longing to serve God at the Temple and at the place God has chosen, vibrates throughout the book. One may question whether today one should follow the same war tactics as Judas and his brothers did; one may be dismayed at the open acceptance of ethnic cleansing as a means to follow God's commandments. But one cannot question whether the Maccabees fought according to their own convictions to keep alive the worship of the God of Israel. For that, their name will be remembered.

THE SECOND BOOK OF MACCABEES

INTRODUCTION, COMMENTARY, AND REFLECTIONS
BY
ROBERT DORAN

THE SECOND BOOK OF MACCABEES

INTRODUCTION

THE EPITOME, 2 MACCABEES 2:19–15:39

The Second Book of Maccabees is not a continuation of the First Book of Maccabees, but a completely independent work. It covers some of the same material as 1 Maccabees, but in a very different fashion. The story starts during the reign of Seleucus IV Philopator (187–175 BCE) and ends with the defeat of Nicanor in 161 BCE, providing much more detail than 1 Maccabees does about the parties and factions in Jerusalem prior to the persecution by Antiochus IV Epiphanes. The letters preserved in 2 Maccabees 11 are particularly important in reconstructing the events of this period. The book has a formal prologue and epilogue and is structured around three attacks on the Jerusalem Temple: (1) by Heliodorus under Seleucus IV (3:1-39); (2) under Antiochus IV Epiphanes (3:40–10:8); and (3) the final assault by Nicanor under Demetrius I (10:9–15:37).

Style. In contrast to 1 Maccabees, which was originally written in Hebrew and then translated into Greek, the bulk of 2 Maccabees (2:19–15:39, often referred to as the epitome) was written in the typical Greek style of the day. The prologue evidences knowledge of Hellenistic historiographical conventions, as do the reflections that the author (commonly called the epitomist) inserts into the narrative at 4:16-17; 5:17-20; 6:12-17. The narrative reveals an author who loves to indulge in metaphors and word play. The author also strives to heighten the emotional effect of the narrative on his readers or listeners, as in the scene of distress at Heliodorus's approach to the Temple (3:15-22), the attention given to the mother and her seven sons (chap. 7), the emotional turnaround of Antiochus IV (chap. 9), and the distress of the priests at the insults of Nicanor (14:13-36). This emotional heightening is helped by the author's focusing on individual confrontations—Heliodorus and the high priest, and Nicanor and Judas in the first battle (chap. 8).

The narrative also abounds in tales of the miraculous, as in the graphic descriptions of the epiphanies of God's deliverance of the people at 3:24-28; 5:2-4; 10:29-30; 11:8-11. The presentation of these angelic helpers parallels the stories about divine helpers that one finds in Greco-Roman literature and is further evidence of the author's acquaintance with Greek literature. One could argue, in fact, that the narrative of the epitome falls within the Greek literary genre of epiphanic collections, which tell of the way a god defends his or her temple.

Worldview. While the narrative shows the influence of Greco-Roman literary conventions, the author has used these conventions to portray a confrontation between Judaism (2:21; 8:1; 14:38) and Hellenism (4:13). As far as we know, this is the first appearance of the term "Judaism." For this author, the Jews are the civilized norm, whereas the Greeks are barbarians (2:21; 10:4). The Jewish scribe Eleazar, and not his opponents, is the one who acts nobly (6:18-31). This attitude of separation of Jews from non-Jews is particularly evident in the author's discussion of the gymnasium in Jerusalem. For him, this change in educational system symbolizes the destruction of the Jewish ancestral religion, and he is particularly violent toward Jews participating in the gymnasium.

Although the author stresses that it is always non-Jews who instigate troubles against the Jews, who only defend themselves and their ancestral religion (10:12-14; 12:1-2), he goes out of his way to show that Jews and Gentiles can get along harmoniously. Non-Jews protest the execution of Onias (4:35) and the members of the Jewish council (4:49); the people of Scythopolis treat the Jews kindly during bad times (12:30-31). Even Antiochus IV claims that the Jews are good citizens and asks them to maintain their goodwill toward him and his son and heir (9:19-20, 26). Alcimus accuses the Jews under Judas of not being loyal citizens (14:6-10), but events prove him wrong as Judas makes an agreement with Nicanor and settles down to married life (14:20-25). What is striking about this narrative, in fact, is that the Jews are not portrayed as seeking to set up an independent realm. Rather, the story ends with the Jews able to celebrate their religion in peace, not with political independence. Judas seems quite happy to live a settled life under the Seleucids. This is in sharp contrast to the outlook of the author of 1 Maccabees, who views all Seleucids with suspicion.

The theology of the author has a distinctly deuteronomistic flavor about it. As long as the Jews obey the laws, God keeps them in peace, and they flourish. When they disobey, punishment comes (3:1; 4:16-17; 6:12-17). The author, therefore, shows Judas and his followers as strict observers of the sabbath (8:27) and other festivals (12:31) and links the Festival of Hanukkah to the older Feast of Tabernacles (10:6). The author is a strong believer in punishment fitting the crime, as seen in the fates of Jason and Menelaus, in the execution of Andronicus on the same spot where he had killed Onias (4:38), in the dismemberment of Nicanor (15:32-33), and in the providential care of God, who restores temple worship on the anniversary of the day that it had been profaned (10:5-6).

Date. The epitome of 2 Maccabees (2:19–15:39) is a shortened version of a no longer extant five-volume work by Jason of Cyrene. Scholars have speculated on how to reconstruct Jason's work and when he might have written it. At present, no sure answers to these questions can be given because all we have is the work of the epitomist. Scholars have also tried to reconstruct a "life of Judas" from the events common to both 1 and 2 Maccabees. One can certainly plot out from both books a sequence of battles in which Judas had engaged. But each book has its distinctive way of describing events. The fact that one account is a Greek translation of an original Hebrew text, whereas the other was written originally in Greek, is further reason to make one feel less than sanguine that any source document, in a meaningful sense of the term, can be recovered.

Who, then, was the epitomist of 2 Maccabees, and when and where did he write? We have even fewer clues to go on than with 1 Maccabees. Dates range from the second century BCE to the first century CE. Perhaps, since the text shows a friendly attitude toward the Romans, it might have been written before Pompey's entry into Jerusalem in 63 BCE. Momigliano has suggested that the epitome was written to accompany the first prefixed letter; therefore, the epitome would have been written in 124 BCE.[1] Yet, although one can make connections between the prefixed letters and the epitome, the author of the epitome makes no mention in his prologue that he was writing it to accompany a letter.

---

1. Momigliano, "The Second Book of Maccabees," *CP* 70 (1975) 83-84.

If there are no indications as to the date of the epitome, can one then suggest where it might have been written? Scholars have suggested, because it was written in Greek, that it must have come out of the diaspora, possibly from Alexandria, (given the great deal of literary activity by Jews there) or Antioch (since the Maccabean martyrs were celebrated there). The author's knowledge of events affecting Jews in Babylonia (8:20) and the author's polemic against Jews attending a gymnasium lend support to such a theory. Later inscriptional evidence from Cyrene shows that Jews did attend the gymnasium there. Therefore, one might conclude that the work was written by someone in the diaspora who was concerned that young Jewish men were beginning to attend the local gymnasium. The author wanted to write against that practice and yet still insist that Jews can be good and loyal residents wherever they live. But there is no reason why someone living in Jerusalem who was fluent in Greek could not have written it. The temptation to attend a gymnasium could be present anywhere in the Hellenistic world.

THE PREFIXED LETTERS, 1:1–2:18

The position of the two letters at the beginning of 2 Maccabees is quite perplexing. What is their connection to the epitome? Why were they added? From where do they come? Since the two letters are addressed to Alexandrian Jews, were they part of some letter archive in Alexandria? Each letter is quite different from the other. Most scholars would see the first letter as authentic but have serious questions regarding the authenticity of the second one. While the first letter follows the conventions of letters written in Aramaic/Hebrew, the second does not and yet abounds in Semitisms. As mentioned above, Momigliano suggested that the epitome was written to accompany the first letter, but there is no explicit mention of this in either the letter or the prologue to the epitome. Also, the account of the death of Antiochus IV in the epitome cannot be reconciled with the account of his death in the second letter.

Yet connections can be seen between the letters and the epitome. While in 1 Maccabees Judas and his followers celebrate the purification of the Temple for eight days (1 Macc 5:56), only in the epitome and in the prefixed letters of 2 Maccabees is the festival explicitly connected with the Feast of Tabernacles (2 Macc 1:10, 18; 10:6). One might also note how both the first prefixed letter and the epitome use a Greek form—"to reconcile," "reconciliation" (καταλλάσσω *katallassō*; καταλλαγή *katallagē*)—which is very unusual in the LXX (2 Macc 1:5; 5:20; 7:33; 8:29). Finally, at the climactic battle against Nicanor, Judas's mission is divinely sanctioned and approved through the figure of the prophet Jeremiah (15:14-16), and Jeremiah figures prominently in the second letter (2:1-8). One should note, of course, that in the epitome the figure of Jeremiah is used to connect Judas with Israel's past, whereas in the letter Jeremiah's hiding of the temple vessels speaks of a discontinuity with the First Temple.

What binds the letters to the epitome most strongly is the connection between the Festival of Hanukkah and the Feast of Tabernacles in Kislev. The second letter dates itself to the lifetime of Judas (between 164 and 160 BCE), the first to 124 BCE. Perhaps the letters were added to the epitome sometime after 124 BCE, but exactly when is unknown. The most likely location of the writing, given the addressees of the letters, is Alexandria.

Finally, it is interesting to speculate whether the letters affect the message of the epitome. The addition of the first letter does not change the message much. The second letter, however, adds to the message of the epitome in several ways. Its emphasis on the continuity between the First and Second Temples and the connections it forges between Judas and Nehemiah underline God's concern with the covenant people and for their following covenant laws. In addition, the second letter concludes with a prayer for the ingathering of God's holy people (2 Macc 2:18). This prayer, which resonates with that of the priests at the miraculous rekindling of the temple fire (1:26-29), has eschatological overtones, especially given the concern that the Jews of the diaspora return to the holy land. The writer of the epitome, however, shows no concern for eschatology.

For more discussion of the historical background of 1 and 2 Maccabees, of the ethics of violence in both books, and of the place of 1 and 2 Maccabees in Jewish and Christian tradition, see the Introduction to 1 Maccabees. See also the annotated bibliography located there.

OUTLINE OF 2 MACCABEES

I. 2 Maccabees 1:1–2:18, The Prefixed Letters

    A. 1:1-9, The First Letter
    B. 1:10–2:18, The Second Letter
        1:10-17, The Letter to Aristobulus
        1:18–2:18, The Holiness of the Second Temple

II. 2 Maccabees 2:19-32, The Prologue

III. 2 Maccabees 3:1-40, The First Crisis

    A. 3:1-8, The Problem
    B. 3:9-14a, The Attack on the Temple
    C. 3:14b-21, The Cry for Help
    D. 3:22-30, The Lord Defends His Temple
    E. 3:31-40, The Effect on Heliodorus

IV. 2 Maccabees 4:1–10:8, The Second Attack on the Temple

    A. 4:1–6:17, The Attack on the Traditional Way of Life
        4:1-6, The Removal of Onias
        4:7-22, The High Priesthood of Jason
        4:23-50, Menelaus in Control
        5:1-27, Antiochus Takes Control of Jerusalem
        6:1-11, The Pagan Cult Imposed in Jerusalem
        6:12-17, Punishment Seen as Discipline
    B. 6:18–7:42, The Reaction to the Persecutions
        6:18-31, Eleazar
        7:1-42, The Mother and Her Seven Sons
    C. 8:1–10:8, God's Defense of the People
        8:1-36, The First Victory
        9:1-29, The Death of Antiochus IV
        10:1-8, The Purification of the Temple

V. 2 Maccabees 10:9–15:36, The Third Act: Further Defense of the Temple

    A. 10:9–13:26, The Attacks Under Antiochus V
        10:9-13, Dynastic Changes
        10:14-23, Campaigns in Idumea
        10:24-38, The Defeat of Timothy

11:1-12, The Campaign of Lysias
   11:13-38, Peace Negotiations
   12:1-45, Further Local Hostilities
   13:1-26, The Second Expedition of Lysias
  B. 14:1–15:36, The Invasion by Nicanor
   14:1-2, Demetrius Becomes King
   14:3-25, Nicanor's Expedition
   14:26-36, The Change in Nicanor
   14:37-46, The Razis Affair
   15:1-36, The Victory over Nicanor

VI. 2 Maccabees 15:37-39, The Epilogue

2 MACCABEES 1:1–2:18

THE PREFIXED LETTERS

OVERVIEW

As mentioned in the Introduction, the epitome of events surrounding the successful rebellion of the Jews under Judas Maccabeus against their Seleucid overlords is preceded by two letters, 1:1-9 and 1:10–2:18. It is not known when or by whom these letters were prefixed, and so it is difficult to evaluate exactly what is the relationship between the letters and between the letters and the epitome. Some scholars have argued that the epitome was written to accompany the first letter; the Introduction suggests ways in which connections may be made between the language and themes of the letters and the epitome. But no explicit connection is made in the documents themselves, thus one could argue that the letters and the epitome circulated independently and that no intrinsic connection between the letters and the narrative should be sought.

2 MACCABEES 1:1-9, THE FIRST LETTER

COMMENTARY

1:1-6, Initial Greetings and Well Wishes. The first letter contains an initial indication of the addressees and the senders of the letter and greetings (v. 1), the well wishes (vv. 2-6), the body of the letter (vv. 7-9), and the concluding date (v. 10*a*), thus following the normal structure of a letter. The letter can be dated to the year 124 BCE (v. 9), which had seen in Egypt an uneasy end to the bitter civil war between Ptolemy VIII Euergetes II and his sister/wife Cleopatra II.

1:1. Cleopatra may have been helped in her struggle by Jewish generals, as they played a role in earlier and later debates.[2] But no mention is made of specific leaders in the letter, however, as the emphasis lies on strengthening the ties that bind all the Jews together; note in the initial greeting the repetition of "brothers" and "Jews," as the Jews in Egypt and in Judea are placed on an equal footing. The initial greeting formula "To X, Y," is often found in Aramaic letters. The present text of v. 1 has a double greeting—"greetings and true peace." The first is what one normally finds in Greek letters; the second is more Jewish.

1:2-6. Following this initial greeting is a long prayer of well wishing for the Egyptian Jews, similar to prayers in the openings of Pauline letters (see, e.g., Phil 1:9-11). The prayer is full of general wishes and hopes. The writers stress the covenant of God with the patriarchs as the common ground of their faith (v. 2). Just as God had heard the groaning of the Israelites while they were slaves in Egypt and had "remembered his covenant with Abraham, Isaac, and Jacob" and looked upon them to take notice of them (Exod 2:24-25 NRSV), so also the writers of this letter ask that God remember the covenant with the Egyptian Jews, a resonance no doubt that the Egyptian readers would have picked up on (cf. Exod 6:4-5; Lev 26:42; Ps 105:8-10; see also Deut 4:31). They ask that God give their brethren a "heart" (v. 3), i.e., understanding; the letter resonates with the language of Ezek 36:26-27 where God promises that, at the renewal of Israel, God will give the Israelites a new heart and spirit so that they will walk in God's

---

2. Josephus *Against Apion* 2.49-52; *Antiquities of the Jews* 13.284-287, 348-355.

statutes and observe God's ordinances (cf. Jer 31:33-34; Ezek 18:31). The Egyptian Jews are to serve God, whose will is known through Moses' law (cf. Ps 103:7), wholeheartedly and willingly, a phrase similar to that in 1 Chr 28:9, where David instructs his son Solomon to serve God. In contrast to that passage, however, the emphasis in the prayer before us is all on God's action. Verse 4 gives the same message as v. 3 but makes explicit the connection with the Torah and its ordinances; instead of God's giving them a heart, God will open their hearts/minds, a phrase in Acts, when God "opened the heart" of Lydia to listen to what Paul had to say (Acts 16:14) and in Luke, when the risen Jesus is said to appear to his disciples and to open their minds to understand the scriptures (Luke 24:45). God is the one who grants peace.

The verb for "be reconciled" (καταλλάσσω katallassō, v. 5) is unusual in the rest of the LXX, but is used at 2 Macc 7:33 and 8:29 as God's response to prayers. The same notion is found when Solomon, at the dedication of the Temple, prays that God will listen to the people's prayers and forgive them (2 Chr 6:19). As in Ps 20:1-4, God is asked to answer on the day of trouble and to grant the heart's desire and the plans of the one who prays. Sirach 51:10-12 states that Sirach himself prayed so that the Lord would not forsake him in his days of trouble; Sirach's prayer was heard, and he was delivered from an evil time. Some scholars have seen in this verse an allusion to specific events in Egypt: the civil war between Ptolemy VIII Euergetes and Cleopatra II. Some have also proposed that the reference to reconciliation is an oblique reference to the Egyptians' need for reconciliation because of the sin that Onias IV had committed in building a temple to Yahweh at Leontopolis in Egypt. Josephus, the Jewish historian of the first century CE, records that Onias IV, the son of Onias III, fled to Ptolemy Philometor for refuge after his uncle, the high priest Menelaus, was murdered. In Egypt Onias IV had requested permission from Ptolemy to build a temple in Egypt similar to that in Jerusalem, perhaps to fulfill the prophecy of Isa 19:19: "On that day there will be an altar to the LORD in the center of the land of Egypt" (NRSV). This temple, however, was set up for the Jewish military colony at Leontopolis under Onias IV.[3] It is not likely that it was set up as a temple for Egyptian Jews to rival that in Jerusalem, as it has such a remote location and receives no attention in other writings of Egyptian Jews. Rather than an oblique reference to Onias's temple the prayer should be viewed as expressing general wishes for the well-being of the Jews in Egypt. Nevertheless, general expressions could be given a specific meaning depending on the reader's own life situation. What is particularly striking in this prayer is the sense of God as the primary agent. The Egyptian Jews are not asked to open their hearts; rather, God is the one who opens hearts. At v. 6, a well-known formula in Aramaic letters, "and now," is used to show the end of this prayer for well-being. The unity of brethren is especially evidenced in the unity of prayer.

1:7-9, The Body of the Letter. 1:7-8a. The body of the letter contains a quotation from a previous letter (v. 7). This letter had been written in the 169th year, according to the Seleucid Babylonian calendar—i.e., between spring 143 and spring 142 BCE. According to 1 Maccabees, the Judean Jews had a checkered relationship with Demetrius II (145–140). After Demetrius came to power, Jonathan the Hasmonean was at first in alliance with him, but later was estranged from him and became a supporter of the young Antiochus VI (145–142). After the treachery of Antiochus's general Trypho, Simon made peace with Demetrius (1 Macc 10:67–13:40). First Maccabees also states that in 170 by the Seleucid Babylonian calendar, Jews in Judea gave the date according to the year of Simon (1 Macc 13:42). The earlier letter, therefore, presumably preceded this lifting of the yoke of the Gentiles. But the text as we now have it is extremely difficult to translate. For example, it is not clear to what event the phrase "critical distress" refers. Since the letter was written in 143–142 BCE, it may refer to the fact that Jonathan had been captured (1 Macc 12:48; 13:23). After the opening well wishes, then, the authors may immediately quote from another letter, with no indication that they were so doing. The NRSV translation, on the other hand, suggests that an introductory statement is made: "In the reign of Demetrius . . . we Jews wrote to you." But the question

---

3. Josephus *Antiquities of the Jews* 12.387; 13.62-73; *The Jewish War* 7.420-432.

still remains as to when the quotation begins, since there are no quotation marks in Greek. The sentence may mean either "During the reign of Demetrius we wrote in the great distress," or "During the reign of Demetrius we wrote, 'In the great distress that came upon us. . . . ' " If the distress had been caused by Jonathan's death, why did the authors refer instead to Jason's withdrawal, which had occurred more than twenty years earlier? Thus, along with the NRSV, the quotation begins "In the great distress. . . ."

Even after settling this issue, problems remain: Who had set fire to the gates and shed innocent blood (v. 8)? Commentators have normally seen the subject as Jason and his followers, since Jason is described in 2 Macc 4:10 as leading Jews away from their ancestral customs. The end of v. 7, therefore, is translated as referring to Jason's revolt from the holy land and the kingdom (of God), with cross-reference to Jason's attack on Menelaus, when Jason slaughtered his fellow citizens relentlessly (2 Macc 5:6). There are some problems with this interpretation, however, both historically and grammatically. The author of 2 Maccabees reports that the gates of Jerusalem were burned by someone other than Jason (2 Macc 8:33; cf. 1 Macc 1:31; 4:38). It is also difficult to say that someone "revolted from" a land and a kingdom; one usually revolts from a person. One of these difficulties would be solved if we understood the Greek verb ἀφίστημι (*aphistēmi*) not as "revolt," but with its basic geographical meaning "to withdraw from." While in the narrative of 2 Maccabees Jason institutes Greek customs, it is only after his withdrawal that Antiochus IV plunders the Temple and attempts to crush Jewish practices in Judea (2 Macc 5:7; 6:1-6). It is probably better, therefore, to understand the third-person plural verbs (ἐνεπύρισαν *enepyrisan*; ἐξέχεαν *exechean*), as frequently in Hellenistic Greek, in an impersonal sense: "the gate was burned and innocent blood shed." The reference would then be to the events of Antiochus IV's persecution. Burnt gates traditionally indicate a defenseless, plundered city. However one translates the verse, it is striking that the writers of the letter presuppose that their addressees know who Jason was, a figure who had left the scene over twenty-five years before the letter was sent, and also that there is no need to mention the name of Antiochus IV. One could contrast this shorthand version of events with those in 1 Maccabees, where Jason is not named and Antiochus IV is the evil force behind the persecution.

1:8b. The tumultuous events of the Hasmonean revolt and the rededication of the Temple in Jerusalem are summed up in this verse: We prayed. We were heard. We offered sacrifices. Once again the emphasis falls on God's action. Later in the narrative, emphasis will be placed on the martyrdoms as bringing about God's mercy. Here it is simply stated, "We prayed." The ritual actions referred to are the daily burnt offering (Exod 29:38-42), the continuously burning lamps (Exod 27:20-21), and the showbread, which was to be on the table before the Lord always (Exod 25:30; Lev 24:5-9). It is interesting that no mention is made of the daily offering of incense (Exod 30:7-8), whereas it is mentioned at the rededication of the Temple in 1 Macc 4:50 and 2 Macc 10:3 (Dan 11:31 mentions the suppression of the daily burnt offering by Antiochus IV).

1:9. The formula "and now" is used as at v. 6 as a dividing marker, here indicating the end of the quotation. The Feast of Booths (Sukkot) was celebrated in the seventh month of Tishri, not the ninth month of Chislev, as the author here states. Only here and at 2 Macc 1:18 and 10:6 is a connection made between the Feast of Booths and Hanukkah, the festival in Chislev to celebrate the rededication of the Temple. Hanukkah is said to last for eight days (2 Macc 10:6; cf. Lev 23:36; Num 29:35). According to 2 Chr 7:8-9, the dedication of Solomon's Temple, celebrated in conjunction with Booths, followed this model (although in 1 Kgs 8:65-66 Solomon sends the people away on the eighth day). The returning exiles followed it also when they celebrated Booths (Neh 8:18). Sukkot reminds the people of the Israelites who lived in the wilderness during the exodus from Egypt (Lev 23:42-43), and likewise the festival in Chislev recalls how Judas and his followers lived away from civilization (2 Macc 10:6). All of these connotations combine to allow the feast in the ninth month (Chislev) to be called the Feast of Sukkot. The date is given at the end of the letter: 124 BCE.

REFLECTIONS

This letter as it now stands has a very cryptic quality. If we did not possess the narrative of 2 Maccabees, we would not know who Jason was, or what was meant by celebrating the Feast of Tabernacles in the ninth month. Would the addressees of this letter, written over forty years after Jason's tenure as high priest, have had a clear grasp of what the letter was referring to? If they did, then we must presuppose a strongly held cultural tradition whereby the events of the Maccabean revolt were transmitted and kept alive. One can surmise that it was during the eight-day celebration of Hanukkah that the stories and traditions would have been related and retold. This context of community celebration and storytelling is not mentioned in our sources, but if we are to realize what life must have been like in the second century BCE, we have to use our imaginations to reconstruct the scene. Parents must have told the traditional stories to their children time and again; the children must have heard and seen them reenacted at liturgical celebrations, and so it must have penetrated into their consciousness.

This living reality of how traditions and cultures are transmitted often eludes us, but it is going on day after day in the stories we tell to our children, in the way our children see us behave toward others. We must learn to value and to recognize the importance of this teaching and transmission of values, a family- and community-based teaching that takes place not in the classroom, but in daily living. We must also recognize that there are other means by which values are being imparted to our children and must strive to filter out what is good from what is bad.

The letter also forces us to reflect on how important liturgical activity is to preserving a sense of community between geographically distant groups. It is central to the forging of familial relations. Can one hope that different religious communities would learn to celebrate together? Would this not help to strengthen bonds across communities and to dispel prejudice? At the same time, the letter stresses that this liturgical activity is dependent on God's action in moving human hearts and minds to action. This emphasis on God's grace, on God's being present in human affairs, is precious testimony to the strong belief of second-century BCE Judaism in God's gracious action. It should counterbalance any claim that Judaism before the time of Jesus was legalistic and barren. The belief in God's grace and in God's graciously covenanting with the Jews was still alive and strong.

2 MACCABEES 1:10–2:18, THE SECOND LETTER

OVERVIEW

While the length of the first letter is known from the initial greetings and the concluding date in 1:9, the extent of the second letter is quite problematic. At 1:18 the letter seems about to end with an exhortation to the addressees to celebrate the purification of the Temple on the twenty-fifth day of the month Chislev, but it then suddenly launches into an extended apologetic on the holiness of the Second Temple; at 2:16 one finds almost exactly the same phrase as at 1:18: "we shall celebrate the purification." No concluding date is given to the letter there. Should one consider the section 1:18–2:15 a digression or an insertion? Problems also arise concerning the authenticity of this letter. If it was written at the time of Judas Maccabeus and after the death of Antiochus IV, it must be dated between 164 BCE (Antiochus's death) and 160 BCE (Judas's death). Why, then, is no mention made of this letter by the writers of the first letter, written in 124 BCE, who quote an otherwise unknown letter from 143 BCE? More difficult to solve would be the chronology involved. If Antiochus IV died between November 20 and December 18, 164, near Isfahan, how could the news of his death have reached Jerusalem in time for the council to convene a meeting, draft this letter, and then send it to Egypt so that it would reach there before mid-December 164 (25 Chislev)? Even if one dates the events to 165 BCE, the problem still remains. Scholars have attempted to solve this difficulty by suggesting that the letter was written so that the Egyptian Jews would celebrate the anniversary of the first feast of purification, but the language of 1:18, following on the account of Antiochus's death, suggests rather a first celebration. The most likely solution is that this letter was not written by Judas and his followers, but is an attempt by some later writer to show that two well-known Jewish contemporaries, Judas Maccabeus and Aristobulus, had dealings with each other.

2 Maccabees 1:10-17, The Letter to Aristobulus

COMMENTARY

1:10. The initial greeting has the form: X to Y. In contrast to the first letter, the addressees are not called "brothers." A senate in Jerusalem is first mentioned during the time of Antiochus III.[4] The chiastic structure of the greeting places Judas in contact with Aristobulus, the only person about whom further information is given. Fragments of the works of a Jewish author named Aristobulus, who presented a work to Ptolemy VI Philometor (180–145 BCE), are known from the later Christian writer Eusebius.[5] Aristobulus argued that Greek authors, like Homer and Hesiod, were dependent on the wisdom contained in the Torah. The author of this letter calls Aristobulus a tutor of the Ptolemaic king and an Aaronide (Exod 29:7, 29). The prestige of Judas is thus enhanced by connecting him with such a respected figure.

This formula "greetings and good health" is unusual. It appears in a letter from the fourth century BCE and then disappears until the middle of the first century BCE, and is then used only infrequently. This epigraphic silence, however, is not conclusive for dating the letter.

1:11-12. The account of the death of Antiochus is prefaced by a general statement about God's care for Jerusalem; God is the one who always expels those who attack the holy city (cf. 2 Macc 3:39). Here as elsewhere in the Hebrew Scriptures, God fights for Israel as a divine warrior (see, e.g., Exod 14:25; Deut 3:22).

1:13-16. This account of the death of Antiochus IV differs from that found in other contemporary sources (and 1 Macc 6:16; 2 Maccabees 9) in that they all agree that Antiochus did not die at the temple of Nanea.[6] The divergence here is similar to that of accounts of the death of Antiochus III. According to Diodorus Siculus, Antiochus III plundered a temple at Elymais and was later punished by the gods;[7] Justin, however, reports that Antiochus III died with his whole army in his attack on the temple.[8] The author of this account mentions the temple is that of Nanea, a goddess of fertility, which is similar to Polybius's account. In Polybius's version, Antiochus makes an expedition against the temple of Artemis in Elymais, but is foiled by the local tribes and dies while retreating. Polybius states that some say Antiochus was smitten with madness and that there were manifestations of divine displeasure at his attempt on the sanctuary.[9] What is interesting is how different the account in this letter is from that in 2 Macc 9:19-27. In that chapter, the author describes Antiochus's attempt to rob the temples in Persepolis. The people resist, and Antiochus retreats. At Ecbatana,

---

4. Josephus *Antiquities of the Jews* 12:142.
5. Eusebius *Preparation for the Gospel* 7.32.16-18; 8.9.28–8.10.17; 13.12.1-16.
6. See Polybius 31:9; Appian *Syriaca* 66.
7. Diodorus Siculus 29.15.
8. Justin *Epitome* 32.2.1-2.
9. Polybius 31:9.

Antiochus learns of Judas's success, rushes to return to defeat the Jews, but dies on the journey when he is smitten by an incurable disease. One cannot reconcile these accounts. The places are different, the manner of death is different. One must conclude, therefore, that this letter and the epitome were produced independently of each other. This does not mean, however, that they do not have common themes which connect them, as we shall see below.

Antiochus came to the temple of Nanea on the pretext of marrying the goddess. The marriage of a king to a goddess (v. 14) was an ancient ritual. Antiochus IV is elsewhere reported to have married Atargatis of Hierapolis-Bambyke in Syria and to have claimed as dowry the temple treasury. The priests of Nanea are portrayed as being particularly deceptive (vv. 15-16; cf. the hidden doors in Bel and the Dragon 21; Dan 14:21 LXX). The author seems to suggest ironically that the priests kill Antiochus IV with thunderbolts à la Zeus through a hidden door in the ceiling (the word translated "struck down" [συνεκεραύνωσαν *synekeraunōsan*]

literally means "strike with a thunderbolt"), and he enjoys recounting the grisly details. The author of the epitome will recount how Nicanor's head was cut off and hung up on the citadel in Jerusalem (2 Macc 15:30-35). In a similar way, Judith is said to have cut off the head of the invading general Holofernes and had his head hung up on the wall of the city (Judith 13–14), and the people of Abel of Beth-maacah cut off the head of Sheba, son of Bichri, who rebelled against David, and tossed his head out to Joab (2 Sam 20:22). In the book of Daniel, King Nebuchadnezzar threatens dismemberment to any of his dream interpreters who cannot tell the king what he had dreamed and its interpretation (Dan 2:5).

1:17. This verse recalls Ahimaz's report that the revolt of Absalom against David has been defeated (2 Sam 18:28). Does the impiety refer only to Antiochus's attack on Israel and Jerusalem (1:11-12), or does it include his attack on other temples as well? Given the context, it seems that the author sees the attack on other temples as improper behavior.

2 Maccabees 1:18–2:18, The Holiness of the Second Temple

COMMENTARY

There are several components in this section: a discussion of fire at the time of Nehemiah (1:18-36); a section on Jeremiah (2:1-8); a comparison of Moses and Solomon (2:9-12); the founding of a library by Nehemiah and Judas's imitation of this (2:13-15); and a conclusion (2:16-18).

1:18-36. The first section is concerned to show the continuity between the Temple of Nehemiah with that of Solomon. Verse 18 is very difficult to translate, as the Greek is very elliptical and requires that something be added to the text to make it intelligible. The author attempts to provide precedents for celebrating the purification of the Temple under Judas Maccabeus, and therefore connects it both to the Feast of Booths/Sukkot, during which Solomon dedicated the Temple (1 Kgs 8:1-2; cf. 2 Macc 1:9; 10:6), and to

Nehemiah, during whose reign the festival was reinstituted (Neh 8:13-18). Three Nehemiahs are found in the Bible: (1) a leader of the Jewish community who returned to Judea with Zerubbabel at the end of the Babylonian exile, shortly after 538 BCE (Ezra 2:2; Neh 7:7; 1 Esd 5:8); (2) a ruler around Beth-zur (Neh 3:16); and (3) Nehemiah, son of Hacaliah, the central figure in the book of Nehemiah, who began his reform activity in Jerusalem in 445 BCE (Neh 1:1; 2:1-11) and who rebuilt the walls of Jerusalem. The reference here is to the person last mentioned, as 2 Macc 1:20 refers to his being commissioned by the king of the Persians (cf. Neh 2:6-8). However, this figure is to be conflated with the first Nehemiah, as 2 Macc 1:20 presumes the condition of the first exile. This conflation was probably helped by the opening scene in Neh 1:1-3 which, set in the month of Chislev, describes a destruction of Jerusalem. Noteworthy is the fact that Nehemiah is credited with restoring temple worship, and not Jeshua or Zerubbabel (Ezra 3-6; cf. Sir 49:12-13). The author of 2 Maccabees may have identified Nehemiah with Zerubbabel, who is said in 1 Esd 4:47 to be commissioned to build the Temple, but such motifs can easily cluster around important individuals. It is interesting that Nehemiah is stressed as well in 2 Macc 2:13-14. One might suggest that Nehemiah, as governor of Judea (Neh 5:14), provided a model for Judas.

1:19-23. Fire is an important symbol of God's power. God led the Israelites out of Egypt as a pillar of fire by night (Exod 13:21-22). When God acts as divine warrior and thunders from the heavens, God sends through the clouds hailstones and coals of fire (Ps 18:11-12) and flashes forth flames of fire (Ps 29:7). In Elijah's competition with the priests of Baal, the god of fertility and rain, Elijah's sacrifice is consumed by God's fire from heaven, which shows that it is God who brings fertility to the land (1 Kings 18). The fire on God's altar was never to go out (Lev 6:12-13), and the sacrifices offered at the inauguration of the public ritual were miraculously consumed by fire that "came out from the LORD" (Lev 9:24 NRSV). So to establish the holiness of the Second Temple, which some disputed (Ezra 3:12; *1 Enoch* 89:73; *2 Bar* 68:5-6; and frequently in the Qumran literature), it was important to establish the continuity of the eternal fire. The author uses the motif of the finding of a hidden sacred object, as in the story of the finding of the book of the law (2 Kgs 22:8). The author stresses that the exact place where the fire was hidden was unknown, so as to bring out the miraculous aspect of the event. The place of exile was Babylonia, not Persia (v. 19), but Babylon had later become part of the Persian Empire. The "thick liquid" (or naphtha; see 1:36), a kind of petroleum, was well known to Hellenistic scientists and geographers.[10] A plausible etymology shows that the word derives from the Persian *naft* ; "nephthar" (2 Macc 1:36) is an adaptation of the Hebrew word טהרה (*ṭohŏrâ*; cf. Lev 14:11). The ancients saw the nature of naphtha as to draw fire to itself. Plutarch, in his *Life of Alexander the Great,* tells the story of the boy Stephanus, who smeared himself with naphtha, caught fire, and barely escaped with his life. Plutarch comments: "This naphtha . . . is so liable to catch fire, that before it touches the flame it will kindle at the very light that surrounds it, and often inflame the intermediate air also."[11] Naphtha is said to be able to draw fire from a distance as well.[12] So in this story, the naphtha blazes from the very light at the sudden appearance of the previously hidden sun. The effect of this miraculous sprinkling of the thick liquid resonates with the story of Elijah, in which the wood was wet so that it would seem impossible to catch fire (1 Kgs 18:33-38); here the liquid used draws the fire of the sun to itself. This power to catch on fire is also noted in 2 Macc 1:32, where the light from the blazing altar causes the naphtha on the rocks to be consumed.

The reference to Jonathan (v. 23) may be to either the high priest named Jonathan mentioned at Neh 12:11 or to Mattaniah, "who was the leader to begin the thanksgiving in prayer" (Neh 11:17 NRSV), since both names mean "God's gift" in Hebrew. But one cannot be certain about which Jonathan is intended.

1:24-29. Jonathan leads the people in a prayer that emphasizes God's power and mercy (cf. Neh 9:31-32). Its repetition of "alone . . . alone . . . alone" highlights God's singularity as creator. Its stress on God's election of Israel (cf. Deut 14:2; Sir 36:13-19; *Ps Sol* 8:28), leads into a plea that the people, who are God's own possession or "portion" (Deut 9:26; 32:9; 1 Kgs 8:53) might be consecrated and might return to the land (Deut 30:1-10; Isa 41:8-20; 49:7-26). They are to be replanted as God had first planted them on Mt. Zion (see Exod 15:17; 2 Sam 7:10; Amos 9:15), and the taunts of their enemies (Ps 42:3, 10; 79:10; 115:2; Joel 2:17; Mic 7:10) are to be answered. The image of God as the divine warrior runs throughout this prayer, as do the motifs of victory for the people and defeat of their enemies.

1:30-32. As when Zerubbabel and Jeshua laid the foundation of the Temple

---

10. Dioscorides *De materia medica* 1.73; Strabo *Geog* 15.3.15; 16.1.15 (quoting Eratosthenes); Plutarch *The Life of Alexander* 35.
11. Plutarch *The Life of Alexander* 35.
12. Dioscorides *De materia medica* 1.73.

(Ezra 3:10-11), so now hymns are sung. The Greek of vv. 31-32 is difficult, but the meaning seems to be that, with the sacrifices resumed and the eternal fire burning again, the naphtha has served its purpose and is consumed.

1:33-36. The miracle is proclaimed, and the Persian king verifies and acknowledges its truth. Nehemiah then gives the liquid a name: "nephthar." Nehemiah is thus shown to be the discoverer of naphtha, and so the story must be classed with other stories of inventors of things beneficial to humans.[13] It would be going too far to say that Nehemiah is described here as the founder of Persian religion, with its reverence for fire, but there is a hint of the derivation of Persian religion from Jewish temple worship.

2:1-8. Other stories are clustered around this one in an associative fashion. Verses 1-3 specify that Jeremiah had ordered that some of the fire be taken into exile by the priests and had admonished them not to forget the law. The exhortations against idolatry are similar to those found in the Letter of Jeremiah. A second story about Jeremiah (vv. 4-8) recounts how he saved the tabernacle and the ark from being captured. Eupolemus, a Jewish writer possibly sent on an embassy to Rome by Judas Maccabeus (1 Macc 8:17-18; 2 Macc 4:11), also states that Jeremiah preserved the ark and the tablets in it from being taken by the Babylonians.[14] The mountain mentioned in v. 4 is Mt. Nebo. The tent and ark recall the whole exodus story as the ark and the tent of meeting are described and outfitted at Sinai (Exodus 36–40) and go before the Israelites on their journey through the desert (Num 10:33-36). Just as Moses never entered the promised land but could only see it from Mt. Nebo (Deut 32:48-52; 34:1-6), so also in this story these ritual items are returned to the desert wandering state, away from the land of Israel. In the wilderness of Moab, at Mt. Nebo, the author of this letter reports, the tent and the ark and the altar of incense have been placed in hiding until God gathers in the people and again sends the glory and the cloud (other constant components of the desert wandering [Exod 40:34-38]) to bring them back to the Temple when God restores the land fully (v. 8).[15] Verse 5 mentions the incense altar for the first time. Since it stood in the holy place and was most holy to the Lord (Exod 30:1-10), it too must not be despoiled, and so it is taken back to the desert. The secrecy of the hiding place is emphasized (vv. 6-8). Just as the place where Moses was buried is unknown (Deut 34:6), so also now these ritual vessels are to be kept in an unknown place until there is a new entry into the promised land. The ingathering of the people repeats the prayer of 1:27. "The glory and the cloud" refer to the exodus story also, as at Exod 40:34-38, where God's glory fills the tabernacle and the cloud leads the Israelites on their journey. When the priests brought the ark and its tablets into the Temple that Solomon built, a cloud filled the house of the Lord (1 Kgs 8:10). This story then stresses the continuity between the worship of Moses and that of the First Temple, but maintains a discontinuity between them; the tablets were not found. This story thus is in contrast with the previous story that emphasized the continuity between Solomon's Temple and the Second Temple.

2:9-12. These verses further develop the continuity between Moses and Solomon. First it is recalled (v. 9) how Solomon was granted wisdom (1 Kgs 3:5-15) and how he sacrificed before and after the ark was taken into the Temple (1 Kgs 8:5, 62). When Aaron was being inaugurated into the priesthood, he laid out the purification offering for himself and for the people, the burnt offering and the sacrifice for well-being (Lev 9:1-22). Moses is not said to have prayed, but both he and Aaron entered the tent of meeting; when they came out, they blessed the people, and "fire came out from the LORD and consumed the burnt offering and the fat on the altar" (Lev 9:24 NRSV). Thus the priesthood of Aaron was legitimized, and proper sacrifice commenced. At 2 Chr 7:1, fire is said to come down after Solomon's prayer

---

13. Among Jewish authors, Pseudo-Eupolemus claims Abraham as the inventor of astrology and mathematics (Eusebius *Preparation for the Gospel* 9.17.3). Artapanus suggests that Moses invented ships, earth-moving equipment, and military weapons and portrays him as the founder of Egyptian religion (Eusebius *Preparation for the Gospel* 9.27.4-6).

14. Eusebius *Preparation for the Gospel* 9.39.5.

15. At 2 Baruch 6, angels are said to take the veil, the holy ephod, the mercy seat, the two tables, the holy raiment of the priests, the altar of incense, the forty-eight precious stones with which the priests were clothed, and all the holy vessels of the tabernacle and to consign them to the earth, which swallows them up, until the time of its restoration. See also the *Lives of the Prophets* 2:11-19.

and consume the burnt offering and the sacrifices. In this way, the chronicler legitimates sacrifice at Solomon's Temple. The saying of Moses (v. 11) is not found elsewhere in the Hebrew Scriptures, but seems to derive from the scene in Lev 10:16-20, where Moses agrees that it was all right for Aaron not to eat the sin offering that time. After this saying, a reference to the command given to Moses at Lev 23:33-36 concerning the celebration of the Feast of Tabernacles for eight days may be missing. Solomon celebrated the dedication of the old Temple for eight days at this feast, according to 2 Chr 7:8-9, although the writer of 1 Kgs 8:65-66 states that Solomon sent the people away on the eighth day.

2:13-15. The mention of Solomon's celebration leads back to the story of Nehemiah (1:18-32). The mention of the consumption of Solomon's sacrifice (2:11) resonates with the account given earlier (1:31). In addition, Solomon's celebration of the eight days (2:12) leads the author to allude again to a similar celebration by Nehemiah (v. 14; see 1:31), although no such celebration has been recorded. These references most likely refer to the celebration of the Feast of Booths under Jeshua and Zerubbabel (Ezra 3:1-4) or Ezra (Neh 8:13-18). The phrase "memoirs of Nehemiah" refers to Nehemiah 1–7; 11–13; these memoirs, however, do not refer to some of the events mentioned or alluded to in 2 Maccabees 1–2, such as the building of the Temple, the finding of the fire, or the construction of a library.

After Seleucus I founded the great library at Alexandria, other kings, particularly the Attalids at Pergamon, followed suit. The author is thus attributing to Nehemiah what one expected a ruler to do in Hellenistic times. The author places in Nehemiah's library books about the kings and prophets, David's works, and letters of kings about votive offerings. There has been much discussion about the precise reference here. Do books about the kings refer to 1 Samuel through 2 Kings, the prophets from Isaiah to Malachi (with the possible exception of Daniel), David's works to the psalms, and the king's letters to those contained in Ezra and Nehemiah? The finds at Qumran have shown us that such equations are not so neat and that many works were available in the second century about which we know little today. For example, Eupolemus tells us that Moses and Joshua were prophets and provides letters exchanged between Solomon and the king of Tyre and Sidon about supplies for building the Temple.[16] Non-canonical psalms have been found at Qumran as well. So it is best not to make too precise an identification of what Nehemiah's library contained. It is interesting to note that in 4 Ezra 14, Ezra is inspired to write the twenty-four public books, as well as seventy books that were to be shown only to the wise. A comparison of these accounts shows an emphasis on Nehemiah as ruler in the line of David, whereas Ezra's role is placed among the wise teachers.

In 1 Macc 1:56-57, the author describes how books of the law were torn to pieces and burned if found, whereas here the author notes how some had been hidden away from the persecutors. Judas, therefore, is cast as restoring the work of Nehemiah, and so with the connection between Judas and Nehemiah we return to the theme started at 1:18. Does the author hint in v. 15 that the books in Jerusalem are in better shape than those in Alexandria? (*Epistle of Aristeas* 30 seems to refer to unreliable Hebrew manuscripts in Egypt. The prologue to Sirach also stresses the superiority of knowing the works in the original Hebrew language as opposed to translations.)

2:16-18. The author returns to his request of 1:18. God again is addressed as the savior of the people, as at 1:25, to whom God gave the land of Israel as an inheritance (Exod 15:17; Deut 2:12; 1 Kgs 8:36). The people also are God's inheritance (Deut 9:26; 32:9; 1 Kgs 8:51-53). Once again the theme of ingathering appears (cf. 1:27-29; 2:7, following Deut 30:3-5). The repeated reference to all the people suggests hope for an end to the diaspora.

The end of v. 18 takes one back to the opening of this letter; recalling that God has rescued the people from great dangers (1:11) and has purified the Temple (1:18). No conclusion is given to the letter.

---

16. Eusebius *Preparation for the Gospel* 9:30.1-34.18.

REFLECTIONS

Throughout these two letters we see references to liturgical actions and, in particular, to prayers, hymns, and sacrifices. In the prayers, God's gracious choosing of the people and care for them are stressed. What these letters bring before us is the vibrant faith and belief of their authors. The second letter shows that part of that faith was a keen hope that God would bring about a new beginning, a new return to the promised land when all would be well, an ingathering of all the Jewish people scattered over the world. This utopian desire was animated by a sense that life could be made better, and this hope should be ours as we fight to make living conditions for all better and more humane.

What is especially noteworthy in the second letter is the way the author is so concerned to relate present actions to earlier traditions. What is happening now continues on the line of tradition from Moses through Solomon and Nehemiah to Judas. We need to reflect on how our present religious and cultural communities maintain and cherish their own traditional values. Here the role of a vibrant community and family setting in which children are told the stories of their past is vital. We should encourage parents to talk to their children and grandparents to their grandchildren about their lives when they were young to keep alive an oral history so that each child can see and learn his or her roots. As a country built on immigration, the United States often saw the children of first-generation immigrants discarding their cultural traditions as inappropriate in their new homeland. How can we foster the maintenance of cultural traditions different from our own, and yet not fragment into a splintered society?

The debate over whether one language should be declared official is a classic case where proponents of both sides of the issue need to be sensitive to the proposals of the other side. It is important for children to learn, and that may require schooling in languages other than the one used by the majority. But if the ultimate goal of education is for a person to become a functioning member of society, then each student has to be able to communicate clearly and well in the nation's predominant language. So the problem is to maintain traditions, and yet balance the claims of different traditions harmoniously within a single society.

Yet we also must be cautious, for sometimes traditions can become set in concrete. Traditions, if they are living, must grow. We also need to be alert to when traditions must be discarded. Traditions, like habits, can be good or bad. The authors of these letters, for example, maintain the image of the divine warrior, and so one sees the author caught in a war metaphor in which his side, to be victorious, must defeat and crush its enemies. Can we find another image to replace that of God the Warrior? Should we not ask for mutual understanding, instead of the annihilation of our enemies? Traditions should not close us in and keep others out, but we must learn to cherish traditions that are not exclusive.

2 MACCABEES 2:19-32

THE PROLOGUE

COMMENTARY

The author writes an elegant prologue to his work in which he states his source (v. 23), the contents (vv. 19-22), his aims (vv. 24-25), and his methods (vv. 26-31). He states that he is condensing into one volume the five-volume work of Jason of Cyrene (v. 23), of whom nothing else is known. A group of Jews was said to have been settled on the North African coast in Cyrenaica by Ptolemy I Lagus,[17] and a large number of Jewish inscriptions, from a later date, have been found there. Josephus quotes Strabo as saying that at the time of Sulla (around 85 BCE), the city of Cyrene had four components: citizens, farmers, resident aliens, and Jews.[18] Jason would thus have been a Greek-speaking Jew from Cyrenaica, which was ruled by the Ptolemies.

Curiously the prologue does not mention Seleucus IV (2 Maccabees 3) or Demetrius I (2 Maccabees 14–15), both of whom are included in the later narrative. The word "appearance" (ἐπιφάνεια *epiphaneia*, v. 21) occurs, however, at 3:24; 14:15; and 15:27 and is a theme throughout the work. The author, who enjoys word plays, thus may have highlighted Antiochus *Epiphanes* in opposition to the *epiphanies* God had performed on behalf of the Jews. The author further contrasts Judaism with barbarism (v. 21). "Barbarian" (βάρβαρος *barbaros*) was the word Greeks used for non-Greeks; here the author turns the usage topsy-turvy and portrays the Greek Seleucids as barbarians. This is the first known occurrence of the word "Judaism," perhaps coined in opposition to Hellenism (2 Macc 4:13) and allophylism—foreign ways (2 Macc 4:13; 6:25). At 15:37, the author states that he ends his story where he does as the city has been in possession of the Hebrews since the defeat of Nicanor. The graciousness of the Lord is particularly shown at the turning point in the story, when the prayer for God's graciousness/mercy by the youngest martyr (7:37) is answered by God's turning from wrath to mercy (8:5).

The author describes his aims as pleasure and profit and ease for those who wish to memorize (v. 25). Memory is helped by clear organization, and so the history is structured around three important epiphanies. These aims are all rhetorical topoi for Hellenistic historians, and the author places himself squarely within this historiographical tradition. Sirach notes that the master of a feast should first take care of the guests before sitting down. "When you have fulfilled all your duties, take your place,/ so that you may be merry along with them/ and receive a wreath for your excellent leadership" (Sir 32:2 NRSV).

To achieve his aims, the author is going to epitomize the five books of Jason of Cyrene (v. 23). The motif of hard work willingly undertaken for one's readers' benefit (vv. 25-26) is a standard ploy to gain the readers' sympathetic hearing. "Flood of statistics" (τὸ χύμα τῶν ἀριθμῶν *to chyma tōn arithmōn*, v. 24) should be translated "large number of lines." The length of books was counted in terms of written lines, and the number of written lines given at the end of the papyrus roll as a comprehensive number. The author is saying that Jason's book had too many pages. Hellenistic historians tried various analogies to explain how their work differed from other writings. Lucian of Samosata, a writer of the second century CE, held that the historian works like a sculptor on raw material; a bare record of events was not enough, but one had to write them up in as fine a style as possible.[19] The Greek historian Timaeus (c. 356–260 BCE), to show that collecting the data required for writing history was a more

---

17. Josephus *Against Apion* 2.44.
18. Josephus *Antiquities of the Jews* 14.115.

19. Lucian of Samosata *On How to Write History* 16.50-51.

serious task than declamatory writing, used the analogy of the difference between real buildings or furniture and the views seen in scene paintings.[20] Polybius (c. 200–after 188 BCE) states that "the difference between real buildings and scene paintings or between history and declamatory speech-making is not so great as is, in the case of all works, the difference between an account founded on participation, active or passive, in the occurrences and one composed from report and the narratives of others."[21] The author of 2 Maccabees, however, is not contrasting two different crafts—for example, unfinished and finished products—but rather contrasts two functions within the same craft—one that deals with the whole project and one that is more specialized, contrasting a full exposition versus a selective presentation. Plutarch had also used the image of a portrait painter capturing a subject's character through few select strokes versus an exhaustive model.[22]

20. Polybius 12.28a.1-2.
21. Polybius 12.28a.6.
22. Plutarch *Alexander* 1.

2 MACCABEES 3:1-40

THE FIRST CRISIS

OVERVIEW

This scene is complete in itself as shown by v. 40. It describes the first attack on the Temple during the time of Seleucus IV Philopator, who succeeded Antiochus III and ruled from 187–175 BCE. This is the first of the epiphanies of God related in the epitome. It is placed as an anti-type to what is to happen under Antiochus IV, when the high priests and the people are entangled in sin (5:18). The story has all the characteristics of accounts written in praise of a deity who defends his or her temple: attackers approach, the defenders ask for help from the deity, the deity responds, the attackers are repulsed, and the defenders rejoice. Within the biblical tradition, one has the repulsion of Sennacherib from Jerusalem (2 Chr 32:1-22; 2 Kgs 18:17–19:36). In 701 BCE, King Sennacherib of Assyria invaded Judea in retaliation for the revolt of King Hezekiah against him. Hezekiah set about strengthening the walls, but the chronicler also portrays him as exhorting the people to trust in God, who would defend them. Envoys from Sennacherib came to Jerusalem and taunted the king, saying, "Who among all the gods of those nations that my ancestors utterly destroyed was able to save his people from my hand, that your God should be able to save you from my hand?" (2 Chr 32:14 NRSV). Such contempt of God, speaking as if the God of Israel were like other gods, brought swift retribution as the Lord sent an angel into the Assyrians' camp to destroy the mighty warriors of the Assyrians; the king has to return to Assyria in disgrace, where he is then assassinated. The God of Israel has defended the Temple and Jerusalem, God's city, from the boastful attack of its adversaries. Within the Greek tradition, Herodotus describes how the temple of Apollo was preserved from the army of Xerxes in 480 BCE,[23] while Apollo is celebrated for repulsing the Gauls from Delphi in 179 BCE.[24] At Nippur, around the sixth century BCE, Enlil and the other gods saved the Ekur temple from Kuturnaḫḫunte, king of Elam. The general pattern is widespread.

23. Herodotus 8.37-39.
24. Pausanias 10.23.2.

2 MACCABEES 3:1-8, THE PROBLEM

COMMENTARY

3:1-3. The author portrays the city as being idyllically at peace (v. 1). Such a utopian picture is credited by the author to the piety and hatred of wickedness of the high priest, Onias III, son of the high priest Simon. Note that the peace of the land depends on the leader, a theme that is found earlier in God's warning to Solomon to follow God's commandments. If Solomon and his descendants did not keep God's statutes, God would cast the Temple down (1 Kgs 9:1-9). The thrust ultimately becomes the explanation for the destruction of the northern kingdom (2 Kgs 17:7-8), the fall of Jerusalem, and the exile (2 Kgs 21:11-15). The piety of Onias will contrast sharply with that of his rivals and successors—Jason, Menelaus, and Alcimus—who all bring ruin upon the Temple. The author states his belief clearly at 5:19: The Lord did not choose the nation for the sake of the holy place, but the holy place for the sake of the nation. The well-being of the Temple depends on the

2 MACCABEES 3:1-8 COMMENTARY

holiness of the people, as stated so forcibly by the prophets (e.g., Jeremiah 19). The utopian quality of the description is at variance with the description of conflict and division that one finds in *1 Enoch* 1–11 and in the history of the Qumran covenanters (CD 1). In these works, Israel is described as being divided between the elect and the ungodly, between the faithful remnant and those who forsake the covenant.

The idyllic picture is enhanced by the author's recounting the preferable treatment and lavish gifts that Jerusalem and the Temple had received (vv. 2-3). Antiochus III, when he had recaptured Judea and Coelesyria from the Ptolemies (198 BCE), had bestowed tax exemptions and privileges on Jerusalem. In this action, he was following what the Ptolemies had done.[25] Before that, the Persian kings had provided for the sacrificial cult (Ezra 6:9-10; 7:20-23). Antiochus's generosity is said by the author to have continued under his son Seleucus IV Philopator. Note that Seleucus defrays expenses for the sacrifices; this will be the bone of contention in the following verse.

3:4-8. Just as Satan enters to destroy the pretty picture in Job 1:6, so also here a troublemaker comes on the scene. Simon probably belonged to one of the priestly families in Jerusalem, from the clan of Bilgah (Neh 12:5, 18; 1 Chr 24:14), following the Latin and Armenian translations, not of the tribe of Benjamin (so the Greek). His brothers were Menelaus and Lysimachus. Simon's exact position is not known, as the term for "captain" (προστάτις *prostatis*) can encompass civil and military as well as religious affairs. Nor do we know by whom he was appointed—whether by the high priest or by the Seleucid governor. He was certainly an important person.

The author does not specify what caused the disagreement between Simon and Onias. Perhaps Simon wanted to install one of his own followers as clerk of the city market to supervise all aspects of buying and selling. Perhaps Onias disagreed with Simon as to what precisely the duties of the market supervisor should be. Or perhaps it involved the interpretation of purity rules for the market. The *Temple Scroll* stipulates that the only animal hides allowed in Jerusalem were those from animals sacrificed in Jerusalem,[26] a much tighter restriction than that found in the decree of Antiochus III, where only the skins of unclean animals were forbidden.[27] Such a restriction obviously had economic repercussions. More likely, the disagreement reflected a power play between two factions in the small city-state. The historical romance of the Tobiads suggests that earlier in the Ptolemaic period there had been a division of powers among important families in Jerusalem.[28] In any case, Simon went over Onias's head to the governor of Coelesyria and Phoenicia (vv. 5-6), the region between the Euphrates and Egypt (see 1 Macc 7:8). The governor, Apollonius son of Tharseas, was most likely a brother or relative of the holder of the same office from 201 to 195 BCE under Antiochus III.[29] Since the Seleucids had capitulated to the Romans and a huge indemnity had been placed on them at the Peace of Apamea in 188 BCE, they had been short of funds. Simon, therefore, cleverly plays on their need by telling Apollonius about the large sums of money available that the king could seize (v. 6). Simon clearly does not want to infringe on the sacrificial cult in Jerusalem, but simply to undermine the position of Onias III. Apollonius was not about to interfere in temple affairs on his own initiative, and so he relayed the information to the king (v. 7). Seleucus approved of the suggestion, since it did not involve any sacrilege as the money dedicated to the temple cult was not involved. He appoints Heliodorus to seize the money. Heliodorus, brought up with the king, was chancellor of the realm. Later he had the king assassinated on September 3, 175.

The author sees all events as revolving around the Temple, so while Heliodorus may have been inspecting the province, this inspection is simply seen as subterfuge.

---

25. Josephus *Antiquities of the Jews* 12.50, 58, 138-144; *Against Apion* 2.48.
26. See 11QTemple 47:7-18.
27. Josephus *Antiquities of the Jews* 12.146.
28. Josephus *Antiquities of the Jews* 12.154-236.
29. See Josephus *Antiquities of the Jews* 12.138-144, in which Antiochus addresses a letter to Ptolemy, son of Thraseas.

2 MACCABEES 3:9-14a, THE ATTACK ON THE TEMPLE

COMMENTARY

3:9-10. The author insists on the friendly attitude of the high priest and the whole city toward the Seleucid minister. The attack on the Temple, therefore, is something quite unexpected. The author has the high priest cleverly respond to Heliodorus by showing how heinous it would be to take the money of the most defenseless in the kingdom: widows and orphans, who are especially protected by God (Ps 146:9); whoever attacks them is cursed and will be punished (Deut 27:19; Isa 1:23; Ezek 22:7). Deposits in temples should not be violated. The combination "widows and orphans" may suggest that the author is referring here to the tithes set aside for them (Deut 14:28-29; 16:11-14; cf. Tob 1:8).

3:11. The mention of Hyrcanus, son of Tobias, has raised many questions. Josephus relates the history of the family of the Tobiads that shows them as closely allied with the Ptolemies.[30] The youngest son, Hyrcanus, son of Joseph, son of Tobias, was forced by his brothers to flee Jerusalem; he escaped to the Transjordan, where he is said to have committed suicide when he realized he could not escape the clutches of Antiochus IV. Many scholars believe that the fact that Onias III has deposits in his temple of a pro-Ptolemaic, anti-Seleucid Hyrcanus shows the pro-Ptolemaic leanings of the high priest and thus that the debate between Onias and Simon was really between parties sympathetic to the Ptolemies and the Seleucids respectively. Such an analysis reads a great deal into one brief mention in a dramatically composed speech. Thucydides (c. 460–400 BCE), the great historian of the Peloponnesian war, laid down the rule that, as it was difficult to remember the exact words a speaker used, the writer should make the speakers say what was appropriate for each occasion.[31] It seems totally out of place that the high priest, when wanting to appease the Seleucids so the temple treasury would not be confiscated, would suddenly flaunt his anti-Seleucid leanings to the Seleucid chancellor. More likely, Hyrcanus, a Tobiad, is mentioned simply as an important person. The reader should not too hastily identify him with the romantic brigand of the Tobiad romance.

3:12. On the general rule for deposits, see Exod 22:7-15. Deposits at the Lord's Temple are doubly inviolate.

---

30. Josephus *Antiquities of the Jews* 12.154-236.

31. Thucydides *The Peloponnesian War* 1.22.

2 MACCABEES 3:14b-21, THE CRY FOR HELP

COMMENTARY

The author uses highly emotional language to describe the reaction to Heliodorus's decision to carry on with the confiscation. The taking of the deposits would not profane the Temple, but it would be an insult—a dishonor (3:18). The word for "distress" (ἀγωνία *agōnia*, v. 14b) is repeated as "anguish" at v. 16 (it can also mean "pain"), and the verb form is found at v. 21: "in great anguish." The emphasis throughout is focused on the way the agony of the high priest mirrors that of the whole populace. Even married women, who are normally excluded from public affairs and restricted to the household, now appear in the streets in mourning. Sackcloth, from which shrouds were made, is the classic symbol of mourning (Neh 9:1; Jonah 3:6; Esth 4:1). Even the unmarried women, kept hidden in the household, are mentioned to show how all the people were involved.

2 MACCABEES 3:22-30, THE LORD DEFENDS HIS TEMPLE

COMMENTARY

Verses 22-23 recapitulate vv. 12-14 and set off the description of the people's distress. The author employs a wide variety of words to describe God—the word "Sovereign" (δυνάστης *dynastēs*, v. 24) is used also at 12:15, 28; 15:4-5, 23, 29; and is picked up at v. 28 in "the sovereign power." (It is found also in 3 Macc 2:3; 6:39; 1 Tim 6:15 and in the context of an epiphany in 1 Tim 6:14.) In Greek, the same word means both "spirit" and "wind" (πνεῦμα *pneuma*). The title "Sovereign of spirits" is similar to the way Heb 1:7, interpreting Ps 104:4, states that God makes angels winds/spirits, and the Wisdom of Solomon says that God knows the powers of spirits/winds (7:20).

This is the first epiphany in the narrative. Some scholars have divided the narrative into two accounts, one with a horseman (vv. 24-25, 27-28, 30) and the other with two young men (vv. 26, 29, 31-34). But the author may also be displaying the power of God through various agents. The description of the avenging figures has all the usual traits of divine interventions in Hellenistic literature: golden armor, handsome young men (see the description in 5:2-3; 10:29; 11:8). To be flogged was humiliating. As the book of Proverbs states, "A whip for the horse, a bridle for the donkey,/ and a rod for the back of fools" (Prov 26:3 NRSV). Flogging was a punishment for wrongdoing, and Jewish law stipulated that no more than forty lashes should be given, for otherwise the person flogged would be degraded (Deut 25:1-3). This punishment could be administered more "mildly," as when the authorities in Caesarea tried to stifle the fights between the Jews and the Greeks in the town by the use of scourges and imprisonment.[32] Paul underwent such punishment at the hands of Jewish and Roman authorities (Acts 16:22-25; 21:24; 2 Cor 11:24-25). A more severe beating could be administered for other crimes, and could sometimes lead to the death of the condemned person. Heliodorus is said to have been flogged continually until he fainted, which suggests the more severe punishment. That someone of his high rank should be subjected to the punishment for criminals would be seen as especially degrading to him. Darkness is often a sign of destruction, as in the ninth plague (Exod 10:21) and for Saul as he was dying (2 Sam 1:9 LXX). The day of the Lord is to be a day of darkness (Amos 5:18; Joel 2:2, 31). The contrast of vv. 22-23 is now reversed in the contrast of vv. 29-30.

32. Josephus *The Jewish War* 2.266-270.

2 MACCABEES 3:31-40, THE EFFECT ON HELIODORUS

COMMENTARY

In contrast to the story in 3 Maccabees 1–2, where Ptolemy IV Philopator attempts to enter the holy of holies and is punished but does not repent, here Heliodorus recognizes the power of the deity. Such recognition of divine power by a former enemy is also found in Greek literature as, for example, in the Lindos Chronicle, which portrays how, before the battle of Marathon, the Persian commander Dates was forced to proclaim the greatness of the goddess Athena through a miraculous thirst she sent on his forces as they besieged the isle of Lindos.

The author emphasizes that this miracle was no tricky ambush played on Heliodorus but the work of God by asserting that the high priest prayed for Heliodorus to assure that the king would not get the wrong impression about what had happened. The text does not specify what kind of sacrifice was offered, but possibly it was an offering concerning deposits (Lev 6:1-7; Num 5:5-10). The importance of the sacrificial cult is underscored as bringing forgiveness to a Gentile and the holiness of the high priest is stressed. Gentiles were healed by Moses (Exod 8:28-29) and Elisha (2 Kgs 5:1-19), and Josephus reports that later sacrifices were offered daily for the emperors.[33]

33. Josephus *Against Apion* 2.77.

Heliodorus in his turn offered sacrifice, presumably a sacrifice of well-being (Lev 7:11-18; 22:21-25). This witness of Heliodorus to the power of God does not mean that Heliodorus has converted, but that he recognizes the power of the deity who resides in Jerusalem. The confession emphasizes the supreme position of the God of Israel. One important theme of the epitome is that Jews and Gentiles can live on good terms with one another (see Introduction); this theme is shown here in the healing of Heliodorus and in his respect for the Jews.

REFLECTIONS

This narrative recalls that the relationship between God and the people is a reciprocal relationship. If the people obey God's laws, God will help them; but if they disobey, God will punish them. Such a relationship demands that each person in the community strive to his or her utmost. The narrative also stresses how one is to combat attacks on the community: The whole community is to be united in its steadfastness. The attack from outside only occurs because of an internal breakdown, a power struggle between community leaders. Envy is a tumor that can eat away, and the desire for personal status must be resisted.

In the political realm, we often see the struggle between what one should do as a partisan politician and what one should do for the well-being of the nation. So it is in the sphere of organized religion as well. Responsible leaders will always opt for what is best for the community. One recalls the response of Jesus to debates among his followers; the true leader is the one who serves (Mark 10:41-45). Paul shamed Corinthian Christians who were so concerned about their status that they began to take one another to court (1 Cor 6:1-11). Placing self before the welfare of the community must be resisted.

What is also striking about the resistance of the community to Heliodorus is that it is a passive resistance, with no attempt to take up arms. Later in the narrative, the author will argue that the Macceabeans' success came through the martyrdoms of Eleazar and the mother and her seven sons. Such a position recalls that of the chronicler as outlined by Susan Niditch.[34] She notes how the authors of 1 and 2 Chronicles are especially fond of having weak and humbled Israelites call upon God for help (e.g., 2 Chr 14:9-15). This theme, as Niditch points out, is at the heart of the exodus tradition. In Chronicles, this theme reemerges in full force alongside a stress on the power of God and the helplessness of human fighters, particularly in the narrative of 2 Chronicles 20. When a great multitude is about to attack Judea, King Jehoshaphat prays, "We are powerless before this vast multitude that comes against us. We are at a loss what to do, hence our eyes are turned toward you" (2 Chr 20:12 NAB). Without any fighting, God delivers the people. The chronicler certainly revels in the death of Israel's enemies, but there are hints that he does not want the Israelites to take part in war but to leave it all up to God. The book of Daniel also stresses the defeat of oppressors by supernatural means. In Daniel 2, the great statue that represents various kingdoms is broken into pieces by a stone not cut by human hands (Dan 2:34). The arrogant beast of Daniel 7 falls under divine judgment and is put to death (Dan 7:11), and the king of Daniel 8 is

34. Susan Niditch, *War in the Hebrew Scriptures: A Study of the Ethics of Violence* (New York: Oxford, 1993) 139-49.

broken, but not by human hands (Dan 8:25). In Daniel 11, the king simply comes to an end, with no one to help him (Dan 11:45).

This same idea of divine intervention is present in this narrative in 2 Maccabees 3. It is also reminiscent of Paul's advice to never avenge oneself, but to leave room for the wrath of God (Rom 12:19). This ideology of non-participation, to use Niditch's phrase, gives the narrative of 2 Maccabees a pacifist tinge unlike 1 Maccabees. The emphasis on confronting evil with defiant passivity rather than with arms, an emphasis that people like Gandhi and Martin Luther King, Jr., evidenced in their lives, is important. Recourse to violence should always be the last resort after all else has failed. We, too, must be willing to follow humbly but persistently what we hold to be right. We will not expect angels to come to our aid, but we must believe that right will win out in the end if we pursue our goals with integrity.

2 MACCABEES 4:1–10:8

THE SECOND ATTACK ON THE TEMPLE

OVERVIEW

The second attack on the Temple in Jerusalem follows the same basic pattern as the attack described in 3:1-40: the attack against Jerusalem and the people's traditional way of life (4:6–6:17); the cry for help (6:18–7:42); God's response (chaps. 8–9); the purification of the Temple (10:1-8).

2 MACCABEES 4:1–6:17, THE ATTACK ON THE TRADITIONAL WAY OF LIFE

OVERVIEW

The attack on Jerusalem comes from both internal and external forces. The internal forces were the removal of Onias from Jerusalem (4:16), which brought changes under the new high priest, Jason (4:7-22), and the events under his replacement, Menelaus (4:23–5:10). The external attack came from Antiochus IV (5:11–6:11). Throughout this section the author reflects on the significance of these events (4:16-17; 5:17-20; 6:12-17). These reflections are important indicators of the worldview of the author—his belief in the election of Israel by God and the necessity that Jews live according to God's covenantal laws.

2 Maccabees 4:1-6, The Removal of Onias

COMMENTARY

The author had insisted that the piety of the high priest Onias was the reason for the well-being of the holy city (3:1), and so, it is an ominous sign if, because of slander, Onias has to leave Jerusalem. In 2 Baruch, a pseudepigraphical work usually dated to around the beginning of the second century CE, Baruch is told by God to tell Jeremiah and all like-minded people to leave Jerusalem, for their works had become a firm pillar for the city and their prayers a strong wall (2 Baruch 2).[35] Then the city will be handed over to be captured. One might also note how the prophet Ezekiel witnesses the departure of the glory of the Lord from Jerusalem before its destruction (Ezekiel 10).

There are close grammatical links between 3:39 and 4:1; 3:39 sums up the events in chapter 3, but 4:1 shows how the underlying problem in chapter 3, the rivalry among the families of the ruling elite, still continues. The concern of Onias that Seleucus not get the wrong idea that the Jews had committed "foul play" (3:32) is shown to be justified as Simon

---
35. A similar account may be found in *Paraleipomena Jeremiou* 1.1-2.

slanders the high priest about this event. The breakdown of civility in the city is dramatically shown by the increase of violence. Simon is shown to be the opposite of Onias, as he instigates murder (v. 3), which goes against the commands of God (Exod 20:13; 21:12; Num 35:30-34). The local rivalry takes on larger dimensions, however, as the Seleucid authorities become involved. The new governor of Coelesyria and Phoenicia does not assume the passive attitude of the previous governor (3:7) but actively supports Simon (4:4). It is not known why, or what benefit a governor might gain from fomenting civil unrest. Whatever the reason, the high priest decides to go over the governor's authority by petitioning the king to decide the case at the royal court at Antioch (v. 5; see also v. 33). Such an appeal could be construed as playing party politics. The author of 2 Maccabees instead insists on Simon's selfishness and on Onias's selflessness. Such concern on Onias's part, not for his own good but for that of the nation, also contrasts with the power-hungry desire the author says drove Menelaus (13:3) and Alcimus (14:3). The section ends with Onias seeking to restore the peace (vv. 5-6) with which the narrative began (3:1).

2 Maccabees 4:7-22, The High Priesthood of Jason

COMMENTARY

4:7-17, Jason's Rise to Power. The author quickly passes over the events of the end of Seleucus's reign on September 3, 175—his assassination by Heliodorus, the installation of Seleucus's young son, and the usurpation of the throne by Seleucus's brother, Antiochus IV Epiphanes, who returned from being held hostage in Rome (cf. Dan 11:20-21; Appian *Syriaca* 45). The author uses a standard formula to describe Seleucus's death (cf. 11:23). At his or her accession a new monarch would appoint or confirm rulers in their position (cf. 1 Macc 11:24-27, 57-58). Jason seizes the opportunity afforded by Antiochus's accession to seek the position of high priest by playing on the need of the Seleucids for money to pay the indemnity to Rome. All in all, Jason promises 590 talents of silver, quite a sizable amount for a small country like Judea. The annual payment imposed by the Romans as a heavy indemnity on the Seleucids was 1,000 talents of silver, and so this extra money is a significant amount. The last installment of the indemnity was to be paid in 173 BCE.

Besides becoming high priest, what Jason asked for in exchange for the money has been the subject of long scholarly debate. The gymnasium was a unique feature of Greek life. Originally designed for athletic activity, it usually consisted of a running track and a wrestling area with perhaps jumping pits and areas for throwing the javelin or discus. Adjacent would be buildings for dressing, bathing, storing oil, etc. Later, gymnasia became centers of both physical and intellectual training, with halls for lectures on music, literature, and philosophy. The exact chronology of this development, however, is unclear, and it is unknown how much of such intellectual training would have been connected with a gymnasium in a city like Jerusalem in the early second century BCE. The same uncertainty surrounds the word translated "body of youth" in the NRSV (ἐφηβεῖον *ephēbeion*). These were boys who had reached the age of puberty. At Athens, for a short period of time in the late fourth century, all young men aged eighteen to twenty, the ephebes, underwent a two-year compulsory military training. Such military exercises as archery and the use of siege engines were still being done by ephebes in the late second century. But few families could afford their sons' not working for two years, so this training period, like most education, was primarily for the sons of rich families. The ephebes, through their training, became involved in the public life of a city, its religious festivals and processions. The reader needs to keep in mind that there was no core curriculum for education in the Hellenistic world, and education was primarily preparation to be a citizen of a particular city with all its particular religious and community responsibilities. The physical exercises, of course, would be common to all, and so cities could compete against each other in games (see 4:18-20). While we cannot be sure what intellectual training took place at the gymnasium in Jerusalem, except no doubt that Greek was taught, the physical training already showed that the people desired to be part of a wider world. Outfitting and maintaining such an athletic facility would have been expensive, and thus one gets a sense of the wealth of the high priestly families. The exact location of the gymnasium is unknown. According to 4:12, the gymnasium lay right under the citadel. If one locates the citadel on the southeastern hill, then the gymnasium would have been either between the city of David and the Temple or in a broad ravine, the Tyropoion, which separated the Lower City from the Upper City.[36]

Besides a gymnasium, Jason also asked for some sort of concession for citizens of Jerusalem (4:9b). The verse has been variously translated: to enroll the people of Jerusalem as Antiochians, i.e., citizens of Antioch; to enroll the Antiochenes in Jerusalem. Who and what are these Antiochenes? Four possibilities have been suggested: that the Hellenized Jews would be made citizens of Antioch in Syria; that Antiochus IV had set up a new republic like the Roman one and that its citizens were to be called Antiochenes;[37] that a Hellenistic corporation would have been set up within Jerusalem and its members called Antiochenes;[38] that Jerusalem itself would now be called Antioch-in-Jerusalem and its citizens called Antiochenes.[39] The first three are unlikely. As regards the first proposition, even the king could not force a city to give citizenship en bloc to citizens of another city. As for the second option, the evidence we do have suggests that Antiochus IV supported local traditions and not that he sought to make a republic. Against the third position, "Antiochene" never refers to a corporation, but to citizenship. Even the last suggestion has its problems; 1 Maccabees does not mention such a change in name and status, nor does the author of 2 Maccabees, even though he knows how to protest a name change (6:2-3), complain openly about it. Nevertheless, many ancient cities received new Greek names, and this seems to be the best explanation of this verse. Did this name change have juridical or constitutional implications? Tcherikover argues that only those who received ephebic training could become citizens and that since Jason controlled the enrollment of the gymnasium, he would now be able to decide who became a citizen of his city. Yet we have no evidence that in the Hellenistic period a city's name change meant constitutional change as well, or that undergoing ephebic training was the only way to become a citizen. Perhaps all one should say is that "to enroll the people of Jerusalem as Antiochenes" means simply that the name of the city was henceforth to be Antioch-in-Jerusalem, and that this does not imply either Jason's control of who was a citizen or a constitutional change in Jerusalem.

However, it is likely that Jason controlled who was enrolled in the gymnasium. And since this educational training would have tracked its students for entrance into higher governmental and diplomatic posts, Jason would have been able to manipulate who would receive this favored treatment as well. This was patronage with a vengeance.

The change of Jerusalem into a Greek city also implies that Jason wanted to integrate Jerusalem into the Seleucid Empire, particularly since his position depended on Antiochus IV's favor. Why would Antiochus have so readily granted the request? He always needed the money for lavish expenditures, but, perhaps just as important, it strengthened his southern region near the border with Egypt at a time of increasing tension.

The author of 2 Maccabees sees what Jason did as the abandonment of traditional Jewish religion (vv. 11, 17). He refers in particular to the privileges bestowed by Antiochus III through the father of Eupolemus, the Jewish ambassador to Rome under Judas Maccabeus (1 Macc 8:17). The author contrasts what is lawful with what is unlawful and uses the word "Hellenization" (v. 13), which formerly meant the use of a pure Greek style of speech, in a new way as the opposite of Judaism (see also 2:21; 8:1; 14:38). The author mocks those concerned with physical exercises rather than spiritual pursuits. Since education

---

36. Josephus *The Jewish War* 5.40.
37. See Jonathan A. Goldstein, *2 Maccabees*, AB 41A (Garden City, N.Y.: Doubleday, 1983).
38. See Elias Bickermann, *The God of the Maccabees: Studies on the Meaning and Origin of the Maccabean Revolt*, SJLA 32 (Leiden: Brill, 1979).
39. See V. Tcherikover, *Hellenistic Civilization and the Jews* (Philadelphia: Jewish Publication Society, 1961).

in the ancient world was so intimately tied to training for citizenship, one can see how the author understands Jason's educational reforms as a denial of Jewish traditions. The athletes wore the Greek-style hat (v. 12), which was a broad-brimmed hat worn to protect them from the sun; it was said to have been similar to the hat worn by Hermes, the god of athletics. The signal (v. 14) was typically to start activity in the gymnasium, not specifically for discus throwing. At vv. 16-17, the author reflects on what was taking place and points forward to the persecutions that will soon happen. The author also introduces his motif of just deserts—punishment meted out is appropriate to the crime committed (see 4:26, 32-33, 38; 5:9-10; 13:8).

4:18-22, Jason's Further Tenure. Every four years games were held at Tyre in honor of the God Melqart/Heracles.[40] Following his capture of Tyre after a long siege in 332 BCE, Alexander celebrated games to Heracles in the spring of 331 BCE.[41] These quadrennial games may have followed that precedent. Antiochus IV, as a supporter of local traditions, was present at these games (v. 18). The envoys sent by Jason (v. 19) were official representatives at another city's festivals. The corollary of Jason's founding a gymnasium is clearly seen here as Antioch-in-Jerusalem now interacts openly with other cities. At the festivals, "sacred envoys" (θεωροί *theōroi*) normally offered sacrifices in the name of their cities. The author sees Jason, the "vile" Jason, as again apostatizing when he sends envoys with three hundred silver drachmas, the price of a sacrificial ox, to offer in sacrifice to the Greek god. Those envoys, however, "thought best not to use it for sacrifice" (v. 19), but use the money to pay for the outfitting of triremes, Greek ships with three rows of oars on each side.

Here again surfaces the issue of self-definition: How were Jews who lived in Greek cities and who interacted with the citizens of these cities to behave toward the deities of those cities? How was Jason, as the leader of the Greek city Antioch-at-Jerusalem, to behave toward his counterparts? Would Jason have insulted other leaders by not recognizing in some way the fact that they paid homage to their patron deity? Jason presumably thought it consistent with Judaism as he understood it to offer such a sacrifice, but his envoys did not.

A similar divergence of opinion emerges in the fragments attributed to the Jewish author Eupolemus, usually identified with the ambassador of Judas Maccabeus to Rome (1 Macc 8:17; 2 Macc 4:11), who wrote that Solomon sent to Souron (i.e., Hiram), king of Tyre, as a gift for his help in building the Temple in Jerusalem "the golden column, which is set up in Tyre in the temple of Zeus."[42] Eupolemus attempted to identify Solomon as the origin of the well-known pillar in Tyre, mentioned by the Greek historian Herodotus as being in a temple to Heracles.[43] Eupolemus thus connects Solomon with votive offerings in a temple of Zeus. Immediately following this fragment of Eupolemus's work in Eusebius is a fragment from another Jewish author, Theophilus, who insists that Solomon simply sent the remaining gold back to Souron. Souron then commissioned a full-length gold statue of his daughter and placed the golden pillar near it as a covering for the statue.[44] We know nothing about Theophilus except that he wrote this fragment. We do not know when or where Theophilus wrote, or whether he wrote in conscious opposition to Eupolemus. We do see him, however, as trying to distance Solomon from any connection with a foreign cult, while that is less of a problem for Eupolemus.

It is also interesting to note how the LXX translates Exod 22:28 as "You shall not revile God." The Hebrew term for "God" (אלהים *ĕlōhîm*) is a plural noun, and the Greek translator has translated it as plural: "You shall not revile the gods." Does this translation imply that the gods of other nations could be honored, but only as subordinate to the supreme God, the God of Israel?

We do not know for precisely what action Apollonius son of Menestheus (4:4) went to Egypt as an envoy of the Seleucids (v. 21). Perhaps it was the first time the young king had presided at a state banquet. Ptolemy VI Philometor, after the death of his father,

---

40. The Tyrian god Melqart came to be regarded as an alias for the Greek deity Heracles.
41. Arrian *Anabasis* 3.6.1.
42. Eusebius *Preparation for the Gospel* 9.34.18.
43. Herodotus 2:44.
44. Eusebius *Preparation for the Gospel* 9.34.19.

Ptolemy V Epiphanes, in 181/180, had been under the control first of his mother, Cleopatra I, who died in 176, and then of guardians; he proclaimed himself to be of age in 170. The event recorded here seems to take place around 172 BCE, and tension had been building for a long time. Ptolemy V Epiphanes might possibly have gone to war with the Seleucids if he had not been assassinated. Antiochus IV, to forestall any invasion, made a tour of his southern areas. Joppa (v. 21) lay on the coast to the northwest of Jerusalem. The language used to describe Antiochus's welcome to Jerusalem (v. 22) is that of the ceremonial reception for Hellenistic kings. One might compare it with the narrative of the arrival of Alexander the Great in Jerusalem, a narrative that also emphasizes the friendly relations between Jews and the Greek rulers.[45]

45. See Josephus *Antiquities of the Jews* 11.329-339.

REFLECTIONS

This section raises in heightened fashion the question of how a religious community is to identify itself and maintain that identity. What boundaries must one not cross if one is to remain part of that community and true to its traditions? The author of the epitome clearly sees Jason as overstepping the boundaries of Jewish identity as the author defines it. Jews, for him, should not participate in the education in gymnasia or have anything to do with the religious activities associated with Greek festivals. Jason thought differently.

We face similar questions about identity and boundaries in contemporary society. Should Christians send their children to public schools, or should they have their own schools to instill their own sense of Christian values? How much television should we expose our children to? Should one study Scripture only within the confines of one's own religious tradition, or does one need to be open to the insights of scholars from differing religious traditions who read it from a very different perspective? How is one to respect other religious traditions, to show respect for the festivals of Islam, of Hinduism, of Buddhism, of Native American religious traditions? How do we maintain our belief in the privileged position of our own religious tradition when we are faced with the idea that people do not come to the knowledge of God by one way alone? These questions come to the surface as we see the Jews of the second century BCE struggling with diverse cultural values. If a multi-cultural society is to survive, the various subgroups that populate it must learn to respect one another's traditions and cultures. This is easy to say, but hard to do. If religion is thought of as something individual, private, that each person has the right to do in his or her own private way, then a simple solution seems attainable. Everyone will be able to worship in his or her own way, but the individual's religion will not impinge on society as a whole. But religious beliefs do have social consequences. The debate over abortion has clearly shown that. The late nineteenth and early twentieth centuries also saw surface a conflict between those who held that following the gospel precepts would bring prosperity and that the poor were therefore lazy sinners, and those who held that the gospel required concern and help for the poor. Religious beliefs *do* have social consequences, and so the task of forming a viable society out of many belief systems requires all of us to work hard at empathizing with those of other faiths.

2 Maccabees 4:23-50, Menelaus in Control

COMMENTARY

4:23-29, Menelaus Gains the High Priesthood. Jason, although a usurper, was of the Oniad family and thus a Zadokite. He is replaced by Menelaus, a brother of Simon and member of the clan of Bilgah (3:4), and thus not a member of the priestly family. Just as Jason had gained the high priesthood by offering money, so also Menelaus, while delivering the annual tribute, promises an annual tribute of six hundred talents of silver (v. 24), which he is unable to deliver (v. 27). The author dehumanizes Menelaus and suggests by the use of the term "orders," or "instructions" (ἐντολή *entolē*), that Menelaus is but a puppet of the king (v. 25). Jason flees across the Jordan (v. 26); the Tobiad Hyrcanus had previously fled there to Araq-el-Emir, about twelve miles east of the Jordan and ten miles northwest of Heshbon.[46]

The author now informs us that there was a Seleucid garrison in the city (v. 28; according to 1 Maccabees, the citadel had not yet been built). Antiochus III had spoken of the expulsion of a Ptolemaic garrison from the citadel in Jerusalem,[47] but this is the first time the reader learns of a Seleucid garrison in Jerusalem. Perhaps it was stationed there in response to the Ptolemaic threat. Since one of Sostratus's duties was to collect revenues, there must have been some division of authority within Jerusalem, with a regular royal functionary operating within and above the city's political structure. Sostratus and Menelaus are summoned by the king to Antioch to resolve the matter (v. 28). Cyprus was at this time a Ptolemaic possession, so Cyprian troops (v. 29) must have been mercenaries.

4:30-38, The Murder of Onias. When Sostratus and Menelaus arrive in Antioch, Antiochus IV is away from Antioch, settling an uprising in the Cilician towns of Tarsus and Mallus caused by an affront to their standing as independent cities (v. 30). The authority of the king in Greek cities, particularly those in strategic Asia Minor, varied from city to city, but in general the Seleucids showed a certain respect for the independence of these cities. For Antiochus to summarily hand them over to his concubine would have been seen as disrespectful.

In the king's absence, Menelaus gives some golden vessels stolen from the Temple to Andronicus, Antiochus's deputy, either as payment of the overdue tribute or as a bribe to have Onias murdered (v. 32). This narrative is quite intriguing. Menelaus, we learn, has been selling temple vessels in Tyre and neighboring cities, perhaps due to his need for cash (v. 27). One might recall how the pious king Hezekiah had paid off Sennacherib with temple silver and gold (2 Kgs 18:13-16; an incident not repeated in the parallel account in 2 Chronicles 32). Menelaus, therefore, may have thought it proper to use the temple furnishings as payment to the king, although he could not have thought that it was right to use the temple treasures to bribe Andronicus. Clearly Onias III, as well as the author, thought Menelaus did not have the authority to sell temple vessels (v. 33). What is intriguing is that, once he has exposed Menelaus's actions, the pious Onias III (3:1) is pictured as taking asylum in the famous temple of Apollo and Artemis in Daphne. What, then, is Onias's view of the power of the Greek gods? Here surfaces another of the motifs of 2 Maccabees: Jews and Gentiles can live in peace together (12:30-31). Andronicus, by murdering Onias (v. 34), is shown as utterly treacherous, a treachery resented even by non-Jews (v. 35). Someone named Andronicus is said by Hellenistic historians to have murdered the son of Seleucus IV, who seems to have been co-regent with Antiochus IV prior to Antiochus's rise to power.[48] (The death of Seleucus's son is dated to July/August 170 BCE from the Babylonian kinglist.) It seems likely that the same Andronicus is meant in both cases. Perhaps Antiochus IV took the opportunity of Onias's murder to do away with an embarrassing accomplice, although Antiochus IV is shown by the author as being

---
46. Josephus *Antiquities of the Jews* 12.229-233.
47. Josephus *Antiquities of the Jews* 12.138.
48. Diodorus Siculus 30.7.2.

concerned only with the death of Onias, and as extremely moved by it (v. 37). Andronicus is stripped of the purple robe, symbol of the order of the Friends of the King (v. 38; see 1 Macc 10:20), and is publicly humiliated. The motif of one's getting one's just deserts thus appears again, while the king does not take action with regard to Menelaus's role in the death.

4:39-50, Further Charges Against Menelaus. The sacrilegious actions of the Bilgah clan result in rioting against Lysimachus. The attack against Lysimachus, Menelaus's brother (vv. 39-42), seems to take place while Menelaus is at Antioch and Lysimachus is in charge in Jerusalem (v. 29). The events narrated here stand in sharp contrast to what occurred earlier (2 Maccabees 3). Onias had protected the money deposited in the Temple, but Lysimachus sells the temple vessels. The people had gathered around the high priest Onias in sympathy; here they accuse Lysimachus. Earlier the action was against outsiders; now it is an internal conflict. Lysimachus resorts to violence (v. 40), just as his brother Simon had done (4:3). The reader may wonder what the Seleucid garrison (4:29) was doing during this confrontation and how Lysimachus could so easily procure arms for three thousand men, a small militia in itself. Lysimachus is supported by an otherwise unknown figure, Auranus, whose description contrasts markedly with that of a later, older man, Eleazar, who suffers martyrdom rather than breach the law (6:18). The author intimates divine help in that an unarmed group puts the three thousand armed men to flight and that Lysimachus dies at the very place he was robbing (v. 42), just as Andronicus was killed on the very spot where he had killed Onias (v. 38).

We do not know how the report about the selling of the temple vessels spread (v. 39), but we can see how the factions mentioned in 4:1-6 still exist. Now, as Onias III had done, the three members of the Jerusalem council (v. 44), a body known from a letter of Antiochus III but whose exact function and responsibilities are unknown,[49] go to the king for justice. We are not told who is in charge of Jerusalem or the outcome of the uprising against Lysimachus. The author insists that the uprising was blamed on Menelaus (c. 43 BCE), but the three high-ranking councilors may have been called to answer questions about the incident. Ptolemy, son of Dorymenes, may already have held the office of governor of Coelesyria and Phoenicia (1 Macc 3:38; 2 Macc 8:8) and may have been present there for the trial. As the previous governor had favored Simon, Menelaus's brother (4:4), and as bribery had won the day before (4:32), so now the author shows the same factors at work. Justice, in the opinion of the author of 1 Maccabees, is perverted (vv. 45-48). The Scythians were a byword for irrational cruelty.[50] As at the murder of Onias, the author depicts here some non-Jews sympathetic to the fate of the executed councilors (v. 49). Once again the contrast with Onias III stands out: Whereas Onias was not an accuser of his compatriots but only sought their welfare, Menelaus is the chief plotter against his compatriots.

49. Josephus *Antiquities of the Jews* 12.142.
50. Herodotus 4.64-75; Polybius 9.34.11.

REFLECTIONS

This section details the intrigues and plots and the breakdown of civility within the Jewish polity. Menelaus uses every means in his power to remain in power: illicitly drawing upon funds that do not belong to him; resorting to violence to quell discontent; silencing the opposition by murder. The story reads almost like the plot for a movie: a politician who steals public monies and then uses his position of power to threaten and get rid of opponents in whatever way is necessary. Unfortunately, art sometimes copies life, and the number of politicians and religious leaders who have been indicted for abuse of trust seems to grow every year. The public figure who can be bribed, like Andronicus, also stands as a warning. Politicians need to be extremely sensitive to even the appearance of a conflict of interest. It does not seem right, for instance, that a senator or member of Congress who owns stocks and shares in oil or gas companies should sit on the committees determining energy policy.

The contrast between the desire for private, short-term gain at the expense of the long-term common welfare of the community is striking in this narrative. It is a contrast each society and each community knows and must deal with. The narrative reminds us of the truth of the maxim cited in 1 Tim 6:10: "The love of money is a root of all kinds of evil" (NRSV). Money donated to charitable works and missions needs to be carefully administered and not squandered on personal affairs or self-aggrandizement. Religious leaders should lead lives of simplicity, and not lord it over their flock. As Jesus said, "You know that among the Gentiles those whom they recognize as their rulers lord it over them, and their great ones are tyrants over them. But it is not so among you; but whoever wishes to become great among you must be your servant" (Mark 10:42-43 NRSV). We should not muzzle the ox while it is treading out the grain (1 Cor 9:8-12), but the ox should not become fat either.

2 Maccabees 5:1-27, Antiochus Takes Control of Jerusalem

COMMENTARY

5:1-10, The Occasion for the Attack on the Temple. The author of 1 Maccabees locates Antiochus IV's attack on the Temple after his second invasion of Egypt (168 BCE), while 2 Maccabees places it after his first invasion of Egypt (170–169 BCE). Daniel 11:28-30 speaks of two invasions of Egypt and two attacks against the Temple, but does not explicitly say that Antiochus IV entered Jerusalem in person on the second attack. In this case, the chronology of 1 Maccabees is to be preferred (1 Macc 1:20-35). Most likely the epitomist has conflated the pillaging of the Temple after the first invasion of Egypt with an armed attack on Jerusalem by the Seleucid Apollonius, captain of the Mysians (1 Macc 1:29; 2 Macc 5:24; note how 1 Maccabees gives a precise date for this attack, "two years later," while 2 Maccabees does not).

5:1-4. Portents or signs in the heavens before a momentous event are frequently reported in Jewish and non-Jewish literature (see esp. Tacitus, the Roman historian [c. 56–115 CE], Pliny the Elder, a Roman writer of the first century CE, and Josephus, the first-century CE Jewish historian).[51] Such portents could, of course, be variously interpreted, and they heightened the narrative tension as to what is in fact to happen (v. 4).

5:5-10. The outcome of battles was always questionable, and so rumors of defeats could easily circulate. The rebuff of Antiochus IV by the Romans after his second invasion of Egypt in 168 BCE would be an appropriate occasion for the rise of such a rumor (v. 5). Lysimachus had been able to muster three thousand men (4:40), but now Jason, with only a thousand men, successfully makes an unexpected attack on Jerusalem and forces Menelaus to take refuge in the citadel, presumably with the Seleucid garrison. Jason must have hoped that, with Menelaus defeated, the successor of Antiochus IV would see him as the strong man of Judea, just as Menelaus had gained the high priesthood by presenting himself as powerful (v. 24). Jason, like Menelaus, attacks his compatriots (v. 6). The author does not tell us why Jason failed in his attempt to gain control (v. 7). Some scholars have suggested that a third force, neither Jason nor Menelaus, but the crowds (see 4:40), rose up in a popular uprising. It is more likely, however, that the citadel was well stocked and ably defended by the Seleucid garrison and could hold out against Jason while waiting for reinforcements. Possibly Jason fled in the face of a Seleucid force sent to reestablish order.

---

51. Tacitus *Histories* 2.50.2; 2.78.2; cf. Pliny *Natural History* 2.148. Josephus *The Jewish War* 6.288-309.

The author is only concerned to draw out the moral of the story, and not to provide the details. Jason is forced to return to Ammon (4:26). That Jason fled to Egypt presumes that Egypt was no longer under Seleucid control, but these events may have taken place either just before or after Antiochus IV's second invasion of Egypt. The author indulges in a series of contrasts to show how God brings just deserts upon sinners.

The fictive kinship of the Jews with the Lacedaemonians, or Spartans (v. 9), found also in the exchange of letters cited at 1 Macc 12:6, 18, 20-23, parallels the attempt of many Hellenistic cities to attach themselves to famous events and cities from the Golden Age of Greece (e.g., the Romans traced their origins to Aeneas the Trojan). The Spartans were legendary for their austere way of life and for their military prowess, particularly as exhibited in the wars against the invading Persian army of Xerxes in 480 BCE. The Spartan way of life and educational system were quite different from that of other Greek cities, particularly Athens. Hecataeus of Abdera, a Greek historian (c. 300 BCE), wrote that in ancient times foreigners dwelling among the Egyptians were driven out because it was thought that the strangers had disrupted the traditional services to the Egyptian gods. Among those driven out, some went to Greece, while most went to Judea under Moses.[52] So some connection was being made between the Greeks and the Jews—although very slight. A more direct connection between the Jews and the Spartans may be through the legendary hero Heracles, to whom Spartan kings traced their ancestry. The Hellenistic-Jewish writer Cleodemus Malchus stated that Afera and Iafra, sons of Abraham through Keturah (Gen 25:4, Ephah and Epher), fought alongside Heracles in his campaign against Antaios and that Africa was named after them. Heracles is said to have married one of the daughters of Afera.[53] This makes a closer connection between the Spartans and the Jews, but does not explain why the Jews and the Spartans were thought to be kin. Perhaps the separation of the Spartans from the rest of the Greeks in their way of life and educational system allowed for a similarity to be drawn between them and the Jews, who were also distinctive in their way of life.

To die far from one's ancestral tomb (v. 10) was a heavy punishment. When a prophet was tricked into disobeying the command that God had laid on him not to eat or drink, he was told that he would not come to his ancestral tomb (1 Kgs 13:22). When Saul's and his sons' bodies were ignominiously displayed on the walls of Beth-shan, the people of Jabesh-Gilead took them down (1 Sam 31:10-13), and later David transferred the bones of Saul and his son Jonathan back to Saul's father's tomb in the land of Benjamin (2 Sam 21:10-14).

5:11-16, The Attack. The narrative parallels 1 Macc 1:20-24. Here, in contrast to 1 Maccabees, Antiochus acts to suppress a revolt. As mentioned earlier, according to 1 Macc 1:20, Antiochus plundered the Temple in Jerusalem after his first invasion of Egypt. The author of 2 Maccabees, however, places the plunder of the Temple after the second invasion in 168 BCE, when Antiochus was forced to leave Egypt at the intervention of the Romans. In addition, the author of 2 Maccabees makes no mention of the reversal Antiochus had suffered at the hands of the Romans, but implies that the only reason why Antiochus left Egypt was to put down the revolt in Jerusalem. The problem of determining in exactly what order the events occurred is further complicated by the version in Dan 11:28-31:

> He [Antiochus IV] shall return to his land with great wealth, but his heart shall be set against the holy covenant. He shall work his will, and return to his own land. At the time appointed he shall return and come into the south, but this time it shall not be as it was before. For ships of Kittim shall come against him, and he shall lose heart and withdraw. He shall be enraged and take action against the holy covenant. He shall turn back and pay heed to those who forsake the holy covenant. Forces sent by him shall occupy and profane the temple and fortress. (NRSV)

Here in cryptic form are outlined the first and second invasions of Antiochus IV against

---

52. See Diodorus Siculus 40.3.1-3.
53. See Josephus *Antiquities of the Jews* 1.239-41.

Egypt. That he "works his will" seems to refer to the plundering of the Temple. After his aborted second invasion, Antiochus is enraged and sends forces to despoil the Temple. This chronology seems to be the same as that of 1 Macc 1:20-35, which speaks of the plunder of the Temple after the first invasion of Egypt in 169 BCE and then reports that two years later, in 167, Antiochus sent forces against Jerusalem, although 1 Maccabees does not speak of the second invasion of Egypt by Antiochus or of his rebuff by the Romans (i.e., the Kittim). The author of 2 Maccabees thus seems to have run together two events: the plunder of the Temple after the first invasion and the second Syrian attack on the Temple.

There is also a problem with the first invasion of Egypt. We do not know why Antiochus IV withdrew from Egypt. He had not captured Alexandria, but had set up a protectorate of sorts with himself as guardian of his nephew, Ptolemy VI Philometor. Some scholars have suggested that Antiochus withdrew to garner more forces, but a Babylonian text records that he celebrated his victory in Egypt with a great festival in August/September 169 BCE. Here again a chronological problem surfaces. The Greek historian Polybius speaks of a great festival held by Antiochus IV, the Festival of Daphnae, but this is usually dated to 166 BCE.[54] The problem arises as to whether Antiochus would have celebrated two festivals for his victories in Egypt. The triumphal festival recorded in the Babylonian diaries appears to be the act of someone satisfied with the results of his invasion, or at least of someone who wants to appear satisfied with the results, since we do not know why he left Egypt. Perhaps Antiochus left because he had settled for a divided, and therefore weakened, Ptolemaic Empire.

The account in 2 Maccabees suggests that the only reason why Antiochus IV left Egypt was to put down the revolt in Jerusalem (v. 11). He is portrayed as being furious that someone should revolt against him. Once again the author of 2 Maccabees dehumanizes the enemy of the Jews by using bestial descriptions—"inwardly raging" is literally "wild beast-like in soul" (τεθηριωμένος τῇ ψυχῇ *tethēriōmenos tē psychē*). Such descriptions show that Antiochus is not in control of himself, not properly human. The author is not concerned with exact chronology so much as with rhetorical flourish. The numbers of those slaughtered and enslaved are exaggerated (v. 14). The text of Dan 11:30 also describes Antiochus as enraged, but there his rage seems rather the result of being humiliated by the Romans. Scholars sometimes explain the harsh treatment of Jerusalem at the hands of Antiochus as a response to his humiliation by the Romans in Egypt in 168 BCE and his wanting to show that he was still a force to be reckoned with. The same motivation would lie behind his ostentatious festival of Daphnae if it is dated to 166 BCE. But Antiochus did not plunder the Temple out of rage after the success of his first invasion of Egypt. Rather, at about the same time in 169 BCE, he was forcibly extracting treasures from the temple in Babylon, so his plunder of the Jerusalem Temple should not be seen as a special case. If his rage at his humiliation by the Romans is seen as a motivating factor for his subsequent actions, it is a rather delayed reaction for the festival— which, if dated to 166 BCE, took place two years later—and also for the persecution of the Jews, which occurred almost a year after Antiochus's rebuff by the Romans. No doubt Antiochus smarted at the humiliation, but this still does not seem a sufficient reason for the slow buildup of measures against the Jews, which culminated in the attempted suppression of their cultural and religious traditions.

After plundering Egypt (1 Macc 1:19),[55] Antiochus must have thought Jerusalem was small pickings. Antiochus's liberal gifts to Greek cities, particularly Athens, where he wished to complete the magnificent temple of Olympian Zeus, made him always glad of further revenue. In contrast to Onias III, whose piety brought it about that kings honored and glorified the Temple (3:1-2), Menelaus now helps Antiochus despoil the Temple. The role of Menelaus is not mentioned in the parallel account in 1 Maccabees.

5:17-20, The Author's Reflections. At this disastrous turn of events the author feels compelled to comment. He stresses the dichotomy between what Antiochus thinks and what God proposes. Antiochus is "puffed

---

54. Polybius 30.25-26.

55. See also Polybius 30.26.9.

up in spirit," an attitude against which he will be warned in 7:34, and thinks he is special (cf. 5:21; 9:8, 10), whereas God is using Antiochus as the instrument of God's anger. This misperception of one's role is also ascribed to the king of Assyria at Isa 10:5-15. In addition, the author has the same theology that is found in Deuteronomy, where, if the people disobey God's laws, they will be punished (Deut 11:13-17, 28; cf. 2 Macc 6:12-17). The author stresses that the welfare of Jerusalem, the place God chose (Deut 12:5-7), depends on the people's keeping the covenant with its blessings and curses. The author, in v. 20, looks forward to the turnaround of the misfortune of the people, which will take place in chapter 8, and reflects on the prayer of Solomon at the dedication of the Temple (1 Kgs 8:46-53; 2 Chr 7:12-22; see also Isa 54:7-8; Jer 7:3-15; Zech 1:12-17 for examples of God's anger turning to compassion).

5:21-26, Antiochus's Measures in Jerusalem. In his arrogance (stressed in 1 Maccabees also; see 1 Macc 1:21), Antiochus carries off 1,800 talents from the Temple, quite a large sum. The way the king is described calls to mind the Persian king Xerxes, who dared to bridge the Hellespont and cut a canal through Mt. Athos.[56] Antiochus is being depicted as someone who fights against God (see 7:19).

Philip (who appears again in 6:11 and 8:8), a Phrygian (in Asia Minor), possibly was in charge of the Seleucid garrison in Jerusalem, from which he could make forays into the countryside. Again, note how this enemy of the Jews is described: "more barbarous than the man who appointed him" (v. 22). The Greek official is termed a barbarian, the exact reversal of normal Greek usage, in which non-Greeks are the barbarians (cf. 2:21). Andronicus was left in charge of Gerizim, the center of Samaria. Note how the Samaritans are included in "the race"/"people" (v. 22; 6:2). The author does not see any conflict between the Jews and the Samaritans.[57] Andronicus, a Mysian (in northwestern Asia Minor), was perhaps the predecessor of Apollonius in Samaria (1 Macc 3:10). Menelaus remains high priest and is described as being even worse than these non-Jewish officials. The description of Apollonius's attack parallels that of 1 Macc 1:29-40, although the author here states that the attack took place on the sabbath, thereby heightening the offense.[58] An army of 22,000 seems much too large for an attack force against unarmed Jerusalem. The purpose of the attack, to kill all the men and sell the women and children as slaves, appears to replicate what Antiochus had already done (5:13-14). The attack of Apollonius, as narrated by the epitomist, appears completely unprovoked and a senseless act of cruelty. The parallel account in 1 Maccabees provides the purpose for Apollonius's attack: to install and fortify a strong Seleucid garrison in the city. As the author of 1 Maccabees dates the event to two years after Antiochus's first invasion of Egypt (i.e., 167 BCE), he thus locates it not long after Antiochus's humiliation at the hands of the Romans in Egypt. So the reader might see these reinforced fortifications as part of an attempt to strengthen the Seleucid Empire's southern border. Throughout all this activity, where was Menelaus? Was he away from the city at Antioch, or was he a witness to the power of the Seleucid army?

5:27. In the midst of this destruction, the author again sounds a hopeful note: Judas Maccabeus appears on the scene (v. 27). The author of 2 Maccabees makes no mention of Mattathias, although, like the author of 1 Maccabees, he has the Hasmoneans first living in Jerusalem (1 Macc 2:1). The author of 1 Maccabees has placed the exit from Jerusalem of Mattathias and his family after the narrative of the religious persecution (1 Macc 1:41-62), whereas the author of 2 Maccabees places Judas's exit before the persecution (2 Macc 6:1-11). However, these differences can perhaps be accounted for by the goals of the two authors. The author of 1 Maccabees introduces his account with the vague phrase "in those days," so an exact chronology cannot be determined. Since the purpose of this author is to concentrate on the reaction to the persecution in Mattathias and his sons, he accentuates Mattathias's grief by including a lament (2:7-13), while giving little space to the martyrdoms (1 Macc 1:60-63). The author of 2 Maccabees, on the other hand,

---

56. See Herodotus 7:22-24, 34-37; Aeschylus *Persians* 69-72, 744-51.
57. Josephus records a letter from some Samaritans arguing against classifying them with the Jews. See *Antiquities of the Jews* 5.260-61.

58. Cf. Josephus *Against Apion* 1:209-11.

emphasizes martyrdom as the appropriate reaction to persecution (6:10–7:42), and for him it is the martyrdoms that bring God's mercy (7:38; 8:5). Therefore, he places the story of Judas's exit from Jerusalem so as to offer the reader a glimpse of hope. The wilderness was a traditional place of refuge, where Moses had fled from Pharaoh (Exod 3:1), David had fled from Saul (1 Sam 23:14), and Elijah had fled from Jezebel (1 Kgs 19:1-9). Judas escapes from the pollution of the city life into the more natural life in the mountains (cf. Hos 2:14-15; Mark 1:12). The final clause of v. 27, "so that they might not share in the defilement," qualifies their living apart from the city as escaping evil influences and not simply eating "what grew wild."

REFLECTIONS

The author of 2 Maccabees, as noted, provides his own comments on what was happening in Jerusalem (5:17-20) and in the way he portrays the just deserts meted out to Jason. What the reader might ponder here is that so often we are caught up in the leading personalities of the conflict. How terrible were Jason and Menelaus? How arrogant was Antiochus? What we sometimes forget is the fate of those slaughtered and enslaved, however inaccurate the figures might be (80,000, 5:14; "great numbers," 5:26). These are the ordinary people who so often bear the brunt of their leaders' pride and ambition. Even in an age when missiles can be targeted with pinpoint accuracy, it is still so often the civilian population that suffers. Here the problem of what constitutes a just war arises again. Can the slaughter of civilians ever be tolerated, however accidental? What level of killing can be tolerated in the prosecution of a war? Can there ever be a just nuclear war? These horrific war stories from the second century BCE should make us reflect on the equally horrible atrocities of our age.

2 Maccabees 6:1-11, The Pagan Cult Imposed in Jerusalem

COMMENTARY

Antiochus IV now takes further measures against the Jews in Jerusalem. As noted in the Introduction, the motives behind this action remain unknown, although many theories abound. What one notes is that these measures are the final step in a process of attempting to control what was going on in Jerusalem and presumably to stabilize conditions in this southern region of the kingdom. The measures against Judaism were directed at Jews in Judea, and not empire-wide. For some reason, Antiochus must have considered the Jewish cult in Judea, centered around the Temple, to be a focal point of resistance to the smooth running of the Seleucid administration of the city, even though his friend Menelaus was high priest. Were opposition and resistance to the Seleucid government and the regime of Menelaus already growing before the rise of the Maccabees? The parallel account in 1 Macc 1:41-64 stresses the megalomania of the king, but, since the decree mentioned at 1 Macc 1:41 is not confirmed by other evidence, one should try to find an explanation that fits the particular situation in Judea. What is intriguing is the silence about the role of Menelaus. Some scholars have suggested that he instigated the persecution. As will be noted later on, the reference to Menelaus in the letter of Antiochus IV, which repeals the persecution (11:27-33), could be taken to mean that Menelaus was instrumental in the repeal of the persecution. He, therefore, may have been overruled when the king decided, for whatever reasons and prompted by whatever advisers, to suppress Judaism in Judea and install paganism. (See also Commentary on 2 Maccabees 11.)

6:1-2. The king's agent is named Geron the Athenian. The Jews are no longer to follow the religious customs of their ancestors. Such a decree might indicate that the Jews could not follow them in public but possibly could in private. However, the instances of people's ignoring the ban show that private observance was also forbidden. The first change is one of nomenclature: the temples in Jerusalem and Gerizim are given new names, Zeus Olympios and Zeus Xenios (i.e., friend of strangers) respectively. Olympios and Xenios were both common epithets for Zeus (Antiochus IV had undertaken to complete the temple in Athens dedicated to Zeus Olympios). The author gives a reason for the change to Zeus Xenios at Gerizim, but the meaning is uncertain. Scholars frequently emend the text to bring it into line with a petition from some Samaritans to Antiochus IV requesting that their temple be renamed Zeus Hellenios and translate v. 2*b* as in the NAB: "as the inhabitants of the place requested."[59] However, since the author has previously linked what happens at Jerusalem with what happens at Gerizim (5:22-23) and seems to hold no antipathy to the Samaritans, one might keep the text as is and translate "as those who live there are, i.e., hospitable." A Hellenistic-Jewish writer, in retelling Genesis 14, describes how Abraham was "hospitably received" (ξενίζω *xenizō*) by the city at the temple of Gerizim,[60] and this may reflect a positive view of the Samaritans.

6:3-6. The author offers a description of the imposed cult that is not found in other contemporary sources. Cult prostitution was prohibited in Israelite religion (Deut 23:17), and various kings were praised for ridding the land of cult prostitutes (1 Kgs 15:12; 22:46; 2 Kgs 23:7), and the presence of cult prostitutes is a sign of the evil reign of Rehoboam (1 Kgs 14:24). The author of 2 Maccabees is using stereotypical accusations to show that what the Gentiles were doing was barbaric. While Antiochus III had issued a proclamation forbidding improper sacrificial animals to be brought to the city and allowed only the sacrificial animals known to their ancestors,[61] now unfit sacrificial offerings are introduced.

What is noteworthy is that the author does not mention the desolating sacrilege of Dan 11:31; 1 Macc 1:54. Also, it is unclear what exactly is meant by "nor even admit that he was a Jew" (v. 6). Does the term "Jew" here have simply a geographical designation so that people who used to live in or originate from Judea were called Jews, but now were going to be called after the new name for the area, a name derived from the name change of Jerusalem to Antioch-in-Jerusalem (2 Macc 4:9, 19)? Would such a geographical name change be applied even to those people originally from Judea who were living outside Judea, or only to those living in Judea? Or does "Jew" here mean more than a geographical designation—i.e., one who follows the Torah? Given the context of the suppression of distinctive religious and cultural traditions derived from the Torah, probably it means the latter. When discussing Exod 20:6, which speaks of those who love God and keep the commandments, a rabbinic commentator writes: "Rabbi Nathan says: 'Of them that love me and keep my commandments' refers to those who dwell in the land of Israel and risk their lives for the sake of the commandments."[62]

6:7-9. The cult imposed was not for one particular divinity, but responded to paganism in general, here to the cult of the king and to the cult of Dionysus, the Greek god of wine and harvest. The author insists that the Jews were forced to take part in these festivals, but 1 Macc 1:52 suggests that many were eager to follow the new practices. The monthly celebration of Antiochus IV's birthday was on the twenty-fifth of the month (1 Macc 1:58-59). The persecution, or attempt to force neighboring Jews to follow Greek ways, is extended to neighboring cities, most probably those immediately bordering on Judea so that the Judeans could not easily cross the border to practice their religion. The translation of v. 8 is difficult; the verb can mean either "suggest" or, more strongly, "enjoin," and the manuscripts read both "of Ptolemy" (i.e., Ptolemy son of Dorymenes the governor of Coelesyria and Phoenicia; 4:45; 8:8) and "of Ptolemais" (i.e., the coastal city in Phoenicia also known as Acco). Ptolemais seems a good distance from the borders of Judea, as it lies near Galilee. However, 1 Macc 5:15

---

59. Josephus *Antiquities of the Jews* 12.261.
60. Eusebius *Preparation for the Gospel* 9.17.5.
61. Josephus *Antiquities of the Jews* 12.145-146.
62. Mekilta de Rabbi Ishmael. *Tractate Baḥodesh* 6.

reports that the people of Ptolemais and Tyre and Sidon and all Galilee of the Gentiles had gathered together against the Jews. Only one decree is said to be issued, whereas each Greek city should pass its own vote. We must imagine, therefore, either that Ptolemy, hostile to the Jews in 2 Macc 4:45; 8:8, strongly recommended to the cities around Judea that they persecute the Jews, or that the citizens of Ptolemais so acted on their own accord and induced other cities to follow their lead. The latter reading makes the persecution a more "grassroots" movement than does the former.

6:10-11. Two examples of the suffering imposed are then adduced (cf. 1 Macc 1:60-61; 2:31-38). Note the use of political language: the women are led publicly through the "city" (πόλις *polis*) and thrown down from the wall (which protects the city). The victims are described as women with babies at their breasts—here women and their babies, the basis for the continued growth and prosperity of any city, are paraded as antithetical to the city values Antiochus IV is espousing.

Immediately following the execution of the women and their babies is an account of some men who were meeting outside the city, out of sight, to "observe the sabbath day" (v. 11). Yet they are betrayed to Philip and are burned to death.[63] Their actions are depicted as anti-social and anti-*polis*. Plato had argued that no one should possess shrines in private houses and that anyone who disobeyed was to be executed.[64] The rites of Dionysus were suppressed in Rome in 186 BCE because, as the Roman historian Livy states, they are secret/hidden rites performed at night. They are alien rites.[65] So here the rituals of the Jews are attacked as anti-*polis*, as a threat to the state and as if they were foreign, and yet the reader knows that the observance of the sabbath, the most holy day, is part and parcel of ancestral Jewish tradition and that Philip, a Phrygian (2 Macc 5:22), is the foreigner.

63. *Assumption of Moses* 8; Josephus *The Jewish War* 1.312-313.
64. Plato *Laws* 10.909-910D.
65. Livy 39.14.8.

2 Maccabees 6:12-17, Punishment Seen as Discipline

COMMENTARY

The author interprets the persecution against the Jews as God's training/education of the people. As a parent disciplines a child, so God disciplines Israel (Deut 8:5). God regards Israel as a mother nursing her child (Isa 49:14-16); God may be angry, but God's love is everlasting (Isa 54:7-8). Israel is God's chosen people, treated differently from the way other nations are treated.

Such a reflection is in line with later rabbinic teaching on the goodness of suffering.

Rabbi Akiba says: "You shall not do with me" (Exod 20:20). You shall not behave towards Me in the manner in which others behave towards their deities. When good comes to them they honor their gods, as it is said: "Therefore they sacrifice unto their net," etc. (Hab 1:16). But when evil comes to them they curse their gods, as it is said: "And it shall come to pass that when they shall be hungry they shall fret themselves and curse their king and their god" (Isa 8:21). But you, if I bring good upon you, give thanks, and when I bring suffering upon you, give thanks.... Furthermore, a man should even rejoice when in adversity more than when in prosperity. For even if a man lives in prosperity all his life, it does not mean that his sins have been forgiven him. But what is it that does bring a man forgiveness? You must say, suffering. Rabbi Eliezer the son of Jacob says: Behold it says: "My son, despise not the chastening of the Lord" (Prov 3:11). Why? "For whom the Lord loves He corrects," etc. You must reason: Go out and see what was it that made this son a delight to his father? You must say, suffering . . . Rabbi Jose the son of Rabbi Judah says: Precious are chastisements, for the name of God rests upon him to whom chastisements come.[66]

In some ways the teaching here differs from that in Sirach, which emphasizes how slow to

66. Mekilta de Rabbi Ishmael *Tractate Baḥodesh* 10.

anger the Lord is and warns against counting on God's indulgence (Sir 5:4-9; cf. 18:10-14). The Wisdom of Solomon also teaches that the righteous receive benefit through punishments (Wis 11:1-14), but it also speaks of God's allowing other nations time to repent: "Though you were not unable to/ give the ungodly into the/ hands of the righteous in battle,/ or to destroy them at one blow by/ dread wild animals or your stern word,/ But judging them little by little/ you gave them an/ opportunity to repent" (Wis 12:9-10 NRSV; cf. 12:20).

2 MACCABEES 6:18–7:42, THE REACTION TO THE PERSECUTIONS

2 Maccabees 6:18-31, Eleazar

COMMENTARY

The story of Eleazar is retold in greater detail in 4 Maccabees 5–7, where he is called a priest (4 Macc 5:4). The word translated "scribe" (γραμματεύς *grammateus*) often in the OT refers to officers of the people (e.g., Num 11:16; Josh 8:33; 23:2; 24:1; 1 Chr 23:4 LXX), so one should see him as a leading official. Since he is said to be well known to those in charge of the unlawful sacrifice, are these officials Jews or non-Jews? Like all heroes, Eleazar is described as being handsome. He is also dignified and from a noble family (v. 23). The author relates that Eleazar was forced to violate the Torah prohibition of eating pork (Lev 11:7-8; Deut 14:8; cf. 1 Macc 1:47, 62-63). But when he refuses to eat the pork, "welcoming death with honor rather than life with pollution" (v. 19), he is sentenced to be tortured on the rack (so the NRSV). Exactly what the torture was is unclear; the Greek word (τύμπανον *tympanon*, v. 19) can be translated "drum," "stick," or "wagon wheel," and so it connotes something turning around—i.e., a rack. Eleazar refuses to act ignobly, for he knows that God knows all things (v. 30). The narrative, in fact, is full of fine rhetorical passages that are common in Greek literature, in which the person's last words before dying bravely are designed to arouse emotion in the reader. But the narrative also resonates with the contrasts, also common in Greek literature, of honor and dishonor (vv. 19, 25). Eleazar eschews any contradiction between his private and his public behavior. His life is to be marked with consistency, not hypocrisy, an example of nobility, a memorial or ἀρετή (*aretē*, "virtue"/"valor"/"excellence"). To die well is the better part of *aretē*. This classical virtue is found in this narrative in a Jew rather than in the officials who counsel pretense to prolong life. Eleazar is not victimized; rather he willingly chooses honor. There is no mention of restoration to life, only to the bleak world of Hades/Sheol. Eleazar, however, is not seeking a reward, only to live nobly.

2 Maccabees 7:1-42, The Mother and Her Seven Sons

COMMENTARY

After the noble death of an honorable man comes the emotionally charged story of a mother and her seven sons who are martyred for their faith. Such stories of whole families perishing under attack are found both in Jewish and Greek literature.[67] The particular motif of a mother's dying with her seven sons was a favorite

---

67. Examples from Jewish literature: the story of Taxo and his seven sons (*Assumption of Moses* 9), and the account of the Galilean martyrs (Josephus *The Jewish War* 1.312-313; *Antiquities of the Jews* 14.429-430). Examples from Greek literature: the deaths of Theoxena and her sister's children under Philip V of Macedon (Polybius 23.10; Livy 40.4).

one in later Jewish literature, where the event takes place either before a Roman emperor[68] or "in the days of persecution."[69] The folktale motif of the youngest son's being the most important is also present, as we see the tortures crescendo until finally the seventh son gives the longest and most effective speech and undergoes the worst torture. This suggests a more popular type of narrative. Some scholars have suggested that the story originally circulated independent of 2 Maccabees and was inserted into the narrative. However, the closing sentence of the chapter (7:42) links the stories of Eleazar and the mother under the rubrics of "eating of sacrifices" (6:18) and extreme tortures (7:1, 13, 15). The pattern of a mother and her seven sons dying may be traditional and have existed independently, but the author of 2 Maccabees has skillfully woven it into his narrative.

Although there is no indication of a change of scene from the previous story, scholars have speculated as to where these events took place. Later tradition, both Christian and Jewish, located them at Antioch, where Antiochus would have held court, since there is no indication that Antiochus ever visited Jerusalem again. The traditional folktale, in which a ruler is bested by a wiser subject, seems to spotlight the evil character of Antiochus. Throughout the scene, the martyrs respond calmly while the king loses control (7:3, 39).

7:1-6. Like Eleazar, the mother and her sons are arrested and ordered to eat pork (v. 1). The first son, who expresses the family's willingness to suffer martyrdom rather than disobey the law (v. 2), is forced to suffer dehumanizing torture by order of the king (vv. 3-5). His tongue, the instrument of speech and of human communication, his hands, and his feet are cut off, and he is scalped. Pans and caldrons are heated, and he is placed inside one to fry as one would cook animal flesh. Thus he is completely dehumanized. Each son, in turn, will suffer the same fate.

As they look on, the mother and the other sons confess that God also is watching (v. 6), and that God "has compassion" (παρακαλέω *parakaleō*). They allude to Moses' declaration that his song will comfort the people as a witness when terrible troubles come upon them (Deut 32:21). The quotation is from the Song of Moses (Deut 32:36), in which God, after chastising the people for their apostasy, begins to take vengeance on the instruments of God's anger who overstep the mark.

7:7-9. The second son is even more painfully scalped. The contrast between the torturers and the tortured person is further brought out by his responding to the torturers in Hebrew, the ancestral language (v. 8; see also vv. 21-27). He tells them that God will "raise us up to an everlasting renewal of life, because we have died for his laws" (v. 9). The title he uses for God, "King of the universe," clearly contrasts with the limited power of the earthly king Antiochus.

The confident reliance upon God demonstrated by this son evidences that the persecution of Antiochus Epiphanes gave impetus to the development of a belief in resurrection and judgment after death. The story of Eleazar reflected the traditional belief in a shade-like existence in Sheol/Hades (v. 23; see Pss 6:5; 30:9; 88:11-12; 115:16-17; Eccl 3:21; Sir 17:27-28; 41:4). In that story, the author had been concerned to emphasize the nobility and dignity of Eleazar as he underwent torture, so there is no discussion of afterlife. In the story of the mother and her seven sons, however, the author concentrates on contrasting the fate of the martyrs with the eventual fate of the king. Drawing on the notion of a life for the righteous after this life, the author highlights the paradox that the dying martyrs are in fact happier than the supposedly successful king.

There are passages in the OT, particularly in Psalms (Pss 16:9-11; 73:23-26; 84:10), in which the faithful practically long for a continued enjoyment of God, and passages that speak of resurrection in the context of national restoration (Isa 26:19; Ezekiel 37; Hos 6:2). The first Jewish discussion of an after-death judgment is found in the earliest parts of *1 Enoch* (*1 Enoch* 22:27; 90:33; 91:10; 93:2; 104:1-6). And Dan 12:2-3 is a clear expression of a belief in resurrection. One should also note how the Greek translators of passages like Isa 26:19; Job 19:24-26, and Job 14:14 had great difficulty and seem to move toward a sense of individual renewal.

---

68. See *b. Git* 57*b*; m.Lam 1:16.
69. See *Pesiq. R.* 43.

So the belief in resurrection pre-dates the persecution of Antiochus. The author of 2 Maccabees, with his threefold repetition of the first-person plural in v. 9, shows that he is speaking of individual resurrection. The language is similar to, though not identical with, Dan 12:2.

The belief portrayed in 2 Maccabees 7 should be distinguished from the earlier tradition about the shades in Sheol, of which a hint is preserved in Isa 14:9-22. The burial customs unearthed by archaeologists suggest a widespread cult of the dead. It was thought that sometimes these shades could be brought back from Sheol, where they may be called divine beings, but they do not like to be disturbed (1 Sam 28:8-19). It is a different kind of existence from this present life, however, and the shades do not return (Job 14:7-22). What v. 9 asserts is that the dead will be given life again, presumably life on this earth as it is described at v. 23 in language resonating with the creation of the first human (Gen 2:7). This hope of the return of a bodily existence should be distinguished from the hope expressed by an author like that of the Wisdom of Solomon. For that author, in human existence "a perishable body weighs down the soul, and this earthly tent burdens the thoughtful mind" (Wis 9:14-15). The author of the Wisdom of Solomon betrays here how he has been influenced by Platonic philosophy with its distinction between the body and the soul. For such an author, "the souls of the righteous are in the hand of God, and no torment will ever touch them" (Wis 3:1). The author is looking forward to a renewed bodily existence, not the continued existence of an immortal soul.

7:10-12. The third son also meets his fate courageously, again expressing a belief in bodily resurrection. "Heaven" here is an epithet for God. The amazement of onlookers at the endurance of suffering was a common topos in Hellenistic literature.[70] Hecataeus of Abdera stated that the Jews deserve admiration because of their willingness to undergo any torture rather than transgress their ancestral laws,[71] and in the story of Aristeas the Exegete, God is amazed at Job's courage.[72] Recall also the amazement of kings at the suffering servant (Isa 52:15).

7:13-14. The fourth son's dying words deny Antiochus the opportunity of resurrection. For the first time, Antiochus is threatened with punishment. Given the belief in the divinity of kings, this statement is quite radical (cf. the end of the ungodly in Wis 3:10-13, 16-19).

7:15-17. The fifth son warns Antiochus that his authority and power are not due to the abandonment of Israel by God. Punishment is now threatened not only on Antiochus but on his descendants as well.

7:18-19. The sixth son warns Antiochus that, even though God is using Antiochus to punish the people, Antiochus should not be arrogant. Israel's sins have brought this punishment. The Lord promised Solomon that if the people did not keep the commandments, Israel would become a taunt among the nations, and they would conclude that Judea was ruined because the people had forsaken the Lord (1 Kgs 9:6-9). Deutero-Isaiah promised that Zion would no longer be called "Forsaken" (Isa 62:4, 12; cf. Isa 49:14-15; 54:5-6; 60:14-15). Anyone who fights against God is sure to lose.

7:20-23. This story of the mother, as noted above, was retold in rabbinic literature. In Midrash Lamentations 1:16, the mother of seven tells her youngest son to tell Abraham not to be proud because he had offered only one son as a test while she offered her seven sons indeed. Here her attachment to ancestral traditions is stressed through her use of the ancestral language, Hebrew. In a patriarchal culture, her nobility is shown through her possessing "a man's courage" (v. 21). The origin of human life is unknown (Ps 139:13-16; Eccl 11:5), but the author plays on the language of Gen 2:7 to explain how God will recreate her sons: God, the creator of the world, forms humans by breathing into their nostrils the breath of life.

7:24-29. Often in traditional literature, when dealing with a powerful opponent the hero or heroine resorts to trickery to outsmart the official. Antiochus does not know what the mother says in Hebrew, but he catches the tone (v. 24). He resorts to bribing the

---

70. E.g., the death of Calanus, the Indian gymnosophist. See Aelian *Varia Historia* 5.6; Arrian *Anabasis* 7.2.
71. Josephus *Against Apion* 1.190-193.
72. Eusebius *Preparation for the Gospel* 9.25.4.

youngest son to change his mind, even offering to make him a Friend, the official title of the king's advisers (1 Maccabees records that such an offer was made to Mattathias [1 Macc 2:18]). The young man's refusal is symbolized by his not even listening to the king (v. 25). The king tries to make the mother act as his advocate, but she cleverly agrees to persuade her son, but does not specify what she will persuade him to do (v. 26). Her "manly" courage (vv. 20-21) is shown as she asks her son to show her pity, not by sparing himself, but by suffering cruel torments and death. The mother refers, as before (vv. 22-23), to God's creating power (v. 28). She states that God did not create from what previously existed—i.e., as properly formed—but that God shaped the unformed world (see Gen 1:2, especially in the LXX). Christian writers and the Latin translator of 2 Maccabees took this to mean that God had created everything out of nothing (*ex nihilo*).[73] The mother further insults the king by calling him a public executioner (v. 29), a job usually performed by slaves.

7:30-38. The last and most impressive speech is given to the youngest son; in traditional literature, the youngest son is always the most important. His speech rehearses the themes met before: The Hebrews suffer because of their sins, as God disciplines them (vv. 32-33; see 5:17-20; 6:12-17); the king should not be elated or arrogant (v. 34; see 4:17, 21; 7:15); God will surely punish Antiochus (vv. 31, 35; see 7:14-19). The sons' discipline at the hands of Antiochus is short, but Antiochus's punishment will be long (v. 36; see 6:12-17). Note how the Jews are called "the heavenly children" (v. 34; "heaven" was used as an epithet for God at v. 11), and so Antiochus is again accused of fighting against God (v. 19). The text of v. 36 is difficult to translate; it may be read either as "endured a brief suffering in exchange for everlasting life and have fallen under God's covenant" or "endured a brief suffering and have fallen to everlasting life under God's covenant." The meaning reflects their earlier statements that God will renew their life because they have followed God's laws (7:9, 23). The youngest son ends his speech by foretelling what the following narrative will show (vv. 37-38): God's just anger does turn to mercy (8:5, 27; cf. 2:22). Antiochus will learn through sickness to confess the power of God (9:5-18).

7:39-41. The king again rages as he had done at the beginning of the chapter. The last son is said to die "pure" (καθαρός *katharos*), perhaps suggesting not only the separation from the unclean Gentiles, but also the purification of the Temple, which will occur soon (10:3-7). Here the mother is said to die, but we are not told how—a classic example of patriarchal neglect. Throughout the story, the reader may wonder where the woman's husband is, but the author omits all reference to him to focus the reader's attention on the maternal role of the woman.

7:42. This verse sums up the martyrdoms of both Eleazar and the seven sons by the use of the phrase "eating of sacrifices" (σπλαγχνισμός *splanchnismos*), a term found only in the account of Eleazar's martyrdom (6:7-8, 21), and "tortures" (αἰκίαι *aikiai*), a word whose root is found in the account of the mother and her seven sons (7:1, 13, 15).

73. See, e.g., Origen *On First Principles* 2.1.5.

REFLECTIONS

Martyr stories are filled with highly charged emotional rhetoric in which the opposition between the martyrs and their opponents is driven home again and again. The author presents the reader with a public, well-born official and a private family forced into the spotlight. All sectors of society are represented and thus symbolize the attempted destruction of the city and its culture. Eleazar presents the picture of a person choosing death because it is the right and honorable thing to do; the family chooses death because God will reward them with life. But God will also have compassion on the nation because of its suffering. The motif of suffering's bringing salvation has a long history. In Judges 11, Jephthah vows that, if the Lord would give the enemy into his hands, he would offer up as a burnt offering to the Lord whoever came out of the doors of his house to meet him (Judg 11:30-31). Jephthah is victorious, but it is his daughter who first greets him and whom Jephthah has to sacrifice. Victory came at the price of her suffering. In the Suffering Servant song of Isa 52:13–53:12, the suffering servant "was wounded for our transgressions,/ crushed for our iniquities;/ upon him was the punishment that made us whole,/ and by his bruises we are healed" (Isa 53:5 NRSV). In the Council of the Community at Qumran there were to be twelve men and three priests who would atone for sin by practicing justice and by suffering the sorrows of affliction.[74] Similarly, when the Moabites were being defeated by the Israelites, the king of Moab "took his firstborn son who was to succeed him, and offered him as a burnt offering on the wall. And great wrath came upon Israel, so they withdrew from him and returned to their own land" (2 Kgs 3:27 NRSV). The same motif is found in Greek literature also, for example, in the story of Iphigenia in Aeschylus's tragedy *Agamemnon*. In this drama, Agamemnon angers the goddess Artemis, who delays the sailing of the Greek fleet against Troy until his daughter Iphigenia is sacrificed. Such stories, of course, have disturbing overtones, for they carry the notion of the efficacy of human sacrifice in appeasing an angry God. Is that an image of God we can be comfortable with today?

Yet these stories of heroic endurance and constancy of faith were extremely influential in Christian tradition. The author of the pseudepigraphical book of 4 Maccabees, writing possibly in the first century CE, uses the martyrdoms as prime examples of how devout reason can master the passions. A tradition grew that the martyrdoms occurred in the city of Antioch, and already in pre-Constantinian times there was a grave associated with the martyrs near the synagogue in a suburb of Antioch. Sometime before 386 CE this synagogue had been taken over by Christians, for John Chrysostom preached four homilies on the Maccabean martyrs and implied Christian possession of their relics. Ambrose and Augustine both record the influence of the stories of the Maccabean martyrs. Bishop Gregory of Nazianzos (c. 329–390), in his 26th Oration "On the Maccabees," defends their veneration against some members of his congregation who opposed it because the Maccabees were not Christians. Gregory argued that those who gained perfection before the coming of Christ did so through faith in Christ. Within Syrian Christianity, the mother was called "Shmuni," first attested in the Christian writer Aphrahat in his Fifth Demonstration, while a fresco (c. 650 CE) in the church of Santa Maria Antiqua in Rome gives her name as "Salomone." Their festival was celebrated usually on August 1.

The stories also stress the clash of traditions. All of us hope that if we were placed in a situation as unambiguous as these martyrs were, we would choose death rather than capitulation. We, too, are confronted not only with the question of what we would be willing to die for but also with what we consider so central to our own religious tradition and culture that to do away with it would be to lose our self-identity. Living in a multi-cultural society, we have to decide when to draw the line. Most likely, the decision will be in a situation not quite so unambiguous as eating pork sacrificed to idols. What is also interesting about these stories is that both Eleazar and the family do not come forward on their own accord but that the confrontation is forced upon them. In early Christianity, church leaders often had to warn against Christians' volunteering for martyrdom and asking Roman governors to kill them.[75] Can we maintain our traditions and values without forcing a confrontation?

---

74. 1QS 8:1-3.
75. See, e.g., *Martyrdom of Polycarp*; Tertullian *To Scapula* 5.1.

2 MACCABEES 8:1–10:8, GOD'S DEFENSE OF THE PEOPLE

OVERVIEW

After describing the disasters that came upon the people after they abandoned their ancestral laws (chaps. 4–7), the author now describes how, following the covenantal obedience of the martyrs, God helps the people (chap. 8), afflicts the archenemy Antiochus IV (chap. 9), and regains and purifies the Temple (10:1-8).

2 Maccabees 8:1-36, The First Victory

COMMENTARY

To present dramatically how God's anger has changed to mercy, the author singles out one battle and one opponent. The dramatization can easily be seen by comparing this account with that in 1 Maccabees. After describing the onset of Judas's guerrilla tactics, 1 Maccabees describes two battles, one against Apollonius (1 Macc 3:10-12) and one against Seron (1 Macc 3:13-26), before the account most like that of 2 Maccabees 8 (cf. 1 Macc 3:38–4:25). In particular, 1 Maccabees emphasizes the tactical maneuvers: a surprise attack by Gorgias, Judas's escape and his surprise attack on Gorgias's camp, and the subsequent flight of Gorgias (1 Macc 4:1-25). In 2 Maccabees, there are no such maneuvers, but one pitched battle decides all. The battles with Apollonius and Seron receive only the vaguest mention; Judas "captured strategic positions and put to flight not a few of the enemy" (8:6). In addition, although 1 Maccabees reports that Lysias sent Ptolemy, Nicanor, and Gorgias (1 Macc 3:38), with the main villain being Gorgias, in 2 Maccabees Ptolemy sends Nicanor and Gorgias, and Nicanor is the main villain. The author may have highlighted this name to balance and reflect the Nicanor in chaps. 14–15, as both are called thrice-wretched (8:34; 15:3). The account then is highly stylized.

8:1-7, The Rise of Judas. Last mentioned as being in the desert (5:27), Judas and his companions now begin to gather their kindred, most likely referring not to near relatives but to Israelites of the same persuasion. Once again the author uses the term "Judaism" (2:21; 14:38) as opposed to "Jewish faith." The number 6,000, the total of people gathered (v. 1), is later repeated (8:16), although some of Judas's force is said to have left (see 1 Macc 4:6, where Judas marches against Gorgias with 3,000 men). The group appeals to the Lord as the last of the martyred sons had done (7:37). The prayer employs traditional language. The blood crying out from the ground (v. 3) recalls the blood of the innocent Abel (Gen 4:10; cf. Deut 32:43; Heb 12:24). The reference to the imminent leveling of the city looks forward to Antiochus's vow (9:13). Once God is with Judas, he is unstoppable (v. 5), although his activity probably consisted of surprise raids and ambushes by night, nuisance raids as the "little by little" of v. 8 suggests.

8:8-11, The Response of the Seleucids. Philip the Phrygian, the governor of Jerusalem (5:22; 6:11), alerts Ptolemy, the son of Dorymenes (4:45), to Judas's success. Ptolemy appoints Nicanor and Gorgias to deal with these guerrillas. First Maccabees reports that Antiochus was informed of the matter (1 Macc 3:27), but the account in 2 Maccabees, which restricts handling of the insurrection to lower echelon officials and subordinates Nicanor and Gorgias to Ptolemy, seems more likely. Someone named Nicanor is mentioned in the letter of the Sidonians in Shechem to Antiochus IV as a royal agent.[76] Later, another

---
76. Josephus *Antiquities of the Jews* 12.257-264.

Nicanor was in Rome with Demetrius, son of Seleucus IV, and was one of the closest of his friends when he became Demetrius I in 161 BCE,[77] and there was also a Nicanor the Cyprian (2 Macc 12:2). "Nicanor" was thus a common name, and it is unlikely that all these references are to the same person. Gorgias was later governor of Idumea (2 Macc 10:14; 12:32), and it seems prudent that Nicanor would be joined by someone with local experience.

The author notes the ethnic mix of the army (v. 9). His estimate of the size (20,000) is half that of 1 Macc 3:38, but still high. The aim, payment of the tribute to Rome (v. 10), is the same as stated in 1 Macc 3:35, 52, 58. By 165 BCE, the time of Antiochus's march on Persia, the Seleucid indemnity to Rome had already been paid, but Antiochus was well-known as desiring money to pay for his extravagant generosity. In order to raise money, Nicanor intends to sell the captured Jews into slavery. Ninety slaves per talent (v. 11) was a low price, perhaps expressing contempt for the Jews. At that rate, Nicanor would need to sell 180,000 slaves to pay the tribute, many more than those already taken from Jerusalem (5:41). In 1 Macc 3:41, the traders come of their own free will, whereas here Nicanor is the instigator of the plan for slavery. Nicanor is thus seen in 2 Maccabees as the source of all evil designs against the Jews. Such a portrayal prepares the way for the dénouement of the story, as Nicanor has to flee like a runaway slave (8:35). This reversal of affairs fits in with the author's desire to make the punishment fit the crime.

8:12-20, Judas's Preparation. The author, in order to magnify Judas's courage, emphasizes the fear of the Jews, outnumbered more than three to one. One wonders why those around Judas sold all they had (v. 14)—in order to run away? They pray for God to remember the covenants with the ancestors (v. 15; note the list in Sir 44:16–45:25), as God has promised (Lev 26:42; cf. Wis 18:22), for they are a people called by God's name (1 Sam 12:22; Dan 9:19; cf. Deut 28:10). Judas, by contrast, is not afraid (v. 16). The Gentiles act with hubris, reflecting the arrogance of Antiochus (5:17-21). The phrase "torture of the derided city" (v. 17) reflects the language used about the martyrs (7:1, 7, 10, 13, 15, 42), while the overthrow of the ancestral way of life recalls what was said about Jason (4:11). The overwhelming power of God is captured in the image of "one nod" (v. 18). As any good speechmaker, Judas proffers examples of God's help. The first is the defeat of Sennacherib in 701 BCE (2 Kgs 19:35-36; Isa 37:36; see also 1 Macc 7:41; 2 Macc 15:22). The second example (vv. 19-20) is taken from more recent history, but the precise reference is unknown. The "Galatians" were the Celts, who, due to unrest in western and central Europe, were forced to migrate to the east and southeast. In 280/79, some Celts marched through Macedonia and Thrace and invaded Greece, while others, complete tribal groups, went to Asia Minor in 278/77 and overran many Greek cities. After a long struggle, they were confined to an area north of Phrygia, later called Galatia. Scholars have suggested that the incident in 2 Maccabees may refer to the battle of Antiochus I against the Celts in the 270s (although this took place in Asia Minor, which would cause the text of 2 Maccabees to be emended from *Babulonia* to *Bagadaonia*), near the Taurus mountains in Cilicia; to an incident in the suppression of the rebellion of Molon, governor-general of the eastern satrapies, by Antiochus III in 220 BCE; or to the rebellion in 227–26 of Antiochus Hierax, who used Galatian mercenaries, in the east against his brother Seleucus III. The latter seems the most likely scenario. The Galatian invasion made a lasting impression on the cities of Asia Minor. What this passage shows is that Jewish soldiers served under the Seleucids, and it supports the report of Josephus that Antiochus III transferred Jewish soldiers from Babylonia to Phrygia and Lydia.[78]

8:21-29, The Defeat of Nicanor. Judas is the counterpart to Menelaus, who was a traitor to laws and country. The division of troops described here (v. 22) is different from that of 1 Macc 3:55. The text (vv. 22-23) is very difficult to translate. Major manuscripts read as if Judas appointed his four brothers, Simon, Joseph, Jonathan, and Eleazar, to lead the four 1,500-man units and that Judas read to them from the Scriptures. In this case, it is unclear whether the first division

---

77. Polybius 31.14.4; Josephus *Antiquities of the Jews* 12.402.

78. Josephus *Antiquities of the Jews* 12:147-153.

(σπεῖρα [*speira*]) refers to a phalanx of 256 men) was part of one of these four 1,500-man units. Other manuscripts suggest, and are followed by the NRSV, that Eleazar read aloud from the Scriptures (the Latin manuscripts read Ezra instead of Eleazar). The names of Judas's brothers in 1 Macc 2:3-5 are John, Simon, Eleazar, and Jonathan. But this account lists Joseph instead of John; some scholars have suggested that this is a reference to the envious couple Joseph and Azariah of 1 Macc 5:18, 55-62, but there Joseph is called "son of Zechariah." Eleazar seems to play the role of priest (Deut 20:2); it is interesting that "Eleazar," in Hebrew, means "help of God" (אלעזר *ʾelʿāzār*). On the reading of the Scriptures, see the parallel statement at 1 Macc 3:48. The *War Scroll* from Qumran indicates that "God's help" was one of the insignia on the standards of God's army,[79] and such watchwords were common in the Hellenistic world.[80] Whatever the intended meaning for vv. 22-23, the author insists that Judas calls on God for aid and that Judas's whole family is involved in the enterprise. To this end, he divides the forces based on the number of brothers in a way that has no parallel in Jewish or Hellenistic tactical tradition. The concern of the author is clearly not about tactical maneuvers, for the description of the battle takes up only one verse (v. 24). What is important is that God is their ally. That connection with God is reinforced by the description of the Jews' observance of the sabbath (vv. 26-27). The last two verses (vv. 28-29) refer to the story of the martyrs; the spoils are to be distributed not only to widows and orphans but also to the tortured (2 Macc 7:1, 42). Here not only the fighters benefit from their victory but so also do those whose prayer for them has great efficacy—i.e., widows and orphans (Deut 14:29; 26:12-15) and those who have been persecuted (2 Macc 7:37-38; 8:3). The language of v. 29 reflects that of the prayer of the seventh son in the martyrdom stories (7:33).

8:30-33, The Defeat of Timothy and Bacchides. The nature of 2 Maccabees as an epitome is evident in this section. People and events are mentioned without any preparation, and these accounts of other campaigns disrupt the focus on Nicanor, whose story is picked up in v. 34.

In 1 Maccabees, Bacchides is a much more important figure than the quick mention at 2 Macc 8:30 would suggest. He was the governor of the province Beyond the River, i.e., between the Euphrates and Egypt. He is sent by Demetrius I to subdue Judea, which he does (1 Macc 7:8-20). After the later defeat of Nicanor, he returns again and defeats Judas, who dies in the battle. Then Bacchides pursues Judas's brother Jonathan but finally comes to terms with him (1 Macc 9:1-70). His activity is completely absent from the corresponding narrative in 2 Maccabees. It is unlikely that such a high-ranking personage would be listed after the middle-level commander Timothy, and so one wonders whether another Bacchides is meant here.

The death of Timothy is recorded at 2 Macc 9:3 and 10:24-38, but 2 Macc 12:10-25 records Timothy's escape; so there seem to be two Timothys involved in 2 Maccabees. However, in 1 Maccabees there is only one Timothy who fights with Judas's forces on three occasions: (1) when Judas defeats Timothy, captures Iazer, and returns to Judea (1 Macc 5:6-8); (2) when Timothy's men are surprised by Judas (1 Macc 5:28-34); and (3) when Timothy, having regrouped his forces, challenges Judas again and is defeated near Carnaim (1 Macc 5:37-44). All three meetings in 1 Maccabees occur after the purification of the Temple. One will note the specific parallels between the accounts of 1 and 2 Maccabees, if the accounts in 2 Maccabees are accepted as being out of order. If one accepts as more historically reliable the outline of events in 1 Maccabees, then the author of 2 Maccabees has misplaced events. Most scholars agree that 2 Macc 12:1-25 parallels the battles in Gilead recounted in 1 Macc 5:28-44. There are also parallels between 2 Macc 10:24-38 and the account in 1 Macc 5:6-8, although 2 Maccabees records that Timothy dies in that battle, whereas 1 Maccabees does not. The events in 2 Macc 8:30-33 also seem out of order: Judas seems to be in control of Jerusalem (v. 31) even though the Jews do not recapture the city until 10:1-8; mention of strongholds (v. 30) reflects the account of 2 Macc 12:10-25. It would thus

---

79. 1QM 4.15.
80. See, e.g., Vegetius 3.5; Xenophon *Anabasis* 1.8.16; *Cyropaedia* 3.3.58.

seem as if vv. 30-32 summarize the Gilead campaign told later in 2 Maccabees 12.

This summary, however, has been well woven into the context. The author refers to the same groups—the tortured, the widows, and the orphans—in vv. 28 and 30. The same word is used for collecting the arms of the enemy at vv. 27 and 31. Just as the author uses the theme of appropriate retribution for Nicanor when he is forced to flee as a slave, so also in this section the burners are burned. The author of 2 Maccabees narrates these events possibly to suggest that there were other campaigns before the purification of the Temple or to note how Judas's men behave after victories and also to heighten the dramatic tension as one wonders what happened to Nicanor. The spoil taken to Jerusalem (v. 31) is probably God's portion (Num 31:28). The word for "commander" (φύλαρχος *phylarchos*, v. 32) is sometimes taken as a proper name, Phylarchos. The Greek word does not refer to the city, Jerusalem, but to the "fatherland" (πατρίς *patris*; see 4:1; 5:8, 9, 15; 8:21; 13:3, 11, 14; 14:18). Nothing else is known about Callisthenes (v. 33).

8:34-36, The Fate of Nicanor. The epithet "thrice accursed" will be used again of the Nicanor in the last battle in 2 Maccabees (15:13). His plan (v. 11) backfires, and he receives the appropriate punishment (v. 35). The author sarcastically contrasts his "success" (v. 35) with that of Judas's (8:8). The help of the Lord (v. 35) resonates with the watchword given to the army (8:23), and the word for "defender" (ὑπέρμαχος *hypermachos*, v. 36) is related to the word for "ally" (σύμμαχος *symmachos*, v. 24). The author returns to the theme enunciated at 3:1: The Jews are invincible once they follow God's law. Nicanor, as Heliodorus had done before him (3:35-39), proclaims the power of God.

REFLECTIONS

Throughout this chapter, the author emphasizes the power of prayer and the need to keep God's covenant; these are the sure ways to victory. His emphasis on fidelity to one's religious convictions and traditions needs to be repeated. But one must also be careful, for in this war context, the stress on standing by one's own traditions, on knowing who one is, at times results in denigrating the opponent. Throughout this chapter, the author seeks to dramatize his story by contrasting the two foes, Judas and Nicanor, almost as light and darkness, but this rhetorical presentation at times obscures what actually happened. So we must not let our rhetoric lead us to paint those who disagree with us as "the enemy," "godless" people.

2 Maccabees 9:1-29, The Death of Antiochus IV

COMMENTARY

Following the defeat of Nicanor and Timothy, the gruesome death of Antiochus IV is described. This arrangement ignores the more complex order of events as they can be pieced together. In 1 Maccabees, after the defeat of the expedition of Nicanor and Gorgias, Judea is invaded by Lysias, the regent left behind in charge of affairs by Antiochus IV while he went on campaign in the eastern part of his empire (1 Macc 5:26-35). There also seems to have been an attempt to negotiate a peaceable settlement of the rebellion as seen in the letter of Antiochus IV (2 Macc 11:27-33), which 2 Maccabees has put out of order, and possibly in the replacement of Ptolemy son of Dorymenes, an enemy of the Jews, by Ptolemy Macron, who was more friendly to the Jews (2 Macc 10:12-13). The author of 2 Maccabees has arranged events for the best dramatic effect. He wants to show no change of heart in the archenemy Antiochus IV until he is humiliated by God's power. His humiliation brings about his regret at his actions against the Jews and the Temple. He then dies, and only after his death is the Temple purified. Dramatically speaking, the death of the one who brought on the initial misfortune has to occur before things can be put right again and the Temple purified. According to 1 Maccabees, Antiochus IV dies after the purification of the Temple (1 Macc 6:5-7). According to a Babylonian chronicle, news of Antiochus IV's death reached Babylonia in the month Kislev in the year 148 according to the Babylonian calendar (between November 20 and December 18 165 BCE). It thus seems that the sequence in 2 Maccabees, where the king dies before the purification of the Temple, is correct, although some scholars still dispute this, suggesting that chapter 9 has been inserted into the narrative and that 10:1-8 should be placed before chapter 9. The connections between 2 Macc 9:3 and the events in chapter 8, as well as the similar threat mentioned at 8:3 and 9:14, suggests that the two chapters work together dramatically. A major threat to the Temple is averted, and then the purification of the Temple can be accomplished.

9:1-4, Antiochus IV Receives News of the Defeat of Nicanor. The geographical and historical data provided in these verses are confusing and conflict with other sources. Persepolis was the old capital of the Persian Empire, while Ecbatana lies in Media, hundreds of miles away to the northwest. According to other sources, Antiochus attempted to rob the temple of Nanaia in Eylmais, to the south of Ecbatana (see 1 Macc 6:1; 2 Macc 1:13-15).[81] Here, however, Antiochus attempts to gain control of Persepolis and to plunder its temples. In addition, this chapter contains only one of several ancient versions of the death of Antiochus IV (see, e.g., 1 Macc 6:1-16; 2 Macc 1:13-14).

Antiochus IV had set out in mid to late 165 BCE to consolidate his rule in the eastern satrapies. A local dynasty of priests and princes had risen to power around Persepolis and Istakhr and had won their independence in the early years of Antiochus IV. Antiochus's reputation for plundering temples is at play here, and he no doubt would have welcomed the money to finance his campaign to regain control of the eastern satrapies. In this temple attack, in contrast to the attack on the Temple at Jerusalem, no divine epiphany is described. Verse 3 links this story to chapter 8, including the out-of-place reference to Timothy. The last time the king appeared in the narrative, he was in a rage (7:39). Here his rage continues, and he is portrayed as a bully wanting to show how tough he is to those weaker than he. The seventh son had prayed that the arrogance of Antiochus would be justly punished (7:36; cf. 5:21), and it begins to happen. The irony of Antiochus's threat to turn Jerusalem into a cemetery (v. 4) is revealed in v. 14.

9:5-12, The Punishment of Antiochus. As so often in 2 Maccabees, the punishment fits the crime (vv. 5-6). Yet Antiochus remains arrogant in spite of his illness, and his mad rage is the cause of his downfall (v. 7). The description of his arrogant self-importance (v. 8; see also 5:21) reflects feats that only God can accomplish (Isa 40:12). The cruel punishment he suffers of death by putrefaction is found in Greek writings as well;[82] the mention of worms recalls Isa 66:24 and Jdt 16:17. The author relishes relating the gruesome torments and accords well with other stories of the deaths of scoffers against the gods. Verse 10 captures marvelously the foolishness of humans thinking they are gods and not mortals (cf. the hymns against proud kings in Isa 14:4-21, particularly the boast of the king of Babylon in vv. 13-14; Ezek 28:12-19). Antiochus, under the flogging of God, comes to knowledge (v. 11). His confession is almost proverbial. One must not fight against God (2 Macc 7:19).

9:13-27, The Repentance of Antiochus. 9:13-17. Although Antiochus makes a vow to the Lord, his prayer will no longer be heard (v. 13). Although Jason (4:18) and Nicanor (15:32) were also said to be "abominable," Antiochus is the worst of all (7:34). The word translated "abominable" (μιαρός *miaros*) also has the connotation of "polluted," "defiled with blood," and thus raises the issue of blood guilt as the reason why God refuses to have mercy on Antiochus (see Isa 1:15). The phrases "level to the ground" (as in 8:3) and "make a cemetery" (as at 9:4) recall Antiochus's earlier misdeeds against Jerusalem and heighten the irony of his current condition (v. 14). Antiochus's earlier threat not to allow the burial of corpses

---

81. See also Polybius 31.9.
82. See Herodotus 3.66; Diodorus Siculus 21.16.4-5.

(v. 15) was a great anti-social, dehumanizing action as well (cf. David's boast to Goliath that David will give "the dead bodies of the Philistine army this very day to the birds of the air and to the wild animals of the earth" [1 Sam 17:46 NRSV]; see also Isa 56:9-11; Jer 7:33; 12:9; 15:3; 16:4; 19:7; 34:20; Ezek 29:5; 39:4, 17). It is not sure exactly what declaring Jerusalem "free" means in this context. It seems to imply more than freedom from taxes (1 Macc 10:31). Freedom in the sense of autonomy was always a slogan of great appeal in any propaganda war (as, for example, the counterclaims of Antigonus Gonatas and Ptolemy I to set all Greek cities free and the declaration by the Roman Senate in 196 BCE that all Greeks were to be free). But the relationship between the monarch and each "free" city, which had its own traditions and system of government, was a special one. It is not clear exactly what is meant by making the Jews equal to the Athenians. Athens was considered the guardian of classical culture, and during the second century the Parthenon was restored and the Agora reconstructed. In 174 BCE, Antiochus IV had promised to finish the unfinished temple of Olympia Zeus. Similarly, Antiochus vows to restore the Temple in Jerusalem to even more grandeur than at the time of Onias III (v. 16; see 2 Macc 3:1). Antiochus's promise to proclaim the power of God worldwide (v. 17) exceeds what Heliodorus had done (3:34, 36). Antiochus even promises to become a Jew. What exactly this means is unclear, although it probably did not mean becoming a Judean (a citizen of Judea). The word "Jew" here is not a geographical designation, but a religious one. What would be required in the second century BCE to become a Jew? Would it mean more than did the worship of Naaman (2 Kgs 5:15-18) or the confession of Nebuchadnezzar (Dan 4:34-37)? Does the author of 2 Maccabees envisage that Antiochus would be circumcised and follow all the laws of the Torah? We do not know. Josephus, the first-century CE Jewish historian, recounts a story in which Izates, the king of Adiabene, wishes to convert to Judaism and thus to be circumcised. However, his mother, who had earlier converted to Judaism, and the Jew who had converted her, Ananias, dissuade him. Later, Eleazar, another Jew, comes to Adiabene and insists that he be circumcised. Izates follows Eleazar's advice.[83]

9:18-27. The author reemphasizes that Antiochus will not escape God's judgment (v. 18), and thus the king, although in such pain, pens a letter. Since the writing of a deathbed testament was a well-known literary device in Hellenistic literature, the authenticity of the letter that follows has been greatly debated. Those who affirm its authenticity agree that the original letter has been added to; those who deny its authenticity agree that it is modeled on a genuine letter, possibly to the army, whose support would have been crucial in any change of leadership. Whatever its origins, the letter has been adapted so as to further the rhetorical aims of the author. This is most easily seen in the way the addressees of the letter, the Jewish citizens, are mentioned before the king and are addressed as "esteemed" or "worthy" (v. 19). It is not specified to whom the term "citizens" refers, whether to the people of Antioch-in-Jerusalem or to those Jews who were citizens of various cities throughout the Seleucid Empire. Since the Jews as a whole were never given citizen rights in any community in which they lived (see, e.g., 2 Macc 12:3, where the citizens of Joppa are distinguished from the Jews living among them), the letter is most likely addressed to the former. The phrasing, however, if imprecise, suits the aim of the author: to show that the Jews can be good citizens, that they are not anti-social. The greeting formula is quite extravagant with its threefold wish of hearty greetings, health, and prosperity (more so than the greeting in 1:10b). The addition of the term "general" (στρατηγός *stratēgos*) supports the suggestion that the letter may have been, or was modeled on, a letter to the army. At vv. 20-21 come the usual well wishes for the recipient's health, although the text itself is variously transmitted in the manuscripts. Note how the king remembers with affection the esteem and goodwill of the Jews (v. 21)! Given that this letter comes after the events narrated in 9:1-12, to describe the king's condition as an annoying illness is a marvelous understatement and shows that this letter, authentic or not, does not really belong with the situation of 9:1-8. Rather, vv. 23-25 make clear that the

---

83. Josephus *Antiquities of the Jews* 20.34-48.

letter originally concerned the orderly transfer of power. Antiochus IV's father, Antiochus III the Great, had appointed his son Seleucus IV as his successor. Following Antiochus III's death, while attempting to raise money in the east after his defeat by Rome, Seleucus took the throne. Following this precedent, Antiochus IV names his own son, Antiochus V Eupator (who was still a young boy and needed a regent; see 1 Macc 3:33; 6:14-15), as heir to the throne. What is astonishing is that in this context, Antiochus places his trust in the Jews for the success of this transfer of power and the stability of the realm (v. 25). The Jews are asked to continue their goodwill toward Antiochus and his son (9:26). Verse 27 is also incongruous in the context, as Antiochus IV was in no way moderate and kind to the Jews. Needless to say, the advice will not be followed. The thrust of this letter in this context is to argue that the Jews are not anti-social, as so many stories circulating in the Hellenistic world suggested.

9:28-29, The Death of Antiochus. Antiochus dies in a strange land (see 5:9-10, the death of Jason). Philip, who has the title σύντροφος (*syntrophos*), meaning "brought up with"—but in the Seleucid hierarchy has the meaning "intimate friend"—takes Antiochus's body home. In contrast to 1 Maccabees, in the account in 2 Maccabees, Philip flees to Egypt because he fears Antiochus V, not Lysias. According to 1 Maccabees, the dying Antiochus IV replaces Lysias by Philip as guardian of Antiochus V (3:32-33; 6:14-15). When Philip returns from the east, he takes control of Antioch, but Lysias forces him out (6:55-56, 63). Philip's unsuccessful attempt is mentioned at 2 Macc 13:23, although, since the author of 2 Maccabees has the Philip who was with the dying Antiochus IV flee to Egypt, he seems to distinguish him from the Philip of the coup attempt in 13:23. Ptolemy VI Philometor, to whom Philip is said to flee, had been driven out of Alexandria to Rome in October 164, just before Antiochus IV's death, and did not return until the middle of 163. The conflict between Philip and Lysias, therefore, must have taken place in the first half of 163. According to Josephus, Lysias had Philip murdered before he could reach Egypt.[84]

84. Josephus *Antiquities of the Jews* 12.386.

REFLECTIONS

The account of the punishment of Antiochus IV draws on a well-attested theme in the Bible: the sharp distinction between humans and God. The serpent had tempted Eve in the Garden of Eden to eat of the fruit of the forbidden tree (Gen 3:5). So the prohibition was broken, and the humans were expelled from the garden for trying to be like God. In the story of the tower of Babel, humans had thought to breach the distance separating them from the heavens and for their pains had been scattered over the face of the earth, speaking different languages (Gen 11:1-9). The hymns of Isaiah against the hubris of the kings of Babylon and how it would result in their humiliation (Isa 14:4-7) and the sayings of Ezekiel over the king of Tyre (Ezek 28:2) are eloquent testimony to the need to maintain this high, exalted notion of God. The story in Daniel 4 tells how King Nebuchadnezzar fell from his place of honor and dignity and was driven away from human society to become like an animal, eating grass like oxen and having hair as long as eagle feathers and fingernails like bird claws. Humans are shown to be stupid if they try to "play God."

These stories raise important issues for our own time. We have had enormous advances in medicine, science, and technology. Yet we have not yet grasped the ethical implications of these advances, especially in the area of human biology. For instance, how are we to use responsibly the technology for gene manipulation in medicine? Clearly it will be a great advantage if doctors are someday able to eradicate genetic disorders, like muscular dystrophy. But what limits should be put on the use of these techniques? Will parents want to manipulate what kind of child they will have, what sex, hair or eye color, body size? Religious communities will need to pay careful attention to such issues. With all of our advances, we still need to recognize our limitations and weaknesses. We must not try to play God.

2 Maccabees 10:1-8, The Purification of the Temple

COMMENTARY

After the elimination of the prime antagonist against the Temple, Antiochus IV, the author now describes the people's joy at righting the wrong Antiochus had done. As mentioned in the Commentary on chap. 9, some scholars suggest that this section has been misplaced from going before chapter 9, but the joy belongs after the death of the enemy (as in the victory-enthronement pattern in Exodus 15). In contrast to the blasphemer Antiochus IV, whose body is "brought back" (παρεκομίζετο *parekomizeto*) to Antioch (9:29), Judas and his companions "bring back" for themselves—i.e., "recover" (ἐκομίσαντο *ekomisanto*, v. 1)—the Temple and the city. The parallel passage in 1 Macc 4:36-59 puts emphasis not only on the purification of the sanctuary, but also on its dedication (as in 1 Kgs 8:63; 2 Chr 7:5; Ezra 6:16-17). The author of 2 Maccabees also recognizes the action as a dedication (2:19), but as he has stressed that the Temple was overthrown because of the sins of the people (5:17-20; 6:12-17), he now stresses the purification of the Temple and the sin of the people. No mention is made of the priests who performed the sacrifices, whereas 1 Macc 4:42 stresses the choice of blameless priests.

The author makes no mention of the citadel (2 Macc 4:28), although it is mentioned later (15:31). In contrast, 1 Maccabees stresses the need to defend the Temple from the troops at the citadel (1 Macc 4:41, 60). The description of altars around the agora (v. 2) reflects Greek custom and supports the notion that Antiochus IV had simply instituted pagan worship practices in Jerusalem rather than one particular cult. The sacrifices (v. 3) most probably refer to the continual daily sacrifice (see Exod 29:38-42; Num 28:3-8). The incense offering (Exod 30:7-8), the lighting of lamps (Exod 27:20-21; Lev 24:2-3), and the setting out of the showbread (Exod 25:30; Lev 24:5-9) show the concern of the author to portray Judas as following the Torah (2 Chr 13:11; 1 Macc 4:50-51). In contrast to the two-year lapse in Jewish sacrifices in the Temple (2 Macc 10:3), 1 Maccabees has an interval of three years (1 Macc 1:54; 4:52), while Dan 12:7 has three and a half years. Most likely 1 Maccabees is correct. The language of v. 4 is similar to that of 6:12-17. Once again the nations are described as barbarous (2:21). The prayer recalls that of Solomon at the dedication of the Temple, where he also prays for mercy for the people's sin (1 Kgs 8:46-50).

To show the providential care of God, the author emphasizes that the renewed sacrifice took place on the anniversary of the day of the defilement (v. 5; see also 2 Macc 6:7; cf. 1 Macc 4:52). The author then refers to Judas's flight to the mountains (v. 6; 5:27). The connection with the Feast of Tabernacles (vv. 6-7) is found in the prefixed letters (1:9, 18), but is not made in 1 Maccabees. The carrying of branches, signifying fertility, is commanded at Lev 23:40. The word translated "ivy-wreathed wands" (θύρσοι *thyrsoi*, v. 7) was also used for what was carried in processions of Dionysus, and the author may be showing once again the reversal from the persecution when the Jews were forced in procession to Dionysus (2 Macc 6:7). The language at v. 8 is repeated almost word for word at 15:36, and so binds the two festivals together.

REFLECTIONS

The second act of this story finishes as the first had done, with the Jews celebrating the power of God in their Temple. Two major opponents of "proper" Jewish behavior have been defeated, the high priest Jason and the Seleucid king Antiochus IV. The reader can anticipate that any further attack on the Temple in Jerusalem will also be unsuccessful, and can also expect that there will be such an attack, since one opponent, the high priest Menelaus, still remains. This has been a much more serious attack on the Temple than that of Heliodorus in 2 Maccabees 3. The first attack had been on the Jewish educational system because Jason had built a gymnasium, thereby attempting to erase any distinction between the Jews and their neighbors. Menelaus had also despoiled the Temple for his own private gain. Finally, Antiochus IV had attempted to wipe out the very practice of Judaism within Judea. The author of 2 Maccabees shows how these attempts had been foiled by God after the martyrs had offered up their lives rather than transgress God's commandments.

The story stresses the need for covenantal loyalty on the part of the Jews. Because they aped Greek ways, disaster had befallen them. Because the martyrs showed their faithfulness to God, God had come to Israel's aid. The martyrs provide a striking example of how death can be fruitful, whereas Antiochus IV dies without accomplishing anything.

The story is one of great heroism, but it is one in which it is easy to tell who are the villains. As in western movies where the bad guys wear black hats and the good guys wear white hats, the author of this narrative shows clearly who he thinks the bad guys are. Where one group is trying to oppress another and suppress their right to worship, it is a pretty clear call. When religion was outlawed, or at least put under very tight rein, in the Soviet Union and in China, it was easy to see that the authorities were in the wrong. Opposition and oppression have a way of helping us to define what we stand for. They have a way of demarcating a believing community from those who wish to suppress or curtail its activities. The blood of martyrs is said to have watered the seeds of Christianity. We all hope that if we were put in such a position we would have the courage and conviction to stand up for our beliefs.

But how are we to keep a sense of community when we are not under attack? When Judea's national symbol, the Temple, was polluted, when the distinctive markers of Judaism—the Torah scrolls, circumcision, the Jewish festivals—were forbidden, it was clear that those who wished to maintain their religious practices had to take a stand. But once the threat has passed, how will a community maintain its sense of identity? The history of sectarian strife within Christianity suggests that the answer may not lie in the direction of trying to define who is and who is not a "proper" member of the community. We can see the beginning of this problem in the attitude of the author of 2 Maccabees. It would appear that, for him, a "true" Jew did not attend a gymnasium. When a community tries to make these kinds of distinctions, problems will always arise, for all of us are different with different backgrounds and different educational and life experiences. When a community is not under threat or attack, perhaps the best solution to maintaining it is to celebrate the various gifts that each member of the community brings to it, to revel in the "rainbow" quality of our community. The apostle Paul speaks to all of our communities when he says, "Love is patient; love is kind; love is not envious or boastful or arrogant or rude. It does not insist on its own way" (1 Cor 13:4-5 NRSV). The moral character of the high priests Jason and Menelaus, as portrayed in this narrative, is shown to be such that they sought only their own aggrandizement, sought ways that they could keep their positions of power and important status. They insisted on their own way to the detriment of the community. They are the anti-type of the high priest Onias, who sought only what was good for the community.

2 MACCABEES 10:9–15:36
THE THIRD ACT: FURTHER DEFENSE OF THE TEMPLE

OVERVIEW

This third section of the epitome deals with further attacks on the Temple under the successors of Antiochus IV. There is a marked contrast between the rather condensed account of many campaigns in 10:14–13:26 and the more expansive account of Nicanor's expedition in chaps. 14–15.

2 MACCABEES 10:9–13:26, THE ATTACKS UNDER ANTIOCHUS V

OVERVIEW

This section of 2 Maccabees seems to be structured around a pattern whereby first attacks by local leaders occur (10:14-38; 12:3-45), then come a major expedition and peace (2 Maccabees 11; 13).

2 Maccabees 10:9-13, Dynastic Changes

COMMENTARY

10:9-11. As at 3:40–4:1, the author provides a transitional sentence to the next episode, the reign of Antiochus V Eupator. Antiochus V was only nine years old and was, in fact, under the guardianship of Lysias (1 Macc 3:33).[85] Lysias had been placed in charge of the area from the Euphrates to the border of Egypt by Antiochus IV (1 Macc 3:32). In contrast to the NRSV translation, v. 11 should be translated "appointed one Lysias to have charge of the government, and Protarchos as governor of Coelesyria and Phoenicia," since the offices of chief minister of the empire and governor of Coelesyria did not overlap.

10:12-13. The situation described in these verses is similar to that at 13:24. Ptolemy Macron, as governor of Cyprus, had been loyal to Ptolemy VI Philometor of Egypt, but the botched maneuverings of the Ptolemaic court and the subsequent loss of the Ptolemies to Antiochus IV in the war of 170/169 had led him to go over to the Seleucid side (c. 168 BCE) when Antiochus IV's fleet invaded Cyprus. The description of Ptolemy Macron as being friendly towards the Jews should not be seen as simply a peaceful disposition. As previous governors of Coelesyria and Phoenicia had been hostile to the pious Jews (Apollonius son of Menestheus, 4:4; Ptolemy son of Dorymenes, 4:45; 8:8) and their stance seems to reflect court policy, this change in attitude should be seen as reflecting the policy of the governor's superiors. Since such

---
85. See Appian *Syriaca* 46.66.

a change in attitude would probably have occurred after the peace negotiations following the first expedition of Lysias (2 Macc 11:14, 16-21), which actually took place during the reign of Antiochus IV (1 Macc 4:28-29; 2 Macc 11:27-33), these events have been misplaced by the author of 2 Maccabees in order to portray Antiochus IV as the evil opponent of the Jews, and not as someone who entered into peace negotiations with them. The court gossip mentioned at 2 Macc 10:13 no doubt reflects the intrigues at court following the restoration of the Temple and preceding Lysias's second expedition (1 Macc 6:21-28). The last part of v. 13 is very corrupt; the conjecture of the NRSV translation is as good as any.

2 Maccabees 10:14-23, Campaigns in Idumea

COMMENTARY

10:14-17. Gorgias was governor of Idumea (2 Macc 12:32) and seems also to have been in control of Jamnia (1 Macc 5:59). He is characterized as being experienced in military affairs and had already taken part in an attack on the Jews (2 Macc 8:9). The author makes sure to mention that it was not the Jews who initiated the attacks, but the Seleucid forces (1 Macc 5:3-5 also has the Idumeans as hostile to Judas and his forces). The Jews who have been banned from Jerusalem (v. 15) are presumably followers of Menelaus, although the author does not explicitly say so and does not mention the garrison in the citadel or use the term "ungodly Israelites" (1 Macc 6:18-27). In fact, the whole account is very sparse on geographical details, not specifying which Idumean strongholds were attacked and captured (vv. 16-17). The author's main concern is not in those details but in stressing that the Jews pray to God to be their ally (v. 16; see 2 Macc 8:24). The figure of 20,000 dead (v. 17) is high, as are the figures 9,000 for those who "took refuge" in the towers (v. 18) and 20,000 for those whom Judas is said to have killed "in the two strongholds" (v. 23; cf. the numbers at 2 Macc 8:30).

10:18-23. The three commanders left in charge of the siege (v. 19) are most likely two brothers of Judas, Simon and Joseph (8:22), and an otherwise unknown Zacchaeus. Scholars have suggested that this episode is a doublet of 1 Macc 5:18, 55-61, where two commanders—Joseph son of Zechariah and Azariah—became jealous of the successes of Judas and Simon and attempted to capture Jamnia but were defeated. The siege fails because of the treachery of some of Simon's men, who are described as "lovers of money" (v. 20; cf. Luke 16:14), a common accusation against opponents. Since Simon is glorified in the account of 1 Maccabees, but not here, some scholars have further concluded that the author is anti-Hasmonean in bent. The author of 2 Maccabees, however, includes many stories of deception (2 Macc 13:21), compromise (12:24-25), and backsliding (12:39-40), so this episode need not be taken as anti-Hasmonean propaganda. What it does is show the faithfulness and incorruptibility of Judas. He summons the leaders of the people (v. 21), perhaps the commanders of the army (following Deut 1:15). The men are accused of treachery (similarly to Menelaus, 2 Macc 5:15) and are executed (v. 22). With that transgression done away with, Judas quickly captures the two towers.

2 Maccabees 10:24-38, The Defeat of Timothy

COMMENTARY

This campaign, also sparse in chronological and geographical details, is often seen as reporting the same events as 1 Macc 5:6-8, an even sparser description of a campaign into

Ammonite territory. But there are major differences in this passage: Timothy's death, not mentioned in 1 Maccabees, is described with considerable detail (10:37). Here Timothy invades Judea (vv. 24-25), whereas in 1 Maccabees Judas crosses over the Jordan to attack the Ammonites (1 Macc 5:6). Second Maccabees describes a single battle that seems to take place in Judea (although Judas and his forces go out "a considerable distance" from the city to engage Timothy [10:27]), whereas 1 Macc 5:7 mentions "many battles" with the Ammonites. And the account in 2 Maccabees describes in detail the siege and capture of Gazara (Gezer), whereas 1 Maccabees recounts only the capture of Jazer, in the Transjordan (5:8; according to 1 Maccabees, Gazara was not conquered until the reign of Simon [1 Macc 13:43-48]).

10:24. As mentioned previously, the author of 2 Maccabees must have thought that there were two Timothys, the one here and at 8:30-33, the other at 12:17-25. Whether there were two or whether one should follow the order of 1 Maccabees and only have one Timothy is disputed, but most likely there was only one. The author does not specify the number of mercenaries but, since over 21,000 die in the battle (v. 31), the author means the numbers to be frightening.

10:25-28. The Jews in their distress turn to supplicate God (v. 25; cf. 10:4), using the traditional signs of national mourning by putting earth on their heads as if they were buried and wearing sackcloth, from which shrouds are cut (Neh 9:1; Esth 4:1-3; Jer 6:26; Dan 9:3). Gathered around the new altar, they ask for God's mercy (v. 26; Joel 2:17). The reference to the law is from Exod 23:22, which specifies that God will act this way if the people obey the commandments (cf. 1 Kgs 8:37-39). The calm confidence of the Jews (v. 28) is contrasted with the animal rage of their opponents.

10:29-31. The epiphany to defend Judas and to scatter the enemy has many Greek elements. Often in the *Iliad*, for example, a hero is protected by a god. When Delphi was defended against the Persians and the Gauls, gigantic figures pursued the fleeing attackers while thunderbolts crashed down on them.[86] Zeus is pre-eminently Zeus Keraunos who hurls thunderbolts at his enemies.[87] No one has satisfactorily explained the number five for the supernatural figures (v. 29). One might note how the following siege lasts five days (v. 35).

10:32-38. According to 1 Macc 5:8, the defeat of the army led by Timothy took place in Jazer in Transjordan, not Gazara on the border of Judea to the west of Jerusalem. The motif of the taunting defenders (v. 34), found again at 12:14-16, mirrors the taunts of the Jebusites during David's siege of Jerusalem (2 Sam 5:6-9). A cistern (v. 37), a large pit with plastered walls for storing water, was a perfect hiding place. The victory hymn (v. 38) may be compared to the song of Miriam after the defeat of Pharaoh (Exod 15:20-21), or to the song after David's defeat of Goliath (1 Sam 18:6-7).

---

86. See Herodotus 8.36-39; Pausanias 1.4.4; 10.23.1-6.
87. See Homer *Odyssey* 23.330; Hesiod *Theogony* 854.

REFLECTIONS

Throughout this narrative, the opponents of the Jews are shown to instigate the problems. While the Jews wish to be left alone to follow their own ancestral customs, the non-Jews will not let them. When someone does try to help them, as in the case of Ptolemy Macron, he is dismissed. The local governors, Gorgias and Timothy, constantly seek to attack the forces of Judas Maccabeus. Here again we see the Maccabees behaving in line with just-war principles, acting only out of self-defense. The reader may be particularly intrigued as to what Ptolemy Macron's peace proposals would have been, but the story reminds us that the peacemakers are often the first casualties of war as more extreme voices for violence drown out the calls for peace.

Yet even while the Maccabees are only acting in self-defense, there are also uglier overtones in these stories. Simon's followers, who let enemy forces go (2 Macc 10:20-21), are portrayed as mercenaries, money-lovers, as not looking for the welfare of the community but only for their self-interest. The assumption behind this telling, however, seems to be that the only good enemy is a dead enemy, for Judas immediately sets out to destroy all those who were left besieged. Such an attitude of taking no hostages, of accepting no ransom for prisoners, is disturbing. It violates the later-formulated principles of just war. These stories are told by someone who definitely thinks that God is on the Maccabees' side, and that their enemies are to be destroyed. Such a cavalier attitude toward human life and its dignity is one that we must seriously question. Even in battle, the object should be not to kill, but to render harmless.

2 Maccabees 11:1-12, The Campaign of Lysias

COMMENTARY

The story of the first expedition of Lysias is told here as having occurred during the reign of Antiochus V (who was only nine years old at this time). It actually occurred, however, under Antiochus IV. As mentioned before, the author did not wish to shift focus away from Antiochus IV as the main and constant antagonist of the Jews, and the author narrated one major battle (chap. 8) before the death of Antiochus IV. First Maccabees reports that Lysias, as chancellor of Antiochus IV, sent out the expedition of Nicanor (1 Macc 3:32, 38) before himself invading (4:24-35).

11:1-3. For the first time, Lysias is described as the guardian of Antiochus V (v. 1; see 1 Macc 3:33). He is also described as being "in charge of the government," a position he held under Antiochus IV (1 Macc 3:32), and is given the high title "kinsman" (Lysias is said to be of royal lineage, probably a reference to this title; see 1 Macc 3:32). Jonathan, Judas's brother, was later given the same title (1 Macc 10:89). The full description of Lysias here, after the brief mention at 2 Macc 10:10, suggests some misplaced order. The figure of 80,000 infantry and "all the cavalry" (v. 2) exceeds the numbers at 1 Macc 4:28. The author of 1 Maccabees reports that Lysias sent the expedition of Nicanor to destroy the people (1 Macc 3:38, 42), as Antiochus IV had commanded him, which contrasts with the description of Lysias's intentions here. The events described here—enforced Hellenization, taxing the temple revenue, and selling the high priesthood (vv. 2-3)—seem closer to what happened during the high priesthood of Jason (2 Macc 4:11-15), who purchased the office (2 Macc 4:7-9). Lysias's actions also seem to presuppose that the Temple and the city were controlled by Judas, and not by the followers of Menelaus.

11:4-5. The author enjoys contrasting the might of humans with the power of God (v. 4; 3:34; 10:28). Here, he states that Lysias "did not take God's power into account at all, but felt exultant confidence" in his own troops (v. 4). The treaty of Apamea with the Romans in 188 had forbidden the Seleucids to use elephants in future battles, but Lysias has eighty; elephants could be quite successful against peoples who had no experience of them. As in 1 Macc 4:29, Lysias approaches Jerusalem from the south (v. 5); 2 Maccabees describes Beth-zur as being five *schoinoi* (σχοινοί), not *stadia* (στάδια), as the NRSV translates, from Jerusalem. The *schoinos*, a Persian measure, could equal thirty, forty, or sixty *stadia*. Since a *stadium* is about one-fifth of a kilometer, five *schoinoi* of thirty *stadia* would locate Beth-zur about 30 kms south of Jerusalem (it is actually 28.5 kms south).

11:6-12. Once again, prayer precedes the battle (v. 6), and Judas sets the example (v. 7). As God had sent an angel before the Israelites in the past (Exod 23:20; 33:2; Josh 5:13-15; 2 Kgs 19:35), so now they pray for God to do likewise for them. The closest parallels to this scene, however, are from nonbiblical accounts: the battle between the Romans and the Latins, when the Dioscuri, the twin gods, charged at the head of the Roman force and forced the Latins to flee;[88] Athena's help to the citizens of Cyzicus;[89] and Theseus, who at Marathon rushed before the Greeks at the barbarians.[90] In this account, the role of the

---
88. Dionysius of Halicarnassus *Roman Antiquities* 6.13.
89. Plutarch *Lucillus* 10.3.
90. Plutarch *Theseus* 35.

divine heroes of the Greeks has been taken over by an angel of the Lord. God's mercy is again praised (2 Macc 8:3, 5; 10:26), and God is described as Israel's ally (v. 10; 8:24; 10:16), giving them the courage to win a convincing victory (v. 11). Lysias saves himself by a disgraceful flight, as had Nicanor (2 Macc 8:34-35). According to 1 Maccabees, the numbers of those killed are much smaller (1 Macc 4:34), and Lysias made an orderly retreat.

2 Maccabees 11:13-38, Peace Negotiations

COMMENTARY

While Lysias is said in 1 Maccabees to retreat to Antioch in order to regroup and gather an even larger force (1 Macc 4:35), here, continuing under the assumption that these events occurred during the reign of Antiochus V, Lysias recognizes, even as Heliodorus had done (2 Macc 3:38-39), that the Hebrews were invincible while God was their ally (v. 13). Such a realization leads Lysias to negotiate for peace (v. 14; cf. the request of the Hasideans at 1 Macc 7:12, where the same phrase "just terms" [δίκαιοι *dikaioi*] is used). The end of v. 14 is difficult, as two verbs "persuade" (πείθω *peithō*) and "compel" (ἀναγκάζω *anagkazō*) are found. The verse should be translated: "promising that he would compel the king to be their friend." Most likely scribes found it doubtful that a minister could compel a king to do anything and so inserted the verb for "to persuade." Just as Onias III had the people's welfare in view (2 Macc 4:6), so too does Judas (v. 15), who sets down the terms in writing.

The context allows the author to insert four documents, the dating, content, and order of which have been much discussed. Three of the letters, the first (vv. 16-21), the third (vv. 27-33), and the fourth (vv. 34-38), are dated to the 148th year, which precedes the death of Antiochus IV. The second letter (vv. 22-26) is undated. The dates given in the documents also represent problems. The month mentioned in the first letter, Dioscorinthius (v. 21), is otherwise unknown in the Macedonian calendar. In addition, both the third and the fourth letters are dated 15 Xanthicus (vv. 33, 38), although their respective contents make it improbable that they were written on the same day. According to the third letter, it was Menelaus and not Judas who conducted the negotiations with Lysias (v. 32), whereas the first and fourth letters seem unlikely to have originated from Menelaus's followers. The order of the letters does not seem correct, as the fourth letter precedes the decision of the king, while the second and third are decisions of a king.

Accordingly, scholars have sought the correct dating and occasion for these letters. Such a search, however, depends on the way one reconstructs the sequence of events. According to C. Habicht's reconstruction, letter three reflects a mission of peace by Menelaus to Antiochus IV before setting out on his eastern expedition.[91] When this mission failed, Lysias made his first attack on Judea, but when it in turn failed, he entered into negotiations with the rebels. The negotiations broke down when Antiochus IV died, thus letter two grants amnesty to the rebels on Antiochus V's accession to the throne. According to Bar-Kochva's reconstruction, after the defeat of Nicanor and Gorgias, Ptolemy son of Dorymenes, an enemy of the Jews, was replaced by Ptolemy Macron, friendly to the Jews (2 Macc 10:12), and negotiations with the rebels began.[92] The first letter thus represents an interim report on the negotiations, and letter four a sign of Roman willingness to help negotiate. According to Bar-Kochva, Antiochus IV refused to negotiate, but Menelaus's request for conditional amnesty was allowed (letter three). Letter two is the official reprieve of the persecution by Antiochus V. In general, the arguments of Bar-Kochva are very plausible, although letter three should probably be placed earlier. After the failure of local initiatives against the rebels in 166/165 BCE (1 Macc 3:10-26; 2 Maccabees 8), Menelaus saw the opportunity to

---

91. C. Habicht, "Royal Documents in Maccabees II," *Harvard Studies in Classical Philology* 80 (1976) 1-18.
92. B. Bar-Kochva, *Judas Maccabeus* (Cambridge: Cambridge University Press, 1989) 516-42.

convince Antiochus IV that his measures in Jerusalem were ill-conceived and that a conditional amnesty and the end of the religious persecutions should take place. Antiochus IV agreed while on his expedition to the eastern satrapies (March 164 BCE; letter three). For some unknown reason, possibly because of the popular hatred of Menelaus and the belief that he was a traitor (2 Macc 4:39-50; 5:15), the amnesty offer was rejected. Lysias took up peace negotiations again after his first expedition (letter one), and the Roman emissaries asked Judas's group for a report on the negotiations (letter four). Either at the death of Antiochus IV or at the end of Lysias's second expedition, after the Seleucids had recaptured Jerusalem (1 Macc 6:48-59), letter two returned to the Jews the Temple and the repeal of the edicts against the ancestral religion.

11:16-21, The First Letter. Lysias chooses a neutral term, πλῆθος (*plethos*, which may mean "multitude" or "mass," sometimes "people"; cf. 1 Macc 8:20), to refer to the addressees (v. 16), rather than the formal "nation" (ἔθνος *ethnos*), "senate" (γερουσία *gerousia*), or "people" (δῆμος *dēmos*). Such a neutral address suggests that the letter was not written to a formally recognized group within the Seleucid Empire. The envoys of this group, John and Absalom (v. 17), are otherwise unknown, but it is interesting that they bear Hebrew, not Greek, names. Two sons of an Absalom, Mattathias (1 Macc 11:70) and Jonathan (1 Macc 13:11), fight alongside Judas's successors, Jonathan and Simon. The document referred to in v. 17 is said to be "appended below" (ἐπιδόντες *epidontes*) to this letter, not "delivered" (NRSV) or "presented" (NAB). Verse 18 distinguishes between those issues that had to be referred to the king and those that Lysias felt competent to grant. The verse should not be translated "he has agreed to what was possible" (NRSV) but rather "what lies within my competence, I have agreed to" (author's trans.). Lysias leaves the working out of further specifics to his subordinates (v. 20). "Goodwill" (εὔνοια *eunoia*, v. 19) is the same word used in the letter of Antiochus IV (2 Macc 9:21, 26). The year 148 in the Macedonian Seleucid calendar (v. 21) would lie between October 165 and September 164 BCE. Dioscorinthius has been interpreted as Dios, the first month in the Macedonian calendar, or Dystros, the fifth month, or Daisios, the eight month.

11:22-26, The Second Letter. This letter is undated. Verse 23 uses a phrase that was customarily used at the death of a king (cf. 2 Macc 4:7) and would suggest a time near the accession of Antiochus V. As such, the letter would be a granting of amnesty at the start of a reign. Yet Bar-Kochva suggests that the writer uses vague, "diplomatic" wording to cover recent negative actions and to point to a new start; thus he dates the letter after the second campaign of Lysias (the negotiations mentioned at 1 Macc 6:59).[93]

Antiochus's addressing Lysias as "brother" is normal court language, and does not infer a close relationship between them; Lysias held the rank of kinsman (2 Macc 11:1). The desire for one's kingdom to be undisturbed is found also in the Greek Esth 3:13, but there it is given as a reason for destroying the disturbing Jews. Although the author of 2 Maccabees saw the reforms initiated by Jason as the adoption of Greek customs (2 Macc 4:10-11), the letter here (v. 24) refers most probably to the decrees of Antiochus IV (1 Macc 1:41-59; 2 Macc 6:1 uses the same verb "conduct their lives," "live" [πολιτεύομαι *politeuomai*] found in v. 25). The language in v. 25 is very similar to that of the letter of Antiochus III, when the king declared that the Jews should live by their ancestral religion.[94] According to v. 25, the letter also stipulates the restoration of the Temple. However, if this letter is dated to the beginning of Antiochus V's reign, the Temple already was under Judas's control, and this is simply a diplomatic recognition of the status quo. If the letter is dated to the end of the second expedition (1 Macc 6:55-62), it is a real concession.

11:27-33, The Third Letter. The "senate" (*gerousia*, v. 27) is known from the same letter of Antiochus III (see above) and was the official municipal body in Jerusalem (2 Macc 4:44). The mention of Menelaus (v. 29) raises the question of whether the letter was addressed only to his supporters. The accompanying phrase, "to other Jews," seems to be quite general. As at v. 23, the Jews are said to wish to return to normality (vv. 29, 31).

---

93. Bar-Kochva, *Judas Maccabeus*, 523-25.
94. See Josephus *Antiquities of the Jews* 12.142.

The letter mentions two dates, 30 Xanthicus (i.e., the end of March 164 BCE), and 15 Xanthicus, the middle of March 164 BCE. In the later *Megillat Ta'anit,* the *Scroll of Fasting,* an entry dated 28 Adar (February/March) states that the good news reached the Jews that they did not have to depart from the Torah. Given that the date of this entry is March 164, then the king must be Antiochus IV, as it seems unlikely that his nine-year-old son would have written such a letter, even at the direction of Lysias. Since Antiochus IV had left for the eastern campaign in late 165 BCE, Menelaus must have accompanied him or perhaps visited him during his first stop in Greater Armenia, to the northeast of Syria. Fifteen days to deliver this document from Greater Armenia (or from Media) to Jerusalem and to announce the amnesty would be cutting it very close. Perhaps Antiochus agreed to Menelaus's request in principle and the letter was dated from the chancery at Antioch. Nevertheless, the amnesty ends the persecution, allowing the Jews to follow their own customs (vv. 30-31; emending the text to διαιτήματα [*diaitēmata*], rather than to δαπανήματα [*dapanēmata*], as the Kosher laws would have been included in the reference to the Torah). But amnesty is conditional upon the cessation of hostilities and the return home of the rebels. If this condition was not met, hostility would break out again.

This letter is very important and intriguing for the role it gives to Menelaus. Since the rest of 2 Maccabees portrays Menelaus as a traitor to Judaism, it is difficult to determine what role he is playing. Perhaps he supported Antiochus's suppression of Judaism in the beginning but later saw that policy as losing ground. Or perhaps he recognized that if he was to remain as civil as well as religious leader of Judea, he would have to switch position and try reconciliation before things got too out of hand in Judea. Or does this letter reveal him as someone who, a little over two years after Antiochus IV had forcibly attempted to suppress Judaism in Judea, succeeded in showing him the stupidity of these measures and convinced him to allow the Jews in Judea to follow their ancestral customs? Does Menelaus comes across, not as a traitor to Judaism, but as an advocate for his people who tries to change the monarch's will not by armed confrontation but by slowly working on him diplomatically? Was it his diplomacy combined with the Maccabean successes that won the day?

11:34-38, The Fourth Letter. After the Romans had forced Antiochus IV from Egypt in 168, they had kept a wary eye on Antiochus IV and his ambitions and did not want him cooperating with Eumenes II of Pergamum. An embassy had been sent to Antioch in 166 BCE, led by T. Sempronius Gracchus. A third embassy would be sent in 163/62, during which the Roman ambassador Octavius would be killed after ordering the Seleucid fleet burned and the Seleucid war elephants hamstrung, since they had contravened the peace treaty of Apamea. The embassy referred to in this letter probably took place in autumn 164, so the date appended to the letter should be disregarded as having been copied from the third letter. The embassy contacted the Jewish forces under Judas, addressing them as "a people" (δῆμος *dēmos*) rather than "a multitude" (*plēthos*; the same term is found in official correspondence in 1 Macc 8:29; 12:6; 14:20, 23; 15:17). Such a recognition was tacit support of the rebels. Rome enjoyed putting a cat among the chickens; also in 164 the Roman commissioner G. Sulpicius Gallus publicly invited accusations against Eumenes II of Pergamum in his own capital at Sardis.[95]

95. Polybius 31.6.

REFLECTIONS

This chapter raises interesting questions about how one is to confront aggression. It is noteworthy that 1 Maccabees is completely silent about these first peace negotiations of Menelaus and Lysias; when the author does mention peace attempts after Lysias's second expedition, it is only to point out that one cannot trust the Seleucids, since they always break their word (1 Macc 6:55-63). In fact, the author of 1 Maccabees shows distinct reserve about relations with the Seleucids and seems always to argue that Judea was able to defend itself independently against its neighbors, who were always suspect. On the other hand, 2 Maccabees is open to negotiations with the Seleucid central government, but argues that these always fail because of jealous minor officials (2 Macc 12:2; 14:26). It also denigrates the memory of Menelaus, who attempted to restore the ancestral customs. What one has to ponder again is when and if one has to resort to armed resistance to counter naked aggression. Under what conditions does non-violent resistance work, and when will it only lead to annihilation of the people and its culture? The third letter suggests that a balanced combination of diplomacy and show of force may be the most pragmatic approach in an armed world for nations to settle disputes.

The fourth letter suggests that the intervention of an outside force may be required to get negotiations going. Such intervention usually does not work, however, if the parties do not want to negotiate. If people want to kill one another, it is exceedingly difficult to stop them. The Romans were not at all altruistic in their intervention. They were seeking to extend their power base. But an organization such as the United Nations can be helpful in bringing opposing parties to the bargaining table and in helping to limit disputes. Its power is limited, however, by the will of the parties involved in the conflict. When all sides have become sickened by the killing, then a mediator like the U.N. can be of most assistance—not when warring factions insist on continuing the conflict.

2 Maccabees 12:1-45, Further Local Hostilities

COMMENTARY

12:1-2. This chapter details hostilities with local officials. The author insists, as he often does, that the Jews are peaceful (10:14-15; 14:25), only desirous of following their own customs undisturbed (v. 1). However, their enemies will not leave them alone (v. 2). The author of 2 Maccabees regards the Timothy in these verses as distinct from the Timothy who earlier invaded Judea and whose death is recorded in 10:37, but most likely the author is mistaken. The Apollonius mentioned here is distinguished from others of the same name (Apollonius captain of the Mysians [2 Macc 5:24] and Apollonius from Samaria [1 Macc 3:10-11]). Hieronymus and Demophon are otherwise unknown. Nicanor was not "governor of Cyprus," which was then part of the Ptolemaic Empire, but was the commander of Cypriot troops, like Crates (2 Macc 4:29), and thus of quite a lower rank from the Nicanor mentioned in chaps. 8 and 14–15.

12:3-9. The incident of the drowning of the Jews of Joppa is not found in 1 Maccabees. Joppa was an important coastal harbor town, about thirty-two miles from Jerusalem (see 4:21). The Jews were not citizens, but lived in the town. Perhaps the Jews thought they were being given a pleasure cruise; v. 4 seems to suggest that they did not know the reason for the voyage, but obeyed simply to keep the peace, since the whole citizen body had voted in favor of it. Would a non-citizen minority group have had any say in the matter? Once again, in response to this tragedy, Judas and his forces call on God (cf. Ps 7:6-11). Judas is unable to take full revenge, however. Later his brother Simon will drive out the inhabitants of Joppa and settle there (1 Macc 13:11; 14:5). Jamnia lay about twelve miles south of Joppa, about thirty-four miles in a straight line from Jerusalem, but much farther by road. Thus it is doubtful that a fire in Jamnia could actually have been seen in Jerusalem, but it is a nice hyperbole.

12:10-12. From this point on, the events in this chapter loosely parallel the account of Judas's campaign in Gilead as recorded in 1 Macc 5:9-36. This section begins awkwardly: A mile away from Jamnia and the west coast, the Israelites begin to march against Timothy in Transjordan (1 Macc 5:24), when they are attacked by Arabs (1 Macc 5:39 reports that Arabs served as mercenaries in Timothy's forces, but records that the first encounter with the Nabateans was a peaceful one [1 Macc 5:24-25]). The author of 2 Maccabees stresses God's help in the battle (v. 11). Judas again shows a willingness to negotiate peace (vv. 11-12). Later, Judas's brother Jonathan will draw on this friendship (1 Macc 9:35).

12:13-16. Although a town named Chaspho is mentioned at 1 Macc 5:36 as one of several cities captured by Judas in Gilead, here the author provides a more elaborate story of the capture of Caspin, which is probably the same city. The strength of the city is stressed as the basis for the inhabitants' arrogance (v. 14). As usual, the author contrasts the blasphemous behavior of the Gentiles with Judas's piety (v. 15; see also 10:34; 15:4-5). The reference to Joshua's attack on Jericho (Josh 6:1-21) provides a biblical example for the following destruction and slaughter. The gruesome image of the blood-filled lake (v. 16) is emotionally powerful and is similar to the image of how, in the war against Syracuse, the defeated Athenians were drinking the river stained with their own blood (cf. 2 Kgs 3:22-23).[96]

12:17-26. Judas and his men travel about ninety miles south to the area around Araq-el-Emir, where Hyrcanus the Tobiad had built a fort (see 3:11). Since the battle with Timothy occurs at Carnaim, near Caspin, this account seems to have been misplaced. According to 1 Macc 5:13, all the male Jews in the "land of Tobiani" (ἐν τοῖς Τουβίου *en tois Toubiou*) had been killed as part of the persecution of the Jews that had prompted Judas's expedition into Gilead. The author of 2 Maccabees, to the contrary, insists that Timothy had not accomplished anything except to leave a garrison behind (v. 18), perhaps at one of the deserted strongholds of the Toubiani. At this point in the narrative of 1 Maccabees, Judas divides his forces into three parts, one under Simon to go to Galilee, another under himself and Jonathan to go into Gilead, the third under Joseph and Azariah to be left in Judah (1 Macc 5:17-18). The author of 2 Maccabees may allude to this in v. 20. The parallel account of the battle with Timothy (vv. 20-26) is found at 1 Macc 5:37-43. Although both engagements take place around Carnaim, the two accounts vary greatly. The size of Timothy's forces is greatly exaggerated (v. 20; see 1 Macc 5:38). According to the author, another epiphany of God takes place (v. 22). Timothy's army reacts in terror and fear (cf. Exod 15:16; Deut 2:25; 11:25) and flees in panic (cf. Josh 10:10; 1 Sam 7:10; 2 Kgs 7:6-7; the description of God as "the one who sees all things" is also found at 2 Macc 15:2; see also Exod 2:25; 2 Macc 7:6). Judas's victory (v. 23) is not complete, since Dositheus and Sosipater, who had successfully destroyed Timothy's garrison (v. 19) are deceived by Timothy (vv. 24-25). Their motive, however, is praiseworthy in contrast to that of the troops under Simon, who had accepted bribes to allow their enemies to escape (2 Macc 10:20).

Judas now destroys Carnaim, where the women and children of Timothy's camp had taken refuge (v. 21), and the temple of Atargatis (v. 26). Atargatis, the Syrian goddess and consort of Hadad, was identified with the Canaanite goddess Astarte. The meaning of "Carnaim" is "two horns," which may reflect the iconography of the goddess, where the horns symbolize power (cf. 1 Kgs 22:11; Zech 1:18-21).

12:27-28. According to 1 Macc 5:45-51, Judas escorted all the Jews in Gilead back to Judea. In these verses, he marches toward Ephron, which lay on the road back to Judea. The townspeople, however, will not let the army through, whereupon Judas besieges and destroys the city. This account suggests that Lysias, the chancellor of Syria, had a residence in this Transjordanian town (v. 27), which prompts the attack. The story seems typecast like that of the siege of Caspin (12:13-16): a mixed multitude in a well-defended town (v. 27), the prayer of the Jews (v. 28), the sovereign who shatters the enemy (cf. Exod 15:3, 7; Josh 10:10). The number killed is the same as at Carnaim, 25,000 (vv. 26, 28).

12:29-31. Scythopolis, or Beth-shean, is mentioned at 1 Macc 5:52 as a place the refugees from Gilead simply pass by. Here, no reason is given for Judas's "hastening" there (v. 29). Perhaps the reason is that the author of 2 Maccabees enjoys recounting the goodwill between Gentiles and Jews (vv. 30-31; 2 Macc 9:21, 26). The Festival of Weeks, or Shabuot, was a harvest celebration (Exod 23:16; Lev 23:15-22) called Pentecost in

---

96. Thucydides 7.84.

Greek—i.e., the fifty days after Passover. The author stresses the piety of Judas's forces in that they break off their campaigning to celebrate the festival.

12:32-42a. The emphasis on the piety of Judas's forces (v. 31) is balanced by a story highlighting what happens to those who are not pious. Compare this passage with 1 Macc 5:55-68, which recounts an encounter with Gorgias near Jamnia in which Joseph and Azariah join battle with Gorgias on their own initiative and are defeated. The author of 1 Maccabees used the story as propaganda for the Hasmonean family.

12:32-37. After recounting battles to the east, the author now turns to activities in the south. Gorgias was already mentioned as harassing the Jews (10:14). The actual size of the battle is not given. The battle starts out poorly for the Jews (v. 34), until the heroic actions of Dositheus (v. 35), a cavalryman who should not be identified with the commander mentioned earlier (12:19, 24; the NRSV identifies him as one of Bacenor's men, but the better reading would have him as one of the Toubiani). The story here belongs to a bardic tradition of hero stories, like the roster of David's warriors in 2 Samuel 23. Whereas in the encounter in 1 Macc 5:55-61 Gorgias is victorious, here the author has him fleeing from the battle scene (v. 35) like Nicanor (8:34-35) and Lysias (1:12), to Marisa, one of the major cities in Idumea. The commander Esdris is mentioned without any preparation (v. 36), another sign of the shorthand nature of the work. Some scholars have suggested that he should be identified with the Eleazar of 8:23. As he and his men tire, Judas calls on the Lord to be their ally and leader. The author again stresses the piety of Judas by noting his use of the ancestral language (v. 37), as had the martyred mother and her seven sons (7:21-27). The sudden frenzied onrush catches Gorgias's troops unawares. Some part of the battle description seems to have been left out, since it is unlikely that Gorgias's troops would have remained fighting after Gorgias had fled (v. 35).

12:38-42a. Judas, ever observant, goes to Adullam, about eight miles northeast of Marisa, and he and his soldiers purify themselves and keep the sabbath (v. 38). Since there is no specific need to purify oneself, to become ritually clean so that one can participate in temple service, before honoring the sabbath so far from the Temple, their purification seems, therefore, to refer to purifying oneself after coming into contact with a dead body (Num 19:10-22; 31:24).[97] As opposed to Jason (2 Macc 5:10), these fallen Israelite soldiers are to be buried in their ancestral tomb (v. 39)—not to be so buried was a punishment (1 Kgs 13:22). While 1 Maccabees explains the death of some of Judas's forces as being due to their jealousy of Judas and his brothers (1 Macc 5:56-62, 67), the author of 2 Maccabees explains it as their lack of Torah observance (v. 40). Under the tunic of each dead man was found "sacred tokens of the idols of Jamnia." These sacred objects may have been taken during the raid on Jamnia (12:8-9); such objects were forbidden to Jews (Deut 7:25-26). Greek inscriptions from Delos set up by people from Jamnia honor Heracles and Horon, two Phoenician deities. Would the soldiers have carried booty into battle with them? More likely what they had were amulets used to protect the wearer. The proverbial wisdom that God sees all things is applied here (v. 41; see also 12:22; cf. Prov 15:11; 16:2; 24:12; Mark 4:22).

12:42b-45. These verses are difficult textually and also difficult to translate. Verse 42b seems to reflect a sacrifice for the reparation of the community, whose sin has come to light, similar to the reparation offering (Lev 4:13-35; the language of Lev 4:26, 35 is similar to that of 2 Macc 12:45). The community aspect of the sacrifice is shown by each man's contributing to the sacrifice (v. 43). The phrase "taking account of the resurrection" is a comment by the author that interprets Judas's action. As seen in chap. 7, the author believes in the resurrection. The language there (particularly 7:23) evokes the language of creation. The hope of the brothers (7:11, 14) is that they will live again in a newly created world. In this passage, vv. 44-45 offer two alternatives: *either* Judas does not think that the dead rise and believes that it is foolish to pray for them, *or* he believes that a reward awaits those who die piously, a holy and pious thought. Some scholars

---

97. In the *War Scroll* from Qumran, the soldiers, after having left their dead enemies, all sing the Psalm of Return and, the morning after, wash their garments and cleanse themselves of the blood of the bodies of the ungodly. See 1QM 14:1-2.

have suggested that the expressions "superfluous and foolish to pray for the dead" and "holy and pious thought" are later insertions. However, in the light of recent research on rituals for the dead in Israel (e.g., those rites underlying Isaiah 57), "to pray for the dead" may in fact reflect a custom of which only traces can be discerned. The Israelites clearly believed that the dead had another existence (see, e.g., Deut 18:11-12, which forbids seeking oracles from the dead; 1 Sam 28:14-19; Isa 65:4, which rails against those "who sit inside tombs,/ and spend the night in secret places" [NRSV]). The customs and rituals surrounding the dead suggest the belief that there is a community that stretches beyond death. The author argues that these customs and rituals mean that one can make atonement for those who have died; such practices presuppose a resurrection of the dead.

REFLECTIONS

The story of the complicity of the citizens of Joppa in the murder of the Jews living among them has fearful resonances for us who live with the memories of the Holocaust of World War II, the ethnic cleansing in Bosnia, and the genocide in Rwanda. We are not told in 2 Maccabees why the peoples round about took offensive action against the Jews. What we are forced to consider is how prejudice can grow and be present in traditional stories about the relations of peoples and how this prejudice can be kindled into active hatred by unscrupulous leaders. One way to prevent that might be to examine what stories we tell our children and whether they may contain unsympathetic portraits of other groups. Are ethnic jokes really all that funny? Should statements demeaning women or minority groups be tolerated?

One particular area in which this problem surfaces is the way the term οἱ Ἰουδαῖοι *hoi Ioudaioi* should be translated in the New Testament. The literal translation, "the Jews," most frequently occurs in the Gospel of John and the Acts of the Apostles, and in these two books it is regularly used to characterize those who oppose Jesus or the early movement of Jesus' followers after his death. The result is that "the Jews" appear as the villains in these books. An unsophisticated reader might even get the impression that Jesus and his followers were not even Jews. Such a reader would not grasp that not all Jews in the first century opposed Jesus' movement, and that often the people who did oppose Jesus were simply other Jews who did not accept Jesus as Messiah. Not all Jews were involved in the death of Jesus; the responsibility for Jesus' crucifixion falls on the Roman officials in Judea, as well as on some Jewish leaders at that time. Certainly "the Jews" as a blanket group are not Christ-killers, as the second-century Christian polemic against them would state and as they would be labeled throughout the medieval period. How, then, are we to translate *hoi Ioudaioi*? If we are to translate the term as "the Jews," we must be sure to point out that this term does not refer to all Jews, not even all Jews in the first century CE.

2 Maccabees 13:1-26, The Second Expedition of Lysias

COMMENTARY

The author of 2 Maccabees, like the author of 1 Maccabees, records two expeditions of Lysias against the Jews. The account in 2 Maccabees 13 parallels the one in 1 Macc 6:28-63, which dates the invasion to the 150th year in the Seleucid Babylonian calendar, or 162 BCE (1 Macc 6:20). Second Maccabees, however, which seems to use the Seleucid Macedonian calendar, places this invasion in 149, or between September 164 and October 163 BCE. The epitome in 2 Maccabees gives only two dates aside from those in the letters in chap. 11. Some scholars prefer the dating in 2 Maccabees, while others follow 1 Maccabees and propose that, since the letters in chap. 11 all carry the date of 148 Seleucid era, either Jason or the epitomist placed the second expedition a year later.

13:1-2. No explanation is given for the change of attitude toward the Jews after the supposed agreements in chap. 11, except that the young king wanted to do worse things than his father had done (13:9). As the expedition comes after the events of chap. 12, these Seleucid setbacks must have been thought by the author sufficient reason. The force assembled is enormous and exaggerated, and the text followed by the NRSV should be emended. It is unreasonable that both Antiochus and Lysias would each have his own force, particularly since Antiochus V was a minor. Instead of reading "each of them" (ἕκαστος *hekastos*), the text should preferably be read as "besides" or "as well" (ἐκτός *ektos*), and thus translated "coming with Lysias, his guardian and chancellor, and he had as well a Greek force. . . . " It is also unlikely that scythed chariots would have been used, as they would have been useless in the hilly terrain of Judea.

13:3-8. Menelaus, who has not been mentioned for some time, now reappears. His role in attempting peace negotiations (11:29, 32) is completely reversed here: Menelaus now "encourages" Antiochus V in his invasion (v. 3; see 11:32) as he had helped his father (5:15). He resumes the role he had played before, a plotter against his fellow citizens (4:50; 5:23). He is the opposite of the good high priest Onias III, who only had in mind the welfare of all the people (4:5). The author stresses that God rules all events and so uses the epithet "King of kings" for God (v. 4; see *1 Enoch* 9:4), an epithet used of Persian kings (Ezra 7:12; Dan 2:37) and of Nebuchadnezzar (Ezek 26:7). Since it seems unlikely that Lysias and his charge would have executed Menelaus before an expedition to regain control of Judea, it has been suggested that this description of Menelaus's death (vv. 5-6) may belong after the expedition of Lysias. The author has placed the account here, just as Jason's death is told at the time of his attack on Jerusalem (5:5-10), even though it took place later. Josephus places Menelaus's death after the expedition.[98] The failure of Menelaus's peace overtures (11:29, 32) may have convinced Lysias that Menelaus, who had been supported by Antiochus IV, was now a liability and could be removed. Beroea (v. 4) was the name given to Aleppo in Syria by Seleucus I. Death by ashes was a Persian punishment. If the ashes were cold, the criminal would be suffocated; if they were hot, he would burn to death. Menelaus had been accused of sacrilege earlier (vv. 7-8; see 4:39). The author's motif of appropriate retribution surfaces again (see 4:26; 5:9-10; 9:6, 28), as does the cruel fate of no burial. The holiness of the altar fire was illustrated in the punishment of Aaron's two sons, Nadab and Abihu (Lev 10:1-5). There was a special dump for the sacrificial ashes in Jerusalem (Lev 4:12; Jer 31:40).

13:9-17, The Engagement with Lysias at Modein. 13:9-12. The depiction of Antiochus V as being worse than his father recalls Rehoboam's statements (1 Kgs 12:13-14). Antiochus's intent is the opposite of the desire stated in his letter that the Jews be undisturbed and live according to their customs (11:25). Once again, the Seleucid king is said to be barbarous (2:21; 4:25). The response of Judas is, as expected, ceaseless prayer (v. 10). Judas had earlier exhorted his followers to be ready to die for their laws and their country (8:21). Here is added the holy Temple, and the prayer in v. 11 echoes the supplication at the purification of the Temple (10:4). The emphasis on the whole community at prayer (v. 12) recalls the community response before the entrance of Heliodorus to the Temple (3:14-22). Fasting and weeping and mourning are the classical ritual acts of repentance to ask the Lord's mercy (e.g., Jer 36:9; Joel 2:12-17; Dan 9:3).

13:13. The elders with whom Judas consults (v. 13) are either members of a council or senate (4:44; 11:27) or some consultative body. According to the *Temple Scroll* from Qumran, the king should always have with him twelve princes of his people, twelve priests, and twelve Levites, without whom he should make no decision; before going to war, he should have the high priest consult the Urim and Thummim.[99] At Qumran the

---

98. Josephus *Antiquities of the Jews* 12.383-385.
99. See 11QTemple 57-58.

role of the priest was stressed, but the thrust was to limit the power of the king. Judas in 2 Maccabees is also portrayed as not acting arrogantly, as opposed to his enemies.

13:14-17. The account of the engagement with Lysias is colored by the theological stance of the author. With God on their side, the Jews are invincible and Judea cannot be overrun. So what was really a defeat for the Jews at Beth-zechariah (1 Macc 6:32-47), resulting in the Seleucids regaining control of Jerusalem (1 Macc 6:48-62), is depicted as a victory for the Jews instead. With the addition of the term "commonwealth," or "way of life" (πολιτεία *politeia*), to the list of what the Jews are fighting for (v. 14), the crisis is placed in the same category as when Jason overthrew their way of life (4:11) and when Antiochus IV sent Geron to compel the Jews to live no longer by the laws of God (6:1). Modein, which in 1 Maccabees is the hometown of the Maccabees (1 Macc 2:1), is mentioned only here in 2 Maccabees. Modein is seven miles east of Lydda, seventeen miles northwest of Jerusalem, and lies at the northeastern end of the Low Shephela, the hilly region between the Judean hills and the coastal plain. It is not far from the Gophna Hills and the ascent of Beth-horon to the mountain plateau near Jerusalem. The author seems to suggest that Judas made a surprise attack on the Seleucid forces as they marched down the coastal plain to enter Judea from the south (1 Macc 6:31; cf. the movement of John Hyrcanus in 1 Macc 16:4-5 to Modein from where he could march into the plain). The author of 1 Maccabees depicts no such surprise attack on Lysias's forces.

Judas gives a watchword (v. 15), just as he had before the battle with Nicanor (8:23). "God's victory" is what the Sons of Light are to write on their standards when they return from battle.[100] The author of 2 Maccabees delights in tales of heroic achievements. Here Judas, with "a picked force," kills more than 2,000 of the enemy; he also kills the leading elephant and fills the camp with confusion (v. 15) and retires safely (v. 16). Judas's feat parallels that of Eleazar (1 Macc 6:43-46), but Eleazar's occurred in the midst of a disastrous battle during which he lost his life. Verse 17 contains the poetic image of Judas under God's shelter (cf. Pss 91:1; 121:5; Isa 25:4; as well as in the phrase "under the shelter of God's wings," Pss 17:8; 36:7; 61:4; 63:7).

13:18-26, Antiochus V's Treaty. The king, recognizing the strength of the Jewish troops (as had Lysias in his first expedition [11:13]), now tries deceit (v. 18). According to 1 Maccabees, the Jews at Beth-zur fought courageously but eventually capitulated through lack of provisions (1 Macc 6:31, 49-50). Here the king's forces are defeated (v. 19), the defenders of Beth-zur get whatever provisions are necessary from Judas (v. 20), and the king eventually withdraws after making a separate peace treaty with the people of Beth-zur (v. 22; did the people of Beth-zur agree not to attack the king's forces from behind?). In the middle of this account of what occurred at Beth-zur is another exciting tale of deception by a Jew that failed (v. 21). In 1 Macc 6:32-47, the battle of Beth-zechariah is described in detail, and the defeat of the Jews is noted. In 2 Maccabees, Beth-zechariah is not mentioned by name, and it is only briefly stated that when the king attacked Judas's forces he was defeated (v. 21*b*). This may be an inversion of what really happened, or it could refer to the fact that Lysias and the king were unsuccessful in their siege of the Temple and thus decided to make peace (1 Macc 6:51-61). Second Maccabees shows the invasion of the king and Lysias to be unsuccessful and the Jews undefeated. Both 1 and 2 Maccabees agree that Lysias and the king break off their attack because of an attempt by Philip to seize control of the government. However, in 1 Maccabees, Antiochus IV appoints Philip to be in charge of the kingdom and guardian of Antiochus V Eupator (1 Macc 6:14-15). Since 2 Maccabees has reported that this Philip fled to Egypt following Antiochus IV's death (9:29), in the condensed statement of 2 Macc 13:23, one might suppose that someone else named Philip had been left in charge of affairs in Antioch by Antiochus V and was now leading a revolt.

According to 2 Maccabees, Antiochus V behaves honorably, agrees to just terms, honors the Temple, and gives gifts to it (v. 23). In doing so, Antiochus is acting as kings had done before him (3:1). He also sacrifices in the Temple, as had Alexander the Great and Ptolemy IV Philopator.[101] In 1 Maccabees,

---

100. See 1QM 4:13.

101. For Alexander, see Josephus *Antiquities of the Jews* 11.336; for Ptolemy IV Philopator, see 3 Macc 1:9.

the king breaks his oath and has the walls of Jerusalem torn down (1 Macc 6:62). Most interestingly, here Antiochus meets Judas graciously (v. 24), whereas in 1 Maccabees Judas does not seem to be anywhere near Jerusalem. The author seems to continue the theme of the Jews' being willing to act as good citizens and be on good terms with Gentiles if they are allowed to do so (12:29-31; 14:24-25). A new governor is installed for the region of Ptolemais to the land of the Gerrenians. The location of land of the Gerrenians is uncertain; some scholars place it southward from Gaza and west of Beersheba, others as far south as Lake Sirbonis, near Pelusium (even though this area was then under Ptolemaic control); still others suggest that it be placed north of Ptolemais at Gerrha, southeast of Beirut. The change of administrators perhaps reflects a more sympathetic policy toward the Jews, as earlier with Ptolemy Macron (10:12), and in opposition to the role local governors had taken (12:2). If the area covered by Hegemonides lay south of Ptolemais, he would have controlled Jamnia, Joppa, and possibly part of Idumea; he may have replaced Gorgias (12:32-37). If the area of his control lay northward, Hegemonides would have controlled Ptolemais, Tyre, and Sidon (1 Macc 5:15). The citizens of Ptolemais, possibly already described as instigators of anti-Jewish decrees (1 Macc 5:15; 2 Macc 6:8), do not like the agreement, as later Alcimus does not like the peaceful arrangements between Nicanor and Judas (14:20, 26). With Philip in revolt, Lysias had to appease the citizens of Ptolemais so that his rear guard would be secure.

REFLECTIONS

This chapter shows again the power of a historian to determine the way history is written. Guided by his worldview that Torah-observant Jews could not be defeated by any enemy, the author of 2 Maccabees has selected his facts, embellished them, and distorted what actually happened. The narrative surely is a warning to us to examine the assumptions we bring to any discussion as well as the ways we have told our cultural histories. Have we looked at our religion's past through rose-colored spectacles and not attempted to see what drove our opponents or to empathize with their views? If we begin every discussion with the entrenched view that we are right and our opponents are wrong, how can we ever advance beyond conflict? It is easy to see the speck in our neighbor's eye and not notice the log in our own (Matt 7:3-5), but we must learn to examine ourselves and our traditions with clear vision.

2 MACCABEES 14:1–15:36, THE INVASION BY NICANOR

2 Maccabees 14:1-2, Demetrius Becomes King

COMMENTARY

The last two chapters of 2 Maccabees parallel 1 Maccabees 7. The author swiftly shifts to the new ruler, Demetrius I. Demetrius, son of Seleucus IV and nephew of Antiochus IV, had been held hostage in Rome in accordance with the Treaty of Apamea. He had replaced Antiochus IV in 178 on the latter's succession to the throne and had been kept in Rome even after the indemnity had been paid off in 173. On the death of Antiochus IV, Demetrius had argued it was useless to keep him a hostage and requested permission to leave, but the Roman senate had refused, no doubt preferring to deal with an underage king like Antiochus V. After the murder of the Roman envoy in Laodicea in 163 BCE, Demetrius applied again for permission to leave, was again refused, and then slipped away to wrest control of the kingdom. The author of 2 Maccabees specifies that he landed in Tripolis and was acclaimed king by the end of 162 BCE (the "three years" of v. 1 means within the third year). The last date given in 2 Maccabees (13:1) was the 149th year; the next date is the 151st year (14:4), so the events of vv. 1-2 come within that span. According to both 1 Macc 7:1 and Polybius,[102] Demetrius arrived in Tripolis with only a handful of supporters.

102. See Polybius 31.14.8-13.

2 Maccabees 14:3-25, Nicanor's Expedition

COMMENTARY

14:3-5. The peace gained at the end of chap. 13 is now to be broken, just as the peace at the end of chap. 11 had been. Alcimus, also called Yakim, had been appointed high priest after Menelaus.[103] Alcimus is said to have "defiled" himself in the "times of separation" (ἀμειξίας χρόνοις *ameixias chronois*, v. 3). Scholars have puzzled over this characterization. Some have noted that, since Alcimus was initially acceptable to the Hasidim (1 Macc 7:12-18), he could not have defiled himself the way Menelaus had done and, therefore, that his defilement resulted from the incident in which sixty Hasidim were executed (1 Macc 7:12-18). Some have further suggested that "the time of separation" mentioned here thus refers to the disagreement between the Hasidim and Judas over Alcimus. Other scholars accept that the massacre is the incident referred to by 2 Maccabees, but follow a different manuscript reading and translate "in times of peace" (ἐπιμιξία *epimixia*), that is, in the time following the treaty with Antiochus V. The execution of the sixty Hasidim, however, occurs in 1 Maccabees after Alcimus's installation by Demetrius I, and so after the events being reported here. But describing Alcimus as "defiled" does not necessarily indicate ritual defilement; the term translated "defile" (μολύνω *molynō*) can have the general meaning of "disgrace": "A whisperer degrades himself/ and is hated in his neighborhood" (Sir 21:28 NRSV). The term may be used here in a general way to contrast Alcimus's behavior to that of Judas, who left Jerusalem so as not to share in the defilement (2 Macc 5:27), and with that of Razis, who had risked his life by remaining obedient to the law during the persecution (14:38). The description of Alcimus thus is the author's character assassination, since Alcimus was not one of Judas's followers and had not (like Razis) risked body and soul for Judaism. We should perhaps not look for a more specific way in which Alcimus had defiled himself—e.g., by eating non-kosher food or by persecuting those who did not obey the emperor's orders. The statement that Alcimus could not be safe suggests that he had been forced out of Jerusalem (cf. 1 Macc 7:6). At the installation of a new king, he had come for confirmation in his office (v. 4; 1 Macc 10:60-64; 11:23-27) and brought the requisite gifts: a gold crown, a palm, and olive branches from the Temple (cf. 1 Macc 13:36-37; "olive branches" [θαλλοί *thalloi*] may be translated by the more general "gifts"). Alcimus, although his folly is like Simon's (4:6), cunningly bides his time. When the king seeks the advice of those Friends of his at hand, it is natural for him to include the high priest in the discussions on Judea (v. 5).

14:6-10. The author provides Alcimus with an appropriate speech for the circumstances. He first answers the king's questions (v. 6), then claims to have the king's and his own country's best interests at heart (vv. 7-8) and requests help (v. 9). In 1 Macc 2:42 and 7:13, the Hasideans are distinguished from the Maccabeans. Here Judas is portrayed as their leader, and the group is distinguished from the rest of the nation (v. 8). The accusation against Judas and his followers is exactly the opposite of what the reader knows to be

103. See Josephus *Antiquities of the Jews* 12.385-87.

true from the narrative: It is not Judas and his followers but Gorgias and those who were banished from Jerusalem who keep up the war (10:14-15); it is the local military commanders who will not let the Jews live in peace (12:2). Judas, in fact, will make peace with Nicanor (vv. 18-25) and settle down, the opposite of what Alcimus charges (v. 6). The charge that the state will never enjoy peace (v. 10) parallels the charge made by Onias III against the original troublemaker Simon (2 Macc 4:6). In several late Jewish narratives we find the pattern whereby the accusation is made that Jews are disturbers of the realm, and this accusation is later disproved (Esth 3:13; 3 Macc 3:26; 6:28; 7:4-7 LXX).

Verse 7 has been interpreted to mean that Alcimus has had the high priesthood taken away from him. That the phrase would have this meaning where Alcimus is presenting himself as humbly seeking the best interests of his people seems out of context. Since the verb ἀφαιρέω (*aphaireō*) can mean "take off a garment" (Esth 4:4; Esth 4:17*k* LXX), it might suggest that Alcimus is claiming that, because of his concern for his people, he has left behind his high priestly duties to come to the king (cf. Onias III at 4:5-6). The glory here would refer to the glorious robe of the high priesthood (Sir 45:8; 50:5-11). The motives Alcimus gives for coming to the king resemble those of Onias III (4:5-6).

14:11-14. The king's Friends instigate action against Judas (cf. 10:13). The Nicanor involved here is unlikely to have been the same Nicanor mentioned earlier (8:9; 12:2), but the author assimilates the two by giving the same epithet to both (8:34; 15:3). The author of 2 Maccabees makes no mention of the expedition of Bacchides and Alcimus or of Alcimus's tenure as high priest (1 Macc 7:8-25). Such an imposition of Seleucid control would have spoiled his depiction of Judea and Judas as invincible. Since the Roman ambassador C. Octavius had had the Seleucid elephants hamstrung in early 162 BCE, perhaps Nicanor was out of a job. Only here, when Nicanor is appointed, is mention made of a governor of Judea (v. 12). The same rank was used earlier to describe local military commanders (12:2), which is probably what is meant here. Nicanor's orders are to do away with Judas (v. 13), as Antiochus V and Lysias had been done away with, to "scatter" his forces (at 1 Macc 7:6, Judas's opponents claim that he had "scattered" them out of the land), and to install Alcimus as high priest. At v. 14, one should probably delete "Gentiles," since the group the author intends seems to be the Israelites who opposed Judas and had been driven out of Judea (10:15). The contrast of prosperity and calamities resembles that made by the author regarding Jason's slaughter of his fellow Israelites (5:6).

14:15-25. As customary, before going into the battle the Jews pray to God (v. 15; see 10:25), who "established his own people forever" by awesome deeds, who "upholds his own heritage by manifesting himself" (cf. Deut 9:26-29; 2 Macc 1:26; literally "with an epiphany"; see 2:21). The place at which the Jews pray and from which they set out (v. 16) seems to be presupposed by the author to be Jerusalem. The location of Dessau, at which the battle takes place, is unknown, but it seems to have been within Judea. Simon, one of the commanders (8:22; 10:19), receives a slight check (v. 17), but Nicanor decides to negotiate (v. 18; there is no mention in 1 Maccabees of an engagement at Dessau or of any contact before Nicanor opens peace negotiations). In 1 Maccabees 7:27, the Seleucid commander from the beginning planned treachery (a motif that occurs frequently in 1 Maccabees [1:30; 7:10-18], as the author is suspicious of any peace settlement with the Seleucids). Here a different picture is given, much like the description of Antiochus V's dealings with Jerusalem (13:23-24): Nicanor acts honorably (vv. 19-20), and Judas acts with commendable caution (v. 22), although no specific reason is given for it. It is also noteworthy how Judas consults with the people before agreeing to the treaty (v. 20). The ambassadors mentioned in v. 19 are otherwise unknown. The scene for the signing of the agreement is vividly drawn (v. 21), with the two chariots coming toward each other and the two leaders sitting on facing chairs. The description of Nicanor given here, that he becomes a friend of Judas and stays on in Jerusalem, completely contradicts that of 1 Maccabees. Nicanor dismissed the group of enemies of Judas (v. 23; note the play between "flocked" [ἀγεληδόν *ageledon*], v. 14, and "flocks" [ἀγελαίους *agelaious*], v.

23). One might suspect that Nicanor kept Judas near him (v. 24) so that Judas could not get up to any mischief, but the author insists on the warm attachment of Nicanor to Judas. Verse 25 shows signs of having been shortened, as three verbs follow one after another (see also 13:19, 22-23, 26). No better peace could be imagined than the fiery soldier Judas married with children and taking part in normal community life.

REFLECTIONS

Judas is shown here as the model citizen. He is not aggressive against the Seleucids, as Alcimus had suggested. When honorable peace conditions can be achieved, he agrees to them and then retires to private life. He does not try to usurp Alcimus's position, but is content with the restoration of peace under the Seleucid government. He is not ambitious and does not seek to use his armed backers as a tool for advancement. He makes the transition from soldier to civilian with apparent ease. There are two lessons for us here. One is again the counsel against ambition. The ambition of Jason and Menelaus had rent apart the social fabric earlier, and Alcimus was about to do it again. In a free-market economy, such as that of the United States, competitiveness is instilled in children from the very first days at school. It is good to be competitive, to be as good as one can be, to excel in intellectual pursuits and in sports. But we do well to remind ourselves and our children that we should not try to win at all costs, that ambition should not make us trample down others.

We should also be reminded as we read about Judas's return to private life how difficult such a transition can be. In today's world, a soldier who returns to civilian life after having fought in a war requires all the support and help he or she can get to move back to normal family life. The horrors of war can be imprinted on the subconscious, and we have to show ourselves as caring for those who have defended our homes and way of life.

Finally, 1 and 2 Maccabees give two very different accounts of Nicanor's behavior, and we should reflect on what that signifies for our appreciation of biblical literature. In 1 Maccabees, Nicanor is treacherous from the start, and Judas is rightly seen to be suspicious of him and his intentions. The mistrust grows and hostilities ensue. The endemic mistrust that the author of 1 Maccabees depicts between the Maccabees and the Seleucids seems as if it could only be resolved by the independence of Judea. In 2 Maccabees, however, Nicanor is depicted as an admirer of Judas. Judas is properly cautious in meeting with him, but the two are said to strike up a friendship. The Jew and the Gentile live on good terms. Proper worship is being performed at the Temple, since its purification and restoration. Judas seems content that normalcy has returned, a normalcy that includes Judea's being part of the Seleucid Empire. Judas does not seek independence for Judea, but appears satisfied with the situation.

Such a strong difference between the two accounts should not be explained away by claiming that one is more accurate than the other, that one deserves to be believed more than the other. Rather, the two accounts remind us of how the same event can be retold in completely different ways even by eyewitnesses of the event. The telling depends on the perspective of the account. This sense of different perspective is one that we should be sensitive to in our reading of the Scriptures. The two accounts of God's creation of the universe in Genesis 1 and Genesis 2–3 show us two different perspectives on the origins of humanity. The four different Gospels allow us to see how different communities at the beginning of the Jesus movement viewed him and his teaching in diverse ways. Difference does not mean contradiction; it simply means diversity of viewpoint.

2 Maccabees 14:26-36, The Change in Nicanor

COMMENTARY

The relations between Nicanor and Judas are characterized as ideal ("goodwill," v. 26; see 9:21, 26; 11:19), but Alcimus intervenes to ruin the peace, as had been done earlier against Ptolemy Macron (10:13). The account presupposes that Alcimus is in Jerusalem, so he must have been installed as high priest as part of the negotiations. He accuses Nicanor with the same accusation Simon had made against Onias III (4:2). Nicanor had appointed Judas as his "deputy," or "substitute" (διάδοχος *diadochos*; see 4:29), rather than successor, for only the king could nominate the governor of an area. If this is not a trumped-up charge on the part of Alcimus, it implies that Judas had become a part of the normal bureaucracy of Jerusalem. Just as the false accusations of the wicked Simon had caused Seleucus IV to send Heliodorus to remove funds from the Jerusalem treasury (3:7), so also false accusations work their evil now. The king acts unwisely, as his anger shows (cf. 7:3, 39) and he annuls the terms of the agreement (v. 27; cf. 13:25). The author notes the distress of Nicanor, an honorable man, at having to break covenant when Judas was innocent, but he obeys orders (v. 28). The author of 1 Maccabees simply states that Judas came to know of Nicanor's treachery (1 Macc 7:30). Here, in vv. 29-30, a whole scene is played out, as Judas is shown to be observant in outwitting Nicanor (v. 30). In the narrative at 1 Maccabees, Judas's escape is followed by his victory over Nicanor at Caphar-salama (1 Macc 7:31-32). The author of 2 Maccabees makes no mention of this battle, but moves directly to Nicanor's attack on the Temple (v. 31). Why would Nicanor think that the priests would know where Judas had hidden? Does he think they will follow the principle that it is better for one man to die than for the nation to be destroyed (2 Sam 20:14-22; John 11:50)? At this point, Nicanor's character changes; by obeying the king's unjust orders, he turns into someone who fights against God. The author deliberately and effectively contrasts Nicanor's stretching out his right hand toward the Temple (v. 33) and the priests' stretching out their hands in prayer (v. 34). As Antiochus had threatened to level the holy city (9:13; 8:3), so Nicanor threatens to level the shrine to the ground (14:33; the altars of the Lord had been thrown down in King Ahab's time [1 Kgs 18:31], and the reader might recall the taunt of Gideon after he pulled down the altar of Baal [Judg 6:28-32]). If Judas is not handed over to him, Nicanor threatens, he will build a "splendid" (ἐπιφανές *epiphanes*) temple to Dionysus, foreshadowing ironically God's "manifestation" (ἐπιφάνεια *epiphaneia*) in defeating Nicanor (15:27). The priests in their prayer call on God as the defender of the nation (8:36); Jerusalem is the place that God chose (Deut 12:5-11). The author has chosen the Greek term σκηνόω (*skēnoō*, lit., "tenting") to describe God's presence, reflecting the term for God's tent of meeting in the wilderness (Exod 25:8-9), which was placed in Solomon's Temple (1 Kgs 8:4; Pss 15:1; 43:3; 61:4; 74:7; 84:1; see also 1 Kgs 6:1; 7:51; 8:16-21, 41-43; Ps 26:8; Sir 24:8). The prayer of the priests, which refers to the purification (10:1-4), will be fulfilled; the blessing at 15:34 will repeat the language of 14:36.

REFLECTIONS

The slander of Alcimus and its acceptance by the king remind us that we must never believe everything we hear, particularly bad news. If we need to know what happened, we should check out all parties to hear every side of the story. But we are also confronted in this narrative with a more serious issue: the question of obedience to authority. The chapter is fascinating in its development of Nicanor's character. First he is portrayed as a soldier who, on seeing the commitment and readiness to die on the part of Judas and his forces, has the wisdom to settle the dispute and gain the main objective of the king, Alcimus's installation as high priest, through a negotiated settlement. Nicanor is not a stubborn, stupid man who can settle things only by violence. But then occurs a moral crisis for Nicanor: Should he obey the unjust decision of the king? He is troubled, but eventually decides that he must obey the king. One would not want to be in his shoes, for what were his alternatives? Could he try to reason with the king, who already had shown signs of anger? If he disobeyed, he would no doubt have been executed, and someone else would have been sent to carry out the king's wishes. So Nicanor obeyed an order he knew was unjust. From that point on his character changes for the worse, and he is shown as fighting against God. His excuse echoes throughout history: He was only following orders. It was heard at the Nuremberg trials after World War II. It was given for what occurred at My Lai during the Vietnam war. And it will always be the excuse for not exercising moral autonomy, for thinking that we are not responsible if we can blame someone else. The ethical issue posed by Nicanor's problem is far-reaching: How can one tell if the order of a superior is "unjust"? Yet how can we "train" people to be morally autonomous and to have the courage to blow the whistle on moral violations they witness in the companies they work for? How can an army operate if every soldier has to decide that the action is morally justified? Lurking under the narrative of Nicanor's actions is the whole issue of conscience and authority, an issue that will always keep surfacing.

2 Maccabees 14:37-46, The Razis Affair

COMMENTARY

The episode of Razis' martyrdom interrupts the focus on Nicanor and Judas. Just as the martyrdom accounts in 6:17–7:42 were placed after the desecration of the Temple and brought about God's mercy, so also the author places Razis' death after Nicanor's threat against the Temple. After Razis' willing death comes the removal of the threat.

14:37-40. Razis, an unusual name, is an elder, perhaps one of those consulted earlier by Judas (13:13). He is a lover of his compatriots, quite the opposite of Alcimus, who claims to be looking out for his compatriots (14:8), but he is not. The title "father of the Jews" is unexpected, but it may be a position similar to benefactor of the city, held by Onias III (4:2). No reason is given for why Razis was denounced to Nicanor. Was he one of those who had gone into hiding with Judas (14:30) because of his former zeal for Judaism at the time of persecution (v. 38)? Nicanor is now said to hate the Jews (v. 39). This is in accordance with the way 1 Macc 7:26 characterizes Nicanor from the first. Sending 500 soldiers to arrest one man seems a bit exaggerated; the author stresses by this figure the importance of Razis.

14:41-42. This scene seems to take place in a private house in which there was a tower overlooking a courtyard. Presumably Razis has been betrayed and surprised in someone's house. Surrounded on all sides, Razis attempts to kill himself. Like Eleazar (6:23), he prefers to die "nobly" (εὐγενῶς *eugenōs*) rather than be insulted "unworthily" (ἀναξίως *anaxiōs*) of his proper ability. The Mediterranean code of honor and disgrace is strongly at play here. Plato, in the ninth book of his *Laws,* states that suicide is allowable under judicial constraint, under the constraint of unavoidable misfortune, and to avoid participating in a dishonorable deed. In 2 Maccabees 8, Nicanor had been defeated and had run away under the guise of a slave. He chose to act dishonorably, fleeing like a slave, when he might have committed suicide under the third condition of the code. Razis does choose to kill himself under the second condition of the code; he has no means of escape from his enemies, who are rushing to take him.

14:43-46. The suicide act is stretched out to draw the reader in with its vivid description; the sword doesn't do the trick, Razis' throwing himself off a wall doesn't, so he tears out his entrails and throws them on the troops—his blood is literally upon them. The intensity of his commitment is clear in this last grisly act. His last prayer (v. 46) recalls the prayers of the martyrs (7:11, 22-23).

REFLECTIONS

Once again the narrative forces us to confront a contemporary ethical issue: the right to die. Within first-century Judaism, "honorable" suicide was debated. After the town of Jotapata had fallen, Josephus's men urged suicide while he opposed it, although Josephus praised Phasael, who committed suicide rather than be in the power of his enemy Antigonus.[104] Philo of Alexandria supported those Jews who were willing to kill themselves rather than see the statue of Emperor Caligula placed in the Temple.[105] According to 4 Maccabees, the mother of the seven martyred sons committed suicide rather than let the king's men touch her.[106] Within fourth-century Christianity, as well, there was a great debate between Donatist Christians, who advocated suicide, and their opponents who did not.[107] These debates over suicide raise the question of whether a believer in God, who gives life, can honestly take his or her life. Must one endure unbearable suffering or the certainty of a painful death through an incurable disease or can one muster moral arguments in support of suicide? It is a vital question in medical ethics today, and one about which we must all inform ourselves.

104. See Josephus *The Jewish War* 1.271-272; 3.355-391; *Antiquities of the Jews* 13.367-369; 15.13. See also the account of the suicides at Masada, in Josephus *The Jewish War* 7.320-401.
105. Philo *Embassy to Gaius* 228-242, 308.
106. See 4 Macc 17:1.
107. See Augustine *Against Gaudentius* 1.28-32 (PL 43.725-732); Letter 204.

2 Maccabees 15:1-36, The Victory over Nicanor

COMMENTARY

15:1-5, Nicanor's Arrogance. The narrative of Nicanor's search for Judas continues. Nicanor hears that Judas is in the region around Samaria (v. 1), possibly referring to the Gophna hills just northeast of Modein and bordering Samaria, where Mattathias and his sons had fled in the first stages of the revolt (1 Macc 2:28). There is no specific mention of this search in 1 Maccabees, but 1 Macc 7:39 has Nicanor encamping in Bethhoron, just south of the Gophna hills. Taking advantage of the sabbath rest to attack the Jews had been a tactic used by the enemy in the early days of the revolt (1 Macc 2:29-38), so the Hasmoneans and their supporters had decided that they would defend themselves even if attacked on the sabbath (1 Macc 2:4-41). The Jewish observance of the sabbath was well known to non-Jews, and was portrayed as a superstition that allowed them to be taken unawares. The author of 2 Maccabees has stressed the observance of the sabbath by Judas and his followers (2 Macc 8:26-27). The incident reported here is designed to stress Nicanor's battle against God. The Jews in Nicanor's company (v. 2) may refer to those mentioned earlier who opposed Judas (10:15; 14:14), but the author, in characterizing them as forced to be with Nicanor, seems to introduce them as a foil to point out Nicanor's arrogance. As often with non-Jews, Nicanor's attitude is characterized as barbarous (2:21; 4:25; 10:4; 11:9). God is described as the all-seeing one (12:22; cf. 7:35; 9:5). Nicanor, the thrice-accursed wretch (v. 3; see 8:34), now taunts/challenges God, as Goliath taunted the Israelites (1 Sam 17:8-10, 26) and as Pharaoh's army had boasted in pursuing Moses and the Israelites (Exod 15:9; at Exod 20:8-11, the observance of the sabbath is grounded in

God's creating heaven and earth). Nicanor's strategy does not work.

15:6-10, The Battle Preparations. The arrogance of Nicanor resembles that of Antiochus IV (9:8). As so often (12:14-15, 27-28), the author contrasts the two sides (cf. 15:20-26). Judas, like Moses (Exod 14:13) and Joshua (Josh 10:25; cf. Josh 8:1), exhorts his men not to fear and follows the speech proposed at Deut 20:1-4. Judas cites victories from the Torah and the Prophets, but also reminds his troops of their own prowess and skill. The perfidy of the Gentiles refers to Nicanor's violation of the covenant he had made (14:20-22, 28). In any competition, after all the training has been done, it is mental toughness that counts, and this is what Judas is instilling in his men (v. 11).

15:11-16, Judas's Vision. In antiquity, dreams were believed to be a means by which humans kept company with the gods. People were aware that not all dreams were heaven sent, but rather were a way the gods visited humans. Dreams are reported frequently in the narrative of Genesis as a way of learning God's will (e.g., Gen 15:12; 20:3; 40–41), whereas Jeremiah polemizes against the lying dreams of prophets (Jer 23:23-32). Daniel is both a dream interpreter (Daniel 2; 4) and a dreamer himself (Dan 7:1). The author of 2 Maccabees characterizes Judas's dream as "a certain waking reality" (v. 11; reading ὕπαρ τι [*hypar ti*] instead of ὕπερ τι [*hyper ti*], "beyond measure"). Such a term was as old as Homer[108] and applies either to the fact that the figures in the dream are so realistic or to the significance of the details that will come to pass. The detailed description of the dream suggests the first possibility here: The elements in the dream are so realistic that Judas thinks he is awake.

The characters in the dream are significant. Onias III (v. 12) takes the reader back to the beginning of the narrative (3:1–4:6); he is described using the expression to denote a perfect Greek gentleman, one trained in "all that belongs to excellence" (ἀρετη *aretē*; see also the lists describing Eleazar [6:18, 23] and Razis [14:37-38, 42]). Just as the priests had stretched out their hands (14:34), so also does Onias. The author stresses Onias's concern for the whole community. Whereas in 12:42-45 the living pray for the dead, here the dead Onias prays for the living. There is thus a continuance of existence beyond the grave. A second person of even more majestic mien appears but does not speak (v. 13). He is identified by Onias as Jeremiah (v. 14). Jeremiah's message was often one of doom and destruction to Judah, but he was also sent to build and to plant (Jer 1:10). Although commanded at one stage of his ministry not to pray for the people (Jer 7:16; 11:14; 14:11), once his prediction of destruction had come true (Jeremiah 42) Jeremiah was asked to pray for the remnant of the people. At 2 Macc 2:1-8, he is portrayed as hiding the temple vessels until God discloses their whereabouts. Here he gives Judas a golden sword (v. 15; see 3:25; 5:2), the giving of which reflects that this is a battle against one who fights against God, and thus it is divine assurance of victory.[109]

15:17-19. The forces determine either "not to encamp" or "not merely to march" (v. 17). In either case, the effect of Judas's dream is shown as arousing the adrenalin of the soldiers. The author strives for emotional effect by picturing the anxiety of those in the city, but insisting that the main concern was for the Temple, and not the relatives (v. 18). The image almost suggests that those inside the city could see what was happening out in the open (v. 19), but that would be impossible for a battle at Adasa (see 1 Macc 7:40; the location of the battle is not given in 2 Maccabees). Earlier the author had claimed that the fires in Jamnia could be seen in Jerusalem (12:9).

15:20-27, The Battle. The tactics of this battle are not described in detail in 1 Maccabees. The deployment of the Seleucid army, described here, seems based on standard practice in Hellenistic armies (v. 20). It is unlikely the elephants were employed, as Octavius had had the Seleucid war elephants hamstrung in 162 BCE, before Demetrius ascended as king. The two sides are contrasted. While the Seleucid force draws on battle array (15:20), Judas prays for help (15:21-24), stretching out his hands to heaven (cf. 14:34),

---

108. See Homer *Odyssey* 19.547; 20.90.

109. The giving of special weapons to a hero is found widely in traditional literature. In the *Enuma Elish*, the Babylonian creation epic, Marduk is given special magic to subdue Tiamat. In the *Iliad*, Achilles is given special weapons to fight Hector. In Egyptian accounts, a god often gives a sword to Pharaoh to defeat his enemy.

reciting Scripture (v. 21). In his prayer, Judas mentions the defeat of Sennacherib (v. 22; 2 Kgs 18:13–19:35; Isaiah 36–37), to which the author already alluded during the battle against the first Nicanor (8:19; cf. 1 Macc 7:41-42). Judas addresses God as "Sovereign of the heavens" (v. 23), playing off the boast of Nicanor (15:4-5). Judas asks that God send an angel (see 11:6) and that God send fear and trembling on the enemy (see Exod 23:20; 2 Kgs 19:35). The reference to "God's mighty arm" (v. 24) recalls the victory hymn at Exod 15:16, which recounts God's triumph over those who attack the people. The battle songs of the Seleucids (v. 25; παιάνων *paianōn*, "paeans") were often addressed to Apollo as soldiers went into battle; these songs are contrasted here with the prayers of Judas's forces (v. 26; see 12:37). God once again is manifested (v. 26; see 2:21) in helping the people. The numbers killed are exaggerated.

15:28-36, The Dismemberment of Nicanor. The success of the Sovereign (15:4-5, 23), who is God of the Jews, is again signaled through the use of the ancestral language, Hebrew (v. 29; see 7:8, 12, 27; 12:37). The army returns from the battlefield toward Jerusalem (v. 28), recalling the victory procession of the divine Warrior to God's abode (Exod 15:17). Judas is described in glowing terms (v. 30), reminiscent of Onias III's concern for his compatriots (4:2, 5).

Judas orders his men to "cut off Nicanor's head and arm and carry them to Jerusalem" (v. 30). Decapitation and cutting off the right hand, the sword hand, was a custom found among the Persians,[110] but dismemberment is also found among the Greeks[111] and the Romans.[112] In Jewish tradition, David had brought the head of Goliath into Jerusalem (1 Sam 17:54), Judith displayed the head of Holofernes on the walls of Bethulia (Jdt 14:1, 11), and the Philistines cut off Saul's head and fastened his body to the wall of Beth-shan (1 Sam 31:9-10). The details of the narrative here may have been influenced by heroic tales like these. Certainly the punishment is seen to fit the crime (vv. 32, 34; see 14:33, 36). While the author distinguishes those in the citadel from Judas's compatriots (v. 31), he has all the groups blessing the Lord (v. 34). The fact that Judas can hang Nicanor's head from the citadel (v. 35) suggests that it is in Judas's control. All this is effective literarily, but probably incorrect historically, since the citadel remained under the control of the enemies of the Hasmoneans (1 Macc 9:53; 10:9); although Jonathan tried to gain control of it, he could not (1 Macc 11:20, 41), and it was not until 141 BCE that Simon conquered it (1 Macc 13:49-52). According to the author of 1 Maccabees, the Jews displayed Nicanor's head and right hand just outside Jerusalem (1 Macc 7:47). It seems unlikely that the corpse of an unclean Gentile could be brought into the view of the priests around the altar; if a Gentile was not to enter the Temple, and the skins of unclean animals were forbidden in Jerusalem, how much more so would a dead Gentile render the Temple unclean?[113]

The wording of v. 36 is exceedingly similar to that of 10:8, suggesting how the book was structured. The Jewish calendar begins at Nisan (March/April), and the last month, Adar, falls in February/March. It is interesting that the author of 2 Maccabees helps to identify the feast day by reference to Mordecai's day, known from the book of Esther (Esth 3:7; 9:20-23). The feast of Mordecai is thus acknowledged as well-established for the author of 2 Maccabees. Since the author of 2 Maccabees shows knowledge of otherwise unknown events in Babylonia (8:20), he may also have known about this popular celebration.

---

110. See, e.g., Xenophon *Anabasis* 1.10.1; 3.1.17; Plutarch *Aratus* 13.2.
111. See, e.g., Plutarch *Nicias* 27-28; Cleomenes 38.
112. See, e.g., Plutarch *Cicero* 48-49.

113. There is a debate among scholars as to whether some later rabbinic texts would allow a corpse into the court of women, although *Mishnah Kelim* 1.7 explicitly forbids burial within towns.

REFLECTIONS

The author himself drives home the point remorselessly that Torah obedience brings God's salvation. This last battle of the war books of 1 and 2 Maccabees brings us back, however, to reflect on how one can wage war justly. The dehumanizing treatment of Nicanor—cutting out his tongue, his right hand, leaving only the decapitated torso—recalls what the first of the seven martyrs underwent (7:4). The author revels in the maltreatment of Nicanor, but can we? Will such enjoyment not make us like our enemies? The difficult question is always, How do we resist the temptation to turn our enemy into a non-human, a monster, a tool of Satan? As we end the reading of these wars, let us take that problem with us.

2 MACCABEES 15:37-39
THE EPILOGUE

COMMENTARY

The author chooses to end his account here, even though in his narrative he seems to at least mention events that occurred after Judas's defeat of Nicanor in March 161 BCE. For example, the author seems to know of the embassy of Eupolemus to Rome after this victory (2 Macc 4:11; cf. 1 Macc 8:17), although this is not certain, as there may have been earlier contacts with Rome that prompted the letter in 2 Macc 11:34-38. It is hard to reconcile the epitomist's statement that from the defeat of Nicanor the city was in the possession of the Hebrews (v. 37). Only a year after the defeat of Nicanor, Bacchides came back to Judea and conquered it, defeating and killing Judas and reinstalling Alcimus (1 Macc 9:1-57). The absence of any reference to Bacchides' first expedition (1 Macc 7:8-20) in 2 Maccabees supports the notion that the epitomist suppressed what did not fit into his program of profiting his readers. This book is propaganda history, and it should not be judged by any other criteria. It is a tightly structured story to praise the God of the Hebrews, who defends the Temple.

The last verses recall the different images the epitomist had used in his prologue (2:29-31) and his humble posture (2:26-27). Wines in the ancient world were so strong that they were usually mixed with water.

REFLECTIONS

One wonders at the end of the book whether it has been a bit too sweet a drink. It is patently a laudatory work, a work of aggrandizement. To the victor belong the spoils, and the historian of the victor helps to perpetuate the victor's point of view. But sometimes truth is despoiled as well. Yet the author of 2 Maccabees was following the conventions of Hellenistic historiography. The author of 2 Maccabees has centered his narrative around the Jerusalem Temple, the attempts to despoil it and the heroic deeds to save it. He may have been a trifle enthusiastic, however, in describing the valorous actions of Judas and his men.

The enduring contribution of 2 Maccabees lies in its affirmation of the ability of humans to have moral autonomy, to say no to oppression even at the cost of one's life, to hold to God's covenant even in the bleakest moments. The narratives of the martyrs are paradoxical, for these most gruesome descriptions of hideous deaths bring forth life and hope. Razis' exuberant tearing out of his entrails leads into the story of Nicanor's defeat and the safety of the Temple. Judas, against more numerous foes, risks all for God's glory. In this willingness to risk all, heroism shines forth, for God backs up the gamble.

The narrative is about events in history, but it is a history wherein God is the principal operator. The covenant faithfulness of the Jews brings God's defense of the Temple; their waywardness brings God's wrath. In the brokenness of this existence, God guides the people. This message of the presence of God within the events of human history, with all its suffering and toil, is one we must listen to. We do not expect to see men on horses with golden bridles fighting to protect us, but we do know that whatever our pain and travail, God is present in this world.

THE BOOK OF WISDOM
INTRODUCTION, COMMENTARY, AND REFLECTIONS
BY
MICHAEL KOLARCIK, S.J.

THE BOOK OF WISDOM

INTRODUCTION

This book has been referred to over the centuries and still today as the book of Wisdom (from the Vulgate) or the Wisdom of Solomon (from the Septuagint). The latter title derives from the middle section of the book where the unnamed speaker is immediately recognized as Solomon—the king who preferred the wisdom of God to fame and riches. In Jewish tradition, Solomon became a model for the "true sage" in whom the best of human wisdom and the most ardent faithfulness to the ways of God were joined. Standing under the authority of this figure of Solomon, the unknown author of this work presents us with a dramatic exhortation to seek justice. It is the gift of wisdom that makes it possible to live justly and to receive friendship with God. The extraordinary deliverance of the Israelites from Egypt and the subsequent guidance through the desert testify to the strength of justice and to the wisdom of God. These three concerns—the exhortation to justice, the gift of wisdom, and the deliverance from Egypt—make up the rich tapestry of the three main sections of the Wisdom of Solomon.

The style of writing is clearly poetic with a strong emphasis on paradoxical and forceful images rather than on logical arguments. Yet the images are arranged and orchestrated in such a way as to sustain an argument for justice and faithfulness. In the first part of the book, the Hebrew poetic device of parallelism between lines is used to great effect—so much so that earlier scholars presumed the text had been written first in Hebrew and subsequently translated into Greek, as in the case of Sirach. But the use of such Greek words as those representing "immortality" (ἀθανασία *athanasia*) and "incorruptibility" (ἀφθαρσία *aphtharsia*) makes it difficult to imagine a Hebrew original. In any event, we have no references to a Hebrew text of Wisdom, and the most ancient manuscripts that relate the book of Wisdom are in Greek. Furthermore, the latter part of the book makes use of a freer prosaic style of writing that reveals the author's familiarity and ease with Greek prose.

AUTHOR, DATE, AND PLACE OF COMPOSITION

The first unambiguous reference to the book of Wisdom stems from the second century CE in the writings of Irenaeus (c. 140–202 CE). Two references are made to Wis 2:24 and 12:10: "Everyone follows the desires of his depraved heart, nurturing a wicked jealousy through which death entered the world";[1] "from generation to generation the Lord gives an opportunity to repent to all those who desire to return."[2] References become multiple in the writings of Clement of Alexandria (c. 175–230 CE), who continuously refers to the book of Wisdom and treats it as a canonical book. The book of Wisdom is cited among the list of books held to be canonical by the church in the Muratorian Canon (c. 180–190 CE). Interestingly, in the Muratorian Canon, the book of Wisdom is located among the canonical books of the New Testament.

Although Origen (c. 185–255 CE) cites the book of Wisdom among his writings and commentaries on Scripture, he shares the uncertainty of its canonical status with others. Jerome follows Origen's hesitancy and accepts as canonical the twenty-two books of the Hebrew canon (according to a certain combination of books), the number of which corresponds to the twenty-two letters of the Hebrew alphabet. The greatest impetus for the formal inclusion of the book of Wisdom in the canon of Scripture came from Augustine (354–430 CE). For Augustine, the long and venerable reading of the book of Wisdom in the liturgy by all Christians revealed its veritable canonical status.[3]

However, it was very clear to early Christian writers like Origen and Augustine that the Solomonic authorship of the book was practically impossible. Although many candidates had been proposed (from the nephew of Ben Sira to Philo of Alexandria), there was no consensus regarding the authorship of this fascinating work.

The great affinity between many phrases in the book of Wisdom and in the writings of Philo (c. 20 BCE–50 CE) has brought attention to their relationship. Although they share a common set of concerns and many phraseological affinities, there are no clear citations between them. It would be tempting to see in the book of Wisdom the result of Philo's personal attempt to write a more religious and poetic work over and above the philosophical and allegorical works for which he is famous. The greatest stumbling block to identifying Philo as the author of the book of Wisdom is his penchant for allegorical interpretation and its absence in Wisdom. Similarly, although Wisdom's personification of wisdom bears similarities to the Logos theology of Philo, the former does not employ platonic philosophical categories as Philo does. Still, the affinities between the two testify to the distinct likelihood that they shared a common cultural background and could not have been far apart in time.

The relationship of the book of Wisdom to Philo suggests the Roman period of Alexandria to be the likely time frame for the book's composition (30 BCE–40 CE). There are many factors to support this time frame and the location of Alexandria in Egypt for the book's composition. The particular nuances of numerous Greek words and phrases, for example, in the book of Wisdom belong to the first century CE.[4]

The tension between the Jewish community and the Greeks in Alexandria under Roman rule explains the many concerns for justice that abound in the book of Wisdom. Moreover, the author's familiarity with Greek poetry and philosophy as well as the author's presupposition that the reader is conversant with Hellenism would suggest a cultural center with strong Jewish participation. Alexandria provides precisely such a cultural context. Under Ptolemy I (323–285), Alexandria became the capital of Egypt. With its museum and library, Alexandria soon became the leading center of Hellenistic philosophy and art. It is not surprising, then, that Alexandria became the focus for the translation of the Hebrew Bible into Greek.[5]

---

1. Irenaeus *Against Heresies* 3:4.
2. Irenaeus *Against Heresies* 7:5.
3. Augustine *Patrologia latina* 44.979-980.
4. For a discussion on the time frame for many words and phrases employed in the Wisdom of Solomon, see David Winston, *The Wisdom of Solomon*, AB 43 (New York: Doubleday, 1979) 20-25. Winston places the date for the composition of Wisdom around the reign of Caligula (37–41 CE), though it could very well have been written over a longer period of time.
5. See *The Letter of Aristeas* c. 150–100 BCE.

According to Philo, the Jewish population in Egypt reached one million,[6] and much of it lived in Alexandria. Although that number may be an exaggeration, there is no doubt that the Jewish community was a major force in the economic and cultural fabric of the city. The Jews formed their own *politeuma,* an organization with economic and educational rights. Such Jewish literary figures as Aristobulos (180–145 BCE) and Philo show how far the Jewish community had integrated many aspects of Hellenism into its own tradition. Whether they gained access to the gymnasium or established their own educational centers parallel to those of the Greeks is difficult to establish. What is certain is that their leading figures were thoroughly conversant with Hellenism.

The tension that the author of the book of Wisdom highlights between justice and injustice, between the Egyptians and the righteous, also mirrors the tension between the Jewish community and other inhabitants of Alexandria. Although Alexandrian Jews had been granted certain rights by Emperor Augustus in continuity with the policies of the Ptolemies, the poll tax that was introduced in 24 BCE threw the status of the Jewish community into question. The criteria for applying the tax made a distinction among Greek citizens, who were exempt; Hellenes, who paid a lower tax; and the Egyptian natives, who paid the tax in full. The Jews of Alexandria sought to establish Greek citizenship, and the Greeks vehemently barred them from doing so.

The tension reached tragic proportions in 38 CE when the Jews were attacked in a pogrom-like manner. Synagogues were destroyed or desecrated with portraits of Caligula bearing divine titles. The following year, Philo himself led the Jewish delegation to Emperor Caligula to argue for the rights that had originally been granted them by Augustus. But no positive results were forthcoming. With the assassination of Caligula in 41 CE, the Jews revolted in Alexandria. This led the new emperor, Claudius, to settle the dispute once and for all with his forceful letter to the Alexandrians in 41 CE. The letter of Claudius essentially maintained the status quo. Greeks were reprimanded for their hostility toward the Jewish community, but the Jews were told to be satisfied with their position and not to strive for Greek citizenship. In effect, even though the letter brought a certain peace to Alexandria, it was a bitter blow to the Jewish community. Without access to the gymnasium, the Jews had no access to Alexandrian citizenship. This restriction paved the way for future strife and rebellion, which would eventually see the annihilation of the Jewish community in Alexandria during Trajan's suppression of the Jewish revolt in 115–117 CE.[7]

This combination of a thorough familiarity with and respect for the best in Hellenism that the Jewish community manifested, as well as the tension between the Greeks and the Jewish community, makes Alexandria the likely site for the composition of the book of Wisdom. The argument that Wisdom could not have been written in Alexandria if Philo does not mention it or quote it is quite weak if, in fact, Philo and the writer of Wisdom were contemporaries.

The question as to whether the New Testament writers were familiar with the book of Wisdom is difficult to resolve. There are, however, special affinities between Paul and John and the book of Wisdom. But the common phraseology and ideas are general enough to suggest that they arise from common concerns and values rather than from literary dependency.

INFLUENCES

The two major influences on the author's thought and arguments in the book of Wisdom are Hellenism and the Hebrew Bible itself. Throughout the argumentation and imaginative language employed in the work, the author essentially retains a Hebrew mentality while conversing in language familiar to various strains within Hellenism. The author has not gone as far as Philo did in applying philosophical categories from Middle Platonism to the interpretation of the biblical stories. Yet, as in the case of Philo, Middle Platonism provided distinctions and concepts that the Wisdom author employed.

---

6. Philo *Flaccus* 43.
7. For a thorough treatment of the ambiguous status of the Jews in Alexandria during the Roman period, see Martin Hengel, *Judaism and Hellenism*, trans. J. Bowden (Philadelphia: Fortress, 1974).

Hellenism is, of course, a wide cultural umbrella that covers diverse philosophical systems and cultural values. With Platonism we can see points of contact all through the author's argumentation: the respect for beauty, the advantage of virtue, the superiority of the soul, the relationship between body and soul, the ethical perspective on justice and injustice. A certain contact may exist between Epicureanism and the author's presentation of the wicked person's project in life (Wisdom 2). In this case, the author was making reference to a popular ethical stance of pleasure that the disciples of Epicurus postulated. The author seems to have borrowed a number of terms and phrases from Stoic philosophers without using them in the precise manner of the Stoics. The Stoic concern to convey a coherent presentation of reality that is permanent and in flux is reflected in the interpretation of the plagues. The Neo-Pythagoreans especially flourished in Alexandria in the Roman period and, with their insistence on heavenly immortality, offered a counterbalance to the Stoics. Other motifs that are close to the Pythagoreans find an echo in the imagery of the book of Wisdom: the order of numbers (Wis 11:20*b*), the metaphor of music for order and harmony in the universe (Wis 19:18), the seriousness of perjury (Wis 14:28-31).

However, the prime source for the author of Wisdom is Scripture itself. Throughout every section of the book of Wisdom, the author makes reference to authoritative images, concepts, and stories from the Torah, the Prophets, and the Writings.

In the first section, Wis 1:1–6:21, the images from the creation and fall episodes form a veritable backdrop for the author's arguments on justice, death, and immortality (Genesis 1–3). Moreover, there is a particular concentration on successive images from Isaiah 52–58 that highlights the author's arguments against injustice and in favor of justice (the suffering servant, the sterile woman, the eunuch, the just, divine judgment).

In the second section, Wis 6:22–11:1, the author builds on the personification of wisdom exemplified in Proverbs 8 and Sirach 24. The prayer for wisdom that the figure of Solomon articulates in Wisdom 9 is formulated through the author's adaptation of Solomon's night vision in 1 Kings 3 and 2 Chronicles 1. Finally, Wisdom 10 is a eulogy of salvation history that recounts wisdom's role in saving and guiding humanity from the time of creation right up to the events of the exodus from Egypt.

The third and largest section, Wis 11:2–19:22, has been termed a "midrash" on the events of the exodus from Egypt and the journeying in the desert. The books of Exodus and Numbers provide the backdrop for the author's extended treatment of the liberation of the Israelites from Egypt. There are two large digressions on God's power and mercy and on the critique of false worship. In the course of these digressions, the author makes continuous reference to the prophets. Although the image of the covenant itself does not command a central focus in the book, such related features to the covenant as election, God's faithfulness, and the responsibility of humans to decide and act constantly emerge throughout all sections of the book.

UNITY

One feature that may be striking, at first, from a surface reading of the book of Wisdom is the great divergence of imagery and style among its three large sections. The first section displays a dramatic struggle between injustice and virtue, against which the images of life and death constantly emerge. It is a forceful exhortation to justice, as if the issue of justice is a matter of life and death for the author and the reader alike. The second section moves almost indiscernibly to a contemplative tranquility. Here the author offers eloquent praise to the wisdom that comes from God and that guides humans effortlessly in their journeys. In the third section, the positive role of wisdom appears to recede into the background, and it is God who intervenes directly in the affairs of the wicked and the righteous during the exodus events. The conflict between the wicked and the just, which we found already in the first part of the book, is exemplified again in the exodus narrative.

All of these differences between the major sections of the book of Wisdom have led scholars to postulate divergent authors for the respective sections. However, studies on the unity of the language have essentially dispelled the theories of diverse authorship, even though different styles of writing were employed. At most, the author may have written these sections over a longer period of time. The surface dissimilarities among the three sections are matched by their deep unity of imagery and purpose.

One particular image that is used throughout all three sections of the book is the positive role of the cosmos. In the first section, the positive function of the forces of creation is set in relief against the backdrop of the struggle between justice and injustice. It is the cosmos itself that God arms to wage a battle against injustice. In the second section, wisdom's role to save humanity is assured through wisdom's presence at the creation of the world and humanity. Wisdom and the cosmos are intertwined in order to bring life and prosperity to the just and the wise. In the third section, the author emphasizes the role of the forces of creation in bringing justice to the wicked and sustenance to the righteous.

In terms of the unity of purpose, each section focuses on a particular concern within the author's overarching argument. The author is attempting to bolster the faith of the Jewish community under attack by powerful forces (such as those present in the Alexandrian community during Roman rule). The first section is an exhortation to justice that attempts to strip away the facade of the power of injustice and unfaithfulness. It would have been attractive to many Jews to give up their tradition in favor of Greek citizenship. The author counters such deprecation of the Jewish tradition by unmasking the powerlessness of injustice in the face of virtuous justice. Essentially, it is a dissuasion from injustice and death. The second section is more of a persuasion to the faith through the beauty and power of wisdom and virtue. Finally, the last part of the second section (chap. 10) and the midrashic treatment of the exodus events (chaps. 11–19) give historical support to the author's message. The wisdom of God has continuously accompanied humanity to bring the righteous to prosperity and well-being even through trials and tribulation (chap. 10). God has intervened with the forces of the cosmos itself to bring the wicked to justice and to sustain the righteous (chaps. 11–19).

GENRE

The book of Wisdom in its entirety does not fit into any particular genre. The work is the result of a creative and imaginative writer who has produced a rather unique piece of literature. Two forms of discourse that stem from Aristotelian rhetoric have been proposed: *Protreptic* discourse, which is governed by exhortation and persuasion, and the *Epideictic* discourse of the *Encomium,* which praises a figure and entertains throughout a sustained argument.[8] Both genres, however, include exhortation and praise. The question is, Which is at the service of the other? Since we are lacking extant sources and examples of these forms of literature from the time of the book of Wisdom, it is not an issue that can be easily decided. David Winston has summarized well the situation regarding the genre: "It is thus extremely difficult to determine whether Wisdom is an epideictic composition with an admixture of protreptic, or essentially a protreptic with a considerable element of epideictic."[9]

The author makes use of several forms of writing throughout the work. There is the *diatribe,* especially noticeable in the first part, where the author sets up speakers in order to critique their arguments. There are *literary diptychs,* which make use of the comparing and contrasting features of *synkrisis.* These are especially noticeable in the first part of the book, where the lives of the just are contrasted with the lives of the wicked, and in the later part of the book, where the Egyptians are contrasted with the Israelites. The second part of the work makes use of the *eulogy* in order to sustain the contemplation of the beauty and attractiveness of wisdom. Finally, though it is difficult to call the style of writing known as a *midrash* a genre because of its loose structure, it is clear that the author makes use of this general style of interpretation when treating biblical texts. In the first part of the book, the author employs a series of images from Isaiah

---

8. Aristotle *The Art of Rhetoric* III.xiv. 10-xv.9.
9. D. Winston, book review, *CBQ* 48 (1986) 527.

in a manner that has been called midrashic or homiletic.[10] In commenting on the events of the exodus in the last part of the book, the author is clearly following the events as recounted in Exodus and Numbers and attempting to give them a specific interpretation from a unique point of view. This is typical of midrashic writing. All of these styles of writing have been combined by a skilled writer who was able to make use of devices and forms according to the movement of the argument.

STRUCTURE

The book of Wisdom is a highly structured literary work. It is helpful for the interpretation of specific passages to keep in mind the overall structure of the book and the structure of individual sections. The structures that give shape to the author's argument and arrangement of images are often dense. They help to bring images in relation to each other, both for comparison and for contrast.

There are two literary structures that the author particularly favors: the concentric structure and the parallel structure of literary diptychs. A concentric structure derives its name from the geometric image of circles sharing a common center (ABCDD´C´B´A´). By paralleling phrases, images, or types of speech at the beginning of a unit to the end, the author skillfully draws the reader's attention to comparisons, to contrasts, and to development. Often the center of such a unit contains a focus of concentration. Parallel structures draw together images or ideas in parallel fashion (ABCDA´B´C´D´). The term *literary diptych* is derived from iconography, where two images are set side by side for the purpose of complementarity or contrast. The parallel structure of literary diptychs is particularly suited for developing and emphasizing contrasts.

The opening section of the book is formulated in a rather elegant concentric structure:

A		1:1-15	exhortation to justice warning against death
	B	1:16–2:24	speech of the wicked their defense of injustice through power and might
		C 3:1–4:20	three diptychs contrast the just with the wicked the defense of injustice by the wicked is dismantled
	B´	5:1-23	speech of the wicked their confession of error
A´		6:1-21	exhortation to wisdom warning against injustice

Even within this concentric structure, the parallel diptych system is used in the central unit, where the situation of the just is contrasted with that of the wicked:

3:1-13*a*	——	the just are in the hand of God
	——	the wicked will be punished
3:13*b*–4:6	——	the just who appear fruitless will bear much fruit
	——	the wicked who appear fruitful will not benefit from their wickedness
4:7-20	——	the virtuous youth who dies is with God
	——	the aged wicked will be condemned by the youth

The second section of the book of Wisdom contains two concentric structures—7:1–8:21, Solomon's desire for wisdom; and 9:1-18, Solomon's prayer for wisdom—and a parallel structure of diptychs—10:1-21, where God's wisdom is shown to have intervened in the life of humanity in order to save the just.

---

10. J. Suggs, "Book of Wisdom II, 10-V: A Homily Based on the Fourth Servant Song," *JBL* 76 (1957) 26-33.

```
A          7:1-6        Solomon is mortal and limited
 B         7:7-12       Wisdom is superior to all goods
  C        7:13-22a     God is the guide of wisdom
                        God gives knowledge and wealth
   D       7:22b–8:1    eulogy of wisdom
                        twenty-one attributes of wisdom
  C′       8:2-9        Solomon desires to have wisdom as a bride
                        Wisdom knows all things and is a source of wealth
 B′        8:10-16      Wisdom grants success and fame
A′         8:17-21      as a child, Solomon was gifted but still needs
                        God's wisdom
```

The concentric structure of chapter 9:

```
A           9:1-3       God has formed humanity through wisdom
 B          9:4         Solomon asks for the wisdom that sits beside
                        God's throne
  C         9:5-6       Solomon is weak and limited
   D        9:7-8       yet called to be king and judge over God's people
    E       9:9         Wisdom knows what is pleasing to God
     F      9:10ab      prayer for God to send wisdom
    E′      9:10c-11    so that Solomon may learn what is pleasing to God
   D′       9:12        Solomon will judge God's people justly
  C′        9:13-17a    for human beings are weak and burdened
 B′         9:17b       unless God's wisdom and Spirit come from on high
A′          9:18        and through wisdom humanity is saved
```

Chapter 10 consists of seven brief diptychs that show how wisdom accompanied various persons from the Torah and helped them against adversaries: (1) 10:1-3, Adam/Cain; (2) 10:4, Noah/those who perished in the flood; (3) 10:5, Abraham/the nations of Babel; (4) 10:6-8, Lot/those who perished in the cities of the plain and his wife; (5) 10:6-12, Jacob/Esau and his personal enemies; (6) 10:13-14, Joseph/his brothers and Potiphar's wife; (7) 10:15-21, the Israelites and Moses/their oppressors.

The final section of the book is a rather developed series of five diptychs that relate the punishment of the plagues to a particular sin of the Egyptians. The contrast in each diptych focuses on the means of punishment against the oppressors and the means of salvation in favor of the righteous. In addition, two major digressions occur within the second diptych. The digression on false worship (chaps. 13–15) is formulated in three parts that progress from the least blameworthy to the most blameworthy: (1) 13:1-9, philosophers incur slight blame; (2) 13:10–15:13, idol worship is condemned; (3) 15:14-19, the idol and animal worship of Egypt is severely condemned.

The central section of the critique that treats idol worship specifically is organized concentrically:

```
A          13:10-19     gold, silver, stone, wooden idols—carpenter
 B         14:1-10      reflection on God's providential care
  C        14:11-31     invention and result of idolatry
                        punishment of idolatry
 B′        15:1-6       reflection on God's mercy and power
A′         15:7-13      clay idols—potter
```

Figure 1: The Five Diptychs and the Seven Antitheses in the Book of Wisdom

	Causal relationship 11:16		Antithetical relationship 11:5, 13
	Sins	Plagues	Blessings
1.	11:6-14 killing of infants	1. 11:6-14 undrinkable water	water in the desert
2.	11:15–16:14 animals adored	2. 16:1-4 animals suppress the appetite	delicious animals (quails)

1st digression 11:17–12:27 — God's power and mercy to save and to punish
2nd digression 13–15 — the origins of false worship
minor digression 16:5-14 — the brazen serpent; God has power over life and death

		3. 16:5-14 animals that kill	the saving brazen serpent
3.	16:15-29 refusal to recognize the true God	4. 16:15-29 rain, hail; creation destroys by fire; lack of food	creation saves; the manna resists burning by fire
4.	17:1–18:4 enslaving the Hebrews	5. 17:1–18:4 captivity by darkness	pillar of fire in the darkness Aaron stops the destroyer
5.	18:5–19:21 killing of infants in river	6. 18:5-25 death of the firstborn	Israel passes through the Red Sea
		7. 19:1-9 drowning in the sea	

minor digression 18:20-25 —
minor digression 19:6-12 — Creation

MAJOR CONTRIBUTIONS

Death, Immortality, Justice. The author advances significantly the formal treatment of the status of an individual human being after death. Although the problem of God's faithfulness to the just who suffer arose in such works as Job and Ecclesiastes, the unambiguous declaration of the survival of the individual is a late phenomenon (Dan 12:2-3; 2 Macc 7:9). The background for the author's unambiguous declaration of human immortality is the covenantal faithfulness of God to the just. God is faithful to the just, and no torment will destroy them; God's grace and mercy remain with the elect (3:1-9).

Although the language the author employs to convey the belief in an afterlife is Greek, a uniquely Hebraic ethical understanding is given to that language. The author sustains the idea of the survival of the just after death with such words as *immortal* (Wis 1:15; 3:4; 4:1; 8:17; 15:3) and *incorruptible* (2:23; 6:18-19). But an ethical perspective is brought in to condition this notion of immortality. The author is not positing an inherent immortality that all humans possess. Rather, immortality depends on the inner life of virtue. Immortality is the divine life toward which all human beings have been destined from the dawn of creation (Wis 2:23). But the decisions and actions of human beings that affect others determine the quality of final life.

A life of justice and virtue leads to immortality (Wis 3:4; 6:17-20). A life of injustice and wickedness leads to death (Wis 1:16; 2:24; 5:17-23). Death here is understood not simply as the experience of mortality, which the just experience as well, but as divine judgment. Similarly, the immortal life of the just is not presented as an inherent quality, but as the result of a positive divine judgment over one's decisions and actions (Wis 5:15-16). Although the author's presentation of the immortality of the just could be reconciled with the notion of a bodily resurrection, nowhere is a bodily resurrection formally posited in the book of Wisdom.

Even the notion of justice, which figures so dominantly throughout the book, retains its Hebraic nuances rather than the Greek qualities of balance and equality that are associated with justice. The two perspectives are not incompatible, but for the author of the book of Wisdom justice involves the support and respect for the weak. Solomon asks for wisdom to be able to judge

God's people justly (Wis 9:12). Injustice is identified as oppressing and exploiting the weak and defenseless. The wicked employ their power to oppress the widow, the aged, the poor, and the just (Wis 2:12-20).

Personification of Wisdom. In focusing on the wisdom of God through personification, the author picks up the sapiential traditions from Proverbs 8 and Sirach 24. However, what is unique to the author of the book of Wisdom is the emphasis on the specific role of wisdom both in creation and in human affairs. The wisdom that comes from God is able to help humans because it was present at creation. As a result of this, wisdom is a bridge between humans and God. Wisdom knows God's works, knows what is pleasing to God, and brings friendship with God.

The author integrates the current Greek views of wisdom with the Hebrew sapiential tradition of the personification of wisdom. For the Greeks, wisdom is essentially a means of gaining knowledge, both cosmic and divine. For the Wisdom author, wisdom lives with God and is revealed and given to humans by God. The wisdom that comes from God is a gift that brings to completion the wisdom through which humans were formed at creation. According to the author's anthropology, human beings have been shaped and formed by the wisdom of God in such a way that they yearn to be completed by the wisdom of God, which comes only as a gift. Solomon provided the ideal figure through which the author presents this anthropology. He is presented as naturally gifted, yet as realizing the limitations of his being and yearning for the wisdom that comes from God.

It is not surprising, then, to see how the author attaches the wisdom of God to the just. Injustice is inimical both to the structures of the cosmos and to the human heart. Wisdom flees from the unjust and the wicked, but waits for the just and actively seeks them out.

The author has gone as far as possible in the personification of God's wisdom without creating a separate entity as an intermediate being between human beings and God. Wisdom is the manner in which God has created the world and fashioned the human heart. Wisdom is the manner in which God continuously intervenes in history both to save the just and to thwart the designs of injustice.

CANONICAL STATUS

The canonical status of the book of Wisdom differs among the Christian communities. Discussion regarding the book's status hinged essentially on the acceptance or rejection of the wider canon of the LXX, the Greek version of the Old Testament. The doubt regarding its acceptance can be traced to the strong voice of Jerome (345–419 CE), who preferred the smaller canon of the Hebrew Scriptures. The authoritative voice of Augustine provided the greatest impetus for acceptance. In the ambit of the Latin Church, the Council of Carthage (397 CE) and the letter of Innocent I to the Bishop of Toulouse (405 CE) follow the list of canonical books presented by Augustine.[11]

The acceptance of the wider canon was settled definitively in the Roman Church at the Council of Trent (1546 CE). The Orthodox Church accepted the Roman canons of Scripture at the Council of Jerusalem in 1672. But since the eighteenth century a renewed discussion has emerged among the Orthodox communities regarding the inspiration of the deuterocanonical books. The Protestant and Reformed traditions follow the lead of Martin Luther, who was inspired by Jerome's preference for the smaller canon. However, even Martin Luther accepted the deuterocanonical/apocryphal books as inspirational reading while withholding their canonical status. So it is not surprising to note that one of Wisdom's best modern commentaries stems from the pen of a Protestant scholar.[12] Since there is little doubt as to the Jewish origin of the work, Jewish scholars also study Wisdom as a source for understanding the currents of Jewish thought during the Hellenistic period.[13]

---

11. Augustine, *De Doctrina Christiana* 2,8; *PL* 34,40.
12. C. L. W. Grimm, *Das Buch der Weisheit* (Leipzig: Hirzel, 1837).
13. Y. Amir, "The Figure of Death in 'The Book of Wisdom,'" *JJS* 30 (1979) 154-78.

BIBLIOGRAPHY

Kolarcik, Michael. *The Ambiguity of Death in the Book of Wisdom (1–6)*. AnBib 127. Rome: Pontifical Biblical Institute, 1991. Explores the various levels of meaning that the image of death presents to the reader in the first part of the book of Wisdom.

Larcher, C. *Le Livre de la Sagesse ou La Sagesse de Salomon*. Vols. 1-3. Études Biblique, nouvelle série. 1, 3, 5. Paris: Gabalda, 1983–85. The most extensive treatment by a single author on the book of Wisdom stems from a French exegete. The three-volume commentary was preceded by a collection of studies by the author on the cultural backdrop for the book of Wisdom (*Études sur le Livre de la Sagesse*. Études Bibliques. Paris: Gabalda, 1969).

Nickelsburg, George W. E. *Resurrection, Immortality and Eternal Life in Intertestamental Judaism*. HTS 26. Cambridge, Mass.: Harvard University Press, 1972. This work sets the context for the Wisdom author's views of immortality in the larger picture of Judaism. Of particular interest for the book of Wisdom is chapter 2, "Religious Persecution: The Story of the Persecution and Exaltation of the Righteous Man," 48-92.

Reese, James M. *Hellenistic Influence on the Book of Wisdom and Its Consequences*. AnBib 41. Rome: Pontifical Biblical Institute, 1970. The precise influence of Hellenism on the author of Wisdom is difficult to determine. Reese explains that though the Wisdom author employs language and images from Hellenistic culture, the mentality of the author remains Hebraic.

Taylor, Richard J. "The Eschatological Meaning of Life and Death in the Book of Wisdom I-V," *ETL* 42 (1966) 72-137. Examines the notion of the afterlife that can be discerned in the first five chapters of the book of Wisdom.

Vílchez, Jose. *Sabiduría*. Sapienciales V. Nueva Biblia Española. Estella: Editorial Verbo Divino, 1990. Complete commentary on the book of Wisdom that combines textual analysis with an examination of sources and with theological interpretation. The extensive introduction and appendixes treat the cultural milieu of Judaism in the diaspora. Vílchez's work has been of great help in the writing of this commentary.

Winston, David. *The Wisdom of Solomon*. AB 43. New York: Doubleday, 1979. Provides an excellent introduction with an overview of the main themes in Wisdom; includes a thorough treatment of the difficulties of translating obscure words and phrases. One of its greatest uses lies in the many references to other parts of Scripture, to Hellenistic philosophy and literature, and to rabbinic sources.

Wright, Addison G. "Wisdom." *NJBC*. Englewood Cliffs, N.J.: Prentice Hall, 1990. Synthesizes various insights into the structure of the book of Wisdom that Wright has presented in other articles.

OUTLINE OF WISDOM

I. Wisdom 1:1–6:21, Exhortation to Justice

    A. 1:1-15, Love Righteousness
    B. 1:16–2:24, The Reasoning of the Unjust
    C. 3:1–4:20, In Defense of Virtue and Justice
        3:1-13*a*, The Just Are in the Hand of God
        3:13*b*–4:6, The Moral Strength of the Virtuous
        4:7-20, The Death of a Virtuous Youth
    D. 5:1-23, The Final Judgment
    E. 6:1-21, Exhortation to Wisdom

II. Wisdom 6:22–10:21, In Praise of Wisdom

    A. 6:22–8:21, Solomon's Desire for Wisdom
        6:22–7:12, The Sage Seeks Wisdom
        7:13–8:1, The Nature and Qualities of Wisdom
        8:2-21, Solomon's Love for Wisdom
    B. 9:1-18, Solomon's Prayer for Wisdom
    C. 10:1-21, Wisdom Accompanies the Righteous

III. Wisdom 11:1–19:22, The Justice of God Revealed in the Exodus

    A. 11:1-5, The Wilderness
    B. 11:6-14, The Nile Defiled with Blood—Abundant Waters
    C. 11:15–16:14, Animals Punish Egypt, and Quails Are Fed to the Righteous
        11:15–12:27, The Moderation of God
        13:1–15:19, Critique of Pagan Cults
            13:1-9, Nature Worship
            13:10–15:13, Origin and Consequences of Idolatry
                13:10-19, The Carpenter and Idols
                14:1-10, The Navigator and Idols
                14:11-31, Origins and Evils of Idolatry
                15:1-6, Reflection on God's Mercy and Power
                15:7-13, The Potter and Clay Idols
            15:14-19, Idolatry and Animal Worship in Egypt
            16:1-14, The Plague of Animals and Delicacies for the Righteous
    D. 16:15-29, The Plague of Storms and Manna from Heaven
    E. 17:1–18:4, Plague of Darkness and a Pillar of Fire
    F. 18:5–19:12, Death of the Enemies and Israel's Deliverance
    G. 19:13-22, Final Reflections

WISDOM 1:1–6:21

EXHORTATION TO JUSTICE

OVERVIEW

The opening chapters of the book of Wisdom appeal to the mind and the heart. We are presented with a spectacle of human life filled with tragedy and great hope. The author, speaking like a sage, invites the reader to look behind the scenes and below the surface of appearances to appreciate fundamental truths. The agonizing mystery we confront in the dramatic presentation of a condensed slice of human life is the struggle between justice and injustice. How do we interpret the reality of injustice in life? Why should we value integrity and authenticity in the face of the apparent power of injustice? The author offers us a dramatic scene to lend us eyes that perceive beyond the surface and behind appearances. By weaving a concise nexus between the practice of injustice and the consequence of death, the argumentation exhorts the reader to reject injustice and embrace virtue. What is at stake is nothing less than life and death. Arguments of thought unfold to engage the heart to choose justice and life. The section opens with an exhortation to love justice (1:1), and it closes with a parallel exhortation to learn wisdom (6:9-11). But what transpires throughout the body of the exhortation is a dynamic argument that attempts to uncover the insidious source of injustice as well as the transforming power of virtue.

Although the exhortation at the outset points to a positive value—namely, that of loving justice—it quickly turns to a warning against bringing on death (1:12). Death is presented as a fundamental obstacle to the practice of justice. This death implies a nihilistic judgment on human dignity viewed from the side of mortality, human weakness, and suffering that reduces ethical perspectives to those of evasive pleasure, arrogant power, and brutal violence (2:6-20). By uncovering the false reasoning implied in the nihilistic judgment on human dignity, the argument attempts to liberate the reader from the fear of death to the love of justice and wisdom.

A major innovation in the argument of this work is the unambiguous declaration of a life after death (3:1; 4:10, 16). Although the declaration is unambiguous, the precise when, where, and how are left open and undefined. This eternal life is not simply a state of being but a relationship with the divine. It is the result of God's faithfulness to those who have been faithful (3:9). Humans were created for incorruption (2:23). The practice of injustice destroys a person's relationship with God and even with the cosmos. The practice of virtue, despite appearances to the contrary, issues in an indissoluble relationship with God and with the cosmos.[14] Immortality is the positive motive for dissuading the reader from a life of injustice.

Death is the prime negative motive for loving justice and seeking God. In these opening chapters, the image of death retains the contours of its threatening ambiguity in life. Death may signify an end, but it may also signify a new beginning. There is the death of mortality in general, which for the wicked renders life meaningless (2:1-5); for the righteous, mortality is a stepping-stone to divine life (3:2-6). There is the death that is experienced as the consequence of unjust actions (5:9-14). Finally, there is a death that is ultimate, a final judgment of God and the cosmos against injustice (5:20-23).

Both eternal life and ultimate death are viewed from the perspective of ethical decisions. The author is not so much concerned with states of being inherent in nature as with decisions that lead to just or unjust actions

---

14. See Richard J. Taylor, "The Eschatological Meaning of Life and Death in the Book of Wisdom I–V," *ETL* 42 (1966) 72-137; J. J. Collins, "The Root of Immortality: Death in the Context of Jewish Wisdom (Sir WisSol)," *HTR* 71 (1978) 177-92.

toward others, toward oneself, and toward God. In this regard, the book of Wisdom continues the great Israelite heritage of stressing the value of ethical conduct.

The first section of the book of Wisdom actually takes the shape of the procedures of a trial. First, there is an accusation against the unjust, expressed through a statement: Lawlessness leads to death (1:1-11). Second, the wicked, who represent lawlessness, put forth a defense for their lives of pleasure, power, and violence (2:1-20). The conclusion of their defense issues in a counteraccusation of the incoherence of the lives of the just. Third, the author dismantles both the wicked's defense and their counteraccusation through a deliberation and examination of the evidence. In four series of comparisons and contrasts, the author sifts through the evidence of appearances and reality (3:1–4:20). Fourth, the wicked confess to their error and guilt (5:2-14). Fifth, the verdict and sentencing are conveyed through an apocalyptic judgment in which the just receive a royal award and the unjust are hurled to oblivion (5:15-23). Finally, the concluding exhortation to rulers calls the readers to apply the judgment rendered during the metaphorical trial to their own lives (6:1-21).[15]

The stylistic device that gives formal shape to the opening section of Wisdom is that of a concentric structure (see the section on Structure in the Introduction). This is a favorite device used throughout the book of Wisdom. A concentric, or chiastic, structure has the effect of intensifying the images used during the argumentation by rendering them parallel in the reader's imagination. In this way, we more readily notice the repetitions and transformations in the flow of the statements.

15. Michael Kolarcik, *The Ambiguity of Death in the Book of Wisdom 1–6*, AnBib 127 (Rome: 1991) 111-12.

WISDOM 1:1-15, LOVE RIGHTEOUSNESS

COMMENTARY

This opening exhortation places before the imagination of the reader the lofty value of righteousness. The conclusion to the exhortation buttresses the importance for humans of embracing this value through the bold assertion that righteousness is immortal (v. 15).[16] "Righteousness" (δικαιοσύνη *dikaiosynē*) is a word that aptly describes an aspect of Israelite heritage that highly values ethical conduct. In the Torah and the Prophets, righteousness engulfed an ethical perspective regarding all facets of life: relationships to God, to oneself, and to others. The nuances of this word are colored by the subject, whether God or Israel, and by the specific relationship to which it refers.[17] It is a value that demands or presumes a conscious choice and a course of action. When God is righteous, human beings are saved through the deliberate actions of God. When humans are said to be righteous, they have made decisions for justice (Abram, Gen 15:6) or carried out righteous conduct as in response to the law (Deut 16:19-20). More than a mere concept, righteousness denotes an entire program of conduct in life that demands commitment and clarity of vision.

The idea of immortality that is introduced at the conclusion of this exhortation is a key concept for the Wisdom author. This is the only occurrence of the adjective "immortal" (ἀθάνατος *athanatos*) in the entire book. The noun "immortality" (ἀθανασία *athanasia*) is employed on several occasions (3:4 in relation to hope; 4:1 in relation to the memory of virtue; 8:13 in relation to remembrance; 8:17 in relation to wisdom; 15:3 in relation to righteousness). It does not refer to an independent quality of being as much as to an aspect of the enduring relationship between the just and the realm of the divine achieved through virtue. This idea of immortality achieved in relation to God through virtue will constitute the author's

16. The Vg added a contrasting colon to 1:15: Righteousness is immortal; injustice is the acquisition of death.
17. For an excellent treatment of the various senses of "righteousness" in the OT, see J. J. Scullion, "Righteousness, Old Testament," *Anchor Bible Dictionary*, 6 vols. (New York: Doubleday, 1992) 5:724-36.

main argument for dismantling the reasoning of the unjust.[18]

The exhortation itself is reminiscent of the call of personified wisdom in Proverbs who goes about the streets exhorting people to learn (Proverbs 8). All the words of her mouth are said to be righteous; they will help humans find life. In Proverbs the exhortation is directed to all who are willing to hear. With a similar universalistic aim, the Wisdom exhortation is directed to the rulers of the earth.

Opening exhortations on the value of ethical conduct are typical of sapiential writings. A Hebrew wisdom writing from the Cairo Geniza (probably written during the Middle Ages) begins its proverbial type of teaching with an exhortation similar to the Wisdom text: "Seek wisdom and the right path so that you will be great in the eyes of God and people. All those who remove foolishness and haughtiness from their lives will become wise and strong."[19]

The addressees are referred to as "the rulers of the earth." This title is parallel to that in the closing exhortation, where the addressees are called "kings" and "judges of the ends of the earth," those who "rule over multitudes and boast of many nations" (6:1-2 NRSV). Although it is possible to see in these titles an allusion to Roman or at least to foreign powers, we should not overlook the function of the royal image to denote humanity. Humans are human precisely in their ability to reign over their thoughts and actions. This royal image is not lacking in the Genesis account of creation, in which God generously gives to humanity the command to fill the earth and the task to have dominion and care over the animals (Gen 1:26, 28). The royal image will extend to the reward of the just when they receive the royal gifts of a "glorious crown" and a "beautiful diadem" (5:16 NRSV). In the second major section of the book of Wisdom, we will soon identify the unnamed speaker as the wise Solomon, pre-eminent in judgment. The reader is being addressed as one who reigns over thoughts and actions, words and deeds. The reader, then, is ultimately one who bears kingly responsibility for both just and unjust actions.

Although the exhortation begins and ends on the positive note of the value of righteousness, sets of opposites dominate the body of the exhortation. There is resistance to righteousness. On one side are righteousness, the Lord, God, wisdom, a holy and disciplined spirit, a kindly spirit, the Spirit of the Lord (vv. 1-7). On the other side are perverse thoughts, a deceitful soul, foolish thoughts, unrighteousness, blasphemers, and death (vv. 3-13). These sets of opposites raise the stakes in the exhortation. They are antagonistic to one another. To love righteousness and to seek the Lord with sincerity imply the burden of overcoming resistance to justice.

In setting up these series of opposites, the Wisdom author is delving into the cherished sapiential doctrine of the two ways (Psalm 1). The way of wisdom and virtue leads to life; the way of foolishness and injustice leads to death. And there is opposition between the two ways. The sets of opposites exclude each other. Both correct and wrong thinking have serious repercussions on one's social life. People with perverse thoughts are separated from God. Wisdom will not enter a deceitful soul. A disciplined spirit flees from deceit and is ashamed at the very approach of unrighteousness (1:2-5). The opposition that is being described between these two ways of justice and injustice sets the scene for a more dramatic confrontation.

Other sapiential biblical works, such as Job and Ecclesiastes, highlight the incongruity between the doctrine of the two ways and life experiences in which the wicked thrive and the just perish. This was an observation as disturbing in ancient times as it remains today. The book of Wisdom confronts this particular incongruity through the lenses of appearance and reality. What appears to be the case in fact is not. What appears not to be the case in fact is. The focus of the author's argument is to look beyond appearances to the heart of the matter.

The anticipation of a confrontation between justice and injustice is heightened as the arena for the sets of opposites subtly shifts to that of a trial. Opposition is now expressed in images

---

18. For a review of the development of the belief in immortality in the intertestamental period, see G. W. E. Nickelsburg, *Resurrection, Immortality and Eternal Life in Intertestamental Judaism*, HTS 26 (Cambridge, Mass.: Harvard University Press, 1972). Nickelsburg treats Wisdom 2 and 5 specifically among other apocalyptic works.

19. *The Wisdom Writing from the Cairo Geniza* 1:1, in Klaus Berger, *Die Weisheitsschrift aus der Kairoer Geniza* (Tübingen: Francke Verlag, 1989).

borrowed from juridical terminology (1:6-11). The kindly spirit will not free blasphemers from the guilt of their words (v. 6). God is a witness, a true observer. Justice will punish. An inquiry or report will be made. The unjust will be convicted of their lawless deeds. Much of the emphasis in these allusions to forensic procedures focuses on the eventual revelation of what is done in secret. Because God pervades the cosmos as a witness and an observer, nothing will remain hidden (cf. Mark 4:22; Luke 8:17: "For there is nothing hidden, except to be disclosed; nor is anything secret, except to come to light" [NRSV]). This metaphor of the trial is strengthened through images relating to the power of speech: "words," "jealous ear," "sound of grumbling," "tongue," "slander," "lying mouth."

Speech is considered a powerful force. Therefore, to speak untruth is understood to have serious consequences for the speaker. There is a consistency between thought and action that is taken for granted and presumed. Bad thinking leads to destructive actions. The ominous warning against "useless grumbling" and against a "lying mouth which destroys the soul" (v. 11) prepares the reader to view critically the speech of the wicked, which will follow the opening exhortation.

What is at stake in loving justice is nothing short of avoiding death (vv. 12-15). What had begun as a positive exhortation is now being transformed into a warning against bringing on death. To find life through justice demands the explicit rejection of all that leads to death. From now on, death and its parallel side, injustice, are seen as prime obstacles to the practice of justice and to the life that ensues.

A rather daring statement is made that radically separates God from death: "God did not make death" (v. 13). On the one hand, the fact that God is said not to "delight in the death of the living" (v. 13) is consistent with the parallel phrases in Ezekiel, "I have no pleasure in the death of the wicked, but that the wicked turn from their ways and live" (Ezek 33:11 NRSV; cf. Ezek 18:23). On the other hand, traditionally, God is understood to be the author of both life and death, the one who makes alive and kills (Deut 32:39; Sir 11:14). The question then arises as to which death is radically opposed to God. Is it mortality in general that God did not make? Is it death as punishment for injustice? Is it the ultimate death that signifies an ultimate separation?

In the opening of the next unit, a direct parallel is made between death and the wicked (v. 16). The ungodly are said to summon death, "they consider him a friend," they "made a covenant with him," "they are fit to belong to his company." This parallel would suggest that the death God did not make is not the death of mortality, which applies to the righteous and to all the living; rather, it is the death of an ultimate judgment that signifies a broken relationship with both God and the cosmos.

Creation itself is being drawn into close parallel with God. God is said to have created all things for good. This close parallel between God and the cosmos prepares the reader for the positive role the cosmos will play in helping the cause of the just in the rest of the book. At the same time, the realm of death is being separated from the realm of creation and the cosmos. All that exists is described as wholesome. There is no destructive poison in creation, and the power of Hades does not reside on earth (v. 14). The death that the author dissuades the reader from bringing on through injustice is not some destructive power that resides somewhat magically in the forces of the cosmos. Rather, the power to bring on such a death resides in the free decision of human beings.

The author may very well be criticizing some contemporary positions among the Hellenists or the native Egyptians that viewed the world in a dualism of forces of good and evil. Such a critique is pointedly aimed at placing the responsibility of injustice squarely on people who make decisions and not on some controlling or deterministic cosmic power.

The contrast to this death brought about through injustice is the immortality of righteousness (vv. 12-15). Individuals who are free to choose and to reject bear the responsibility for receiving the gift of immortality or for bringing on death. This personal responsibility makes the exhortation to justice so urgent and the need to uncover the masks of injustice so compelling. The effect of the sets of oppositions that have been created in the exhortation is to build up an expectation of resolution.

REFLECTIONS

1. A word in our own contemporary setting that conveys perhaps some of the evocative force that *righteousness* has for biblical faith is *integrity*. A person of integrity is one who adheres to given values even in the face of opposition. In one sense, integrity is tested and known only through opposition. We know whether we adhere to the values of honesty, justice, and respect for others and our world by facing the test of resistance to such values.

The opposition that the Wisdom text envisages between justice and injustice is one that permeates life. It is a part of the human situation and predicament that choices be made for the sake of justice and integrity. Failing to make such choices, human beings collapse into the structures of silence, passivity, and injustice, which ultimately lead to death. Not to speak out against injustice is to succumb to its lure. Much of the drama of human greatness and tragedy devolves on the choices human beings make.

2. It is tempting to shirk responsibility in the face of overwhelming social, environmental, and structural problems. What can one person do in the face of massive injustice? What can one person do in the face of years of environmental abuse? But the voice of one person does matter. The Wisdom text refuses to displace the responsibility for injustice onto foreign cosmic powers or onto an inherent determinism. By the "error of our lives" and by the "works of our hands" we invite death into our world (1:12). Responsibility for greatness and for tragedy ultimately resides in the concrete choices of human beings. We do need to take sides in the polarity of justice and injustice.

3. The author presents a profound basis for optimism in the human struggle against injustice. A rather unique emphasis in the book of Wisdom is placed on the "wholesomeness" of the cosmos (1:14). We have here in the forces of nature an ally in the struggle for authenticity and for maintaining integrity.

This positive view of the cosmos is evidently the author's interpretation of the Priestly account of creation: "God saw everything that he had made, and indeed, it was very good" (Gen 1:31 NRSV). The idea that the cosmos is an ally to the cause of justice is introduced in the opening exhortation, and it will recur with added force throughout the entire book. The basis for this positive outlook lies in God, the creator. Since God is the creator of all things, the existence of all things ultimately is wholesome. Injustice, though it pervades human existence, essentially remains foreign to human life. As an intruder, it dismantles what is essentially wholesome and good.

WISDOM 1:16–2:24, THE REASONING OF THE UNJUST

COMMENTARY

1:16, Introduction to the Speech of the Wicked. The author introduces the speech of the wicked with an explanation as to the way they bring ultimate death upon themselves. Through their words and deeds, which flow from unsound reasoning, the wicked beckon the stark, negative reality of death. Personalistic language is employed to highlight the personal responsibility they bear for inviting death. They summon death through their words and actions; they consider death a friend; they pine away in longing for death; they even make a covenant with death, for they belong to death's company. This last image encloses the entire unit of 1:16–2:24. In both the opening and the closing of the unit, the wicked are said to belong to the company of death (1:16d; 2:24).

The idea of making a covenant with death highlights the deliberate and responsible choice implied in achieving an alliance. This death has not sought out the wicked; rather, through their thoughts and actions they have sought out death. The phrase is reminiscent of that in Isa 28:15: "We have made a covenant with death, and with Sheol we have an agreement" (NRSV). Here Isaiah is criticizing the ruling classes during Hezekiah's reign (716–686 BCE) for placing their trust in an alliance with Egypt, famous for its respect for the dead.

The inner reflection of the wicked constitutes their defense for a project in a life of injustice. The author has the wicked speak for themselves, and this they do with an elegance and poetic flare that belie the nihilism and violence that seethe underneath.

The defense has four major parts: (1) the wicked's reflection on the ephemeral value of life that portrays their nihilistic judgment (2:1-5), (2) a despairing exhortation to pleasure (2:6-9), (3) an exhortation to power (2:10-11), and (4) an exhortation to oppose the righteous one (2:12-20).

2:1-5, The Ephemeral Value of Life. This reflection on the fleeting value of human life is portrayed in uncommonly rich, poetic imagery. It will be matched in the wicked's confession of guilt with a parallel reflection using similar imagery to depict their lack of moral virtue (5:9-14). Much of the imagery echoes the depiction of human sorrow and limitations that can be found in other sapiential works, such as Job and Ecclesiastes. The books of Psalms and Proverbs also provide parallels for the imagery used in this reflection. Still, a number of images and concepts throughout this section depicting the reasoning of the wicked can be seen to have been borrowed from Hellenistic thought.[20]

The very first line states the wicked person's negative judgment on life. It is short and sorrowful. Job, in his laments, utters similar phrases that touch upon the fragility and evanescence of life: "Are not the days of my life few?" (Job 10:20 NRSV); "A mortal, born of woman, few of days and full of trouble, comes up like a flower and withers" (Job 14:1-2 NRSV).

All the images used in this unit illustrate the irrevocability of death without the word *death* ever passing through the lips of the wicked. Instead of the usual word for "death," they use metaphors to portray what they judge to be the destroyer of human value ("end," vv. 1, 5; "Hades," v. 1; "we shall be as though we had never been," v. 2; "extinguish," "dissolve," v. 3; "pass away," "scattered," v. 4). It is as if the unspeakable reality of death cannot be named.[21]

The wicked insist upon the irreversibility of death. There is no remedy for it. No one has been known to free us from Hades. There is no return from our fate; it is sealed, and no one turns back. Just as our fate and end are judged to be insignificant and pointless, so too is our beginning. We have come into being by mere chance. In order to portray as vividly as possible the evanescence of life, the wicked compare aspects and elements of the body—such as breath, the heartbeat, reason, the soul—to smoke, mist, a spark, and air. All of these are described as vanishing or dissolving without a trace.

Again, these statements echo similar biblical descriptions of the fragility of life. Qohelet's speeches abound with such ruminations: "No one has . . . power over the day of death" (Eccl 8:8 NRSV); "in the days to come all will have been long forgotten" (Eccl 2:16 NRSV); "For who knows what is good for mortals while they live the few days of their vain life, which they pass like a shadow?" (Eccl 6:12 NRSV). The psalms, especially the laments, also share similar sentiments: "For my days pass away like smoke, and my bones burn like a furnace" (Ps 102:3 NRSV); "For the ransom of life is costly, and can never suffice that one should live on forever and never see the grave" (Ps 49:8-9 NRSV).

Several images in this unit have no biblical parallels but can be related to contemporary currents in Greek philosophical thought and

---

20. There are several excellent works that study the sources used for the speech of the wicked. See Winston, *The Wisdom of Solomon*, 113-23; Kolarcik, *The Ambiguity of Death in the Book of Wisdom (1–6)*, 114-23.

21. In v. 2:5b, "there is no return from our death," the NRSV is translating the Greek word for "end" (τελευτή *teleutē*) as "death." The word *teleutē* actually functions as the image that encloses this entire unit of 2:1-5. It stands parallel to the statement "There is no remedy when a life comes to its end" (2:1).

literature. The Wisdom author has the wicked use these images to depict their denial of an afterlife, which abrogates the context for ethical conduct. The idea of coming into being by mere chance (v. 2) was a common explanation for the origin of the cosmos and all life in late Epicurean thought and was found as well in preceding authors, such as Leucippus and Democritus.

The idea that human thought is but a spark in the beating of our heart (v. 2*d*) is a unique formulation of the Wisdom author. In the ancient world, both Greek and Hebrew, it was common to locate the reasoning processes with the heart ("there were great searchings of heart" [Judg 5:15 NRSV]). In Epicurean and Stoic thought, the association of the soul with fire was meant to express the superiority of reasoning to matter. But the Wisdom author uses the image of reason's being but a spark in the heart to show its transitoriness and perhaps even its insignificance. When the spark is extinguished, every function ceases. The body turns to ashes, and the soul dissolves like empty air.

Since much of the imagery employed in this unit has concrete parallels to other biblical sources, we can legitimately ask, Where is the difficulty or fallacy in reasoning? The author has alerted the reader at the outset that the wicked reason unsoundly. The difficulty in their logic does not rest in the assertion of the inevitability of mortality, but in the negative judgment of purposelessness that they ascribe to it.

Here is the crux of the erroneous reasoning of the wicked. They claim that we have come into the world by mere chance and afterward we will be as though we had never been. The wicked espouse a purely mechanistic concept of life. They deny any form of life beyond mortality and any form of divine intervention at death. Just as no divine being gives purpose to life at the beginning, so also there is no divine reality that awaits humans at the end. Perhaps it is for this denial of divine relevance that the wicked are introduced as the "ungodly" (ἀσεβής *asebēs*, 1:16); this designation for the wicked will continue throughout the author's rebuttal (3:10; 4:3, 16). Essentially what the wicked's rumination on life expresses, couched as it is in poetic imagery, is that human life in the face of death is void of meaning. The wicked's preoccupation with physical death issues in a judgment that portrays despair and hopelessness.

The author chooses to have the wicked speak in eloquent language for a reason. By presenting the wicked's judgment on life in expressive and poignant imagery, the author is holding up for careful scrutiny what could be construed as a tenable and convincing philosophy of life. Of course, since the wicked speak in their own defense, we would expect their positions on life to be presented in as positive a light as possible. The background image of the trial warns the reader to look below the surface, to sift through appearances to understand the heart of the matter. If the wicked's judgment on life is described in poetic language that only masks their negative judgment, in the end it will be revealed for what it is: unrelenting despair.

2:6-9, A Despairing Exhortation to Pleasure. The negative judgment on life provides the wicked with a philosophical basis for their project in life. They exhort each other to enjoy life's apparently innocent pleasures. The series of subjunctives through which they exhort one another serves as a counterpoint to the author's imperatives that inaugurate the opening exhortation to love righteousness and to seek the Lord. Poetic imagery carries over from the previous unit.

Although the exhortation of the wicked appears positive enough, it soon takes on frenetic proportions that belie the appearance of healthy pleasure. The wicked call for the enjoyment of the good things that exist, and they encourage each other to make use of creation as they did in youth. Luxurious items are the order of the day: costly wines, perfumes, and rosebuds (vv. 7-8). A crown of rosebuds is to be worn before they fade and wither. The memory of the evanescence of life in reference to the fading rosebuds carries over from the negative judgment of life. An exaggerated call to revelry betrays signs of strain and despair, almost as if the wicked need to suffocate the cries of despair with frenzied activity. Everyone should take part in revelry and leave signs of diversion everywhere (v. 9). What began as a call to innocent pleasures appears to be heading toward a sinister end.

The conclusion of the wicked's exhortation to pleasure boasts in such revelry to be their due "portion and lot in life" (v. 9c). The phrase parallels the author's critique of the speech of the wicked both at the beginning ("they belong to his *company*," 1:16d) and at the end ("those who belong to his *company*," 2:24b). In both cases, when the wicked are said to belong to death, the same Greek word for "portion" or "company" (μερίς *meris*) is employed. By making evasive pleasure that leads to a grasping for power through violence their project in life, the wicked unwittingly bring upon themselves the very realities they so despise: weakness and death.

Two main proponents have been proposed as the target of the Wisdom author's criticism in this section: Qohelet and the Epicureans. On the one hand, the exhortation to enjoy life does have certain parallels to that of Qohelet (Ecclesiastes), but they are quite minimal. Qohelet on numerous occasions calls for the enjoyment of life: "There is nothing better for mortals than to eat and drink, and find enjoyment in their toil. This also, I saw, is from the hand of God" (Eccl 2:24 NRSV; cf. Eccl 3:13; 5:18; 8:15; 9:7-9; 11:9). In each case where Qohelet exhorts the reader to enjoy life, God's presence is assured. Either pleasure is seen as God's gift or God is understood as one who sets a limit and calls excess into judgment (Eccl 11:9). Since the very presence or relevance of God is denied rather forcibly by the wicked in Wisdom, only with a strained effort could one construe the Wisdom speech as a critique of the preacher in Ecclesiastes.

On the other hand, the call to enjoy life is so diffused in the literature of the ancient world that it is difficult to pinpoint a single source for the Wisdom author. It was a favorite motto for funerary inscriptions. On a tomb inscription from the XIth Dynasty in Egypt we read, "Follow your heart as long as you live. Sprinkle perfumes on your head; clothe yourself in fine linen, anoint yourself with the most marvelous of essences" (author's trans.).

The exhortation to pleasure became closely identified with Epicurus, who gave enjoyment noble stature as the end to be sought in life. But when Epicurus postulates pleasure as the goal to strive for, he does not identify pleasure with a dissipated life, but understands pleasure to be the result of sober reasoning. Even the garden gatherings associated with followers of Epicurus were renowned for their simplicity and frugality.[22]

Other disciples of Epicurus promoted the famous "discussion-dinner party," whose attendees perhaps on occasion fell into excesses of drinking special wines and eating lavish foods. Marc Anthony and Cleopatra adopted the customs of the symposium in Alexandria. It became customary on such occasions to spice the best of wines with fragrances and for attendees to adorn themselves in flowers. Lucian criticizes the waste associated with such gatherings. His description contains resemblances to the Wisdom author's portrayal of the wicked people's exhortation to pleasure. "It is they," said he, "who buy expensive dainties and let wine flow freely at dinners in an atmosphere of saffron and perfumes, who glut themselves with roses in midwinter, loving their rarity and unseasonableness and despising what is seasonable and natural because of its cheapness, it is they who drink myrrh."[23]

It would appear that the author is culling ideas from various representatives of hedonism of his day to portray the dynamic of false reasoning. Although some of the Epicurean ideas, such as the finality of death, the denial of divine presence, and the legitimacy of pleasure, have been used to portray the hedonism of the wicked, it is not possible to single out a specific group as the target of the Wisdom author's criticism.[24] It is the reasoning process of the wicked that is being criticized rather than a philosophical group or political faction contemporaneous to the author.

2:10-11, An Exhortation to Power. A sudden and menacing turn of events has the wicked extolling the oppression of the poor, widows, and the elderly. The call for oppression finally betrays the appearance of innocent pleasures that followed from the judgment on the ephemeral value of life. The sinister reality of despair that was masked in poetic imagery is raising its head. The call to oppress the weak in society stands in clear contradiction to the law, which protects the weaker members of Israelite society.

---

22. Diogenes Laertius 10-11.
23. Lucian *Nigrinus* 31.
24. D. Winston summarizes well the various arguments for not postulating a single group as the target of the Wisdom author's criticism. See Winston, *The Wisdom of Solomon*, 114.

This combination of the poor, the widow, and the elderly to designate the weak and the helpless in society is unique in the OT. To be sure, all three groups, along with the sojourner and the orphan, were especially protected under Israelite law (for sojourners, orphans, and widows, see Deut 14:29; for the poor, see Exod 23:6; for the respect of the elderly, see Lev 19:32).

The combination of the poor and the widow occurs more often with the orphan or the sojourner to designate the weak person who stands under special protection (Job 24:3-4; 29:12-13; 31:16-18; Isa 10:2; Jer 7:6; Zech 7:10). The triad of the poor, the widow, and the orphan has the closest parallel to the Wisdom designation of the poor, the widow, and the elderly. Why the Wisdom author has replaced the more usual designation of the orphan with the aged will become clear in the ensuing argumentation. But the wicked persons' adulation of youthful strength (v. 6) anticipates this derogatory view of old age. In other biblical references, the aged are represented as being vulnerable and in need of protection in various associations with orphans, widows, and the needy (2 Chr 36:17; Jer 6:11; 2 Macc 8:30).

The wicked justify the arbitrary oppression of the weak with a double-sided principle: Power makes right; weakness is useless (v. 11). This idea of power and strength making right is as old as the stars and has found justification in many circles throughout history. The nihilistic judgment of the wicked that the value of life is ephemeral lends its support to the principle that might makes right. On the one hand, if there is no divine reality that gives purpose to human origins or human destination, then the basis for ethical conduct devolves on arbitrary power. On the other hand, if life's value is radically depressed by the limitations of space and time, then any manifestation of mortality in weakness, sickness, and death should be curtailed and held in derision. What surfaces unmistakably is that the victorious tone of the wicked only serves to mask an abysmal despair in the value of human life.

2:12-20, An Exhortation to Oppose the Righteous One. The reasoning of the wicked takes on a life of its own and focuses with a frightening consistency on the righteous, who oppose their way of life. If might makes right and what is weak is useless, then whoever opposes the wicked will be subject to the weapons of their wrath. What had begun as an exhortation to seemingly innocent pleasure (vv. 6-9) ends in calling for an unambiguous act of injustice, the brutal death of the just (vv. 17-20).

For the first time, the image of the just one comes onto the scene. In tension with the wicked and the godless, the just will occupy center stage for the rest of the first section of Wisdom. The idea of the wicked "ambushing" the just or "lying in wait" (ἐνεδρεύω *enedreuō*) for the righteous is a familiar description of the wicked in the psalms, particularly the psalms of lament. In Ps 10:8-11 the wicked are presented as a lion lying in wait for the helpless and to seize the poor (cf. Pss 17:8-12; 37:12; 59:3-4; 64:2-6).[25] The wicked are always many. The just stand alone.

The opening motive for the wicked's oppression of the just one is the opposition directed against them (v. 12). It is the just who are inconvenient in that they oppose the actions of the wicked; they reproach them for sins against the law and accuse them of sins against their training. This motif of antagonism between the just and the wicked echoes the radical separation between God and justice in the opening exhortation. It confirms the standard of the "two ways" in that the just are encouraged to separate themselves from the ways of the wicked (see Pss 1:1; 6:4-5; 38:20; 139:21-22).

The second series of motives for oppressing the just focuses on the claims of the just, which contradict the wicked's judgment on life and death (2:13-16). The just claim to have knowledge of God. They are children of God; their end will be happy; and they boast that God is their father. These claims are interpreted by the wicked with disdain as opposing their way of life. Hence, the just one is considered to be reproof of their thoughts, a burden for them simply to behold.

Two of the claims of the just that fundamentally contradict the nihilistic judgment of

---

25. Wisdom 2:12*a* is almost identical to a sentence added in the LXX version of Isaiah 3:10, "Let us kill the righteous man because he is inconvenient to us." But it is more likely that the Wisdom text influenced the Greek writing of Isaiah, rather than Isaiah's being the source for Wisdom in this instance.

the wicked are the fatherhood of God (v. 16) and the sonship of the just (vv. 13, 18). Moreover, the particular aspect of this filial and paternal relationship that the wicked question in their counteraccusation is the just's *trust* in God.

All three themes of God's fatherhood, the sonship of the just, and their trust in God have their root in the psalms of lament. The fundamental stance of the one who laments is to trust in God despite all odds: "But I trusted in your steadfast love; my heart shall rejoice in your salvation" (Ps 13:5 NRSV); "I believe I shall see the goodness of the LORD in the land of the living" (Ps 27:13 NRSV).

Just as the wicked in Wisdom accuse the just of unfounded trust in God (vv. 17-20), so also the wicked in the psalms of lament deride the just for their trust in God. "Many are saying to me, / 'There is no help for you in God'" (Ps 3:2 NRSV). "Commit your cause to the LORD; let him deliver—let him rescue the one in whom he delights!" (Ps 22:8 NRSV). "They say, 'Pursue and seize that person whom God has forsaken, for there is no one to deliver'" (Ps 71:11 NRSV).

The fatherhood of God is an image that has its sources in the devout and religious prayer of the psalms and in the messianic texts in which the king/messiah is the adopted son of God. To describe God's loving care for the weak, the psalms speak of God as a caring father: "Father of orphans and protector of widows is God in his holy habitation" (Ps 68:5 NRSV). "As a father has compassion for his children, so the LORD has compassion for those who fear him" (Ps 103:13 NRSV; cf. Deut 1:30-31; 8:5; 32:6; Isa 63:16; 64:8; Jer 3:19; Mal 1:6).

The theme of adoption that marked Israel's relationship to God in monarchic theology stresses the fatherhood of God: "He said to me, 'You are my son; / today I have begotten you'" (Ps 2:7 NRSV). "He shall cry to me, 'You are my Father, my God, and the Rock of my salvation'" (Ps 89:26 NRSV; cf. 2 Sam 7:14).

Various formulations for the phrase "son of God" (v. 18) are attested throughout Scripture with differing nuances (a holy people, Deut 14:1-2; restoration of Israel, Hos 2:10-11; vocation, Hos 11:1). Still, one particular prophetic source can be identified in the author's formulation of the opposition between the wicked and the just: the suffering servant of Isaiah, especially the fourth servant song (Isa 52:13–53:12).[26] In Wis 2:13, the wicked recall the just's claim to be children of God. The Greek word for "child" (παῖς *pais*) can also mean "servant"; in fact, the LXX translates the Hebrew word for "servant" (עבד *'ebed*) in Isaiah alternately as "child" (*pais*) and as "servant" (δοῦλος *doulos*). The term is meant to express a special relationship between the Lord and the servant. It is precisely this special relationship of the just to God that the wicked hold in derision. Just as the servant suffers a shameful death and is despised by others (Isa 53:3, 7), so also the wicked propose to inflict a shameful death on the just. A major difference between the persecution of the just in Wisdom and the servant in Isaiah is the vicarious suffering of the servant. For the obvious reason of the developed antagonism between the just and the wicked in Wisdom, the theme of the vicarious suffering of the servant in Isaiah was dropped.

The final part of the wicked's speech constitutes their counteraccusation against the just (vv. 17-20). They decide to put the just one through the trial of an ignoble death to test whether his claims are true. Of course, the test is a rhetorical one. The wicked inflict on the just the experience of mortality, which they have judged to be the destroyer of human value. Since the just stand for a way of life with ethical parameters that contradicts their project in life, the wicked inflict on others the very conditions of mortality that led them to their nihilistic judgment on life.

Taken as a whole, the speech of the wicked contains a logic that involves a progressive dynamic of evil. The negative judgment on mortality, expressed through poetic imagery, provides a basis for an amoral perspective on life. The commitment to transient, youthful pleasure simply masks the underlying despair that is dimmed or softened through the clamor of busy activity. The other side of the adulation of youthful pleasure is the despising of

---

26. The Wisdom author's use of texts from Isaiah is virtually certain. In fact, an entire series of images from Isaiah 42–56 is borrowed for the author's arguments in Wisdom 2–5. See Patrick W. Skehan, "Isaiah and the Teaching of the Book of Wisdom," *CBQ* 2 (1940) 289-99; M. J. Suggs, "Wisdom of Solomon II, 10-V: A Homily Based on the Fourth Servant Song," *JBL* 76 (1957) 26-33.

human weakness and the reliance on power. The sinister side of the nihilistic judgment on life emerges with frightening clarity, until the blatant and brutal project to kill the just reaches the climax. What had begun as a poetic rumination on mortality ends with a frightful project to inflict a shameful death on the just. The wicked's speech progresses from a nihilistic judgment on life to a project in life that embraces sensuality, that in its turn despises weakness and relies on power, and that finally, when challenged, unmasks itself as an unbridled license to brutal violence.

Since the speech of the wicked provides an explanation and defense of their way of life, it also constitutes the author's attack against a project of injustice, which brings death. The wicked are being accused of a false judgment on human life, of a pointless sensuality, of a ruthless reliance on power, and of a blatant and brutal act of violence. Their principal line of defense rests in the claim that death renders life meaningless. Therefore, the author will have to explain the shameful death of the just in order to prove effectively that the reasoning process of the wicked is false. The wicked's call for the death of the just as proof of the validity of their life of despair is the climax of their speech. In the context of the trial scene, it raises an expectation of resolution for the reader.

2:21-24, Conclusion to the Speech of the Wicked. The author reiterates the falseness of the wicked's reasoning (cf. 2:1). In both the introduction and the conclusion, the author stresses that through their injustice the wicked bring death upon themselves. The author introduces an etiology for both immortality and death to prepare for the dismantling of the false reasoning of the wicked.

However, a new basis for their false thinking is added. Their evil ways have blinded them (v. 21). Their blindness has caused the wicked to overlook three essential realities: the secret purposes of God, the wages of holiness, and the prize for blameless souls. In other words, their wickedness has brought about a blindness to a fundamental truth. This metaphor of blindness prepares the reader for the author's rebuttal, which will depend heavily on sifting through appearances and reality.

The fundamental reality the wicked overlook is the destiny for which God created human beings: incorruption (v. 23). This declaration contradicts the wicked's claim that human beings have come to exist arbitrarily and that after death it will be as though they had never been. To sustain the bold claim for immortality, the author appeals to the powerful "image of God" in the Genesis narrative (Gen 1:26-27; 5:1). God has created human beings for immortality because we are made in the image of God's identity or eternity (v. 23b).[27]

If the origin of human immortality is based on the image of God, then where does death originate? The author has already declared that God did not make death (1:13). Human beings bring on death through their own words and actions. Since the human destiny of immortality is rooted in creation itself, the author appeals to the Genesis narrative to give an etiology for death as well. Through the envy of the adversary, death has entered the cosmos (2:24).[28] The adversary,[29] like the serpent in Genesis 3 or the satan in Job, is opposed to the liberal act of God's generosity to human beings. It is the adversary who occasions the human option for wickedness, and those who belong to the adversary experience death (2:24b).

The author presents a nuanced idea of immortality. Human beings are not created immortal; they are created *for* immortality. In other words, human beings, who are created in the image of God, form or shape the original image into God's identity of immortality through their ethical conduct. With a

---

27. With a change of a single letter, different versions offer a word that means either God's "identity" (ἰδιότης *idiotēs*) or God's "eternity" (ἀιδιότης *aidiotēs*). The idea of eternity draws out more explicitly the author's claim that life does not end with physical death. For an excellent review of the import of the image of God in the history of interpretation, see Gunnlaugur A. Jonsson, *The Image of God: Gen 1:26-28 in a Century of Old Testament Research*, ConBOT 26 (Stockholm: Almqvist & Wiksell International, 1988).

28. Several legends that recount the creation and fall narratives in haggadic fashion actually ascribe envy to the devil (*Enoch, Apocalypse of Moses, Life of Adam and Eve*): "And the devil sighed and said, 'O Adam, all my enmity and envy and sorrow concern you, since because of you I am expelled and deprived of my glory which I had in the heavens in the midst of angels, and because of you I was cast out onto the earth'" (*Life of Adam and Eve*, 12:1). It is probable that the Wisdom author was familiar with one or more of these stories. Paul used a similar phrase in which death is replaced by sin: "Therefore, just as sin came into the world through one man, and death came through sin, and so death spread to all because all have sinned" (Rom 5:12 NRSV).

29. The original meaning of the Greek word διάβολος (*diabolos*), from which the English word *devil* derives, is "accuser" or "slanderer." This is the usual manner in which the LXX translates the Hebrew word for "the satan," "the adversary" (השטן *haśśāṭān*; Job 1:6; 2:1).

life of injustice, the initial figure of God can be deformed into death, which God did not create. The death that is presumed here signifies a total separation from God and the cosmos, not the experience of mortality that all human beings, even the virtuous, experience.

Sirach relates the image of God to human mortality in a similar fashion to that of Wisdom. It does not, however, draw out the ethical implications for life and death: "The Lord created human beings out of earth, and makes them return to it again . . . He endowed them with strength like his own, and made them in his own image" (Sir 17:1-3 NRSV).

In terms of the trial image that has been subtly working in the background, the speech of the wicked constitutes the defense of their purpose in life, which in its turn ends in the counteraccusation of the incoherence of the just's purpose in life. For the wicked, the rhetorical test of death is proof enough of the validity of their entire reasoning process. To disprove the false reasoning of the wicked, the author must resolve the issue of the tragic death of the righteous.

If the death of the just is resolved, then the entire reasoning process of the wicked, beginning with the end, falls apart. If the death of the just is not a tragic manifestation of meaninglessness, then the limitations of human mortality do not render human life worthless and empty. If human life is not worthless, then the experience of youthful pleasures is not merely an evasion of underlying despair. If the experience of youthful pleasure is not meant to smother despair, then power over the weak, who remind us of mortality, does not make any right. The original nihilistic judgment on the vacuity of human mortality, which is the basis for the wicked's project of injustice, will be proved false.

REFLECTIONS

1. In the speech of the wicked, the author provides us with a rather profound understanding of the psychology involved in the dynamic of injustice. Self-justification for blatant violence does not rest on mere rationalization but has its source in a fundamental judgment on the value we place on life. The nihilistic stance of the wicked flows from despair. Like a chain reaction, their despair elicits a form of escapism from the manifestations of human limitations. At first, in this form of escapism they turn to evasive sensuality. In the case of the wicked, the adulation of youthful pleasure serves only to mask and to deny the underlying despair. The victorious tone in their voice is more like a clamoring noise that tries to fill a deafening silence. It is as if their ensuing project in life is simply to blunt and mask the reality of human limitations and suffering.

Another form of escapism opposes manifestations of mortality. The call of the wicked to exercise power over others, especially over the weak, who remind them of the "uselessness" of a life stamped with mortality, is only a brief and tenuous denial of the "weakness" that awaits everyone in the face of mortality.

Finally the blatant expression of injustice over one who opposes them reveals the full consequence of the wicked's original judgment on mortality. In their call to kill the just, the wicked only affirm their nihilistic despair and inflict it on others.

There are serious consequences in our lives that flow from the fundamental value we attribute to life. The dynamic of injustice in the wicked's project shows how difficult it is to isolate one decision from another.

A concrete example of a similar dynamic of injustice can be gleaned from the story of David and Bathsheba (2 Samuel 11–12). One decision on the part of David leads to another. What appears relatively trivial at the beginning is revealed to be quite hideous at the end. The conclusion of the dynamic is a blatant and unjust killing of an innocent person. But whereas the Wisdom author stresses the initial nihilistic judgment as the source for the spiral of violence, the story of David and Bathsheba concentrates on the final outcome of the dynamic of evil.

2. The author chooses to portray the wicked's nihilistic judgment on life through poetic imagery. There is a tremendous difference between the reflection on the ephemeral value of life by the wicked in Wisdom and the reflections on human limitations and suffering in the books of Job and Ecclesiastes. The reflection of the wicked issues in despair; that of Job and Qohelet issues in hope. What is constant in both is that the experience of human limitations and suffering elicits an important and fundamental human response. On the one hand, the experience of sickness, failure, loss, and death can elicit a destructive despair as it does in the case of the wicked; on the other hand, it can elicit a response of sustaining hope, as it does in the case of the just. Suffering is not neutral. In the end, our response, whether it be the silence of despair or the serenity of respect, will be revealed in our actions.

3. Human dignity resides in our relationship to the divine. The author of Wisdom sustains the value of human dignity in the face of the wicked's deadening ruminations on mortality. This value is maintained by the affirmation of a relationship with a transcendent being. The ungodly deny a divine presence both in our origins and in our finality. From that denial issues the wicked's despair and judgment on life, which in turn elicits the final turn to violence.

Both prior to the speech of the wicked (1:12-15) and afterward (2:22-23), the author affirms the dignity of the universe itself and the dignity of human beings in their relationship to the divine creative act. All the generative forces of the world are wholesome. Human beings were created for incorruption and were made in the image of God.

The denial of divine relevance opens the problematic and enduring issue of power constituting right. If there is no God, why do power and might not constitute the only right? We have not substantially advanced the arguments presented in Wisdom over the years. In the face of arbitrary and relative laws based on power, the dignity of human beings becomes arbitrary and relative.

I recall the arguments of Alexander Solzhenitsyn and Vadim Borisov in their analyses of the regime of power in the Soviet Union. If the concept of the human personality is deprived of divine authority, then the personality can be defined conditionally and inevitably arbitrarily. If the personality is not absolute but conditional, then respect for humans is something one can disregard or claim at whim.[30] Of course, various agnostic or humanistic philosophies still try to maintain an ethic that does not reduce the human being to arbitrary power. But to do so they still appeal to a larger framework, such as society, the community of humanity, or the universe, for the basis of their ethic.

30. See Vadim Borisov, "Personality and National Awareness," in *From Under the Rubble*, ed. Alexander Solzhenitsyn (Toronto: Little, Brown, 1975) 200.

WISDOM 3:1–4:20, IN DEFENSE OF VIRTUE AND JUSTICE

OVERVIEW

In the conclusion of the wicked's defense, the righteous one is accused of incoherence. The wicked's proof for such incoherence is the projected death of the righteous. This tragic death is meant to belie the claim of the just that their end is full of hope. In this way, the entire reasoning process of the wicked and their life project of exploiting creation, oppressing the weak, and doing violence against the just depends on the interpretation of the tragic death of the just. The author must disprove this interpretation for the entire argument of the wicked to collapse. The author examines the evidence by sifting through the appearance of tragedy in the lives of the just and the appearance of strength in the case of the wicked.

In three diptychs, the author examines the way of virtue in the case of the just, who suffer, and the way of the wicked, who appear to thrive over the just. Each diptych begins with a picture of the just, who appear to have suffered, and then turns to the other side to examine the picture of the wicked, who appear to have thrived. The examination constitutes the author's defense of the virtuous life and an attack against a project of life that consists of injustice.

Each diptych picks up the themes within the speech of the wicked in exactly the reverse order in which they appear. The shameful and tragic death of the just is picked up in the very first diptych (3:1-12), which declares the life of the virtuous to be in the hand of God. The call to oppress the poor man and the widow and the aged is treated in the second diptych (3:13–4:6), which deals with the barren woman, the eunuch, and the virtuous who are childless. This second diptych actually contains two sets of comparisons and contrasts on each side. The one side deals with the barren woman and the eunuch (3:13-19), and the second deals with virtuous people who are childless (4:1-6). What unites them into a single diptych with four parts is the image of the fruit of virtue and wickedness (3:13; 4:5). Finally, the wicked's call to exploit creation as "in youth" is confounded in the third diptych (4:7-20), which elaborates the blessing of the virtuous youth who has had an early death.

The argumentation of the author cannot be considered purely philosophical or logical. More than not, the critique is based on declarative statements that show the strength of the wicked to be false in the light of the blessedness of the just. The key technique in the criticism is the examination of appearances and reality. This perspective is particularly suitable to the background image of the trial, which examines appearances, reality, and intentionality. What really happened? Why did it happen? And what are the consequences? Such are the questions the author explores within the declarative statements regarding the just and the wicked. The author defends the virtuous life of the just and attacks the unjust lives of the wicked.

The unraveling of the argumentation of the wicked reveals their entire reasoning process as flawed. The death of the just is not the dreaded tragedy the wicked claim it to be. The oppression of the old, the widow, and the poor does not in the end confine the virtuous, who had "little strength to show" during their life. The call to exploit life "as in youth" is shown to be groundless in the face of a youth who has died an early death, yet is blessed in the presence of God. In its turn, the wicked's nihilistic judgment on the mortality of human beings is shown to be the true cause of a death that goes far beyond the contours of mortality, which they despise.

Wisdom 3:1-13a, The Just Are in the Hand of God

COMMENTARY

The Reward of the Just. 3:1-4. As opposed to the shameful death the wicked projected for the just one, the author declares the just to be in the hand of God. Three images are used to create a sharp contrast between the blessedness of the just and the anticipated tragedy and shame projected by the wicked. The just are in the hand of God (v. 1); they are in peace (v. 3); and their hope is the fullness of immortality (v. 4). The hand of God traditionally signifies divine power and protection (Ps 95:4). To be in peace intimates the fullness of rest and well-being (Pss 4:8; 29:11). The hope of immortality refers to the author's declaration that justice is immortal (1:15). This noun "justice" (δικαιοσύνη *dikaiosynē*), along with its adjective, "immortal" (ἀθάνατός *athanatos*), is late and quite rare in the LXX (cf. Wis 3:4; 4:1; 8:13, 17; 15:3; 4 Macc 14:5; 16:13). It is a concept borrowed from the Greek that expresses Israel's hope in God's faithfulness to the promises of the covenant.[31]

The author concedes the appearance of tragedy and shame, but contends that the reality of the just is one of blessedness (vv. 2-4). Only from the perspective of the foolish do the just seem to have died, and their death seems to have been disaster, destruction, and even punishment.

3:5. By creating this disjunction between appearances and reality, the author is inviting the reader to look behind appearances for enduring values. The author introduces the idea of God's "testing" the just and offers two traditional metaphors of transformation and applies them to the case of the just who have died.

The idea of God's testing the people is often associated with the wanderings in the desert after the exodus from Egypt. In the theology of Deuteronomy, the desert experience of Israel is presented as a time of testing and an opportunity for inculcating discipline and knowledge (Deut 4:36; 8:2-5). This theme will be picked up in the later part of the book, when the specific history of the exodus will be treated. The sapiential tradition developed the notion of "testing in order to teach" as a means of passing on the insights of wisdom (Prov 3:11-12; Sir 2:1-5; 4:17-18).

3:6. The two metaphors that facilitate the notion of the transformation of the just in the context of God's testing are borrowed from metallurgy and the temple cult. Both metaphors share the image of fire as the element that causes transformation. The transformation of the just is compared to gold's being tested or purified in fire (v. 6; cf. Ps 66:10; Prov 17:3; Zech 13:9; Mal 3:2-3; Sir 2:5). The testing of gold in fire has the double function of verification and purification. The second metaphor, the burnt offering, accentuates the union between the just and God. The just are literally compared to a burnt offering that, though consumed by fire, is accepted by God as a pleasant fragrance (see Gen 8:21). If the metaphor of gold's being tested in fire stresses transformation and purification, the second metaphor stresses God's acceptance and union with the just.

3:7-8. The transformation of the just includes also a heightening of their activity at the time of judgment (vv. 7-8). Until now, the just have been passive, both during the wicked's speech and during the author's declaration of their blessedness. They are at peace in the hand of God. But at the time of judgment they will "shine forth"; they will run like "sparks through the stubble"; they will "govern nations." This idea of the righteous shining with brilliance is often associated with the vindication of the just at the time of judgment in apocalyptic writings. In Dan 12:3, for instance, the wise and the righteous are described as shining forth like the brightness of the sky and the stars (cf. Matt 13:43).

Several descriptions in the wicked's speech are reversed in the author's presentation of the just. The just were in the hands of the wicked, but now they are in the hands of God (2:18–3:1). The wicked were to put the just to torment, but now no torment will touch them (2:19–3:1). The wicked planned to test what would happen to the just, but it was really God who had tested the just and found them worthy (2:17–3:5). The wicked were to try the forbearance of the just, but God is the one who has tried them like gold in the furnace (2:19–3:6).

3:9. The final brief comments on the just reiterate the faithfulness of God in covenantal terms. The just abide with God in love. Grace and mercy rest on the holy ones, and God's providence watches over the elect. The author's belief in an afterlife is rooted more deeply in covenantal theology than in Greek philosophical ideas concerning the immortality of the soul.[32]

The Punishment of the Wicked. 3:10-11. In contrast to the active blessedness of the just, the author declares the hope and strength of the wicked to be

---

31. Although the book of Wisdom presents an unambiguous belief in an afterlife, it does not affirm a clear belief in the resurrection (though other sources already affirm such a belief; cf. 2 Macc 7:9). Richard J. Taylor argues concisely that the Wisdom author's belief in an afterlife follows more from the theology of Israel's covenant than it does from Greek philosophical positions. The presence of specifically covenantal terms such as "grace," "mercy," and "the elect" (ἐκλεκτός *eklektos*, Wis 3:9) would indicate the value the author attributes to covenantal realities. See Taylor, "The Eschatological Meaning of Life and Death in the Book of Wisdom I-V," 72-137.

32. Scholars once thought that the Wisdom author was deeply entrenched in Greek philosophy and anthropology. The fact that the work was written in Greek, including unique words with no Hebrew counterparts, lent substance to such a view. However, with careful analysis it is evident that the author is thoroughly established in Hebrew anthropology with a great deal of sympathy for Greek philosophy and literature. See J. M. Reese, *Hellenistic Influence on the Book of Wisdom and Its Consequences*, AnBib 41 (Rome: Pontifical Biblical Institute, 1970).

empty and useless (v. 11). As a result of their injustice, the wicked will be punished according to their reasoning (v. 10). The wicked will not be punished simply because they have sinned. Rather, in the very manner of their wickedness, they will experience the punishment of their own reasoning.

The author draws a close connection between the false reasoning of the wicked and the experience of punishment. This is a unique perspective in the work that once again reveals the author's profound psychological understanding of the relationship among thought, praxis, and consequences. The entire reasoning process of the wicked contains the seeds of their own destruction. The nihilistic judgment on life, the invitation to evasive pleasure, the beckoning to oppress the weak, and the call to kill the just—all of these principles informing their view are understood by the author to turn against the wicked.

It is not as if the punishment is an external penalization that has no bearing on the manner of the injustice perpetrated. The author envisages an internal coherence between one's actions and their consequences. This will be particularly emphasized in the latter half of the book, where the author treats the issues of idol worship (11:16; 12:23-27; 14:30-31) and the punishment of the enemies of the righteous ones in the plague episodes (15:18–16:1; 18:4-5). An explicit relationship will be drawn between their sin and the punishment for it.

This idea of a relationship between sin and punishment is implicit in several psalms of lament in which the psalmist calls on God for liberation and for the wicked's punishment according to their very means of wickedness: "Their mischief returns upon their own heads, and on their own heads their violence descends" (Ps 7:16 NRSV; cf. Pss 5:10; 9:15; 35:8; 37:14-15; 109:29; 141:10).

Although the punishment of the wicked for their false reasoning and injustice is envisaged as taking place in the future (they "will be punished as their reasoning deserves," v. 10), the seeds of destruction are already operative in their lives. Their lives really are miserable, their hope is vain, their labors are unprofitable, and their works are useless. These images are the very antitheses of the experience of the just, who are in peace, whose hope is the fullness of immortality, and whose future is to govern nations and rule over peoples.

3:12-13a. The concluding declaration of the first diptych focuses on the fruit of the wicked, the topic for the next diptych. The wives of the wicked are foolish, their children are evil, and their offspring are cursed. The author's judgment of punishment for the wicked here is rather harsh and comprehensive, without distinctions and exceptions. Even the children and the wives of the wicked will experience destruction.

The author takes pains to attribute the cause of ultimate death to the words and actions of the wicked. Why does the curse of the wicked extend to wives and children who may not have any guilt? Of course, the author is continuing in a long-standing tradition that claimed that blessings and curses continue to the fourth generation (cf. Exod 20:5; 34:7; Num 14:18; Deut 5:9; Sir 41:5-10). Actions do have consequences on other people, for better or for worse. If the wicked hope to accumulate advantages and wealth through injustice, they will be sorely dismayed. This irony introduces the contrast in the next diptych between the hopeless fruitfulness of the wicked and the hopeful sterility of the just.

REFLECTIONS

1. This passage, which declares the hope of the just who have died (3:1-9), is one of the many biblical texts offered for selection at funerals. The author encourages the embracing of pain and loss, but offers hope as well. The declarations and images in the text have the unique capability of offering hope without bypassing or diminishing the pain of loss. Recognition is given to the suffering and death of others in the image of gold's being tested and purified in fire and in the image of the burnt offering. To lament and mourn the loss of family and friends is an important element in human relations, and it is not wise to pass over mourning lightly.

Yet, at the same time, pain and loss may be transformed into hope. The purification of gold leads to brilliance; the burnt offering signifies union. This is the unique perspective the author wishes to bring to the tragedies of life. In contrast to the perspective of the wicked, who see in human tragedy a destroyer of human value, the author focuses on the relationship between the just and God that emerges from their experience of tragedy. Far from being destructive tragedies, experiences of pain and loss can become moments of purification, resolution, and even deeper union with others.

2. The interpretation of tragedy in our own lives and in the lives of others remains ambivalent. Perhaps it is almost an instinctive reaction to interpret tragedy as punishment and a consequence of guilt. Instead of seeing tragedy, loss, sickness, and even death as a call to care and to be concerned for union, we judge either other people or ourselves as being accursed. Perhaps we simply try to avoid the realities of those who suffer altogether.

"Though in the sight of others they were punished,/ their hope is full of immortality" (3:4 NRSV). The Wisdom text offers a different perspective on the reality of tragedy and limitations in human life. Tragedy, loss, and death are not the destroyers of ultimate human value. The book of Job is the great precursor to the Wisdom text for modulating the perception and interpretation of tragedy in life. The tragedy of Job's life and family was not the result of his guilt, no matter how much the tradition and the three friends tried to impose such an interpretation on his experience. Christ, likewise, modulated the interpretation of tragedy in the case of the man who was blind from birth. The disciples presumed guilt to have been the cause of his blindness: "Rabbi, who sinned, this man or his parents, that he was born blind?" (John 9:2 NRSV). Jesus' response transformed the perspective on tragedy. He denied sin to be the cause for that tragedy and instead stated that the response to the man's blindness will be the manifestation of God's works (John 9:1-3).

3. In the author's critique of the lives of the wicked, a parallel is drawn between their sin and their punishment. Implicit in this parallel lies the age-old belief that injustice will finally catch up with the perpetrators. The reward of justice and the punishment of injustice too easily may be understood as extrinsic to moral conduct. For the Wisdom author, the fruit of a moral life is already implicit in the concrete decisions and actions of individuals. Even if the explicit or public revelation of justice and injustice resides in the future, the personal consequences of moral acts, like planted seeds, are active from the start.

Wisdom 3:13b–4:6, The Moral Strength of the Virtuous

COMMENTARY

The Moral Fruit of Virtue. 3:13b-14. This central diptych is aimed at dismantling the wicked's despising of everything that is weak and useless (2:10-11). Again, the issues of appearance and reality in the case of the just and the wicked are paraded before the reader for critical examination. This is done in two sets of comparisons and contrasts of the childless, who are righteous, and the wicked, who thrive. The particular image that unites the elements of this double comparison and contrast is "fruit" (καρπός *karpos*). The sterile woman will have "fruit" in the day of accounting (v. 13b), whereas the "fruit" of the wicked will be useless (4:5). Where there appears to be fruitlessness in the virtuous, there will be fruit. Where there appears to be fruit in injustice, there is no lasting fruit.

In order to recast the reader's perspective on human tragedy, the author chooses two traditional images of the accursed and raises them to a status of "blessedness." Because of the virtue of the barren woman and the eunuch, what appears to be human weakness and tragedy turns out to be a stage or a passage toward blessedness.

The barren woman and the eunuch are traditional images of curse and misfortune. The corollary image of blessing is that of fruitfulness. The abundance of children was considered a major sign of God's blessing. The initial divine blessing and command at creation, "Be fruitful and multiply . . ." (Gen 1:28), constitutes procreation as one of the intrinsic blessings of humanity (cf. Psalm 128). The gift of children was a sign of blessing associated with the Abrahamic covenant (Gen 12:2; 15:3-5; 17:15-21) and also in a particular manner with the deuteronomic covenant (Deut 30:16). Sterility for both women and men was considered a grave misfortune (Gen 30:23; 1 Sam 1:4-8). The eunuch was barred from the priesthood and the assembly of the Lord (Lev 21:20; Deut 23:2). As such, the images of the barren woman and the eunuch are extreme examples of human limitation and weakness.

In a turnabout of events, the author declares both the barren woman and the eunuch to be blessed because of their moral integrity. The barren woman who is undefiled will bear fruit during the final judgment (v. 13b); the eunuch who has done no lawless deed will have a place of great delight in the temple of the Lord (v. 14). In this way the reader is being challenged to evaluate what constitutes true blessedness. The author has not flinched from choosing traditional images of curse as possible examples of blessedness.

Although there is no other biblical passage in which these two traditional images of curse are transformed precisely into declarations of blessedness, it is evident that the Wisdom author is borrowing themes from Isaiah.[33] In Isaiah 54, the prophet exhorts the barren woman, who represents Jerusalem, to rejoice, for she will have many children (Isa 54:1-3). In Isaiah, the city of Jerusalem is referred to as a barren woman (Isa 54:1) and a widow (Isa 54:4); Jerusalem is like a wife abandoned by her husband (Isa 54:6-7); the city is afflicted (Isa 54:11) and oppressed (Isa 54:14). In each case, the image of affliction is transformed into an image of restoration. Jerusalem will have many children; God is declared to be her husband; the covenant of peace shall not be taken away; the city will be rebuilt with magnificent stones; the city will become a safe haven. The author of Wisdom has condensed and focused on the image of the barren woman from the Isaiah passage. But the added perspective is that of her virtue. Because of her virtue, which is stated in negative terms ("undefiled," "not entered into a sinful union"), the barren woman will have fruit.

Similarly, the idea of righteous eunuchs' receiving a place in the Temple is borrowed from Isaiah. In Isaiah 56, the covenant of the Lord is extended to all who maintain justice and who keep the sabbath. Specifically this includes the foreigner who loves the name of the Lord, eunuchs who hold fast to the covenant, and the outcasts of Israel.

3:15. The temporal fruitlessness of the virtuous barren woman and the virtuous eunuch is reduced to mere appearance when compared to the fruitfulness they will have in their virtue. The author continues the attack on the reasoning of the wicked by transforming the perspectives on ordinary human limitations and weaknesses. Just as the death of the just appeared to be a final tragic event only in the eyes of the foolish, so too is the fruitlessness of virtuous individuals who hold to their integrity only apparent. In fact, the virtuous, who bear little or no temporal fruit, have the root of understanding, which ultimately does not fail. Perhaps no other biblical author has pushed the concept of blessedness so far as to exclude from it material goods and to include within it the experience of suffering.

3:16-19, The Apparent Fruit of the Wicked. In direct contrast to the moral fruitfulness of the just, the author declares the temporal fruit of the wicked to be of no account. On the day of judgment there will be no consolation for the unrighteous generation. Whatever temporal fruit they have acquired through unrighteous means will

---

33. Two works draw the parallels that can be found between Isaiah and the Wisdom of Solomon: Suggs, "Wisdom of Solomon II,10-V," 26-33; J. Schaberg, "Major Midrashic Traditions in Wisdom 1,1-6,25," *JSJ* 13 (1982) 75-101.

not come to the hoped-for maturity. The final outcome of the unrighteous generation is grievous.

If we understand the expression "children of adulterers" literally as the children of the unrighteous, then the author's reasoning would appear to be entering a rather awkward position. Innocent children would appear to be punished for the sins of their parents. As in the case of vv. 12-13, the author's argument has more nuances than the literal sense would suggest. In prophetic literature, terms relating to adultery signify Israel's faithlessness to God, idolatry, and abandonment of the law (cf. Isa 57:3-13; Jer 5:7-9; 7:8-10; Ezekiel 16; Hos 2:2-13; 3:1-5; 4:2-19). Adultery referred to the whole complexity of Israel's faithlessness to God.[34] Children from such an "adulterous" relationship signified the advantages and privileges gained from alliances and cultic practices. Instead of relying on the covenantal promises, Israel adopted cultic practices and entered political intrigues through which Israel hoped to secure advantages and privileges; thus the children of adultery represent these advantages. Even within prophetic teaching, the judgment of God is presented as demolishing the children of adultery—that is, the advantages that Israel hoped to secure through idolatry, foreign alliances, and cultic practices (cf. Jer 5:8-9; Hos 9:12).

The particular nuance that the Wisdom author is deriving from the image of the hopelessness of the children of adultery is that the wicked's hoped-for consolation will turn to nothing. Children represent hope and strength. They provide a guarantee for the future. However, for those who practice injustice, all the apparent advantages that have been thus gained will fail, like children of an adulterous relationship. The fruit of wickedness, contrary to its appearance of blessedness, will become a curse.

The wicked had declared might to be their right, and they judged weakness to be useless (2:11). The author is focusing on the image of fruitfulness as an external sign of might and strength and fruitlessness as an external sign of weakness and helplessness. The apparent fruit of unjust actions will not bring the hoped-for consolation. The apparent fruitlessness of the righteous will in fact bring forth the fruit of virtue.

4:1-2, The Advantage of Virtue. Unlike the opening and closing diptychs, the central diptych contrasts the hope of the virtuous who are childless with that of the wicked in a double set of comparisons. In this second half of the diptych, the author declares the particular advantage of virtue to be immortality. Parents live on in their children. But how do the childless continue? Through their virtue and honor, the just will live on in relation to God and to others. In virtue there is immortality. Therefore, it is better to be childless and virtuous than to have the abundance of the wicked (cf. Ps 37:16: "Better is a little that the righteous person has than the abundance of many wicked" [NRSV]).

What was stated negatively for the barren woman and the eunuch is stated positively in the case of virtuous people who are childless. The righteousness of the barren consisted of their refraining from unlawful conduct, whereas the righteousness of the childless consists of being rooted in virtue.

The author has adapted familiar Greek ideas on the value of virtue to the case of the just who are childless. For Plato, the life of the soul was far more important than the life of the body. In the examination of justice from the point of view of who is happier, the just or the unjust, Plato champions the enduring value of virtue, which lives on.[35]

Virtue is personified as a victorious athlete who marches with the crown of victory after having won spotless prizes (v. 2). In 1:8, justice was personified as one who punishes. In the following section of the book, wisdom will be personified as the object of the unnamed Solomon's admiration.

4:3-6, The Disadvantage of the Wicked. In contrast to the advantage of virtue, the prolific brood of the wicked is declared to be of no use. Whereas virtue was compared to a victorious athlete, the results of wickedness are compared to a doomed tree and a rootless plant.

Vegetation is used often in Scripture as a metaphor for the flourishing of moral life. The righteous are compared to trees that are planted by streams of water and that yield

---

34. For a concise treatment of the nuances of adultery in prophetic literature, see Elaine A. Goodfriend, "Adultery," *Anchor Bible Dictionary*, 6 vols. (New York: Doubleday, 1992) 1:82-86.

35. Plato *Republic* 2:362.

their fruit in due time (Ps 1:3; Jer 17:7-8). Perhaps even more frequently, especially in the prophetic writings, we find the image of vegetation, and particularly the vine, as a metaphor for judgment against the unfaithful (Isa 5:1-7; 27:1-6; Jer 2:21; 5:10-11; 8:13; 12:10-13; Ezekiel 15; Amos 4:9). The destruction of the vine, which is ordinarily a symbol of life and abundance, is a striking image that portrays the precariousness of an immoral and unfaithful life.

The author of Wisdom adapts the vegetation metaphor for the life of the wicked to include the progressive stages of growth: seedlings, roots, boughs, branches, fruit. By following the progressive growth of the plant from the illegitimate seedling to its useless fruit, the author stresses the thoroughness of the plant's ineffectiveness. Even if the seedlings take root, those roots will not be deep; even if they put forth boughs, they will be shaken by the wind; even if they sprout branches, they will be broken off; and even if they should provide a semblance of fruit, it will be useless (vv. 4-5).

The metaphor for the children of adultery veers away from vegetation and returns to that of a trial. Even more useless than fruit, the children of the wicked become witnesses against their parents when God examines them (v. 6). This is the pivotal issue in the author's argument on the apparent fruit of the wicked. The author is unmasking the illusion of strength and power that the wicked gain through injustice. Not only are the advantages and privileges of the wicked said to be useless, like unripe fruit that cannot be digested, but also this fruit actually testifies against them for their injustice.

Since the wicked had regarded weakness as useless and power as making right, then the fruit of their injustice would appear to be a vindication for their stance in life. The author counters this erroneous reasoning by declaring the fruit of the wicked to be both useless and accusatory. The wicked will fail not because they will not achieve success from their injustice, but because their supposed success will not bring them the hoped-for security; instead, it will be a source for their own condemnation at the time of accounting.

To elucidate the change in perspective from appearance to reality, the author provides several reversals of fortune in the case of the just and the wicked. The barren woman and the eunuch who are virtuous have the "root" of understanding (3:15), whereas the wicked do not plant deep "roots" (4:3). The wicked lamented that there would be no "memory" (μνημονεύω *mnēmoneuō*) of them after their death (2:4), whereas in the "memory" of virtue there is immortality (4:1). In their frenetic boasting, the wicked called for wearing "crowns" of roses before they fade (2:8), whereas it is virtue that marches victoriously carrying the "crown" (στέφανος *stephanos*, 4:2). The wicked claimed evasive pleasure to be their lot in life (2:9), whereas it is the righteous eunuch who will have a "lot" (κλῆρος *klēros*) in the Temple (3:14). The wicked had planned to inflict a shameful death on the just one to see what the end of his life would be (2:17), whereas the "end" (τέλος *telos*) of the unrighteous generation is said to be grievous (3:19). The wicked had judged weakness to be useless (2:11), whereas the apparent success of the wicked is shown ultimately to be "useless" (ἄχρηστος *achrēstos*, 4:5).

The reversal of fortune regarding the apparent fruitlessness of the just and the supposed fruitfulness of the wicked is aimed at countering the wicked's despising of what is weak and extolling the virtue of sheer might and success. The author's counterattack relies heavily on the distinction between appearance and reality. What appears to be a weakness of the righteous in the end turns out to be the strength of their virtue. What appears to be a strength of the ungodly—namely, all the benefits and privileges accrued from injustice—in the end turns against them and reveals their moral weakness and depravity.

REFLECTIONS

The author's treatment of the theme of childlessness points to a more general and universal problem: How do we interpret the many forms of human weakness and limitations that we encounter in ourselves and in our world? If the first diptych aimed at facing the issue of the human tragedy of a violent and unjust death, the second diptych focuses on the less obvious tragedies that the unfulfillment of human possibilities presents.

In ancient Israel, children were considered one of the great gifts and rewards in life. They were a sign of God's blessing. Childlessness was considered to be a lack and even a curse. The image of the "fruit" of the wicked and the righteous relies on the presence of children, but goes beyond the metaphor of procreation to include all the consequences of injustice. The fruit of one's actions includes all the strengths, achievements, and failures of one's labor of righteousness or of injustice. The Wisdom author explores the apparent lack of the "fruit" of the righteous and the apparent strength of the "fruit" of the wicked to face the issue of the meaning of human weakness and the propensity for false hope.

1. The strength of injustice is only apparent and illusory. The seeming strength of injustice is one of the great problems that emerges with growing intensity among the sapiential circles of Israel. The wicked appear to thrive while the just appear to founder. The apparent thriving of injustice runs head-on against the covenantal promises. Obedience and faithfulness to the law bring life; injustice and faithlessness bring death (Deut 30:11-20).

A number of eloquent voices in Scripture speak to this perennial problem. Psalm 73 is dedicated entirely to the theme of the apparent success of injustice. The psalmist confesses to having been sorely tempted to envy the arrogant for their prosperity. What saves the psalmist from succumbing to this temptation is the realization of the ultimate end of the wicked at the time of judgment. Job, in confronting the accusation of his three friends, contemplates the bitter paradox of the just who perish and the wicked who thrive (Job 21). Qohelet continuously raises the issue of the apparent strength of folly or injustice to jolt the reader from reducing reward and punishment to an automatic consequence of one's actions (Eccl 2:12-17; 4:1-3; 7:15; 8:10-17).

The particular nuance that the Wisdom author brings to the paradox is the dichotomy between appearance and reality. The author concedes the appearance of strength to the practice of injustice but denies its strength to be effective in the long run. Moreover, the effect of the author's reversal of images between the just and the wicked is to raise the importance of being critical of appearances. For our culture, which relies so heavily on appearances and first impressions, this exhortation to reflect on the essentials and arrive at the heart of the matter can be a significant voice for integrity. It calls for a critical examination of the fruit of one's action and its effect in the long run: "Thus you will know them by their fruits" (Matt 7:20 NRSV). Although the fruit of injustice may appear strong in the short term, in the long run it reveals its origins in nihilism. Success, strength, and achievements brought about unjustly are false sources of hope. In the end, these very strengths will reveal their function of simply masking the abysmal despair that breeds injustice.

2. The weakness of integrity is only apparent. In antithesis to the paradox of the seeming strength of injustice is the apparent weakness of integrity. What benefit is there to following a way of life of justice and integrity? Weakness, limitations, and surface failure put integrity and justice as a way of life to a sore test.

But the author challenges the reader to set his or her gaze beyond the immediate, beyond appearances, to view the result of justice in the long run. Virtue is respected by God and by people (4:1). A life of virtue places one in relationship to God and in a relationship of integrity with others. Again, it is in the long run that the true strength of justice is grasped with all its clarity. What cannot be destroyed in a life of integrity is the enduring relationship with God and others.

Ultimately, the author is affirming the covenantal promises. Faithfulness to God's way of justice does bring life; the way of injustice does bring death. But this defense is not sustained in a naive or superficial manner. The defense of justice and the critique of injustice are sustained by an examination of the ultimate fruit that is derived from ethical conduct. For a critical assessment of the strength and weakness of justice, one has to go all the way. What is the ultimate result of having achieved success, security, and temporary glory through a life of injustice? What is the ultimate result of clinging to a life of integrity and justice while enduring failure, threat, and a seeming anonymity? In the long run, a life of injustice leads to the alienation it presumes, whereas a life of justice places one into relationship with others.

Wisdom 4:7-20, The Death of a Virtuous Youth

COMMENTARY

4:7-15, The Righteous Are Pleasing to God. The final diptych contrasts the death of a virtuous youth with the prolonged life of the wicked. Just as children in ancient Israel were a sign of great blessing, so too was a ripe old age considered to be a blessing (Gen 15:15; 25:8; 35:29; Exod 20:12; Deut 4:40; Judg 8:32). Old age was presented as a sign of wisdom and as a reward for right conduct in the sapiential traditions as well (Job 42:17; Prov 3:1-2; 10:27; 16:31; Sir 1:12). Again, as with the case of the barren, the author has not shrunk away from choosing an image that ordinarily evokes tragedy and misfortune to propel the reader to seek out the deeper source of human dignity. What is truly disastrous is not a brief life lived out with integrity, but a long life filled with the perpetration of injustice.

An early death was considered a great calamity; it was a curse one wished only on enemies (Ps 109:8). But viewed from the perspective of virtue, an early death may even signify a blessing. The author is advocating the same change in perspective as in the case of the violent death of the just and the fruitless lives of the righteous. From the point of view of justice and integrity, what appears tragic is only a stage in further growth.

The author argues that an honorable old age is not something that can be established by external signs of age, such as gray hair. Neither can it be measured by number of years. Rather, an honorable age is achieved in a life of innocence, understanding, and inner maturity (vv. 8-9). The idea of progressive internal growth is portrayed through the images of "a life become pleasing to God" (v. 10) and "coming to perfection in a short time" (v. 13).

Pushing away even further the interpretation of an early death as necessarily tragic, the author goes so far as to consider the early death of a virtuous youth to be an expression of divine favor (vv. 10-15). This certainly is a novel position within the biblical writings. More than likely, the idea was facilitated by the popular axiom in Greek and Roman literature, "He whom the gods love dies young."[36] It is parallel to our own popular expression, "The good die young." The Wisdom author is adapting this idea in the light of the Enoch stories in Genesis and Sirach. Two links to the Genesis account of Enoch (LXX) exist in the Wisdom text: The idea of Enoch's pleasing God and the idea of transference: "Enoch was pleasing to God, then he was found no more, for God transferred him" (Gen 5:24). Notice that in the Hebrew Bible the opening phrase reads, "Enoch walked with God . . ." unlike the Greek text, which Wisdom employs. Sirach makes a similar reference to the Enoch account of the Greek version of Genesis in the hymn that honors the ancestors: "Enoch pleased the Lord and was taken up, an example of repentance to all generations" (Sir 44:16 NRSV; cf. Heb 11:5).

The particular nuance attributed to God's pleasure in the case of the virtuous youth's being removed from the world is that of saving the youth from evil and calamity. God has taken up the virtuous youth, who has achieved maturity early, lest the future corrupt him (vv. 11-12). This idea was also present in Greek, Roman, and rabbinic literature: "For who knows but that God, having a fatherly care for the human race, and

---

36. Menander 425; cf. Plautus *Bacchides* IV.816.

foreseeing future events, early removes some persons from life untimely."[37]

The Wisdom author stresses God's motivation of care and love in the early death of the virtuous youth. As with the case of the tragic and violent death of the just in the first diptych, people misinterpret the untimely death as tragic and void of divine care (v. 15). But from a perspective of justice and virtue, even events of seeming tragedy are interpreted in the light of God's grace, mercy, and providence.

4:16-20, The Righteous Youth and the Aged Wicked. The conviction of the wicked frames the second half of the diptych. At the outset, the righteous ones and the just youth are said to condemn the ungodly and the prolonged age of the unrighteous (v. 16). In the conclusion, the lawless deeds of the wicked will convict them to their face (v. 20). The author stresses the quality of judgment in the righteous youth. It is the youth, ordinarily not renowned for judgment, who will condemn the aged, who are commonly associated with wisdom, for their wickedness.

There are biblical precedents for the image of a wise youth who criticizes the wicked or foolish people who have the respect that belongs to elders. In the book of Job, Elihu defends his right to speak out because the source of wisdom resides in the breath of God and not in length of years. As a younger man, inspired by the Spirit of God, Elihu is critical of his elders for not responding effectively to the laments of their friend Job (Job 32:6-9). Qohelet speaks of the advantages of a poor and wise youth over an old and foolish king (Eccl 4:13). God is said to have aroused Daniel, a youth with a holy spirit, in order to confound the wicked elders and liberate Susanna from false judgment (Sus 45).

The author's judgment against the wicked is expressed in apocalyptic language. This language anticipates the similar expression of the formal judgment that occurs after the wicked's confession (5:17-23). In part, the language of destruction may have been inspired by Isaiah's judgment on the downfall of the king of Babylon (Isa 14:3-21). The Lord "will laugh" the wicked to scorn; they will become "dishonored corpses"; they will be "dashed, shaken," and "left utterly dry" (vv. 18-19). At the time of reckoning, the lawless deeds of the wicked will convict them.

The issue of appearance versus reality is applied to the case of the virtuous youth who dies an early death. Although it appears to be a tragedy, such a death need not be interpreted as a calamity or disaster. On the contrary, from the perspective of virtue and maturity, such a death may be a sign of God's special favor. People may see such events and not understand their true meaning or take such ideas into consideration (v. 15).

A number of images are taken up by the author from the original speech of the wicked and the previous diptychs in order to dismantle the reasoning of the wicked and counter their false accusation of the just. The wicked wanted to see whether the claims of the just were true, and so test him to the end (2:17); now the wicked will see the end of the wise and still not understand (v. 17). Just as the righteous were to become active and govern nations and peoples in the first diptych (3:7-8), so too the just and the righteous youth condemn the wicked in the third diptych (v. 16). Just as the children of the wicked become witnesses against them at the time of accounting in the second diptych (v. 6), so too the lawless deeds of the unrighteous convict them at the day of reckoning in the third diptych (v. 20).

By taking up another image of disaster and tragedy—namely, that of the early death of a virtuous youth—the author is countering the wicked persons' adulation of youthful pleasures (2:6-9) and their negative judgment on the transience of human life (2:1-5). In this way, all three diptychs counter the judgment and exhortation to injustice that reflect the wicked's approach to life. And this they do in reverse order as they appear in the wicked's speech.

During the sifting of appearances and reality, the author systematically uncovers the true meaning of the violent death of the just, the final fruitfulness of the barren woman and the eunuch, the special divine favor shown to the virtuous youth. The first diptych refutes the challenge of the wicked, who project the shameful death of the just one to be

---

37. Plutarch *Consolatio ad Apollonium* 117D. David Winston provides several sources in rabbinic, Roman, and Greek literature that give expression to this idea, developed by the Wisdom author, whereby God "removes" those who are at the prime of their virtuous life, lest they change their minds. See Winston, *The Wisdom of Solomon*, 140-41.

a confirmation of the validity of their stance toward life. The second diptych counters the wicked's decision to make might their right and to oppress those who are weak: the poor, the widow, and the elderly. The third diptych on the wise youth refutes the negative view of the wicked's judgment on physical death, which had led to their initial exhortation to evasive youthful pleasures. The interpretation of physical death plays a critical role in the author's refutation of a style of life that justifies injustice. The entire reasoning process of the wicked falls apart and prepares the reader for the day of judgment, when they will confess the error of their ways and their sin.

REFLECTIONS

1. The author's declaration of the blessedness of the wise youth who has died is not meant to be an answer to someone who is grieving the loss of a child or young friend. The death of a young person increases the poignancy of the loss of life, the waste of human possibilities, and the transience of life. Precisely for this reason, the author chose this common enough experience of human affliction to heighten the appreciation of a life of virtue and justice. Far from being an ultimate tragedy, even a short life can be considered a full life if it is measured by integrity and not by the ordinary standards of human strength. By looking behind the appearance of loss, in the case of a youth who has died, the author celebrates the power of virtue, justice, and inner maturity.

2. Wisdom and virtue can be found in the most unlikely places. The author holds up the example of a virtuous and wise youth in contrast to the wicked elderly in a manner that challenges our ordinary perspectives on wisdom and virtue. Wisdom and virtue traditionally are associated with the tried, the experienced, and the aged. But it is more important to assess the acts and judgments of human beings in the light of wisdom and virtue than it is to assess their appearances and places in society. Christ would proclaim a similar change in perspective in even more drastic terms: "Truly I tell you, the tax collectors and the prostitutes are going into the kingdom of God ahead of you" (Matt 21:31 NRSV; cf. Luke 18:9-14).

3. In the context of the author's refutation of the wicked's argument, the image of the death of a youth calls into question an absolutely negative judgment of the loss of youthful energies. The wicked regard the experience of the loss of life so negatively that this judgment justifies their escape to youthful pleasures. If youthful pleasures are pursued simply to evade the limitations and afflictions of life, they will never completely satisfy the desire for communion. Communion and integrity can be achieved even when youthful energies are diminished to the point of death.

4. The negative interpretation of an early death is mitigated by two realizations. The first is communion with God. God's faithfulness to the promises of the covenant has elicited the faith in an afterlife (4:15). The communion that is envisaged between the youth that has died an early death and God depends not so much on the immortality of the human being as much as on the enduring covenantal relationship. This communion is realized through the virtuous life of a youth that has been found pleasing to God.

The second is the idea of the inner maturity of virtue, whereby the essence of life reaches its completion. What is critical for the author of Wisdom is the inner life of virtue. The failings and shortcomings of life in their physical contours—even including early death—pale in comparison to the dignity of a life lived out with integrity.

5. The appearance of wisdom and achievement of the aged is not to be confused with virtue. As with the earlier cases of the tragic death of a virtuous person and the apparent fruitlessness of a barren person, the author calls for an examination of the true nature of human strength and wisdom. What appears to be a tragic loss of life in the case of the wise youth indeed is not. Presumably the author could have chosen other figures to signify human strength, such as people of wealth or those with educational and political might. Instead he uses three extreme examples of human misfortune to highlight with clarity the significant values of virtue and justice for determining the dignity of human beings. The true failures, tragedies, and disasters in life are not what the wicked think they are. Moral vacuity expressed through a life of evasive pleasure, exploiting the weak, and perpetrating violence brings on a death and destruction that is far more devastating than the experience of mortality, which all human beings encounter.

WISDOM 5:1-23, THE FINAL JUDGMENT

COMMENTARY

5:1-3, Introduction to the Scene of Judgment. The author has refuted the entire reasoning process of the wicked in a series of diptychs that uphold the integrity of the just and condemn the ways of the unjust. Despite appearances to the contrary, the blessedness of the just is assured by virtue of their relationship with God, whereas the downfall of the wicked is guaranteed by the vacuity of their moral life. The linchpin in the wicked's argument was their final project to condemn the just one to a shameful death (2:20). In their minds, a shameful death would disprove the just's pretensions to an enduring divine relationship and would confirm their own negative judgment on the transiency of life. In turn, the negative interpretation of life justified their flight to evasive pleasure, their grasping of power, and their exercising of violence. By having the just one stand with confidence before the oppressors in a final judgment, the author strips away any vestiges of the wicked's claim to truth. The author brings the reader to the lofty heights of a divine perspective whereby the blessedness of the just shines clearly against the moral tragedy of the wicked. The power of injustice and the impotence of virtue are reversed. The just one will stand before the oppressors.

The theme of a final judgment has continuously been brought to the fore by the author. In a sense, a final judgment functions as a "trump card" for eliciting in the present a reflection on the eventual outcome of one's judgments and actions. The terms of this judgment are general and descriptive. It is called an "inquiry" and a "report" that will be brought to God (1:9). The author's favored term ἐπισκοπή (*episkopē*) refers to God's day of visitation or accounting, in which God cares for the just and punishes the wicked (2:20; 3:7, 9, 13; 4:15; cf. Isa 10:3; 23:17; 29:6). But this day of judgment is also described as a time when God will examine or judge human beings (3:18; 4:6).

The mere presence of the just one who stands before the oppressors constitutes irrefutable evidence against the wicked. The very act of standing up has juridical overtones. A judge stands in order to inquire and to pronounce judgment (Job 31:14; Ps 82:1). A witness stands to accuse or to defend (Deut 19:15-16; Job 33:5). A person who cannot stand has nothing further to add for his or her defense (Ps 1:5). Therefore, the very presence of the just one constitutes a condemnation. Not a word need be spoken, yet the wicked are accused and condemned. The wicked had wanted "to see" whether the words of the just were true (2:17); now in divine judgment they "see" the end of the just and are overtaken with fear (v. 2).

The wicked confess their guilt. Just as the author provided the reader with the privileged position of following the wicked persons' perspective on life, so too is the reader allowed to listen in on the wicked's confession of guilt. A confession can have one of two purposes. In the context of a relationship, confessing one's sins or wrongdoing can have the function of expressing conversion or a change of heart that seeks reconciliation. We confess our sins in order to elicit the forgiveness of God (Ps 32:5). In the context of a trial, the confession confirms the validity of the accusation and justifies the condemnation (see the story of Achan, who confesses his sin of taking booty and is promptly executed after the misdeed is verified, Josh 7:10-26).

The confession of the wicked in the book of Wisdom takes place only among themselves. It does not take place in the presence of God and not even in the presence of the just one. The wicked are not seeking reconciliation through their confession. They simply are admitting to their error among themselves. Even though they are said to speak with remorse and in anguish, the purpose of the confession is not to indicate a change of heart but to provide incontrovertible evidence that their reasoning has been false. After the three diptychs that defend the just and accuse the wicked, even the unrighteous admit they are wrong.

5:4-14, Confession of the Wicked. Just as the author's defense of the just in three diptychs unraveled the wicked's argumentation in the reverse order of their project in life, so too does the wicked's confession disclaim their project in reverse order. The death of the just is not their final and tragic end (vv. 4-5); the wicked's paths of lawlessness and exploitation brought only destruction (vv. 6-7). Their arrogance and wealth have not provided profit (v. 8). As a result, their lives have become the meaningless and hopeless reality that they feared mortality had decreed for all human beings (vv. 9-14).

The wicked's confession of error covers their entire reasoning process, not just their miscalculation of the final end of the just one. A shadow is cast right back onto their original ruminations on the transience of life, and it covers their evasive pleasures, exploitation of the weak, and violence.

There are several touches of irony in the wicked's confession in phrases referring to images employed in their project of life. The wicked had derided the just one for claiming to be a "child of God" (2:13); now they acknowledge that the just one is counted among "the children of God" (υἱοὶ θεοῦ *huioi theou*, v. 5). The wicked had described revelry as their proper "lot" (κλῆρος *klēros*, 2:9) in life, but now they acknowledge that the just have their "lot" among the saints (v. 5). The wicked acknowledge that they have "taken their fill" (ἐμπίμπλημι *empimplēmi*) of lawlessness and destruction (v. 7), whereas they had exhorted one another "to take their fill" of costly wines and perfumes (2:7).

The recognition of their error and guilt leads the wicked to a lengthy reflection on the vacuity of their moral lives (vv. 9-14). This reflection stands in parallel fashion to the opening reflection on the transience of life (2:1-5). Both sections are marked by poetic images. Just as the wicked had judged their lives to be stamped fatally by the sign of mortality, so now they recognize that their moral conduct is stamped by hopelessness as well. Whereas in the first reflection the wicked ruminated on the transience of their physical existence, now they lament the transience of their moral existence. Their hopelessness and rootlessness in the moral sphere are parallel to their judgment of meaninglessness in the physical sphere. They are being punished according to their very own reasoning (3:10).

Two brief images open the disclosure of the illusory nature of their project in life. All the appearances of their wealth have vanished like a shadow and like a rumor (v. 9). These images are followed by the elaboration of several metaphors depicting the transience of their project. First comes the metaphor of the boat with its oars, which after its passing leaves no sign of its presence (v. 10). Next comes the metaphor of the bird that pushes itself through the air and leaves no sign of its coming (v. 11; cf. Job 9:26). Finally there is the metaphor of the arrow shot through the air toward a target whose trajectory cannot even be recognized (v. 12). All of these metaphors emphasize the common feature that no trace is left of an object's passing.

The wicked profess what they had denied in their opening reflection: There is an enduring value in the transience of life—virtue. But as a result of their unjust actions, they have nothing of it. Four poetic images conclude the wicked's confession whereby the rootlessness of their hope is emphasized. Without virtue, their hope is like chaff in the wind, frost in a storm, smoke in the wind, and the passing memory of an occasional guest (v. 14). It is possible that this last image of an occasional guest is formulated in the light of the Near Eastern custom of traveling in the evening and spending the day in hostels so as to avoid the heat of the day. Such guests would come and go and not be noticed.

The confession of the wicked continues to follow the pattern in Isaiah. Just as the author borrowed themes of the suffering servant, the barren woman, the eunuch, and the wise one from Isaiah, so too do we find a confession from Israel that precedes a scene of God's judgment. In Isa 59:9-13, the people confess their sin with at least one image similar to that employed by the wicked in Wisdom: They recognize how they walk in darkness and how they grope like the blind because of injustice (Isa 59:9-10; cf. Wis 5:6-7). Similarly, various parts of the wicked's confession allude to sections of the suffering servant of Isaiah ("hold in derision," Wis 5:3-4 = Isa 53:3; "we have strayed," Wis 5:6 = Isa 53:6).

The author has chosen to express the confession of the wicked in eloquent language similar to the wicked's ways of injustice. On the surface, the reasoning of the wicked remains polished, erudite, and even sophisticated. For the sake of the reader, the author does not wish to strip away from the wicked the attractive facade of their erroneous positions. The effect of the eloquent language of the confession is to underscore the importance of judging not on the surface appearance, but according to the results of judgments and actions. Although the wicked can speak with eloquence and even though they have the appearance of strength, their injustice is heading them toward a death that is far more devastating than the physical death they lament in their opening ruminations.

5:15-23, The Apocalyptic Scene of Judgment. The confession of the wicked confirms the author's argument in the three diptychs. It prepares the way for judgment to be established with respect to both the just and the wicked. The image of a royal reward is used to depict the victory of the just (vv. 15-16), whereas the image of a final and cosmic conflagration is employed to depict the punishment of the wicked (vv. 17-23).

In sharp contrast to the transience of the wicked's hope, the righteous are said to live forever (v. 15). The author here confirms the destiny that God has determined for human beings (1:15; 2:23). Faith in an enduring relationship with God is the hallmark of the just (3:1; 4:7; 5:1). The transcendent image of God as "the most high" is joined to the image of God's immanent "care," which reflects the concern of a parent watching over his or her child (v. 15b).

Two royal images are used to convey the dignity of the just person's future and eschatological reward: the crown and the diadem (v. 16). The author's use of these two images may have been inspired by Isa 62:3, where the downcast of Zion are assured that they will become a "crown of beauty" and a "royal diadem" in the hand of the Lord. The royal reward is consistent with the opening address, in which kings and rulers are exhorted to justice (1:1), and it anticipates the final address, in which kings are encouraged to listen and judge correctly (6:1).

God protects the just like a warrior whose hand covers them and whose arm shields them. The image of the divine warrior who prepares for battle is an adaptation of the metaphor that occurs in Isa 59:17-19. The analogy is expanded somewhat from Isaiah's use of breastplate, helmet, garments, and mantle to the use of the full armor of a *hoplite* in Wisdom. Each weapon of a hoplite is compared to a divine attribute: zeal = armor, justice = breastplate, impartial judgment = helmet, holiness = shield, wrath = sword.

Particularly innovative in the metaphor of the divine warrior in Wisdom is the role of the cosmos.[38] The Lord is arming creation as well (vv. 17, 20), and creation will join God in battle against the enemy (vv. 20-23). This positive role of creation on the side of justice is consistent with the author's declaration of the positive forces of the cosmos (1:14). The forces of creation are on the side of the righteous against injustice.

---

38. In all three parts of the book of Wisdom, the author displays consistency in portraying the positive role of the cosmos: in relation to God's judgment in the first, in relation to wisdom in the second, and in relation to the exodus in the third. See John J. Collins, "Cosmos and Salvation: Jewish Wisdom and Apocalyptic in the Hellenistic Age," *HR* 17 (1977) 121-42.

The ultimate conflagration is depicted in a limited apocalyptic fashion in which meteorological phenomena bring about the destruction of wickedness.[39] The forces of the cosmos—lightning, hail, water, rivers, winds, storms—will ravish the earth as a result of lawlessness (cf. Pss 18:7-15; 97:1-5; Isa 29:6).

Little can be deduced regarding the specific eschatological beliefs of the author from this restrained apocalyptic account. Such beliefs as the resurrection of the body, a definitive annihilation of the physical cosmos, and the location of blessedness cannot be presumed. In this respect, the apocalyptic judgment in Wisdom differs from other presentations of the ultimate conflagration in its brevity and in its restrained descriptions. The author is not so much interested in focusing on the end times as in portraying the importance of living a life based on justice and virtue in the present. The final conflagration simply affirms the royal reward of the just and the destruction of wickedness. It functions as the cosmic sentencing in the context of the trial that has been working in the background of the author's debate (cf. Job 34:21-30).

This somber but noble account of God's judgment brings to a close the tension that was raised in the opening exhortation between justice and injustice. It is this ultimate death portrayed in apocalyptic fashion that became the negative motive for the author's exhortation to love justice and to seek God. This death is the result of the deliberate judgments and actions of the wicked, which they have brought upon themselves through their words and deeds. This is the undesirable destiny of alienation from God and the cosmos that the author dissuades the readers from bringing upon themselves. Through a false reasoning on mortality that leads to a life of evasive pleasure, exploitation of the weak, and reliance on violence, a death far worse than mortality is experienced.

---

39. For a thorough review of the genre and language of apocalyptic sources, see John J. Collins, *The Apocalyptic Imagination* (New York: Crossroad, 1989). The judgment and destruction of the wicked is one of the dominant and consistent features of apocalypses (Collins, *The Apocalyptic Imagination*, 6).

REFLECTIONS

1. Considering the final day of judgment is relevant for the present. It may appear that the consolation for the just and the punishment of the wicked reside in a future so distant that the day of judgment is irrelevant for the present moment. This could become a difficulty if the issue of time becomes the overriding factor. But for the author of Wisdom, the consideration of the ultimate judgment is meant to focus the reader on the present situation. Judgments and actions of virtue or of injustice already initiate the dynamics of immortality and of moral death. By bringing the reader to the lofty heights of a divine perspective at an ultimate judgment, the author is focusing the lens on the true outcome of a life of virtue and a life of injustice.

2. The fruit of injustice has no enduring significance. This hard truth is one that the author argues in the three diptychs and is confirmed in the wicked's confession. The contrast between appearances and reality is heightened from the perspective of the ultimate judgment. When we examine the final outcome, what remains of our actions and relationships in the long term says a great deal about the quality of life in the present. In the case of the wicked, the strength and benefits of injustice disappear, and their status is shown to be transient.

The wicked are said to perceive this dissonance from the perspective of the enduring relationship between the just and God. What the wicked had embraced as signs of pleasure, strength, and power turn out to be hollow and transient benefits from the perspective of justice. The illusion of strength that accrues from unjust actions is built on a false hope that eventually is revealed for what it is. False hope leaves them rootless and hopeless.

3. The forces of the cosmos have both a positive and a negative function. They are positive toward justice and negative toward injustice. The unique viewpoint of the author of Wisdom interprets the forces of creation as having a concrete function for the human world. This is an extension, or perhaps an adaptation, of the creation story in Genesis. God saw everything that had been created and declared it good. For the author of Wisdom, then, the source of evil resides in the human heart and not in the forces of the world. In fact, even the forces of creation aid human beings in the pursuit of justice and hinder the practice of injustice. The exodus event will be interpreted in the latter half of the work as an instance in history of the forces of the cosmos coming to the aid of the just and hindering those who pursue injustice.

4. A good example in our own time of the principle that justice is an inherent aspect of the cosmos is our concern for the conservation of the environment. Perhaps at no other time in history have human beings been more acutely aware of the consequences of exploiting the resources of nature. Nature does have its way of reconstituting a balance with powerful and even cataclysmic events. Actions in the present, along with all of the negligence of the past, do have serious consequences for the future. We can either align ourselves with the forces that balance nature or set ourselves over and against the environment. In either case the environment will work for us or against us.

WISDOM 6:1-21, EXHORTATION TO WISDOM

COMMENTARY

In returning to words of exhortation similar to those of the opening, the author is bringing to a conclusion the first part of the work. Almost immediately, the opening exhortation to love justice and to seek God turned into a warning against a way of life that would hinder those values. The main negative image behind the warning is death: "Do not invite death by the error of your life" (1:12 NRSV).

The defense of the wicked for an unjust way of life was motivated by the negative judgment on mortality and human weakness. Their counteraccusation envisaged a shameful death for the just one. This would disprove the claims of the just and conclusively prove the validity of their own position. Through the metaphor of a trial, the author has paraded before the imagination of the reader the various scenes of the just in the hand of God—the barren woman, the eunuch, and the virtuous youth. In the examination of these scenes, the author has cut through the appearance of tragedy and injustice. These scenes function, therefore, as witnesses for justice against injustice. Finally, the scene of a final judgment elicits the confession of the wicked. They retract their entire reasoning process, which exemplified the defense of the way of injustice. The wicked are sentenced to annihilation, and the just are vindicated.

But the exhortation does not conclude with the sentencing. In suitable sapiential fashion, the author invites the reader to learn and to appropriate the lessons of the trial scene. These lessons are a matter of vital importance—the dissuasion from death, the persuasion to life. By appropriating the lessons of a warning against death, the reader can then pursue the love of justice and wisdom. With an uncluttered mind that is not mesmerized by the appearance of the power of injustice and the impotency of virtue, the attractiveness of wisdom will be readily accessible.

Exhortation to Kings. 6:1-2. The addressees of the exhortation are formally referred to as "kings" (βασιλεῖς *basileis*) and "judges" (δικασταί *dikastai*) who rule over multitudes (vv. 1-2; cf. "monarchs" [τύραννοι *tyrannoi*] in vv. 9, 21). These terms pick up the opening scene where the addressees are called "rulers of the earth" (1:1). As is the case in the opening address, the exhortation "to listen," "to learn," and "to give ear" is reminiscent of personified wisdom, who goes about the streets to convince listeners of the importance of her message (Proverbs 8). Sages would introduce their wisdom with similar exhortations (Job 13:6; 21:2; Prov 4:1; Eccl 3:1). There is a sense of urgency in the plea that has been accruing since the author introduced the stark image of death (1:12).

On the one hand, there is no need to look to specific contemporary rulers, kings, or emperors as if they are the direct addressees of the book of Wisdom. The "king" is a metaphor for human beings who are human insofar as they judge, act, and rule (Gen 1:26-27). Especially in sapiential circles, the royal image becomes the metaphor of the sage who understands and knows how to judge and to act. This royal metaphor, which begins explicitly in the closing exhortation, will become concrete in the unnamed king and sage, Solomon, for the second part of the book.

On the other hand, this does not mean that the author is not intending a critique of political power. The function of the ruler is important to understand from the point of view of faith for subjects as well as for rulers. The declaration "you that rule over multitudes and boast of many nations" (v. 2) could very well have been inspired by the extension of Roman authority during the diaspora. This does not, however, make the Roman emperor the addressee of the entire work. The Jewish community in the diaspora also had to come to terms with the meaning of such power in their cities and the role of Roman authority in their own self-understanding.

6:3-4. The author introduces a key element of the faith of Israel regarding the true source of kingship and sovereignty. The Lord is the one who confers dominion; the Most High is the source of sovereignty (cf. Judg 8:22-23; 1 Chr 29:10-13; Prov 8:15-17; Dan 2:20-23). As such, the Lord remains the unrelenting defender of justice before those who administer power in the world. God is the guarantor of justice, the one who inquires into the dealings of human beings (cf. v. 8). Therefore, the same judgment against the wicked that the author has presented in the trial scene awaits anyone who does not rule rightly and who transgresses the law and the purposes of God.

6:5-8. A corresponding theme that the author develops in the exhortation is the heightened responsibility of those in power (cf. Luke 12:48). The greater the power, the greater the accountability. To heighten the effect of this axiom, the author appeals to the long-standing tradition of God's not deferring to the powerful and the mighty. This is especially consistent with the author's penchant of looking behind appearances to the heart of judgment and action. Judgment is not partial to appearances. Since God is the source of all, everyone is accountable to God (cf. Deut 1:17; Job 34:19; Ps 104:27-30; Prov 22:2). God holds all accountable, especially those with greater responsibility. The lowly may find some leniency, but the mighty will be judged with severity (v. 6; cf. Luke 12:47-48).

6:9-11. The final purpose of the exhortation is to learn wisdom in order not to transgress. The reader is challenged to appropriate the insights and the understanding that emerge from the entire sequence of the trial scene in the earlier chapters. If we do not appropriate the importance of loving justice, then the death from which the author has dissuaded the reader will come with its full force as God's justice.

This short counsel within the larger exhortation (vv. 1-21) marks the switch from the author's warning against bringing on death to the persuasion to love wisdom as a means of practicing justice. The first part has concentrated on what one must not do to avoid the judgment of God. The second part concentrates on what must one do (learn wisdom, observe holy things, set one's desire on the words of the sage). If the reader has appropriated the insights and understanding that follow from the results of the wicked's ruminations on life, then all the more important will it be to learn wisdom. To avoid death, one must pursue wisdom so as to learn justice.

6:12-21, The Qualities of Wisdom. Wisdom is presented as a person who seeks out the sage. The author is freely adapting the personification of wisdom from the book of Proverbs (Prov 8:1-17). The literary device of personification is frequently employed by the sages (cf. Proverbs 8; Sir 6:18-31). Very briefly the author had employed the personification of justice in the opening exhortation (1:8). With this introduction to wisdom, the author is anticipating the second part of the work, which focuses on the sage Solomon, who seeks out wisdom as a bride.

The double movement of the encounter between wisdom and the sage characterizes this opening presentation of wisdom. An encounter may take place with one person moving to another, or by two people moving toward each other. The author uses the double movement of both the sage and wisdom for the meeting. The sage is instructed at first to seek wisdom, to rise up early to meet her, to fix his thought on her, to be vigilant. But wisdom is not passive. She does not simply wait for the sage. She "hastens to make herself known"; "she sits at the gate"; "she goes about seeking those who are worthy of her"; "she appears to them in their paths"; "she meets them in every thought." Since wisdom is intimately connected to God, it is not difficult to recognize the author's understanding of divine grace and intervention operating in the figure of wisdom.

Two adjectives characterize the quality of wisdom. She is "radiant" (λαμπρά *lampra*) and "unfading" (ἀμάραντος *amarantos*, v. 12). Both adjectives serve to describe the encounter between wisdom and the sage. Wisdom as radiant light is easily discernible to the one who seeks her. Wisdom as unfading light shows her constancy and permanence, her immortality. One has time to meditate and concentrate on her with one's whole mind and heart. Both images reflect the double movement of the encounter between wisdom and the sage. Wisdom actively seeks out human beings, and she lets herself be discovered by those who seek her.

A chain syllogism (*sorites*) encapsulates the surprising conclusion that the love of wisdom leads to a kingdom (vv. 17-20). Chain syllogisms were a popular literary device used to condense insights and propositions with a playful effect. The classical sorites was a six-part chain syllogism in which each proposition led to another and finally concluded with a surprise declaration.[40] But there were many variations of it. The end of each proposition would become the opening for the next. The playfulness in these syllogisms was meant to lead the reader along with several propositions that one could easily give assent to and then surprise the reader with a more difficult proposition. In our case, the surprise ending consists of the proposition that the desire for wisdom leads to a kingdom. The kingdom is an appropriate goal for the addressees, who are described as kings, judges, and monarchs.

With the offering of a kingdom through wisdom, the exhortation of the first part reaches its conclusion. The reader has been encouraged to divest a way of life of injustice, which leads to death. The argumentation of the diptychs is subtle. By sifting through appearances and reality, the author has enhanced a change in perspective according to the light of virtue and justice. The dissuasion from death has now been transformed into a persuasion toward life. Wisdom is an illuminating source for justice that brings one into proximity to God and to immortality. For the second part of the book, wisdom becomes the central concern. The focus will concentrate on the wisdom that comes from God and how it accompanies human beings throughout their struggles for a just life.

---

40. See Linda Claire Burns, *Vagueness: An Investigation into Natural Languages and the Sorites Paradox* (Boston: Kluwer Academic, 1991); H. A. Fischel, "The Uses of Sorites in the Tannaitic Period," *HUCA* 44 (1973) 119-51.

REFLECTIONS

1. God is the source of power. The exhortation by the author for kings and judges to learn and understand puts matters of authority into perspective. Throughout the diptychs and in the trial scenes, the author has stripped away the appearance of the strength of injustice as well as the apparent weakness of virtue. In the final exhortation, even the act of ruling and judging is declared to be rooted in the sovereignty of God. The mere fact that one has authority over others is no reason to attribute such power to oneself. Such a misconception opens the way for the abuse of power. The forms of injustice that follow are subject to the same judgment of God and creation. The author cautions everyone who acts with authority not to be mesmerized by the appearance of strength as if it were rooted in oneself.

The tendency to attribute strength and authority to oneself is recognized within the Torah, and so too is the need to be reminded of the ultimate source of governance in God. The homilies of Moses in the book of Deuteronomy offer a point of comparison with Wisdom's exhortation. The Israelites are poignantly reminded of their relative insignificance before crossing the Jordan River. It was not their strength in numbers or even their moral conduct that prompted God to elect them and to bring them success and blessings in the land. It was out of God's love that Israel was chosen. Only by remaining rooted in God will Israel be blessed in the land (Deut 8:1–9:7).

2. Responsibility brings accountability. This reflection concretely places the function of authority into greater perspective. For whatever reason one is given authority, one will be held accountable for the exercising of that authority. The theme of judgment permeates the exhortation. In fact, it is the perspective of the ultimate judgment that allows the author to critique the ways of injustice in the present. Similarly, in the case of authority, the more authority a person has, the more justice will be expected from that person. The Wisdom author foreshadows Christ's parable of the unfaithful slave: "From everyone to whom much has been given, much will be required; and from the one to whom much has been entrusted, even more will be demanded" (Luke 12:48 NRSV; cf. Matt 25:14-30; Luke 19:11-27).

3. There is a paradox in the experience of seeking God and discovering in the encounter that it is the seeker who has been sought and found by God. The Wisdom author recognizes the double movement in the human relationship to God. The background metaphor of encounter is used to portray the movements of the sage who seeks wisdom. The sage and personified wisdom strive to meet each other. They each set out to encounter the other. The sage "seeks" wisdom, "desires" her, "gets up early" to find her, and "fixes the mind" on her. But wisdom also "hastens to make herself known," "she goes about seeking those worthy of her," "she graciously appears . . . and meets them in every thought" (6:12-16 NRSV). No matter how hard we strive to find God in our lives and in our world, the moment of encounter often reveals how, in fact, it is God who has been seeking us out, speaking to us through others with many words and in different languages of silence and action.

4. Wisdom makes one intimate with God. A life of injustice brings death, but a life of justice brings one into union with God. The way to a life of justice is through wisdom. Wisdom is a value to be sought even as God seeks out human beings to give them wisdom. The way is clear for the author to advance a way of understanding the human condition in a manner other than that of the wicked. The second part of the book becomes a eulogy of wisdom that began in the conclusion of the exhortation. Wisdom is on intimate terms with God, and it is through wisdom that human beings come close to God.

If anything, the complexity of human life and the challenge of discerning between justice and injustice should bring about a humble desire for wisdom to guide us through life.

WISDOM 6:22–10:21

IN PRAISE OF WISDOM

OVERVIEW

On the surface, the tone of these chapters is quite different from the first part of the book. Speech in the first person signals the main shift in perspective and in emphasis. The various scenes of the trial that mediated an argument against injustice had been presented through a narrator speaking in the third person. Now, the author speaks personally, "I will tell you what wisdom is and how she came to be" (6:22), as if to heighten the understanding of the author's personal knowledge of wisdom.

If the first part of the book can be understood as the tense drama between justice and injustice, represented in the conflict between the righteous and the wicked, the second part can be understood as the creative drama between wisdom and the righteous, represented in Solomon's love of and desire for wisdom. The first section of Wisdom presented an argument against a life of injustice and death. The second part presents a persuasion to the wisdom that comes from God. Understood in this light, the sections complement each other.

The main shift in perspective focuses on the unnamed speaker: Solomon. By attributing the eulogy and praise of wisdom to Solomon, the author is garnishing authority for the values of wisdom. The Hebrew tradition idealized Solomon as the wise sage who was able to govern through wisdom. The well-known story of Solomon's first act of judgment, which uncovered the true mother of a child, formed a basis for the process of idealization (1 Kgs 3:16-28).

In keeping with the policy of not naming names throughout the book, the author uses descriptions that lead the reader to identify the speaker as Solomon. This feature is well known in certain genres of Greek writing that belong to protreptic discourse and to the encomium.[41] It is a stylistic feature that is meant to engage the reader's mind playfully to make judgments of identification.

The significance of Solomon, who praises wisdom, is that he offers a counterpart to the wicked in the first part of the book. Like the wicked, Solomon offers a perspective on mortality that issues in a concrete project in life. Unlike the wicked, Solomon's ruminations on mortality lead to a profound desire for wisdom so as to govern justly.

The main shift in emphasis from the first part focuses on personified wisdom. These chapters are permeated with Solomon's desire for, praise of, and love of wisdom. The personification of wisdom is perhaps the unique contribution of the sapiential tradition to Israel's theological heritage. In the book of Wisdom, wisdom is presented through the imagery of romantic courtship.[42] Solomon desires to win wisdom over as a suitor who woos his lover. In the other sapiential sources for the personification of wisdom (Proverbs 1–9; Sirach 24), wisdom speaks on her own behalf. But all three sources share the common feature of relating wisdom to the act of God's creation.

The author highlights two functions of wisdom in the process of personification: (1) the creative role of wisdom for humans (7:12, 22; 8:5-6; 9:2, 10-11, 18; 10); and (2) the cosmic function of wisdom in the universe (7:24; 8:1). These emphases contrast with the Hellenistic concept, whereby wisdom is primarily understood as a means of attaining knowledge and of contemplating God. For the Wisdom author, wisdom is a gift and a revelation of God that works with humans and in creation.

---

41. For examples of the technique of "riddling speech" in Hellenistic writings, see Winston, *The Wisdom of Solomon*, 141-42.

42. For an excellent treatment of the personification of wisdom in the Wisdom of Solomon, see John S. Kloppenborg, "Isis and Sophia in the Book of Wisdom," *HTR* 75 (1982) 57-84. This work compares the Hellenistic version of the Isis cult (as opposed to the Egyptian version, which celebrates the healing power of the goddess Isis over the poisonous forces in the world) to the qualities of wisdom as presented in the book of Wisdom.

As in the first part of the book, the technique of concentric structuring abounds in this central section of Wisdom. Chapters 7–8 are concentrically structured with the description of the nature of wisdom standing at the center:

```
A    7:1-6
 B    7:7-12
  C    7:13-22a
   D    7:22b–8:1
  C´   8:2-9
 B´   8:10-16
A´   8:17-21
```

The extreme sections describe what prompts Solomon to pray for wisdom. In the two midsections, Solomon extols wisdom by comparing her favorably to other commonly recognized goods.

Chapter 9 presents the climax of Solomon's eulogy of wisdom. Here he adamantly prays for the wisdom that is a gift of God. The prayer begins with his recalling how the world and human beings were created through wisdom, and it ends declaring wisdom to be the one who has saved humans continuously throughout history. In the center stands the request for God to send forth wisdom from the holy heavens and from the throne of God's glory.

```
A    9:1-3
 B    9:4
  C    9:5-6
   D    9:7-8
    E    9:9
     F    9:10a
    E´   9:10b-11
   D´   9:12
  C´   9:13-17a
 B´   9:17b
A´   9:18
```

In addition, the unit C´, 9:13-17a, is also arranged concentrically within itself.

The conclusion of Solomon's prayer provides the theme for the rest of the work. Wisdom is the one who saves the righteous in their difficult conditions of life. Chapter 10 specifically describes how wisdom accompanies righteous persons throughout history to prompt them through the crises and difficulties of life. Beginning with Adam and ending with Moses, the author tersely charts wisdom's saving role in history. As in the case of Enoch (Wis 4:10) and Solomon (Wisdom 7–9), the biblical characters remain unnamed, but their descriptions allow for relatively easy identification.

Chapter 10 provides the link between the eulogy of wisdom (chaps. 6–9) and the midrashic treatment of the exodus and the desert experience in the concluding part of the work (chaps. 11–19). The concluding part picks up the thread of the argument from wisdom's role in raising up Moses to save the troubled people and compares the Israelites in the desert to the plague-ridden Egyptians. The subject of the last part of Wisdom is not personified wisdom, but God. Wisdom recedes into the background, having completed her function of drawing the righteous into an immediate relationship with God.

WISDOM 6:22–8:21, SOLOMON'S DESIRE FOR WISDOM

Wisdom 6:22–7:12, The Sage Seeks Wisdom

COMMENTARY

6:22-25, Introduction to Solomon's Discourse. This passage displays the author's literary penchant for linking major units with transitional sections. As such, it has striking parallels of phrases to the first part of Wisdom and to the eulogy of wisdom in the second. Royal imagery from vv. 9 and 21 is continued in the reference to a sensible king's being the stability of the people (v. 24). The exhortation to "honor wisdom" recalls the enclosing exhortations of the first part to rulers, judges, and kings (vv. 21, 25; cf. "my words," vv. 11, 25). Solomon will not hide any "secrets" (μυστήρια *mystēria*, v. 22; cf. 2:22, "they did not know the secret purposes of God" [NRSV]). Envy is dissociated from wisdom (v. 23; cf. 2:24, through the devil's envy death entered the world). Of course, the unit has even stronger links to the eulogy of wisdom of the second part. The origins and qualities of wisdom, which Solomon promises to reveal in the introductory speech, become the focus and the subject for the ensuing chapters.

The unique theological perspective in this short introduction to Solomon's eulogy on wisdom rests with the author's emphasis on the universality and openness of the revelation of wisdom. Solomon will tell of wisdom's origins and her function in history. No secrets will be hidden, and the truth will not be sidestepped. This openness to the gifts of personified wisdom is consistent with the figure of wisdom in Proverbs and Sirach, in which wisdom proclaims openly her values and gifts.

Solomon's insistence on revealing wisdom's origins freely without reservation is the author's counterpoint to the secretive initiation procedures of the mystery cults. In such cults, such as those developed in Egypt around the veneration of Isis and Osiris, there would be a combination of public expressions of celebration (processions, rituals of purification and sacrifice) and secretive rites of initiation of which very little is known.[43] In contrast to the value of secrecy in the mystery cults, the Wisdom author champions the openness of wisdom's revelation. Wisdom has a universal appeal that is readily available for all who have the disposition of virtue.

A proverbial saying that highlights the value of wisdom ends the introduction. Many wise people and a sensible king are said to be the salvation of the world and the stability of the people (v. 24). This proverbial statement echoes Prov 29:4, where justice replaces wisdom as the virtue that brings stability: "By justice a king gives stability to the land" (NRSV; cf. Eccl 10:16-17; Sir 10:1-50).

Since the first part of the work identified the just with the wise, especially in the diptych on the virtuous youth (cf. 4:16-18), the multitude of the wise and the sensible king represent those who have learned justice through wisdom. They are the source of salvation. Wisdom's positive role in the salvation of humanity throughout history in general and in the case of Israel specifically (9:18; 10:1-21) is consistent with the author's positive stance toward the world (1:14).

7:1-6, Solomon Is Mortal and Limited. Solomon's resolve to pursue the wisdom that comes from God is preceded by a brief, yet touching, reflection on his mortal condition. This reflection serves as a direct counterpart to the ruminations of the wicked on the transience of life (2:1-5).

Solomon recognizes his common lot with humanity. The reflection is not evasive. Solomon declares his mortality (v. 1). But what accompanies the recognition of the mortal condition is the solidarity of Solomon with the rest of humanity. Solomon is mortal, equal to and like everyone else. Since he is

---

43. For a concise treatment of the mystery religions that flourished during the Greco-Roman period, see Marvin W. Meyer, "Mystery Religions," *Anchor Bible Dictionary*, 6 vols. (New York: Doubleday, 1992) 4:941-45.

a son of Adam, he belongs to humanity. His origin is described not like that of the wicked, by mere chance, but out of the desire of his mother and father, "from the pleasure of marriage" (v. 2).

The author's description of the formation of the embryo is informed especially by Greek science. The idea of the embryo's being molded into flesh in the mother's womb through the compacting, or "curdling," of the semen in the blood was common in Greek writings.[44] In Ps 139:13-16 and in Job 10:10 we have references to the formation of the embryo in which God is said to be the author of life or the creator who knows intimately the workings of human beings.

Solomon's formation in the womb for a period of ten months is like that of all other people. The Hebrew tradition understood the time of human gestation to be nine solar months ("I carried you nine months in my womb" [2 Macc 7:27 NRSV]; but see 4 Macc 16:7, where pregnancy translates the Greek word δεκαμηνιαῖος [dekamēniaios] to mean "a ten-month period"). The Greeks and the Romans often referred to a ten-month period for pregnancy; Roman law understood ten lunar months to comprise the period of gestation. Aristotle noted that for human beings the period of gestation differs from seven to eleven months, with the ninth month being the most common for birth.[45]

Solomon recalls how at his birth he breathed the "common" air and fell upon the "kindred" earth. The world is not presented as a hostile, transient environment. Rather, the earth constitutes a home that is "common" and compassionate. Even though his first sound was a cry, like that of all healthy newborns, he was cared for and nursed in swaddling clothes. Solomon recognizes that his first cry of need was met by the care of another human being.

The conclusion of the reflection stresses Solomon's equality with everyone else. For everyone there is one entrance into life and one exit from it (7:6). Solomon's egalitarian status could very well be an implicit critique of the divine status attributed to Egyptian pharaohs and to the kings of the Hellenistic period. But the author's purpose of stressing Solomon's commonality with humans has a more immediate aim. Solomon does not have a status separate from other humans that guarantees special wisdom. The wisdom that Solomon will seek and attain is open to everyone.

Instead of issuing in despair, as is the case with the wicked, Solomon's ruminations on mortality bring him into solidarity with humanity. The world is not perceived as a hostile environment in which might makes right. Rather, the experience of human limitations, like the first cry of a newborn, elicits care and concern for others. Recognizing the common limitations of all human beings, Solomon is led to yearn for the transcendent reality of God.

7:7-12, Solomon Prays, and Wisdom Is Given. Whereas the wicked's negative judgment on the value of human life led to a project of evasive pleasure, power, and violence, Solomon's recognition of the solidarity among humans in their limitations leads to an openness to God.

The reference to prayer and wisdom in v. 7 unmistakably employs the dream episode of 1 Kings (cf. 2 Chr 1:6-12), where Solomon came to Gibeon to offer sacrifices, and God appears in a dream to offer him a choice (1 Kgs 3:1-15). In the dream, Solomon recognizes the great task of being king and his own need to be guided in government and in judgment. Therefore, he requests an understanding mind and the ability to discern between good and evil. God responds by giving Solomon a wise and discerning mind, and God also grants him what he did not request: riches and honor.

Similarly, in the Wisdom text, Solomon recalls how he prayed and called out. The reflection on his smallness, fragility, and commonality with humanity leads him to search for a source to guide him. Understanding and a spirit of wisdom are given to him so that he will prefer wisdom to all else. Yet, all good things come to him as well through wisdom.

The author relates the gift of wisdom to the human goods that became associated with the life of Solomon (1 Kgs 4:20-34; 7:1-51). First, wisdom is declared to be superior to all that is most esteemed among humans: power and wealth (v. 8); precious stones and wealth (v. 9); health, beauty, and light (v.

---

44. See, e.g., Aristotle *Generation of Animals* 739b21.
45. See, e.g., Aristotle *Generation of Animals*, VII 4, 584ab.

10). This technique of comparing wisdom to riches, gems, and honor for exalting the benefits of wisdom was common in the sapiential tradition (Job 28:12-19; Prov 3:13-18; 8:10-11, 19).

At the same time, through wisdom, all good things have come to Solomon, and he rejoices in them. Solomon's delight in the natural qualities of health, riches, and beauty serves as a counterpoint to the wicked's evasive adulation of sensual pleasure (2:6-9). The author is adding nuances to the notion of blessedness, offered in the first part of the work. Earlier, in the diptychs, the author had argued that blessedness rooted in virtue endures even in the face of suffering and in the lack of natural human goods. The author is not pessimistic or strictly ascetic toward the pleasures of human life. Pleasure is not meant to be evaded; it is a gift of wisdom. The Preacher's exhortation in Ecclesiastes to enjoy life as God's gift finds an echo in the Wisdom text (see Eccl 2:24; 3:13; 5:18; 8:15; 9:7-9; 11:9).

The relationship between physical goods and virtue was much discussed in Greek philosophy. The Stoics held a position whereby virtue is considered the only quality necessary for human happiness. Aristotle offered a notion of happiness that integrates the good functioning of the three fundamental aspects of human life: the outside world, the body, and the soul.[46] Philo offered positions on human happiness that resemble those of Wisdom: A person attains happiness and bliss, "when there is welfare outside us, welfare in the body, welfare in the soul, the first bringing ease of circumstance and good repute, the second health and strength, the third delight in virtue."[47]

The conclusion of the passage adds a nuance to the relationship between wisdom and human goods that supersedes the source in 1 Kings. In 1 Kgs 3:10-13, the gifts of "riches and honor" are given in addition to the gift of a wise and discerning heart. The Wisdom author refers to wisdom as the engenderer of human goods (the rarely used Greek word γενέτις [*genetis*, v. 12*b*] is the feminine form of γενέτης [*genetēs*], which means "the begetter" or "father"). The image of the mother is a rare metaphor for wisdom. Ordinarily, wisdom is presented as a lover. In Sir 15:2, wisdom is compared to a mother in parallel fashion to the young bride: "She will come to meet him like a mother, and like a young bride she will welcome him" (NRSV). In Proverbs, personified wisdom is not called a mother; yet she exhorts others as a mother would her children (cf. Prov 7:24; 8:32). Philo describes wisdom as a mother and nurse.[48] As is the case with the author's view on the internal consistency between sin and punishment, the author postulates an intimate and intrinsic connection between wisdom and human goods. Wisdom is not passive in the world; rather, like a mother, wisdom actively engenders the human possibilities for happiness.

The fact that Solomon comments on not having known that wisdom was the mother of all goods singles out his pristine love for wisdom. He did not pursue wisdom in order to have these goods. Rather, in discovering and receiving wisdom he has unearthed a value that goes far beyond his desires and expectations.

---

46. Aristotle *Nicomachean Ethics* 1098b.
47. Philo *Who Is the Heir* 285-86. For other Greek and Latin references to the various definitions of human happiness, see Winston, *The Wisdom of Solomon*, 168.
48. Philo *On Drunkenness* 31.

REFLECTIONS

1. Gratitude leads to generosity. The eulogy for wisdom is introduced with Solomon's desire to impart knowledge of her freely and without restriction (6:22-25). This unfettered placement of knowledge at the disposition of others corresponds to the universal accessibility of the wisdom that comes from God. The figure of wisdom in the sapiential writings who proclaims the ways of God from the rooftops and in the marketplace is consistent with the figure of Solomon, who imparts wisdom freely (Prov 1:20-21; 8:1-4; Sir 16:24-25). Another strain in the sapiential tradition will insist on the limits of human wisdom and will stress its inaccessibility (Job 28:1-28; Eccl 7:23-25; 8:16-17).

In the case of the Wisdom author, what has been freely given to Solomon is likewise given freely in return. This attitude of generosity is explicitly and concisely formulated in the preaching of Jesus: "You received without payment, give without payment" (Matt 10:8 NRSV). Jesus' exhortation to the disciples not to hold their light under a bushel basket but to put it on a stand for all to see likewise is concretely exemplified in Solomon's disposition to impart freely the knowledge of wisdom (cf. Matt 5:15; Mark 4:21; Luke 11:33).

2. Solomon's appreciation of human weakness elicits a sense of solidarity with humanity. It is interesting to notice how both the wicked (2:1-5) and Solomon (7:1-6) provide short reflections on the human condition of mortality prior to elucidating their projects in life. What for the wicked leads to despair for Solomon leads to solidarity with humanity.

Solomon's reflection on his own mortality and smallness constitutes his commonness with humanity. Recalling his frailty as a crying infant is not something that belittles him. Instead, his memory serves to remind him of the care and solicitude shown to him in his fragile state: "I was nursed with care in swaddling cloths" (7:4 NRSV). A reflection on the limitations of human life in space and time need not lead to despair if the experience of suffering and weakness draws human beings together. On the one hand, suffering and weakness can remind us of our commonness with humanity. On the other hand, perceiving another person's need may draw out of us the care and solicitude that issues in unbreakable bonds.

3. Human weakness may open a person to transcendence. A parallel result of Solomon's reflection on mortality is his openness to transcendence. The realization of his "smallness" not only solidifies Solomon's commonness with the rest of humanity, but it also leads him to search, to desire, and to reach out. Again, in Solomon's outreach is the counterpoint to the inner despair of the wicked. Their negative judgment on life leads them to collapse in on themselves to mask the abyss with evasive pleasure and violence. Solomon's acceptance of his limitations leads him to pray and to call out.

4. A spirituality for suffering can be found in Solomon's two responses to his reflection on mortality: solidarity and desire. These responses provide the author's counterpoint to the response of the wicked. Suffering will always remain a mystery that cannot be resolved by conceptual formulations. But the author's treatment of the wicked's and Solomon's responses to human mortality provides clues for approaching the mystery of suffering both in ourselves and in others. Human suffering elicits solicitude and care. The anguish of human limitations reminds us of our solidarity with all of humanity. In facing the suffering of others, we sense the need to speak a word of solidarity and to reach out with solicitude. Finally, suffering in its many forms, from the normal experience of human finitude to the horrendous displays of despair and violence, invites or even shocks a person to reach out for answers. Suffering leaves us restless. Instead of collapsing in on himself in despair, like the wicked, however, Solomon accepts his "commonness" with all of humanity. He remembers the solicitude and care shown to him in his fragility. He looks beyond the self through prayer to find a response to the enigma of his situation in life.

5. Wisdom abounds with gifts. The description of wisdom's many attributes exemplifies the principle of abundance. Solomon recognizes that in wisdom all of life is ordered to bring forth the best of human goods. Solomon's response to receiving wisdom is the fullness of gratitude that rejoices in all of wisdom's gifts. Gratitude issues in his generosity to impart knowledge of wisdom without restriction. The figure of the wise Solomon epitomizes the principle of abundance. The more he has, the more he receives and the more he gives. When Solomon pursues wisdom first, all other gifts are showered on him with wisdom. A similar perspective on abundance is found in the teaching of Christ. The figure of wisdom is replaced with the kingdom of God and righteousness: "But strive first for the kingdom of God and his righteousness, and all these things will be given to you as well" (Matt 6:33 NRSV; cf. Luke 12:31).

Wisdom 7:13–8:1, The Nature and Qualities of Wisdom

COMMENTARY

God Is the Guide of Wisdom. 7:13. The author had affirmed the relationship among wisdom, justice, and God in the opening exhortation (1:1-4). Now that the speaker is to divulge ungrudgingly and without guile what has been learned (v. 13), the relationship between wisdom and God comes to the fore with striking emphasis. The repetition of the idea of not holding back or hiding the wealth of wisdom reiterates the author's critique of the secretive methods of induction into the mystery cults (cf. 6:22-23; Sir 20:30-31).

7:14. Through the gift of wisdom comes friendship with God (v. 14; cf. vv. 27-28). Friendship was highly valued in the wisdom tradition, and it became an ideal for fostering a faithful and personal relationship with God (Job 29:4; Ps 25:14; Prov 7:14; 18:24; 27:10; Sir 6:5-17). Friendship with God was one of the highest epithets that could be given to a person. Abraham received the appellation of God's friend, and Moses spoke to God as a friend (Abraham, 2 Chr 20:7; Isa 41:8; Jas 10:23; Moses, Exod 33:11; cf. Christ and the disciples, John 15:13-15).

7:15-16. In the preceding passage, the author had just finished highlighting the superiority of wisdom to all human goods. Wisdom is described as the author or mother of good things. Now the intimate relationship between wisdom and God is laid bare. God is declared to be the source and guide of wisdom, the corrector of the wise (v. 15). Although wisdom has been personified according to the tradition of Proverbs and Sirach, the image of wisdom does not have a separate status apart from God. This intimate relationship between wisdom and God will allow the author to drop references to wisdom in the third part of the work as the subject who acts and to replace the subject with God, who acts on behalf of Israel. God is the giver of wisdom, and wisdom brings one into unity with God.

To impart the wisdom that comes from God, the sage asks for God's help and inspiration (v. 15). To be able to speak well and to express oneself with convincing artistry was a particular value of the sapiential tradition, as its literary activity testifies (Eccl 12:9-12). Yet the sage calls upon God and recognizes that even this acquired talent is a gift to be sought from God. Wisdom was described as the source of all human goods; yet, wisdom itself has its source in God. Therefore, all the gifts that belong to wisdom, "our words," "all understanding," and "skill in crafts," are in God's hand.

7:17-20. The knowledge that the sage attests contains several references to the Hellenistic philosophy and science of the day. The range in knowledge covers chronology and astronomy (vv. 18-19), zoology, demonology, the human psyche, botany, and pharmacology (v. 20). The author is appealing to the traditional motif of extraordinary wisdom and knowledge that became associated with Solomon, considered pre-eminent among sages (1 Kgs 4:29-34).

On the one hand, such phrases as "structure of the world," "activity of the elements," "the beginning and end and middle of times," "alternations of the solstices," and "cycles of the year" (v. 19) belong to technical and popular Hellenistic ideas on the universe. Alexandrian astronomy was famous for calculating the corrections needed for the public calendar to match the solar calendar. It was under Ptolemy III Euergetes (246–221 BCE) that an extra day was added to the calendar every four years so that the seasons would fall into regular cycles. In 45 BCE, Julius Caesar employed the Alexandrian astronomer Sosigenes to oversee the implementation of the Julian calendar.

On the other hand, such phrases as "the natures of animals," "the varieties of plants," and "the virtues of roots" (v. 20), point to the traditional knowledge attributed to Solomon. In the eulogy of Solomon's wisdom, both botany and zoology are included in his vast knowledge: "He would speak of trees, from the cedar that is in the Lebanon to the hyssop that grows in the wall; he would speak of animals, and birds, and reptiles, and fish" (1 Kgs 4:33 NRSV). Ordinarily, God is presented as the one who understands the thoughts of human beings (Ps 94:11; Jer 17:9-10). Yet this knowledge is attributed to Solomon, based perhaps on the "discerning mind" he received in the dream sequence (1 Kgs 3:12). The phrase "powers of spirits" (or "of winds") can be understood either as meteorological or magical knowledge. Magical knowledge would appear to be somewhat out of place in a list of specialties that reflect Hellenistic concerns, but later Jewish tradition attributed to Solomon knowledge of magical arts. Josephus, for example, describes Solomon's magical knowledge and how it was used against demonic spirits for the purpose of healing the sick.[49]

7:21-22a. The concluding sentence forms an inclusion to the opening part of the passage with the idea of learning (vv. 13, 21). Solomon learned and taught because wisdom, the fashioner of all things, taught him. The book of Wisdom is the only book in Scripture in which wisdom is presented as the fashioner of the cosmos (cf. 8:6, where she is the fashioner of what exists). But this idea is in continuity with the presentation of wisdom in Proverbs. There wisdom is the first act of God's creation, present to God and to the cosmos as it is being created and formed (Prov 8:22-36; cf. Wis 9:9). Wisdom is personified as a master worker or a darling child taking delight in the creation of the cosmos.[50]

By attributing a stronger nuance of creation to personified wisdom, the author is once again bridging the distance between the transcendent God, creator of all, and the palpable experience of the cosmos.

7:22b–8:1, Wisdom Is Praised. Through the figure of Solomon, the author had promised to reveal the origins of wisdom and to trace her activities from the dawn of creation (6:22). This is precisely what takes place in the very center of the second part of the book of Wisdom. Wisdom is praised both for who she is and for what she does. This eulogistic passage forms the central unit of the concentric structure of 7:1–8:21. The author eulogizes wisdom through a description of her innate, natural qualities (7:22b-23), through an explanation of her origins in God (7:24-26), and through a presentation of her activities in the world and in history (7:27–8:1).

7:22b-23. The description of wisdom's innate and natural qualities takes the form of a list of attributes. There are numerous examples of this device for eulogies or for praise in both Hellenistic and rabbinic writings. The goddess Isis, for example, has so many names attributed to her that one epithet for her is "countlessnames."[51] In similar fashion, Philo attributes the epithet "manynames" to wisdom, referring to the several names given to wisdom by Moses.[52]

In this passage, the number of qualities attributed to wisdom, twenty-one (vv. 22-23), is not arbitrary. Three sets of the perfect number seven signify complete perfection. For the most part, the adjectives or qualities are borrowed from Greek thought, especially that of the Stoics. Of themselves the terms do not offer precise connotations. Rather, they are approximations and nuances that point to the subtlety, authenticity, and permeation of wisdom in the cosmos.

Intelligent, holy, unique, manifold, subtle, mobile, clear; unpolluted, distinct, invulnerable, loving the good, keen, irresistible, beneficent; humane, steadfast, sure, free from anxiety, all-powerful, overseeing, penetrating—it is not easy to discern a clear-cut pattern in the list of attributes, but three general concentrations of qualities can be recognized in

---

49. Josephus *Antiquities of the Jews* 8.2.5.
50. For a discussion on the images behind the personification of wisdom in Proverbs, see Mitchell Dahood, "Proverbs 8:22-31," *CBQ* 30 (1968) 512-21; Gale A. Yee, "The Theology of Creation in Proverbs 8:22-31," in *Creation in the Biblical Traditions,* ed. Richard J. Clifford and John J. Collins, CBQMS 24 (1992) 85-96.

51. *The Oxyrhynchus Papyri* XI 1380.
52. Philo *Allegorical Interpretation* 1.43.

the three sets of seven attributes. The qualities of the first set point to the mobility and transparency of wisdom. Appropriately, this series begins with the image of intelligence. Wisdom will be described as "an initiate in the knowledge of God" (8:4 NRSV), who "knows and understands all things" (9:11 NRSV). The second set points to the moral good associated with wisdom. Wisdom is dissociated from the opposite of the good, as in the opening exhortation (1:4). She is unpolluted and loves the good. The third set begins to point to wisdom's indomitable relationship to humanity. Wisdom is humane, pervading and permeating all that exists. Wisdom's pervasiveness in the cosmos makes her immediate and immanent to human beings.

7:24-26. Of the twenty-one attributes, the mobility and the pervasiveness of wisdom in the cosmos are singled out for special attention (v. 24). The idea that thought is faster than any physical motion was a common reflection in Greek philosophy. Philo likewise made use of the idea of swiftness in praising the speed of the Logos[53] and commented on the speed of the mind: "For the mind moves at the same moment to many things material and immaterial with indescribable rapidity."[54] The idea of the pervasiveness of knowledge that penetrates all things was a typically Stoic idea. Even the use of the double verbs "pervade" (διήκω *diēkō*) and "permeate" (χωρέω *chōreō*) points to its Stoic source, which makes use of these verbs to describe the presence of the spirit.[55] Because of its mobility and pervasiveness, wisdom is readily accessible to human beings as a source of right conduct.

Five metaphors are used in the central part of the unit to indicate the relationship of wisdom to God (vv. 25-26). Each metaphor attempts to relate wisdom to an aspect of God. Wisdom is the breath of God's "power" (δύναμις *dynamis*), an emanation of the "glory" (δόξα *doxa*) of the Almighty, a reflection of the eternal "light" (φῶς *phōs*) of God, a mirror of the "working" (ἐνέργεια *energeia*) of God, and an image of the "goodness" (ἀγαθότης *agathotēs*) of God. All of these varied metaphors attempt to root wisdom in God through images that point to wisdom's flowing, emanating, or originating from an aspect of God.

The metaphors themselves are quite an innovation for the Wisdom author, in comparison to the descriptions of the origins of wisdom in Proverbs 8 and Sirach 24. The author is combining various terms and metaphors that refer to divine or spiritual activity from Greek and Hellenistic sources.[56] Yet, the author is evidently applying such metaphors to the traditional Jewish concept of wisdom.[57]

The use of "breath," which in general denotes exhalation, signifies the close connection between wisdom and the power of God. The Greek word for "breath" (ἀτμίς *atmis*) comes closer to signifying the effect of the mist on our nostrils than it does to the breath of God in the Genesis creation accounts. As such, it often refers to the fragrance of incense (Lev 16:13; Sir 24:15). Wisdom, then, is like the fragrance of the power of God. The metaphor of the pure emanation (NRSV) or effusion (NAB) of God's glory brings us into the semantic range of water, although light can be said to flow as well (Ezek 1:13, lightning issues from the fire). Wisdom is being compared to the flowing of water from the source, which is God's glory. With the qualification of wisdom as being a pure flowing, the author is intensifying the authenticity of wisdom's relationship to God. Just as pure water flows freely from a good source, so too nothing defiled or impure contaminates wisdom, whose source is God (cf. 1:4; 6:23).

The comparison of God to various forms of light is a frequent and effective image in the OT, especially as light relates to the theophanies of God (Exod 24:17; Isa 60:1-3; Ezek 1:27-28; Hab 3:4). The psalms often speak of God's light and the light of God's countenance brightening up the life and path of humans (Pss 4:6; 27:1; 36:8; 43:3; 44:3; 89:15; 104:2). The author has already applied images of light to wisdom. Wisdom is radiant and unfading (6:12). Wisdom is said

---

53. Philo *On the Cherubim* 28.
54. Philo *On the Change of Names* 179.
55. *Stoicorum Veterum Fragmenta*, ed J. von Arnim, 4 vols. (Leipzig, 1903-24; reprint Stuttgart, 1966; New York, 1986) 2.416: "the spirit pervades all things"; 2.1021: "the spirit permeates the whole."
56. For a source of multiple references to Philo's metaphors for the relationship of the Logos to God and for those of the Isis cult, see Winston, *The Wisdom of Solomon*, 184-87.
57. For an excellent presentation on the Wisdom author's sympathy for Greek thought and for attempting to express traditional Israelite faith through Hellenistic forms, see Alexander A. Di Lella, "Conservative and Progressive Theology: Sirach and Wisdom," *CBQ* 28 (1966) 139-54, also in *Studies in Ancient Israelite Wisdom*, ed. James L. Crenshaw (New York: KTAV, 1976) 401-16.

to surpass the brightness of light and the sun (7:10, 29). But here, wisdom is presented as the reflection of the eternal light. The same idea is continued in the following metaphor, which employs the image of a spotless mirror reflecting the activity of God (v. 26b). Philo also uses the metaphor of the mirror to describe how the activity of order and management in the cosmos mirrors the powers of God.[58] Wisdom, essentially, is busy with the activity of God (7:22; 8:6).

The metaphor of the image of God's goodness confirms the attribute of goodness and friendship that has continuously been applied to wisdom. Wisdom has been called a "kindly spirit" (1:6), the mother of all good things (7:11-12) who provides "friendship with God" (7:14; cf. 7:27) and who "loves the good" (7:22). The metaphor of "image" is biblical, used to convey the relationship between humans and God (2:23; cf. Gen 1:27; 5:1; 9:6). But with the specific nuance of explaining the relationship of God's goodness to wisdom, the metaphor in Wisdom is particularly at home with the platonic metaphor of a copy, "It is wholly necessary that this Cosmos should be a copy of something,"[59] and with Philo's application of the metaphor to relate the Logos to God, "The Divine Logos is himself the Image of God."[60]

The novelty for the author of Wisdom in identifying the proximity of wisdom to God lies in the density of the images, not in creating a new personality for wisdom. No other biblical source provides the variety of metaphors for relating personified wisdom to God. Yet all of these metaphors of fragrance, flowing, reflection, mirroring, and image relate only aspects of God (God's power, glory, light, activity, and goodness) to wisdom. The Wisdom author is expanding the traditional images of God's Word and God's deed—which relate the transcendent God to the life of Israel—to include images that portray causality and relation in God's dealings with humanity.

7:27–8:1. This unit explains the activity of wisdom in the life of the cosmos and humanity. Here the author highlights wisdom's effective influence on humanity. Cognizant of wisdom's effective role in the cosmos and in the lives of the just, Solomon will proceed to desire her above all else and to discover how to obtain wisdom (8:2-21).

The paradox of wisdom's being one, yet able to do all things, perhaps is inspired by the Greek paradox of the one and the many, or the problem of change and permanence, as put forward by Parmenides (504–456 BCE). It was a paradox applied to the many faces of Isis, who is described as being one, yet able to do everything.[61] However, the same general idea is not absent in Scripture: "You [God] change them like clothing, and they pass away; but you are the same" (Ps 102:26-27 NRSV). The simplicity of wisdom is comparable to the unicity of God (Deut 6:4). Similarly, the parallel idea in the same verse has its roots in Greek philosophy. While remaining in herself, wisdom renews all things. In Greek philosophy, God is described as the "unmoved mover," who "remains in the same place," "not moving at all."[62] However, the idea that wisdom renews all things has particular biblical overtones. Making things new is the activity of God's Spirit: "When you send forth your spirit, they are created; / and you renew the face of the ground" (Ps 104:30 NRSV). The author is drawing close parallels between wisdom and the activity of God in creation. Wisdom is God's activity in the cosmos and in humanity that renews the earth and restores human beings.

The turn to the specific focus on wisdom's relationship to humanity (7:27c) is consistent with the image of wisdom in Prov 8:31, where wisdom is said to rejoice in the inhabited world and to take delight in the human race. Wisdom enters into holy ones to make them friends and prophets of God. Both ideas have already been asserted by the author. Divine providence especially cares for the just (3:9), and those who have wisdom obtain God's friendship (7:14). What had been stated negatively in 1:3-6—namely, that wisdom flees from deceit—is now stated positively. Wisdom collaborates with the holy ones. Both friend and prophet refer to relationships of personal friendship and affiliation (Isa 6:1-9; Jer 1:4-10; Ezek 2:1–3:11).

---

58. Philo *Questions and Answers on Genesis* 1.57.
59. Plato *Timaeus* 29B.
60. Philo *On Flight and Finding* 101.
61. *Isis Aretalogy* Cyrene 6,15.
62. See Plato *Timaeus* 42E; Aristotle *Physica* 156b25.

The notion of God's loving the person who lives with wisdom anticipates the following unit, in which Solomon seeks to obtain wisdom as his spouse. The image of "living with wisdom" conjures up the parallel that the relationship between the just and wisdom is comparable to that of husband and wife (cf. Isa 62:5). They are completely faithful to each other, and their mutual love reaches a completion that goes beyond themselves.

To complete the eulogy, the author returns to the superiority of wisdom over light and ends with wisdom's pervasiveness over the earth, which effectively orders all things well. What is particularly striking and new in the comparison (from that of 7:8-10 and 7:24) is the introduction of a moral perspective. Wisdom is superior to light not because of brightness, since night follows day, but because evil does not prevail over wisdom. The tension between injustice and wisdom that dominated the first part of the work resurfaces, but with the emphatic superiority of wisdom assured.

The concluding remark also contains echoes of the Stoic belief in God's providence. The author has prepared for the conclusion that wisdom reaches from one end of the earth to the other and orders everything well in the description of wisdom and in the metaphors relating wisdom to aspects of God. Wisdom is mobile and actively present in the world and in humans. However, the image of wisdom stretching through the universe is similar to the Stoic belief of the *pneuma* stretching from one end of the universe to the other. Similarly, the idea of wisdom's ordering all things well is parallel to the Platonic and Stoic ideas that God orders the universe continuously.

REFLECTIONS

1. Knowledge of the cosmos is consistent with the wisdom of God. The author of Wisdom presents, essentially, a positive view of the cosmos, of human beings, and of human knowledge. The role of God and God's wisdom in creation confers upon the cosmos and human beings a primary dignity that endures even during the conflicts between justice and injustice. The author, therefore, welcomes the insights of Greek and Hellenistic philosophy and integrates them into Israel's faith. Within the controversy of faith and science, the book of Wisdom comes down on the side of the integration of faith and knowledge. Since God has created the cosmos through wisdom, then knowledge of the cosmos leads to God.

In praising the origin of knowledge in God, the author's list of insights into the cosmos, into nature, and into the thoughts of human beings seems like a litany of praise for God and wisdom. It is as if the wonder and amazement of the intricate functioning of the cosmos lead to the awe and the astonishment of the source, who is God (7:17) and God's wisdom (7:22). The list of insights embraces the major fields of Greek knowledge: the activity of the elements, the calculation of time through astronomy, the variety of animal species, vegetation, human psychology, and medicine. At the beginning of the list of various forms of knowledge, God is praised as the originator of knowledge. At the end of the list, wisdom, the fashioner of all, is praised as the teacher. In the reflection on the origin of false worship, the author will reiterate the consistency between knowledge of the cosmos and divine origin (13:1-9) with greater philosophical precision.

The constant growth and expansion of our knowledge of science, of human psychology, of medicine, and of technology can appear rather daunting in terms of faith in a personal creator. Other voices in Scripture warn humans of the folly of holding one's own knowledge up with arrogance, thereby considering humans the center of the universe. The story of the Tower of Babel in Genesis signals the danger of truncating knowledge of the universe from the purposes of the creator. At the same time, the belief in the creation of the world by a personal God reminds us that the cosmos is imprinted with signs that point to a divine origin. The voice we hear in the book of Wisdom reminds us that the wonder we experience in understanding the universe can lead to the contemplation of the source of God's wisdom.

2. The eulogy of wisdom shows signs of attempting to bridge the distance between God's transcendence and God's immanence. The distance yet proximity of God is a paradox at the heart of Israel's faith. God, at once, is understood as reigning high in the heavens, beyond human understanding, yet intervening in human history to call Israel and to save the just (see Psalms 33; 113; 136). God's face cannot be seen; yet God is the one who cares for Israel as a parent. Traditional images that bridged the distance between God Almighty and God, compassionate love, rested on God's Word and deed. Through Word and deed, God would reach into human history to save the just and destroy resistance.

Personified wisdom is the later sapiential contribution to theology that bridges the gap between God's distance and God's proximity. The author understands God's proximity to human beings as being realized in the signs of intelligence in creation itself. The twenty-one attributes of wisdom attempt to describe wisdom's pervasiveness in and through the universe and the solicitude for human beings in calling them to the moral good. Wisdom is not personified to the point of becoming a separate entity. Rather, through five metaphors, wisdom is presented as God's intervention in history: a breath of God's power, a flowing of God's glory, a reflection of eternal light, a mirror of God's activity, and an image of God's goodness. The whole point of wisdom's activity is to bring human beings into proximity to God. It is wisdom who makes humans friends of God.

3. Although it remains unclear whether the NT writers were familiar with the book of Wisdom, some of the christological formulations in the letters associated with Paul have strikingly close parallels to the metaphors for wisdom's relationship to God in 7:25-26. Paul employs the image of a mirror reflecting the glory of the Lord to portray the manner in which God's glory transforms human beings in Christ:

> And all of us, with unveiled faces, seeing the glory of the Lord as though reflected in a mirror, are being transformed into the same image from one degree of glory to another. (2 Cor 3:18 NRSV)

Just as wisdom is called the image of God's goodness (7:26*c*), so too does Paul refer to Christ as "the image of God" (2 Cor 4:4 NRSV). Similarly, in Col 1:15, Christ is referred to as "the image of the invisible God" (NRSV) through whom all things were created. The author of Hebrews employs the rare Greek word for "reflection" to explain how Christ "is the *reflection* of God's glory and the exact imprint of God's very being" (Heb 1:3 NRSV, italics added; cf. Wisdom 7). Since the personification of wisdom became a literary device for presenting the immanence of God in human history, it was natural enough for the NT writers to employ similar language in presenting Christ as the image of God.

Wisdom 8:2-21, Solomon's Love for Wisdom

COMMENTARY

8:2-9, Solomon Desires Wisdom. This passage corresponds to the unit 7:13-22 within the concentric structure through a parallel of several themes and images (i.e., wealth, riches, understanding, wisdom as fashioner of what exists, as knower of the seasons). After praising wisdom's nature, her origin in God, and her effect on humanity, the figure of Solomon turns to a more personal note. It is for these reasons that Solomon is personally caught up in the pursuit of wisdom. There is a return to speech in the first person. The language changes to that of love, courtship, and marriage. The same issues of wisdom's nature, relationship to God, and benefits for humanity are pursued, but now from Solomon's personal point of view. It is as if the speaker is contemplating the precious moments of falling in love with a value of extreme importance.

8:2. The underlying metaphor of courtship is unmistakable. Solomon recounts how he had sought wisdom from his youth, desired to take her as a bride, and became enamored of her beauty. The literary device of treating wisdom or other abstract values as a lover and wife who is to be sought and cherished was common in both the Israelite and the Greek traditions.[63] Both Proverbs and Sirach provide excellent examples in the sapiential tradition of offering advice on the importance of choosing a good wife (Proverbs 31; Sirach 25–26). In Proverbs, wisdom is personified as a woman calling attention to her values in the streets (Prov 1:20-33; 8:1-21), as the woman of a household who prepares a feast for those who are willing to hear insight (Prov 9:1-6), as a sister and an intimate friend (Prov 7:4). Sirach uses several metaphors for the pursuit of wisdom: a hunter (Sir 14:22), a suitor (Sir 14:23-25), a youth in quest (Sir 51:13-22). In a very brief metaphor, wisdom is presented as a bride and a steadfast wife (Sir 15:2-6).

The Wisdom author extends the treatment of the personification of wisdom as a lover and a bride. The figure of Solomon, whom tradition held to have cherished wisdom (1 Kgs 3:9), lends itself to the metaphor of courting wisdom as a lover. The metaphor of human sexual love to connote the passionate pursuit of values or faithfulness to God has its precursors in the Song of Songs and in the extensive metaphor of Israel's being the bride of God (Isa 62:4-5; Hos 2:14-23). Here the metaphor is held up to the reader's imagination to contemplate the values associated with wisdom.

8:3-4. The metaphor is applied not only to Solomon and wisdom, but also to God and wisdom. Wisdom's divine origin is dignified through a symbiosis of God and wisdom. Wisdom lives with God. The Lord loves her. The term used to characterize wisdom's relationship to God as an "initiate" (μύστις *mystis*) in knowledge is a technical term used in the mystery cults to designate the highest level of illumination for their members.[64]

8:5-8. Four conditional sentences introduce wisdom's effective role for humanity in creation. If riches are a value to be pursued, then even more so is wisdom the source of wealth. If understanding is a value, then even more so is wisdom, the fashioner of whatever exists. The author appeals to wisdom's enduring role in creation to highlight her benefits (cf. 7:11, 22).

If righteousness is a value to be loved, then so much more so is wisdom, the origin of the four virtues: self-control, which moderates the use of pleasure; prudence, which discerns the means for ends; justice, which determines what belongs to each; and courage, which gives strength to surmount difficulties and trials. This is the first clear reference in Scripture to the famous debate of the four virtues in Greek literature. Plato classified virtue into four categories as expressing the harmony or health of the soul.[65] Although the Epicureans rejected the platonic division, they discussed all four virtues in the pursuit of pleasure.[66] The Stoics and Philo continued to speak of the four virtues, and Philo attributed the origin of the virtues to the divine Logos very much as our author attributes them to wisdom.[67] The author may very well have been inspired to integrate the Greek philosophical debate on the virtues with the traditional understanding of wisdom. In Proverbs 2, for example, wisdom is presented as the origin and bestower of several virtues (cf. 4 Macc 1:18).

Finally, if wide experience is a value, then so much more so is wisdom, who knows the

---

63. For several examples of the wife metaphor for virtue or wisdom in Greek literature, see Winston, *The Wisdom of Solomon*, 192-93.

64. The initiate (*mystis*) is one who has experienced the mysteries of the cult and is bound by a vow of silence not to divulge its secrets. See Meyer, "Mystery Religions," 4:941-42. Wisdom, however, is one who has the complete experience of the mysteries of God, but divulges the secrets to the just.

65. Plato *Republic* 443D-E, 444D.

66. Cicero *De Finibus bonorum* 1.42-54.

67. Philo *Allegorical Interpretation* 1.63-65.

past and the future, who understands speech and riddles, and who has foreknowledge of signs and wonders. The underlying allusion here is to Solomon's ability to solve riddles and enigmas (1 Kgs 5:9-14; 10:1-9). Among the sages, the ability to communicate with effective speech was highly regarded. The disciples of Qohelet valued this particular ability in their master (Eccl 12:9-13).

The common word pair "signs and wonders" (σημεῖα καὶ τέρατα *sēmeia kai terata*, 8:8) is ordinarily associated with the great events surrounding the exodus (Exod 7:3; Deut 4:34; 6:22; 7:19; Ps 135:9). In reverse order, it appears in 10:16 referring precisely to the great events of liberation that wisdom inspired through Moses. These signs and wonders associated with the exodus will become the focus in the last part of the book. The phraseology here anticipates the wisdom of God to be the one who saves the people and guides them through the desert with signs and wonders.

8:9. To conclude the series of conditional sentences, Solomon expresses his decision to have wisdom live with him. This decision continues the metaphor of courting wisdom as a lover in the opening sentence of the unit (v. 2). For the author, to accept wisdom into one's life is like engaging oneself in marriage. The commitment to live with wisdom will assure Solomon good counsel and encouragement in the trials of life.

8:10-16, Wisdom Grants Success. This unit corresponds to the declaration of wisdom's superiority over all goods within the concentric structure (7:8-12). The image that is treated throughout the unit is Solomon's fame, both during his life and after his death. Two phrases introduce the alleged fame Solomon will have through wisdom. The first addresses the fame he will have during his rule (v. 10), and the second introduces the fame of immortality that will belong to him (v. 13). The time frame focuses on the future, and the form of discussion is a personal and interior reflection of the unnamed speaker, Solomon.

The allusion to Solomon's fame is based on two features in the historical accounts of Solomon's rise to power. The first is to the youthfulness of Solomon, who recognizes his need for experience and wise counsel. In the dream sequence, Solomon confesses that he is but a child and does not know how to govern. Therefore, he asks for an understanding mind so that he can govern wisely and continue in the footsteps of his father, David (1 Kgs 3:7-9). In his reflection on Wisdom, Solomon realizes how he will have glory and respect before the multitudes and his elders, even though he is young. The idea of youths having understanding beyond their years was already addressed in the third diptych (4:7-20). Other examples in Scripture would be those of Joseph, who could interpret dreams (Gen 41:33-45); Elihu, who confronts the elders (Job 32:6-14); and Daniel, whose wisdom saved Susanna (Sus 44-46, 64). Solomon confesses that the reputation he has acquired is based on his commitment to wisdom.

The second feature in the historical accounts to which the author makes an allusion is the reputation Solomon will earn as a wise statesman both in Israel and beyond. His keen judgment is represented in the astute action he took to determine the true mother of a child (1 Kgs 3:16-28). His fame is alleged to have spread throughout all the neighboring lands (1 Kgs 4:29-34), and his rule extended far and wide (1 Kgs 4:20-21). Even the Queen of Sheba came to Solomon to verify his fame as the wisest of kings (1 Kgs 10:1-13). For the author of Wisdom, Solomon's reputation as a wise and powerful statesman was made possible because of the gift of wisdom that he received from God.

The claim that wisdom will confer immortality on Solomon is consistent with the previous association of wisdom with immortality (6:17-20). Wisdom brings one close to God and confers immortality. In the Isis cult, the goddess Isis was considered to have been the conferrer of immortality, which she conferred on her husband, Osiris, and on her son Horus. The immortality Solomon will enjoy is the honored reputation that will last even after his death. This reputation of immortality stands in sharp contrast to the reflection of the wicked, who were denied any lasting memory after death (2:2-5).

Finally, the metaphor of loving wisdom as a wife concludes this part of Solomon's inner reflection on the advantages of living according to wisdom. Wisdom is the one who brings complete rest and joy. All of Solomon's activity in planning and ruling finds its culmination in rest and peace through wisdom (v. 16). Both Solomon's public life and his private life will become well ordered so that he may enjoy in peace the fruit of his labor.

8:17-21, Wisdom Is a Gift of God. This unit corresponds to the opening unit of the concentric structure (7:1-6). The opening of Solomon's reflection on his human limitations and mortality led to the realization of his solidarity with all humanity and his openness to the transcendence of God. Here at the conclusion of Solomon's reflection and eulogy for wisdom, we return to the concrete awareness of his need to ask from God the wisdom that is graciously bestowed as a gift.

8:17-18. The speaker recaps the essential features of the lengthy reflection on wisdom (vv. 17-18). In kinship with wisdom, there is immortality (cf. v. 13); in friendship with her, pure delight (cf. v. 16); in laboring with her, unfailing wealth (cf. 7:11); and in the experience of her companionship, understanding and knowledge (cf. 7:21-22). The conclusion of the summary leads to Solomon's awareness that he must actively seek the gift of wisdom.

8:19-20. The theme of Solomon's birth and childhood binds the unit to the opening reflection on his first cry as an infant (7:3). What is critical to the author of Wisdom is Solomon's awareness that even his good corporeal and spiritual nature needs to be completed by the wisdom that comes from God. The author is balancing the positive dynamic of the human structure against the incompleteness of human nature. It is as if the wisdom of God has fashioned human beings in such a way that they are complemented by the wisdom that is bestowed as a gift. The very structure of human beings is oriented to being completed by the transcendence of God (cf. 9:5-6, 13-17).

The controversial theory of the pre-existence of the soul has played a part in the formulation of the author's positive view of Solomon's nature.[68] A good soul fell to Solomon's lot—or, rather, being good, Solomon entered an undefiled body (vv. 19-20). The author's qualification of the priority of the soul over the body was probably influenced by nuances of Greek ideas treating the pre-existence of the soul. The notion of pre-existence had already worked its way into Jewish thought as exemplified in Philo and Josephus. But, in both formulations of vv. 19-20, the author is asserting the natural harmony that exists between Solomon's soul and body. What the qualification stresses is not so much the pre-existence of the soul as the moral perspective of the relationship between body and soul. By the virtue of "being good," Solomon entered an undefiled body. This is consistent with the author's ethical stance toward immortality.

8:21. Even though Solomon's natural disposition is as good as anyone could expect, he realizes that he will achieve the goal of his desires only through the gift of the wisdom that comes from God. Solomon's naturally good disposition gives him the insight that there is a gift from God that completes his desires.

At the beginning of the reflection, Solomon ponders the aspects of wisdom in his heart (v. 17), and at the end he prays to God with all his heart (v. 21). The idea of praying to God with all one's heart and soul and might was firmly ensconced in Hebrew piety. The author may very well be alluding to the shema in describing the ardor in which Solomon prays to God for wisdom, "You shall love the LORD your God with all your heart, and with all your soul, and with all your might" (Deut 6:5 NRSV).

---

68. The pre-existence of the soul received its authoritative expression in Plato's complex doctrine (see *Phaedo; Republic*). The Wisdom author is clearly referring to the primacy of the soul with a notion of its pre-existence without reference to the more complex and negative aspects of Plato's doctrine—the transmigration of souls and the "fall" of the soul into matter. The negative interpretation of matter and the "fall" of the soul into a material body is quite foreign to the author of Wisdom. But, as David Winston points out, a few Middle Platonists already offered the perspective of a positive view of the joining of souls to bodies. For a thorough discussion of the various views of the pre-existence of the soul in Platonism, in Stoicism, and in rabbinic and apocalyptic writings, see Winston, *The Wisdom of Solomon*, 25-32.

REFLECTIONS

1. The effect of Solomon's reflection on the beauty of wisdom provides an insight into the self-appropriation of values. Solomon's pursuit of wisdom does not issue from a blind obedience or from outside pressure. Rather, by contemplating the reality of the wisdom that comes from God, the author engages the intellectual and the affective capacities of the mind and the heart. The author provides the reader with the inner dispositions of the unnamed Solomon that lead him to embrace the value of wisdom: the appreciation of beauty, wealth, intelligence, the virtues, and the desire for wisdom's intimacy with God, and even the knowledge of human experience. The pursuit of wisdom leads to the balance and harmony of a full human life.

The appropriation of the value of wisdom with all of its associated virtues in the figure of Solomon provides a contrast to what the wicked do with their lives (2:1-20). Despair motivates their judgments and actions in life. Love motivates Solomon's decision to embrace wisdom.

2. The mystical marriage between Solomon and wisdom continues a long-standing tradition of highlighting the personal engagement involved in choosing and appropriating values through the metaphor of human love. Just as courtship and marriage fully engage the entire spectrum of our intellectual and affective concerns, so too does the pursuit of God's wisdom demand the engagement of the entire person. The relationship between Israel and God is portrayed often enough through the image of a marriage. Hosea made extensive use of courtship and marriage to portray the painful consequences of unfaithfulness as well as the freshness, intimacy, and beauty of God's "first love" for Israel (Hos 2:1-23), and Paul used the metaphor to depict the relationship between Christ and the church (Eph 5:22-33). This marriage metaphor, then, both heightens the beauty of the exchange of love in the covenant and sharpens the pain of loss due to unfaithfulness.

In Christian mysticism, the use of language of human love to express divine love was inspired by these metaphors from the scriptures. John of the Cross rewrote the Canticle of Canticles based on a contemplative discussion between God as the bridegroom and the soul as the bride:

Bridegroom
She has entered in, the bride,
To the long desired and pleasant garden,
And at her ease she lies,
Her neck reclined
To rest upon the Loved One's gentle arms.[69]

Teresa of Avila spoke of the final stage in one's relationship with God in terms of a spiritual marriage. In the *Interior Castle,* she sets out to explain the progression of the soul in its spiritual journey as being led by God through a series of mansions. The seventh mansion represents the complete fusion of the soul with God through the image of a spiritual marriage.[70] Human friendship, love, and commitment provide images through which we can grasp both the challenge of wisdom and its gifts of rest, completion, and intimacy.

3. A spirituality from abundance emerges through Solomon's eulogy of wisdom. Solomon's awareness of his natural gifts does not lead to arrogance or complacency, but

---
69. John of the Cross *The Spiritual Canticle* 28.
70. Teresa of Avila *The Interior Castle*, Seventh Mansion II.

to the contemplation of the origin of his being. The awareness of having been given abundant gifts brings him to recognize the source of those gifts. In his final reflection on wisdom's many benefits (8:17-21), Solomon offers the counterpoint to his opening reflection on mortality and limitations (7:1-6), which offers a spirituality of privation and suffering. The final reflection offers a spirituality of abundance. Human limitation can be the birth of desire and longing. Solomon's realization of his mortality led him to yearn for completion in God. The experience of life in abundance also can lead to a yearning for union with the source of all gifts.

The eulogy of wisdom suggests that there is also a proper way to live with abundance. In the wicked, despair brought forth a plan in which abundance and power simply masked a nihilistic stance in life. They used the natural gifts of life to cover the abyss of weakness and mortality. Solomon's many gifts, which he received from his natural environment, however, lead him to reflect on the source of his blessedness. Instead of collapsing in on himself, Solomon reaches out to the source of blessedness.

What do we have that we have not received as a gift? Even the most personal achievements of insight or works of art never occur in a vacuum. Someone gave us encouragement or provided the right conditions for us to receive insight or inspiration. It may be easy to forget the giver in the experience of abundance (see Deut 8:1-20), but to reflect on the source of prosperity brings the purpose of abundance to its completion: union between the lover and the beloved.

WISDOM 9:1-18, SOLOMON'S PRAYER FOR WISDOM

COMMENTARY

This eloquent prayer for wisdom has been recognized by many commentators as the climax of the book of Wisdom. The eulogy of wisdom, which began at the end of chap. 6, flows into a dramatic appeal to God by the unnamed Solomon for the gift of wisdom. Throughout the chapters that dissuaded the reader from bringing on the reality of death by living a life of injustice (chaps. 1–6), the need for guidance in the turbulent sea of life has been coming to the fore. The wisdom of God offers the context of a positive vision for creation and humanity. With the wisdom that comes from God, humans find completion for their energies. And so Solomon pleads with God for the gift of wisdom.

The prayer is located near the central position of the book, especially when considered from the point of view of lines in the manuscripts.[71] It is modeled on the dream sequence in 1 Kgs 3:1-15 and the nocturnal appearance of the Lord in 2 Chronicles 1. Both stories relate how God appeared to Solomon in a dream or in a vision to grant him any request. Instead of choosing riches, fame, or a long life, the standard values, Solomon asks for a discerning mind and wisdom. The significant difference between Wisdom and those accounts is that the original context of a dream or a vision has been changed into a prayer initiated by Solomon.[72]

The prayer is crafted exquisitely from a literary perspective. It is as if the density of insight and feeling enclosed in the prayer needs an appropriate form to express and contain what otherwise would be dissipated. A curious fact is that the most moving passages of Scripture, upon a little probing, turn out to have been crafted with great artistic

---

71. For a discussion on the central position of Solomon's prayer for wisdom in the book of Wisdom, see A. G. Wright, "The Structure of the Book of Wisdom," *Bib* 48 (1967) 165-84. Chapter 9 concludes the first half of the book, with chap. 10 added as link to balance the two halves of the book: chaps. 1–9; 10; 11–19.

72. Maurice Gilbert uncovered the concentric structure of Solomon's prayer and pointed out the author's creative transformation of the sources from 1 Kings and 2 Chronicles. See Maurice Gilbert, "La structure de la prière de Salomon (Sg 9)," *Bib* 51 (1970) 301-31. For a treatment of this work in English, see Kolarcik, *The Ambiguity of Death in the Book of Wisdom (1–6)*, 17-18.

care.[73] It would appear that insight and profundity favor an aesthetic expression.

The three sections of the concentric structure of 9:1-18 may be outlined as follows:

```
A   9:1-3                    A´  18
   B   4                       B´  17b
      C   5-6                     C´  13-17a
         ─────────────────────────────────
            D   7-8      D´  12
               E   9     E´  10b-11
                  F   10a
```

Through this structure, the author balances ideas and images within the prayer. The first section within the structure (vv. 1-6) speaks of wisdom's role in creation for all humanity. This section stands parallel to the last section (vv. 13-18), in which the tasks of life in general again are addressed. In the beginning, it is wisdom's role in creation that assures wisdom's intimacy with God (v. 1). At the end, it is wisdom's role in salvation history that assures humanity its intimacy with God (v. 18). The middle section (vv. 7-12) concentrates specifically on the task of kingship placed on the shoulders of Solomon. In itself, it is balanced by two halves that treat Solomon's call to govern, and in its center rests the formal request that God send to him the wisdom that is with God (v. 10). The prayer synthesizes the broad perspectives of the author's view of the human relationship to God and to the cosmos. It balances the reflection on human limitations and potential with the essential function of wisdom in creation and in salvation.

9:1-6, Wisdom Fashioned Humanity. Key themes are touched upon in the opening address of the prayer: the God of the ancestors, the God of creation, the creation of humanity through wisdom, the call of humanity to rule over the world in justice, the limitations of humanity for this great task, the need for human knowledge to be completed by the wisdom of God.

God is addressed in traditional Hebrew fashion as the God of the ancestors and the God of mercy (v. 1). The image of the God of the ancestors recapitulates the providence and care shown to Israel through the history of the patriarchs Abraham, Isaac, and Jacob (cf. Gen 26:24; 28:13; 32:10; Exod 3:13-16; 4:5; Deut 1:11, 21; 4:1; 12:1). During the divine intervention into the life of Moses in the desert, God's name is revealed precisely through the image of the God of the ancestors (Exod 3:13-16). But immediately the image of the God who saves is juxtaposed to the image of the God who creates the world (v. 1) and humanity (v. 2).[74] God is the savior and the creator.

The reference to the Priestly account of creation is unmistakable. God creates by the spoken word (Gen 1:3-29; cf. Ps 33:6). Humanity is given dominion over God's creatures and the task to rule the world (Gen 1:26-28). This task represents the ideal of God's plan for humanity: to rule as God rules, through justice and mercy. The author adds a clarification of wisdom's role in creation. Humanity has been formed by God's wisdom (cf. Ps 104:24; Prov 3:19; Jer 10:12, the same verb for "to form" is used in Wis 13:4). The relation of God's wisdom to creation and to humanity has already been addressed by the author on several occasions (Wis 1:6; 6:12-20; 7:14, 22, 27; 8:6, 13). It is a key idea that guarantees the efficacy of wisdom in bringing humanity continuously into union with God.

In the light of the great task that belongs to humanity, Solomon recalls the limitations and weaknesses that humanity equally shares. Humans are weak and short-lived, with little understanding in comparison to the complexities of the world (vv. 4-6). As in the earlier instances of this reflection on human weakness (7:1-6; 8:19-21), the awareness of limitations is no cause for despair. Rather, the reflection propels Solomon outside himself to seek wisdom in someone greater. The reflection is double-sided. Humans are limited, yet these limitations are subsumed by the wisdom of God (9:4-6). Humans also have many

---

73. The concentric structure, which relates images and expressions through a mirror-like reflection from top to bottom, is only one literary device employed frequently throughout Scripture. Several key passages in both the OT and the NT contain elements of concentric structuring: e.g., the Priestly creation account, Gen 1:1–2:3; the Priestly Abrahamic covenant, Gen 17:1-27; the sacrifice of Isaac, Gen 22:1-19; the disciples on the road to Emmaus, Luke 24:1-33.

74. Ordinarily, Scripture seems to give precedence to the saving interventions of God as the fundamental bedrock of Israelite faith. Creation theology takes second place as a development from salvation theology. In an interesting article, Walter Vogels points out that the author of Wisdom appears to reverse this perspective. See Walter Vogels, "The God Who Creates Is the God Who Saves: The Book of Wisdom's Reversal of the Biblical Pattern," *Église et Théologie* 22 (1991) 315-35.

strengths. But if the wisdom of God is lacking, then even these gifts and strengths will lack their full power (v. 6). From the point of view both of human weakness and of human strength, Solomon realizes the efficacy of the wisdom that comes from God.

Solomon Needs God's Wisdom. 9:7-8. The prayer turns to the great tasks that have been placed on the shoulders of Solomon. First there is the call for him to be king over Israel (see 1 Kgs 1:28-40; 3:7), and, second, there is the call to build the Temple on the holy mountain (see 2 Sam 7:12-14; 1 Chr 28:11-19). The various terms employed for the construction of the Temple combine the image of the tabernacle in the desert with that of the Temple in Jerusalem ("a temple on your holy mountain," v. 8; "an altar in the city of your habitation," v. 8*b*; "a copy of the holy tent," v. 8*c*).

The instruction to Solomon to build the Temple is parallel to the instruction to Moses to build the tabernacle (tent of meeting) so that God may dwell among the people (Exod 25:8-22). The tabernacle housed the ark and the incense altar as well as a table, a candelabrum, an eternal flame, Aaron's staff, the priestly vessels, and a book written by Moses. The Temple in Jerusalem was meant to function as the tabernacle had done throughout Israel's early history. It became God's dwelling place (Psalm 84). When Solomon dedicated the Temple after its completion, the ark and the tent of meeting were placed in it (1 Kgs 8:4; 2 Chr 5:5). The relationship between the tent of meeting and the Temple was already implicit in David's plan to build a temple to house the ark (2 Samuel 7).

It would appear that a platonic concept enters the author's formulation when the Temple is described as a "copy of the holy tent" prepared by God from the beginning (v. 8*c*). The chronicler speaks of a "plan" for the Temple that David gave to Solomon, which likewise was given to David by the Lord (1 Chr 28:11-19). Sirach also may contain an allusion to a heavenly tent where personified wisdom is said to minister to God and that, therefore, was established in Jerusalem (Sir 24:10).

Although the precise formulation may very well be under platonic influence, the idea of an earthly temple reflecting a heavenly one is old, indeed. Gudea, the governor of Lagash in the second millennium BCE, spoke of the ground plan of a temple to be built, given to him in a dream.[75] Sennacherib (704–681 BCE) likewise spoke of the founding of the city of Nineveh as having been planned long ago in heaven. Philo made use of the platonic theory of forms to explain how the tabernacle envisaged by Moses was modeled on a prototype produced by immaterial and invisible forms.[76]

9:9. The abrupt switch to the theme of wisdom in the prayer has been prepared in the opening reference to wisdom. Because Solomon has been given such a great task and is so limited, he needs the wisdom that has fashioned human beings and, therefore, understands what is right. The author contends once again that wisdom is with God (cf. 7:21; 8:3, 21). But the particular nuance that adds force to the affirmation is wisdom's presence at creation. Wisdom knows God's works, was present at creation, and, therefore, understands what is pleasing to God. The author is continuing in the sapiential tradition of Proverbs and Sirach regarding wisdom's presence in creation (Prov 3:19-20; 8:22-31; Sir 1:1-10; 24:1-7).

9:10. At the very center of the prayer stands the formal request that God send forth wisdom to Solomon from heaven. The phrase is formulated chiastically:

A   send her forth
    B   from the holy heavens
    B´   from the throne of your glory
A´   send her

The purpose of receiving the gift of wisdom is that wisdom "labor" at the side of Solomon, thereby enabling him to be united to God in his life and in his work. Wisdom is the one who makes friends with God (cf. 7:27), because she is intimately in union with God and a collaborator with human beings (cf. 6:12-16; 8:16-18; 9:2). The emphasis on learning what is pleasing to God (vv. 9, 10*d*, 18) may well be an echo of the central statement in the dream narrative of 1 Kgs 3:1-15, where Solomon's request for a discerning

---

75. *Inscription of Gudea, CAH* 1, part 2, 103.
76. Philo *Moses* 2.74-76. For other references in Greek and rabbinic literature to the idea of the Temple's being a copy of a heavenly prototype, see Winston, *The Wisdom of Solomon*, 202-5.

mind is described as "pleasing" the Lord (1 Kgs 3:10).

9:11-12. Wisdom's presence at creation (v. 9) guarantees efficacy in her collaboration with Solomon. Since wisdom knows all things, she will guide and protect Solomon in his decisions and actions. The idea of the glory of wisdom guiding and protecting Solomon may be an allusion to the pillar of cloud and fire that guided the Israelites in their flight from Egypt (Exod 13:17-22; 14:19-20). The theme of Solomon's task to rule and to judge is picked up positively in the second half of the prayer. With wisdom, his works will be acceptable; he will be able to judge justly; he will be a king worthy to follow in the footsteps of his father, David.

9:13-18, Wisdom Saves Humanity. Completing the concentric structure of the opening section of the prayer, the author addresses the phenomenon of human limitation with the concluding summary of wisdom's role in salvation. Just as the opening dealt with both wisdom's role in creation and a reflection on human weakness, so too does the conclusion show how human weakness is taken up and compensated for by the teaching and saving wisdom of God.

On first reading, it would appear that the author's formulation of human weakness in this section combines Greek and sapiential ideas on the limits of human knowledge. Greek philosophy holds the idea of the body burdening down or hindering the mind's activity.[77] However, for the Wisdom author it is not matter that separates humans from God but injustice (5:1-23). The idea of the soul's being imprisoned in matter would be quite foreign to the author of the book of Wisdom (see 1:14; 8:19-20).[78] The Hebraic notion of the "flesh" symbolizing human weakness and fragility comes much closer to the author's understanding of human limitations than do the precise nuances of the Platonic distinction between the body and the soul (see the use of the term "flesh" throughout the flood narrative in Genesis 6–9).

From the sapiential tradition, the author makes reference to the limits of human knowledge with respect to the wisdom of God. The poem to wisdom in Job 28 emphasizes the human incapability of finding wisdom (Job 28:12-15). The preacher in Ecclesiastes likewise emphasizes the limits of human wisdom: "That which is, is far off, and deep, very deep; who can find it out" (Eccl 7:24 NRSV). Whereas the sages caution against arrogance and hubris in their emphasis on the limits of wisdom, however, the Wisdom author stresses that human knowledge *is* completed by the wisdom that comes from God. The reflection on human weakness is formulated through a series of apparently rhetorical questions: Who can learn? Who can discern? Who has traced out what is in the heavens? Who has learned God's counsel? The surprising answer is affirmative when God grants wisdom. The conclusion to the reflection is that with the wisdom that is given by God all of these endeavors are possible (v. 17). This is consistent with the author's view of the function of human weakness, treated earlier. Human limitation and suffering need not be interpreted as signs of human despair and meaninglessness, as the wicked interpret them (2:1-11). Rather, like Solomon, the experience of fragility and weakness can propel one to seek the wisdom that comes from God (7:1-7; 9:4-6).

The conclusion to the prayer draws a direct parallel between creation and salvation.[79] It is through wisdom that human paths are set right, and people are saved by wisdom. Just as wisdom was present at creation (vv. 1-2), then, so too is wisdom continuously present to save human beings (v. 18). Salvation is the theme that will dominate the remaining part of the book (10:4; 14:4-5; 16:7, 11; 18:5). Chapter 10 will follow wisdom's role in saving the just ones in their trials from the time of Adam right up to Moses. Then in the last section of the book, the focus will be on the exodus events, the foundational saving event for Israel.

---

77. The most notable reference would be in Plato *The Phaedo* 81C, where the soul is described as being burdened by the body.

78. Richard J. Taylor examines in detail the links and differences of the Wisdom author's anthropology to that of Platonic and Neo-Platonic philosophies. The conclusion is that although many terms are borrowed from Greek philosophy, the characteristic underpinning of the author's philosophy is essentially Hebraic. See Taylor, "The Eschatological Meaning of Life and Death in the Book of Wisdom I-V," 92-95.

79. The author has broadened the perspective of salvation throughout the entire book of Wisdom to include creation, exodus, and ultimate judgment. For the author of Wisdom, salvation is understood as God's effort to bring humanity to the point of realizing the original intentions of creation. See Michael Kolarcik, "Creation and Salvation in the Book of Wisdom," in *Creation in the Biblical Traditions*, ed. Richard J. Clifford and John J. Collins, CBQMS 24 (1992) 97-107.

REFLECTIONS

1. Wisdom is not the same as knowledge. Solomon's recognition of his need for wisdom is a paradigm for humanity, particularly for our own time, when our technical knowledge has grown exponentially. There is a fundamental distinction in Solomon's prayer between knowledge and wisdom. Solomon is acutely aware of both the limits and the strength of his knowledge. Knowledge represents the human familiarity with the world that enables people to move and act within it. It bestows the power to act. But how will Solomon act? How will he act out of both the limits and the strengths of his knowledge? How will he assess and judge rightly the tasks before him? How will he choose the good from the myriad possibilities open to him?

It is through the divine wisdom given as a gift and welcomed as a friend that Solomon hopes to use wisely the power entrusted to him. This wisdom is elusive, and the author has attempted to describe its many facets throughout the eulogy of wisdom. It is close to the human mind and heart. It is divine. Because humans have been "fashioned" by wisdom, it enables people to judge well and act for the good.

Our contemporary situation is not essentially different from that of Solomon, described in the prayer. Our knowledge in the areas of technology, medicine, and psychology is more extensive than at any time in history. At the same time, it has become evident that without the will to act wisely, we leave behind a wake of turmoil in the environment and in the social fabric of life. Both our knowledge and our awareness of our limitations should propel us like the unnamed Solomon to seek with humility and with passion the wisdom that judges wisely and acts with respect for the world.

2. Divine wisdom is not set over and against human knowledge. It is not as if Solomon must deny his knowledge to embrace the wisdom that comes from God. The prayer affirms with a particular nuance the essential relationship between humans and God presented in the account of creation (see Gen 1:27). Humans were fashioned according to God's wisdom (Wis 9:2). It is as if human energy is directed to being completed by the wisdom that comes from God. This means that without this wisdom, human knowledge becomes truncated from its divine source and will fail (Wis 9:6). But with the gift of wisdom that comes from God, human knowledge reaches its full potential (Wis 9:13-17).

3. Both human weakness and human strength lead to God. In the prayer, Solomon's view of his own weakness and his strength supplements what was already treated in 7:1-7; 8:19-21. Together these passages form a contrast with the view of weakness and strength offered by the author through the perspective of the wicked (2:1-20). For the wicked, human weakness in all of its forms is a cause for despair, and human strength is an occasion for hubris and exploitation. The portrait of Solomon painted by the author offers the very antithesis to such an interpretation. Solomon viewed his limitations and weakness (9:5) from the perspective of his tasks in life and his relationship to God. Instead of collapsing in on himself, Solomon confesses his limitations and seeks wisdom to overcome his limitations. Similarly, Solomon recognizes the strengths of his standing before others and in his selection to be king and judge. This is no occasion for hubris. He recognizes that without right judgment and action these strengths will come to nothing (9:6). The interpretation we give to weakness and strength is a perennial gauge of our moral perspective.

4. The prayer's enclosure of themes that relate creation and salvation reveals a synthetic theological panorama. God is the creator who has fashioned humans according to wisdom. And it is through the wisdom of God that humanity is continuously being saved. In some circles it has become customary to view creation theology and salvation theology as somewhat in opposition. Salvation theology emphasizes the unique interventions of God in history to liberate and redeem humanity from oppression and sin. Creation theology emphasizes the immanence of God's presence through the structure of the universe and humanity as continuously calling humanity to its original dignity and harmony with God and the world.

In older biblical scholarship, it was thought that creation theology was a very late addition to Israelite faith.[80] In more recent theological scholarship, it has been suggested that the salvation theology of the Bible has so dominated the last centuries of Christiandom that we need to recover the creational perspective.[81] The two perspectives of creation and salvation are not in opposition in the Bible. Certainly, the author of Wisdom envisions a harmony between the God who has created the world and humanity through wisdom and the God who continuously saves humanity through wisdom. Precisely because God is the creator and fashioner of the human heart, this same God intervenes to bring humanity to freedom and liberation. In the last part of the book, which deals with the saving event of the exodus, for example, the author presents the exodus as a new creation (19:6, 18).

80. Gerhard von Rad, *Old Testament Theology*, 2 vols., trans. D. M. G. Stalker (London: SCM,1975). Von Rad's basic approach to understanding Israel's faith is to explore the creedal statements within the biblical narrative. Since these statements are expressed in the form of praising God for salvation, it is only natural that the salvational perspective of Israel's faith would be highlighted. In a later book, Von Rad explores the theme of creation within the wisdom tradition. See Gerhard von Rad, *Wisdom in Israel*, trans. J. D. Martin (London: SCM, 1978).

81. Thomas Berry captures the importance of a holistic approach to creation through a renewed understanding of the context of growth—the earth. The creational perspective is present in the symbolic representations of our understanding of the earth in the Bible, but it can be overshadowed by the salvational perspective. See Thomas Berry, *The Dream of the Earth* (San Francisco: Sierra Club, 1988); Thomas Berry and Thomas Clarke, *Befriending the Earth: A Theology of Reconciliation Between Humans and the Earth* (Mystic, Conn: Twenty-Third, 1991).

WISDOM 10:1-21, WISDOM ACCOMPANIES THE RIGHTEOUS

COMMENTARY

Most commentators understand the function of chap. 10 as a link that joins the eulogy of wisdom in chaps. 6–9 to the midrashic treatment of the exodus events in chaps. 11–12. This it does admirably well by continuing the praise of wisdom through examples of her accompanying the righteous of humanity from Adam to Moses and by introducing the final theme of the book: the exodus. Specifically, the concluding reference in the prayer to people's being saved by wisdom is concretely exemplified through biblical support. Of the author's three approaches to personified wisdom (7:22b–8:1; 8:2-8)—namely, to expound on her beauty, on her rootedness in God, and on her beneficial qualities for humanity—the latter is highlighted to conclude the eulogy on wisdom.

Seven loose sets of contrasts from personages in the Torah are brought forward to emphasize the positive function of wisdom in the lives of the just: (1) Adam/Cain (vv. 1-3); (2) Noah/the flooded earth (v. 4); (3) Abraham/the nations put to confusion (v. 5); (4) Lot/the five cities and Lot's wife (vv. 6-8); (5) Jacob/Esau and Laban (vv. 9-12); (6) Joseph/Potiphar's wife (vv. 13-14); (7) Israel-Moses/Pharaoh-enemies (vv. 15-21). In each case, wisdom is understood to have accompanied the righteous in their trials in order to protect them and bring them success. The contrasts are grouped into six sections (vv. 1, 5-6, 13, 15-16), each beginning with the pronoun "she" (αὕτη *hautē*). All the noble personages in the contrasts are described as "righteous," except for the first—Adam. The reason why the author does not describe him as righteous is likely that it was precisely from his transgression that wisdom had delivered him. The contrast between the righteous and their enemies or oppressors continues the contrast from the first section of the book, where the apparent fate of the righteous was contrasted with the fate of the wicked. At times, the contrast emphasizes the debilitating result of evading wisdom, as is the case with Cain, the enemies of Lot, and the Egyptians. Other contrasts focus on the positive guiding force of wisdom, as in the case of Jacob and Joseph especially.

The passage looks upon God's interventions in history in typical sapiential fashion. In wisdom literature, God is seen to act in history from within creation, so to speak. Through wisdom, God works within historical events and within the cosmos to bring the plan of creation to completion. There is a difference of emphasis in the prophetic perspective, which tends to look upon God's interventions as extraordinary acts of power that break into human history.[82] In the prophetic view, we see God reaching out into the cosmos and into human history. In the sapiential view, we see the cosmos and humanity reaching out toward God with the aid of divine wisdom. Covenantal theology forms the backdrop for prophetic literature, whereas creation theology forms the backdrop for wisdom literature.

The form of writing in this chapter (and for a good part of the remainder of the book) is midrashic. Because of its loose style, it is difficult to call midrash a literary genre (it is a rabbinic term meaning "investigation"). In its broadest definition, a midrash is a type of literature that contains explicit allusions to the fixed canonical text.[83] The author is presuming knowledge of the accepted text and interprets the events of the Torah in a manner that attributes them to the wisdom of God. (For other examples of midrashic praises of illustrious persons in the Bible, see Sirach 44–50; 1 Macc 2:49-64; Heb 11:4-40.)

10:1-3, Adam/Cain. Three details from the Genesis accounts of Adam are singled out to show wisdom's protective role for all humanity: (1) he had been created alone, (2) he transgressed, (3) he received the strength to rule over all things. Adam's "aloneness" alludes to the second creation account, in which the creation of humanity is described through a double process: First, Adam is created and then Eve, and together they constitute the beginning of humanity (Gen 2:4-24). The transgression alludes to Adam's eating of the fruit in disobedience to the divine command (Gen 3:6). The third point reaches back to the first creation account, in which humanity is given the task of ruling over the living creatures (Gen 1:26, 28). Wisdom's protective role encompasses both the weaknesses and the strengths of humanity.

Adam is called the father of the world (v. 1). Although an abundance of literature surrounding the figure of Adam had arisen in the mystery cults and in gnostic writings, it is unlikely that the Wisdom author is alluding to some "ideal man" or demiurge through whom the creation of the world took place.[84] Adam is immediately described as the "first-formed" father of the world who was created alone. The term "world" (κόσμος *kosmos*) most likely refers to the world of humanity. As the father of Cain and Abel, Adam is called the father of humanity.

In contrast to Adam, Cain is described as having departed from wisdom in anger, and as a result he is said to have perished. When his sacrifice of the fruit of the ground was not accepted by God, Cain became exceedingly angry and plotted to kill his brother Abel (Gen 4:3-8). For the author, Cain is a figure of unrighteousness; consequently the tradition of God's protective mark on Cain and his family is ignored (Gen 4:15-17).[85]

10:4, Noah/the Flooded Earth. The author mentions Cain's sin as the cause of wickedness that occasions the flood. Actually, in the Genesis narrative, Cain's murder of Abel is treated only as the first expression of violence among humans, which eventually leads to the wickedness that occasions divine wrath in the form of a flood. The earth is described as being saved by wisdom, who steers Noah, a righteous man, on "a paltry piece of wood." The author singles out the fragility of "a piece of wood," referring to the ark, to highlight the directive quality of wisdom's action for humanity (cf. Gen 7:17-24).

10:5, Abraham/the Nations. Three events from Abraham's life are depicted as being directed by wisdom: the Tower of Babel (Gen 11:1-9), Abraham's righteousness

---

82. For a discussion on the unique function of wisdom in relation to history, see Collins, "Cosmos and Salvation," 121-42.
83. See Gary G. Porton, "Midrash," *Anchor Bible Dictionary*, 6 vols. (New York: Doubleday, 1992) 4:818-22.
84. See Plato *Timaeus* 28C, where the demiurge is described as the "father of this world." See also *Life of Adam and Eve*, *Apocalypse of Adam*, *Apocalypse of Moses*.
85. Conspicuously absent from the list of righteous persons is Enoch, who had become one of the biblical characters who personified the sage and the beloved of God. Perhaps his absence is due to the fact that the author had already alluded to Enoch in the diptych regarding the untimely death of a just youth (Wis 4:10-15).

(Gen 15:6), and the sacrifice of Isaac (Gen 22:1-19). The description of the nations that are put to confusion because of their wicked agreement refers to the episode at the tower of Babel (11:1-9). Although in the Genesis narrative there is no mention of Abraham's being involved in those events, the genealogy that follows the episode leads up to Terah, the father of "Abram." The rabbinic tradition, moreover, made Abraham contemporaneous to those events: "Abraham said to the men of the generation of the Tower of Babel: What do you seek from God? Has He said to you, 'Come and provide for me?' He created and He provides; He made and He sustains."[86]

Wisdom is said to have recognized Abraham's righteousness and to have maintained his integrity before God. This is a reference to the covenant episode between God and Abram (Genesis 15), where Abram expresses hope in God's promises and this action is reckoned to him as righteousness. With respect to the testing of Abraham (Genesis 22), the author explains how it was the wisdom of God that strengthened Abraham to follow God's command in the face of sacrificing his own son Isaac. The author had described wisdom as a friend of humans who seeks out those who are just in order to guide them and to make them friends of God. The references to famous persons of the Torah are meant to be concrete examples of what the author has argued in general terms.

10:6-9, Lot/the Five Cities. Although Lot is not presented in exemplary fashion in the Genesis narrative, the Wisdom author attributes the divine intervention of the two angels who save him to the working of wisdom (cf. Gen 19:1-29). Two features from the Genesis story of Sodom and Gomorrah are put into relief: the destruction of the cities by fire and the fateful glance backward of Lot's wife, who turns into a pillar of salt. The Genesis narrative mentions only three cities of the plain by name, Sodom, Gomorrah, and Zoar (the city that was spared for Lot). In the previous battle between the two groups of five kings against four, all five cities are mentioned (Gen 14:1-2). Although the accepted tradition understands only four of the cities to have been destroyed (see Deut 29:23), other traditions generalize the destruction as affecting the five cities of the plain (cf. Gen 19:24-25).[87]

The story of the destruction of Sodom and Gomorrah had become a proverbial epithet to characterize the ensuing devastation of wickedness (Deut 29:33; Isa 13:19; Jer 50:40; Amos 4:11; Matt 10:15; 2 Pet 2:6; Rev 11:8). It gives occasion for the author to elaborate the connection between devastation and wickedness. The desolate land around the southwestern part of the Dead Sea had given rise to many legends regarding its rocky, inhospitable terrain. The wisdom author refers to two of these legends: the destruction by fire, which renders the land hostile to cultivation, and the pillar of salt. The mention of the plant whose fruit does not ripen echoes the author's earlier critique of the "brood of the ungodly" (4:3-5 NRSV). The pillar of salt refers to the legend of Lot's wife, who was punished for her unbelieving gesture of turning back (Gen 19:26). This legend playfully explained the erosion in the salty rock around the Dead Sea that created all sorts of eerie forms, one of which resembles a human being and is called "the wife of Lot." The author uses these images to drive home the importance of collaborating with wisdom. Because these people passed wisdom by, they could not recognize the good (cf. 2:21-22). In contrast to the folly of the wicked, the passage concludes on a positive note, highlighting the manner in which those who serve wisdom are rescued from their troubles. This theme of wisdom's protecting the righteous in their trials will be picked up in the examples of Jacob and Joseph.

10:10-12, Jacob/Esau and Laban. A series of events from the life of Jacob are picked up in order to illustrate the positive working of divine wisdom: Jacob's flight from his brother, Esau (Gen 27:41-45); Jacob's vision of the ladder at Bethel (Gen 28:10-17); Jacob's growing prosperity despite Laban's restrictions (Gen 30:25–31:54); Jacob's wrestling with the divine at Peniel (Gen 32:22-32). In each instance, wisdom is shown to be working in the background to bring about success for Jacob against those who would have harmed him. Wisdom guides him; shows him the kingdom of God; helps him to prosper at

---

86. *Tanhuma*, Wayera, 50a.

87. See also Josephus *The Jewish War* 4.8.4; *Antiquities of the Jews* 1.11.4.

the expense of Laban, who had been oppressing him; and even gives him the victory in his arduous contest with the "angel." Jacob's vision at Bethel had been expanded in pseudepigraphal works to include explanations of divine plans.[88] The emphasis in the Jacob/Esau contrast is not on the negative source of wickedness, as with Lot, but on the positive accompaniment of wisdom that brings success out of trying circumstances.

10:13-14, Joseph/Potiphar's Wife. One might have expected Isaac to have been listed among the illustrious personages whom wisdom has aided. The author selected Joseph, perhaps, because the trials he faced in life were more amenable to showing wisdom's creative power to transform situations of distress into occasions of divine blessing. Joseph was known for his sagacity in his interpretation of dreams and in his rising to great heights within the ranks of the Egyptian government. However, the author passes over the sapiential themes already present in the Genesis narrative (Genesis 37–50) and concentrates instead on two episodes: the attempted seduction of Joseph by Potiphar's wife, which eventually caused his imprisonment, and his rising out of prison to the heights of power in Egypt.

Wisdom did not abandon Joseph in his solitary position. Wisdom accompanied him to protect his righteousness and to be with him in the pit and in the dungeon. His resistance to the seduction of Potiphar's wife is attributed to wisdom. Wisdom is described as staying with him right to the point of reversing his misfortune. He ends up having authority over his previous masters (his brothers), and his accusers (Potiphar and his wife) are shown to be false. As a result of wisdom's accompanying presence, Joseph receives "everlasting honor." Wisdom was described by the unnamed speaker Solomon as one who leads people to a kingdom (6:20) and who confers an everlasting remembrance (8:13). Not only is this the case for Solomon, but also, according to the author, history itself has already exemplified wisdom's creative role.

10:15-21, Israel-Moses/Pharaoh-Enemies. The final contrast is more complex than the previous one in that the righteous consist of the entire people Israel and their singular leader, Moses. By contrast, the enemies are the Egyptian oppressors and their leader, the pharaoh. The protagonist throughout the contrast is wisdom. Wisdom delivers Israel by entering into Moses to guide the people and bring them over the Red Sea. Likewise, wisdom is the protagonist in thwarting the resistance to Israel's liberation. It is wisdom who drowned the enemies and cast them up. Wisdom is the one who inspires praise for God's marvelous liberation from the mouths of mutes and infants.

10:15. The Israelites are called "holy and blameless" and later in the passage "righteous" (v. 20). This is not to say that the author is unaware of the memory of Israel's own resistance to liberation, which is entrenched in the tradition. The book of Exodus insists on a triple source of resistance to God's intervention: Moses (Exod 4:1-17), the people themselves (Exod 6:9; 14:11-12), and, of course, the pharaoh (Exod 14:5-9). Later in the book of Wisdom, the author alludes to Israel's resistance in the desert and to the punishment inflicted on the people as a result of Korah's rebellion (18:20-25; cf. Num 16:25-35; 17:1-15). But for the purpose of an effective contrast here, the author singles out Israel's righteousness under Egyptian oppression.

10:16. Moses is designated the Lord's servant, which is a much-used title for Moses in the Torah (Exod 4:10; 14:31; Num 11:11; 12:7-8; Deut 3:24; 34:5). The ancestors as well as Israel as a whole are referred to as God's servants (Exod 32:13; Deut 9:27; Lev 25:42, 55). In Isa 63:11, God is described as the protagonist of liberation who put his Spirit into the people and raised up Moses. Similarly, the author of Wisdom attributes the power of the Spirit that enters into Moses to the workings of God's wisdom.

10:17-19. Various events from the exodus narrative are attributed to the guiding and inspiring activity of wisdom: Moses and Aaron bargaining with Pharaoh using signs and wonders (Exodus 7–11); the acquisition/reception of goods from the Egyptians (Exod 11:2-3; 12:33-36); the remarkable journey from under Pharaoh's power guided by the cloud by day and by fire at night (Exod 13:17-22); the crossing of the Red Sea (Exod 14:13-25); the destruction of the army in the waters (Exod 14:26-31; 15:19); the song

---

88. See, e.g., *Testament of Levi* 9:3.

of praise by Moses, the people, and Miriam (Exod 15:1-21).

10:20-21. Two details in the Wisdom account are based on later interpretations of the events surrounding the exodus: the plundering of the Egyptian army (v. 20) and the singing of praises to God by mutes and infants (v. 21). The first detail, the plundering of the Egyptian army, was developed to explain how the Israelites acquired arms to thwart Amalek's attack at Rephidim (Exod 17:8-13). Josephus gives an account of this interpretation:

> On the morrow, the arms of the Egyptians having been carried up to the Hebrews' camp by the tide and the force of the wind setting in that direction, Moses, surmising that this too was due to the providence of God, to ensure that even in weapons they should not be wanting, collected them and, having accoutred the Hebrews therein led them forward to Mount Sinai.[89]

The reference to wisdom's opening the mouths of the mute may be the author's clever reference to the song of Moses, which praises God's liberation (Exod 15:1-18). When God called Moses forth to lead the Hebrews out of Egypt, Moses resisted by claiming he did not know how to speak (Exod 4:10-16). The author thus attributes to wisdom God's concrete intervention to give Moses the power of speech and the ability to sing spontaneous praise.

Even the infants are singled out as singing God's praise under wisdom's inspiration (v. 21). Inspired, perhaps, by Ps 8:2, "Out of the mouths of babes and infants you have founded a bulwark because of your foes, to silence the enemy and the avenger" (NRSV), a very early rabbinic tradition attributes the singing of God's praises to infants: "When the babe lying on its mother's lap and the suckling at his mother's breast saw the divine presence, the former raised his neck, and the latter let go of his mother's breasts, and they all responded with a song of praise, saying, 'This is my God, and I will glorify him.'"[90]

89. Josephus *Antiquities of the Jews* 2.16.6.

90. *Tosefta Sotah* 6.4.

REFLECTIONS

1. Through wisdom God provides providential care for humanity. The sweeping survey of biblical figures from Adam to Moses is meant to expound on the saving role of wisdom. This saving role formulated the concluding remark of Solomon's prayer: Through wisdom God has fashioned the human heart, and through wisdom God saves humanity continuously (cf. 9:1, 18). The author has chosen familiar biblical characters to illustrate how the difficult circumstances of their lives fell under the providential gaze of God. In each case the saving activity of God is attributed to God's wisdom.

The providential care of God rests on the immanent workings of wisdom in creation. Providential care is at work in the forces of the cosmos, in the human heart, and in the history of human events. Where the standard biblical texts envisage God as intervening in the affairs of the ancestors, often dramatically and against the course of events, the sages understand God's interventions to be implicit in the ordinary activities of human decisions for justice or for injustice.

The Wisdom author's commentary on the ark that is guided by wisdom is a good case in point. The Genesis narrative highlights God's majestic command for Noah to build the ark to save humanity and the various animal species (Gen 6:11-22). The Wisdom author emphasizes the implicit guiding hand of wisdom that "steers" the fragile piece of wood to safety. God's providence need not be seen simply in the extraordinary events that bring liberation, but in the everyday circumstances that allow for injustice to be redressed as well.

2. Through wisdom, God reverses the misfortune of the just. The saving activity of wisdom not only intervenes on behalf of the righteous but also thwarts the plans of the unjust. The contrasts of righteous biblical figures and their wicked counterparts mirror the author's treatment of the just and the wicked in the first part of the book (3:1–4:20). In each case, the author recalls the trying situations of the righteous to show how, in fact, through wisdom the lingering threat is transformed into fortune. Only in the first case, Adam, is the trying situation brought about by one's own transgression. In this way, all of humanity, which originates from Adam, can be understood to be under the guiding providence of God's wisdom.

Wisdom had already been associated with righteousness in the opening part of the book. So it comes as no surprise that the author argues for wisdom's being God's means of saving the just and hindering the wicked. Cain is described as having "departed from" wisdom (v. 3); the populations of the destroyed cities "passed wisdom by" (v. 8); wisdom had shown Joseph's accusers to be false (v. 14); and to wisdom is ascribed the role of having drowned the enemies of the Hebrews at the Red Sea (v. 20).

3. History is a forum for discovering God's action toward humanity. In the first part of the book, the author had argued out of principles. The reversal of fortune in the case of the righteous and the wicked was established through a series of declarations. The fortune of the wicked and the misfortune of the just were stripped of their appearances. In large part, the redress of injustice took place by the author's postulation of an ultimate judgment. It is the ultimate judgment that reveals the true nature of the reward of the righteous and the moral vacuity of the wicked. But what is the author's basis for postulating an ultimate judgment? In chap. 10 and throughout the rest of the book, history provides the data to argue for the merits of justice and the peril of injustice.

The series of incidents from the ancestral stories is presented to our imaginations with a particular intent. We see concrete examples of the righteous, who are rewarded by wisdom for justice during their own lifetime. These references to past incidents that are open to reflective scrutiny form the basis for contemplating the relationships between justice and wisdom and between wisdom and life. Contemplating the stories with the connections the author draws leads to an appreciation of wisdom and to a respect for justice. Since these connections are palpable in the illustrious persons of the tradition, there is hope that they are valid for the future.

The technique of recasting faith history to establish fundamental truths lies at the heart of the biblical narrative.[91] The particular examples of recasting ancestral history, besides the Wisdom text, are few: Sirach 44–50; 1 Macc 2:49-64; Heb 11:4-40. Sirach, the most extensive of the ancestral eulogies, begins with Enoch and ends with Simon son of Onias. In 1 Maccabees, Mattathias recounts stories of ancestral heroes from Abraham to Daniel to show how they were rewarded or saved for their virtue. The eulogy of the ancestors in Hebrews is the closest parallel to Wisdom. Faith replaces personified wisdom as the architect of salvation. Hebrews begins with the sacrifice of Abel and concludes by mentioning Samuel and the prophets to show how they had all been protected and saved by faith.

---

91. For an interesting discussion of the function of history in the articulation of Israel's faith, see Claus Westermann, *Praise and Lament in the Psalms*, trans. K. R. Crim and R. N. Soulen (Edinburgh: T. & T. Clark, 1981) esp. "The 'Re-presentation' of History in the Psalms," 214-49.

WISDOM 11:1–19:22

THE JUSTICE OF GOD REVEALED IN THE EXODUS

OVERVIEW

The praise of wisdom's role in the history of the ancestors leads to the reflection of the foundational saving event for Israel: the exodus. The events of the exodus, ranging from the plagues of Egypt to God's providence for the Israelites in the desert, are presented as signs of God's wisdom and commitment to justice. As different as this final section of the book appears on the surface from the first two parts, the inner cohesion is nonetheless striking as well. This is the most "Israelite" section of the book, focusing as it does on the foundational event of Israel's consciousness. In it the author integrates God's commitment to justice, from the first section of the book, and the wisdom of God working through creation to bring union between humans and God, from the second part of the book. In the first two parts, the dramatic personae are individuals: the just one who suffers unjustly and Solomon, the seeker of wisdom. This initial focus on individuals allows the author to generalize and to philosophize on the nature of justice, life, death, wisdom, and God. In the third part, the forum for the conflict between justice and injustice is the collective unity of Israel. In God's action on behalf of the righteous in the exodus, the author draws out the confirmation of the principle of justice from the first part of the book and the sagacity of God's interventions from the second part of the book.

Given the author's tendency to organize literary units in dense forms, it is not surprising to see the further use of intricate concentric structures (chaps. 13–15). However, the major organizing device of the entire section is comparison and contrast, which is similar to the diptychs of the first part of the book. The various means of punishment of people who resist Israel's liberation are set in relief to the ways God intervenes on behalf of the just. The similarity to the diptychs that compare the just and the wicked in the first part of the book is noticeable.

This form of writing shows remarkable similarities to the literary genre *syncrisis*, which involves a comparison and contrast of antitheses.[92] In the classical forms of *syncrisis*, there are only two elements that are both compared and contrasted. The Wisdom author has adapted this Greek literary device to include a third party—namely, God, who intervenes in the case of the Egyptians and on behalf of the Israelites.

Since the basis for the author's comparisons and contrast is the story of the exodus as presented in the Torah, the form of writing is midrashic.[93] A midrash is an interpretation of a text that follows the contents and events of the narrative or poetic text explicitly or implicitly. In the book of Wisdom, the author follows carefully, though at times loosely, the events as related in the text of Exodus and interprets them as signs of God's justice. The author has made use of the older Scripture in both previous parts of the book (part 1 relies on Isaiah 42–60; part 2, 1 Kings 3). However, these biblical references in the first half functioned more as allusions to authoritative figures than as the organizing basis for interpretation. Here, in the third part, the references to selected events of the exodus are sustained throughout the entire section.

---

92. See James M. Reese, "Plan and Structure in the Book of Wisdom," *CBQ* 27 (1965) 391-99.

93. See R. T. Siebeneck, "The Midrash of Wisdom 10–19," *CBQ* 22 (1960) 176-82.

Exegetes have noticed two organizing features for the author's interpretation of the plagues associated with the exodus (see Fig. 1, p. 434). One is a system of antitheses that compare and contrast the Egyptian punishments with Israel's blessings.[94] This system follows a moral principle enunciated in 11:5, 13: The very means that God uses to punish the Egyptians are used to save the Israelites. Thus seven plagues are chosen for these diptychs; notice how these plagues compare loosely with the ten plagues and the final destruction of the army in Exodus.

94. Reese, "Plan and Structure in the Book of Wisdom," 391-99.

Wisdom		Exodus
1. water turned to blood	—	1. water turned to blood (Exod 7:14-25)
2. animals suppress the appetite	—	2. frogs (Exod 8:1-15)
3. animals that kill	—	3. gnats (Exod 8:16-19)
	—	4. flies (Exod 8:20-32)
	—	5. livestock diseased (Exod 9:1-7)
	—	6. boils (Exod 9:8-12)
4. rain, hail, and fire	—	7. thunder and hail (Exod 9:13-35)
	—	8. locusts (Exod 10:1-20)
5. darkness	—	9. darkness (Exod 10:21-29)
6. death of the firstborn	—	10. the firstborn die (Exod 12:29-32)
7. drowning in the Red Sea	—	Pharaoh's army drowns (Exod 14:26-29)

The other system consists of five diptychs that draw a parallel between Egypt's sins and the ensuing punishments of the plagues.[95] This system follows the moral principle enunciated in 11:16: God punishes the Egyptians according to the very manner in which they sin. This principle is consistent with that of the first part of the book, where the author declares that the wicked are punished according to their false reasoning (3:10-13).

The contrasts within the first four diptychs are introduced by the adverb "instead" (ἀντί *anti*; 11:6; 16:2; 16:20; 18:3). The last diptych is more complex. Instead of there being a single punishment for one sin, there is a sin with two punishments. The sin of killing the Israelite infants elicits both the death of the Egyptian firstborn and the drowning in the sea of the Egyptian army. Both the first and the last diptychs concentrate on the identical sin of the Egyptians, the killing of the Israelite newborn.

The comparison and contrast within the diptychs afford the author the opportunity to reflect on and interpret the significance of the enemy's sins, the blessings for Israel, and God's actions. These reflections have been coined "digressions" whenever they are sustained for a longer period. Two major digressions occur within the second diptych, which treats the worship of animals. The first major digression deals with God's grace and moderation (11:17–12:27). The second concentrates on the origins of false worship (chaps. 13–15). From within the five-diptych system, three other minor digressions can be noted: the digression on God's power over life and death, derived from the episode of the brazen serpent (16:5-14); a digression on the death experienced also by the righteous, which Aaron stops (18:20-25); and a concluding digression on creation (19:6-21).

One of the reasons why a number of exegetes earlier had posited different authors for the three sections of the book is the absence of personified wisdom in the midrash on the exodus. Indeed, on the surface this absence appears rather striking. Wisdom is the protagonist in the sweeping review of the history of illustrious figures from the book of Genesis until Moses (10:1–11:1). Afterward (11:2–19:22), God alone is the protagonist who acts in favor of the righteous and in opposition to the enemies of the righteous. Moses and Aaron function as mediators, but it is always God who is presented as the actor

95. See Wright, "The Structure of Wisdom 11-19," 28-34.

who inspires even the mediators to act. Wisdom is mentioned only twice in the third part of the book in the reflection on the origin of idolatry (14:2, 5).

There remains the convenient explanation that the Wisdom author may very well have written the various sections of the book at different intervals. This distance in time, then, might account for the different focus in images and themes within a style of writing that bears striking consistency of vocabulary. However, there is a theological consistency in the relative silence on wisdom in the third part that should not be overlooked. For the author, personified wisdom is not a separate entity from the divine sphere. Wisdom is the particular outreach of God to humans in the cosmos. The purpose of wisdom for humans is to guide them to God. Wisdom is described as making people friends of God (7:27). Therefore, for the author to focus on God as the protagonist in the events of the exodus shows the transparency of personified wisdom. Wisdom recedes into the background, but it permeates the exodus events because of wisdom's subdued role in the first two sections of the book. Philo likewise would alternate between speaking of personified wisdom or the Divine Mind as the outreach of God in the world and the personal God who acts immediately in the affairs of human history.[96]

One of the unifying features throughout the diptychs on the plagues that relates the third part to the first is God's justice and judgment. The author's interpretation of the exodus event applies the principle of justice from the first part of the book to the foundational experience of Israel. God intervenes in Israel's history to restore justice. Justice implies the restoration of life to the Israelites and the thwarting of the resistance to liberation in the case of the Egyptians. The Israelites are constantly named the righteous, whereas the Egyptians are often called the enemies. The polarity between the righteous and the enemies in the exodus interpretation parallels the polarity between the wicked/godless and the righteous in the first part.

In fact, there is a deliberate correlation between God's ultimate judgment in the first part of Wisdom and the judgment of God against the enemies of the righteous and in behalf of Israel in the third part. In both cases, the cosmos acts in unison with God's activity of justice. God makes use of the cosmos to bless and to punish. The author had posited an ultimate judgment that would reveal the true nature of the blessedness of the just and the empty hope of the wicked. The basis for positing such an ultimate judgment lies in Israel's own history. Since God has acted to restore life and to thwart resistance to life in Israel's history, then there is hope that this is the guiding principle of God's justice in the present time and in the future.

Another theological consistency in the author's unique interpretation of the exodus event and in the first two parts of Wisdom centers on the role of the cosmos in sustaining the creative activity of God. Salvation and creation become fused into a continuum of God's activity. The unique saving event of Israel, the liberation of the Israelites from Egypt, is portrayed as a new creation (19:9-22). God used the cosmos to thwart the resistance of the lawless in the apocalyptic judgment of the first part of the book. In the second part of the book, it is wisdom's work in and through the cosmos at the time of creation that allows wisdom to save the righteous throughout history. Through wisdom, God is able to direct the positive force of creation to establish justice continuously. The author derives proof for such divine activity in the reflection on the episodes of the exodus drawn from the Torah.

---

96. David Winston notes Philo's tendency to move almost unconsciously from speech about wisdom to speech about God. See Philo *On the Sacrifices of Abel and Cain* 98 and *On the Migration of Abraham* 128. See also Winston, *The Wisdom of Solomon*, 226.

WISDOM 11:1-5, THE WILDERNESS

COMMENTARY

11:1. The exposition on the role of personified wisdom in the lives of the righteous leads the author to the contemplation of the activity of God in the events of the exodus. Wisdom is said to be the one who prospers the activities of the righteous through the prophet Moses (v. 1). This verse brings to a conclusion the exposition of wisdom's role in the lives of the righteous and introduces specifically the events of the exodus from Egypt and the wandering in the desert. The figure of Moses towers over the events of the exodus. The wisdom author, however, attributes the guiding hand of God for the entire people and for their mediators to personified wisdom.

11:2-4. Interestingly, the introduction to the exodus events focuses on the image of the wilderness, which actually follows those events as narrated in Exodus. After the extraordinary deliverance at the Red Sea, the Israelites face the antagonism of the desert. The wilderness refers to a space that is hostile to life and to a time that is volatile and unsure. It is described as being uninhabited and untrodden (v. 2). There is a threat to life not only from the natural circumstances of drought in the wilderness, but also from the deliberate hostility of enemies (v. 3). The combination of drought and enemies that the author employs to characterize Israel's existence in the desert is more than likely a reference to Exodus 17, where the two episodes of thirsting in the desert and of waging war with Amalek are narrated side by side. However, the entire period of Israel's life in the desert was characterized by thirst and hunger (Exod 15:22-27; 16:1-26; 17:1-7; Num 11:1-14; 11:31-35; 20:1-13) and by threat from enemies (Exod 17:8-16; 21:1-33; Deut 2:1–3:22). The threat to life in the wilderness actually highlights the extraordinary intervention of God for the benefit of the righteous. They call upon God because they are thirsty, and water is given through the flinty rock (v. 4).

11:5. The reflection on the source of water in the wilderness brings the author to one of the two key principles through which the exodus events will be interpreted. The very means of punishment against the Egyptians are the means of salvation for the Israelites. In this case, water was used to punish the enemies of the Israelites both when the Nile was turned to blood and when the Egyptian army drowned in the Red Sea. But for the righteous, the gift of water in the wilderness brings the quenching of thirst and survival.

The use of identical means of blessing and punishment is rare in biblical literature. In Sirach we find a similar idea, although it is formulated differently. In a comparison between the gifts given to the righteous and the punishments given to sinners, the author notes: "All these are good for the godly, but for sinners they turn into evils" (Sir 39:27 NRSV). In a rabbinic source, the same idea is formulated much in the way the Wisdom author understands it: "The Holy One blessed be He heals by the same means whereby He smites."[97]

The principle implies that God is the Lord of both creation and history. The elements of creation are ambivalent. God can use them to bless and to punish. Creation itself, as noted in the first half of the book, is on the side of justice and the righteous. The events of the exodus, viewed from this perspective, become the author's clinching proof for the judgment that justice and wisdom bring life.

97. *Wayyikra Rabba* 18.5.

REFLECTIONS

1. The backdrop of the wilderness experience highlights the gift of life. No matter how much the Israelites may have struggled for survival against the harshness of the environment and against the threat of enemies, their memory records their survival as

a gift and as an extraordinary deliverance. The Wisdom author introduces the exodus events by setting them in the context of this wilderness experience. Where the threat to life is extreme, so much more does the awareness of life and its gift become acute. The purpose of the comparisons between the acts of deliverance of the righteous and the acts of punishment of the enemies is to heighten the appreciation of the gift of life.

In the book of Deuteronomy we see how a tradition within Israel had idealized the wilderness experience as Israel's privileged moment of faith and trust in God (see Deut 8:1-20). Exodus and Numbers record the "grumbling in the desert" and the acts of "faithlessness" even in the leadership of Moses, Aaron, and Miriam. The authors of Deuteronomy interpret the wilderness experience after the great acts of rebellion as the in-between time of learning trust and faith in God (Deuteronomy 1–3). The Wisdom author shares this perspective on the wilderness experience. To reflect on the difficulties and tragedies in life is not a morbid or depressing exercise. What is extracted from the memories of the threat to existence is the energy and the gift of life.

2. The principle enunciated by the author reinforces the positive function of the energies of the cosmos. Through the very elements in which the Egyptians experienced punishment, the righteous experienced benefit in their need. There is an inherent parallel between the apocalyptic judgment presented in the first part of the book and the continuous judgment exercised throughout the midrash on the exodus and wilderness episodes. Just as all of creation was understood to be armed by God to wage battle against lawlessness (Wis 5:15-23), so too are the elements of the cosmos used to bring punishment to the enemies and life to the righteous.

The ambiguity of the elements of the cosmos, as symbolized by water and fire, elicits a healthy respect for the environment. The forces of the cosmos cannot be possessed through knowledge or manipulation without regard to justice. Because creation is guided continuously by the wisdom of God, the relationship between justice and the forces of the cosmos remains dynamic. In the case of the exodus episodes, the captivity and enslavement of the Hebrews in Egypt elicit even from the forces of the cosmos the redressing of injustice.

WISDOM 11:6-14, THE NILE DEFILED WITH BLOOD—ABUNDANT WATERS

COMMENTARY

The first diptych contrasts the thirst of the Egyptians due to the defilement of the Nile (Exod 7:14-24) with the abundant waters the righteous received in the wilderness (Exod 15:22-27; 17:1-7). The brief introduction to the diptychs prepares for the elaboration on the first plague with the reference to the Israelites' calling out to God from their thirst (Wis 11:4).

11:6-7. An explanation is given for the specific punishment the Egyptians experience by means of the Nile's defilement (v. 7). The Nile is defiled in rebuke to Pharaoh's decree that the newborn males be drowned in the Nile (Exod 1:22). This explanation for the first plague inaugurates the author's technique of relating the specific plague experienced by Egypt to a correlating sin. For the author, there is an inherent relationship between sin and punishment. This principle will be formally announced in the second diptych: "so that they might learn that one is punished by the very things by which one sins" (v. 16 NRSV). This correlation between sin and punishment was also present in the author's argumentation in the first part of the book. The wicked, who had reasoned falsely, were said to have experienced punishment according to to their reasoning (3:10). Since they judged mortality to be meaningless and decided to subject the righteous to a shameful death, the wicked finally will experience an ultimate death as punishment.

11:8-10. One difficulty the author faces throughout the contrast between the righteous and their enemies is the experience of suffering on Israel's part as well as that of Egypt. Whereas in the diptychs of the first part of the book the suffering of the righteous was not the result of their sin, the suffering of the Israelites in the wilderness at times was caused by their own rebellion. In the case of the first plague, the author notes how Israel also experienced thirst. But even here the author contrasts the thirst of the Israelites with that of the Egyptians. Israel's thirst is meant to be disciplinary. The thirst of the enemies is punitive. The deuteronomic interpretation of Israel's suffering in the wilderness is harnessed to appreciate the Israelites' desert trials (Deuteronomy 8). Israel's suffering is a time for learning God's faithfulness and power. God tests the righteous as a parent does in warning, but the Lord tests the ungodly as a stern king in judgment (11:10; cf. Deut 8:5). This positive function of God's testing the righteous is parallel to the author's explanation of the suffering of the just in the first part (3:4-6). There, too, the righteous were tested by God as gold would be tested in fire. They were found to be worthy and acceptable as an offering to God.

11:11-13. The thirsting of the righteous gives them an appreciation of God's judgment against Egypt. The anguish of the Egyptians' punishment by thirst is twofold. In addition to the plague ruining the water supply while the Israelites were present in Egypt, the Egyptians suffer further from the realization that the Israelites receive abundant water in the desert. The author is telescoping the events of the exodus and the wilderness and imagining what the Egyptians would experience by realizing that blessings are bestowed on the righteous. The first principle is elaborated (vv. 5, 13). When the ungodly realize that the righteous are blessed through the very means by which the wicked are punished, their anguish doubly increases.

The turn to direct speech toward God (vv. 7-10) signals the quality of laudatory prayer. The entire midrash on the exodus is enclosed by the author's direct praise of God (vv. 7-10; 19:22). Throughout the midrash, the author turns to God in praise of the marvelous interventions in Israel's history.

11:14. The conclusion to the diptych focuses on Moses, on both his tenuous clinging to life at birth and his power as an adult. Moses had narrowly escaped the death sentence decreed by the pharaoh. Now, at the end, the Egyptians are forced to marvel at the events wrought by Moses both in Egypt and in the desert. The formulation of this scene is reminiscent of the scene of judgment in the first part of the book. In the final scene of judgment, the ungodly are amazed at the salvation of the righteous. With anguish they recognize that those whom they had held in derision are numbered among the children of God (5:1-5). Similarly with Moses, the Egyptians marvel at the one they had cast out and exposed to death.

REFLECTIONS

1. The principle whereby one is punished by the very means by which one has sinned presumes an inner coherency between sin and punishment. This idea was introduced in the first part of the book when the author declared that the wicked are punished according to their reasoning (3:10). The author constantly applies this principle throughout the diptychs that deal with the plagues preceding the exodus. The Wisdom author is advocating a psychological truth. Often enough, both blessing and punishment are conceived of as being extraneous to the activities that are being rewarded or penalized. On many levels, this is an adequate representation. But in the case of both faithfulness and sinfulness, there is an internal consistency between acts of faithfulness and acts of sinfulness and their corresponding consequences. The author is stressing this consistency between the sin of injustice and the suffering that the Egyptians experience as a result of their sin. There is an internal reward for faithfulness that, in the long run, even against all appearances, reveals itself through abundance and joy. There is an internal destruction of the source of injustice that, in the long run, despite appearances to the contrary, reveals itself in despair and anguish. The very earth lets the blood of Abel cry out to God for a murder done in secret (Gen 4:10-11). The arguments the author labored to maintain in the first part of the book regarding the blessedness of the righteous and the wretchedness of the unjust are sustained through a reflection on Israel's salvation history. An act of injustice, as small as it may appear, eventually finds a way of raising its head toward destruction. Even a small act of kindness, as unnoticeable as it may be, carries with it the expression of love.

2. God tests the righteous in order to bring discipline and knowledge to them (11:6-10). The author explains the suffering of the righteous, both deserved and undeserved, as a process of purification and learning. The model is that of a parent who disciplines children for their benefit, a procedure enshrined in the Torah (Deut 8:5). It is always difficult to attribute human suffering to God without making God appear to be a tyrant or a merciless taskmaster. The writer of the book of Job rebels against a rigid application of the laws of retribution to all forms of human suffering. But, at the same time, the God who speaks from the whirlwind does not shy away from praising Behemoth and Leviathan, the symbols of enduring chaos (Job 40:6–41:34). Perhaps the very function of chaos and human limitations within creation is that they constitute a condition for freedom and decision.

For the author of the book of Wisdom, human limitations are not the destroyer of value. Suffering and tragedy do not destroy the soul, but injustice does. On the contrary, the awareness of his limitations propels Solomon to seek God and wisdom. According to the book of Wisdom, the God who tries and tests the righteous is the God who out of love attempts to stir them to knowledge and discipline. The end result is that Solomon's relationship to God is assured through wisdom—wisdom makes humans friends of God.

WISDOM 11:15–16:14, ANIMALS PUNISH EGYPT, AND QUAILS ARE FED TO THE RIGHTEOUS

OVERVIEW

The second diptych contrasts the plaguing of Egypt with various animals to the special foods provided the Israelites in the wilderness. Although in itself the contrast is quite brief, the entire diptych is rather lengthy. The image of animals in the plagues elicits the two major digressions or theological reflections of the last part of the book (the reflection on the moderation of God, 11:17–12:27; the reflection on false worship, chaps. 13–15), as well as a minor digression that treats God's power over creation in the episode of the brazen serpent (16:5-14). The two major digressions are well composed and theologically dense. Therefore, an understanding of their structure will facilitate their interpretation.

The first reflection on the moderation of God toward both the enemies of Israel as well as Israel itself is elicited by the awareness of the progressive infliction of the plagues. God sent various plagues against Egypt. The author reasons that since God could have destroyed Egypt in a single show of might (11:17-21), then God's reluctance to use the full force of power expresses the moderation and mercy of God (11:26–12:2). Through moderation and mercy, God provides room for human conversion.

The treatment of the moderation and mercy of God is composed in three parts: (1) God's moderation in dealing with the Egyptians, 11:15–12:2; (2) God's moderation in dealing with the Canaanites, 12:3-18; and (3) a double lesson for Israel, 12:19-27.

The first two sections, on the moderation of God with the Egyptians and the Canaanites, are parallel in theme and in structure:

11:15-20   the Egyptians—the Canaanites   12:3-11
11:21–12:2   God is sovereign and merciful   12:12-18

By noticing how God treats the weak and the haughty from the examples of the exodus, the wilderness, and the conquest, the righteous are to learn and to appropriate the same compassion and mercy of God.

The second reflection or digression is more directly motivated by the central image of the second diptych. The main contrast of the diptych fluctuates between the animal worship of Egypt and the animals that become a source of food for Israel. Egypt's sin of animal worship occasions a thoughtful critique of false worship in general. The entire critique progresses in three parts from the least blameworthy form of false worship to the most blameworthy: (1) philosophers incur slight blame, 13:1-9; (2) idol worship is condemned, 13:10–15:13; (3) both the idol worship and the animal worship of Egypt are severely condemned, 15:14-19.

The first critique centers on the various forms of nature worship, from worship of the elements of nature to worship of the heavenly bodies. Only slight blame, but blame nonetheless, is attributed to such persons who come to identify the divine with natural phenomena.

The most extensive part of the critique concentrates on the central section, which deals with idol worship. Here the critique attempts to explain the origins of the worship of idols and the dreadful moral consequences of such worship in life. The critique (13:10–15:13) is arranged concentrically:

A   13:10-19   gold, silver,
                     stone, wooden
                     idols—carpenter
B   14:1-7   reflection on God's
                     providential care
                   ⎡ punishment of idols
C   14:8-31   ⎢ invention and result of
                   ⎢ idolatry
                   ⎣ punishment of idolatry
B' 15:1-6   reflection on God's
                     mercy and power
A' 15:7-13   clay idols—potter

In addition to the progressive blame attributed to forms of false worship within the overall structure of the critique (chaps. 13–15), we can notice a progression in the matter of the idols (13:10–15:13). The overall progression moves from the least blameworthy to the most blameworthy. The internal progression moves from precious metals, like gold and silver, to the common, lower-value substance clay.

In the third and final critique of animal worship, the author is at a loss to find a conceivable explanation or source of such worship. Therefore, the most severe condemnation is attributed to animal worship. This return to the image of animals, which occasioned the two reflections on God's moderation and on false worship, continues the thread of the argument in the second diptych. Animals torment the enemies of Israel, yet animals provide sustenance to the righteous.

Wisdom 11:15–12:27, The Moderation of God

COMMENTARY

11:15-16. The second diptych contrasts the animals that were sent to punish Egypt with the quails that were sent to feed Israel in the desert (Wis 11:15-16; 16:1-4). Direct speech to God signals the quality of prayer that the reflection is taking for the author

(11:15-17). The diptych continues to emphasize the relation between sin and its inherent punishment. In the case of the Egyptians, the worship of animals is perceived to be the cause of plagues of various animals. The author is conflating into a single diptych the several plagues of animals and insects from Exodus (frogs, gnats, flies, pestilence in livestock, locusts).

The author's explanation that irrational animals were sent to plague Egypt for their sin of animal worship reinforces the inherent relationship between sin and punishment. Again, the author is exerting great effort to explain that punishment is not extrinsic to thought and action, but is implicit in the very structure of sin. Since for the author the worship of animals is irrational, then irrationality seizes the minds of the Egyptians as irrational animals plague the land.

This principle is both similar to and distinct from the long-standing principle of taliation (*lex talionis,* "an eye for an eye, a tooth for a tooth"). In the law of talion, the damage to or injury of the claimant is equated with the punishment of the culprit (see Exod 21:23-25; Deut 19:18-21).[98] For the author of Wisdom, the principle of retaliation equates the means of punishment to the sin. The idea of the similarity of the means of punishment to the means of the injury emphasizes the inherent relationship between sin and its consequences. As a clearly enunciated principle, it is an idea that is seen infrequently in ancient texts. Perhaps the closest parallel to the author's principle can be found in the *Testament of the Twelve Patriarchs*: "For by whatever capacity anyone transgresses, by that also is he chastised."[99]

11:17–12:2, Moderation Toward the Egyptians. This brief introduction to the second diptych elicits a reflection on God's treatment of the Egyptians in the plague episodes. The author focuses on God's moderation. The progressive harshness of the plagues reveals God's attempt to teach the Egyptians through the experience of lack and suffering that their injustice brings. To highlight God's moderation, the author notes that the enemies of Israel could have been destroyed by a single show of force (11:20) and by horrendous and unimaginable animals. Instead, they are tormented by rather insignificant pests.

11:17-20. God's reign over the universe through creation is one of moderation and balance. The author employs a platonic term to paraphrase God's creation of the heavens and the earth in Genesis. The image of "formless matter" (11:17) corresponds to the "formless void" of Gen 1:2. This image, which opens the reflection, is parallel to another platonic idea that closes the unit before the contemplation of God's mercy. As if to summarize the moderation of God's reign, the author in 11:20 harnesses the popular platonic triad of "measure, number and weight."[100] These references to elements of physics were employed by many classical writers to denote the harmony and balance of the universe. In Scripture, similar terms were used to indicate the harmony and balance of God's creation (weight, measure, decree, way, Job 28:25-26; measured, weighed, Isa 40:12).

11:21–12:2. The contemplation of God's moderation combines the two poles of God's power and mercy. God is powerful yet merciful. The two poetic images that contrast the smallness of the world with the majesty of God are reminiscent of Solomon's description of his own transience (7:1-6). Just as Solomon's reflection on his insignificant stature propelled him to seek God and wisdom, so too the author's reflection on the smallness of the universe elicits the contemplation of God's mercy and compassion. The world is compared to a speck that tips the scales and to a drop of morning dew. Both images point out the smallness and insignificance of the universe in comparison to the majesty of God. Similar images are used in Isaiah to illustrate the smallness of the nations ("a drop from a bucket, dust on the scales" [Isa 40:15 NRSV]).

The power and majesty of God highlight the Lord's compassion and mercy (11:23). The purpose of the moderation of God is to give space for conversion and repentance. The author recalls the relationship between God and the universe, enunciated in the

---

98. *Laws of Hammurabi,* 196, 200; For the varieties of the principle of retaliation found in Ancient Law Codes and in the Bible, see the brief treatment by H. B. Huffmon in "Lex Talionis," *ABD,* 4:321-22.

99. The *Testament of the Twelve Patriarchs, Gad, the ninth son,* 5:10.

100. Plato *Philebus* 55E, measurement and weights are essential for art; *Republic* 602D, measuring, counting and weighing are correctives to illusory art; *Laws* 757B, the equality determined by measure, weight, and number is meant to ensure good politics.

beginning of the book. God loves all that exists and does not detest anything that has been created (11:24-26; cf. 1:14). The earlier reflection on the irrationality of animals has probably elicited this reaffirmation of the positive qualities of creation. It is not the animals that are detested by the author, even if their appearance may be repulsive (15:18-19); rather, the author abhors the falsity of animal worship.

The passage 11:21–12:2 is stamped through and through with the value of universalism, which characterizes sapiential literature in general. God is merciful to all, loves all things that exist, and spares all things. The universal goodness of God is affirmed within the polemic against Israel's opponents. The power and mercy of God extend to all of creation. This is quite remarkable for a work that clearly is marked with polemics against the injustice suffered by the Jewish community in the diaspora.

God's mercy is expressed in moderation. As harsh as the polemic appears in the midrashic treatment of the narrative of the plagues in Exodus, the author of Wisdom interprets the punishments within the context of God's compassion and moderation. The unit closes with the purpose of God's moderation in the administration of punishment. Punishments are meant to elicit conversion. Those who sin are reminded of their sin precisely in order that they may be freed from sin (12:2).

12:3-18, Moderation Toward the Canaanites. The same principle of moderation is applied to God's treatment of the Canaanites. Here the author is interpreting the events of the conquest and the infiltration of the promised land as predicted in Exodus and Deuteronomy. The idea of God's punishing the Canaanites for their sins gradually and in stages, sending "wasps" as forerunners, is an interpretation of Exod 23:20-33. The description of the various forms of the sins of the Canaanites that result in their losing the land in favor of the Israelites is an interpretation of Deut 18:9-14 (cf. Deut 9:5). Their sins include child sacrifice, divination, and sorcery (cf. Wis 12:3-6). Although the author is evidently making reference to human sacrifices in the cult of Moloch, as described in the biblical texts (Lev 18:21; Deut 12:31; Jer 32:35), it is also true that human sacrifice extended well into the Roman period, at least among some groups, even in Egypt.[101]

The author's purpose in recalling the destruction of the pre-Israelite dwellers of the land is to highlight the moderation and mercy of God. As with the Egyptians, God could have destroyed them in one blow (v. 9). Instead, they were judged little by little, precisely to give them an opportunity to repent (v. 10). The author appeals to the very same image of wasps or hornets being sent out before the invading Israelites to weaken the enemies of Israel as related in Exod 23:28 (cf. Deut 7:20; Josh 24:12). The Hebrew word for "hornets" or "wasps" is unclear, and it could very well refer to disease or pestilence, as the root meaning would suggest. The LXX translates the Hebrew by the Greek word σφήξ (*sphēx*), which means "wasps" or "hornets." Interestingly, a difference in the comparison between the Egyptians and the Canaanites is that the suppression of the means of punishment is equal to the means of their sin. The author is content to stress that the reason for the Canaanites' loss of the land is their sin. Perhaps the author could not think of an immediate correlation between the forms of sin and the punishment of the loss of land.

The reflection on the plight of the first dwellers of the land serves to underscore the sovereignty of God (vv. 12-18). God cannot be accused of acting unjustly, since no one is condemned without recognition of his or her sin (v. 15). But precisely because God is sovereign over creation and history, God acts with care, mildness, and forbearance. God's motive for such moderation is love for all people. The universal aspect of God's love for what exists (11:24-26) is reiterated in the reflection on the treatment of the Canaanites (vv. 15-18).

Just as the reflection on the destruction of Egypt elicited the author's praise of God's power and mercy, so too the reflection on the destruction of the Canaanites elicits the praise of God's sovereignty and compassion (vv. 12-18). The two sections stand parallel, 11:21–12:2 = 12:12-18. In both cases, the reflection on God's treatment of Israel's

---

101. For references to the debate on cannibalism and the practice of human sacrifice, see Winston, *The Wisdom of Solomon*, 239-40.

enemies leads to the perception of God's universal love and moderation.

A Double Lesson for Israel. 12:19-22. What the righteous are to learn from the meditation on the plight of the unrighteous is summarized succinctly in v. 22. They are to learn to be compassionate and moderate, and they are to trust in the mercy of God. The double lesson touches upon their relationship to God and their relationship to enemies. The points in the argument the author has constructed regarding the treatment of the unrighteous are now applied to the righteous as well. The main issue the author holds up for consideration is the moderation of God (vv. 19-21). God provides repentance for sinners and gives time and space for the unrighteous to turn from their injustice.

12:23-27. The concluding section of the first reflection on the moderation of God returns to the punishment of the Egyptians. In its context, this unit returns to the theme of the opening section of the digression and prepares for the second digression on false worship. In itself, it continues the theme of the second diptych—namely, the animals that torment Egypt are understood as a punishment in accord with the sin of animal worship. This section could very well have been a part of the second diptych before the two major theological reflections were inserted into the text (11:15-16; 12:23-27; 16:1-14).

The language applied to the Egyptians is reminiscent of the language applied to the wicked in the scene of judgment in the first part of Wisdom. Just as the wicked recognized that they had strayed from the way of truth and had taken their fill of the paths of lawlessness (5:6-7), so too are the Egyptians described as straying onto the paths of error (12:24). Just as the wicked reproached themselves for their folly (5:4), so too are the Egyptians accused of living unjustly in a life of folly (v. 23). Just as the wicked recognized the blessed end of the just (5:5), so too do the Egyptians finally recognize the true God, whom they hitherto refused to acknowledge (v. 27). The final verse, which introduces the idea of recognizing the true God, allows the argument of the author to pass smoothly onto the next major digression on false worship.

REFLECTIONS

1. There is an ethical difficulty in reflecting on the fall of one's enemy. How does one reflect on the demise of anyone, even one's enemies or opponents, without gloating over their fall in such a manner as to take on their very attributes and values? The oppressed only too easily becomes the oppressor, the victim the victimizer. How does one face injustice without falling into the pitfalls of destructive anger and revenge? The difficulties inherent in this reflection are similar to those found in the psalms of complaint, in which the just lament over the power of the enemies and plead with God for salvation and vindication (e.g., Psalms 5; 10; 17; 35; 58; 59). Only a fine line, indeed, separates the righteous anger of the oppressed from destructive thoughts and desires for revenge. Throughout the latter part of Wisdom, the author reflects on the demise of Israel's enemies. But instead of this reflection building up a sense of arrogance and self-righteousness over their demise, it leads to an appreciation of God's sovereignty and mercy. The reflection on the power and tolerance of God provides a necessary context for pondering the power and folly of the unjust.

It should be borne in mind that the polemical character of the latter part of Wisdom reflects the situation of a Jewish community under siege in the diaspora. Although at times Jewish communities achieved great autonomy and flourished in the fields of philosophy, art, and commerce, especially in Alexandria, they often fell prey to the jealousy of local centers of power. The careful reflection the author is offering over the demise of the unjust powerful is not meant to foster gloating over the fall of one's enemies. Rather, the examples of an unjust and unfair use of power from Israel's history are brought to the fore in order to bolster commitment to and trust in justice. The example of the exodus is set forth by the author as historical proof for the vindication of justice over the appearance of the power and might of injustice. What had been argued in the first part of Wisdom regarding the folly of injustice and the strength of virtue is now bolstered by examples from Israel's history. Injustice *does* lead to death. Justice *does* lead to life. The exodus is the author's supreme example that constitutes Israel's hope in virtue and justice for the present and the future.

2. Ironically, perhaps, the examples of the demise of Egyptian and Canaanite power are used to foster compassion and mercy. The focus is not so much on the fall of Egypt and Canaan as it is on God's treatment of the just and the unjust. Using the example of the punishment of the wicked, the author continuously asserts the inner dynamic of the self-destruction of injustice. The unjust are punished by the very means by which they sin. From the example of God's treatment of those who wield power unjustly, the author derives the tolerance and mercy of God. Like Ezekiel, the author interprets the activity of God toward sinners as a call to conversion: "Have I any pleasure in the death of the wicked, says the Lord GOD, and not rather that they should turn from their ways and live?" (Ezek 18:23 NRSV; cf. 33:11-16).

3. The moderation of God toward Egypt and Canaan teaches the Israelites to be tolerant. Israel is to be compassionate and kind because that is God's approach, even to Israel's enemies. The author's reflection on the universal love of God instills an ethical imperative toward one's opponents. The author may very well have had in mind the extraordinary extension of God's blessing to Israel's traditional enemies, Egypt and Assyria, as narrated in Isa 19:18-25: "Blessed be Egypt my people, and Assyria the work of my hands, and Israel my heritage" (NRSV). This openness to opponents, or at least to the stranger in one's midst, is also consistent with the deuteronomic call to be kind to the sojourner in the midst of Israel because the Israelites were sojourners in the land of Egypt (Deut 10:18-19; 23:7; 24:21).

The way one treats one's opponents in life reveals a great deal about one's appropriation of the virtue of justice. The tolerance and moderation proposed by God's treatment of Egypt and Canaan is similar to the tolerance proclaimed by Christ. Tolerance is not a sign of weakness, but of strength and compassion. In the parable of weeds among the wheat, there is the concern of uprooting the wheat along with the weeds, the good along with the bad (Matt 13:24-30). Although the parable is more directly concerned with the final judgment, which separates the weeds from the wheat, it also gives space to the coexistence of good and evil. In this in-between time, the wicked subsist along with the good and are not to be eliminated but tolerated. The Wisdom author's explanation for God's tolerance is the desire for conversion, as is the case with Ezekiel (Ezek 18:23). The parable's explanation for tolerance is the protection of the good. Both, of course, recognize the final judgment as a time of reckoning.

The theme that true power is sublimely expressed through love or mercy has been cast into the cinematic form. In *Schindler's List*,[102] the ruthless commanding officer at Plaszow boasts to Oscar Schindler that power is control. Schindler, the business tycoon who feels compelled to save the Jews who had worked for him, responds with a story. He relates how a common thief who was unmistakably guilty was given the death sentence. But the emperor, who had every right and all the power to confirm the sentence, for no apparent gain acquitted the thief out of mercy toward him. "Now that is power," ruminates Schindler to the officer.

---

102. Steven Spielberg, director and producer, *Schindler's List*, Universal City Studios and Amblin Entertainment, 1993.

Wisdom 13:1–15:19, Critique of Pagan Cults

OVERVIEW

The principle of the means of punishment being equal to the form of sin generates a second major theological reflection in the second diptych: a critique of pagan cults. Egypt is punished by animals for the sin of worshiping animals. The theme of Egypt's animal cult elicits the critique of pagan cults in general. The critique is carefully balanced into three parts, the largest of which deals with idolatry in the very center. There is a qualitative progression from the least blameworthy (the foolish, who cannot recognize God, 13:1), to the more blameworthy (the miserable, who put their hope in dead idols, 13:10), finally to the most blameworthy (the most foolish, who go further and, in addition to dead idols, worship the most hateful animals, 15:14). The *Letter of Aristeas* (134-141) from the second century BCE (c. 150–100) also contrasts two forms of worship—namely, idol worship, attributed to the Greeks, and animal worship, attributed to the Egyptians.

The division of various forms of cultic worship into two or three types is also well-known within Hellenistic/Jewish writings contemporaneous to the book of Wisdom. Philo makes a distinction between the worship of natural elements or celestial bodies and the worship of idols or animals.[103] The Stoics made a threefold distinction in forms of worship: the mythical type, the philosophical type, and the legislative type.

103. See Philo *On the Decalogue* 52; *On the Special Laws* 1.13.

Wisdom 13:1-9, Nature Worship

COMMENTARY

The author's main argument against nature worship rests on the failure to recognize God, the creator, in the beauty of creation. The prime metaphor used throughout the argument is the image of the artist and the artifact. One may recognize the artist in the quality of the work of art (vv. 1, 5). This critique is done with a great deal of sympathy for the natural desire to search for God in the forces of creation (vv. 6-7). Since creation itself is the work of God, the author acknowledges the naturalness of recognizing the beauty of creation inherent in the various forms of nature worship. The fault in nature worship is the failure to recognize the creator behind the works of creation. In contrast to this failure, the believer moves easily from the contemplation of the beauty of nature to the personal God who is the creator (v. 9; cf. Psalm 8).

The relationship between the artist and the artifact was a frequent metaphor in Greek philosophical circles: "Assuredly from the very structure of all made objects we are accustomed to prove that the work is certainly the product of some artificer and has not been constructed at random."[104] Similarly, as a work of art, the universe was the workplace of the divine artist for Stoic philosophers.[105]

God is explicitly called the artisan (τεχνίτης *technitēs*, v. 1), the same term the author had used earlier for personified wisdom (7:22; 8:6). Wisdom will be called the artisan who builds the vessels in which people put their trust on the raging waters of the sea (14:2). The term used for God as artisan in the first half of the unit is parallel to "Creator" (v. 5), "God" (v. 6), and "the Lord" (v. 9) in the second half. Otherwise, God is never referred to as artisan in Scripture. Applying the term "artisan" to God is another sign of the author's deliberate joining together of the role of wisdom in human affairs to that of God in the exodus in the final part of the book of Wisdom.

104. Epictetus 1.6.7.
105. Cicero *De Natura Deorum* 1.20.53.

The two general forms of nature worship that are singled out are those of the natural forces (fire, wind, air, water) and that of celestial bodies (circle of the stars and luminaries of heaven, v. 2). The author is combining the traditional biblical critique of luminary cults (cf. Deut 17:3; Job 31:26-28; Jer 8:2; 19:13; Ezek 8:16) to the particular critique of the deification of natural forces, associated loosely with Stoic tenets. In particular, the author of Wisdom pays attention to the polyvalent understanding of the *pneuma* in Stoic writings. In Stoic philosophy, the *pneuma* is the unifying principle of the universe. For the Stoic philosopher Chrysippus, *pneuma* consists of fire and air, which on occasion appear to be deified.[106] All three elements that focus on the concept of *pneuma* in Stoic philosophy—fire, wind, and air—are represented in v. 2.

The fundamental argument of the author is that if people are swayed by the beauty of the created universe, so much more should they come to appreciate the creator who stands behind it (vv. 3-9). The search for the divine reality in the universe among peoples who worship natural phenomena, therefore, receives the author's sympathy and approbation (vv. 6-7). Philo likewise apportions less blame to those who magnify the subject above the ruler in nature worship than to those who worship dead idols.[107] What is lacking in the many forms of nature worship is the further step of recognizing the personal creator God behind the beauty of the universe (13:8-9).

---

106. Chrysippus *Stoicorum Veterum Fragmenta* 2.310.442.786.

107. Philo *On the Decalogue* 66.

REFLECTIONS

1. The reason for the author's reticent and limited critique against adherents of nature cults resides in their implicit desire to seek God in creation. Behind this reticence we can recognize the author's admiration for some of the noble features of Greek philosophy and religious tenets: the relentless search for truth, the desire to understand human society and the universe, and the respect for principles and laws in nature. While the author does not exculpate them for their failure to take the final step and recognize the creator of the universe, there is strong recognition of the inherent goodness and appropriateness of groups who genuinely seek God and meaning in life (13:7).

The author recognizes a certain affinity to biblical faith in the search for God manifested among the Greeks. This restrained attitude on the part of the author, even within criticism, can serve as a good reminder of the fact that faith in an ultimate being is based on a search for meaning and desire. Faith involves a journey, a search, and a willingness to find God. The author lauds the desire to search for God in creation, but criticizes the failure of adherents of nature cults for being satisfied with the gifts of the giver and not reaching the beauty of the creator.

2. The author's metaphor of the artisan, in which the artist is recognized in an admired artifact, is a powerful analogy for the process of recognizing the creator behind the beauty of the universe. God is understood inherently as the artist who has fashioned a great work of art in the universe. Aesthetics and faith have been allies for a long time. Take the covenant with Abram. To assure Abram that the promise of progeny would be fulfilled, God called Abram to contemplate the heavens and the stars, "Look toward heaven and count the stars, if you are able to count them" (Gen 15:5 NRSV). Even more to the point is the contemplation of God's love for humanity through a reflection on the beauty of the heavens: "When I look at your heavens, the work of your fingers, the moon and the stars that you have established; what are human beings that you are mindful of them, mortals that you care for them?" (Ps 8:3-4 NRSV). Even in the NT, which is more prone to advancing the "cross of Christ" as the privileged moment of encounter between humans and God, the contemplation of the beauty of nature elicits wonder in God's care for humanity:

> Consider the lilies of the field, how they grow; they neither toil nor spin, yet I tell you, even Solomon in all his glory was not clothed like one of these. But if God so clothes the grass of the field, which is alive today and tomorrow is thrown into the oven, will he not much more clothe you—you of little faith? (Matt 6:28-30 NRSV)

It was quite fashionable until recently, perhaps, for many scientists and artists to declare their agnosticism (if not direct hostility) with respect to belief in an ultimate being guiding the universe. Yet, many scientists who face the beauty and intricacy of the universe every day in their routine experimentation, from analyzing the constellations of the stars to the mapping of the genetic code, are led to a mystery behind the universe that cannot be denied. The sheer majesty of the universe continues to evoke questions of faith and ultimate meaning.

3. Perhaps the closest parallel in our own time to the author's ambivalent critique of nature cults is the Christian response to secular humanism. Although many of the values promoted by secular humanism are based on Judeo-Christian values—such as the dignity of the person, the right to education and health, and social justice—there remains a fundamental antagonism between the two approaches on the issue of belief and commitment to a personal divine being. Extremists on both sides have argued that the respective approaches of each side belittle humanity. On the one hand, for some secular humanists, positing a divine being unnecessarily reduces human beings to the category of servants or slaves. On the other hand, Christian critics have argued that if the authority of a divine being is not acknowledged, human beings are easily discounted and subjected to the whims of the majority and the powerful.

The author of Wisdom is not willing to compromise the values that the nature cults and Israelite faith have in common—namely, respect and admiration for the universe. At the same time, the critique is a challenge to anyone who may be tempted to remain within the sphere of the natural and, in the author's words, "fail to find sooner the Lord of these things" (13:9). Similarly, in the debate between secular humanism and the Judeo-Christian tradition, the antagonisms should not blind us to the values shared in common. The mysterious and beautiful voice of creation should be allowed to speak of the artist behind the great works.

Wisdom 13:10–15:13, Origin and Consequences of Idolatry

WISDOM 13:10-19, THE CARPENTER AND IDOLS

COMMENTARY

The more serious nature of idol worship is signaled at the outset of the critique. Miserable are those who worship "dead things" (v. 10). This critique against idol worship continues a long tradition in the biblical writings. The making of idols counters the supreme prohibition against creating a graven image of God (Deut 5:8, "You shall not make for yourself an idol, whether in the form of anything that is in heaven above, or that is on the earth beneath, or that is in the water under the earth" [NRSV]; cf. Lev 26:1). The author's ridicule of the making and worshiping of idols is formulated in a manner similar to that found in several other scriptural passages (e.g., Pss 97:7; 115:3-8; 135:15-18; Isa 2:8-20; 40:18-20; 44:9-20; 45:16-20; 46:5-7; Jer 10:1-16; Hab 2:18; Bar 6:8-73).

What is emphasized throughout the author's sustained critique is the origin behind the practice of making and worshiping idols. Just as the author attempted to portray the process whereby humans came to deify the elements of the universe, so too is there an attempt to understand the process whereby idol worship came into practice.

The language applied to the creators of idols is reminiscent of the language applied to the wicked in the first part of Wisdom. The points of contact focus on the origin of idol worship, the moral depravity associated with idol worship, the deserved punishment for idol worshipers, and the judgment against both idol makers and the idols.

The author is deliberately drawing parallels between the perpetrators of injustice in the first part and the idol makers and worshipers in the second part. For instance, death was said to have entered the world through the adversary's envy (2:24). Here it is said that idols have entered the world through human vanity (14:14). The wicked's project in life was described through images of moral corruption and injustice (2:6-20). Even more so are the consequences of idol worship presented through images of moral depravity and licentiousness (14:22-29). The wicked were described as being fit to belong to the company of death (1:16). The idol worshipers are said to be fit for the dead objects they worship (15:6). The day of reckoning for the wicked was presented vividly, where the righteous were rewarded with royal dignity, whereas wickedness was utterly demolished through a cosmic upheaval (4:18–5:14). Similarly in the critique against idolatry, a day of divine reckoning is assured for both idol makers and their idols (14:8-11).

The pejorative language used to speak of the cult of idols is highlighted at the outset with the emphasis on the lifeless quality of idols. At least in nature worship the human mind is taken up with the beauty of God's creation. In idol worship, the human mind is mesmerized by the lifeless works of human hands, works of gold, silver, stone, and wood (vv. 10-11). The progression from quality metals to less valuable materials used in fashioning idols accentuates the author's criticism. Idol worship represents for the author a movement of degradation. To worship idols made of precious metals like gold and silver or made of valuable stone is deplorable, but to worship items made of useless bits of wood and of odd pieces of clay reveals the moral vacuity of such worship.

The focus of the critique rests on the carpenter who from the less valuable commodity of wood makes all sorts of useful utensils with artistry. The ridicule is based on the distance between the useful tools made from wood for daily needs and the "cast-off" pieces of wood chosen for idols. Not being useful for anything practical, such crooked and knotted blocks of wood are then carefully shaped into human or animal form, their blemishes are covered with paint, and they are set in a niche in the wall.

The author highlights the helplessness and lifelessness of the idol, which sets up the irony of praying for human values and needs to a lifeless thing. The idol cannot walk or stand by itself and must be fastened in the niche. To such a helpless image the idol worshiper entrusts things of great value: marriage and children, health, life, a safe journey, a prosperous business transaction (vv. 16-19). The final statement clinches the essential argument: Idol worshipers ask for strength from something whose hands have no strength at all.

The author is adapting at least two biblical arguments against idols into a unified argument: the process of making the idol and the lifeless qualities of the idol. In Isa 44:9-20 is a critique of ironsmiths and carpenters who make practical objects from the same substance from which they make idols. The prophet concentrates on the same process used in the book of Wisdom whereby a carpenter fashions both practical utensils and lifeless idols from the same block of wood (see also Isa 40:18-20; Jer 10:3-5). Psalm 115:3-8 is a poetic analysis of the lifelessness of idols made of silver and gold. They have a mouth that cannot speak, eyes that cannot see, ears that cannot hear, a nose that cannot smell, hands that cannot grasp, and feet that cannot walk (see also Deut 4:27-28; Ps 135:15-18; Bar 6:8-16, 53-59). These idols need to be fixed into a niche and fastened so that they will not topple over (vv. 15-16; cf. Isa 40:18-20).

The author of Wisdom highlights, in a similar manner, the lifeless qualities of the statue. At this point, however, instead of using the metaphor of the bodily senses (as will be done in 15:15), the author juxtaposes the prayers for human needs against the lack of human vitality in idols. The prayer for possessions, marriage, and children is juxtaposed to the lifelessness of an idol; praying for health is juxtaposed to the weakness of an idol; praying for life to the "deadness" of an idol; praying for help in life to the utter inexperience of idols; praying for a prosperous journey to an idol that cannot move; praying for success in business and work to an image whose hands have no strength (vv. 17-19).

It should be pointed out that in Greek and Hellenistic circles there was both a critique of the naïveté of idol worship and a defense for a more sophisticated view of an idol's function in prayer. The author's critique presumed a parody of idol worship. The lifeless quality of images and statues of worship was a subject of scorn for Heraclitus and Timaeus of Tauromenium.[108] But Plato defended the use of idols to remind humans of the living gods. The idol is to the living god what the shadow is to the object in Plato's allegory of the shadows in the cave: "The ancient laws of all men concerning the gods are two-fold: some of the gods whom we honor we see clearly, but of others we set up statues as images, and we believe that when we worship these, lifeless though they be, the living gods beyond feel great good-will towards us and gratitude."[109]

In terms of the author's overall argument, it should be noted that the image of wood continues to be used in the next part of the critique (14:1-10), when the fearful sailor prays to a wooden idol for protection aboard the wooden vessel. The theme of the carpenter who fashions idols is matched at the outer level of the concentric structure with the theme of the potter who gives shape to statues from clay (15:7-13).

---

108. See Winston, *The Wisdom of Solomon*, 259-61, for references to the practice of idol worship in Egypt and in Greek writings.

109. Plato *Laws* 931A.

REFLECTIONS

The author gives a name to a disorder that stifles human growth: idolatry. This disorder, which can be described in so many different ways, essentially seeks life where in fact there is no life. Appropriately, at the beginning of the critique the idol is described as "dead" (13:10). At the end of the critique what is highlighted is the discrepancy between the worshiper's attempt to secure values of life through idols and the "lifeless" quality of the idols themselves (13:17-19). Idolatry rests on a false hope, much as the wicked's reckless purposes and projects in life in the earlier chapters of the work rest on their false understanding of power and might (2:1-24).

With respect to the idol worshiper, the idol is described as the work of "human hands" (13:10). Herein lies the author's essential criticism of idolatry. It involves a lifeless absorption with the "self." Those who worship an idol made of human hands are locked into a preoccupation with the self that stifles transcendence. In the author's argument, there is in nature worship at least the minimal amount of transcendence involved because of its appreciation of the beautiful works of creation. But in the worship of idols made by human hands, the focus of the worshiper is drawn more and more toward the self.

Although it would be rather difficult to find idol worshipers in the strict sense in our contemporary societies and cultures, the essential function of idol worship still abounds. The idols of our own time may not be ones fashioned into images of gold, silver, or wood. There are the idols of consumerism with their many faces through which an entire generation has been trained to focus on the self. The resulting alienation and purposelessness that arise from not living out one's life for another are as lifeless as the helpless idols the author of Wisdom holds up for ridicule.

WISDOM 14:1-10, THE NAVIGATOR AND IDOLS

COMMENTARY

The critique of worshiping a wooden idol focuses on the contrast between entrusting one's survival on the sea to a piece of wood and calling upon an idol made of wood that is more fragile than the ship itself. Entrusting one's life to the forces of creation and to one's knowledge of them is rooted in the goodness of creation. The artistry involved in the fashioning of the ship is praised as the work of wisdom, the artisan (v. 2). It is God's providence that steers the the ship through the laws governing the winds and the currents.

As an example of genuine human trust in the forces of creation, the author presents the ark of Noah, which provided a saving benefit to all humanity (vv. 3-7). Trust in this piece of wood was rooted in God's providence. God supplements the natural disposition of human intelligence with a providence that brings to completion the desired goal of safety (v. 5). By highlighting the wood in the ark as a means of rescue, the author is drawing a distinction between the goodness of the materials of creation and the corruption of misusing those materials to make idols. God is being praised for the gift of wood that sustains human beings in precarious moments on the sea. The reflection takes on the quality of thankful praise to God for the wonders of creation and for God's providential care in and through creation.

The praise to God ends in a statement of beatitude reminiscent of the declaration of blessedness for the virtuous sterile woman and the eunuch (3:13-14, different Greek words for "blessedness" are used in each passage). The very wood by which the righteousness of Noah brought salvation to humanity is proclaimed blessed.

It is quite understandable how the early church, which on occasion favored an allegorical interpretation of Scripture as exemplified in Origen of Alexandria, recognized in this statement a reference to the blessedness of the cross of Christ. Ambrose comments on Wis 14:7-8 by juxtaposing the matter that is considered blessed with matter that is considered accursed. He explains the reference to wood as representing the cross of Christ and the reference to the work of human hands as representing wooden idols.[110]

The NT employed the same Greek word to designate "cross" that can be translated as "wood" in general or even "tree" (ξύλον *xylon*; Acts 5:30; 10:39; 13:29; Gal 3:13; 1 Pet 2:24). The tree of life and the tree of the knowledge of good and evil are represented by the same Greek word in the creation text (Gen 2:9). The book of Revelation also employs the same word for references to the tree of life (Rev 2:7; 22:2; 22:14, 19). The Wisdom author had already employed the same word in an evident reference to the ark of Noah ("wisdom again saved it, steering the righteous man by a paltry piece of wood" [Wis 10:4 NRSV]). Since there was an evident interpolation to the cross in Ps 96:10 LXX, "The Lord reigns from the wood," which the oldest Greek MSS (B, S, and A) had already expunged, it was thought that perhaps the text of Wis 14:7 was also a Christian insert. The Muratori Canon (c. 180–190 CE) includes the Wisdom of Solomon in its list of NT writings, and this could very well have been the verse that caused the compiler to include it on the oldest list of NT writings that we have. However, as reflecting a reference to the ark of Noah, the verse fits well into the argument of the author, which lauds the matter through which human beings come to salvation and to justice. The author's firm assertion of the health and beauty of creation perhaps elicited this emphasis on the integrity of matter itself to distinguish the matter of wood from the idols made of wood that are accursed (vv. 8-11).

The turn to direct speech (vv. 3-7), which is found throughout the midrashic treatment of the exodus, points to the contemplative nature of the reflection. God is invoked directly as Father (v. 3). Although the image of father is used for God throughout Scripture, the address to God as Father in direct prayer is very late.[111] God is described through various images as a father (as father of orphans,

---

110. Ambrose *Sermon* 8,23; *Patrologia latina* 15, 130A.
111. On the fatherhood of God in direct prayer, see Eileen M. Schuller, "The Psalm of 4Q372 1 Within the Context of Second Temple Prayer," *CBQ* 54 (1992) 67-79.

Ps 68:5; as a father who has compassion or provides discipline, Ps 103:13; Prov 3:12; cf. Deut 8:5). At times God wishes that Israel would call upon the Lord as a father (Jer 3:4; 3:19; 31:9; Mal 1:6; 2:10).

There are occurrences of God's being addressed directly as a father in the texts representing the Davidic covenant (Ps 89:26), whereby the king is understood to be the adopted son of God (2 Sam 7:14). The closest parallels to the Wisdom text to God's being called father in direct speech is in Isa 63:16: "For you are our father . . . you O LORD are our father; our Redeemer from of old is your name" (NRSV; cf. Isa 64:8), and in Sir 23:1, "O Lord, Father and Master of my life" (NRSV; cf. Sir 23:4). It was common in rabbinical stories for God to be addressed as a father, "Hanin ha-Nehba was the son of the daughter of Honi the Circle-drawer. When the world needed rain, the Rabbis would send schoolchildren to him, who would pull him by the corners of his garments, and say to him: 'Father, Father! Give us rain!' Said Hanin: 'Master of the world! Do it for the sake of these who do not distinguish between the Father who gives rain and a father who does not give rain.' And the rain came."[112]

112. *Babylonian Talmud, Ta'an*, 23b.

Philo and Josephus employ the metaphor of father for God in a universal manner, as does the author of Wisdom. The ambiance, therefore, was already very fertile indeed for Jesus of Nazareth to address God through the personal designation of God as "Abba, father" (Matt 5:16; 6:1-32; Mark 19:36).

In contrast to the blessedness of the wood that saves, the author declares the idols made by human hands to be accursed (vv. 8-10). Both the makers of idols and the idols themselves fall under the disapproval of God. Since the author had declared that all creatures stand under God's providential care (1:14; 11:24-26), a distinction is made between the material of the idol and its function of "snaring" human souls and "trapping" the feet of the gullible (v. 11). Human beings, through their deliberate choices, have transformed a material that is part of God's creation into something that is not. Just as the responsibility for bringing on death lies squarely on the shoulders of human beings, according to the first part of the book, so too does the responsibility for transforming something blessed into a thing accursed rest on the idol makers.

REFLECTIONS

1. The author's critique of sailors who beseech for safety a wooden idol more fragile than the ship that carries them elicits the author's contrasting admiration of God's providence. This admiration is occasioned by the juxtaposition of the groundless trust in a wooden idol and the marvelous trust exemplified by Noah, who entrusted the future of the living also to a "piece of wood" (14:5). The piece of wood is one of God's "many works of wisdom" through which human beings can develop their potential for life. The author recognizes the providential care of God within the works of creation that are placed at the service of human beings. Creation itself is there for human beings to find sustenance and security. The author's positive view of the forces of creation that stand under God's providence surfaces again and again throughout the work. The reflection ends in a declaration of praise of the very material of creation, "Blessed is the wood by which righteousness comes" (14:7 NRSV).

2. But the positive forces of creation are open to abuse from human manipulation. The idol symbolizes the human abuse of the created material of the universe. Instead of using wood for its many positive functions, the idol makers transform it into objects that misguide and ensnare human beings so that they do not perceive the originator of the universe. The particular nuance of this critique against idol makers highlights the importance of reflecting on our use of material goods, of the environment, and of the earth itself.

WISDOM 14:11-31, ORIGINS AND EVILS OF IDOLATRY

COMMENTARY

14:11-14. The idols fashioned by human hands fall under the same judgment as their makers and worshipers. This argument, which relies on a distinction between the function of the idol and the material of the idol itself, is similar to that found in the first part of the book. Human beings have been made for immortality. Their rightful destiny is to be in union with God. But they can choose a life of justice that brings immortality or a life of injustice that brings death. The case with idols is similar. From their very material they are part of what God had created. Yet through human choice they have become an abomination because they have led people astray. The final judgment includes God's visitation not only on the makers and worshipers of idols, but also on the idols themselves.

Nonetheless, the argument appears somewhat forced and awkward. It would appear that the author is including the idols under the judgment of God in continuity with the prohibition against idols that arose during the prophetic period. One of the arguments for the validity of the idol is that it endures in time and space. Judgment against the false worship of idolatry includes the revelation of the idol's worthlessness or ineffectiveness. The story of the statue of Dagon that stood beside the ark in captivity is a case in point. Twice it had fallen before the ark as a judgment against its worshipers (1 Sam 5:1-5).

An interesting reflection on the problem of the endurance of idols occurs in the Mishnah, where some Romans questioned the rabbis about idols: "The elders in Rome were asked, 'If your God has no pleasure in the worship of idols, why does he not destroy them?' They replied, 'If men had worshiped the things which the world does not need, He would have destroyed them. But, they worship sun, moon, stars and planets; is He to destroy His world because of the fools?'"[113] God spares the wicked, providing a time for conversion (Wis 11:26–12:1-2, 10). The idols belong to their worshipers and fall under the cloud of the final judgment along with them.

The explanation for the origin of idolatry (vv. 12-21) continues the author's tendency to probe under the surface to arrive at the causes of injustice and death. In the first part of the book, the author provided an explanation for the origin of sin and death. Human beings bring on death through living unjustly (1:12-15). Through the envy of the adversary, death had entered the cosmos (2:24). In the critique of nature worship, the author probed the origins of identifying the forces of creation with divine reality (13:1-9). The critique of the carpenter ridiculed the idol-making process, but it did not offer an explanation for idolatry. In the very center of the concentric structure, the author attempts to enter into the mind-set of those who have come to worship an idol made by human hands.

The language that introduces the explanation for idol worship reflects the author's previous concerns and explanations: the essential goodness of all that exists and the entrance of idol worship into the world. Since God loves all that exists, the author reiterates how idols did not exist at the beginning. God is not their creator. They entered the cosmos through human vanity (v. 14); therefore, their end is assured (cf. Isa 45:16; Jer 16:19-21).

The relationship between idol worship and fornication (v. 12) is one that the author adapts primarily from prophetic teaching. The Greek word representing "fornication" (πορνεία *porneia*) refers to various forms of sexual disorders. The corresponding Hebrew term is often used to designate more precisely the worship of false gods, as is the case with

---
113. Quoting this, the Gemara adds, "The world maintains its course, but the fools who have corrupted their ways, will be judged hereafter." *Aboda Zara* 4.7.

the Wisdom author. The image of marital infidelity is implied in the prophetic use of the metaphor of fornication with idols (Jer 3:6-8; Ezek 16:15-43; Hosea 1–2; 4:11-19; cf. Exod 34:15-17; Judg 2:16-23). Infidelity to the faithful God of the covenant is understood as a breach of the covenant agreement. The author is adapting the uniquely Israelite understanding of fidelity to the One God for its application to all humanity in the explanation of the origin of idol worship.

14:15-21. Two brief examples of the origin of idol worship are presented in the story of a father who is bereft over the sudden death of a child (vv. 15-16) and the monarch who commands the worship of carved images (vv. 16-17). The latter example is further developed with the illustration of the artisan who, perhaps not even having known the monarch, embellishes the likeness with a charm that attracts a multitude (vv. 18-21). Neither example is attested in Scripture as an explanation for the cult of idols, but each relates to general practice in the Greco-Roman age of setting up images of either one's beloved or monarchs.

Many of the clear examples of the Greco-Roman practice of idol worship are posterior to the book of Wisdom. For example, there is the cult of Antinoos, which the emperor Hadrian set up in memory of his young friend who drowned tragically in Egypt (c. 130 CE). There is a story from the fourth century CE that explains how a statue became an idol that is very similar to the case envisaged in Wisdom. In that story, an Egyptian named Syropahnes sets up a statue of his dead son in his house in order to ease the family's grief at their loss. The family members decorate the statue to please the father, and eventually the household slaves begin to flee to it for protection. In this way, a statue honoring the memory of a son was understood to have become eventually the object of cultic worship.[114]

The author adds to the critique of the origin of such idol worship the falsity of the artist's embellishment of the idol. Plato had expressed a certain ambivalence toward art that was motivated primarily by the tendency of artists to embellish their subjects. For Plato such a tendency led to a falsification of the true form and represented an aberration from true art itself.[115] Philo added the same argument found in Wisdom, which ridicules the artist's embellishment of the subject, in his critique of idol worship, "Further, too, they have brought in sculpture and painting to cooperate in the deception, in order that with the colors and shapes and artistic qualities wrought by their fine workmanship they may enthrall the spectators and so beguile the two leading senses, sight and hearing."[116] The attraction to works of art is viewed as a snare that entraps humans to worship idols made of stone or wood (v. 21).

14:22-26. What follows is a list of vices that arise from not having knowledge of God. The passage is reminiscent of the speech of the wicked, in the first part of the book, who perpetrated injustice against the just one (chap. 2). The wicked have no knowledge of God, and this lack of knowledge blinds them to the gifts of justice and wisdom. Whereas the author's presentation of the wicked's aberration to injustice was subtle, with a progressive and sinister momentum, the author's invectives are unrestrained with respect to idol worshipers.

The list of vices follows a much-used literary device in which disorders and aberrations are accumulated to highlight the perversions that stem from a single cause. In the Greek *Apocalypse of Baruch* is a series of disorders attributed to the fall and to drunkenness: "Brother does not have mercy on brother, nor father on son, nor children on parents, but by means of the Fall through wine come forth all (these): murder, adultery, fornication, perjury, theft, and similar things."[117]

The combination of blood, murder, theft, and deceit in v. 25 is a reference to Hos 4:1-2, where the list of vices follows the similar declaration of a lack of knowledge of God: "There is no faithfulness or loyalty, and no knowledge of God in the land. Swearing, lying, and murder, and stealing and adultery break out; bloodshed follows bloodshed" (NRSV). The list of vices, in the Greek translation of Hosea especially, appears to be structured according to a section of the decalogue

---

114. For several examples of the custom of honoring the dead and monarchs in the Greco-Roman world, see the references in Winston, *The Wisdom of Solomon*, 270-78.

115. Plato *Republic* 604D.
116. Philo *On the Special Laws* 1.29.
117. 3 Bar 4:17; see also Philo *On the Decalogue* 168 and *Who Is the Heir* 173.

in Exod 20:13-16 (LXX): "You shall not murder. You shall not commit adultery. You shall not steal. You shall not bear false witness against your neighbor" (cf. Matt 15:19; Mark 7:21-22). Paul made frequent use of a list of vices in his letters (Rom 1:24-32; 1 Cor 5:9-11; 2 Cor 12:20-21; Gal 5:19-21; Col 3:5-9; 1 Tim 1:9-10), at times juxtaposing them to a list of virtues (Gal 5:22-23; Col 3:11-17).

At the outset of the list of vices, the author highlights one particular feature that had surfaced earlier in the book: The lack of virtue confuses the perspective on the good (vv. 22b, 26). In the concluding summary, regarding the reasoning of the wicked (2:21-24), the author explained how the injustice of the wicked blinded them to the purposes of God, the wages of holiness, and the prize for blameless souls. When the figure of Solomon speaks in the second part of Wisdom, emphasis is placed on the openness of wisdom and on the revelatory character of Solomon's teaching (6:22-23). All good things came to Solomon through wisdom, who makes people friends with God (7:11, 27). In the criticism of idol worship, the author postulates that the lack of knowledge of the true God confuses the perception of the good and devolves into secrecy and disorder.

The theme of mistaking war for peace was immortalized in the famous epithet of Tacitus (c. 55–117 CE): "To plunder, butcher, steal, these things they misname empire; they make a desolation and they call it peace."[118] Tacitus was criticizing the *Pax Romana,* which was often achieved through a brutal exercising of power through violence. For the victors, the outcome is called peace, but for the victims it is sheer desolation. Just as injustice blinds the wicked from perceiving the plan of God, so also the lack of knowledge of God in idol worship confuses the perception of the good (v. 26). Idol worshipers consider the internal and external disorders that throw them into great strife as peace (v. 22).

The critique of idolatry includes an attack on the secret mystery cults (v. 23). In the second part of the book, the author implied a critique of the mystery cults by deliberately presenting personified wisdom as transparent and open (7:22–8:1). Likewise, Solomon was presented as having transmitted his knowledge acquired through friendship with wisdom openly, ungrudgingly, and without restriction (6:22-23; 7:13-14). This open style of pedagogy on the part of personified wisdom and exemplified in the persona of Solomon stands in stark contrast to the secretive initiation rites common to mystery cults in the Greco-Roman world.

14:27-31. The concluding section on the origin and evils of idolatry focuses on the cause of disorders and the accompanying judgment against idolatry. In this way, we are brought back to the themes in the beginning of the unit by the repetition of the image of the origin of evils (v. 12 = v. 27), and the image of judgment and punishment for idol worshipers (v. 11 = vv. 30-31). The unit begins with the declaration of the punishment of the idols themselves and the connection between the origin of evil and the making of idols. The unit concludes with the declaration of the origin of every evil residing in idolatry and the punishment of idol worshipers.

One of the criticisms of idol worship in this unit focuses on the Israelite prohibition of the naming of idols and swearing oaths by them (cf. Exod 23:13; Josh 23:7; Ps 16:4). But the particular nuance that the Wisdom author emphasizes in this critique is the loss of moral direction that results from the worshiping of false gods made by human hands.

In effect, the worship of idols brings about a life of injustice (v. 28). Without moral direction, the idolater's life is easily caught in false "exultation," "prophesying lies," "living unrighteously," "committing perjury," "swearing unjust oaths" without realizing the destructive consequences of such actions (vv. 28-29). The tension between justice and injustice is brought to the fore with six words in the Greek text: "unrighteously" (ἀδίκως *adikōs*, v. 28), "wicked oaths" (κακῶς ὁμόσαντες *kakōs omosantes*, v. 29), "just penalties" (δίκαια *dikaia*, v. 30), "unrighteously" (ἀδίκως *adikōs*, v. 30), "just penalty" (δίκη *dikē*, v. 31), and "unrighteous" (ἄδικοι *adikoi*, v. 31).

The generalization whereby the origin of every evil is said to reside in idolatry (v. 27) parallels the generalization in the first part of the book whereby injustice is described as being the cause of death (1:12-16). More immediately, the phrase parallels the opening volley against the making of idols in v. 12: "For

---

118. Tacitus *Agricola* 30.

the idea of making idols was the beginning of fornication, and the invention of them was the corruption of life." The generalizations are not meant to exclude each other. Rather, they intensify the level of disorder that the author judges injustice and idolatry to cause.

REFLECTIONS

1. The declaration of divine judgment against idols and their worshipers (14:11) recalls the author's assertion of divine judgment against the wicked in the first part of the book. The wicked had placed their hope in the apparent "fruit" of their injustice. But on the day of judgment the very fruit of the wicked accuses them and, therefore, does not bring its hoped-for strength (3:13–4:9). The idols that entrap and snare human beings fall under the same divine judgment (14:11). Whatever prevents human beings from realizing their relationship with God and with one another is to be destroyed.

The severity of the judgment the author extends to the idols is based on their continuous entrapping function. Idols are like structures of injustice. They have become somewhat independent from their originators, the hands that crafted them; yet they continue to be a snare and a trap that hinder people from achieving a more just and equitable balance in society.

2. The aberration of idol worship produces a confusion over what is good: "They call such great evils peace" (14:22 NRSV); "and all is . . . confusion over what is good" (14:25-26 NRSV). The author offers insight into the moral confusion that results from the sin of idolatry. Sin brings about a confusion over what is good and what is evil. This same misdirection was evident in the author's critique of the reasoning of the wicked in the first part of the book. The wicked's judgment, that mortality renders life arbitrary, caused them to value power and might and to despise weakness and frailty (2:11). As a result, they perceived death in weakness when in fact the weakness of the virtuous is transformed into life; they perceived life in their exercise of unjust power when, in fact, the power of the wicked is revealed as being groundless and empty of virtue.

A similar understanding of the confusion over good and evil, and life and death, that results from unfaithfulness to God is presented in the book of Deuteronomy. When the spies had returned from reconnoitering the promised land, they announced that the land God was giving them was a good land (Deut 1:25). But instead of perceiving life in the new land as good, the people thought only of death: "It is because the Lord hates us that he has brought us out of the land of Egypt, to hand us over to the Amorites to destroy us" (Deut 1:27 NRSV). The nonsequitur that stands between the spies' positive assessment of the land and the people's interpretation of the divine motive can be explained only by the blindness and confusion caused by their sin of faithlessness.

The same lack of trust prompted the people to announce their preference for life as slaves in Egypt to the tenuous existence in the wilderness, where they perceived death. At the imminent moment of deliverance the people accused Moses of bringing them to the desert to die (Exod 14:10-14). The author of Wisdom attributes the same confusion over the good to the idolatry that focuses on the self, symbolized in the idol, "the work of human hands." Those caught in idolatry perceive the turmoil of misdirection as peace. Sin carries with it the consequence of a moral blindness that induces a misinterpretation of what is good and brings life in the long term and of what is evil and brings death in the long run. Only the shock of a tragedy or an amazing expression of love and respect can jolt the one who is blind into reexamining the moral consequences of his or her actions.

3. A just punishment pursues those who devote themselves to idolatry (14:30). This idea affirms the author's particular understanding that punishment arises from seeds of destruction inherent in the paths of injustice or untruth. It is not as if the punishment comes from the outside and somehow could be avoided if the perpetrators of injustice or followers of untruth go unseen or are not caught by the legal authorities. The seeds of turmoil are inherent in a path of life that focuses on the self (on the works of human hands). Such a life excludes the transcendence (going beyond oneself) that brings human beings into communion with one another. As in the case of an addiction, whatever semblance of human fulfillment may appear to be in the beginning, eventually the relentlessness of the addiction brings about the evident signs of destruction.

WISDOM 15:1-6, REFLECTION ON GOD'S MERCY AND POWER

COMMENTARY

Within the concentric structure of the critique of idolatry, the author turns briefly to praise God for the mercy and power shown to the righteous. The unit stands parallel to the prayerful reflection on God's providential care in the treatment of the sailor who prays to a wooden idol (14:1-10). The difference in tone is noted immediately by the use of direct speech. God is addressed directly in the second person and is praised for the merciful sovereignty exercised over creation.

15:1-3. One notable difference in the language of this reflection from that on God's providence is the author's explicit identification with the people of God. This sense of identification with the community under divine protection is inaugurated in v. 1 with the image of "*our* God," and it continues with the persistent use of the first-person plural in v. 2: "even if *we* sin, *we* are yours . . . but *we* will not sin, because *we* know that you acknowledge *us* as yours" (italics added). The vocabulary depicting this personal bond between the righteous and God is reminiscent of the terms describing the bond between Israel and God in covenantal language:

> They shall know that I, the LORD their God, am with them, and that they, the house of Israel, are my people, says the Lord GOD. You are my sheep, the sheep of my pasture and I am your God, says the Lord GOD.
> (Ezek 34:30-31 NRSV; cf. Ezek 11:20; 14:11; 37:27; 39:7)

The bond between the righteous and God is highlighted and intensified by the contrast to the relationship between idolaters and their lifeless idols (vv. 4-6). The God of the righteous is full of power and mercy (v. 1); the many gods of the idolatrous are powerless (13:17-19).

The opening phrase of the unit, "But you, our God," contrasts the personal God of the righteous to the previously described lifeless idols of the unrighteous. A series of four descriptive words and phrases characterizes the mercy and power God exercises over creation and the righteous. God is depicted as kind, true, patient, and ruling all things in mercy. Verse 1 evidently was inspired by the poetic vocabulary of God's declaration to Moses in the giving of the second set of tablets. As God passed before Moses,

> The LORD, the LORD,
> a God merciful and gracious,
> slow to anger,
> and abounding in steadfast love
>   and faithfulness,
> keeping steadfast love for the
>   thousandth generation.
> (Exod 34:6-7 NRSV)

Three of the four descriptive expressions in the Wisdom text are found in the Greek text of the Exodus source: "true" = "faithfulness" (Exod 34:6); "patient" = "slow to anger" (Exod 34:6); "ruling all things in mercy" = "merciful" (Exod 34:6). The first adjective, "kind" (χρηστός *chrēstos*) is not found in Exod 34:6, but it is frequently used in the psalms as a translation of the Hebrew word for "good" (טוב *ṭôb*; Pss 25:8; 34:9; 86:5; 100:5; 106:1). Moreover, the same root in the adverbial form was used by the Wisdom author to describe the manner in which wisdom guides the cosmos, wisdom "guides" all things *well* (8:1).

The phrase "ruling all things" (v. 1), had already been employed by the author in 8:1, where personified wisdom was described as "guiding all things well." The Greek phrase was particularly in common use among the Stoics. The Wisdom author is applying the coined phrase to the gracious manner in which God guides the cosmos without the pantheistic and materialistic overtones of Stoic philosophy. The covenantal language of the verse maintains the tension between God's transcendence and God's care for all things.

This tension was maintained by the author in several previous passages in which God's mercy and power are held together to portray the marvelous manner in which God guides the cosmos. In 8:1, personified wisdom is described as "reaching mightily from one end of the earth to the other" as well as "ordering all things well." In 11:21-24, both God's power and God's mercy are praised as giving expression to God's love for all things that exist. In 12:15-18, the description of God's justice concentrates on the consistency between God's righteousness and God's power: "You rule all things righteously, deeming it alien to your power to condemn anyone who does not deserve to be punished" (12:15 NRSV). The sovereignty of God is described as combining strength and mildness, power and forbearance.

The bond between God and the righteous is said to be stronger than sin itself (v. 2). Even if the righteous sin, they still belong to God. This awareness of the indissoluble covenantal bond prompts the author's declaration that the righteous will not sin. It is rare in the book of Wisdom for the author to treat the sin of the righteous. Of course, the biblical traditions from which the author heavily draws support, particularly Isaiah and Deuteronomy, are filled with an explicit awareness of the sin of Israel. In the diptychs of the first part of Wisdom, which contrasted the righteous and the wicked, the author employed Isaiah's image of the suffering servant. Yet the feature of the vicarious suffering of the servant in Isaiah was suppressed by the Wisdom author. The reason for this suppression is evident when one considers that the author is contrasting the righteous one who suffers unjustly with the powerful wicked who oppress. In Isaiah the servant suffers for the sake of Israel. The themes of conversion and reconciliation associated with the suffering servant are replaced with themes of judgment against the wicked and the integrity of the righteous by the Wisdom author. The issue of the righteous person's also experiencing punishment for infidelity will surface again later in the diptychs. The author will have to face the possible objections or protests that naturally arise in the contrast between the enemies of Israel and the righteous. Not only the enemies of the Israelites but also the righteous themselves experience the tragic consequences of injustice (16:5-6; 18:20-25).

The reference to the sin of the righteous was more than likely prompted by the same source (Exod 34:6-7) that was used for the image of God's mercy and compassion in v. 1. The merciful and gracious God of Moses is also a forgiving God who pardons iniquity, transgression, and sin (Exod 34:7). Israel had committed the sin of idolatry by worshiping the golden calf immediately after the giving of the law to Moses at Sinai. Yet, this sin did not eradicate their belonging to God. Because of God's mercy and faithfulness, Israel remained God's special people before whom great wonders would be done (Exod 34:8-10).

Since the author of Wisdom is criticizing the worship of false gods in the broader context of the argument, the particular sin being alluded to is probably idolatry. The supreme demand of the covenantal bond for Israel is to worship the Lord alone and not bow down to false gods (Exod 20:2; 34:11-17; Deut 5:6-11). The prophetic voice that continually reprimands Israel for apostasy and idolatry testifies to the tenacious rootedness that idolatry had in ancient Israel.

The author's confidence that the righteous will not fall into the sin of idolatry stems from the general belief in the eradication of idolatry among the Jews at the time of the author's writing. This belief was voiced in the book of Judith: "For never in our generation, nor in these present days, has there been any tribe or family or people or town of ours that worships gods made with hands, as was done in days gone by" (Jdt 8:18 NRSV). Even Tacitus (55–117 CE) acknowledges that the Jewish cult showed no signs whatsoever of tolerating idolatry as an expression of faith: "The Jews conceive of one god only, and that with the mind alone: they regard as impious those who make from perishable materials representations of god in man's image; that supreme and eternal being is to them incapable of representation and without end."[119] The tone of confidence is not one of arrogance arising from merit on the side of Israel, but is one of humility arising from the realization of God's continuous expression of mercy and forgiveness.

The effective result of the covenantal bond between the righteous and their merciful God is perfect justice and possession of the root of immortality. The verse expresses its thought through complete parallelism. To know God is righteousness; to know God's sovereignty is the root of immortality. As in the first part of Wisdom, justice and immortality meet once again (3:1-4; 4:1; 6:17-20).

The nuance that the verb "to know" (εἴδω *eidō*) carries in the verse is twofold, "to be intimate with" and "to acknowledge." In v. 2*b* the force of the verb "to know" in the phrase "knowing your power" is that of acknowledging or recognizing the power and sovereignty of God. Even if they sin, the righteous still will acknowledge and recognize the dominion of God. This acknowledgment of God's sovereignty follows from knowing that God claims them.

The author has made frequent use of the verb "to know" in the triple relationship among Solomon, wisdom, and God in the second part of Wisdom. Personified wisdom is described as an initiate in the ways of God (8:2-8). Solomon prays to God for the gift of wisdom, who knows the works of God and, therefore, can guide him wisely in his actions (9:9-12). In effect, one sees in the prayerful reflection on God's mercy and power the results of Solomon's prayer for the wisdom that comes from God. Wisdom brings a knowledge of God that makes one an intimate friend of God and enables one to acknowledge God's dominion.

Acknowledging the sovereignty of God is the root of immortality. The gift of immortality is as inchoate as a tree with its root growing in the soil. Eventually the tree will come to full maturity. Whereas in the first part of the book immortality was presented more as a gift in response to the fidelity of the righteous, here the inchoate presence of immortality is more explicitly seen to exist as a root that will come to a complete fullness of union with God. In the case of the barren woman and the faithful eunuch, a similar image was employed to show the eventual fruitfulness of virtue: "The root of understanding does not fail" (3:15 NRSV). It is not simply the sovereignty of God that assures immortality; rather, the acknowledgment of God's dominion is the root of immortality.

A different line of interpretation of the expression "to know your power is the root of immortality" would understand the force of meaning to be that God is the one who has power over death.[120] In this case, God's power over death is the source of immortality. God's power, of course, is open to signifying either a concrete expression of God's sovereignty or the general dominion of God. Interpreting the verb "to know" as "to acknowledge" would suggest that God's power refers to the general dominion of God over all creation. It is not simply God's power that is the root of immortality. Rather, God's dominion is the context, the soil for the root of immortality. Those who acknowledge God's sovereignty and who have come to experience the fidelity of God even in the face of their own resistance have the root of immortality.

15:4-6. The concluding part of the unit contrasts the root of immortality, which the righteous have in recognizing the true God, with the hopeless situation of idolaters. The righteous have not been led into idolatry by the misguided attempts of artistry that embellishes the lifelessness of the idols (v. 4).

The author has already criticized the duplicity of artists who embellish the surface

---

119. Tacitus *Histories* 5.5.

120. R. E. Murphy, "To Know Your Might Is the Root of Immortality (Wisd 15:3)," *CBQ* 25 (1963) 88-93. Murphy understands God's power specifically as God's power over death. This interpretation explains the reference to immortality and ties the argument to the first part of the book, where death is seen as the obstacle to justice and virtue. Even this interpretation can be broadened to include the general dominion of God over life and death, indeed, over all creation.

of idols (13:13-15; 14:18-21). The author's own critique in this regard parallels the criticism of such practices by Plato and the Stoics.[121] At this point the author focuses briefly on the sexual aberrations associated with idolatry. The embellishment of the idols goes so far as to bring about an aberrant yearning for the lifeless idol. Stories and legends were in circulation at the author's time regarding such behavior. One such story, that of Pygmalion, was known in several versions. This legendary king of Cyprus had a statue of a woman made from ivory whose form was so real and beautiful that he fell in love with it.[122]

The author stresses the lifeless and dead qualities of the idol that become the source of affection in the idolater: "they desire the lifeless form of a dead image" (v. 5). The idolater is called a "lover of evil things" who is worthy of the object that is loved. The parallel to the wicked in the opening part of the book is unmistakable. There the wicked were described as the friends of death who pined away and made a covenant with death (1:16). In turn, this passage contrasts the "lovers of evil things" (v. 6) and Solomon's love for wisdom (8:2; cf. Prov 8:36, "all who hate me love death" [NRSV]). Just as the wicked are said to be worthy of death, so too are idolaters worthy of the lifeless idols in which they base their hopes (v. 6).

121. Plato *Republic* 602D-603B; Seneca *Letters* 88:18.
122. Ovid *Metamorphoses* 10.243-297.

REFLECTIONS

1. Four descriptive terms for "God" initiate the author's praise of God for the mercy and kindness shown to the righteous. God is kind, true, and patient, ruling all things in mercy (15:1). God's transcendent power and immanent compassion are held together in these descriptive images. The power of God is balanced by compassion and mercy. The compassion of God is expressed through God's ruling all things in mercy. What a contrast to the idols, which have no power! They cannot even stand up on their own, but have to be fastened to a niche in the wall (13:15-16). Neither do they afford mercy and kindness, because they are lifeless, weak, inexperienced, and dead (13:17-18).

2. The praise of the powerful and merciful God of the righteous conveys a sense of communal pride. God's power and mercy created a people and sustains them even in their rising and falling fortunes. The turn to the first-person plural in the verbal forms points to the author's being caught up in the praise of God's mercy and compassion shown to the righteous. This is one of the few occurrences in the entire book in which the author formally identifies with the righteous through the first-person plural form of "we" and "us." In the first part of the book, the author as narrator has an objective viewpoint. In the second part of the book, the subjective viewpoint takes over as the author identifies with the figure of Solomon and speaks in the first person. In the third part of the book, the author speaks through both the objective viewpoint of a narrator and the subjective viewpoint in the first-person singular. Only rarely, as in this brief unit, does the author's identification with the righteous surface explicitly (cf. 12:18-22; 18:8).

The communal sense of pride in the God of power and mercy that the author expresses in this passage has parallels in the book of Deuteronomy. The reflection on the history that brought the people to the land of Moab elicits from the figure of Moses the praise of God for the gift of the Torah and for the extraordinary interventions of mercy and power: "For what other great nation has a god so near to it as the LORD our God is whenever we call to him? And what other great nation has statutes and ordinances as just as this entire law that I am setting before you today?" (Deut 4:7-8 NRSV; cf. Deut 4:32-40). If we are correct in locating the time of composition of this passage from Deuteronomy during the exile, then the similarity of the function of praise here is like that in the book of Wisdom. A community under siege, feeling weak and threatened, becomes cognizant of the great strength of its tradition. A reflection on the living tradition becomes a source of strength and pride. Although the author of Wisdom is sympathetic to the best of Hellenistic contributions to literature and culture, and incorporates terminology and philosophical arguments from them, the author is attempting here to strengthen the Jewish community in the diaspora. It is a community under siege and weakened both from without and from within, not unlike the community in exile. The sense of pride the author expresses in belonging to a special people is based on a reflection of history and the quality of faith. Thus the author offers this reflection to strengthen the community's faith. The values that accrue from being faithful to the true God overshadow the dismal facade of trust in idols.

3. We receive what we love. In contrast to the sure hope of immortality for the righteous, the idolaters receive what they love in idolatry: lifeless hope. Again, the author's understanding of punishment comes to the foreground. The form of punishment is intimately connected to the false hope in which the idolater trusts. On one side, we have Solomon, who loves wisdom; wisdom makes one a friend of God and brings the assurance of immortality (6:18-19; 7:27; 8:2). On the other side, we have idolaters, who desire "the lifeless form of a dead image" (15:5). Such lovers of evil things are fit for the lifelessness that idols represent. The author uses the similar phrase that was employed for the wicked in the first part of the book, describing them as being fit for death, with which they make a covenant, pining away for it as for a friend (1:16).

The idea that one receives what one loves is taken up in several forms in the teaching of Christ. In the teaching concerning treasures, Jesus contrasts the treasures of earth, which can be stolen or consumed by moths or rust, to the treasures of heaven. Wherever people place their treasure, they will find that their heart is there as well (Matt 6:19-21; Luke 12:33-34). They receive what, in fact, they love. In one case they receive something perishable; in the other, they receive something enduring.

The parables regarding the talents to be invested (Matt 25:14-30; Luke 19:11-27) and stories about the measure that is given out (Matt 7:1-5; Mark 4:21-25; Luke 6:37-38) make a direct correlation between what one gives and what one receives. Here as well there is a continuity between what one actually receives and what one has given or invested. The reward or punishment does not come from the outside, but is a direct consequence of the fruit of one's own decisions and actions. Giving and investing are the themes that replace "loving." But in all three cases, a direct correlation is made between the fruit of one's actions and the intention behind the decision to love, to give, or to invest.

For the author of Wisdom, it is important to pay attention to what one seeks and loves. If one seeks and loves, like Solomon, the wisdom that makes one close to God, then the gift of immortality is assured. If one seeks and loves the lifeless security of idolatry, then one's own hope becomes as lifeless and dead as idols.

WISDOM 15:7-13, THE POTTER AND CLAY IDOLS

COMMENTARY

Within the concentric structure of the author's treatment of idolatry, the judgment of the potter stands parallel to the critique of the carpenter (13:10-19). Both the carpenter and the potter form a natural substance into many shapes, including ones that eventually become objects of worship. The author moves from gold, silver, stone, and wood in the critique of the carpenter to the less valuable clay in the critique of the potter. As a result of this progression of blameworthiness, the critique of the clay idols and the potter is more severe than that of the carpenter. The author offered no motives for the carpenter's slipping into the fabrication of idols. But in the case of the potters, they are described as forging counterfeits, motivated by greed and profit (v. 12).

The unit is enclosed by images that capture the theme of the critique: "earth," "earthy" (vv. 7, 13); "vessels," "vessel" (vv. 7, 13). The very substance of these idols as "earthy vessels" is the same matter from which humans were formed and to which they return (v. 8). Several of the themes from the critique of idolatry and even the critique of the wicked from the first part of the book are condensed in this judgment of the potter: the motive of profit, the idols as counterfeit, the distinction between useful vessels and useless idols, the contrast between the lifeless clay idol and the dignity of the human being who is made of clay. A contrast is developed between the duplicitous creativity of the potter and the creativity of God, who has molded human beings out of the earth. There is a clear emphasis on the personal responsibility of the makers of clay idols. Because of their full knowledge of the process of deception, these idol makers know what they are doing in setting up works of clay as idols.

The opening description of the technique of molding clay is as innocuous as the opening description of the technique of carpentry (13:11-12 = 15:7). Of itself, the description betrays no signs of criticism at first. Only when the ordinary labor of fashioning utensils is applied to idols does the discrepancy between useful tools and deified objects leap into view. Elsewhere in Scripture, the technique of the potter is used positively to describe God's care for Israel or to highlight Israel's unfaithfulness to such care (e.g., Jer 18:1-11; cf. Gen 2:7; Isa 64:8; Job 10:9; Sir 33:13). The carpenter and the potter alike give shape to useful vessels for noble and necessary needs. However, both become misguided when they use their skill to form idols.

In the case of clay idols, the author draws attention to the existence of the same earthly substance in the clay idol and in the human being who fashions it. In fashioning clay idols, the potter is falsely imitating the work of the Creator. Potters make idols from earth, the very substance from which they have been made and to which they will return upon death.

The moment of death is described through an image that appears in only late canonical texts. The soul is described as being on lease and as returning to the Creator at death (v. 8b; cf. v. 16). In the famous passage on death in Ecclesiastes, the moment of death is depicted through the double movement of the body's returning to the earth and the spirit's returning to God, who had originally given it (Eccl 12:6-7; cf. 3:20-21). The Wisdom text describes death as the body returning to the earth (from which it was taken) when the time comes for the soul that was borrowed to be returned. The obvious source for such imagery is the Yahwist version of the creation of Adam. Adam was formed from the earth, and the breath of life was breathed into his nostrils so that he became a living being (Gen 2:7). But in the account of the punishment for his and Eve's disobedience, the Genesis text speaks only of the return of Adam to the earth. Nothing is said of the living breath returning to God. In the Gospel of Luke, such an image sways in the background when the rich fool is reprimanded: "This very night your life is being demanded of you" (Luke 12:20 NRSV). Only in v. 8 do we have the explicit comparison of death to the return on a lease.

The idea that life is borrowed and that death constitutes the return of life to the proprietor was known in both Greek and Roman literature as well. "Life is granted to no one as formal possession, but to all on lease."[123] Philo employs the same idea on several occasions: "Now, the creator of life has given you on loan life, speech and sensation."[124] Josephus appeals to the same idea when he explains to his fellow Jews why he did not commit suicide and, as a result, was captured by the Romans: "Those who die at the time when the Creator demands it by following the natural law and give back to God the loan they had received, they will obtain immortal glory."[125]

---

123. Lucretius 3.971.
124. Philo *Who Is the Heir* 104-108.
125. Josephus *The Jewish War* 3.374.

The author criticizes the clay-idol makers for not recognizing the limits of the span of human life (v. 9a). The clay should be a reminder to the potter that human beings are made of clay, to which they return at death. From the very substance that defines human mortality, the idol makers conceive idols that are but pale imitations of those made of gold, silver, and copper (v. 9b). The counterfeit is doublefold; not only are the clay idols false in themselves, but also they are doubly so as imitations of idols made of precious metals.

The author juxtaposes three images of clay to three images of the interior life in order to highlight the lack of life in the clay idol makers: Their hearts are ashes, their hope is dirt, their lives are clay. By choosing the very image through which the idol makers sin to characterize their moral bankruptcy, the author continues to draw a link between sin and the lifelessness that ensues from it.

The guilt of the idol makers is highlighted by their failure to recognize in their work and skill the Creator (cf. 13:9), who like a potter fashioned human beings from clay and breathed a living spirit into them. Instead, they consider human existence to be an "idle game" in which one must gain profit through whatever means possible. The imagery contains allusions to the wicked in the first part of the book. Since they had declared that human beings come into the world by mere chance (2:2), their project in life took on the form of a festival (2:6-9), which in turn led to the conclusion that their might makes them right (2:11).

The motive of might is transformed in the case of the clay-idol makers into the motive of gain and money. The author is attributing to the clay-idol makers the motive of gain and profit regardless of the source (v. 12b). The theme regarding dishonorable gain appears quite frequently in Greek and Roman literature. Creon declares that it is "not well to love gain from every source."[126] Horace argues for the merit of virtue over the gain of those who say, "Make money, money by fair means if you can, if not, by any means money."[127]

The author attributes greater responsibility for sin to the clay-idol makers (v. 13). Since they know very well that the objects they fashion are made from clay and perishable materials, they bear greater responsibility for the counterfeit than do those who worship the lifeless objects.

---

126. Sophocles *Antigone* 312.
127. Horace *Letters* 1.1.65.

REFLECTIONS

1. Most of the author's arguments regarding idol creation and idol worship have already been covered in the treatment of the carpenter (13:10–14:10) and in the explorations of the origin of idolatry (14:11-31). Essentially, the arguments revolve around the inexplicable tendency of those who practice idolatry to deify a lifeless object that is less valuable than the human being, who has received the gift of life. The author continually highlights the discrepancy between the lifeless object and its worshiper, who is alive. In the case of the carpenter, the idol was described through the very antitheses to the prayers of the idolater—prayers for family, health, life, help, a prosperous journey, success, and strength. The misguided sailor puts trust in a wooden idol more fragile than the marvelous piece of wood crafted by wisdom that keeps the sailor afloat. The clay-idol makers fashion images from the earth, the very substance God had used to fashion Adam. But God has breathed into humans the gift of life, something the potter cannot do for the idol.

2. The critique of the potters marks an intensification of responsibility through the potter's obvious motive of gain and profit. It is out of personal gain that the potter fashions counterfeit images. With respect to the carpenter and to the explanations of the origin of idolatry, ordinary human needs and tragedies formed the basis of the misguided deification of images and statues. But in the case of those who make clay idols, the author draws attention to the willful and deliberate fashioning of counterfeit objects for personal profit and gain. Greater responsibility rests on those who deliberately misguide people into placing their hope on unfounded principles. Consequently, greater guilt resides with them as well. Their own hope is less than the very substance they use to fashion the counterfeit image. They are not unlike the ungodly in the first part of the book whose hope is compared to dust carried by the wind or to frost driven away by a storm (5:14).

Wisdom 15:14-19, Idolatry and Animal Worship in Egypt

COMMENTARY

In all its brevity, this passage brings to a close the author's critique of idolatry. The particular idolaters under discussion are identified as the enemies of God's people (v. 14). This is the typical designation for the Egyptians throughout the midrashic treatment of the exodus from Egypt (e.g., 11:5; 12:20; 16:8; 18:1). Other designations for the Egyptians link the oppressors of Israel to the wicked in the first part of the book ("wicked," 12:10-11; "ungodly," 16:16; "unjust," 12:23; "foolish," 15:14; 19:3).

The quality of the false worship exhibited by the enemies of God's people elicits the most severe reprimand from the author of Wisdom. Within the concentric structure of the passage on idolatry (chaps. 13–15), the worship of the Egyptian gods and goddesses is contrasted with the worship of the elements of nature and the heavenly bodies (13:1-9). This contrast intensifies the reprehensible form of zoolatry. Those who deify the elements of creation are at least making divine the great works of God. But those who deify the visually abhorrent species have lost touch even with the aesthetics of creation. The intensification of the reprimand is noticeable also in the progression throughout the entire critique: the worship of nature and heavenly bodies made by God, counterfeit images of God's creation made by humans (gold, silver, copper, clay), and finally the inexplicable deification of animals.

The return to the image of animal worship brings the author's argument right back to the punishment of the Egyptians through animals, which occasioned the two major digressions on God's power (11:17–12:27) and false worship (chaps. 13–15). This return at the end of the critique against false worship also allows for the continuation of the second diptych, which deals with the animals that punish the Egyptians and the animals that help sustain the righteous (16:1-14).

The critique against the Egyptians' false worship focuses on two forms: syncretistic idolatry (15:14-17) and zoolatry (15:18-19). The acceptance of all the idols of the nations, and not merely one's own, condenses the author's critique of idolatry. Various arguments already alluded to in the earlier treatment of idolatry provide proof for the most severe judgment reserved to the Egyptians (13:10-19; 14:4-5; 15:7-8). This tendency to attribute divine status to the various idols was particularly acute in Hellenism. It was especially predominant in Ptolemaic Egypt. The lifelessness of all such idols is again recounted in traditional fashion. Although the idols may appear in bodily form, they have no organs of sight, smell, hearing, or touch. They are not able even to walk (cf. Pss 115:3-8; 135:15-18; Isa 44:18).

More important, the author concentrates on the discrepancy between the life of the human being who makes an idol and the lifelessness of the idol (v. 16). The idol maker has a spirit that is borrowed (cf. v. 8), but he or she cannot give the gift of life to the idol. The author's perplexity revolves around the obvious irony that is present in idolatry. The idol makers are human beings—that is, they are alive and have been given the gift of life and thus are more valuable than the lifeless objects they create. Philo is perplexed by the same inconsistency in idolatry: "In their general ignorance they have failed to perceive even that most obvious truth which even 'a witless infant knows,' that the craftsman is superior to the product of his craft both in time, since he is older than what he makes and in a sense its father, and in value, since the efficient element is held in higher esteem than the passive effect."[128]

The final two verses of the critique focus on a particular form of idolatry—namely, animal worship (vv. 18-19). As mentioned at the outset, the theme of animal worship occasioned the major digressions within the second diptych. These two verses refer to 11:15, where the enemies are described as being led astray to worship irrational serpents and worthless animals, and to 12:27, where it is recalled how the Egyptians were punished by the very animals they thought to be gods.

The idea that these animals worshiped as deity are so abhorrent that they have escaped divine blessing (v. 19b) appears to go against much of what the author has previously stated on the essential dignity of all creation (1:14; 11:24). In Zoroastrianism, which presumes a radical dualism between good and evil, certain animals, such as reptiles and dangerous insects, along with poisonous plants, were considered evil creatures. To destroy such creatures was the equivalent of destroying evil and wickedness.[129] Although the author does not adhere to such a dualism of good and evil as that of Zoroastrianism, it is possible that some of the formulations of its ideas have influenced the author's argument.

For an explanation of this judgment against the deified reptiles, it is helpful to recognize the parallel the author is drawing between idols and deified animals. In the critique against the carpenter and the sailor who worships a wooden idol, the author concluded with the divine judgment against idols. Although they are a part of God's creation, they have become an abomination through their deliberate fabrication by human beings (14:8-11). The author's purpose in highlighting the lack of intelligence of the animals worshiped in Egypt's zoolatry is to put into relief the misguided nature of false worship. Like the idols, the sacred animals stand under God's judgment. But instead of turning to the judgment against such animals, the author focuses on the inexplicable choice of human beings to deify the lesser animals of God's creation.

---

128. Philo *On the Decalogue* 69.

129. For a presentation of Zoroastrian thought, see Robert Charles Zaehner, *The Dawn and Twilight of Zoroastrianism* (London: Weidenfeld and Nicolson, 1961).

REFLECTIONS

1. The author's rather lengthy digression, which offers a severe critique of false worship, concludes with the utter foolishness of idolatry. The brevity of this final passage within the entire concentric structure (chaps. 13–15) reveals the author to be at a loss to explain the aberration of syncretistic idolatry and zoolatry. The progression from the least blameworthy form of false worship of natural phenomena to the most blameworthy—namely, zoolatry—reflects a progression similar to that found in the wicked's reflection on their project in life (2:1-20). What had begun in the wicked as a rather innocuous reflection on human mortality ended in the blatant and sinister plot to humiliate and destroy the just one. In a similar manner, the author presents the tendency of false worship to move from the beautiful works of God's creation to the inexplicable adoration of the strangest and most dangerous animals.

2. The opposite side of the critique highlights the importance of being rooted in the worship of the true God. Just as the practice of justice through the gift of wisdom in the first part of the book brings the assurance of immortality, so also the worship of the true God brings protection in danger and immortality to the righteous (14:2-7; 15:1-4). The author's critique of the seduction of injustice and of false worship is meant to present before the imagination of the reader the compelling attraction of justice and the true God. The incoherence of idolatry and the aesthetic repugnance of zoolatry render the worshiping of the true God much more plausible.

Wisdom 16:1-14, The Plague of Animals and Delicacies for the Righteous

COMMENTARY

16:1-4. The final critique of zoolatry brings the argument back to the second diptych, which had begun in 11:15. The diptych contrasts the plagues of the various animals upon Egypt with the marvelous gift of quails for the righteous in the desert. The argument of the diptych picks up exactly where it left off regarding the principle of punishment through the very means of one's sin (11:5, 16). Since the enemies of the righteous reached the extreme form of idolatry and worshiped animals, it is only to be expected that through animals they will experience the consequences of their sin. The short unit that focuses the diptych on the hunger of the Egyptians is enclosed by the image of torment: They "were tormented by a multitude of animals" (v. 1); "their enemies were being tormented" (v. 4).

The turn in the diptych contrasts the torment of the enemies by animals with the marvelous gift of quails provided to the righteous in the desert (v. 2). The author is condensing the several plague episodes of the exodus that deal with animals into a single diptych (v. 2, frogs; v. 3, gnats; v. 4, flies; v. 5, diseased livestock; v. 8, locusts). In order to provide a contrast with the gift of quails in the desert, the author adds one particular element to the Exodus narrative—namely, that of the Egyptians' hunger. Although in the plague narratives Egypt's sources of water, food, and livestock had been destroyed by the plagues, nowhere does the book of Exodus mention that the Egyptians actually hungered. However, this is a reasonable assumption the Wisdom author is making in condensing the stories of the plagues in Exodus 8:1–9:7.

In response to the Israelites' hunger, God provides them with quails. The author is following episodes from the narrative of the Israelites in the desert from Exod 16:1-13 and from Num 11:4-35. In both sources, the meager signs of food and water in the desert contrast sharply with the abundance of food in Egypt (Exod 16:3; Num 11:5). The people complain. They demand food, and they are given the extraordinary gift of manna and quails.

The motif of the people's grumbling and complaining in the desert is suppressed in the author's contrast of the Egyptians' hunger with that of the righteous. The suppression of the theme of Israel's sin and need for repentance regarding the desert wandering is consistent with the author's suppression of the theme of the vicarious suffering of God's servant in the wicked's plan to kill the just one (2:12-25). But the theme of Israel's resistance to God's law will emerge in a subtle manner through the experience of punishment and death that the author feels compelled to address later in the diptychs (16:5-6; 18:20-25). The righteous will hunger for a short while to enable them to appreciate the depth of hunger their enemies will experience.

16:5-14. This reflection on the hunger of the righteous moves the author to another digression within the diptych on animals. The author is reminded of the threat to life that the Israelites experienced in the desert, as recounted in Num 21:6-9. The reflection of Israel's salvation from the venomous serpents occasions the author's praise of God's power over life and death. Some exegetes understand the unit to be another comparison or antithesis that contrasts the killing of the Egyptians through the bites of locusts and flies with the saving symbol of the brazen serpent for the righteous.[130] But the author does not use the word for "instead" (ἀντί *anti*), which introduces the contrast. A type of antithesis is introduced in a negative form in v. 10: "But your children were not conquered even by the fangs of venomous serpents." Instead of considering the passage a full diptych, A. G. Wright perceives the unit's digressional form of reflection and praise within the second diptych.[131]

---

130. Reese, "Plan and Structure in the Book of Wisdom," 391-99.
131. Wright, "The Structure of the Book of Wisdom," 165-84.

In the book of Numbers, the episode of the poisonous serpents in the desert is narrated as God's response to the people's continuous complaints: "Why have you brought us up out of Egypt to die in the wilderness? For there is no food and no water, and we detest this miserable food" (Num 21:5 NRSV). After many Israelites had died from the bites of venomous snakes, the people confessed their sin and pleaded with Moses to beseech God for healing. In response to God's command, Moses formed a bronze serpent, put it on a pole, and whoever looked upon it was healed. We come across the bronze serpent again far later in the historical books, where Hezekiah is noted to have broken in pieces the bronze serpent Moses had made (2 Kgs 18:4).[132]

The author of Wisdom is interpreting this event within the second diptych from two points of view: The people's suffering in the desert is a warning that is meant to prevent them from being unresponsive to God's kindness, and the extraordinary healing of the people is a sign of the power of God's healing word.

The author does not focus directly on the sin of the righteous that evoked the punishment by the serpents in the desert. To focus on Israel's sin in a work that contrasts the righteous and the wicked on the one hand, and Israel and Egypt, on the other, would be out of place within the style of the diptychs. But the author alludes to the wrath of God and interprets its beneficial results for the righteous (v. 5). Instead of continuing to the end, God's wrath provides punishment, which serves as a warning (v. 6). The bronze serpent is interpreted as a symbol of deliverance that is meant to remind the Israelites of the command of the law. Similarly, the punishment is meant to remind them of God's commands and word (v. 11; cf. 12:2).

Since the image of the bronze serpent comes very close to that of the idols the author has just criticized, an explanation for the serpent is provided. The author draws attention to the power of God's Word. The people were not healed by the image they had beheld but by God, the savior of all (v. 7; cf. 9:18, where wisdom is the one who saves). It was God's mercy that came to help them and heal them. The bronze serpent does not contain in itself a cure for sickness. Medicine was not applied to the bite wounds (neither herb nor poultice cured them, v. 12). Rather, God cured them through the Word: "It was your word, O Lord, that heals all people" (v. 12; cf. Exod 15:26).

Both Philo and the Mishnah interpret the healing of the Israelites as recounted in Num 21:6-9 in a spiritual manner, like that of the author of Wisdom: "He, then, who has looked with fixed gaze on the form of patient endurance, even though he should perchance have been previously bitten by the wiles of pleasure, cannot but live; for, whereas pleasure menaces the soul with inevitable death, self-control holds out to it health and safety for life."[133] "But could the serpent kill or could the serpent keep alive? But rather, whenever Israel looked on high and subjected their heart to their Father in heaven were they healed, but if not, they perished."[134] *Targums Pseudo-Jonathan* and *Neophyti I* on Num 21:8 also add to the canonical text the idea that all those who looked upon the bronze serpent also lifted their hearts to God in heaven and lived. The entire reflection focuses finally on the merciful power of God. God alone has power over life and death, to bring people to Hades and back again (v. 13). The author is alluding to a traditional formulation regarding God's power over life and death (cf. Deut 32:39; 1 Sam 2:6; Ps 49:15; Hos 6:1-2; Tob 13:2). The power of God is contrasted with the human powerlessness to bring people to life. Although human beings can kill others, they cannot bring them back to life (v. 14).

---

132. For a brief outline on the serpent as a religious symbol in the ancient Near East, see Lowell K. Handy, "Serpent (Religious Symbol)," *Anchor Bible Dictionary*, 6 vols. (New York: Doubleday, 1992) 5:1113-1116.

133. Philo *On Husbandry* 98.

134. Mishnah *Rosh Hashanah* 3.8.

REFLECTIONS

1. The author's reflection on the plague narratives focuses on discernment between good and evil. The source of evil is concentrated in the enemies of the righteous. The source of good is concentrated in the hand of God, who intervenes constantly to direct events in favor of the righteous. By holding up before the imagination of the reader the conflict between good and evil in the plague episodes, the author is laying bare the ultimate tragedy of injustice and the eventual success of integrity. Oppression leads to the loss of one's own source of life, as in the case of the oppressing Egyptians. Integrity leads to unexpected sources of life, as in the case of the faithful righteous. The author uses the episodes from Israel's distant history, as recorded in the Torah, as the basis for learning the consequences of injustice and the success of integrity. What was argued from a more philosophical position in the first part of the book is confirmed in the reflection of Israel's foundational history.

2. The righteous are called to learn from their suffering. Although the author does not touch directly upon the sin of the righteous, the suffering that results from the wrath of God in response to their sin is addressed (16:5-6). The righteous also experienced hunger, and they were ravaged by venomous serpents. What the author asks the reader to conclude from this experience is the purpose of God's punishment to bring back and to heal ("they were troubled for a little while as a warning" [16:6 NRSV]; "To remind them of your oracles they were bitten, and then were quickly delivered" [16:11 NRSV]; cf. 11:21-24; 12:2; 12:10).

Human suffering is paradoxical and ambiguous at best. Much of the pain and injustice people endure results from others' disregard for life or unscrupulous desire for gain. It is not easy to differentiate the suffering that comes from outside from the suffering that results from one's own injustice or failure. Still, so much pain is associated with the mere fact of living, of growing, and of dying. Yet, the suffering that the righteous are said to experience is meant to be a source of learning. They are asked to learn from the consequences of their resistance to God's ways with the assurance of God's mercy and power.

The author's perspective on the suffering of the righteous is consistent with that of the writers of Deuteronomy. The curses of the covenant are meant to be a source of conversion:

> When all these things have happened to you, the blessings and the curses that I have set before you, if you call them to mind among all the nations where the Lord your God has driven you, and return to the Lord your God, and you and your children obey him with all your heart and with all your soul, just as I am commanding you today, then the Lord your God will restore your fortunes and have compassion on you. (Deut 30:1-3 NRSV)

Similarly, from the perspective of Deuteronomy, the period of wandering in the desert is the privileged moment of learning God's ways. Where resources for life are so feeble, the perception of life is intensified (Deuteronomy 8).

For the author of Wisdom, the reflection on the suffering of the righteous, which is due to their own resistance, leads to a reminder of the purpose of God's interventions. God is powerful and merciful. Even in the midst of trying situations, such as those of the Israelites in the desert, the unexpected can occur to bring healing and sustenance.

WISDOM 16:15-29, THE PLAGUE OF STORMS AND MANNA FROM HEAVEN

COMMENTARY

This third diptych is located centrally within the diptych system of the midrashic commentary. Its theological import matches its centrality. The author's positive view of the forces of the universe, which had been touched upon earlier (1:14; 5:17-23; 7:15-22; 9:1-3, 9), reaches its sharpest focus. The forces of the cosmos reside under the sway of divine providence in order to save the just and to thwart the wicked. Essentially, the author contrasts the plague of storms against the Egyptians with the extraordinary rain of manna for the Israelites in the desert. The sources for this contrast are the seventh plague of thunder and hail from Exod 9:13-35 and the episode of the manna's being provided to the people from Exod 16:1-36 and Num 11:4-9.

16:15-23. All three principles that the author employs throughout the interpretation of the plague narratives coalesce into a unified argument in the third diptych: (1) the source of one's sin becomes the source of one's punishment; (2) the very means by which the ungodly are punished are the means of salvation for the just; (3) the cosmos exerts itself on behalf of the righteous and against the ungodly. The main principle being applied in the contrast is that of 11:5; the very source of punishment for the Egyptians becomes the source of blessing for the Israelites. The density of the theological perspective is achieved in the joining of this principle to that of the positive view of creation and the cosmos. Creation itself labors to bring life to the just and justice to the wicked. Finally, the justice of God, which wreaks havoc from the heavens upon the ungodly, is a response to their refusal to recognize God (v. 16).

The particular elements of the cosmos that the author adapts for the plague and manna episodes are those of fire and water. The author interprets these episodes to show how the forces of creation become transformed in order to bring about salvation for the Israelites. Against the ungodly, fire is transformed so that in one case water cannot extinguish it (v. 17); yet in another story water actually intensifies the fire's heat and destructive power (v. 19). In favor of God's people, water (snow and ice) withstands the fire (v. 22), and fire itself, even as it is destroying the crops of the ungodly, forgets its natural destructive power regarding the food sent from heaven (v. 23). Some of the Stoic theories contemporary to the author of Wisdom regarding the transforming qualities of the elements are joined to the traditional theme of God's overriding providence in creation and history.

The opening phrase of the diptych actually links the unit to the preceding reflection of the power of God (v. 15). The idea that it is impossible to escape from God's hand alludes to Deut 32:39, "no one can deliver from my hand" (NRSV), and to Tob 13:2, "there is nothing that can escape his hand" (NRSV).

In response to their sin of refusing to recognize God, the ungodly are pursued by the strength of God's power from the heavens in the form of rain and fire. The author extracts two primal elements of the cosmos, water and fire, from the natural phenomenon of the storm with its rain and lightning in the seventh plague of Exodus. The unusual characteristic of these opposing forces is that they unite in destruction (v. 17). On the one hand, fire had an even greater effect within water, its very opposite. On the other hand, not even water could quench the fire so that it might not destroy the other creatures sent against Egypt. The author is supposing the punishments of animals and storms to be taking place contemporaneously, whereas in Exodus they occur sequentially.

The idea that the universe defends the righteous in the symbols of fire and water (v. 17*b*) is consistent with the positive view of the cosmos the author expounded in the first part of the work. The corollary statement that the universe punishes the unrighteous is made in the second half of the diptych (v. 24). In this way a careful balance is achieved: The ungodly are punished through the cosmos, for the universe defends the righteous (vv. 15-19); the ungodly know this is the judgment of God (v. 18). The righteous are sustained by the cosmos, for creation exerts itself to punish the unrighteous (vv. 20-24). The people of God know that the same destruction relaxed on their behalf that they might be fed (v. 23).

The turn in the diptych (v. 20) contrasts the ravaging storms sent against Egypt with the special food provided to God's people in the desert. The author employs images of ease, abundance, and rest in association with the bread that came from heaven. They did not toil for it; it provided every pleasure suited to every taste; it was expressive of God's kindness to them (cf. Deut 6:10-11; 8:3-10).

The contrast of the manna from heaven with the storms from the heavens continues with the images of water and fire. The manna is compared to snow and ice that would not melt in the face of burning fire. The author is exploiting the metaphor of frost, which is employed for the manna in Exod 16:14: "When the layer of dew lifted, there on the surface of the wilderness was a fine flaky substance, as fine as frost on the ground" (NRSV). The comparison of manna to snow based on the metaphor of frost in Exodus is made by Philo and Josephus as well.[135] The miraculous endurance of the manna in the threat of fire allows the righteous to know that the fire has relaxed (forgotten its own power) in order that they might survive (vv. 22-23). Just as the ungodly came to know that they were being pursued by the judgment of God (v. 18), so also the righteous came to know that fire was transformed so that they might live.

16:24-29. The final part of the diptych is a theological reflection on the transforming qualities of creation in the light of the gift of manna in the desert. The notion of creation's exerting itself to punish the wicked is in direct continuity with the ultimate judgment recounted in the first part of Wisdom (5:17-23). There the image of an apocalyptic storm was the author's vehicle for declaring the eventual demise of lawlessness and injustice. This image of the storm unites the plague diptych of storms and manna to the storm of destruction in the apocalyptic judgment.

A new feature that is articulated clearly in the function of the cosmos is that it actively labors on behalf of those who trust in God (v. 24). Although the idea is expressed in a new formation within the book, it is consistent with the author's positive view of the universe. Moreover, the direct relationship that was drawn between personified wisdom and creation in the second part of the book (9:1-2, 9-11, 18) prepares for the transference of the positive function of wisdom from human beings to the cosmos. It was through wisdom that human beings were made; wisdom was present at the creation of the world. As a result of its relationship to creation, wisdom knows God's works and can guide humans to set their paths straight so they may be saved. The wisdom of God and the forces of creation are intimately connected for the wisdom author. Creation is the work of God through wisdom, so that the forces of the cosmos stand on the side of the just and against the wicked (cf. 14:2-7).

The author's background metaphor for the adaptation of creation to justice and injustice employs two verbs, "exert" (ἐπιτείνω *epiteinō*) and "release" (ἀνίημι *aniēmi*). Creation exerts or tenses itself against the unrighteous, but relaxes or releases itself on behalf of the just. These verbs connote the tension and release of a cord, whether for a bow or for a musical instrument. Tonal assonance and dissonance were used frequently in Greek philosophical circles. It was a favorite metaphor employed by the Stoics to describe the harmony or disharmony of the constitution of the *pneuma*.[136] The right tension constituted health; the wrong tension involved sickness. The wisdom author will return to the metaphor of musical tones to describe the transforming qualities of creation that make a many-faceted harmony (19:18-21).

The author finally draws forth from the argument of the transformation of creation its intent and purpose, which the just will learn from their experience. The focus on the intent "to know" was already made within the diptych, with respect both to the unjust and to the righteous (vv. 18, 22). The just are to learn and take to heart the fact that

---

135. Philo *Moses* 1.200; Josephus *Antiquities of the Jews* 3.1.6.

136. *Stoicorum Veterum Fragmenta*, ed. J. von Arnim, 4 vols. (Leipzig, 1903–24; reprint Stuttgart, 1966; New York, 1986) 3.92,525,259,471.

the source of sustenance and life for human beings is the Word of God (v. 26).

The author's turn of phrase is a more rigorous adaptation of the declaration in Deut 8:3 that human beings do not live on bread alone but by every word that comes from the mouth of God (cf. Matt 4:4). Although the manna that is referred to in Deuteronomy did not come directly from the mouth of God, God's Word commanded its presence. What is stated as a gradation in Deuteronomy is articulated through antithesis in Wisdom. It is not the production of crops that feeds humans, but the Word of God that sustains those who trust in God. Philo adapted the phrase in Deut 8:3 into a similar antithetical formulation, making a formal distinction between the body and the soul, which the Wisdom author presumes: "You see that the soul is fed not with things of earth that decay, but with such words as God shall have poured like rain out of that lofty and pure region of life to which the prophet has given the title 'heaven.'"[137]

The author draws one final moral conclusion from observing the adapting qualities of the manna to fire and to the rays of the sun.

137. Philo *Allegorical Interpretations* 3.162-163.

It is important to be grateful to God for the marvelous interventions in one's life. The manna could not be destroyed by fire, yet a single ray of sunlight would melt it at the appropriate time (v. 27). The mention of the rays of the sun melting the manna is an allusion to Exod 16:21. Moses commanded that the manna be collected by the Israelites in the morning, according to the need of each person, for when the sun grew hot the manna would melt. From this observation the author draws forth an exhortation to observe the pious practice expressed in the psalms: The faithful rise before the sun to express their prayer of thanksgiving or lament to God (Pss 5:3; 55:17; 57:8-9; 88:13).

The concluding remark in which the hopelessness of an ungrateful heart is compared to melting frost (v. 29) is occasioned by the previous image of the melting manna (v. 27). It recalls the language and imagery associated with the wicked in the first part of the book. The wicked had compared the evanescence of their lives to mist that is chased away by the rays of the sun (2:4). After their confession of guilt, the hope of the ungodly is compared to thistledown carried by the wind and to a frost driven away by a storm (5:14).

REFLECTIONS

1. The particular virtue that the author expounds from the diptych on the plague of storms and the gift of manna is gratitude. Although gratitude has not been a particular focus throughout the arguments and presentations of the author, the author's disposition of praising God throughout the midrashic treatment of the exodus is certainly marked by a pervading attitude of thanksgiving. It is out of thanksgiving that the author turns to God directly throughout the final part of Wisdom in order to express praise and wonder (10:20-21; 11:21-26; 12:15-16; 14:3-7; 15:1-3; 16:12-13; 19:9, 22). Reflection on Israel's blessed history brings knowledge of the extraordinary interventions of God and the workings of creation on behalf of the faithful.

2. The forces of creation are on the side of justice. Even though this principle marks the entire book of Wisdom, nowhere is the author's theological perspective on creation enunciated with greater clarity. Creation rests in service of God, who formed it by battling injustice and coming to the aid of the righteous (16:24). Assertions on the positive function of creation dominate all three parts of the book. It is one of the unifying themes of the three divergent sections (chaps. 1–6; 7–10; 11–19) that form the author's argument into a coherent whole. The forces of creation are declared to be wholesome (1:14). Creation itself is armed by God to redress injustice (5:17-23). Personified wisdom is able to direct human beings on their paths because it was present at the creation of the universe and knows all of God's works (9:9). Throughout the author's presentation of the exodus events, the principle of the goodness of creation becomes the interpretative key for explaining the plight of the oppressors and the sustenance of the faithful.

3. Are natural phenomena an expression of moral integrity or dissolution? The third diptych presents the principle of the goodness of creation in terms of the punishment of the ungodly and the sustenance of the faithful through the natural phenomena of atmospheric storms and food. Does the author imply that all natural disasters are creation's response to human moral bankruptcy? Conversely, are all forms of deliverance and sustenance creation's response to human moral virtue? The answer must be an unequivocal no.

In the first part of Wisdom, the author argued vehemently against the apparent success of injustice and the apparent fruitlessness and failure of virtue. There the author argued that, in the long run, the moral vacuity of unjust people would be laid bare. In the long run, the moral fruitfulness of the virtuous would bring immortality. But tragedies, failures, and death itself befall all human beings. The experience of death for the just was tragic, like a holocaust and like gold tested in fire. Even Solomon recognizes the fragility of his life through the image of his cry at birth, which was like that of all human beings.

The emphasis on the author's application of the principle of the goodness of creation is consistent with the argument in the first part of the book. Eventually, moral vacuity is laid bare for what it is. There are consequences to a life of injustice. Injustice bears within it the seeds of its own destruction. Similarly, there are consequences to a life of justice. Although appearances may be to the contrary, a life of justice contains within it the seeds that eventually will blossom into union with God. The author employs the exodus events as a sign of divine judgment from Israel's foundational history. The interpretation of the plagues against the oppressors of Israel and the extraordinary interventions of God on behalf of the faithful are meant to assure the reader of the eventual consequences of injustice and justice.

WISDOM 17:1–18:4, PLAGUE OF DARKNESS AND A PILLAR OF FIRE

COMMENTARY

The fourth diptych contrasts the plague of darkness that engulfed the Egyptians during the ninth plague with the light that accompanied the Israelites in the desert. This diptych shows the author's imaginative, interpretative, and poetic skills at their highest level. The source from Exodus regarding the ninth plague is brief, indeed (Exod 10:21-23). Yet, the fourth diptych, which is inspired by it, is of considerable length. The passage contains a varied vocabulary with more than fifty words occurring only in this unit within the entire book. Some words are familiar, but others are rare and carefully selected.

The author combines several literary and stylistic features that betray a complex style of Alexandrian writing. Often, it is difficult to recognize or appreciate these features in translation. Hebrew does not make extensive use of adjectives, but the author employs the Greek technique of using adjectival phrases throughout the diptych ("a dark curtain," 17:3; "the powerless night," 17:14; "the inescapable fate," 17:17; "a whistling wind," 17:18). Nouns are employed as qualities ("curtain of forgetfulness," 17:3; "power of fire," 17:5; "the rush of water," 17:18). Metaphors abound throughout the passage ("self-kindled fire," 17:6; "one chain of darkness," 17:17; "the heavy night," 17:21). Antitheses are used with dramatic effect ("lawless people"/"holy nation," 17:2; "brilliant flames"/"hateful night," 17:5). Use is made of a seven-part linked series of images of terror in 17:18-19, which is reminiscent of the six-part chain syllogism of the sorites employed in 6:17-20.

In addition, the relative brevity of the description of the ninth plague in Exodus invites the author to explore the symbolism and the psychological drama of the terror of darkness. This entrance into the symbolism and drama of the fear caused by the heavy darkness parallels the author's entrance into the reasoning process and confession of the wicked in the first part of the book (5:2-14). The two passages are made parallel by the concentration of the dramatic result of terror and fear: "they will be shaken with dreadful fear" (5:2 NRSV); "they perished in trembling fear" (17:10). The author may very well have been familiar with the literary genre known as "descents into Hades," which at one point attempted to portray the terror and fear of those who are burdened with guilt.[138]

Although this is the only diptych in which God or the Lord is not explicitly mentioned, the direct speech both at the beginning (17:1) and at the end of the unit (18:15) retains the quality of praise directed to God.

17:2-6. The sin of the oppressors, which elicits the punishment of the imprisoning night, is described through two images: the imprisonment of the holy nation and the hiding of their sin behind the dark curtain of forgetfulness (vv. 2-3). Again the author attempts to show how the particular punishment of the ninth plague corresponds to the manner in which the oppressors sinned against the righteous. Since the righteous have been imprisoned, the oppressors experience an imprisonment of paralyzing fear arising from darkness.

A considerable amount of effort is spent to dramatize the elusive form of terror that has stricken the Egyptians. The author makes up for the relative brevity of the ninth plague with a vivid imagination of the terrors of the night. But all of the images of fear and terror are interpreted by the author finally as metaphorical language. The terror of the night represents the burden of guilt the oppressors are to themselves (v. 21). The author displays a great deal of psychological dexterity in exploring the debilitating effects of fear and hopelessness caused by a guilty conscience.

The idea of the Egyptians' hiding or concealing their oppression (v. 3) recalls Adam and Eve hiding in the garden after their disobedience (Gen 3:8; cf. Cain's disclaimer of knowing the whereabouts of his brother, Gen 4:9). The terrible darkness that engulfs them cannot be illumined either by fire or by the shining stars (vv. 3-6). In this way the author continues the theme that the elements change their normal qualities and functions for the purpose of redressing injustice, from the third diptych. Their inner fear is described by the author as a "self-kindled fire" (v. 6), which emphasizes their personal responsibility for their punishment.

17:7-10. The idea that the magic art and wisdom of the Egyptians was humbled with their failure to dispel the darkness depends on a contrast between the first few plagues and the later ones. The Egyptian magicians were able to match the signs and wonders of the first two plagues of blood and frogs (Exod 7:22; 8:7; cf. Exod 7:11). But during the third plague, that of gnats, the magicians failed to reproduce the signs of Moses and Aaron and admitted that the finger of God was present (Exod 8:18-19). The magicians themselves would become helplessly covered with boils in the sixth plague (Exod 9:11).

17:11-15. The author enters into a quasi-philosophical presentation of the fear that pursued the oppressors in the darkness (vv. 11-13). The punishing fear is brought into moral perspective. It is the result of wickedness, which is condemned by its own testimony of cowardice. It is compared to the burden of conscience that exaggerates the difficulties at hand. Fear is defined as the abrogation of reason, which prefers the stupor of not knowing the cause of punishment.

Where exactly the author derives such reflections is unclear. The idea of the conscience is more at home in the Greek philosophical schools than in Hebrew thought. However, the reflection is consistent with the views the author has enunciated throughout the work regarding the responsibility of wickedness and the positive function of reason. The idea that wickedness is condemned by

---

138. See, e.g., Virgil Aeneid 6.

its own testimony parallels the author's declaration regarding the fruit of the wicked, which will bear witness against the parents at the time of accounting (4:4-6). The idea that wickedness gives up on reason and prefers ignorance contrasts well with the positive function of wisdom, which is the source of understanding and virtue (7:7-14; 8:2-8).

The philosophical currents of Hellenism, particularly of the moralists, such as the Epicureans and the Stoics, gave considerable space to the anguish that a guilty conscience could exercise.[139] The author of the book of Wisdom appears to be arguing that the resulting fear and cowardice of the oppressing conscience prefers ignorance, which actually compounds the torment of the one plagued by guilt. Plutarch relates a similar idea: "But fear alone, lacking no less in boldness than in power to reason, keeps its irrationality impotent, helpless and hopeless."[140]

17:16-17. The author continues with a series of images that are meant to describe and even mimic the perplexing and debilitating fear that resulted from the punishing darkness. Fear is described as an imprisoning power ("a prison not made of iron," v. 16), which contrasts with the power Egypt exercised over the holy nation (v. 2). It is all inclusive. The Exodus narrative insists on the general application of the plagues on humans, animals, and the land itself. Here the author chooses three specific walks of life to characterize the all-encompassing darkness. Darkness strikes farmers, shepherds, and laborers (v. 17). The qualification of the laborer who toils in the wilderness has led to several conjectures. What would a worker be doing in the wilderness? The Greek noun that signifies "wilderness" (ἐρημία *erēmia*) also refers to solitude. Thus it could very well refer to a qualitative aspect of laboring in solitude rather than to one of location, laboring in the desert. David Winston offers another possibility that could have arisen from the social conditions of Egypt in the first century CE. Due to heavy taxes levied on the inhabitants during the Ptolemaic period, but especially in the Roman period, workers escaped to the desert as a form of protest.[141] In any event, the import of the author's argument is that the chain of darkness bound all who were part of the oppression against the holy nation.

17:18-19. The seven-part linked series of images of terror describes through poetic imagery the paralysis of terror. Images from the animal world and from the elements of creation describe poetically a cause of terror that goes beyond all expectations: whistling wind, the sound of birds, rushing water, crash of rocks, leaping animals, roaring beasts, and the echo from mountains. This concentration of poetic imagery to convey the punishment of the wicked is reminiscent of the poetic imagery used by the wicked in the first part of the book. There the author employed poetic imagery from nature to describe the transience and the hopelessness of the wicked (2:1-5; 5:9-14).

17:20-21. The final reflection on the all-encompassing darkness contrasts the darkness that fell on the Egyptians with the light of the whole world. Everyone else goes about his or her work unhindered, whereas the Egyptians are plagued with the heaviness of darkness. As if to single out the personal responsibility of those who have oppressed the holy nation, the author emphasizes that on them alone the heavy night had spread. This is consistent with the events as described briefly in the ninth plague in Exod 10:21-23. Even heavier than this all-encompassing darkness are the guilty to themselves. This perception of personal guilt parallels the confession of the wicked in the first part of the book. After seeing the deliverance of the righteous, the wicked are tormented by a dreadful fear (5:2).

18:1-2. While the dreadful darkness plagued Egypt, the righteous experienced a very great light (v. 1). The reference to this light for Israel is the same as that mentioned in 17:20. While the Egyptians were experiencing darkness, the holy ones experienced a great light. The positive response of the Egyptians to the Israelites' escape from the darkness (vv. 1-2) is an interpretation of Exod 11:2-3 and 12:33-36. After the tenth plague, the Egyptians themselves urged the Israelites to flee. They even gave the Israelites the silver and gold they asked for. The author interprets this external gesture as a brief sign of

---
139. Lucretius 3:1011; Seneca *Epistulae* 41, 97.15.
140. Plutarch *Moralia* 165D.
141. Winston, *The Wisdom of Solomon*, 309-10.

repentance before the foolish decision to pursue them once again is made (19:3).

18:3. The theme of light leads the author to reflect on the pillar of fire that accompanied Israel in the desert during the night and on the harmless sun during the day. The pillar of fire constitutes the prime antithesis to the plague of darkness. In this way, the righteous experience a blessing through the light in darkness just as the oppressors experience a punishment through the all-encompassing darkness. The source for the image of the pillar of fire is Exod 13:21-22. Only in this passage from Exodus in addition to the Wisdom text is the source of fire described as a "pillar." Elsewhere the source of light is described as a "cloud" or as a "fiery light" (Exod 40:38; Num 9:15-16; Ps 78:14, the fiery light is parallel to the cloud by day; cf. Ps 105:39).

The author makes no reference to the pillar of cloud by day (Exod 13:21), perhaps in order to sustain the theme of light. The sun was the source of light during the day, and it had no scorching or burning effect (cf. Isa 49:10).

18:4. The conclusion to the diptych reaffirms the connection between the oppressors' sin of imprisoning the righteous and the ensuing punishment of imprisoning darkness. It illustrates one of the main principles the author has been expounding throughout the diptychs: One is punished in accordance with one's sins. The very seed of punishment is contained in the sin. In this way, the diptych is enclosed by the inclusion of the theme of imprisoning darkness (17:2; 18:4).

The theme of light is reintroduced through the image of the universality of the law. The imprisoned people were the ones through whom the light of the law was to be given to the world. The author interprets the gift of the law as a light not only for Israel but also for the world. This understanding of the universality of the law follows that of Isaiah and Micah: "All nations shall stream to the holy mountain, for out of Zion shall go forth instruction" (Isa 2:2-3; Mic 4:1-4, author's trans.). Philo likewise stressed the universal purpose of the law by describing it as "a law for the world."[142] Earlier the author of Wisdom described the wicked as not walking in the light of justice (5:6). The light of the law will illuminate the paths of truth. The responsibility of the righteous, then, is to transmit the law of justice to the world.

---

142. Philo *Questions and Answers on Exodus* 2.42.

REFLECTIONS

1. The fourth diptych explores primarily the psychologically damaging effect of injustice as it is conveyed through fear and hopelessness. The antithesis regarding the pillar of light is treated briefly in comparison to the imprisoning darkness that engulfs the enemies. One of the interesting features the author picks up from the exodus narrative to emphasize the unguided nature of injustice is the absence of reason. Through fear the unjust give up the help of reason. The author is interpreting the resistance of Pharaoh from the exodus narrative as the absence of reason. Despite all the evidence accumulated from the plagues, and despite the advice of his own wise counselors, Pharaoh persists in a policy of injustice that leads to destruction. Whereas Exodus attributes this folly to the hardening of Pharaoh's heart, the Wisdom author attributes this action on the part of the oppressors as resulting from the absence of reason (17:12-13). By refusing to read the signs of the times and interpret them with humility, the oppressors prefer ignorance. This ignorance begins to weigh heavily on them in the form of fear and guilt. In the Gospels, Christ also is said to interpret the refusal to read the signs of the times as a consequence of wickedness or moral blindness (Matt 16:1-4; Mark 8:11-13; Luke 12:54-56).

2. The theme of the first half of the diptych revolves around irony. The oppressors who imprison the righteous become imprisoned by terror and darkness themselves. This irony is reflective of the situation of the wicked in the first part of the book. There the wicked had formulated a plot whereby they would test the claims of the just by subjecting them to a "shameful death" (2:20). Yet in the end, at the time of accounting, the wicked experience terror and fear over their lack of virtue when they face the blessing of the righteous. They describe their state of anguish through images of death (5:9-14). They planned to subject the just one to a shameful death, yet they become subjected to the shame of their virtueless lives. Similarly, with the oppressors of the "holy nation," those who imprison the righteous are themselves in a prison of darkness. The master becomes enslaved in the process of enslaving others. The very form of one's injustice determines one's punishment.

3. Another side to this irony is the distance between the bravado and apparent strength of the oppressors and their cowardly behavior before seemingly innocent natural phenomena and harmless animals. This state also parallels the wicked in the first part of the book, whose apparent bravado with respect to the pleasures of life only masked the underlying despair and terror they finally revealed.

4. The extraordinary deliverance of the just through light parallels the deliverance of the just in the first part of the book. The author postulates firm hope in the promises of life for the just because of the great memories of deliverance of the righteous from the past. What takes place in history is seen to form a basis for imagining the unseen future. Although the author did not explain the where, when, and how of the deliverance of the just in the first part of the book, the firm belief in such a deliverance is postulated through a reflection on Israel's foundational history.

WISDOM 18:5–19:12, DEATH OF THE ENEMIES AND ISRAEL'S DELIVERANCE

COMMENTARY

The fifth and final diptych contrasts the death of the Egyptians with the extraordinary deliverance of the Israelites. The antithesis is presented in two stages: (1) The death of the firstborn in Egypt contrasts with the deliverance of the Israelites at the hands of Aaron's intercession in the desert (18:5-25); (2) the death of the ungodly in the sea contrasts with the extraordinary deliverance of the Israelites through the sea (19:1-12).[143] The sin of the oppressors, which the author cites as the root for the double-pronged punishment, is the killing of the Hebrew children by drowning them in the Nile (18:5). The oppressors experience a punishment according to the manner in which they mete out injustice. For the killing of the children, they will lose their own children. For killing the children by drowning, they will experience punishment by drowning in the sea. The book of *Jubilees* draws the same connection between the killing of the Hebrew infants and the punishment by drowning in the sea:

> And all of the people whom he brought out to pursue after Israel the LORD our God threw into the middle of the sea into the depths of the abyss beneath the children of Israel. Just as the men of Egypt cast their sons into the river he avenged one million. And one thousand strong and ardent men perished on account of one infant whom they threw into the midst of the river from the sons of your people. (*Jub.* 48:14)

Note the parallelism drawn between the first and the final diptych. Both diptychs deal with the same sin of the oppressors against

---

143. A. G. Wright argues for a single, double-pronged diptych stating that the author of Wisdom explores one event with two results. The tenth plague of death and the destruction of Pharaoh's army at sea are joined together as a response to the decree to kill the infants in the Nile (18:5). See Wright, "The Structure of Wisdom 11–19," 28-34.

the righteous. The sin the author cites as eliciting the punishment of water turning to blood is the decree that the infants be killed in the Nile (11:6-7). In this way, the entire series of diptychs (chaps. 11–19) is enclosed by the theme of water. The Nile itself became a source of punishment at the beginning of the cycle of plagues, and the sea turns into a source of punishment at the very end. Just as the righteous experienced a blessing through the gift of water in the desert, so too did they experience their foundational deliverance by a safe passage through the sea. Moreover, the theme of water returns the reader to the conclusion of the history of wisdom's interventions on behalf of the just in chap. 10. It was the theme of the extraordinary deliverance at the Red Sea that occasioned the lengthy midrashic treatment of the exodus events (10:15-21).

18:5-19, Death of the Firstborn. At the very beginning of the diptych, the author brings together the double response of God's punishment to Pharaoh's decree regarding the Hebrew infants (v. 5). The first response refers to the tenth plague, the death of the firstborn among the Egyptians. The second response refers to the destruction of Pharaoh's army at the Red Sea. The brief reference to the abandonment and rescue of the infant Moses provides a familiar link to Pharaoh's decree (Exod 1:22; 2:1-10). The threat and deliverance of the infant Moses prefigure the threat and extraordinary deliverance of the entire people.

The theme of the ancestors' foreknowledge of both the destruction of Egyptian oppression and their own deliverance underscores the continuous providence of God. In addition to the ancestors at the time of Moses, the author is alluding to the ancestors of the patriarchs. The ancestors' foreknowledge (v. 6) alludes to the covenant with Abram during the terrifying darkness that descended upon him. The message given to Abram after the "fire pot" descends and passes between the animal parts offered for sacrifice includes the history of Israel's four-hundred-year oppression. That period of oppression will be followed by judgment against the Egyptians and by the Israelites' extraordinary deliverance (Gen 15:12-16).

The author contrasts the situations of the righteous and the oppressors just before the administration of the tenth plague. The reference to the offering of sacrifices by the holy children in accordance with the divine law alludes to the institution of the passover feast (Exod 12:1-28). The paschal meal is understood as an expression of the praise of God in anticipation of the blessings and dangers that all would share and witness (v. 9). The image of "holy children of good people" is a new formulation for designating the righteous.

In contrast to this sacrifice of praise on the part of the holy ones, the oppressors' lament at the loss of their children passes throughout the land, from the greatest to the least. The universality of the tragedy is presented through word pairs, slave and master, commoner and king (vv. 10-12). The image of the tragedy's being so massive that the oppressors can hardly bury their dead (v. 12) is not present in Exodus. It may very well have been inspired by Num 33:3-4: "the Israelites went out boldly in the sight of all the Egyptians, while the Egyptians were burying all their firstborn, whom the Lord had struck down among them" (NRSV).

The particular wording the author employs to describe the release of God's people after the experience of the tenth plague is reminiscent of the speech of the wicked. The oppressors acknowledged the just to be "God's child" (v. 13). The author attributes the Egyptians' reluctance to release the Hebrews to their magic arts. Only the death of their firstborn forced the Egyptians to recognize their slaves as "God's children." In the first part of the book, the wicked had derided the just one for claiming God's paternity (2:16). Moreover, they planned to subject the just one to a shameful death because of this claim (2:18-20). Just as the wicked had to acknowledge that the just are counted among the "children of God" (5:5), so too do the oppressors of God's people acknowledge those whom they had oppressed to be "God's child." The author's use of this image in the tenth plague is facilitated by the reason given in Exodus for the release of the Hebrews: "Thus says the Lord: Israel is my firstborn son. I said to you, 'Let my son go that he may worship me'" (Exod 4:22-23 NRSV).

The parallel between the judgment of death in the fifth diptych and the judgment against the wicked in the first part of the book continues with the description of the "destroyer" from Exod 12:23 (5:17-23; 18:15-16). The destroyer is described as God's "all-powerful word" and as "a stern warrior" stretching from heaven to earth (v. 15), who wields a sharp sword filling all things with death (v. 16; cf. 5:20). Wickedness undergoes a judgment of cosmic proportions in the first part of the book, just as the oppressors of the holy ones meet their judgment of death in the final part.

Finally, the author alludes to the previous plague of darkness in the fourth diptych. The purpose of this is to highlight the effect of judgment to reveal the purpose of the punishment. The same apparitions, dreadful dreams, and unexpected fears as in the plague of darkness came upon them to remind them of their function of forewarning. In this way they understood why death had touched them and why they suffered (vv. 18-19).

18:20-25, Aaron's Intercession. The contrast to the destruction of the oppressors' firstborn is markedly different from the previous contrasts of the four diptychs. The contrast ordinarily presents the principle that the very means used to punish the Egyptians are used in some manner to deliver the just. In this case, the punishment that befalls the destroyer will occur to the just for their rebellion in the desert. The contrast consists of the saving intervention on the part of Aaron.

It would appear that the author is addressing a possible objection that might arise in the mind of the reader. It is true that Israel experienced extraordinary acts of deliverance in the desert. However, the Israelites also experienced death and destruction in response to their stubbornness and rebellious spirits. The author addresses their punishment without dwelling on the spirit of rebellion. The situation of the righteous differs from that of the oppressors in that the punishment of the righteous was not total. Because of the intercession of Aaron, the hand of the destroyer was stayed.

The episode being addressed is the punishment of the plague, which the Israelites experienced in the desert (Num 16:1-50). In response to the punishment meted out for the levitical rebellion of Korah, Dathan, and Abiram, the people assembled against Moses and Aaron. The plague destroyed 14,700 people before Aaron stopped it by making atonement for the people.

This episode picked up by the author in the fifth diptych is similar to the episode of the venomous serpents, treated as a digression in the second diptych. In both cases, the punishment of the just, which is only temporary, is a response to their rebellion. It was stopped by the intercession of Moses (through the brazen serpent) and Aaron. Similarly, in both cases, the punishment is addressed without stressing the sinfulness of the people that had given rise to the experience of death. The reason for this is probably that the author judged it unfitting to be overtly critical of the righteous while contrasting their plight to that of their oppressors. Nonetheless, the recognition of the punishment in the episode of the venomous serpents and the plague in the desert reaffirms the author's judgment from the first part of the book: Punishment and ultimate death are brought upon people through their unjust decisions and actions.

The author employs a number of images for the plague that struck the righteous to make it parallel to the tenth plague against the Egyptians. The plague is referred to as "the experience of death" (v. 20; cf. 2:24). In both cases, the end result of the plague was numerous dead ("corpses too many to count," v. 12; "when the dead had already fallen on one another in heaps," v. 23).

The contrast between the punishment of the oppressors and the punishment of the righteous also is related through similar imagery. Whereas God's word against the oppressors was described as a "stern warrior" who carried a "sharp sword" (vv. 15-16), Aaron's intercession is described as a "shield" that subdued "the avenger" through his "word" (vv. 21-22).

To supplement the brief description of Aaron's atonement with the censer of atonement from Num 16:47, the author describes Aaron's intervention as an appeal to God's oaths and promises. In Numbers, Aaron does not intercede for the people. Rather, in response to Moses' command, he conducts a ritual of atonement with the censer for the people. The idea of intercession is borrowed from the intercessory interventions of Moses to save the people from God's wrath. In order to stave off the wrath of God against the people, Moses appeals to the promises of God sworn to the ancestors (Exod 32:11-14; cf. Num 14:13-24).

Finally, the author alludes to the priestly robe of Aaron, with its ephod, and the diadem before which the destroyer yielded (vv. 24-25). The ephod, which was placed on Aaron's priestly robe, was to contain two onyx stones on which "all the names of the sons of Israel" were to be engraved (Exod 28:6-14). The idea that the robe contained a depiction of the world (v. 24) expresses the author's universalistic perception of God's rule. The cosmos is on the side of God, for God is its creator. Philo makes a similar point with allegorical overtones that the Wisdom author is less prone to make. The robe of the high priest is described as a likeness and copy of the entire universe. Its dark blue color symbolizes the air, its full length symbolizing the recesses of the earth; its breastplate symbolizes heaven; the twelve precious stones arranged in four rows symbolize the twelve signs of the zodiac.[144]

19:1-5, The Strange Death. In contrast to the temporary anger of God against the righteous, the oppressors experienced the pitiless anger of God to the end (v. 1). The author alludes to Pharaoh's foolish decision to change his mind despite the release granted to the Israelites. The underlying dynamic here is that the oppressors' injustice is to reach completion in their punishment (v. 4). This idea is consistent with the author's emphasis throughout the work that injustice bears the seeds of its own destruction. Very little is said regarding the final judgment against the oppressors. It is summarized in the concise image of "a strange death." In contrast to the strange death of the oppressors, the righteous experience an incredible journey.

19:6-12, Creation Is Fashioned Anew. The contrast with the strange death of the oppressors is dramatized through the extraordinary moment of deliverance at the Red Sea. The author harnesses the positive function of the cosmos to highlight the final moment of salvation for God's people. Creation itself was transformed in order to redress injustice (cf. 16:24). It is as if the crossing of the sea unhindered on "a grassy plain" summarizes succinctly both the punishments of the oppressors and all the acts of deliverance recounted in the diptychs. Just as the sea was the means of the ultimate judgment against the oppressors (18:5), so too is the sea the means of the ultimate deliverance of the righteous (v. 7).

The praise of God expressed through images of ranging horses and leaping lambs (v. 9) recalls the joy expressed for deliverance in the Song of Moses (Exod 15:1-18) and in the Song of Miriam (Exod 15:20-21). Psalm 114 employs the image of skipping rams and lambs (Ps 114:4-6) to express the joy of creation at the deliverance of Israel. The comparison of the joyful righteous to ranging horses may be a contrast to the traditional image of the destruction of the "horse and rider" (Exod 15:1, 21 NRSV). Isaiah speaks of Israel's passing through the depths like "a horse in a desert" (Isa 63:13 NRSV).

In experiencing the extraordinary deliverance through the sea, the righteous remember the manner in which creation had come continuously to their aid against the unjust (v. 10). Against the unrighteous, the earth produced gnats and the river spewed forth frogs instead of fish, recalling the third (Exod 8:16) and second plagues (Exod 8:1-6). In favor of the righteous, a new kind of bird came up from the sea to give them relief when they desire food (v. 12; cf. Num 11:31). The creation of animals, as recounted in Gen 1:20-25, undergoes a metamorphosis in the exodus event in favor of the righteous.

---

144. Philo *Moses* 2.1117-1135; *On the Cherubim* 100; *Questions and Answers on Exodus* 2.73, 76, 91.

REFLECTIONS

1. The author has been drawing a parallel between the wicked in the first part of the book and the Egyptian oppressors in the latter half of the book. That parallel is all the more evident in the final diptych with the judgment of the final plague and the strange death at the Red Sea. Just as the judgment against wickedness is exercised through the arming of creation, so too is the final judgment against the oppressors of God's people exercised through the transformation of creation itself. The images that highlight the parallelism in the two sections are the following: creation's being armed to repel the enemies (5:17); "stern wrath for a sword" (5:20 NRSV); "the water of the sea" (5:22 NRSV); "the whole creation in its nature was fashioned anew" (19:6 NRSV); "a stern warrior carrying the sharp sword" (18:15-16 NRSV); "you destroyed them all together by a mighty flood" (18:5 NRSV).

Note the pedagogical function of the author's interpretation of the final plague. In the first part of the book, the author labored to defend a life of virtue and justice in the face of apparent failure and weakness. The virtue and justice of the righteous appeared to be weak and fruitless compared with the apparent strength of the unjust. Death, in its many expressions of mortality, punishment, and ultimate judgment, was uncovered as being an obstacle to the exercise of justice. The wicked feared and despised a life stamped by mortality and weakness. By postulating an ultimate judgment, the author strips away the apparent weakness of the just as well as the facade of the wicked's power. The entire midrashic treatment of the exodus interprets the foundational experience of Israel's liberation as the basis for postulating the final judgment. Just as creation labors on the side of the just to bring salvation and judgment to the righteous and to the wicked, as seen throughout the exodus narrative, so also then will there be an ultimate judgment that reveals the ultimate power and fruitfulness of a virtuous and just life.

2. A further parallelism is drawn between the Word of God in the final diptych and personified wisdom in the center of the book. Wisdom was described as residing beside the throne of God (9:10), as being all powerful (7:22). In the final diptych, God's all-powerful word leaps from heaven, from the royal throne (18:15). Although wisdom by name does not play a crucial role in the final part of the book, the saving activity of wisdom continues to be present. The activity of wisdom is to guide, to protect, and to rescue human beings on their paths in life (7:27; 8:2-8; 9:18; 10:1-21). In the final diptych, the activity of wisdom is fulfilled through God's Word and in the forces of creation, which were made through wisdom. The forces of the cosmos fulfill the function of wisdom, and wisdom becomes transparent in the struggle for justice between the righteous and their oppressors.

3. The experience of death touches the righteous as well as the wicked (18:20). The author does not develop to a great extent the theme of conversion. Perhaps the literary technique of comparing and contrasting the wicked and the righteous did not lend itself to developing the theme of conversion. In the digression on God's power and mercy, the issue of conversion was addressed at least in part. The experiences of punishment are interpreted as providing an opportunity for a change of heart and for conversion in one's life (11:23; 12:2, 10, 20). However, the recognition that the righteous experience punishment underscores the life-and-death consequences of decisions and actions. Even the righteous, treated collectively, rebelled against God and experienced the consequences of their actions. But it was a punishment that did not lead to an ultimate, tragic judgment. Aaron's intercession is a sign of the people's conversion. Just to test the wrath of God was enough (18:25).

4. The theme of creation's being fashioned anew highlights the author's positive view of the forces of creation. This reflection has accompanied the reader throughout the midrashic treatment of the exodus narrative. It is one of the unitive themes that weave a thread throughout the three diverse parts of the book. The elements of creation that served to thwart the resistance of the oppressors are transformed continuously to guide and protect the righteous in their struggle for life. The locus for evil and tragedy is not to be found in the forces of creation. Rather, tragedy resides in the decisions and actions of human beings. Creation itself is a creature of God whose energies are ultimately directed to bringing life to completion. The function of wisdom to guide, to protect, and to save is exercised by creation, which was made according to God's wisdom.

WISDOM 19:13-22, FINAL REFLECTIONS

COMMENTARY

The final reflections of the author can be divided into three brief sections: (1) vv. 13-17, the punishment of the Egyptians; (2) vv. 18-21, the transformation of creation; and (3) v. 22, a concluding summary of praise to God. The author is distilling the essential features from the reflections of the extraordinary deliverance of the Israelites from Egypt. The oppressors suffered justly because of their wickedness toward the righteous (v. 13). The elements of the cosmos underwent a transformation in order to maintain harmony (v. 18). God's faithfulness has exalted and glorified the righteous (v. 22). Although the author is bringing the reflection on the exodus to a close, new themes are introduced to emphasize the extraordinary salvation of the just.

The statement that declares the punishment of the oppressors to be just corresponds to the ethical perspective the author has been pursuing throughout the book. There were signs that warned the wicked of the sinister results of their actions (v. 13; cf. 12:1-2, 10; 14:30-31). The successive plagues in the exodus narrative were meant to warn the oppressors of the inherent tragedy of their injustice.

19:13-17. A new argument for the just punishment of the oppressors is introduced with the theme of hospitality to guests and strangers (vv. 13*d*-14). The author interprets the Israelites' sojourn in Egypt as their being strangers and guests who originally were welcome benefactors, yet became enslaved. The background detail for the author's observation on hospitality is the story of Joseph and his brothers, who were welcomed in Egypt as strangers. The children of these strangers became the benefactors of the Egyptians in the governorship of Joseph. They became enslaved, however, by the very people who had benefited from his services (Genesis 41–42; 46–47; Exodus 1). The reference covers a large span of history. The book of Exodus recounts how after Jacob's family had multiplied and grown strong in Egypt, a pharaoh arose who did not know Joseph. This pharaoh set a policy in motion that treated the Hebrews as slaves.

The guilt of the Egyptian oppressors is highlighted by the comparison between those who did not welcome guests in the first place and those who welcome them only to enslave them. The author is alluding to the inhabitants of Sodom who wanted to abuse the guests of Lot (Gen 19:1-11). The punishment of the inhabitants of Sodom became a paradigmatic motif of sin and punishment in Scripture (cf. Deut 29:23; 32:32; Isa 1:9; 3:9; 13:19; Jer 23:14; 50:40; Lam 4:6; Ezek 16:48-56; Matt 10:15; 11:23; Luke 17:29; 2 Pet 2:6; Jude 7). Often the comparison of a contemporary sin to that of Sodom is made in order to highlight the greater culpability of the contemporary generation (cf. Lam 4:6; Matt 10:15). This greater seriousness and culpability of the sin of Egypt is exactly what the Wisdom author wishes to emphasize by comparing Egypt to Sodom. If it is a great sin not to receive a stranger with hospitality, as in the case of the inhabitants of Sodom, so much greater is the sin of receiving strangers only to enslave them, as in the case of Egypt.

Corresponding to the sins of both Sodom and Egypt is the punishment of darkness. The author draws a comparison between the forms of punishment for the sins of inhospitality and slavery. The Egyptians were stricken with the loss of sight in the ninth plague (Exod 10:21-23; cf. Wis 17:1-21). The aggressors against Lot were struck by blindness so that they could not find the entrance to the door (Gen 19:11).

Two details in the author's treatment of the hostility of Sodom and Egypt toward strangers possibly relate to the contemporary situation of the author. These details consist of the theme of hospitality to strangers (vv. 13-14) and the notice of someone's being enslaved who had shared the same rights as those who enslave him (v. 16).

Reference to the inhospitality of Egypt to the ancestors may be the author's reversal of the polemic levied against Jews by contemporary pagans. The Jews were often accused of secluding themselves from people of other nationalities and fostering a hatred of aliens.[145] Philo vehemently attacked such false accusations and interpreted the slavery of the Hebrews in Egypt in the same manner as did the Wisdom author:

> So, then, these strangers, who had left their own country and came to Egypt hoping to live there in safety as in a second fatherland, were made slaves by the ruler of the country. . . . And in thus making serfs of men who were not only free but guests, suppliants, and settlers, he showed no shame or fear of the God of liberty and hospitality and of justice to guests and suppliants.[146]

The reference to the Hebrews' being reduced to slavery after having shared equal rights (v. 16) possibly alludes to the polemic for equal rights and citizenship that Alexandrian Jews waged under Roman rule. Originally, the Jews welcomed Roman authority, to the consternation of the Egyptian natives and Greeks alike. According to Philo, Augustus confirmed the right for the Jewish community in Alexandria to maintain its autonomous status.[147]

Between the death of Augustus in 14 CE and the letter of Claudius (41–54 CE) to the Alexandrians, confirming the status quo, the Jewish community was in serious conflict with the Greek population in Alexandria. Not only was a special tax imposed on all non-Greek citizens by the Romans in 24 BCE, but also Emperor Caligula (37–41 CE) demanded divine status for himself. Both burdens were rejected by the faithful within the Jewish community. This put them into conflict with the Greeks, who successfully barred those who were demanding access to the gymnasia from attaining Greek citizenship. Philo headed the delegation sent to Caligula to reestablish equal rights, but without success. Caligula's successor, Claudius, finally intervened to stop the arguments and mutual recrimination in Alexandria by imposing the status quo.

It is possible that the Wisdom author is not limiting the reference of "sharing the same rights" to the equal status enjoyed by the Hebrews under Joseph in ancient Egypt. The reference could equally apply to the autonomous status of the Jews in Ptolemaic Egypt who then subsequently became the object of attack by an aggressive Hellenism.

19:18-21. The second reflection in the concluding remarks picks up the theme of the metamorphosis of the elements. Creation is transformed for the benefit of the righteous. The metaphor the author uses to convey the quasi-mystical harmony of the exodus event is the symphony of sound. The elements of nature are compared to the varying notes played on a harp. Although the sound of a musical instrument is a new metaphor in the work, there was a fleeting reference to the same idea of creation's adjusting itself for different effects. In the third diptych, the author appealed to the transforming elements of creation to explain the paradoxical food of manna from heaven. Creation was described as tensing and relaxing itself to punish the unjust and to help those who trust in God (16:24). The author wishes to account for the transformation of the permanent elements of creation using the metaphor of a symphonic melody. Just as the notes of a melody may vary or stay the same to give shape to a harmonious tune, so too does creation exert itself to bring about a harmony of creation and salvation.

The various schools of Greek philosophy habitually spoke of four elements of nature: water, earth, fire, and air. The author's subsequent explanation of the transforming elements in the exodus deals with only three of these: land, water, and fire (vv. 19-21). Although the author may appear to be using technical language from physics and music to forge harmony, the argument is essentially a poetic one lacking the precision of both physics and musical science.

In order to present an account of permanence and variation for the "miracle

---

145. For references to allegations and polemics against Jewish views of aliens by pagan authors, see Winston, *The Wisdom of Solomon*, 327-28.
146. Philo *Moses* 1.36.
147. Philo *Moses* 1.36.

stories" of the exodus, the author appeals to an ancient Greek tradition. Under the influence of the Pythagoreans, various Greek philosophical schools would use the analogy of musical harmony to explain or to present the order of the universe.[148] Although the author may lack detail and precision in presenting the metaphor, the choice of the concept of a musical harmony is a felicitous one. The author makes use of the analogy of music to explain the creativity of divine action. Through the metaphor of music, God is imagined as an instrumentalist (or even a composer) who plays the various components and multiple variations of human history into a unity and a harmony. The entire midrashic treatment of the exodus is transformed before our eyes into a perspective on a new creation. Harmony is achieved through the transformation of notes in melodies and tones. Injustice is redressed through the salvation of the righteous, which is presented through the lens of a new creation.

The various images the author holds up briefly as a sign of the transforming qualities of creation are taken from the previous diptychs. They are all paradoxical images that deal with land, water, and fire to express punishment of the oppressors and salvation of the righteous. The image of land animals who are transformed into water creatures is a clever description of the passage of the Israelites through the sea (v. 19a). The swimming creatures that moved over to land refer to the plague of frogs that invaded all the land of Egypt (v. 19b).

The following two verses contain images that highlight the transformed functions of fire and water (vv. 20-21). These images are all taken from the third diptych, which contrasted the plague of rains, storm, and hail to the gift of manna in the desert (16:18-27). Fire burned more strongly in the hail, which rained down upon the crops of the oppressors (16:22); the function of water to quench fire was transformed so that the fire would burn even more strongly (16:17). On the contrary, in favor of the righteous, flames did not consume the flesh of the animals that were sent to plague the oppressors (16:18), nor did the rays of the sun melt the special gift of manna (16:23).

Note that the author concludes the images of the metamorphosis of creation with that of the gift of "heavenly food" (lit., "food of ambrosia"). The author used two different metaphors for the gift of manna in 16:20, "food of angels" and "bread from heaven" (NAB). In this final image, the "ambrosia" is employed (the food of the gods that brings immortality). The sixth day of creation came to completion with the gift of food to humans and to animals alike: "See, I have given you every plant yielding seed that is upon the face of all the earth, and every tree with seed in its fruit; you shall have them for food" (Gen 1:29 NRSV). In Wisdom, the gift of manna as "heavenly food" occurs also after the transformation of creation through water, land, and animals. This situation of the gift of food parallels the situation in Genesis where God's generous gift of vegetation to humanity for food takes place at the end of creation, on the sixth day, after the separation of light and darkness, earth and waters, and the creation of the animals. By mentioning the gift of the manna as the culmination of the reflection on the exodus, the author places the exodus into the context of a new creation. Just as a life of justice achieved through the gift of wisdom brings immortality, so also divine intervention on behalf of the righteous brings the gift of immortality.

19:22. The author's final word is directed personally to God as a final hymn of praise. The doxology is formulated through a double, antithetical statement. The first half states the praise of God positively: "you have exalted and glorified your people." The second half states the praise of God negatively: "and you have not neglected to help them at all times and in all places." This final doxology forms a great inclusion to the doxology that was begun at the outset of the re-reading of the exodus narrative (10:20-21). It is an apt ending that focuses on the fidelity of God to a people who have experienced trials and hardship. The doxology is a confirmation of the validity of the opening exhortation of the entire work: "Love righteousness, you rulers of the earth . . . and seek the Lord with uprightness of heart" (1:1, author's trans.). The author's praise of God at the end of the

---

148. Aristotle *Metaphysica* I 5,986a3; *De mundo* 5,396b,7; Plato *Republic* VII 12,530d.

book does not refer only to the divine interventions throughout the exodus (chaps. 11–19). Since the midrashic treatment of the exodus is meant to be a concrete example of the author's argument supporting God's fidelity to the just and of the author's praise of divine wisdom, the doxology refers to God's fidelity, expressed in all three parts of the book. It includes the praise of God's fidelity to the just who suffer unjustly throughout history (chaps. 1–6). And it includes the praise of God's wisdom, which continuously accompanies humanity (chaps. 6–10). The midrashic treatment of the exodus confirms God's fidelity to the just and reveals the wisdom of God that forges a harmony of creation and salvation. What begins as an exhortation to seek God and love justice ends with a personal dialogue of praise to God.

REFLECTIONS

1. The author describes the extraordinary deliverance of the Israelites in the exodus through the imagery of a new creation. The very elements and creatures of the universe undergo transformation to effect a harmony of justice. Although this is not necessarily an innovation on the part of the author (cf. God as creator and redeemer, Isaiah 48; a new creation, Isa 65:17-25; the valley of dry bones, Ezek 37:1-14), this idea has followed the author's reflection throughout the work. There is a continuity in the mind of the author between the positive forces of God's creation and the extraordinary interventions of salvation.

This continuity, perhaps, has not been so boldly depicted in any other biblical work. Moments of salvation and deliverance are understood as being rooted in the positive forces of creation itself. Creation wages a battle against injustice and strives to support the efforts of the just. The explanation for the positive role of the universe is provided in the first two parts of the book. The universe is God's creature, and there is no "destructive poison" in its forces (1:14). It has been fashioned according to God's Word and divine wisdom (9:1-2). The author's tangible example of the world's positive forces is the foundational experience of the exodus. From a reflection on God's fidelity to the righteous in history, the author formulates a paradigm of creation and salvation for the present and the future.

One concrete effect that this continuity of creation and salvation offers is a set of criteria for assessing perspectives of theology. It is relatively easy to truncate creation from salvation, and vice versa, in our visions and theologies of life. A theological perspective that is one-sided in favor of salvation and redemption may offer a pessimistic and derogatory view of the natural forces of creation, and even of the human spirit. Creation and humanity become crushed at the expense of maintaining the extraordinary signs of God's redemption. On the contrary, a theological perspective that is one-sided in favor of creation and the harmonious force of the human spirit may neglect to assess the horrors of injustice. The book of Wisdom has an extraordinary coherence that allows the reader to view the horrors of injustice in the context of a world that is marked through and through with the beauty and wisdom of God.

2. The image of the symphonic harmony at the end of the book is an invitation to contemplate the extraordinary fidelity of God. Where the author has earlier provided somewhat philosophical arguments for the defense of virtue and the critique of injustice, the author now moves to the level of quasi-mystical language. Music has that capacity of suppressing one level of thought in order to heighten another level. The image of the symphonic harmony that God achieves in orchestrating the universe is an image that raises us to the level of contemplating God's fidelity tangibly in our lives. God's fidelity engulfs the paradoxes involved in life and death, in virtue and injustice, in apparent strength and weakness.

3. The final doxology bolsters the hope of those who suffer unjustly. The entire series of reflections in the book is brought to a conclusion that focuses on the enduring relationship between God and the righteous. God is the faithful one. God has not abandoned the just who suffered an ignoble death at the hands of the wicked. God has not abandoned the righteous in the course of their tenuous journey through the wilderness. Through the wisdom of God, which directs the forces of creation (7:7–8:21) and illumines the paths of humans (9:9-18), people are taught to trust in the path of justice. Despite weakness, despite the apparent power of injustice, people who follow the path of justice are not abandoned to the despair of death. Instead of ultimate death, the just will find themselves giving thanks to God in the community of the faithful.

THE BOOK OF SIRACH
INTRODUCTION, COMMENTARY, AND REFLECTIONS
BY
JAMES L. CRENSHAW

THE BOOK OF
SIRACH

INTRODUCTION

In English Bibles the titles for the book under consideration lack consistency. The NRSV calls it "Ecclesiasticus, or the Wisdom of Jesus Son of Sirach." The TNK, or new Jewish translation, opts for "Ecclesiasticus," a title derived from many Latin Vulgate manuscripts. The GNB uses "Sirach: The Wisdom of Jesus, Son of Sirach (Ecclesiasticus)," and the REB has "Ecclesiasticus or the Wisdom of Jesus son of Sirach." This commentary refers to the book as Sirach and designates its author as Ben Sira.

WISDOM LITERATURE IN THE BIBLE

The books of Proverbs, Job, and Ecclesiastes differ markedly from the rest of the Old Testament, in both style and content. Their closest parallels occur outside the Bible, particularly in ancient Egyptian and Mesopotamian literature associated with educational contexts, either in the training of courtiers or in the instruction of temple personnel. On the basis of sustained interest in wisdom within these biblical texts, scholars have labeled them "wisdom literature."[1] Specialists in Egyptian and Mesopotamian literature have adopted this nomenclature,[2] although it brings together texts with quite different settings and purposes.

Egyptian literature in this genre arose in the third millennium BCE in connection with the instruction of rulers, at first given by pharaohs and later by counselors who taught potential rulers. Several texts have survived the ravages of time, including *The Instruction of Ptah-hotep*, *The Instruction of Amenemope*, *The Instruction of Ani*, *The Instruction of Ankhsheshanky*, and

---

1. One can obtain entry into this realm of discourse from several introductions, most notably James L. Crenshaw, *Old Testament Wisdom* (Atlanta: John Knox, 1981); Gerhard von Rad, *Wisdom in Israel* (Nashville: Abingdon, 1972); and Roland E. Murphy, *The Tree of Life* (New York: Doubleday, 1990). Several volumes of collected essays cover the entire spectrum of ancient wisdom, particularly *The Sage in Israel and the Ancient Near East*, eds. John G. Gammie and Leo G. Perdue (Winona Lake: Eisenbrauns, 1990); *In Search of Wisdom*, eds. Leo G. Perdue, Bernard Brandon Scott, and William Johnson Wiseman (Louisville: Westminster/John Knox, 1993); James L. Crenshaw, *Urgent Advice and Probing Questions* (Macon, Ga.: Mercer University Press, 1995); and *Wisdom in Ancient Israel*, eds. John Day, Robert P. Gordon, and H. G. M. Williamson (Cambridge: Cambridge University Press, 1995).
2. W. G. Lambert, *Babylonian Wisdom Literature* (Oxford: Clarendon, 1960); and Miriam Lichtheim, *Late Egyptian Wisdom Literature in the International Context: A Study of Demotic Instructions*, OBO 52 (Fribourg: Fribourg University Press, 1983).

Papyrus Insinger. In addition, several scribal texts illuminate the educational enterprise, attesting to lazy students and vigorous disciplinary measures by teachers. A text called *A Satire of the Trades* or *The Teaching for Duauf* makes fun of several occupations and praises the profession of the scribe above all others.[3]

Scribal texts from Sumerian times in ancient Mesopotamia describe conditions at the school house (*edubba*) and indicate that similar conditions existed there as in Egypt. A Sumerian instruction attributed to Šuruppak advises his son about the duties of kingship. An early prototype of the book of Job and a collection of Sumerian proverbs round out this early literature from Sumer.[4] Babylonian texts of this kind include *Counsels to a Prince*, various collections of proverbs, and parallels to the books of Job (*I Will Praise the Lord of Wisdom, The Babylonian Theodicy*) and Ecclesiastes (*The Dialogue of a Master and His Slave*).[5] *The Sayings of Ahiqar*, an Aramaic document, purports to have come from an adviser to an Assyrian king, Sennacherib (704–681 BCE). This text of early "Jewish" wisdom was enormously popular, being translated into several languages.[6] Although very little evidence of Canaanite wisdom has been preserved, many interpreters think that these peoples must also have had such texts.[7]

Resemblances between biblical wisdom and these extra-biblical texts from Egypt and Mesopotamia sometimes are so striking that a relationship of some kind appears likely. Most noteworthy is the case of *The Instruction of Amenemope* and a collection within the book of Proverbs, specifically Prov 22:17–23:33, where eleven sayings overlap.[8] The similarities between the book of Job and earlier prototypes from Mesopotamia are only slightly less remarkable, as is the affinity of Ecclesiastes with the ideas put forward in *The Dialogue of a Master and His Slave* and the *Epic of Gilgamesh*, a story about a hero who goes in search of eternal life and retrieves a branch from the tree of life, thanks to advice from the survivor of the flood, Utnapishtim, only to lose it to a serpent.[9]

These close similarities in teachings from three distinct environments in the ancient Near East illustrate a characteristic of wisdom literature: its tendency to present ideas in a universalistic context, one grounded in creation.[10] To the sages, truth was not bound by national ties. Nothing specifically Israelite appears in the books of Proverbs, Job, and Ecclesiastes. Scholars have often noted an absence in these texts of anything about the patriarchs Abraham, Isaac, and Jacob; nothing about early leaders like Moses, Joshua, Samuel; no mention of the judges; no celebration of Israelite kings—except to attribute wisdom literature to Solomon—and no mention of the prophets or a covenant between the Lord and Israel, a special people. In short, the entire history of salvation is missing from these texts. For this reason, wisdom literature has been largely ignored until recently in efforts to describe the theology of the Bible.[11]

---

3. Miriam Lichtheim, *Ancient Egyptian Literature*, 3 vols. (Berkeley: University of California Press, 1973, 1976, 1980), includes wisdom literature among other genres, offering fresh translations of all the texts referred to above.

4. In addition to Lambert's translation of these texts, see Bendt Alster, *The Instructions of Šuruppak: A Sumerian Proverb Collection*, Mesopotamia 2 (Copenhagen: Akademisk Forlag, 1974); *Studies in Sumerian Proverbs*, Mesopotamia 3 (Copenhagen: Akademisk Forlag, 1975); and *Proverbs of Ancient Sumer: The World's Earliest Proverb Collection* (Bethesda, Md.: CDL, 1996).

5. Translations can be found in *Ancient Near Eastern Texts Relating to the Old Testament*, ed. James B. Pritchard, 3rd ed. (Princeton, N.J.: Princeton University Press, 1969).

6. James M. Lindenberger, *The Aramaic Proverbs of Ahiqar* (Baltimore: Johns Hopkins University Press, 1983).

7. No satisfactory study exists, as one can readily see from Loren R. Mack-Fisher's two entries in Gammie and Perdue, *The Sage in Israel and the Ancient Near East*. The first, "A Survey and Reading Guide to the Didactic Literature of Ugarit: Prolegomenon to a Study on the Sage" (67-80), suffers badly from an ill-defined grasp of wisdom literature, and the second, "The Scribe (and Sage) in the Royal Court at Ugarit" (109-15), fares no better.

8. See Harold C. Washington, *Wealth and Poverty in the Instruction of Amenemope and the Hebrew Proverbs*, SBLDS 142 (Atlanta: Scholars Press, 1994); Glendon E. Bryce, *A Legacy of Wisdom: The Egyptian Contribution to the Wisdom of Israel* (Lewisburg: Bucknell University Press, 1979). Both assess the relationship between these two texts from different countries. Nili Shupak, *Where Can Wisdom Be Found? The Sage's Language in the Bible and in Ancient Egyptian Literature*, OBO 130 (Friburg & Göttlingen: University Press & Vandenhoeck & Ruprecht, 1993), offers a valuable analysis of linguistic affinities between Israelite and Egyptian sages.

9. Alexander Heidel, *The Gilgamesh Epic and Old Testament Parallels* (Chicago: University of Chicago Press, 1946); Jeffrey Tigay, *The Evolution of the Gilgamesh Epic* (Philadelphia: Fortress, 1982); Jeffrey Tigay, *Empirical Models for Biblical Criticism* (Philadelphia: Fortress, 1985); Jack M. Sasson, "Gilgamesh Epic," *ABD* 2:1024-1027; William L. Moran, "The Gilgamesh Epic: A Masterpiece from Ancient Mesopotamia," in *Civilizations of the Ancient Near East*, ed. Jack M. Sasson (New York: Scribner's, 1995) 4:2327-2336.

10. Leo G. Perdue, *Wisdom and Creation: The Theology of Wisdom Literature* (Nashville: Abingdon, 1994).

11. No reference to the last-cited work, see Ronald E. Clements, *Wisdom in Theology* (Grand Rapids: Eerdmans, 1992). William P. Brown, *Character in Crisis: A Fresh Approach to the Wisdom Literature of the Old Testament* (Grand Rapids: Eerdmans, 1996), emphasizes the development of moral character in the sapiential literature; Joseph Blenkinsopp, *Wisdom and Law in the Old Testament* (Oxford: Oxford University Press, 1995), draws attention to the ordering of society in ancient Israel, one dubiously located in the school by E. W. Heaton, *The School Tradition of the Old Testament* (Oxford: Clarendon, 1994). Lennart Boström, *The God of the Sages: The Portrayal of God in the Book of Proverbs*, CBOTS 29 (Lund: Almqvist & Wiksell, 1990); James L. Crenshaw, "The Concept of God in Old Testament Wisdom," in Perdue et al., *In Search of Wisdom*, 1-18 (reprinted in Crenshaw, *Urgent Advice and Probing Questions*, 191-205), and James L. Crenshaw, "The Contemplative Life," in Sasson, *Civilizations of the Ancient Near East*, 4:2445-2457.

Besides being applicable to all people, wisdom literature addresses the fundamental question, "What promotes well-being?" It offers advice on coping with difficult circumstances, in a sense giving parental counsel to growing children, but also offering popular advice to people of all ages. One type of wisdom literature explores existential questions, chiefly the matter of innocent suffering and what this implies about divine justice. Naturally, this questioning attitude does not stop short of asking about death and its consequences.[12]

Another characteristic of this literature is its preoccupation with the search for wisdom, which appears as a feminine personification associated with God in the creative process. She also actively woos young men to deeper intellectual and moral pursuits; in this endeavor she has a rival, folly, also personified as a woman. Often called a foreign woman, or strange, she seduces young men with the aid of powerful rhetoric (cf. Prov 9:17).[13]

The extent of biblical wisdom has elicited considerable debate, some interpreters wishing to broaden the category to include much of the Bible (e.g., Genesis 1–11; Deuteronomy; the story of David's rise to power and the succession, 2 Samuel 9–20; 1 Kings 1–2; Esther; Jonah).[14] These attempts merely demonstrate the fact that sages did not own a distinct vocabulary but used the ordinary language of their time. Their influence does seem to manifest itself in the book of Psalms, especially in 37; 49; and 73.

Sirach definitely belongs to biblical wisdom, although its teachings represent a transition from a nonspecific national audience to Jewish hearers whose intellectual heritage faces obliteration by Hellenism. Its author, Ben Sira, unites the unique legacy of Israel's saving history to the wisdom tradition. Although the language echoes that within the book of Proverbs, the content weaves together an account of the merciful guidance of Israel's Lord with advice on coping with life's eventualities. Like the book of Proverbs, Sirach also praises personified wisdom, further elaborating a myth of her activity at creation and identifying her with the accessible Mosaic law. Ben Sira describes the various professions, like *The Satire of the Trades,* and evidences a strong personal piety resembling that in *The Instruction of Ani.*[15]

A new dimension in Sirach, the praise of Israel's "saints" (men of piety), relates Israelite spiritual leadership to the guidance of wisdom. The other wisdom text, also from the Apocrypha, that develops this approach to Israel's history is the book of Wisdom. Its author praises personified wisdom, now a hypostasis (or manifestation) of God's essential character, and describes the period of the exodus from Egypt as one during which wisdom guided God's people into freedom. Prayer and praise unite in this thoroughly Hellenistic text, one composed in Greek and making extensive use of Greek rhetoric.[16]

THE ORIGINAL TITLE OF THE BOOK AND ITS CONTENTS

The title of this book in most Greek manuscripts identifies its genre and author: Σοφία Ἰησοῦ υἱοῦ Σιραχ (*Sophia Iēsou huiou S(e)irach*, "the Wisdom of Jesus the son of Sirach"). A shorter form occurs in the Syriac text: the Wisdom of Bar Sira (the Wisdom of the Son of Sira). And an altogether different title appears in the Latin tradition, where one finds such descriptive categories as the church book (Ecclesiasticus) in the Vulgate and *Parabolae* ("Wise Sayings") in a Hebrew copy, according to Jerome. On two occasions later Jewish writers preface a citation from Sirach with the words המשל אמר (*hammōšēl 'āmar*, "the one who spoke in Proverbs"). The tenth-century Jewish scholar Saadia refers to Sirach as ספר מוסר (*sēper mûsār*, "the book of Discipline/Instruction"), and Rabbi Joseph calls it משלי בן סרא (*mišlê ben sirā'*, "The Proverbs of the Son of Sira").

---

12. James L. Crenshaw, "The Shadow of Death in Qoheleth," in *Israelite Wisdom* (Philadelphia: Fortress, 1979) 205-16; reprinted in Crenshaw, *Urgent Advice and Probing Questions,* 573-85.
13. J. N. Aletti, "Seduction et parole en Proverbs 1–9," *VT* 27 (1977) 129-44.
14. Donn F. Morgan, *Wisdom in the Old Testament Traditions* (Atlanta: John Knox, 1981). James L. Crenshaw, "Method in Determining Wisdom Influence upon 'Historical' Literature," *JBL* 88 (1969) 129-42 (= Crenshaw, *Urgent Advice and Probing Questions,* 312-25), evaluates such attempts to find wisdom in various parts of the OT.
15. A shift from confident self-reliance, characteristic of early Egyptian wisdom, seems to occur in the new kingdom with Ani and Amenemope and to grow stronger with the passing of time, as evidenced by demotic instructions (Papyrus Insinger and the *Instruction of Ankhsheshanky*).
16. See James L. Crenshaw, "The Restraint of Reason, the Humility of Prayer," in Crenshaw, *Urgent Advice and Probing Questions,* 206-21.

Although the opening chapter of Sirach has not survived in the Hebrew manuscripts, a remark in Sir 50:27 attributes the book to Simeon ben Eleazar ben Sira, and Sir 51:30 adds: "Thus far the words of Simeon, the son of Jeshua, who is called Ben Sira. The Wisdom of Simeon, the son of Jeshua, the son of Eleazar, the son of Sira." The name "Simeon" (Σίμων *Simōn*) seems to have come from Sir 50:1, 24*a*; the probable name of the author is Jeshua ben Eleazar ben Sira. Most Greek and Latin manuscripts partially confirm the identity of the author, reading "the Wisdom of Jesus son of Sira" and "the book of Jesus son of Sirach" respectively. The *ch* ending on Sirach in Greek manuscripts represents either a Greek χ (*chi*), indicating an indeclinable word, or the Hebrew א (*'aleph*).

The prologue to the book, written by Ben Sira's grandson, confirms the tradition that identifies the author's name with Jeshua (Jesus). Ben Sira's patronymic includes the name of his father (Eleazar) and his grandfather (Sira). Within the book several self-references occur, identifying Ben Sira as a professional wise man, describing his disciplined life-style, and inviting young boys to study in his academy.[17]

The first of several authorial self-references, 24:30-34 (cf. 34:12-13; 39:12-15, 32-35; 41:16; 43:32; 50:25-29; 51:1-30) implies that Ben Sira understood his teachings as inspired utterances that began small but grew unexpectedly, like a canal expanding into a huge stream. His own learning, directed initially toward personal enjoyment ("I will water my garden/ and drench my flower-beds" [24:31 NRSV]), soon lost its selfish character and became available to everyone ("Observe that I have not labored for myself alone,/ but for all who seek wisdom" [24:34 NRSV]). In 33:16-18, Ben Sira repeats the latter remark; in doing so he compares himself to gleaners following grape pickers. This image suggests an awareness that the period of divine inspiration is rapidly coming to an end ("Now I was the last to keep vigil," 33:16). Later rabbinic teaching limited the era of divine inspiration to that begun by Moses and ended by Ezra. In the context of discussing the wide experience of educated persons, he mentions extensive travel and the danger associated with journeys in the ancient world (34:9-13).

Within an elaborate treatment of various professions in his day, Ben Sira demonstrates the advantages of being a scholar (38:24–39:11). The similarities to a popular Egyptian text, *The Instruction for Duauf*, often called *A Satire of the Trades*, has long been known and commented on, although the texts differ in tone and subject matter. (Ben Sira does not satirize, and his list of vocations is much shorter.) Having given his strong endorsement of the scribe's profession, yet without disparaging the works of one's hands, Ben Sira states that he has more to say, being full like the full moon, and invites students to blossom comparably, joining knowledge and worship (39:12-15). He proceeds to sing praise to the Creator:

So from the beginning I have
  been convinced of all this
  and have thought it out and
    left it in writing:
All the works of the Lord are good,
  and he will supply every need in its time.
(39:32-33 NRSV)

Expressing a teacher's desire for respect, Ben Sira urges students to observe his instruction (41:16). In the Greek text of 43:32 (but not in the Hebrew, which has the plural "we"), Ben Sira acknowledges the inevitable mystery that humans encounter when reflecting on transcendence: "Many things greater than these lie hidden,/ for I have seen but few of his works" (NRSV). An epilogue, 50:25-29, expresses Ben Sira's extreme animosity toward Samaritans, Idumeans, and

---

17. Wolfgang Roth, "Sirach: The First Graded Curriculum," *The Bible Today* 29 (1991) 298-302, thinks the book was used as a textbook. The curious silence about circumcision and the sabbath, noted by J. Marböck, *Weisheit im Wandel: Untersuchungen zur Weisheitstheologie bei Ben Sira*, BBB 37 (Bonn: Peter Hanstein, 1971) 93, shows that, whatever its use, a certain haphazardness exists. The same principle was operative in law codes in the Bible, where significant gaps occur, and in ethical texts, such as Proverbs, that omit many important areas of life.

Philistines (Hellenists), along with some comments reflecting an entirely novel idea in Hebraic thought: pride of authorship.

> Instruction in understanding and knowledge
>   I have written in this book,
> Jesus son of Eleazar son of
>   Sirach of Jerusalem,
>   whose mind poured forth wisdom.
> Happy are those who concern
>   themselves with these things,
>   and those who lay them to
>   heart will become wise.
> For if they put them into practice,
>   they will be equal to anything,
>   for the fear of the Lord is their path.
> (50:27-29 NRSV)

The final chapter, consisting of a prayer, an autobiographical poem on wisdom, and an appeal to readers (51:1-30), is rich with personal references, although employing literary conventions. This practice of using traditional language of self-reference already appears in the book of Proverbs (cf. Prov 4:1-9) and Ecclesiastes (Eccl 1:12–2:2 and throughout the book).[18] For this reason, some of the self-references in Sirach may reveal nothing about the author's personal experiences (e.g., adventures during traveling).

The information that Ben Sira enjoyed the leisurely status of a professional teacher suggests that one can find in Sirach the sort of teachings he conveyed to his students. The book stands in the tradition of Proverbs and Ecclesiastes, especially the former. It consists, therefore, of brief aphorisms, maxims, and clever statements in poetic form having to do with practical daily existence.[19] Like the initial collection in Proverbs (Proverbs 1–9), the sayings in Sirach frequently make up brief paragraphs on a particular topic. The subjects range widely, extending from inner feelings, like a sense of shame,[20] to external behavior, such as slander, from deeply religious acts of charity to self-serving conduct at banquets, from proper attitudes toward money to the disgrace of being reduced to begging, from various kinds of friends to the trouble occasioned by bad daughters, and much more.

The teachings also take up existential issues, such as sickness and death,[21] wrestling with the ethical question of whether one should consult a physician, who in popular imagination was seen to interfere with divine punishment for sin. Ben Sira takes no refuge in belief in a future life, and that refusal to do so allows the matter of divine justice—or more correctly its absence—to press heavily on him, as it did on the author of the book of Job.[22] This vexing problem surfaces frequently in argumentative contexts, suggesting that Ben Sira encountered a vocal group who denied God's just governance of the world. Ben Sira subscribed to traditional religious teachings and expressed his own faith quite tangibly, either in prayer or in hymnic praise. Moreover, he identified the divine revelation in the Torah with the figure of wisdom, who descended from heaven to dwell in Jerusalem. True knowledge, as he saw it, consisted of worship, its origin and destination.

---

18. For different views about the frequency of first-person language in Ecclesiastes and its function, see James L. Crenshaw, *Ecclesiastes*, OTL (Philadelphia: Westminster, 1987); and Michael V. Fox, *Qoheleth and His Contradictions*, JSOTSup 71 (Sheffield: Almond, 1989).

19. Research in the area of OT wisdom has made significant progress, yet without actually clarifying the precise sociological context within which ancient sages worked. For an understanding of the complex issues, see von Rad, *Wisdom in Israel*; Crenshaw, *Old Testament Wisdom*; Murphy, *The Tree of Life*; R. N. Whybray, *The Intellectual Tradition in the Old Testament* (Berlin: Walter de Gruyter, 1974); Claus Westermann, *Roots of Wisdom: The Oldest Proverbs of Israel and Other Peoples* (Louisville: Westminster/John Knox, 1995); Claus Westermann, *Forschungsgeschichte zur Weisheitsliteratur 1950–1990*, AzT 71 (Stuttgart: Calwer, 1991); Stuart Weeks, *Israelite Wisdom*, OTM (Oxford: Clarendon, 1994).

20. Jack T. Sanders, "Ben Sira's Ethics of Caution," *HUCA* 50 (1979) 73-106.

21. Friedrich Vinzenz Reiterer, "Deutung und Wertung des Todes durch Ben Sira," *Die Alttestamentliche Botschaft als Wegweisung: Festschrift für Heinz Reinelt*, ed. Josef Zmijemski (Stuttgart: Katholisches Bibelwerk, 1990) 203-36; the focus of attention in this article falls on Sir 41:1-4. L. J. Prockter, "'His Yesterday and Yours Today' (Sir 38:22): Reflections on Ben Sira's View of Death," *J Sem* 2 (1990) 44-56, claims that Ben Sira combines Jewish piety with the best of popular Hellenistic philosophy, accepting life and death as part of God's providential order, like a good Stoic.

22. On theodicy as perceived by biblical authors, see James L. Crenshaw, ed., *Theodicy in the Old Testament* (Philadelphia: Fortress, 1983), particularly the opening essay, "Introduction: The Shift from Theodicy to Anthropodicy," 1-16. See also Crenshaw, *Urgent Advice and Probing Questions*, 141-54.

Ben Sira's teachings have no discernible order, except for the lengthy section praising faithful men (אנשי חסד 'anšê ḥesed; 44:1–50:24), and even there some confusion occurs as to actual sequence.[23] Occasional vocatives ("my son") give the book an appearance of actual classroom use, although this form of address is standard in wisdom literature, occurring in ancient Sumerian and Egyptian instructions and in Proverbs. The expressions "father" and "son" eventually came to be used for "teacher" and "student." The advice in the book of Sirach certainly accords with the supposition that a professional teacher is busily at work in Jerusalem preparing his Jewish students to cope with reality in a Hellenistic environment (50:27).

Viewing the book as a text for the academy, Wolfgang Roth understands the book in terms of "seven teaching units set off from each other through brief passages that reassure and encourage the struggling student."[24] In his view, the book moves from simple matters to more complex ones on the assumption that students learn by stages. Moreover, Ben Sira uses himself as an example, describing his own progress from early discipline to later success. Marking the stages of a student's progress, an exhortation to prepare for testing (2:1-18) leads to instruction about filial devotion and duty to associates (2:7–4:10). A call to cling to wisdom (4:11-19) then introduces section two, an instruction on sincerity and justice, on humility, consistency, and friendship (4:20–6:17). An exhortation to accept wisdom's fetters follows introducing section three, teaching about social issues (7:1–14:19). The fourth section (15:11–23:27) praises students for staying in Wisdom's shelter, debates the matter of free will, and closes with a discourse by Wisdom (24:1-27). The fifth section (25:1–33:15) deals with social relationships in general, giving a "mini-sociology of early Judaism." The sixth section (33:19–39:11), introduced by a report on Ben Sira's progress (33:16-18), deals with such intimate issues as dreams and the inner springs of piety (providence, prayer, temperance, and illness), "a sort of mini-psychology." The seventh section (39:16–50:24) begins with a reflection on divine presence in human thinking and experience (39:16–42:14) and treats God's presence in the universe (42:15–43:35), reaching its climax in the praise of faithful Israelites (44:1–50:24), "a theological survey."[25]

THE HISTORICAL SETTING

A prologue introduces the Greek translation of Sirach. Ben Sira's grandson, who rendered the Hebrew text into Greek for the Jewish community in Egypt, gives the precise date of his arrival in Egypt as the thirty-eighth year of Euergetes. That epithet was applied to only two Lagid rulers, Ptolemy III Euergetes I (246–221 BCE) and Ptolemy VII Physkon Euergetes II (170–164, and 146–117 BCE). Only the latter king held office long enough to meet the translator's specified thirty-eight years; the date 132 BCE, therefore, marks his entry into Egypt. The translation was completed after the death of Euergetes II in 117 BCE (note the participle συγχρονίσας [sygchronisas], which ordinarily implies simultaneity, hence, "I was there as long as Euergetes reigned").[26]

Ben Sira lavishly praises a high priest named Simeon, son of Jochanan (called Onias in some Greek MSS). From 219 to 196 BCE, Simeon II was high priest in Jerusalem, which accords well with the information provided by Ben Sira's grandson. The grandfather lived during Simeon's

---

23. Interpreters usually emphasize the random character of the teachings in Sirach, viewing the book as a compendium of the accumulated lectures of a lifetime of work, with no fundamental structure. Rejecting a theory of accidental juxtaposition of wholly unrelated teachings, Wolfgang Roth, "On the Gnomic-Discursive Wisdom of Jesus Ben Sirach," *Semeia*, 17 (1980) 59-79, thinks Ben Sira wrote an original book consisting of 1:1–23:27 and 51:1-30, later supplementing this first edition with three additional units (24:1–32:13; 32:14–38:23; 38:24–50:24, 29). A prologue introduces each new section (24:1-29; 32:14–33:15; 38:24–39:11), and an autobiographical note intervenes between the prologue and the body of the unit (in contrast to the original edition, where prologues occur [1:1–2:18; 4:11-19; 6:18-37; 14:20–15:10], but no autobiographical note). Roth sees 39:2-3 as programmatic for Ben Sira's "hermeneutic-pedagogic theory: from understanding to explanation, from assimilation to exposition, from learning to teaching, from apprenticeship to mastery" (Roth, "On the Gnomic-Discursive Wisdom of Jesus Ben Sirach," 63). In Ben Sira's oral instructions (e.g., 6:35; 17:10; 25:9; 42:15–43:33; 44–50), he sees a forerunner to *haggadah* (homiletic discourse); in other teachings (18:30–19:30; 20:27-31; 31:12–32:13) he recognizes early *halakah* (legal instruction). Roth thinks Ben Sira's warning against exceeding the scope of assignments (3:21-22) means exactly that: Stick to the day's lesson (Roth, "On the Gnomic-Discursive Wisdom of Jesus Ben Sirach," 64). Roth also believes that Ben Sira organized the original four sections alphabetically: אב ('āb, "father") in 3:1-16; בשת (bōšet, "shame") in 4:20-28; גאות (gā'ôt, "arrogance") in 7:17 and 10:5-18; דעת (da'at, "knowledge") in 16:25b–23:27, following the order of the first four letters in the Hebrew alphabet (Roth, "On the Gnomic-Discursive Wisdom of Jesus Ben Sirach," 74). The first two sections comprise, in Roth's view, elementary instruction; the third section "is more hortative-ethical and society oriented in character," while the fourth is more explorative-theological and individualistic (Roth, "On the Gnomic-Discursive Wisdom of Jesus Ben Sirach," 74-75).
24. Roth, "On the Gnomic-Discursive Wisdom of Jesus Ben Sirach," 302.
25. Roth, "On the Gnomic-Discursive Wisdom of Jesus Ben Sirach," 298-302.
26. Rudolf Smend, *Die Weisheit des Jesus Sirach erklärt* (Berlin: Reimer, 1906) 3-4.

rule over the religious life of the Jews, and Ben Sira vividly describes an occasion in which the high priest presided over the ritual at the Temple on a special holy day, perhaps the Day of Atonement, or possibly the daily whole offering.[27] The tone of Ben Sira's remarks about Simeon suggests that he had already died.

Assuming that Ben Sira lived during Simeon's tenure as high priest, when did he die? One thing is certain: He does not mention the social chaos that erupted during the Maccabean revolt against Syrian oppression in 167 BCE, although that seethed for some time prior to open resistance. In 175 BCE the Seleucid ruler Antiochus IV Epiphanes came to power, intensifying the policy of Hellenization already in force. Jason, the son of the high priest Simeon, joined in this effort, having replaced his own brother, Onias III, in that office, a prize secured through a bribe of 360 silver talents, plus the promise to hasten Hellenization through the construction of a gymnasium in Jerusalem. According to 2 Macc 4:23-26, the prize of the office of high priest later went to Menelaus, who offered an even higher sum to Antiochus.

In 167 BCE, this Seleucid king went so far as to proscribe Judaism, forbidding the celebration of festivals and sacrifices, the practice of circumcision and observance of dietary laws, and setting up a statue of Zeus over the altar in the Temple at Jerusalem. The horrified author of Dan 8:13; 9:27; 11:31; and 12:11 designates this statue "the abomination of desolation." Ben Sira has nothing to say about these disturbing events, and one can plausibly assume that he died before they took place. On the basis of a somewhat nostalgic depiction of Simeon, seemingly directed at his successor, Onias, and urging him to imitate his father's good deeds, scholars generally date Sirach in the period between 195 and 180 BCE. A date c. 185 BCE seems likely.[28]

Seleucid kings had not always looked on Jews as enemies. Antiochus III the Great (223–187 BCE) waged aggressive campaigns from Asia Minor to India, then turned his attention to Egypt. He was defeated at Raphia in 217 by Ptolemy IV Philopator, but succeeded in crushing the Egyptian army at Panium in 198 during the reign of Ptolemy V Epiphanes (203–181 BCE). The Jewish historian Josephus claims that the Jews assisted Antiochus in these early years, providing supplies and elephants and fighting to remove the garrison of Egyptian soldiers in the citadel at Jerusalem.

In gratitude, Antiochus made a number of concessions: (1) to help defray the cost of daily sacrifices; (2) to exempt from taxation the materials for building the Temple; (3) to obligate the people to live according to the Torah; (4) to exempt from taxation the senate, priests, scribes, and sacred singers; (5) to exempt Jerusalem citizens from taxation for three years; and (6) to let the remaining citizens reduce their taxes by a third and to emancipate slaves.[29] When the Syrians were routed by Romans at Magnesia in 190 BCE, the situation changed noticeably, and, pressed for revenues, Antiochus rescinded the exemptions from taxes and reduced the privileges previously granted to Jews. In 187, Antiochus was assassinated at Elymais while attacking one of Bel's sacred places to make payment to Rome. His son, Seleucus IV Philopator (187–175 BCE), succeeded him. Seleucus's treatment of the Jews was somewhat ambiguous, at first restoring the privileges earlier granted them by his father, but later sending Heliodorus to confiscate the treasures in the Temple at Jerusalem (2 Macc 3:4-40). In 175, Seleucus IV Philopator was

---

27. F. O'Fearghail, "Sir 50, 5-21: Yom Kippur or The Daily Whole Offering," *Bib* 59 (1978) 301-16, argues that Ben Sira describes the daily whole offering rather than the Day of Atonement. Alexander Di Lella accepts this view; see Patrick W. Skehan and Alexander A. Di Lella, *The Wisdom of Ben Sira*, AB 39 (New York: Doubleday, 1987) 550-51.

28. James D. Martin, "Ben Sira—A Child of His Time," in *A Word in Season: Essays in Honour of William McKane*, eds. James D. Martin and Philip R. Davies, JSOTSup 42 (Sheffield: JSOT, 1986) 141-61, examines Ben Sira's teachings in the light of emerging apocalypticism in the Jewish world. The changing circumstances associated with the Babylonian defeat of Jerusalem and dislocation of a large segment of the Judean populace contributed to an attitude quite different from earlier optimism. Portions of the books of Ezekiel (chaps. 38–39), Isaiah (chaps. 26–29), and Zechariah (chaps. 9–14) reflect an early apocalypticism (sometimes called proto-apocalypticism). Full-blown developments occur in the books of Daniel and Revelation. Apocalyptic thought includes, among other things, a belief in a transcendent God (momentarily inactive in Israel's history), the temporary victory of evil, and imminent judgment on all peoples. This message assumes the form of revelation attributed to ancient worthies but kept hidden for years, strange imagery involving animals and beasts, coded language, heavenly journeys, visions, and martial conflicts. Sometimes a work asks difficult questions and ponders the existence of wickedness in a world supposedly ruled by a benevolent deity (cf. 2 Esdras, a masterpiece that asks why God's people are subjected to such harsh treatment from persons less devout than they). The idea of a final battle between the forces of good and the forces of evil finds expression in *The Wars of the Sons of Light Against the Sons of Darkness*, a text from Qumran; earlier expressions of this conflict occur in Ezekiel 38–39 and Joel 3–4 (Eng. 2:28-32; 3:1-21). The closest kinship with Ben Sira's panegyric of the fathers exists, in Martin's view, in Wisdom and 1 Maccabees (Martin, "Ben Sira," 145); such cult-centered historiography may thus be the origin of apocalyptic's historical expression (Martin, "Ben Sira,"147), although Ben Sira opposes idle speculation and apocalyptic excesses (Martin, "Ben Sira," 154). For Ben Sira in the Hellenistic context, see Martin Hengel, *Judaism and Hellenism*, I-II (Philadelphia: Fortress, 1974) 131-53.

29. Josephus *Antiquities of the Jews* 12.138-144.

assassinated, and Antiochus IV Epiphanes (175–164 BCE) assumed the reins. Among Jews he earned the nickname "Epimanes" ("Madman") from his cruel treatment of them.[30]

The internal situation reflected the political climate abroad. Opportunists chose sides, hoping to find themselves on the side of the eventual winners in the struggle for power. Competing families—Tobiads and Oniads—strove for popular support, and old rivalries—Jews versus Samaritans–extended the dissension beyond the streets of Jerusalem. Avarice and greed ran free, touching the highest office, turning the religious priesthood into a coveted prize up for grabs to the highest bidder. Jason's and Menelaus's willingness to compromise ancestral practices in favor of Greek ways demonstrates the degradation of the priesthood and explains Ben Sira's glowing praise of Simeon, who stood as a sharp contrast to the weak son, Onias III. Antiochus IV Epiphanes' removal of Onias showed how far a foreign ruler was willing to go in carrying out his policy of Hellenization.

A few allusions in Sirach may suggest the volatile situation. In 50:25-26, Ben Sira voices contempt for Idumeans, Philistines (Hellenizers), and Samaritans, and in 7:4-7; 40:25-26; and 50:1, 23-24 (Hebrew text), he may criticize contenders for the office of high priest. Finally, the prayer for renewed deeds of deliverance and signs of divine leadership (36:1-22) suggests that Ben Sira thought that belief in the ancient experience of divine watchcare could soon disappear from the collective memory.[31] Nevertheless, such remarks fall readily within the historical situation envisioned by an activity for Ben Sira between 200 and 180 BCE.

FORMS OF EXPRESSION

Ben Sira stands in a venerable tradition of wisdom teachers.[32] His speech forms resemble those in Proverbs, Job, and Ecclesiastes, which he studied thoroughly (along with the Torah and prophetic literature).[33] Truth statements and instruction, the base forms of the משל (*māšāl*), loosely translated "proverb" but etymologically implying a likeness and an authoritative word, occur with great frequency.

Truth Statements. Often called sentences, truth statements capture fleeting insights and express them in poetic form so as to seize the imagination and linger in memory. They capture the experience of many and couch it in words that individualize the discovery, giving it a timeless quality. Such aphorisms and maxims have the force of legal injunction in some societies;[34] ancient Israelites employed them as incontrovertible evidence. They need only be spoken to command assent: "A new friend is like new wine;/ when it has aged, you can drink it with pleasure" (9:10*b* NRSV). Who can deny that "all living beings become old like a garment,/ for the decree from of old is, 'You must die!'" (14:17 NRSV)? These sentences pronounce judgment on human nature: "A rich person does wrong, and even adds insults;/ a poor person suffers wrong, and must add apologies" (13:3 NRSV); "Like music in time of mourning is ill-timed conversation,/

---

30. Skehan and Di Lella, *The Wisdom of Ben Sira*, 8-16, sketches this history and locates Ben Sira within the general period 250–175 BCE, with Sirach being written when Ben Sira was an old man, probably about 180 BCE. This interpretation of the data has obtained the status of consensus, rare among biblical critics.

31. J. Marböck, "Das Gebet um die Rettung Zions Sir 36, 1-22 (Gr: 33.9-13a; 36, 16b-22) im zusammenhang der Geschichtsschau ben Siras," in *Memoria Jerusalem*, ed. J. B. Bauer (Jerusalem and Graz: Akademische Druck-und Verlagsanstalt, 1977) 93-116. In examining this remarkable prayer, Marböck points out that Ben Sira's appeal for renewed action on behalf of an elect people accords with Sir 17:17, which refers to Israel as Yahweh's special portion.

32. Walter Baumgartner, "Die literarischen Gattungen in der Weisheit des Jesus Sirach," *ZAW* 34 (1914) 161-98; James L. Crenshaw, "Sirach," *Harper Bible Commentary* (San Francisco: Harper & Row, 1988) 836-54; James L. Crenshaw, "Wisdom," in *Old Testament Form Criticism*, ed. John H. Hayes, TUMS 2 (San Antonio: Trinity University Press, 1974) 225-64. See also Crenshaw, *Urgent Advice and Probing Questions*.

33. J. L. Koole, "Die Bibel des Ben-Sira," *OTS* 14 (1965) 374-96; Douglas E. Fox, "Ben Sira on OT Canon Again: The Date of Daniel," *WTJ* 49 (1987) 335-50; T. Middendorp, *Die Stellung Jesu Ben Siras zwischen Judentum und Hellenismus* (Leiden: Brill, 1973); Eckhard J. Schnabel, *Law and Wisdom from Ben Sira to Paul: A Tradition-Historical Enquiry into the Relation of Law, Wisdom, and Ethics* (Tübingen: J. C. B. Mohr, 1985). The last two authors calculate the extent of Ben Sira's allusions to scripture (70 allusions to the Torah, 46 to historical books, 51 to prophetic books, and over 160 to the writings, according to Middendorp's reckoning). A more exacting criterion for establishing an allusion would reduce the number appreciably.

34. The advisory nature of sentences, as opposed to mandatory instructions, can no longer be maintained. See James L. Crenshaw, *Prophetic Conflict*, BZAW 124 (Berlin and New York; Walter de Gruyter, 1971), excursus B, "*'eṣa* and *dabar*: The Problem of Authority/Certitude in Wisdom and Prophetic Literature," 116-23; James L. Crenshaw, "Wisdom and Authority: Sapiential Rhetoric and Its Warrants," *Congress Volume Vienna 1980*, SVTP 32 (Leiden: Brill, 1981) 10-29 (see also Crenshaw, *Urgent Advice and Probing Questions*, 326-43); Claus Westermann, "Weisheit im Sprichwort," *Schalom. Festschrift A. Jepsen* (Stuttgart: Calwer Verlag, 1971) 73-85; Westermann, *The Roots of Wisdom*; Friedemann W. Golka, *The Leopard's Spots* (Edinburgh: T. & T. Clark, 1993).

but a thrashing and discipline are at all times wisdom" (22:6 NRSV).[35] Long experience with poor learners rests behind this one: "Whoever teaches a fool is like one who glues potsherds together,/ or who rouses a sleeper from deep slumber" (22:9 NRSV). Fools in biblical wisdom were morally bankrupt, not devoid of intellect.

These ancient truth statements came in various forms: "Better are the God-fearing who lack understanding/ than the highly intelligent who transgress the law" (19:24 NRSV). Echoing a sentiment within Proverbs, this truth statement expresses the pathos of being dependent on others: "Better is the life of the poor under their own crude roof/ than sumptuous food in the house of others" (29:22 NRSV). Failing to speak at the right time evokes the following comment: "Better are those who hide their folly/ than those who hide their wisdom" (41:15 NRSV).

Numerical sayings enable teachers to combine similar things to achieve maximum effect when the last item finally appears:

> I take pleasure in three things,
>   and they are beautiful in the sight of God
>   and of mortals:
> agreement among brothers and sisters,
>   friendship among neighbors,
> and a wife and a husband who
>   live in harmony. (25:1 NRSV)

Sometimes these sayings become somewhat wordy:

> Two kinds of individuals multiply sins,
>   and a third incurs wrath.
> Hot passion that blazes like a fire
>   will not be quenched until it
>   burns itself out;
> one who commits fornication with
>   his near of kin
> will never cease until the fire
>   burns him up. (23:16 NRSV)

> At two things my heart is grieved,
>   and because of a third anger comes over me:
> a warrior in want through poverty,
>   intelligent men who are treated contemptuously,
> and a man who turns back from
>   righteousness to sin—
>   the Lord will prepare him for the sword! (26:28 NRSV)

Some truth statements are introduced by a particle of existence; e.g., יֵשׁ (*yēš*, "there is").[36]

> Some [*yēš*] people keep silent and are
>   thought to be wise,
>   while others are detested for being talkative.

---

35. John J. Pilch, "'Beat His Ribs While He Is Young' (Sir 30:12): A Window on the Mediterranean World," *BTB* 23 (1993) 101-13, examines the ancient understanding of parenting, concluding that respect for parents was more important than actual deeds and that strict (harsh) discipline fit nicely into such a worldview. His use of modern Mediterranean concepts raises the question of how appropriate is the analogy. Modern educators question the universality of the statement about the value of corporal punishment.

36. On this type of proverbial saying, see Pancratius C. Beentjes, "'Full Wisdom Is Fear of the Lord.' Ben Sira 19, 20-20, 31: Context, Composition and Concept," *EstBib* 47 (1989) 27-45, esp. 37-40. In the existing Hebrew manuscripts, יֵשׁ (*yēš*) occurs 64 times, involving 46 different verse lines; in 20:5-6, 22-23 they appear in "absolute condensation" (Beentjes, "'Full Wisdom Is Fear of the Lord.' Ben Sira 19, 20-20, 31," 37).

Some people keep silent because
>   they have nothing to say,
> while others keep silent because
>   they know when to speak. (20:5-6 NRSV)

> There are those who work and
>   struggle and hurry,
>   but are so much the more in want.
> There are others who are slow and need help,
>   who lack strength and abound in poverty;
> but the eyes of the Lord look
>   kindly upon them;
>   he lifts them out of their lowly condition
> and raises up their heads
>   to the amazement of the many.
> (11:11-13 NRSV)

> There is the gift that profits you nothing,
>   and the gift to be paid back double. (20:10 NRSV)

Some truth statements take the form of benediction or malediction, blessing and curse: "Happy are those who do not blunder with their lips,/ and need not suffer remorse for sin./ Happy are those whose hearts do not condemn them,/ and who have not given up their hope" (14:1-2 NRSV). Ben Sira characterizes pursuit of wisdom in this manner:

> Happy is the person who meditates on wisdom
>   and reasons intelligently,
> who reflects in his heart on her ways
>   and ponders her secrets,[37]
>
> pursuing her like a hunter,
>   and lying in wait on her paths;
> who peers through her windows
>   and listens at her doors;
> who camps near her house
>   and fastens his tent peg to her walls;
> who pitches his tent near her,
>   and so occupies an excellent lodging place;
> who places his children under her shelter,
>   and lodges under her boughs;
> who is sheltered by her from the heat,
>   and dwells in the midst of her glory.
> (14:20-27 NRSV)

The benedictions contrast mightily with these maledictions: "Woe to timid hearts and to slack hands,/ and to the sinner who walks a double path!/ Woe to the fainthearted who have no trust!/ Therefore they have no shelter./ Woe to you who have lost your nerve!/ What will you do when the Lord's reckoning comes?" (2:12-14 NRSV). These two forms reflect the sapiential tendency to think in polarities, making clear distinctions between the wise and fools, good and evil.

The simple sentence, or *māšāl,* also occurs as a rhetorical question: "Whose offspring are worthy of honor?/ Human offspring./ Whose offspring are worthy of honor?/ Those who

---

37. Martin, "Ben Sira—A Child of His Time," 154, thinks of the warning against seeking hidden things as being aimed at apocalyptic speculation. Others think it refers to Hellenistic philosophy.

fear the Lord./ Whose offspring are unworthy of honor?/ Human offspring./ Whose offspring are unworthy of honor?/ Those who break the commandments" (10:19 NRSV). Apostrophe, direct rhetorical address, livens the speech about death in 41:1-2: "O death, how bitter is the thought of you/ to the one at peace among possessions,/ who has nothing to worry about and is prosperous in everything,/ and still is vigorous enough to enjoy food!/ O death, how welcome is your sentence/ to one who is needy and failing in strength,/ worn down by age and anxious about everything;/ to one who is contrary, and has lost all patience!" (NRSV).[38]

Instruction. The other base form, instruction, sets the tone for Ben Sira's teaching, for he speaks as an authoritative figure addressing students. The direct address varies from the usual בני (*běnî*), "my son," to "holy sons" (39:13), "children" (3:1), "my children" (23:7; 41:14), and "you who need instruction" (51:23). His prescriptive advice, often resembling brief paragraphs on specific topics, is reinforced with warnings and admonitions, the proverbial dangling carrot employed to motivate people. Frequently, refrains set this material apart from what precedes or follows.

Throughout the book positively expressed instructions alternate with negative ones: "Honor your father by word and deed,/ that his blessing may come upon you" (3:8 NRSV); "Do not glorify yourself by dishonoring your father,/ for your father's dishonor is no glory to you" (3:10 NRSV). Frequently these instructions lack motivation, e.g., "Do not be ashamed to confess your sins,/ and do not try to stop the current of a river" (4:26 NRSV). Sometimes a series of instructions is followed by a single motivating clause: "My child, do not cheat the poor of their living,/ and do not keep needy eyes waiting./ Do not grieve the hungry/ or anger one in need./ Do not add to the troubles of the desperate,/ or delay giving to the needy . . . for if in bitterness of soul some should curse you,/ their Creator will hear their prayer" (4:1-6 NRSV). The appeal to reward for good conduct balances threats aimed at misbehavior: "Give to the Most High as he has given to you,/ and as generously as you can afford./ For the Lord is the one who repays,/ and he will repay you sevenfold" (35:12-13 NRSV).

Ben Sira demonstrates a fondness for refrains and repetitive phrases, as if stopping the readers in midthought and suspending them there: "You who fear the Lord, wait for his mercy;/ do not stray, or else you may fall./ You who fear the Lord, trust in him,/ and your reward will not be lost./ You who fear the Lord, hope for good things,/ for lasting joy and mercy" (2:7-9 NRSV; cf. 2:15-17). Similarly:

> Question a friend; perhaps he did not do it;
>   or if he did, so that he may not do it again.
> Question a neighbor; perhaps he did not say it;
>   or if he said it, so that he may not repeat it.
> Question a friend, for often it is slander;
>   so do not believe everything you hear.
> . . . .
> Question your neighbor before you threaten him;
>   and let the law of the Most High take its course.
> (19:13-15, 17 NRSV)

Other Literary Forms. Besides the two base forms, truth statement and instruction, several other forms of literary expression liven Ben Sira's teaching. He includes two prayers, a rare feature in earlier wisdom (cf. Prov 30:7-9 for a profound invocation of help, presumably from above).[39] In 22:27–23:6, Ben Sira asks for effective control over his speech and thoughts, as well as mastery of pride and illicit sensual desire. This moving expression of piety addresses God as "O Lord, Father and Master of my life" and as "O Lord, Father and God of my life" (23:1, 4 NRSV). Ben Sira welcomes divine chastisement as early warning against repeating one's sins, lest one also become subject to human mockers. The other prayer, 36:1-22, invokes the "God

---

38. The rhetorical device apostrophe occurs in the final acrostic (alphabetic poem) to capture students' interest and to give the impression of intimacy.
39. On prayer in wisdom literature, especially in Sirach, see James L. Crenshaw, "The Restraint of Reason, the Humility of Prayer," in Crenshaw, *Urgent Advice and Probing Questions*, 206-21. See also James L. Crenshaw, *Origins: Early Judaism and Christianity in Historical and Ecumenical Perspective*, Brown Judaic Studies, forthcoming.

of All," Yahweh, the sacred name of the deity in Jewish literature, and the "God of the ages." Here Ben Sira gives vent to frustration over God's apparent inactivity, praying for renewed signs and defeat of enemies, hastening the day of reckoning.[40] He longs for the return of all exiled Jews, and he asks for pity on Zion. Remembering ancient recitations of Yahweh's mighty deeds on Israel's behalf, together with prophetic promises yet unfulfilled, Ben Sira begs the Lord to confirm the truth of both in his own time.

Several hymns also appear in Sirach, most notably 42:15–43:33 and 51:1-12 (the Hebrew text of MS B after 51:12 has another hymn of sixteen verses modeled on Psalm 136).[41] In these hymns, Ben Sira extols the wonders of the created world in the same way the author of Job did. The awesome power of the Creator and a humble awareness of mystery, still unseen, establish the mood for these hymns. Ben Sira knows that human eyes merely touch the surface, but his exquisite use of poetic imagery suggests that even this limited knowledge is something marvelous. He mentions the way pools put on ice like a breastplate, and he describes frost as pointed thorns. The rapid descent of snow reminds him of birds in the sky. Such poetic flourish does not detract from the impression of order and precision, the existence of complementary pairs, and the purposive attention to design and function where the heavenly bodies are concerned.[42]

Two didactic compositions resemble the hymns, but their mood places more distance between the singer and the Creator (16:24–17:14; 39:12-35). One has the feeling that these learned meditations grew out of rational reflection and studious instruction. Exploring the place of human beings in the universe, they affirm a legitimate role for everything, even those things that seem out of place in a harmonious universe. These didactic compositions function as a defense of divine justice, like the debate form,[43] which Ben Sira uses freely.

Also known from Egyptian wisdom literature, this device to stave off dissent first appears within the Bible in Ecclesiastes: "Do not say, 'Who can have power over me?'/ for the Lord will surely punish you./ Do not say, 'I sinned, yet what has happened to me?'/ for the Lord is slow to anger. . . . Do not say, 'His mercy is great,/ he will forgive the multitude of my sins,'/ for both mercy and wrath are with him,/ and his anger will rest on sinners" (Eccl 5:3-4, 6 NRSV). This debate form warns against presuming too much about God's patience, mercy, and sovereignty. It challenges those who think they can sin with impunity: "Do not say, 'I am hidden from the Lord,/ and who from on high has me in mind?/ Among so many people I am unknown,/ for what am I in a boundless creation?'" (16:17 NRSV).

In two places Ben Sira sings wisdom's praise (1:1-10; 24:1-23), moving beyond Job 28, where wisdom remains altogether inaccessible to human beings, and Prov 8:1-36, where she is present alongside Yahweh as the first act of creation. Ben Sira affirms this earlier tradition, attesting to her innate inaccessibility and declaring her the initial creative act. At the same time, he insists that the Lord dispensed wisdom on all God's works and on those who love God (1:1-10). According to Sirach 24, wisdom searched the whole world for a suitable resting place until the Creator chose Israel as her place of residence. In Zion she blossomed and produced fruit, inviting those who desired her to eat their fill. Ben Sira identifies wisdom with the Mosaic law, making it accessible to everyone in Israel. The universal motif of wisdom's covering the earth like mist gives way to a particularistic tradition. The erotic relationship between wisdom and students,

---

40. Several scholars have addressed the issue of eschatology and messianism in Sirach, usually reaching a minimalist position that only hints of each appear. See James D. Martin, "Ben Sira's Hymn to the Fathers: A Messianic Perspective," in *Crises and Perspectives: Studies in Ancient Near Eastern Polytheism, Biblical Theology, Palestinian Archaeology and Intertestamental Literature: Papers Read at the Joint British-Dutch Old Testament Conference Held at Cambridge, U.K., 1985,* Oudtestamentische Studien, deel 24, ed. A. S. Van der Woude (Leiden: E. J. Brill, 1986) 107-23; Stanley Frost, "Who Were the Heroes? An Exercise in Bitestamentary Exegesis, with Christological Implications," in *The Glory of Christ in the New Testament,* eds. L. D. Hurst and N. T. Wright (Oxford: Clarendon, 1987) 65-172; Burton L. Mack, "Wisdom Makes a Difference: Alternatives to 'Messianic' Configuration," in *Judaisms and Their Messiahs at the Turn of the Christian Era,* eds. Jacob Neusner, William Scott Green, and Ernest S. Frerichs (Cambridge: Cambridge University Press, 1987) 15-48; Robert Hayward, "The New Jerusalem in the Wisdom of Jesus Ben Sira," *ScanJT* 6 (1992) 123-38. A. Caquot, "Ben Sira et le Messianisme, *Sem* 16 (1966) 43-68, finds no evidence for messianism in Sirach. Hayward contrasts the lackluster Greek translation of Sirach 36 with the vibrant Hebrew, arguing that the grandson thought too much emphasis had been put on Zion in the past, an era that was "dead and gone" (Hayward, "The New Jerusalem in the Wisdom of Jesus Ben Sira," 137).

41. C. Deutsch, "The Sirach 51 Acrostic: Confession and Exhortation," *ZAW* 94 (1982) 400-409, studies "the passage as the statement of the sage, the focus of the acrostic." Deutsch emphasizes the affective language and lessons from Ben Sira's own life. Pamela F. Foulkes, "'To Expound Discipline': The Portrait of the Scribe in Ben Sira," *Pacifica* 7 (1994) 75-84, thinks of Ben Sira as a reflective scholar fit for judicial or ambassadorial posts.

42. Marböck calls it "very abstract, indeed almost philosophical." See Marböck, *Weisheit im Wandel,* 137.

43. On the debate form, see James L. Crenshaw, "The Problem of Theodicy in Sirach: On Human Bondage," *JBL* 94 (1975) 47-64. See also Crenshaw, *Urgent Advice and Probing Questions,* 155-74.

present in Proverbs 8–9, achieves new expression in an acrostic poem that concludes Sirach (51:13-20, 30), an earlier form of which was discovered in cave 11 at Qumran.[44]

Ben Sira also heaps praise on a select group of ancestral heroes (Sir 44:1–50:24).[45] He walks through the gallery of biblical characters, and in doing so prepares the way for a eulogy on the high priest of his day, Simeon. These descriptions resemble Greek encomia in some respects,[46] but suitable antecedents from biblical literature exist.[47] The choice of heroes, highly selective, betrays a decided preference for priestly figures[48] and for others who contributed to Israel's cult in some material way. One looks in vain for a woman in the list, despite the presence of remarkable females in the sacred traditions (e.g., Deborah, Huldah, Hannah, Samson's mother, Ruth). Pride of position goes to Aaron and Phinehas, with Moses, David, Solomon, Hezekiah, Josiah, Zerubbabel, and Joshua being invoked for their part in reforming and strengthening the cult of the temple. Prophets who make the list do so on the basis of miraculous acts rather than oracular proclamations. The sequence of heroes follows the canonical divisions, first those characters whose lives are recorded in the Pentateuch; then prophets, including Job; and finally Nehemiah, from the writings. An afterthought leads Ben Sira to return to the beginning, Enoch, and work backward to Adam.

BEN SIRA'S USE OF BIBLICAL TRADITIONS

Although Ben Sira patterns his teaching after Israel's wisdom literature, the extensive praise of ancestral heroes moves outside that body of texts to embrace the whole Hebrew canon.[49] This appeal to special revelation and its confessional attestations marks a radical departure from the books of Proverbs, Job, and Ecclesiastes. Sacred history thus becomes subject matter for consideration, and that shift compromises the fundamental character of wisdom as accessible to all people, regardless of nationality or geographical location.

To be sure, the author of Proverbs 1–9 introduces the notion of divine legislation (תורה *tôrâ*) and discipline (מוסר *mûsār*), together with the concept of reprehensible conduct (תועבה *tôʿēbâ*), all of which come perilously close to providing a link with Deuteronomy. Their non-specific use with reference to the will of God and its punitive action against despicable behavior complicates matters and prevents firm resolution of the question of whether the author had Deuteronomy in mind when using these ideas. With Ben Sira, the issue is no longer ambiguous.

The integration of sacred history and wisdom instruction pervades the entire book of Sirach, not just 44:1–50:24. Allusions to Israel's history as recorded in the canon of his day function as examples of praiseworthy conduct and as warnings against deeds that provoke divine anger. No longer content to study nature and human nature in search of instructive analogies, Ben Sira draws freely on the special relationship between an elect people and its deity. He actually quotes King David's response to divine anger occasioned by obedience to a command to number the

---

44. James A. Sanders, *The Dead Sea Psalms Scroll* (Ithaca, N.Y.: Cornell University Press, 1967); James A. Sanders, *The Psalms Scroll of Qumran Cave 11 (11 Q Psa)*, DJD 4 (Oxford: Clarendon, 1965). Sanders interprets the psalm as highly erotic, but see T. Muraoka, "Sir 51:13-30. An Erotic Hymn to Wisdom?" *JSJ* 10 (1979) 166-78.

45. The panegyric on ancestral worthies has generated considerable discussion, the most thorough recent studies being those of Burton L. Mack, *Wisdom and the Hebrew Epic: Ben Sira's Hymn in Praise of the Fathers*, Chicago Studies in the History of Judaism (Chicago: University of Chicago Press, 1985); Thomas R. Lee, *Studies in the Form of Sirach 44–50*, SBLDS 75 (Atlanta: Scholars Press, 1986). Other important essays include Maurice Gilbert, "L'eloge de la Sagesse [Siracide 24]," *Revue Théologique* 5 (1974) 326-48; Edmond Jacob, "L'Histoire d'Israel vue par Ben Sira," in *Mélanges bibliques rédigés en l'honneur de André Robert* (Paris: Bloud and Gay, 1958) 288-94.

46. Lee understands the section lauding Israel's heroes as an encomium (a Greek device praising a notable figure; it consisted of a prooemium, a genealogy, a narration of the person's accomplishments, and an epilogue with its concluding exhortation). The object of praise, in this view, is Simeon, not Israel's ancestors. See Lee, *Studies in the Form of Sirach 44–50*, 81. The record of Simeon's predecessors is proof from example. Mack thinks in terms of a hymn with decidedly encomiastic features (*Wisdom and the Hebrew Epic*). Chris A. Rollston, "The Non-Encomiastic Features of Ben Sira 44–0" (M.A. thesis, Emmanuel School of Religion, Johnson City, Tennessee, 1992), challenges their interpretation.

47. The unknown authors of the book of Wisdom and 1 Maccabees imitate Ben Sira's recitation of ancient history with emphasis on human accomplishments. Biblical antecedents of Ben Sira glorify God even when referring to similar history (cf. Psalms 68; 77–78).

48. J. G. Snaith, "Ben Sira's Supposed Love of Liturgy," *VT* 25 (1975) 167-74, plays down the author's priestly interests in favor of prophetic social justice, but John F. A. Sawyer, "Was Jeshua Ben Sira a Priest?" *Proceedings of the Eighth World Congress of Jewish Studies*, Div. A. (Jerusalem: World Union of Jewish Studies, 1982) 65-71, and Saul M. Olyan, "Ben Sira's Relationship to the Priesthood," *HTR* 80 (1987) 261-86, argue persuasively for identifying Ben Sira as a priest/sage. H. Stadelmann, *Ben Sira als Schriftgelehrter*, WUNT 6 (Tübingen: Mohr-Siebeck, 1980), develops the thesis that Ben Sira was a priestly, learned scribe.

49. J. G. Snaith, "Quotations in Ecclesiasticus," *TThS* 18 (1967) 1-12, finds very little citation of Scripture in Sirach. Other interpreters think Ben Sira made use of an anthological style, using brief phrases with telling effect. On the larger problem of citations, see *It Is Written: Scripture Citing Scripture. Essays in Honour of Barnabas Lindars, SSF*, eds. D. A. Carson and H. G. M. Williamson (Cambridge: Cambridge University Press, 1986).

people, a perplexing story of a vacillating deity that prompted the chronicler to introduce Satan as the instigator of David's action. According to 2 Sam 24:14, David opted to take his chances with an angry Yahweh in preference to three years of famine or three months of fleeing from enemies. Ben Sira observes: "Let us fall into the hands of the Lord,/ but not into the hands of mortals;/ for equal to his majesty is his mercy,/ and equal to his name are his works" (2:18 NRSV).

From the book of Genesis, Ben Sira alludes to Adam (Sir 33:10; 40:1), to Eve (Sir 25:24),[50] to Lot (Sir 16:8), to Sodom and Gomorrah (Sir 39:23), to the fallen angels (Sir 16:7), to the flood (Sir 40:10), to the covenant with Noah (Sir 17:12), to the image of God (Sir 17:3), to the creation account (Sir 39:16, 21), and to Jacob's descendants (Sir 23:12). Given the dearth of biblical references to Adam and Eve outside Genesis, Ben Sira's clear mention of Adam in 40:1—only the Greek text has the proper name in 33:10—and his placing on Eve the sole responsibility for the origin of sin show that he was influenced by a growing trend to speculate about such biblical persons as Adam, Eve, and Enoch.

Allusions to incidents associated with the signal event of Israelite history, the exodus, also occur. Ben Sira mentions the six hundred thousand Israelites who perished in the wilderness because of their idolatrous conduct (Sir 16:9-10), as well as the tree that turned bitter water sweet (Sir 38:5). He refers to Yahweh as the "Holy One" (Sir 4:14) and mentions the Sinaitic legislation transmitted through Moses to the people (Sir 24:23).

Sometimes Ben Sira alludes to a cluster of ideas from specific biblical themes. In 24:1-12, he refers to the Yahwistic notion of creation by means of a heavenly mist; to the pillar of cloud that symbolized Yahweh's guiding presence with the Israelites under Moses' leadership; to the tabernacle, also a sign of Yahweh's coming to meet the chosen spokesman for the wandering people; to sacred names—Israel/Jacob, Jerusalem—and to an elect people. Similarly, 36:1-17 mentions divine signs and wonders, echoing those associated with the exodus from Egypt and its immediate aftermath; the regular cultic recitation of Yahweh's "mighty deeds" (צדקות *ṣĕdāqôt*); the tribes of Jacob and their inheritance, the land promised to Abraham; the people on whom the divine name Yahweh had been pronounced; Israel, the firstborn of God; Zion, the city of God's sanctuary; unfulfilled prophecies uttered in Yahweh's name; and Aaron's priestly blessing.

Such allusions to the major sacral traditions, creation and exodus, also appear within didactic psalms, becoming at times somewhat tedious. Ben Sira stops short of giving a detailed account of these historical events connected with the wilderness, thus avoiding the tedium of learned psalmography (cf. Psalms 78; 105; 106; 136). The surprising aspect of his selection from Israel's sacred story is what he does not choose. Given the illustrative force of Joseph's refusal to succumb to seduction, the powerful negative potential of Saul, the perennial temptation to idolatry afforded by the story about Balaam, and so forth, one marvels at Ben Sira's reticence. When warning against the dangers of uncontrolled passion, he does not appeal to the examples of David and Bathsheba or Amnon and Tamar (cf. 6:2-4). To combat the strong lure of Hellenism, especially for young men, Ben Sira does not use the episode about Balaam or even the incident involving Elijah and the prophets of Baal.[51]

Ben Sira may very well have alluded to far more biblical texts than suggested thus far, inasmuch as his language frequently echoes ideas from them. For example, the designation of the Lord as compassionate and merciful (2:11)[52] undoubtedly reflects an abbreviated version of

---

50. Jack Levison, "Is Eve to Blame? A Contextual Analysis of Sirach 25:24," *CBQ* 47 (1985) 617-23, makes an interesting case for understanding the reference in this verse (Sir 25:24) as being directed to wicked wives, no thanks to whom husbands die. Levison rightly observes that elsewhere Ben Sira implies that death belongs to the natural order of things. An allusion to Eve in the context of discussing evil wives seems entirely natural, however, and Levison must assume remarkable gaps in Ben Sira's expression, which are supplied by brackets in Levison's translation: "From the [evil] wife is the beginning of sin, / and because of her we [husbands] all die." Moreover, the evidence from the use of γυνή *gynē* (ἀπὸ γυναικός *apò gynaikos*) is inconclusive, for the word refers to "wife" and to "woman" generally. Levison's claim that women are depraved is then canceled by a recognition that good wives benefit husbands. Finally, the text from Cave 4 at Qumran entitled "The Wiles of the Wicked Woman," to which Levison alludes, deals with a mythic reality, personified evil, just as Sir 25:24, on the traditional reading, refers to the primal myth. See R. Moore, "Personification of the Seduction of Evil: 'The Wiles of the Wicked Woman,'" *RevQ* 10 (1979–81) 505-19. Levison's attempt to reorient scholarly thinking about Sir 25:24 resembles Norbert Lohfink's reading of Eccl 7:23-29: "War Kohelet ein Frauenfeind?" in *La Sagesse de l'Ancien Testament,* ed. Maurice Gilbert (Leuven: University Press, 1979) 259-87.

51. Mary Douglas, *In the Wilderness: The Doctrine of Defilement in the Book of Numbers* (Sheffield: Academic Press Limited, 1995), interprets the Balaam story as satire directed at the harsh policies of Ezra and Nehemiah. A recently found text from Deir 'Alla attests the popularity of the prophetic legend in relatively late times.

52. See James L. Crenshaw, "Who Knows What YHWH Will Do? The Character of God in the Book of Joel," in *Fortunate the Eyes That See: Essays in Honor of David Noel Freedman in Celebration of His Seventieth Birthday,* eds. Astrid B. Beck et al. (Grand Rapids: Eerdmans, 1995) 185-96.

Exod 34:6-7, the ancient proclamation to Moses of the divine attributes. This oft-cited creed—only the positive attributes—left an indelible print on subsequent characterizations of Yahweh. Ben Sira often offers advice that has its point of reference in ancient teachings, such as the command to honor one's parents (Sir 3:3), although he provides a different rationale for such filial allegiance than one finds in the Decalogue.

Comparison with a wisdom text later than Ben Sira is instructive, for the author of the book of Wisdom also weaves sacred story into his instructions, always without specific names of the persons being recalled (Wis 10:1–19:22). He traces the long account of Israel in Egypt and the escape into the wilderness without ever naming anyone. The clear implication is that the audience knew the story intimately and filled in the missing names. This author adheres to the story line from beginning to end. The resulting treatment approaches the type of interpretation known as midrash, a running commentary on a biblical text. Furthermore, this midrash-like interpretation heightens the psychological features of a divine drama between Israel's God and the Egyptians. Their offense, idolatry, provides focus for the entire analysis.

The characters behind the story in Wis 10:1–19:22 include Adam, Cain, Abel, Noah, Abraham, Isaac, Lot, Lot's wife, Jacob, Esau, Joseph, and Moses. The full narrative explores the familiar events in considerable detail, leaving little to the imagination. Nevertheless, the incidents lead up to and set the stage for a sharp attack on idolatry, including three explanations for its appeal to the popular imagination (the aesthetic, a parent's grief over a son, a desire to honor a distant emperor).

With a single exception, Ben Sira withholds the names of persons to whom he refers in 1:1–43:33. That one specific reference is Lot (Sir 16:8). Ben Sira does mention Jacob, but the reference seems always to be national, hence synonymous with Israel. In the section praising ancestral heroes (Sir 44:1–50:24), Ben Sira specifically names the individuals under discussion. The difference probably relates to the literary form being employed; one mentions the name of the deceased in a "eulogy."

The practice of rehearsing ancient history by means of allusions raises the question, "Who was the intended audience?" In the light of the expense of owning scrolls of the entire Bible, one may reasonably conclude that both Ben Sira and the author of the book of Wisdom directed their teachings to a small group of prospective scribes. These young men would have studied the Scriptures just as Ben Sira is said to have done. Still, one cannot rule out the possibility that communal worship, especially singing the didactic psalms, and parental teaching may have familiarized the people with certain biblical traditions, particularly the story of the beginnings.

In some ways, Sirach resembles the book of Tobit, Baruch, the *Testament of the Twelve Patriarchs,* and *Pirqe 'Abot,* devotional literature from the wider Jewish environment. The author of Tobit emphasizes acts of piety as an expression of loyalty to the Mosaic law and regularly lifts up a voice in prayer. In Tob 12:6-10 the angel Raphael assumes the venerable role of wisdom teacher, insisting that "a little with righteousness is better than wealth with wrongdoing" (Tob 12:8 NRSV) and promising reward for virtuous living. Tobit both prays for and experiences divine activity; like Job, his misfortune was eventually reversed. The poem on wisdom in Bar 3:9–4:4 does not integrate mythic themes concerning wisdom's function at creation with the notion that wisdom finds concrete expression in the law of Moses. Instead, it proceeds in the manner of Job 28, stressing the inaccessibility of wisdom to all but God, who passed it on to Israel in the Torah.[53] The *Testament of the Twelve Patriarchs* transcends the ritual features of worship in favor of ethical dimensions to an unprecedented degree; Ben Sira endeavors to combine the two.[54] Like *Pirqe 'Abot,* Ben Sira offers ethical advice to students steeped in torah piety.

---

53. Lewis J. Prockter, "Torah as a Fence Against Apocalyptic Speculation: Ben Sira 3:17-24," *Proceedings of the Tenth World Congress of Jewish Studies,* Div. A (Jerusalem: World Union of Jewish Studies, 1990) 245-52. Prockter writes: "To seek in heaven what is already on earth, namely Torah given once and for all to Moses, is not only foolish but perilous. To seek what is 'beyond you' is to display pride, and by so doing to wilfully cut yourself off from God, who reveals his will to the humble here below, not to those trying to ascend to the heavenly *hekhalot* (3:17-20)" (Prockter, "Torah as a Fence Against Apocalyptic Speculation," 251). On the limitations to knowledge generally, see James L. Crenshaw, "Wisdom and the Sage: On Knowing and Not Knowing," *Proceedings of the Eleventh World Congress of Jewish Studies,* Div. A (Jerusalem: World Union of Jewish Studies, 1994) 137-44.

54. J. G. Snaith, "Ben Sira's Supposed Love of Liturgy," *VT* 25 (1975), emphasizes the teachings about social justice in Sirach. Ben Sira maintains a healthy balance between observing the niceties of cultic ritual and deeds of kindness, and he provides theological underpinnings for both in divine commands and the nature of Yahweh as merciful. Otto Kaiser, "Die Begrundung der Sittlichkeit im Buche Jesus Sirach," *ZTK* 55 (1958) 51-63, examines the basis for ethical actions in Sirach.

BEN SIRA AND HELLENISM

Occasional similarities between Sirach and Greek authors raise the issue of Ben Sira's dependence on popular Hellenistic philosophers.[55] The comparison of death to falling leaves in 14:18 (and in the *Iliad* vi.146-149) belongs to folk wisdom. The image would naturally occur to anyone who gave much thought to the process of growth and decay in nature and among humans. Ben Sira proclaims at one point: "He is the All." This expression was common in Stoic philosophy, but Ben Sira could easily have arrived at such an understanding of God on the basis of his reading of Isa 45:5-7 and Deut 32:39. Unlike Stoic thinkers, Ben Sira did not equate God with the created universe. The Stoic ideal of world citizenship did not drive out Ben Sira's conviction that God had chosen Israel as a special heritage.[56]

Ben Sira's affirmation of physicians shows that he did not reject Greek ideas without careful consideration (Sir 38:1-15). He combines traditional Jewish belief about sin and disease with Hellenistic teachings, although the two seem mutually contradictory. In the end, piety prevailed, and because both Greeks and Jews prayed for healing, he could argue for combining the physician's treatment with fervent prayer. Greek customs and ideas filled the air Ben Sira breathed, expressing themselves in many ways: a eulogy of ancestors, the notion of a rational universe with perfectly balanced pairs, human freedom and divine providence, dining customs, pride of authorship, and much more.

The last two deserve further comment. Ben Sira refers to the Hellenistic practice of selecting a person to preside over a banquet, and he gives advice on fulfilling that honor in an acceptable manner (Sir 32:1-13). He even mentions the reward for good service, the customary wreath awarded for leadership. His advice on table etiquette in 31:12-24 presupposes dinners like Greek banquets followed by symposia. Such dinners included contests at drinking wine, musical entertainment, speeches demonstrating wit and wisdom, seating of guests according to rank, and a blessing to the gods at the end of the dinner.

Greek pride of authorship influenced Ben Sira so strongly that he departed from the usual anonymity or pseudonymity of those who composed the books of Proverbs, Job, and Ecclesiastes. He saw no particular virtue in attributing his teachings to King Solomon; given the nature of the book, he could not have done so, for the praise of ancestral heroes required an author from a much later time than the Solomonic era. The author of the book of Wisdom avoided a historical resume that would place him in the second or first centuries.

Egyptian influence can probably be detected in the comparison of professions in 38:24–39:11, although this text differs fundamentally from the *Satire of the Trades*. Ben Sira offers no hint of satire in describing the work of the farmer, the artisan, the smith, and the potter. Instead, he merely points out that their work consumes both time and energy, leaving no opportunity for study. In no way does he disparage their contribution to society, which he thinks depends on what they do for survival. The Egyptian *Instruction for Duauf*, or the *Satire of the Trades*, ridicules considerably more occupations than the four Ben Sira mentions. Both Ben Sira and the Egyptian author contrast the scribe's profession with all other kinds of work; their intent was to attract students to intellectual pursuits.

The ethic of caution based on shame and regard for one's reputation as expressed in Sirach closely resembles that in Papyrus Insinger; similarities also exist between this late Egyptian

---

55. T. Middendorp, *Die Stellung Jesus ben Siras zwischen Judentum und Hellenismus*, overstresses Ben Sira's dependence on Hellenistic thinkers. The fault lies in his method, for similarities in phrases and ideas between Sirach and various Greek philosophers indicate literary dependence only when (1) the language and concepts are otherwise unique to Hellenism and (2) similarities in biblical literature are lacking. Moreover, two other factors enter the picture: Only a limited sample of Jewish literature from the ancient world has survived, and intelligent people can arrive at similar ideas independently. Even the expression "He is the all" does not necessarily derive from Stoic thinkers, for biblical precedent exists (Deut 32:39; Isa 45:5-7). These caveats notwithstanding, Ben Sira does show Hellenistic influence in the way he understands the universe as an orderly arrangement of complementary pairs. His almost mathematical tone in describing the universe, his endorsement of physicians, his description of banquets and symposia, and his pride of authorship place him squarely within the Hellenistic world. On the broader issue, see Jonathan Goldstein, "Jewish Acceptance and Rejection of Hellenism," in *Jewish and Christian Self-Definition*, eds. E. P. Sanders et al. (Philadelphia: Fortress, 1981) 2:64-87.

56. Stoic influence on Ben Sira has also been exaggerated; for a sober assessment, see David Winston, "Theodicy in Ben Sira and Stoic Philosophy," in *Of Scholars, Savants, and Their Texts*, ed. Ruth Link-Salinger (New York: Peter Lang, 1989) 239-49. An earlier study, Raymond Paultrel, "Ben Sira et le Stoicisme," *RSR* 51 (1963) 535-49, challenges Smend's claim that Ben Sira declares war against Hellenism. Paultrel also remarks on the omissions within such a long work as Sirach, noting Ben Sira's silence about angels, the Messiah, and the prohibition against images (Paultrel, "Ben Sira et le Stoicisme," 547).

instruction and Ecclesiastes.[57] If Ben Sira relies on this work, he varies it in significant ways (cf. Sir 6:13; 13:1–42:2; 32:23; 41:11-13). His allusion to the bee to illustrate the importance of tiny things hardly confirms dependence on Papyrus Insinger, for such an analogy seems like a natural conclusion to an observant reader.

Links with Aramaean wisdom through the *Sayings of Ahiqar*, although possible, may derive from folk tradition: the futility of opposing a turbulent stream (*Ahiqar* 3.83 and Sir 4:26) and the revelation of character through the clothes one wears (*Ahiqar* 2.39 and Sir 19:29-30).[58] Anyone could easily draw these conclusions without having heard or read either work.

This meager evidence of Greek influence on Ben Sira[59] indicates that he drew far more extensively from biblical literature than from extra-biblical, even when trying to persuade Jews that their legacy was just as universal as Greek philosophy. That was the point of identifying the Mosaic law with cosmic wisdom. Ben Sira's teachings demonstrate an awareness of the seductive power of Hellenism, especially to young people, and he wages battle for the next generation of Jews. This struggle introduces new types of discourse: psychological and philosophical arguments in the service of theodicy, discussion of free will and determinism, reflection about two ways (Sir 2:12). In essence, he sought to provide rational backing for his ancestral heritage.[60] The assertion that wisdom comes from the Lord constitutes a declaration of war against Hellenism, where it was a product of human inquiry. Ben Sira dismisses all astrological speculation—and apocalyptic—as sheer arrogance or pride. "Be content with the knowledge God has bestowed on you" sums up his attitude toward striving to unlock hidden mysteries.[61]

Did Ben Sira venture forth into the Hellenistic world as an ambassador like John, the father of Eupolemus, who was sent to Rome to negotiate a treaty (cf. 2 Macc 4:11), or Philo, who represented the Jews of Alexandria before Caligula? Did Ben Sira occupy a position as judge or counselor in the *gerousia*? Did he work as a scribe in the Temple? Perhaps one could say more about his relationship with Hellenism if these questions could be answered.

RELIGIOUS TEACHINGS IN SIRACH

The two primary themes in the book, fear of the Lord[62] and wisdom,[63] are interwoven from first to last, making it difficult to determine the dominant one. The author of Proverbs 1–9 subjugated piety to knowledge, viewing the fear of the Lord as the main ingredient and first principle of learning. Wisdom thus consisted of something above and beyond obedience to God, although religion comprised its very core. For Ben Sira, fear of the Lord has no rival, not even the acquisition of wisdom: "How great is the one who finds wisdom!/ But none is superior to the one who fears the Lord./ Fear of the Lord surpasses everything;/ to whom can we compare the one who has it?" (25:10-11 NRSV). Like the word translated "wisdom" (חכם *ḥākam*), the expression "fear of the Lord" (יראי יהוה *yir'ê yhwh*) appears often in Sirach (over fifty times).

Such elevation of religion prompts Ben Sira to conclude that wisdom's garland and root exist in the fear of the Lord, making religious achievement the sole justification for pride (Sir 10:22).

---

57. Sanders, "Ben Sira's Ethics of Caution"; *Ben Sira and Demotic Wisdom*, SBLMS 28 (Chico, Calif.: Scholars Press, 1983). On the influence of "Papyrus Insinger" on Qoheleth, see Crenshaw, *Ecclesiastes*; and for a modern translation of the Egyptian text, see Lichtheim, *Ancient Egyptian Literature*, 3:184-217.

58. These references come from Edmond Jacob, "Wisdom and Religion in Sirach," in *Israelite Wisdom: Theological and Literary Essays in Honor of Samuel Terrien*, eds. John G. Gammie et al. (Missoula: Scholars Press, 1978) 250. They do not appear in Lindenberger, *The Aramaic Proverbs of Ahiqar*, but the popular sayings attributed to Ahiqar have survived in various translations, chiefly Syriac, Armenian, Arabic, and Slavonic. See Lindenberger, *The Aramaic Proverbs of Ahiqar*, 354. The saying about stopping a river occurs frequently in ancient literature.

59. Hengel, *Judaism and Hellenism*, 1:115-254, examines the extent of Hellenistic influence on Jewish literature of the last three centuries before the emergence of the church.

60. Ryan thinks of Ben Sira's "holistic response to the divisions within Israel" as a "comprehensive act of identification." See Michael D. Ryan, "The Act of Religious Identification in Ben Sirach and Paul," *The Drew Gateway* 54 (1983) 4-16.

61. Ben Sira acknowledges that the intellect can only touch the surface of divine mystery; at the same time, he wishes to assert that God has revealed to Israel all that is necessary for living in obedience to Yahweh. Maintaining a balance so as to discourage idle speculation, whatever its nature, was no easy matter. This struggle to appreciate the revelation of Torah without discrediting a sense of the unknown and unknowable has persisted in Judaism. Michael Fishbane, *The Garments of Torah: Essays in Biblical Hermeneutics* (Bloomington: Indiana University Press, 1989), treats this problem with his usual freshness and passion.

62. Joseph Haspecker, *Gottesfurcht bei Jesus Sirach: Ihre religiöse Struktur und ihre literarische und doctainäre Bedeutung*, AnBib 30 (Rome: Pontifical Biblical Institute, 1967), argues forcefully that the fear of God, not wisdom, occupies the prominent position in Sirach.

63. Von Rad, *Wisdom in Israel*, 242, insists that wisdom subordinates everything else to it. The summary statement in 50:27 that Ben Sira poured forth wisdom from his heart does not settle the issue, for 50:29 balances knowledge with action. For Ben Sira, wisdom expressed itself in religious devotion ("fear of the Lord").

Human wisdom expresses itself in deeds of kindness, true obedience to the law of Moses. Divine wisdom manifests itself in the Torah. Whereas the later wisdom has assumed the form of legal statute and passionate exhortation, men and women have no excuse for choosing folly. It has been said that wisdom manifests itself subjectively as fear of the Lord and objectively as the law of Moses.[64]

Ben Sira urges submission to the yoke of divine discipline (מוסר *mûsār*), noting that it withholds itself like its name. Acknowledging the difficulty encountered by most students when they first endeavor to become wise, he describes wisdom as a hard taskmaster until people have demonstrated their worth. In time, however, she shows herself as the ardent lover, making them consider her earlier afflictions as nothing. This erotic language for intellectual curiosity and obedience to the Lord links up with the passionate discourse about love for God in the book of Deuteronomy.

Another theme pervading Sirach concerns God's justice and mercy. Ben Sira subscribes to the traditional belief in God's justice, but he knows that skepticism has imprinted itself indelibly on the minds of his audience. He uses the standard arguments—that God waits patiently, giving sinners an opportunity to repent; that things can change in a moment; that the hour of death will settle the score; that suffering serves as a test of character or as discipline; that human knowledge is partial; that praise is the proper response—and seeks to improve on them from Greek arguments about the design of the universe and punishment by mental and psychological anxiety.[65] He refuses to endorse an answer that seems to have been emerging slowly in the Jewish community: the conviction that righteous individuals will receive eternal life (17:27-28).[66] The Greek and Syriac texts introduce this belief at crucial junctures (Sir 7:17*b*; 48:11*b*; Greek II, Sir 2:9*c*; 16:22*c*; 19:19; Syriac, Sir 1:12*b*, 20; 3:1*b*). In this respect, Ben Sira resembles later Sadducees rather than Pharisees, who believed in life after death. That conservative tendency on the part of Ben Sira explains why he places so much emphasis on preserving honor or reputation, the one thing that survives after a person dies (Sir 41:11-13).

The origin of sin in a perfect universe placed a special burden on defenders of divine justice, particularly when it was attributed to the Creator. The serpent's presence in the garden indirectly indicted the Lord. Later biblical texts compromise divine justice further, insisting that God overrides human freedom, forcing pharaohs and others to persist in obstinacy. Ben Sira stoutly resisted such ideas, for he believed that everyone acts with absolute freedom (Sir 15:11-20). Nevertheless, he realized that irresistible forces put extraordinary pressure on free will (Sir 33:11-13). That ambiguity characterizes much biblical thinking about sin, but Ben Sira brings the issue of free will into the arena of public discussion.

Ben Sira's frequent attribution of mercy to the deity stands out when one observes the rarity of this idea in earlier wisdom literature. If an individual can rely on reward for virtuous conduct, the presupposition of much earlier wisdom, then divine mercy really does not fit into the picture. That understanding probably explains why sages did not characterize God as merciful. The shift takes place in Sirach, perhaps because earlier optimism had faded under the barrage of questions in the books of Job and Ecclesiastes.[67] Historical circumstances no longer favored such optimistic reading of the human situation, if they ever did, and a greater consciousness of human frailty produces existential anxiety. The extent of alarm over sinful dominance and the sorry future of the human race, both in this life and in the next, can be grasped by studying 2 Esdras. In the light of the weighty burden hanging over humanity, Ben Sira takes some comfort in divine compassion. The source of his confidence in God's mercy lies outside the wisdom literature, most likely in the ancient creedal confession in Exod 34:6-7.

---

64. "Subjectively, wisdom is the fear of God; objectively, the Mosaic lawbook (chapter 24)." ("Subjektiv ist die Weisheit daher die Gottesfurcht, objektiv ist sie das Gesetzbuch Moses, c 24.") This succinct statement appears in Smend, *Die Weisheit des Jesus Sirach erklärt*, xxiii.

65. See these works by Crenshaw: *Theodicy in the Old Testament*; "Theodicy," in *Anchor Bible Dictionary*, 6 vols. (New York: Doubleday, 1992) 6:444-47; and "The Problem of Theodicy in Sirach."

66. Vincenz Hamp, "Zukunft und Jenseits im Buche Sirach," *Alttestamentliche Studien, Festschrift Nötscher*, BBB 1 (Bonn: Hanstein, 1950) 86-97. Hamp finds no evidence that Ben Sira thought of retribution in the next life.

67. Crenshaw, "The Concept of God in Old Testament Wisdom," 1-18, explores the function of the idea of mercy in Sirach. Earlier optimism has given way to a sense of utter dependence on God's compassion; obedience has become more difficult and temptations harder to resist, perhaps because of declining influence from the family. Moreover, confidence in divine sovereignty, as well as faith that God works wonders on Israel's behalf, has begun to fade.

The God whom Ben Sira worshiped was the Creator, a concept at the very heart of wisdom thinking.[68] This majestic fashioner of an orderly universe saw whatever transpired and therefore ruled with exact justice. This sovereign demanded social justice (Sir 4:8-10) and the demonstration of one's true worship through ritual *and* charitable deeds, as well as pure thoughts. Ben Sira honors God as father, shepherd, and judge (Sir 18:13, 40; 23:1, 4; 51:10; 16:12-14).

It was noted earlier that Ben Sira did not believe in life beyond the grave, and in this regard he could be labeled a proto-Sadducee. Rejecting a meaningful existence after death alone hardly suffices to place him in the camp with later Sadducees, for he shared this skepticism with virtually all OT authors (Psalm 73; Isa 26:19; and Dan 12:2 being the only exceptions). Like the Sadducees of the first century CE, Ben Sira had strong interests, if not actual membership, in the priesthood. Moreover, he belonged to the elite ranks of upper-class citizens, and with this status came ultraconservatism aimed at maintaining the status quo. In addition, the temple cult represented the center of religious life for him, despite a commendable concern for doing acts of kindness when the occasion presented itself. In a sense, he understood the fundamentals of hasidic piety, but he never let the emotions seize control.

Later Pharisaism lacked this elitism and the strong attachment to the temple cult; it also appealed to the masses much more readily than did Sadduceeism. The destruction of the Temple in 70 CE brought the sacrificial cult to an end, as well as placing the priesthood in jeopardy. The Pharisees were able to continue their worship in synagogues, which offered a natural setting for prayer and religious training of the young. Ben Sira's influence may well have suffered along with the priests whose life centered in the Temple. The sectarians at Qumran also cared deeply about the temple cult, but Ben Sira did not share their strong attention to divine mystery. Nor did he subscribe to their apocalyptic fervor, midrashic exegesis, celibacy, and so much more.

BEN SIRA'S ATTITUDE TOWARD WOMEN

Much has been said about biblical patriarchalism,[69] a subjecting of women to their husbands' whims and placing them in the category of property to be disposed of at will. Daughters depended on their fathers to arrange marriages, husbands could negate solemn oaths taken by their wives, and women usually did not inherit property. Husbands could marry more than one wife, but women had no such freedom. Two standards operated in the area of sexual misconduct, and husbands punished wives for infidelity. In a sense, primary responsibility for sin's origin fell to a woman, and a prophet could even personify evil as a woman (Zech 5:5-11). In traditional lore, if not also in fact, a father could sacrifice his daughter if he so wished (Jephthah), but sons were equally vulnerable (Isaac).

We should not lose sight of the fact that the male authors of the biblical texts often portrayed women in a highly favorable light (cf. the depiction of Samson's mother over against that of Manoah,[70] Ruth, Deborah, and Susanna). They may have acknowledged the threat presented by the notorious foreign woman of Proverbs,[71] but they balanced this figure with wisdom, personified as a woman, and with the portrait of an ideal wife. To be sure, they also personified folly as a female and praised the wife in Prov 31:10-31, largely from the point of view of the husband whom she benefits. Numerous instances of mutual love between husband and wife in the Bible suggest that not all women considered themselves oppressed. Sages considered good wives gifts of God, and the unknown author of 1 Esdr 3:1–4:41 praises woman as the strongest thing on earth, exceeded only by truth and its Author.[72] The erotic passion expressed in Song of Songs testifies to a society that values the power stronger than death that draws men and women to each other.

---

68. See the recent analysis of creation theology in Perdue, *Wisdom and Creation*.
69. Phyllis Trible, *God and the Rhetoric of Sexuality* (Philadelphia: Fortress, 1978); Trible, "Depatriarchalizing in Biblical Interpretation," JAAR 41 (1973): 30-48.
70. James L. Crenshaw, *Samson* (Atlanta: John Knox, 1978) 65-98.
71. Carol A. Newsom, "Woman and the Discourse of Patriarchal Wisdom: A Study of Proverbs 1–9," in *Gender and Difference in Ancient Israel*, ed. Peggy L. Day (Minneapolis: Fortress, 1989) 142-60; Joseph Blenkinsopp, "The Social Context of the 'Outsider Woman' in Proverbs 1–9," *Bib* 72 (1991) 457-73.
72. James L. Crenshaw, "The Contest of Darius' Guards in 1 Esdras 3:1-5:3," in *Images of Man and God: The Old Testament Short Story in Literary Focus*, ed. Burke O. Long (Sheffield: Almond, 1981) 74-88, 119-20. See also Crenshaw, *Urgent Advice and Probing Questions*, 222-34.

Nevertheless, rare expressions of misogynism reveal the darker side of Israelite society, the result of centuries of double standards and jokes that have long since lost their humor. The author of Ecclesiastes expresses disdain over his, or someone else's, inability to discover a single trustworthy woman, although he does proceed to indict men almost equally, giving them only one one-thousandth of an advantage over women (Eccl 7:23-29). The heroine Judith stands above all the men in the little town of Bethulia as courageous, virtuous, and pious (Jdt 8:1-34; 15:8-10). In the book of Tobit, both Anna and Sarah appear above reproach (Tob 2:11-14; 3:7-15), suggesting that misogynistic views may have been less dispersed than has often been claimed. Examination of the Greco-Roman environment and of rabbinic Judaism reveals rampant misogynism, making the attitude of the Bible toward women look tame by comparison.[73]

Ben Sira inherits the mixed biblical tradition with respect to women, but he may be subject to Hellenistic views as well. In any event, he adds a new dimension, the discussion of daughters as a separate category.[74] Moreover, he places the adjective "wicked" (רעה *rā'â*) before the noun "daughters" (בנות *bānôt*). His obscene characterization of them as opening their quiver for every arrow (Sir 26:12) represents the ultimate in disrespect, and his rancorous opinion that the birth of a daughter is a loss (Sir 22:3) can hardly be justified by anxiety over what that entails—finding a husband for her, securing her virginity until marriage and her faithfulness afterward, worrying about her ability to bear children. Worse still, he places the entire blame for sin and death on the first woman (Sir 25:24) and apparently makes the ridiculous statement that a man's wickedness is better than a woman's goodness.[75]

The positive evaluation of woman also finds expression in Sirach, demonstrating Ben Sira's awareness that life without women would be drab, indeed. He recognizes the value of a faithful wife, and he sees the pathos of impossible "love" (using the image of a eunuch who beholds a desirable young woman and groans). Ben Sira scolds foolish old men who stray from their nests like birds, and he mentions restless sighing brought on by loneliness. His erotic appreciation for a woman's physical beauty seems boundless, issuing in effusive language based on the holy artifacts in the Temple ("Like the shining lamp on the holy lampstand,/ so is a beautiful face on a stately figure./ Like golden pillars on silver bases;/ so are shapely legs and steadfast feet" [Sir 26:17-18 NRSV]).

THE PRAISE OF ANCESTRAL HEROES

Such lavish praise of women did not induce Ben Sira to include a woman in his praise of loyal people, which comprises the last major section of the book, 44:1–50:24. If his primary criterion for selection relates to their contribution to and active participation in the temple cult, then silence with regard to women is mandated. That particular perspective certainly applies to Moses, Aaron, Phinehas, David, Solomon, Hezekiah, Josiah, Zerubbabel, Jeshua, Nehemiah, and Simeon. A secondary criterion, the desire to achieve canonical coverage, may explain the inclusion of Joshua and Caleb, along with the unnamed Judges, and the prophetic figures Nathan, Elijah, Elisha, Isaiah, Ezekiel, Job(!), and the unnamed twelve. That leaves two royal reprobates, Rehoboam and Jeroboam, and three priestly villains (Korah, Dathan, and Abiram) who merely stand out because of their infamy. Perhaps the addition of pre-Israelite worthies—Enoch, Noah, Abraham, Isaac, Jacob at first, then Enoch, Joseph, Shem, Seth, Enosh, and Adam later—represents a feeble effort to universalize the list.

This unusual journey through the portrait gallery of notables has recently been described as a complete reading of epic history that served as a mythic etiology for Judaism in the period of the

---

73. Charles E. Carlston, "Proverbs, Maxims, and the Historical Jesus," *JBL* 99 (1980) 87-105, esp. 95-97, gives some examples of maxims in the Greco-Roman world that denigrate women. Skehan and Di Lella, *The Wisdom of Ben Sira*, 91, also give some repugnant maxims about women culled from M. R. Lefkowitz and M. B. Fant, *Women's Life in Greece and Rome* (Baltimore: Johns Hopkins University Press, 1982). Di Lella wishes to judge Ben Sira in the light of attitudes prevalent in his own time, a valid procedure.

74. Karla G. Bohmbach, "With Her Hands on the Threshold: Daughters and Space in the Hebrew Bible" (Ph.D. diss., Duke University, 1996).

75. W. C. Trenchard, *Ben Sira's View of Women: A Literary Analysis*, BJS 38 (Chico, Calif.: Scholars Press, 1982), goes too far in condemning Ben Sira for hostility to women. The positive treatment of some women, like the negative attitude toward some others, requires proper nuancing. On this problem, see Maurice Gilbert, "Ben Sira et le femme," *RTL* 7 (1967) 426-42. Modern corrective to such thinking receives impetus from Brenner, ed., *A Feminist Companion to Wisdom Literature* (Sheffield: Sheffield Academic Press, 1995).

Second Temple.⁷⁶ The hypothesis runs like this: The hymn consists of a tripartite architectonic structure with transitional units: (1) the establishment of covenants with the conquest of the land as transition; (2) the history of the prophets and kings, with the story of the restoration as transition; and (3) the climax in Simeon the high priest. Themes unite the figures within each major unit, for example, the promise of a blessing joins together the individuals from Abraham to Jacob. The poem resembles an encomium with four parts: (1) a prooemium in 44:1-15, (2) a genealogy in 44:17–49:16, (3) the narration of the subject's achievements in 50:1-21, and (4) an epilogue in 50:22-24.

According to this theory, Sir 49:14-16 serves as a bridge linking past and present, juxtaposing Adam and Simeon in a manner that renders praise of the latter both appropriate and effective. This praise commemorates rather than entertains, although many rhetorical encomiastic devices occur, such as amplification by syncrisis (the juxtaposition of opposites for rhetorical effect), hyperbole, rhetorical questions, appeal to experience acquired through traveling, a reference to a person's character and reputation for good deeds, the claim that words cannot adequately describe an individual, and an assertion that a person's contribution to society lacks precedent. Thus far, the theory.

The hypothesis would be more persuasive if Ben Sira had used the four essential characteristics of encomia (prooemium, ancestry, deeds, epilogue) in proper proportion and in a manner so that they could easily be recognized.⁷⁷ Stated differently, if Ben Sira borrowed the form of an encomium, he changed it radically. Moreover, the chronicler provides a number of parallels to Ben Sira's use of biblical material, remaining silent about embarrassing aspects of David's character and dropping people from the record. Everything in the list could easily have occurred to a Jewish sage with no knowledge of Greek encomia. Most of the rhetorical features above occur in the Samson narrative, as well as in numerous other stories in the Hebrew Bible.

Why does Ben Sira overlook Ezra?⁷⁸ Was the omission intentional? At least five competing explanations for this anomaly deserve consideration. First, the socioeconomic circumstances had changed radically between the late fourth and early second centuries BCE in Jerusalem, making mixed marriage a matter of indifference."⁷⁹ This view assumes that Ezra's strict legislation concerning marriage with foreigners failed because it did not take into account long-standing practice among the Jews. Ben Sira, on this view, remained quiet about Ezra out of embarrassment over his strict policy and the ensuing suffering it generated.

A second explanation focuses on the venerable profession of scribes, to which Ben Sira belonged. In Ezra's day scribes had become narrowly and exclusively oriented toward the Mosaic law, but Ben Sira understands the scribal profession much more broadly. For him, an interest in the law went hand in hand with research in the tradition of the wise. To some degree, Ben Sira transforms the office of priest-scribe into that of teacher, whose authority rests ultimately on scholarship, insights, and communicative ability.⁸⁰

A third response to the silence about Ezra focuses on the state of the priestly office during the immediate period after Simeon's death. Although Simeon's son and successor, Onias III, was a pious leader, he lacked the qualities of bold leadership. Like Ezra, he was a political quietist. For this reason, Ben Sira did not want to laud Ezra as someone whom Onias could emulate. Instead,

---

76. Mack, *Wisdom and the Hebrew Epic*. R. A. F. MacKenzie, "Ben Sira as Historian," in *Trinification of the World: A Festschrift in Honor of F. E. Crowe*, eds. T. A. Dunne and J. M. Laport (Toronto: Regis College Press, 1978) 313-27. MacKenzie observes that Ben Sira does not mention the Babylonian exile in his account of Israel's heroes. Was there any compelling reason to do so? After all, he concentrates on the high points, illustrating them with the names of persons involved in those momentous events.

77. Rollston illustrates the difficulty of proving literary dependence when an author adapts material or exercises exceptional selectivity. The resulting product differs appreciably from the presumed source, casting doubt on the presumption itself. See Rollston, "The Non-Encomiastic Features of Ben Sira 44–50."

78. Peter Höffken, "Warum schwieg Jesus Sirach über Esra," *ZAW* 87 (1975) 184-201, argues that Ben Sira omitted Ezra from the list of ancestral worthies because of his championing of Levites. Ben Sira rejects the chronicler's plea for the levitical priesthood and returns to the earlier priestly emphasis on the Aaronide line. Höffken understands the choice of the priestly tradition as theological. Christopher Begg, "Ben Sirach's Non-Mention of Ezra," *BN* 42 (1988) 14-18, finds the key to Ben Sira's silence about Ezra in his absence from participation in building projects related to the Temple. Begg detects no anti-Levitical polemic in Sirach.

79. Changing socioeconomic circumstances may explain many emphases in Sirach, on which see Hengel, *Judaism and Hellenism*.

80. Ben Sira does not stand in the direct line of Ezra, whose responsibility for instructing the people in the law of their God was tantamount, and yet both men were teachers. Ben Sira links up much more closely with the unknown authors of Proverbs, but with decisive differences. He embraces the entire sacral tradition and integrates it into wisdom instruction.

Ben Sira skips over Ezra and commends Onias's father, hoping to stimulate a desire on the son's part to pattern his actions after his father and predecessor in the office of high priest.[81]

A fourth explanation for Ben Sira's omission of Ezra in the list of ancestral heroes takes its cue from a feature common to several individuals—active participation in constructing or repairing the Temple.[82] In this view, Ezra was omitted in favor of Nehemiah, whose vital role in repairing the wall of the city was essential to the successful operation of the cult.

A fifth attempt to explain Ben Sira's failure to mention Ezra focuses on the chronicler's championing of Levites, which did not accord with the elevation of the Aaronide priestly lineage in Ben Sira. For this reason, he did not wish to mention a scribe who championed the cause of a rival priestly group.[83]

Two other prominent omissions call for comment, Joseph and Saul. In the body of the poem, one expects a reference to Joseph after the mention of Jacob, but it does not occur. The name "Joseph" appears in a brief "afterthought," along with the pre-deluvians Shem, Seth, and Adam (Sir 49:14-16; Enoch occurs here for a second time but is missing in the Masada text and the Syriac). Perhaps Joseph's connection with the northern tribes of Ephraim and Manasseh and his blessing of these sons gave the appearance of approving the despised Samaritans, who now occupied the area originally granted to Ephraim and Manasseh. The active campaign waged by the Tobiads in Transjordan and the leaders of Samaria against the policies of Simeon II and the Tobiads in Jerusalem may have generated sufficient antipathy to cause Ben Sira to remain silent about Joseph. Alternatively, Ben Sira may have removed the name of Joseph to blot out any record of his role as adviser to the pharaoh. Again, in the light of Onias III's switch of allegiance from the Seleucids to the Ptolemaic ruler, Ben Sira may have avoided giving the impression that he approved this shift.

Naturally, these attempts to explain Ben Sira's silence about Joseph presuppose the secondary character of the name in Sir 49:15. Viewing his presence in the latter text as comparison rather than praise lacks persuasiveness; excising the entire unit of 49:14-16 as secondary solely to restore a sequence of two persons, Nehemiah and Simeon II, who were responsible for engineering improvements in Jerusalem, seems problematic at best.[84]

One further notable omission is the first king, Saul. The biblical story ascribes enough negative features to his character to explain the lack of any reference to him. In addition, his rivalry with David and his connection with northern tribal groups made Saul an unlikely candidate for Ben Sira's list of worthy men.

SIRACH AND THE CANON

The preface to Sirach, written by Ben Sira's grandson, refers to the law, the prophets, and the other writings, suggesting that the first two divisions of the Hebrew Bible existed as distinct entities and that the third group may or may not have been relatively fixed in his day. Ben Sira's praise of ancestral heroes supports this evidence, pushing the date back to the early second century BCE for at least two closed units, the law and the prophets.[85] He knows the chief characters in Genesis through Deuteronomy, and he mentions Isaiah, Jeremiah, Ezekiel, and the Twelve, as well as prominent persons from the Former Prophets (Joshua, Judges, Samuel, and Kings). Unfortunately, he does not provide enough information to enable scholars to identify the exact books making up the third category. Among them he mentions Job and Nehemiah, but he probably knew Psalms and other books as well.[86]

---

81. With the assassination of the weak Onias III, Simeon's line came to an end. According to P. C. Beentjes, "'The Countries Marveled at You.' King Solomon in Ben Sira 47:12-22," *BTfuT* 45 (1984) 13, Ben Sira's goal in writing the history of Israel was "the perpetuation of and the succession of the priestly dynasty of Simeon and his descendants," their rule signifying divine activity.

82. P. C. Beentjes, "Hezekiah and Isaiah: A Study on Ben Sira xlviii 15-25," *OTS* 25 (1989) 77-88, esp. 81-82, calls attention to differences between the biblical account of Hezekiah's fortifications and that by Ben Sira.

83. Höffken, "Warum schwieg Jesus Sirach über Esra."

84. Begg, "Ben Sirach's Non-Mention of Ezra."

85. Harry M. Orlinsky, "Some Terms in the Prologue to Ben Sira and the Hebrew Canon," *JBL* 110 (1991) 483-90, insists that the first two divisions of the HB were already fixed in the time of Ben Sira's grandson, hence should be capitalized—Law and Prophets.

86. The inclusion of Job among the prophets accords with an ancient Jewish tradition, although the book usually appears, in varying sequence, among the Writings.

Although Sirach was excluded from the Hebrew Bible, it was frequently cited in rabbinic circles until the tenth century CE, occasionally introduced by the formula "it is written," which indicates Scripture.[87] Akiba, the noted rabbi of the second century (d. c. 132 CE), thought it belonged among the חסנים (*ḥisōnîm*, "outside"), or extra-canonical books, those that did not, in the language of the day, "defile the hands." A severe penalty accompanied their reading, forfeiture of any participation in the next life.[88] The same assessment of Sirach appears in *Tosephta*,[89] which states that the book does not defile the hands. Nevertheless, Sirach is quoted eighty-two times in the Talmud and other rabbinical writings.

Recent evidence from Masada and Qumran confirms that the Jewish communities in the area of the Dead Sea viewed the book as sacred, for the copy from Masada and the two tiny fragments from Cave 2 at Qumran are written stichometrically, with parallel columns, the first half of each colon beginning on the right side and the second half appearing on the left side. Moreover, the inclusion of Sirach in the Septuagint and the Palestinian revisions of this Greek text and the Hebrew indicate its acceptance as sacred. The formulation of specific criteria for canonicity, resulting from the debates associated with the so-called council of Jamnia and related discussions, automatically excluded Sirach, if one limits inspiration to the period from Moses to Ezra. In addition, several aspects of the book are closer to Sadducaic teaching than to Pharisaic, and this may have influenced its checkered history.

The situation is equally ambiguous in Christian tradition. The presence of the book of Sirach in the Septuagint implied at least quasi-sacred character, but the translator of the Vulgate, Jerome, denied a place in the canon to the additional books, labeling them deuterocanonical.[90] These books include 1–2 Esdras, Tobit, Judith, the Additions to Esther, the book of Wisdom, Sirach, Baruch, the Letter of Jeremiah, the Song of the Three Jews, Susanna, Bel and the Dragon, the Prayer of Manasseh, and 1–2 Maccabees. Augustine disagreed with Jerome's estimate, considering all the books in the Septuagint equally authoritative.

Following Jerome, Martin Luther rejected the sacred character of the additional books in the Septuagint, which he called apocrypha and placed in a separate group between the two Testaments in his German translation of 1534. John Calvin rejected these books altogether. Nevertheless, the Apocrypha appeared in the King James translation in English until the third decade of the nineteenth century, when they were removed for a combination of reasons, partly theological and partly economic. The Roman Catholic Church still considers these books sacred, but deuterocanonical, except for 1–2 Esdras and the Prayer of Manasseh.

The author of the Epistle of James was particularly fond of Sirach.[91] Other works of the early church used Sirach as a source of inspiration, including the *Didache*, the *Shepherd of Hermas*, and the *Epistle of Barnabas*. So did the church father Clement of Alexandria. The early Latin fathers included Sirach as one of the five books written by Solomon, and Cyprian accepted its sacred character. This position eventually prevailed at the Council of Trent.

THE TEXT

Slightly more than two-thirds of Sirach has survived in Hebrew manuscripts (approx. 68 percent).[92] Between 1896 and 1900, the Cairo Geniza, a place for discarded sacred texts in the old synagogue in Cairo, yielded four distinct manuscripts of Sirach (A, B, C, D), dating from the tenth to the twelfth centuries. Another leaf (E) was discovered in 1931, and additional fragments of B and C came to light in 1958 and 1960. Three years later a fragmentary and mutilated

---

87. Israel Levi, "Sirach, the Wisdom of Jesus the Son of," *The Jewish Encyclopedia* 11 (New York and London: Funk and Wagnalls, 1905) 390-92, discusses the book's popularity among Jews and Christians.
88. *Sanhedrin* 28a.
89. *Yadayim* 2. 13.
90. According to Gilbert, "The Book of Ben Sira: Implications for Jewish and Christian Traditions," in *Jewish Civilization in the Hellenistic-Roman Period*, ed. Shamaryahu Talmon (Sheffield: JSOT, 1991) 87, Jerome quotes Ben Sira eighty times in his works.
91. Luke Timothy Johnson, *The Letter of James*, AB 37A (New York: Doubleday, 1995) 33-34, calls attention to similarities and differences between wisdom literature generally and the Epistle of James. Hubert Frankemolle, "Zum Thema des Jakobusbriefes im Kontext der Rezeption von Sir 2:1-18 und 15:11-20," *BN* 48 (1989) 21-49, stresses the affinities, at least in one respect.
92. Skehan and Di Lella, *The Wisdom of Ben Sira*, 53.

scroll, resembling B, was discovered at Masada. In 1982 a new leaf of Sirach from the Cairo Geniza was identified (F). These manuscripts contain the following texts from Sirach:[93]

A		3:6b–16:26 (six leaves)
B		30:11–33:3; 35:11; 38:27b; 39:15c–51:30
		(nineteen leaves, written stichometrically)
	C	4:23, 30-31; 5:4-7, 9-13; 6:18b-19, 28, 35;
		7:1-2, 4, 6, 17, 20-21, 23-25; 18:31b–19:3b;
		20:5-7; 37:19, 22, 24, 26; 20:13; 25:8, 13, 17-24;
		26:1-2a (a florilegium)
	D	36:29–38:1a (one leaf)
	E	32:16–34:1 (one leaf, written stichometrically)
	F	31:24–32:7; 32:12–33:8 (one leaf, written stichometrically)

A fragment from Cave 2 at Qumran has Sir 6:20-31 in stichometric arrangement (only the ends of the lines have survived).

The Greek text exists in two forms: (1) codices such as the four major uncials: Sinaiticus, Vaticanus, Alexandrinas, and Ephraemi; and (2) a longer form in the Lucianic rescension and Origen's recension of the Septuagint. The Old Latin and Vulgate used the Greek text of Sirach, which has also influenced the *Peshitta* to some degree.

Both the Greek and the Hebrew texts contain titles for individual sections (Greek, 20:27; 23:7; 24:1; 30:1, 16; 44:1; 51:1; Hebrew, 31:12 = Greek 34:12; 41:14; 44:1) and transitions (42:25 to 43:1; 43:33 to 44:1; 49:16 to 50:1). In the Hebrew text an extra psalm resembling Psalm 136 follows Sir 51:12 (cf. 11QPs^a). The sequence from Sirach 31 to 36 differs in the Hebrew, the Vulgate, and the Syriac from the Greek, which offers a less likely order at this point.

---
93. Skehan and Di Lella, *The Wisdom of Ben Sira*, 52.

SELECT BIBLIOGRAPHY

Commentaries, Concordances, Monographs:

Barthelemy, D., and O. Rickenbacher. *Konkordanz zum hebräischen Sirach.* Göttingen: Vandenhoeck & Ruprecht, 1973. A comprehensive survey of the vocabulary in the Hebrew text of Sirach.

Hengel, Martin. *Judaism and Hellenism.* 2 vols. Philadelphia: Fortress, 1974. Illuminates the interplay of cultures during the period in which Ben Sira lived.

Lee, T. R. *Studies in the Form of Sirach 44–50.* SBLDS 75. Atlanta: Scholars Press, 1986. Views the Greek encomium as the literary model for Ben Sira's praise of honorable men.

Mack, Burton L. *Wisdom and the Hebrew Epic: Ben Sira's Hymn in Praise of the Fathers.* Chicago Studies in the History of Judaism. Chicago: University of Chicago Press, 1985. Claims that Ben Sira fashions a national epic from the lives of past heroes.

Marböck, J. *Weisheit im Wandel: Untersuchungen zur Weisheitstheologie Bei Ben Sira.* BBB 37. Bonn: Peter Hanstein, 1971. Emphasizes the changes in wisdom represented by Sirach over against earlier texts, specifically Proverbs, Job, and Ecclesiastes.

Oesterley, W. O. E. *The Wisdom of Jesus the Son of Sirach or Ecclesiasticus.* Cambridge: Cambridge University Press, 1912. An excellent commentary on Sirach, particularly rich with respect to Jewish sources.

Sanders, J. T. *Ben Sira and Demotic Wisdom.* SBLMS 28. Chico, Calif.: Scholars Press, 1983. Finds traces of Egyptian influence on Ben Sira, especially Papyrus Insinger.

Schrader, Lutz. *Leiden und Gerechtigkeit. Studien zu Theologie und Textgeschichte des Sirachbuches.* BBET 27. Frankfurt am Main: Peter Lang, 1994. Examines the themes of suffering and justice in Sirach.

Skehan, Patrick, and Alexander A. Di Lella. *The Wisdom of Ben Sira.* AB 39. New York: Doubleday, 1987. The best commentary on Sirach, although better in treating stylistic matters than in theological analysis.

Snaith, John G. *Ecclesiasticus or The Wisdom of Jesus, Son of Sirach.* CBC, NEB. Cambridge: Cambridge University Press, 1974. Brief notes on Sirach.

Stadelmann, Helga. *Ben Sira als Schriftgelehrter: Eine Untersuchung zum Berufsbild des vor-Maccabäischen Sofer unter Berucksichtigung seines Verhältnisses zu Priester-, Propheten und Weisheitslehretum.* WUNT 2/6. Tübingen: Mohr, 1981. Stresses Ben Sira's occupation as a learned scribe.

Trenchard, W. C. *Ben Sira's View of Women: A Literary Analysis.* Brown Judaic Studies 38. Chico, Calif.: Scholars Press, 1982. Emphasizes Ben Sira's misogyny, although in need of more nuancing.

Wischmeyer, Oda. *Die Kultur des Buches Jesus Sirach.* BZNW 77. Berlin: Walter de Gruyter, 1994. Examines the cultural setting of Ben Sira.

Yadin, Yigael. *The Ben Sira Scroll from Masada.* Jerusalem: Israel Exploration Society, 1965. Textual notes on the portion of Sirach discovered at Masada.

Ziegler, J. *Sapientia Iesu Filii Sirach.* Septuaginta 12/2. Göttingen: Vandenhoeck & Ruprecht, 1965. The Greek text of Sirach.

For Further Reading:

Crenshaw, James L. *Old Testament Wisdom.* Atlanta: John Knox, 1981. Provides a general introduction to the wisdom literature in the Bible and in neighboring cultures, Egypt and Mesopotamia.

———. "Sirach." *Harper Bible Commentary.* San Francisco: Harper & Row, 1988.

———. *Urgent Advice and Probing Questions: Collected Writings on Old Testament Wisdom.* Macon, Ga.: Mercer University Press, 1995. Extensive articles on various aspects of biblical wisdom.

Day, John, Robert P. Gordon, and H. G. M. Williams, eds. *Wisdom in Ancient Israel.* Cambridge: Cambridge University Press, 1995. Treats a wide variety of topics related to ancient wisdom.

Duesberg, H. *Les Scribes Inspirés: Introduction aux livres sapientiaux de la Bible.* 2 vols. Paris: Maredsous, 1966. Attention to intra- and extra-biblical parallels to wisdom literature.

Gammie, John G., and Leo G. Perdue, eds. *The Sage in Israel and the Ancient Near East.* Winona Lake: Eisenbrauns, 1990. A comprehensive look at professional sages and their literature.

Levine, Amy-Jill, ed. *"Women Like This": New Perspectives on Jewish Women in the Greco-Roman World.* Atlanta: Scholars Press, 1991. Claudia Camp's article on Ben Sira's view of women (pp. 1-39) is particularly valuable.

Murphy, Roland E. *The Tree of Life: An Exploration of Biblical Wisdom Literature.* ABRL. New York: Doubleday, 1990. An introduction to wisdom literature.

Nickelsburg, G. W. E. *Jewish Literature Between the Bible and the Mishnah: A Historical and Literary Introduction.* Philadelphia: Fortress, 1981. A good introduction to the rich corpus of Jewish literature from the general period in which Ben Sira lived.

Perdue, Leo G., Bernard Brandon Scott, and Wiliam Johnston Wiseman, eds. *In Search of Wisdom: Essays in Memory of John Gammie.* Louisville: Westminster/John Knox, 1993. Articles on wisdom in both Testaments.

Rad, Gerhard von. *Wisdom in Israel.* Nashville: Abingdon, 1972. An introduction to wisdom literature, with special emphasis on the limits of knowledge.

Schnabel, E. J. *Law and Wisdom from Ben Sira to Paul: A Traditional Historical Inquiry into the Relation of Law, Wisdom, and Ethics.* WUNT 2/16. Tübingen: Mohr, 1985. A comprehensive examination of the relationship between law and wisdom.

OUTLINE OF SIRACH

The Prologue

I. Sirach 1:1–4:10, Part I

    A. 1:1-10, A Hymn to Wisdom
    B. 1:11-30, The Meaning and Value of the Fear of the Lord
    C. 2:1-18, Faithfulness During Testing
    D. 3:1-16, Filial Duty
    E. 3:17–4:10, Humility and Almsgiving

II. Sirach 4:11–6:17, Part II

    A. 4:11-19, In Praise of Wisdom
    B. 4:20-31, Social Status, Shame, and Speech
    C. 5:1-8, On Presuming Too Much
    D. 5:9–6:1, On Dissimulation Through Speech
    E. 6:2-4, On Uncontrolled Passions
    F. 6:5-17, On Friendship

III. Sirach 6:18–14:19, Part III

    A. 6:18-37, Wisdom's Rigorous Discipline
    B. 7:1-17, The Consequences of Sin
    C. 7:18-28, Domestic Advice
    D. 7:29-36, Obligations to Priests and to the Poor
    E. 8:1-19, Some Things to Avoid
    F. 9:1-9, Relationships with Women
    G. 9:10-16, Friends and Neighbors
    H. 9:17–10:5, On Rulers
    I. 10:6–11:1, Pride and Honor
    J. 11:2-28, Deceptive Appearances
    K. 11:29–14:19, On Friendship and Wealth

IV. Sirach 14:20–23:27, Part IV

    A. 14:20–15:10, Seeking Wisdom and Being Welcomed by Her
    B. 15:11–16:23, On Free Will and Divine Recompense
    C. 16:24–18:14, The Relationship Between the Creator-Judge and Humankind
    D. 18:15-18, On Giving Alms
    E. 18:19-29, On Caution
    F. 18:30–19:19, On Self-Control

G. 19:20-30, Wisdom and Cleverness
H. 20:1-31, On Speech and Silence
I. 21:1-10, Sin's Smooth Path
J. 21:11–22:18, The Wise and the Foolish
K. 22:19-26, Preserving Friendship
L. 22:27–23:6, A Prayer for Self-Control
M. 23:7-15, The Proper Use of Language
N. 23:16-27, On Fornication and Adultery

VI. Sirach 24:1–33:19, Part V

A. 24:1-34, The Praise of Wisdom
B. 25:1-12, Some Numerical Proverbs
C. 25:13–26:27, On Wives, Both Bad and Good
D. 26:28–27:15, On Integrity
E. 27:16–28:26, Offenses Against Companions
F. 29:1-20, On Lending and Providing Collateral
G. 29:21-28, On Being Independent
H. 30:1-13, On Rearing Children
I. 30:14-25, On Health
J. 31:1-11, On Riches
K. 31:12–32:13, On Proper Etiquette
L. 32:14–33:19, On Divine Providence

VI. Sirach 33:20–39:11, Part VI

A. 33:20-24, The Advantage of Independence
B. 33:25-33, On Slaves
C. 34:1-8, On Dreams
D. 34:9-20, On the Dangers of Travel and God's Protection
E. 34:21–35:26, On Sacrifices
F. 36:1-22, A Prayer for National Deliverance
G. 36:23–37:31, On Making Discriminating Choices
H. 38:1-15, On Physicians
I. 38:16-23, On Mourning
J. 38:24–39:11, The Superiority of the Scribal Profession

VII. Sirach 39:12–43:33, Part VII

A. 39:12-35, In Praise of the Creator
B. 40:1–41:13, Life's Wretchedness
C. 41:14–42:8, On Shame
D. 42:9-14, On Protecting Daughters' Honor
E. 42:15–43:33, The Wonders of Creation

VIII. Sirach 44:1–51:30, Part VIII

A. 44:1-15, Introduction
B. 44:16–45:26, The Seven Covenantal Figures
C. 46:1-20, Joshua, Caleb, the Judges, and Samuel
D. 47:1-25, Nathan, David, Solomon, and Rehoboam/Jeroboam

E. 48:1-16, The Prophets Elijah and Elisha
F. 48:17-25, Hezekiah and Isaiah
G. 49:1-16, Josiah and Subsequent Heroes
H. 50:1-24, Simeon the High Priest
I. 50:25-29, A Numerical Proverb and an Epilogue
J. 51:1-30, A Prayer of Thanksgiving, a Hymn of Praise, and an Acrostic Poem About Wisdom

THE PROLOGUE

COMMENTARY

Like Greek historical expositions by Herodotus, Thucydides, and Polybius and treatises by Dioscorides Pedamus, Hippocrates, Aristeas, and Josephus, the book of Sirach begins with a brief prologue, to which may also be compared Luke 1:1-4. Written in three elegant sentences by Ben Sira's grandson, the prologue demonstrates the author's mastery of Greek rhetoric to an extent not found in the rest of the book, where he translates in a manner that reflects the style of the original Hebrew being rendered into Greek. The three sentences (1) explain Ben Sira's reasons for writing the book; (2) request readers to study it in its Greek form, making allowances for infelicities in translation; and (3) provide an autobiographical note about the actual date of the translation and the extent of care involved in producing it.

The grandson, who does not give his own name, identifies the author of the book he is translating as "Jesus," which is the Greek form of the popular Hebrew name "Jeshua," and characterizes him as a learned teacher of sacred writings. The author views these texts as channels of divine instruction and for the first time in extant literature refers to Scripture in the tripartite division that came to characterize the Hebrew Bible—the law, the prophets, and the later writings. This initial sentence also mentions the law, the prophets, and the other books of the ancestors; the second sentence varies the expression further, mentioning the law, the prophets, and the rest of the books. Like this loose language, the third group remained open as late as the first century CE (cf. Luke 24:44; in Matt 22:40, Luke 16:16, and Acts 13:15 the expression stops with the mention of the law and the prophets). The Greek text contains a suggestion of discipleship in the reference to the other books that followed. Like Deut 4:6, the author of the prologue sounds a strong note of ethnic pride to encourage readers living in the Egyptian dispersion.

The reference to "those who read the scriptures" echoes the technical expression for professional scribes entrusted with the preservation and transmission of sacred texts. In 1 Esdras the expression takes several forms, always with reference to Ezra: "priest and reader of the law of the Lord" (1 Esdr 8:8-9 NRSV); "priest and reader of the law of Most High God" (1 Esdr 8:19 NRSV); "priest and reader" (1 Esdr 9:39 NRSV); "priest and reader of the law" (1 Esdr 9:42 NRSV); "chief priest and reader" (1 Esdr 9:49 NRSV; cf. Neh 8:8-12). Such "readers" explained the meaning of Scripture written in a language that had ceased to be the vernacular—for Ezra's compatriots, Hebrew texts and Aramaic as the spoken language; for the present readers, a Greek translation of a Hebrew text for outsiders. This reference to non-Jews implies an effort to foster among Egyptians an appreciation for the religious insights of the Jewish tradition. The author attributes inspiration to his learned grandfather, whose book continues the legacy of sacred texts, and views the finished product as progress, the wise teacher adding to the accumulated insights of the ancestors.

The second sentence in Greek voices the anxiety felt by most, if not all, conscientious translators. The early rabbis formulated the problem concisely, attributing the witticism to Eliezer: "Whoever translates literally is a liar, and whoever adds to the text is guilty of blasphemy." Modern translators phrase the issue similarly, juxtaposing two fundamentally different principles—formal correspondence or dynamic equivalence. In brief, should the grammar and syntax of the source language prevail in the target language, or should the idiom of the target language dominate? W. O. E. Oesterley observed that "the numerous instances in which the translator misunderstood the original . . . show that his misgivings were fully justified."[94] In his own defense, the grandson of Ben Sira charged the translators of the Septuagint with similar unintentional misrepresentation of the

---

94. W. O. E. Oesterley, *The Wisdom of Jesus the Son of Sirach or Ecclesiasticus* (Cambridge: Cambridge University Press, 1912) 3.

original sense of the Hebrew text. That translation, probably completed in the mid-second century BCE in Alexandria, was necessitated by the large Jewish population in Egypt.

Jewish presence was felt in Egypt as early as the sixth century BCE; according to the biblical account, the prophet Jeremiah ended his long career there (Jeremiah 43–45). A Jewish community at Elephantine near Aswan has yielded important papyri from the fifth century, one of which mentions a celebration of the Passover; the Zenon papyri provide much information about the economic life of Jews in the second century BCE. In 162 BCE the priest Onias was exiled to Egypt and proceeded to build a rival temple at Leontopolis. From the late third century, when one of Alexander the Great's generals, Ptolemy, assumed control in Egypt, Jewish citizens assisted in maintaining authority over the indigenous population. The first-century CE Jewish philosopher Philo claimed that the Jewish population in Egypt totaled nearly one million.[95] The city of Alexandria granted Jewish citizens full rights, although conflicts in various areas of the country occasionally erupted, such as the burning of the temple to Yahweh at Elephantine. Two quite opposite responses to living in dispersion are evident within Jewish literature of the period: (1) harsh polemic as found in the book of Wisdom; and (2) apologetic as exemplified by Josephus's *Antiquities of the Jews* and *Against Apion,* as well as Philo's many writings.

The third sentence in the Greek prologue states that the translator arrived in Egypt during the reign of Euergetes II Ptolemy VIII Physkon, who ruled Egypt from 170 to 164 and 146 to 117 BCE. The Greek word συγχρονίσας (*sygchronisas,* "a synchronizing") indicates that the grandson lived in Egypt from 132 to 117 BCE, completing the translation after Euergetes' death. The translator states that he had access to a copy of the book, ἀφομοιόν (*aphomoion,* "like"), but some manuscripts read ἀφορμήν (*aphormēn,* "opportunity"), implying "access to" and thus opportunity (cf. the different translations in the NRSV text and note).

The three sentences in this prologue employ three thematic expressions: (1) the law, the prophets, and later books (or the variants on the third category, the other writings, the rest of the books); (2) discipline and wisdom; and (3) law. The first of these occurs three times, the other two only two times. Alexander A. Di Lella overlooks the symmetry of these three expressions, for he views the first and last reference to "law" as an inclusio, a statement, a phrase, or a word occurring at the beginning and end of a bracketed unit of thought.[96] Actually, the first sentence uses all three thematic expressions, the first two twice. The second sentence refers to the law, the prophets, and the rest of the books, whereas the third sentence mentions only the law. The phrase "instruction and wisdom" identifies the two major components of the book of Sirach, the teachings of the Mosaic law and proverbial instructions, here linked together for the first time.

---

95. Philo *Flaccus* VI.43.

96. Skehan and Di Lella, *The Wisdom of Ben Sira,* 135.

REFLECTIONS

For everyone except the original recipients, God's Word is always at least once removed. This introduces a human element into all Scripture. Those to whom God entrusted a message were required to pass that word along to others whose vocabulary, experience, and psyche differed to some extent. In transmitting the revelation, these human spokespersons for the deity reflected on what they heard and then clothed the message in appropriate rhetoric, along with motive clauses and warnings. In short, they did their best to communicate the essence of the message from God to those who themselves had no direct access to the deity.

Christians today may find it extraordinary that God actually communicated with human beings; most of us would undoubtedly lift an eyebrow if confronted with someone who claims receiving a direct message from God. We should remember that the ancients were not all that different, for not everyone who asserted that God had spoken in his or her life was automatically accepted as an authentic messenger of transcendence. The mere affirmation that the living God, the source of all life and mystery, broke the silence of eternity and entered into dialogue with humans, made in the divine likeness, must surely be as bold a thought as humans can imagine. Viewed in this way, the testimony to this divine-human encounter becomes precious beyond measure. At the same time, its present form cautions against an idolatry that honors the literary medium rather than the God to whom all words point.

By its very nature, every revelation necessitates translation into the language of ordinary discourse. That is no easy task, for a vast chasm separates the two realms, human and divine. We know far more about the former than the latter, and we endeavor to use our greater knowledge to understand the less well-known. The primary means of relating the two realms is analogy. On the basis of the better-known constitutive element, often called *the vehicle* by literary critics, we try to grasp the meaning of the unknown, which critics designate *the tenor*. For Ben Sira and for subsequent interpreters, the Mosaic legislation, particularly the Ten Commandments, functions as the vehicle. The contents of the law are well known, for the legislation touches on matters of everyday experience. The tenor, however, is a construct of the human imagination. It goes by the name of divine wisdom. We know far more about the specific statutes than we do about the broad concept of divine instruction. Nevertheless, together the law and divine wisdom enable us to understand something about God's solicitous concern in guiding humans along safe paths.

In the important task of translating the revealed Word to society at large, faithful transmitters of the tradition were required to preserve accuracy through the ages. The ancient guardians of sacred texts were governed by the spiritual needs of various communities rather than any rigid concern to repeat verbatim earlier versions of the communicative effort. As a result, the tradition grew and retained vitality; in essence, religious texts took on the character of the living Word, a divine communication always both old and new. At the same time, these sacred texts bore witness to the human response to them, often questioning and protesting but, in the end, yielding to divine mystery.

This interrogative mood punctuates prophetic literature and occasionally makes an unexpected appearance in the narrative material in the Torah. The third division of the Hebrew Bible, the writings, witnesses an eruption of protest against the heavens that reaches a crescendo with the books of Job and Ecclesiastes. Ben Sira's teachings belong to this third division; appropriately they combine features of both perspectives, affirming praise and doubt about divine justice. In this extensive collection of a teacher's advice to professional sages, one comes face-to-face with human wit and wisdom, as in the book of Proverbs, but Ben Sira places this exploration of reality from below within the larger context of divine disclosure.

The language of the prologue, which describes the necessary process of transmitting religious texts across generations and cultures, calls attention to professionals from the religious establishment and to people entirely outside the community of believers. Although regrettable, not all members of a religious group have the inclination or capacity to become proficient in its sacred texts. Consequently, professional interpreters, here called readers, immerse themselves thoroughly in the texts and devote their lives to explaining the hidden meanings of God's interactions with the community. According to the unknown author of the prologue to the book of Sirach, Ben Sira belonged to this elite class of readers. His task was to assist in worship by explaining the meaning of the sacred text in the language of ordinary speech. A danger inherent in this practice is obvious: Others in the religious community relax their natural curiosity and leave the matter of interpretation to specialists.

This tendency to leave the Scriptures to the experts is buttressed by the mysterious character of so many texts, linguistic difficulties, and cultural gaps. Nevertheless, some rabbis spun stories that gave voice to the desire of numerous ordinary people to sit down together and discuss Torah from dawn to dusk. One extraordinary vision of heavenly existence pictured those who love Torah spending eternity while the true meaning of God's gift in sacred words unfolded before their eyes.

In the real world, there will always be outsiders and insiders; perhaps religious people should take heart from the fact that this situation offers an occasion for proclaiming the good news of God at work in human lives. Although the missionary endeavor was not central to ancient Israel, rare insights do acknowledge the need to be a blessing or a light to all nations. By nature evangelistic, Christians feel compelled to declare the good news that is transforming their lives. Often the most effective witness comes through example, not words. The goal to bring outsiders into the fellowship entails faithfulness to the integrity of a religious community; otherwise dissension and ultimately a rift within the body will result.

Possibly the most instructive feature of this prologue to Sirach is the apology for mistakes in translating the original Hebrew text into Greek. Concern over authentic rendering of one language into another has not disappeared from the scene, despite a lapse of over two millennia. The difficulty involved in translation should temper heated contemporary controversies over the inerrancy of Scripture. Because a certain amount of interpretation takes place in every translation, we would do well to adopt a stance of humility with respect to all renderings of the Bible into a language other than the originals. Today we are particularly fortunate in having several excellent translations, among which three stand out as superb representatives of two different principles: the NRSV (cf. also the NIV) for formal correspondence, the TNK, and the REB for dynamic equivalance. Because languages change with time, the task of translation never ends.

The prologue implies that God's people invariably move about from one country to another, often placing them in an alien context, imposing special demands. Existence in exile presents unusual temptations at the same time it offers considerable potential for good, especially the dissemination of the good news. This proclamation takes place through voluntary or involuntary exile, for God's people declare the Word in altogether new settings and unfamiliar languages. That religious message always occurs in the midst of political realities, as the mention of Pharaoh Euergetes suggests. The sacred text emerged in quite particular cultural contexts, a fact we ought always to keep in mind. God's Word certainly includes universal and absolute claims, but these claims are clothed in temporal garb. Separating the timeless from the temporal is exceedingly difficult.

The last verse of the prologue poses an intriguing problem. It can be read in two entirely different ways, one of which has stronger theological resonance. Which of the two should one treat as original? One actually does not need to choose, inasmuch as both readings address God's people, although at different times and in different settings. In one context, the emphasis on God's maternal love spoke with particular force, as it does once more. Another setting took special comfort in connecting God's compassion with scriptural warrant, in this instance the praise of God in Exod 34:6-7. Whether maternal feelings or sacred texts, the allusion captures the poignancy of God's affection for those who lovingly assist victims of a cruel society.

SIRACH 1:1–4:10

PART I

OVERVIEW

Like the book of Proverbs and, to some extent, Ecclesiastes, Sirach has no clear logical progression. Scholars, therefore, have difficulty when trying to divide its contents into distinct units. A few ancient manuscripts have topical headings here and there, although they lack consistency. The divisions that follow represent but one of many possible readings of the material.

Part I consists of five smaller units: (1) 1:1-10, an opening hymn to wisdom; (2) 1:11-30, the meaning and value of the fear of the Lord; (3) 2:1-18, faithfulness during testing; (4) 3:1-16, filial duty; and (5) 3:17–4:10, humility and almsgiving. The hymn to wisdom anticipates a far more elaborate celebration of divine wisdom in chap. 24, and the remarks about the fear of the Lord function as a theological statement for the whole book. The next two sections elaborate on the implications of the first and fifth commandments. The last section deals with responsibilities toward God and fellow human beings, particularly the social mandate to provide aid and comfort for needy persons in the community.

SIRACH 1:1-10, A HYMN TO WISDOM

COMMENTARY

Marböck concludes his analysis of the opening hymn to wisdom (vv. 1-10) with these words: "the hymnic introduction... contains the outline and most significant elements for a theology of wisdom in Ben Sira."[97] To be sure, Marböck's observations are directed at refuting the thesis of Josef Haspecker that the fear of Yahweh, not wisdom, lies at the heart of Sirach and that the hymn in vv. 1-10 introduces only 1:1–2:18, a treatise on the fear of God.[98] Both of these scholars have clearly observed the signal importance of the opening hymn to divine wisdom.

The language and mood of this hymn are charged with polemical overtones, probably resulting from Ben Sira's encounter with Hellenistic philosophy, especially the Stoic philosophers' emphasis on the antiquity of their wisdom. For Ben Sira, only one God could rightly be called wise, and that one was Yahweh, the personal God of the Jews. Ben Sira attributes all wisdom to this God and concedes that humans acquire knowledge solely as a divine gift. With one sweep of the pen, he rules out human experience as a valid means of discovering the hidden subtleties of God's wisdom. The only bridge from human to divine knowledge starts with God's initiative, in which wisdom serves as a medium of divine presence and a revelation to human beings. In the words of C. J. Kearns, wisdom is "the multifareous gift that He has made of Himself, personified so as to be rendered comprehensible."[99]

Ben Sira reaches back into prophetic tradition to describe Yahweh's generous dispersal of wisdom on all flesh, but particularly on the elect. The expectation of an outpouring of the divine spirit, first articulated by Moses (Num 11:29) and subsequently endorsed by Ezekiel

---

97. Marböck, *Weisheit im Wandel*, 34.
98. Marböck, *Weisheit im Wandel*, 93-104; and Haspecker, *Gottesfurcht bei Jesus Sirach*.
99. C. J. Kearns, "La vie intérieure à l'école de l'Ecclésiastique," *La Vie Spirituelle* 82 (1950) 146.

(Ezek 39:29) and Joel (Joel 3:1-5 [Eng. 2:28-32]), furnishes the language for God's gift of wisdom to all flesh (μετὰ πάσης σαρκὸς *meta pasēs sarkos,* 1:10*a*). Just as Joel 3:1[2:28] restricts the outpouring of the divine vitality to Jews, so also Ben Sira places "those whom Yahweh loves" in a special category. Similarly, Ben Sira borrows traditional language from prophecy and wisdom to describe the inaccessibility of wisdom. The rhetorical questions in vv. 2-3 and 6 recall Job 38:4; Prov 30:4; Isa 40:12-14; and Bar 3:15. Even the expressions "the sand of the seashore" and "drops of rain" echo Gen 32:12; 1 Sam 13:5; Ps 78:27; and Job 36:27 respectively. The creation of wisdom recalls the hymn in Prov 8:22-30, while wisdom's hiddenness is remarked on in Job 28:28. Ben Sira's use of impossible questions (vv. 2-3) gives expression to a cosmology that seems strange to modern readers, one composed of spatially limited heavens, a flat earth floating on top of underground waters, the circuit of which can be traversed in a day by the sun god (Ps 19:4*b*-6). The form of the impossible questions resembles numerical proverbs.[100]

The rare Greek word in v. 6 for wisdom's subtleties (πανουργεύματα *panourgeumata,* "secrets") occurs elsewhere in Sirach only at 42:18; together with σοφία (*sophia*) and ἐπιστήμη (*epistēmē,* vv. 6*a*, 7*a,* "wisdom" and "understanding"), it occurs also in Jdt 11:8, the only other place these three words appear in close proximity.[101] Ben Sira uses "root" and "subtleties" to indicate the origin and essence of divine wisdom; the Hebrew word ראשית (*rēʾšît*) in Prov 1:7 includes the ideas of "source," "essence," and "primacy." Like the unknown author of the prologue to the first collection of the book of Proverbs (Proverbs 1–9; or to the whole book), Ben Sira associates fear of the Lord with wisdom, but in reverse sequence if one takes *rēʾšît* to be temporal, a moment of beginning.

The interpretative addition to v. 4, found in some manuscripts, anticipates Ben Sira's later discourse on his inspiration that began as a small stream and grew to unexpected size (24:23-33). It reads: "The source of wisdom is God's word in the highest heaven, and her ways are the eternal commandments" (v. 5 NRSV). The gloss after v. 6 is repetitive: "The knowledge of wisdom—to whom was it manifested? And her abundant experience—who has understood it?" (v. 7). The addition to v. 10*ab* elaborates on the notion of God's friends (lit., "those who love God"). Marböck rightly focuses on vv. 1 and 8-10, the former verse as a great superscription and the latter verses as its obvious development.[102] Certain features of the original hymn in vv. 1-4, 6, 8-10*b* (omitting the two interpretative glosses in vv. 5 and 7) anticipate ideas that Ben Sira will take up later, specifically in the rest of chap. 1 and in chap. 18. The hymn extols different forms of wisdom, creation, and the fear of God. The brief allusion in v. 9 to mercy provides a clue for the interpretation of the entire first chapter, and indeed for the whole book. Marböck recognizes the importance of divine mercy to Ben Sira, although without adequate discussion of the tension thus produced with older sapiential views, according to which individuals received exactly what they deserved.[103] The centrality of mercy in the brief hymn in 18:1-13 and similarities with the initial one under discussion here, especially the idea of divine largess to all, suggest that Ben Sira considered these themes crucial to his teaching. The hymn in vv. 1-4, 6, 8-10*b* also clearly relates to vv. 25-27, which unites the themes of wisdom and fear of the Lord. The latter concept occupies center stage in vv. 11-30.

This opening hymn to wisdom actually extols its Creator, who alone has complete access to its mysteries and thus deserves the epithet "Wise." By enumerating various secrets of the universe that continue to mystify humans, the author contrasts our limited knowledge with God's immediate control of such facts as those that defy human inquiry. As the first created one, wisdom was subsequently mediated to other creatures, particularly to those who love God. Here in this simple observation Ben Sira sums up the exquisite praise of wisdom in Prov 8:22-31

---

100. Cf. James L. Crenshaw, "Impossible Questions and Tasks in Israelite Wisdom," *Gnomic Wisdom,* Semeia 7 (1981) 19-34 (also in Crenshaw, *Urgent Advice and Probing Questions,* 265-78), and "Questions, Dictons et Épreuves Impossibles," in *La Sagesse de l'Ancien Testament,* ed. Maurice Gilbert, BETL 51 (Leuven: Duculot, 1979) 96-111.
101. Skehan and Di Lella, *The Wisdom of Ben Sira,* 138.
102. Marböck, *Weisheit im Wandel,* 23.
103. Marböck, *Weisheit im Wandel,* 28-30; and Crenshaw, "The Concept of God in Old Testament Wisdom," 1-18. See also Crenshaw, *Urgent Advice and Probing Questions,* 191-205.

and Job 28, to which he will return (cf. Sirach 24), using considerably more lavish language. The present hymn strikes a note of awe, in the references to both the unknown and the unknowable, and in the reminder that the Wise Sovereign must be revered.

REFLECTIONS

The hymn about wisdom's true source arises from recognition that mystery always remains in any intellectual quest. Critical inquiry can do no more than touch the hem of the garment of truth. Jewish mystics spoke about the world as the garments of Torah, an insight Christians would do well to acknowledge. Such an understanding of reality gives the world a sacred character, including the declaration that the universe consists of divine disclosure, an accommodation necessitated by human weakness and ignorance. Ben Sira intimates that the universe conceals sufficient mystery to satisfy the curiosity of average citizens as well as gifted overachievers in intellectual quests. Whereas God has access to all wisdom, that unique possession does not create in the deity a wish to keep it for selfish purposes. Instead, God freely offers bits and pieces of this knowledge to deserving human beings. Here, too, humility is in order, for individuals who acquire huge amounts of knowledge owe much of it to divine generosity. Seminal thinkers know this fact well.

SIRACH 1:11-30, THE MEANING AND VALUE OF THE FEAR OF THE LORD

COMMENTARY

A poem of twenty-two bicola (a line of poetry with two half-lines as separate cola), the same number of letters in the Hebrew alphabet, serves as a programmatic statement for the entire book. It identifies wisdom with the fear of God—that is, religion—and enumerates the fruits of living according to wisdom's dictates. Ben Sira infuses his statements about the fear of the Lord with the warmth of personal piety. The expression "fear of the LORD" and its variant occur ten times in this poem (twelve times if one counts the addition to v. 12, together with v. 21) and function as an inclusio to delimit the unit (vv. 11, 30). The heart of the poem equates wisdom, fear of the Lord, discipline, and observing the Mosaic law (vv. 25-27). A thematic statement (v. 11) leads to a promise of a long and blessed life to those who fear the Lord (vv. 12-20, where "long life" in vv. 12, 20 forms an inclusio), which abruptly veers off into warnings against loss of self-control (vv. 22-24) before returning to stress the need for keeping the commandments (vv. 25-27) and avoiding duplicity (vv. 28-30).

For the most part, Ben Sira's teachings in this poem derive from the book of Proverbs, especially the introductory collection Proverbs 1–9, which gives prominence to personified wisdom, but also the final praise of the woman in Prov 31:10-31. Some of these images of wisdom as a crown, a garland, a tree, health and life, happiness, produce, root and branches came to prominence in later wisdom texts also (e.g., Wis 6:17-21; 7:1–9:18). At least two expressions in Ben Sira's poem about the identification of wisdom as fear of the Lord echo the larger canon, Torah and the Prophets. The concept of abomination (v. 25) is a cultic expression in Deuteronomy, although the notion belongs to the wisdom tradition in Egypt and the book of Proverbs as well. The connection in v. 26 with the commandments points to the original deuteronomic context in which God's law is proclaimed (cf. Exod 20:2-17; Deut 5:1-21) in capsular form. Ben Sira may actually allude to the entire Mosaic legislation. In v. 14, Ben Sira expresses a concept that was regularly associated with the birth of a prophet or a special servant of Yahweh in Israel (Isa 44:24; Jer 1:5) and with royal births in Mesopotamia. In this view, God chooses special persons to carry out individual assignments, whether prophetic or royal.

The reference to a happy end to life (v. 13) does not imply anything beyond the grave, for in this respect Ben Sira sides with those who later formed the party of the Sadducees. He accepts the usual teaching about the end (אחרית *'aḥărît*) in the OT—that a person dies and joins the ancestors in a ghost-like existence in Sheol, the body returning to dust whence it came, according to hallowed narrative. Ben Sira's reference to the dead being blessed lacks any indication of the one doing the blessing, whether God or the human survivors (cf. 11:25-28, however, where Ben Sira attributes the blessing to God). According to the wisdom teachers who composed the book of Proverbs, an intimate connection existed between morality and happiness, with rare exceptions. These exceptions became the rule for the authors of the books of Job and Ecclesiastes, and yet Ben Sira was hardly touched by their poignant attacks on traditional wisdom. Events soon after he wrote his book threw an even greater question mark on this optimism, for the frequency of martyrdom during the Maccabean revolt (167–164 BCE) made it difficult to describe the end of such faithful ones as blessed. The author of Dan 12:2 breaks sharply with Hebrew tradition in a desperate effort to salvage divine reputation for justice and to provide comfort for those who either faced a martyr's end or grieved for someone who had.

Many features of this poem manifest an exuberance equal to that of the final verse in the prologue, which speaks of God's lavishing gifts on friends. Drawing on the poem about personified wisdom's building her house and inviting guests to a feast (Prov 9:1-6), Ben Sira actually uses a word for "inebriation" (μεθύσκω *methyskō*, v. 16). The allusion in v. 15 to her building a nest (ἐνόσσευσεν *enosseusen*) anticipates 24:8-12, a section on wisdom's coming to dwell in Jerusalem that reaches a crescendo at the close of the first half of the book. At the same time, this allusion looks back on the similar poem about personified wisdom in Prov 8:22-31.

The resemblances between this figure of wisdom and the Egyptian goddess *ma'at* have been acknowledged for some time, especially the picture of her holding the *ankh*, a symbol of long life, in one hand and riches in the other. That idea certainly resembles Ben Sira's description of wisdom's gifts. In addition, Egyptian wisdom emphasizes silence so much that the word becomes a technical term for the person of character, one who controls anger and is, therefore, the opposite of the heated person. Egyptian instructions also describe the good person as one who is like a tree with well-watered roots (cf. v. 20 and more fully 24:13-14, 16-17), and they characterize wise behavior in terms of restraint, eloquence, timing, and integrity. The wise person thus practices self-discipline, speaks effectively at the appropriate moment, and declares the truth. In vv. 22-24, Ben Sira refers to self-control and the right time (καιρός *kairos*) for speaking. The image of wisdom as a garland and a crown has its exact counterpart in Egyptian wisdom literature.

The interplay between free will and divine gift finds expression in v. 26, where human initiative evokes divine largess. To the unspoken question, "How can one become wise?" Ben Sira answers, "Keep the commandments." The author of the Epistle of James offers yet another response to this query: "Ask God for wisdom" (Jas 1:5 NRSV). The closing section of Ben Sira's poem introduces a powerful element of social control in the ancient world: honor and shame, one that he returns to several times (3:2-11; 4:21; 7:7; 10:19–11:6; 41:17–42:8). In his first reference to the loss of honor (v. 30), Ben Sira probably reflects on a text in Proverbs in which a dying victim of the "strange woman" confesses his mistake:

Oh, how I hated discipline,
    and my heart despised reproof!
I did not listen to the voice of my teachers
    or incline my ear to my instructors.
Now I am at the point of utter ruin
    in the public assembly.
(Prov 5:12-14 NRSV)

Presumably, Ben Sira thinks of disgrace in the context of the synagogue, although the greater Jewish community functioned as a social arena dispensing honor or shame. The language of duplicity, a double heart, occurs in Ps 12:3 and Jas 1:8; 4:8, and the notion of watching over one's lips recalls Ps 141:3, a theme that recurs in Sir 23:2-3.

Ben Sira's deep piety comes to expression in vv. 25-27, where the Greek words σοφία (*sophia*, "wisdom"), παιδεία (*paideia*, "instruction"), πίστις (*pistis*, "faith"), and πραότης (*praotēs*, "humility") recall venerable Hebrew terms for "wisdom" (חכמה *ḥokmâ*), "instruction" (מוסר *mûsār*), "faithfulness" (אמונה *'ĕmûnâ*), and "humility" (ענוה *'ănāwâ*). The noun *'ĕmûnâ* consists of active fidelity and passive trustworthiness, senses conveyed by various renderings in the Septuagint (πίστις *pistis,* "faith"; πιστός *pistos,* "faithful"; ἀλήθεια *alētheia,* "truth"; ἀληθινός *alēthinos,* "truthful"; ἀξιόπιστος *axiopistos,* "reliable"). It thus becomes clear that the word includes far more than the cognitive dimension; mere intellectual assent expresses itself by means of appropriate action, as the author of the Epistle of James recognized.

To reiterate, this elaboration of the primacy of religious devotion within intellectual inquiry leaves no doubt about Ben Sira's allegiance. He elevates piety above all else, but it is an informed piety. Wisdom determines one's speech and actions, as it were, watching over those who fear God and keep the divine commandments. Such wisdom embraces every dimension of human existence, in Ben Sira's opinion. It informs one's silence, bringing rich dividends both in material wealth and in prestige among one's peers. It shapes virtue and strenghtens one in the fight against vice. Wisdom also gives loyal followers integrity, enabling them to avoid hypocrisy. Under its instruction, the faithful learn to compose wise sayings and thus to transmit a valuable legacy to others. Ben Sira will spell out these insights, and more, in what follows.

REFLECTIONS

For Ben Sira, genuine religious faith is the clearest indication of wisdom. A person cannot, in his view, be wise without acknowledging the priority of God in one's life. Possibly the most daring suggestion of all concerns the personification of wisdom as a woman, given the frequent disparaging of women in ancient proverbial sayings. This bold move was undoubtedly dictated by two factors: the circumstances of instruction, where boys comprised the students; and the feminine form of abstractions, such as wisdom, truth, and righteousness in the Hebrew and Greek languages. Viewing wisdom as feminine definitely introduced an erotic component into learning precisely at a stage in the life of young boys when they could make optimal use of attraction to the opposite sex.

This practice, while potentially enervating, is also fraught with danger. The natural curiosity about the opposite sex among young people easily leads to conduct that threatens both their spiritual well-being and their physical safety. At the same time, this heightening of the erotic brings the whole realm of sex into the clear light of day, requiring youth to come to terms with powerful feelings while striving to discover God's will for their lives. This struggle, begun in tender years, lasts into later years as well, and the church will do well to harness erotic energy so as to channel it into productive endeavors. Sacred dance and drama can add a powerful dimension to worship, particularly when one sees the body as a place of residence for the divine.

SIRACH 2:1-18, FAITHFULNESS DURING TESTING

COMMENTARY

This section consists of three stanzas and a concluding couplet (vv. 1-6, 7-11, 12-16 + 17-18). Its ornate rhetorical style—three verses beginning with "You who fear the Lord" (vv. 7-9), three rhetorical questions (v. 10), three verses with introductory "woe to" (vv. 12-14), and three verses with an initial phrase consisting of "Those who fear the Lord" (vv. 15-17)—suggests oral use in classrooms. These *repetits* (refrain-like phrases) aided the memory and enhanced the rhetorical style of the unit. The key to understanding the first stanza, v. 6 has the catchwords *trust* (πιστεύω *pisteuō*) and *hope* (ἐλπίς *elpis*), whereas *mercy* (ἔλεος *eleos*) in vv. 7-9 provides a cohesion for the second stanza, and the correspondence between vv. 11 and 18 links the last two stanzas.

2:1-6. The idea of testing, discipline attributed to a loving father in Prov 3:11-12, follows naturally from the previous poem, which ends by warning against hypocrisy. Adversity has the potential for unmasking such insincere religion. The literature on divine testing in the OT is set within such a context (e.g., the offering of Isaac, Gen 22:1-18; the trials of Joseph in Egypt, Genesis 37–50; and the afflictions of Job). Biblical texts frequently describe this testing in the language of separating impure dross from precious metal (cf. Prov 17:3; Wis 3:6; Jas 1:12). The biblical writers maintain firm confidence that genuinely virtuous people will emerge victoriously in the end, just as the worst-case scenario, Job, exemplifies. Only the author of Ecclesiastes resolutely refuses to view testing in positive terms (perhaps also the author of Jeremiah's laments in Jer 11:18–12:6; 15:10-21; 17:14-18; 18:18-23; 20:7-18). The three young men who enter the furnace, according to the devotional legend in Daniel 3, confess their readiness to die even if God elects not to rescue them (Dan 3:16-18). In some instances, these experiences of testing forged a special bond between the worshiper and God, eliciting profound expressions of piety.[104]

An important manuscript, MS 248, sets this unit apart by means of a heading, "On Patience" (περὶ ὑπομονῆς *peri hypomonēs*). The initial vocative, "my son" (τέκνον *teknon*) appears frequently in the book (3:12, 17; 4:1; 6:32; 10:28; 11:10; 14:11; 31:22; in the plural, 3:1; 23:7; 39:13; 41:14). This direct address of a son is typical of wisdom instruction throughout the ancient Near East, beginning as early as the third-millennium Sumerian *Instructions of Šuruppak* and Egyptian royal instructions. In this same vein, Israelite teachers directed their words to sons ("my son," Prov 1:8, 10, 15; 2:1; often in Proverbs 1–9; occasionally in Prov 22:17–24:22; "sons," Prov 4:1; 5:7). From earliest times this language of "father" and "son" was used in educational settings to designate "teacher" and "student." Sumerian schools also had a monitor who went by the title of "big brother." At first this familial language referred to kinship, but over the years the terms "father" and "son" lost their original connotations entirely and came to designate "teachers" and "students" only. That is exactly how בני (*běnî*, τέκνον *teknon*) functions for Ben Sira.

One of the most difficult aspects of testing was the necessity of holding firm in one's expectation of promised gratification for faithful conduct. Hence the necessity for encouraging words like Ben Sira's; "Trust in him, and he will help you" (v. 6*a*). Hoping in God's eventual deliverance of the worshiper occupies central place in much of the Bible, although sounding a rare note in wisdom literature, which emphasized human achievement. Ben Sira unites the traditional piety of psalms, prophecy, and sacred narrative with the more down-to-earth teachings of the sages. In this respect, Ben Sira continues

---

104. Cf. Ps 73:23-28. On these texts, see James L. Crenshaw, *A Whirlpool of Torment* (Philadelphia: Fortress, 1984) 99-100, 106-9.

the views attributed to Job's three friends who urge him to place his hope in God.[105]

2:7-11. In v. 10, Ben Sira uses a traditional argument of the sages, the appeal to accumulated experience. His long rhetorical question:

Has anyone trusted in the Lord
    and been disappointed?
Or has anyone persevered in the
    fear of the Lord and been forsaken?
Or has anyone called upon him
    and been neglected?

anticipates a negative response (cf. Ps 22:4-5). This answer scarcely follows if one actually examines Israel's recorded past, particularly the tragic disappointment ending King Josiah's faithful reliance on the promises articulated in the book of Deuteronomy. Religious belief seldom coincides, however, with brutal reality, and people always seem capable of interpreting even the most adverse circumstances as confirmation of dogmatic expectations (cf. Ps 37:25-26).

Like numerous worshipers who preceded him in Israel, Ben Sira bases his confidence on Yahweh's much-cited proclamation to Moses of the divine attributes:

The LORD, the LORD,
a God merciful and gracious,
slow to anger,
and abounding in steadfast love and
    faithfulness,
keeping steadfast love for the thousandth
    generation,
forgiving iniquity and transgression
    and sin,
yet by no means clearing the guilty,
but visiting the iniquity of the parents
    upon the children
and the children's children,
to the third and the fourth generation.
(Exod 34:6-7 NRSV; cf., e.g., Pss 86:5; 103:3-4; 145:8-9; Joel 2:13; Jonah 4:2; Neh 9:17)

Predictably, later citations of this text omit the threatening traits of the divine character and appeal to the Lord's compassionate nature (except for Nah 1:2-3, directed against Nineveh). Liturgical use of this text extends beyond the Bible to the contemporary Jewish Passover seder, in which children respond to their parents' question, "Who knows?" (מי ידע *mî yôdēaʿ*), in numerical gradations from one to thirteen, ultimately reaching a devotional crescendo with the recitation of the thirteen divine attributes. Modern interpreters have understandably mined this biblical text as a mother lode of theological insight.[106]

2:12-14. For Jewish compatriots who consider Hellenistic thought and culture superior to ancestral traditions of the Jews, Ben Sira reserves the strongest language. Three times in these verses he utters the language of curse ("woe to" [הוי *hôy*; οὐαι *ouai*]). Persons whose hands slacken in observing the Mosaic statutes and who neglect to lift them in prayer occasion the first of these harsh curses. The other two uses of the curse accentuate cowardice and loss of nerve. All three refer to the body: heart and hand, heart, and nerve, respectively. The Lord's reckoning to which Ben Sira refers is entirely this-worldly; it manifests itself in various forms of sickness and disaster. The image of walking a double path, almost comic, underlines the absurdity of all attempts to reconcile Jewish and Hellenistic worldviews, according to Ben Sira. He was prepared to make modest compromises to accommodate those who valued Hellenistic ways, but that principle did not extend to matters affecting the divine commandments concerning good deeds. He willingly adopted Greek views and practices without any real drawing of the line. Perhaps the political situation permitted him such freedom. That changed with the oppressive policies inaugurated by Antiochus IV.

2:15-17. The concluding stanza stresses the interior motive for serving God and enjoins humility. The author of the saying in the Jewish tractate *Pirqe 'Abot* ("The Sayings of the Fathers") that elevates the love of God over desire for reward ("Be not as slaves that minister to their master in order to receive reward; but be as slaves that minister to their

---

105. For this theme in the HB, see Walther Zimmerli, *Hope in the Old Testament* (London: SCM, 1971).

106. See Michael Fishbane, *Biblical Interpretation in Ancient Israel* (Oxford: Clarendon, 1985) 335-50; Thomas B. Dozeman, "Inner-Biblical Interpretation of Yahweh's Gracious and Compassionate Character," *JBL* 108 (1989) 207-23; David Noel Freedman, "God Compassionate and Gracious," *Western Watch* 6 (1955) 6-24; and Crenshaw, "Who Knows What YHWH Will Do?," 185-96.

master without a view of receiving reward," *Pirqe 'Abot* 1:3) follows the clear teaching of Ben Sira. According to v. 16, religious devotion arises out of desire to please God. The keeping of the law, suspect to those Jews who have fallen under Hellenism's seduction, issues from love for God. This theme will recur many times throughout the book. For now, however, Ben Sira endeavors to put the fear of God into his hearers—and readers.

2:18. The final couplet evokes an episode in King David's life when he became vulnerable to divine wrath by, of all things, obeying Yahweh's explicit order to take a census of the people. Ben Sira quotes, not entirely accurately, David's decision to take his chances with God's wrath rather than endure three years of famine or three months of fleeing before enemies (cf. 2 Sam 24:1-17, esp. vv. 13-14). Choosing a three-day pestilence, David entertains the hope that Yahweh's unpredictable anger will give way before the reliable divine compassion: "I am in great distress; let us fall into the hand of the LORD, for his mercy is great; but let me not fall into human hands" (2 Sam 24:14 NRSV). The appeal to this text, like so much application of Scripture to later situations, stretches it to the limits, for an innocent David awaits divine punishment, whereas Ben Sira appears to view dependence on Yahweh as a means of *escaping* wrath. In any event, he closes this unit with a pun on the Hebrew word from Exod 34:6 for divine compassion, רחום (*raḥûm*; cf. 50:19), which he equates with God's name.

To sum up, in this section Ben Sira acknowledges that all who strive to do good inevitably encounter obstacles along the way. They need not despair, however, for the author of such trials uses difficulty to build character. Facing tests of various kinds, one should faithfully rely on divine assistance, knowing that the outcome will be favorable. This confidence rests above all in the nature of God, whose compassion is well known and whose faithfulness is attested from of old. Nevertheless, one's trust should have a solid basis in piety, for God's mercy is exacting.

REFLECTIONS

Ben Sira was convinced that true wisdom accompanied the keeping of the law. In Christian terms, this means that we become wise as a direct result of obeying God's will. True knowledge depends on faithfulness to divine guidance. To be sure, some people only pretend to be religious, necessitating rigorous examination of the conduct of those who claim to be wise. True religion is evident in those who worship God alone; Ben Sira knew that such devotion was difficult, for moments of testing inevitably arise. To stave off such temptation, he urged people to become thoroughly familiar with religious history. In his view, the testimony of predecessors provided adequate support for believing in divine mercy. In Hasidic Judaism and in Christian worship of the recent past, at least among some fellowships, testimony to God's faithfulness became a significant part of communal life. We may not wish to revert to this practice liturgically, but we can surely benefit from conversations with elderly members of congregations in which they bear witness to God's faithfulness during their days in our midst. The active participation of the elderly in worship thus provides an inspiration and a model for younger people, for whom the older generation stands as a permanent witness to the truth of the gospel and its claims on their lives.

Ben Sira's brief reference to David's struggle to endure divine anger in the least destructive manner introduces readers to a valuable means of relating to Scripture. In this instance, readers are instructed to search the sacred texts for occasions when someone experienced something similar to the circumstances confronting them. The assumption underlying this anecdote is that God is faithful. If in David's case God's fury was clothed in mercy, God will most probably behave similarly now.

SIRACH 3:1-16, FILIAL DUTY

COMMENTARY

Whereas the preceding poem takes up human obligation, expressed in the first commandment—honor the Lord—the present unit much more self-consciously provides a commentary on the fifth commandment—honor your parents (Exod 20:2-3, 12; Deut 5:6-7, 16). Many ideas in these three sub-units (vv. 1-6, 7-11, 12-16) derive from the book of Proverbs, where duty toward parents is mentioned often.[107]

Ben Sira's sharp comments (cf. v. 16) may have been provoked by changing economic conditions that put enormous pressure on the stability of the large family. Carol A. Newsom has perceived the beginnings of this conflict in Proverbs 1–9, the latest collection within the book of Proverbs. There the younger generation is tempted to adopt extreme measures to obtain its heritage without the delay occasioned by the long life of parents.[108] New ideas about longevity also began to surface, perhaps in the wake of Hellenistic influence, in the late third and second centuries BCE, particularly elevating youth and questioning the value of long life. A telling instance of this attitude occurs in 2 Macc 4:40, which refers to a certain Auranus as "advanced in years and no less advanced in folly." Ben Sira endeavors to preserve the traditional Jewish value of a definite hierarchy in the family structure, where parents and children relate to one another, in regard to power, in the same way masters and slaves do (v. 7).

The fifth commandment is the first to introduce reinforcements, specifically the promise of prolonged existence on earth (Exod 20:12) and well-being (Deut 5:16). This emphasis in ancient Israel on showing honor for one's parents reflects a sociological context where adult sons continued to live in the family complex long after marrying. This situation naturally increased the occasions for conflict between grown sons and their aging parents.

The fifth commandment, therefore, covers more than the obligations of young children to their parents. In vv. 12-13, Ben Sira reinforces this broader understanding of the obligation to parents, for he urges his readers to remain constant in their respect for parents even when decrepitude and senility place extraordinary strains on the relationship.

3:1-6. The first unit opens with the conventional appeal from a teacher to a student, in this instance, but originally the language of father and son was literal. The probable Hebrew verb (שמע *šāmaʿ*, "Listen to me your father, O children"), when followed by the preposition ב (*bĕ*), implies obedience; here Ben Sira explicitly urges action in accord with the advice. The Greek purpose clause "so that you may be saved" (ἵνα σωθῆτε *hina sōthēte*) should not be understood in its New Testament sense, for it probably translates the Hebrew expression for "faring well" (cf. Deut 5:16: יטב [*yāṭab*, "that you may be kept in safety"]). The second verse attributes the authority of parents over their children to a divine gift rather than to societal convention. Nothing in this section indicates that honor for mothers was secondary, which should give pause to interpreters inclined to decry ancient Israel as an unmitigated patriarchal society.

Something relatively new in Hebraic thought, the atoning power of good deeds and the amassing of credit in the heavenly record book, finds expression in vv. 3-4. The emphasis on the efficacy of charitable acts arose as a consequence of the increased esteem in which piety was held during the second and first centuries BCE. The book of Tobit frequently acknowledges the positive correlation between acts of kindness and divine approval (cf. Tob 14:10-11). The notion of laying up treasure in God's sight, familiar to students of the NT, has an analogue in rabbinic literature that refers to meritorious conduct, both inherited and personally acquired. According to *The Sayings of the Fathers* (*Pirqe ʾAbot*), charitable works and repentance erect a

---

107. In the Vg text a verse precedes the entire poem: "The children of wisdom are the congregation of the just; obedience and love are what they beget." A Christian interpolation in the LXX of v. 1 extends the promise of long life to existence beyond the grave.
108. Newsom, "Woman and the Discourse of Patriarchal Wisdom," 142-60.

shield against evil.[109] Presuming too much, earlier sages carried such promises of divine blessing for faithful service to the limit and refused to acknowledge huge cracks in this system of theological accounts. Such calculating morality, challenged by the books of Job and Ecclesiastes, continues unabated in Sirach. The Greek expression for laying up treasure occurs elsewhere only in 1 Tim 6:19, although the idea itself occurs also in Matt 6:9-20 and Luke 12:21.

Ben Sira moves beyond a meritocracy based entirely on almsgiving and charitable works, for he knows that all such human deeds count in God's sight only when accompanied by prayer. Therefore, Ben Sira promises those who honor their parents that their own children will bring joy and that God will hear the parents' prayer (v. 5). In v. 6, Ben Sira returns to the motivation for honoring parents in the fifth commandment, specifically the prolonging of life, but he places selfish interests in a broader context of religious devotion: Those who honor their parents obey the Lord.[110]

3:7-11. The second unit (if indeed a separate entity) begins with a break in the text at v. 7, which MS 248 fills with typical teaching from Sirach, now applied to the subject under consideration ("Whoever fears the Lord will honor his father"). The description of children's service to parents uses the Greek word for the work of slaves, although with a qualifying expression "just like": "he will follow his parents just like masters" (ὡς δεσπόταις δουλεύσει *hōs despotais douleusei*). The singular form of the word for "masters" (δεσπότης *despotēs*) designates "God" in the LXX of 23:1 and 34:29. The next two verses (vv. 8-9) echo an earlier concept of patriarchal blessing, one that provides an important ingredient of the plot in the stories about Isaac and his two sons, Jacob and Esau (Genesis 27; cf. Genesis 48). Ben Sira knows that children can dissimulate, like Jacob, saying one thing while behaving in a deceptive manner. True honor for parents, Ben Sira insists, unites practice with speech. The image of a deeply rooted plant in v. 8 conveys Ben Sira's idea of the beneficent paternal blessing, just as Psalm 1 conveys the Lord's blessing by means of the image of a tree planted beside abundant waters. The second half of v. 9 states that not even such well-fed roots can protect a plant from a maternal curse (cf. Prov 20:20 for the reverse idea that a son who curses his parents will lose his lamp, a metaphor for life).

The final two verses of this subunit (vv. 10-11) introduce the concept of rivalry between a father and a son. Ben Sira observes that sons gain nothing through exalting themselves at their fathers' expense but that they benefit from their fathers' honor. He extends this notion to include respect for mothers as well. Alexander Di Lella quotes Sophocles' *Antigone* (703-4), for a similar idea: "For me, my father, no treasure is so precious as your welfare. What, indeed, is a nobler ornament for children than a prospering father's fair fame, or for father than son's?"[111] Sophocles' last observation goes considerably beyond Ben Sira's exclusive emphasis on deriving benefit from a *father's* honor, with no mention of a father's benefiting from a son's honor.

3:12-16. The third subunit takes up special circumstances in which aging parents become a source of acute exasperation, tempting sons to seize authority. What should one do when parents lose control of their faculties, whether physical, emotional, or intellectual? Returning to the form of address "my son," perhaps to regain a sense of intimacy, Ben Sira urges the son to assist his father and not to stoop to the level of a father who has lost his ability to reason anymore.[112]

The next two verses (vv. 14-15) describe the atoning power of respect for parents. From early times, ancient Egyptians pictured the heart being weighed on scales against a feather, which represented justice. Israelites believed that God kept a book in which were recorded the names of those persons reckoned for life (cf. Exod 32:32, Moses' bold request to have his name blotted out of that book if the Lord did not forgive the sinful people). Later rabbinic literature also alludes to "that which balances."[113] Presumably, the people thought God kept a careful record

---

109. *Pirqe 'Abot* 4:11.
110. The promise of rest for the mother (cf. Prov 29:17) marks the beginning of the Hebrew text in MS A. The Hebrew runs to Sir 16:25.
111. See Skehan and Di Lella, *The Wisdom of Ben Sira*, 156.
112. The Hebrew has "Do not abandon him all the days of your life," whereas the Greek has "his life."
113. *Qiddushin* 40b.

of people's actions, whether good or evil, to assure that divine judgment was completely impartial—like blind justice. Naturally, such an idea stood in tension with an equally widespread belief in God's mercy. Believing that deeds of kindness atoned for sin, the author of the saying in the rabbinic tractate *Sukka* 49*b* concludes that almsgiving is superior even to sacrifice. In the same vein, Ben Sira remarks that the accumulation of credit for honoring one's parents will pay off in time of calamity, sins melting like frost in warm weather. The Greek ἐλεημοσύνη (*eleēmosynē*) of v. 14 translates a similarly technical Hebrew word, צדקות (*sĕdāqôt*), signifying "deeds of kindness."

The final verse in this unit under discussion presupposes the harsh legal statute that condemns to death anyone who curses his or her parents (Exod 21:17; Lev 20:9). Ben Sira equates dishonoring one's parents with blasphemy; the way one behaves toward parents thus becomes an indicator of religious allegiance.[114]

114. The two Hebrew mss, C and A, have different verbs for the son's treatment of parents: "abandon" (זאב *z'b*) and "despise" (בזה *bāzâ*), respectively. The Hebrew of the second half of v. 16 reads: "and whoever curses his mother provokes his Creator."

REFLECTIONS

Looking back over these sixteen verses, one is struck by the way Ben Sira comments from several perspectives on a particular commandment: Honor your father and your mother. The tendency of members of an extended family to reside in close quarters must have put enormous strain on younger family members when parents became old and lacking in judgment. Kindness to such individuals yields rich dividends, according to Ben Sira, atoning for earlier offenses.

True religion moves beyond love of God; it includes love for one's fellows, too. The recipients of acts of love are personalized here—parents in their waning years when they may become difficult and excessively demanding. In this way need becomes highly visible, and one cannot escape responsibility by entering the realm of an idealized and vague love of humankind.

SIRACH 3:17–4:10, HUMILITY AND ALMSGIVING

COMMENTARY

The present unit consists of two distinct subunits, 3:17-31 and 4:1-10, each of which begins with the traditional appeal, "my son." Verses 30-31 provide a transition from a discussion of humility and pride to consideration of almsgiving. Two sayings (vv. 25, 29) offer self-conscious reflection on wisdom, in this regard resembling Hos 14:9 and similar reflective comments ("Those who are wise understand these things;/ those who are discerning know them" [Hos 14:9 NRSV]). The best Greek mss actually lack v. 25, although it appears in ms 248.

3:17-31. The section on humility begins with conventional teaching about the virtue of humility, specifically that it incurs favor with humans and God. Ben Sira observes that persons in authority ought to be especially humble, because the Lord is honored by the lowly. The argument from the greater to the lesser is not entirely consistent, inasmuch as the supremely powerful One does not offer an example of humility. Nevertheless, various traditionists in ancient Israel acknowledged the centrality of humility—from Mosaic legislation and the description of the meek Moses to prophetic summaries of essential piety, such as Mic 6:6-8. Similarly, wisdom sayings link humility and piety ("The reward for humility and fear of the LORD/ is riches and honor and life" [Prov 22:4 NRSV]).

Perhaps the greatest temptation confronting sages was intellectual pride, particularly in a Hellenistic environment that encouraged the pursuit of every imaginable mystery. Traditional Judaism combined revelatory knowledge with human achievement but gave precedence to the former. Jewish leaders acknowledged the significance of intellectual inquiry, although imposing certain restrictions as a result of dangerous speculations into the unknown and unknowable. For example, they prohibited liturgical reading or study of the creation narrative, the mystifying description of Ezekiel's vision recorded in Ezek 1:4-28, and the list of sexual transgressions in Lev 18:6-18.

On the basis of Deut 30:11-14 and similar texts, one may conclude that some Israelites assumed that nothing worthwhile came cheaply, for the speaker insists that God's gift of the law requires no human effort at all beyond willing acceptance. The presumption that the people were prepared to ascend mountains or cross perilous seas to attain such a valuable treasure makes the announcement of a free gift all the more noteworthy. The gracious instruction leading to life could be had for the asking, but such an arrangement seemed too simple for persons accustomed to rigorous intellectual pursuits with minimal results.

Ben Sira recognizes the appeal of the unknown to the young students whom he addresses, but he also understands the hidden dangers inherent in astrological calculations among the Greeks and some forms of wisdom speculation in Jewish circles (cf. Sir 18:4-7). Hence he cautions against probing into areas that resist analysis, for in his view God has made known everything that human beings need to know.

One finds here no inkling of dissatisfaction like that expressed by Qohelet over God's restriction of knowledge (Eccl 3:11). This poignant complaint in the midst of praise for an orderly universe and a vigorous intellectual curiosity (if that is the real meaning of the obscure Hebrew word העלם [*hāʿōlām*]) contrasts mightily with Ben Sira's stern warning against investigating the secrets of the universe. In a sense, however, he merely serves as a guardian of sanity, inasmuch as some facts will forever remain locked in mystery, and as a reminder that sacred tradition already contains enough mystery to keep most students occupied for the remainder of their lives. As for anything else, a statement in Deut 29:29[28] suffices: "The secret things belong to the LORD our God, but the revealed things belong to us and to our children forever, to observe all the words of this law" (NRSV).

The psalmist recognizes the need for controlling intellectual pride and boasts about mastering that temptation (Psalm 131). This modest person pleads not guilty to preoccupation with things too great and marvelous. The dominant image in v. 2 is either that of an infant cuddling against its mother's breast, suggesting that the probing mind has finally achieved rest, or that of a weaned child who has begun to venture forth on his or her own, a fine image for intellectual progress toward independent thought. This attitude, too, differs greatly from that of Qohelet, who complains that knowledge lies beyond human perception (Eccl 7:24).

The language of these texts on the proper scope of intellectual inquiry includes a wide range of expression, but a few words stand out. Among them are the ordinary word for "seeking" (דרש *dāraš*), a verb expressing penetrating study (חקר *ḥāqar*), and four adjectives for the hidden (נסתרת *nistārôt*), the wonderful (פלאות *pĕlāʾôt*; נפלאות *niplāʾôt*), the deep (עמק *ʿāmōq*), and the distant (רחוק *rāḥôq*). Ben Sira's use of this weighty vocabulary lends credence to the hypothesis that he has in mind Greek speculation of a cosmogonic and theosophical character. Cosmogonic speculation centered in the question of the governance of the universe, and theosophical ruminations explored the hidden or mystical nature of the deity. The psalmist who composed Psalm 139 marvels that, unlike human knowledge, God's knowledge of the worshiper has no limit; here one finds some of the same vocabulary listed above, specifically the verb for rigorous investigation (*ḥāqar*) and the adjectives for "distant" (מרחוק *mērāḥôq*), "wonderful" (פליאה *pĕlîʾâ*; cf. v. 14), and "secret" (בסתר *bassēter*). One can easily concur in the exuberant conclusion that such divine knowledge is too wonderful, beyond human grasp (v. 6).

Verses 25-31 contrast obstinate individuals with persons who listen to sound advice, attributing salvific generosity to sages who experience the joy of helping needy persons.[115]

Ben Sira characterizes obdurate persons as sinners who lack enough good deeds to ward off inevitable calamity, whereas responsive individuals perform acts of kindness that prevent harm from striking them. The concept of reward and retribution underlies such thinking, and the language echoes the description of Pharaoh as hard-hearted in Exod 7:14 and the sage par excellence, Solomon, who requested a hearing heart to equip him for the task of ruling the nation. The Hebrew for an obdurate mind or will ("a hard heart" [לב כבד *lēb kābēd*]) indicates a heavy weight of arrogance that increases with every obstinate act; and its opposite ("a wise heart" [לב חכם *lēb ḥākām*]) becomes even lighter when overcome by joy.

Ben Sira's notion of retribution has no reference to a future life; "at the end," therefore, indicates disaster in this present existence. The scorner (לץ *lēṣ*) frequently provoked scathing rebuke in the book of Proverbs, but to no avail. Ben Sira even associates such persons with madness and describes them as active lovers of evil, not merely acquiescing in loathsome conduct. From such scoundrels only evil can proceed, so deep-rooted have their misdeeds become.

According to 3:29, an obedient will understands the sayings of the wise, and an attentive ear brings joy to a sage. Both qualities apply to teachers and to students, the former needing obedient listeners and the latter becoming wise through obedience.

Like fire, obstinate conduct threatens the existence of sinners. Ben Sira lacks confidence in the judgment of sinners to take advantage of the available antidote to sin, although the wise provide examples of almsgiving that atones for wrongdoing. Belief in the efficacy of charitable deeds led to an expression, attributed to Rabbi Aqiba, that God placed the poor on earth to provide a means for the rich to attain salvation through almsgiving.[116]

4:1-10. The final section of Part I (1:1–4:10) takes up the matter of duties toward marginalized citizens of the community, specifically the poor, widows, orphans, and sojourners. Ben Sira grounds social ethics in God's conduct toward the needy and promises divine approval for acts of kindness. The teacher recognizes the facts of life, the temptation for rulers to curry favor among powerful citizens, but he offsets this reality with the reminder that God hears the cry of the oppressed when they curse those who spurn them.

The Hebrew text of v. 1 has "mock" (לעג *lā'ag*) instead of "defraud" (ἀποστερέω *apostereō*) as in the Greek text, recalling Prov 17:5 ("Those who mock the poor insult their Maker" [NRSV]; cf. Prov 14:31, "Those who oppress the poor insult their Maker" [NRSV]). This verse also has a reference to embittered eyes, presumably made that way through harsh experience. Ben Sira urges his listeners to offer assistance without delay (cf. 29:8), thus conferring dignity on persons reduced to poverty. In v. 3, the Hebrew reads "boil" (חמר *ḥāmar*) and "bowels of the oppressed" (דך *m'y dk*), conveying the idea of seething emotions. Ancient Israelites thought of the intestines as the seat of turbulent feelings.

Verses 4-6 warn against incurring the wrath of needy persons through outright rejection of their petition or a furtive glance away so as to avoid eye contact with them. The operative words in v. 6, "cry out" (צעק *ṣā'aq*) and "cry" (צעקה *ṣě'āqâ*), belong to liturgical tradition (cf. Exod 22:23[22], "If you do abuse them, when they cry out to me, I will surely heed their cry" [NRSV]; Ps 22:25).[117]

Verses 7-10 treat the relationships among the several social classes in the Jewish community. Ben Sira offers advice on how to ingratiate oneself to the entire "congregation" (עדה *'ēdâ*). That includes proper respect for the ruling aristocracy as well as for those in need. Under the Ptolemaic rulers in Egypt, Jerusalem had a number of officials, a pattern that continued in the Sanhedrin. These aristocrats demanded respect, which

---

115. The place of v. 25 varies in the MS tradition; it occurs after v. 27 in the Hebrew and Syriac texts.
116. Baba Bathra 10a.

117. The Hebrew of v. 6, צורו (*ṣûrô*, "his Rock"), may be a mistake for יוצרו (*yôṣěrô*, "his Maker"), which the Greek MSS attest (ὁ ποιήσας αὐτόν *ho poiēsas auton*).

was easy enough to give; as for the poor, one should acknowledge their salutation, which preceded a request for alms. Ben Sira's reference to rescuing the oppressed recalls similar advice from Lemuel's mother in Prov 31:8-9, for royal ideology demanded that kings rescue the needy. This ideal seldom found expression in actual practice; most kings occupied themselves with military ventures aimed at securing—or improving—their political situation. The allusion to courageous rendering of a verdict does not necessarily imply membership in the legal profession, for ordinary citizens were often called upon to render judicial decisions.

Ben Sira presses his point home by calling upon everyone to assume parental responsibility for those in need. The reward makes such behavior worth the effort, according to Ben Sira. He promises that God will call these surrogate parents "children." Such imagery of God as parent, although rare, occurs enough times to make it particularly poignant.[118] The section closes on a high note, the staggering assurance that "God will be gracious and deliver you from harm," or if one follows the Greek, "God will love you more than your mother does."

118. Cf. Job 29:16; 31:18; Ps 68:6; Isa 1:17; 49:15; 66:13. See M. J. Lagrange, "La Paternité de Dieu dans l'ancien Testament," *RB* 5 (1908) 481-99.

REFLECTIONS

In this section, Ben Sira addresses an issue that was dear to the pious in Israel: the role of humility in the presence of divine mystery and human need. Beginning with appreciation for the humble by their peers, the unit closes by asserting that God, too, looks with favor on the humble. Two areas in which humility finds expression are highlighted: (1) intellectual inquiry and (2) the attitude toward marginalized citizens. Ben Sira recognizes the enormous gulf between human and divine knowledge, indeed the utter reliance of people on God for insight, here understood as the gift of Torah; but the teacher also perceives the practical implications of humility. Anyone who truly understands the meaning of humility will perform acts of kindness in a way that allows recipients to retain their dignity.

SIRACH 4:11–6:17

PART II

OVERVIEW

This section consists of discrete proverbs concerning relationships, both private and public. A brief poem in praise of wisdom (4:11-19) introduces the sayings, with alternating third- and first-person narrative. (The Greek text lacks this particular feature, describing wisdom throughout in third person.)

SIRACH 4:11-19, IN PRAISE OF WISDOM

COMMENTARY

The Hebrew of this poem is patterned after Prov 1:22-33 and 8:4-36, where Wisdom extols her virtues. This mode of address returns in Sir 24:3-22. The first-person account in the Greek echoes the style of comparable poems praising Isis (aretologies). A remarkable link between serving wisdom and serving God occurs in v. 14. Moreover, wisdom possesses the power to turn over those who resist her instruction to their own destruction. Such a figure is no ordinary person, and the poem comes close to hymnic praise of deity.

Using the image of treacherous paths and rigorous testing, Ben Sira acknowledges the difficulty of acquiring wisdom, but he insists that persistence pays off eventually. Earlier religious thinkers attributed testing to Yahweh, assuming that genuine faithfulness could best be ascertained when believers faced adversity and triumphed. Only as loyal servants demonstrated integrity could one be sure that religious devotion would endure, regardless of the circumstances. Ben Sira closely associates loyalty to wisdom and divine service (v. 14).

4:11. The initial verse in the Greek text echoes Prov 4:8, which promises that wisdom will exalt those who value her. The Hebrew and Syriac texts in v. 11 have a different verb, "to teach" (למד *lāmad*), as if to emphasize the stage of learning rather than the end result of respect among peers. The spelling of "wisdom" as חכמות (*ḥokmôt*) rather than the more usual חכמה (*ḥokmâ*) resembles Prov 1:20 and 9:1, which state that wisdom cries out in the busy streets and that she has built a house containing seven pillars.[119] A pun on the two consonants, ב (*b*) and נ (*n*), occurs in the Hebrew words for "sons" and their activity ("her sons" [בניה *bānêhâ*]) and מבינים (*mĕbînîm*), a participle from the verb בין (*bîn*, "to understand"). The NRSV's "her children" captures the wider sense of the expression *bānêhâ,* although in the context of the classroom it had the more restricted meaning of "sons" and "students."[120]

4:12. In keeping with wisdom's hiddenness and her readiness to put individuals to a test, this verse assures those who actively search for wisdom that they will obtain favor. The Hebrew text identifies the Lord as the source of favor, agreeing with the statement in Prov 8:35 ("For whoever finds me finds life and obtains favor from the Lord"), where the first colon uses the verb מצא (*māṣā'*) and a participle from the same root with the sense of "finding" instead of בקש (*bāqaš*), as here, "to seek." The Greek text does not indicate

---

119. Patrick W. Skehan, "The Seven Columns of Wisdom's House in Proverbs 1–9," *CBQ* (1947) 190-98, and in revised form Skehan, *Studies in Israelite Poetry and Wisdom*, CBQMS 1 (Washington, D.C.: Catholic Biblical Association of America, 1971) 9-14.
120. B. Couroyer, "Un Égyptianisme dans Ben Sira IV,11," *RB* 82 (1975) 206-17.

whether the favor derives from God, from wisdom, or from human beings. In the thinking of Israel's sages, conformity with wisdom's dictates entitles persons to rewards from all three sources. An epithet for Yahweh, "the living one," can be viewed in the context of Canaanite religion in which Baal dies and rises again in accord with seasonal patterns. The divine title "the living one" asserts that Israel's God does not die and consequently must be reckoned with at all times. The concept of a deity who transcends natural seasons reinforces notions of both justice and mercy in that Yahweh always observes human conduct and watches over the faithful.

4:13. This verse moves beyond the images of loving and seeking wisdom to holding her fast. Together, these three ideas refer to an individual's prizing the life of the intellect, expending enormous energy to acquire an education, and building moral character that embodies the learning. The persons who embrace woman wisdom, an idea implicit in loving her (v. 12), and hold on to her for dear life will discover honor. Here Ben Sira uses the verb *māṣā'*, along with כבוד (*kābôd*, "glory," "honor"; δόξα *doxa*) as the direct object of the verb. In this instance, both the Hebrew and the Greek indicate that the Lord bestows blessing on faithful individuals. The concept of blessing (ברכות *běrākôt*, plural) included long life, a loving family, and prosperity. The benefits that accrue from successful pursuit of wisdom thus pertain to one's status in the community and to the privacy of a family. The Greek text states that the Lord blesses every place wisdom enters, whereas the Hebrew concentrates on wisdom's followers.

According to Prov 9:1-6, wisdom has constructed a grand house with seven columns and invites guests to a banquet. Naturally, her house is believed to be a dwelling in which blessing abounds. In a later poem (14:20-27), Ben Sira describes those who meditate on wisdom as being blessed and urges them to pursue her like hunters on a chase, daring to pitch their tents near her house.

Ancient peoples imagined blessing and curse as states of mind and body subject to outside control. Professional cursers like Balaam, whom Balak, king of Moab, hired to denounce Israel in the story preserved in Numbers 22–24, were thought to have possessed considerable power. This tradition about Balaam survived outside the Bible and has been confirmed by a stroke of good fortune that yielded a text, discovered at Deir 'Alla near the Dead Sea, that actually refers to a prophet named Balaam. Such professionals were naturally feared, although the biblical narrative portrays this prophet as being subject to a greater power, the will of Yahweh.

Blessings, too, carried immense weight.[121] They also inspired certain incidents in the Bible, notably the story about Jacob's deceit of his father and receipt of the paternal blessing, to Esau's great dismay. The contravening divine will entered the picture, too, when human wishes did not coincide with Yahweh's plans; the strange scene describing Jacob's last words in Gen 48:8-22 sets aged father against son and ignores once more the right of primogeniture, giving the blessing to Ephraim rather than to Manasseh, the firstborn. These stories suggest that neither the curse nor the blessing automatically achieved its goal, contrary to much that has been written over the years.

4:14. The image moves beyond "seeking," "loving," and "holding" to that of "serving." The language belongs to Israel's cultic life; a noun formed from the verb שרת (*šārat*) applies to priestly ministers of the altar (משרתי מזבח *měšārtê mizbēaḥ;* cf. Joel 1:13, also called "ministers of Yahweh" [משרתי יהוה *měšārtê YHWH*] in Joel 1:9 and 2:17). Similarly, the verb בקש (*bāqaš*, "to seek") belongs alongside other terms like דרש (*dāraš*) in describing inquiry of the Lord at the cultic center. The verb for "loving" (אהב *'āhab*), also functions as liturgical vocabulary in addition to its use in the secular realm. These verbs from the experience of worship indicate how Ben Sira allowed his personal piety to shape his everyday language. In vv. 11-13, the religious dimension of these verbs remains obscure, whereas it comes to prominence in v. 14. Now Ben Sira equates divine service with intellectual pursuit. This idea differs appreciably from the earlier notion that religion both orients knowledge and makes it possible, or that spiritual insight crowns

---

121. The classic analysis of blessing and curse appears in Johannes Pedersen's monumental work, *Israel,* vols. 1-2 (London: Oxford University Press, 1926) 182-212, 411-52. In the context of Yahweh's covenant with Israel, blessings are promised to those who serve the Lord faithfully, and those who turn away are threatened with curses.

all true knowledge. The older formulation, "The fear of God is the beginning/first principle of knowledge," has yielded an even bolder claim: Devotion to a life of the mind is identical to that of religious leaders. Both scholars and priests minister to the Lord, each in his or her own way.

The epithet "the Holy One"[122] occurs often in the Isaianic corpus, especially in the longer form, "the holy one of Israel." One can read the Hebrew for "Holiness" (קדוש *qādôš*, or קדש *qōdeš*) as a reference to a person or to a place. This title for God became the favorite of rabbinic Judaism, where it is often followed by "Blessed be He." Like v. 12, where a participle form of the operative verb occurs (those who *love* her *love* life), this verse employs a verb and a noun from the same root (those who *serve* the Holy One *serve* her). This feature of Hebrew syntax occurs frequently, indicating no aversion to repeating an idea in close proximity. Unlike the second colon of v. 14 in Hebrew, the Greek is perfectly clear: "and the Lord loves those who love her."[123]

4:15. The next verse continues the general topic of the preceding four, although shifting in the Hebrew to first-person address. In the thought of ancient Israelites, as also in Egyptian wisdom, the verb שמע (*šāmaʿ*, "to hear") indicates obedience. "Those who hear me" are persons who conduct their lives in compliance with wisdom's proclamation. Such persons, Ben Sira avers, will judge accurately, with integrity; the Hebrew אמת (*ʾĕmet*) suggests "truth" or "reliability." The idea that the righteous will judge nations, which the Greek declares, derives from an ingenious reading of the Hebrew word for "truth," *ʾĕmet*. By repointing the consonants to אמת (*ʾummōt*), a rare expression for nations results. In this way, the translator introduces a concept that was more at home in the Alexandrian context, specifically Israel's relationship to non-Jews. The same idea that wise Jews will judge nations appears in Wis 3:8 (cf. the Prov 29:9*a* LXX). In popular Hellenistic thought, the wise were entitled to rule over the people (cf. the idea of philosopher kings associated with Plato). The initial verb in the second colon of v. 15 parallels the verb for "hearing" in the first colon: "Those who listen to me" // "Those who obey me." The sentence concludes with a promise of secure dwelling in the inner recesses of wisdom's house. The language has an erotic undertone, implying that obedient ones will reside in wisdom's bedroom. Such fantasy enjoyed free rein in ancient speculation about wisdom.[124] Reading ישכן (*yiškan*) as "dwells," one can translate as follows: "Whoever obeys me dwells in safety; whoever listens to me resides in the inner chamber of my house."

4:16. This verse is lacking in the Hebrew. The Greek text, which turned the idea of faithfulness in v. 15 into an entirely different notion (*ʾemet*, "truth" to אמת [*ummōt*, "nations"]), now introduces faithfulness. In doing so, it promises an inheritance to those who remain loyal to wisdom, extending the legacy to their descendants. That inheritance consists of personified wisdom, who freely bestows herself and all accompanying blessings on faithful lovers. Because the Hebrew of this verse is not extant, we cannot tell whether the language was intended to evoke ancient sentiment connected with the divine promise that Israel constituted Yahweh's private possession (see, e.g., Exod 19:5-6).

4:17-19. The last section in this unit issues a somber warning that pursuit of wisdom's blessings entails arduous effort and not a little danger. The image of testing suggests that wisdom will intentionally lead people along false paths in order to determine their worth, in the end returning to a straight path and rewarding the faithful but abandoning others to thieves. The difficult experiences in classrooms probably inspired this talk about trials, for the life of students included numerous unpleasantries ranging from harsh whippings to painful thinking. The latter included tedious memorization of texts, extensive practice of calligraphy, copious recitations, and rigorous thinking—all at the expense of frivolity and fun with persons of the opposite sex.

---

122. Rudolf Otto, *The Idea of the Holy* (New York: Oxford University Press, 1958; originally 1923), made the concept of the numinous a household word in theological discourse. His analysis of holiness, which he described as a *mysterium tremendum et fascinans*, an awesome yet alluring mystery, brings Isa 6:1-13 into the heart of the discussion of all religious experience.

123. By transposing two consonants, the Syriac rendering of this colon, "and God loves her dwellings," misreads the present Hebrew "and his God" as "her tent" (ואלהו *wʾlhw* = ואהלו *wʾhlw*).

124. By changing two consonants in the verb פת (*pat*), Rudolf Smend arrives at two perfectly synonymous cola: "whoever obeys" // "whoever listens." See Smend, *Die Weisheit des Jesus Sirach*, 40.

The excessively long initial verse (v. 17) cannot stand alone, although it introduces the situation that vv. 18-19 resolve. It states that wisdom disguises herself, accompanying her followers and putting them to tests. Earlier sages often spoke of discipline as an unpleasantry that must be endured in the educational task. The Hebrew verb signifying "disguise" has the basic sense of forgiveness; the word recalls the notorious נכריה (*nokriyyâ*, "strange or foreign woman") in Proverbs 1–9, which Joseph Blenkinsopp plausibly interprets in the light of exclusivism during the time of Ezra and Nehemiah.[125] Another term for this dangerous foe in Proverbs 1–9 is אשה זרה (*'iššâ zārâ*), "the foreign woman."

The exact nature of her alienness is unclear, but possibilities include ethnicity, spirituality, and moral character. In short, the foreign woman may have been a non-Israelite whose strange ways and relative freedom set her apart and enhanced her seductive powers; she may have been a practitioner of a rival cult to Yahwism, particularly one associated with sexual license; she may have been an Israelite with loose morals. Ben Sira's choice of vocabulary brings all this speculation to bear on the experience of acquiring knowledge.

The language of v. 17 emphasizes wisdom's active involvement in testing her followers, first by specifying that she walks alongside them and then by indicating that she probes them directly (lit., "to their face"). Furthermore, the noun for "trials" (מסה *massâ*) contains the consonants of the verb "to test" (נסה *nāsâ*), which occurs in Gen 22:1 to describe God's action in testing Abraham by demanding that he sacrifice his son Isaac. The same verb appears in the story about King Ahaz, recorded in Isaiah 7, this time in the mouth of the outwardly pious Judean ruler. His smug, hypocritical remark, "I should not petition nor test Yahweh" (Isa 7:12, author's trans.), outraged the prophet Isaiah, who endeavored to persuade the king to rely on the Lord rather than on the might of Assyrian soldiers.[126]

The Hebrew text of vv. 17-18 completes the thought as follows: "when his mind concurs with mine, I will once more put him on a straight path and make known to him my secrets." The Greek expands the idea of trials, noting that wisdom will bring fear and dread (cf. Exod 15:16), testing followers with discipline (παιδεία *paideia*). Here the Greek verb βάσανισει (*basanisei*) suggests "rubbing on a touchstone" to determine an object's authenticity.[127]

The imagery in the Hebrew involves the heart's becoming full of wisdom and the person's then being led on an accurate ("straight") route, until full disclosure takes place. Occasional hints of esoteric lore surface in biblical literature, e.g., Job 11:6a "that [God] would tell you the secrets of wisdom" (NRSV), and Dan 2:22, "He reveals deep and hidden things;/ he knows what is in the darkness,/ and light dwells with him" (NRSV). Similarly, Qohelet speaks about obscurity and deep mystery, first in Eccl 3:11 ("He has made everything beautiful in its time; also he has put the unknown[128] in their mind, because of which no one can find out the work God has done from beginning to end"), and later in Eccl 7:24 ("Distant—whatever is—and extraordinarily deep; who can find it?").

The Greek text adds what is surely implicit in the Hebrew of v. 18: "and she will gladden him." The last verse (v. 19) returns again to the threatening posture, wisdom's final words here. If he turns away from her, she warns, she will cast him off, abandoning him to destruction. The image of a simpleton attempting to negotiate life on his own and ending up like the ruins of a deserted village or in the hands of robbers (cf. Obad 5, "plunderers by night" [NRSV]) brings this unit to an effective conclusion. The doublet in Hebrew makes the warning even more poignant.

In sum, this poem praises wisdom by associating her with life and its divine source. It asserts that wisdom's loyal followers attain joy, exalted position, and honor. Ben Sira's language inclines toward the sacral when describing wisdom's devotees as ministers—i.e., priests at the altar. The picture is not completely rosy, for Ben Sira acknowledges the unpleasant fact that intellectual inquiry

---

125. Blenkinsopp, "The Social Context of the 'Outsider Woman' in Proverbs 1–9," 457-73.
126. For discussion of testing in the HB, see Crenshaw, *A Whirlpool of Torment*, 1-7, indeed throughout the book.
127. Skehan and Di Lella, *The Wisdom of Ben Sira*, 172.
128. A nominal form of the verb עלם (*'elem*, "to be dark, obscure") occurs in Job 11:6 and Eccl 3:11. This use of עלם (*'elem*) has also shown up in Ugaritic texts.

demands arduous toil, particularly in the early stages until the pursuit becomes natural. Ben Sira understands this initial hardship as wisdom's testing of individuals to determine whether they will remain resolute in their study. The dire consequences of turning away from wisdom contrast with an unveiling of secrets to the faithful.

REFLECTIONS

A significant feature of this section is the place of the intellect in biblical religion. The modern tendency to disdain intellectual pursuits as the domain of nerds and eggheads has made a negative impact on the church at every level. Social pressure on bright young people often places demands on them to hide their intellectual achievements and aspirations rather than risk rejection by less motivated peers. Society's refusal to value education has forced potential teachers to enter more lucrative professions like medicine, law, business, and scientific research. School standards, therefore, continue to decline, threatening society at large. The lowering of the reading level in textbooks, known in the trade as "dumbing down," and the constant pressure from competing interest groups to highlight private readings worsen the situation. Addiction to television compounds the problem, contributing to vastly shortened attention spans and mental laziness.

In years past, pastors belonged to the intellectually elite members of society, having received formal education in the classics. The situation has changed dramatically today, and many intellectually gifted individuals choose more lucrative professions. Few pastors now excel in the life of the mind, partly because of disinterest, but also because of mounting pressure on every hand to attend to all kinds of professional responsibilities. Moreover, many highly successful televangelists fill the airwaves with messages that extol the life of the Spirit at the expense of the mind. Some of these preachers even consider intellectual pursuits alien to spirituality, partly because of residual fallout from the historical-critical study of the Bible and partly because of well-known extremists in some universities.

Ben Sira elevates the life of the mind, equating divine service with devotion to the pursuit of knowledge. This attitude suggests that religious people need to take another look at the way they spend leisure time, as well as their commitment to education. Perhaps one can serve the Creator by studying just as effectively as one can by doing good deeds. Using the brain to explore the unknown may please God just as much as any number of acts, and applying the intellect to devout meditation may be looked upon with even more favor than some deeds of kindness. Both intellectual rigor and moral rectitude belong in the arsenal of religious people.

Furthermore, childlike curiosity should be encouraged in intellectual research. Ben Sira's stress on active seeking furnishes a vivid contrast to contemporary passive education. The beauty of intellectual pursuit is its open-endedness, for no one actually ever achieves the goal. The treasure at rainbow's end simply sits there, always beckoning but ever receding in the distance. Most of the excitement comes from the search; those individuals who sit at home and wait for wisdom to drop down upon them miss everything. In a similar vein, Mary L. Caldwell proposes that much of the value in prayer comes in the act itself, not in the answer.[129]

---

129. Mary L. Caldwell, *Praying for Fishhooks* (Macon, Ga.: Smyth & Helwys, 1994). The title for this book on intercessory prayer is taken from an incident in Twain's *The Adventures of Huckleberry Finn*, in which Huck prays for fishhooks and gets fishing line instead.

SIRACH 4:20-31, SOCIAL STATUS, SHAME, AND SPEECH

COMMENTARY

This section contains practical advice, largely stated negatively, on speaking one's mind regardless of the social classes involved, and on generosity. Ben Sira distinguishes two kinds of shame, one desirable and the other undesirable. He will discuss shame more thoroughly in later chaps. (41:14–42:8; cf. 20:22-23).

4:20. The customary address by a teacher to a student, derived from that of parent to child, opens this unit in the Hebrew and the Latin. The first observation, "Guard the time and noise," reverses usual sentence order in Hebrew, perhaps to emphasize the objects, which usually come after verbs. On the basis of Eccl 3:1, where the nouns for "season" and "time" (זמן ועת *zĕmān wěʿēt*) occur, one may conjecture that המון (*hāmôn*, "noise") is a corruption of an original *zĕmān*. The verb שמר (*šāmar*), the imperative of which is translated "guard," also has the sense of "observe." Ben Sira urges students to watch over the occasions that come along, alert to opportune moments (καιροί *kairoi*). The Greek term καιρός (*kairos*) distinguishes these quality times from uneventful ordinary times (χρόνος *chronos*). Wise students inspect the different situations that emerge over the course of a day and seize the opportune moment for action.

This simple admonition to watch for promising moments possibly relates to the venerable practice of observing the times in order to control events magically. Specialists who knew the times are mentioned in Daniel; such individuals who studied the stars and chronicled seasonal changes sought mastery of astrology for the purpose of controlling events for themselves and their clients. The practice thrived in Mesopotamia, where wisdom has been plausibly defined as magic,[130] and in Egypt, where the well-known *Book of the Dead* was compiled. Priestly groups in Israel, particularly those belonging to the sect at Qumran, devoted much energy to calendrical matters. They believed that God had specified exact times for sacred observances.

Precisely what "the evil" had to do with the times remains unclear, unless it signifies a misfortune for which omens were sought. Ben Sira continues with "And fear the evil," without elaborating on the nature of this object of dread. Alexander Di Lella understands the potential threat as Hellenism, the tendency to glorify Greek customs and ideas at the expense of Jewish practices and thoughts.[131] Nothing in this context points in such a specific direction, however deplorable attempts to become more Greek than Jewish may have been reckoned in later literature. In contrast to the unknown author of 1 Macc 1:11-15, who expresses chagrin over the efforts of Jews in the time of Antiochus IV Epiphanes (175–164 BCE) to efface all evidence of circumcision so they could participate in athletic contests in gymnasia, Ben Sira remains silent about such activity. Similar contempt for priests who highly prized Greek honors while despising Jewish values issues from the pen of the writer of 2 Macc 4:13-15.

Ben Sira warns against conduct that prevents students from standing up for what they believe. Being ashamed of taking a stand covers any number of situations, although embarrassment over identification with people whose customs seem backward and uncultured certainly fits the context. So does reticence to espouse unpopular causes when persons of power and influence resist them. Ben Sira may have in mind the many different ways influential, but corrupt, people pressure the wise to keep silent for fear of unwelcome consequences, for their livelihood often depended on the goodwill of the affluent. He urges students to guard their integrity in the same way they watch over opportune moments.

4:21. This verse reminds the reader that not all shame is the same, some being an

---

130. See Lambert, *Babylonian Wisdom Literature*, 1.

131. Skehan and Di Lella, *The Wisdom of Ben Sira*, 175-76.

indication of honor while other instances signify disgrace. One ought to be ashamed of deplorable conduct, which entails sin ("iniquity" [עוון ʿāwôn; ἁμαρτία hamartia]), but a person should not be ashamed of actions worthy of honor and favor (כבוד וחן kābôd wĕḥen; δόξα καὶ χάρις doxa kai charis). The literary form of this statement consists of a particle of existence, "there is" (יש yēš), followed by predicate nominatives. In this instance, the two cola use synonymous parallelism but specify opposite types of shame: "For there is a shame that leads to sin,/ and there is a shame that is glory and favor." The LXX adds this verse after Prov 26:11.

At some point during the transmission of the HB, the divine name "Baal" caused sufficient unease to prompt changes in some personal names using this appellation. The name "Ishbosheth" thus resulted (2 Sam 1:1), with the implausible meaning "man of shame" instead of "man of Baal." In at least one instance, the change did not take place in every occurrence of the name, for Saul's son Meribbaal (1 Chr 8:34) is also called Mephibosheth (2 Sam 4:4). Clearly, Ben Sira's sensitivity toward shame has ancient precedent in Jewish scribal circles and does not, therefore, necessarily reflect the influence of Mediterranean culture, with its strong emphasis on honor and shame.

4:22. "Show no favoritism to the detriment of your true self" seems to represent the sense of v. 22a, although the Hebrew may warn against partiality toward oneself—i.e., selfishness. The Hebrew phrase "to lift up your face" implies showing favor toward someone, often in warning against being unduly influenced by wealth (cf. 42:1b and 35:16a for additional uses in Sirach). The second colon in v. 22 may advise against a sense of shame that leads to one's downfall. The Hebrew "do not stumble at your stumblings" can be improved by adopting the verb from the Greek, "do not be ashamed" (μὴ ἐντραπῇς mē entrapēs). The verse then warns against a shame that leads to ruin, but it does not indicate what Ben Sira has in mind. This generality leaves the saying open to many applications.

4:23. This verse counsels against withholding comment when the occasion for speech presents itself, thereby concealing one's intelligence. The use of the weighty expression for time in v. 23 (עולם ʿôlām instead of עת ʿēt) might indicate that speculation about the world to come and this age has already begun. Ben Sira has no use for such optimistic hopes of existence after death, but he knows that some moments are filled with potential, and he does not want his students to let them pass unnoticed. On the basis of 8:9 in Greek, "to give answer in time of need" (ἐν καιρῷ χρείας δοῦναι ἀπόκρισιν en kairō chreias dounai apokrisin), Rudolf Smend reads χρεία (chreia) for σωτηρία (sōtēria, "need" for "safety").[132] The author of Eccl 3:7 also recognizes a time for speech—indeed a time for everything under the sun.

The second colon in v. 23 acknowledges that wisdom can go unnoticed if one lacks the courage to speak up or the ability to recognize an opportune moment. To be sure, the adage that "remaining quiet and being thought a fool is better than opening one's mouth and removing all doubt" possesses some truth. One aim of ancient education was to equip young people for effective speech, which entails a capacity to discern the right time to respond.

4:24. The adverb כי (kî; γάρ gar) signals an explanation of the sentiment expressed in v. 23: "Through speech intelligence is made known and understanding through the tongue's response." This artful literary inclusio ABB´A´:

A "through speech"
  B intelligence (חכמה ḥokmâ)
  B´ understanding (תבונה tĕbûnâ)
A´ "tongue's response"

employs technical vocabulary of the sages and gives voice to traditional beliefs in their circles. Despite this extraordinary praise of eloquence (cf. Prov 15:23; 16:1), these intellectuals knew that successful rogues also possessed smooth tongues. This theme found expression in the frequent warnings within the book of Proverbs about a seductress with her smooth line.[133] Quick answers and glib answers often go hand in hand, indicating that one needs to analyze the content of what is said and not just its eloquence.

---

132. Smend, *Die Weisheit des Jesus Sirach erklärt*, 44.
133. Aletti, "Seduction et Parole en Proverbes I–IX," 129-44.

4:25. The Hebrew here has contrasting parallelism: "Do not contradict God [האל *hāʾēl*] but bow before God [אלהים *ʾĕlōhîm*]." An Aramaic loan word, סרב (*sārab*), connotes verbal lying, a bold resistance to the truth. The Greek has "Do not oppose the truth" (μὴ ἀντίλεγε τῇ ἀληθείᾳ *mē antilege tē alētheia*). In Jewish piety of the first century CE, "truth" (אמת *ʾĕmet*) actually served as a divine appellation; the Gospel of John has Jesus identify himself as "the way, the truth, and the life." Similarly, the Babylonian Talmud Sanhedrin 1:18*a* mentions Truth as one of God's names.[134]

In contrast to the Hebrew of this verse, the Greek second colon introduces the concept of folly and returns to the earlier notion of shame. According to this version, one ought to be ashamed of foolishness.

4:26. Here Ben Sira advises against pride that prevents persons from confessing fault. In these circumstances, embarrassment facilitates remorse, enabling one to admit guilt. The verb שוב (*šûb*) signifies an about-face, a turning from iniquity to true confession and moral resolve confirmed by subsequent conduct. In rabbinic times a noun form, תשובה (*tĕšûbâ*), indicated the act of repentance. The second colon in v. 26 probably alludes to an ancient proverb pointing to the futility of trying to resist the inevitable—in this instance God. "Do not stand in front of a flood" calls attention to the impossibility of resisting God's will. The image of an overflowing river occurs in Isaiah 8 with reference to Assyria's might. An Eygptian proverb about the impossibility of concealing a river appears several times, attesting the popularity of such thinking. The Syriac translation of the Aramaic collection of aphorisms titled *The Sayings of Ahiqar* includes the following comment: "My son, struggle not against a man in his day, and oppose not the current of a river."

4:27-28. Ben Sira next advises against spineless surrender before fools, "spreading

---

[134]. Oesterley, *The Wisdom of Jesus the Son of Sirach or Ecclesiasticus*, 32.

oneself out" to be walked on, and showing favoritism to rulers (v. 27). At this point the Hebrew has a variant of 8:14, which states the obvious fact that litigation against a judge stands little chance of succeeding. The remark about rulers leads naturally to v. 28, which admonishes sages to fight to the death for righteousness (Greek and Syriac, "for truth") and promises assistance from above. The Hebrew adds 5:14*a* at this point.

4:29-30. Speech and actions form the two subjects of v. 29. Ben Sira advises against hasty—or haughty—speech and slovenly actions. The next verse resists the display of power in the presence of subjects: "Do not rage like a lion [or a dog] in your house or be wily and suspicious among servants." The rare expression for "your servants" (עבדתך *ʿăbuddātāk*) appears elsewhere only in Job 1:3 and Gen 26:14. According to Eccl 7:21-22, suspicion about slaves' criticism of their masters was fully justified.

4:31. The final aphorism in this unit addresses the problem of stinginess and greed by ridiculing persons whose hands open wide to receive gifts but clamp shut when others beg for alms. A hypothetical situation in Deut 15:7-8 mentions the same concept of an open and a closed hand. The idea persists into the early second century CE, for example in *Did.* 4:5 and the *Epistle of Barnabas* 19:9, where the expression is exactly the same in Greek: "Be not one who stretches out his hands to receive, but shuts them when it comes to giving."

To recapitulate, this brief section concentrates on speech, both its timing and its integrity. It warns against concealing one's intelligence, but also against exposing ignorance. Because life seldom unfolds in simple patterns, one needs to cultivate the ability to discriminate between a time for speech and a time for silence. The same discernment applies to shame, which can be both positive and negative. In all circumstances, courage plays a role, and the person who possesses power is advised to practice restraint.

REFLECTIONS

1. The issue of shame seldom surfaces today. There once was a time when honor and shame governed human conduct, particularly in the ancient Near East, as it still does in modern Asian communities. Pilch and Malina contend that this code survives in the Mediterranean world today.[135] They and others find this ancient viewpoint among obscure villagers. When asked which son in Jesus' story did the right thing, the one who said yes but did nothing or the one who said no and later obeyed his father, modern Arabs praise the first son because he honored his dad in public. They denounce the other son for dishonoring his father openly.[136]

We live in a society whose people have forgotten how to blush. Honor and shame have little value to countless individuals. The parading of private lives on television talk shows, the restoration to respectability of junk bond traders on Wall Street, and contributing to the fortunes of criminals by purchasing their stories—all these and more bear witness to a loss of the concept of honor. Christians have an obligation to recapture the virtue of honor and reinstitute the notion of shame. Any society that ignores or rewards reprehensible behavior has a terrible mark against it. Shameless individuals who disgrace public office and cavalierly run again bear witness to our moral bankruptcy. Christians who reward such candidates by helping to elect them seriously compromise the office and demonstrate shameful disregard for honor.

Ben Sira recognized different kinds of shame. Christians rightly feel shame when the nation embarks on activities that bring death and starvation to people elsewhere. A sense of outrage may, indeed, be the strongest reaction one can make to military aggression, sales of weapons, and unjust economic policies that supplement the income of a few rich citizens.

2. The most reliable indication of intellectual acumen is found in deeds, for wisdom manifests itself in moral character. In the view of ancient sages, anyone who truly listened and understood the teaching acted in accordance with its demands.

This emphasis on deeds as the evidence of wisdom provides a balance for the earlier elevation of the intellect. Ben Sira realized the necessity of complementary pairs, for some truth resides in each side. Both doing and knowing are vital components of wisdom. In religious matters, one easily slips into a type of thinking that offers simplistic answers, for consistency seems desirable at all costs. Unfortunately, most such thinking distorts the truth while lulling people to sleep. Rather than taking comfort in single-minded answers, religious people need to be reminded of faith's complexity and fragility. A false sense of ease, a pseudo-simplicity, thus characterizes many Christians' approach to crucial issues precisely when they should be forced to work out the intricacies of their faith with fear and trembling.

3. This section also makes a point that Jesus subsequently reiterated: Money can capture the heart and push God out (see also 5:1-8). The ultimate longing of the heart, whether God or mammon, determines the character of joy and the nature of security. Modern society measures a secure future in terms of a good job, adequate medical coverage, and access to a good education. Without promise of these things, people become anxious about what is denied them, bestowing unreasonable importance on the missing element.

Those who have a disproportionate share of the world's wealth have great difficulty imagining the way basic things like daily food and shelter occupy the attention of Third World peoples from dawn to dusk. We who can reasonably expect to have adequate food and a place to sleep are fortunate in that our minds are freed from the cares of subsistence. Christians have an opportunity to demonstrate gratitude by easing the burdens on those who have less.

Ben Sira knew that wealth influences those who lack it in unhealthy ways. Like so many ethicists of the ancient world, he tried to counter the temptation to curry the favor of influential citizens. The author of the Epistle of James also brought this matter

---

135. John J. Pilch and Bruce J. Malina, *Dictionary of New Testament Culture* (Peabody, Mass.: Hendrickson, 1993).
136. Pilch, " 'Beat His Ribs While He Is Young,' " 104.

to the attention of early Christians, many of whom displayed favoritism whenever rich visitors arrived in their midst. He reminded Christians that their worst enemies were wealthy citizens.

The modern church has considerable difficulty living up to the ideals of a people who do not show partiality toward those persons with money and prestige. One reason why, surely, is the need for money to fund an operating budget. Most churches need a certain number of reasonably affluent members whose generosity enables them to carry out a program. A potential problem arises, however, when persons who will undoubtedly be a drain on the budget apply for church membership. Many congregations find themselves torn between a desire for security and status, on the one hand, and a sincere wish to minister to the needy, on the other hand. Ben Sira was sufficiently observant to know that the scales naturally tilt in favor of the rich. Perhaps we should be thankful for the visible presence of those who represent real need, for they give those who have sufficient resources an occasion to be truly generous.

SIRACH 5:1-8, ON PRESUMING TOO MUCH

COMMENTARY

The author of the profound prayer in Prov 30:7-9 knew that wealthy people face a special temptation to rely on their own resources rather than trusting in God. Ben Sira also recognizes this danger, but he links it to certain additional attitudes that deny divine sovereignty. These attitudes fall into the category of theodicy, for they assert that God does not really punish evil people. In this brief section on theodicy,[137] Ben Sira takes up at least three arguments that sinners often use in defense of their presumption with regard to God's mercy: (1) Acquired wealth proves divine favor; (2) expected retribution for sin has not fallen; and (3) God's readiness to forgive gives one ample time to repent. The mention of wealth in v. 8 provides an inclusio with the first verse in chap. 5 and brings the unit to a close.

The language of this entire section assumes a combative posture, an authoritative figure issuing negative commands or prohibitions. The operative command "Do not" occurs at least once in every verse, twice in vv. 1 and 7. Ben Sira adopts an ancient formula from debates, "Do not say," which is then followed by proscribed sentiments.[138] He appears to address distinct attitudes toward the relationship between sin and punishment.

5:1-3. The first of these commands relates to possessions. One who has amassed a fortune tends to lean on it rather than trust in God. The Hebrew word for "wealth" (חיל *ḥayil*) implies vigor, hence it fits nicely into a context of self-reliance. The pregnant expression is matched by an idiom for control over one's destiny, "There is power in my hand."[139] The second verse reiterates the thought, repeating the verb "to lean" (שען *šāʿan*), but using a different word for "his strength" (כחו *kōḥô*) before the final phrase about pursuing one's desire (cf. Job 31:7*b*). Confident in his or her own might, the bold sinner is thought to boast, "Who can prevail over my strength?" Ben Sira reminds those who would speak in this way that Yahweh will seek out the persecuted, which must mean that the oppressors cannot escape punishment. The same expression occurs in Eccl 3:15.

5:4. A second attitude toward delayed punishment surfaces in this verse. Ben Sira warns against saying, "I sinned and what has happpened to me?" Here we come up against an age-old dilemma: People do wrong and appear to suffer no ill consequences for

---

137. On this "compendium" of theodicy, see G. L. Prato, *Il problema della teodicea in Ben Sira*, AnBib 65 (Rome: Pontifical Biblical Institute, 1975) 367-69; and Crenshaw, "The Problem of Theodicy in Sirach," 47-64. See also Crenshaw, *Urgent Advice and Probing Questions*, 155-74.
138. Crenshaw, "The Problem of Theodicy in Sirach," 48-51.
139. W. G. E. Watson, "Reclustering לאליד *l'lyd*," *Bib* 58 (1977) 213-15, claims that לאה (*lāʾâ*, "to be strong") has yielded a noun, לא (*lāʾ*, "power"). He divides לאליד (*l'lyd*) as לאליד (*l'leyād*) and translates "power in the hand of."

their actions. As time elapses and nothing unpleasant comes their way, they conclude that God does not punish the wicked. To counter such skepticism, Ben Sira reaffirms traditional belief that God is longsuffering. The expression "God is longsuffering" (אל ארך אפים הוא *'ēl 'erek 'appayim hû*) echoes the liturgical confession in Exod 34:6-7, in this instance the divine patience. The image "long of nose" suggests that God's anger does not flare up quickly but requires considerable provocation. Here, again, comparison with Ecclesiastes is instructive: "Because sentence against an evil deed is not executed speedily, the human heart is fully set to do evil" (Eccl 8:11 NRSV).

5:5-6. A third presumptive attitude concerns God's readiness to forgive. According to this opinion, the scope of one's sins does not really matter so long as they are atoned for by sacrifice and good works. Thinking forgiveness a light matter, the sinner freely indulges, "multiplying iniquity." Ben Sira warns against this kind of overconfidence, which trusts in Yahweh's compassionate nature to forgive an abundance of sin. Here, too, the decisive language for divine compassion (רחום *raḥûm*) derives from Exod 34:6-7. The apostle Paul combats a similar view in Rom 6:1; it seems that some Christians argued that the greater the sin, the more copiously God's forgiveness manifests itself. Such reasoning provides a dubious justification for continuing in a state of rebellion, indeed, for excelling in evil. The Mishnah offers evidence of similar presumption, warning against thinking that one can sin and ask forgiveness only to repeat the offense.[140] The rabbi responsible for this saying believed that for such persons the Day of Atonement had no efficacy.

5:7. Another attitude that Ben Sira rejects outright consists of calculated delay in the act of repentance. Assuming that God's wrath comes rather slowly, people hope for enough warning to enable them to repent at the last moment. In this way, they do not miss out on any fun, having the best of both worlds. Ben Sira reminds such thinkers that God's vengeance strikes suddenly, without warning, for at the time of reckoning they will perish.

5:8. Returning to the previously mentioned reliance on wealth to protect one from danger, Ben Sira insists that such ill-gotten wealth will not secure anyone in the day of God's vengeance. Trusting in lies ("deceitful riches" [נכסי שקר] *nĕkāsê šeqer*]), the sinners will be completely vulnerable when divine fury "passes over" them (cf. Prov 11:4).

Verses 1-8 bracket presumptuous thoughts within overreliance on wealth. Ben Sira warns against ill-placed confidence, one based on faulty reasoning about delayed punishment. Both mercy and wrath belong to God, he insists, and one should act accordingly.

---

140. *M. Yoma* 8:8-9.

REFLECTIONS

This text probes the human psyche, exploring the rationale for shifting the blame for people's conduct to an unjust God. The several defenses given for adopting a life of sin imply fuller knowledge of the universe than is accessible to anyone except God. Such attacks on divine justice, and ultimately on God's benevolence, grow out of an unwillingness to accept the inevitable status of creature. Being finite means living in a condition of limited potential, and that limitedness includes such important qualities as power and knowledge. The arrogance of Job and all others like him becomes ludicrous when faced with the real problem of evil, mythologically symbolized in the two creatures Behemoth and Leviathan.

No human being can obtain sufficient distance from the scene to observe everything that transpires in the universe and to pass judgment on its appropriateness. Our view always takes place from below, as it were, and suffers from severe myopia. Even if one could bring together all human perspectives into a single view of things, the result would still lack the one essential ingredient for understanding the whole picture— *telos*, "the end." Hidden from our eyes is the larger picture in which God's purpose plays itself out on the earthly stage.

In some ways our lives resemble a great patchwork quilt. The individual pieces of cloth that make up the final design vary considerably in aesthetic appeal, with some actually falling into the category of ugly. Once the quilt maker finishes the design, the total picture completely transforms former unattractive pieces. The viewer now sees each individual square of cloth as it contributes to the beauty of the whole quilt.[141] Perhaps God weaves together the separate strings of human existence, intricately mixing and matching the different colors and textures so that they ultimately form a beautiful garment.

Biblical imagery suggests a similar analogy. If our bodies constitute a temple in which God resides, perhaps the master builder takes the individual stones and constructs an edifice from the different sizes, shapes, and colors. Together these building blocks make up a splendid house, God's dwelling place. In the final design, every single stone contributes to the whole just as every piece of cloth adds something necessary to the patchwork quilt.

This argument implies that the ugly incidents of our lives, those events that cause us to question divine justice, may fit into the larger picture in a way that our limited perspective obscures. In any event, most arguments for rebelling against God are so self-serving that they scarcely convince those using them, much less anyone else. The ones that Ben Sira cites lack the grandeur and power of struggles by loyal servants to comprehend things so thoroughly incongruent with belief in a loving God.

141. See *A Quilter's Wisdom: Conversations With Aunt Jane* (San Francisco: Chronicle Books, 1994), based on a Historical Text by Eliza Calvert Hall.

SIRACH 5:9–6:1, ON DISSIMULATION THROUGH SPEECH

COMMENTARY

Two images from popular proverbs in 5:9 provide a fitting transition to a new theme that evokes a triple use of the idiom "master of two" with reference to duplicity in speech. The remarks about winnowing indiscriminately, regardless of the direction of the wind, and trying out various paths apply equally well to the preceding discussion of different attitudes to retribution as they do to what follows. Another widespread expression, "to put the hand to the mouth," indicates humility and respect in the presence of greatness, perhaps also the lack of an adequate response. This symbolic gesture is mentioned in Job 21:5; 29:9; 40:4 and elsewhere in the OT (Prov 30:32; Mic 7:16; cf. Wis 8:12). Like so much in wisdom literature, it also appears in Egyptian texts.[142]

142. See B. Couroyer, "Mettre la main sur la bouche en Égypte et dans la Bible," *RB* 67 (1960) 197-209.

Ben Sira recommends quickness in hearing but a considered response, one "long in spirit" (the same advice can be found in Jas 1:19). The necessity of hearing rightly before responding captured popular imagination much earlier, for it finds expression in Prov 18:13. Years later Qohelet contrasts a patient person with an arrogant individual in Eccl 7:8.

The slanderer comes in for Ben Sira's strongest censure. The double-tongued person resembles a thief in robbing innocent people of their good reputation. Just as speech with integrity brings honor in its wake, so also deceitful remarks cause shame. The purpose of such duplicity is described in the language of hunting—lying in wait. Thus the double-tongued person lays a trap for the unwary. The significant terms in 5:14 comprise an ABB´A´ pattern: double-tongued/shame/reproach/double-tongued. The next verse combines two opposites: minute and large, friend and enemy. A third occurrence of "double-tongued" for emphasis or completion, plus the combination of "shame" and "reproach," offers a suitable conclusion to the section.

SIRACH 6:2-4, ON UNCONTROLLED PASSIONS

COMMENTARY

The subject of this short unit probably falls into the realm of sexual misconduct. The warning applies generally to powerful passions of all kinds, but the images for the consequences apply particularly well to sins of the flesh. Ben Sira likens illicit sex to a raging bull, all the more apt because of the association of bulls with fertility, and he warns that sexual misbehavior destroys a tree, causing its fruit and leaves to drop off. The description elsewhere of a eunuch as a dry tree (Isa 56:3) indicates the dire consequences of ungoverned lust. Like the mighty Samson, the person who loses control of his or her passions falls into the hands of the enemy (Judg 15:18), the same expression used here in v. 2.

Later on Ben Sira uses the popular image of leaves falling from a tree as a powerful reminder of death.[143] This graphic image contrasts with that of a healthy tree situated near an abundance of water (Ps 1:3). The closing reference in v. 4 to an insatiable desire (נפש עזה *nepeš 'azzâ*) acknowedges the strength of sexual lust, an appetite similar to hunger for essential nourishment. Uncontrolled, this desire turns one into an object of ridicule. According to Anderson's interpretation of שמחה (*śimḥâ*) as a rabbinic cipher for legitimate sex within marriage,[144] Ben Sira's choice of this noun to indicate enemies' happiness ("rejoicing") is especially fortuitous. The subject of sexual lust will occupy Ben Sira's attention again (cf. 18:30–19:3).

---

143. Homer uses this same image in discussing death (*Iliad* 6.146ff.), but one need not draw the conclusion that Ben Sira knew the *Iliad*. The idea would naturally have occurred to anyone who reflected on nature's transformation each year.

144. Gary A. Anderson, *A Time to Mourn, a Time to Dance* (University Park: Pennsylvania State University Press, 1991) 27-45.

SIRACH 6:5-17, ON FRIENDSHIP

COMMENTARY

This section on the value of faithful friends is the first of several in the book dealing with a subject that was widely discussed in Hellenistic literature of the time. Jack T. Sanders has examined the affinities between this advice from Ben Sira and similar counsel in Theognis's elegiac poems of Book 1 and Phibis, another name for Papyrus Insinger.[145] Sanders's analysis demonstrates extensive cross-fertilization of ideas throughout the Greek world. Popular philosophers wandered from town to town and taught anyone who would listen to their ideas, and merchants traveled from port to port and inland, exchanging both goods and concepts. Ben Sira's frequent use of "lover" (אוהב *'ôhēb*) instead of the usual word for "friend" (רע *rēaʿ*) probably betrays an unconscious influence from the Greek world.

Nevertheless, two expressions clearly mark this advice as authentically Hebraic. The language of greeting, "to ask about one's well-being" (שאל שלום *šāʾal šālôm*), characterizes genuine friendship, according to v. 5. In v. 16, the image of the soul's residing in a

---

145. Sanders, *Ben Sira and Demotic Wisdom*, 27-59, esp. 30 (for Theognis), 69-100 (for Phibis/Papyrus Insinger). The primary text of Theognis is *Elegy and Iambus with the Anacreontea I*, LCL (Cambridge, Mass.: Harvard University Press, 1968).

protective vessel, "the bag of the living" (צרור חיים *ṣĕrôr ḥayyîm*), recalls ancient folklore from 1 Sam 25:29, Abigail's rhetorical flourish about divine protection for David. Although the expression "one in a thousand" occurs in Job 9:3 and Eccl 7:28, it also appears in Egyptian wisdom literature and thus cannot be considered exclusively Hebraic. Ben Sira connects this expression with an interesting collocation, "lord of your counsel" (בעל סודך *baʿal sôdekā*). He therefore advises his students to have many companions ("persons of your well-being") but to restrict their intimates to one in a thousand (v. 16). The same advice is found in *Sanhedrin* 100*b*: "Let the men of thy peace be many; reveal thy secret to one out of a thousand."

Just as wisdom withholds her secrets from her followers until she has submitted them to various trials, so also should Ben Sira's students do. He suggests that they not share confidences with friends hastily, waiting until circumstances have tested their reliability. The reason for such caution concerns the harsh reality that some friends stay around only during fair weather. In Ben Sira's language, they do not withstand calamity with you, but they hang around as long as things go well. Furthermore, some friends become enemies for whatever reason and proceed to tarnish one's reputation by divulging embarrassing intimate details to everyone eager to devour delicious morsels of slander. The fact that this former friend once shared food at table seems to mean nothing, despite the rich symbolism of eating together in ancient Israel. The former table companion cannot be found to assist one in an evil day (v. 10). In the light of questionable character in friends, Ben Sira urges caution in every instance pertaining to friends but extraordinary wariness in the presence of enemies.

Despite its pitfalls, Ben Sira certainly esteems friendship highly. He likens a friend to treasure (הון *hôn*, a word much loved by the sages), and he recognizes the high cost of obtaining (קנה *qānâ*, "to purchase," "to acquire") a true friend. The threefold use of "a faithful friend" (אוהב אמונה *ʾôhēb ʾĕmûnâ*) in vv. 14-16 has almost a touch of fantasy, as if Ben Sira wished to describe a perfect state of things on earth. Only deeply religious people, he asserts, will experience such friendship. Naturally, he understands true friends as God's gift for faithful service in spiritual living.

In contrast to the unit about deceptive speech in 5:9–6:1, this one emphasizes the positive power of language to foster friendship. The section opens with a beautiful expression for courteous greeting, "gracious lips" (שפתי חן *šiptê ḥēn*), the pleasant response to a sweet palate (היך ערב *hêkʿārēb*). The adjective *ʿārēb* is as rare in the Bible as the sweet palate itself, occurring only in Prov 20:17 and Cant 2:14. Other links to the unit on duplicitous language include the word *reproach* (חרפה *ḥerpâ*) and the thrice-repeated particle of existence, "there is" (יש *yēš*), in vv. 8-9.

The Greek text of v. 16 changes the image of "a bag of the living," which the translator probably did not understand (or he considered "bundle," "bag" [צרור *ṣĕrôr*] a mistake for צרי [*ṣŏrî*]), to an expression compatible with Hellenistic thought. The resulting statement, "a faithful friend is a medicine of life" (φίλος πιστὸς φάρμακον ζωῆς *philos pistos pharmakon zoēs*), illustrates the way changes occur whenever texts are translated into a language with entirely different concepts and images.

The realization that even intimate friends sometimes "change into" enemies (the Hebrew verb הפך [*hāpak*] has this meaning in v. 9) does not give Ben Sira a jaundiced view of friendship. The ease with which a wisdom teacher could move over into suspicion of all relationships can be seen in *The Instruction of Amenemhet*: "Trust not a brother, know not a friend, make no intimates, it is worthless."

The Jewish tractate *Pirqe ʾAbot* sums up the value of friends as follows: "Let a man buy himself a friend who will eat and drink with him, who will study with him the written and the oral law, and to whom he will entrust all his secrets."[146] Ben Sira would surely concur in these sentiments, as his return to this topic again and again suggests (cf. 11:29–12:18; 22:19-26; 37:1-6).

---

146. *T. Pirqe ʾAbot* 1:6. See Oesterley, *The Wisdom of Jesus the Son of Sirach or Ecclesiasticus*, 41. Oesterley is quoting from Solomon Schechter, *Studies in Judaism* (Philadelphia: Jewish Publication Society of America, 1924) 93.

REFLECTIONS

The importance of true friendship can hardly be overemphasized. Modern patterns of work put enormous strain on friendships, for people constantly change locations, making it difficult to maintain long-term relationships. Awareness that one will likely move to a new location in a few years works against the formation of close friendships, as does the time factor itself. To quote Ben Sira, "True friends are like wine; when it [friendship] has aged, you will enjoy it." Genuine friendship grows with the passing of time as two people share experiences and confidences over the years.

Extending a hand in friendship always makes one vulnerable. Ben Sira certainly recognized this unwelcome aspect of friendship, as did Jesus, who addressed his betrayer with the stinging word *friend*. Many victims of false friends walk around and pose a staggering problem for trusting Christians. How much should a person divulge of his or her own hurts and joys? How far should an individual go toward cultivating friendships with those who have a long history of wearing their feelings on their sleeves? If friendship implies vulnerability, then Christians willingly become vulnerable by being friends at tremendous cost.

SIRACH 6:18–14:19
PART III

OVERVIEW

The third major unit in Sirach begins, like the first two, with a reflection on wisdom (6:18-37). It concludes with a solemn reminder of death's universality and urges young men to make the most of life by applying the advantages derived from wisdom (14:11-19). The final observations return to the contrasting stages of life, youth and old age, that introduce the initial poem (6:18), and reiterate the notion of fruits from one's labor (6:19; 14:15). Between the opening and closing sections, Ben Sira offers random advice about appropriate behavior; various responsibilities; warnings about different types of people, particularly women; caution in selecting associates; and unreliable friends.

SIRACH 6:18-37, WISDOM'S RIGOROUS DISCIPLINE

COMMENTARY

Three distinct sections make up the larger unit of twenty-two bicola: 6:18-22, 23-31, 32-37 (for the entire section, the Vg supplies the title *De Doctrina Sapientia*, "On Wise Teaching"). An inclusio, built on the noun "wisdom" (חכמה *ḥokmâ*), links vv. 18 and 37. An introductory "my son" (בני *běnî*) sets each of the three subsections apart. A single theme unites the whole discussion: the necessity for and rewards of seeking wisdom regardless of the obstacles one may encounter. Images of farming and hunting consistently dominate the material in the first two subsections; the third, vv. 32-37, shifts to the picture of lively conversation and deep thought.

The Hebrew of v. 18 is lacking in MS A, and only the last two words appear in MS C. For vv. 23-24, the Hebrew has 27:5-6, and vv. 26 and 34 are completely missing. In v. 19, the twin images of plowing and sowing are broken up in the Hebrew, but not in the Greek; an unlikely sowing and *reaping* occur in Hebrew, the context calling only for the preparatory stage of planting. This brief unit demonstrates the difficulty of determining precisely what the original Hebrew text of Sirach actually included. Often, as here, insufficient clues exist to enable interpreters to decide which option comes closer to the autograph.

6:18-22. Ancient Israelites believed that wisdom accompanied old age, the result of long experience. Naturally, because young people lacked exposure to the tradition and to the realities of life, they also could make no legitimate claim on knowledge. The sole means of attaining this worthy goal was by submitting to discipline and by persevering through all difficulties. Young people, like Elihu in the book of Job, were expected to listen while their elders gave their view of things and were to speak only briefly, if at all.

The weight of this preference for the aged in intellectual matters fell heavily on the prophet Jeremiah, who unsuccessfully pleaded youthful innocence as a way of escaping the divine commission. In his case, the narrative reports, the one who summoned him to prophesy would grant eloquence and courage so that he could stand up to ridicule (Jer 1:5-10). Within wisdom circles, the elevation of a young man or woman to a position of authority and leadership was unlikely.

Wisdom and its advantages came at the end of much hard work; gray hairs signaled to others that one had lived long enough to acquire some valuable insights. This claim becomes problematic in the book of Job, for Elihu rejects it outright, and Job insists that he knows as much as his older friends.

The Bible often uses agricultural imagery, primarily because Scripture arose in an agrarian society. Claus Westermann has emphasized this aspect of wisdom literature, especially the older sayings in the book of Proverbs.[147] In his plausible view, this instruction is the product of simple villagers whose central concern was the family and its survival. Their discourse revolved around the daily routine in the fields and vineyards, at the gates, and in the intimacy of tents and small dwellings.

Although Ben Sira appears to have lived in a city, probably Jerusalem, he continues to use agricultural images, partly because of his conservative nature and partly because even in his day many city dwellers owned small plots outside Jerusalem and worked them daily during the growing season. He issues an invitation to approach wisdom in the same way one begins the day in the fields. Just as workers go about various tasks, here symbolized by plowing and sowing, with eager expectation of a successful yield, so also young students can start their long journey with confidence that the harvest will, indeed, be a time of rejoicing.

For ancient peoples, the metaphor of plowing and sowing often functioned as a euphemism for sexual relations, and a woman was described as a fruitful field to be plowed by her husband. This widespread metaphor, familiar to readers of the Samson narrative, in which one of his riddle-like sayings accuses the Philistine companions of dallying with his wife ("plowing with his heifer"), links up with the rich and varied imagery of eroticism associated with personified wisdom.[148] In addition, such language of explicit sexual expectation was fully at home at harvesttime, as the beautiful story about Ruth and Boaz demonstrates.[149] The eating of wisdom's bountiful produce, like the enjoyment of sexual union, makes the work involved in all former cultivation seem inconsequential, almost trivial. In Prov 8:19, Wisdom boasts that her fruit surpasses gold and silver in value; a similar point is made in 1 Esdr 4:18-19 with reference to a man's delight in a woman. Dropping precious ore like refuse, he stares at a beautiful woman with mouth agape.[150]

Ben Sira urges young boys to draw near to wisdom, eagerly anticipating her produce (v. 19); the verb קוה ($q\bar{a}w\hat{a}$) connotes lively hope, a confidence born out of experience and reinforced by hard work. Simpletons and uninformed individuals, indicated by traditional terms from the book of Proverbs ("foolish" [אויל '$\check{e}w\hat{\imath}l$] and "unintelligent" [קצר לב $q\bar{a}\d{s}ar\ l\bar{e}b$]), encounter her like an uneven path, unless the idea of plowing continues in v. 20 and suggests rocky terrain. Stopping momentarily to pick up a heavy stone, they quickly throw it down rather than moving it to an area in the field where its bulk would be useful, probably in helping to form a terrace to slow erosion and to retain water for agricultural use.

Verse 22 offers an explanation for such shortsightedness in persons of insufficient intellect and consequently inadequate resolve, and in doing so it draws on views about wisdom's hiddenness. Although Ben Sira's play on words is not entirely clear to modern interpreters, it probably involves מוסר ($m\hat{u}s\bar{a}r$), a synonym for "wisdom," and a participle form of the verb סור ($s\hat{u}r$, "to turn away") with passive force, "withdrawn."[151] The same root returns in the verb תוסר ($tiwasser$) of v. 33, "you will become wise."

This puzzling observation that wisdom, like her name, is not manifest to the crowds sounds somewhat elitist, particularly in its Greek translation, "and is not manifest to the populace" (καὶ οὐ πολλοῖς ἐστιν φανερά *kai ou pollois estin phanera*). She does not

---

147. Westermann, *Roots of Wisdom.*
148. On the metaphor "plowing with my heifer," see Crenshaw, *Samson,* 118-20; and for personified wisdom, see Bernhard Lang, *Wisdom and the Book of Proverbs* (New York: Pilgrim, 1986); Samuel Terrien, *Till the Heart Sings* (Philadelphia: Fortress, 1985); Claudia V. Camp, *Wisdom and the Feminine in the Book of Proverbs,* BLS (Sheffield: Almond, 1985).
149. A stimulating and unconventional interpretation has recently come from Danna Nolan Fewell and David Miller Gunn, *Compromising Redemption* (Louisville: Westminster/John Knox, 1990).
150. James L. Crenshaw, "The Contest of Darius' Guards in 1 Esdras 3:1–5:3," in *Images of Man and God: The Old Testament Short Story in Literary Focus,* ed. Burke O. Long (Sheffield: Almond, 1981) 74-88, 119-20. See also Crenshaw, *Urgent Advice and Probing Questions,* 222-34.
151. John G. Snaith, *Ecclesiasticus,* CBC (Cambridge: Cambridge University Press, 1974) 39. Snaith thinks the pun occurs between מוסר ($m\hat{u}s\bar{a}r$) and מוסר ($m\hat{o}s\bar{e}r$), "bond," "halter," and provides a link with "fetters" of v. 24.

appear to ordinary citizens, *hoi polloi*. The Hebrew text has "obvious" or "plain" (נכחה *nōkḥâ* or נכחה *nĕkōḥâ*), perhaps continuing the idea of a path or furrow. The form is laid out in an ABB´A´ pattern: wisdom: she: she: not straight. Ancient peoples believed that a name encapsulated one's essence, hence should be carefully guarded. A deity who divulged his or her name risked being controlled by magical incantation, which probably explains the story about Yahweh's reluctance to share the divine name with Moses (Exod 4:13-15). Other traditionists did not subscribe to this theory about the divine name and, therefore, used "Yahweh" freely.

6:23-31. Whereas the first section emphasizes the harsh discipline involved in acquiring an education, the second unit continues its emphasis but moves beyond the idea of toil in splendid fashion. What once appeared to be fetters and a yoke will be transformed into royal garments. Now at last those students who persisted realize that wisdom only *seemed* harsh but was actually acting in their best interests. Like the symmetry in the book of Joel, where the destructive results of invading locusts are replaced in every detail by their opposite,[152] each unpleasant feature connected with trials imposed by wisdom on young students will be changed into highly desirable attire (Joel 1:2–2:17 // 2:18-27). The language of putting on moral traits like clothing was common in Israel and Greece at this time.

The form of v. 23, an imperative followed by its opposite with a negation, recalled earlier teaching in the book of Proverbs ("listen, accept // do not reject"). The teacher asserts his authority by means of a threefold possessive pronoun, "my" (אתי *'ōtî*) in the Hebrew; the Greek translator drops one of these but makes up for the loss with an intensive verb, "do not refuse" (μὴ ἀπαναίνου *mē apanainou*).

The dominant image in v. 24 comes from plowing; imagining an ox submitting to a yoke and collar, Ben Sira uses this symbol for the process of getting an education. This idea caught on rapidly in the Jewish community, for it appears prominently both in rabbinic literature and in the New Testament. According to Matt 11:29, Jesus invited followers to take his yoke upon their necks and learn from him; he promised, however, that his yoke would be easy and his burden light.[153] A passage in *Pirqe 'Abot* reads as follows: "Every one who receives on himself the yoke of Torah, they remove from him the yoke of the kingdom and the yoke of worldly occupation. But every one who breaks off from him the yoke of Torah, they lay upon him the yoke of the kingdom and the yoke of worldly occupation."[154] According to *Erubin* 54a of the Babylonian Talmud, whoever brings the neck under the yoke of Torah will enjoy her protective care.[155]

The reference to bonds or fetters in v. 24 is difficult; the Hebrew text actually has a word for "net" in v. 28. Perhaps the language suggests the stocks that were used to punish uncooperative slaves or weights that athletes employed during practice to strengthen their ankles and increase their speed. The expression may even be a rather loose way of describing the cords that secured yokes around the necks of oxen. In any event, v. 25 continues the image of an ox willingly submitting to a yoke. The following verse recalls deuteronomic language of resolve ("with your whole mind [heart] and strength").

Three imperatives describing the quest for wisdom signal the importance Ben Sira placed on the hunt. Lying between two imperatives for searching, דרש (*dĕrāš*) and בקש (*baqqēš*), the imperative of חקר (*ḥāqar*) suggests tracing out a route. Together the three verbs indicate thorough research,[156] a probing into the realm of the unknown. Actually, a fourth imperative appears in the initial colon of the Hebrew text, but the Greek translator probably read a verb, "and you will discover" (ותמצא *wĕtimṣā'*). The language of the second colon in this verse (v. 27) derives from Prov 4:13; once you have taken hold of (חזק *ḥāzaq*) wisdom, do not relinquish her. This verse furnishes a contrast to the conduct of the uninformed who abruptly threw away the

---

152. Discussed in James L. Crenshaw, *Joel*, AB (New York: Doubleday, 1995) 83-163.

153. M. Jack Suggs, *Wisdom, Christology, and Law in Matthew's Gospel* (Cambridge, Mass.: Harvard University Press, 1970) 99-127.

154. *Pirqe 'Abot* 3:6.

155. Quoted in Oesterley, *The Wisdom of Jesus the Son of Sirach*, 44.

156. The term *midrash* comes from the verb דרש (*dāraš*) and refers to the act of searching for the meaning of a sacred text. In the Middle Ages, Jews and Christians employed a fourfold method of interpretation. In Jewish circles, an acronymn, PaRDeS, indicated פשת (*peš̌at*, the literal meaning), רמז (*remez*, the allegorical meaning), דרש (*deraš*, the tropological and moral meaning), and סוד (*sôd*, the mystical meaning).

tone he had picked up, presumably because of its heavy weight (v. 21).

Completely transformed, wisdom will present herself as rest and exquisite delight. Two verbs stand out here, "to find" (מצא *māṣā*) and "to overturn" (הפך *hāpak*).[157] The former is governed by an adverb of time, "at last," while the latter is qualified by the personal pronoun "for you." Finally, worthy students see wisdom as she truly is and as she has always been. Verses 29-31 describe the splendid clothing that, with the cooperation of her industrious students, she has woven for them. The collar has become a beautiful robe, the yoke a golden ornament, the bonds a purple cord. Royal imagery abounds in this fanciful description, and even the color purple signifies kingship. The expression "purple cord" comes from Num 15:38-39 and later played into rabbinic speculation about a determent from adultery, the cord becoming visible when clothes are removed and serving as a reminder that God observes everything one does.

6:32-37. The third subsection, which proclaims that "where there is a will there also exists a way," offers useful advice about seizing every opportunity to learn, and provides a religious interpretation of the intellectual journey. The conclusion to the Egyptian "Instruction of Anii" demonstrates that some students seriously doubted their ability to live up to their teacher's moral requirements. Here the son, Khonshotep, objects that he lacks his father's moral stamina, although approving the teachings. Anii responds that everyone can learn, and he reinforces this view with specific examples taken from nature and society in general. Ben Sira, too, has full confidence in his students' ability. Having settled the matter of motivation, he encourages them to look for learned sources of knowledge among older people and become willing followers. The idea of peripatetic teachers flourished in the Greek environment, and Jewish teachers of the first century CE established rival schools, those of Hillel and his rival, Shammai.

Two things stand out in this bit of advice. First, education takes place by listening to intelligent discourse rather than through reading texts, and second, it assumes the form of a witty saying (משל *māšāl*; proverb, aphorism, witticism, allegory, riddle). The Hebrew שיחה (*śîḥâ*, "meditation") occurs only three times in the OT, Job 15:4 and Ps 119:97, 99. It conveys a sense of wonder and gratitude in the presence of God's mystery and statutes (cf. Amos 4:13, where a related form occurs [שחו *śēḥô*, "his thoughts"]). Verse 36 almost urges students to make a nuisance of themselves, rising early and wearing out the stone at the entrance of a wise man's house. The Hebrew imperative of v. 36 further stresses the active responsibility to observe (ראה *rĕ'ēh*) intelligent behavior.

The final verse in this unit reveals Ben Sira's extensive theological bent. He urges students to ponder the fear of the Most High and to meditate on the statutes continually ("daily" [תמיד *tāmîd*]). The ABB´A´ structure returns in the first bicolon of v. 37 ("reflect on/the fear of Elyon/his state/meditate on") and persists to the end ("and he/will give insight to your mind/what you desire/he will make you wise").

---

157. Jack Sasson, *Jonah*, AB (New York: Doubleday, 1990) 234-35, illustrates the rich ambiguity of this word הפך (*hāpak*) in Jonah 3:4 (in the feminine form). When Jonah proclaimed that Nineveh would be overturned (*nehpak*) in forty days, the word conveyed two possibilities: "destroyed" and "converted." Jonah understood the former sense of the verb, and the Ninevites heard the latter sense.

REFLECTIONS

1. Ben Sira's remarks about cultivating a sense of self-worth are hardly needed in modern American society, which seems almost obsessed with universal self-congratulation, regardless of ethical character. The growth of the human potential movement and the widespread popularity of self-help literature have encouraged people toward an uncritical self-esteem and self-acceptance. The important thing, feeling good about yourself, has virtually extinguished the concept of guilt and banished the notion of sin. This attitude has led to disastrous pedagogy, ruling out the idea of learning from one's mistakes and accepting mediocrity, laziness, and slovenly habits.

While in the moral sphere, as well as the educational, the contemporary message promotes accepting the status quo and even glorying in it; in the area of body building and diet precisely the opposite message goes forth: "No pain, no gain." Here nothing worthwhile comes without effort, and no one tries to conceal this reality. To lose weight and to tone the muscles, one must submit to a rigorous regimen of food and exercise. The judgment that we are not always and completely okay underlies the entire enterprise.

The latter understanding of things resembles the ancient worldview, one in which discipline played a central role. Without practice, no one becomes really good at anything, whether sports, music, dance, cooking, parenting, or anything else. The apostle Paul applied this principle to the spiritual life, acknowledging that one begins as an infant and then grows in faith and knowledge through diligent study and moral discipline. Ancient moralists adopted images from sports, the martial arts, and agriculture in the effort to encourage people to grow in character.

2. Jesus, like Paul, made strict demands on his disciples, warning against an enthusiastic initial surrender followed by a slackening of resolve (Luke 9:62). He expected followers to forsake everything they valued and to take his yoke on their shoulders. Nevertheless, he did promise that, in retrospect, they would recognize his burden as easy and his yoke as light (Matt 11:29-30). The sect at Qumran also emphasized the difficult discipline facing initiates, and to ease that process the religious teacher provided a manual of discipline by which to organize their daily lives.

Christians today can profit from plain directions about living, particularly because absolutes have fallen under attack from every quarter. We may no longer render a categorical no about this or that practice, but one thing surely remains as fixed as ever: Growth in Christian discipleship comes only as a result of constant effort. In this struggle to become mature in faith, only Christians who exercise self-discipline will make any ascertainable progress. Jesus' exclusive language made the price of following him absolutely clear; the symbolism of a narrow way, and straight, implied that discipleship was only for the select few. That exclusive language clashes with the legitimate need to be inclusive today, and many Christians merely bypass the rigorous demands. The result is a brand of Christian witness lacking moral commitment.

SIRACH 7:1-17, THE CONSEQUENCES OF SIN

COMMENTARY

This section opens with a thematic sentence about how to avoid trouble and closes with a graphic description of punishment for evil. In between these powerful motivators, Ben Sira gives some advice about aspiring to a position of power and responsibility, warns against presumption and loose speech, and recommends manual labor. The grammatical form, the negative particle אל (*'al*) plus a jussive, runs through the entire section, except for v. 17, actually extending through v. 20. The repeated negative command builds up to a crescendo, emphasizing the teacher's concern for students' welfare. Two features of vv. 1-17 require comment, first the personification of evil and, second, the difference between the Hebrew and Greek texts.

Like wisdom, evil is personified in vv. 1-2 and thus capable of chasing someone and overtaking a hapless victim or turning its back on persons who show no interest in it. Such a move had already occurred in Prov 9:13-18, which describes a personified folly as a seductress who invites young boys to a banquet, reminding them of the pleasure derived from eating forbidden fruit. Interpreters generally consider this personification of evil to have been modeled on wisdom, although the reverse sequence has been proposed.[158] This descriptive language of personification characterizes prophetic speech, too, the prophet Amos likening the fallen nation Israel to a raped virgin (Amos 5:2), and Jeremiah threatening destruction from pestilence, sword, famine, and captivity (Jer 15:2). Similarly, a psalmist referred to righteousness and truth as kissing each other (Ps 85:10).

7:1-17. The most striking difference between the Hebrew and the Greek texts in this unit occurs in this verse. Whereas the Hebrew only mentions the natural decomposition of the body ("worms") as the destiny of evil people, the Greek translator wrote "fire and worms" (πῦρ καὶ σκώληξ *pur kai skōlēx*). Critics usually see the addition of "fire" as evidence that Hellenism strongly influenced Ben Sira's grandson in Egypt. The Greek concept of perdition has thus invaded the thinking of pious Jews in the late second century BCE, according to this view. One should probably not make so much of this textual difference, for the expectation of "fire and worms" as punishment for rebels against the Lord occurs already in Isa 66:24: "for their worm shall not die, their fire shall not be quenched, and they shall be an abhorrence to all flesh" (NRSV). Nevertheless, the shorter version of Sir 7:17 (without any reference to fire) probably represents Ben Sira's view and, therefore, will be followed here.

7:1-3. The thematic sentence "Do no evil, and evil [misfortune] will never overtake you" struck later Jewish religionists as worthy of wider dissemination, for it is quoted several times in midrashic literature. The optimistic worldview underlying the sentiment owes nothing to the questioning of divine justice pursued in the books of Job and Ecclesiastes, as well as in Psalm 73. Instead, Ben Sira here reaffirms the dominant view of earlier wisdom within the book of Proverbs—namely, that individuals can control their own fate by the way they conduct their lives (Prov 10:16; 12:14; 13:18; 22:4). The agricultural metaphor in v. 3 about sowing "in the furrows of injustice" and reaping "a sevenfold crop" sounds like a popular aphorism. An erotic nuance probably clung to the saying, given the customary use of the metaphor for sexual relationships and the personification of evil as a woman.

7:4-7. The attempt by Ben Sira to dissuade young boys from aspiring to high office comes as a total surprise, for elsewhere he praises the office of sage above all other professions and states that they will serve among rulers (39:4; cf. 8:8). Martin Hengel has viewed the negative counsel against the dark background of Seleucid politics,[159] which is characterized in the book of 2 Maccabees as thoroughly corrupt (2 Macc 4:1-20). Where high office goes to the highest bidder and foreign control over internal Jewish decisions existed, service as judge or in any one of a number of official positions would have seriously compromised an individual. The more positive advice in the latter part of the book could have arisen in an earlier period, perhaps during the Ptolemaic rule prior to 198 BCE or early in the Seleucid era before a hostile attitude developed toward the Jews.

Less probably, in vv. 4-7 Ben Sira simply enjoins humility: "Don't seek office, but be prepared to serve if it searches you out." The warning against boasting about goodness to God and calling the king's attention to your intelligence supports the latter alternative. Verse 6 points away from that reading, suggesting that the demands of the office would be so taxing that the individual would inevitably fail. Either he would lack authority to expel wickedness, or he would be vulnerable to bribery and to the subtle influence of persons in power.

This brief section concerns four distinct entities: God, king, judge, and people. The first two, God and king, are brought together as supreme (heavenly) and terrestrial authorities respectively. By Ben Sira's time, the older concept of judge as warrior had given way to a more modern understanding of one who pronounces verdicts in litigation. The fourth category, the public at large, lacks the power inherent to the king and the judge, but it

---

158. Boström, *The God of the Sages*, 56.

159. Hengel, *Judaism and Hellenism*, 1:133-34.

controls people in a much subtler fashion, through withholding honor and imposing shame.

7:8-14. The third subdivision deals with presumption. Ben Sira describes arrogant people who think they can treat everybody lightly, indeed contemptuously, with impunity. They even treat God in this manner. Ben Sira warns against doing the same sinful act twice, the sinner presumably gathering courage from the absence of immediate punishment (cf. v. 16). Verse 9, missing in Hebrew, offers another rationale for sin, specifically that generosity toward God atones for one's deeds. The notion that money can buy anything, even forgiveness, has often lurked in the nooks and crannies of the religious mind. In v. 8 the image suggesting conspiracy is that of "binding up," the opposite of binding the precepts of the law on the hands and forehead (cf. Deut 6:8; 11:18).

Ben Sira advises against taking prayer lightly and uttering the same thing over and over (cf. Eccl 5:2). Finding the right balance between liturgical petition through refrains and offering spontaneous adoration did not come easily in the ancient world, any more than today. Warnings against excessive use of epithets for God and adjectives for divine attributes occur in rabbinic literature, and Jesus is quoted as cautioning against empty repetitions in prayer (Matt 6:7). At the same time, he teaches a model prayer to his followers and is pictured as repeating himself three times at prayer during his final hours in the garden of Gethsemane (Matt 26:39-44). For Ben Sira, the proper combination seemed to have been energetic prayer followed by the dispensing of alms to the needy.

The power of the spoken word for good and ill seems to have occupied Ben Sira's mind here. The negative side of speech, both ridicule and outright falsehood, provokes his ire, as does loose talk generally. Because the assembly of elders conducts important business, one's talk ought to be to the point and circumspect.

7:15-16. In the Hebrew text, v. 15 replaces v. 9 and belongs to the present subsection. Unique in subject matter, the verse reflects a viewpoint that will be explored more thoroughly in 38:24–39:11. Ben Sira recognizes manual labor as divinely ordained and therefore honorable; he derives this positive assessment of work from the ancient story about Adam and Eve in the garden of Eden before their sin. The changed sociological environment in the early second century BCE, with the opening up of numerous professions besides farming and the commercial situation that rewarded venturesome investments, may have prompted Ben Sira to come to the defense of traditional values here. He knew that society could not survive without products from the farm, and he also understood the reluctance of young boys to work with animals when they could avoid such backbreaking toil.

Ben Sira's favorable attitude toward work was also shared by the rabbis, finding expression in *Pirqe 'Abot* 2:2, "Excellent is Torah study together with worldly business . . . all Torah without work [i.e., manual labor] must fail at length, and occasion iniquity," and in Qiddushin 99*a*, "Whoever does not teach his son work, teaches him to rob."

SIRACH 7:18-28, DOMESTIC ADVICE

COMMENTARY

7:18-21. With this section Ben Sira moves into the privacy of the home, mentioning brother, wife, slaves, children, and parents. The opening statement about the exceptional worth of a brother sets the tone for the entire discussion of the family circle. Ophir, the source of the gold that was most valued in biblical literature, was either in southern Arabia or in Egypt (1 Kgs 9:28; 10:11; 22:48; Job 22:24; 28:16; Ps 45:9). Ben Sira places an intelligent and good wife alongside a brother as worth more than gold. His remarks about slaves reflect both Hebraic and Greek ideas, Hebraic in the reaffirmation of the ancient legislation enjoining owners to release slaves after six years (Exod 21:2; Deut 15:12-15), and Greek in the comment about intelligent slaves. Often Hellenistic slaves were learned educators acquired through conquest.

7:22-26. The sequence in these verses is somewhat jarring, particularly the abrupt move from mentioning cattle to mentioning children, but one observes a similar, although reverse, movement in the prologue to the book of Job (Job 1:2-3). To some degree, children and wives were understood as a man's property, although this does not rule out deep affection on both sides.

Ben Sira uses a rhetorical question four times: "Do you have cattle . . . children . . . daughters . . . a wife?" After each question he offers some timely advice, always from the standpoint of self-interest. Take care of valuable cattle, discipline children, protect a daughter's virginity and choose a sensible husband for her, and keep a wife whom you love. Conceivably, fathers chose husbands for their daughters without soliciting their wishes, but one can naturally assume that many young girls made their desires known. Ben Sira will have much more to say about daughters, not all positive (42:9-14). The Hebrew text has strong language for disciplining sons: "bend their necks," but it adds "and acquire wives for them while they are young"—that is, before awakening lust gets them in trouble.

7:27-28. These verses do not appear in the Hebrew text; they were probably omitted through a scribal error—after the scribe wrote, "with the whole heart" in v. 27, his eye then may have fallen on the similar phrase in v. 29. The sentiment expressed in these verses moves from the greater to the lesser. Your parents gave life to you; how can you ever match that gift?

SIRACH 7:29-36, OBLIGATIONS TO PRIESTS AND TO THE POOR

COMMENTARY

7:29-31. Ben Sira's fondness for the priestly office finds frequent expression in the book, particularly within the section praising biblical heroes and ending with a magnificent poem eulogizing the high priest, Simeon II. The social status of priests varied over the centuries; because of competing sacerdotal families, the rise to power of one group naturally marked the decline of another in rank and privilege (1 Sam 3:10-14). The Levites endured this kind of demotion at one time, prompting the author of the book of Chronicles to come to their defense. Similarly, the family of Abiathar had fallen from royal favor in earlier days (1 Kgs 2:26-27). It follows that one can hardly describe all priests as privileged, although their status had certainly risen considerably during Ben Sira's time.[160] He urges his readers to obey biblical legislation with respect to supporting priests (cf. Deut 14:28-29; Lev 6:14-18). The two verbs, פחד (*pāḥad*) and כבד (*kābēd*), imply awe and high regard respectively. An ancient epithet for Yahweh was "the Fear of Isaac" (Gen 31:42), although an alternative translation of פחד יצחק (*paḥad yiṣḥāq*) is "kinsman of Isaac." Either rendering of the phrase emphasizes Yahweh's protection of Isaac in times of danger. The careful delineation of different types of sacrifice involving gifts to priests suggests that Ben Sira left little to chance where priests were concerned.

7:32-36. The addition of some remarks about responsibilities toward the needy shows that Ben Sira linked duties to God and to human beings. The positive evaluation of offerings to the dead is surprising, for the funerary cult fell into disfavor quite early in Israelite history. Nevertheless, ancient and venerable practices such as this one survived through the centuries because of strong feelings for departed loved ones. One explanation for idolatry points to a parent's grief over a lost child and the desire to have a reminder in tangible form (Wis 14:15). The cult,

---

160. M. Stern, "The Social and Governmental Structure of Judea Under the Ptolemies and Seleucids," in *A History of the Jewish People,* ed. H. H. Ben-Sasson (Cambridge, Mass.: Harvard University Press, 1976) 194.

widely practiced among Greeks and Romans, persisted into Christian times, according to F. X. Murphy. Catacombs of St. Sebastian have yielded a banquet room with graffiti on the walls "signifying that pilgrims had satisfied a vow by celebrating a memorial banquet in honor of Sts. Peter and Paul."[161] The Greek text tones down the reference to a cult of the dead, turning the remark into an admonition to attend burial rites, so important to the pious Tobit (Tob 1:16-20; 2:3-9).

161. F. X. Murphy, "Refrigerium," *New Catholic Encyclopedia*, ed. M. R. R. McGuire (1967) 12:197. See also Charles A. Kennedy, "Dead, Cult of the," *ABD*, 2:105-8; Theodore J. Lewis, *Cults of the Dead in Ancient Israel and Ugarit*, HSM 21 (Cambridge, Mass.: Harvard University Press, 1989); and Paola Xella, "Death and the Afterlife in Canaanite and Hebrew Thought," in *Civilizations of the Ancient Near East* (New York: Charles Scribner's Sons, 1995) 3:2059-2070.

SIRACH 8:1-19, SOME THINGS TO AVOID

COMMENTARY

8:1-7. The central theme of this unit, competing against someone with vastly more resources than you have, reminds Ben Sira of some related dangers, such as associating with violent people and revealing one's intimate secrets to strangers. The Hebrew verb ריב (*rîb*) is primarily juridical, connoting litigation in the court, but it also implies competition in other ways. Ben Sira deals with aging and the prospect of death in a humorous vein, quite differently from Qohelet's treatment of these issues in Eccl 11:7–12:7.[162] The eternal decree, "You must die," did not carry terror for Ben Sira, unless he managed to hide it successfully. For him, death meant "a gathering in" just as earlier narrators spoke of the patriarchs' being gathered to the ancestors (Gen 25:8, 17; 49:29).

8:8-9. The next subsection emphasizes the importance of tradition, a point that *Pirqe 'Abot* dramatizes by imagining a great chain of tradition spanning the generations. In this way, the link between past and present was assured, as was the accuracy of what was transmitted. Ben Sira uses technical terms for careful pondering (שׂיח *śîaḥ*), riddles (חידות *ḥîdôt*), and teaching (למד *lāmad*) in v. 8 and for accepting the instruction (שמע *šāmaʿ*) in v. 9. The primary source of wisdom is aged people; according to *Pirqe 'Abot* 4:26, "He who learns from the old, to what is he like? To one who eats ripe grapes and drinks old wine." Similarly, in *Pirqe 'Abot* 4:1 the question is asked, "Who is wise?" and answered, "He who learns from every man."

8:18-19. In v. 18, Ben Sira achieves a striking pun through reversing the consonants of the Hebrew word for "stranger" (זר *zār*, yielding רז *rāz*, "secret"). The latter word plays an important role in the *War Scroll* from Qumran with its esoteric knowledge and strong emphasis on being initiated into divine knowledge of mysteries that was not available to ordinary citizens.[163] The word *rāz* also occurs in the book of Daniel (2:18-19, 27-30, 47; 4:6), where a mystery must be unveiled by God's special representative. For Ben Sira, the secrecy implied by *rāz* had nothing to do with celestial mysteries.

162. Crenshaw, "The Shadow of Death in Qoheleth," 205-16. See also Crenshaw, *Urgent Advice and Probing Questions*, 573-85.

163. 1QM 3:9; 14:9; 16:11.

SIRACH 9:1-9, RELATIONSHIPS WITH WOMEN

COMMENTARY

Such recognition of dangers inherent to interaction between males and females characterizes wisdom literature from the very beginning, although the later Jewish concern for purity of lineage gave more bite to the warnings. Ben Sira cautions against jealous suspicions on the basis that they might become self-fulfilling prophecy, and he uses an ancient metaphor for dominance, treading on one's back (cf. the advice to her son Lemuel by the Queen Mother in Prov 31:3).[164] This entire section reflects the perspective of a male who views women as dangerous seductresses. That was true of all women, in Ben Sira's view, but particularly was the case with dancing women, prostitutes, and partygoers. A gloss on v. 4 reads: "Do not sleep with singing women lest they burn you with their mouths."

The allusion to fire in the context of seduction recalls the extended treatment of passion in Prov 6:20-35, where a probable pun occurs between "fire" (אש 'ēš) and "woman" (אשה 'iššâ). Here, too, the adulterer is threatened with ruin, for the cuckolded husband will have no mercy on the offender. In this text from Proverbs, two images are juxtaposed, that of a cozy lamp guiding one's eyes and that of a burning fire destroying one's very existence (cf. Job 31:9, 12). The former is parental teaching, the latter an adulteress. Ben Sira's discussion of this danger is more prosaic and comprehensive than Prov 6:20-35. He takes up this issue again in 25:13–26:27, where more emphasis is put on loyal wives than in 9:1-9.

The astonishing tendency to blame the woman even in cases not involving active seductresses places Ben Sira among a host of other male teachers of his day. If men could not control their lust when a beautiful woman came into view, it was not the woman's fault. Like the rabbi who advised against walking behind a woman, Ben Sira blamed the victim of passion.

---

164. James L. Crenshaw, "wĕdōrēk al bamôtê 'āreṣ," *CBQ* 34 (1972) 39-53; and "A Mother's Instruction to Her Son (Prov 31:1-9)," in *Perspectives in the Hebrew Bible* (Macon, Ga.: Mercer University Press, 1988) 9-22. See also Crenshaw, *Urgent Advice and Probing Questions*, 383-95.

REFLECTIONS

In Ben Sira's teaching, a negative understanding of women in society outweighs his few positive comments. Modern sensibilities about sexual harassment have brought about an enormously complex situation. In such a context, the church can function as an agent of reconciliation, helping to maintain pressure on those who think the issue is trivial and to encourage women and men to learn how to relate in a manner that guarantees dignity to both sexes. In coming to terms with the relationship between males and females, one does well to remember that Jesus' attitude toward women contrasted sharply with that of most others in the first century, in both the Jewish and the Greco-Roman worlds. The modern elevation of women owes much to his openness to them regardless of their reputation, as Charles E. Carlston pointed out some years ago.[165]

---

165. Carlston, "Proverbs, Maxims, and the Historical Jesus," 87-105.

SIRACH 9:10-16, FRIENDS AND NEIGHBORS

COMMENTARY

Returning to some topics already treated in 8:1-9, Ben Sira uses an arresting simile: Friendship resembles wine in that both need time before they can be fully enjoyed. This saying may be a proverb that he quotes for effect, but he may actually have coined the saying himself. The delay in retribution can be misleading, he insists, and one should be careful about associating with powerful people whose anger can spell one's end. Ben Sira never seemed to tire of using the language of snares and nets. Here he offers an antidote to sin: constant conversation about Torah and religion in the presence of wise and good people.

SIRACH 9:17–10:5, ON RULERS

COMMENTARY

Two things stand out here, the positive correlation between eloquence and success in rulers and the optimistic view of providence in appointing wise individuals to govern. The Greek text focuses on the way clever speech reflects an artisan's craft, whereas the Hebrew emphasizes the manipulative power of language. The persistence of belief in universal providence regardless of the political situation is testimony to the force of tradition, and Ben Sira's readiness to compromise universalism with particularist views about special divine interest in scribes (in the Greek text, at least) shows how both understandings of providence often co-existed. One wonders whether Ben Sira would have affirmed God's hand in appointing Antiochus IV Epiphanes to the Seleucid throne. This ruler proceeded to wage a campaign to destroy Jewish identity, proscribing the observance of the law and legislating the practice of idolatry. Ben Sira could not have forseen any of this. Perhaps one could view Ben Sira's remarks as applicable only to Judah, for ארץ ('ereṣ, "land") can have this restricted meaning, but the sages usually cast their nets much more widely than this reading allows. He appears to have framed his statement with thought only of the relative freedom enjoyed by Jerusalem under the Ptolemies.

SIRACH 10:6–11:1, PRIDE AND HONOR

COMMENTARY

10:6-18. The essential question posed for interpreters of this section, "Does the language have a specific referent?" cannot be answered. To be sure, certain events in the political world of the day resemble Ben Sira's remarks rather closely. They could refer to Antiochus III's victory over Ptolemy Philopator at Panium in 198 BCE, as well as to the story about the excruciating death of the latter king. The comment in v. 14 makes one think of Joseph, the "ruler" who rose from a lowly state to a place of honor (Genesis 39–50), but the resemblance is minor. Even if Ben Sira wished to describe the situation involving political jockeying for control of Judea, he would have veiled his language to avoid arousing the rulers' ire. The description is sufficiently general to apply in any number of contexts, and it may never have been intended as satire against the ruling Seleucids or Ptolemies.

Similarly, the remark about someone who became ill and died promptly, either because the physician did not recognize its seriousness (the Greek text) or because he was helpless to stop its progress (the Hebrew), does not necessarily relate to a specific instance in Ben Sira's memory. Transference of power, helplessness in the face of illness, and eventual decomposition represent general occurrences of which almost everyone would be aware. Ben Sira uses these powerful illustrations to emphasize the universal and personal nature of defeat. Every vestige of pride becomes ludicrous in the light of human makeup ("dust and ashes" [עפר ואפר *'āpār wā'ēpēr*]; cf. 17:32; 40:3; Gen 18:27).

Having witnessed a transferral of power of great magnitude, Ben Sira knew that even "pretend-gods" succcumbed to death's grim horror. Today's king is tomorrow's corpse. That realization, together with the anecdote about a worthless physician, prompted Ben Sira to write that, in the face of boundless pride, God turns things upside down. Egyptian wisdom literature often deals with a topsy-turvy world of societal unrest, but it lacks Ben Sira's optimism. The price of pride, according to Ben Sira, exceeds loss of life in a most humiliating manner; it also involves total extinction, even with all recollection of an individual being erased.

10:19-25. Verses 19-22 employ a rhetorical device, catechetical instruction (v. 19), that became popular in later times, both in Jewish pedagogy and in the Christian church. The simple question, "Whose offspring are worthy of honor?" is matched by its opposite, and the first answer fits both questions. Human beings deserve both honor and dishonor. The device permits the teacher to contrast the two types, rebels and God-fearers. Social status actually means nothing where honor is concerned. The comment about despising a poor wise man echoes Eccl 9:15-16. The Hebrew sociological categories in v. 22, largely monosyllabic, imply meager existence ("sojourner," "stranger," "foreigner," "impoverished" [גר *gēr*, זר *zār*, נכרי *nokrî*, רש *rāš*]). Ben Sira acknowledges their worth on the basis of a religious standard, whether they fear God or not.

Lest this graphic description of the fate awaiting all humans, proud or not, the concentration on divine intervention to frustrate human efforts, and the attention paid marginalized citizens lead to self-contempt, Ben Sira moves ahead to salvage personal esteem and to base self-worth on intelligence. He recognizes the necessity for a certain measure of pride lest others treat one like a doormat.

SIRACH 11:2-28, DECEPTIVE APPEARANCES

COMMENTARY

The international character of wisdom literature comes through nicely in this section. The Egyptian Papyrus Insinger uses the illustration about the bee's smallness and the wonderful delicacy it produces. The entire twentieth instruction warns against overlooking small things (e.g., a small illness, a little fire, a tiny lie, a small snake) and mentions some advantageous small things such as bread, dew, wind, and good news. Similarly, the *Instruction of Ankhsheshanky* has this comment: "Do not disdain a small document, a small fire, a small soldier."[166]

Several Greek writers observe that one's life cannot be evaluated until death. Solon, for instance, wrote: "Until he is dead, do not yet call a man happy, but only lucky"; Aeschylus stated, "Only when man's life comes to its end in prosperity can one call that man happy"; and Sophocles declared:

Let every man in mankind's frailty
Consider his last day; and let none
Presume on his good fortune until he find
Life, at his death, a memory without pain.[167]

Ben Sira may well have heard a popular saying like one of these, but the ideas are sufficiently

---

166. *Instruction of Ankhsheshanky* 16.25. See Lichtheim, *Ancient Egyptian Literature*, 3:172.

167. The quote from Solon is preserved by Herodotus *Histories* I.32, Aeschylus's remark occurs in his *Agamemnon* l.928, and Sophocles' observation appears in *Oedipus Rex* l.1529. Each is cited in Skehan and Di Lella, *The Wisdom of Ben Sira*, 241.

general to occur in any cultural context. His formulation of the matter speaks volumes in few words: "A man's end tells about him."

The similarity between the teaching in v. 2 and the biblical story about Yahweh's selection of David to rule over Israel instead of Saul (1 Sam 16:6-13) does not necessarily indicate that Ben Sira had that incident in mind. Remarkably, the account of David's anointing takes pains to add, "Now he was ruddy, and had beautiful eyes, and was handsome" (1 Sam 16:12 NRSV), after having discounted external appearance on the basis of the Lord's penetrating sight (1 Sam 16:7). Perhaps the narrator merely acknowledged a natural preference among human beings for attractive features. Ben Sira tries to overcome this tendency.

The enigmatic remark about concealed divine works probably plays on an epithet for Yahweh, the "Worker of Wonders" (Exod 15:11; Ps 77:14; cf. Judg 13:19). The reference may be to God's activity in human lives—the exalting of the lowly and the humbling of the proud—rather than the works of creation, which are for the most part gloriously manifest. Ben Sira gives several examples of God's hidden work, particularly in changing the lives of paupers, but also by mocking arrogance among the wealthy.

In the ancient world, the deity, or deities, were said to be responsible for everything, whether good or evil. Ben Sira accepts this belief without expressing the slightest reservation (v. 14). The fuller exposition in vv. 15-16, widely attested, suggests that a later editor thought Ben Sira's straightforward remark needed further elaboration in the direction of spiritual qualities. This practice attests to the vitality of the interpretive community and to the biblical text's character as a living tradition.

The idea that work does not necessarily pay dividends (v. 11) runs counter to the fundamental teaching of early wisdom in the book of Proverbs. Sometime later, Qohelet certainly doubted the lasting value of human toil. Ben Sira's point, that God's peculiar actions defy human standard, arises from a strong concept of divine freedom. The allusion to the eyes of the Lord does not reflect Persian influence in this instance, although the notion of personified eyes roving the empire seems to be found in the book of Zechariah, but expressed differently (Zech 1:8-17, horsemen patrolling the earth).

Once again, Ben Sira returns to the issue of theodicy (vv. 20-28) and mocks the rich, who rely on their wealth to protect them from adversity. Like the rich fool whom Jesus ridiculed for overlooking one small matter (Luke 12:13-21), the fact of death, these powerful individuals take their ease and wait for more good to come their way. The debate formula, "Do not say," occurs twice (vv. 23-24) and a variant as well, "Do not wonder" (v. 21). Ben Sira points out that appearances often deceive, for instantaneous changes can reverse present circumstances. The final declaration of a person's character, the balancing of virtuous deeds against wicked works (cf. Dan 5:27), was thought to take place at the hour of death. The reward for faithful service was an honorable name that survived in children (so the Greek translation of באחריתו [$bĕ'aḥărîtô$, "at the end of his life"]) and in grateful memories of the entire community. The word סוף ($sôp$, "end") as an indication of life's termination occurs in Eccl 7:2. The idea of an exact balancing of the account soon took on great importance among the Pharisees, who enthusiastically endorsed belief in life after death.

SIRACH 11:29–14:19, ON FRIENDSHIP AND WEALTH

COMMENTARY

This section vividly illustrates the difficulty of dividing the contents of Sirach into discrete units. A glance at the commentaries reveals little agreement on this and many other larger units, each interpreter viewing the material from a different perspective.

Riches, the unifying theme of 11:29–14:19, provokes various thoughts from Ben Sira, chiefly cautionary advice about the dangers involved in trying to relate to wealthy people. He uses several arresting images to convey his insights.

11:29–12:9. The first picture comes from a hunter's practice of placing a bird in a cage to lure other birds into it (11:30). The cage has a special entrance that opens from below; once another bird has entered the enclosed place, it cannot spring the door from above and is thus trapped. Ben Sira likens the proud to a decoy bird attracting the attention of its victims, perhaps also to the hunter who watches from a hiding place until its prey has entered the cage. As if this image of vulnerability were not sufficient, Ben Sira observes that a single spark ignites coals (11:32). An ancient proverb warned against underestimating a little fire, a tiny rumor, a small soldier. Experience had taught society that some small things did enormous harm. A "worthless person" (איש בליעל 'îš bĕliyya'al) lurks in the shadows to shed blood (cf. Prov 1:11, "to lie in wait, to ambush" [ארב 'rb]). This use of the expression 'îš bĕliyya 'al is unique in Sirach, but it occurs elsewhere in Job 38:18 and Prov 6:12; 16:27; 19:28. The application of these images to the problem at hand, inviting strangers into one's home, uses a wordplay for "stranger"/"estrange" (זהיר/זר zār/zāhîr).

12:10-12. Another image in this unit compares enemies to a corrosive pot or to a "magic mirror" that was thought to divulge the identity of friend and foe when carefully polished and examined. Ben Sira advises caution, taking the form of constantly polishing the metal surface of a mirror to prevent its copper from becoming discolored (12:10-11). The reference to the right hand (12:12) implies the place of honor, which should be zealously protected from impostors.

12:13-18. The picture of a snake charmer, once bitten, pleading for sympathy from onlookers, or a thoughtless daredevil who tempts ferocious beasts and then asks for pity when they have mauled him, accurately describes the behavior of anyone who gets cozy with an enemy. Shedding insincere tears and whispering feigned affection (12:16), the enemy awaits an opportunity to throw a victim into a pit (cf. Joseph's brothers in Gen 37:12-24).

13:1-20. The principle that the person who touches tar becomes dirty (13:1) gave rise to a proverb long before Ben Sira's day, for the idea of being tainted through association with base fellows already appears in a text by Theognis.[168] Its popularity has persisted to the present, occurring in two of Shakespeare's works.[169] Similarly, the concept of "like associating with like" was enunciated frequently in various forms (cf. the Latin "like delights in like," *Similis simili gaudet*). In Isa 11:6, the prophet envisions a total reversal of the usual pattern of things, an era when a wolf will lie down with a lamb, a leopard with a goat, a calf with a lion, a cow with a bear, and when an infant will play over the hole of an asp, a weaned child will touch an adder's den. The real world, one in which a clay vessel that collides with an iron kettle shatters (13:2), does not deal gently with opposites who try to forge close friendship. Ben Sira lays out some areas of vulnerability when people of ordinary material resources attempt to become close friends with persons who possess extraordinary wealth.

In the first place, he argues, "like loves like" (13:15). The argument from analogy with animals like wolves, hyenas, dogs, wild asses, and lions contains a fundamental flaw, for rich and poor belong to the same genus. Ben Sira selects predatory animals to make his point: hyenas, wolves, lions. Their prey—or natural enemy, in the case of dogs (cf. Job 30:1; Isa 56:10; Jer 12:9)—illustrates the precarious position of people who aspire to be friends with the rich. Once the poor have served their purpose, whether for amusement or for their meager resources, they are promptly cast off like refuse. Moreover, in the process of responding to the hospitality of the wealthy by the customary follow-up, people of modest means deplete their resources through an endless round of entertainment.

In the second place, Ben Sira observes, those who befriend the wealthy walk a difficult tightrope, trying to be noticed without being too conspicuous and inviting contempt. The situation has been compared to sitting at

---
168. Theognis #35.
169. See William Shakespeare *Much Ado About Nothing* III.3.61 and *King Henry IV*, Part I II.4.460.

a fire; one needs to get close enough to feel the warmth of the flame, but must remain far enough away to avoid getting burned.[170]

A third point of vulnerability issues from the inevitable self-denial demanded by limited resources, now stretched to the limit by competing with people who have greater wealth. One has to adopt a miserly life-style, and that, says Ben Sira, makes absolutely no sense for any number of reasons. The third and second centuries BCE, with surging interest in amassing a fortune, also produced advocates of personal enjoyment, such as Qohelet, Ben Sira, and the rabbi who insisted that everyone must give an account of every good thing not enjoyed. One can infer from the heated attack in Wis 1:16–2:24 on such indulgence that things quickly got out of hand, leading to lawless conduct by young robbers. Qohelet's sevenfold encouragement to enjoy life had found a receptive audience, one prepared to do so without any consideration for those harmed by this commitment to gathering rosebuds before they wither.

13:21–14:2. Yet another source of difficulty lay in society's natural disposition, a bias in favor of the rich. The plain fact must be faced, Ben Sira observes (13:23), that the crowds praise the wealthy even when the latter utter nonsense, and the masses condemn the lowly who may speak eloquently; the word for "ridiculing" in 13:22 (גע גע *gaʿ gaʿ*) imitates the croaking of frogs; if one reads גגע (*gagaʿ*), it may refer to cackling. In other words, people who endeavor to cross that invisible line between poverty and riches only fool themselves. As Qohelet rightly perceived, the poor wise man received no one's gratitude (Eccl 9:16). Small wonder a clever individual wryly observed that "God loves the poor but helps the rich."

The judgment that riches in themselves are not evil (13:24) introduces a wholly unexpected sentiment. Just as Ben Sira's advice about charitable giving in 12:1-7 presents an insuperable challenge—ascertaining authentic goodness in others—his opinion of the wealthy requires a similar looking into the hearts of others. Happily, he believed that goodness was reflected in one's countenance (13:26; cf. Prov 15:13; Ps 104:15; Eccl 8:1; Matt 6:16-18).

14:3-19. Finally, Ben Sira points to the absurdity of being stingy, "small of heart" (לב קטן *lēb qāṭān*), and denying oneself life's pleasure when standing under a sentence of death. This allusion to the story about Adam and Eve and the divine decree, "You must die!" (14:17), is virtually without precedent. Ben Sira will take the reflection one additional step, blaming the woman for all subsequent misfortune. For now, he restricts himself to drawing a comparison between leaves falling from a tree and people dying. The analogy, although appropriate in the case of individual people, becomes strained when applied to generations, for usually when leaves fall from a tree on their own, others do not take their place until the seasons have changed. Ben Sira's expression for humankind, "flesh and blood" (בשר ודם *bāśār wĕdām*), occurs often in rabbinic literature.

When leaves fall to the ground, they decompose, enriching the soil. Human beings also rot (the verb רקב [*rāqēb*] occurs here and in two other places, Prov 10:7 and Isa 40:20), but the Israelites thought of the deceased as somehow existing in Sheol. The reference to this shadowy domain in 14:12 is the first one in Sirach. It was originally thought to be outside Yahweh's realm, but the prophet Amos recognized no such limit to God's authority (Amos 9:2). The unknown author of Job believed that a certain leveling of social distinctions occurred there, resulting in rest for the weary (Job 3:13-19). In the opinion of at least one psalmist, the residents of Sheol do not chant Yahweh's praises (Ps 6:5). Those who entered Sheol, so it was thought, took up permanent residence.[171] This opinion was replaced in NT times by a conviction that Sheol was only a temporary resting place, at least for the righteous. A change also took place in the character of Sheol, perhaps under Persian influence, in common thinking. No longer a neutral domicile, Sheol came to be depicted as hell, a realm of punishment by fire.

---

170. Gracian notes the skepticism regarding the political life: "First make an obligation, of what you are paid for afterwards; it is a trick of the political giants, to yield favor before it is earned, for it betokens that the men concerned are men of honor. The favor thus advanced, has double merit, for in the readiness with which it was bestowed, it lays greater obligation upon him who receives it, and if later it is mere pay, given earlier, it constitutes a promissory note." See Baltasar Gracian, *The Art of Worldly Wisdom* (New York: Barnes and Noble, 1993) 236.

171. Theodore J. Lewis, "Dead, Abode of the," *ABD* 2 (New York: Doubleday, 1972); and N. J. Tromp, *Primitive Conceptions of Death and the Nether World in the Old Testament*, BibOr 21 (Rome: Pontifical Biblical Institute, 1969).

REFLECTIONS

1. Still another area in which Ben Sira's views have suffered over time concerns wealth. For the most part, he looked on rich people as enemies; the author of the Epistle of James shared this suspicion (Jas 2:1-7). Given the social context producing the Scriptures, such an attitude is understandable. Ben Sira does qualify his criticism of wealth in the end, observing that riches not associated with wickedness cannot be totally bad. Perhaps that appreciation for wealth rightly used should become a mainstay of Christian teaching—particularly in the light of the enormous financial resources in the coffers of the church. One can scarcely imagine modern society apart from the contributions of philanthropists who have donated funds for private hospitals, colleges and universities, churches, foundations that bestow seed money on all kinds of worthy causes, and the like.

Furthermore, many persons who have prospered materially encounter a problem peculiar to the wealthy: the difficulty of distinguishing between genuine friends and others who seek to use them for personal gain. The church serves these people faithfully when it also recognizes this problem and welcomes the rich into its circle in the same way it does the poor—that is, as persons needing Christian love. In this way, churches can help wealthy people learn to use their resources for worthy causes just as they teach those with meager possessions to be stewards of their resources.

2. Ben Sira has a few observations about death's inevitability that ring true today just as they did long ago, although the church has introduced the *hope* of the resurrection that alters the situation emphatically. This hope, fundamental to Pauline theology and to the early Christians generally, rests in God's character and in the belief that God raised Jesus from the dead. Ultimately, the hope in the resurrection symbolizes an unwillingness to believe in the victory of evil over good. No one really knows what happens at death, and Christians need to face up to that fact, readily admitting that they live by faith. In the meantime, the church can bear faithful witness to the hope of the resurrection by helping those who stare death in the face more immediately than the average individual. By providing hospices, visiting the dying, helping people die with dignity, preparing members to face the inevitable reality, remembering the dead, and teaching Christian workers to deal comfortably with the terminally ill, churches can demonstrate to society at large that their members take death seriously but do not let it paralyze them into inaction.

SIRACH 14:20–23:27

PART IV

OVERVIEW

Reminiscent of Psalm 1, with its language of blessing and the imagery of a flourishing tree, the opening poem about wisdom lays the groundwork for serious reflection on free will and divine retribution for wickedness. This discussion leads naturally to thoughts about God as judge, a concept that arose often in the volatile ancient Near East. Confident that God rewards virtue and punishes sin, Ben Sira urges his hearers to exercise their free will wisely, attending to small matters like giving alms to the needy, exercising caution and self-discipline, gaining control over speech by avoiding harmful utterances and by skillful elocution when speech was preferable to silence. He recognizes the favorable circumstances afforded wickedness and distinguishes between the wise and fools, who take different paths to distinct destinies. Ben Sira stresses the importance of long-term friendships, the proper use of language, and entering exclusively into appropriate sexual relationships. A prayer focuses his compelling desire to utter only what issues in favor from both God and humans.

SIRACH 14:20–15:10, SEEKING WISDOM AND BEING WELCOMED BY HER

COMMENTARY

This praise of wisdom consists of two parts, 14:20-27 and 15:1-10; 15:1 then provides a thematic verse uniting the description of those who pursue wisdom with that of her receiving them with open arms. The remarkable resemblance between this hymn and Psalm 1 is both linguistic and theological. Each begins with the formula of blessing, "Blessed are" (אשרי *'ašrê*), then goes on to describe the behavior of the happy ones—their meditating on Torah and subsequent prosperity—while using the image of a flourishing tree. Each one also contrasts two groups, the favored ones and the unfortunate victims of their own wickedness and folly.

14:20-27. The opening section focuses on the lively pursuit of wisdom; it does so by concentrating at first on the images of spies (in the Hebrew) or hunters (in the Greek), then shifting to that of a passionate lover, only in the end changing the metaphor for wisdom to that of a tree with birds building nests in its branches and finding refuge from the scorching sun. All of this comprises a single sentence in Hebrew with various linking devices in the explanatory appositional clauses. The Greek reading in v. 20, "will die" (τελευτήσει *teleutēsei*), may have arisen through reflection on 11:28, the insistence that only at death can one really consider anyone happy. The verb "to meditate" (הגה *hāgâ*) also occurs in 6:37 and 50:28. In v. 22, the Greek manuscripts have "ways" (ὁδοῖς *hodois*), with only Codex Vaticanus reading "in her entrances" (ἐν ταῖς εἰσόδοις αὐτῆς *en tais eisodois autēs*), which agrees with the Hebrew. The idea suggests that spies observe every single entrance to wisdom's dwelling. The dominant image in the Greek text, that of hunting, implies that wisdom's pursuers lie in wait at all her paths and demonstrate their skill at tracking wild animals.

The change to lover occurs in vv. 23-25, where his action demonstrates strong passion at the expense of proper decorum, at least to the modern way of thinking, where peering into a window of a beloved hardly accords with acceptable conduct. On the basis of Cant 2:9, which has the young woman rejoice that her beloved stands outside and peers into her window, one may assume that the practice did not offend some segments in ancient society. Wishing to be near the object of his ardor, the young man in v. 24 pitches his tent against the wall of her house. The word אהלו (*'ŏhŏlô*, "his tent") has both a literal and a figurative meaning here and in Job 8:22; 22:23; and 29:4, approximating the sense of one's physical and psychological existence.

In vv. 26-27, the earlier image of wisdom as a shade tree recurs, with the lover now being described as a bird. The Hebrew text has "its nest" (קנו *qinnô*) in v. 26, whereas the Greek has "his children" (τέκνα αὐτοῦ *tekna autou*). The idea of wisdom's providing shelter occupies the thought of Qohelet in Eccl 7:12, an extremely enigmatic verse. The divine object lesson in Jonah 4:6-11 dramatizes the deep feelings generated by adequate protection from the sun's sweltering rays in the ancient Near East.

15:1-10. Part two of this poem shifts the point of view to the object of hot pursuit. As this section illustrates, wisdom gladly lets herself be captured by worthy pursuers but holds herself at a distance from those lacking intelligence. The thematic verse equates fear of Yahweh—that is, "piety"—with keeping the law and then relates both to wisdom. The expression "the one who handles the law" (תופש תורה *tôpēś tôrâ*) refers to a scribe in 15:1, but in Jer 2:8 it indicates a priest (alongside rulers [shepherds] and prophets). The verb תפש (*tāpaś*) connotes catching and holding an object securely, hence skill at warfare (cf. Num 31:27) and expertise at interpreting the law, as here.

The tame imagery of wisdom as a mother in v. 2 quickly yields to the more customary picture of a passionate young bride ("a wife of youth"; cf. Prov 5:18). Both Deutero- and Trito-Isaiah compare Yahweh to a mother who cannot forget her children and who offers comfort (Isa 49:14-15; 66:13). Verse 3 echoes the ancient tradition about wisdom's feast as proclaimed in Prov 9:1-6, but the language comes closer to that uttered by wisdom's rival, folly, in 9:13-18. Although wisdom is said to serve bread and wine, folly offers stolen water and bread consumed in secret (v. 17). Ben Sira carefully specifies the nature of the bread and water ("bread of astuteness" and "water of understanding"). The clandestine and erotic features of illicit sex in Prov 9:17 have given way here to intellectual categories. This symbolic use of bread and water for religious instruction and its rewards gained popularity in Jewish literature after Ben Sira.[172] The idea has a long history, beginning as early as the period of return from Babylonian exile. In Isa 55:1-2, Yahweh offers water, milk, and bread to the hungry.

The literary structure of vv. 1-4 merits closer attention. In vv. 1 and 4 an ABA´B´ parallelism reigns: "one who fears Yahweh/ will do this // one who handles torah/will obtain her" (v. 1); "whoever leans on her/ will not totter // whoever trusts her/will not be shamed" (v. 4). The ruling pattern of vv. 2-3 differs greatly, an ABB´A´ structure obtaining: "she will meet him/like a mother // like a woman of youth; she will receive him" (v. 2); "and she will feed him/bread of astuteness // and water of understanding/she will give him to drink" (v. 3). Besides essential spiritual nourishment, wisdom grants honor and eloquence (v. 5). The explosion of sibilants in v. 6 almost gives the impression that Ben Sira wished to demonstrate his own skill at persuasive and pleasant communication: ששון (*śāśôn*, "joy"), ושמחה (*wĕśimḥâ*, "and rejoicing"), ימצה (*yimṣâ*, "he will discover"), ושם עולם (*wĕśēm 'ôlām*, "and an everlasting name"), תורישנו (*tôrîšennû*, "she will bequeath to him"). The teasing sound of the consonants is balanced by content that evokes a desirable mood.

The poem ends on a threatening note: Sinners will not even catch a glimpse of wisdom. The contrast between the fate of foolish people and the reward of persistent lovers could hardly be starker. On the one hand, the lover camps beside wisdom's house and "nests" in her branches, and wisdom receives him with open arms, treating him to a sumptuous meal. On the other hand, the fool stands in

---

172. W. O. E. Oesterley cites several references (in the Midrashim: an early Tannaitic reference, *Sifre* 84a, as well as sayings from the Amoraim, Shir Rabba i 2, Bereshith Rabba lxxi, and in the Babylonian Talmud: *Shabbath* 120a). See Oesterley, *The Wisdom of Jesus the Son of Sirach or Ecclesiasticus*.

the remote distance, having failed to capture her. Such arrogant sinners are not worthy of singing her praise (v. 9), and only divinely sent praise enjoys God's blessing.

REFLECTIONS

One of the most useful symbols for human existence is that of pilgrimage. We are *homo viator,* people on the road. Ben Sira's use of imagery from Bedouin who dwell in tents reminds us all of the temporary nature of earthly existence. "This world is not my home, I'm just passing through"—the words of this spiritual touch a responsive chord, describing how we are embarking on a journey, with its final destination by no means certain.

Whether we subscribe to that hope grounded in Jesus' resurrection or limit our concerns to the present existence, we can undoubtedly profit from clear signs laid by the trailblazer from Nazareth, for the journey will take us along dangerous routes. Ancient Romans set up milestones along the way, some of which survive to this day. As Christians, we can begin to think of ways to erect markers that indicate progress in coming to terms with ourselves and with God—over and above the customary moments of birth and conversion. Careful chronicling of spiritual progress, together with an honest listing of the unfortunate byways we frequently take, will serve as useful road maps for us and, at times, for others. We are not alone after all, and we bear some responsibility for fellow travelers.

The symbol of a pitched tent also suggests that every illusion of permanency will be exposed. In God's world, we do not own the land but merely occupy it for a short time and then move on to another place. Moreover, those committed to pilgrimage travel light, even in a day when success is measured in terms of material wealth. A readiness to go where need arises and to take up our tent pegs in God's service comes much more easily when one views life as a journey and sees every dwelling as temporary. Then the plight of dispossessed persons throughout the world becomes one every person can comprehend.

SIRACH 15:11–16:23, ON FREE WILL AND DIVINE RECOMPENSE

COMMENTARY

In a fictional debate, Ben Sira tries to answer some accusations against God and to counter justification for wicked conduct.[173] Several biblical texts come very close to blaming Yahweh for human rebellion, especially Exod 11:10, Yahweh's hardening of Pharaoh's heart; 2 Sam 24:1, Yahweh's prompting David to carry out a census of young men who were eligible for conscription into the army; Jer 6:21 and Ezek 3:20, Yahweh's imposing obstacles to life; and Isa 6:9-13, Yahweh's use of the prophet to hinder repentance on the part of the nation. Furthermore, the claim that both weal and woe come from the Lord in Deut 32:39 and Isa 45:7, when coupled with a firm denial of any rival deities, can easily lead to belief that both good and evil human beings derive from God.

The fundamental problem arose from widespread belief that Israel's God had created a world in which sin was a live possibility. The skeptic asked why such a universe was formed when a deity capable of creation could surely have made one that rendered transgression impossible. Three possibilities

---

173. Readers can quickly recognize the complexity of the problem of theodicy and become familiar with various ways of dealing with it in Crenshaw, *Theodicy in the Old Testament.*

for the origin of evil naturally came to mind: (1) God created both good and evil; (2) Satan introduced sin into the world; and (3) human beings brought evil into a perfect world. At this point, Ben Sira strongly attaches blame to men and women, who willingly opt to rebel against their maker. In three verses, he uses the Hebrew word חפץ (ḥāpēṣ, "to desire," "to choose") as many times, emphasizing human choice (15:15-17). In his view, any attempt to shift blame from humans to God ignored one essential fact: God cannot do that which God despises.

Skepticism about divine recompense for sinful deeds seemed to support the claim that Yahweh either approved of evil or simply overlooked it. When a delay in divine visitation coincided with reverse expectation, such as numerous children being born to wicked people, traditional understandings of divine justice became suspect. That situation existed in early second-century BCE Jerusalem and demanded a thoughtful response from a teacher like Ben Sira. In offering a rebuttal to such skepticism, he put forth at least one bold statement at odds with tradition: Barrenness with virtue surpasses a large family of wicked children (16:1-4). To overcome doubt about divine punishment, he lets Scripture demonstrate the reality of God's wrath on sinners of all sorts. Ben Sira's answer to those who considered their little actions inconsequential in God's eyes amounts to a teacher's harsh rebuke for sloppy thinking.

15:11-20. The initial section echoes Moses' speech in Deut 30:15, 19, which offers the people of Israel a choice between good and evil, life and death. This unit also draws on Gen 1:1 and insists that *from the beginning* God has opposed sin absolutely. The formula of debate, "do not say" (אל תאמר 'al tōmar), and a variant, "lest you say" (פן תאמר pen tōmar), appear in vv. 10-12 ('al tōmar in 16:17). The attribution of rebellion (פשע pešaʿ) and violence (חמס ḥāmās) to God evokes in Ben Sira a twofold use of the word שנא (śānēʾ, "to hate"; cf. vv. 11, 13; in the latter instance, רעה [rāʿâ, "wicked"] in hendiadys with ותועבה [wětôʿēbâ, "abomination"] precedes the verb). The Epistle of James also refutes a claim that God incites sinners to do evil; it, too, stresses human desire as the origin of sin (Jas 1:13-15).

Verses 15-16 breathe the spirit of Hab 2:4, where human faithfulness is said to bring justification before God. The strong intellectual component in faith thus finds a worthy complement in actions demonstrating one's convictions. Fire and water (v. 16) serve as metaphors for life's destruction and generation; and the idea of two ways was familiar in the Hellenistic world, as well as in Judaism. The rabbis frequently refer to two inclinations, the יצר הרע (yēṣer hārāʾ) and the יצר הטוב (yēṣer haṭṭôb). The first, the evil disposition, antedates the second, the good tendency, by a dozen years, according to rabbinic speculation. Biblical grounds for two inclinations existed in Gen 6:5 and 8:21 (for the evil bias) and 1 Chr 29:28 and Isa 26:3 (for the good inclination). The rabbis even noticed two spellings of the crucial nouns for mental disposition, לב (lēb) and לבב (lēbāb, "heart") and יצר (yēṣer, "inclination") in the biblical text.

16:1-23. In the second unit, which the Vg titles *De filiis impiis* ("On Wicked Children"), Ben Sira draws the consequences of his belief in an all-seeing God: Sinners will pay dearly for their offenses. He first takes up the mistaken notion that numerous progeny demonstrate God's favor. That is true, Ben Sira says, only when the children fear God. Indeed, one good person is better than a thousand sinners (cf. Eccl 9:15), and a single worthy individual can generate enough children to fill a city. Here Ben Sira probably alludes to Gen 15:1-5, the promise to Abraham that he will be the father of countless descendants.

Verse 5 raises a provocative issue for interpreters of wisdom literature: When does the personal ego surface? Peter Höffken has discussed this problem as it pertains to Qohelet, where the authorial "I" occurs often.[174] Does Ben Sira appeal to his own private experience in alluding to what he has seen and heard, or does he merely transmit information by means of a literary convention? Interestingly, he stops short of recording these personal insights; instead he promptly enters into an allusive account of divine wrath in biblical narrative. He recalls the punishment of

---

174. Peter Höffken, "Das Ego des Weisen," *Theologische Zeitschrift* 4 (1985) 121-35. Occasionally, an author of brief proverbial sayings in the book of Proverbs slips into an "autobiographical style" (cf. the imagined speech in Prov 5:12-14, but also 25:30-34; and 30:18-19; the instructions naturally use the first-person address of a teacher, as in Prov 22:19-21; 30:1-14; and 31:1-9).

Korah, Dathan, and Abiram in Num 16:1-35, that of the rebellious giants in Gen 6:1-4, the destruction of Sodom and Gomorrah in Gen 19:1-28, and the erasure of a whole generation of Israelites in the wilderness (cf. Exod 12:37 for the number 600,000).

The avoidance of the Hebrew word for "giants" (נפלים *nĕpilîm*) may represent Ben Sira's aversion to speculation about their role in the fall of humankind that characterized the Enochic literature and the book of *Jubilees*.[175] Ben Sira's choice of "giants of old" (נסיכי קדם *nĕsîkê qedem*) may also allude to the myths preserved in Isaiah 14 and Ezekiel 28.[176]

Several psalms take up the problem of doubters who emphasize the vastness of the universe and the inconsequentiality of human deeds, whether good or bad (cf. Pss 10:4, 11, 13; 14:1; 53:2). Ben Sira combines such skepticism with vocabulary taken from theophanic descriptions of earth's response to God's coming, the prayers attributed to Solomon at the dedication of the Temple and to Jonah in the belly of the fish (1 Kgs 8:27; Jonah 2:6), and acknowledgment of mystery where God's actions are concerned. The exact grammatical relationship from vv. 17-23 is unclear, although vv. 18-19 may be parenthetical. In the Hebrew text, v. 20 links up with v. 17, whereas the Greek has v. 20 as a continuation of v. 19. The glosses on this unit (vv. 15-16) and the many variants in other languages attest to the lively debate generated by such skepticism (cf. 17:15-20; 23:18; Wis 3:7; 14:11). For now, Ben Sira seems content to adopt the practice of diatribe, a vibrant form of persuasive discourse in which an imaginary audience is addressed directly, often going so far as to label his opponents "misguided, senseless, and foolish."

---

[175]. James VanderKam, *Enoch: A Man for All Generations* (Columbia: University of South Carolina Press, 1995), has examined this growth of a corpus of literature about Enoch in great detail; in doing so, he has thrown considerable light on the context of second- and first-century BCE Judaism.

[176]. Mythical language abounds in Isaiah 14 (Day Star, Dawn, Mountain of the North, the Pit, the Most High), all of it reminiscent of Canaanite mythology. The unspecified object of ridicule—Nebuchadrezzar? Babylon? Persia?—is depicted as having fallen because of extreme pride. The king of Tyre, according to Ezekiel 28, also was brought low because of overweening pride. Here, too, mythological concepts from Ugaritic literature occur, but so do Israelite mythic ideas (the wise Dan'el, the Pit, Mount Saphon, the garden of Eden, cherubim).

REFLECTIONS

Generation after generation of religious people have struggled to understand the implications of divine knowledge and sovereignty. Does God know everything that happens even before it takes place, and does divine power leave any room for human freedom? Experience teaches us that we make free choices when confronted with alternatives, but we also know that those decisions are shaped to a great extent by genetics and culture. How free, then, are people? In the religious realm, a similar ambiguity reigns. We choose God or spurn the divine invitation to holiness, but how much real choice do we have in that decision?

The biblical manner of addressing this problem began with the result and argued backward to causal factors. When people turned their backs on God, that action must surely have been willed by God, whose intention cannot be frustrated, given the operative understanding of divine power. The real difficulty with this view came in incidents involving people who desired to change but whose will was subjected to a contrary divine power (e.g., Pharaoh) or in circumstances where it was believed that God blocked human inclinations to repent (e.g., Isa 6:9-10; Mark 4:10-12). Possibly these texts represent mistaken assessments of the situation, but how can the church hold in proper tension our potential for good or ill and God's sovereignty? That struggle has divided the church and continues to baffle theologians, who usually take their cue from the rabbinic affirmation of free will *and* divine authority. That mystery is not the only one in the religious life of modern Christians.

SIRACH 16:24–18:14, THE RELATIONSHIP BETWEEN THE CREATOR-JUDGE AND HUMANKIND

COMMENTARY

This section consists of four (or five) distinct poems: 16:24-30; 17:1-24 (or 17:1-14 and 17:15-24); 17:25-32; 18:1-14. It treats the dual themes of God's creative and judicial functions, especially divine retribution, extends an invitation to repent, and elaborates on God's compassion for frail human beings. The former resembles a midrash on Genesis 1, while much of the language recalls Psalms 8 and 104. The brief unit in 17:15-24 provides further response to the earlier skeptical attitude articulated in 16:17-22.

16:24-30. The initial poem praises the Creator for the orderliness of the universe, its appropriateness in every detail. The detached language and mathematical precision emphasize the divine plan (κοσμέω *kosmeō*, "to order," "to arrange") in Greek, from which comes the noun "cosmos." The Greek text has a vocative in v. 24, "my son," lacking in both Hebrew and Syriac. Verses 24-25 serve as an introduction to this initial poem, perhaps also to the larger section. Ben Sira stresses the reliability of his teaching by such terms as "weighing" (שקל *šāqal*) and "preserving" (צנע *ṣn'*). He implies that he has carefully examined God's works and retained his findings for posterity. From Prov 1:23 he borrows the concept of pouring out God's Spirit (אביעה *'abbî'â*), although in 50:27 he uses the causative form of the verb (נבע *nāba'*).

The poem describing God's creative act that brought forth the universe (vv. 26-30) reflects on the narrative in Gen 1:1-25, but the Hebrew is fragmentary from the second bicolon of v. 26 to 30:11. The Greek κρίσει (*krisei*, "judged") is a mistake for κτίσει (*ktisei*, "created"), for which the Hebrew has an infinitive construct form of the verb ברא (*bārā'*, "to create"), a verb used only with God as subject in the Bible. Whereas Gen 1:1 has בראשית ברא אלהים (*běrē'šît bārā 'ĕlōhîm*),[177] Ben Sira used the syntactically correct בברא אל (*bibrā' 'ēl*, "when God created") plus מראש (*mērōš*, "from the beginning"). These works, in contrast to human beings, always obey God's commands; indeed, they deserve the divine affirmation of extraordinary goodness (cf. the refrain in Genesis 1, where God makes this judgment often). Still, these creatures must return to the earth whence they came (cf. 40:11).

17:1-24. In 17:1-14, Ben Sira turns to the account of God's creation of human beings, merging the two different descriptions in Genesis 1–2 with the separate tradition from Sinai about the giving of the commandments. Ben Sira understands the image of God to imply authority over the animals comparable to God's sovereignty in the heavens. The Greek concept of the five senses (sight, touch, smell, sound, and taste), together with two additional faculties from Stoic philosophy, knowledge and reason, have evoked a gloss in v. 5, perhaps prompted by the listing of gifts in v. 6. The abrupt shift to the Sinaitic theophany in v. 13 follows the notion of fearing God, an accompaniment of praise, and emphasizes responsibility toward neighbors. The reference is probably to the second tablet of the Decalogue.

Contrary to the opinions expressed by "foolish persons" in 16:17-22, Ben Sira is convinced that God does see every human being and rewards or punishes each according to his or her actions. That assurance comprises the next seven verses, which conclude with a promise of forgiveness to the repentant.

---

177. Because of the peculiar pointing of the first two words in the Bible, interpreters have had difficulty deciding whether to translate the initial construction as absolute or temporal, both being possible grammatically. Context often leads scholars to understand the words temporally, thus "When God began to create the heavens and the earth, the earth was already waste and void." This translation, adopted by the NRSV, although phrased differently, seems to have more to recommend it than the alternative, "In the beginning God created the heavens and the earth."

Verse 17 refers to ancient speculation about Israel's special relationship to God. Whereas God appointed secular rulers for the other nations (or angelic mediators with Yahweh on their behalf), Ben Sira observes, as God's portion, Israel has direct access to God. In short, Israel exists as the private people of God. Ben Sira's high esteem for good works shows in the metaphors employed in v. 22, where both a "signet ring" and "the apple of the eye" describe almsgiving. The signet ring, or seal, worn on the finger or around the neck, when pressed in wax, left a person's insignia on important papers (cf. Gen 38:18; Cant 8:6; Jer 22:24). The other metaphor appears in Deut 32:10; Ps 17:8; Prov 7:2; and Zech 2:12, the first and last of these references with regard to Israel and Judah as God's special portion.

Jewish reflection on the relationship of other peoples to God acknowledged their place in the divine scheme of things. *Sifre* 40 states that "God does not provide for Israel alone, but for all people," and the Targum to Pseudo Jonathan at Gen 11:7-8 observes that every nation has its own guardian angel (cf. Deut 32:8-9 LXX). Ben Sira believed in the universal domain of Israel's God, but he also considered some nations inveterate foes. His harshest comments occur in 50:25-26 with reference to Idumeans, Philistines, and Samaritans.

The threat of retribution in v. 23 resembles that in Joel 4:4-7[3:4-7, Eng.], where the prophet stresses an exact recompense for offenses against the Judeans. Ben Sira implies that God may remain inactive for the time being, as the skeptics in 16:17-22 suspected, but that patient waiting will eventually give way to divine visitation. Nevertheless, Ben Sira offers hope to the despairing.

17:25-32. The Latin text sets the next section apart with the title *De Conversione* ("On Repentance"); these verses urge mortals to repent in order to sing Yahweh's praises. Extolling the Lord's glory represented for Sirach the highest form of life (cf. 15:9-10; 17:10; 18:4-7; 39:8, 15, 35; 43:28-30; 51:1, 22), one forbidden those in Sheol. Ben Sira uses an analogy in v. 31 that also occurs in 1 Esdr 4:33-41 and in a fragmentary Sumerian text, specifically that if even the sun is eclipsed, how much more the feeble light of humankind. The contest of Darius's guards appropriately concludes with praise of the Lord of truth, just as this poem sings of divine mercy in the context of human dust and ashes.

18:1-14. The final unit characterizes Yahweh as a righteous and merciful judge whose majesty surpasses human imagination. This thought prompts Ben Sira to reflect momentarily on the lowliness of men and women when compared with God's grandeur. The frailty of humankind even moves the Lord to compassion, according to Ben Sira, and evokes in the deity a shepherding role. This image of the divine shepherd enjoyed wide coverage in the Bible (cf. Psalms 2; 23; 80; Isa 40:11; Ezek 34:11-16; John 10:11-18; Heb 13:20; 1 Pet 2:25; Rev 7:17).

The title in v. 1 for Yahweh, "the One who lives forever," occurs in Dan 4:31; 6:27; and 12:17. This epithet probably constitutes the author's reaction against predominant extra-Israelite views of gods who die and rise each year. It follows that none could possibly adequately grasp Yahweh's mystery; Ben Sira expresses this point beautifully: When one has finished, one is actually still at the very beginning, having progressed little in recounting God's glory (cf. 1:3, 6; 42:17; Job 9:10; Ps 145:3). The rhetorical question in v. 8 links this verse with Pss 8:5; 144:3; and Job 7:17. Papyrus Insinger also likens the human life span to a grain of sand (see v. 10), and Egyptian texts generally calculate one's existence on earth as a maximum of one hundred years (see v. 9; cf. Ps 90:10; Isa 65:20). Ben Sira concedes in v. 13 that human beings limit their compassion to immediate neighbors, while Yahweh extends a merciful hand to everyone.

REFLECTIONS

The religious life stands under the promise of divine blessing, which comes in the midst of a broken world and makes life tolerable. A significant number of texts in the

Bible either invite God's people to rejoice or actually characterize them as wholly surrendering to joyful praise. The sound of benediction, the blessing, may have served as the concluding note of congregational gatherings, but that affirmation had its basis in the earlier happiness created by God's presence in the company of good people. The "positive thinking" preachers of modern Christianity have rightly seized this feature of religion, although often by overlooking the biblical realism that gives that joy a moral obligation to ease others' suffering.

The church has an unenviable record of suppressing happiness, although unwittingly. Emphasis on negatives in one's personal moral conduct arose from purely good intentions, a desire to avoid every appearance of evil. Applying the Johannine principle of residing in the world without being a party to its values has never been easy. Too often the church has chosen withdrawal from the world as the safer option, despite the clear rejection of this approach in the New Testament.

Good Friday and Easter Sunday serve in the liturgical calendar as perennial reminders that both sadness and joy belong to the very center of Christian experience. Reflecting on the prevalence of sin and suffering in society, as well as contemplating the cost in human lives and in the divine economy, brings streams of tears. Nevertheless, meditating on God's bountiful love and acceptance of transgressors who turn away from their self-centered ways, along with thinking about the beauty and goodness in God's creatures, elicits rapturous songs of joy. The challenge is to give equal rein to each feeling. The long face must not become permanently fixed, for happiness comes with the dawn. That hope springs eternal in the human breast, awakened by every pronouncement of blessing on the people of God.

SIRACH 18:15-18, ON GIVING ALMS

COMMENTARY

The elaborate praise of God for unlimited generosity in the preceding section leads to some observations about acts of kindness among humans. They are to model their giving on that of the Lord (cf. Jas 1:5). Ben Sira realizes that the prevalent view about God's blessing on good persons and the opposite on sinners implies that prosperous people deserve their wealth just as the poor suffer appropriately for laziness or wickedness. The temptation, therefore, was to look on the poor with contempt, even when giving them a handout. Ben Sira advises that words should match deeds, a charitable act being accompanied by gentle remarks.

The analogy from daily experience—relief from oppressive heat that dew brings to plants suffering distress—prompts an exuberant overstatement, which Ben Sira hastens to qualify. A (kind) word is better than a gift, *but* a truly gracious individual unites both word and action. Ignorant persons do just the opposite, they compound a miserly gift by harsh language. The Babylonian Talmud makes the point effectively: "Whoever gives a farthing is blessed sixfold, but the one who adds words elevenfold."[178]

178. *Baba Bathra* 96.

SIRACH 18:19-29, ON CAUTION

COMMENTARY

This brief unit may also have been inspired by the poem on divine mercy and forgiveness in 18:1-14. Ben Sira encourages his readers to plan for unpleasant intrusions, particularly sickness and death. The Syriac of v. 19 urges readers to consult a physician; because illness was thought to strike those who had offended God, one could not get well until obtaining forgiveness. Physicians did not fit into this understanding of sin and its consequences very well, for they interfered with that process. Ben Sira wrestles with this vexing problem in 38:1-15, where he combines the traditional view of sin's relationship to sickness with a more modern concept of doctors and medicines.

Reflection on the day of God's visitation and the prospect of rejection puts the fear of the Lord in people, according to v. 24. One should observe a similar caution in making vows (cf. Eccl 5:3), for one's circumstances may change quickly, rendering it impossible to fulfill a promise despite its accompanying solemn oath. Ben Sira reverses the usual order in the phrase "from morning to evening" (see similar usage in late texts, such as 1 Chr 16:40; 2 Chr 2:4; but cf. Gen 1:5; Ps 55:7; Dan 8:26), perhaps because political decisions and commercial transactions, the primary means of quick reversals, occurred during the daylight hours.[179]

In Judaism, various ways to obtain forgiveness were advocated. Sickness and its accompanying suffering atone for sin, according to a Tannaitic source,[180] if one also repents. In this regard, W. O. E. Oesterley refers to *Bereshith Rabba* (chap. 65), which states that Isaac prayed to be given suffering to turn away divine judgment in the next life.[181] Another means of forgiveness, according to *Yoma* 86b, is repentance, and almsgiving was yet another (*Baba Bathra* 10a). Death, the supreme suffering, also brought reconciliation (*Sifre* 33a). These texts reveal an eagerness to find ways to make God's forgiveness as far-reaching as possible.

---

179. Frank Crüsemann, "The Unchangeable World: Reflections on the 'Crisis of Wisdom' in Koheleth," in *The God of the Lowly*, eds. Willi Schottroff and Wolfgang Stegemann (Maryknoll, N.Y.: Orbis, 1984) 57-77, has emphasized the excessive concern to get rich during the time of Qohelet, although he overemphasizes the author's greed.
180. *Sifre* 73b.
181. Oesterley, *The Wisdom of Jesus the Son of Sirach or Ecclesiasticus*, 125-26.

SIRACH 18:30–19:19, ON SELF-CONTROL

COMMENTARY

Before v. 30, the Greek has a title, "Self-control of the Disposition" (ἐγκράτεια ψυχῆς *egkrateia psychēs*), a title that appeared at v. 15 in Codex Sinaiticus. Such headings occur elsewhere at 19:29; 20:27; 24:1; 30:1, 16; 44:1; and 51:1. This section contains brief poems about sensual desire (18:30–19:3) and gossip (19:4-17). The chapter division interrupts a unit of thought (v. 1), indicating the consequences of living beyond one's means.

18:30–19:3. The surrender to extravagant lust impoverishes a person and brings mockery and contempt. Ben Sira associates lavish parties with sexual license, here symbolized by an expression that has become proverbial, "wine and women." He knows the power of carnal lust, a desire so strong as to tempt men to squander savings and to borrow with abandon in order to satisfy their lust. He warns that such debased conduct often brings venereal disease in its wake, although the reference could be to an untimely death by other means. The Hebrew emphasizes the complete exposure of the one who indulges in such conduct: "He will become utterly naked," probably a metaphor for an impoverished condition.

19:4-17. The unit on gossip urges those who hear unpleasant tales about others to put an end to the vicious rumor and to report what has been said only to the person about whom the gossip has revolved. The purpose is to warn that individual to be more circumspect or to repent, if the gossip contained any truth. The one exception to remaining silent (v. 8) alludes to Lev 5:1, legislation concerning testimony when someone knows a fact that bears on another's guilt or innocence. The graphic illustrations (bursting from holding a word inside; writhing, as if feeling the pains of giving birth; suffering from an arrow that has penetrated one's thigh) mock the ludicrous behavior of avid gossipmongers.

The anaphrous style of vv. 13-15, referring to a previously mentioned person or object (e.g., "friend . . . he"), with the repeated imperative, "Question . . . perhaps . . . or if . . . so that" with a variant in the third and fourth instances, arrests the attention of those who hear the successive items. In this manner, Ben Sira achieves maximum effect for the rhetorical question, "Who has not sinned with his tongue?" and the admonition to give free rein to the law (cf. Lev 19:17-18). The generous attitude toward the subject of gossip alone can successfully counter a natural tendency to believe the worst in others.

SIRACH 19:20-30, WISDOM AND CLEVERNESS

COMMENTARY

The reference to the law links this short poem to the preceding one. Ben Sira observes that wisdom can be both positive and negative, hence one who fears God is better than a shrewd sinner. Such a statement in a Hellenistic context invited mockery, given the Greek emphasis on intelligence. Earlier Jewish tradition illustrates the evil potential of knowledge—e.g., the serpent's craftiness in Gen 3:1 and Jonadab's clever but unscrupulous use of intelligence to enable Amnon to seduce his sister (2 Sam 13:3). In this brief section, Ben Sira unites the two fundamental themes of the book: wisdom and the fear of the Lord.

The insights in vv. 26-28 reveal profound psychological awareness; the outward demeanor of an unscrupulous person masks an inner hostility awaiting a chance to express itself openly, and the juxtaposition of competing claims about judging someone by external appearance. Although Ben Sira realizes that appearances can deceive, he insists that one can know another person by examining three things: clothing, laughter, and gait. Whoever maintains this cautious realism refuses to give up on the necessary task of making judgments about the character of those with whom one comes into contact. Some books *can* be judged by their covers, as everyone knows all too well.

SIRACH 20:1-31, ON SPEECH AND SILENCE

COMMENTARY

Random sayings comprise this unit, often juxtaposing an idea and its "opposite" in the two bicola. The central issue, the right use of speech, stands over against appropriate and inappropriate, or misleading, silence, on the one hand, and lying, on the other hand. The paradoxical circumstances involving speaking and refraining from talk lead to a discussion of paradoxes in general. The Greek heading, "Proverbial Sayings," before v. 27 indicates that an ancient scribe divided this section differently from that suggested here.

Sirach 20:1-31 Commentary

20:1-8. The sages in Israel and Egypt spoke often about right speech and silence, the latter idea serving to characterize a professional sage, among others, in Egypt as "the silent one." Egyptian instructions develop a concept of rhetoric to serve as an ideal for the wise to aspire to in their study, one characterized by timing, restraint, accuracy, and eloquence. Israelite sages, too, recognized the importance of knowing when to speak and when to be silent; they also praised truthfulness and eloquence. These qualities were not limited to the wise, however, for some people possessed an innate gift of eloquence. Nor was this appreciation for silence limited to Israel and Egypt. Alexander Di Lella cites the following extra-biblical aphorisms: "A sage thing is timely silence, and better than any speech" (Plutarch, c. 100 CE); "Let a fool hold his tongue and he will pass for a sage" (Publilius Syrus, first cent. BCE); "Let your speech be better than silence, or be silent" (Dionysius the Elder, fourth cent. BCE).[182] Apparently, many thinkers prized silence as golden.

Matters were not quite so simple, as the contrasting sayings in Prov 26:4-5 reveal. In some situations, neither speech nor silence is unambiguous, for responding to a stupid remark bestows more dignity on it than the comment deserves, and failing to answer may appear to indicate ineptness, an inability to offer better counsel than that given by the fool. Ben Sira knows the tradition represented by this attempt to point out the difficulty in interpreting silence, and he acknowledges that refraining from speech does not always demonstrate wisdom. Some people merely have nothing worthwhile to say.

The analogy in v. 4, although graphic, is not entirely clear. Ben Sira pictures a eunuch being overwhelmed by lust for a young woman, passion that by the very nature of his condition will lead the eunuch nowhere. To that scene, Ben Sira compares the attempt to force an individual devoid of moral formation to behave ethically. Lacking inner motivation, the person can make no progress in doing the right thing.

20:9-17. These verses interrupt the discussion of speech and offer some observations on various oddities of existence: an unexpected windfall that costs much more than its value, honorable losses, so-called bargains that actually amount to a drain on one's finances, and a lender who repeatedly demands repayment before its due date. Anyone who has purchased a used automobile at a "good price," only to discover its actual condition and the expense involved in repairing it, can understand Ben Sira's point. His allusion to persons who rose from humble circumstances to positions of power represents a literary topos in the ancient world, as the story about Joseph demonstrates.

20:18-20. The original topic of this unit returns in v. 18; this "better saying" about the greater damage inflicted by slander than by falling down is widespread.[183] The image in the Greek of v. 19 is lost on modern readers who do not realize that the fatty tail of a sheep was considered a delicacy in the ancient Near East. The saying in v. 20 serves as an instance when timing rather than content renders a remark worthless. Everyone who has suffered in silence, only later to think of an appropriate response, appreciates the significance of timing. The observation in v. 21 that absence of sin does not necessarily indicate virtue resembles an Egyptian saying that only a man's purse prevents him from satisfying his insatiable lust.[184]

20:21-26. These verses take up the matter of shame, especially that resulting from misstating the truth. The stakes in honor and shame are high; one's reputation and life hang in the balance. Persons whose humble circumstances evoke embarrassment and cause them to make promises they cannot keep (v. 23) and liars earn the same reputation as a thief. All three suffer disgrace.

20:27-31. The final unit consists of traditional teachings about the scribal profession—the sages will serve rulers (like Daniel, Ahiqar, Mordecai, and Joseph)—and about special temptations they encounter, such as bribes and unpredictable anger. The concluding couplet states that, like hidden treasure, concealed wisdom is worthless and that hiding one's ignorance is superior to hiding one's intelligence.

---

182. Skehan and Di Lella, *The Wisdom of Ben Sira*, 300-301.

183. Cf. Zeno's remark, "Better to slip with the foot than with the tongue." Cited in Diogenes Laërtius *Lives and Opinions of Eminent Phyilosophers* vii.26.

184. "Man is more eager to copulate than a donkey; his purse is what restrains him" (*Ankhsheshanky* 24:10).

SIRACH 21:1-10, SIN'S SMOOTH PATH

COMMENTARY

Three images conjure up the horror of sinful action for Ben Sira's audience, here addressed as "my child." They consist of two threats from the realm of nature—the serpent's bite (cf. Gen 3:1-5; Prov 23:32, which likens the sting of strong drink to that of a snake) and a lion's teeth (cf. 27:10 and Joel 1:6 for the same language)—and one threat from the human domain—a dreaded two-edged sword in the agile hands of someone bent on destruction.

The allusion to the prayer of the poor in v. 5 demonstrates Ben Sira's positive attitude toward God's rule of the world. As affirmed in ancient religious tradition, God hears the cries of persons in need; the doubts expressed in the book of Job and in Ecclesiastes have not dampened Ben Sira's spirit in the least. The point of v. 8 varies with the manuscript traditions; the Septuagint has "for the winter" (εἰς χειμῶνα *eis cheimōna*), whereas the important MS 248 has "for a tomb" (εἰς χῶμα *eis chōma*). The former implies that one gathers stones instead of wood in preparation for cold weather; the latter reading may suggest that payment on the loan becomes due before the burial mound is complete. The audial pun in v. 9 in the Greek, "a bundle of tow is like a band of lawless ones" (στιππύον συνηγμένον συναγωγὴ ἀνόμων *stippuon synēgmenon synagōgē anomōn*) and the probable reference to techniques employed by the later Romans in the construction of roads in v. 10 bring this brief unit to a close.

REFLECTIONS

In 1 Pet 5:8 the description of the devil evokes all three of the horrors cited in Sir 21:2-3 by combining the old notion of the serpent with that of Satan who resembles a raging lion ready to devour, the usual language for the sword's activity in the OT.

SIRACH 21:11–22:18, THE WISE AND THE FOOLISH

COMMENTARY

21:11–22:2. Ancient sages never tired of drawing a sharp contrast between themselves and ignorant ruffians, whom they called fools. One decisive difference between the two groups concerned the value of education.[185] Because they failed to appreciate the worth of knowledge, fools were impossible to educate, information entering their minds and flowing right through into oblivion. The wise place a value on education like ornaments worn by royalty (v. 21); when they learn something, they promptly add to it (v. 15). Here Ben Sira recognizes the importance of preserving the tradition intact, but he balances that idea with the necessity of contributing to the fund of knowledge. Mere retention of ancestral tradition did not make one wise; that instruction from the past had to be thoroughly adapted to new conditions and to personal experience.

Verse 12 recalls the earlier distinction between wisdom and shrewdness, and v. 13 introduces an image that Ben Sira will use again to signify his own effort to write a second volume of instruction (24:30-34).

---

185. The HB has preserved minimal information pertinent to ancient formal education, but that has not prevented extravagant claims about schools throughout the land. For cautious assessments of the evidence, see James L. Crenshaw, "Education in Ancient Israel," *JBL* 104 (1985) 601-15, and a forthcoming volume in the Anchor Bible Reference Library, entitled *Across the Deafening Silence: Education in Ancient Israel*; and Stuart Weeks, *Early Israelite Wisdom*, OTM (Oxford: Clarendon, 1994) 132-56.

The same symbolism, knowledge as a mighty stream and a life-giving spring, occurs in *Pirqe 'Abot* 6:1, where one who studies Torah for its own sake is described in this way.[186]

This entire unit characterizes fools more fully than wise persons. Fools hear sensible remarks and toss them aside, behave in altogether uncivilized ways, inspire hatred, resent discipline, and babble incessantly. Ben Sira compares their idle chatter to a heavy burden on a journey (v. 14). The harsh criticism of sluggards within the book of Proverbs continues in 22:1-2, where Ben Sira uses a coarse image to describe them, that of a smooth rock used in the ancient world after a bowel movement.

22:3-6. Here Ben Sira utters one of his most misogynistic statements;[187] his opinion, regrettably, was shared by many at the time.[188] Precisely what inspired the observation that "the birth of a daughter is a loss" can only be surmised, although the context may suggest that he had in mind the difficulty and cost involved in obtaining a suitable husband for her. Elsewhere his comments about daughters imply suspicion about their morals and show that he did not think highly of them—at least not of a certain kind of daughter. One can see how such an opinion of girls would fit nicely into a society that exposes infant daughters to the elements in order for them to die. Echoes of this horrible practice occur within the OT.[189] In its liturgical practice, later Judaism continued this negative attitude toward women. A daily prayer, recommended for all men, stated: "Blessed are you, O Lord our God, King of the Universe, who have not made me a woman," and every man was urged to thank God daily for not making him a woman or a slave.[190] This sentiment reflects the numerous regulations in Jewish law strictly regulating the life of a woman.[191]

22:9-15. Ben Sira uses strong images to describe fools in these verses. Teaching them is futile, like gluing the pieces of a broken pot together or communicating with a sleepy person. Long experience with dull students probably taught Ben Sira the accuracy of this analogy; the slow student simply misses the point as if half asleep. No wonder Ben Sira recommends perpetual tears for such fools, as opposed to the more usual seven-day mourning for the dead. The image in v. 13 moves one step further than that of fools as the ancient equivalent of toilet paper. Here they shake themselves like pigs (the Hebrew original probably had "dogs") and spread their filth on all bystanders. The comparison of debt and a foreigner to a heavy load occurs also in *Ahiqar*.[192]

22:16-18. The closing unit praises intelligence as both strong and beautiful. The final thought, that fences (or pebbles) cannot withstand a strong wind, may allude to the practice of placing small rocks on a wall enclosing a vineyard or garden so that when a jackal or a fox invaded a garden, the animal would knock them off and alert the farmer. This entire section, 21:11–22:18, is remarkably free of religious teaching, except for the opening verse.

---

186. Cf. also 1QH 8:4-15.
187. Trenchard, *Ben Sira's View of Women*, has discussed misogynistic elements in the book, without tempering his criticism in the light of the ancient context.
188. Carlston, "Proverbs, Maxims, and the Historical Jesus," 87-105.
189. The most obvious instance concerns the old story about Yahweh's discovery of an infant girl in the wilderness and nurturing the child until she had reached a marriageable age, at which time the Lord married her (Ezek 16:1-14). The theological point, God's choice of Israel when it had done nothing to deserve it, turns on Israel's existence as an infant that someone had cast out to die.
190. *Menahot* 43b.
191. One whole division (out of six) in the Mishnah is devoted to "women."
192. See Sayings 29 and 30 in Lindenberger, *The Aramaic Proverbs of Ahiqar*, 98-99.

REFLECTIONS

Just as Ben Sira's understanding of women reflected a society in which women were born under a curse, so also some modern views of women relegate them to secondary status. The present disparity in pay between women and men, where it still exists, results from various economic factors, chief of which is the understanding of men as providers for families. The subtle shifting of women to lower-paying jobs and assessing them by standards that more appropriately apply to men place women in a disadvantaged position. Pregnancy and its attendant obligations make it more difficult for females to advance in their workplace. Differences in women's temperament and style strike many males as signs of inferiority or lack of motivation. All this and more fuels misogynistic and chauvinistic sentiments today.

For anyone who values human worth and believes such attitudes should vanish like dinosaurs, one can think of no challenge that, if successfully met, offers more reward. First, men can finally begin to treat women in the same revolutionary manner Jesus did. Second, men can start to learn from women in more ways than imaginable, even if it means radically questioning the very foundations of modern society. Third, women can be elevated to senior leadership roles within the church and its ministry. This move alone holds the potential for revolutionizing the devotional life of God's people.

SIRACH 22:19-26, PRESERVING FRIENDSHIP

COMMENTARY

In this short section, Ben Sira returns to the topic of friendship (cf. 6:5-17) and comments on the remarkable resiliency of affections. He understands that the severe strain produced by personal insults can cause genuine friendships to snap. Two clear images for inflicting pain and driving friends away—jabbing one's eye and, by analogy, throwing a rock at birds—draw attention to the harm caused by hurtful words. Nevertheless, he believes the constancy of genuine friendship can stand serious offenses such as threatened physical violence and verbal abuse. Ben Sira does not recommend that one count on this strong bond in all instances of abuse because some things (e.g., divulging secrets and treachery) will drive any friend away.

The test of true friendship comes when one cannot do anything to help those befriending him or her. Ben Sira advises his readers to begin a friendship with someone in difficult circumstances and then take pleasure when that person's financial situation improves. The closing observation in the first-person pledges personal loyalty—in the context of a veiled threat, should harm befall the speaker. That is, others will avoid the person who caused the injury, for they will know that he or she cannot be trusted.

SIRACH 22:27–23:6, A PRAYER FOR SELF-CONTROL

COMMENTARY

This moving prayer[193] for control over wrongful speech and carnal lust introduces the two following units, 23:7-15, 16-26. The final verse (v. 27) sums up this section and, indeed, everything up to this point in the book. Other prayers appear in 36:1-13a, 16-22; 51:1-12.

The opening request for a sentry to be perched on the speaker's lips uses a Hebraic expression, מי יתן (*mî yittēn*, lit., "who will set?"). Ben Sira's double request for a sentry and a seal demonstrates the urgency of the need. Anyone with this much protection would not fall into sin through speech. The image of a guard for one's mouth also occurs in Ps 141:3 and *Ahiqar* 14b-15. In Sir 28:24-26, Ben Sira extends the image considerably, recommending a door and a bolt for the mouth and balances and scales for words.

The threefold address to God in 23:1 includes the tetragrammaton (YHWH), Father, and Master of my life. The OT refers to God as Father of the nation of Israel (1 Chr

---

193. For a discussion of prayer in Ben Sira and the rest of wisdom literature, see Crenshaw, "The Restraint of Reason, the Humility of Prayer." See also Crenshaw, *Urgent Advice and Probing Questions*, 206-21.

29:10; Isa 63:16; Mal 2:10). Ben Sira personalizes that form of address (23:1, 4; 51:1, 10). The third epithet, "Master of my life," gives way to "God of my life" in v. 4. The expression "our Father, our King" (אבינו מלכנו 'ābînû malkēnû) became popular in Jewish prayers, for the twin ideas cover the immediacy of parental love and the sovereignty of a transcendent ruler of the universe.

The abrupt reference to "their designs" in 23:1 without a clear antecedent prompted W. O. E. Oesterley to rearrange the prayer in the following sequence:

27	. . . and that my tongue destroy me not,
2	O that scourges were set over my thoughts . . .
3	that mine ignorance be not multiplied . . .
4	O Lord, Father, and God of my life,
1	Abandon me not to their counsel, Suffer me not to fall by them.

5 Give me not a proud look,
   and turn away concupiscence from me.[194]

The manuscript evidence indicates considerable disarray, with the Syriac and the Vg reading v. 1b after v. 4a. The rearrangement is not necessary, for Hebrew poetry often introduces unanticipated pronouns for which the reader must supply an appropriate antecedent.

Verse 2 asks for whips to subject thoughts to their control. Thus doubly protected—from sins of the tongue and from thought—Ben Sira can avoid becoming the object of ridicule. The prayer now takes up one further danger, which might result from success in avoiding sins of speech and thought. He asks for protection from "giant-like eyes," pride; for good measure, he repeats the request for power over sinful lust.

194. Oesterley, *The Wisdom of Jesus the Son of Sirach or Ecclesiasticus*, 150-51.

SIRACH 23:7-15, THE PROPER USE OF LANGUAGE

COMMENTARY

This section, which many Greek manuscripts label "Instruction Concerning the Mouth," takes up two types of language that get people into deep trouble, the one religious and the other secular. First, Ben Sira discusses the lavish use of oaths, which constantly place one under divine scrutiny just like a slave who requires close watch. The implication is that continual supervision will inevitably reveal flaws in character that demand punishment. Oath-taking alone includes the danger of swearing unknowingly to a lie, using the divine name loosely, and placing oneself in danger through excessive obligations that reduce one to poverty. Second, the person who habitually uses lewd speech will inadvertently slip into this manner of talking in circumstances where it will bring disgrace. Ben Sira thinks that such foul language does not belong in the Jewish community ("the inheritance of Jacob," v. 12). This expression usually refers to the land in which Israel dwelled.

SIRACH 23:16-27, ON FORNICATION AND ADULTERY

COMMENTARY

Ben Sira adopts a common form in wisdom literature, the numerical proverb, to describe those who give themselves over to sexual sins of various kinds. Elsewhere he uses numerical sayings in 25:1-2, 7-11; 26:5-6, 28; 50:25-26. They are found often in Proverbs (Prov

6:16-19; 30:15b-16, 18-19, 21-23, 29-31) and Job (Job 5:19-22; 13:20-22; 33:14-15), and are also in prophetic literature (Amos 1:3–2:16) and in Ugaritic texts. Like the book of Amos, Sirach does not list the full quota of sins (three here, four in Amos) but pauses to explore a single offense, carnal lust.

The section sparkles with psychological insight as Ben Sira describes the insatiable hunger of fornicators, to whom all bread is sweet (cf. Prov 9:17, where the seductress calls stolen water "sweet" and bread eaten in secret "pleasant"), and the endless rationalizations for surrendering to the primal urge. The feeble excuses for adultery—no one will ever know, and God is forgetful—do not reckon with an all-seeing deity who knows the future intimately. Ben Sira comes perilously close to stating a doctrine of predestination in v. 20, which conflicts with his earlier stress on free will.

Having dealt with adulterers in the first part of this treatise on carnal lust, Ben Sira moves on to talk about adulteresses. Their crime consists of breaking the divine legislation, betraying a marital relationship, and bringing children into the world where they will not be wanted.[195] This threefold offense, arranged to emphasize a descending order of gravity, also applies to the adulterer, but Ben Sira does not explicitly say so. The punishment of adultery, according to Lev 20:10 and Deut 22:21-22, was death, and Talmudic law continued this punishment, at least theoretically. Verse 24 extends the punishment to children, which suggests that the death penalty was no longer in force at this time.

The last verse uses the adjectives "better" and "sweeter" to suggest that faithful service to Yahweh held far greater appeal than surrendering to one's sexual passions. The key word *survive* provides the clue to Ben Sira's reasoning, for loyalty to the Lord brings life, but surrendering to passions issues in death.

195. Children of an adulterous union could not belong to the congregation of Israel, according to *Qiddushin* 78b.

REFLECTIONS

The appeal of sexual satisfaction, even with inappropriate partners, will always characterize human existence, as it certainly did in Ben Sira's time. The difficult task of remaining monogamous when bombarded with temptation on every hand or of refraining from sex until the right time and place tests one and all. The knowledge among advertisers that sex pays rich dividends and the active role of fantasy leave many people in the grip of a destructive force. Children are particularly vulnerable. Increased mobility and privacy make liaisons with an attractive other both tempting and possible.

In such a volatile environment, how do Christians negotiate the waters of change? Perhaps the story in Genesis 39 of Joseph's resistance to a seductive summons from Potiphar's wife offers a starting point. Joseph's reason for saying no to the attractive offer was first and foremost theological: "How then could I do this great wickedness, and sin against God?" (Gen 39:9 NRSV). Admittedly, such an act as sleeping with Potiphar's wife would have represented betrayal of his master's trust and bed, but Joseph's only stated concern was quite different. He did not want to prove false to his relationship with God. Moreover, the adulterous act also affects the partner, in this instance, Potiphar. And such conduct inevitably takes a heavy toll on the offenders, for it undermines integrity and weakens character. This satisfaction of carnal desire becomes habitual, as Ben Sira perceived, and in the end it depersonalizes everyone involved, turning them into objects of pleasure.

How can the church encourage interaction between women and men while discouraging obsessive fascination with obtaining the forbidden and avoiding an attitude of indifference to sexual mores? The old obsession with sex as *the* sin, which occupied the church for centuries, has done far more harm than can be recounted here, but new guidelines are essential to assist young Christians in the never-ending struggle to deal responsibly with sexual desires.

SIRACH 24:1–33:19
PART V

OVERVIEW

Beginning with an elaborate poem extolling wisdom's virtues and identifying wisdom with divine revelation to Moses, and thus to Israel, this section of Sirach ends on a comparable note affirming divine providence. Between these lofty religious sentiments lie observations and advice from Ben Sira concerning the inner sanctum of the family and the heart of individual character, integrity. He characterizes despicable people in general, as well as wives—both desirable and undesirable. This leads to a broader discussion of offenses against companions, as well as the important, yet potentially devastating, matter of lending money and providing collateral for persons needing it. Ben Sira gives his views on rearing children, etiquette, and wealth; these topics, although traditional within wisdom literature, take on added significance in the Hellenistic environment, with its quite different customs and values where public dining and commerce were concerned.

SIRACH 24:1-34, THE PRAISE OF WISDOM

COMMENTARY

Like the four major parts in the first half of the book, this section—the first of four parts—begins with an elegant poem about wisdom in three stanzas, vv. 3-7, 8-12, 13-17. Most Greek manuscripts have the title "The Praise of Wisdom." An introduction to the poem (vv. 1-2) and a conclusion (vv. 19-22) give this poem the same number of lines as letters in the Hebrew alphabet. An identification of wisdom with the Mosaic law follows in vv. 23-29, and a personal claim for the author's inspiration from wisdom (vv. 30-34) concludes the chapter. Some interpreters (e.g., John Snaith) see chap. 24 as the conclusion to part one of the book, with vv. 30-34 justifying Ben Sira's addition of a second part, chaps. 25–43.[196] In Snaith's view, a similar hymn in 42:15–43:33 concludes part two, just as a hymn in 51:13-30 concludes a third part and also the whole book.

The praise of wisdom in vv. 1-22 draws freely on Prov 8:1-36 (cf. Job 28; Prov 1:20-33) for its language and ideas, although similar hymns occur in ancient Egypt, primarily in aretalogies associated with the goddess Isis.[197] These texts recite her virtues or accomplishments in the first person, praising Isis as creator and ruler of the universe. These same ideas appear in Ben Sira's praise of wisdom, but they already characterize her in the biblical precedents.

24:1-2. The introductory speech mentions wisdom's people and the assembly of the hosts of the Most High. The natural way to understand these references places them in a heavenly context; they represent the angelic hosts attending God's court. Nevertheless, "her people" subsequently takes on a special sense, the nation Israel, even if in these verses it connotes heavenly companions.

24:3-7. The initial stanza uses images from the Priestly creation account in Gen 1:1–2:4*a* and from the Israelite sojourn in

---

196. Snaith, *Ecclesiasticus or The Wisdom of Jesus, Son of Sirach*, 120.

197. On these aretalogies—i.e., hymns in praise of a god or goddess (in this instance, the Egyptian Isis)—see Hans Conzelmann, "Die Mutter der Weisheit [Sir 24:3-7]," in *Festschrift Rudolph Bultmann* (Tübingen: J. C. B. Mohr, 1964) 2:225-34.

the wilderness. That wisdom issues from the divine mouth and settles like a mist on the entire earth accords with the claim that God spoke the world into existence and that the Spirit hovered over the chaotic mass from which order evolved. Wisdom identifies herself as the pillar of cloud mentioned in Exod 13:21-22, accompanying the Israelites and confirming for them God's watchful eye. Picturing the universe as a vault with circumscribed limits, wisdom claims to have walked around its entire area in a creative act. The reference to plumbing the depths of Sheol amounts to an assertion of sovereignty over its citizens.

Verse 7 introduces the subject of the second stanza: wisdom's search for a resting place. Other traditions picture her as unable to find a home on earth, whereas iniquity was successful in its quest for a suitable residence there, settling like rain or dew in the desert (cf. *1 Enoch* 42:1-2). These two attitudes to the hiddenness of wisdom represent the tension between particularism and universalism within the community. The author of *1 Enoch* did not grant any people exclusive access to divine knowledge, but Ben Sira attributes true wisdom to the Jews.

24:8-12. The second stanza identifies wisdom's resting place as Jerusalem and suggests that the favorable location encouraged her to grow deep roots. Wisdom's selection of the inheritance of Jacob resulted from a divine decree, not from some accident of time or place. The universe came into existence through a divine word, and wisdom pitched her tent in Israel because of God's command. The possessive pronoun "my" attached to the word *Creator* links up with the notion in Prov 8:22 that Yahweh created wisdom first of all, and the mention of dwelling in a tent recalls the tabernacle, or tent of meeting, in the wilderness. Verse 10 introduces an entirely new concept: Wisdom ministers before God in the Temple at Zion, the ancient name for the city of David. Ben Sira's priestly interests successfully link wisdom with the daily sacrificial service, something no previous sage had been willing to do.

24:13-17. The idea of wisdom's taking root leads immediately to the theme of the third stanza, which describes her as various trees in the land of Israel: durable and majestic like the cedar of Lebanon or tall as the cypress on Mount Hermon; beautiful as the palm in Engedi or oleanders in Jericho; useful as the ever-present olive; rare as the plane tree; fragrant as trees yielding spices, perfumes, and incense; sprawling like the huge terebinth. The choice of these trees suggests wisdom's omnipresence; she dwells in the mountains to the north and in the valleys and gorges to the south.[198] This sensual imagery concludes with a somewhat different, although related, simile: Wisdom grew like a vine and gave forth abundant clusters of grapes.

Ben Sira's choice of cassia and myrrh relates to their function, when mixed with cinnamon and fragrant cane, in preparing an ointment essential for the ritual involving the sacred ark. Similarly, galbanum (an aromatic, though bitter, gum), mastic (an aromatic resin), and onycha (an extraction from a marine mollusk) in combination with frankincense produced incense for use in the liturgy. Despite the frequent association of the terebinth with idolatrous cults and sacred prostitution (e.g., 1 Kgs 14:23; 2 Kgs 17:10; 18:4; 23:14; Isa 17:8; 27:9; Jer 17:2; Mic 5:13[Eng., 5:14]), Ben Sira dares to incorporate the image of this splendid shade tree into his description of wisdom.

24:18-22. The concluding invitation develops the notion of viticulture and its fruit; wisdom summons everyone to a feast, as in Prov 9:1-6. She offers food and drink that makes one return for more, and she promises protection from shame and its cause, missing the mark. Patrick Skehan thinks this (conjectured!) use of the verb יחטאו (*yeḥeṭāʾû*) and חטאי (*ḥōṭĕʾî*) in Prov 8:36 are the only instances in the Bible where חטא (*ḥāṭāʾ*) has its original meaning of "missing the mark."[199]

24:23-29. With v. 23, a new section begins, momentarily in third-person *narrative,* descending into prose. Ben Sira makes an astonishing statement: that divine wisdom, here described, is identical to Israel's prize possession, the Mosaic law. In other words, access to wisdom comes through reflection on the divine commandments, no longer through studying nature and human

---

198. Merism is the use of opposites to express completeness. Thus the merism "mountains and valleys" reinforces the sense of wisdom's omnipresence.

199. Patrick Skehan, "Structures in Poems on Wisdom: Proverbs 8 and Sirach 24," *CBQ* 41 (1979) 378.

experience as maintained in Proverbs, the book of Job, and Ecclesiastes. To convey the immensity of its coverage, Ben Sira evokes the ancient myth of the four rivers flowing through the garden of Eden. The Mosaic law is inexhaustible, like those rivers, ever spilling over their banks with beneficial gifts to those who depend on water for survival. The Pishon, the Tigris, the Euphrates, the Jordan, the Nile, and the Gihon comprise the major rivers with which the Israelites were acquainted in fact and in fiction. According to Gen 2:10-14, four rivers—Pishon, Gihon, Tigris, and Euphrates—watered the whole land. To these, Ben Sira adds the Jordan and the Nile. He alludes to the effort on the part of Adam and Eve to grasp knowledge, labeling the result of that first initiative partial. Like the first couple, all those who follow will also fail to capture wisdom's full contents. First and last constitute a merism here—i.e., opposite parts of something representing the whole. No one can contain a river, and none can comprehend the full extent of Torah. The ABB´A´ symmetry of v. 29 is total:

A   her thoughts
  B   her counsel;
A´ more abundant than the sea
  B´ deeper than the great abyss.

24:30-34. The final section constitutes Ben Sira's personal claim to having been moved by prophetic and sapiential inspiration to write his book, which also became a mighty river spilling over its banks. At first he resembled an irrigation canal watering a small garden, but later he became a river and, even greater yet, a sea. No longer a derivative body, he now pours forth original teaching like prophecy for all who desire it. The final verse claims a selfless motive for his labor, a desire to share his insights with others worthy of their contents (cf. 33:18, where this verse is repeated). The idea that teaching as a light occurs with respect to the law in Ps 119:105; Prov 4:18; 6:23. The author of the book of Wisdom understands wisdom as light (Wis 7:26, 29). In Ps 19:10, the law is said to be sweeter than honey and drippings from the honeycomb; wisdom takes over this imagery and applies it to herself in v. 20.

Some of the ideas in this chapter found expression in Judaism generally. The Alexandrian philosopher Philo Judaeus (c. 15 BCE–45 CE) identified wisdom with the pillar of cloud, and *m. Pesiqta* 186*a* states that God offered the law to all nations but only Israel was willing to accept its stipulations.[200] Homiletical use of this imagined refusal to accept the Torah naturally appealed to the moral imperative and a sense of ethnic superiority.

200. Cf. the similar comment in the Babylonian Talmud, *Abodah Zara* 2*b*.

REFLECTIONS

Ancient peoples developed authenticating stories (or myths) to confirm their own views, thus functioning primarily within closed walls, and only secondarily as a defense of these views directed to outsiders. Some of these stories reinforced ethnic claims comparable to contemporary slogans, such as "the noble savage," "the prostitute with a heart of gold," "the land of the free and the home of the brave," etc. Ordinarily, these myths arise to counter less than complimentary value judgments. Compared to an intellectually vigorous Greek culture, the religious tradition of Israel, represented by its legal transmitters like Ezra, gave an appearance of mental softness. Particularistic claims flew in the face of Greek universalism, and monotheism seemed pitifully restrictive over against a rich pantheon.

Ben Sira's response to potential, if not actual, mockery anchors Jewish ethnicity in a universal context. The Creator of the cosmos chose provincial Judah as the appropriate location for divine instructions in right living, a law that applies equally to every citizen in God's special kingdom. For some unspecified reason, God's *logos* rejected all nations except Judah and took up residence at Jerusalem. The consequences of that claim extend to the present era, when opposing factions vie for that sacred ground. Accompanying features of the myth complicate matters beyond repair, especially the belief that God has given this holy land to the Jews and taken it away from its previous owners, the Canaanites.

Perhaps the primary value of such efforts to justify national and religious convictions is negative. They point to the paucity of really persuasive arguments on behalf of particularistic claims, thus calling all groups to abandon imperialistic notions in favor of humble confession alone. Moreover, the sensual delights and visceral level on which the myth operates summon us all to celebrate the beauty of the natural order and its unending mystery rather than wasting time and energy quarreling over religious dogma.

SIRACH 25:1-12, SOME NUMERICAL PROVERBS

COMMENTARY

In this brief section, Ben Sira returns to the form introduced in 23:16-17, numerical proverb, varying it in the first of two by omitting the smaller number. Verse 1 refers to three sources of pleasure; all have in common an emotion that creates harmony. The first relates to the larger family, the second to people living in the immediate vicinity, and the third moves into the inner sanctum of the home. The next verse names three loathsome types: the pauper who is too proud to accept help, the rich person who lies (the assumption being that wealthy people have no need to dissemble), and an old lecher. The following four verses reflect on the responsibility of acting one's age. The comment that one who failed to gather anything during youth cannot reasonably expect to do so in advancing years may apply directly to a lecherous desire to recapture the amorous past with a vengeance. Ben Sira notes that old age should be characterized by signs of wisdom and religious devotion, for the aged have the advantage of wide experience. The folly of old lechers is beautifully illustrated in the book of Susanna, which tells of two men who try to blackmail Susanna into complying with their wishes.

Verses 7-12 deal with ten fortunate types of people. Among these, the second and fourth deserve further comment. The wish to see one's enemies' downfall belonged to the piety of biblical psalms (Pss 18:38-43, 48-49; 54:7; 112:8) and laments generally, although the attitude did not enjoy universal acceptance (Prov 17:5; 24:17-18; cf. Matt 5:43-44). The allusion to plowing with incompatible animals (cf. Deut 22:10) assumes a polygamous environment, the husband having sexual relations with two wives who cannot get along with each other. Ben Sira's elevation of piety over knowledge goes beyond traditional views, in which fear of the Lord was both the originating force and the essence of wisdom. Verse 11 states that worship *surpasses* wisdom.

SIRACH 25:13–26:27, ON WIVES, BOTH BAD AND GOOD

COMMENTARY

Having momentarily introduced the topic of a good wife in 25:1, Ben Sira now turns to a discussion of virtuous and wicked wives, beginning with the latter (25:13-26) and interrupting this strong censure with a brief section on a good wife (26:1-4), only to return to the less complimentary assessment of wives (26:5-12) before concluding on a positive note (26:13-18). In the cursive MSS 70 and 248, as well as Syriac, a section combining positive and negative comments about wives sums up the discussion, ending with an image of a garrulous wife as the sound of a battle cry (תרועה *tĕrû'â*) and the accompanying confusion.

25:13-26. Hyperbole sets the tone for Ben Sira's treatment of the traditional topic about bad wives, and this fact needs to be taken into account when evaluating his attitude toward women. The unpleasantries—severe blows, villainy, suffering, and revenge—provide a semantic and psychological context within which to view the grief caused by a wicked woman. Thus far the language refers to bad women generally, not just to wives. The association of evil women with snakes and their venom was balanced in the ancient world by a positive celebration of the rejuvenating power and virility of these creatures. The reference to "vengeance of enemies" in v. 14 may actually reflect a polygamous setting in which wives jockey for position and harbor grudges that lead to aggressive acts of vengeance in the same way Jacob's wives, Leah and Rachel, expressed rivalry (Gen 29:31–30:24).

The exaggerated speech continues in v. 16 with the first-person expression of preference. The comparison, absurd in the extreme, for no one could live with a lion or a dragon, calls to mind the unbearable situation of dwelling in the same house with an incorrigible woman. Whereas wisdom brightens the countenance, according to Eccl 8:1, for Ben Sira wickedness has the opposite result, darkening the face. To indicate the full effect of such evil, Ben Sira evokes the thought of a bear, perhaps because lions and bears were often associated (cf. Amos 5:18-19). Driven from his own house, the unfortunate husband hangs out with friends and seeks consolation (v. 18). The next verse uses the same hyperbole of vv. 13-14, "*any* iniquity," although phrased differently to stress the minuteness.

The image in v. 20 emphasizes the difficulty encountered by old people when the terrain does not permit them to plant their feet firmly. A sandy slope is both slippery and hard to negotiate. Ben Sira thinks a complaining wife makes life equally challenging to that of a sandy hill. The following two verses (vv. 21-22) take up the subject of two different ways by which women trap men, in Ben Sira's view: with their beauty and their wealth. Only the latter attraction provokes further comment, the assertion that a man who depends on his wife's assets for daily survival is also subjected to constant abuse.

The bold claim in v. 24 that sin originated with woman, presumably an allusion to Eve's disobedience of the divine decree, and that all subsequent people die because of Eve's sin represents but one of three different viewpoints in ancient Israel regarding sin and death. The usual explanation for death in Judaism focused on Adam's unrepentant attitude rather than on Eve's original disobedience,[201] when it did not assume that human beings were by nature mortal (41:4). In the ancient story of the fall, Eve's disobedience preceded Adam's chronologically (cf. 2 Cor 11:3; 1 Tim 2:14), but Adam's presence and complicity implicate him equally. John Levison has endeavored to exonerate Eve in Ben Sira's eyes; Levison thinks v. 24 refers to an evil wife and to husbands who die because of such terrible spouses,[202] but the contextual evidence and the fragment from Qumran do not make a strong case for the argument. The third source of evil, along with Eve and Adam, was Satan, at least in popular thought.

Verses 25-26 project a patriarchal worldview completely at odds with the modern one, particularly in the West. Ben Sira advises husbands to suppress evil wives' freedom to express themselves just as one builds a dam to prevent the free flow of water. Failing in that endeavor, husbands can then resort to the ultimate contingency, divorce (cf. Deut 24:1). The language implies severing her from her husband's flesh, which recalls the statement in Gen 2:24 that husband and wife become one flesh. Within Judaism, two opposing attitudes to divorce vied for acceptance, the one lenient—for something as trivial as burnt bread—and the other quite restrictive, allowing divorce only for instances of adultery or other sexual offense. The lenient view merely acknowledges a fact: If one is prepared to divorce a wife over burnt bread, then the

---

201. *Bemidbar Rabba* 13; cf. Rom 5:12, 14-29; 1 Cor 15:22.
202. Levison, "Is Eve to Blame?" 617-23.

marriage is already dead. Ben Sira's view falls into the former camp; a husband can divorce a wife who refuses to bow down before his wishes.

26:1-4. These extreme comments about wicked wives do not constitute the sum of Ben Sira's remarks about wives, for he knows that good women also exist. The praise of virtuous wives, like the charges against bad ones, represents the view of the husband. Good wives bring longevity, peace, blessing, and happiness that expresses itself openly in their husbands' faces. These gifts resemble those that wisdom bestows on her lovers. One can scarcely imagine higher praise than this. Even poverty loses its sting when a man has a good wife, according to Ben Sira.

26:5-12. Having registered strong appreciation for good wives, Ben Sira reverts to the earlier topic of undesirable wives. Although the Greek of v. 10 refers to a daughter, the Syriac reading ("wife") probably retains the Hebrew original. The entire section bristles with arresting images and obscenities, particularly the references to an ill-fitting yoke that rubs the skin of an ox raw, a dreaded scorpion, and the euphemisms for sexual relations—a thirsty traveler drinking from any available stream, sitting (lying) in front of every tent peg (penis) and opening her quiver (vagina) for every arrow (penis). In addition, allusions to drunken and flirtatious conduct make this litany of undesirable behavior extremely uncomplimentary to *some* wives. In Ben Sira's mind, their harm ranks alongside false accusations leading to mob action; v. 5 refers to slander, gang action, and false charges. The form of this verse—only the first part of a numerical saying—is false, like the behavior itself.

26:13-18. These verses take up the subject of good wives once more, this time using comparisons from the Temple to convey their incomparable beauty. When a virtuous wife also possesses good looks, she resembles a menorah, a seven-branched candelabra, and golden and silver pedestals (or ornaments, if one reads "breasts" with Alexandrinus and Vaticanus instead of "feet"). Ben Sira observes that a good wife fattens her husband up, an indication of good health in the ancient Jewish environment, and that such a woman comes as a divine gift, a view shared by the authors of some sayings in the book of Proverbs. The attributes of a good wife include modesty, self-discipline, and orderliness, but they also embrace physical beauty. Ben Sira shows a remarkable appreciation for the external appearance of a woman, although his comments belong in the larger context of character. The remark that the value of chastity cannot be weighed on existing scales indicates where he really places the emphasis. The notion of weighing virtue or vice was widespread in the ancient Near East (cf. the divine judgment on Belshazzar in Dan 5:27 and the Egyptian concept of weighing the soul against a feather representing justice).

Nothing in the final section demands an understanding of it as secondary, despite its absence in the shorter Greek translation (and Hebrew; it is preserved in the expanded Greek version and in Syriac). Nevertheless, much of the material either repeats what Ben Sira has already said or echoes similar remarks in the book of Proverbs. The reference to a wife as daughter in v. 24 strengthens the understanding of v. 10 as an allusion to a wife. This section warns against squandering one's vitality on foreign women, a common theme in wisdom literature, and advises young men to plow their own fields, sowing worthy seed. This euphemism for sexual relations becomes for Ben Sira a way of assuring patrimony. His disdain for prostitutes and adulteresses, as well as his conviction that men get the sort of wives they deserve, places Ben Sira in the mainstream of wisdom's exponents. The suggestion in v. 24 that a modest daughter always retains an element of embarrassment, even in the presence of her husband, appears to press beyond anything prior to this time, when mutual enjoyment of sex was the rule. At the very least, this ideal of modesty differs radically from the exuberance of the young sister ("lover") in the Song of Songs.

REFLECTIONS

The family lies at the center of society today, just as it did long ago. Ben Sira undercuts this significant institution while endeavoring to strengthen it, for he harbored misogynistic sentiments even while singing women's praises. His comments about wicked women raise a significant question: Can praise ever make amends for damaging criticism?

In fairness to him, one must acknowledge the fact that Ben Sira certainly has strong words of approval for good wives. Nevertheless, the crude remarks and generalizing condemnation of a certain kind of woman, together with his suspicion concerning woman's lascivious nature, make an indelible impression on readers' minds. Like violent images that linger long after the fact, these unfavorable comments leave unwelcome vestiges. Words can hurt even more grievously than do sticks and stones, particularly when directed against persons lacking power and prestige. Here, too, the sensual expressions of delight go a long way toward salvaging Ben Sira's reputation as a sage—but not far enough.

In the light of this, Christians may wish to take inventory of their use of language about groups who lack the authority to challenge unwelcome remarks. Over the centuries, the English language has become freighted with derisive terms and unflattering expressions, each of which brings pain to innocent victims. By consulting compendia that isolate such offensive terms, and by studiously avoiding their use, concerned Christians can make a difference in a society that seems to know no limits where offensive speech is concerned.

SIRACH 26:28–27:15, ON INTEGRITY

COMMENTARY

A variety of sayings discusses the general topic of honesty, beginning with a numerical proverb about three problematic instances of persons trapped in the opposite state from the expected one (26:28) and ending with a few comments about offensive speech (27:11-15).

26:28. The initial saying refers to a rich person reduced to poverty, intelligence that fails to elicit respect, and a person who forsakes virtue for its opposite. The Greek text has "warrior" (ἀνὴρ πολεμιστής *anēr polemistēs*) for the first of these, probably through a misunderstanding of an original איש חיל (*'iš ḥayil*) or גבור חיל (*gibbôr ḥayil*), "a wealthy man" or "person of substance." In the HB, גבור *gibbôr* means "a mighty person," "a warrior."

26:29–27:3. Ben Sira's suspicion that commerce by its very nature participates in sin grows out of the fact that the very premise of trading consisted of gain at the buyer's expense. In his day, commerce flourished, taking Jews to many places and reducing their leisure. According to *Erubin* 55*b* (cf. *Qiddushin* 82*a*, which calls such trading "the handicraft of robbery"), such preoccupation with business adversely affected the study of Torah.

Ben Sira credits merchants with sufficient conscience to necessitate turning the eye, an inability to look their victim in the eye. Such body language was already recognized in the book of Proverbs (cf. Prov 6:12-19; 28:27). The bartering process had led to humorous posturing by the buyer, who would protest the exorbitant price at first but subsequently brag to others about the purchase, but Ben Sira's evaluation of the new merchant class lacks humor. He thinks of sin as an inevitable consequence of selling, one as firmly fixed as a tent peg wedged between two rocks to secure it against the wind. In this view he was not alone, as this quote from the Egyptian "Instruction of Ankhsheshanky" 28.4

reveals: "Do not have a merchant for a friend; [he] lives for taking a slice."

27:4-7. The three images that illustrate the manner in which speech demonstrates the discipline of one's mind derive from ordinary farm life in ancient Palestine. After oxen had threshed grain, it was placed in a sieve that retained the husks and dung while allowing the kernels to pass through for immediate use or temporary storage. The analogy suffers somewhat, for one expects the speech to represent pure grain, whereas Ben Sira observes that talk demonstrates flaws, bringing them to the surface. The second comparison is more apt: Just as a kiln tests a potter's vessels, bringing imperfections into the open, so also conversation reveals faulty logic. The third comparison rests on the assumption that a well-tended vine or fruit tree will produce appropriate fruit, but this principle does not always apply (cf. Isa 5:1-7 for acknowledgment that one cannot count on a positive correlation between effort and result, as any farmer knew well).

27:8-10. These observations about perverse expectations, commerce, and testing through speech assert a principle of divine reward and retribution. That idea comes to expression again in vv. 8-10, where Ben Sira observes that one who practices justice and integrity will succeed royally, just as surely as the wicked will encounter a lion in their path.

27:11-15. This thought leads Ben Sira to deplore the offensive banter of the wicked, which is unstable and anarchic. Naturally, he urges good people to associate with others like them, a principle that gave rise to the proverb in v. 9: "Birds roost with their own kind." The adverse effect of offensive language, "causing the hair to stand on end," is the same as that resulting from a divine revelation in Job 4:15. (See Reflections at 27:16–28:26.)

SIRACH 27:16–28:26, OFFENSES AGAINST COMPANIONS

COMMENTARY

This section consists of poems about betraying another's trust (27:16-21), retribution (27:22-29), vengeance (27:30–28:11), and slander (28:12-26).

27:16-21. Two images from hunting, that of a released bird or a gazelle, emphasize the futility of trying to repair the damage resulting from betrayal of trust (cf. Prov 6:5). Once a bird or a gazelle has left its trap, no one can easily recapture it. Ben Sira stresses the ultimate cost of revealing secrets about an intimate friend; nobody will ever trust you again. The introductory clause, "whoever betrays secrets" (v. 16), recurs in the final verse of this poem, forming a neat inclusio (v. 21) bracketing the unit of thought.

27:22-29. The poem about retribution evokes Ben Sira's ire for an individual who feigns friendship to your face but plunges a verbal dagger in your back when out of your range of hearing. The language describing the hypocrite's action is noteworthy; he sweetens his words while in your presence but twists his mouth in other people's midst. Ben Sira shares earlier sages' disdain for the practice of winking, viewing it as malicious (cf. Prov 6:13; 10:10). In this context of discussing someone who uses your own words to condemn you by perverting their original meaning, the first person returns once more; but here Ben Sira aligns himself with God. Both of them hate such dissemblers.

Verses 25-29 cite traditional proverbs that assert a relationship between cause and effect, here focusing on the dire consequences of particular actions: throwing a rock straight up (cf. Prov 26:27*b*), digging a pit (cf. Prov 26:27*a*; Eccl 10:8), and setting a trap (Ps 9:15-16). Such wishful thinking characterizes much of wisdom literature, largely because the sages believed that God guaranteed justice in society. As numerous proverbial sayings demonstrate, the sages' faith was not naive. The incisive questions in the books of Job (e.g., Job 10:3-7; 24:1) and Qohelet (Eccl 2:16; 3:21) develop some ideas already present in the earlier sayings.

27:30–28:11. The treatment of vengeance links up with the previous discussion, asserting divine retribution based on an accurate record of sinful deeds. Sirach 28:2-5 insists that anyone who desires forgiveness from the Lord must first exercise that compassion toward human enemies (cf. Matt 6:12, 14-15; 18:32-35; Mark 11:5; Luke 21:4; Jas 2:13). This sentiment also appears in Jewish literature generally. For example, God forgives whoever forgives his or her "neighbor";[203] "So long as we are merciful, God is merciful to us; but if we are not merciful to others, God is not merciful to us";[204] "Whoever has pity on men, to him will God be merciful";[205] "Only the one who is merciful with mankind may expect mercy from Heaven."[206] The concluding verses (28:6-7) appeal to the prospect of death as sufficient reason for extending forgiveness to others and remind readers of the supreme commandment: to love God *and* neighbor (Lev 19:18).

The next section (28:8-11) warns against letting sharp words escalate into blows. It quotes a proverbial saying about the amount of wood to use on a fire (Prov 26:20; cf. Jas 3:5). This citation leads to a similar one in 28:12, which observes that at a certain point when a coal is glowing one can blow on it and start a fire or spit on it and extinguish the ember.[207] This thought leads naturally into a discussion of gossip, for like breath and spit, words proceed from the mouth. This transitional verse demonstrates the difficulty of dividing Ben Sira's teaching into distinct units (cf. the Vg's title at 28:1, "On the Forgiveness of Sins" [*De remissione peccatorum*]).

28:12-26. The most striking feature of the discussion of gossip is the claim that slander has destroyed more people than has the sword (v. 18) and that the verbal lash breaks bones (cf. Prov 25:15). In v. 14, the Greek Codex Alexandrinus has "third tongue," a technical expression in rabbinic literature for slander that, according to '*Arak.* 15*b*, slays three people—the slanderer, the slandered, and the person who believes the slanderer. Ben Sira specifically refers to the rupture of marriages resulting from slanderous allegations about innocent wives (v. 15), and he likens slander to an iron yoke (cf. Jer 28:14). A particular example of slander's effect comes from the time of Herod the Great, who believed such reports on his wife Mariamne and had her executed, only to regret his action to the point of near madness. Returning to the earlier teaching about retribution, Ben Sira claims immunity from slander's power for the godly but asserts that wild animals will pounce on the wicked. As a precaution against falling prey to the temptation to slander others, he advises putting a strong bolt on the door of one's mouth and using accurate scales to weigh every utterance prior to speaking. The images of a yoke and chains also occur in Prov 6:24-25, 29-30 with regard to the discipline of wisdom.

---

203. *Rosh Ha-shanah* 17*a*.
204. *Megillah* 28*a*; cf. also *The Testament of the Twelve Patriarchs*, Gad 6:3-7; Zebulon 5:3.
205. *Erubin* 17:72.
206. *Sifre* 93*b*. See also Oesterley, *The Wisdom of Jesus the Son of Sirach or Ecclesiasticus*, 178-79.
207. Cf. *Wayyikra Rabba* 33.

REFLECTIONS

Many observations in this part of Sirach move outside the family structure to the broad realm of economic and social relations. On the basis of what is said, one can legitimately conclude that ancient Israel, like much of the West, was overcome by greed. Ben Sira's indictment of merchants leaves little, if any, room for fair trading practice. In earlier times, when the economy was based on bartering, little opportunity existed for making excessive profits through exchange of goods. With the emergence of currency and speculation in commerce, that situation changed forever. Greed has come to characterize our entire society, and cynicism has replaced trust with each revelation of unchecked lust for money.

In addition, confidences are readily broken, and the social fabric tears a little with every betrayal of trust. People profit from slandering others and from exposing every peccadillo to a curious populace. The rules of polite society have given way as more and more parents shirk their responsibility to train young children in the way they should walk. The church has a rare opportunity to take up the slack, nurturing neglected youth in the art of living. Christians who traditionally promise to assist in bringing up new converts in the family of God need to broaden their understanding of nurturing to include rudimentary matters of etiquette, indeed socialization in every aspect.

SIRACH 29:1-20, ON LENDING AND PROVIDING COLLATERAL

COMMENTARY

The book of Proverbs advises strongly against guaranteeing loans for someone else (Prov 6:1-5; 11:15; 17:18; 20:16; 22:26-27; 27:13), but Ben Sira urges the opposite, although in a responsible manner. His motive for this practice and for lending money to the poor, as well as for almsgiving, derives from religious duty, the commandment to be generous to the needy. In accord with the prohibition against charging Jews interest on loans (Exod 22:24; Lev 25:36-37), it plays no role in this discussion of loans. (In the later Talmudic tractate *B. Bat. 90* it is said that "a userer is comparable to a murderer, for the crimes of both are equally irremediable.") Polonius's counsel to Laertes, "Neither a borrower nor a lender be; for loan oft loses both itself and friend,"[208] lacks this theological mandate that drove Ben Sira to risk abuse and loss of money. Nevertheless, he enters into the negotiation with open eyes, knowing that borrowers humbly "kiss profusely" (καταφιλέω *kataphileō*) and feign appreciation before acquiring a loan but become obstinate and abusive when payment comes due. Borrowers either blame hard times for failure to meet the deadline, or they accuse the lender of setting the date too early. Irony fills the observation

208. William Shakespeare *Hamlet* I.iii.75-76.

in v. 6 that by lending money to someone the lender acquires an enemy at no extra charge ("freely" [δωρεά *dōrea*]).

The strong "nevertheless" (πλήν *plēn*) in v. 8 places the poor in a different category from the unappreciative, abusive borrower. Rather than hiding silver under a rock and letting it rust (cf. Isa 45:3; Matt 25:18), one should, in Ben Sira's opinion, obey the commandments and put the money to good use. In this way, one lays up treasure and attains protection from harm (cf. Matt 6:19; 19:21; Jas 5:3). The Vg has the title "On Compassion" (*De misericordia*) at v. 12.

The cautious remarks on guaranteeing a loan or covering a debt for someone indicate that Ben Sira knows the consequences of covering a bad debt. He acknowledges that some generous people have been driven into penury and forced to travel to distant lands because of extending themselves too far out of compassion. He also recognizes unscrupulous and illegal practices, such as seizing collateral when someone has failed to repay a debt at the appointed time (cf. Exod 22:25; Deut 24:12-13; Amos 2:8). Ben Sira's description of the plight of those who engage in careless surety, tossing like the boisterous sea, offers a sober warning to all who consider standing in for a creditor.

SIRACH 29:21-28, ON BEING INDEPENDENT

COMMENTARY

This brief unit is best understood against the background of Greco-Roman culture, in which certain individuals stayed in the

homes of wealthy people as unpaying guests. These parasitic persons were obliged to do menial chores to earn their food and lodging, and in the process they encountered considerable abuse. Ben Sira urges people to be content with their status, whether prosperous or humble, and thus to keep their independence. The initial verse mentions life's essentials: water, bread, clothing, a house for privacy (cf. 39:26, where a different list occurs). The remark in v. 25 about playing the host is ironic, for abuse instead of gratitude greets the "host's" action, making him a virtual slave. The unexpected reference in v. 28 to a creditor links this unit to the preceding one.

SIRACH 30:1-13, ON REARING CHILDREN

COMMENTARY

The essential point to remember in assessing the harsh discipline of children in ancient Israel (cf. Prov 13:24; 19:18; 22:15; 23:13-14; 29:15) is the belief that children provide continuity after their parents' deaths, both in defending the family's rights and in carrying the name forward into the next generation. Moreover, the severe treatment of children was common throughout the ancient Near East; a very old Sumerian school text, numerous Egyptian school texts from a somewhat later era, and the Aramaic *Sayings of Ahiqar* (perhaps seventh century BCE) provide copious evidence of this pedagogical practice over millennia. Ben Sira offers a curious justification for avoiding familiarity with one's children: They will lose respect for you. The reference in v. 10 to a parent gnashing teeth reverses the proverb in Ezek 18:2 and Jer 31:29, where children's teeth are set on edge because of their parents' deeds.

Verse 7 suggests that coddling a son will make a parent vulnerable to grief whenever a cry is heard in the streets, causing their anxious query, "Is that my child in pain?" The advice against playing with children assumes paramount importance in the light of the silence within the Bible about playful interaction between children and their parents. The entire section presupposes that children, like wild horses, must be tamed—one might even say subdued. The language of a heavy yoke accords with this understanding of children. The Hebrew, which is missing from 26:2a, resumes again at 30:11. The following verse catches the spirit of the entire discussion: "As a python pounces on a wild beast, so crush a son's loins while he is young." This harsh image probably suggests severe punishment for all offenses, particularly sexual ones—the reason for referring to chastising the boy's loins.

SIRACH 30:14-25, ON HEALTH

COMMENTARY

Codex Vaticanus has the titles "On Health" above v. 14 and "On Goods" over v. 16. The brief section states a truism that robust health is preferable to wealth accompanied by sickness and momentarily dwells on the futility of giving delicacies to those unable to enjoy them, before concluding with encouragement to enjoy life. Ben Sira considers death, with its grim finality, better than constant illness. The Greek translators shied away from his pessimism with regard to life beyond the grave; accordingly, they omit the phrase "eternal sleep." Verse 18 alludes to the practice of offering food and drink to dead ancestors (cf. Tob 4:17), but an apparent interpretive gloss in v. 19 shifts the thought to another familiar ritual, the giving of sacrifices to idols. Allusions to the latter type of worship occur in Deut 4:28; Ps 115:4-7; Isa 44:9-11; 57:6; Wisdom 13; Bel and the Dragon 3:22; and Letter of Jeremiah 27, while Tob 4:17 possibly refers to the placing of food and the pouring of drink offerings on memorial stones (but cf. the attitude in Deut 26:14).

Biblical authors never appreciated the practice among their neighbors of treating idols as if they were alive—dressing them, feeding them, and taking them for a walk. Like so much in the OT as well as in the NT (cf. John 9:2), verses 19-20 understand sickness as divine punishment. Elsewhere Ben Sira offers a more nuanced interpretation of illness, one informed by Hellenistic attitudes to physicians and medicines rather than responding to criticism of this popular notion by the author of the book of Job (cf. Job 38:1-15, but note the resurgence of the popular view in the Greek text of v. 15, "Let him fall into the hands of a physician." The Hebrew text has "Whoever sins before his Maker will behave proudly before the physician"). The graphic portrayal in v. 20 of a eunuch embracing a young woman and groaning captures the utter futility of combining grievous illness with enjoyment of rich foods (cf. 20:4a).

A healthy attitude toward maintaining beneficial psychological states occurs in vv. 21-25. In recognizing the danger of harboring resentment and nursing grief over a prolonged period, Ben Sira resembles Qohelet (cf. Eccl 11:9-10; Matt 6:34). The rabbinic tractate *Sanh.* 100b cites a portion of v. 23: "Do not let sorrow enter your heart, for sorrow has killed mighty men." Many ancient thinkers have registered similar ideas, for example, "Anger would inflict punishment on another; meanwhile, it tortures itself."[209]

The order of the Greek text becomes confused after v. 24; two pairs of leaves containing respectively 30:25–33:13a and 33:13b–36:12 have been transposed. A more natural order, placing 33:13b–36:12 before 30:25–33:13a, is retained in the Hebrew, the Vg, and *Peshitta.*

---

209. Publilius Syrus *Moral Sayings* 1009 (first cent. CE). Cf. the more recent (sixteenth cent. CE) aphorisms by Baltasar Gracian: "The envious die not once, but as oft as the envied win applause," and by Friedrich Nietzsche: "Nothing on earth consumes a man more quickly than the passion of resentment" (*Ecce Homo*). The last reference cited is from Skehan and Di Lella, *The Wisdom of Ben Sira*, 382.

SIRACH 31:1-11, ON RICHES

COMMENTARY

In this unit about the difficulty of being rich and also virtuous, Ben Sira uses rhetorical questions and emphatic language that comes close in meaning to "miracle." The prayer attributed to Agur in Prov 30:8-9 captures the danger inherent to the wealthy, a temptation to forget God as a result of (deceptive) self-sufficiency. Others in ancient Israel shared the sentiment expressed in v. 10. This criticism of wealth was also common among Hellenistic authors of this time. Ben Sira's understanding of riches was complicated by contradictory impulses—the destructive effect of pursuing money as if it were the ultimate thing in life and the belief that God commanded the Israelite people to do works of charity by helping the needy. Extreme poverty, like excessive wealth, brought special temptations.

Verses 3-4 contrast rich and poor in terms of the results of a common activity, "toiling."

In the one instance, toil yields plenty, whereas in the other the labor only brings need. The first known use in the Bible of the Aramaic loan word *mammon* (ממון *mammôn*) occurs in v. 8, although later texts use it often (cf. Matt 6:24; Luke 16:9, 11, 13; and *Pirqe 'Abot* 2.16, "Rabbi Jose said, 'Let your friend's wealth [*mammôn*] be as precious to you as your own'"). Verse 9 probably expresses irony, following an unlikely blessing, one pronounced on a non-existent entity. The next verse suggests that only one who has withstood the ethical test that comes with a fortune has the right to boast, for others do not know how they would deal with the temptation. The final verse alludes to the practice of proclaiming aloud the names of benefactors in the gathered assembly or in writing on the walls of synagogues.

SIRACH 31:12–32:13, ON PROPER ETIQUETTE

COMMENTARY

This extensive section consists of three discrete topics dealing with conduct in eating (31:12-24), self-control in drinking wine (31:25-31), and behavior at banquets (32:1-13). Egyptian instructional literature devotes considerable space to these subjects, largely because of its use in preparing young men for life at court. In the book of Proverbs, only the brief section in Prov 22:17–24:33, which depends on the *Instruction of Amenemope*, takes up these matters (cf. Prov 23:1-3). Ben Sira's remarks came at a time when Greco-Roman banquets were notorious occasions for gluttony.

31:12-24. Ben Sira offers advice that falls in the category of common courtesy. In his culture, the host praised the food and guests exercised restraint, lest they appear greedy. The curious argument about the evil eye—that is, an insatiable appetite—and the appropriateness of tears flowing from this instrument needs to be balanced by recognizing the positive contribution of the eye. Ben Sira bases his advice on courtesy and self-interest, arguing that eating in moderation enables one to sleep. In context, the suggestion that one get up and vomit seems better suited as a relief from indigestion than advice during meals to excuse oneself long enough to vomit so as to continue eating everything provided by the host.

31:25-31. The counsel to drink wine in moderation appears in conjunction with lavish praise for this contributor to human happiness. The rhetorical question in v. 27 implies that life without wine is hardly worth living. Nevertheless, Ben Sira knows how wine, drunk in excess, brings misery beyond comprehension. This description of drunken conduct pales in comparison with that in 1 Esdr 3:17-24, which praises wine as the strongest thing in the world.

32:1-13. Hellenistic banquets (symposia) were governed by a strict set of rules. A banquet master was selected for the occasion and may have worn a wreath of flowers (cf. 2 Macc 2:27). Musical entertainment was provided, and senior guests displayed their wisdom; only occasionally were younger guests expected to speak, and that quite briefly.

In v. 13, Ben Sira manages to combine such Hellenistic partying with his own religious inclination, although Greeks also praised their gods at the end of a feast. He demonstrates astute insights about proper social conduct in the advice to go home promptly, even if out of courtesy the host invites you to stay beyond the appointed hour. Ben Sira's knowledge of natural phenomena—the association of thunder with previous lightning—leads to unsupported claims about popular approval of modest persons. The key to this statement lies in one's support group; Ben Sira's fellow scribes would probably have praised modesty. They certainly would not have approved of drinking contests like those in Greek symposia (cf. Isa 5:22 for similar language), for the perils of drunkenness were well known to the authors of Proverbs (cf. Prov 23:29-35).

SIRACH 32:14–33:19, ON DIVINE PROVIDENCE

COMMENTARY

32:14-18. This section on divine providence deals with the positive role of the law in individual lives and posits a theodicy based on polarities in nature and among humans. Five variants in the Hebrew of v. 14 yield virtually the same idea—that whoever seeks

God submits to discipline, and the one rising early to pray (cf. 39:50) enjoys divine favor. Praying at sunrise was an act of piety with enormous symbolic power, a sanctioning of each new day. Ever conscious of sinners, Ben Sira acknowledges this vulnerability before the law's curses. Knowing the contents of divine instruction, these reckless persons (the Greek has "hypocrite" [ὑποκρινόμενος *hypokrinomenos*]) refuse to observe them, preferring their own wishes to God's. The image of light in v. 16 does not necessarily indicate Ben Sira's familiarity with the lighthouse of Pharos of Alexandria,[210] for biblical literature abounds in such language (Ps 119:105; Prov 6:23).

32:19-24. Verse 19, at which the Vg has the title "Do Everything with Counsel" (*cum consilio omnia facienda*), uses an old idea but gives it a new twist: Think before acting, and having done so, put an end to second-guessing. Ben Sira recognizes the psychological stress generated by constant anxiety over whether one has made the right decision. At the same time, he warns against a sort of brash confidence that ignores real danger such as that posed by brigands lying in ambush on the open roads, and he expects people to learn from past mistakes. Verses 23-24 apply the verb "to keep," "to observe" (שמר *šāmar*) to the Torah as well as to one's life (נפש *nepeš*). According to v. 23, guarding one's ways (or deeds) is tantamount to observing a statute (מצוה *miṣwâ*), while v. 24 varies the verb with reference to Torah (נצר *nāṣar*) but repeats "watches over himself" (שומר נפשו *šōmēr napšô*).

33:1-3. The assertion in 33:1 flies in the face of reality, although many sages subscribed to this simplistic theology. From a certain perspective, however, even the experience of Job can be harmonized with the claim that God rescues good people from tests. The same cannot be said for Job's children and servants, who perished through no fault of their own. The description of sinners as a boat without a rudder, tossing at sea in a tumultuous storm, occurs widely in ancient ethical teachings (cf. Jas 1:6). The belief that a divine oracle, predictive by nature, is reliable like the priestly throw of dice (Urim and Thummim) indicates that Ben Sira trusted heavily in God's control of such minute details as the way these sacred "rocks" fell.

33:4-6. Two images characterize fools, according to vv. 5-6. They repeat themselves incessantly, like a cart wheel and axle, and they lack any discrimination at all, like a rutting stallion scenting for a mare. In v. 4, the Hebrew MS E advises people to give careful attention to what they wish to say, whereas the Greek verb "gather" (συνδέω *syndeō*) suggests a colorful image of a person binding up clothes and essential supplies in a bundle before setting out on a journey.[211]

33:7-15. Ben Sira tries to explain why people divide into two distinct groups, which he labels wise and foolish, righteous and wicked. First, he notes that in God's wisdom not all days have the same significance in the liturgical calendar, despite their enjoying a common source of light and warmth. Second, Ben Sira concedes that all people derive from the same source, dust, but the potter decides what value to place on the completed vessel. Some people, like Abraham, receive divine blessing; others, like priests, are brought near to the Holy One; still others, like Canaanites, are cursed. From such comparisons, Ben Sira concludes that God made the whole universe like this, each entity having an opposite—good and evil, life and death.[212] This idea of constitutive pairs goes beyond Qohelet's teaching of a time for everything under the sun (Eccl 3:1-8). In this section, Ben Sira probably responds to Jewish Hellenizers who doubted the special place of Israel in the divine economy.

33:16-19. The last four verses of this unit comprise the second authorial self-reference in the book (cf. 24:30-34; 34:12-13; 39:12-15, 32-35; 41:16; 43:32; 50:25-29; 51:1-30). Ben Sira allies himself with the prophets, using the metaphor of a watcher guarding the people against enemy attack (cf. Ezek 3:17; 33:7; Hab 2:1), and with wisdom teachers (cf. Wis 6:12-20). Conscious of his position

---

210. Skehan and Di Lella think Rudolf Smend may be right in seeing an allusion to the lighthouse of Pharos in Sir 32:16. See Skehan and Di Lella, *The Wisdom of Ben Sira*, 397.

211. Cf. Theodotion's use of this verb in Prov 6:21 and Aquila's in Prov 3:3; 6:21; and 7:3 to translate the Hebrew קשר (*qasar*, "to bind").

212. Cf. the *Testament of the Twelve Patriarchs*, Asher 1:3-4: "God has granted two ways to the sons of men, two mind-sets, two lines of action, two models, and two goals" (accordingly, everything is in pairs, the one over against the other); 5:1-2: "Children, you see how in everything there are two factors, one against the other, one concealed by the other. . . . Death is successor to life, dishonor to glory, night to day, darkness to light, but all these things lead ultimately to day: righteous actions to life, unjust actions to death since eternal life wards off death."

at the end of a long line of inspired persons, he seeks to overcome the stigma of being last by excelling in knowledge, thus making the last become first. The image of filling his winepress suggests success in learning Torah. Verse 18 repeats the claim of altruism already made in 24:34, and v. 19 asks influential citizens to reflect on his teaching (cf. Wis 1:1; 6:1-2 for this rhetorical form).

Like their modern counterparts, ancient teachers felt the need to capture the attention of their students; to do so, they made direct appeals to be heard. Both Ben Sira and the unknown author of the book of Wisdom flattered their audience by identifying them as rulers and officials, the important decision makers in the community. According to the sages' ideology, their students could look forward to appointment in high office, hence the language here is not simply rhetorical flourish.

REFLECTIONS

1. Doubt about the actual operation of a principle of reward and retribution provoked Ben Sira to affirm divine providential care and to make an audacious claim that tilts perilously close to cosmic dualism. Inherent to ethical monotheism is a perennial problem: how to harmonize belief in a benevolent Creator with the presence of so much evil. A moment's thought suggests that a good God would surely have made things capable of running more smoothly—that is, acting in conformity with the divine will. Ben Sira offers a reasonable answer—namely, free will—but then he places this partial resolution of the problem in jeopardy by insisting on something approaching divine determinism. Modern apologists fare little better, even when profiting from Ben Sira's bold endeavor.

2. Anyone who hopes to persuade others to adopt a certain life-style must be prepared for questions about credentials. What right do you have to offer advice? Where did you acquire insights into the nature of reality? Ben Sira asserts the right to teach others, claiming total immersion in Israel's sacred traditions and exceptional success in that study. The sages' authoritative introduction, "Listen, my son, to your dad's advice," functions precisely like the prophetic oracular formula, "Thus has the Lord spoken." Neither the one nor the other actually required others to pay attention, for successful counsel depends on the disposition of the person to whom it is addressed. Learning, therefore, is a mutual process involving teacher and student, one characterized by trust.

This principle applies at every level of instruction. Parents, relatives, friends, and pastors can no longer assume that the mere assertion of authority commands obedience, for respect of that magnitude must be earned. Even the right to share intimate feelings is not automatic, for privacy needs to be honored. Nevertheless, many individuals desperately long for worthy persons to shatter their wall of isolation and construct a relationship of trust and fidelity. Like Ben Sira, unselfish Christians can bring a ray of hope to such lonely children of God.

3. Perhaps the time has come for Christians to acknowledge a need for lifelong education. In the past, emphasis has fallen on the teaching role, so that whatever learning took place came as a result of preparing to instruct others, often children. Society in general has begun to place greater emphasis on continuing education, with major universities offering stimulating and intellectually demanding classes for persons enjoying longer years of retirement. This opportunity for instruction in later life bodes well for active minds and earnest learners among the aged. The church is beginning to recognize this shift among its members and to encourage lifelong learning about spiritual matters, but more needs to be done in this vein.

The present interest among many Protestants in the spiritual life of mystics and in meditation as practiced by monastics of the Roman Catholic Church offers yet another challenge. The potential for spiritual enrichment is almost unlimited, and the combination of meditation and secular existence opens up new ways of dealing with reality. Those persons who allow the deep spiritual life of meditation to shape their decisions have much to gain.

SIRACH 33:20–39:11

PART VI

OVERVIEW

This section begins with an appeal stressing the advantage of maintaining one's independence until the moment of death. The unit concludes with a lengthy comparison of various vocations to that of professional teachers of wisdom. Between introductory and concluding units, one finds quite distinct treatments of several topics of interest to sages generally and some sentiment specific to Ben Sira's own day, but until then foreign to wisdom literature.

SIRACH 33:20-24, THE ADVANTAGE OF INDEPENDENCE

COMMENTARY

The advice in vv. 20-24 to hold on to one's possessions until just prior to death may have been prompted by pious Jews who gave away their wealth in the interest of acquiring credit with God for performing deeds of kindness (מצוות *miṣwôt*). The unfortunate consequence of such generosity, an impoverishment that placed unnecessary hardships on family members of the charitable individual, carried with it an embarrassing need to request assistance. Ben Sira's silence about daughters in this list of family members stands out, for he mentions son, wife, brother, and friend but says nothing about a daughter. The advice to distribute one's goods just before death implies that the practice of writing a last will and testament had not yet become normative. This literary form came to be an important vehicle for ethical instruction, for in it a revered figure approaching the end of life handed down the insights about life acquired through long experience. The well-known *Testament of the Twelve Patriarchs* demonstrates the usefulness of this literary device in Jewish ethical instruction.

REFLECTIONS

In Jesus' day life's unpredictability prompted many Jews to worry about the future in a way that he considered counterproductive, particularly in the light of human inability to control so many factors that shape destiny. His call to trust the heavenly Father notwithstanding, modern Christians join their secular compatriots in worrying about becoming dependent in their later years. Social Security and Medicare may have reduced people's anxiety somewhat, but many persons approaching that period in life when their earning potential goes down and their expenses for medical care skyrocket find themselves frequently worrying about the future.

This anxiety increases as taxes rise, inflation and medical care eat away at people's savings, and they can see no end to the rising spiral of costs. That worry is further heightened by a sense of vulnerability to numerous forces that seem wholly out of control, particularly violence and crime of all sorts. No longer able-bodied, many elderly persons feel like prisoners in their own homes, unable to venture very far for fear of attack. Moreover, the fast pace of society places them at risk, for failing sight, waning dexterity, and slower reaction time increase their chances of having an accident. In addition, they cannot understand the younger generation's lack of respect for their elders. Time appears to have passed them by as so many cherished values go up in smoke.

Ben Sira understood this type of anxiety and suggested a practical way of dealing with it in his time. The secret as he saw things was to hang on to possessions until death, in that way avoiding the necessity of depending on one's family for primary care. He correctly perceived the blow to personal dignity when one must rely on others' goodwill, even when the caregivers belong to one's own family.

The theological conviction that God hears the petition of those in need should not prevent caring individuals from addressing the root causes of such anxiety. Ben Sira's partially humorous remark that one should not make fun of old people for "some of us are growing old" personalizes the problem in precisely the right manner. Everyone has a stake in solving the dilemma, for sooner or later each individual will internalize the feelings that generate such anxiety. In this struggle to find answers to a vexing problem, the first consideration may be, by necessity, the strengthening of familial bonds. Perhaps the time has come to recognize children's responsibility to repay parents for their years of generous care. In this regard, we can learn valuable lessons from other cultures, particularly the Arabs and Asians, both of which honor those who have lived a long time.

SIRACH 33:25-33, ON SLAVES

COMMENTARY

Both religious and social legitimation for slavery existed in the ancient world, and Ben Sira did not question these sanctions. The slaves of Israelites possessed minimal rights; for example, Deut 23:15-16 protects a runaway slave from being returned to an abusive owner; Exod 21:2 states that slaves must be set free in the seventh year (cf. Deut 15:12-18); and Exod 21:26-27 lists compensation for the loss of an eye or a tooth as a result of cruel treatment by an owner. Such laws may never have been obeyed, but at the very least they indicate awareness that slaves were in fact qualitatively different from animals, even if they are mentioned frequently in lists alongside oxen, asses, and other cattle (cf. Exod 20:10, 17). Ben Sira's advice to keep slaves busy assumes that "an idle mind is the devil's workshop." But that principle can be pressed too far, and Ben Sira cautions against harsh treatment—beyond, that is, the demeaning use of stocks and chains for unmanageable slaves.[213]

Ben Sira's concluding advice for those modestly well-to-do owners of only one slave would appear to be self-evident. Because you have but one slave, you should be particularly generous to prevent that slave's displeasure and to assure that he or she will not run away. The remark that the owner purchased the slave with his own blood must be understood figuratively as representing one's life's savings. The motive underlying this conduct is entirely one of self-interest. Several narratives in the Bible indicate that slaves often rose to high places and contributed greatly to the well-being of households, their loyalty to masters often leading to exceptional behavior (cf. Joseph in Genesis 37–50, Eliezer in Genesis 24, and Naaman's Israelite slave in 2 Kings 5).

213. Similar counsel occurs in Papyrus Insinger 14:6-11.

SIRACH 34:1-8, ON DREAMS

COMMENTARY

Although revelatory dreams are reported favorably in the patriarchal narratives (Genesis 37–50), in the stories about the judges (Judg 7:13-15), in the book of Job (Job 4:12-21; 33:15-18), and even as late as the period when the popular tales preserved in the first six chapters of the second-century BCE book of Daniel took shape, this means of ascertaining the divine will came under sharp attack from several prophets, most notably Jeremiah (cf. Jer 29:8). Ben Sira concurs in this negative assessment of dreams, but he reserves space for legitimate dreams sent by God (cf. the NT dreams of Joseph, of the magi, and of Pilate's wife, Matt 1:20; 2:12-13, 20; 27:19). Such a judgment begs the question, however, for no means existed for determining which one had its origin in divine revelation as opposed to those arising in human fantasy. The same situation pertained in prophecy, for no adequate criterion for distinguishing true prophetic words from false could be found (cf. Deut 18:15-22).[214]

The basis for rejecting dreams, in Ben Sira's view, was their lack of any foundation in tangible reality. They resemble idols in that they possess no link with the realm to which they supposedly point.[215] Ben Sira uses graphic images of utter futility, trying either to take hold of a shadow or to catch the wind in the palm of a hand (cf. Hos 12:1 and Qohelet's use of the latter image as an apt description of human existence, Eccl 1:14; 2:11, 17, 26; 4:6, 16; 6:9). In addition, Ben Sira compares dreams to looking at oneself in a mirror; the pale reflection in a mirror fashioned from polished metal lacked the qualities intrinsic to life itself. The apostle Paul uses this thought to indicate that what one sees in a mirror is only a partial, and necessarily distorted, although to some extent trustworthy, proclamation of God's promise awaiting Christians (1 Cor 13:12). Ben Sira's further line of argument against dreams calls attention to their adverse effect and unreliability; according to the laws of purity and impurity, something ritually clean cannot come from an unclean object, just as truth cannot derive from lies. Rhetoricians in ancient Greece used a similar argument with regard to ethos, insisting on moral character as an essential ingredient in persuasive speech.[216]

Verse 5 enlarges the discussion to include two other significant ritual functions in the ancient world, particularly in Mesopotamia and Egypt, but certainly present in Israelite culture as well. These highly valued modes of finding out what lay in store for a person were divination and omens. Considerable literature about omens has survived, and even the OT preserves allusions to a number of different kinds of divination (e.g., casting sacred dice, 1 Sam 14:42; shooting arrows, 2 Kgs 13:15-19; observing the flight of birds, drinking a sacred potion, etc.). The vast number of clay livers discovered in Mesopotamia testifies to the enormous significance of hepatoscopy to the Babylonians. Priests observed the livers of animals sacrificed at altars as a means of discovering the will of the gods as it pertained to the person offering the sacrifice. Whereas a considerable population viewed dreams, omens, and divination as reliable and understood the study of these manipulative practices as "scientific," to use a modern term, Ben Sira thought they merely equipped fools for a wild ride, one characterized by an unchecked imagination.

The last verse states Ben Sira's real reason for discrediting these familiar means of discovering the future. In his view, the Mosaic law contained God's complete revelation to the Israelite people, and such unreliable probings as dreams, omens, and divination prevented the divine legislation from attaining

---

214. Crenshaw, *Prophetic Conflict*, examines the criteria within the Bible for distinguishing true from false prophets and discusses their inadequacy.

215. Robert K. Gnuse, *The Dream Theophany of Samuel* (Lanham, Md.: University Press of America, 1984), looks at ancient Near Eastern interpretation of dreams. Sigmund Freud's reading of dreams as sexual pathology represents a new departure.

216. George A. Kennedy, *Classical Rhetoric and Its Christian and Secular Tradition from Ancient to Modern Times* (Chapel Hill: University of North Carolina Press, 1980). This resource contains numerous insights into persuasive speech. Alongside ethos, Kennedy posits pathos and logos (passion and logic). For the OT, see Crenshaw, "Wisdom and Authority," 10-29. See also Crenshaw, *Urgent Advice and Probing Questions*, 326-43.

its full scope. The faithful exposition of the Torah by a sage provided everything the people needed, Ben Sira insisted, so that no one need resort to proscribed or fundamentally foreign avenues of inquiring about the unknown.

SIRACH 34:9-20, ON THE DANGERS OF TRAVEL AND GOD'S PROTECTION

COMMENTARY

Ancient sages recognized the broadening experience of travel to foreign lands, but they also knew the accompanying perils. Resorting to first-person narration, Ben Sira discusses these dangers in the context of God's protective care. Interestingly, Ben Sira does not offer any details about the dangers from which his cleverness delivered him (cf. the account of Paul's shipwreck as told in Acts 27:13-44; 2 Cor 11:24-27, 32-33). The remainder of this unit, vv. 14-20, encourages readers to trust the Lord, presumably in undertaking dangerous journeys where brigands, unfamiliar diet and customs, and countless other obstacles to safe travel await the inexperienced traveler.

SIRACH 34:21–35:26, ON SACRIFICES

COMMENTARY

Historical necessity taught ancient Israelites to think of other means of atonement than sacrifices on the altar in the Solomonic Temple, for during their stay in captivity and for sometime after their return to Judah, circumstances made it impossible for them to carry out the prescribed offerings. Moreover, a strong prophetic voice beginning with Amos and enduring for many years called into question the entire cultic apparatus, at least as practiced in Jerusalem. A rabbinic anecdote from the late first century CE reveals a similar attitude, for when Joshua ben Hannaniah lamented the destruction of the Temple in 70 CE and simultaneously the disappearance of the place of atonement, Johanan ben Zakkai responded that an equally valid means of forgiveness, deeds of kindness, remained, as acknowledged in Hos 6:6: "For I desire steadfast love and not sacrifice,/ the knowledge of God rather than burnt offerings" (NRSV).

34:21-27. In this section Ben Sira tries to do justice to this revolutionary criticism of the sacrificial cult while at the same time granting the binding authority of earlier laws requiring Israelites to bring specific offerings to the Lord. He begins by reinforcing the prophetic indictment of flawed offerings, using the prohibition against giving a blemished animal to the Lord and applying the principle underlying the law to include gifts obtained at the expense of marginalized citizens. Such gifts, he says, resemble heinous acts of murder (cf. 2 Kgs 25:6-7, the execution of King Zedekiah's sons in his sight); whoever deprives the poor of food are in reality murderers, and the one who delays payment of wages beyond nightfall is likewise guilty of homicide (cf. Lev 19:13; Deut 24:14-15; *Baba Metzia* 112*a*, "Everyone who withholds an employee's wages is as though he deprived him of his life").

34:28-31. These verses emphasize the necessity of genuine transformation, a radical reversal of one's conduct, if one expects to receive God's forgiveness. Unless one's actions accord with the inner attitude, the two work at cross-purposes, accomplishing nothing. One builds; another tears down. One prays; another curses—and the result is negligible. Similarly, Ben Sira insists, one who has become impure by touching a corpse and who has undergone ritual lustration has gained nothing unless he or she avoids corpses thereafter. On that principle, Ben Sira boldly insists that only those who forsake their sins obtain forgiveness, for fasting alone has no atoning power.

35:1-13. The next section weaves together this ethical transformation of the sacrificial cult and a literal understanding of the requirements concerning tithes and offerings (cf. Tob 1:6-8). Ben Sira equates charitable deeds with the meal offering and thanksgiving offering. Having insisted on the moral requisite for acceptable offerings, he goes on to recommend generosity toward the Most High, who rewards the faithful much more unstintingly.

35:14-26. These verses describe the Lord as champion of widows and orphans (cf. Ps 68:5; Jas 1:27), but one who stands for impartial justice, and they utter a fervent psalm praising God for crushing the wicked. The latter provides a fine point of transition to the prayer in 36:1-22, which reiterates the sentiment about destroying evildoers, in this instance foreigners. Ben Sira assures his readers that imprecation issuing from the lips of the powerless will reach heaven, calling attention to a widow's tears. Whereas Lam 3:44 accuses God of being wrapped in an impenetrable cloud, Ben Sira asserts that the prayer of humble people pierces the clouds and keeps knocking at the door of the Most High until provoking a favorable response. The rapid rehearsal of divine punishment against guilty humans, unexpected in a text of this sort, may reflect the chaotic political situation under the new Seleucid rulers. According to Isa 55:10-11, Yahweh's Word will not return empty but will accomplish its purpose on earth; Ben Sira applies the same reasoning to the prayer of the lowly.

REFLECTIONS

An interesting feature in studying different religions is the effort to maintain specific regulations, believed to be divinely ordained, when historical circumstances change so drastically as to make them obsolete or questionable at best. Such requirements may once have made sense, but now their arbitrary character stands out. One thinks immediately of Jewish dietary laws and restrictions relating to observing the sabbath. Religious leaders confronted with the question about the permanence of divine laws often look for enduring principles that enable them to salvage the essence of sacred commands while discarding the external trappings.

Naturally, this sort of situation arose in ancient Israel after the Temple in Jerusalem was destroyed, making it impossible to fulfill the laws about sacrificing at the sacred altar. During their stay in Babylonia, exiled Judeans were forced to find other ways of obeying their God; in doing so, they resorted to a spiritualization of divine regulations. Back in Judah, the prophet Jeremiah spoke of circumcizing the heart, along with the actual bodily circumcision. Similarly, Joel pleaded with the people of Judah to rend their hearts rather than their garments, and a poetic Hosea referred to prayer and praise as "the bulls of the mouth" (sacrifices, Hos 14:2).

Such transformation of religious language also occurred in respect to specific offerings intended for the temple cult. Religious leaders gradually realized that sacrifices alone had no redemptive power; without repentant attitudes, even multiple offerings achieved nothing beneficial. By the time of Ben Sira, this novel way of looking at age-old ritual obligations existed alongside strong desire to fulfill the letter of the law, once more possible because of the restored Temple. He held both notions in a delicate balance, insisting that charitable deeds and sacrificial offerings brought divine favor.

Christians face the same issue, although focused differently. Over the years the church has constructed a heavy chain of tradition containing numerous obligations that have been given divine sanction. Tithing, specific observance of the Christian sabbath, and loyalty to orthodoxy and orthopraxy specific to a denomination often assume roles like those occupied by Jewish dietary laws and requirements for offering sacrifices in the Temple. Faced with such externals, many Christians search for the spiritual meaning of these rituals. In this quest, Ben Sira provides sound leadership, for he realized that religious ritual devoid of loving deeds was empty and that people need specific ordinances to remind them that love of fellow human beings becomes complete when that love also directs itself to God.

However profound this spiritualization of legal obligations, it runs the risk of dissolving into pious generalities and vague practice. The orthodox Jewish argument that dietary laws, for example, must be observed because people owe allegiance to God carries considerable force, even if we cannot go further and accept such arbitrary regulations as divine law. Individuals from many different cultures have attributed their laws to a particular deity, perhaps primarily as a means of sanctioning them after the fact. Nevertheless, their willingness to submit to "divine legislation" indicates that they felt constrained to recognize an authority beyond their own, and in that regard they were surely worthy examples for moderns.

SIRACH 36:1-22, A PRAYER FOR NATIONAL DELIVERANCE

COMMENTARY

This prayer seems entirely foreign to wisdom literature as traditionally understood, for nowhere in the books of Proverbs, Job, and Ecclesiastes do such sentiments appear. Ben Sira prays in the tone of laments within the psalter, with one decisive difference: the absence of any praise of God (e.g., Psalms 12–13; 25–26). There, too, however, some laments stand alone (cf. Psalm 38), and elsewhere the book of Sirach has elaborate expressions of praise for the Creator. This prayer begins with a cry for rescue, especially in the Hebrew ("Save us" [הושיענו *hôšî'ēnû*]) and addresses God as lord of all (cf. 45:23 and 50:22 in the Greek and Rom 9:5); it ends with a similar thought, that everyone will know that Yahweh is God of all time (cf. the Prayer of Azariah). A psalm from Qumran uses a similar expression, "Lord of all" (אדון הכל *'ādôn hakkōl*) and "God of all" (אלה הכל *'ĕlôah hakkōl* [Ps 151:4 = 11QPs^a 28:7-8]), which reproduces the title of Baal, "Lord of earth" (אדון ארץ *'ādôn 'ereṣ*) and "Lord of all the earth" (אדון כל הארץ *'ādôn kol hā'āreṣ*), attributed to Yahweh.

The language of the prayer echoes traditional texts from Israel's liturgical repertoire as well as more recent eschatology and apocalyptic. Ben Sira cautiously veils his allusions to Seleucid rulers, perhaps concealing a direct reference to Antiochus III the Great, who, according to Dan 11:18, arrogantly claimed to be unique in power ("There is no one besides me"). The anthological style recalls Ezekiel's oft-used formula about the nations' knowing that Yahweh is God (v. 5), which the prophet Joel also uses more than once (Joel 2:27; 3:17). He, too, spoke of signs and wonders when Yahweh renewed the saving activity heralded by Israel's ancestors (Joel 2:28-32; 3:1-5 in Hebrew). Ben Sira implores God to let the end come quickly, that day when the Lord acts in judgment against all the nations (v. 10, קץ *qēṣ*). Then people will recite Yahweh's mighty deeds, צדקות (*ṣidqôt*), as they did in bygone days.

For the moment, the ethic of forgiveness that Ben Sira taught elsewhere has flown out the window, and desire to see revenge poured out on foreigners dominates. That human wish to see the wicked pay for their crimes reaches a peak in vv. 8-12, after which Ben Sira concentrates on the people of God, some of whom are scattered in other countries, with one minor exception in v. 22 (the formula of acknowledgment). He recalls Israel's unique position in Yahweh's eyes, symbolized above all by Zion, and reminds the Lord that some prophecies have not yet come to fruition. The underlying premise of this argument was that ultimately every divine word will be fulfilled.

This plea for deliverance does not mention a messiah, although the language definitely suggests that the eschatological era is being described. Oesterley has noted that silence with respect to a messiah is not unique to Ben Sira in such contexts.[217]

Several features of this prayer resemble the *Shemoneh 'Esreh,* "The Eighteen Benedictions," in the Jewish prayer book. In the first century CE, the first three benedictions and the last three praises were recited in every synagogue service.

---

217. Oesterley, *The Wisdom of Jesus the Son of Sirach or Ecclesiasticus,* 232. A late first-century CE text, Pss Sol 17:23, gives a prayer for deliverance through the Messiah and identifies this person as the son of David.

REFLECTIONS

1. Fear of vulnerability in old age is matched by a xenophobia that feeds on partial truths and prejudices, when ample cause for such hatred does not exist. Citizens of the United States boast that their country has historically welcomed everyone to its shores, intent on creating a single society from the resulting melting pot. In periods of heightened conscience, the doors have been thrown open to receive immigrants from numerous oppressive societies, and at other times greed has prevailed—the desire for cheap workers in agricultural areas during recent decades is one example. Once welfare programs and other entitlements fell to these masses and the costs more and more fell to local governments, some people began to question the advisability of such open policies. In the end, economics reveals itself as the decisive issue.

Ben Sira was heir to a similar struggle, chiefly that between returning exiles from Babylonia and the people who had occupied the land of Judah for the previous seventy years or so. Descendants of Joseph who lived in Samaria also pleaded for inclusion in the new state, to no avail. Both the religious authority, Ezra, and the secular governor, Nehemiah, rebuffed the petition and protest of these foreigners, whose claim on the land certainly had merit. Instead, these two leaders enforced a rigorous policy that excluded everyone except returning exiles. That isolationism appealed to Ben Sira, and in this respect placed him at odds with his predecessors in the wisdom tradition.

Fear of those with different skin color, language, and customs comes easily, even in our moments of prayer. Perhaps if such sentiments must surface, that setting is the best one of all, for the self-examination when communicating with God offers an opportunity to purge such hatred. Like Ben Sira, we are forced to rub shoulders daily with people from many different cultures. That necessity can be taken as an opportunity for broadening one's experience in numerous ways without having to travel to distant lands. Assuming that Christians mean what they say about all creatures being children of God, modern society assists the family of God in getting to know their brothers and sisters. From this perspective, we can transform the source of our fears into cause for rejoicing as we endeavor to be the family of God to others.

2. How should we balance idealism and realism in grasping the nature of the universe? On the one hand, so much evidence in our daily lives seems to confirm a skeptical realism, and at the same time denying that truth and beauty stand a chance in this world. On the other hand, we seem unable to relinquish a conviction that God has something better in store for us all. The biblical prophets gave voice to this optimistic hope of an era when God would establish divine rule, transforming creatures into appropriate subjects for this kingdom.

Realism forced religious thinkers to search for a credible explanation for evil; the most natural one suggested equal powers, good and evil, in charge of the universe. Binary thinking as represented by this sharp opposition of the forces of good to the forces of evil has characterized ancient peoples from various cultures, as anthropologists and literary theorists have demonstrated in great detail.[218] Ben Sira drew on Hellenistic theories about complementary pairs, one of which encouraged virtue and rewarded it, the other functioning similarly by punishing wickedness. In this view, the universe itself assisted the Creator in achieving the divine purpose for creation.

Modern believers will probably stop short of such optimism, although they cling tenaciously to belief in a benevolent God who will ultimately, in some mysterious way, tie all the loose ends together. Ben Sira lived in a time of enormous changes but held tightly to his trust in the God of Israel despite apparent evidence that foreign powers could act with impunity against the chosen people. Christians today live in comparable circumstances, with the evidence seeming to indicate that God has abandoned the church and perhaps even the universe. In such a time, we can learn a valuable lesson from Ben Sira, who refused to give up on God. Here is realism tinged with idealism, no small achievement.

218. Douglas, *In the Wilderness*, relies on such thinking, among other things, to open up a fresh way of understanding the structure and context of the book of Numbers. She believes that its author deliberately fashioned a satire on the ruling hierarchy, Ezra and Nehemiah, one held together in a complex manner with parallel interlocking panels.

SIRACH 36:23–37:31, ON MAKING DISCRIMINATING CHOICES

COMMENTARY

36:23-31. After the passionate expression of concern that Yahweh inaugurate the messianic era, exalting Israel and bringing its foreign rulers low, Ben Sira returns to deal with mundane affairs of daily existence. First, he discusses the matter of choosing a partner in marriage. His initial remark, grounded in the social restrictions placed on women—that is, their dependence on arranged marriages—sounds cruel (v. 26). The limited choice open to a woman explains her readiness to accept any man; in contrast, men could be more selective in choosing a wife. Ben Sira's opening remarks about a discriminating palate and foods of different quality illustrate his analogical thinking.

Although he has already commented on good and bad wives, in vv. 27-29 Ben Sira lavishes high praise on beautiful and kind wives. The language echoes the eulogy of personified wisdom in Prov 8:22-36 and the description in Gen 2:18, 20 of Eve as Adam's helper.[219] The remark in v. 30 that a man without a wife wanders about like a fugitive recalls the exact expression applied to the first murderer, Cain

219. Carol Meyers, *Discovering Eve* (New York: Oxford University Press, 1988), offers a stimulating exploration of ancient Israelite women in cultural context.

(Gen 4:12, 14, נע ונד [*nāʿ wānād*], "a fugitive and a wanderer"). Ben Sira credits wives with protecting property and bestowing credibility on husbands. The allusion to robbers in v. 31 probably points to mercenary soldiers who traveled wherever clients wanted them to engage an enemy in combat; the point of this reference is the comparison with a "footloose and fancy-free" male.

37:1-6. The brief unit about unreliable friends distinguishes between speech and action. Pledges of friendship do not necessarily carry conviction, according to Ben Sira, and former friends sometimes become enemies. Moreover, adversity may prompt friends to abandon the individual whose fortunes have shifted, for most people act in their own self-interest (vv. 4-5). The closing remark may relate to experience in battle, but the Greek text makes the more general point that a friend who merits inner thoughts deserves to enjoy one's prosperity.

37:7-15. By far the most extraordinary section, these verses consist of Ben Sira's astute advice about seeking counsel from others. "Be suspicious of all counselors," he warns, "for they operate from the standpoint of their own selfish interests." Above all, do not seek advice from anyone who looks on you with suspicion. Anyone needing that counsel is naive beyond belief. In v. 11, Ben Sira lists nine kinds of people to avoid when soliciting advice; all of them would naturally render biased judgments, whether from self-interest or from character flaws. In vv. 12-15, Ben Sira suggests a hierarchy of advisers, beginning with a reliable observer of the law, then moving to self-reliance and ultimately to divine guidance through prayer. The remark that one's own mind is superior to seven sentinels may debunk Hellenistic astrologers,[220] although the hyperbole probably refers to persons on a watchtower who alert citizens of an approaching army.

37:16-31. Verses 16-26 address the matter of effective speech, with emphasis on God's gift and popular applause. The national sentiment expressed in the prayer in 36:1-22 recurs in v. 25, which contrasts the limited life span of individual persons with the endless duration of the nation of Israel (cf. 2 Macc 14:15). Just as this brief opening refers back to the preceding discussion of counsel (v. 16), the unit concludes (vv. 27-31) with a comment about sickness, which becomes the topic for the following major section. Ben Sira offers some self-evident advice: Beware of foods that harm you and avoid overeating. The vocative "my child" seems especially appropriate to such banal teaching. As vv. 16-26 imply, teachers differed in their knowledge and its application to life, some divorcing the two and suffering the consequences, others enjoying the grace (charm) that elicits praise, and still others offending through arrogance, unfortunate speech patterns, and choice of words.

220. Skehan and Di Lella, *The Wisdom of Ben Sira*, 433, following Smend, *Die Weisheit des Jesus Sirach erklärt*, 332.

SIRACH 38:1-15, ON PHYSICIANS

COMMENTARY

Because ancient Israelites associated sickness with sin, the place of doctors in society presented a problem to the pious, many of whom understood illness as God's punishment of guilty people. According to 2 Chr 16:12, King Asa had a serious ailment of the foot and consulted physicians for the malady, to no avail. The chronicler condemns him for relying on doctors rather than trusting God to heal him. A weighty tradition identified Israel's Lord as healer (Exod 15:26; cf. Job 5:18; Hos 6:1), conceding at the same time that Yahweh brought disease on the unfortunate Egyptians.

Ben Sira endeavors to hold together both concepts, belief in a deity who punishes violators of the divine will by causing them to become sick and a conviction that God actively works to overcome illness in repentant people. In doing so, Ben Sira draws on religious tradition and practical knowledge. Citing an episode in the story of Israel's wandering in the wilderness when Moses purified dangerous ("bitter") water by throwing wood into it (Exod 15:23-25), Ben Sira attributes healing properties to the branch from an unspecified tree. He also appealed to the best pharmaceutical information of the early second century BCE, which untrained (professionally) practitioners of healing arts had accumulated over the years through trial and error. These individuals learned that some roots and herbs have medicinal value, and they transmitted that vital information from generation to generation.

Ben Sira was probably not the first to draw the conclusion that if certain plants possess healing properties, then their Creator must have intended it that way. Carried to its logical conclusion, this line of reasoning indirectly challenges the popular notion that sickness and sin go hand in hand. Ben Sira makes that step hesitantly, and in the end he returns to this former position, perhaps flinching from giving up the powerful motivation for ethical conduct residing in threatened sickness.

In Ben Sira's view, doctors work closely with God and the various remedies the Creator placed at human disposal. Naturally, prayer enters the picture here, the physicians humbly invoking divine sanction on their efforts to bring healing to their clients. In this way, Ben Sira endorsed the exalted social status of physicians in the Hellenistic environment but subjected the medical profession to a humbling ritual at the heart of Jewish piety. Thus tradition sanctioned innovation, and everyone gained something in the process.[221]

In the light of vv. 9-15, it seems likely that some devout Jews spurned physicians and thus jeopardized their own health. Ben Sira gently urges them to combine traditional remedies, specifically prayer and sacrifice, with more modern approaches to sickness. This section reeks with old-fashioned views: confession of sin as a prerequisite for healing, offering generous sacrifices as atonement for fault, and the belief that sinners risk divine punishment in the form of disease. Whereas the Hebrew text emphasizes the divine ordaining of physicians (lit., "to allocate" [חלק *ḥālaq*]) and stresses the deity's activity in handing over sinners to illness, the Greek has "created" (κτίσις *ktisis*), with doctors as objects, and refers to defiance toward physicians by those persons incurring God's anger.

Jewish ambiguity toward physicians persists into later times. The telling allusion in the New Testament to one who had exhausted all funds on physicians with no beneficial results (Luke 8:43) probably reflects more than a sense of monetary loss. A saying in the *Mishnah Kiddushin* 4:14 goes much further: "the best among physicians is destined for Gehenna." In Jewish rabbinic literature, hyperbole is common and is not to be pressed literally. That sentiment has continued into more recent times, as Di Lella's citations from Benjamin Franklin, John Donne, and others demonstrate.[222] On the other hand, a rabbinic comment on Exod 21:19 in *Baba Qamma* 85*b* gives tacit approval to physicians, for it observes that the law gave permission to the physician to practice his art. The reference in Col 4:4 to greetings from "our dear friend Luke, the physician" reveals a similar appreciation for someone in the profession of healing.

This entire discussion of physicians indicates Ben Sira's skill in diplomacy. He avoids offending pious Jews whose understanding of sickness and its remedy was rooted in popular belief, but he also manages to accept radically new views about the cause of sickness and its cure. In the process he underscores the cooperative efforts of pharmacists, doctors, and God in bringing healing to the patient. This attitude takes into account the enormous energy expended on discovering medicinal value in roots and herbs, which is attested in ancient Egyptian papyri listing over five hundred such plants.[223] Ben Sira acknowledges the necessity for divine instruction in assisting physicians to reach correct diagnoses (cf. v. 14, where the Hebrew has a rare loan word from Aramaic, *interpretation* [פשר *pešer*], also meaning "discovery," "diagnosis," otherwise attested in the Bible only in Eccl 8:1).

---

221. Von Rad, *Wisdom in Israel*, emphasizes Ben Sira's sophisticated awareness of the complex nature of experience, the fact that very few things in life are unambiguous.

222. Skehan and Di Lella, *The Wisdom of Ben Sira*, 441.
223. C. Spicq, "L'Ecclesiastique," *La Sainte Bible* 6, eds. L. Pirot and A. Clamer (Paris: Letouzey et Ane, 1951) 758.

SIRACH 38:16-23, ON MOURNING

COMMENTARY

Ancient Israelites had no mortuaries in which to prepare corpses for burial. The body was laid out in the home, leading to ritual contamination of those residing there. Custom dictated the length of lamentation for the dead, and special laws regulated purification rites for those who became ritually impure. Ben Sira expresses concern over extended grief, suggesting that one shorten its duration for reasons of health. Excessive grief, he argues, threatens well-being, a thoroughly modern insight into the detrimental effects of psychological states on physical health. Ben Sira urges mourners to practice elemental courtesy for the sake of appearance but to get on with life, letting the memory of the deceased rest. Elsewhere he gives more credence to the traditional notion that one should keep the memory of the dead alive and thus ensure a kind of immortality to that person (44:8).

Ben Sira does not seem to address professional mourners, who, accompanied by the music of the flute, cried aloud in the public display of grief (Amos 5:16; cf. Mark 5:38 // Matt 11:17). Their lament (גנה *ginâ*) took a distinctive form in Hebrew verse, a limping meter characterized by three beats that ensued in two further beats. Originally, the shrill cries and beating of breasts may have been aimed at driving away evil spirits associated with the dead. Later rabbinic directives mention three days of weeping, seven days of mourning (cf. 22:12; Gen 50:10; Jdt 16:24), and thirty days of letting the hair and beard grow (*Moed Katan* 27*b*). This same text states that "whoever indulges in grief to excess over his dead will weep for another" (i.e., his own).

For this unit the Vulgate has the title *De exeguiis* ("On Mourning Rites"), just as it designated the previous section with the words *De medico* ("On Physicians"). Ben Sira's silence with regard to prayers for the dead contrasts with 2 Macc 12:43-45, where praying for the dead is commended. For Ben Sira, death had an element of finality; he mentions one's destiny as matter-of-fact. What was yours yesterday will be mine today—period (v. 22). Furthermore, the occasion of someone else's demise obliges one to contemplate one's own departure, but not in any debilitating fashion (v. 20).

SIRACH 38:24–39:11, THE SUPERIORITY OF THE SCRIBAL PROFESSION

COMMENTARY

38:24-34a. This section contrasts four professions—farmer, artisan, smith, and potter—with that of the wise. The opening verse specifies the essential requirement for anyone hoping to become a scribe—namely, leisure time. The four trades other than that of scribe consume the workers' time and energy, making it impossible for them to study religious texts and converse with informed persons. Nevertheless, these workers contribute to the well-being of society, even if the various honors of a community regularly fall to others. These honors belong to the scribes, who offer counsel, attain public office, and associate with rulers.

An Egyptian instruction from the Twelfth Dynasty (about 1991–1786 BCE) entitled *The Instruction for Duauf*, written by an otherwise unknown Khety and often copied, ridicules numerous occupations in Egypt so as to exalt the scribal profession. Because of the tone of this text, scholars often call it "The Satire of the Trades." The author belittles all occupations except that of scribes; he characterizes the harsh realities associated with sculptors, smiths, carpenters, jewelsmiths, barbers, merchants, brickmakers, builders, farmers, weavers, arrowmakers, couriers, embalmers, cobblers, launderers, fowlers, and fishers. Khety emphasizes the scribes' freedom from a boss, in contrast to all other workers. If Ben Sira knew of this satire, he completely avoided mockery in his remarks about the four professions other than that of scribe.[224] Moreover, he credits them with maintaining the fabric of the world, something entirely absent from Khety's ridicule. Consistent with his previously stated view of greedy merchants, Ben Sira omits this occupation from the list to be compared with the scribal profession.

The Hebrew text of v. 25 has the farmer conversing with cattle rather than with the wise, although the Greek suggests that he talks about their pedigree. The emphasis on "being occupied with, setting his heart on, and being careful about" conveys the idea that farmers are totally consumed by their work, so that they can never find time or strength to improve their minds. The same emphasis occurs in the description of the artisan, the

---

224. Sanders, *Ben Sira and Demotic Wisdom*, 69, writes, "that the 'satire of occupations' in 38:24–39:11 relies on an Egyptian antecedent seems beyond doubt."

smith, and the potter. The expression "set their heart on" appears in all four accounts; other comparable phrases are "labors by night as well as day" (v. 27), "is diligent" (v. 27), and "is always deeply concerned" (v. 29). Manual skill has one advantage, according to v. 32: Those who possess it will never lack adequate food, for society cannot do without their wares. Each of them deals with something that is in great demand because of a principle of obsolescence. Food is consumed, seals and pottery are broken, implements wear out. Daily routines in towns and villages thus created sufficient need for the services of farmers, artisans, smiths, and potters.

38:34b–39:11. In contrast to these, the scribe concentrates on one thing: study. Interpreters have understood the object of this intellectual curiosity as threefold—the law, wisdom, and prophecy—corresponding to the three divisions of the Hebrew Bible, but in a different order from that of the prologue, which has law, prophecy, and the other books.[225] The two different sequences are represented in the Hebrew Bible (law, prophets, writings) and the Septuagint (law, writings, prophets; cf. the Latin Vulgate also). The context suggests a different interpretation of 39:1-3. Ben Sira indicates that the scribes not only concentrate on the law but also apply their minds to insights from various sources: traditional wisdom, oracles, sayings, similes, and proverbs. The introduction to the initial collection in the book of Proverbs uses the following four terms: "proverb," "simile," "wise saying," and "riddle" (Prov 1:6).

Exalting the scribes as confidants of rulers, Ben Sira mentions their experience, acquired through extensive travel, which informs them about human nature. Above all, he praises the wise for their piety, which evokes divine favor and renown among humans. To communicate the exceptional reward for such devotion to learning and virtue, Ben Sira uses the expression "greater than a thousand" (v. 11), which recalls "one in a thousand" in Job (Job 9:3; 33:23) and Ecclesiastes (Eccl 7:28). The unusual divine epithet in v. 6, "the Great Lord" (cf. 46:5; Jas 4:15) occurs in a context that recalls a phrase in Isa 11:2, the promise that the Davidic ruler would be filled with an understanding spirit.

Ancient Judaism endeavored to hold together a belief in the value of manual labor and a conviction that one was obligated to study Torah. On the one hand, the following observation was attributed to Rabbi Gamaliel: "Excellent is study of the law together with worldly occupation, for toil in them both puts sin out of mind. But all study of the law without (worldly) labor comes to nothing and occasions sin."[226] On the other hand, Rabbi Meir was remembered for a quite different view: "Do little in business and be busy with Torah, and be humble in spirit before all men."[227] In Sir 7:15, 22 Ben Sira implies that the wise should also work at manual labor.

---

225. Oesterley, *The Wisdom of Jesus the Son of Sirach or Ecclesiasticus*, 256.

226. *Pirqe 'Abot* 2:2.
227. *Pirqe 'Abot* 2:2, 4:12.

REFLECTIONS

Modern technology increasingly reinforces vocational elitism, at the same time elevating professions that require advanced education and sophisticated knowledge. In this process, cerebral occupations such as law, medicine, university teaching, and comparable professions in business are placed in prestigious categories of work, whereas manual labor is demeaned. From the perspective of the elite, the nature of much manual labor contributes to their contempt; moreover, in this elitist view, minimal intelligence, skill, or ambition allows these workers to be content with assembly lines, service employment, and menial chores.

Ben Sira's attitude toward the workers of his own day, and Khety's before him, reveals the early roots of elitism. In Ben Sira's defense, it should be recognized that he was fighting for an elevated understanding of intellectual pursuits in a society that valued expertise in various crafts far more than the acquisition of literary skills. His apologetic was written on behalf of poorly paid and barely respected scribes at a time when society had begun to rely on written documents more and more. Art for art's sake hardly commended itself then any more than today; a utilitarian criterion alone seemed to justify expenditure of great time and effort. Using this measuring stick, the professions Ben Sira considers inferior to that of scribes receive high marks. For him, however, other standards canceled this advantage, particularly access to power and fame.

Contemporary disdain for menial laborers has even less to commend it, for this pejorative understanding of the work of one's hands is based primarily on economic factors. Elitists in contemporary North America consider monetary earnings the significant factor in dismissing many occupations as beneath their dignity. This attitude has been internalized by countless workers who labor in jobs from which they receive no personal satisfaction. Lacking adequate self-respect, they take little or no pride in the finished product of their labor. Consequently, the prophecy by elitists becomes self-fulfilling, and people fall into a kind of "treadmill" existence—living out existentially the myth of Sisyphus.

Although some early Christians succumbed to the seductive lure of pre-eminence, both Jesus and the apostle Paul resisted the disciples' desire to be first in rank. Their arguments in rejecting such efforts to attain honor and authority recommend subservience and emphasize the mutual interdependence of the corporate body, the church. Whoever wishes to be first in rank must serve others, for that kind of pre-eminence alone accords with God's will for Christians. Moreover, just as no part of the body can boast that it is more important than another, so also all vocations in the church are complementary and, therefore, equally important.

This understanding of spiritual calling can be meaningfully applied to the diverse ways by which Christians earn a living. All worthy labor, manual or otherwise, contributes to the body politic. No type of profession has more inherent worth than another, although society still tends to value some types of work more highly than others. Manual labor is just as important as its intellectual counterpart. The important thing is that Christians do their work, whatever its nature, with pride and dignity. Having done so, they need not yield to anyone who insinuates that manual labor lacks worth. Perhaps in this way Christians can resist the debilitating trend to connect earnings and self-worth. It is worth recalling that the apostle Paul boasts that he worked night and day (1 Thess 2:9) so that he could preach the gospel without charge (cf. 1 Corinthians 9).

SIRACH 39:12–43:33

PART VII

OVERVIEW

A carefully crafted hymn extolling the Creator for a well-ordered universe sits awkwardly alongside a harrowing assessment of life as nightmarish. On the one hand, a smooth-running world would appear to offer no refuge for evil and its woeful consequences. On the other hand, human existence is fraught with ambiguity and outright wickedness. Ben Sira endeavors to provide a rational defense of things along the same lines offered by Hellenistic philosophers of his day. The wretchedness of daily existence was compounded by the possibility of falling into shame, both as a result of one's own failure and as a consequence of conduct by one's daughters. Because of the economic value placed on the virginity of eligible wives and their ability to conceive, any behavior that jeopardized either was condemned by society in the strongest way possible. Ben Sira shared this concern. This topic gives way, however, to more elevated thoughts about the beauty of the created world—its wonderful mystery, the Creator's intimate knowledge of all aspects of creation, and a summons to praise.

SIRACH 39:12-35, IN PRAISE OF THE CREATOR

COMMENTARY

This hymn in praise of the Creator (vv. 16-31), together with its introduction (vv. 12-15) and personal conclusion (vv. 32-35), is essentially a theodicy. The "very academic hymn"[228] addresses the question about apparent anomalies in the world, specifically "What is this or why is that?" (vv. 17, 21). As we have seen, in dealing with the general problem of evil Ben Sira employs traditional arguments; for example, he promises eventual rectification, interprets undeserved suffering as disciplinary, and points out that appearances often deceive. Failing to arrive at a satisfactory answer to theodicy, he insists that God is just despite all evidence to the contrary, and humans should, therefore, acknowledge divine mystery by raising their voices in praise rather than in protest.

In addition to such traditional responses to the problem of theodicy, Ben Sira offers at least two new ways of looking at this vexing issue, one philosophical, the other psychological. He takes up the Greek rational argument that the cosmos consists of complementary pairs, good things that promote virtue and harmful things that punish wickedness. Moreover, Ben Sira insists that inner psychological states determine how people view outer experiences and that wicked persons are afflicted with anxiety. The unknown author of the book of Wisdom develops the latter idea more fully in Wis 16:24–19:22, which describes the manner in which fear transforms ordinary things into frightening sources of terror.[229]

39:12-15. Ben Sira's invitation to sing God's praises mentions "faithful children"

---

228. Snaith observes that "this learned discussion, typical of the lecture room... thus becomes a very academic hymn, with the doctrinal lesson that 'All that the Lord... commands will happen in due time' repeated almost like a refrain." See Snaith, *Ecclesiasticus or The Wisdom of Jesus, Son of Sirach*, 195.

229. Crenshaw, "The Problem of Theodicy in Sirach," 47-64, examines the various responses to apparent injustice in Ben Sira's teaching and in the book of Wisdom, where the psychological answer dominates. See also Crenshaw, *Urgent Advice and Probing Questions*, 155-74.

(υἱοὶ ὅσιοι *huioi hosioi*), a departure from the usual vocative without a qualifying adjective (v. 13) following an appeal for attention. Furthermore, he actually states that this particular hymn should be recited (v. 15). The admission in v. 12 that the author has not exhausted his teachings echoes the initial remarks at the opening of book two, where Ben Sira describes his renewed effort to deal responsibly with a mighty stream of ideas (24:30-34).

The dominant image there was that of a canal that grew into a river and then into a sea; here the emphasis falls on the full moon and flowers growing alongside a flowing stream. There the imagery was restricted to the author; here he moves a step further to include his students in the circle of praise, recalling in the process the pleasant fragrances of nature and also those associated with worship. He likens hymnody and the accompanying music to the beauty and fragrance of oleanders, lilies, and incense. Just as personified wisdom flourished in 24:13-34, so also the scribe, who in 39:1-11 represents Ben Sira's ideal, thrives in the same way.

39:16-31. The hymn in these verses echoes the refrain in Genesis 1, affirming the goodness of everything that God created. Such an extraordinary claim in the face of so many things that seem out of place in an orderly universe must surely have encountered resistance. In the end, claim and counterclaim seem to cancel each other out, just like Ezekiel and his vocal opponents who insisted that Yahweh was unjust (Ezek 18:25-29). Ben Sira has learned a valuable lesson from Qohelet that everything is good in its time (vv. 16-17; cf. Eccl 3:11). The allusion to waters piling up, usually applied to the story about Yahweh's victory over the pursuing Egyptian army (Exod 15:8), may actually recall the separating of waters in Gen 1:9-10.

The stress on divine power and clarity of sight functions to reinforce Ben Sira's theodicy. Because no one can limit God's ability to reward virtuous people (the actual Hebrew word is תשועתו [*tĕšû'ātô*], "his saving deeds") and nothing can obscure God's vision, nothing stands in the way of dispensing accurate justice. To accomplish that end, Ben Sira insists, the Lord looks on human beings in blessing and wrath, depending on which is appropriate at a given moment. The beneficial things, intended for the faithful, consist of ten basic ingredients to a good life—an extension from the four necessities of life mentioned in 29:21 (water, bread, clothing, and a house).[230] The six additional items raise the level of comfort: fire for warmth and cooking; iron (and fire) for the making of tools and weapons; salt for flavor; milk, honey, wine, and oil to complement bread. Curiously, Ben Sira thinks that even these necessities bring misfortune to the wicked (the Hebrew word הפך [*hāpak*] implies a total overthrow as at Sodom and Gomorrah or Nineveh).[231] This language links up with v. 23, perhaps an allusion to Gen 19:24-28.

Like the blessings, which manifest themselves as basic necessities and for which Ben Sira uses the image of the Nile and the Euphrates rivers, the wrath of God comes to expression in nine natural elements (vv. 28-31). Powerful sirocco winds, a mighty tempest from the southeast, wreak havoc even on solid mountains; fire, hail, famine, pestilence, wild animals, scorpions, vipers, and the sword do the divine bidding to execute sinners. The last of these alone involves human agents. Ben Sira implies that all of nature stands ready to carry out God's wrathful decrees, as do human armies. A contrast may be implied between an obedient nature and willful human beings. To some extent, this list of natural calamities resembles that found in the account of plagues affecting Egypt in the book of Exodus (Exod 7:14–12:32).

39:32-35. In an epilogue to the hymn, Ben Sira reaffirms his long-held conviction that all of God's works are good, and he reiterates the invitation to praise the Creator. This time, at least in the Greek text, he formulates popular sentiment denying divine justice as a statement, "This is not as good as that," instead of repeating the earlier interrogative form, "What is this? What is that?" Pride of authorship prompts him to boast about leaving a written legacy of his intellectual conclusions. Although the Greek text has "Lord" (κύριος *kyrios*) in vv. 16 and 33, the Hebrew

---

230. The effort to discover the fundamental elements of the universe represents a similar concern—e.g., the supposition that the universe consists of earth, air, fire, and water.

231. Sasson, *Jonah*, 234-35, 267, discusses the ambiguity of the niphal use of this verb and thinks the prophet implied that the city would turn over (reform).

has "God" (אל *'ēl*); in v. 35 a marginal note to the Hebrew has "his holy name" (שם קדשו *šēm qodšô*; cf. שם הקדוש *šēm haqqādôš* in the text), while the Greek uses *kyrios* (the Hebrew text has survived in MS B from 39:15, beginning with the reference to songs, to the end of the book). In the Talmudic tractate *Sabb.* 77*b* a similar statement to Ben Sira's affirmation uses the customary rabbinic epithet, "the Holy One." It reads: "Not a single thing of those which the Holy One created in this world has been created in vain, as though it did not fulfil its purpose."

REFLECTIONS

1. The primary basis for lauding the Creator, according to Ben Sira, is the goodness of creation. That optimism does not come easily, for some things seem out of place in an orderly universe. Even persons who believe in the essential harmony of creation occasionally adopt the interrogative mode: Why do bad things happen to decent people? What possible justification for cancer cells can one posit?

The beauty of Ben Sira's position resides in the way he situates doubting questions within the framework of spontaneous praise. This manner of facing up to the anomalies of existence prevents skepticism from becoming counterproductive. Confident that the maladies of existence, which Ben Sira calls curses, are divine instruments for punishing sinners, he assumes that time alone will convey fuller knowledge to doubters who refuse to turn away from their Creator.

2. The familiar phrase from *The Rubáiyát* of Omar Khayyám, "A loaf of bread, a jug of wine, and thou," sums up a famous lover's effort to articulate the bare necessities of life. Perhaps Ben Sira's version of the essentials in terms of bread, water, clothing, and a home (Sir 29:21) is more realistic, although his additional reflection expands this list further still. The move from four necessities to ten (Sir 39:26) speaks volumes about human nature, for it reflects the desire to make life not merely tolerable but to some degree comfortable as well. People who have enjoyed the pleasures of the good life may have moments of nostalgia in thinking about a simpler existence, but rarely do they voluntarily relinquish the comforts they have come to know.

In some ways Ben Sira's list strikes modern readers as somewhat one-sided, for it is slanted entirely toward the needs and desires of the body. For an intellectual, as he surely was, the absence of anything cerebral, spiritual, or aesthetic in this list of essentials for living is surprising. Can one imagine life without a book, worship, or music? Whether one agrees with Ben Sira in this regard or wishes to extend the list even further, religious enthusiasts ought to give him credit for asking an important question: What absolute minimum can one possess and still live? Because many citizens of impoverished countries face this question every day, the issue for them is existential rather than hypothetical. Our pondering of the matter may open up the floodgates of compassion as we grasp the magnitude of the gulf between them and us.

The enormous pressure to buy more and more will undoubtedly continue, for it fuels the international economy. So will pangs of guilt when Christians succumb to its persuasive power. Caught in the middle between external forces and inner compulsion, thoughtful individuals grope for adequate criteria for deciding how to spend their financial assets. Asking Ben Sira's unstated question and reaching a conclusion about the essentials for living will equip them to act morally in this situation.

SIRACH 40:1–41:13, LIFE'S WRETCHEDNESS

COMMENTARY

Ben Sira's description of human bondage to sin and death is broken only by a series of comparisons in which the second-mentioned item is preferred (40:18-27), and to some degree by a brief unit about contrasts in conduct, the second of which brings lasting joy (40:12-17; in 40:14, however, the positive one appears first). This grim depiction of the human situation stands in the shadow of Ben Sira's lofty expression of praise for the goodness of creation.

40:1-11. The initial section depicts the heavy yoke worn by all creatures but felt seven times more severely by the wicked. Ben Sira observes that the yoke cannot be lifted from birth to death; he uses the expression "mother of all the living" with reference to the earth. Naturally, this thought echoes the ancient story about the creation of Adam and Eve from dust and the identification of Eve as the mother of all living persons. The language, now traditional, occurs also in the prologue to the book of Job: "Naked I came from my mother's womb, and naked shall I return there" (Job 1:21 NRSV). In this instance, "there" is probably a euphemism for Sheol, not a reference to the mother's womb. Not only do people endure trouble (this word, עסק [ʿōseq], does not occur in the HB) and anxiety during their waking hours, but at night they have dreadful nightmares, waking at their moment of greatest need (reading χρεία [chreia] for σωτηρία [sōtēria], "salvation"). No one escapes this yoke, neither the ruler nor the subject, neither rich nor poor. Ben Sira associates the flood with other calamities that God created especially for the wicked. The only relief comes at death, according to v. 11, when dust returns to dust (Gen 3:19), and lifebreath goes back to its divine source (Eccl 12:7).

The poetic niceties of this poem include interlinear parallelism: "the one who sits on a splendid throne" (v. 3) and "the one who wears purple and a crown" (v. 4); "the one who grovels in the dust and ashes" (v. 3) and "the one who is clothed in burlap" (v. 4); the symbolic reference to seven sources of misery (v. 5), signifying fullness, and the explicit statement in v. 8; the portrayal of inner anxiety and the comparable depiction of external dangers; the reference in v. 3a to the civil authority and in v. 4a to the religious authority.[232]

In this section Ben Sira borrows ideas from a tradition about the miserable lot entrusted to humans: e.g., the curse on rebellious Adam in Gen 3:17-20; Job's reflections about the awful plight of human beings in Job 7 and 14; and the unflattering opinion about the human imagination in Gen 6:5. Although these ancient texts describe a universal human bondage, Ben Sira qualifies this misfortune by attributing far more trouble to sinners than to good people. For Job, divine watchfulness exacerbated suffering, whereas Ben Sira thinks of God's surveillance as assurance of justice.

40:12-17. These verses reaffirm Ben Sira's belief in the divine ordering of things to benefit the righteous on earth. True to precedent, he employs images from nature to reinforce his point. Wealth unjustly acquired resembles wadis in winter, temporarily filled with water from torrential downpours, only to dry up in summer. Similarly, possessions are like deafening thunder, all sound and fury and soon vanished. Children of evil parents are like trees growing on a rocky precipice, their roots clinging to unsubstantial soil and lacking adequate moisture, or like reeds along a riverbank inviting passersby to pull them up (cf. Job 8:11-12). Deeds of kindness, however, flourish for a long time, like a well-tended garden.

40:18-27. Ben Sira introduces ten comparative sayings that lead up to his favorite concept, fear of the Lord. Ancient sages were fond of this device, which modern interpreters label "better-than proverbs."[233] Each of these sayings juxtaposes two ideas, the second of which is deemed more desirable than the first. Such sayings greatly assist scholars

---

232. Skehan and Di Lella, *The Wisdom of Ben Sira,* 470.
233. On the forms of sapiential discourse, see Crenshaw, "Wisdom," 225-64. See also Crenshaw, *Urgent Advice and Probing Questions,* 45-77.

in understanding a relative scale of values in a prominent sage from second-century BCE Judah. The positive valence of good wives, mentioned twice in the superior category (vv. 19, 23), and of friendship (v. 20; cf. the Greek, which has "wisdom") is noteworthy. Some of the sayings occasion no surprise; the discovery of hidden treasure is better than having to work for one's fortune; help from God (as reward for almsgiving) is superior to assistance from family and friends.

Other sayings make one raise an eyebrow, at least momentarily: Intelligent advice is preferable to wealth; a pleasant voice is better than music; green shoots of grain bring more pleasure than grace and beauty (because they indicate a bountiful harvest); wisdom is preferable to progeny and an honorable reputation, acquired through building a city. Ben Sira may reflect the Greek practice of naming cities after prominent figures in society (e.g., Philippi, named after Philip of Macedon; Alexandria, named after Alexander the Great; Antioch, named after Antiochus III).

The threefold use of the phrase "the fear of the Lord" in the final couplet (vv. 26-27) reinforces the importance of piety to Ben Sira, a note already struck indirectly in v. 24, perhaps also in the initial allusion to wisdom, inasmuch as fear of the Lord both leads to and comprises the essence of wisdom. Ben Sira emphasizes the sufficiency of religious devotion; safe in divine solicitude, the one who fears the Lord flourishes like a garden and basks in honor.

40:28-30. Verse 28 introduces the two subjects of the next section as begging and death. In 29:24-27 Ben Sira discussed the indignity of having to eat at someone else's table. Here he raises that topic again, reiterating the loss of respect associated with such dependence. Verse 30 highlights the hypocrisy involved in begging, the necessary self-effacement that masks a bitter resentment within, aptly likened to a fire. Reduced to such non-life, one would be better off dead (v. 28). Burton Mack has conjectured that Ben Sira may have in mind the Cynic practice of begging as a form of social critique.[234] Even if one assumes that Ben Sira's audience comprised an elite group, it does not follow that he would remain silent about the subject of self-reliance. Advice against begging may simply be a traditional topic in such sapiential advice.

41:1-4. Two different particles in Hebrew, the one (הוי *hôy*) signifying grudging reluctance in the face of an unpleasant decree (הק *ḥōq*) and the other (האח *he'āḥ*) connoting open arms, contrast reactions to death by people in opposite circumstances. The first interjection refers to a person who has adequate resources, personal and otherwise, to enjoy life, whereas the second indicates someone whose aged body "stumbles and trips," having grown weary of the accompanying aches and privations. Naturally, death appears differently to these persons. One thing they have in common, however, is a date with the Grim Reaper. Ben Sira, therefore, urges acceptance of the divine decree as universal and implies that questioning the wisdom of that statute makes no sense. The Hebrew of this verse in MS A has "individual decree" or "statute" (חק *ḥōq*) and "laws," "instruction" (תורות *tôrôt*), but the scroll from Masada reads "end" (קץ *qēṣ*), as does the Syriac (MS B has "portion" [חלק *ḥēleq*]). Presumably, he thinks the interrogative mode, so typical of existence on earth, vanishes at death, whether it comes early or late. Ben Sira assumes that all distinctions, and hence inequities, disappear in Sheol.

41:5-13. This disquisition on death prompts Ben Sira to reflect on those left behind, particularly children, in his view a person's only access to a kind of immortality. The emphasis falls on offspring of the wicked who have spurned the Most High God, for to them clings a heavy curse. Ben Sira turns to describe the opposite situation of parents whose virtue endures in memory long after their bodies have returned to dust. True to form, he praises reputation over gold, which disappears long before an honorable name does. The three uses of "memorial" (שם *šēm*, lit., "name") in vv. 11-13 reflect Ben Sira's high assessment of reputation. The contrast between the ungodly and a lasting name could hardly be starker. According to v. 10, the wicked will vanish into nothingness ("waste" [תהו *tōhû*]; cf. Gen 1:2; Isa 40:17 for *tōhû* and אפס [*'epes*], "cessation" together as here).

---

234. Burton Mack, "Annotations to Sirach," in *The HarperCollins Study Bible*, ed. Wayne A. Meeks (New York: HarperCollins, 1993) 1595.

REFLECTIONS

1. For Ben Sira the highest priority went to religious devotion, which he called "the fear of the Lord." In two ways he signaled the importance of religion, first by mentioning it three times and, second, by leading up to the subject as a sort of crescendo. Closely behind religious service were wisdom and reliable counsel, which Ben Sira prized more than a lasting memory or wealth respectively.[235] Next came a good wife, followed by love, pleasant speech, and the early signs of a bountiful harvest. This corrective to the essentials of life shows that Ben Sira did not let physical appetites dictate important decisions.

From the items he uses in comparing favored things with less desirable ones, Ben Sira opens a door into his own system of values. None of the less-desirables deserve to be labeled as undesirable, least of all children—the only immortality accessible to Jews in ancient times. Likewise, gold and silver, wine and music, grace and beauty belong to the good things in life.

If one really can be known by what one treasures most dearly, then we would do well to explore Ben Sira's question of priorities for ourselves. Precisely where does our treasure lie? In spiritual things or in material comforts? Once we have settled that question decisively and honestly, we shall be ready to go a step farther and ask how the newly ascertained list of priorities can transform our lives and enrich our spirits.

Ben Sira did not conceal the fact that a religious value system often clashes with the dominant mores of society, but when that occurred he urged people to dare to be different. In Christian terms, that may mean courageously saying no to any number of activities, such as excessive spending, unethical financial dealings, cheating in school, immoderate drinking, casual sex, supporting political candidates who are racist or otherwise corrupt, voting for those who think the United States should traffic in weapons. Positively, daring to be different may mean spending time working at unselfish causes and volunteering to help those members of society who have difficulty fending for themselves.

2. What explanation for this treadmill existence makes the most sense? Ben Sira could not make up his mind. Some of his remarks point toward death and the unpleasantries leading up to it as part and parcel of the human condition from the very beginning, whereas other comments place the blame on Eve for disobeying a divine prohibition. Perhaps his inability to opt for one or the other testifies to Ben Sira's awareness of the complexity of the problem.

In one sense, the failure to resolve this dilemma leaves human beings vulnerable to enormous anxiety about death, when ready acceptance of mortality as the human condition has the potential of reducing such concern greatly. To Ben Sira's credit, he realized that the lion's share of worry is self-generated, like a nightmare. In our time, a decisive shift is taking place in that many people worry more about the manner of death than the fact of death itself. Death with dignity has introduced a new factor into the discussion of one's eventual demise. If a person views death as something other than punishment, then death's stigma disappears.

For Christians, death does not signify the ultimate word, for they place their hope in God's gracious activity aimed at drawing humankind into a kingdom of the redeemed. The last word, according to Christian hope, is one of divine acceptance, symbolized by the story of Jesus' resurrection and the anticipation of a resurrection of believers. If that hope is firmly grounded, Christians have a far better reason than Ben Sira had to lift up their voices in constant praise of the Creator and redeemer.

---

235. This arrangement of priorities is not specifically stated in the text but constitutes Ben Sira's probable scale of values, when seen in the overall context of the book.

SIRACH 41:14–42:8, ON SHAME

COMMENTARY

Honor and its negative counterpart, shame, were strong motivating forces in ancient Mediterranean cultures. Ben Sira demonstrates the appeal this ethical system had on the Jewish world, although he seems to represent the minority opinion on several specifics. After underscoring the areas in which Jewish readers ought to feel shame (41:17–42:1a), he mentions some types of behavior that, he thinks, should occasion no sense of embarrassment (42:1b-8). Some of these may have been disputed because they represent a clash between Hellenistic and Jewish values.

42:1b-8. First and foremost, the Mosaic legislation made demands on Jews that set them apart from their Hellenized compatriots and gave the impression of provincialism. Ben Sira admonishes Jews not to be ashamed of the law and covenantal obligations. In a highly mercenary environment, the temptation to make a profit through unethical means must have overtaken many individuals. Ben Sira urges them to keep accurate records of expenses and to give honest measures, keeping weights and scales completely free of the slightest particles of dust or grain. This concern for accuracy of weights is reinforced in the *m. B. Bat.* 5:10, where merchants are enjoined to clean their measures twice a week, polish weights every week, and clean their scales after every business transaction.[236] Ben Sira also reinforces traditional sexual mores in an era of free attitudes toward sensuality; moralists, he says, ought not to be ashamed of rebuking even their elders for sexual impropriety.

This section actually treats merchants neutrally, accepts profit as appropriate in dealing with them, and insists on written records for deposits or withdrawals. The Zenon papyri from third-century BCE Egypt furnish exceptional evidence of at least one royal official's obsession with an exact account of all business transactions.[237] Ben Sira's own students were probably literate, but the extent of literacy among average citizens is unclear. If it never exceeded 10 percent in classical Greece,[238] not many Jewish citizens in Ben Sira's day likely would have known how to read and write, for the agrarian economy offered few incentives to literacy.

The remarkable comment in 42:1b about sinning to save face reveals the dilemma in which many Jews found themselves at this time. Rather than following Jewish custom and calling attention to their foreignness to Greek culture, those Jews who sought a place of honor in the eyes of Hellenists found themselves breaking the Mosaic law for the sake of appearing to be like their cultured rulers. Ben Sira thinks that such Jews should not be ashamed to be different.

41:17–42:1a. The list of conduct unbecoming to Ben Sira's students contains no surprises, unless it be the paucity of sins mentioned.[239] Ben Sira includes some observations about social location, specifically the authoritative figures in second-century BCE Judah—parents, rulers, judges, the assembled congregation, friends. The list begins in the family circle and ends there: "the place where you live" (v. 19). As usual in sapiential literature, sexual sins dominate, perhaps because of the youthful age of the students, but not entirely so, because sages also warn against the sexual follies of old men. Even lust—for a prostitute or for another man's wife—is included here, because it leads to unfortunate consequences. Notably, Ben Sira mentions abuse of authority, the use of a slave girl for sexual purposes (v. 22), and poor table manners (v. 19).

The Greek translator seems to have misunderstood v. 19, reading אלה (*'ālâ*, "oath") as אלה (*'ĕlōâ*, "God"), and then rendering the phrase "before the truth of God and the covenant."[240]

---

236. Oesterley, *The Wisdom of Jesus the Son of Sirach or Ecclesiasticus*, 279, refers to *B. Bat.* 88a for the same stipulation.

237. C. Robert Harrison, Jr., "Quoheleth in Social-Historical Perspective" (Ph.D. diss., Duke University, 1991), uses the Zenon papyri as a partial means of illuminating the context within which Ecclesiastes was written. They preserve in part the returns from landed estates in the Ptolemaic province of Judea that were worked by tenant-farmers.

238. After an exhaustive study of literacy in classical Greece, William V. Harris reaches this conservative conclusion. See Harris, *Ancient Literacy* (Cambridge, Mass.: Harvard University Press, 1989) 65-115.

239. Biblical laws and proverbs are never exhaustive, suggesting that they serve a representative function.

240. Marginal notes in the Hebrew text suggest that an earlier version has been compared to the present MS B and that corrective glosses have been added to the latter. See Oesterley, *Ecclesiasticus*, 279.

41:14-16. The introduction to this section on shame includes two verses that also occur in 20:30-31, except for the vocative and accompanying imperatives with their objects ("My children, be true to your training and be at peace"). The Hebrew text has a title above v. 16, "Instruction Concerning Shame" (מוסר בשת *mûsār bōšet*).

SIRACH 42:9-14, ON PROTECTING DAUGHTERS' HONOR

COMMENTARY

This brief section takes up one additional area in which unwanted shame easily arises: the disgraceful conduct of a young woman. Ben Sira fails to note that a man is also implicated in her offense, and even if one emends the text of v. 14 to read "Better a religious daughter than a shameless son," the misogynism remains nonetheless.[241] In this regard, Ben Sira was by no means alone, as shown by the Jewish prayer thanking God that the male speaking the words is not a Gentile, a slave, or a woman.

Ben Sira's observations grew out of the importance Jewish society attached to virginity, primarily because of its value when young women entered into marriage. Fathers, whose role in selecting husbands for their daughters became precarious in cases of lost virginity, worried prior to the wedding date, and even subsequent to it, lest the bride be either unfaithful or barren. To protect unmarried daughters, Ben Sira advises parents to guard them closely and thus prevent them from becoming known as women of easy morals, a byword. To hide a young daughter from a male's gaze and resulting seduction, Ben Sira urges precautionary measures such as preventing her from looking out a window and enjoying the relative freedom—and conversation—of married women. The well-known ivory carving depicting a woman peering from a window reveals this religious motif as common in the ancient Near East, although its full implications are still unclear (cf. Prov 7:6).[242]

The concluding remarks in vv. 13-14, which are textually uncertain, leave no doubt that Ben Sira held a low opinion of women. The analogy of moths may mean that just as garments attract moths, so also wickedness lures women, or that insects fly from one piece of cloth to another and women go from man to man. Ben Sira's comment that a man's wickedness is better than a woman's goodness invites modern readers to suspect that he has taken leave of his senses at this point. True, some women bring shame and disgrace, but they have not seized a monopoly on such conduct. Many men do the same, as Ben Sira surely knew. Perhaps his extreme remarks reveal how far an ancient Jewish teacher would go to protect ethnic identity in a context of cultural and personal subservience.

---

241. Skehan and Di Lella, examine emendations and readings suggested by J. Strugnell and F. M. Cross, the latter of whom translates as follows: "but better a daughter of a religious wife than a son of the shameless one." See Skehan and Di Lella, *The Wisdom of Ben Sira*, 480.

242. A photograph of an ivory carving of a woman at a window, dating from the first half of the eighth century BCE, can be found in James B. Pritchard, ed., *The Ancient Near East in Pictures* (Princeton, N.J.: Princeton University Press, 1954) 39, pl. 131.

SIRACH 42:15–43:33, THE WONDERS OF CREATION

COMMENTARY

This majestic hymn about the wonders of creation introduces the much longer praise of famous men in 44:1–50:24, as the probable use of "to the pious" (לחסידים *lĕḥăsîdîm*) in v. 33 (cf. the Greek "to the devout ones" [τοῖς εὐσεβέσιν *tois eusebesin*]) and "men of kindness" (= "pious men" [אנשי חסד *'anšê ḥesed*]) in 44:1 makes clear.[243] This hymn consists of a poem on the inscrutable knowledge of the Creator (42:15-21), a long section describing the wonders of nature (42:22–43:26), and a conclusion inviting readers to praise the sovereign Lord (43:27-33). In many respects this hymn resembles Psalms 29; 104–105; and Job 38:1-38, as well as noun lists (onomastica) from Egypt and Mesopotamia, which include, among other things, lists of astrophysical phenomena. Such lists were used in educational circles to teach foreign languages and knowledge about the natural world.

42:15-21. The idea that the universe came into existence as a result of divine utterance recalls Gen 1:1-31, a concept that comes to prominence in Wis 9:1; 2 Esdr 6:38; Jdt 16:14; and in the prologue to the Gospel of John. Ben Sira concedes that the task of declaring the full scope of God's works exceeds the capacity of the angelic hosts, specifically astrophysical phenomena enlisted in divine service (cf. *1 Enoch* 1:9). Even the abyss (תהום *tĕhôm*, "Tiamat," the chaos dragon of the deep) and the depths of the human heart lie open before the Most High's penetrating gaze, Ben Sira asserts, and nothing is hidden. That includes the future, which God knows as intimately as the past, without benefit of counselors (cf. Isa 40:14). This theme echoes a similar one in Deutero-Isaiah. Such bold claims function as a theodicy, one based on the view that the Creator sees everything. The Persian notion of the roving eyes of the deity and the Egyptian concept of the eye of Ra, the sun god, reinforced the belief in a harmonious universe. Believing that the Creator is the same yesterday, today, and forever, Ben Sira found reason to trust in divine consistency.

42:22–43:26. The idea of opposites, expressed already in 33:15, recurs in 42:24, in this instance connoting variety and thus contributing to the beauty of the universe. Beginning in 43:1, Ben Sira describes astrophysical phenomena (sun, moon, and stars) before turning to geophysical phenomena, such as the rainbow, lightning, clouds, winds, snow, frost, ice, and dew. Finally, he mentions the ocean, that unexplored abyss in which mythological beings were believed to cavort, according to Job 38:8-11; 40–41 and various mythological texts in Deutero-Isaiah (Isa 51:9-10; cf. Isa 27:1; 30:7; Ezek 29:3) and Psalms.

Although the sun is the first to be introduced, the emphasis falls on the moon, presumably because of its determination of the religious calendar. Biblical precedent observed the solar calendar, as did the community at Qumran, whose opponents observed the lunar calendar. Verse 8 contains a play on the words for "moon" (חדש *ḥōdeš*) and "renew" (חדש *ḥādaš*), while using the analogy of a fire signal indicating an army's beginning to march at night. Ben Sira waxes poetic in comparing snow to the deft and orderly descent of birds and locusts, icicles to thorns, frost to ashes scattered on the ground, and a frozen pond to a warrior's breastplate. He concludes this section by returning to the thought of the creative word, this time extending the idea to its cohesive power (43:26).

43:27-33. The final admission that such praise only touches the surface makes a daring assertion: "Let the final word be: 'He is the all'" (cf. Eccl 12:13). The similarity of this confession to Stoic pantheism is undeniable, although Ben Sira goes on to insist that the Creator is greater than all the wonders of the universe (v. 28). In Ben Sira's view, a single divine principle holds the universe together, but God is not encompassed by

---

243. The Hebrew text has only the initial (*lamedh*); the Greek translator seems to have read either *lĕḥăsîdîm* or *l'anšê ḥesed*.

that entity (cf. the Vg's *ipse est in omnibus,* "He is in all"). This hymn utilizes both Jewish and Stoic ideas of creation and the ordering of things. According to Stoic philosophy, the *logos* (divine rationality) permeates the cosmos and holds it together. In the ancient world, mythological creatures representing chaos were thought to have threatened the divine order; according to v. 23, the Creator brought these creatures, here called Rahab, under control (cf. Job 9:13; 26:12). The God of such power and exquisite artistry justly deserves Ben Sira's adjective "awesome" (נורא מאד ונפלאות *nôrāʾ měʾōd wěniplāʾôt,* "exceedingly terrifying and wondrous," v. 29; cf. Joel 2:11, ונורא מאד [*wěnôrāʾ měʾōd,* "exceedingly dreadful"]).

REFLECTIONS

Anyone who genuinely cherishes the spiritual dimension of reality finds it impossible to restrain songs of praise, for we are surrounded by signs of grace from our waking moment to the second our eyes close in sleep. Grateful hearts seem capable of bursting if we do not express appreciation for the supreme gift of life.

Traditionally, believers have tried to buttress their faith by using the argument from design, believing that the Creator planted in the created world witnesses to the source of all things. We know today that equally cogent arguments against the existence of God can be mustered from apparent flaws in nature and that adaptability is the very nature of things as they evolve. Nevertheless, believers are encompassed by a vast universe almost as mysterious as the God they worship.

The ancient world, like certain segments of the modern population, believed that the mysteries of the universe were revealed to a small band of initiates, who guarded that knowledge zealously from that time forward. Ben Sira acknowledged no such sect, choosing instead to confess his own ignorance in the face of overwhelming mystery. That lack of knowledge did not rule out personal acquaintance with God in some small way, and he readily claimed to have direct experience of the Holy One. Nevertheless, in the end he confessed that his best effort to praise God only scratched the surface, that the moment he arrived at the end of his song he had merely reached the beginning. That perceptive insight cautions modern worshipers against assuming that we have exhausted what can and should be said about the one who dwells in utter darkness.

Ben Sira's endeavor to provide an easy guide to extolling the Creator unites him with countless writers of hymns that have enriched worship over the years. Poets, theologians, and musicians have collaborated to provide a rich repertoire of hymnody that both instructs and motivates, songs that express the unutterable and lead to noble aspirations and deeds.

SIRACH 44:1–51:30
PART VIII

OVERVIEW

This poetic section praising Israel's ancestors follows naturally from the hymn extolling God's creative activity (39:12–43:33), for Ben Sira emphasizes divine election of the heroes lifted up for memorializing. The long account of past worthies concludes with an encomium of Simeon II, the high priest contemporary with Ben Sira (50:1-21), and a brief personal word from Ben Sira (50:22-24). An introduction (44:1-15) mentions a dozen categories of leaders deserving commendation, which then leads to a selective record of Israel's history, beginning with Enoch. The following names complete the list: Noah; Abraham; Isaac and Jacob; Moses; Aaron; Phinehas; Joshua and Caleb; the judges, with specific reference to Samuel only; Nathan; David; Solomon; Rehoboam and Jeroboam; Elijah; Elisha; Hezekiah; Isaiah; Josiah; Jeremiah; Ezekiel; Job; the Twelve Prophets (unnamed individually); Zerubbabel; Jeshua the son of Josadak; and Nehemiah—with a sort of "lest we forget" Enoch, Joseph, Shem, Seth, Enosh, and Adam.

SIRACH 44:1-15, INTRODUCTION

COMMENTARY

The Hebrew text (MS B) has the title "Praise of the Ancestors of Old"; a shorter title, "Praise of the Ancestors," appears in most Greek, Latin, and Syriac manuscripts. The phrase "in their generations" (v. 1) implies a listing in chronological order. Verses 3-6 specify twelve categories of greatness: rulers, men of valor, counselors, prophets, wise leaders, guardians of tradition ("lawgivers"), instructors, compilers of wise sayings, composers, authors, the rich, and the peaceful. This entire unit has a striking end rhyme, תם (*tām*; except for ם [*ām*] in v. 2 and תב [*tāb*] in v. 5). Ben Sira makes a surprising concession in vv. 8-9 that some pious individuals died without leaving a "name," despite his earlier assurance that good people can count on a living memory. Presumably, he offers this brief introduction as a eulogy to these forgotten and nameless persons, together with all others who will be mentioned in the body of the epic poem. The latter have received appropriate burial and are called to memory by the assembled congregation.

The choice of the number twelve to indicate classes of people probably derives from its general use to designate completeness, as in twelve tribes of Israel, twelve months, twelve memorial stones, twelve disciples. All of these men are called "devout persons" (אנשי חסד *'anšê ḥesed*), the legacy of Elyon, the Most High.[244]

The emphasis on sages in vv. 3-5 reflects Ben Sira's particular bias, one that does not manifest itself in the actual selection of heroes that follows. A priestly preference easily surfaces in that portrait of great figures of the past with whom God has worked, and this sacerdotal interest expresses itself in both content and scope. This type of historical retrospect has remote antecedents in Neh 9:6-37; Psalms 78; 105–106; 135–136;

---

244. The expression "those who lift up a proverb in writing" (v. 5) is peculiar, but an emendation to במכתם (*bemiktam*, "lyric") to restore a conjectured end rhyme *tam* has nothing to commend it. See Skehan and Di Lella, *The Wisdom of Ben Sira*, 499.

Ezek 20:4-44 (cf. Jdt 5:5-21; 1 Macc 2:51-64), although none of these texts focuses on specific human figures. The closest text is Wis 10:1–12:27, which traces Israel's early history by means of allusions to easily identified persons, beginning with Adam. The other historical surveys differ qualitatively in the manner of extolling God, and any human being mentioned is incidental. Some interpreters think Hellenistic encomia serve as the model for this historical survey, although conceding that Ben Sira has made many adjustments in the process.[245] (See Reflections at 50:1-24.)

245. On the affinities between Sirach 44–50 and encomia, see Mack, *Wisdom and the Hebrew Epic*; Lee, *Studies in the Form of Sirach 44–50*. Rollston challenges this interpretation of the text in Sirach in "The Non-Encomiastic Features of Ben Sira 44–50."

SIRACH 44:16–45:26, THE SEVEN COVENANTAL FIGURES

COMMENTARY

44:16. Beginning with Noah, seven recipients of covenant promises are praised: Noah, Abraham, Isaac, Jacob, Moses, Aaron, and Phinehas. Actually, the section opens with a brief comment about Enoch, an increasingly popular biblical character because of the implication that he escaped death. Later speculation credited him with heavenly journeys, during which time he received revelations of divine mysteries. Ben Sira ignores all this extra-biblical tradition, contenting himself with repeating biblical language about Enoch's pleasing the Lord and being taken up (cf. Wis 4:10; Heb 11:5). An unusual aspect of this reference to Enoch sets it apart: He is said to be an example of repentance, or knowledge. The Greek text implies that Enoch's acquisition of mysteries led to pride, for which he repented. The other figures are not lifted up as examples for readers in this way. The Hebrew fragments of Sirach from Masada do not refer to Enoch; neither does the Syriac text. This evidence suggests that the remark about him may not derive from Ben Sira, although the comment on Enoch seems rather tame. One expects more lavish praise of the kind found in later speculation about heavenly journeys and remarkable wisdom. Its absence in the text from Masada and the Syriac, therefore, may be accidental.

44:17-18. If the praise really starts with Noah, and if v. 16 constitutes a later addition, the entire section begins and ends with the two founders of civilization, Noah and Adam (v. 17; 49:16). Noah's blameless conduct elicits praise—he is "just" (צדיק *ṣaddîq*) and "perfect" (תמים *tāmîm*)—and his name gives rise to a pun on the word *remnant* (נוח *nûaḥ*). Ben Sira explicitly refers to the covenant in Gen 9:8-17, of which the rainbow served as a perpetual reminder.

44:19-21. Ben Sira cites a phrase from Gen 17:4 describing Abraham as "father of a host of nations" and attributes to him a life of obedience to the law, although God had not yet revealed the Sinaitic legislation. The covenant refers to the act of circumcision (Gen 17:9-14), which was widely practiced in the ancient world. Because the Philistines did not submit to this practice, they received the nickname "the uncircumcised" (1 Sam 17:26, 36). The test that Abraham passed alludes to Gen 22:1-19, which is specifically called a divine test (Gen 22:1). Later traditionists developed various features of this incident, interpreting the binding of Isaac as an atonement for sins. The divine oath, reiterated in Gen 22:15-18, incorporates promissory language from Gen 15:5 (cf. Ps 72:8).

44:22-23a. The observations about Isaac and Jacob derive from Gen 17:19; 28:1-4, as well as the poetic blessing in Gen 49:1-27. The Hebrew text of v. 22 reads "son" (בן *bēn*), but the margin has "in like manner" (כן *kēn*), for Isaac did not have a son for Abraham's sake. Curiously, Ben Sira says nothing about Joseph at this juncture (cf. 49:15), and this omission accords with this patriarch's minor role in subsequent tradition. At least one feature of the text applies better to Joseph than to Moses, specifically the acknowledgment that he won everyone's approval (cf.

Gen 39:4, 21, but see also Exod 2:5-10; 11:3).

44:23b–45:5. Although Ben Sira uses a variant of the traditional invocation for blessed memory ("Moses of blessed memory," rather than "may his name be blessed"), the nine bicola (five verses), as opposed to thirty-two (17 verses) for Aaron and ten (4 verses) for Phinehas, reveal Ben Sira's preference for priestly matters. The Greek translator weakened the comparison of Moses to God, rendering אלהים (ʾĕlōhîm) as "angels" (v. 2; cf. the Greek text of Ps 8:5). Moses' ability to terminate the plagues (cf. Exodus 8–10), his receipt of the Decalogue, indeed the entire Sinaitic legislation, and his unique admittance into the divine presence (Exod 33:18) place in relief the ancient assessment of him as the humblest of men (Num 12:3). The rest of the observations are more general, including direct conversation with the Lord and the commission to instruct Israel from life-giving commandments.

45:6-22. The long section praising the priest Aaron is matched only by that extolling Simeon II in 50:1-24. According to Exod 29:9; 40:15, God established a perpetual covenant of priesthood with Aaron, Moses' brother. Psalm 106:15 calls Aaron a holy man, as Ben Sira does in v. 6. The description of priestly vestments in Exodus 28–29 includes four that were worn by all priests (tunic, trousers, turban, girdle) and four worn exclusively by the high priest (breastplate, apron, the upper garment, and the frontlet). Ben Sira omits the girdle, while emphasizing such decorative features as pomegranates, the golden bell, embroidery of various kinds, precious stones, and a gold crown. He thinks of the bells as a reminder to the people, unless the Hebrew implies that the sound calls God's attention to the people, for whom the high priest makes intercession in the holy of holies. This whole description throws little light on the nature of the ephod, which seems to have been a sort of apron with a pouch for holding the Urim and the Thummim, sacred stones. These garments could not be worn by outsiders (v. 13), although soon after Ben Sira made this claim the office of high priest became a prize to be granted by Antiochus IV to the highest bidder (2 Macc 4:7-8, 23-27).

Verses 14-17 describe the priestly duties, and vv. 18-22 mention the rewards for faithful service. First, Ben Sira refers to the two daily offerings, called Tamid in his time. Second, the priests pronounce blessings on the people (cf. Num 6:23-27). The instructional responsibility comes next (v. 17), and nothing is said of the rendering of judgment by means of the sacred Urim and Thummim. Instead, Ben Sira mentions a heinous conspiracy, the offering of strange fire by Korah, Dathan, and Abiram (Num 16:1–17:15), as a contrast to Aaron's faithfulness. Ben Sira concludes by referring to the legitimate portion of offerings that belong to the priestly functionaries, a kind of compensation for the omission of the tribe of Levi during the allocation of the land to the twelve tribes.

Ben Sira's generous remarks about an everlasting covenant with Aaron (vv. 7, 15) suggest that the earlier rivalry between Zadokites and Aaronites has been settled, with Zadokites now incorporated into the line of Aaron. The HB mentions an eternal covenant with Phinehas, and not with Aaron (Num 25:12-13). Under King David, the Zadokites gained sole control of priestly duties and privileges.

45:23-26. The following section jumps over Aaron's son Eleazar in favor of the grandson Phinehas, as if to settle the dispute over priestly lineage once and for all. The struggle for control of the priesthood by the Oniads and the Tobiads illuminates this particular observation. The Oniads were related to Aaron on the paternal side, but the Tobiads laid claim to Aaronite ancestry through the maternal side. The latter group sought to wrest the priesthood from the Oniads in the early second century BCE. Ben Sira's reference in v. 25 to a covenant with David, though out of place here, nevertheless legitimates priesthood alongside royalty as the important social institutions of the day with divinely ordained succession. The expression "third in glory" alludes to Phinehas's place in a line of succession including Moses and Aaron. His zeal, recorded in Num 25:11, earned Phinehas a covenant of peace. This unusual praise of Phinehas as "third in glory" indicates that he was far more important in certain Jewish circles than among Christians, who hardly recognize the name (cf. Ps 106:30-31, a recollection of his zeal, which earned him righteousness for endless generations). The concluding call to bless the Lord, the "Good" (cf. 2 Chr 30:18), also wishes that divine favor will fall on the kingly figure—namely, the high priest, who in Ben Sira's time had acquired considerable political power. In essence, the high priest had become ethnarch. Verse 25 suggests that Davidic kingship was transmitted by direct succession to a single son, whereas the priestly heritage belonged to all descendants of Aaron. (See Reflections at 50:1-24.)

SIRACH 46:1-20, JOSHUA, CALEB, THE JUDGES, AND SAMUEL

COMMENTARY

This unit divides naturally into vv. 1-10 and vv. 11-20, the former praising Joshua and Caleb, the latter lauding unnamed judges and Samuel. Ben Sira unites both of these with puns on the names "Joshua" and "Samuel": v. 1, "Yahweh is salvation"; v. 13, "obtained by request."

46:1-10. Moses' two lieutenants succeeded in one respect where he failed: Joshua and Caleb were allowed to enter the land of milk and honey. Joshua's expertise in battle consisted of timely signals (Josh 8:18, 26); his intercession caused the sun to pause (Josh 13:13; cf. the LXX, which mistakenly has the sun go backward as the shadow does in Isa 38:8) and brought hailstones upon the enemy (Josh 10:11). Together with Caleb, Joshua brought a favorable report about the land of promise and urged Moses to advance there in the hope of defeating its occupants (Num 14:6-10). The number 600,000 appears in various accounts (cf. 16:10; Num 11:21; 14:38; 26:65; Deut 1:36, 38). Caleb's extraordinary strength in advanced years (Josh 14:7, 10-11) enabled him to gain mastery over his enemies, the meaning of the expression "to tread on the high places of the land" (cf. Deut 33:29).

The epithet for God in v. 5 ("the Most High, the Mighty One") occurs here for the first time in Sirach. The Hebrew אל עליון (*'ēl 'elyôn*) is used in v. 5 (twice); 47:5, 8; 48:20; 50:15 (where the Hebrew is missing, but the Greek has ὕψιστος παμβασιλεύς [*hypsistos pambasileus*, "the Most High, the king of all"]). The Hebrew title *Elyôn* occurs nine times by itself in Sirach (41:4; 42:2; 44:20; 50:16; 49:4; 41:8; 44:2; 50:17; 50:14). Before chap. 41, the names יהוה (*Yahweh*) and אלהים (*'ĕlōhîm*) occur, the former usually abbreviated ווו (*yyy*).

46:11-20. The two most prominent judges, Gideon and Samson, probably prompted Ben Sira to discuss the larger group without naming anyone, for these two men certainly succumbed to deceit (v. 11). The remark about their bones flourishing (cf. 49:10) implies that ancient Israelites believed that bones, like roots, could extend themselves vigorously (cf. the vision of dry bones in Ezekiel 37 and the story in 2 Kgs 13:21 about the power of Elisha's bones to revivify a corpse).[246]

Samuel's claim to fame is based on his extraordinary birth, his role in anointing both Saul and David to kingship, his priestly function, his prophetic office, and his unimpeachable integrity. Even his appearance after death to a frightened Saul only confirmed for Ben Sira Samuel's prophetic office, already affirmed by the deuteronomistic criterion of accuracy in predicting future events. The failure to mention Saul by name reveals how little regard Ben Sira had for Israel's first king. (See Reflections at 50:1-24.)

---

246. Cf. the Semitic ritual of pouring water on the bones of ancestors. See Oesterley, *The Wisdom of Jesus the Son of Sirach*, 316.

SIRACH 47:1-25, NATHAN, DAVID, SOLOMON, AND REHOBOAM/JEROBOAM

COMMENTARY

47:1-11. Eager to indicate prophetic continuity, Ben Sira briefly refers to Nathan, who served ("stood before") David, according to the Hebrew (the Greek has "prophesied in the days of David"). The description of David, almost entirely favorable, resembles that in 1 Chronicles 11–29, a selective use of available traditions. The opening image in v. 2 derives from the sacrificial cult; David is set apart in the same way the choice fat of an offering was lifted off for priestly consumption (Lev 4:8, 10, 19; cf. Ps 89:19). From the story about David's defeat of Goliath, Ben Sira chooses several incidents, particularly David's skill in killing lions and bears, here euphemistically called "play" (1 Sam 17:34-36); the victory over the Philistine champion (1 Sam 17:32-51); the exuberant song of triumph by local women (1 Sam 18:7); and the suppression of surrounding enemies—Moabites, Aramaeans, Edomites, Ammonites, and Philistines—as recorded in 2 Samuel 5–21. Ben Sira mentions the Philistines as the supreme instance of hostile neighbors, noting that their defeat at David's hands was permanent. That is the function of the traditional expression "until our own day" (v. 7).

Beginning with v. 8, Ben Sira concentrates on David's contribution to religious worship, especially his composition of psalms and his musical interests. The chronicler also credits David with musical instruments associated with the chanting of psalms (1 Chr 23:5; cf. Amos 6:5), as well as solemnizing religious festivals (1 Chr 23:31-32). Not until the final verse does Ben Sira acknowledge David's sins, and then only generally as a recipient of divine pardon. Like the chronicler, who does not even mention David's adultery with Bathsheba and murder of Uriah, Ben Sira prefers to dwell on David's virtues—after all, the genre requires praise rather than blame. The last word, however, remains one of grace, the perpetual covenant of kingship (v. 11; cf. 2 Samuel 7).

47:12-22. Ben Sira attributes Solomon's peaceful reign to his father's influence, although he seizes the opportunity to create a pun on the meaning of Solomon's name ("peace"). The chronicler goes so far as to credit David with making preparations for building the Temple in Jerusalem; Ben Sira merely suggests that peaceful conditions, the result of David's victories, made it possible for Solomon to build the sanctuary. Defying all odds, Solomon is reputed to have received wisdom as a youth—utterly impossible in traditional sapiential texts, which assume that wisdom can be acquired only through wide experience and over a long period.[247] Ben Sira alludes to the traditions pertaining to Solomon's wisdom preserved in 1 Kgs 3:9-12, 16-28; 5:9-11; 10:1-12. The reference to his fame's having reached distant islands probably echoes the story about the queen of Sheba, and the observation about the composition of songs, proverbs, riddles, and answers (v. 17) refers to the ancient tradition that Solomon spoke 3,000 proverbs and composed 1,005 songs (1 Kgs 5:12 [Eng. 4:32]). Later traditionists credited Solomon with considerably more compositions: Proverbs, Ecclesiastes, Song of Songs, the book of Wisdom of Solomon, the Odes of Solomon, and the Psalms of Solomon, to name a few.

The legendary traditions in 1 Kings also speak of huge sums of gold and silver that the king amassed from distant lands, and Ben Sira does not overlook this feature of Solomon's fame, despite the condemnation in Deut 17:17 of such royal practice. Only with v. 19 does Ben Sira allow himself to mention Solomon's weakness for women, for which the author of 1 Kgs 11:1-10 faults him (cf. Prov 31:3, "Give not your vigor to women, nor your strength to women who ruin kings"). Curiously, Ben Sira ignores the other complaint in 1 Kgs 11:1-13, 33: the sin of idolatry.

---
247. James L. Crenshaw, "Youth and Old Age in Qoheleth," *HAR* 10 (1986) 1-13. See also Crenshaw, *Urgent Advice and Probing Questions*, 535-47.

Verses 21-22 concede the grief occasioned by Solomon's sins and the ensuing rupture in the kingdom, but not without an emphatic affirmation of the Davidic dynasty. That explains the reference to a remnant of Jacob's descendants and a root from David's own family (v. 22).

47:23-25. These verses describe the division of David and Solomon's kingdom into two national states led by Rehoboam in the south and Jeroboam in the north. Ben Sira plays on the meaning of the name of the former, calling him "great in folly" (from רחב [*rāḥab*, "to be wide"]). The contrast between Solomon's wideness of heart (1 Kgs 5:9 [Eng. 4:29]) and his son's arrogance could hardly be greater. In the Hebrew, Ben Sira omits the name "Rehoboam," using instead the adjective for "broad, open place" (*rāḥāb*) plus the noun "people" (עַם *ʿam*) to indicate the king, whose folly consisted of increasing forced labor against the advice of senior statesmen (1 Kgs 12:1-24). Instead of naming Jeroboam, archvillain in the deuteronomistic history, Ben Sira uses a clever formula, "let his name not be mentioned" (אל יהי לו זכר *ʾal yěhî lô zēker*). The present Hebrew text has the names of both kings written out. Jeroboam's chief offense was the construction of the two rival sanctuaries at Bethel and Dan, the southernmost and northernmost borders of the new kingdom, each featuring a golden bull. (See Reflections at 50:1-24.)

SIRACH 48:1-16, THE PROPHETS ELIJAH AND ELISHA

COMMENTARY

The transition in 47:25 sets the stage for Elijah's appearance. Unlike the chronicler, who virtually ignores the history of the northern kingdom, Ben Sira focuses on the activity of the two prophets from the ninth century, passing over in silence the prophetic ministry of Amos and Hosea a century later.

48:1-11. Verse 1 continues the thought of 47:25. Wickedness ran unchecked "until a prophet arose." Ben Sira withholds the prophet's name until v. 4, once more creating a pun from familiar epithets for Elijah, "man of God" (איש אלהים *ʾîš ʾĕlōhîm*), who called down fire from God upon his enemies (אש אלהים *ʾēš ʾĕlōhîm*). From Mal 3:19, Ben Sira derives the metaphor for Elijah's word as a hot furnace, but most of the references come from 1 Kings 17–19 and 2 Kings 1–2. That includes the famine Elijah announced to the Omride ruler Ahab (1 Kgs 18:3); his zeal (1 Kgs 19:10, 14); his summoning of fire three times (1 Kgs 18:38; 2 Kgs 1:10, 12); his resuscitation of the son of the widow from Zarephath (1 Kgs 17:17-22); his condemnation of kings (1 Kgs 21:19-24); the divine rebuke at Horeb (1 Kgs 19:8-18); the anointing of kings (indirectly through Elisha; 2 Kgs 8:7-15; 9:1-13); and his ascension into heaven (2 Kgs 2:1-11). In v. 10, Ben Sira uses the formula for citing Scripture, "it is written," with reference to Mal 3:23-24 (cf. Luke 1:17; Matt 11:10, 14; 17:10-13). The phrase "to reestablish the tribes of Israel" appears in Isa 49:6. In Sir 48:10-11 it gives way to uncertain speculation about people who saw Elijah. Apparently it contains a play on the ancient account of Elisha's persistence in seeing his master ascend to heaven, but in the present form it is confused with a blessing on those who might see Elijah's return to earth. The later popular idea that Elijah would precede the Messiah does not find expression here. The strange gloss in v. 11 shifts away from the unusual form of address, which began in v. 4. This second-person speech has a precedent in 47:14-21, where Ben Sira addresses Solomon directly. In Ben Sira's view, Elijah lived up to his name, "Yahweh is my God," for his deeds were awe-inspiring (v. 4).

48:12-16. Verse 12 serves as a transition from praising Elijah to lauding his successor, but Ben Sira misunderstands the concept of inheriting a double portion to mean twice as much rather than twice one's equal share, the portion received by the oldest son. This confusion leads Ben Sira to say that Elisha performed twice as many signs as did his master (see 2 Kgs 2:9-15 for the idea that Elisha was filled with the Spirit). The story about the extraordinary power of his bones—giving life to a corpse that had come in contact with them—shows once more that Ben Sira understood prophetic activity as miraculous power rather than the communication of the divine word (cf. 2 Kgs 13:20-21). He endorses the earlier explanation for the dispersion of the ten tribes, specifically their refusal to repent (2 Kgs 18:11-12). The Hebrew text states that Judah was left—that is, continued under the rule of a legitimate descendant of David. (See Reflections at 50:1-24.)

SIRACH 48:17-25, HEZEKIAH AND ISAIAH

COMMENTARY

48:17-19. Although the deuteronomistic history gives qualified approval to six kings in Judah (Asa, Jehoshaphat, Joash, Azariah, Hezekiah, and Josiah), Ben Sira's less generous assessment restricts itself to Hezekiah and Josiah. A wordplay on the name "Hezekiah" (חזקיהו *ḥizqiyyāhû*) enables Ben Sira to speak about the king's strengthening of the capital city, Jerusalem ("he fortified" [חזק *ḥāzaq*]). To provide water for the inhabitants of the city, Hezekiah ordered workers to dig a tunnel 1,749 feet from the Spring of Gihon to the Pool of Siloam (2 Kgs 20:20; 2 Chr 32:30). In 1880, this tunnel was discovered, along with an inscription describing how this remarkable feat was accomplished.[248]

Ben Sira mentions the legendary account of Sennacherib's invasion of Judah during Hezekiah's reign, one for which three different versions have survived (2 Kgs 18:13-27, retold in 2 Chr 32:1-20; Isa 36:1-22; and the altogether different account in the annals of Sennacherib).[249] Whereas the biblical story attributes Sennacherib's withdrawal and the death of 185,000 of his soldiers to the Lord's angel, Ben Sira states that a plague ravaged the invading camp. The reference in Herodotus to a bubonic plague, often used to support the account in Isa 36:1-22, lacks evidentiary force. Such a plague would not have been restricted to the invading army, assuming that Herodotus recalled the incident. The account in 2 Kgs 18:17-35 and 19:14-19 (cf. Isa 37:15-20) about the arrogance of the Rabshakeh ascribes the prayer to Hezekiah, but Ben Sira credits the people with this invocation.

48:20-25. Spreading the hands was the usual gesture during prayer (v. 20); Ben Sira attributes the deliverance of Zion to Isaiah's mediation. The rare title for God in this verse, "the Holy One," reflects Isaianic terminology; Ben Sira probably used "Most High" (עליון *'elyôn*), as "From heaven" (ἐξ οὐρανοῦ *ex ouranou*) in the Greek suggests. In v. 22, another pun on the name "Hezekiah" occurs: "he kept firmly to the ways of David." The reference to Isaiah's visions (cf. Isa 6:1-13) introduces specific praise of the prophet: the sign that promised an extended life span to the king—namely, the backward movement of the shadow on a stairway (2 Kgs 20:6-11; Isa 38:5-8); the proclamation of comfort (Isa 40:1); and the revelation of future events (Isa 40:3-11; 42:9, 24-27). Various legends about Isaiah arose in later Judaism and survive in *The Ascension of Isaiah* and *The Martyrdom of Isaiah* (cf. Heb 11:37, "they were sawn in two," NRSV).[250] (See Reflections at 50:1-24.)

---

248. James B. Pritchard gives this inscription in translation. See Pritchard, *Ancient Near Eastern Texts Relating to the Old Testament*, 321.

249. James B. Pritchard gives this inscription in translation. See Pritchard, *Ancient Near Eastern Texts Relating to the Old Testament*, 287-88.

250. M. A. Knibb, "Martyrdom and Ascension of Isaiah," in *The Old Testament Pseudepigrapha*, ed. James H. Charlesworth (Garden City, N.Y.: Doubleday, 1985) 143-76.

SIRACH 49:1-16, JOSIAH AND SUBSEQUENT HEROES

COMMENTARY

49:1-7. A poem consisting of twenty-two bicola concludes Ben Sira's eulogy of Israel's heroes. Josiah's eradication of idolatrous worship throughout Judah earned him the approval of the deuteronomist and the chronicler (2 Kgs 23:4-24; 2 Chr 34:33), and moved Ben Sira to liken Josiah's memory to incense and honey. The remark that he grieved over Judah's betrayals refers to Josiah's reaction upon hearing the contents of the book of the law, reportedly uncovered during repairs to the Temple (2 Kgs 22:10-19). In v. 4, Ben Sira sums up the monarchy as being wicked, with three exceptions: David, Hezekiah, and Josiah. Consequently, God had given the holy city and its inhabitants into the hands of the Babylonians (vv. 4-6), as Jeremiah had prophesied (v. 7). Ben Sira refers specifically to Jeremiah's call and uses the language of the divine commission (Jer 1:5, 10). The designation of Jerusalem as "the holy city" occurs elsewhere in Neh 11:1, 8; Isa 48:2; 52:1; and Dan 9:24.

49:8-10. Ben Sira's allusion to Ezekiel comes from the visionary account in Ezek 1:4-28, which describes a sort of chariot. He mentions Job, whom Ezekiel also refers to as a righteous individual from ancient times, along with Noah and Daniel. The inclusion of Job among the other great prophets accords with the loose sense of the word *prophet* in Gen 20:7 with respect to Abraham; with the view of Josephus, who includes the book of Job among the prophets; and with later rabbinic literature.[251] The other prophets appear in Ben Sira's list as a single entity, like the book of the Twelve in the HB. He uses for the second time the formula "May their bones send forth new life from where they lie" (cf. 46:12, with reference to unnamed judges). The assertion that the so-called minor prophets overwhelmingly provided hope places extraordinary weight on such passages as Amos 9:11-15; Joel 3:1-21; and Zech 9:9-17.

49:11-13. Ben Sira mentions only three people from the post-exilic period, all of them associated with restoring the Temple (Zerubbabel and Jeshua) and the walls of Jerusalem (Nehemiah). The designation of Zerubbabel as a signet ring derives from the messianic aspirations reflected in Hag 2:23, which seem to have surfaced in connection with the newly founded community and its cult in 516 BCE.[252] Ben Sira's silence about Ezra in v. 13 has occasioned much discussion,[253] although the individuals mentioned here—Zerubbabel, Jeshua, and Nehemiah—actively participated in rebuilding the city of Jerusalem and restoring its cult. Ezra's activity resembled that of Josiah, for he endeavored to purge the worship of everything foreign. That zeal should have earned him honorable mention at least.

49:14-16. To provide transition from the heroes of the past to the high priest during his own time, Ben Sira gives a brief survey of global history. First, he mentions Enoch, that subject of endless speculation; then Joseph, the patriarch whose body was so painstakingly cared for and transported from Egypt to the land of promise; next Shem, the ancestor of the Semites; Seth, the son of Adam; Enosh, Seth's son in whose day people first began to call on the name of Yahweh (Gen 4:26);[254] and finally Adam. The expression "the splendor of Adam" (תפארת אדם *tip'eret 'ādām*) eventually led to speculation about a second Adam who would appear in the messianic age. In addition, the word translated "splendor" links v. 16 with 50:1, "the splendor of his people" (תפארת עמו *tip'eret 'ammô*). (See Reflections at 50:1-24.)

---

251. E.g., *Baba Bathra* 15*b*: "God raised up seven prophets for the gentiles," one of whom is Job.

252. Carol C. Meyers and Eric M. Meyers, *Haggai, Zechariah 1–8*, AB 25B (Garden City, N.Y.: Doubleday, 1987) 47-84; David L. Petersen, *Haggai and Zechariah 1–8*, OTL (Philadelphia: Westminster, 1984) 96-106.

253. Höffken, "Warum schweig Jesus Sirach über Esra?" 184-201.

254. Steven D. Fraade, *Enosh and His Generation*, SBLMS 30 (Chico, Calif.: Scholars Press, 1984).

SIRACH 50:1-24, SIMEON THE HIGH PRIEST

COMMENTARY

Evidently the last of Israel's heroes whom Ben Sira eulogizes has recently passed from the scene, having served as high priest 219–196 BCE. The language of v. 1 implies that Simeon was deceased (cf. the Greek for "in whose life" [ὃς ἐν ζωῇ αὐτοῦ *hos en zōē autou*]). Simeon II, called "the Just," made an indelible impression on Ben Sira, which he conveys by means of exquisite similes and sensory language. Verses 1-4 continue the dominant theme of the praise of Hezekiah, Josiah, and Nehemiah—the strengthening of the city and improvement of its supply of water. A similar account of repairs in the early second century appears in Josephus,[255] who quotes a letter attributed to Antiochus III to the governor of Palestine after the Battle of Paneas in 199 BCE. If these reports are trustworthy, they indicate enormous political power resting in the hands of the religious leader at this time. The Hebrew words for "temple," בית (*bayit*) and היכל (*hêkāl*), although often used synonymously, can refer to the Temple and to a house generally. The inner sanctuary was called the דביר (*děbîr*), usually translated "Holy of Holies."

In vv. 5-21, Ben Sira describes Simeon's appearance on a special occasion in the Temple, either on Yom Kippur (the Day of Atonement) or at a celebration of the Daily Whole-Offering. Most interpreters opt for the first of these,[256] largely on the basis of the proclamation of the ineffable name (v. 20). Naturally, this view rests on the assumption that by Ben Sira's day the divine name "Yahweh" had become so holy that no one pronounced it, with a single exception: the high priest on the Day of Atonement. This interpretation has recently been challenged,[257] primarily on the basis of the description of the Tamid offering in the Mishnah tractate *Tamid* 6:3–7:3, but this new understanding of Ben Sira's text makes two major assumptions: (1) that the later tractate accurately describes the sacrificial ritual from the second century BCE and (2) that the differences between the two accounts (the omission of the incense offering and the placing of the blessing last instead of third) derive from an accident (the incense offering) or from an intentional change to achieve dramatic effect. The issue cannot be decided on the basis of the evidence available today, and the description in vv. 5-21 may be purposely general.

The emotional language of vv. 6-10 draws on the realms of nature and religious worship to convey Ben Sira's awe at witnessing the high priest in splendid vestments. Ben Sira's exuberance is contagious, as the similes show. Simeon is like a star, the full moon (which governed the timing of festivals), the sun, the rainbow, blossoms, a lily, the lush growth of Lebanon, incense, gold vessels, precious stones, an olive tree. Verses 11-13 describe the scene when a host of priestly attendants hand Simeon the carcasses and other offerings, reminding Ben Sira of a circle of trees.[258] Verse 14 emphasizes the proper ordering of the sacrifice, and v. 15 mentions the drink offering poured out at the foot of the altar. At a blast of the trumpets, everyone falls to the ground. Verse 18 mentions singing, and shouts of joy follow. Then the high priest, having completed the offerings, blesses the people and utters the name "Yahweh." Martin Rinckart's hymn "Nun danket alle Gott" ("Now Thank We All Our God") captures the religious intensity of this text magnificently.[259]

According to Josephus, "the sacred trumpets were long straight metal tubes of hammered silver . . . about a half a yard long . . . composed of a narrow tube, somewhat thicker than a flute and ended in the form of a bell, like common trumpets."[260] The people's response to hearing the name "Yahweh" is underscored in the Mishnah tractate *Yoma* 6.2: "And the priests and the people, who

---

255. Josephus *Antiquities of the Jews* 12.138-144.
256. Oesterley, *The Wisdom of Jesus the Son of Sirach or Ecclesiasticus*, 342-43; Snaith, *Ecclesiasticus or The Wisdom of Jesus, Son of Sirach*, 251-53.
257. O'Fearghall, "Sir 50, 5-21," 301-16.

258. Snaith, *Ecclesiasticus*, 252, thinks of the analogy with students and nurses surrounding a surgeon at the operating table.
259. Oesterley, *Ecclesiasticus*, 343.
260. Oesterley, *Ecclesiasticus*, 341.

are standing in the court, when they hear the 'Ineffable Name' proceeding forth out of the mouth of the High-priest, bow down and worship, and fall upon their faces saying: 'Blessed be the Name of the glory of His kingdom for ever and ever.'" The expression "people of the land" (עם הארץ ʿam hāʾāreṣ, v. 19) originally referred to persons who had high social standing, but eventually it came to refer to those lacking society's esteem. Here they represent the congregation, singing and praying in the presence of the merciful God.

Ben Sira concludes this eulogy of Simeon with a short personal blessing (vv. 22-24). Because of the gracious gift of life, he calls on God to grant permanent well-being to Simeon and his descendants from the line of Phinehas. That wish was quickly frustrated with the assassination of his son Onias III (cf. 2 Macc 4:34); hence the translator removes this hope entirely from the Greek text, making the specific reference a general one applying to all Israel.

REFLECTIONS

1. The people whom one admires reveal much about oneself. A nation whose young people choose only celebrities for celebrity's sake as idols—sports heroes, movie stars, and rock musicians—has done a poor job of educating its public to appreciate those who contribute to the improvement of the human race. When the names of people like Jonas Salk, Marie Curie, Mahatma Gandhi, Albert Schweitzer, and countless others do not move young and old to expressions of gratitude for noble actions, something seriously wrong has infected the populace.

The deeper problem rests in the loss of imagination, the failure to seek challenges that inspire conduct of an extraordinary nature borne of discipline, achievement, and courage. Belief that God works in and through those who make significant strides toward nobler lives and who help to eradicate disease, crime, and poverty may require unconventional assumptions, but surely such thoughts merit serious consideration.

In looking around for heroes, we seldom pause long enough at home to reflect on our parents' qualifications in this regard. The obvious reason why is immediacy, the fact that we know their flaws too well as a result of constant exposure to them. Discovery that mothers and fathers have feet of clay often comes as a rude awakening, removing them permanently from the list of potential heroes. Ben Sira's willingness to weigh his heroes' complete lives and to make concessions for momentary lapses, some quite serious, stands as a marvelous example for contemporary readers.

Furthermore, he offers another clue with respect to a valid resource for locating heroes. For him, the written tradition of sacred texts—his Bible—contained the list of persons whom he most admired. Naturally, one must choose persons for such a list with care, and in doing so the operative criterion makes a world of difference. Religious persons who ponder seriously the definitive criteria for selecting heroes, and honestly give thought to various alternative criteria, will gain insight into their own values and character. Such meditation could well become a companion piece to annual reassessments at the turn of the year.

In a very real sense, our choice of heroes becomes a kind of sacred story, a record of temptations overcome, obstacles bypassed, goals achieved, and dreams realized. Together their stories move us to greater resolve, warm our souls, and open our eyes to needs and opportunities.

2. The author of the Epistle to the Hebrews acknowledged the presence of a cloud of witnesses hovering over us, a holy memory that lives on in our minds and evokes feelings of solidarity with the past (Heb 12:1-2). Modern believers also sense a presence of the extended family, persons who have preceded us into the great unknown. Those whom we especially cherish continue to have an important place in our lives.

In trying to link up with representatives of a bygone era, we tend to employ expressions from the past that communicated effectively at that time but may have become dead metaphors over the years. Ben Sira's contrivances, such as alphabetic hymns and ancient titles, certainly evoked an earlier time, while risking the alienation of persons in his own day whose language of discourse had become highly charged with Hellenistic ideas and expressions. Religious leaders almost inevitably face this sort of situation. Wishing to recapture the idyllic past, they use concepts appropriate to that period; at the same time, they hope such language has not lost its capacity to communicate in a new context.

Sometimes conservative by nature, religious people can tend to reject new ideas and expressions, and thus to lose touch with much of the population, particularly the young. Here, too, we need to be ever alert to the reasons for conservatism and to abandon this rejection of new ideas if the basis for refusing to change lacks merit. Knowing what to preserve and what to discard may be one of the most significant achievements in life.

3. What place do pomp and circumstance have in worship? Few people have reached a satisfactory answer to this vexing question. On the one hand, it seems entirely appropriate to honor God in as lavish a manner as possible; that includes a whole range of things, such as majestic cathedrals and places of worship; elaborate and expensive vestments; copious means of enrichment, including incense, intonation, music, dance, and so forth. On the other hand, simplicity has extraordinary appeal too. Combining the two, whenever attempted, has not been particularly successful, and yet we respond to both approaches to the holy.

Then, too, the place of religious fervor and a sense of the numinous come into play. Unless devotion to God gives birth to overwhelming gratitude and reminds one of ultimate dependency, it does not seem sufficiently compelling to deserve one's total allegiance. Ben Sira shamelessly gives voice to his religious passion, ultimately bowing before divine mystery. That degree of self-abandonment in the presence of the living God and celebration of gracious divine character challenges ordinary worshipers to ponder why so many days of worship lack this sense of ultimacy and fail to evoke zeal and awe.

SIRACH 50:25-29, A NUMERICAL PROVERB AND AN EPILOGUE

COMMENTARY

The internationalism of the sage vanishes in this bitter invective about three of Judah's neighbors: Canaanites, Edomites, and Samaritans, for whom Ben Sira uses ancient designations. The Philistines, who gave their name to the land of Palestine, had vanished long before Ben Sira's time, thus he may be referring to the pro-Hellenistic people dwelling along the seacoast. By Seir he indicates the Idumeans, loathed because of their ancestors' treatment of Jews during the Babylonian conquest of Jerusalem; soon after Ben Sira's time, they were forcibly converted to Judaism by John Hyrcanus. The Samaritans, inhabitants of the area around Shechem, had intermarried with the population settled in the vicinity after the expulsion of the Jewish landowners into Babylonian captivity. In the fourth century BCE, Ezra and Nehemiah rebuffed the Samaritans' offer to help restore the sanctuary at Jerusalem. Hostilities between the two groups increased because of the existence of a rival temple on Mt. Gerizim near Shechem, exacerbated by their claim to be the legitimate descendants of Phinehas. The extent of the Jews' hatred of the Samaritans can be measured by a comment in *The Testament of the Twelve Patriarchs*: "From this day forward Shechem will be called a city of imbeciles, for as one mocks a fool, so we mocked them" (*Testament of Levi* 7.2; cf. Deut 32:21, "a foolish nation" [גוי נבל *gôy nābāl*]; Luke 9:51-55; John 4:9). Such intense dislike led to the destruction of the temple on Mt. Gerizim in 128 BCE.

The epilogue (vv. 27-29) contains Ben Sira's full name and a sort of summary of the advantages that come to those who study his teachings and embody them in their lives. Both meditation (cf. Ps 1:1) and praxis (cf. Eccl 7:2; 9:1) come into play here, and Ben Sira echoes the introduction to the book of Proverbs (1:1-3) and the epilogue to Ecclesiastes (12:9-10).

REFLECTIONS

Even good people have weak moments and blind spots that lead them into embarrassing situations, for which they genuinely repent. Ben Sira's hatred for three neighboring peoples may have been entirely justified, humanly speaking, by their repeated offenses. Nevertheless, his attitude toward Samaritans, Idumeans, and Hellenists along the coastal strip seriously compromised his teachings, for sages should have been able to rise above such petty hatred. The very context of this sentiment, so terribly out of place, corresponds to its place in Ben Sira's life. It did not belong anywhere if he truly lived up to his teaching.

From this text we easily observe that even great men, and by extension women, at some time will have to rely on others' tolerance. No one need hurl the first stone at Ben Sira, for we all are guilty. Such momentary lapses bring dishonor, to be sure, but they should not destroy one's reputation. In judging Ben Sira's character, one needs to consider the total picture rather than a single moment.

Besides the psychological release and honest confession before God, the positive contribution of such expression of hatred may be found in what it generates in good people, specifically extensive self-examination. Perhaps this soul-searching will enable us all to see the error in judging others by nationality, class, or whatever group they belong to rather than seeing each individual as a person deserving the same respect.

SIRACH 51:1-30, A PRAYER OF THANKSGIVING, A HYMN OF PRAISE, AND AN ACROSTIC POEM ABOUT WISDOM

COMMENTARY

51:1-12. The first twelve verses of this chapter comprise a prayer in which Ben Sira employs traditional language to give thanks for deliverance from an unspecified threat. The prayer is sufficiently general to be used by almost any worshiper. An anthological style draws on the language of biblical psalms to recount the author's subjection to verbal abuse, his descent into the abyss of despair, and his remembering the Lord's mercy. Addressing Yahweh as "my father" (אבי *'ābî*), Ben Sira begs God not to forsake him. The prayer concludes with the declaration that the Lord listened to the plea and acted on behalf of the supplicant (cf. Pss 17:9; 30:3; 55:9; 116:8). In a study on the poetic structure of this declarative psalm of praise, Di Lella identifies six stanzas and isolates instances of artistic balance or correspondence, inclusion, chiasm, breakup of stereotyped phrases, rhyme, and parallelism.[261]

---

261. Alexander A. Di Lella, "Sirach 51:1-12: Poetic Structure and Analysis of Ben Sira's Psalm," *CBQ* 48 (1986) 395-407.

The dual epithet for God, "Lord and King" (v. 1), together with "Father" (v. 10) recall common expressions in ancient Jewish prayers, e.g., "Our Father, our Sovereign" in the prayer by that name, in "Great Love," and in "The Eighteen Benedictions," where the clauses begin with "Our Father" and "Our King" alternately.[262]

A litany of praise follows this prayer in MS B, but it does not appear in the Greek, the Syriac, or any translations based on them. Moreover, the Greek text has a title for the entire chapter, "The Prayer of Jesus, son of Sirach," which applies only to vv. 1-12. Although the litany does not appear to have been written by Ben Sira, it dates from before 152 BCE, when the Hasmonean Jonathan received the high priesthood as a reward for supporting Alexander Balas of Syria (cf. 51:12 ix, which implies that Zadokites are still in control of the priesthood). Di Lella conjectures that a member of the Essene community at Qumran wrote the psalm and inserted it into a copy of Sirach that found its way into a cave near Jericho and eventually into the hands of Qaraites, who made copies that were discovered in the Cairo Geniza between 1896 and 1900.[263]

Like Psalm 136, this psalm contains the refrain "for his mercy endures forever" in fourteen of the sixteen verses (cf. Pss 106:1; 107:1; 118:1, 29 for the same expression). The language is entirely biblical ("the Guardian of Israel" in Ps 121:4; "who fashioned everything" in Jer 10:16; 51:19; "the Redeemer of Israel" in Isa 49:7; "who gathered Israel's dispersed" in Isa 56:8; "who rebuilt his city" in Isa 60:13; "who makes a horn to sprout for David's house" in Ps 132:17; Ezek 29:21). Similarly, the divine epithets in 51:12 x-xii derive from the patriarchal narratives—the Shield of Abraham, Rock of Isaac, Mighty One of Jacob.

51:13-30. An alphabetical poem about wisdom concludes the book of Sirach, as in Prov 31:10-31—even though Ben Sira never uses the noun "wisdom" in the poem. Verses 13-21 describe Ben Sira's search for wisdom, and vv. 22-30 contain a personal appeal to others to follow his example. A copy of this poem has been found in a scroll from Qumran (11QPs^a) containing lines א (*aleph*) through כ (*kaph*; ll. 1-20). In the translation by J. A. Sanders, this poem is interpreted as an erotic text,[264] and various scholars have offered alternative readings.[265] An erotic understanding of personified wisdom certainly exists in Proverbs 8 and Wisdom 7, however one views Ben Sira's acrostic.

The poem tells how a young Ben Sira determined to cultivate wisdom from youth to old age and how wisdom gave herself to him as he pursued her paths and set his heart on her. As reward for faithfulness, he received a gift of eloquence (cf. Isa 50:4), which equipped him to teach others. He thus invites people to come to his house of learning (MS B has "into my house of instruction" [בבית מדרשי *bĕbêt midrāšî*]; Di Lella claims that both the Greek and the Syriac texts demand a reading of "into the house of learning" [בבית מוסר *bĕbêt mûsār*] and sees a play on words based on סור [*sûr*, "to be remote"]).[266] Ben Sira's language about money, reward, and thirst may be purely metaphorical, like Prov 4:5-7; Isa 55:1-3; Amos 8:11. Too little is known about education in second-century BCE Israel to ascertain whether one should assume that Ben Sira received payment for instructing students.[267]

The final two verses nicely juxtapose the complementary theological concepts of grace and merit. Remembering the Lord's mercy, one ought to do good works and await a reward in God's own time. In this short statement, Ben Sira effectively combines religious and social teachings.

The Hebrew manuscript closes with a long subscript stating that the work has reached its conclusion and identifying its author as Simeon, the son of Jeshua who is called Ben Sira. It adds: "The Wisdom of Simeon, the son of Jeshua, the son of Eleasar, the son of Sira. May Yahweh's name be blessed from now unto the ages" (cf. Ps 113:2).

---

262. Oesterley, *The Wisdom of Jesus the Son of Sirach or Ecclesiasticus*, 346.
263. Skehan and Di Lella, *The Wisdom of Ben Sira*, 569.
264. Sanders, *The Psalms Scroll of Qumran Cave II (11QPsa)*, DJD 4 70-85; and *The Dead Sea Psalms Scroll*, 112-17.
265. J. Muraoka, "Sir 51:13-20: An Erotic Hymn to Wisdom?" *JSJ* 10 (1979) 166-78; and C. Deutsch, "The Sirach 51 Acrostic: Confession and Exhortation," *ZAW* 94 (1982) 400-409.
266. See Skehan and Di Lella, *The Wisdom of Ben Sira*, 578.
267. Cf. *Pirqe 'Abot* 4:9.

Introduction to Apocalyptic Literature
Frederick J. Murphy

The terms *apocalypticism, apocalypse,* and *apocalyptic* are widely used within biblical scholarship, and they also appear in more popular settings—literature, film, and the news media, for example. The words derive from the Greek ἀποκάλυψις (*apokalypsis*), which means "revelation." Modern use of these words to describe a certain kind of literature and a specific worldview is due to the book of Revelation, which begins, "The revelation [*apokalypsis*] of Jesus Christ." The book of Revelation is often called the Apocalypse, and the title "Revelation" is simply a translation of that term. Beginning in the nineteenth century, scholars perceived similarities of form and content between Revelation and other ancient Jewish and Christian works, so they began to call such works "apocalypses" by analogy. Other ancient works written after Revelation explicitly call themselves apocalypses, but none before. Nonetheless, many Jewish works written before Revelation share its literary genre.

Until the 1970s, the word *apocalyptic* was used as a noun, denoting a rather amorphous entity made up of certain texts, a specific kind of imagery, vision reports, a variety of worldviews, and particular social groups. A wide range of Jewish and Christian texts, many of them not apocalypses, were used in this construction of "apocalyptic." The resulting construct was then used to interpret specific texts, persons, and events. Ideas like "apocalyptic movement" emerged, implying that there was a single movement that could be called apocalyptic in which the various expressions of the phenomenon were included. The problem with this approach is that the theoretical "apocalyptic" that results does not always fit the apocalypses. There is tremendous variation in apocalypses with respect to form and content, beliefs, expectations, historical circumstances, political positions, and so on. Nothing like a single apocalyptic movement ever existed. A basic worldview is common to all apocalypses, but it is common in the Hellenistic world even outside apocalypses, leaving room for a wide spectrum of particular apocalyptic theologies and ideologies.

Greater precision is attained through distinguishing between apocalypse as a literary genre, apocalypticism as a worldview, and "apocalyptic" as an adjective applied in the first instance to apocalypses and in a derivative way to texts and ideas that have much in common with apocalypses. What is apocalyptic is first of all what one finds in apocalypses. Anything else is apocalyptic by comparison. Further, it is no longer assumed that a given text necessarily represents a historical community or movement, rather than the point of view of an individual or of a small group fairly indistinguishable from society as a whole. The basics of the apocalyptic worldview were widespread enough in the Hellenistic world that apocalypses do not necessarily imply a sectarian group that produced and preserved them. The judgment about whether a sect stands behind a given apocalypse must be made anew for each text.

The book of Daniel in the Hebrew Bible and the book of Revelation in the New Testament are the only biblical examples of apocalypses. But apocalyptic influence in the Bible is far broader than that fact suggests. A number of prophetic texts written during and after the Babylonian exile share features of content and form with the apocalypses, so they are sometimes called "proto-apocalyptic." Apocalyptic influence is also evident throughout most of the New Testament. Of course, the Bible presents only aspects of ancient Judaism and Christianity, thus it is part of the task of biblical scholars to look beyond the canon to situate the biblical texts within their original contexts. In this connection, it is noteworthy that a substantial proportion of Jewish literature written between 300 BCE and 200 CE is either in the form of apocalypses or displays apocalyptic features. Likewise, apocalypses and apocalyptic thought played a prominent role in early Christianity. This article concentrates on the period between 300 BCE and 200 CE. References to and analyses of specific apocalypses are illustrative rather than exhaustive.

THE APOCALYPTIC GENRE

The first step in discussing apocalyptic literature is to decide which texts are apocalypses. In the late 1970s, a group of scholars examined all documents considered apocalypses and constructed a definition that fits all of them and distinguishes them from other sorts of ancient literature.[1] All apocalypses are narratives, stories describing the disclosure of otherwise inaccessible secrets to a human seer by a heavenly being. The disclosures are usually through visions. (The term *seer* literally means "see-er," one who sees visions.) Often the visions themselves are enigmatic and must be interpreted by a heavenly being, usually an angel. There are two main kinds of apocalyptic narratives. In the first, the seer travels to the heavenly realm or to parts of the cosmos usually inaccessible to human beings. The second type contains no otherworldly journey. This type often incorporates a review of history, culminating in an eschatological crisis and resolution, such as a conflict between the forces of good and evil, resulting in evil's defeat. That review is frequently in the form of fictive "prediction" of history (actually, the past of the real author) by the pseudonymous seer, a device known as *vaticinia ex eventu,* "prophecies after the event." At the end of such reviews is genuine prediction of things to happen in the author's future. A Jewish apocalypse from the end of the first century CE, the *Apocalypse of Abraham,* contains both an otherworldly journey and a review of history, but such a combination is unusual.

Apocalyptic revelation has temporal and spatial dimensions. The spatial aspect deals with the supernatural world, often conceived of as being above or below this world. It sometimes involves a heaven divided into levels, and it discloses the activities of supernatural beings, such as angels and demons. The natural and supernatural realms are closely interrelated. Decisions made in the supernatural realm or events that transpire there affect and sometimes determine what happens on earth. Conversely, earthly events can have repercussions in the supernatural world. True understanding of historical events and concrete earthly circumstances requires knowledge of the heavenly world not generally available. The temporal aspect of apocalyptic revelation concerns eschatological judgment. That judgment can involve cosmic catastrophe and public judgment of all humanity, a scenario that conforms to what is popularly termed apocalyptic, but it might involve only individual judgment after death. The element common to all apocalypses is postmortem rewards and punishments, an idea that enters Judaism through the medium of apocalypticism, since it does not occur elsewhere in the Hebrew Bible. Israel's religion as presented in

---

1. See John J. Collins, ed., *Apocalypse: The Morphology of a Genre,* Semeia 14 (Missoula, Mont.: Scholars Press, 1979).

the Hebrew Bible is focused on this life. After death, good and bad alike descend into Sheol and live a shadowy existence that bears little resemblance to later concepts of heaven and hell. Daniel is the only biblical book in which transcendence of death through resurrection is clearly attested, and it is the last-written book to be included in the Hebrew Bible (c. 165 BCE). Even before Daniel, transcendence of death is expressed in the *Book of the Watchers,* a Jewish apocalypse from the third century BCE, now preserved as *1 Enoch* 1–36. Resurrection becomes a regular feature of apocalyptic scenarios of the eschaton. The future life is often conceived of as taking place in the supernatural realm. In Daniel 12 and *2 Baruch* 51, for example, the righteous join the stars. In other instances, there is a new heaven and a new earth in which the saved live. In Revelation 21–22, the new Jerusalem descends to earth, and God and Christ live on the new earth with the righteous.

All Jewish apocalypses and many Christian ones are pseudonymous. The seer is an ancient hero, such as Enoch, Abraham, Moses, Baruch, or Ezra. Such attributions enhance the authority of the works. The specific choice of seer is often appropriate. Three Jewish apocalypses were written as responses to the destruction of the Jerusalem Temple by the Romans in 70 CE. *Second Baruch* is attributed to a writer who lived through the earlier destruction of the Temple by the Babylonians in 587 BCE. Fourth Ezra is credited to the scribe who brought the Torah back to Israel after the Babylonian exile, and the work ends with Ezra reconstituting the Torah, which was burned in the destruction, by dictating it to scribes (4 Ezra 14). The *Apocalypse of Abraham* takes the vision experienced by Abraham in Genesis 15 as the occasion of a sweeping view of world history that puts the destruction of the Temple into perspective. A large number of apocalypses were assigned to Enoch. At least five such apocalypses are now preserved in a collection called *1 Enoch,* preserved in Ethiopic, in Aramaic fragments from Qumran, in several Greek fragments, and in one Latin fragment. Enoch appears in Gen 5:24 as one who walked with God—i.e., as righteous. It is stated enigmatically that "God took him," a phrase later interpreted as God's taking him to heaven. Enoch thus became an appropriate figure to whom heavenly revelations could be given. In *1 Enoch* 14, he makes a trip to the heavenly throne room, and in chaps. 17–36 he tours parts of the cosmos not accessible to other humans.

Although apocalypses are often permeated by scriptural language, images, and patterns, they do not try to convince their readers through exegesis of Scripture. Nor is rational persuasion their technique. Rather, the authority of an apocalypse comes from the seer's direct reception of revelation. In effect, the author claims divine authority for the content of the apocalypse. Apocalypses are the more compelling in that they do not merely relay information, but allow their readers to accompany the seer through the process of revelation by describing that process in detail. So, for example, the readers experience Enoch's awe as he enters the heavenly sanctuary (*1 Enoch* 14), Daniel's terror as he sees mysterious beasts arising from the sea and a powerful angel descending from heaven (Daniel 7; 10), John's wonder as he sees the great harlot dressed in crimson and purple and riding on the seven-headed, ten-horned beast (Revelation 17). Through such means, apocalypses do more than convey information or demand specific behavior. They also contain a powerful emotional element that cannot be translated into other terms. They allow the reader to experience the supernatural world that affects this one and to see firsthand the coming eschatological judgment. Through that experience they can put their own circumstances into perspective. Through historical apocalypses, readers can contemplate history as a whole and understand their place in it. Apocalypses concerned with politics can allow readers to perceive their struggles with evil rulers as part of a larger struggle between good and evil forces. They derive hope from the knowledge that as in the mythological combat between the most high God and forces inimical to divine order, good will be victorious.

Discussions of apocalyptic genre have been complicated by the fact that apocalypses are sometimes found embedded in other genres, that they frequently incorporate other genres, and that apocalyptic elements can be found in a variety of texts. Two other genres show particular affinities with apocalypses:

testaments and oracle collections. Testaments are last words of major figures before their deaths. The form was popular in the period under consideration. A common element in testaments is prediction of the future. Such predictions often include eschatological scenarios and so are suited for apocalyptic predictions. There are many such passages in the *Testaments of the Twelve Patriarchs,* and one of the texts in that collection, the *Testament of Levi,* contains a short apocalypse in chaps. 2–5. In the *Testament of Moses,* Moses predicts the course of Israel's history, culminating in the appearance of God's kingdom (chap. 10). Satan is destroyed, and God comes as the divine warrior to put an end to idols and to vindicate Israel.

The prophetic books in the Hebrew Bible are for the most part oracle collections. Their relevance for the apocalypses will be examined below. Another oracle collection that is very significant for the study of Jewish apocalyptic literature is the *Sibylline Oracles.* The notion of a woman prophet (sibyl) who utters prophecies of a political nature was taken over by the Jews from their environment in the Hellenistic period. Sibylline collections also figured largely in Greek and Roman settings. The *Sibylline Oracles* in standard editions are Jewish (books 3–5 and 11–14) and Christian (only books 6 and 7 were originally Christian; the others adapt Jewish works). Although the form of revelation is quite different from that found in apocalypses, they contain political prophecy that resembles what is found in many historical apocalypses. They employ mythological elements; criticize the present state of affairs, particularly Roman rulers; and predict future disaster.

WORLDVIEW

The form and content of apocalypses imply a basic worldview common to all of them. There is a supernatural world that is closely related to this one, and there is an eschatological judgment for humans and often for supernatural beings as well. This basic foundation allows for a wide variety of theologies, messages, and social ideologies.

Most past scholarship on apocalypticism has been dominated by Christian concerns. Since eschatology and messianism are so important to early Christian thought, those aspects of apocalypses, both Jewish and Christian, have often attracted attention disproportionate to their actual importance in apocalyptic literature. That imbalance is now being addressed by studies that do greater justice to the noneschatological and nonmessianic nature of many of the revelations in particular apocalypses. The heavenly journey apocalypses in particular show an interest in a wide range of topics—cosmology, meteorology, astronomy, astrology, calendar, angelology, etc.—in addition to eschatology. Many of the topics addressed by such apocalypses do not receive much attention in the Hebrew Bible. Such apocalypses may not conform to what is popularly thought of as apocalyptic, because they do not always contain cosmic upheavals or eschatological sufferings. But they share with the historical apocalypses interest in the supernatural world, a world that is crucial for understanding this one, and belief in rewards and punishments after death.

Apocalypses frequently display some degree of dualism. A distinction is drawn between this world and the supernatural realm and between life before and life after death. Some apocalypses go beyond these dualisms to see a cosmic dualism consisting of an opposition between supernatural forces of good and evil. This is not a thoroughgoing dualism, positing an evil entity equal to God. Rather, it opposes lesser forces, such as Michael against Satan (Revelation 12), Michael against Belial,[2] Gabriel and Michael against the heavenly patrons of Persia and Greece (Daniel 10; cf. Jesus against Satan in the Gospel of Mark). God is always supreme. The degree of cosmic dualism varies across the apocalypses, and so it cannot be taken as a universal characteristic of them.

Social dualism is also frequent in apocalypses and is correlated with cosmic dualism when present. Humanity is divided into good and evil, the elect and the rest, those who are being saved and those who are perishing (see 1 Cor 1:18). There is a final struggle between good and evil, which usually involves supernatural powers. The nature of human participation in that struggle varies. In Daniel,

2. See 1QM 17.

it is God who destroys Judaism's enemy, the Seleucid king Antiochus IV Epiphanes, and the heavenly patrons of various nations clash with Gabriel and Michael. In Revelation, Christians participate in the battle against Satan and Rome only through their witness to Christ and their refusal to accommodate themselves to Hellenistic culture and to the imperial cult. Christ has already defeated Satan in his death and resurrection. Satan has been ejected from heaven by Michael and the good angels (Revelation 12) and now wages war against Christians on earth. The final military victory is fought between Christ and his heavenly armies on the one side and Satan and his allies on the other.

All apocalypses involve eschatology, but some forms of apocalypticism have a strong eschatological focus. The conflict between good and evil will be resolved through victory for the forces of good. That victory is conceptualized in many ways. It may be renewal of the earth, where life will be lived as it should be, in union with God and without evil of any sort, or it may be a future heavenly existence for humans.

THE ORIGINS OF APOCALYPTICISM

The origins of apocalypses and apocalypticism have been a major preoccupation of scholars. The main debate has been between those who consider apocalypses to be a natural development of elements already existent within Judaism and those who see apocalypticism as a foreign entity, imported from the Gentile world. The most widely accepted position today is that apocalypses resulted from a complex interplay of foreign and domestic elements. The debate over whether apocalypticism is authentically Jewish can be misleading. Israel was always to some degree open to outside influences. Israelite and Jewish religion was full of elements adapted from its environment. The Hellenistic age saw a particularly fertile interaction of different cultures and national and ethnic heritages, and Judaism shared in that interaction. Writers of Jewish apocalypses responded to the new conditions and circumstances of the Hellenistic and Roman periods, and they used both domestic and foreign elements to do so.

The Hebrew Bible furnishes much raw material for apocalypticism. The idea that God communicates in mysterious dreams or visions that require inspired interpretation is found in the story of Joseph in Egypt (Genesis 40–41) as well as in the books of Zechariah and Ezekiel. That God controls human events from the heavenly court is clear in the story of the prophet Micaiah ben Imlah, who is granted a view of God deciding to send a lying spirit into Ahab's prophets so as to mislead him (1 Kings 22). The apocalyptic picture of a warrior God who intervenes in history to defeat evil has its roots in the notion of the divine warrior, a common biblical idea.

Efforts to find the origins of Jewish apocalypticism in Israel's proverbial and speculative wisdom tradition have not won many supporters, but the exilic and post-exilic prophets are a particularly fruitful source of comparison. Zechariah attests to the vision-reaction-interpretation pattern common in apocalypses. Ezekiel contains extended metaphors, such as the prostitute of chap. 16, which Revelation uses in chap. 17 (see also the oracles against Babylon in Jeremiah 50–51). Ezekiel's vision in chaps. 40–48 of the restored Jerusalem inspired later apocalyptic visions. The visions of the heavenly throne room found in texts such as *1 Enoch* 14, Daniel 7, and Revelation 4–5 find counterparts in the earlier visions of Isaiah 6 and Ezekiel 1. Beyond formal similarities there are also similarities of content. Although prophetic texts never contain the idea of postmortem rewards and punishments, they do provide elements that were used in apocalyptic eschatological scenarios. A good example is Isaiah 24–27, often called the Isaiah Apocalypse, although it is not written in the form of an apocalypse. Isaiah 24:21-23 speaks of punishment of the heavenly host and earthly kings who are shut up in prison until a final punishment. This is like the scheme found in the *Book of the Watchers* (see also Revelation 20). Isaiah 26:19 calls for the rising of those who dwell in the dust, an apparent reference to resurrection. This may be simply a metaphor, as is the revivification of dry bones in Ezekiel 37, but it at least hints at the later apocalyptic idea of resurrection. Zechariah 14 and Ezekiel 38–39 speak of a great eschatological battle, and those texts inspired later versions of the final battle between forces for and against God.

Apocalypses differ from prophetic texts in their combination of heavy use of techniques like vision-reaction-interpretation and heavenly journeys, intense interest in the supernatural world, and eschatology that includes transcendence of death. Each of these elements was common in the Hellenistic world, as were pseudepigraphy, periodization of history, and *ex eventu* prophecy.

Scholars have noted phenomena in Persian, Egyptian, and Mesopotamian texts that correspond to features of Jewish apocalypses. Persian sources contain evidence of resurrection, postmortem judgment, division of history into periods, eschatological tumult, dualistic conflict between the forces of good and evil, and the ascent of the soul. Although the Persian sources are difficult to date, it is likely that many of these ideas go back at least to the Hellenistic period, if not before. Egyptian sources provide examples of political prophecy, as do Mesopotamian texts. Mesopotamia also furnishes examples of *ex eventu* prophecy combined with authentic prediction, as is found in Daniel 11. Daniel 8 betrays the influence of Mesopotamian astrology.

It is difficult to know precisely how these influences fed into Israel's traditions so as to emerge in apocalypses. It is possible that Jews in the eastern diaspora were the first to incorporate such features into their works and worldview. The seer of the two earliest extant Jewish apocalypses, the *Book of the Watchers* and the *Astronomical Book* (*1 Enoch* 72–82), is Enoch. The figure of Enoch originates in Gen 5:18-24, but it has been developed according to the model of the Enmeduranki, who was the seventh of the kings on the Sumerian king list. Enmeduranki founded an association of Babylonian diviners. The book of Daniel shows various Eastern influences, and the stories in the first six chapters of the book are set in the royal courts of Babylonia, Media, and Persia. Those stories may have originally existed independently of the book of Daniel and have come from the eastern diaspora. But given the fluid interchange of ideas, symbolism, and traditions that marked the Hellenistic age in general and the amount of Hellenistic influence that occurred even among Palestinian Jews, it is unwise to draw too sharp a distinction between the Jews in the diaspora and those who remained in the homeland. Both groups were influenced by their Hellenistic environment, thus both can be called Hellenistic Jews, although perhaps to different degrees and in different ways.

Apocalypses make creative use of mythology. Indeed, they are more heavily mythological than is the Hebrew Bible itself. Although the Hebrew Bible contains mythological elements, they are often historicized. They are not related as full myths, but are used to comment on or to embellish Israel's history. Nonetheless, some parts of the Hebrew Bible, the book of Psalms and Second Isaiah, for example, do attest to a certain vitality of mythology in Israel. Apocalypses tap into the deep wellsprings of ancient Near Eastern mythology. In doing so, they render fuller versions of some myths that are used more sparingly in the Hebrew Bible. For example, Gen 6:1-4 briefly recounts the descent of angels to have intercourse with human women, resulting in offspring who were giants. The story is mentioned, but not developed. A much fuller version of this story appears in the *Book of the Watchers,* where the watchers' development of their plan, their descent, and its consequences are related in much more detail. The angels' descent becomes the explanation for the existence of evil in the world. Another example of a more developed mythology concerns the punishment of humans and supernatural figures mentioned in passing in Isa 24:21-23. They "will be gathered together like prisoners in a pit" and "shut up in a prison" (Isa 24:22 NRSV) until the time of their punishment. This pattern is found in much greater detail in the *Book of the Watchers,* and it may have influenced the story of the binding, releasing, and defeat of Satan in Revelation 20. A last example involves the combat myth, the notion that there once was a great battle between supernatural figures that determined the subsequent course of the universe. One finds that myth in various forms throughout the ancient Near East. It serves as a model for Revelation 12 and Dan 8:10.

The proximate sources for the mythological traditions found in Jewish and Christian apocalypses are something of an open question. The cult may well have preserved mythological elements that are not entirely clear through our extant texts. Israel may also have passed down such elements in its general culture or adopted them from its environment at different stages of its history. Since Jews lived in the Hellenistic world, which was characterized by a fertile interaction of cultures, their literature may have received many elements from that interaction. In any case, scholarship will not grasp the meaning of apocalypses merely by tracing the origin of their individual traditions. Apocalypses must be read as whole units and as creative responses to the new conditions of the Hellenistic world.

Another open question is to what extent apocalypses attest to actual visions experienced by their authors. There is not enough evidence to decide the answer to this question definitively. The descriptions of preparations to receive revelations found in some apocalypses suggest genuine techniques to induce visions. Some scholars have pointed to the scribal nature of apocalypses and their heavy use of tradition to argue against this position, but apocalypses may be the results of learned elaboration of an original experience rather than a simple description of what actually happened to the seer. Some scholars have attempted to develop criteria by which it might be decided which apocalyptic passages represent real visions and which are stylized accounts, but no set of criteria has won general approval. What is clear is that the authors of apocalypses expected their claims to visionary experience to be taken seriously and to affect their audiences profoundly.

Apocalypses have often been considered crisis literature, composed during times of oppression or even persecution. Two crises in the Second Temple period led to the production of apocalypses. When Antiochus IV Epiphanes, the Seleucid king, tried to outlaw Judaism in 167 BCE, one result was the Maccabean revolt, and another was the writing of apocalypses. Daniel dates to this time, as does a small apocalypse embedded in the collection called *1 Enoch:* the *Animal Apocalypse* (*1 Enoch* 85–90). The *Apocalypse of Weeks* (*1 Enoch* 93:1-10; 91:12-17) probably dates from about the same time. The *Animal Apocalypse* clearly supports the militant resistance of the Maccabees and sees it as the culmination of history, leading to the messianic era. But Daniel takes a more quietistic stand. Humans are not expected to take up arms, a fact that makes it seem unlikely that the author had much enthusiasm for the revolt. Daniel 11:34 may refer to the Maccabees as "a little help" (NRSV), judging them to be ultimately irrelevant to the solution of the problem. The real solution will be provided by God's direct intervention. The differing stands taken by these contemporary apocalypses show that the apocalyptic worldview does not imply any special political ideology. Another crisis that led to the writing of apocalypses was the Roman destruction of Jerusalem and its Temple in 70 CE. Shortly afterward, four apocalypses appeared: *4 Ezra, 2 Baruch,* the *Apocalypse of Abraham,* and probably *3 Baruch.*

Although many apocalypses clearly arise from circumstances of crisis, that is not so clear for others. No public crisis is obvious in the *Similitudes of Enoch* (*1 Enoch* 37–71), the *Testament of Abraham, 2 Enoch,* or the *Apocalypse of Zephaniah,* for example. Of course, what constitutes a crisis may be in the eye of the beholder. What might look like a period of prosperity and peace from the viewpoint of the well-to-do can appear as a time of oppression and suffering to those at the bottom of the social hierarchy. Even those who are not poor or obviously oppressed might see a crisis in the fact that a foreign power rules their land. Recent research on Revelation and its social and political setting agrees that there was no large-scale persecution of Christianity in the late first century under Emperor Domitian, when Revelation was written. Opposition to Christianity, where it existed at all, was probably local and resulted not in Christians' being thrown to the beasts, but in informal social and economic sanctions on a small scale. The function of Revelation may have been less to comfort Christians at the onset of a major persecution than to warn them of the demonic nature of the Roman Empire so as to discourage the accommodation to Hellenistic and Roman culture that the author observed going on around him.

Although a crisis setting is not provable or even probable for many apocalypses, they all express, at least implicitly, a dissatisfaction with the temporal world. The impulse to explore the supernatural world and to look beyond death is due at least in part to a perception that all is not as it should be on earth. The wrong king may be on the throne, a foreign power may occupy the land, there may be laxity in ordering society according to God's will.

APOCALYPTIC DISCOURSE

The way that apocalypses make meaning is foreign to most modern people. Scholars have often dealt with the strangeness of apocalypticism by reducing it to more understandable terms. At times, apocalypses have been treated as encoded forms of exhortation, timeless truths, or descriptions of historical situations. At other times, they have been treated as sources from which to extract bits of information about topics of interest, such as messianism and eschatology. These approaches to understanding apocalypses are not without some justification. Apocalypses do make references to historical events and circumstances, and they sometimes express truths that speak to ages other than their own, and they can be used to supply information about messianic and eschatological beliefs. But to appreciate apocalypses for what they are, one must read them on their own terms.

Apocalyptic discourse has been called poetic and even mythopoetic. Apocalypses project experience onto a cosmic screen, using all the resources at their disposal, including elements from their own religious traditions as well as from their broader environment. The result is imaginative literature, which uses symbolic language to evoke aspects of reality that are beyond our powers of literal description. They allow their readers to see their own situations from the perspectives of the supernatural world and from the vantage point of life after death. This change of perspective allows a different consciousness to emerge, thereby changing experience itself. Human experience is found to be connected to larger, even cosmic realities. One's own historical period or personal life is viewed within a broad vista and can thereby be ordered correctly. This does not just make experience more tolerable; it actually changes experience, since experience is inseparable from perception. To change perception is to change the world.

A consideration of the use of mythology displayed in apocalypses can produce insight into the ways in which they make meaning. Ancient Near Eastern myths were stories about supernatural figures. Those stories shed light on human life, its institutions, hopes, fears, and struggles. Myths incorporate patterns that correspond to deeply held convictions, profound emotions, and basic attitudes toward life. To tap into this sort of discourse is to access the power of such stories and the images and symbols they contain. For many people, the beasts from the sea and the Son of Man coming on the clouds in Daniel 7 are still potent symbols of the victory of good over evil. The same is true of the battle between Christ and Satan depicted in Revelation and in the Gospels. If the strength of such symbols can still be felt today, the effect they had in ancient Mediterranean and Near Eastern cultures where they originated can be imagined as well.

Because apocalypses project human experience onto a broad screen, temporally and spatially, they have something to say not just to the particular circumstances in which they were written, but also to other times and situations. The history of interpretation of the two canonical apocalypses, Daniel and Revelation, bears eloquent testimony to the adaptability of apocalypses. Daniel itself was crucial to the writing of parts of the Enochic literature, and it was also important to Revelation and 4 Ezra, for example. Revelation supported the hopes of the early Christians who expected a thousand-year period of blessedness, was interpreted as a description of Christian life between Christ's resurrection and the parousia (by Augustine and many others), served as a map of church history, and has been seen by some contemporary Christians as the key to current events and a disclosure of the future. A solid understanding of the genre, the worldview, and the original historical circumstances of apocalypses can enable today's believers to benefit from their spiritual insights and strange beauty without being misled by simplistic and sometimes dangerous interpretations.

THE CANONICAL APOCALYPSES: DANIEL AND REVELATION

The two biblical apocalypses, Daniel and Revelation, are similar in many respects. Each responds to a specific crisis—Daniel to the persecution of the Jews by Antiochus IV Epiphanes in the second century BCE, Revelation to what the author perceives as an impending persecution of true Christians by the Roman Empire in the first century CE. Each document provides typically apocalyptic solutions to its crisis. In each case a revelation is granted to a human seer in which the seer has visions of the supernatural world—visions at least partially explained by an angelic interpreter. The visions reveal that the supernatural world determines the natural world and human history. It is disclosed that the earthly adversary of God's people will be defeated through divine intervention, and the righteous will live in union with God forever after. Each text anticipates resurrection. Each attempts to persuade readers of its viewpoint. Because Daniel and Revelation supply insights into the heavenly world and into God's own decisions, the points of view that each book advocates receive divine sanction and attain the status of divine revelation.

Daniel and Revelation receive detailed analysis elsewhere in *The New Interpreter's Bible* volumes. This article looks at only a few selected passages that illustrate how the works are apocalyptic.

Daniel. This book falls into two parts. Chapters 1–6 are a prologue to the apocalypse proper, which occupies chaps. 7–12. Chapters 1–6 are set in the royal courts of the Babylonian, Median, and Persian empires, where Daniel distinguishes himself both as a champion of Jewish piety and as a divinely inspired interpreter of dreams and signs. This portrait of Daniel makes him an ideal mediator of heavenly secrets. This is true particularly because Daniel credits God with his dream interpretations and does not attribute them to his own talents or efforts (2:28, 30). In chaps. 7–12, Daniel has his own visions in the night, interpreted for him by an angel. His vision in chap. 7 contains the essential elements of the other dreams. He sees a succession of four beasts rising out of the sea. In the ancient Near East and in Israel, the sea represented the powers of chaos, a cosmic force opposed to God and to God's order. The beasts' origin in the sea reveals their nature as opponents of God. They are both like and unlike earthly animals. Because the beasts are in some ways similar to earthly creatures, the readers can get some idea of the strength and fearful qualities of these beasts. Since as a whole they correspond to no earthly creature but are a bizarre combination of known beasts, they assume an otherworldly and awful aspect. They are suitable, therefore, to represent powers that are both this-worldly and cosmic.

Later in the vision, Daniel learns that the beasts represent four kings (7:17), but in 7:23-24 it is clear that the fourth beast is also a kingdom and that its horns are individual kings. The fluidity of the imagery here should be a warning not to insist on a rigid, one-to-one correspondence between elements of the visions and the natural or supernatural realities to which they refer (see also Revelation 17). Such correspondences do occur, but the visions are mythopoetic, so their full import always exceeds such simple references. The fourth beast differs from those that precede it in its destructiveness. Then a horn arises on the fourth beast that supplants three other horns and begins to speak arrogantly. Commentators agree that the arrogant horn is Antiochus IV Epiphanes, whose rise to power was at the expense of other royal pretenders and whose persecution of Judaism was arrogant in the extreme, since by it he opposed God.

After the vision of the four beasts, the focus suddenly shifts to God's heavenly court, where God, the Ancient of Days, sits on a throne. As the court sits in judgment, books are opened. Abruptly, the focus leaves the heavenly court and is back on the fourth beast, who is slain. After some words about the fate of the other beasts, the scene again jumps to heaven, where one like a "son of man" comes on the clouds and is presented before God and receives kingship. The rest of the chapter indicates that just as the one like a son of man and the holy ones receive the kingdom in heaven, so also their people, Israel, receive sovereignty on earth. The holy ones are angels, and the one like a son of man is a prominent angel, probably Michael, Israel's heavenly patron (see Dan 10:21).

Daniel 8–11 covers much the same material as Daniel 7, but there is more detail concerning the Seleucids, especially Antiochus IV Epiphanes. In chap. 10, the mode of revelation shifts from vision and interpretation to direct instruction of Daniel by an angel, probably Gabriel. The angel tells Daniel that an angelic war is being waged in which he is fighting against a series of "princes" representing earthly empires (10:13, 20-21; 11:1). Gabriel has only Michael, Israel's heavenly patron (10:21), as an ally. The angel's words assume that each nation has its own patron angel and that conflicts between earthly nations reflect struggles between their supernatural patrons. This notion builds on ancient Near Eastern mythology as glimpsed in Psalms 82; 89:5-7; Deut 32:8-9, and serves apocalyptic purposes by emphasizing the close connection between entities and events in the natural and supernatural realms. In Daniel 12, Israel's protector, Michael, appears, and there is turmoil such as has never been seen in the world's history. There is a resurrection that does not seem to include all of humanity, but only certain select good and evil persons, and some of the elect "shine . . . like the stars" (Dan 12:3 NRSV) forever. Daniel is then told to seal up his book until the end.

This brief review of Daniel 7–12 highlights several elements typical of apocalypses. Daniel, a human seer, is granted visions mediated by an angel. He is allowed to see the supernatural world, even heaven itself, and to know of the divine decree for the eschatological defeat of Israel's enemy, Antiochus. Daniel thus learns the truth behind the historical events in the time of the actual author. True interpretation of events depends on divine revelation. Daniel does not come to this understanding through his own talents or insight. His understanding comes through the unveiling of heavenly mysteries.

In addition to features that Daniel shares with all apocalypses, there are a number of ways in which it fits the subgenre of historical apocalypses. There is a review of events that are actually in the real author's past, such as the rise of the Babylonian, Median, Persian, and Greek empires in the form of *ex eventu* prophecy, made possible by the attribution of the work to the ancient seer. When the review reaches Antiochus's persecution, in the real author's present, it shifts to genuine prediction. In fact, the prediction of Antiochus's death in chap. 11 is historically inaccurate in a number of ways. The review builds confidence in the real prediction contained in the text by showing how Daniel accurately foretells the rest of history. It also implies God's control of history. Since there are four beasts, history is periodized, another way of saying that it is controlled by God. History is seen as a whole, under the rubric of divine sovereignty and purpose. History leads to the ultimate goal of the defeat of God's (and so God's people's) enemies and the establishment of God's authority over a harmonious cosmos and a faithful people.

There is a complex and intimate connection between the natural and the supernatural worlds, illustrated especially well by Daniel 7. The scene undergoes several sudden and unexplained shifts between the earthly and the supernatural realms. The implication is that there is a close connection between decisions made in heaven and events in human history. The text does not say that explicitly; it demonstrates it graphically. Because Antiochus is judged in the heavenly court, he dies on earth. The earthly realm can also affect the heavenly, as when Antiochus's persecution is portrayed as an attack on heaven and the angels (Dan 8:10-12, 23-25). The lack of literary transition between the heavenly and the earthly parts of the vision reinforces the impression that the two realms are mutually dependent.

Revelation. The book of Revelation is a Christian work written in western Asia Minor at the end of the first century CE, when the Roman emperor Domitian was on the throne. In Revelation's environment, religious devotion to the goddess Roma and to past and present emperors as gods was an expression of loyalty to Rome. The author viewed the imperial cult as symbolic of Christian accommodation to Hellenistic culture. Such accommodation violated the Christian obligation to render worship to God alone. The letters in Revelation 2–3 bear witness to the extent to which some Christians were at home in Hellenistic and Roman culture, but Revelation's author was convinced that the empire that seduced some Christians and threatened others drew its power from Satan and would soon be defeated by God. Indeed, Satan had already been defeated in heaven by Michael and his angels. Satan's dominion on earth was visible in the oppression of the Christian churches, but his ultimate defeat was inevitable.

In Revelation 4, the seer John ascends to the heavenly throne room, where he sees God and the heavenly court. In God's hand is a sealed scroll containing the eschatological events. There is lamentation in heaven that no one is worthy to open the scroll because until the scroll is opened, the eschatological events cannot take place. In chap. 5, a slain lamb appears, representing the crucified and risen Christ. He takes the scroll from God, and the heavenly host sings a hymn that reveals that he is able to take the scroll and open it because of his death. Here we have the traditional Christian notion that the death and resurrection of Christ set in motion the events of the end time. As in Paul's letters, something eschatological has already happened—Satan's defeat through the death of Christ—and something is still to happen—Satan's ultimate defeat at the hands of Christ at the end of time. The conviction that the end time has already been inaugurated in the death and resurrection of Christ is the major point of difference between Jewish and Christian apocalypticism.

As the seals of the scroll are broken, the events of the end time unfold. The point is that God has a plan for the eschatological events—a plan set in motion by the Christ event. The rest of Revelation reinforces the idea that all of the final events on earth are initiated in heaven and implemented by angels. Eschatological judgment is evident throughout the book. In chap. 19, Christ emerges as the heavenly warrior at the head of his army. He defeats the first beast (the Roman Empire and its emperors) and the second beast (leaders of the imperial cult), and he throws them into the lake of fire. Final judgment comes in chap. 20, where the dragon (Satan) is thrown into the fiery lake. Then the righteous live forever in God's and Christ's presence in the new Jerusalem, now descended onto earth.

Revelation never explicitly quotes Scripture, but it is permeated by biblical allusions and patterns. The use of Isaiah, Ezekiel, Jeremiah, Joel, and Daniel is particularly evident. But events in Revelation are never said to fulfill biblical prophecy. As with other apocalypses, Revelation draws its authority not from biblical proof but from the seer's visions. What he sees divulges what is happening in heaven itself, and this special knowledge grounds the entire book. The use of biblical allusions gives Revelation deep roots in Israel's sacred traditions and taps into their power. Revelation contextualizes its own revelations in the vast sweep of God's previous actions and revelations, but its authority remains steadily grounded in the seer's experience.

Although Daniel is a historical apocalypse and Revelation belongs to the otherworldly journey variety, these books are quite similar in form and content. Indeed, the definition of *apocalypticism* employed by many is dependent on the worldview shared by Daniel and Revelation. Eschatology plays a dominant role in both works, as it does in many definitions of *apocalypticism*. Both works expect public upheaval and eschatological woes. Both look forward to resurrection. Both see heavenly events, including conflict between supernatural beings, reflected on earth. Both symbolize evil powers in bizarre beasts coming from the sea (four in Daniel 7, one in Revelation 13). Both see society in somewhat dualistic terms, although both leave room for movement from the category of those who will perish to those who will be saved. Both refer to the Son of Man, a heavenly figure who plays a role in the eschatological events. Given the fact that Daniel and Revelation are the canonical examples of apocalypses, it is not surprising that the elements they share in common have assumed importance in the definition of *apocalypticism* that is in some cases out of proportion to the presence of these elements in apocalypses in general. Nonetheless, the basic elements of the apocalyptic genre and of its implied worldview are, indeed, shared with all other apocalypses from this period.

THE EARLIEST APOCALYPSES

The earliest extant apocalypses are embedded in *1 Enoch*. They are the *Book of the Watchers* (*1 Enoch* 1–36) and the

Astronomical Book (*1 Enoch* 72–82). They both date from the third century BCE, and both involve otherworldly journeys. The *Book of the Watchers* is in three parts. The first part (chaps. 1–5) serves to introduce the *Book of the Watchers* in particular and the whole of *1 Enoch* in general. It describes the coming of the divine warrior in eschatological judgment. God comes to judge because humans have not followed the example of the cosmos in its obedience to divine commands. The second part (chaps. 6–16) concerns the introduction of evil into the world through the activity of angels, called "watchers," a name that may come from their original function as heavenly guards (see also Dan 4:13, 17, 23). Two strands of tradition are discernible here. One concerns intercourse between angels and human women, a tradition similar to but more fully developed than the fragmentary narrative in Gen 6:1-4. The other tradition concentrates on illicit revelation of heavenly secrets to humans by angels. Both strands see catastrophic consequences, including violence, following from these violations. The earth cries to heaven for relief, and the good angels bring the case before God, who decrees punishment. The sinful watchers enlist Enoch to intercede for them, but he is told of God's irrevocable sentence and is brought to the heavenly sanctuary (chap. 14). In chaps. 17–36, Enoch tours the universe. Most of what he sees concerns eschatological judgment. For example, he sees the place of torment prepared for the sinful watchers and the chambers in which human souls await final judgment. Finally, he sees the preparations that have been made for the restoration of Jerusalem, in which the righteous will live.

The precise historical circumstances that led to the writing of the *Book of the Watchers* are unclear. Two suggestions are the suffering caused by the wars between successors of Alexander the Great and dissatisfaction caused by the laxity toward Torah of the Jerusalem priesthood. What is clear is that the author of the book is unhappy with present circumstances and sees their cause as the people's deviance from God's original plans for the cosmos. The solution is typically apocalyptic—sentence is passed in the supernatural world, evidence for which Enoch receives both directly from God and indirectly through his tour of the universe. Eschatological judgment is inevitable.

The *Astronomical Book* is an excellent example of how closely human history is interrelated with the cosmos. Most of the book is a somewhat dry review of astronomical laws. It takes the form of a tour of the cosmos by Enoch, guided by the angel Uriel. Enoch learns that because of human sinfulness, the universe is disrupted (chap. 80). Crops will not grow properly, rain is withheld, and the orbits of the heavenly bodies are disturbed. The book is presently integrated into *1 Enoch*, so it is not in its original form, but Enoch's tour of heaven assumes some sort of ascent as described in *1 Enoch* 14. In chap. 81, Enoch reads heavenly tablets that reveal the course of human history, and he is sent back to earth to write down what he has seen and to warn of eschatological judgment.

LATE APOCALYPSES

Four Jewish apocalypses were written in reaction to the destruction of Jerusalem in 70 CE: *4 Ezra*, *2 Baruch*, the *Apocalypse of Abraham*, and *3 Baruch*. The book of *4 Ezra* is now preserved as 2 Esdras 3–14; 2 Esdras 1–2 and 15–16 are Christian additions to the Jewish work, and 2:42-48 is itself a little apocalypse. Set in the time of the destruction of Solomon's Temple by the Babylonians in 587 BCE, *4 Ezra* was really written after the destruction six and a half centuries later. It consists of seven sections. In the first three, Ezra argues with the angel Uriel and challenges the justice of a God who allows Israel to be punished at the hands of unrighteous Gentiles. Uriel offers Ezra an apocalyptic solution. The angel first stresses the inaccessibility of the heavenly information that is necessary to understand earthly events. Humans can no more achieve such understanding on their own than they can weigh fire, measure wind, or recall days that are past (4 Ezra 4:5). Nonetheless, God can choose to reveal such information, and that is precisely what happens as Uriel speaks to Ezra. Uriel says that God made two worlds, and it is only in the world to come that the righteous will receive their just reward and the wicked their punishment. Ezra protests that there are so few righteous people that the angel's words provide little comfort.

In the fourth section of the book, Ezra receives a vision of a woman weeping, whom he tries to distract by telling her of Zion's destruction. She is then transformed into a marvelous city, and the angel tells Ezra that she is Zion restored. From this point on, Ezra's attitude changes. He accepts God's judgments as expressed by the angel. Then follow two visions predicting the victory of the forces of good over the powers of evil. In the first vision, an eagle represents Rome. It is reproached and defeated by a lion, representing the Messiah. In the second vision, "something like the figure of a man" arises from the sea (a probable allusion to Daniel 7), does battle with the nations at Zion, and emerges victorious. In the last section of the book, Ezra preserves the Torah, which had been burned in the destruction. Under inspiration, he dictates it to scribes. The twenty-four books of the Torah are meant for the public. Ezra also dictates seventy other books that are to be revealed only to the elect, and those books appear to be held in even higher esteem than the Torah itself, "for in them is the spring of understanding, the fountain of wisdom, and the river of knowledge" (14:47). It would appear that these other books are apocalyptic revelations, necessary for true understanding.

An interesting aspect of 4 Ezra is that it polemicizes against the notion, common in other apocalypses, that anyone could possibly ascend to heaven (see John 3:13). It does so to emphasize human beings' inability to understand heavenly realities on their own, an understanding that is necessary to comprehend earthly happenings. Nonetheless, Uriel does reveal those heavenly secrets to Ezra.

A perennial problem of interpreting 4 Ezra is the question of why Ezra changes his attitude during the course of the book. In the first three visions and during part of the fourth, Ezra complains about God's ways, questions the angel sharply, and seems dissatisfied with the angel's answers. Even if, as some interpreters claim, Ezra does show some movement in his position in the first half of the book, there is still a remarkable change in his attitude after the fourth vision. Once he sees the woman transformed into the restored Zion, he accepts God's ways and the angel's answers. A plausible solution to this quandary is that Ezra's religious experience—his encounter with the grieving woman and her transformation into restored Zion—is necessary for him to transcend his sorrowful circumstances and accept the apocalyptic solution offered to him. The angel and the seer may represent two aspects of the real author, a person so anguished by the destruction of Jerusalem that he was torn between acceptance of God's ways and rebellion against them. It was only the author's own religious experience, perhaps the very visions described in this book, that led him to accept and to espouse the solution the book provides. Writing the book allowed the author to impart his experiences to others and lead them through the same process he had undergone. This explanation suggests that a real religious experience, perhaps an authentic vision or set of visions, underlies this apocalypse and perhaps others as well.

Another response to the destruction of the Second Temple in 70 CE is *2 Baruch,* which is also set in the time of the destruction of the previous Temple by the Babylonians in the sixth century BCE. This work stresses the foundational importance of the Torah for the continued existence of Israel, emphasizes the temporary nature of this world, and anticipates an eschatological judgment in which Israel's enemies will be punished and the righteous will be elevated to the positions of the stars. It thereby relativizes the loss of the Temple and helps to provide for Israel's survival without a sacrificial cult.

The *Apocalypse of Abraham* develops Abraham's vision in Genesis 15 into a full-blown apocalypse. The idea that Abraham received more extensive revelation than is narrated in Genesis 15 is also found in *2 Baruch* 4. The apocalypse is in two parts. Chapters 1–8 tell of Abraham's discovery of the falseness of idolatry and his rejection of it. In chaps. 9–32, Abraham makes a heavenly journey assisted by the angel Yaoel. This twofold structure recalls that of Daniel, where the stories about Daniel in chaps. 1–6 prepare for the apocalypse proper in chaps. 7–12. During the cosmic journey, Abraham views the whole of human history. This section of the apocalypse has been adapted by Christians, but most of the material is Jewish.

The review of history leads to eschatological judgment. As with the other apocalypses, the key to understanding human history lies in the supernatural world and is able to be known only through direct revelation.

The book of *3 Baruch* is a Jewish apocalypse dating from the early second century CE. It describes Baruch's ascent through five levels of heaven. Baruch never enters the presence of God. There is a door in the fifth heaven through which the archangel Michael goes to bring the prayers of the faithful to God, but Baruch never passes through that door. Thus the apocalypse may envisage the more common scheme of seven heavens, even though Baruch sees only five. This apocalypse contains no cosmic upheavals, political turmoil, or public eschatology. Baruch observes the places of reward and punishment in heaven reserved for those who have died. Therefore, this apocalypse offers an example of personalized eschatology.

THE *SIMILITUDES OF ENOCH*

The *Similitudes of Enoch* has survived as part of the Ethiopic form of the collection called *1 Enoch* (chaps. 37–71). It is the only one of the five books in that collection not preserved at Qumran. (The Qumran fragments do contain part of another Enochic book called the *Book of the Giants*, not present in the Ethiopic manuscript.) The *Similitudes* is a fascinating document both as a witness to Jewish belief and thought and as a parallel to Christian notions. Because it is not attested in the Aramaic fragments at Qumran and because of its similarity to Christian ideas, some scholars have sought to date it quite late, perhaps in the third century CE. Scholarly opinion now tends strongly to a first century CE date.

The *Similitudes of Enoch* is an otherworldly journey apocalypse. Enoch is caught up to the heavenly throne room and is given revelations that make him understand the way the world is and the inevitability of eschatological judgment. The most common designation for God in this book is "Lord of the Spirits," which appears to be an adaptation of the biblical "Lord of Hosts." The change to "Spirits" indicates the view, common in apocalypticism, that an unseen world of spiritual beings determines what happens in this world. When Enoch first views God in heaven, he also sees another figure, called the "Elect One of righteousness" (*1 Enoch* 39). In chap. 46, the dependence of the *Similitudes* on Daniel 7 for its vision of heaven becomes clear. God is called one with a "head of days" who has a head "white like wool," recalling Dan 7:9, where God is called the Ancient of Days who wears white and has hair like pure wool. With God in *1 Enoch* 46 is one whose "face was like the appearance of a son of man." Elsewhere in the *Similitudes* this mysterious figure is called the Righteous One, the Elect One, and the Messiah. The adjectives *righteous* and *elect* are also applied to faithful humans on earth, who recognize the authority of the Lord of Spirits. Just as the one like a son of man is hidden in heaven, known only to Enoch and to those to whom he reveals him, so also the righteous are hidden on earth, to be recognized only at the eschatological judgment (*1 Enoch* 38:1). The ultimate fate of the righteous will be to live with the one like a son of man forever (*1 Enoch* 62:14). In the *Similitudes*, the relation of the one like a son of man to the elect on earth is analogous to the relation between the one like a son of man and Israel in Daniel 7. In each case, the figure like a son of man is the heavenly patron of the faithful.

Contrasted with the righteous are the sinners. They are portrayed as the powerful and wealthy of the earth, those persons who trust in their own power and riches. They do not acknowledge the Lord of Spirits, nor do they admit that their status is due to the Lord. Therefore, the one like a son of man will judge them. He will sit on a throne to judge them (*1 Enoch* 62:1-12), and he will lift them from their own thrones (*1 Enoch* 46:4-8). Their acknowledgment of the Lord's authority and their pleas for mercy at the final judgment will go unheeded. They will be punished, together with the angels who disobeyed God (*1 Enoch* 67). Eschatological judgment is sure, and it will result in a reversal of fortune between those who are now wealthy, powerful, and arrogant and those who are now righteous and persecuted. This reversal is fairly common in Jewish and Christian eschatological thought of this period (e.g., the *Epistle of Enoch* [*1 Enoch* 91–104]; Matt 19:30; 20:16; Luke 1:46-55; 1 Cor 1:20-25; Revelation), and it is especially powerful in apocalyptic settings. For apocalypses, the certainty of reversal rests on divine revelation and involves rewards and punishments even after death. The *Similitudes* contain the idea that a certain number of righteous people must shed their blood before the eschatological judgment can take place (*1 Enoch* 47:3-4). According to 4 Ezra 4:36 and *2 Bar* 23:4-5; 48:46, the number of humans to be created is fixed, and must be completed before the end can come. Revelation 6:11 adapts that idea to its own purposes by making it a certain number of martyrs that must be fulfilled. The *Similitudes* is close to Revelation here. All such schemes imply that history is determined by God in advance.

Enoch emphasizes the uniqueness of his revelation. He says, "Till the present day such wisdom has never been given by the Lord of Spirits as I have received" (*1 Enoch* 37:4). Chapter 42 claims that when personified Wisdom was sent out by God to find a dwelling place among humans, she had to return to heaven because she could find no such place. This contrasts with Sirach 24, where Wisdom finds a home in Zion and is equated with the Torah. The *Similitudes* claim that true wisdom can be found only in heaven, in the presence of the Lord of Spirits and the one like a son of man. Enoch must go there to find it. While there, he sees the founts of wisdom and reads the heavenly books (see Dan 7:10; Rev 3:5; 20:12). At the end of the apocalypse, Enoch is permanently exalted to heaven after having conveyed his revelations to humans (*1 Enoch* 70). In what is probably a later ending, he is identified with the son of man (*1 Enoch* 71:14).

The *Similitudes of Enoch* is certainly an apocalyptic text, with its otherworldly journey, its disclosure of secrets that explain this world and the next, and its anticipation of postmortem rewards and punishments. Its final judgment is public and involves a strong critique of the powerful and wealthy people of the earth. It is especially interesting for students of early Christianity because of the enigmatic figure of the one like a son of man, the Righteous One and the Elect One, who is to judge the world at the end and with whom the righteous will live forever. The similarities between this figure and the Christ of some early Christian documents have led to theories of Christian dependence on the *Similitudes* and, conversely, to suggestions that the *Similitudes* depend on Christian ideas. Dependence in either direction has never been convincingly argued. It is of great interest, however, that such a mediating figure is attested to in a Jewish document of the first century CE, because it helps to provide a context for early Christian concepts of Christ.

QUMRAN AND CHRISTIANITY AS APOCALYPTIC MOVEMENTS

If discussions of apocalypses and apocalypticism are rife with debates and disagreements, the difficulties increase when the topic is actual apocalyptic groups. Some scholars insist that a group can be considered apocalyptic only if it produces apocalypses. Others opt for a wider definition, considering those groups apocalyptic whose worldview is like that found in the apocalypses. In most cases, this means the particular worldview especially characteristic of historical apocalypses, including public eschatology. A good deal of discussion of this issue centers on two collections of documents: the Dead Sea Scrolls and the New Testament.

Qumran. The Dead Sea Scrolls are a collection of manuscripts, some fairly well preserved and others in fragmentary form, that were found in caves in the Judean desert in a series of discoveries beginning in 1947. They are commonly thought to have been the library of a community that inhabited a settlement nearby, whose ruins are called Qumran. The scrolls fall into three basic categories: biblical manuscripts, texts written by members of the community, and other texts that are neither biblical nor written by the sect. This is a somewhat simplified typology, since the community may have had a complex history involving several groups over time with varying relationships to one another and to the authorities at Jerusalem. To date there is no clear evidence that the sect living at Qumran produced any apocalypses. However, they seem to have had a high regard for Daniel and

1 Enoch, both of which are found in multiple copies among the scrolls. They also possessed the book of *Jubilees,* a work of mixed genres with apocalyptic features, written in the second century BCE.

Although the matter is disputed among scholars, most still consider the community at Qumran to have been an apocalyptic community. Its members were intensely interested in the supernatural world, explaining events in Israel's history and in the history of the sect itself in terms of that other world. They saw their own time as part of what they called the "Age of Wrath," an age dominated by Belial and the human and supernatural beings under his sway. They expected a great eschatological battle to be conducted in a preordained way, which would result in the victory of the forces of good over the powers of evil. The Qumran community thought itself to be allied with the good angels, chief of whom was Michael, who would fight alongside members of the community—the sons of light—against Satan and his supernatural allies and human allies—the sons of darkness. It considered that it had such knowledge through divine mysteries revealed to the Teacher of Righteousness, a key figure in the origins of the community. Because of the revelations made to the Teacher, the community knew the correct interpretation of Torah and therefore was able to please God and able to interpret the prophetic literature accurately. The people at Qumran saw history as culminating in themselves and interpreted the prophets and several psalms as predicting the community's own history.

Parallels between the Qumran community and early Christianity are plentiful and have been explored in depth. Each interpreted Scripture eschatologically and saw it as pointing to itself. Just as the Teacher of Righteousness unlocked the mysteries of Scripture for his followers, so also did Jesus for his own. Each had an authoritative interpretation of Torah that contradicted that of the ruling authorities. Each expected an eschatological resolution to the problems of this sinful world.

The Synoptic Gospels. Revelation is the only apocalypse in the New Testament, but apocalyptic influence is strong throughout the rest of the New Testament as well. The synoptic Gospels have strong apocalyptic attributes. In each of them, Jesus delivers what is usually referred to as an apocalyptic discourse (Mark 13; Matthew 24–25; Luke 21), in which he predicts eschatological sufferings to be endured by his followers, followed by the return of the Son of Man to rescue the elect. Matthew repeatedly refers to the close of the age, and as part of his apocalyptic discourse he has Jesus tell of the last judgment for all humans, followed by eternal rewards and punishments (Matt 25:31-46; see also Matt 13:24-30, 36-43). Matthew associates Jesus' death and resurrection with other eschatological events (Matt 27:51-55). Whether Jesus himself thought in apocalyptic terms is highly debated. No one claims that Jesus wrote apocalypses. Many think that since he began his career as a follower of John the Baptist, an eschatological prophet, and since the New Testament documents present him in an apocalyptic light, Jesus himself probably thought in such terms. Others see the apocalyptic characteristic in the New Testament portrait of Jesus as a later development by the church, and they see Jesus as being similar to a wisdom teacher, a sort of countercultural figure who could be compared to other such teachers and philosophers in the ancient world.

Paul. The apostle Paul is often characterized as having an apocalyptic worldview. He traces his call to a "revelation" (*apokalypsis*; Gal 1:12). He claims to have made a heavenly journey and to have received other visions and revelations (2 Cor 12:1-7). He divides humanity into those being saved and those perishing (1 Cor 1:18). He thinks that his work is being hindered by Satan (1 Thess 2:18). He expects this world to pass away soon (1 Cor 7:26, 31; Rom 13:11). He even presents brief eschatological scenarios. In 1 Thess 4:13-18, he expects Christ to return with a trumpet blast, at which time the faithful dead will rise and be caught up together with the living believers into the clouds, to be with Christ forever. Paul insists, however, that the exact time of the end is unknowable (1 Thess 5:1-11). In 1 Cor 15:20-28, he says that Christ is the firstfruits of the dead. At the end of time, all of the righteous will rise, and then Christ will hand over the kingdom to God, having conquered "every ruler and every authority and power" (1 Cor 15:24 NRSV) and all his enemies. That these enemies are supernatural is supported by the fact that the last enemy to be overcome is death (1 Cor 15:26). In 1 Cor 15:50-57, Paul divulges an eschatological "mystery" about the transformation of the faithful at the end, and in Rom 11:25-32 he shares another "mystery" concerning the inclusion of the Jews among the saved at the end time. In Rom 8:18-25, Paul claims that the entire creation waits for the eschaton and the revelation of the righteous.

CONCLUSION

Apocalypticism played a far greater role in early Judaism and early Christianity than is attested by the presence of only two apocalypses in the Bible. The Jewish and Christian apocalypses written between 300 BCE and 200 CE constitute a substantial body of literature. Consideration of other genres that display features, imagery, patterns, and views typical of apocalypses leads to examination of a still larger body of texts. Discussions of apocalypses and apocalypticism are central to conversations about Second Temple Judaism, earliest Christianity, and the historical Jesus. They have helped to situate various forms of Judaism within both the sweep of Israel's history and culture and the larger Hellenistic world. They have also shed light on Christianity's Jewish roots and on its relation to its Hellenistic environment. Studies of apocalypticism and of individual apocalypses will continue to contribute to biblical studies and to modern assessments of the two ancient religions for some time to come.

BIBLIOGRAPHY

Charlesworth, James H., ed. *The Old Testament Pseudepigrapha.* 2 vols. Garden City, N.Y.: Doubleday, 1983–1985.

Collins, John J., ed. *Apocalypse: The Morphology of a Genre.* Semeia 14. Missoula, Mont.: Scholars Press, 1979.

———. *The Apocalyptic Imagination: An Introduction to the Jewish Matrix of Christianity.* New York: Crossroad, 1984.

Collins, John J., and James H. Charlesworth, eds. *Mysteries and Revelations: Apocalyptic Studies Since the Uppsala Colloquium.* Sheffield: JSOT, 1991.

Hanson, Paul D. *The Dawn of Apocalyptic: The Historical and Sociological Roots of Jewish Apocalyptic Eschatology.* Rev. ed. Philadelphia: Fortress, 1979; orig. ed. 1975.

Hellholm, David. *Apocalypticism in the Mediterranean World and the Near East: Proceedings of the International Colloquium on Apocalypticism, Uppsala, August 12-17, 1979.* Tübingen: Mohr, 1983.

Rowland, Christopher. *The Open Heaven: A Study of Apocalyptic in Judaism and Christianity.* New York: Crossroad, 1982.

Stone, Michael. "Apocalyptic Literature." In *Jewish Writings of the Second Temple Period.* Edited by Michael Stone. Philadelphia: Fortress, 1984.

THE BOOK OF DANIEL
INTRODUCTION, COMMENTARY, AND REFLECTIONS
BY
DANIEL L. SMITH-CHRISTOPHER

THE BOOK OF
DANIEL

INTRODUCTION

The book of Daniel is arguably the most unusual book of the Hebrew Bible. Certainly part of its notoriety can be attributed to the textual and literary problems that have perplexed scholars for generations. But, as we will have occasion to point out in the commentary that follows, some moderns would suggest that Daniel is also a notoriously dangerous book that has fueled religious speculation as well as contributing to social unrest and even revolution. In order to appreciate reading a biblical book of such multifaceted interest, one needs to place Daniel in some literary, historical, and—perhaps just as important—sociological and political context.

LITERARY CONTEXT: THE COURT STORIES (DANIEL 1–6) AND THE APOCALYPTIC VISIONS (DANIEL 7–12)

The book of Daniel comes to us in two different, although related, Semitic languages. Chapters 1:1–2:4a and 8–12 are written in Hebrew, while chaps. 2:4b–7 are written in Aramaic, the *lingua franca* of the ancient Near East, especially in Mesopotamia, in the late Babylonian, Persian, and early Hellenistic periods (before Aramaic was replaced by Greek). There have been some attempts to relate these language changes in the book to stages in the composition of the book (suggesting, e.g., chaps. 2–7 as an original and early version of the text, before chaps. 1; 8–12 were added), but such theories have never achieved a general consensus in textual studies of the book. One of the main reasons for the difficulty is that the language differences do *not* coincide with the literary changes between chaps. 1–6 and 7–12.

Daniel 1–6. It is obvious to any reader of the book of Daniel that the first six chapters differ dramatically from the last six chapters. The first half of the book consists of six stories that have been called, variously, "diaspora novellas/stories,"[1] "court stories,"[2] and even divided more

---

1. A. Meinhold, "Die Diasporanovelle: Eine Alttestamentliche Gattung" (Ph.D. diss., University of Greifswald, 1969).
2. L. Wills, *The Jew in the Court of the Foreign King* (Minneapolis: Fortress, 1990); S. Niditch and R. Doran, "The Success Story of the Wise Courtier: A Formal Approach," *JBL* 96 (1977) 179-93.

specifically into "contest" stories (chaps. 2; 4–5) and "conflict" stories (chaps. 3; 6).[3] These first stories in the book are usually assumed to have derived from the life of the Jewish Eastern diaspora after the time of the exile in 587/586, but usually are assigned to the Persian (539–333 BCE) or Hellenistic (333–63 BCE) periods rather than to the Babylonian period (597–539 BCE).[4] Although some of the court details seem, at first sight, to be impressive, most scholars argue that the Daniel stories as well as the stories of his friends Hananiah, Mishael, and Azariah are fictional accounts that represent the folklore of the diaspora communities. Furthermore, these details are something that a healthy imagination could create, drawing from the gossip and speculation of the surrounding peoples under Persian occupation. There was similar speculation about the pomp and circumstance of the Persian court among the Greeks as well.[5]

Recent attention to the stories in chaps. 1–6 has also emphasized their literary character as stories that recommend a "lifestyle for the Diaspora."[6] Most literary analysis of these stories, however, has tended to overlook their potent sociopolitical power as stories of resistance to cultural and spiritual assimilation of a minority by a dominant foreign power.[7] From this perspective, these stories take on a more ominous shade than from the perspective of purely folkloristic analysis.

Related to these questions is that of who actually wrote these stories. It is often suggested that these stories derived from an upper class of the Eastern diaspora community simply because only a member of the upper classes could aspire to service in the emperor's court. It is further assumed that these stories reflect a somewhat benign view of the foreign emperor and, therefore, are certainly much older than the assumed setting for the second half of the book of Daniel, which is much darker and more pessimistic about worldly powers, because of the persecution of the Palestinian Jewish communities under Antiochus IV Epiphanes, the reigning Seleucid Hellenistic ruler between 167 and 164 BCE.

It will be the perspective of this commentary, however, that the authors of Daniel 1–6 did *not* aspire actually to work for the foreign emperor. Rather, the emperor's court served as an ideal setting for a political and religious folklore that speaks of surviving and flourishing in a foreign land, in a hostile environment. It effectively communicates as well the powerful images of lowly Jewish exiles standing with faith and courage before the very throne of the occupying (and militarily superior) emperor, overcoming his military and political power through the power of God. The perspective of the book of Daniel toward foreign conquerors, even in the first six chapters, is not nearly so benign as is often thought; in fact, it is openly hostile to their authority. This hostile challenge to authority provides one of the major unifying factors of Daniel as a whole, and is not merely an aspect of the latter half of the book.[8] This hostility requires a creative theology of confrontation as an essential aspect of the modern use of the book.

Court story narratives are not, of course, unique to Daniel. Besides the obvious similarities with Esther and the Joseph tales of Genesis (the striking similarities among these three texts were systematically noted as early as 1895) and even Ezra and Nehemiah (Nehemiah is a courtier), we should note the story of Zerubbabel in 1 Esdras. The discovery of the Dead Sea Scrolls and their publication since 1948 has provided other court stories of Jewish courtiers that resemble Daniel in some interesting details. The most dramatic example of such a story is the *Prayer of Nabonidus*, which many scholars believe is a more ancient form of a Daniel legend, even though Daniel is not explicitly mentioned in the fragments that have been found. The fragment reads as follows (with gaps and difficulties indicated by brackets):

---

3. W. L. Humphreys, "A Life-Style for Diaspora: A Study of the Tales of Esther and Daniel," *JBL* 93 (1973) 211-23; John J. Collins, *The Apocalyptic Visions of the Book of Daniel* (Missoula, Mont.: Scholars Press, 1977); and John J. Collins, *Daniel*, FOTL (Grand Rapids: Eerdmans, 1984).

4. Collins dates the "traditions," rather than the texts as we have them, to the late Persian period. The Aramaic of the book of Daniel is older than the Aramaic of the Dead Sea Scrolls. This suggests that the tales should be dated early in the Hellenistic era, which began in 333 BCE with the conquests of Alexander the Great.

5. J. M. Cook, *The Persian Empire* (New York: Schocken, 1983) 132-33.

6. The classic study is Humphreys, "A Life-Style for Diaspora," 211-23.

7. A notable exception is D. N. Fewell, *Circle of Sovereignty: A Story of Stories in Daniel 1–6* (Sheffield: Almond, 1988).

8. Note the perspective of D. Berrigan in his series on Daniel, "Till the End of Empire," in *The Other Side* (July-August 1990) 8-14; (September-October 1990) 8-17; (November-December 1990) 36-42.

1 Words of the prayer which Nabonidus, king of the la[nd of Baby]lon, [the great] king, pra[yed when we were afflicted]
2 by an evil inflammation, by the decree of God the All-Highest, in Teiman. [I Nabonidus] was afflicted [with an evil inflammation]
3 for seven years and was banished far from [men until I prayed to God the All Highest]
4 and an exorcist pardoned my sin. He was a Jewish [man] of the [exiles, and he said to me:]
5 Proclaim and write to the glory, exa[ltation and honor] of the name of Go[d the All-Highest. And I wrote as follows; When]
6 I was afflicted with an evil inflammation and I stayed in Teiman [by the decree of the all Highest God, I]
7 prayed for seven years [to all] Gods of silver and gold, [bronze, of iron]
8 of wood, of stone, of clay, for [I thought] they were Gods.[9]

This fragment contains a number of interesting details that relate to the study of Daniel. First, and most important, it specifically names and, therefore, connects Nabonidus, last king of Babylon, to the Daniel traditions. It is often assumed that the images of Nebuchadnezzar in many of the Daniel stories seem better suited to the historical Nabonidus (who was the historical father of Belshazzar of Daniel chap. 5), and this fragment would seem to confirm that suspicion. That Nebuchadnezzar was eventually substituted is not hard to understand, given that he was, after all, the conqueror of Jerusalem and responsible for the destruction of the Temple—and thus a more powerful symbol of Babylonian rule than was Nabonidus. Second, however, this fragment suggests that many Daniel stories may have circulated among the Jewish people in a kind of Daniel "folklore cycle" and that our present book of Daniel contains only a selection from that folklore tradition. Finally, there are some interesting specifics in this fragment, such as the list of materials in lines 7-8 that resembles lists in the book of Daniel and the story line that the Babylonian king had to learn that God is the true god, and not one of the gods of gold and silver. Although the historicity of many of the biblical and nonbiblical accounts must be doubted, given what we know from other sources, the theology of these stories (and the visions) is not significant for their time alone, but remains significant for modern Christians who seek to construct a biblically informed theology for contemporary living.

Daniel 7–12. The last six chapters of Daniel are the most important example of apocalyptic literature in the Hebrew Bible. A considerable amount of scholarly research has gone into the definition and description of apocalyptic literature, of which we have many examples outside the canon of the Old and the New Testaments.[10] Clearly, apocalyptic was an important style of theological writing for at least 500 years, during the Hellenistic and Roman periods (roughly 333 BCE–200 CE, although it may extend back into the Persian period, if some Persian influences are accepted).[11] We have both Jewish and Christian examples of this type of literature. Apocalyptic is most generally defined as literature that deals with the revelation and understanding of mysteries, but there have been attempts to be even more specific and comprehensive. For example, Collins has proposed the following definition:

"Apocalypse" is a genre of revelatory literature with a narrative framework, in which a revelation is mediated by an otherworldly being to a human recipient, disclosing a transcendent reality which is both temporal, insofar as it envisages eschatological salvation, and spatial insofar as it involves another, supernatural world.

An apocalypse is intended to interpret present earthly circumstances in the light of the supernatural world and of the future, and to influence both the understanding and the behavior of the audience by means of divine authority.[12]

---

9. 4QPrNab. Translation from F. García-Martínez, *Qumran and Apocalyptic: Studies on the Aramaic Texts from Qumran* (Leiden: Brill, 1992) 119-20.
10. See the article in this volume by Frederick J. Murphy, "Introduction to Apocalyptic Literature," 1-16.
11. On Persian influences, see esp. A. Hultgård, "The Bahman Yasht: A Persian Perspective," in *Mysteries and Revelations: Apocalyptic Studies Since the Uppsala Colloquium*, ed. John J. Collins and J. H. Charlesworth (Sheffield: JSOT, 1991).
12. John J. Collins, "Genre, Ideology, and Social Movements in Jewish Apocalypticism," in *Mysteries and Revelations, Apocalyptic Studies Since the Uppsala Colloquium*, ed. J. J. Collins and J. H. Charlesworth (Sheffield: JSOT, 1991) 19.

The advantage of such a definition is not that it is finally complete, but that it gives students and scholars at least some kind of common language in their analysis of actual texts. The point is not to exclude certain texts from consideration (as if to create some kind of informal canon of "real" apocalyptic texts) but to facilitate our understanding of any particular text in all its unique originality as well as formal resemblances to other texts. Daniel, for example, has clear resemblances to books like *1 Enoch,* but they were not issued from some sort of theological or literary mold, and assumptions about their similarity can be hazardous.

Equally hazardous is the attempt to generalize about a sociological context for apocalyptic literature as a whole. Reid, for example, used a sophisticated sociological outline in order to compare *1 Enoch* and Daniel, and he concluded that they have quite different source communities.[13] Other scholars, however, are content to generalize that apocalyptic literature seems to come from "disenfranchised" communities, without being more specific.[14] It is not necessary, however, to suggest that an entire genre has the same sociological setting in every specific case (attractive as such a conclusion may be!). The sociological setting of Daniel must also be determined on the basis of internal evidence as well as the genre of the stories and visions. That the authors of Daniel are hostile to foreign conquerors and to ancient Near Eastern empire building is clear from *what* the book says, and not only from *how* it is said. Furthermore, the social context of the exile itself and the realities of occupation from then on should alert the reader to certain attitudes that are revealed in Daniel. For this reason it is important to review the basic historical background before discussing the meaning of that background for a reading of the book of Daniel.

HISTORICAL BACKGROUND OF DANIEL: THE CONTEXT OF EMPIRE

The independent Jewish kingdom was short lived in the ancient Near East. Allowing for a 200-year period of decentralized tribal existence (roughly 1200–1000 BCE), the united kingdom existed under the Davidic monarchy from 1020 to 922 BCE, with the northern breakaway kingdom lasting until the Assyrian conquest of 722 BCE. The southern state of Judah continued until the Babylonian conquests began in 597 BCE and was completely overrun when Jerusalem was devastated in 587/586 BCE, the beginning of the Babylonian exile. Both the northern and the southern kingdoms ended tragically (but not atypically for the ancient Near East) in military conquest and deportation of a sizable segment of the populace—taken, it appears, from the institutional leadership of royal, military, and religious sectors. We know more about the Babylonian exiles than we do about the Assyrian captives because this community survived the ordeal. With the brief exception of the Hasmonean client state (which, given the realities of Hellenistic and Roman power, is not much of an exception), there was never again a military-royalist state of the ancient Hebrews in Palestine.

Around 539 BCE, Cyrus the Persian conquered Babylon and soon thereafter began allowing parties of Jews to return to Palestine (Ezra 1–6). This action is often interpreted as a freedom policy on the part of the Persians. But it must be kept in mind that these missions back to Palestine had particular Persian goals in mind—particularly the shoring up of the western flank of the Persian Empire when the Greeks became a troublesome presence in the Mediterranean rim.

The Persian period ended with the conquests of Alexander the Great in 333 BCE. After Alexander's death in 323 BCE in Babylon, his massive empire was divided among his generals. After a period of internal warfare, lines were drawn in the Near East between the eastern portion of the empire, based in Syria and Mesopotamia, and Egypt to the west. The Ptolemies ruled Egypt, which included Palestine until 198 BCE, when the Seleucids (Antiochus III), who ruled the eastern section of the empire, annexed Palestine to their region. Alexander's conquests brought

---

13. S. B. Reid, *Enoch and Daniel,* Bibal Monograph Series (Berkeley: Bibal, 1989).
14. G. W. F. Nickelsburg, "Social Aspects of Palestinian Jewish Apocalypticism," in D. Hellholm, ed., *Apocalypticism in the Mediterranean World and the Near East* (Tübingen: Mohr, 1983) 641-54; see also, in the same volume, E. P. Sanders, "The Genre of Palestinian Jewish Apocalypses," 447-59. Note recent disagreements in Stephen L. Cook, *Prophecy and Apocalypticism: The Postexilic Social Setting* (Minneapolis: Fortress, 1995).

an intensification of Hellenistic influence on life, but as Morton Smith has recently pointed out, western influence on Palestine is documented from the Philistine involvement in the early monarchy, and only intensifies in the Babylonian, Persian, and post-Alexandrian historical eras.[15] Following Alexander's death, and until Seleucid rule in 198 BCE, the Ptolemaic rule of Egypt was economically rigid, although most scholars doubt that there was any severe persecution when compared to the Seleucid period that followed. Newsome noted that, according to the Zenon Papyri from the Ptolemaic period, the Jews were "considered little more than serfs in that economic pyramid which placed the Greeks and Macedonians at the top."[16]

The era of Hellenistic rule that is of greatest interest for the study of the book of Daniel is the reign of Antiochus IV Epiphanes (175–164 BCE). Antiochus's father, Antiochus III, had already managed to expel the Ptolemies from Palestine by 200 BCE, and at first the Jewish residents welcomed him as a liberator (especially from Ptolemaic taxation!). Already during the years of Seleucus IV Philopater (187–175 BCE), the immediate successor of Antiochus III, the Jewish community was fractured into rival parties. A certain Simon denounced Onias III, at that time the high priest, and suggested that the high priest should not have such control of the great wealth of the temple treasury. Simon and his allies were pro-Seleucid, while Onias and Hyrcanus (the head of one of the aristocratic families named Tobias) were pro-Ptolemaic. When Onias traveled to Antioch-on-Orantes to appeal to the king, the new successor to the throne, Antiochus IV, imprisoned him. Jason, brother of Onias, paid a large sum of money to Antiochus IV, who promptly made Jason the high priest. Jason was at the head of the move to modernize and Hellenize Jewish life, and he became a significant ally to Antiochus IV's efforts to rule the unruly Jews.

Matters took an even more complex turn when Simon's brother Menelaus, the old rival of Onias, outbid Jason for the office of high priest. So the situation involved two rival Hellenizing factions among the Jewish aristocracy and a third anti-Hellenistic party of Jews, led by the religious resistance known as the Hasidim (the "pious ones," although some have suggested the translation "the committed ones"); there were many other factions among the anti-Hellenistic parties as well. These events took a serious turn for the worse at the end of Antiochus IV's campaigns in Egypt. Antiochus IV managed to destroy the Egyptian army of Ptolemy VI Philometer (180–145 BCE) in 168 BCE. But instead of allowing Antiochus IV to consolidate power even over Egypt, Rome intervened to halt Antiochus IV's advance. Roman intervention is symbolized in the person of Popilius, who forced a humiliated Antiochus to withdraw his forces when they met at Eleusis. Back in Jerusalem, Jason had imprisoned Menelaus after hearing that Antiochus IV had been killed in battle. But the word that Jason had acted on was false, and when Antiochus assessed the situation in Jerusalem, it appeared to be open revolt against his authority, initiated perhaps by those who thought Antiochus was in a weakened position, even if not actually dead. Antiochus IV's response to the disarray in Jerusalem was violent. Not only were many Jews killed or sold into slavery, but also the Temple was violated; eventually certain aspects of Jewish traditional practice were banned as contributing factors to what Antiochus IV perceived as disloyalty. For some scholars, persecution of religiously motivated resisters to Antiochus's Hellenization policies under Jewish leaders like Jason makes sense—even in the context of otherwise tolerant policies that normally allowed diverse religious expressions: "If the revolt was led by Hasidim, for whom the commandments of the Torah were of the utmost sanctity, and if devotion to the Mosaic Law was the watchword of the uprising, then that Law had to be extirpated if the rebellion was to be put down."[17]

These political policies toward the rebellious Jews resulted in an intensification of intracommunal hostility as well as hostility toward the rulers. Antiochus IV's indulgences of rival priests who sought the office of high priest created internal struggles in the Jewish community that are now recognized as important to the strife of 167–164 BCE as were Antiochus IV's own policies. The emperor's endorsement of the move to make the Temple a home for an altar (rather than,

---

15. M. Smith, "Hellenization," in M. Stone and D. Satran, eds., *Emerging Judaism* (Minneapolis: Fortress, 1989) 111-12.
16. J. D. Newsome, *Greeks, Romans, Jews* (Philadelphia: Trinity Press International, 1992) 37.
17. V. Tcherikover, *Hellenistic Civilization and the Jews* (New York: Atheneum, 1970) 198.

most scholars think, an actual image) for Baal Shamem/Zeus Olympios as well as the strengthening of the Greek garrison (the Akra) and the building of such Hellenistic institutions as a gymnasium as a part of the process of Hellenizing the Jews all resulted in violent factionalism in the Jewish community. Part of Antiochus's policies clearly involved the strengthening of the military presence in Jerusalem—the garrison with whom the later Maccabees would have to contend for control of the city. One result of this action was the open Maccabean revolt (along with Josephus, 1 Maccabees is the most reliable source for this period). But the book of Daniel represents other forms of political and religious resistance during this same time. To summarize, scholars have discussed the outbreak of the resistance and the resultant repression of the Jews in different ways. Was it mainly the result of rival factions among the aristocratic Jewish families? Tcherikover, for one, has pointed out that we must not minimize the temptations that Hellenistic wealth and control offered to those members of local aristocracies who could successfully become part of the ruling elite.[18] Was it mainly the result of tensions between Ptolemaic and Seleucid sympathizers? Or was it a symptom of the larger conflict between the Seleucid and the Ptolemaic rulers of the Near East? How much of a role can we attribute to the desire for religious freedom among the Jews themselves, as portrayed in such pious documents as the books of the Maccabees? History, we know, is seldom so simple as a choice among opposing factors— all were clearly elements contributing to this period of severe disturbance, violence, and, for some, horrendous persecution. The precise causes are less significant to us than is the context of uncertainty and instability facing the average person, who then reflected on the words of the apocalyptic dreamers and speakers.

While Daniel 7–12 is usually dated to the time of greatest conflict under Antiochus IV Epiphanes (i.e., between 167, when the Temple was desecrated with the pagan altar, and 164 BCE, when the rule of Antiochus IV ended), it is important to keep in mind that one of the main reasons why so much attention is focused on this episode is because of the existence of 1 Maccabees. This can easily give the impression that Jewish life under the Ptolemies and the Seleucids was otherwise peaceful or without major incident, and therefore any language of resistance or unrest that we find in Daniel must also be from the time of Antiochus IV. This would be a false impression.

Morton Smith recently calculated that in the period between Alexander's conquest in 333 BCE and the Roman takeover of Palestinian affairs around 63 BCE under Pompey, some 200 military campaigns were fought in or around Palestine and that "this military history alone shows that no part of the country can have escaped Greek influence."[19] Thus military conquest, the taking of slaves and the temptations of mercenary service (it appears that some Jews welcomed military opportunities), and Greek settlement would have taken their toll on Jewish traditional life throughout the period from the exile to the Roman occupation of Palestine. The background of Daniel must include the social and political realities of exile and occupation throughout this period, and not only during any specific crisis. Late Hebrew thought, the Bible itself as a document, and both Rabbinic Judaism and Christianity were all formed under one or another system of political domination or occupation. This social and political reality will help to inform our reading of the book of Daniel.

It is common for many biblical scholars of the twentieth century to deal with the exile in a most peculiar manner: as an event that may have begun tragically, but resulted in an exilic existence that "must not have been that bad" under the Babylonians. This situation then improved even more, it is thought, under the benevolent rule of the Persians from the time of Cyrus's conquest of Babylon in 539 BCE until the coming of Alexander the Great in 333 BCE. While the Hellenistic rule that followed Alexander was not exactly political independence, the Hellenistic rulers over Palestine—the Ptolemies first and then after 198 BCE the Seleucids—must not have been so bad with the one exception of Antiochus IV Epiphanes' severe persecution of the Jews. Greek influence allowed for a blossoming of Jewish "philosophy" and the translation of the Septuagint (the Greek version of the Hebrew Bible).

---

18. Tcherikover, *Hellenistic Civilization and the Jews*, 202-3.
19. Smith, "Hellenization," 111-12.

There are a number of severe historical and sociological problems with the (admittedly somewhat exaggerated) summary of this dominant paradigm for understanding the exile and the post-exilic developments within Jewish society. The main problem with this perspective is the lack of sensitivity to, and awareness of, the realities of living in exile and under military occupation. Although we have understood for some time that the exile must have had a dramatic impact on the ancient Jewish communities, we are only recently confronting the wider sociological and political, not to mention psychological, impact of these experiences, largely because we are only recently hearing from modern "exiles," minorities who insist that their stories of disenfranchisement be heard. Even more recently, some of these voices are taking up the scholarly study of the Bible, maintaining their unique perspectives as racial or cultural minorities in a variety of political circumstances.[20] By listening to modern exiles, minorities whose stories reflect the powerlessness of captivity of various kinds, we become far more alive to the meaning of the stories of the Bible—especially stories that reflect the realities of captivity and subordination. Furthermore, these voices are being heard against a new awareness of the historical realities of Persian and Hellenistic imperial politics.

The influence of Hellenism is already under severe reassessment, led by important older works such as S. K. Eddy's *The King Is Dead*[21] and Peter Green, who states that the "civilizing and missionary aspects [of Hellenistic conquests] have been greatly exaggerated, not least by modern historians anxious to find some moral justification for aggressive imperialism."[22] Such a reassessment, however, must also extend to the widespread notion of Persian "benevolence" as well. In a recent popular commentary on Ezra and Nehemiah, Holmgren reflects this general perspective in a most interesting manner. In his comment on Neh 9:36-37, a text that contains one of the most significant and explicit complaints against the Persians, Holmgren recognizes that this passage indicates a measure of resentment and unrest, but then continues at some length to maintain the general assumption about Jewish attitudes to Persian rule:

> To be "almost free" is never enough; if you are a slave, "almost free" means that you are still a slave. Under Persian rule the Jews were "almost free." Jews did not despise this "almost free" existence, however, because under benevolent monarchs the Jews were free to return to the land and there to rebuild the temple and the city of Jerusalem. The writings of both Ezra and Nehemiah portray the Persian rulers as cooperative and fair . . . toward the Jewish community.[23]

Thus the idea of Persian benevolence has become an almost unquestionable doctrine of research on the exilic and post-exilic periods of the Bible, and is obviously relevant to the study of the book of Daniel. Such a positive view is typically considered a reliable collective memory of the Jews in the diaspora. So Collins writes that "the benevolence of the king is assumed" in the court tales,[24] and Wills, in an otherwise very interesting study, further presumes the positive view of the foreign rulers.[25] Blenkinsopp, commenting on Ezra and Nehemiah, also notes "the theme of the benevolence of the Persian kings."[26] Indeed, such a positive view is often used as an argument for dating the Daniel materials in an era other than that of the hated Antiochus Epiphanes IV, because it is hard to accept stories of a benign foreign ruler in that time. It is the argument of this commentary that such an assumption about the benign rulers of either Babylon or Persia overlooks many of the significant symbols of domination that are indicated in the stories themselves—threats of death from the king, fear of the king's rage, name changing as a sign of subordination, symbolic warfare in the visions, etc. Thus that assumption fails to appreciate

---

20. See the volume of essays, *Voices from the Margin: Interpreting the Bible in the Third World*, ed. R. S. Sugirtharajah (New York: Orbis, 1991); and Daniel Smith-Christopher, ed., *Text and Experience: Papers on Cultural Exegesis from the 1992 Casassa Conference* (Sheffield: Sheffield University Press, 1996).
21. S. K. Eddy, *The King Is Dead: Studies in the Near Eastern Resistance to Hellenism 334–31BC* (Lincoln: University of Nebraska Press, 1961).
22. P. Green, "Greek Gifts?" *History Today* (June 1990) 27-34.
23. F. C. Holmgren, *Israel Alive Again* (Grand Rapids: Eerdmans, 1987) 134-35.
24. Collins, *Daniel*, 72.
25. Wills, *The Jew in the Court of the Foreign King*. This view is maintained in recent commentaries, such as that of André Lacocque, *The Book of Daniel*, trans. D. Pellauer (Atlanta: John Knox, 1979) 113; N. Porteous, *Daniel: A Commentary*, OTL (Philadelphia: Westminster, 1965) 90; and O. Plöger, *Daniel*, KAT (Leipzig: Gütersloh, 1965) 98.
26. J. Blenkinsopp, *Ezra–Nehemiah* (London: SCM, 1988) 160.

fully the themes of resistance and opposition that are major aspects of these stories. In short, one need not find calls to open and violent revolution in order to recognize calls to resistance, even if it is nonviolent resistance. It is true that some passages from the Bible would seem to support such assumptions, perhaps most powerfully in the enthusiastic bestowal of the title "Messiah" on Cyrus in Isa 45:1 or the clearly more sympathetic portrayal of Darius in Daniel 6 (but see the commentary below).

Finally, because Jewish names turn up among the Murashu Documents (an archive of business affairs from the Persian period, discovered in the ancient city of Nippur), many scholars have concluded that life must have been profitable for some of the community members. Zadok's studies, however, note that very few Jewish names turn up as officials or members of the upper echelons of society. Nehemiah, he argued, was a clear exception to the rule.[27] While there is nothing in the Elephantine correspondence[28] of Jewish soldiers under Persian mercenary employment in Egypt to suggest resentment, it must not be overlooked that it was a military colony in the service of the Persians, opposed to a hostile local Egyptian populace. What might a new view of Persian imperial policy do for a reading of the book of Daniel?

The "positive attitude" notion is based on very few biblical sources that have nevertheless been allowed to dominate the interpretation of all Persian period biblical literature and the Jewish experience of Achaemenid rule. This has led scholars to overlook important sociological and sociopsychological factors in biblical and nonbiblical literature that are crucial for a modern assessment of the historical and ideological understanding of the Persian period.

In a recent analysis, Root contrasts the Persians' own self-image and propaganda as portrayed in official artwork with actual practice: "The world was at peace on the walls of Persepolis as it never was in actuality. While news of the Persian sack of Miletus was striking terror in the Athenian soul, artisans from near and far were carving dreams in stone for Darius."[29] In her important reassessment of the implications of the famous Cyrus Cylinder, Amelie Kuhrt also warns against allowing "a blatant piece of Persian propaganda" to convince modern historians of the benevolence of Cyrus.[30] Finally, in a recent forum in which the historical image of Cyrus was examined again, Van der Spek also takes issue with the older view on the basis of the historical sources, concluding that "Cyrus and the other Persian kings ruled their empire in a way which was quite common in antiquity. . . . Cyrus introduced no new policy toward subdued nations, but acted in conformity with firmly established traditions, sometimes favorable, sometimes cruel. Under his responsibility temples were destroyed, Ecbatana was plundered, after the battle of Opis Cyrus 'carried off the plunder (and) slaughtered the people.'"[31]

This historical reconsideration is beginning to have an impact on biblical analysis. For example, Jenner considers the Cyrus decree recorded in Ezra 1 to be a falsification by Darius, who needed to legitimate a strong western flank, and the Jewish Temple would certainly serve his purposes. Furthermore, that Cyrus is called "Messiah" should not be overread, since, Jenner suggests, the meaning attached to such a title could have been much cooler than many modern interpreters assume, since "Cyrus, being in a position of dependency and obedience to JHWH, was no more than a useful tool in the service of Jerusalem."[32] This conclusion will have an important impact on a reading of Daniel.

The most important recent voice along these lines is that of Kenneth Hoglund.[33] Hoglund argues convincingly for a reassessment of the role of such Jewish representatives of the Persians as Ezra and Nehemiah, but especially the military leader Nehemiah. Nehemiah, declares Hoglund,

---

27. R. Zadok, *The Jews in Babylonia During the Chaldean and Achaemenid Periods* (Haifa: University of Haifa, 1979) 86-90.
28. Part of a group of papyrus documents and fragments written in Aramaic in the fifth century BCE, originating at Elephantine, an island in the Nile opposite Aswan (ancient Syrene); they were discovered during the nineteenth and twentieth centuries CE.
29. M. C. Root, *The King and Kingship in Achaemenid Art: Essays on the Creation of an Iconography of Empire*, vol. 9 of Acta Iranica, Textes et Memoires (Leiden: Brill, 1979) 311.
30. A. Kuhrt, "The Cyrus Cylinder and Achaemenid Imperial Policy," *JSOT* 25 (1983) 94-95.
31. R. J. van der Spek, "Did Cyrus the Great Introduce a New Policy Towards Subdued Nations? Cyrus in Assyrian Perspective," *Persica* 10 (1982) 278-79, 281-82.
32. K. D. Jenner, "The Old Testament and Its Appreciation of Cyrus," *Persica* 10 (1982) 284.
33. K. G. Hoglund, *Achaemenid Imperial Administration in Syria-Palestine and the Missions of Ezra and Nehemiah*, SBLDS 125 (Atlanta: Scholars Press, 1992). See also Kuhrt, "The Cyrus Cylinder and Achaemenid Imperial Policy," 83-97; van der Spek, "Did Cyrus the Great Introduce a New Policy Towards Subdued Nations?" 278-83.

was a Persian official (courtier?) whose task was more military than spiritual and who was concerned with the further imposition of Persian control over Palestine, not with any supposed free expression of local religion by the Jewish residents there. The Persians built a series of garrisons that represented strong military control of their western flank; thus any Jewish "returns to the land" under the Persians must be seen now as part of this strategic plan and not as the result of enlightened Persian rulership. In short, as Hoglund summarizes, "the appearance of these garrisons in the mid-fifth century is the indelible fingerprint of the hand of the Achaemenid empire tightening its grip on local affairs in the Levant."[34]

How do such historical realities about both Persian and Hellenistic policies influence interpretation of Daniel? Perhaps they simply alert the reader to look for the realities of political occupation and to learn how to see those realities, by reading Daniel in new ways. Given the sociopolitical context of empire in the latter half of the first millennium, the era of world empire, a full understanding of such post-exilic books as Daniel (not to mention Ezra–Nehemiah, Malachi, Esther, and many others) requires an understanding of the meaning and the impact of the exile and the kind of captivity it represented. It also requires that portions of the Bible be read "in the shadows," in order to fully comprehend their meaning and significance to a subordinated minority population. For minorities throughout the world, certain conversations must take place in the shadows, away from the "king's ear"—informers or guards. These conversations include stories, jokes, or tales told in whispers. Where a minority feels subordinated by either tradition or law, these stories can become a creative world of resistance in which heroes are drawn from among their own people, standing against the dominant majority culture.[35]

RETHINKING THE CONDITIONS OF CONQUEST AND EXILE

The exile was an experience of military defeat, deportation, and oppression in a new and strange land, which ended the days of independence for ancient Israel. At the hands of Nebuchadnezzar, Jerusalem, its Temple, and much of the environs were devastated (2 Kings 25). As was their policy, the Babylonians exiled large sections of the conquered population. Josephus, in his review of the history of the prisoners of war taken to Babylon, spoke of their being bound and chained. Whether this report can be taken as historically reliable and how far it is reconstruction on the basis of Josephus's time period is unclear, but note the language about fetters in Jer 40:1 (cf. Nah 3:10). As recounted in 2 Kings 25 and Jeremiah 52, only the poorest of the land were left to be "vinedressers and plowmen."

We know that under imperial rule subject populations and conquered territories were treated as sources of resources and labor; scholars sum this up graphically as a huge military and administrative apparatus designed to secure a constant flow of goods from the periphery to the center. Biblical traditions of proclamation against Babylon lead the reader to believe that Babylonian policies were severe; the oracles in Jeremiah, for example, threaten punishment of Babylon for its severity (Jer 50:15-16, 29; 51:20-22) and idolatry (50:2, 36; 51:44). But clearly the most crushing reality of Babylonian policy was the deportation itself, the disruption of life and the constant reminder of being a conquered people.

As for the actual number of people exiled, the evidence is unclear. Second Kings 24:14 states that there were 10,000 captives, but 2 Kgs 24:26 lists 7,000 "men of valor" and 1,000 craftsmen. Jeremiah claims that in all 4,600 persons were taken to Babylonia, listing them by year as follows: in Nebuchadnezzar's seventh year, 3,023 Jews; in his eighteenth year, 832; and in the twenty-third year, 745 (Jer 52:28-30).

The usual means of calculating the number of exiles is to multiply a "typical family" unit (four to five members of an immediate family) by the number 4,600—who are assumed to have been only men—which results in approximately 20,000–25,000. However, if only "important" men were counted (heads of households, etc.), then the total figure could easily be much higher.

---

34. Hoglund, "Achaemeid Imperial Administration in Syria-Palestine and the Missions of Ezra and Nehemiah," 433.
35. See D. Smith, *The Religion of the Landless* (New York: Meyer-Stone, 1989).

It is often strongly asserted in studies of the Babylonian exile that the exiles were *not* slaves, although at least one important building inscription has Nebuchadnezzar bragging that he "imposed the brick basket" on exiles taken from the western reaches of his empire, most certainly including Palestine.[36] We have noted, even under the rule of the supposedly tolerant Persians, that Ezra mentions in his prayer to God that "we are slaves" (Ezra 9:9 NRSV; cf. Neh 9:36).[37] But do we really know what we are talking about when we say that the exiles were (or were not) slaves? For North Americans, the image of slavery is indelibly marked by African American slavery in the early United States. But that is not the only form slavery has taken throughout history. In his book *Slavery and Social Death*,[38] Orlando Patterson analyzes the structure of slave societies using data from over forty different slave systems from all over the world and in different times. Common to all is the significance of symbolic institutions, what Patterson calls "the symbolic whips of slavery . . . woven from many areas of culture." These symbols include forceable name changes, hair or clothing changes, body markers, and anything that symbolized the death of one's identity at birth by means of a "rebirth" to a new identity given by the dominant authorities. Patterson notes that in different slave systems, a slave may be forced to change his or her name or "eat" the old identity through a food ceremony. Hence, according to Patterson's analysis, slavery is, in essence, the removal of one's identity and a social death. Therefore, the reconstruction and resistance of an ethnic group can be seen as a potential response to just such a threat of social death. One of the ways we see Jewish resistance to the symbols of powerlessness in the exile and afterward is in the telling of stories of Jewish courage in the face of tremendous foreign power. The tales of the book of Daniel are stories and writings of this kind.

Once we consider the significance of the symbols of domination, we are better prepared to note their significance in the Bible. For example, name changing is a common symbol used by foreign rulers in the Bible. Even though the stories of Daniel and his friends come from a late era in their final form, the symbol of name changing is an important factor in their association with the Babylonians and may not be an incidental detail. Furthermore, Nebuchadnezzar also changed the name of Zedekiah, when he placed him on the throne of Judah in Jehoiachin's absence (2 Kgs 24:17). That biblical writers mention these policies seems to reflect an awareness of the symbols of power that the exiles had to live with and struggle against.

Clearly, one element of recognizing these symbols is to note the constant reminders of foreign imperial power over the Jews. Indeed, so often is this context of empire noted in Ezra–Nehemiah, Daniel, and Esther that we may overlook its significance. For example, simply to pay attention to the frequency of the word *decree* in these works is revealing. The vast majority of occurrences of this term in the Bible are commands of foreign emperors dealing with the Jewish minority. The terms translated into English as "decree" in these books have been borrowed from political and administrative vocabulary of Imperial Aramaic or Persian, the official languages of the time. This is hardly surprising, since minorities would learn quickly such words as "police," "papers," "command," "authorized," and "order."

Such terms signal that the Jewish community was trapped by the competing claims to authority made by the local non-Jewish officials and the Persian court ("Who gave you a decree to build this house?" [Ezra 5:3]). They depended on Persian benevolence and support and had to appeal to the Persian court for permission at every turn. The biblical books from this period exhibit a heightened consciousness of a people not in control of their own lives: "I, Darius, make a decree," "You are permitted to go to Jerusalem," "I decree that any of the people . . . may go with you," "the unchangeable law of the Persians." Once again, the exile's legacy casts its shadow—the shadow of the guard tower—whether real or symbolic. Read in the shadows, Daniel becomes a revolutionary book of resistance, albeit nonviolent resistance.

Finally, one of the reasons why the revolutionary nature of the call to resistance in Daniel is not noted more frequently is the tendency among many modern historians to regard only violent

---

36. F. H. Weissbach, *Das Hauptheiligtum des Marduk in Babylon* (Leipzig, 1938) 47. See also S. Langdon, *Building Inscriptions of the Neo-Babylonian Empire* (Paris, 1905) 59, 149.
37. It has been suggested that this refers to the fact that all Persian citizens routinely referred to themselves as slaves of the emperor. But is this what Ezra and Nehemiah were referring to? In the context, it can hardly be read as merely an equivalent term to "citizen." Cook, *The Persian Empire*, 132.
38. Orlando Patterson, *Slavery and Social Death* (Cambridge, Mass.: Harvard University Press, 1982).

forms of resistance as evidence of any kind of resistance activity. If violence is not present, then the literature is deemed unrealistic or fantasy. Yet, 1 Maccabees is seldom criticized as being either, even though it proposes to celebrate the preposterous notion of a military confrontation between a divided Jewish community and a vastly superior force. It would appear that if we do not have texts that explicitly state that the people did not like the conditions under which they lived and that thus they would fight for independence, then some scholars conclude that conditions must not have been so bad. It is hard to avoid the conclusion that more than historical evidence is implicated in such viewpoints. Yet this perspective overlooks the subtleties of spiritual, social, and political resistance, which are not always obvious to those who simply equate violence with resistance. In short, the Maccabean uprising was not the only form of Jewish social resistance to world empire in the Persian and Hellenistic era. A reading of Daniel "in the shadows of empire" greatly facilitates this historical conclusion.

POSTSCRIPT ON READING THE REFLECTIONS IN THIS COMMENTARY

It is somewhat dangerous to ask a Quaker to write a commentary on Daniel. Quaker associations with this book are long and interesting—and not a little controversial. Indeed, there is no other Hebrew biblical book that is more a Quaker's book than Daniel. Quakerism arose, after all, in the throes of the English civil war. The founder of Quakerism, George Fox, was himself offered an officership in Cromwell's anti-Royalist forces. It was not an unusual offer, as there were certainly other (and similarly minded) Christian radicals who believed that dethroning and then beheading the king and fighting for a much wider participation in national affairs, including in some cases the extreme notion of the vote for all persons, was a fulfillment of the book of Daniel. Some of these radicals called themselves "The Fifth Monarchy Men," a term inspired directly from the sequence of four empires named in Daniel 2 and 7. Many of Cromwell's more theologically extreme soldiers, including many Fifth Monarchists, swelled the ranks of Quakerism in its first generation.

Daniel has engendered more bizarre speculations than those of the seventeenth-century Puritan revolutionaries, of course, and part of its continued appeal is precisely the sense of crisis out of which the book arose, which then seems to speak to the frequent recurrence of crises in human society over the centuries. In short, people who sense that the world is not right are drawn to a book that shares their conviction. One of the ways in which we will read Daniel "in the shadows" is to read two authors along the way: Franz Fanon and Albert Memmi. Fanon was an Algerian psychologist who wrote about the Algerian resistance to French colonialism. His work written in 1961, *The Wretched of the Earth,* remains a classic statement of the colonized perspective.[39] Already in 1957, however, the Tunisian Jewish author Albert Memmi had written *The Colonizer and the Colonized* with a similar interest in analyzing the impact of colonization on native peoples.[40] Both works will help us to understand important aspects of reading Daniel as a book that reflects the domination of the Jewish people by Babylonians, Persians, and Greeks. The situations, so different and so far apart historically, are not exactly the same, of course, but Fanon and Memmi provide provocative suggestions for helping us to rethink the implications of social context in a reading of Daniel. We may also draw on the experiences of minority peoples, drawing especially on Native American comments.[41]

The danger inherent in the book of Daniel is clear from the fact that Josephus found himself attempting to tone down the rhetoric, lest it offend his Roman readers. In short, Daniel directs its severe judgment toward human rulers, and a serious assumption of the work is that the people of faith will inevitably find themselves in opposition to the state and its accompanying forms

---

39. F. Fanon, *The Wretched of the Earth* (New York: Grove, 1963).
40. A. Memmi, *The Colonizer and the Colonized* (Boston: Beacon, 1965).
41. During the time I spent in research for this commentary, I was able to sit with Lakota Christians and Traditionalists on the Rosebud Reservation in South Dakota and read chapters from the book of Daniel with them. Some of the comments in the following commentary reflect that research. These interviews form part of an upcoming study on cultural influences on the reading of the Bible.

of political loyalties and idolatrous patriotism. Albert Memmi summarized the position of anyone who would begin to be sympathetic to those who suffer under present political circumstances, which in his context meant the colonized of North Africa. He wrote that a European in North Africa who begins to have sympathy and then to identify with the colonized is to choose "treason" against the values of the powerful.[42] Such a position will generate a reaction: "Wonder has been expressed at the vehemence of colonizers against any among them who put colonization in jeopardy. It is clear that such a colonizer is nothing but a traitor. He challenges their very existence."[43] The book of Daniel calls people of faith to just such a treason against the rule of the powerful, a treason based on loyalty to the rule of God.

Such thoughts should immediately bring pause to any modern pastor who would attempt to preach or teach on Daniel—you are venturing into subversive territory. There is no message of facile patriotism, of "good citizenship," or of merely personal, pietistic faith in Daniel. Thus there can be no such thing as a non-political reading of Daniel, if it is to be true to the living spirit of Scripture and to the suffering of those who wrote it under the inspiration of a God who first delivered slaves from Pharaoh.

Reading Daniel in some contexts raises disturbing questions. How can a book meant to encourage the faith of a politically subordinated people be made meaningful for those of us in a dominant culture, such as European Americans, European Canadians, or European Australians? In short, do we read Daniel as modern "Babylonians," "Persians," and "Greeks," or as their captive peoples?

The frequency with which I draw on the experiences or comments of historically subordinated peoples in this commentary is not intended to be an exercise in collective guilt. The intention is not only to highlight the possible similarities in experience between the writers of Daniel and modern conquered or colonized peoples, but to suggest further that if the Christian faith is to be one that challenges the modern world, then it must accept a certain alienation from the dominant culture and its religious traditions of dominance.

To read the book of Daniel in one hand while holding Fanon or modern Native American works in the other is to suggest that biblical faith will of necessity find significant social and spiritual parallels with the life of alienated peoples. This is because Christians know that they live in Babylon and not in the kingdom of God. To come to that realization means embracing a theology of Christ against culture, particularly where that culture is based on the products of military conquest and economic abuse of conquered peoples.

42. Memmi, *The Colonizer and the Colonized*, 22.
43. Memmi, *The Colonizer and the Colonized*, 21.

BIBLIOGRAPHY

Commentaries:

Bentzen, Aage. *Daniel.* HAT 19. Tübingen: Mohr, 1952. A brief critical commentary that is now somewhat dated.

Collins, John J. *Daniel.* Hermeneia. Minneapolis: Fortress, 1993. This is clearly the new standard-bearer for thorough reading of Daniel. Essential for serious study.

Goldingay, John. *Daniel.* WBC 30. Dallas: Word, 1988. A thorough and helpful work, particularly valuable for its attention to cross-references throughout the Bible.

Hartman, Louis F., and Alexander A. DeLella. *The Book of Daniel.* AB 23. Garden City, N.Y.: Doubleday, 1978. Helpful, but dated, entry in the Anchor Bible series.

Koch, Klaus. *Das Buch Daniel.* Darmstadt: Wissenschaftliche Buchgesellschaft, 1980. Particularly attentive to Jewish tradition.

Lacocque, André. *The Book of Daniel.* Translated by D. Pellauer. Atlanta: John Knox, 1979. An erudite literary masterpiece.

Montgomery, James A. *A Critical and Exegetical Commentary on the Book of Daniel.* ICC. Edinburgh: T. & T. Clark, 1927. An older, but still valuable, contribution.

Porteous, Norman W. *Daniel: A Commentary.* OTL. Philadelphia: Westminster, 1965. Translated from the German original, this is a helpful, brief survey of issues.

Towner, W. Sibley. *Daniel.* Interpretation. Atlanta: John Knox, 1984. Good for preaching and adult education.

Background Information:

Collins, John J. *The Apocalyptic Vision of the Book of Daniel.* Missoula, Mont.: Scholars Press, 1977.

Fewell, Danna Nolan. *Circle of Sovereignty: Plotting Politics in the Book of Daniel.* Nashville: Abingdon, 1991. An excellent literary analysis, sensitive to political issues.

Ginsberg, Harold. "The Oldest Interpretation of the Suffering Servant." *VT* 3 (1953). The classic article that further defends the nonviolence of Daniel.

Hellholm, David, ed. *Apocalypticism in the Mediterranean World and the Near East: Proceedings of the International Colloquium on Apocalypticism.* Tübingen: Mohr-Siebeck, 1983. Excellent collection of scholarly background articles.

Kippenberg, Hans G. *Religions und Klassenbildung im antiken Judaä: Eine Religions-soziologie Studie zum Verhätnes von Tradition und gesellschaftlicher Entwicklung.* Vandenhoeck und Ruprecht: Göttingen, 1982. Controversial work that argues for class conflict in the post-exilic society.

Kvanvig, Helge S. *The Roots of Apocalyptic: The Mesopotamian Background of the Enoch Figure and of the Son of Man.* Neukirchen-Vluyn: Neukirchener Verlag, 1988. Important for analysis of apocalyptic literature.

Otzen, Benedikt. *Judaism in Antiquity: Political Development and Religious Currents from Alexander to Hadrian.* Sheffield: JSOT, 1990. Very good survey of historical background.

Rowland, Christopher. *The Open Heaven: A Study of Apocalyptic in Judaism and Early Christianity.* London: SPCK, 1982. A unique and important theory about apocalyptic literature.

Smith, Daniel. *The Religion of the Landless: The Sociology of the Babylonian Exile.* New York: Meyer-Stone, 1989. A more detailed elaboration of some of the sociological assumptions of this commentary.

Tcherikover, Victor. *Hellenistic Civilization and the Jews.* Atheneum: New York, 1970. The classic survey of the Hellenistic period.

VanderKam, James C. *Enoch and the Growth of an Apocalyptic Tradition.* CBQMS 16. Washington, D.C.: Catholic Biblical Association, 1984. A very important study for Daniel/Enoch comparisons.

Weinberg, Joel. *The Citizen Temple Community.* Sheffield: JSOT, 1992. An important and unique argument with regard to the nature of the post-exilic socioeconomic community setting.

OUTLINE OF DANIEL

I. Daniel 1:1–6:28, The Court Stories

    A. 1:1-21, The Cuisine of Resistance
    B. 2:1-49, Speaking Truth to Power: Daniel and Nebuchadnezzar's Dream
    C. 3:1-30, Political Atheism and Radical Faith
    D. 4:1-37, The True Throne and False Thrones
    E. 5:1-31, The Humiliation of the Conquered: Belshazzar's Feast
    F. 6:1-28, In Defiance of Death: Daniel in the Lion Pit

II. Daniel 7:1–12:13, The Apocalyptic Visions

    A. 7:1-28, Visions of Change
    B. 8:1-27, The Ram and the Goat
    C. 9:1-27, Textual Interpretation and Angelic Revolution
    D. 10:1–12:13, The Final Vision

DANIEL 1:1–6:28

THE COURT STORIES

DANIEL 1:1-21, THE CUISINE OF RESISTANCE

COMMENTARY

1:1-2, The Ideological and Political Significance of the Setting. The first two verses of the first chapter serve notice to the reader that the context of these stories is of paramount importance to the writers and editors of the book of Daniel. These verses introduce the book as a whole and not merely the first story, reminding the reader of the context of dominance from which these stories derive their life and power. The bare facts are that Nebuchadnezzar conquered Jerusalem, captured King Jehoiachin (son of Jehoiakim, who died while Jerusalem was under seige), and took captive not only the king but the temple implements as well. These implements were placed, significantly, in the "treasury of his gods" (v. 2). This is an important note, since we know that the Babylonians were highly aware of the propaganda value of placing captured religious symbols "under" the Babylonian gods in the Babylonian imperial shrines, thus symbolizing the captivity of conquered gods as well as people. Since the Jews did not have an image of their God, the Babylonians used their temple vessels instead. Note that these materials were not merely melted down (see chap. 5), but kept intact so as to serve as symbols of the Jews' subordinate position in relation to Babylonian imperial and religious power.[44]

It has long been noted that the historical details of vv. 1-2 cannot be accepted literally, although attempts have been made to suggest that the author is drawing on a combination of Jer 25:1, 11 and 2 Chr 36:6 in order to arrive at his ideas about a campaign during Jehoiakim's reign[45] as well as conforming to Jeremiah's prediction of a seventy-year exile. It seems conclusive, however, that Nebuchadnezzar did not campaign in Palestine before his success at Carchemish in 605 BCE. Surely it is much more sensible to assume that a folktale is interested not in chronological details, but in the power of the context of exile.[46] Much more interesting, however, is the reference to "Shinar," a name for Babylon that recalls the story of the tower of Babel in Genesis 11 and associates Babylon with the hubris evident in that tale.[47]

Therefore, the introduction serves notice to readers, ancient and modern, that these important facts of life serve as the essential background to the proper appreciation of the stories and the visions of the book of Daniel. As we will see, reminders of the exilic status of the characters in Daniel run through the twelve chapters like a political litany.

1:3-7, The Selection of Jewish Exiles for Training. The first story in the book of Daniel focuses on the treatment of the exiles from the perspective of the Babylonian conquerors. The king requests that members of the captured peoples be selected (specifically from the leadership of the Jewish people) for specialized training in Babylonian language and culture. Note that the assessment of their

---

44. The Persians were especially attuned to the significance of symbols that are directed to mass consumption. See Root, *The King and Kingship in Achaemenid Art.* Note also Porteous, *Daniel*, 26-27; and John Goldingay, *Daniel*, WBC 30 (Dallas: Word, 1988) 15-17.

45. Lacocque, *The Book of Daniel*, 25.
46. Collins, *Daniel*, 132. Collins is rather critical of attempts to mesh the dates in Daniel with some configuration of dates drawn from Chronicles, Jeremiah, or elsewhere.
47. After Lacocque, *The Book of Daniel*, 25. The association of exile, Nebuchadnezzar, and the Tower of Babel is explicit in the enigmatic Dead Sea Scroll fragments designated 4QpsDan a, b, and c in F. García-Martínez, *Qumran and Apocalyptic, Studies on the Aramaic Texts from Qumran* (Leiden: Brill, 1992) 127-61; but also published as 4Q243-245 in R. Eisenman and M. Wise, *The Dead Sea Scrolls Uncovered* (Shaftsbury: Element, 1992) 64-67.

competence to serve in the king's palace is made before they have been trained, implying that they have something to offer the king's court, and that, therefore, their knowledge of Jewish language and culture is what the king is particularly interested in. For what other reason could they be useful other than for maximizing the efficiency of Babylonian rule? If they are actually drawn from the royal families or from the priestly families, as Lacocque has suggested, noting that the ones chosen were "without blemish,"[48] then the Babylonians' interest in them would surely be even greater.

The four Jewish men chosen are to be issued rations of royal food and wine during their three-year course of study. (Many scholars have noted that three years of study is mentioned in Persian sources as the time required for training in knowledge of religious matters.)

Significantly, the four Jewish exiles are carefully introduced with their Jewish names, before it is noted that their names have been changed to Babylonian names. There does not appear to be any particular importance attached to the non-Israelite names, and scholars do not agree on the precise meanings. Roughly, Daniel is renamed "Belteshazzar," or "Protect the king's life"; Azariah's new name becomes "Abednego," "Servant of Nabu"; Hananiah is renamed "Shadrach," or "Shining" (from Persian?); and Mishael becomes Meschach from the Persian religious name "Mithra." Name changing is, of course, a prominent biblical sign of dependent status, thus Abram to Abraham in covenant with God (Gen 17:5); Jehoiakim is renamed by Pharaoh (2 Kgs 23:34); and Zedekiah is renamed by Nebuchadnezzar (2 Kgs 24:17). The practice became common in late biblical literature. While it is true that many observant Jews in the Hellenistic period took on non-Jewish names (Philo), and even earlier there is evidence of names like "Zerubbabel," the issue here is not whether the names are non-Israelite, but that it is done by a power that assumes the authority to make such a change.[49]

1:8-21, Resistance to Partaking of the King's Food and Wine. The planned assimilation of the four Jewish representatives of the exile community runs into a brick wall.

Daniel (Why not the others? Does this imply a division among the Jews on these issues of resistance?) firmly states his refusal to accept the king's offer of food and wine, stating that he would be "polluted" (גאל $gā'al$) by them. This powerful term is highly suggestive for the exilic and post-exilic experience. Ezra the priest would also strongly assert the necessity of maintaining "purity" in the conditions of subordination in the post-exilic community, and we know that the priests involved themselves diligently in the codification of levitical purity law during the exile. Furthermore, purity concerns that even exceeded the specific demands of the priestly purity laws are not unusual in the late biblical and Hellenistic periods (e.g., Tob 1:10-11; Jdt 12:1-4; 2 Maccabees 6–7; *Jub.* 22:16; and Josephus *The Life of Flavius Josephus* 3.14). As Mary Douglas has shown, worries about the purity of the body are symbolic reflections of concerns for the integrity of the social group, and purity laws serve as effective barriers to assimilation. The assertion of purity concerns during the exile served as an important spiritual and social bulwark against the dangers of disappearing as a people, and Daniel 1 obviously maintains this important theological motif.[50]

Scholars have debated the reasons for Daniel's resistance of the rations. Of course, Daniel does accept the "vegetables" (זרעים $zērō'îm$; lit., "pulses" or "seeds") from the royal supply, so the likelihood that he wanted to avoid any Babylonian food that had been dedicated to pagan deities seems not to be the issue. The consumption of wine is clearly not forbidden in levitical purity laws. But as Goldingay has noted, meat and wine are not only the foods of festivity (Isa 22:13), which may need to be avoided when the attitude of exiles ought to be mourning for the destruction of Jerusalem, but they are also the foods of the wealthy rather than the peasants. The issue is dependence on royal largess and wealth—wealth that was not incidentally stolen from the livelihood of the nations conquered by the Babylonian Empire.[51] This point deserves concentrated attention in the following excursus.

---

48. Lacocque, *The Book of Daniel*, 27.
49. Thus, I would respectfully take issue with Goldingay, Collins, and Porteous. On this matter, Lacocque is much more alive to the impact of forced name changes. See Lacocque, *The Book of Daniel*, 29.
50. Mary Douglas, *Purity and Danger* (London: Routledge and Kegan Paul, 1966).
51. Goldingay's discussion of this matter is very helpful. See his *Daniel*, 18-19. See also D. Berrigan, who states: "They must know, these favored ones, that the princely diet offered them is the fruit of murder and oppression" ("Till the End of Empire," 11).

EXCURSUS: FOOD AND POWER

A full appreciation of this story also requires that one keep in mind the prominence of food as a symbol of privilege and wealth and foreign overindulgence. Lacocque notes that Daniel 1 illustrates "the custom in ancient royal courts of introducing important prisoners to the national diet."[52] But if the modern reader is alerted to the significance of food in the context of post-exilic conditions, Daniel 1 takes on added significance.

Throughout biblical history, control of food, especially large amounts of it, is symbolic of power. This can best be summarized in a discussion of feasting and the taxation of foodstuffs (in-kind taxation). This discussion obviously anticipates some of the symbolism of Belshazzar's feast in chap. 5 as well.

A banquet suggests the celebration of a joyful occasion, such as the weaning of Isaac in Gen 21:8, Pharaoh's birthday in Gen 40:22, and Samson's wedding in Judg 14:10. Such feasts were to be occasions for rejoicing and were contrasted with occasions for mourning in Eccl 7:2 and Jer 16:8. But it is clear that feasting is also a symbol of power. In 1 Kgs 3:15, Solomon declares a joyous feast after his "conversation" with God. Job and his sons feast as a symbol of their good fortune (Job 1:4), and the "messianic banquet" in Isaiah 25 carries this theme of celebration into eschatological expectation. The exiled King Jehoiachin "put aside his prison clothes. Every day of his life he dined regularly in the king's presence" (2 Kgs 25:29-30 NRSV).

Improper or impious revelries, by the same token, are seen as symbolic of wealthy excess and oppressive power and are condemned by the prophets Isaiah (Isa 5:8-14) and Amos (Amos 4:1-3). This prophetic condemnation of misplaced revelry is also connected to feasting as a symbol of foreign excess and privilege. Royal largess is thus a motif in the banquets of Pharaoh in Gen 40:20, a portion of the Genesis material that is probably post-exilic.[53] The post-exilic author thus used these banquets to symbolize further the power of the pharaoh.

Over 40 percent of all the occurrences of the word *banquet* (משתה *mišteh*) are in the book of Esther alone. Indeed, banquets appear so frequently in Esther as to suggest a framework for the story as a whole, each feast marking a major step from humble origins to crisis and finally to victory:

A the king's feast (rise of Esther among exiles) 1:3, 5; 2:18
  B Esther's feast (threat to Esther and Jews) 5:5, 8, 12, 14; 6:14
A´ the Jews' feast (victory of Esther and Jews) 8:17; 9:17-18

In her analysis of the book of Esther, Berg elaborates on the centrality of banqueting in the story as a whole: "Esther's author constructed a tale whose beginning, middle, and conclusion center upon the motif of feasting. In addition, each of these banquet pairs recalls the others, simultaneously paralleling and contrasting with them."[54]

Finally, in the late book of Judith, the time of Judith's triumph is at the feast of Holofernes (Jdt 12:10) a reversal of fortune precisely at the time of the foreign king's display of power and extravagance. And within the same book is the assertion that Judith maintained purity from Gentile food!

These examples reveal banqueting to be a potent biblical symbol of power, that moves from a positive symbol of prosperity in the pre-exilic texts and stories to a

---

52. Lacocque, *The Book of Daniel*, 28.
53. The post-exilic dating of portions of the Joseph story was suspected by German scholars as early as the 1890s, but has been impressively argued in detail by D. Redford, *A Study of the Biblical Story of Joseph* (Leiden: Brill, 1970).
54. S. Berg, *The Book of Esther*, SBLDS 44 (Atlanta: Scholars Press, 1979) 35.

Excursus: Food and Power

predominantly negative symbol of foreign oppression in the prophetic and post-exilic contexts, when the oppressors would have feasted on utensils taken from Jewish tables to satisfy their appetite for materials and money.

This final point clearly derives from the fact that taxation of the supply of food was already a source of consternation in the deuteronomic "anti-king" text: "He will take the best of your fields, your vineyards and your olive groves and give them to his officials. He will tithe your crops and vineyards to provide for his courtiers and his officials. . . . He will tithe your flocks, and you yourselves will become his slaves" (1 Sam 8:14-17 NJB).

Taxes were usually paid in kind, the value of such payments being accounted for in monetary equivalents. It is clear that, from at least the deuteronomic period, taxation in kind was a symbol of royal privilege and power. As Hoglund points out, in the Persian and Hellenistic empires, the economics of the imperial systems was rooted in a "tributary mode of production." The rural countryside, the source of such supplies, was heavily taxed in order to maintain tribute to the imperial coffers, feeding the bureaucracy of the imperial program.[55]

Malachi 1:8 undoubtedly refers to in-kind taxation imposed on the Jews by their governors. That taxation of the means of subsistence was common among the governors of the area of Judea between the exile and the mission of Nehemiah is clear both from the complaints of the people in Nehemiah's time about the crippling level of taxation (Neh 5:1-5) and from Nehemiah's own assurances that he intends to lighten their burden (Neh 5:14-16). Furthermore, and most important, in the prayer/poem in Nehemiah 9, foreign control over food materials was clearly understood as a potent symbol of foreign domination and of God's punishment:

> Here we are, slaves to this day—slaves in the land that you gave to our ancestors to enjoy its fruit and its good gifts. Its rich yield goes to the kings whom you have set over us because of our sins; they have power also over our bodies and over our livestock at their pleasure, and we are in great distress. (Neh 9:36-37 NRSV)

Resistance to food in Daniel 1, therefore, and the clear condemnation of Belshazzar, pictured in drunken revelry in chap. 5, clearly relate to symbolic awareness of the meaning of controlling food stores as a key to controlling lives. In short, I agree with Davies' assertion that Daniel 1 is "a symbolic denial of the king's implicit claim to be sole provider,"[56] but when this observation is set within the context of the politicization of food as symbol, Daniel 1 (and chap. 5) is read with more appreciation of the theme of resistance.[57]

---

55. Hoglund, *Achaemenid Imperial Administraion in Syria-Palestine and the Missions of Ezra and Nehemiah*, 9, 11.
56. P. Davies, *Daniel* (Sheffield: JSOT, 1989) 91.
57. My argument here is in contrast to the view that fasting is an ascetic practice. See, e.g., D. Satran, "Daniel: Seer, Philosopher, Holy Man," in G. Nickelsburg and John J. Collins, eds., *Ideal Figures in Ancient Judaism* (Chico, Calif.: Scholars Press, 1980) 33-48.

1:9-10. Verse 9, which asserts that Daniel received protection from God, is an important answer to an obvious question: Why wasn't this upstart captive cut down where he stood for such blatant insubordination? Anyone who might think that this is assuming too much about Babylonian attitudes is clearly forgetting the reminders of vv. 1-2, let alone the destructive anger of the emperors discussed in the entire book!

One answer is that the king was not present, but only the official called Ashpenaz (the name probably derives from the Persian for "Innkeeper," or keeper of the court). Many commentators have noted the sympathy of Ashpenaz toward Daniel and its significance for the continued idea about a positive view of foreigners in Daniel 1–6. But Ashpenaz is not so powerful that he does not have to fear for his life if called before the emperor (v. 10). The friendship between Daniel and Ashpenaz, therefore, is the solidarity of the oppressed, both of whom serve the imperial will under threat of death; and this solidarity crosses ethnic lines, as Ashpenaz obviously admires Daniel's courage. This is hardly a sign of positive attitudes toward Babylonians!

Another answer is that Daniel received God's חסד (*ḥesed*). The NRSV's implication that this *ḥesed*—favor and compassion— came from the palace master is misleading. God influenced events in Daniel's favor by giving Daniel *ḥesed*. The term is typically translated as "steadfast love," but because of Katherine Doob Sakenfeld's detailed work, we understand the full implications of *ḥesed* as "deliverance or protection as a responsible keeping of faith with another with whom one is in a relationship."[58] Although *ḥesed* appears often in the context of praise for the building or rebuilding of the Temple in the psalms (Psalms 100; 106; 107; 118; 136; cf. 1 Chronicles 34; 41; 2 Chr 5:13; 7:3, 6; Ezra 3:11), note that *ḥesed* is the particular power of God to deliver Israel from its enemies (see Psalm 143). In Jer 33:11, the restoration after exile is clearly the intended result of God's *ḥesed*: "For I will restore the fortunes of the land" (NRSV). Finally, the shout of praise for God's *ḥesed* is associated with the miraculous defeat of enemies in 2 Chr 20:21, which is associated (by the act of fasting) with Ezra 8:21-23 (God's deliverance from enemies).[59]

So in v. 9 God makes Daniel the object of *ḥesed* and mercy before Ashpenaz. *Ḥesed* is closely associated with "mercy" (see Neh 1:11, in which Nehemiah requests mercy before "this man," the emperor; cf. Psalm 106). Sakenfeld's concluding statement on the use of *ḥesed* in the psalms is that the term is "predominantly associated with deliverance rather than any special blessing."[60]

---

58. K. Sakenfeld, *The Meaning of Hesed in the Hebrew Bible: A New Inquiry* (Missoula, Mont.: Scholars Press, 1978), 233.
59. My full study on fasting and its military associations in Daniel can be found as "Hebrew Satyagraha: The Politics of Biblical Fasting in the Post-Exilic Period (Sixth to Second Century BCE)," *Food and Foodways: An Interdisciplinary Journal* 5 (1993) 269-92.
60. Sakenfeld, *The Meaning of Hesed in the Hebrew Bible*, 218. See also K. D. Sakenfeld's more recent summary statement of her work on *ḥesed* in the Bible: *Faithfulness in Action: Loyalty in Biblical Perspective* (Minneapolis: Fortress, 1985).

Sakenfeld suggests that *ḥesed* as "delivering power" reaches its height in a series of texts in which it parallels "strength." Prominent among these texts is Exod 15:13:

> You led in your *ḥesed*
> The people whom you redeemed
> You guided in your strength
> to your holy encampment.[61]

Ḥesed and mercy, especially in the context of late biblical theology, are given to those Jews who appear before the Babylonian and Persian monarchs, which forces us to conclude that the passage assumes the necessity for God's delivering action against a presumed enemy. Praise was directed to God's delivering power, not to the Babylonian or Persian monarch's (or an assistant's) good intentions.

1:11-17. These verses summarize the "contest" of this story. The Jewish captives are to be tested and compared to the "young men" (Babylonians? Other captives/non-Babylonians with fewer scruples?) for ten days. The folkloric nature of the story is obvious in the selection of the number ten, although one might have expected a number like seven or forty.

In any case, physical appearance, rather than knowledge or wisdom, is the deciding factor in choosing these young men; however, their wisdom is mentioned (v. 17) as an additional aspect of their superior performance. The last section of v. 17*b*, which mentions Daniel's insights into visions and dreams, is clearly a foreshadowing of the stories to come, further suggesting that this story was a late addition to the series that evolved into the present book of Daniel. Knowledge and wisdom, however, become the crucial factors in the following verses, when the four Jewish men stand before the king.

1:18-20. The story ends with the young men appearing before the king. Standing before the king is a common motif in biblical literature. It is interesting to note the frequency with which the narrators of stories set in the exilic period (and later) emphasize the significance of standing before the foreign king. In vv. 3 and 18, the appearances before

---

61. Sakenfeld, *The Meaning of Hesed in the Hebrew Bible*, 212.

the king are the frame scenes for the story as a whole. Daniel and his friends stood before the king for the first time when introduced with their challenge and again when they are rewarded for their success.[62] In other biblical stories, Esther and Mordecai (who stands rather than bows before Haman), as well as Ezra and Nehemiah, had their turn to stand before the king. The scene is dramatic and crucial. Rarely do these figures stand before some lower official, which would more likely have been the case historically.[63] Incidentally, this is among the most significant indications of the folkloric setting of these stories.

That these scenes are unique is clearer when they are compared to the mention of bowing or doing obeisance, which is more common in the deuteronomic historian (1 Sam 24:8; 28:4; 2 Sam 1:2; 9:6, 8; 14:4, 22, 33). Scholars have noted that the Persian courts especially captured the imagination of the Greeks and certainly seemed a dramatic setting for the Jewish diaspora tales as well.[64] But it was a dreaded fascination, and the wise, according to Proverbs, would avoid such appearances before powerful rulers, unless specifically called upon:

> Do not put yourself forward in
>   the king's presence
> or stand in the place of the great;
> for it is better to be told, "Come
>   up here,"
> than to be put lower in the
>   presence of a noble.
> (Prov 25:6-7 NRSV)

Similarly, both Ezra and Nehemiah include significant appearances before the king. In the Nehemiah text, the relationship of Nehemiah to the king should not distract one from the language of fear. In Neh 2:2, Nehemiah is "very much afraid." Fear of the authorities and their opposition appears in Neh 4:14. Ashpenaz states that he is afraid of the king (v. 10). Like Daniel, Nehemiah is granted mercy before "this man."[65] This term "mercy" is found also in 1 Kgs 8:50; 2 Chr 30:9; and Ps 106:46, all cases of God's assurance before intimidating power.

The implication is that the court of Nebuchadnezzar is a setting of awe and majesty. The king's questions, clearly intended to be a test, are also common features of many of the biblical and post-biblical Jewish writings (note the abundant questioning in the Letter of Aristeas and Zerubbabel's clever solving of problems posed by the king in 2 Esdras). The king's interrogation of the four Jews results in the conclusion that the Jewish exiles are "ten times better" (note the repetition of the theme of multiples of ten from vv. 12-17) than all the magicians and enchanters throughout the kingdom, and not merely the others who were in training. That Babylon was known as a center for magic and enchanters is a theme the Bible will elsewhere affirm, and this passes into Jewish lore from the time of the exile onward, even to the "wise men" tradition of the New Testament Gospels. "Chaldean" (כשׂדים *kaśdîm*) is a term used throughout Daniel to refer to an astrologer as one of the royal court officials, rather than the general term for an ethnic Babylonian.[66]

1:21. The final verse notes that Daniel began his work during the reign of King Nebuchadnezzar and remained in his position until the first year of King Cyrus. This information can be somewhat confusing—even if one has already stated doubts about the historicity of any of these stories. The editor of the material clearly wants to connect Daniel to the fate of the exiles, from the time of the conquest by Nebuchadnezzar (586/587 BCE) to the beginning of the reign of Cyrus as liberator of Babylon (539 BCE). While this is not impossible during a usual life span (roughly fifty years in royal service added to the age of the young Daniel—thirteen? sixteen?—when he was

---

62. Also note that in Dan 2:2, Nebuchadnezzar's advisers come to his presence and stand before the king prior to the introduction of the Jewish resisters. These resisters will stand rather than bow before the image of the king. Similarly, in Dan 10:11-12 Daniel is to stand before God's messenger.

63. There are some "standing before the king" scenes in the deuteronomic historian (note 1 Kgs 1:28, in which Bathsheba is called to stand before the king; 1 Kgs 3:16, where two prostitutes stand before the king; and 1 Kgs 18:15, where Elijah points out that he stands before God [rather than merely the king?]); see also 1 Kgs 17:1; 2 Kgs 3:14.

In the narratives, it is more typical to mention that someone was "before" the king (no mention of standing) or simply going to the king, with no court scene mentioned at all.

64. "In Asia Minor, Mesopotamia, and Israel, the power of the centralized court evidently captured the imagination of the masses. . . . The gracious gifts to be received or the terrible punishments to be inflicted here were greater than anywhere else" (Wills, *The Jew in the Court of the Foreign King*, 19-20).

65. Blenkinsopp wonders whether the use of "this man" is a slightly pejorative term. See Blenkinsopp, *Ezra–Nehemiah*. Kellerman, however, compares it to other uses of courtroom language where one imagines a gesture toward the person being accused. See U. Kellerman, *Nehemia*, BZAW (Berlin: Kaiser, 1967) 85-86.

66. See Herodotus *The History* 1:181-183.

taken into Babylonian service), we must also contend with the fact that the stories have Daniel still active in the court of Darius, who is surely based on the Persian ruler who succeeded Cambyses, as well. The reign of the historical Darius began after considerable turmoil around 522 BCE! The Darius in Daniel, however, was supposed to have been a Mede who ruled *before* the time of Cyrus.

Goldingay notes that chap. 1 begins with Nebuchadnezzar and ends with Cyrus, suggesting a thematic structure that parallels the beginning and the end of the exile, by beginning with the capture of the Jews and ending with Daniel's "victory" over the Babylonians.[67] But as Knibb has shown, Daniel as a whole does not imagine that the exile has ended but rather extends it to seventy weeks of years, or 490 years—far beyond Jeremiah's predicted seventy years (Jer 25:1, 29)![68] Indeed, the book of Daniel does not presume an end to exile at all; thus any reading and theological understanding must begin with the realities of exilic existence. The book comes to us from the midst of resistance, and not from a sense that the danger has passed.

67. Goldingay, *Daniel*, 12.
68. M. Knibb, "The Exile in the Literature of the Intertestamental Period," *The Heythrop Journal* 17 (1976) 253-72.

REFLECTIONS

Christian faith inevitably calls us to active nonconformity with the world, even in the manner in which we daily live our lives—the food we choose to consume, and the clothing we choose to wear. The message of Daniel 1 is a powerful reminder for us to search within ourselves for those aspects of "the king's food and wine" that we ought to resist for the sake of the gospel message. For the writer of Daniel, food was merely one symbol among many others of the resistance to total domination and total assimilation to the culture and ways of dominant powers. So, too, is the Christian life a life of resistance—to the enticements of financial power and control over the destiny of others—such as powerful nations over the developing world—and to the enticements of luxury that come from the abuse of underpaid laborers in struggling societies. For Christians from dominant cultures in North America, Australia, and Europe, a man like Ashpenaz, rather than Daniel, may provide a more apt role model of resistance. Ashpenaz emerges from the power elite to have sympathy for those who suffer and resist. But like Ashpenaz, the faithful among the elite must be aware that their faith borders on treason; hence identification with, let alone sympathy for, the "exiled" peoples may have its cost.[69]

Therefore, the first question one needs to ask in a consideration of a theology of Daniel 1 (and in many ways the book as a whole) is, What is the food and wine that the modern emperors are offering us? The key here is that these enticements can be disguised as necessities, like food! So much of contemporary advertising and marketing is directed toward changing people's habits, to entice them to buy products that will become necessities, that they simply "can't live without." North American consumers especially are not used to asking serious questions about their consumption habits—not only whether it is too much, but also whether it is consumption that supports a living wage and a safe environment for workers. The market entices us to ignore such matters, but we are not to be enticed by the king's food and wine.

John Woolman, the great American Quaker traveling minister of the eighteenth century, asked a powerful question that is relevant to all modern Christian resisters. Woolman himself refused to wear certain articles of clothing that were either dyed or made by means of slave labor. In his essay "A Plea for the Poor," Woolman asks lifestyle questions: "May we look upon our treasures, the furniture of our houses, and the

69. See Memmi, *The Colonizer and the Colonized*. See also Introduction.

garments in which we array ourselves—and ask whether the seeds of war have any nourishment in these our possessions or not."

A call to faithful resistance may require modern Christians to think through whole new approaches to living our lives so that we no longer defile ourselves with the food and wine of kings and their militias, and begin to work with those exiled peoples whom these kings and their militias intended to control.

DANIEL 2:1-49, SPEAKING TRUTH TO POWER: DANIEL AND NEBUCHADNEZZAR'S DREAM

COMMENTARY

2:1a, Chronological Note. Like chap. 1, chap. 2 begins with a somewhat perplexing chronological note that defies modern attempts to treat it seriously. In this case, the "second year of Nebuchadnezzar" would place the story before the year 600 BCE and before the time of the preceding story. Despite many attempts to deal with these chronological indicators in any historical sense, it is best to treat them as further evidence that these stories once circulated independently of one another and that the editor of the collection that now comprises Daniel 1–6 chose to leave some of the enigmatic chronological notes alone, rather than straighten them out. However, as Daniel is apparently reintroduced to the Babylonian monarch in chap. 2, simply rearranging the dates will not do either. Rather than doubt the sophistication (or the attentiveness) of the editor, perhaps the reader is meant to see that the book of Daniel is, after all, to be taken as a collection of stories that were never originally intended to be told together in a single sitting.[70]

The Troubled Emperor in His Court. 2:1b. The emperor cannot sleep. He is troubled—not by the thousands of people he has forceably displaced or the thousands he has massacred on the battlefield or the wealth he has pillaged from the surrounding nations. He is troubled by his dreams, which is perhaps a way of saying that these issues *do* trouble the monarch. As Lacocque has trenchantly commented, the emperor has good reason to be troubled! His dreams announce to him that his powerful regime teeters on a foundation of clay: "Underlying the empires is an insatiable will to destruction; this is why they contain within themselves the seed of their destruction."[71]

The notion that an emperor's dreams conveyed important messages was widely held. Indeed, the dreams of emperors and kings were carefully noted in one of the earliest formalized works of dream interpretation, Artemidorus's *Oneirocritica*.[72] A. L. Oppenheim, in his classic study of dream interpretation in ancient Near Eastern thought, points out that dreams were believed to have evil powers over the dreamer, and one of the reasons why ancient peoples were so anxious to have the dreams interpreted was not only to know what they meant, but also to use that knowledge to conduct appropriate rituals to do away with the evil powers that produced the dream.[73] What is more critical to our consideration here is that the power of dreams must also have been known to the Jewish author of this dream story, which is attributed to Nebuchadnezzar. The reader need not be so enchanted by the story as to forget that it is a Jewish diaspora composition about the Babylonian emperor, and not a court document from Babylonian sources. Thus the reader needs to be attentive to what this dream suggests about the Jewish attitude to

---

70. Collins, typically, does an impressive job of analyzing the various opinions about these chronological notes. See Collins, *Daniel*, 154-56.

71. Lacocque, *The Book of Daniel*, 48.
72. See Artemidorus, *The Interpretation of Dreams*, trans. Robert White (New York: Noyes, 1975) 17.
73. A. L. Oppenheim, *The Interpretation of Dreams in the Ancient Near East* (Philadelphia: American Philosophical Society, 1956) 219.

the Babylonian monarch and his successors, and particularly whether the symbols in the dream refer to succeeding Babylonian monarchs (as some scholars suggest) or to succeeding empires (as the majority of modern scholars hold).

When we are introduced to Nebuchadnezzar as a monarch who is unable to sleep because his "spirit is troubled," it is inevitable that we recall Pharaoh's troubling dreams in Gen 41:8 and his response of calling in his advisers; this is only one of many parallels (sometimes quite strikingly similar) between the Daniel stories and the Joseph stories (cf. Esther). These parallels were systematically noted as early as 1895[74] and ever since have been a common feature of scholarship.[75]

But most important is the fact that the last Neo-Babylonian monarch, Nabonidus, was famous for his inscriptions dealing with his dreams. In his dreams, Nabonidus was instructed to restore the statue of the god Sin in Haran, and he was even reassured in his dreams by appearances of Nebuchadnezzar himself. On the basis of this widely known aspect of Nabonidus, and the fact that we have a Dead Sea Scroll fragment of another Daniel-like story that specifically mentions Nabonidus, many scholars believe that he was the actual ruler upon whom many of the Daniel stories were based, and that the name naturally changed over time to the more well-known and infamous conquerer of Jerusalem.[76] In short, we need not insist that Daniel 2 presupposed Genesis 41, but could equally suggest similar circumstances of authorship for both texts in the same era.[77]

2:2. The list of advisers, "magicians, enchanters, sorcerers, and Chaldeans" is interesting. The term translated "magicians" (חרטמים *ḥarṭummîm*), likely an Egyptian loan word (because it was borrowed from the Joseph stories?), is the same term that is used in the Joseph story in Genesis 41 and in the story of the Egyptian magicians who were able to match Moses' tricks before Pharaoh in Exodus (7:11, 22; 8:3, 14-15; 9:11). Oppenheim, again, strongly suggests that dream interpretation was a serious science in Egypt, while it was of minimal interest in Mesopotamia.[78] "Enchanters" (אשפים *'aššāpîm*), on the other hand, is not a widely used term, although already encountered in Dan 1:20. "Sorcerers" (מכשפים *mĕkaššĕpîm*), also used in Exodus (7:11), is a term with much darker connotations, especially in prophetic literature. Sorcery is mentioned as a sin in the same breath with condemnation of the oppression of the poor. Prophetic interests clearly associate both with the religious influence of Canaanite culture and society (see Jer 27:9, addressed to the surrounding nations of Edom, Moab, Tyre, Sidon, and Ammon; Mic 5:11; Nah 3:4, with reference to Assyria; Mal 3:5). To round out this list with "Chaldeans" is somewhat surprising, although the term has come to mean "astrologer" in most of Daniel (see Commentary on 1:18-20), as in classical Greek literature, long after the specific national association was lost.

Finally, an interesting geographical spread is represented in this list through the inclusion of the wise professionals from Egypt to Babylon (and by association of the terms used, also Canaan). Is the intention, then, to portray the court of Nebuchadnezzar as being composed of an international assembly of advisers and religious practitioners from around the ancient Near East? Oppenheim notes that the Assyrian monarch Esarhaddon mentions Egyptian magicians among his prisoners of war.[79] Thus we are once again alerted to the reach of the empire and its unmistakable power as the context for the full appreciation of this story.

If this cosmopolitan emphasis is intended, then Daniel and his friends, whose wisdom is not of the world (2:30), are set up against the best of the world's advisers. Daniel is facing

---

74. In a series of articles by the German scholar L. A. Rosenthal, beginning with "Die Josephsgeschichte mit den Büchern Ester und Daniel verglichen," *ZAW* 15 (1895) 278-84.

75. Although all scholars recognize the parallels, Lacocque goes a bit far in saying that "all agree" that Daniel 2 is a midrash of Genesis 41. See Lacocque, *The Book of Daniel*, 43-44.

76. C. J. Gadd takes this notion further. On the basis of an inscription discovered in 1956 that mentions foreign troops in Nabonidus's military, Gadd surmises that some of the Daniel stories may well have originated among Nabonidus's Jewish troops. That Nabonidus mentions oases that are later referred to by Islamic sources as having Jewish populations lends even further weight to Gadd's suggestions. See his article "The Harran Inscriptions of Nabonidus," *Anatolian Studies* 8 (1958) 35-92, esp. 85. The *Prayer of Nabonidus* has by now inspired a great deal of comment, the most recent comprehensive treatment being Garcia-Martinez, *Qumran and Apocalyptic*.

77. This view is defended convincingly by Redford, *A Study of the Biblical Story of Joseph*. Goldingay is typically interesting with his suggestion that, just as the Joseph stories pre-figure the exodus, so also the Daniel stories elicit hope for a new exodus. See Goldingay, *Daniel*, 43.

78. Oppenheim, *The Interpretation of Dreams in the Ancient Near East*, 200, 243.

79. Oppenheim, *The Interpretation of Dreams in the Ancient Near East*, 238.

not merely his Babylonian opposition in the king, but also the power and prestige that the Babylonian monarch is able to draw upon throughout the empire. The theme, as many scholars have pointed out, is that the wisdom of the world will prove impotent before knowledge of the true God.

2:3-4. When Nebuchadnezzar makes his request, it is the Chaldeans who reply, speaking Aramaic. From this point until the end of chap. 7, the book of Daniel switches to Aramaic (see Introduction). The opening greeting of the Chaldeans, "Live forever!" (which is used throughout Daniel) is here a particularly clever irony, given the fact that the dream will soon reveal that Nebuchadnezzar will certainly not live forever, and neither will his regime.

2:5. After the Chaldeans have made their perfectly reasonable request to hear the dream so that they might comment on it, Nebuchadnezzar's surprising reply sets up the crisis and the task for Daniel and his Jewish compatriots. Nebuchadnezzar makes a "decree," a "firm matter" (the term is a Persian loan word, borrowed from the official terminology of the Persian Empire). To punctuate this "firm decree," a threat of death and destruction comes before any possibility of reward. The threat, to "be torn limb from limb" if they do not tell him "the dream and its interpretation," is a legal phrase[80] that has been translated variously as "you be cut in pieces" (Lacocque) or "you will be dismembered" (Collins). But if the language is difficult, the point is frighteningly clear. The Babylonian monarch is portrayed as affirming his unchangeable commands and decrees, which are backed up by the authority that all imperial power must ultimately appeal to: brute force, which is not merely lethal, but *spectacularly* lethal. Furthermore, their houses will be destroyed. In short, it is to be public punishment, which totalitarian regimes both past and present are always particularly fond of, since such spectacles are useful in keeping a restive population in check with examples of what might befall them if they attempt to resist. One thinks immediately of the ancient Roman tradition of hanging political prisoners on crosses as a public humiliation.

2:6. These punishments are then contrasted with rewards. Among those things that the king offers in possible reward is "honor." Daniel will later inform the king that this honor is, in fact, a gift from Daniel's God (v. 37), and not inherent in the king's office. We are intended to see in Nebuchadnezzar the arrogance of power: "See how I can punish, or reward, at my pleasure!"

2:7-16. Some scholars have suggested that Nebuchadnezzar's offer of a reward attempts to show a certain fairness or even-handedness. But these rewards are hardly meant to portray the king as even-handed, as is clarified by the fact that the conversation with the Chaldeans takes a more serious turn in vv. 7-12, where the advisers' inability to do as the king (unreasonably) asks drives him into a rage. This rage is noted by Collins as a "stock motif" of court tales (see Esth 1:12; 7:7; Dan 3:13, 19; 3 Macc 3:1; 5:1), but contributes to a sense that power is in the hands of a foolish human being, dangerously susceptible to unrealistic demands.

The king's rage then leads him to decree the destruction of *all* of his advisory department, including Daniel and his companions, who must have been promoted to this position, although that is not stated explicitly in chaps. 1–2. Yet, this is complicated by the fact that Arioch will introduce Daniel as an apparent stranger in v. 25, which is probably the way the original story read, particularly given its resemblance to the *Prayer of Nabonidus* at this point (see Introduction). Perhaps the original Daniel tales always presumed a court setting, and chap. 1, which purports to tell the story of how Daniel and his friends originally arrived in the court, is a later development of the legends.

When Daniel, through the king's official Arioch, requests that he be given time to present an interpretation of the king's dreams, Daniel is challenging both the king and his decree before he has assurance from God as to the nature of the dream. In the face of danger to his life, Daniel does not hesitate to assume that God would prefer matters were otherwise. Note that the Chaldean (and other) advisers had earlier angered the king by attempting to gain time—so thought Nebuchadnezzar (v. 8). This is important, as God is praised by Daniel in v. 21 as "one who changes times," in the same context

---

80. F. Rosenthal, *A Grammar of Biblical Aramaic* (Wiesbaden: Harrassowitz, 1983) 59.

as "deposes kings and sets up kings" (2:21 NRSV). The implication is that God is above the royal authority and is able to change what the world's authorities declare to be unchangeable.

There is a somewhat surprising implication in v. 16 that Daniel simply burst in on the king. Apparently unable to believe that Daniel could have had such easy access to the king, some of the ancient texts add that Daniel sent Arioch to petition the king on his behalf.[81]

2:17-23, The Prayer of Appeal and Praise. One of the crucial centers of this chapter is certainly the prayer for aid and response of praise in these verses. This section follows a well-established pattern of post-exilic literature in which the Jewish people appeal to God in the face of apparently overwhelming odds. The pattern is usually: (1) clarification of the threat; (2) gathering of the community to appeal to God (often associated with fasting), typically for "steadfast love" and "mercy" as aspects of deliverance; (3) songs of praise, rehearsing God's majestic existence and God's mighty power to deliver the people in times of need. This pattern will be fully explicated in the Commentary on chap. 9, but suffice it here to note that it is not merely an insignificant detail that Daniel proceeds to return to his compatriots and gather them together for prayer. Scholars often mention that the three friends are noted here merely to set up chap. 3, but this gathering is crucial for what follows; Daniel is mustering spiritual power for warfare. Note that Ezra also calls on the protection of God by first gathering his community, declaring a fast, and proclaiming God's ability to deliver them (Ezra 8:21-22, 31*b*).

Seen in this post-exilic context of corporate prayers of deliverance, the song of praise in vv. 20-23 is interesting in many respects. The name "God of heaven" (אלה שמיא *ĕlāh šĕmayyā'*, v. 19) is a standard post-exilic term, appearing in Ezra–Nehemiah as well. The blessing of God's name from age to age recalls Isaiah 47, and also recalls the "name theology" of Deuteronomy, particularly when the Temple is discussed as the place where God's name dwells. That wisdom and power belong to God is rehearsed already in Jeremiah 10 and 51. Notably, many of the other biblical contexts where these same motifs are found are hymns directed against foreign powers, and thus fit this hymn of political praise in Daniel 2.

God's power is rehearsed as being over and above the apparent power of the kings of this world. If God can change the times and seasons, God can certainly change whatever the Babylonian monarch declares unchangeable. That God not only places but also unseats kings is a theme found in other Daniel material (cf. the dramatic anti-Roman polemic by Mary in Luke 1:47-55). Further, the expression "knows what is in the darkness" (v. 22) is very similar to Job 12:9, 22. Note, moreover, the highly political context of Job 12:22-25, which discusses God's ability to unseat or otherwise strip of authority kings, counselors, priests, and judges. Job 12 thus contains "reversal of fortune" motifs:[82]

> He makes nations great, then
> destroys them;
> he enlarges nations, then leads them
> away. (Job 12:23 NRSV)

The prayer concludes with a reference to the "God of my ancestors" (אלה אבהתי *ĕlāh 'ăbāhātî*) before praising God's blessing on Daniel. It is instructive to note the increase in popularity of this term in the late biblical literature. Although "God of ancestors" is found four times in Exodus and eleven times throughout the deuteronomic historian, it is used twenty-six times in Chronicles and becomes prominent in prayers of the post-exilic literature of the Hellenistic period as well. The context for the use of the phrase "God of our ancestors" is interesting, particularly in the following:

Ezra 7:27—standing before the Persian king
Tob 8:5—prayer for safety in times of
  trouble
Jdt 10:8—prayer for Judith's success
  against the Assyrian king
3 Macc 7:16—the survival of defilement
  by foreigners
1 Esdr 9:8—breakup of mixed marriages
Prayer of Azariah—survival in the fiery
  furnace

---

81. E.g., Theodotion and the Syriac text; see Porteous, *Daniel*, 41.

82. D. J. Clines, *Job 1–20*, WBC 17 (Dallas: Word, 1989).

To refer to God as a "God of my ancestors," then, is clearly a defining term that is relevant outside the homeland. The term becomes particularly relevant, therefore, when religious matters pit Jewish faith (based on the experience of this God from the ancestors) against the challenges of foreign powers or religious temptations. To assert anything about "the God of my/our ancestors" is to say something equally about that particular God, and the identity of the person using the terminology.

2:24-30, Daniel Before Nebuchadnezzar. As has been noted, the appearance or "audience" before the emperor is an important scene for virtually all of the stories that deal with the foreign court. To stand before the king was a setting of danger and threat. Daniel, therefore, speaks with courage in requesting an audience. His status is clearly established by Arioch: Daniel is from "among the exiles" (v. 25). The Hebrew terms (בני גלות *běnê gālût*) behind this phrase may be significant. The phrase "sons of exile" was a significant indicator of community identity in Ezra, and it may also serve that function here, rather than simply being a conventional way to speak of the Jewish population in the eastern diaspora.[83]

The conversation with Nebuchadnezzar establishes Daniel's credentials to speak before the king. It is a tense moment, and Daniel speaks with disarming respect, given that he knows he is about to tell the king that his regime will not last.

Daniel first dissociates himself from the world's wisdom by pointing out the failure of the "wise men, enchanters, magicians, or diviners" (v. 27; perhaps he diplomatically leaves out Chaldeans). In contrast to the king's powerlessness to call on the wisdom traditions from the far reaches of his empire, there is a God who is able to reveal mysteries. Daniel insists that the point of his appearing before the king is not to prove his own status or wisdom, but so that the king will know of the existence of this God (cf. Genesis 41). Daniel clarifies that the matter is between God and the king. Daniel is only the messenger of God's pronouncement to the foreign king. The theme of God's reigning over "mysteries" is also developed in the Dead Sea Scroll texts, as many scholars have noted.

2:31-35, The Statue. Daniel begins his interpretation of the dream by describing the great statue the king was looking at in the dream, which "was standing before you" (v. 31). The words "you looked, and *behold!*" appear in many dream/vision reports of prophets, beginning with Amos 4:7; 7:2; and Jeremiah through Zech 1:8; 8:3, etc. In short, it was an apparition that demanded the attention of the king by its imposing presence. It was not to be ignored—indeed, it was frightening. Was this merely one aspect of its appearance? Or was it frightening because it was clear even before Daniel's detailed explanation that the various metals that comprise the statue suggested instability?[84]

Oppenheim notes the frequency of large apparitions, like statues, in ancient dream reports. He suggests that this may be partially explained by the ancient practice of seeking dreams at the feet of idols, a form of what the Greeks called incubation (intentionally seeking answers in dreams by sleeping in a shrine). But the size of the images has other suggestions as well. Porteous is on the right track when he notes the monumental scale of Mesopotamian statuary,[85] a form of propagandist art intended as massive public displays of the size, permanence, and strength of a regime (typically depicted as a powerful animal—a lion or a bull). One thinks of the role of the triumphal arch in imperial Roman architecture or a siege-minded Pentagon (see Reflections).

The statue is made of several different metals, each declining in value, from gold, to silver, to bronze, and then finishing with a mixture of iron and clay. Such a calculation of value is interestingly mentioned in 2 Esdr 7:55-57:

> Say to [the earth], "You produce gold and silver and bronze, and also iron, and lead and clay; but silver is more abundant than gold, and bronze than silver, and iron than bronze, and lead than iron, and clay than lead." Judge therefore which things are precious and desirable, those that are abundant or those that are rare? (NRSV)

---

83. The term appears in the Dead Sea Scroll fragments of the Pseudo-Daniel material as well. See Eisenman and Wise, *The Dead Sea Scrolls Uncovered,* 66-67.

84. See J. H. Charlesworth, "Folk Traditions in Jewish Apocalyptic Literature," in *Mysteries and Revelations: Apocalyptic Studies Since the Uppsala Colloquium,* ed. J. J. Collins and J. H. Charlesworth (Sheffield: JSOT, 1991) 91-113.

85. Porteous, *Daniel,* 45.

But what do the metals mean? There is precedent outside the Bible for the use of metals to represent successive empires. Hesiod (700 BCE?) dealt with a succession of four empires represented as metals of declining value. Collins, among others, considers Persian comparisons, also suggesting successive empires, to be even clearer and closer to Nebuchadnezzar's dream.[86]

However, the obsession with gold and silver, yet a further indication of the typical monetary concerns of empire, is interesting in this context. Goldingay surely goes too far in suggesting that the head, being gold, represents "the world power in originally positive terms, impressive and deserving of admiration in its God-given might."[87] After all, gold, silver, and bronze were the metals taken from the Temple (2 Kgs 24:13ff.) when Nebuchadnezzar sacked Jerusalem.[88] That a Jewish author would portray Nebuchadnezzar as dreaming of his regime as golden would hardly bring forth admiration; rather it would be the bitter realization of where at least some of the empire's gold had come from. Gold and silver are the means of trade, accumulation, and wealth. Of course, the essential question is, To whom is gold and silver of more value than iron and clay? To the common person, iron and clay are the materials of daily living and useful materials, whether they be plows or bowls. Who possesses gold but the powerful (cf. Job 3:15)? Gold and silver have their main value as monetary units, or decoration for religious idols or temple vessels. In the later prophetic material, Isaiah mentions gold and silver in the context of decorations for Babylonian/pagan idols (Isa 31:7; 40:9). Silver, especially, was the preferred medium of taxation since the time of Darius, which forced many Jews into poverty when they were forced to trade their agricultural produce for the coin of state (see Nehemiah 5).[89] In short, in the context of the exile, the head of gold was hardly a sign of admiration, but a sign of a Near Eastern empire's insatiable drive to horde precious metals

The focus of interest in Nebuchadnezzar's dream, however, is the stone—not to be associated with any human achievement—that destroys the entire statue. Surely the careful dissociation with humanity rules out an association with Cyrus as the destroyer of the Babylonian regime. Interestingly, Artemidorus notes that dreams of the destruction of cult statues are inauspicious for all people who dream them[90] (although Nebuchadnezzar's dream does not necessarily suggest a religious significance to his statue). The stone, then, is the key (see Reflections).

Daniel Interprets the Dream. 2:36-38.
The interpretation begins with Daniel's reiteration of where the source of true power is to be located. This is a bold statement, even for a religious folktale. The one who claimed power and authority from the Babylonian gods is actually given authority only by the permission of the God of Daniel and his friends. Nebuchadnezzar is allowed to have "power, might, and glory." This is a familiar refrain in late biblical literature; 1 Chr 29:11-12 rehearses similar sentiments: "Riches and honor come from you, and you rule over all. In your hand are power and might" (author's trans.; note also 2 Chr 20:6; Jdt 9:14; 3 Macc 6:12; Tob 13:6). Similar suggestions can be noted in New Testament thought. In John 19:10, Jesus tells Pilate that any authority Pilate might have is given from God, and Paul shares similar sentiments in Romans 13. All of these references can be read in either of two mutually exclusive ways. Either they are an affirmation of authority as granted by God, or they are a challenge to human authority in itself, pointing out that authority is really only in God. The dominant line in Christian circles has been a conservative affirmation of worldly authority as somehow delegated from God. However, a challenge to human pretensions is far more in keeping with the spirit of these passages, both in Daniel and in the New Testament. To suggest that God has ultimate control is to affirm the weakness and the merely utilitarian nature of human authority, which can just as easily be passed

---

86. Collins, *Daniel*, 162-63. Goldingay isn't quite convinced, suggesting that the sequence may well be Babylonian rulers within the Babylonian regime itself; after all, Nebuchadnezzar himself is the head of gold, not Babylon generally. If this is so, then the rock could be read as Cyrus rather than as a direct heavenly intervention. See Goldingay, *Daniel*, 49-50.
87. Goldingay, *Daniel*, 50.
88. This association was already made in later Jewish legend. See Ginzberg, *Legends of the Jews* (New York: Jewish Publication Society, 1910–1938) 4:328.
89. See H. Kippenberg, *Religion und Klassenbildung im antiken Judäa* (Göttingen: Vandenhoeck und Ruprecht, 1982).
90. Artemidorus, *The Interpretation of Dreams*, 112.

to another at God's whim. It is as if worldly power is *not* the central concern!

That Nebuchadnezzar rules over beasts and birds and, according to the LXX, "fish of the sea" has raised interesting speculation among commentators. Does Nebuchadnezzar echo Adam's rule over God's creation? Or does he merely follow the ways of other Mesopotamian rulers, who maintained animals and who were often pictured hunting, suggesting their power even over the animal kingdom?

2:39-45. The king is given to understand that his regime will not be the final power on earth. Indeed, there will be many to come. The kingdoms decline in significance from gold to bronze and then to iron mixed with clay. An interesting amount of attention is given to the statue's feet—the mixing of iron and clay. The incompatibility of iron and clay is an intriguing theme, noted in other late biblical passages. Wisdom 7:9 suggests that clay is worthless compared to silver, and Wis 15:8-10 suggests that idols are made of worthless clay. Consider Sir 13:2-3:

> Do not lift a weight too heavy for you,
>   or associate with one mightier and
>   richer than you.
> How can the clay pot associate with
>   the iron kettle?
> The pot will strike against it and
>   be smashed.
> A rich person does wrong, and even
>   adds insults;
>   a poor person suffers wrong, and must
>   add apologies. (NRSV)

In this passage, we see both the use of the iron/clay contrast and its use as a metaphor. Scholars have suggested that the mixing of iron and clay represents the attempts of the Ptolemaic and Seleucid rulers to cement ties with marriages—Antiochus II to Berenice in 252 or Ptolemy Epiphanes to Cleopatra in 193/194 (also suggested in Dan 11:6, 17). In any case, the amount of attention given to the interpretation of the feet and the mixed iron and clay suggests that this is the era of greatest interest to the writers. As this is almost universally taken to be a reference to the Hellenistic period, we can conclude that the interpretation—perhaps even the dream itself—was a composition of the Hellenistic period.

But as indicated above, the real interest is focused on the mountain of God as the true, everlasting kingdom and thus on the imminent expectation of the end of the Hellenistic regimes over the Jewish people. The use of a mountain to symbolize God's rule is familiar from the great prophecy of world peace in Isaiah 2, where God's rule from the mountain will allow nations (including Israel) to beat their swords and spears into farming tools.

Many scholars have noted that Josephus did not go into much detail about this rock turned mountain, because it might offend his Roman readers.[91] If this is true, then how deeply revealing is Josephus's silence! He is correct, because the mountain of God will end the reign of terror perpetuated by humans. When Goldingay, commenting on v. 44, suggests that God's kingdom also includes "the capacity to crush and shatter [which] is not wicked in itself,"[92] he neglects the important aspect of the stone—precisely that it was not cut by human hands. God's everlasting kingdom will be peaceful (Isaiah 2), and if it involves arresting evil, it will be a striking followed by healing of those who are stricken (Isa 19:22-25). When humans try to cut the stone, even if they do so in God's name, the result is inevitably violent destruction with no healing.

The dream attributed to Nebuchadnezzar by the Jewish author of Daniel 2 is a dream of destruction of world terror and power in the name of God's rule over humanity. It is, furthermore, a striking reminder that God achieves this destruction through means unavailable to human beings. The belief in the destruction of Babylonian, Median, Persian, and Greek rule is a powerful pronouncement to the listener that God will bring these reigns of terror to an end. All forms of inhumanity are destined to end, and it is this destiny that the faithful are invited to know and to act upon by means of an insight into the future of God's plan.

2:46-49. Transformation of the King and Promotion of the Jews. The reaction of the king is somewhat curious. It is affirmed that his regime will not last, and yet he is

---

91. Collins, *Daniel*, 171.
92. Goldingay, *Daniel*, 59.

deeply impressed with Daniel and praises Daniel's God. These are two themes in vv. 46-49 that will recur in the Daniel stories (parts of which are seen in the Joseph and Esther stories as well)—namely, the conversion of the foreign monarch (or at least the impressive affirmation of God by the king) and the attribution of a kingdom's impressive achievements to its Jewish administrators.

The transformation of the king is an important issue. The idea that the Daniel stories have a benign or positive view of the foreign rulers is usually not alive to the fact that the monarch changes in the end. It is a *changed* monarch who is affirmed, not the image that we have had throughout the story before his change. Before the change, the reader is presented with an image of a power-mad ruler who makes commands he thinks are permanent and decrees the massacre of many people. To say that the Daniel stories affirm all aspects of the royal figures is to ignore the significance of the transformation of Nebuchadnezzar, or if not the conversion the significance of his realization of the power of God. In a sense, the monarch finally learns what Daniel has been affirming throughout the story: that God exists and that God has ultimate power over all aspects of life. This is not to say, of course, that such a change in the king transforms his nature completely. Another element of these stories is precisely the element of reversal of fortune, and often the enemies of the Jews are killed rather than the Jews who were earlier threatened (see the book of Esther for the best example of this).

REFLECTIONS

Two themes are particularly interesting in chap. 2: the image of stones and the significance of the dreams of the disenfranchised.

1. Uncut Stones and Moving the Unmovable Stone. God's stone, which turns into a mountain, reminds us of the frequency of the use of stones and rocks in the Bible as symbols of strength and power. In Daniel, the stone is in the hand of God against human authority, but in the New Testament, the stone is in the hand of human authority against God. The contrast is instructive. God's stone in Daniel reminds us of another particular stone that attempted to prevent the founding of God's kingdom. It was a stone of death, sealed with the official insignias of Roman power. In a dramatic act of civil disobedience against the power of the state, God (no human hand!) rolled away this stone to free God's chosen founder of the new kingdom, and at the same time deny worldly powers to stop God's reign. This stone, too, was destined to crush human power. Is there a sense that Daniel calls us to be stones in the hand of God, rather than in the hands of human authority?

The image of uncut stones, suggesting no human involvement, has interesting associations in rabbinic tradition as well. According to the laws of Moses, the stones used to make altars for sacrifice are not to be "cut" (Deut 27:6). This idea is a point of departure for a rabbinic commentary:

For if thou lift up thy sword upon it (Ex. 20:25). In this connection R. Simon b. Eleazar used to say, "The altar is made to prolong the years of man and iron is made to shorten the years of man. It is not right for that which shortens life to be lifted up against that which prolongs life."

R. Yohanan b. Zakkai says, "Behold it says: *Thou shalt build . . . of whole stones (Deut. 27:6).* They are to be stones that establish peace.

"Now, by using the method of *qal vahomer*, you reason: The stones for the altar do not see nor hear nor speak. Yet because they serve to establish peace between Israel and their Father in heaven, the Holy One, blessed be He, said, *Thou shalt lift up no iron tool upon them (v. 5)*. How much the more then should he who establishes peace between man and his fellow-man, between husband and wife, between city and city, between nation and nation, between family and family, between government and government, be protected so that no harm should come to him."[93]

In Daniel 2, the stone "not cut by human hands" teaches us that God is directly involved in the matter of political sovereignty over the symbol of world power: the statue. Daniel 2 suggests that God will bring an end to oppression, but the stone is not cut using tools. God's stone is effective without human involvement, rather like Rabbi Yohanan ben Zakkai's call for the faithful to be God's peaceful altar stones who do not touch the weapons of war.

Note further that the stone, being uncut, has not been mined, like silver and gold. The stone does not have the same value placed on precious metals by humans. A stone cannot be used to pay taxes or to make idols glisten in the sunlight. But this stone is in the hand of God, and its destruction of the human pretense to power is total. God will not rule as humans rule, through the hording of the symbols of labor and achievement, much less by violence. God rules through peaceful altar stones, but God may also hurl them at human pretenses!

2. The Dreams of the Disenfranchised. Is there any significance to the kind of dreams attributed to Babylonian rulers in Daniel 2–6? To speculate on this, one must keep in mind that these dreams are compositions of Jewish authors, attributed to the emperor. Do the oppressed dream about particular themes, or do their dreams feature unique images? If an answer could be established, we might have some general themes to compare to dream content in the Bible, keeping in mind the important cultural and historical contexts involved.

It would help us to understand Daniel and Joseph, for example, if psychologists were to notice a difference in dream content between lower and upper classes of society. However, it is significant to note that there are virtually no studies in contemporary psychology, let alone in ancient dream materials, of whether poor or disenfranchised people dream in the same way that the privileged do. Some psychological researchers have admitted that one of the reasons why there are so few studies of such an interesting social question is the fact that private psychotherapy, a source for much data on dream interpretation, is expensive for the patients involved. Still, a few studies of "ethnic" dreams can give us some ideas of how to settle this issue.[94]

Renaldo Maduro wrote of the prominence of "journey dreams" among modern Mexican Americans who search for their identities because they are often rejected in modern American society.[95] Do dreams, then, provide compensation for being powerless or disenfranchised (as a Jungian might suggest)? On the other hand, a Freudian approach would also emphasize family and sexual dynamics: "Faced with painful, humiliating exigencies that generate feelings of powerlessness and rage the individual welcomes an alternative view of reality, namely the illusion that his enemies will be destroyed and that he will be reborn in a mystical reunion with mother."[96]

The hints provided by such views suggest that dream life is certainly influenced by the sociopolitical realities of waking life. Fanon, in his work as a psychiatrist during the Algerian resistance to French rule, regarded the dreams of the colonized as attempts to gain power by imaging alternative realities:

---

93. *Mekhilta of R. Ishmael*, J. Z. Lauterback, ed. (Philadelphia: Jewish Publication Society, 1933–35) 2:290.

94. Precisely such a theoretical association between the dreams of pre-industrialized societies and those of lower classes in industrialized societies was suggested by Vittorio Lanternari, "Dreams as Charismatic Significants: Their Bearing on the Rise of New Religious Movements," in A. Bharati, ed., *The Realm of the Extra-Human: Ideas and Actions* (The Hague/Paris: Mouton, 1976).

95. R. Maduro, "Journey Dreams in Latino Group Psychotherapy," *Psychotherapy: Theory, Research and Practice* 13 (1976) 148-55; M. Kramer, "Dream Translation: An Approach to Understanding Dreams," in *New Directions in Dream Interpretation*, ed. G. Delaney (New York: SUNY Press, 1993); M. Ullman, "Dreams, the Dreamer, and Society," in Delaney, *New Directions in Dream Interpretation*, 11-40.

96. M. Ostrow, "Archetypes of Apocalypse in Dreams and Fantasies, and in Religious Scripture," *American Imago* 43 (1986) 307-34.

The dreams of the native are always of muscular prowess; his dreams are of action and of aggression. I dream that I am jumping, swimming, running, climbing, I dream that I burst out laughing, that I span a river in one stride, or that I am followed by a flood of motorcars which never catch up to me. During the period of colonization, the native never stops achieving his freedom from nine in the evening until six in the morning.[97]

Roger Bastide's work on the dreams of African Brazilians lends further weight to Fanon's observations, and it adds helpful nuances. Bastide's interviews suggested that the very poor in the slums dreamed only of fulfilling immediate needs—winning lotteries, eating in abundance. It was the more educated Brazilians of African descent, those who began to understand political dynamics and the economic impact of racism, who dreamed of conquest, destruction of European Brazilians and their homes, and reversal of fortune.[98]

On the basis of these suggestions, can we hazard some observations about the book of Daniel, and chap. 2 in particular? The dreams attributed to Nebuchadnezzar are obviously images of an alternative reality—one in which God reverses present conditions. We see how the dreams of the disenfranchised, whether based on actual experiences or on literary products of daytime thought, reveal further elements of a theology composed "in the shadows of empire." Dreams are beyond the control of even a world emperor. As Fanon suggests, dreams reveal uncontrolled worlds of the subordinate person where he or she can, at last, move freely. Bastide's work, however, suggests that the dreamers in the book of Daniel clearly understand the source of their suppression. Their dreams grow from their understanding. But dreams are not in and of themselves revolutionary.

The dreams of the people can be dangerous for those in power. In the first half of the twentieth century, European surrealist artists and philosophers were involved in a movement based on an appropriation of "dream forms," most famously depicted in the bizarre dreamscapes by surrealist painters like Dali. The political message of surrealism, however, is similar to the understanding of the dreams in Daniel. Andre Breton wrote in the *Surrealist Manifesto*: "The dream alone entrusts to man all his rights to freedom." But surrealism runs the risk of staying in dreamland. The question for the modern Christian who reads Daniel as a basis for faith and practice is whether these dreams of an end to human exploitation can be liberated from dreamland to break into reality. In short, can dreams become strategies?

97. Fanon, *The Wretched of the Earth*, 52.
98. R. Bastide, "Reve de noirs," *Psyche: revue internationale des sciences de l'homme et de psychanalyse* 49 (1950) 802-11.

DANIEL 3:1-30, POLITICAL ATHEISM AND RADICAL FAITH

COMMENTARY

3:1, The Statue. This chapter begins abruptly with the construction of a statue. The dimensions of this statue are certainly odd; the height is ten times greater than the width, giving the impression that it is a pole-like structure. Montgomery suggests that we should understand that it is a stele (that is, a tower of stone, like an obelisk) with a carving of a figure or covered with inscriptions. We are not told that the statue is of Nebuchadnezzar himself, but the text certainly allows this impression, particularly noting that the statue in chap. 2 is in the form of a human being. Hippolytus of Rome (c. 220 CE) suggested that Nebuchadnezzar actually sought to build the image that he saw in the previous dream, being overly impressed with his reign's being represented by gold.

This statue, then, is made of gold, the substance of highest commercial value. In his recent work, Dutch theologian Ton Veerkamp speaks powerfully of the use of gold and its meaning, as well as the location of "Dura." Veerkamp believes that the present form of Daniel 3 took its redactional shape in the Seleucid period, and thus writes that the statue portrayed in Daniel 3 is "a golden monstrosity.... Medium of exchange, deposit of value, measure of worth—gold was the gravitational center of the Hellenistic economy. The King of Kings made an image of it—he established the economy and made from it a cult object—he made a fetish of gold. The Empire establishes Gold as a god of the whole world—that is the meaning of what is described here."[99]

Basing his analysis on his proposal that "Dura" (which can mean "plain") is in fact the famous Dura-Europos (270 miles northwest of Babylon), Veerkamp notes that although this Dura was not significant in the Babylonian period, it was a place of significant activity for Antiochus III and Antiochus IV, because it was located along important trade routes and was the site of a temple to Zeus. Veerkamp supposes that the writer unites the crisis of the Jews under Nebuchadnezzar with the height of Seleucid power, the latter's rule being one in which gold reigned; but a Seleucid era insertion of the reference to Dura would have this impact just as effectively. Other scholars, however, are more cautious about the reference to Dura, noting that the term is used for many locations. The Greek historian Herodotus also goes to some length to describe what he had heard about the amount of gold in the religious shrines of the Babylonians, including statues and tables for sacrifice.[100] Finally, Brown has noted that already in the fifth century BCE, gold was becoming the "primary circulating source of value."[101]

Lacocque draws attention to the Greek versions, which insert a date for this event as the eighteenth year of Nebuchadnezzar—in other words, the year of his conquest of Jerusalem. Thus the statue went up in the year the Temple came down—false worship as opposed to true worship.[102]

Although not always using gold, Mesopotamian regimes certainly built monstrous images; this is clear to any visitor to the British Museum, where Nineveh's massive winged bulls are on display and to this day communicate very powerfully the message they were originally meant to convey: the power of an empire. Collins, on the other hand, suggests that a memory of Nabonidus's construction and restoration of the statue of Sin, the moon god, at Haran (which apparently infuriated the priesthood of Marduk in Babylon) may be behind the motif of the Babylonian monarch's erecting the statue.

Is the construction of the statue an act of pride? Does the story suggest that the Babylonian monarch wanted to be divinized? If so, is there any historical precedent for this? Judith 3:8 records a legend that Nebuchadnezzar certainly did want to be looked upon as a god, and the grandiose claims of the Mesopotamian rulers could easily give this impression, even if it is not technically accurate. Whether Nebuchadnezzar ever erected such a statue is totally beside the point. The point was that he could—he could amass that much gold; he could assemble the leaders; he could demand obedience and threaten horrible punishment—and this is the plausibility (that is, a political plausibility) that the stories of Daniel are based on.

The Command of Obedience. 3:2. As if to remove any doubt of what the gold is to symbolize, there follows a gathering of all the highest officials of the government—the representatives of Babylonian power and prestige—called by Nebuchadnezzar to announce his cult of gold. The book communicates the great size of the court, Persian as well as Babylonian, and the various levels of administration by its use of lists of various types of officials. Note also, however, that the Jewish writers are familiar with the terminology of governance. Rosenthal notes that the first few terms are borrowed from Mesopotamian (Akkadian) languages, while most of the others are from Persian terms, such as the words translated in the NRSV as

---

99. My own translation of T. Veerkamp, *Autonomie und Egalität* (Berlin: Alektor-Verlag, 1992) 243-44.
100. Herodotus *The History* 1:183.
101. J. P. Brown, "Proverb-Book, Gold Economy, Alphabet," *JBL* 100 (1981) 177.

102. Lacocque, *The Book of Daniel*, 56.

DANIEL 3:1-30 COMMENTARY

"counselors," "treasurers," "law officials," "magistrates/police chiefs," and the general category of "all who rule/have authority."[103] The presence of treasurers is, of course, particularly interesting for the origin of Nebuchadnezzar's "image of gold." In his attempt to suggest a date, Collins proposes that the use of Persian names requires a long enough period of time for the language of the Persians to sink in to the Jewish population,[104] but all minority peoples learn the vocabulary of authority very quickly (see Introduction).

3:3a. This verse repeats the list, in response to Nebuchadnezzar's command. This frequent repetition of orders, usually repeated word for word, gives the impression that all the minions of the Babylonian emperor obey his whim to the letter. This is what he wanted, and this is exactly what happened.

3:3b-4. The herald cries in a loud voice, a term also used in association with the military; thus it is a commanding voice. The address is directed to the "peoples, nations, and languages." The vastness of the territories under imperial control is suggested here. Empires of the ancient Near East frequently claimed to control massive numbers of the peoples in the known world. The Assyrian monarch Sennacherib wrote: "Sennacherib, the great king, king of the universe, king of Assyria, king of the four quarters . . ."[105] Nebuchadnezzar II, in one of the Wadi-Brisa inscriptions, claims to have made Babylon "foremost among all the countries and every human habitation,"[106] while in the so-called Cyrus Cylinder, Cyrus claims, "I am Cyrus, king of the world, great king, legitimate king, king of Babylon, king of Sumer and Akkad, king of the four rims of the earth."[107] Such is the rhetoric of power, perhaps reaching a zenith in Roman rhetoric of Roman rule: "Cities now gleam in splendor and beauty, and the whole earth is arrayed like a paradise."[108]

3:5. Scholarly comment on the musical instruments is interesting because of the presence of at least one Greek term, συμφωνία (*symphōnia* [סומפניה *sûmpōnyâ*]; NIV, "pipes"; NRSV, "drum"), usually taken to be some primitive form of bagpipe. But Lacocque's comments on the instruments are also interesting. "The flute" (NIV, NRSV, "pipe" [משרוקיתא *mašrôqîtā'*]) was a simple peasant's instrument (Judg 5:16), while the "lyre" (NRSV, NIV, "zither" [קיתרוס *qaytĕrôs*]) would be made of precious metal or ivory and would be an aristocrat's instrument.[109] Both the *sambyka* (NRSV, "trigon"; NIV, "lyre" [סבכא *sabbĕkā*]) and the *symphonia* have bad reputations with the Greeks, the former repudiated by Plato and the latter an instrument that inspired Antiochus IV to dance in what was seen as a shameful public spectacle. It may be that the instruments themselves, and the social class associated with them, suggest a kind of universal demand on all peoples (poor and wealthy) to be obedient to the king.

3:6. Punishment by fire is not entirely unknown, as seen in Jeremiah 29. As Collins notes, punishment by fire became the "eschatological punishment par excellence in the post-exilic prophecy and apocalyptic literature."[110] (Note the destruction of the beast in Revelation as well as in Daniel 7.)

3:7. The peoples are to "fall down" (נפל *nĕpal*, a position of submission) and "do honor" (סגד *sĕgad*; the NRSV translates this as "worship," but this will be somewhat problematic, as noted below) when they hear the music. As earlier in the story, the repetition fits exactly, and the people respond as they are commanded. As Nebuchadnezzar wants it, so shall he have it—except for one slight problem: Jewish resistance breaks out again.

3:8-12, The Denunciation of the Jews. Here, the story begins to get interesting. The setting is the presence of the king. The Chaldeans (the use of this term for Babylonians is perhaps intended to be ethnically specific, rather than to refer to court astrologers) accuse the Jews of disobedience and insolence before the king. The literal phrase used for "accusation" (אכלו קרציהון *'ăkalû qarṣêhôn*) is rather interesting: "they ate bits off," which is an Akkadian idiom meaning "to accuse." The Chaldeans remind the

---

103. Rosenthal, *A Grammar of Biblical Aramaic*.
104. Collins, *Daniel*.
105. D. D. Luckenbill, *The Annals of Sennacherib* (Chicago: University of Chicago Press, 1924) 23. I an indebted to Dr. Millard Lind for reminding me of other examples of this, including the Assyrian cases.
106. Pritchard, *Ancient Near Eastern Texts Relating to the Old Testament*, 307.
107. Pritchard, *Ancient Near Eastern Texts Relating to the Old Testament*, 316.
108. Aelius Aristides *Eulogy of Rome* 103.
109. Lacocque, *The Book of Daniel*, 57.
110. Collins, *Daniel*, 185.

king of the decree he has made, repeating all that was stated before with one interesting exception: The Jews also "do not worship your gods." This was not, of course, part of Nebuchadnezzar's original decree about the statue, but it adds to the sense that the Jews are guilty because they are foreigners—merely conquered exiles—who were trusted by the king (as in Esther). The king's rage is perhaps to be understood to have arisen not only from the disobedience of the command to fall before the statue, but also from the fact that the judgment of the king is brought into question for having appointed these four Jews to positions of importance in the first place. Thus betrayal is added to insubordination.

The motif of the evil counselors vs. the Jewish court officials runs through many of these stories and suggests some ethnic tensions between the tellers, and hearers, of these stories and the surrounding peoples. In his analysis of the Daniel stories, Meinhold was particularly alert to this sociopsychological aspect of the stories.[111]

Interestingly, the term translated "worship" (of your gods [פלח *pĕlaḥ*]) is different from that used for "worship" (of the statue [*sĕgid*]) in v. 5. The latter term can be read as "honor"—that is, that the statue was to be honored. When Nebuchadnezzar fell before Daniel in 2:46, he honored Daniel, but did not worship him in the same sense that the Jews did not worship the gods of Nebuchadnezzar.

It seems odd that the king does not know that these Jews will not worship the Babylonian gods, irrespective of their attitude toward the golden statue. This is further indication of the isolation of these stories from one another at some point before they were joined together. The stubborn refusal to compromise their faith is reintroduced in story after story. It seems that almost each time, the king needs to learn something about these Jews, including those aspects that were introduced already in a previous story. That Daniel and his friends Hananiah, Mishael, and Azariah worshiped the Hebrew God should hardly have been news to Nebuchadnezzar. In any case, as a result of the accusation, the Jews will be brought before the king.

The Appearance Before the King and Jewish Defiance. 3:13-14. The king, once again in a "furious rage," summons the insubordinate Jewish exiles. As with many of the Daniel stories, the turning point occurs in the presence of or before the king. The setting of these crucial scenes is obvious given the power and majesty of the emperor. To actually stand before this ruler who commands such authority and wealth is an awesome fate. Thus in v. 14 the question is put to the young Jewish men, and now regards two accusations: "You do not worship my gods . . . and . . . honor my statue?" (cf. Bel and the Dragon in the Commentary on the Additions to Daniel, 185-94).

3:15. Nebuchadnezzar offers the Jews one last chance; thus this verse is full of the folkloric repetition of lists that is typical of Daniel. What is interesting is the final phrase, which has been translated variously as "and who is the god that will deliver you out of my hands" (NRSV) and "who ever is the god who could rescue you from my power?"[112] Nebuchadnezzar's rule and authority are such that only a god can deliver the accused Jews. The Babylonian ruler is a man of great arrogance. Porteous writes, "We see here the worldly power absolutely confident that there is no limit to its authority."[113]

3:16-18. The reaction of the accused Jews is to declare their independence from royal authority. Their response in v. 17 is a statement of faith, proclaiming the existence of the God who can deliver them—indeed, there is one with greater authority than Nebuchadnezzar. Such is their faith. But their belief has consequences. Verse 18 is a statement of the resulting action: If their God does not deliver them, still they "will not worship the golden statue." They boldly express civil disobedience to the law of the king.

Verse 18 contains one of the most powerful statements in the entire book of Daniel, with consequences reaching far beyond this little story: "But if not . . ." They profess that their God is able to deliver them, but even if not, they will not obey the king's commands. This is a statement of faith against the appearance of defeat. The most infuriating aspect of radical faith is its adamant refusal to be

---

111. Meinhold, "Die Diasporanovelle," 170.

112. Goldingay, *Daniel*, 64.
113. Porteous, *Daniel*, 59.

impressed with the obvious—namely, the subordinated status and powerlessness of the Jews before the mighty emperor—and their steadfast adherence to an alternative reality: God reigns. Nebuchadnezzar's response is hardly unexpected in the face of this open defiance in the name of faith.

3:19-27, The Salvation of the Jews. The strength of those who overpower the Jews in order to cast them into the furnace is impressive. Again, the specific vocabulary used for this action suggests a military association. The garment terminology ("robes, trousers, turbans and other clothes") has caused some difficulty, but the Aramaic has an almost rhythmic, rhyming quality to it, reminding one of a phrase like the English "lock, stock, and barrel." In any case, taking care to point out that they are wearing clothes when they are placed in the furnace will allow the later observation that their garments do not even smell of smoke, let alone look burnt.

A key to this description of their impending execution is the binding. Binding is the symbol of police authority *par excellence.* In his analysis of symbols of power carried by each Roman soldier, Wengst noted that handcuffs "stand for the maintenance of the new situation brought about by force of arms."[114] In Daniel 3, the act of binding the young Jewish men is repeated (1) when the three are cast into the furnace; (2) when the king asks if his order has been fulfilled, including the binding (v. 24); and (3) when Nebuchadnezzar sees the men walking, unbound (v. 25). Furthermore, as in 2:15, the king's decree is punctuated by his hysterical rage, without regard for clear thought. The death of those who would kill the Jewish exiles recalls similar reversals of fortune, such as one finds in the book of Esther, but the motif may be used here to convey the absurdity of the king's rage, which results in the senseless loss of his own officials who were killed by the flames when they threw the three Jews into the furnace.[115]

Verse 24 introduces another of the most interesting aspects of the story. The "fourth person" whom the king sees inside the furnace has given rise to considerable scholarly debate. The Aramaic reads literally "son of god." Was this intended to be a reference to an angel? Perhaps the reference is to a special presence of God with the three young men? The Aramaic word בר־אלהין (*barʾĕlāhîn*) is typically taken to refer to a member of the "sons of god," who are collectively known as the "host of heaven" (Gen 6:2; 1 Kgs 22:19; Job 1:6; 38:7; Ps 148:2). There is also frequent mention of the presence of a court of heaven in the Ugaritic/Canaanite materials.[116] Goldingay suggests that Old Testament promises of heavenly aides to protect God's people become concrete here (cf. Pss 34:8; 91:11).[117] Collins relates the fourth person to the "Angel/Messenger of Yahweh" who protects Israel in Exod 14:19 and who guides Israel (Exod 23:20), helps Elijah (1 Kgs 19:7), and destroys the Assyrian army (2 Kgs 19:35; Isa 37:36).[118] This seems particularly suggestive in the light of the appearances of Michael as the protector of the Israelite people during the exilic experience (Daniel 7; 10–12).

What is further interesting is that the presence of the fourth figure and the survival of the three young men in the fiery furnace brings forth a statement of faith by Nebuchadnezzar, who calls them, "servants of the Most High God" (v. 26). The phrase "Most High God" (עבדוהי די־אלהא *ʿabdôhî dî-ʾĕlāhāʾ*) is a form of reference used for the God of the Jews in many exilic and post-exilic writings.

Many scholars have suggested an interesting resemblance to the near burning of Croesus by Cyrus, who wanted to know if gods would come to Croesus's rescue.[119] But fire imagery has other associations with the exilic experience in the Bible. Isaiah 48:10 refers to the exile itself as a "refining fire," and many scholars have pointed to the imagery of Isa 43:2 as obviously related to this story: "When you walk through fire you shall not be burned,/ and the flame shall not consume you" (NRSV).[120] If this Isaiah passage was in the mind of the storyteller, the implication that the exile (which is compared by Isaiah to

---

114. This observation was based on Josephus's inventory of what the typical Roman soldier carried. See K. Wengst, *Pax Romana and the Peace of Jesus Christ* (London: SCM, 1987) 27.

115. The Septuagint inserts The Song of the Three, or The Prayer of Azariah, at this point in Daniel. That text will be dealt with in this volume in the separate commentary on the Additions to Daniel, 158-70.

116. Lacocque, *The Book of Daniel,* 61.
117. Goldingay, *Daniel,* 68.
118. Collins, *Daniel,* 191.
119. Herodotus *The History* 186.
120. Many scholars go so far as to suggest that Daniel 3 was inspired by the Isaiah passage. I agree, however, with those who suggest that this is too sweeping a statement for a much richer tradition in Daniel 3.

the exodus) was like a fiery threat ought once again to give pause to those who argue that the exile was "not that bad."

Glorification of the Jews, Promotion, and Proclamation. 3:28. Nebuchadnezzar not only honors the trust of the Jews, but also emphasizes that his decree has been successfully disobeyed. This theme of changing the supposedly unchangeable decree of the king is noted throughout Daniel (Dan 2:9; 3:19; 5:6, 9; 6:18; 7:7; note also the theme in Ezra 2:21; 6:9, 11, 16; 7:25). The defiance that appears to be obvious—in other words, the political "atheism" of the Jews in their refusal to bow to the symbols of Babylonian power—is a key point to the teller of the stories. Those who hear these stories learn to see a new reality that is informed by the "Most High God."

3:29-30. Now the proclamation is made throughout the many lands under Babylonian rule that God's signs and wonders are great and mighty. More important, God's kingdom and the sovereignty of God are everlasting. In the face of the mistaken power of Babylon, even Nebuchadnezzar is made to recognize his limitations before this God. But the humbling of the mighty emperor was instigated by the civil disobedience of three who lived by another reality, because they served another sovereign.

REFLECTIONS

1. Fanon reminds the reader of Daniel of the power and impact of symbols of colonialism and imposition of foreign culture: "The colonial world is a world where the settler makes history and is conscious of making it . . . a world of statues: the statue of the general who carried out the conquest, the statue of the engineer who built the bridge. . . . The first thing the native learns is to stay in his place, and not to go beyond certain limits."[121]

Memmi echoes this observation: "The few statues which decorate the city represent (with incredible scorn for the colonized who pass them every day) the great deeds of colonization. The buildings are patterned after the colonizer's own favorite designs; the same is true of the street names, which recall the faraway provinces from which he came. . . . Traditions and acquirements, habits and conquests, deeds and acts of previous generations are thus bequeathed and recorded in history."[122] Memmi insists that there is a certain inevitability to such displays in the mind of the conqueror, because "he loves the most flashy symbols, the most striking demonstrations of the power of his country. He attends all the military parades and he desires and obtains frequent and elaborate ones; he contributes his part by dressing up carefully and ostentatiously. He admires the army and its strength, reverses uniforms and covets decorations . . . this corresponds to a deep necessity . . . to impress the colonized is just as important as to reassure oneself."[123]

It is possible, in the light of what Fanon and Memmi reveal, to look on the ruins of ancient Babylon with a new eye—an eye to the impact that such sights would have had on those whose suffering formed the very bricks of this ancient wonder of the world. Yet, Fanon writes that the *inward* life of the colonized person is quite different: "He is overpowered but not tamed; he is treated as an inferior but he is not convinced of his inferiority . . . the settler pits brute force against the weight of numbers. He is an exhibitionist. His preoccupation with security makes him remind the native out loud that he alone is master. The settler keeps alive in the native an anger which he deprives of outlet."[124]

---

121. Fanon, *The Wretched of the Earth*, 51-52.
122. Memmi, *The Colonizer and the Colonized*, 104.
123. Memmi, *The Colonizer and the Colonized*, 59.
124. Fanon, *The Wretched of the Earth*, 53.

Daniel 3:1-30 Reflections

In Daniel 3, the statue as a symbol of power communicates the power of this story, but Daniel 3 itself communicates the inward conviction that the Jewish population is *not* powerless or without recourse. As is often the case with the Bible, the reader must turn to the world of subordinated peoples, minorities, the displaced and threatened, to learn how to ask socially appropriate questions of a book that reflects an exiled or politically occupied people.

Nebuchadnezzar's statue stands for political and economic power. As such, it only weakens the message of Daniel 3 to reduce it to merely a pious lesson about idolatry or the fall of the proud, as if to relate it to any proud person of any station in life. Daniel 3 is about a particular kind of pride that comes from a system that derives its prestige and power from the suffering of others; in short, it is the unique pride of the wealthy and the powerful. Who else can erect golden monuments? Along this same line, it is perhaps somewhat dangerous to see in chap. 3 any sympathetic portrayal of Nebuchadnezzar (who is portrayed, in the words of Fanon, as both an "exhibitionist" of power and the raging executioner).[125] To suggest that chap. 3 has a sympathetic portrayal of the emperor at the end is merely to point out that in the end the monarch's power is humbled, defeated because of the statue's powerlessness over the Jews; and thus the monarch is transformed. There is no sympathy with tyranny in Daniel 3; there is only the possibility of change.

2. Is Daniel 3 a martyr legend? Porteous suggests that martyr legends can indeed result in the last-minute salvation of the heroes as well as their death,[126] but Collins prefers to suggest that Daniel 3 is an emergent form of a martyr legend that will be fully developed in a test like 2 Maccabees 7.[127] In any case, a martyr legend is intended to promote action—to embolden faith—and in the case of Daniel 3, to call people to active, nonviolent resistance to the symbols of worldly power and its religious expressions. In short, it is a call to political atheism.

In his recent history of Christianity, W. H. C. Frend often refers to the Roman charge of "atheism" directed against the Christians because of their refusal to recognize the Roman state gods.[128] Concomitant to this, of course, was their refusal of military service both because of Jesus' commands to love enemies and because of the pagan worship required of those who took the Roman commands. As he stood before the authorities who demanded to know the reason for his insubordination in refusing to bear arms, it is reported that the Roman centurion Marcellus, a Christian convert, replied, "I am a soldier of Jesus Christ, the eternal king. From now on I cease to serve your emperors and I despise the worship of your gods of wood and stone . . . it is not fitting that a Christian, who fights for Christ his Lord, should be a soldier according to the brutalities of this world." The annals of the radical reformation traditions—Quaker, Mennonite, and Church of the Brethren—are filled with such encounters "before the king," standing in the courts of states. The early Brethren leader John Naas of Nordheim, for example, in the eighteenth century stood before the king of Prussia and refused to bear arms because he was already enlisted in the army of Christ. Likewise, George Fox refused Oliver Cromwell's offer of an officership in his army.

Christian faith involves the refusal to bow before the golden statues of Nebuchadnezzar. But what is critical in the modern era is the realization that in our time Nebuchadnezzar is now perfectly capable of building his statues with the face of Jesus—evil appears as an angel of light. (E.g., a U.S. nuclear submarine capable of dozens of Hiroshimas was named *Corpus Christi*, "the body of Christ"!) For Americans who believe that they live in a "Christian" country, it is far too easy to accept political or economic policies that involve bowing to golden statues in the name of national interests. The

---
125. Fanon, *The Wretched of the Earth*, 53.
126. Porteous, *Daniel*.
127. Collins, *Daniel*, 55.
128. W. H. C. Frend, *The Rise of Christianity* (Philadelphia: Fortress, 1984) 148, 181-82, 234-35.

bombing of Baghdad during the Persian Gulf War resulted in thousands of civilian deaths and continued to wreak havoc for the poor of that society years after the cease-fire through the destruction of a vital infrastructure for distribution of medical supplies, food, water, and other essentials of peaceful existence. Yet, the bombing was accompanied by a political rhetoric of "faith and patriotism" that played as sweetly on international television as did Nebuchadnezzar's orchestra. But the Christian is called to resistance, and to "atheism" in the face of *all* false gods. If chap. 1 was a call to resist the enticements of the king's food and wine, chap. 3 is just as clearly a call not to lose heart before the sight of the monumental self-importance of the conquering regime, both then and now. Modern Christians ought to refuse all attempts to serenade violence and exploitation with the tunes of patriotism. It is precisely the responsibility of Christians to point out the falsehoods of using Christian symbolism and language to defend exploitation and military brutality. The beginning of that task, however, is for us to refuse to be moved by the music of national interest. Mishael, Azariah, and Hananiah, then, are Hebrew apostles of a radical faith that is, at the same time, a political atheism.

3. Sovereignty is a central issue in the book of Daniel. In 3:27, once again the king gathers many of his officers, who share his astonishment that the fire has no sovereignty over the three men. The king's punishment failed. Not even the fire, let alone the king, can rule over them. Traditional Christian suggestions that there is a reference here to a "resurrection motif" may not be theologically acceptable in modern historical-critical discussion, but read as a comparison to the sociopolitical circumstances of first-century Roman Palestine, such comments are near the mark, particularly if Jesus' resurrection is seen as a defiant reversal of the Roman authorities' attempt to impose their will on the subordinated minority Jewish population of first-century Palestine.

DANIEL 4:1-37, THE TRUE THRONE AND FALSE THRONES

COMMENTARY

Chapter 4 is particularly interesting because of two elements. It includes a wealth of potential influences from traditions attested in Greek and Mesopotamian sources (the arrogance of Nebuchadnezzar, the madness and/or absence of the Babylonian ruler in Babylon, dwelling with beasts, etc.). And it reflects a wealth of Jewish sources that are obviously relevant to understanding the chapter.

The nonbiblical sources include a story in Eusebius attributed to Megasthenes (300 BCE?): *Concerning the Assyrians*. In brief, the story portrays Nebuchadnezzar, in a fit of madness or possession, climbing to his roof and predicting the coming of a Persian mule that will enslave the Babylonians. Nebuchadnezzar wishes that this mule would join the wild beasts in the desert and leave him alone. There are intriguing parallels as well as significant differences between this tale and Daniel 4. The significance of this tale, however, is that it may point to certain collective memories of Nebuchadnezzar or Nabonidus that the author of Daniel 4 draws on—e.g., Nebuchadnezzar's odd behavior, the fear of his reign's coming to an end, and the location "on the roof."

A second series of sources surrounds Nabonidus, who left Babylon for a sojourn in the desert, spending time in Teima, an oasis village. Many ancient texts give negative portrayals of him, which most scholars presume to have been written by angry Babylonian religious leaders who resented both the king's absence and his apparent neglect of the Marduk cult in Babylon.[129]

---

129. "Verse Account of Nabonidus," in Pritchard, *Ancient Near Eastern Texts Relating to the Old Testament*, 312-15.

That the historical Nabonidus, rather than Nebuchadnezzar, may be the source of the portrayal of the monarch in Daniel 4 is a view that received a major piece of corroborating evidence with the publication of the Dead Sea Scroll fragment entitled *Prayer of Nabonidus* (see Introduction), which parallels Daniel 4 in many ways and specifically names Nabonidus.

Finally, there are fascinating differences between the Greek and the Aramaic versions of the chapter. The two versions are quite distinct, although clearly covering the same ground. In the Greek, Nebuchadnezzar narrates his dream, and then Daniel interprets it. What is particularly interesting in the Greek, however, is a much stronger confession of faith/conversion by Nebuchadnezzar:

> From now on I will serve him. From fear of him trembling has seized me, and I praise all his holy ones. For the gods of the nations do not have in themselves power to turn over the kingdom of a king to another king, to kill and make alive and to do signs and great and terrible wonders, and to change very great things, as the God of heaven has done in my case. . . . Every day of my reign I will offer sacrifices to the Most High for my life, for a pleasing odor to the Lord, and I will do what is pleasing before him.[130]

This is an important addition, suggesting that the themes of the transformation of Nebuchadnezzar, already suggested in the Aramaic version of the Masoretic Text, were enlarged and made stronger in the Hellenistic period, which is a tendency we also see in the Greek additions to Daniel, especially Bel and the Dragon (see commentary on Additions to Daniel).

4:1-3, Confessional Introduction. Chapter 4 begins with a standard Aramaic letter form, including the wish for *shalom* ("peace") and the clear identification of the sender. The concern to publish the proclamation in "all languages" is reflected in Darius's famous Behistun Inscription, which still survives on the cliff face on which it was carved. The inscription is written in three different languages, and it describes Darius's rise to power as the third Persian monarch.[131]

Chapter 4, then, begins with Nebuchadnezzar speaking in the first person in praise of the Jewish God, and the chapter also ends with his praise of the Jewish God. It is worth noting that dream reports, as well as epistles, are typically cast in the first person.

The key term in the confessional introduction, and the focus of Daniel 4, is the issue that has been raised already in previous stories: sovereignty or political power. The issue of the nature of political authority was obviously a critical one for the exiles and the exiles in the diaspora, who constantly encountered the claims of total sovereignty by their foreign rulers. The Aramaic term that is usually translated "sovereignty" (שלטן *šālṭān*) can be found running through the text of Daniel again and again in chaps. 1–6 and is particularly prominent in the first vision of chap. 7 (see Dan 2:38-39; 3:27, 33; 4:19, 31; 5:7, 16; 6:25; 7:6, 12, 14, 26-27; cf. Ezra 4:20; 7:24).

Nebuchadnezzar Calls His Counselors. 4:4-6. The setting of Nebuchadnezzar's experience is important. He was in his palace, and was "prospering/flourishing." Goldingay provides a very helpful description of the Babylonian setting and Nebuchadnezzar's vantage point over Babylon and its wonders from the palace.[132] The Old Greek text also dates this story to Nebuchadnezzar's eighteenth year, which would, as in the previous chapter, be the year of Nebuchadnezzar's conquest of Jerusalem and the destruction of the Temple. In any case, things were going well for the king—or so he thought. But just as he was enjoying his success, the king has a dream that frightens him, and so he decrees that the "wise of Babylon" be brought in.

4:7. The listing of those who are brought in includes magicians (using an Egyptian term), enchanters (Persian), Chaldeans (here "astrologers"), and exorcists. The term for "exorcist" is unique to this story, and is the same word used to describe the Jew who heals Nabonidus's illness in 4QPrNab (see Introduction). Again, as expected, all of these advisers to the king fail him.

4:8-9. It would be interesting to know why Daniel is delayed in his arrival, but as many scholars have suggested, it certainly serves to build the drama for his entrance.

---

130. Collins, *Daniel*, *Hermeneia*, 213.
131. Cook, *The Persian Empire*, 12-13, 19.

132. Goldingay, *Daniel*, 89-90.

In any case, the delay serves the function of giving Nebuchadnezzar time to realize that he will not be able to get his answers from anyone else in his regime. Notably, Daniel's slave name is repeated by Nebuchadnezzar, "Belteshazzar after the name of my god" (v. 8). Are we to believe, then, that Nebuchadnezzar does not know Daniel's given name? Nebuchadnezzar knows him well enough to say that he is one who is "endowed with a spirit of the holy gods." Nebuchadnezzar appears to lack understanding about where the source of Daniel's great wisdom is to be found. Goldingay notes that this title is not used for the Jewish God elsewhere.[133] This is perhaps the main hint in chap. 4 that once again we are dealing with the separate story that was eventually joined to the series that appears in the book. In v. 9, Nebuchadnezzar realizes his dependence on Daniel and openly attests to Daniel's wisdom and his ability to interpret dreams and mysteries.

The Description of Nebuchadnezzar's Dream. 4:10-11. Nebuchadnezzar then describes the dream to Daniel. In the dream he saw a tree of "great height," like the statue in chap. 2 (note the prevalence of things that are great, tall, mighty, awesome in these dreams). Many scholars suggest that this tree is a reference to the widely held notion of the "cosmic tree" that stretches to the heavens in many different ancient mythologies (and perhaps related also to the tree of life portrayed by sacred poles in the Jerusalem Temple; see 2 Kgs 17:10; 18:4; 23:14), which may be the source of the tree imagery in Ezekiel 31, where Pharaoh is described as a great tree. There are many nonbiblical references similar to this, such as Herodotus's description of the dream of Astyages the Mede in which a vine grows from the womb of his daughter and stretches across the earth (a reference to the birth of Cyrus, the conquerer of the Medes).[134] Note also the portrayal of Babylon as a tree in the Dead Sea Scroll fragments.[135] In v. 11 the emphasis on the height of the tree—reaching into the heavens—is reminiscent of the Tower of Babel story in Genesis 11 (as was the reference to Shinar in Daniel 2). The idea that this tree is "visible to the ends of the earth" is another comment on the megalomania of the emperor.

4:12. The tree's foliage was beautiful, but the issue here is the control of provisions. Twice, the fact is repeated that the tree fed all humanity and then all living things. In this initial description, the impression is given that animals found shade under the tree and that birds lived in it by choice. However, when the imagery changes, another perspective is revealed.

4:13. This verse introduces the concept of a "watchful one" or "watcher." This nomenclature for a representative of heaven is especially prominent in *1 Enoch*. Goldingay associates the watchmen with God's court, but others have also made reference to the Persian officials known as the "King's Eyes," who regularly informed the emperor of matters throughout his empire. It is possible, then, that these watchmen are God's informants, in contradistinction to the Persian secret service. The empire that spies on others is now itself being spied upon by the regime of God! For exiles and foreign immigrants, such an image would be potent, since fear of betrayal to the authorities would be a daily reality. That these informants are themselves matched by even greater watchmen of God would be an interesting source of satisfaction for the exilic hearers of such stories.[136]

4:14. The result of the visit of the heavenly messenger is the near total destruction of the tree. The animals are told to flee. Have they been released? It is hard not to equate them with the captive peoples of Babylon and Persia. For the Persians, especially, the self-delusion that the people dwelt among them peacefully and by their choice was, as already noted, a common notion. For a later period, historians also note the cynicism of the Roman writers who spoke of a "peace of Rome" (*Pax Romana*). This peace referred to a time of opulence that disregarded the suffering at the frontiers of the empire, even though the suffering of the conquered peoples at the

---

133. Goldingay, *Daniel*, 80.
134. Herodotus *The History* 1:108.
135. See 4Q547 in Eisenman and Wise, *The Dead Sea Scrolls Uncovered*, 71-73. It is worth noting in passing that the Dead Sea Scroll fragments 4Q 234-245 include Daniel, Belshazzar, Nebuchadnezzar, the seventy-year period of exile, and the tower of Babel traditions among the historical references cited. See Eisenman and Wise, *The Dead Sea Scrolls Uncovered*, 64-68; García-Martínez, *Qumran and Apocalyptic*, 137-45.

136. For an argument that the "King's Eye" may have existed only in Greek (and apparently Hebrew!) imagination, note Steven Hirsch, *The Friendship of the Barbarians* (Hanover: University Press of New England, 1985) 101-31.

perimeters of the empire made such comforts possible for the elite of Rome.

In the presence of Daniel, the heavenly visitor attacks the central political administration directly by cutting down the great tree. "Let the animals flee" (the jussive form in Aramaic)[137] suggests that the animals are finally released from captivity by the destruction of the tree.

4:15-16. Attempts to explain the significance of the binding of the tree are difficult. Was Nebuchadnezzar to be bound in some fashion? Another difficulty here is that the binding imagery gives way to the animal imagery, which provides the main theme of the dream. The problem derives from the mixing of the images of beasts and trees. Does the tree eat grass? Is the animal bound? Are we perhaps to see that a limitation has been placed on the expansion of this "tree" into the lives of countless thousands in the ancient Near East? Certainly this would agree with what is stated later in v. 27. Many scholars have suspected that two original themes (trees and animals) have been artificially and awkwardly joined at this point, bringing about the confusion. The Greek versions make this shackling of Nebuchadnezzar much clearer.[138] The "mind" (Aramaic, "heart" [לבב *lĕbab*], which is the seat of thought in ancient Semitic psychology) of Nebuchadnezzar is changed to that of an animal, and he must act accordingly, living among the beasts of the field.[139] Attempts to see in this some form of recognizable mental illness (e.g., lycanthropy) push the sense of the story beyond the more common motifs of reversal of fortune and the bringing down of the proud. Finally, the reversal of fortune will last for "seven times" (avoiding the specific "years").

4:17-18. It is now time for a decree by the angel, and not by the emperor. The question of who can give decrees with true authority is answered here. Throughout the book of Daniel the answer is consistent: God alone. The entire point is dramatically summed up in the phrase "in order that all who live may know/ that the Most High is sovereign/ over the kingdom of mortals." "All who live," not merely Nebuchadnezzar himself, will recognize God's sovereignty. The ruler is to be humbled in the sight of all who have suffered at his hands as well as those who believed him to be invincible.

Daniel Delivers the Interpretation. 4:19. At the end of the description of the dream, Nebuchadnezzar is curious, apparently without a clue as to the consequences of what he has seen. In direct contrast to this, Daniel is apparently already fully cognizant of the implications of what he has just heard. The terror of his thoughts is reminiscent of his reactions to other dreams that he experiences (2:25; 3:24; 4:2, 16; 5:6, 9-10; 6:20; 7:15, 28). But Daniel's terror is also the realization of truth and of the fact that this truth will now be spoken against power. In short, it is the terror of the prophet (Jeremiah noted threats against him by quoting his enemies: "Let us destroy the tree with its fruit" [Jer 11:19 NRSV; see also Jer 20:7-18]). Daniel's initial expression does not mask the truth of what he is about to say against the power of the king. Scholars often read far too much into Daniel's reply to the king, as if Daniel is terribly sympathetic to Nebuchadnezzar. As Oppenheim's study reveals, however, actions must be taken or words spoken to counteract the evil of a dream, and this phrase may simply be Daniel's version of his obligatory ritual of neutralizing the evil.[140] But the truth of the dream is not a mere "curse" that can be averted, and to this, Daniel proceeds.

4:20-24. Most of Daniel's interpretation of Nebuchadnezzar's dream is repeated from the description given to Daniel by the king in the first place. The tree is, not unexpectedly, identified as the king himself. If the tree is to be cut down, then its grand expanse into the lives of other people will be curtailed. In v. 24, Daniel interprets the decree from the "Most High." The continued image of the king in heaven versus the king on earth goes with the contrast between the apparent unchangeability of the decrees on earth and their only apparent power, as opposed to the decrees issued from God.

4:25-26. The king will be driven from human society. As the king has done to

---

137. I. Jerusalmi, *The Aramaic Sections of Ezra and Daniel* (Cincinnati: Hebrew Union College, 1972) 99.
138. Collins, *Daniel,* 227.
139. There is a possible influence from the Gilgamesh Epic here, in which Enkidu also "ranges over the hills . . . with the beasts [he feeds on grass]" (*ANET,* 74). But as M. Lind has suggested, Enkidu rises from animal to ruler, whereas Nebuchadnezzar goes in the opposite direction, until he is restored.
140. Oppenheim, *The Interpretation of Dreams in the Ancient Near East,* 218-20.

thousands of subjects, so he will be cast out from human society and will be forced to live among the wild animals. The punishment is to give the king a lesson—"until he has learned" who has true control over the kingdom of humans. It is significant that the kingdom of Nebuchadnezzar will be returned only when he realizes that he does not really have a kingdom; his reign is only by permit from the One who truly reigns over all living beings on the earth. The issue here is sovereignty. In reference to this exile, Lacocque writes that "there is a sort of visceral fear of animality in the book of Daniel"[141] (cf. Nebuchadnezzar's curse to the lions of chap. 6 and the beasts of chap. 7).

4:27. As a result of his exile among the animals, the king is to "tear away" or "break off" (פרק *pĕraq*) his sins, like the branches of a tree (v. 11). But lest we be ill informed as to the nature of Nebuchadnezzar's abuse of power and what it has meant, it is made clear by one of the demands of restitution: "mercy to the oppressed." The Aramaic term meaning "poor" or "oppressed" (ענין *ănāyin*) is related to the more common Hebrew term עני (*'ănî*), which is often found in characteristic prophetic passages about the treatment of the poor (Isa 29:19; 32:7; Amos 2:7; 8:4). Collins notes that later Jewish commentaries relate this treatment to the actual treatment of the Jewish exiles to whom mercy should be extended.[142] Lacocque, also, refers to "the organic ties established by the Law and Prophets between the poor and oppressed, on the one hand, and the community of Israel on the other."[143] In short, the Babylonian emperor must no longer behave like a Babylonian emperor; he must no longer act like the destroyer of Jerusalem and the tyrannical mover of whole populations like pieces on a chess board. The branches of this oppressive tree must be torn away. The animal imagery is similar. To be exiled among the animals is to become *like those who found shade and food from the tree,* but who were able to flee when the tree was destroyed (v. 14). In short, Nebuchadnezzar must identify with the victims of his own rule.

141. Lacocque, *The Book of Daniel*, 86.
142. Collins, *Daniel*, 230.
143. Lacocque, *The Book of Daniel*, 84.

We can follow this association of pride and the treatment of the lowly elsewhere in the Bible. Note, for example, how many of the themes of Daniel 4 are picked up in Psalm 79, about the destruction of Jerusalem: Ps 79:1—the nations who ruined God's temple and destroyed Jerusalem; 79:2—servants of God given as food to birds and wild animals; 79:8—the "low state" of those who are defeated; 79:11—the groans of the prisoners should be heard by God; 79:12—a sevenfold return on the taunts of the neighbors against Jerusalem; 79:13—the remembrance of God "from generation to generation." All of this serves as a reminder that the identification with his victims and the recognition of God's sovereignty are crucial aspects of what Nebuchadnezzar must learn from his exile among the animals (that is, among the conquered).

4:28-33, The Dream Fulfilled. Verses 28-29 are masterful irony. After having read Daniel's interpretation, we are not told how Nebuchadnezzar reacted to it. We are only shown that he continues in his arrogant claims to be sovereign over all the earth. He is pictured as surveying the vastness of his empire and attributing to himself "power," "might," and "glorious majesty/great honor"—all of which are traits attributed to God in 2:37.

A key phrase occurs in v. 32b: "until you have learned that the Most High has sovereignty over the kingdom of mortals and gives it to whom he will." God has the ability to give power to whomever God pleases (note that "doing as one pleases" is a frequent indication of political power in the book of Daniel). The emphasis here is not on Nebuchadnezzar's being for a time the one chosen, but on the tenuous nature of being God's chosen ruler. As the kings of Israel and Judah were to learn (and often fail to learn), God's sovereignty is partially guaranteed by the fact that someone else can be chosen at any time. The threat of recall is real and instantaneous!

In the classic Hebraic sense of reversal of fortune, Nebuchadnezzar's fate befalls him "while the words were still in the king's mouth" (v. 31)—at the moment that the king attributes his power to himself and to what he has built. Nebuchadnezzar's fate is described in precisely the language of Daniel's interpretation (vv. 32-33).

4:34-37, Nebuchadnezzar's Confession. At the beginning of v. 34, Nebuchadnezzar's narration in the first person resumes. The "confession" in vv. 34-35 is the longest such confession in the stories in Daniel, and it includes several important themes: (1) that God's sovereignty lasts forever, "from generation to generation." This involves a reversal of Nebuchadnezzar's statement in 4:3; (2) that God's control extends to all the earth (similar to the extension of the branches of a tree, the image used earlier of Nebuchadnezzar's reign); (3) no one has the power or the ability to question God.

The final verse of chap. 4 reaffirms God's ability to bring down the proud. This repeats a theme found in wisdom literature (see Prov 11:2; 16:18; 29:23; see also Jas 4:6) but is also powerfully found in late prophetic passages (Isa 2:11, 17; 13:11; Ezek 16:49, 56, where pride is associated with mistreatment of the poor specifically).

REFLECTIONS

Two different, but related, theological issues arise from contemporary reflection on Daniel 4: (1) the significance of rulers on earth acting by God's permission; and (2) the significance of Nebuchadnezzar's exile and confession.

1. Rulers on Earth. The words of another arrogant world authority ring from the past: " 'Do you refuse to speak to me? Do you not know that I have power to release you and power to crucify you?' Jesus answered him, 'You would have no power over me unless it had been given you from above' " (John 19:10-11 NRSV).

Beginning with St. Augustine's apologia excusing Christians so that they might wield the power of Rome's thundering legions without guilt, it is amazing how many attempts there have been in Christian history to reverse totally the point of saying that authorities act only as proxies under God. To say that the emperor rules only by God's allowance is *not* an invitation to a total surrender to the state and is hardly to be taken as approval of the power and strength of the state. It is precisely the opposite. To say that God truly reigns is to make human authority tentative, temporary, and always liable to being disregarded in favor of the higher authority. In the Bible it is the *prophet* who wields the symbol of office—the horn of oil—and not the king!

The book of Daniel asks us, What does it mean to say that God rules? How can we speak of the rule of God in a way that is not merely a pious platitude—a platitude that masks more mundane political commitments? The key, according to Daniel 4, is genuine transformation, not pious rhetoric. Nebuchadnezzar actually claimed to be meek and just, as did many of the Mesopotamian rulers in their public inscriptions and official party propaganda. In the annual new year festival, the Babylonian monarch was slapped in the face by a priest as a reminder that he ruled in Marduk's place only. Yet this hardly tempered his passion for conquests. From the perspective of the exiles, such rhetoric would have had a hollow ring, as does any modern reference to a land of the free when spoken in the context of domestic or global poverty. Fanon, in his context of French occupation of Algeria, accused Christianity itself of being such a hollow, self-justifying ideology: "The church in the colonies is the white people's church, the foreigner's church. She does not call the native to God's ways but to the ways of the white man, of the master, of the oppressor. And as we know, in this matter, many are called but few chosen."[144]

The book of Daniel suggests that the mere fact that Christians may find themselves under the rule of an oppressive state (whether overt or more subtle) does not mean that they need bow to its authority. Note the interesting paradox in the words of 1 Pet 2:16 (NRSV): "As servants of God, live as free people"! The modern state is a reality with which Christians must work for more just and peaceful structures in our lives—not

---

144. Fanon, *The Wretched of the Earth*, 42.

to preserve the sanctity of the state, but to uphold justice and peace as the way of the Christian in the world. Because God reigns, the state is merely a tool—sometimes to be used, sometimes to be prophetically condemned, but never to be baptized. In their involvement in the government of the state, whether it be political office or civil service or some other role, Christians should maintain a sense of the tentativeness of the state's role as a tool of God.

2. Nebuchadnezzar's Exile and Lesson. We have had occasion in the commentary to question the scholarly opinion that these stories show a positive attitude of the Jews toward the foreign king. These scholars support their claim by pointing to the confessions of honor or even the belief that the king is made to speak once he has learned his many lessons at the hands of the Jewish exiles. This notion of the confessions of the ruler in Daniel is worth further thought. When we are introduced to Nebuchadnezzar in chap. 4, we recognize the proud and domineering emperor of the Babylonian Empire—a regime built on the extortion and pillage of both people and resources throughout the ancient Near East. But this man undergoes a transformation through being forced to endure what he has inflicted upon others. Furthermore, restitution is demanded from him for his sins, especially his treatment of the dispossessed. In Daniel, it is a humbled and transformed emperor who finally confesses that God's "works are truth," and God's "ways are justice" (Dan 4:37 NRSV).

In short, Daniel does not teach that it is impossible for foreign emperors to be righteous and God-fearing. In order to be so, however, they must not be a "tree" whose military "branches" invade other peoples, nor can they continue to oppress the weak. The book of Daniel teaches that, of course, it is possible for a political leader to be righteous, but he or she must be totally transformed from conventional perspectives and practices and be one who knows the true God. Similarly, it is not the view of Daniel (or Jonah, or Isaiah 19) that a Babylonian or Assyrian is by virtue of race barred from the kingdom of God. But conversion means much more than inward, pious assent to the rule of God. It means no longer being Assyrian or Babylonian in a profound sense. These powers may still rule, but not in the traditional sense. Is it even possible to have a state with such a transformed monarch who is now unwilling to oppress and ruthlessly exercise the power of the state? To even ask this question is evidence that the force of these stories in Daniel is being heard.

In the radical reformation traditions of Christianity (Quakerism, Mennonites, Church of the Brethren, among others), there is a long-standing debate about the possibility of Christian righteousness within the secular political systems of world states. The most radical rejection of this possibility is the nonconformity of such groups as the Amish, whose conception of the church is that it is a social reality in the world, but an entity entirely apart from the world. Such Christian communities would refuse almost any participation in a system that is apart from the church. The Quaker tradition, while aware of the import of these ethical questions, has always taken a more hopeful, and at times utilitarian, approach to this issue. Quakerism is utilitarian in that it accepts the present realities, even if less than ideal, but remains hopeful that God's transforming justice can at least influence partially any system of humanity. Therefore, lobbying, prophetically advocating, and perhaps even running for office within any governmental system may result in a bit more light in the world, even if it is never bright sunshine! A respectful eye on our more radical Christian brothers and sisters is necessary to maintain a clearheaded approach about the reality of the demands of God's justice, which must never be compromised for political expediency. The book of Daniel teaches that transformation is possible, but the very fact that we are dealing with fictional accounts of transformed emperors (which were ironic twists in the stories and must surely have raised a smile among those Jews who first repeated them to one another) makes one wonder whether the possibility for conscientious Christians to "rule" is an ethically viable choice. Perhaps the answer is that when we reach the point at which we find that such participation in the kingdoms of the world involves impossible compromise, Christians become, with Daniel, Hananiah, Mishael, and Azariah, a part of the prophetic resistance.

DANIEL 5:1-31, THE HUMILIATION OF THE CONQUERED: BELSHAZZAR'S FEAST

COMMENTARY

5:1-4, The Revelry of the Powerful. Although there are problems with the historical aspects of this story, we are now certain of the existence of Bel-shar-usur (Belshazzar). He was the son of Nabonidus, and not Nebuchadnezzar, as v. 2 claims. Nabonidus left Babylon for a time and lived in the oasis of Teima, leaving his son in charge of Babylon.[145] It is noted in the Babylonian cuneiform sources that the new year festival was not observed during Nabonidus's absence, which most scholars take to mean that Belshazzar was not recognized as king. It was from Nabonidus that Cyrus seized control of Babylon in 539 BCE.

Chapter 5, like the previous chapters, begins somewhat abruptly, with Belshazzar and his great feast. Note once again the emphasis on the epic setting and number (e.g., "a thousand of his lords," "drinking in front of the thousands") and on the excesses of drunkenness. We certainly do have evidence that Persian kings would occasionally conduct massive banquets,[146] but what is particularly interesting is the fact that this chapter portrays this night as Belshazzar's last—the night of the conquest of Babylon by the Persians. This story may be based on oral traditions about the fall of Babylon, since similar ideas about revelry on the eve of the fall of Babylon are found in both Xenophon and Herodotus.[147] Furthermore, the ease with which the Persians conquered Babylon was taken by the Cyrus Cylinder to be an indication of the blessings of the god Marduk on the Persian conquest.[148]

Describing King Belshazzar as being under the influence of alcohol, (the Aramaic reads "in the taste of the wine"), chap. 5 continues the theme of excess and abuse. We are reminded of the exile by the gold and silver vessels taken from the Jerusalem Temple by Nebuchadnezzar. This is an important point. The Babylonian policy was to commandeer the religious icons or statues of the gods of the conquered people. In the case of the Jews, since no image of their God could be found in the Temple, the ritual vessels were taken instead. Nebuchadnezzar is often noted as the one who took the temple vessels (Ezra 5:14; 6:5). Therefore, the vessels serve as a symbol of the subordinate status of the Jews throughout their exile. They are captives in the same sense that the people are captive. The gold and silver vessels once again highlight the hunger for valuables that symbolizes the appetite for power of conquering empires.[149]

Feasting was typically used in biblical narratives, especially post-exilic writings, to portray the abuse of power and privilege by the wealthy, and especially foreign monarchs. Taxes were paid in kind, and such great feasts would be resented just as much as the waste of tax money to fund government programs! As has been noted, in Esther and Judith feasts or banquets serve as the setting for Jewish victory over foreign power, much in the same way that a royal banquet serves as the backdrop for God's punishment of Babylon in this chapter.

Verses 2-3 repeat the list of people—including "concubines," apparently a pejorative term in Aramaic—who join in defiling the holy implements. People of decidedly

---

145. "The Nabonidus Chronicle" in Pritchard, *Ancient Near Eastern Texts Relating to the Old Testament*, 305-7.
146. Porteus, *Daniel*, 78.
147. Xenophon *Cyropedia* VII.5.15-16; Herodotus *History* 1:191.
148. *ANET*, 315-36.

149. It is interesting that Collins has noted other extra-biblical sources for a Persian preference for gold cups. See Collins, *Daniel*, 245.

unholy reputations despoil these implements. As if to add to the shame of the event, the revelry also includes idolatry and the offering of libations to the gods. Verse 4 lists the materials from which the various Babylonian idols were made, which serves to tie this chapter to the themes of idolatry in other chapters. In v. 4, is it to be understood that these gods were, in fact, statues and idols taken from other conquered peoples? More likely, it is the biblical manner of speaking of foreign images of gods by emphasizing that they are *merely* gold, silver, bronze, etc. The list of elements in v. 4 repeats the elements of the statue in chap. 2, with the one exception of wood.[150] Most scholars have assumed that what is involved here is some sort of libation offered to the gods. Lacocque notes that the Persian custom was to offer such libations after the meal was completed.[151]

5:5-9, The Hand of Judgment. The text clearly emphasizes the abuse of the temple implements, because judgment begins immediately after this abuse is described. There is no waiting, no delay. The message ("writing on the wall") is delivered *during* the revelry. Furthermore, there is a strong emphasis on the public display of the appearance of the fingers of a human hand writing on the wall and the reaction of the king. Repeating a theme that readers are by now familiar with, the writer notes that the countenance of the king falls and that his thoughts "terrified" or "appalled" him (v. 6; cf. 2:29-30; 4:16; 5:6, 10; 7:28; see also Ps 69:24; Isa 21:3; Ezek 21:11; Nah 2:11). Lacocque seems to imply that the king was the only one who saw the apparition,[152] but this is not clear from the text. The writing obviously is seen by others, however, since the various court magicians are not able to interpret it. Collins notes that the strange appearance of the hand is similar to the strange appearance of the fourth person in the fiery furnace of chap. 3.[153] Finally, there is an emphasis on the strength of the king's voice as he calls for "the enchanters, the Chaldeans, and the diviners."

The king sets the challenge and offers the reward, following the contest pattern. It is interesting that a promotion in authority is included among the rewards (the wearing of purple and the promotion to third in authority/sovereignty), which relates this story to the fate of Daniel and his friends in the previous stories; it signals as well the separation of this story from the previous stories. The offering of a purple robe (a sign of authority) and a gold chain is a custom Daniel's audience would have been familiar with. A purple robe was given to Mordecai (Esth 8:15), and a gold chain was presented to Joseph (Gen 41:42). Both items were commonly given as gifts in the Persian period.[154] However, there is some scholarly debate as to the exact nature of the "third position" that is offered as a reward.[155]

These counselors, following the set pattern of the Daniel stories, are not able to interpret the meaning of the event. Belshazzar remains terrified, and the counselors are perplexed.

5:10-12, The Queen Mother's Introduction. Once again, Daniel is reintroduced to the Babylonian ruler—this time by the queen mother herself! The term used here for the king's mother, מלכה (*malkâ*), has been taken to mean "queen mother" by nearly all commentators, who cite not only her extensive knowledge of previous Babylonian administrations but also the important theme of the power of the queen mother in ancient Near Eastern literary traditions.[156] Furthermore, there is a series of intriguing legends about the power of Nebuchadnezzar's wife in Herodotus.[157] She was credited with great wisdom, with the building of Babylon's outer fortifications (where she had herself buried in the wall over one of the entrance gates), and with a humorous cleverness that appears to have impressed Herodotus. It is possible that such legends about this unusual woman were drawn upon for local color in the Belshazzar story.

The queen mother has not appeared in any of the Daniel stories until now, and her introduction here suggests that Daniel's potential promotion to "third" means that he would rank third in authority, after the king and the queen mother. Whether the queen mother actually had such authority is an interesting

---

150. Interestingly, a similar sequence is noted in 4QPrNab.
151. Lacocque, *The Book of Daniel*, 94.
152. Lacocque, *The Book of Daniel*, 95.
153. Collins, *Daniel*, 246.

154. Herodotus *The History* 3:20; Xenophon *Cyropedia* 2.4.6.
155. Lacocque cites the *Testament of Joseph* 13:5, which refers to "Third after Pharaoh," but this is clearly influenced by the Daniel traditions. See Lacocque, *The Book of Daniel*, 92.
156. Collins, *Daniel*, 248.
157. Herodotus *The History* 1:185-186.

historical question, but it is somewhat irrelevant to the point of the story as here presented. Goldingay notes that the queen mother's function in the story is not unlike that of Arioch, who earlier served to introduce Daniel. Daniel's attributes are listed in the queen's speech: He is endowed with a spirit of the holy god(s) (i.e., "excellent spirit"?), enlightened (cf. 2:22), knowledgeable/understanding, wise, experienced (Nebuchadnezzar made him chief of his magicians, enchanters, Chaldeans, and diviners, noting the words of 4:4 exactly; cf. the list in 2:27), able to interpret dreams, explain riddles, and solve problems (figuratively, "untie knots"). The only aspersion cast upon Daniel by the queen mother is the mention of the changing of his name, suggesting a changed status for this Daniel and perhaps reminding Belshazzar of Daniel's exile status.

5:13-16, Daniel Before the King: The Challenge. The all-important scene, "standing before the king," appears next, with Daniel being questioned. After all of his impressive qualifications have been listed by the queen mother, it is Daniel's status as an exile and a conquered foreigner that Belshazzar mentions first, which presumes a conversation much more in keeping with 2:25, where Arioch introduces Daniel as being one from "among the exiles."[158]

The king begins his interrogation of Daniel with a reminder of his station as a prisoner of war before repeating what he has heard about Daniel's abilities. The king then rehearses the fact that nobody else has been able to interpret the handwriting, and then finishes with a restatement of the rewards for the one who can.

5:17-23, Daniel Before the King: The Judgment. Like Nathan before David, Daniel immediately declares his independence from the power and fearsomeness of Belshazzar. Goldingay notes that there is no salutation, such as "O King, Live Forever!"[159] The brash reply, "Keep your gifts, or give them away," signals an attitude on Daniel's part that is considerably more antagonistic than was the case in any of the previous stories (and is particularly interesting, since Daniel appears to accept the gifts at the end of the story).

There are some suggestions that this entire section may not be original to the story. It does not appear in the Old Greek versions of the story. Without it, there is no contradiction with Daniel's acceptance of the gifts at the end. But its presence here signals a serious turn in the polemics directed against authorities, and it further suggests to us how these stories were earlier interpreted in a more negative light than modern readers interpret them. Collins notes that in the Roman era Josephus softened the tone of Daniel here, as he also tried to soften the impact of the "stone uncut by human hands" as God's destruction of human governmental authority in chap. 2.[160]

In any case, Daniel's story of Nebuchadnezzar in vv. 18-21 is very much in the prophetic style. Daniel begins with a story, a true-life parable, much in the same way that Nathan told a story standing before David (2 Samuel 12). Most of this section repeats the previous chapter, except for an interesting assessment of the power of Nebuchadnezzar: Those whom he wanted to kill were killed; those whom he wanted to smite (or spare) were struck down (or spared; the Aramaic [מחא $mah\bar{e}$] is somewhat ambiguous, so both possibilities need to be noted here); those whom he wanted to honor were honored; and those whom he wanted to make low were dishonored. No description of the capricious nature of the head of a Near Eastern empire could be more telling. The ruler claims for himself what are actually God's prerogatives: the ability to give or take life, death, and prosperity. This passage has an intriguing similarity to Job 5:11-16, where these attributes are assigned to God (cf. 1 Sam 2:7; Ps 75:8; Sir 7:11); but it can be further pointed out that included in Job's rehearsal are the powers of God to "[save] the needy . . . / from the hand of the mighty,/ So the poor have hope,/ and injustice shuts its mouth" (Job 5:15-16 NRSV). God is able to give life; Nebuchadnezzar can only kill or refrain from killing. The irony of this description of power by Daniel is the fact that Nebuchadnezzar *thought* he had this ability, but in reality he did not. As did his friends in chap. 2, Daniel stands as the political atheist of radical faith.

---

158. Again, a similar introduction that mentions the status of the individual is noted in 4QPrNab. It is clearly an important detail for these traditions.

159. Goldingay, *Daniel*, 110.

160. Collins, *Daniel*, 249.

Nebuchadnezzar's faulty impression of his power is in stark contrast to the statement that such power is God's alone in the world, as reaffirmed in v. 21. After Daniel's parable, and once again like Nathan (2 Sam 12:7), the judgment falls on the one being addressed: "You, Belshazzar" (v. 22).

"Humbling of the heart" is synonymous with the treatment of the conquered, the "lowly," as noted in v. 27. The mistreatment of the temple vessels is read as an object lesson of Belshazzar's treatment of people. Like Nebuchadnezzar's exile with the animals, Belshazzar is tainted with the injustices of the Babylonian regime.

The accusation about worshiping idols of gold, silver, bronze, wood, iron, and stone is in stark contrast to the lack of honor for the true God, in whose power, says Daniel, is "your breath" and who controls "your ways." Typically eloquent, Lacocque writes, "Whether a Jew serves the government or not, history has a sense and it moves toward its omega, even though men untiringly repeat their choice for nonsense."[161]

5:24-28, The Interpretation of the Writing on the Wall. As one would expect, the meaning of the symbolic terms "mene, mene, tekel, and parsin" has been debated extensively. First, it is important to indicate that the Old Greek version of this text has only three terms, and most scholars believe that a second "mene" was added in order to conform to the "four kingdom" motif that becomes a central aspect of the book of Daniel as a whole, when all the parts have been joined. Porteous takes these words to be an indication of declining value and thus a representation of the value of the kings of Babylon.[162] Finally, Brown has suggested that the words have been borrowed from a money changer's rhyme, heard in the marketplaces of international trade from the fifth century BCE. In its present form, suggests Brown, the message reads as an epitaph for the fall of the Seleucid Empire, attributing the empire's fall to its political and financial policies; but it is possibly derived from an older critique of Babylon, which "merited the critique more than the Seleucids."[163]

Lacocque reads "Babylonians, Belshazzar, Medes" for the original sequence of three, with a fourth entity added later to change the representation to Babylonians, Medes, Persians, and Greeks. This suggestion assumes that Darius "the Mede" is also represented. There is no evidence of a historical "Darius the Mede"; thus the importance of inserting a Median presence into the Daniel stories is usually attributed to the need to fulfill the prophecy that the Medes would precede the Persians.

Goldingay helpfully summarizes many of the different approaches, but he prefers to avoid the notion that this is a judgment on the empire. To him, it is simply "a judgment on one man's sin."[164] Surely this is an unnecessary avoidance of the powerful political critique that is typical of Daniel from beginning to end. Collins believes that the original sequence was one of straight declining value: Mina, Parsin, Tekel (as in the preface to the chapter in Old Greek) and that these words represent the only three Babylonian kings mentioned in the Daniel traditions (including 4QPrNab): Nebuchadnezzar, Nabonidus, and Belshazzar.[165] "Parsin" was subsequently moved to accommodate the wordplay on "Persians."

Whatever these words may represent in terms of a sequence of empires, all scholars agree that they are essentially monetary terms, denoting coins and weights. In fine biblical fashion, the obsessions of the empire (power and monetary gain, tribute payments and accounting) become the symbolic basis for judgment. The judgment takes place not so much in the courtroom as in the bank lobby! The place of judgment and the language used are significant. "Mene" is related to the term for "count," and "Tekel" is related to "weigh." "Peres" is an Akkadian loan word meaning "half-mina," but it is taken also to mean "divide." Thus the king has been counted and weighed in the balances (audited?), and has been judged at a deficit. In short, the interpretation of these words offered by Daniel 5 sounds like the activities of a countinghouse—weighing, counting, and dividing. This chapter, then, parallels the theme of chap. 4: Just as

---

161. Lacocque, *The Book of Daniel,* 101.
162. Porteous, *Daniel,* 82.
163. Brown, "Proverb-Book, Gold Economy, Alphabet," 187.
164. Goldingay, *Daniel,* 111.
165. Collins, *Daniel,* 251.

Nebuchadnezzar suffered the same fate he subjected the exiles to, so also Belshazzar will be audited in the midst of his wasteful, demeaning opulence.

5:29-31, Fulfillment of the Prophecy. As noted, Daniel appears to accept the gifts and rewards that he earlier refused. However, if Daniel had not been rewarded, even if the message he delivered was one of serious judgment, then this story would have diverged from the folkloric form of the tale. Either Daniel's refusal of gifts in v. 17 was part of a later, and politically significant, redaction or the constraints of the story form require that the story end in the traditional manner.

That the Babylonians were conquered by the Persians remains one aspect of historical recollection that is valid in the story of Belshazzar; however, the details appear to have been muddled in the oral retellings of the story before it was finally put to writing. The concluding verse (v. 30) presents the contrast and the reversal of fortune: Daniel is clothed in purple, Belshazzar dies, and the kingdom passes to the Medes ("Darius") and finally, at the end of chap. 6, to Cyrus the Persian.

REFLECTIONS

What is the nature of the "sin" of Belshazzar? Attention in this story focuses on the banquet (a theme also of chap. 1) and on the desecration of the temple vessels. Here we have a significant theme of the abuse of conquered people's culture and values. We see in Daniel 5 one of the most insidious elements of imperial power and oppression: the destruction of faith and identity, the attack on a culture as well as a people. The intoxication of power releases the ruler from maintaining any further pretenses: "We are the conquerors; we are the superior culture. Let us parade their treasures and mock the defeated." Pacific native peoples bitterly recall the desecration of native holy sites by Captain Cook, and today's Cheyenne recount another "Belshazzar's Feast"—the parade of body parts of slain Cheyenne through downtown Denver following the 1864 Sand Creek Massacre, led by the Rev. Col. Chivington of the U.S. Cavalry.[166] Defeat and destruction are never enough for the powerful; they must also glorify themselves with acts of unspeakable humiliation of the defeated. A society based on injustice must find ways to sustain its existence; it must appear to be more civilized, more advanced, more cultured than those conquered, who must, therefore, be portrayed as bloodthirsty, disrespectful of the land, heathen. Humiliating the conquered, then, helps to sustain the myth of superiority.

In 1990, the Congress of the United States finally ended a centuries-long "Belshazzar's feast" by passing the Native American Graves Protection and Repatriation Act. Indigenous peoples across North America have long demanded that their sacred objects be returned to them. For modern Christians, Daniel 5 is a call to understand the humiliation of defeated cultures and peoples, and perhaps to work toward reconciliation and restitution so that finally ours can be a society that appreciates and celebrates the diverse traditions that enrich our life.

Finally, Daniel 5 is a call to modern Christians to involve themselves in prophetic delivery of God's judgment on the gluttony of the hundreds of "Belshazzar's feasts" that have victimized so many people over the centuries. Perhaps it needs to be said that for many Christians who have been born to the privileges afforded by the dominant culture, such a prophetic task begins by excusing ourselves from Belshazzar's table!

---

166. See G. Obeyesekeve, *The Apotheosis of Captain Cook: European Mythmaking in the Pacific* (Princeton: Princeton University Press, 1992). The story of the Sand Creek Massacre was recounted to me by the Rev. Lawrence Hart, a Cheyenne chief of the Southern Cheyenne, Oklahoma. See also Stan Hoig, *The Sand Creek Massacre* (Norman: University of Oklahoma Press, 1961).

DANIEL 6:1-28, IN DEFIANCE OF DEATH: DANIEL IN THE LION PIT

COMMENTARY

6:1-3, Prologue and "Darius the Mede." Many essays have been written on the subject of Darius the Mede. Historically, Darius I Hystaspis (522–486 BCE) certainly was a notable figure, having seized the throne of Persia after political instability in the empire. He was also notable as a great organizer, and the discussion of satrapies in this chapter is a vague but accurate recollection of the fact that the third Persian ruler after Cyrus certainly did divide the Achaemenid territories into administrative units called satrapies. But in no other document has there been a reference to any Median connection. It is typically thought, then, that the Median association is influenced more by the desire to have a Median presence before Persia, in order that earlier biblical prophecy be seen to unfold correctly. But the historical figure alluded to in Daniel 6 must be Darius I, the usurper of the Persian throne after the death of Cambyses. Once again, however, it is undoubtedly fruitless to try to force the folklore of Daniel to fit what we know of the actual circumstances of Persian history. That Darius I was chosen as the historical model for this otherwise fictional character is undoubtedly due to the length of the historical Darius's reign, but also perhaps because of the influence of this same ruler's important role as the defender of the Jewish reconstruction work under Zerubbabel (Ezra 6). Furthermore, the intra-court intrigue may reflect some of the administrative tensions that led to Darius's rise to power,[167] although scholars point out that this is an essential aspect of the folklore form. Other Persian rulers are mentioned in the Greek versions of Daniel, adding to the general confusion.

Verses 2-3 mention 120 satrapies[168] and over them three *sarkin,* a Persian term meaning "chief ministers" (NIV, "administrators"; NRSV, "presidents"). Daniel was appointed one of these *sarkin.* What is interesting by its absence is a story of Daniel's rise in this Median (Persian?) court. We find him assigned there at the outset of this story, without explanation of how he attained that status. Thus the form of this story is much closer to a restoration than to a rags-to-riches story, more typical of the previous chapters.

Daniel is said to have an "excellent spirit" (cf. 5:12, missing the usual, "spirit of the god" form). The story as a whole gives one the impression that excellence of spirit must have to do with trustworthiness or loyalty, as opposed to an endowment of the gods.

6:4-9, The Conspiracy Against Daniel Is Launched. The other two *sarkin,* presumably Persians, conspire with the heads of the satraps against Daniel, thus indicating a sense of tension between the Jewish exiles and the Persian nationals. There has been some scholarly debate as to the possible ethnic overtones of the tension. Lacocque resists the effort to see no anti-Semitism in this story, stating that "the sacred cause is to prevent an alien from assisting in the dismemberment of the empire . . . the Jew is always an alien body in the illusory constructions of the nations."[169] But it is unnecessary to avoid the implication of ethnic tensions in this story, hence the perception of ethnic tensions among the tellers and the hearers of the Daniel stories. These stories certainly include such elements of ethnic and religious tensions in them. Chapter 6 is much more in line with chap. 3, as each story presents the Jewish heroes as facing evil conspirators who seek their defeat, rather than simply solving a riddle or a problem that baffles the other advisers to the king. However, the stories of the Jewish courtiers' success seem essential to a full appreciation of the resentment of the Jewish courtiers in the first place. Apart from the "rise to success" stories, the restoration stories would not have nearly the power and dramatic impact they possess.

---

167. Lacocque, *The Book of Daniel*, 110.
168. Esther 1:1 mentions 127 satrapies; Herodotus (*The History* 3:89) suggests only 20 and Josephus claims 320 (*Antiquities of the Jews* 11.33:127)!
169. Lacocque, *The Book of Daniel*, 111.

The story of Darius has been the prime case for those scholars who have emphasized the benign nature of the representation of the kings in Daniel 1–6. These scholars use this characterization to further the general assumption that the situation of the Jews who told and heard these stories must not have been so terrible. But let us not be hasty about Darius's benevolence. Even Darius "the Mede" is a king who maintains lions to dispose of his enemies, and he will sacrifice a loyal adviser for the sake of the letter of the law, even his own law, as the sovereign principle of the empire. When compared to chap. 3, where the king ruled as absolute monarch, chap. 6 introduces the "rule of law," but it is still the king's own law.

The Aramaic term הרגשו (*hargišû*), used to describe the group of conspirators who approach the king (v. 6), has engendered considerable discussion. Did they "come in a throng" in a raucous mass gathering? The eighteenth-century Quaker Bible translator Anthony Purver rendered it: "they crowded in to the king," which captures the image suggested by the term, which includes the satraps as well as the two other Persian officials.[170] The last phrase in this verse, the basis of their proposed accusation against Daniel, raises an issue that has not arisen yet in the entire book: the matter of the law of the Jews. The mention of the "law" of God was not mentioned even in chap. 3, where one might have expected it. (That the Persian authorities were aware of the religious importance of the law of the Jews is noted in Ezra 7:12, 14, 21, 25-26 and will become an issue in Daniel 7.) A reference to the Jewishness of Daniel by specifically mentioning the laws/traditions of the Jews lends weight to arguments for the significance of ethnic tensions as an important part of the traditions in Daniel.

In contrast to the previous chapters that mention the religious worship practiced by the Jews, Daniel will now be accused because he follows the ethical requirements of his religion. Interestingly enough, the fact that Daniel prays regularly to his God is certainly not a matter of the law. Daniel prays three times daily toward Jerusalem, but this is nowhere mandated in the Torah as we now have it. Does this represent a diaspora innovation? Praying three times a day (morning, noon, and evening) is found in later rabbinic tradition, and certainly it influenced early Christianity; but there is no evidence that it was already in practice this early. Praying toward the Temple is mentioned in 1 Kings 8, itself an early exilic-deuteronomic passage.

The notion that the Persian people should not pray to anyone other than the king is a fanciful aspect of the story that may have more relevance in the Hellenistic era than in the memories of the Persian exile. The historical Darius, especially, carefully attributed his success to Ahura Mazda, the Zoroastrian deity (some scholars suggest that Cyrus was Zoroastrian). But this aspect of the story is clearly a folklore element. The king signs the law and establishes an "edict." The Aramaic term אסר (*'ĕsār*), which is related to the terms for "binding" and for "prison," suggests that what is established here is Persian law and the punishment for violation of that law. The symbolic weight of the state stands behind this new enactment. Daniel 6 repeats the concept of the unchangeable laws of the emperor, which is repeated in Ezra 6:11-12 as well. Lacocque noted that Diodorus of Sicily also made reference to the unchangeable laws of the Persians.[171] We have learned from chap. 2, however, that God changes what humans consider unchangeable (Dan 2:21).

---

170. Collins, *Daniel*, 265-66.

171. Lacocque, *The Book of Daniel*.

EXCURSUS: IMPRISONMENT AND EXILE

It appears to be the advisers' idea that Daniel be thrown to the lions. This deserves careful consideration, since the lions' den may well be an example of an interesting motif of punishment and imprisonment within the Daniel tradition.

It is interesting to note how often the motif of imprisonment occurs in exilic texts, like the book of Daniel. Because imprisonment or confinement is a potent symbol for the exile in other biblical texts, this aspect of Daniel more than any other may help us to understand the circumstances of the writers of these stories.

There are a number of terms in the OT that translators render as "prison," but the most common term for "prisoners" is from the verb "to tie," "to bind," or "to imprison" (אסר *'āsar*), which is frequently used in the late Joseph stories (Gen 39:20; 40:3, 5). It appears also in Isa 42:7; 49:9; 61:1; and Ps 146:7-8 (cf. Ps 107:10); it is interesting to note that in Isa 49:9 and Ps 146:7c-8a, the combination of release from prison, with "opening eyes" or "sight to the blind" is common (cf. Zech 9:12). A "Surpu Hymn" (incantation to Marduk of Babylon) contains the same association:

[beginning "It rests with you, Marduk . . ."]
31 to set free the prisoner, to show (him) daylight
32 him who has been taken captive, to rescue him
33 him whose city is distant, whose road is far away
34 let him go safely to his city
35 to return the prisoner of war and the captive to his people

---

73 may the sick get well, the fallen get up
74 the fettered go free, the captive go free
75 the prisoner see the light (of day).[172]

The "Verse Account of Nabonidus" celebrates the end of his reign with the following passage:

[to the inhabitants of] Babylon, a joyful heart is given,
  [like prisoners] when the prisons are opened
Liberty is restored] to those who were surrounded by oppression.[173]

Here, too, imprisonment is equated with conquest. What do we know about imprisonment in the ancient Near East? In an important article exploring the subject, San Nicolo states, "A prison-punishment in the formal sense is essentially unknown in Near Eastern jurisprudence."[174]

The most common term for "prison" in the OT is an Akkadian loan word, ביה כלא (*bêt kele'*), which relates to the use of the verb "to restrain," "to hold back" (cf. Gen 23:6; Num 11:28; 1 Sam 25:33; Pss 88:9; 119:101; Jer 32:2-3; and in reference to exiles, Isa 43:6). The term is found in the deuteronomic historian (1 Kgs 22:27;

---

172. Erica Reiner, *Surpu: A Collection of Sumerian and Akkadian Incantations* (Graz: Archiv fur Orient Forschung, 1958) 25.
173. *ANET*, 306.
174. M. San Nicolo, "Eine Kleine Gefängnismeuterei in Eanna zur Zeit des Kambyses," *Münchener Beiträge zur Papyrusforschung und Antiken Rechtsgeschichte* (1945) 2.

Excursus: Imprisonment and Exile

2 Kgs 17:4), in direct reference to the Assyrians and to Jehoiachin's internment and release (2 Kgs 25:27). One of the most interesting passages is Jeremiah 37, especially vv. 4, 15-16, where three different terms for "prison" are used. Of particular interest is the fact that the recurring phrase about a pit "where there is no water" occurs in three passages, the first in Genesis 37, the second in Jer 38:6, and the third, in direct reference to exiles, in Zech 9:11. The image of the pit is associated with death in Psalm 88, and in Jer 41:7-9 Gedaliah and his followers are thrown into the pit after their murder. Lamentations 3:53, 55 compares the catastrophe of exile to being thrown into a pit from which the people call on God's name. This has obvious relevance to Daniel in the lion pit.

The vast majority of instances of the use of the term for prisons and imprisonment are cases of unjust imprisonment of the righteous, whether individual prophets or an entire community. Furthermore, most examples, apart from the imprisonment of prophets, are cases of people being detained in foreign prisons. Indeed, it appears that the judicial system of Israel and Judah did not include prisons. They are never mentioned in the legal corpus of the Pentateuch, and (with the exception of 2 Sam 20:3, which is obviously not much of an exception), prisons are mentioned only toward the end of the monarchical era, in Jeremiah 37–38, where Jeremiah is confined by Zedekiah, Nebuchadnezzar's puppet ruler in Jerusalem. But Jeremiah's imprisonment fits the theme of unjust confinement/punishment. Most hero types of the exilic period (Joseph, Jehoiachin, Jeremiah, Daniel, and the Suffering Servant of Isaiah) suffer imprisonment innocently and are eventually delivered.

So, if imprisonment was not a typical form of punishment in Israelite practice, then one may conclude that the images in the biblical material and in other Near Eastern texts more likely refer to punishment or confinement, especially confinement as a result of superior military power. The obvious social significance of the Daniel stories as hero stories leads one to conclude that confinement became an established symbol for the exiles who reflected on their fate in Babylon. The metaphor of imprisonment, whether intended to be confinement or punishment or execution, and references to places of imprisonment do not grow more plentiful during the exilic period by pure chance, especially in view of its foreignness to the Israelite judicial system. The experience of exile was compared to being in prison, and liberation was seen as release from that prison, the "opening of eyes of the imprisoned." Thus the diaspora hero types, whether king, courtier, or collective remnant, had to overcome this social reality. This is the context from which we must understand the wider sociopolitical importance of the theme of the lions' den in the book of Daniel. Daniel's emerging from the lions' den unharmed was a source of hope for surviving the exile itself.

The diaspora hero stories were maintained by a people who compared their social existence to imprisonment, and it is only within the context of this symbolism that the function of these stories as resistance literature makes sense. It is not surprising, therefore, that prison (and the various terms that are used) was a favorite metaphor for the exile experience:

> I have kept you and given you
>   as a covenant to the people,
> to establish the land,
>   to apportion the desolate heritages;
> saying to the prisoners, "Come out,"
>   to those who are in darkness, "Show yourselves."
> (Isa 49:8-9 NRSV)

> The Spirit of the Lord God is upon me,
>   because the Lord has anointed me;
> he has sent me to bring good news to the oppressed,

> to bind up the brokenhearted,
> to proclaim liberty to the captives,
> and release to the prisoners.
> (Isa 61:1 NRSV)

The lions' den experience, then, is to be read as both folktale and a symbol of the exile itself.

❖   ❖   ❖   ❖

6:10-11, Daniel's Civil Disobedience. The focus of these two verses is on two facts: (1) Daniel knows that the law has been signed; and (2) Daniel breaks the law by praying as he always had done before. What is not clear is the meaning of his opening the windows. Had Daniel always opened the windows, or was it an act of civil disobedience? Side issues need not detain us here, such as the implication of his having an upper room (a sign of wealth or prestige?).[175]

Interesting questions arise when one examines the text of Dan 6:10[11], particularly with regard to the presumption that Daniel actually threw open his windows in defiance of Darius's law. The text clearly means to suggest that Daniel disobeys the king's decree. But is he found out or has Daniel openly violated the law? The Aramaic reads in the passive—that is, the windows "were opened," implying that they always were that way. The Theodotian text of the Septuagint reflects the Aramaic passive construction, using a passive participle form. The passive form suggests that, although Daniel was defying the law, he was not intending to defy it in any way that was innovative or different from his routine. However, the Old Greek text reads in the active voice, with Daniel actually throwing open his windows before he prays. The Vulgate also reflects this reading, which is rendered in the Douay as: "Now when Daniel knew . . . that the law was made, he went into his house and, opening the windows in his upper chamber toward Jerusalem, he knelt down three times a day."

The Ethiopic texts (fourth century?)[176] echo this construction, rather than the Theodotion/MT passive voice.[177] Clearly, the active voice tends to emphasize Daniel's prayers as an act of open or public defiance more than does the passive, although the theme of defiance is not thereby totally absent even in the Theodotion/MT reading.

It is interesting that earlier commentators did not see any sense of defiance in Daniel's actions.[178] Montgomery commented on the rituals of the passage (e.g., prayer toward Jerusalem) and summarized that the story was written for the encouragement of the community. That Daniel was praying for mercy, seeking favor from the Lord, suggests that he knew what the implications of his actions would be. Seeking mercy is the usual response of Jewish diaspora communities when confronted with potential tragedy (see chap. 2). Although it is strange that fasting is not mentioned here, given the argument about Jewish fasting in exile (see Commentary on 9:3-19; Excursus "On Fasting, Communal Prayer, and Heavenly Warfare") perhaps this is because Darius himself is depicted as fasting.

The story, in short, represents an act of civil disobedience on Daniel's part, whether that disobedience was public or whether he was spied upon to discover him defying the king's decree. The mention of open windows, however, mitigates against the idea that he was spied upon. Daniel was openly declaring his disobedience by keeping open, or even throwing open, his windows.

6:12-15, The Conspiracy Comes to Fruition. The counselors repeat (note the continued use of repetition throughout the Daniel stories) the decree that the king had

---

175. See Goldingay, *Daniel*. Behrman cites 2 Kgs 13:17 as a comparison of Daniel's opening of the windows. See Georg Behrman, *Das Buch Daniel* (Göttingen: Vandenhoeck und Ruprecht, 1894) 40.

176. Ernst Würthwein, *The Text of the Old Testament* (Grand Rapids: Eerdmans, 1979) 98.

177. O. Löfgren, *Die Äthiopische Übersetzung des Propheten Daniel* (Paris: Librarie Orientaliste Paul Geuthner, 1927) 127.

178. Behrman, *Das Buch Daniel*; R. H. Charles, *A Critical and Exegetical Commentary on the Book of Daniel* (Clarendon: Oxford, 1929).

ordered, almost to entrap the king by means of his answer that the law cannot be changed. Daniel is then charged in words that echo his status and the status of the Jews throughout the book of Daniel: "Daniel, one of the exiles from Judah." Daniel, the foreigner, the defeated, the mere Jew is accused before the king. As in chap. 3, the mixed implication is clear: The foreigner whom the king had trusted has betrayed him by defying his order.[179]

Yet, Darius is troubled by the scenario. Here we have perhaps the most significant piece of evidence for those scholars who argue for the benign image of the foreign rulers in the book of Daniel. Darius "set his mind to deliver Daniel" (author's trans.) and made efforts to release him—presumably trying to determine a legally acceptable way to set Daniel free. As indicated, it is certainly true that the portrayal of the Persians in the Bible is occasionally, but not universally, positive. We will see in Daniel 7–12, however, that the image of the Persians, along with the Greeks and the Babylonians, is painted in significantly darker colors.

6:16-18, Daniel Is Punished. The all-important throne-room scene is presumably in the background of the story because of the nature of Daniel's civil disobedience. But what is there to try and to determine? There does not need to be a trial to determine the guilt of the accused, because he clearly confesses. Both the king and Daniel know that he is guilty, and he is thus immediately sentenced to his fate.

Contrast the sympathetic statement of Darius, "May your God, whom you faithfully serve, deliver you!" (v. 16), with the arrogant statement of Nebuchadnezzar in 3:15: "Who is the god that will deliver you out of my hands?" (NRSV). Once again, Darius is portrayed somewhat sympathetically; yet he carries out the act of state, Daniel's destruction by lions, which will serve as an example to other would-be dissidents. The hope—indeed, the calculation—is that word will spread quickly among the masses about the fate of any who disobey the will of the state. Note the sealing of the stone with the signs of state, including not only that of Darius, but of the counselors as well (including the conspirators?). For Christian readers, this is reminiscent of Matt 27:62, in which the rock used to seal Jesus' tomb includes the official insignia of the emperor. In the cases both of Daniel and of Jesus, life was ensured by God in defiance of the empire. Goldingay also draws attention to the similar delivery of Peter from prison in Acts 12.[180]

The lion imagery has raised interesting suggestions from scholars. In Ps 91:13, lions are symbolic of chaos (see also Pss 22:14; 57:5) and are also noted in 1 Kgs 13:23-26 and Ezek 19:2-9. The older idea that Daniel in the lion pit was somehow representative of an ancient myth of a descent into the underworld is not widely held today, although it is clear that resurrection themes were attributed to this story in both Jewish and Christian traditions.[181] My view on this matter has already been suggested: The lions' den is a metaphor of the exile.

The fasting of Darius may be seen not only as a symptom of his being upset by Daniel's fate, but also in the context of a miraculous delivery from death. There is a sense in which Darius is almost interceding for Daniel by fasting. Darius was not brought any "food" (NRSV) or "entertainment" (NIV); some scholars have suggested that "entertainment" may have implied concubines[182] (note that sexual abstinence is sometimes associated with fasting as a part of military preparation, so Uriah, in the David and Bathsheba affair, protests that he must not eat or drink while his comrades are in battle [2 Sam 11:11]).

6:19-24, The Miraculous Delivery and Reversal of Fortune. Darius goes in haste to the lion pit to check on the fate of Daniel. Presumably a minimum period of time needed to pass before the legal status of Daniel would be changed. Darius cries in a painful voice, "O Daniel, servant of the living God"; a foreign ruler's addressing the God of the Jews as "Most High" is not unusual, but this particular form of address is somewhat unusual.

Daniel begins his answer with respect for the king—a detail that further emphasizes his innocence, which he then proceeds to verify. He has done no "hurtful thing" before God

---

179. On this point, see Goldingay, *Daniel*, 132.
180. Goldingay, *Daniel*, 132.
181. Lacocque, *The Book of Daniel*, 113.
182. Collins, *Daniel*, 270.

or before the king. Verse 24 notes that Daniel was totally unharmed, an emphasis similar to the lack of smoke on the clothes of the three men thrown into the furnace in chap. 3. Goldingay notes that Daniel's calm contrasts nicely with the king's agitation.[183]

The episode is completed with a reversal of fortune: Those who had unjustly accused the innocent are sentenced to the same punishment, their families along with them. This troublesome detail is not made easier by the reference to punishment for false witness in Deut 19:16-19. But this excess in the reversal of fortune is not altogether unusual in the diaspora stories; the ending of the book of Esther is a particularly good example. There is a sense here of the thoroughness of the miraculous acts of God. One can only note that one of the certain effects of oppressive, evil actions is the suffering of the innocent. Are we to applaud the deaths of the innocent in this passage, or, as at the traditional Passover seder, do we set aside a moment to remember the death of innocent Egyptians in the liberation of Israel?

6:25-28, The Restoration of Daniel. The end of the story relates the restoration and elevation of Daniel the hero. This is complete with a powerful confession of faith as decreed by Darius. But this statement goes much further than simply honoring the Jewish God; now Darius appears to be almost a convert to Judaism! God is the living God, and God's kingdom and sovereignty endure forever. What is interesting here is the note about deliverance and rescue as attributes of God. This is the faith response, the doctrinal response if you will, to the parable/story itself. The creator God also delivers and rescues, while the emperors of the world only kill or refrain from killing!

The final verse only adds to modern scholars' misery in trying to date the Daniel stories, as it appears that Cyrus follows Darius. That one historical person's life could span these various reigns, from Nebuchadnezzar to Cyrus, gives further evidence for the folkloric nature of these stories.

In the New Testament (Heb 11:33-34) both Daniel 3 and 6 are referred to in one sentence, anticipating modern scholarly discussion on the similarities between the two chapters. Goldingay suggests a systematic comparison:

Introduction	6:2-9	3:1-7
First Part	10-19	8-23
Second	20-25	24-27
Conclusion	26-29	28-33[184]

Other scholars have made observations about further similarities, as well as pointing out the significant differences between the two stories.

Goldingay notes that there are details in chap. 6 that associate it with either the Babylonian (lions in captivity, Jewish faith under pressure) or Greek periods (divinization of kings), but that the story fits most easily into the Persian period (bureaucratic organization, satrapies, Jews in respected positions, strict law of the Persians, and the dropping of Daniel's Babylonian name).[185] Collins, on the other hand, wants to date it at a time late enough for confusion to occur on the details of the Persian rulers, but before the time of Antiochus IV Epiphanes. The portrayal of Darius hardly fits a symbolic representation of Antiochus, since Darius comes out so positively and sympathetically in this story.[186] The story certainly suggests ethnic tensions and serious threats to life from the power of the state (unjust and arbitrary power at that, because Daniel was innocent!). Finally, we must face the story from the perspective of the hearers of Daniel 6. The court of Darius is a kangaroo court, the kind of justice system that is always suspect in the eyes of the subordinated sections of society. Daniel was innocent; yet Persian law threw him to the lions quite legally and properly. Only among the conquerors are there the reactions of indignation, as if such atrocities are unusual; but the conquered peoples know better.

---

183. Goldingay, *Daniel*, 133.
184. Lacocque, *The Book of Daniel*.
185. Goldingay, *Daniel*, 123.
186. Collins, *Daniel*, 273.

REFLECTIONS

Two issues seem of particular importance when reflecting on Daniel 6: (1) the meaning of nonviolent resistance and (2) the violence of reactions to injustice. Let us begin by reflecting on the fact that Daniel 6 evokes great passion. The story of Daniel facing the lions is one of the most well-known of all biblical tales, frequently portrayed in artistic renderings in children's Bibles. But it is hardly the stuff of children's stories when its full political and theological intentions are realized. Note, for example, John Calvin's strong language in his commentary on Daniel 6: "Earthly princes deprive themselves of all authority when they rise up against God, yea, they are unworthy to be counted amongst the company of men. We ought rather to spit in their faces than to obey them when they . . . spoil God of his right."[187]

1. Daniel 6 and Nonviolent Resistance: Gandhi and Daniel's Prayer. Mahatma Gandhi made interesting comments, between 1909 and 1937, on the book of Daniel in his work in both South Africa and India. Gandhi stated that he had "found much consolation in reading the book of the prophet Daniel in the Bible" and declared Daniel to be "one of the greatest passive resisters that ever lived." Gandhi appears to have been particularly intrigued with chap. 6, the story of Daniel in the lions' den, vv. 10-11 especially. In his earliest article referring to Daniel, Gandhi suggested that Daniel was a model of resistance to South African "pass laws" for Indian South Africans. It is interesting to see how Gandhi used the Daniel theme when he stated that the Indians should "sit with their doors flung wide open and tell those gentlemen [South African authorities] that whatever laws they passed were not for them unless those laws were from God."[188]

Clearly, Gandhi assumed that Daniel had actually flung open the windows in flagrant disregard of Darius's decree against prayers to any god but the king: "When Daniel disregarded the laws of the Medes and Persians which offended his conscience, and meekly suffered the punishment for his disobedience, he offered satyagraha in its purest form."[189] Particularly when dealing with Western audiences, Gandhi returned to his Daniel interpretation, again emphasizing the opening of the windows. Furthermore, however, Gandhi also stressed the idea that Daniel was otherwise portrayed as a model citizen: "It must be remembered, that neither Daniel nor Socrates . . . had any ill will towards their persecutors. Daniel and Socrates are regarded as having been model citizens of the states to which they belonged."[190]

Gandhi's comments suggest a number of possibilities for understanding Daniel 6 and, by implication, the other stories as well. Clearly, a story can have differing circumstances, depending on where one is reading it. From a South African prison, Daniel 6 made perfect sense to one engaged in nonviolent resistance to unjust laws. Here, perhaps, we have an important clue to reordering our own reading of the text in the modern era. Stories of resistance were written by a diaspora community who faced such trials often enough to identify with the fate of the heroes in these stories.

The lions' den, then, serves as a metaphor of both unjust punishment and imprisonment. There is clearly more than initially meets the eye in the early church's use of Daniel 6 (and chap. 3) as resurrection stories. Resurrection itself is a direct threat to imperial power. Putting it bluntly, if the imperial armies cannot keep their executed prisoners dead, where now is their power?

---

187. John Calvin, Commentary on Daniel 6, quoted in C. Hill, *The English Bible and the Seventeenth Century Revolution* (London: Penguin, 1993) 59.
188. M. K. Gandhi, *Gandhi's Complete Writings* (Bombay: Indian Government) Vol. IX, 541 from *Indian Opinion*, London, No. 12, 1909, "Speech at Farewell Meeting." See also Vol. LXXXIV, 1946, "Talk with Missionaries," where Gandhi referred to Daniel's open windows so that all could see him praying, from *Harijan*, 28-4-1946.
189. M. K. Gandhi, *Writings of Gandhi*, Volume XVII, "Congress Report on the Punjab Disorders" (March 25, 1920) 152.
190. Gandhi, *Writings*, Vol. XVII, 152.

2. The Violence of the Reaction to Injustice. One of the main motifs of "reversal of fortune" stories in the Bible, and Daniel especially, is the punishment of those who seek the death of Jewish heroes. Sometimes this theme of the "discomfiture of the Egyptians" reaches disturbing proportions, as it does in Daniel 6, where the entire families of the evil advisers are cast into the lions' den. While such aspects of these stories are disturbing, it is important not to overlook the psychology of the dispossessed—and especially their anger. Fanon writes:

> The settlers' town is a well-fed town, an easygoing town; its belly is always full of good things. The settlers' town is a town of white people, of foreigners.
>
> The town belonging to the colonized people, or at least the native town, the Negro village, the medina, the reservation, is a place of ill fame, peopled by men of evil repute . . . the native town is a crouching village, a town on its knees, a town wallowing in the mire. It is a town of niggers and dirty Arabs. The look that the native turns on the settler's town is a look of lust, a look of envy; it expresses his dreams of possession—all manner of possession: to sit at the settlers' table, to sleep in the settlers' bed, with his wife if possible. The colonized man is an envious man. And this the settler knows very well; when their glances meet he ascertains bitterly, always on the defensive, "They want to take our place." It is true, for there is no native who does not dream at least once a day of setting himself up in the settlers' place.[191]

The punishment of the innocent is definitely an offensive theme in many of the biblical stories, and it is equally offensive in the words of Fanon. But is this element of these stories to be attributed to the anger of the suffering? I would argue that these stories in Daniel often reflect the physical and spiritual crises brought about by the conquerors and rulers in the ancient Near East from 587 through the Hellenistic despots of the second century BCE. It is precisely the angry details that open a historical window onto the emotions of occupied Palestine and diaspora Judaism. It is not the people of God in their finest moment, but it is the reality of social conditions. Their ability eventually to embrace nonviolence and even to welcome the foreigner is all the more amazing—and all the more a witness to the involvement of revelation!

Members of the dominant culture in all times often delude themselves into expecting great praise and thanks for having paid attention to those who suffer injustice. Instead they often find anger and resentment from these suffering people. For many, this initial response is enough to send them back to their comfortable homes behind locked doors in separate neighborhoods. Such expressions of anger are all too often turned against people as evidence of their "irresponsibility" or "unwillingness to compromise." But surely we must patiently listen to the anger of those people who are hurting, in the hope of eventually earning the trust and friendship of people who have so much to teach us. Furthermore, is it not true that even Christians are tempted by such emotional failures of conscience? Are we no less members of the body of Christ despite our occasional failures of moral courage?

Let us be cautious here. This is not an excuse or a plea for understanding the violence of the oppressed. There is no such thing as "righteous" violence, as if brutal actions are somehow transformed by calling them aspects of the struggle for justice. Such manipulation is as offensive in progressive circles as are the more nationalistic versions of justification of violence by using patriotic terms. Both sides only succeed in justifying violence. Christians are correct to reject all such reprehensible special pleading. Our call is to understand anger and to accept it as a reality in people's lives, precisely because our nonviolent action must be based on the realities of human life and not on fantasy worlds.

191. Fanon, *The Wretched of the Earth*, 39.

The popular media bombard the world with the false virtue of vengeance and "paybacks." Thus it is a constant struggle against popular wisdom to maintain the witness that vengeance is not the way of God. It is particularly disturbing when Christians, in false attempts to identify with the sufferers, somehow suspend their convictions of peace and nonviolence and find ways to justify the violence of those who have suffered, saying, "There is no peace without justice." But understanding anger is not an invitation to suspend commitment to the way of peace. Rather, it is an invitation to prophetic endurance of anger while not compromising the gospel of nonviolence. Ultimately, there is no justice without peace.

DANIEL 7:1–12:13

THE APOCALYPTIC VISIONS

DANIEL 7:1-28, VISIONS OF CHANGE

COMMENTARY

Chapter 7 begins a new genre in the book of Daniel. Instead of the king's dreams, now we focus on the dreams, thoughts, and visions of Daniel himself. This chapter has been called "the veritable center of the book"[192] and the "heart" of Daniel.[193] These evaluations derive mainly from the fact that the book has so many connections with the stories in chaps. 1–6 (issues of sovereignty and dominion, negative evaluations of empires, and most especially the sequence of four kingdoms in chap. 2) that it serves almost as a capstone—as if the stories were leading up to this chapter. The fact that chap. 7 was written in Aramaic also gives this interesting impression. Lenglet pointed out a plausible chiastic symmetry to chaps. 2–7:

A chap. 2, vision of four empires
  B chap. 3, faithfulness of the Jews and their rescue
    C chap. 4, judgment on empire (Nebuchadnezzar)
    C´ chap. 5, judgment on empire (Belshazzar)
  B´ chap. 6, faithfulness of a Jew and his rescue
A´ chap. 7, vision of four empires.[194]

The relationships among these chapters have led many scholars to suggest that chaps. 2–7 were, in fact, originally a separate document (which included, of course, the older stories that became chaps. 2–6), to which chaps. 1 and 8–12 were added at a later time. When they were added is a tricky question. Most scholars assign chap. 7 in its present

192. Lacocque, *The Book of Daniel*.
193. Porteous, *Daniel*, 95.
194. A. Lenglet, "La structure litteraire de Daniel 2-7," *Biblica* 53 (1972) 169-90.

form to 167 BCE, just before Antiochus IV desecrated the Temple, since this event would surely have been alluded to in this chapter if it had happened by the time this section was written. (It is referred to later in Daniel 10–12.)

On the other hand, chap. 7 has obvious literary connections to 8–12. It is the first of the clearly apocalyptic chapters of the book of Daniel, and while there are references to earlier phrases and terms, there is no story narrative in chap. 7 that would relate it to the older diaspora stories in chaps. 1–6.

There has always been considerable scholarly debate as to the origins of Daniel 7. Was there an earlier vision that did not mention Antiochus so specifically? If so, then, with many scholars, I might suggest that the references to the "little horn" (referring to Antiochus IV) may have been added at the time chap. 7 took its present shape—i.e., 167 BCE. However, there are many scholars who defend the unity of this chapter, considering vv. 21-22 as the only possible candidates for later additions, if any.

In any case, it will be clear from this analysis that chap. 7 certainly turns the theological/ideological direction of the book as a whole in a dramatic, and darker, direction. The images here are those of struggle and warfare between the forces of evil and chaos against the heavens, the "holy ones," and by implication the Jewish tellers and hearers of the story. Even those scholars who see the kings negatively in chaps. 1–6 also see a change in chap. 7, where the attitude is decidedly angry and alarmed. The hope for a change in the foreign rulers has been abandoned; the empires are revealed for what they always have been: beasts who rose out of chaos and evil.

7:1, In the Time of Belshazzar. The first vision is associated with the time of Belshazzar. This is an interesting move, because it associates this vision with the most negative portrayal of a foreign ruler thus far. We are to understand that this dream (a night dream is clearly implied here because Daniel is lying in bed) is occasioned by the kind of negative political rule that was typified by the story of Belshazzar. This is a significant point. Dreams of deliverance, then, are associated with adverse political rule.

The terminology used for Daniel's dream, "visions of his head," is precisely that used for Nebuchadnezzar earlier. It is interesting that the assumption here is that Daniel is an important interpreter not only of others' dreams, but of his own as well (through the aid of an angelic assistant).

The Rise of the Beasts. 7:2. The narrative shifts to first person as Daniel describes his dream. The "four winds of heaven" (ארבע רוחי שמיא 'arba 'rûḥê šĕmayyā) relate closely to imagery found in *1 Enoch*, where four "angels" of heaven represent the winds from the four directions. In Daniel 7, these winds are "stirring the sea" (מגיחן לימא mĕgîḥān lĕyammā). The Greek suggests "attacked" (προσβάλλω *prosballō*), and the implication is even greater that what this sentence describes is spiritual/mythical warfare between the winds of heaven and the sea. The winds of heaven were part of God's weapons, or tools, in the creation (Job 26:12-13; Ps 89:9-11). This is an echo of the ancient Semitic myth of the storm god (Baal in Canaanite mythology, Marduk in the Babylonian version; the stories are essentially parallel) at battle with the god of the sea (Yam, Canaanite; Tiamat, Babylonian; the sea god was frequently associated with or identified with monsters or dragons from the deep), the latter representing the powers of chaos that must be controlled by the god of the storm. Marduk, for example, uses the four winds as weapons in his struggle against Tiamat.[195] This myth, with its many suggestive echoes in the Bible, is often used creatively to refer to historical struggles of the Israelite people, in which God is a major participant. The most dramatic example of this is Isa 51:8-11 (NRSV), the significant portion of which is:

> Was it not you who cut Rahab in pieces,
>   who pierced the dragon?
> Was it not you who dried up the sea,
>   the waters of the great deep;
> who made the depths of the sea a way,
>   for the redeemed to cross over?

Here the ancient myth is brilliantly used to represent the crossing of the Reed Sea; the ancient Semitic myth becomes historicized as Yahweh's doing battle with the Reed Sea, which the Hebrew slaves then crossed in the exodus. Goldingay points out that "great sea" is *always* used to refer to the Mediterranean Sea—that is, the actual place—rather than a primordial, mythical sea.[196] Such aspects of realism add to the power of the message.

Therefore, 7:2 sets the scene for what follows. Many scholars have suggested that this is the first event in the series that follows, implying that the four winds of heaven are actually the catalyst that brings forth the beasts from the deep and that God initiates that action. But this is not what is intended here. Verse 2 sets the scene of battle, and the following verses then describe what occurs during that battle. God is at war with the sea, not bringing forth the beasts. There is no suggestion here, then, that the beasts rise at God's request.

7:3. During the battle, four great beasts rise from the sea. The sea is the enemy, chaos, the realm of Leviathan (Lotan, Rahab, Tunannu, etc.). And so the beasts, which will be interpreted as world powers, are associated with the forces of chaos in the world and at odds with the powers of heaven. As the rest of the chapter will represent battle and judgment images, it is clear that these beasts arise one by one to do battle. Theologically, the battle is between good and evil. Note that the kingdoms of this world are associated with powers of the sea, with evil. This is a long-standing, though typically neglected, element of biblical tradition that carries through into

---

195. Lacocque, *The Book of Daniel*, 138; see also the "Akkadian Creation Story" (Enuma Elish), in Pritchard, *Ancient Near Eastern Texts Relating to the Old Testament*, 60-72.

196. Goldingay, *Daniel*, 160.

the New Testament, where Jesus is tempted by Satan, who is assumed to have control of the kingdoms of the earth (Matt 4:8-10). Von Rad suggested that the four beasts mean "all the world," referring to Zechariah 1.[197] Certainly we see such animal symbolism in Pss 68:31; 74:13; 87:4; Isa 27:1; Ezek 29:3, 32; and *1 Enoch* 85–90. The most dramatic parallel to this section, however, is Hos 13:6*b*-9, which lists the same animals in succession (though not in the same order):

> they were satisfied, and their heart was proud;
> therefore they forgot me,
> So I will become like a lion to them,
>   like a leopard I will lurk beside the way.
> I will fall upon them like a bear
>   robbed of her cubs,
>   and will tear open the covering of their heart
> there I will devour like a lion,
>   as a wild animal would mangle them.
> I will destroy you, O Israel;
>   who can help you? (NRSV)

Note that the final animal is undefined, as is the fourth beast in Daniel 7 (although in parallel with lion). What is perhaps most interesting in this passage is the fact that these animals are seen as a threat to the northern agricultural and herding society. All, then, are predators, animals of the hunt that become useful as images of God's making war on Israel. But the images in Daniel 7 are *more* than lions, bears, and leopards. The images are mixed, therefore violating the clear categories enumerated in levitical law and further suggesting that they are "unclean."

7:4. The first beast conveys the image of a lion. Lions are frequently used in modern iconography as symbols of courage and strength (particularly by the British), even in children's stories; but it is rare to have such a favorable image of a lion in the Bible, in which they are usually seen as wild threats to civilized life and horrific menaces (Amos 3:12). Although many scholars see this lion image in Daniel as finally a positive representation of Nebuchadnezzar ("a human mind given to it"), this is not likely to be what is intended. That this beast is transformed into a human may signify that this represents human beings—Babylonians at that. In other words, the lion suggests that this first "government" or "ruler" is the personification of the powerful threat represented by lions. If such a positive or specific reference to Nebuchadnezzar's insanity is intended here (cf. chap. 4), then it is appropriate to point out that his fearsomeness and his "wings" (often a symbol of the swiftness of conquest) must be removed before he can have a human mind. Once again, a transformation of the ruler is a way of conquering the enemy!

7:5. The second beast, also associated with threats to human life from wild animals, is a bear. It is portrayed as already devouring; as the Aramaic suggests, it has "ribs" between its teeth, already starting to fulfill the command, "Arise, devour many bodies!" *Who* tells the bear to devour many bodies? Goldingay and others presume that this is God's command,[198] implying that the destructiveness of the empires is also under God's direction—dare I say blessing! But God never speaks in this vision. Contrast the images of Antiochus IV, the "little horn," who speaks too much (vv. 8, 11). The voice here is the antagonistic Chaos, in battle against the forces of heaven.

7:6. The third beast, represented as a leopard, is seen as having great ability because of its numerous wings and heads. Do these four wings and four heads somehow represent the four Persian kings (Darius, Cyrus, Xerxes, Artaxerxes) mentioned in Scripture? Or do they represent the four corners of the earth? The term "sovereignty" (שלטן *šāltān*; NIV, "authority"; NRSV, "dominion") is used often in Daniel, and here is given to the leopard. Of all the beasts, this one alone may be a neutral image, in contrast to the first two—since "dominion" was given to Darius as well. But this interpretation must not be stretched too far; the leopard is hardly benign!

7:7-8. The last beast is not given an earthly association, but is described in strong language: "fearsome," "terrible," "very strong." It has great iron teeth, devouring its victims and trampling all else under its feet. Some scholars have suggested that the beast in mind may well be an elephant, "breaking in pieces, and stamping what was left with

---

197. G. von Rad, *The Message of the Prophets* (New York: Harper & Row, 1962) 278n2.

198. Goldingay, *Daniel,* 160-65.

its feet." Greeks brought the war elephant from the east, and they are mentioned in 1 Macc 1:17; 3:34; and 6:28-47. Note especially 3 Maccabees, a first-century document that describes the threat to faithful Jews by Ptolemy, who ordered them to be trampled by elephants "equipped with horrible implements" (3 Macc 5:45). Whatever kind of beast this may be, its power is purely destructive. The context suggests that this beast differs from the previous three because of the magnitude of its destructive force. Despite its strength, its ten horns are soon overpowered by the force of one who comes later, who speaks arrogantly.

As can be imagined, there has been considerable debate about the meaning of the ten horns and the later three horns. The little horn certainly is meant to represent Antiochus IV, but who are the three who are "plucked up by the roots"? The most likely suggestion is that there were three men in line for the throne upon the death of Antiochus III: Seleucus IV Philopater and his sons, Demetrius and Antiochus. We know that Antiochus IV killed his young nephew Antiochus, but it is not clear whether he can be implicated in the deaths of the other two except indirectly. The variety of options increases dramatically when one tries to figure out who the "ten horns" might refer to. Alexander and six of the Seleucids who followed (so Collins)?[199] Or is "ten" simply to be reckoned as "many"? Does it matter? It is hard to avoid an image of diaspora Jews (even in Palestine) as, in fact, a minority quite disengaged from the powers of the empire and who, in fact, see it taking place over their heads. The frequent change of rulers might then be a basis for cynicism—at which point the ten horns crowding together on an animal become a dark-humored, satirical comment on the constant intrigue in the Hellenistic courts.

Finally, there arises a horn with eyes and a mouth speaking arrogantly—Antiochus IV (for the immodest speech of Antiochus, see 1 Macc 1:24-25; 2 Macc 5:17). Later Christian groups would interpret Rome as the final and great beast, an understandable confusion, given Christian suffering under Roman imperial rule. In 2 Esdr 12:10-12, there is a conscious change to Rome as the last beast, which seems to presume the earlier series of Hellenistic empires. It is clear, however, that Antiochus IV was the original reference, and the earliest interpretation of this passage[200] strongly supports the importance of seeing the beast as a metaphor for Antiochus IV.

The elasticity of these symbols is what lends Daniel one of its enduring points of interest for later generations who were able to fill in the blanks with whatever powers they were opposing at the time (e.g., Rome, England's Charles I during the civil war, George III during the American Revolution, Louis XVI during the French Revolution, etc.; see Reflections below). It seems hardly surprising, then, that there is considerable debate on who the four beasts were meant to signify.

7:9-14, The Heavenly Judgment. As Daniel is trying to understand these events, the battle shifts to the heavenly arena, where an interesting description of God's actions takes place. We are "standing before" another king in another throne room (v. 9). As Daniel watches, "thrones" are set in place. Why is "thrones" plural? Is a heavenly council suggested? Is there a throne for the "one like a son of man" introduced later?[201] What is clear is that we are in the realm of political sovereignty once again—except that this throne room is the one with true authority. The description of the "Ancient of Days" (NIV; "Ancient One," NRSV) is fanciful and impressive, suggesting an old man with great authority (the white robes and white hair are also noted in *1 Enoch* 14:20, resembling descriptions of El, the father/king figure in Canaanite imagery), surrounded by miraculous signs of power, like light and fire. While Canaanite mythology is clearly a part of the resources available to the visionary writer of Daniel, other biblical images certainly verify that these ideas were already well known in Hebrew circles. Consider, especially, portions of the "enthronement of God as king" theme in Ps 97:1-3 (NRSV):

> The LORD is king! Let the earth rejoice;
>   let the many coastlands be glad!
> Clouds and thick darkness are all
>   around him;

---

199. Collins, *Daniel*, 299.
200. See Sibylline Oracles 3:388-400.
201. Collins notes the idea of thrones of judgment in Matt 19:28. See Collins, *Daniel*, 301.

> righteousness and justice are the
> foundation of his throne
> Fire goes before him,
> and consumes his adversaries on
> every side.

As if to magnify the power of this ruler in Daniel 7, "a thousand thousands" attend him (v. 10), much more than the mere thousand that attended Belshazzar in the earlier story. As the "court" is in session, there follows a startlingly brief dispatch of the beasts (vv. 11-12). The worst one, the beast with the horn that speaks arrogantly, is immediately burned in judgment. The speed of this judgment contrasts with our modern fascination for the battle itself. Surely there must be struggle, a matching of power and force until finally good wins over evil. Not so in biblical apocalypticism. Almost as soon as the Ancient of Days arrives, the judgment is settled. Note also Revelation, where the supposedly "great battle" is so easily missed as to be made insignificant. There, too, the beast is dispatched to a fiery destruction (Rev 19:19-21).

The others, made powerless, are allowed to live "for a season and a time" (v. 12). The implication that dominion has been taken from the remaining beasts, although they have been allowed to live for a while, is important. Many scholars have wondered whether this is an indication that when the Hellenistic Empire is destroyed, the former kingdoms would live once again as independent states. But this can hardly be the meaning of this text. Each beast symbolizes an empire, and each one's dominion is removed. The emphasis, then, is on the delay of destruction, even after the beasts are left powerless. That the powers of this earth exist but are already defeated is an important aspect of political atheism and radical faith. What this means is that the apocalyptic writer no longer believes in the power of the empires, but points instead to an alternative reality.

The rationale for rendering the empires powerless, instead of obliterating them, is because authority is given to the mysterious one who is now introduced, the "one like a human being" (vv. 13-14), literally, "son of man" (בר אנש *bar 'ĕnāš*), which is taken to mean "human being," thus "someone who looks like a human being." Given Jesus' use of the "son of man" image, this spectacular entrance at precisely this moment in the vision of Daniel 7 has brought forth torrents of scholarly debate as to the origin and meaning of the term. That the New Testament writers drew on this image of a powerful authority under God is clear. But one must not allow the later Christian use of the term to affect one's understanding of what is meant in the context of the vision of Daniel 7.[202]

Irrespective of the precise origin or meaning of the "son of man" figure, the important aspect of this figure is that he is a heavenly representative, appointed by the source of heavenly authority, the Ancient of Days. Some scholars have pointed out that God "appears on clouds" in Deut 33:26 and Ps 104:3, but in Canaanite mythology, Baal appears on clouds as well. Since Baal is lesser than El, this suggests a closer parallel to Daniel 7.

Some scholars have suggested that the "one like a son of man" is a priestly figure,[203] but this association has not been widely accepted in the most recent commentaries. Attention is focused on the fact that this person has supernatural attributes—he is one who "looks like" a human being, as the other beasts "look like" lions, bears, etc. Also, this person comes from heaven, ruling out an earthly figure. Finally, this person has authority and is part of the preceding judgment/battle scene. As Collins and Goldingay both conclude, the candidate best suited for the identification as "one like a son of man" in Daniel 7 is the angel Michael, who will do battle on Israel's behalf in later visions (Dan 10:13, 21), and is, of course, a supernatural figure. Michael is well known in the New Testament as well, appearing in Matt 16:27; 25:31; and Revelation 12. Furthermore, in the Dead Sea Scrolls Michael is named as one whose "kingdom will be raised up" when the other kingdoms are destroyed.[204]

But there are further implications, if this identification is accepted. Michael is an angelic representation of the people of Israel.

---

202. Jesus is not being "predicted" or "announced" in Daniel 7. Rather, Daniel 7 is among many of the Hebrew images in the OT that the NT, and Jesus himself, draws upon in order to compose a biblically informed picture of Jesus as the Messiah.
203. Lacocque, *The Book of Daniel*.
204. 1QM 17:5-8.

Michael's going to battle, then, is a symbolic representation of the struggles of the people of Israel, much in the same way that God was pictured as fighting when Israel was at war (Exodus 15).

Thus, through this viceroy, heaven is claiming its right to rule. The terms used in reference to the authority of the son of man figure are significant in their direct contrast to the assumed power of the Babylonians and Persians in the previous stories. In other stories in Daniel, these attributes were ultimately assigned to God: sovereignty, 2:20-23; honor/glory, 4:17; kingship, 4:34-37; over all peoples, nations, and languages, 6:25; 3:4, 7, 29; 4:1; 5:19; he shall be served, 3:28; his authority will last forever.

7:15-18, The Summary of the Vision. Daniel is greatly distressed by these visions, presumably because of his own confusion on the matter. He asks one of the attendants for an explanation. It is typical of such apocalyptic visions that there is a conversation between a heavenly mediator and the seer. So Daniel seeks out an interpreter. In reply, he is given a simple summary of the entire vision: The worldly powers will arise ("kingdoms from the earth"; note the interpretation of the earlier image of the beasts coming from the sea), but God will conquer them all and God's kingdom will be everlasting. The conflict and its results are certain. Daniel, however, is more curious about the fourth beast; the writer focuses attention on the beast that undoubtedly has the most importance for the hearers and readers of this visionary experience: the beast with which they are currently contending.

The Elaboration of the Fourth Beast. 7:19-20. In typical fashion for Daniel, these verses repeat precisely what we have read already in vv. 7-8. The new elements that follow, therefore, are of greatest interest—namely, the war with the "holy ones."

7:21-22. Like "one like a son of man," the precise referent of the "holy ones" (קדישיו *qaddîšîn*) has engendered considerable comment. Here, however, the conclusions of recent scholars are on somewhat more solid ground, given the wider evidence of the Dead Sea Scrolls as well as the wider extra-biblical Jewish literature that can be drawn upon.

It would seem, at first glance, that the holy ones might be a name given to the faithful Jews of the community, but it is much more common for this image to refer to supernatural beings (see Deut 33:2; Job 5:1; 15:15; Ps 89:6, 8; Zech 14:5; see also Dan 4:14, compared with "watchers"; 4:20; 8:13) and thus in line with the earlier image of Michael. Both Lacocque and Collins, however, refer to the fact that angels are mixed with real people in combat themes in the Dead Sea documents (esp. the "War Scroll").[205] Goldingay suggests that the holy ones may be either supernatural or a symbol of Israel. It is important to point out that the fate of the holy ones is certainly intended to reflect the fate of the Jewish people themselves, much in the same way that Michael does. Therefore, we should understand the close association between the holy ones and the people of Israel suffering under Hellenistic domination. Furthermore, these holy ones are associated with "the Most High," which is the term diaspora Jews often used for God and, in turn, was used by non-Jews in reference to the Jewish God. Furthermore, to these holy ones some authority is given within the everlasting kingdom that is inaugurated by the Ancient of Days.

Whoever the holy ones are assumed to be, they are suffering near defeat. Surely this is the moment of greatest relevance for the reader—and strongly suggests that the writer identified strongly with the holy ones and felt powerfully their near defeat. The war is specifically against the "arrogant horn" of the final beast.

7:23-25. The beast is described in more detail in these verses, before a repetition of the heavenly court that defeats the beast finally in vv. 26-27. The attributes of the beast are worldwide dominion, destructive power,[206] division of leadership within the empire, and the eventual success of one of the leaders within the empire.

Although most scholars consider this last beast to be the Hellenistic Empire inaugurated by Alexander, it is interesting to note that some of the beast's attributes are

---

205. Lacocque, *The Book of Daniel*, 131; Collins, *Daniel*, 314-15. They are opposed, among others, by V. S. Poythress, "The Holy Ones of the Most High in Daniel VII," *VT* 26 (1976) 208-13.

206. Note the use of the same term "crush" in the eschatological fragment 4Q246, Col 2, Line 3, "shooting stars who crush people, and nation (will crush) nation." See Eisenman and Wise, *The Dead Sea Scrolls Uncovered*, 68-70.

reminiscent of images associated with Cyrus in Isa 41:25b: "He shall trample on rulers as on mortar, as the potter treads clay." One is cautious about reading such descriptions positively!

Furthermore, this final leader is also described as: different from the former ones (more powerful?); one who will make war with the holy ones and nearly win; someone who will attempt to change "sacred seasons and law" (undoubtedly a reference to attempts by Antiochus IV to change the religious observances of the Jewish people); one who will rule for only a time, and one who will be the last to rule. It will be his power that is given to the holy ones. As Porteous writes: "It is a sobering reflection that it was this empire, for all that it mediated to the ancient peoples of East the achievements of Greek culture, that could appear, in the eyes of a member of a subject people, to be the worst of all tyrannies."[207] Yet, this view of oppressive power is precisely what one finds in v. 23, where the beast is said to be "devouring," "trampling," and "breaking."

7:26-27. In the end, the holy ones will rule in God's everlasting kingdom, and all nations will serve and obey them. The final sense of a rule of the holy ones echoes some of the reversal-of-fortune motif that is found not only throughout the book of Daniel to this point, but also in such important passages as Isa 19:16-25. Thus to the holy ones will be given "kingship," "dominion," "the greatness of the kingdoms." However, one should not be too quick to assume that this is merely a reversal-of-fortune motif that presumes that the former slaves will be the masters of the rest of the world. While it is true that some biblical passages have a more vengeful tone (including Daniel 2 and 6), it is also true that in other passages the rule of the holy ones, or God's final rule, will be one of peace and worldwide healing. Isaiah speaks of Assyrians and Egyptians worshiping together (Isa 19:23-25) and then sharing equally with the Israelites in the blessings of God (Isaiah 2; Zech 9:10, where dominion from sea to sea means that God will "command peace to the nations" [NRSV]).

7:28. Finally, Daniel remains alarmed and concerned about what he has seen. His reaction is interesting, given the somewhat positive nature of what he has seen. Are we to presume that the experience of seeing such a vision of holiness and power itself, though positive, gives rise to fearful awe? That such a vision would be, at the very least, exhausting is hardly surprising.

207. Porteous, *Daniel*, 113.

REFLECTIONS

It is easy for scholars, who are used to categorizing apocalyptic texts according to such characteristics as visions, dreams, and otherworldly visits, to overlook the significance of the vision/dream as a medium of communication for the subordinated people of Palestine in the Hellenistic period. It was a powerful medium of communication that encouraged the people by drawing on a reservoir of possibilities beyond current realities. It is the nature of faith to look beyond the powers of this world to ask not only about the meaning of these powers, but also about their ultimate reality. Dreams are the beginning of the release from oppression. Dreams are images of what could be, what may be, and, most dramatically, what will be!

In a widely read and influential study of biblical apocalyptic literature, Paul Hanson articulated a view of biblical apocalyptic that represents it as the literature of those who suffered so severely that they began to lose their moorings in reality. Apocalyptic is disengaged from the realities of this world, as the earlier prophets were not. In such a view, dreams and visions are signs of sociopsychological breakdown, and thus apocalyptic is the literature of desperation: "When separated from the realism, the vision leads to a retreat into the world of ecstasy and dreams and to an abdication of the social responsibility of translating the vision of the divine order into the realm of everyday earthly concerns."[208]

208. P. Hanson, *The Dawn of Apocalyptic* (Minneapolis: Fortress, 1986) 30.

Apocalyptic, according to such a view, is often a "flight into the timeless repose of myth."[209] One only hopes that God will miraculously, and irrationally, intervene to halt the suffering and the horror. Perhaps apocalyptic, then, is passive, waiting, and resigned, thus allowing the oppression to continue. It is a small step to see apocalyptic as a slave religion, what Karl Marx described as an opiate to salve the wounds of political dominance rather than actually engaging in resistance or other action to change matters. But in Marx himself we see the beginnings of the great flaw in this assessment of apocalypticism. Marx, after all, propounded a view of revolution that was supposedly scientific, and thus inevitable. There would inevitably be a struggle between the workers and the owners of the means of production—the great class war. However, this inevitability hardly resulted in the workers of the world sitting back and desperately waiting for scientific certainties to come to pass. Yet, can anyone now dispute the fact that Marx's descriptions of a stateless society were as "timeless a flight into myth" as was Daniel 7–12? I would argue that apocalyptic consciousness, like Marx's scientific inevitabilities, need not result in a resigned invitation for God to intervene unilaterally in reality.

Fanon speaks of the "updating" of national myths and legends in the process of resistance to the colonizer by bringing "conflicts up to date and modernizing the kinds of struggle which the stories evoke, together with the names of heroes and the types of weapons."[210] Such is the power, for example, of rethinking the appearance of the angel Michael in the social circumstances of the book of Daniel.

As a result of the westward movement of European American settlers, Native American societies experienced horrible convulsions of change, violence, deportation, unknown disease, and desperation. In such circumstances and across tribal lines many prophet-like figures arose who delivered messages based on visions. One thinks of the famous Ghost Dance religion across many tribal lines, or the Handsome Lake religion among the Seneca/Iroquois, or the Indian Shaker church from northwest Indian John Slocum's visions. In many cases, these visions imagined the intervention of supernatural forces to drive away the European settlers and restore the old ways of tribal life. The results of these visions were varied—sometimes revolutionary violence (the Ghost Dance alone was expressed in various ways among different Native American nations), sometimes a new cultural adjustment in tribal traditions that allowed the people to survive and flourish even under grim circumstances. But the result was not passivity or withdrawal—the result of the vision was a new approach to reality, a new opening of a way forward for the people.

Native American philosopher Vine Deloria writes of this function of reasserting traditions and visions:

> We might therefore expect American Indians to discern out of the chaos of their shattered lives, the same kind of message and mission that inspired the Hebrew prophets. Indians would, in this situation, begin to develop a new interpretation of their religious tradition with a universal application. They would further begin to seek out areas in which they could communicate with sympathetic people in larger society, and put their own house in order. A process of intense commitment to certain social goals might then emerge in which the traditional values of pre-contact days would be seen as religious principles having a universal application. Most important, Indians would begin to probe deeper into their own past and view their remembered history as a primordial covenant.[211]

Such transformation of apocalyptic into action can also be illustrated in the Radical Reformation traditions (esp. Quakers and Mennonites), which have deep roots in

---
209. Hanson, *The Dawn of Apocalyptic*, 134.
210. Fanon, *The Wretched of the Earth*, 240.
211. V. Deloria, Jr., "Out of Chaos," *Parabola* 10 (1985) 3-11.

European apocalyptic traditions. Many of the early Quakers were involved with a revolutionary group supporting Oliver Cromwell's seventeenth-century English new model army, a group that called itself the Fifth Monarchy Men. The Fifth Monarchists derived their name directly from Daniel 2 and 7, and they believed that in removing Charles I and asserting the power of parliament controlled by the faithful, they were bringing about the coming rule of "holy ones": the fifth empire of the "one like a son of man." Their reading of the Bible's apocalyptic visions hardly engendered passivity; yet the books of Daniel and Revelation were read with a consuming passion and were debated with great zeal around the campfires of the Roundhead forces who faced the royalist armies. Vavasor Powell (1617–1670), a Fifth Monarchist leader, noted Dan 4:17 (similar to chap. 7) in reference to the lower classes ruling instead of the monarchy. Another Fifth Monarchist sermon, commenting on the assassinations of France's Henri III and Henri IV, noted that "such princes might read their destiny in . . . Daniel 11:20."[212]

The struggle for peace and justice that is traditional in Mennonite and Quaker traditions draws part of its fire from a visionary openness to what may be possible, even if modern representatives of these traditions are embarrassed in polite theological company by their historical roots in such apocalyptic events as Thomas Müntzer's rebellion or George Fox's dreams and visions. Frank Borchardt makes the interesting observation that "there is no sense in mocking Doomsday speculation for its countless failures to predict the end of the world accurately. The system does not continue to seize the minds of great numbers of people on account of its failures. It must succeed somewhere. It must conform to experience sufficiently to survive as a system, indeed to flourish. *It does so in its evaluation of the present.*"[213]

Historians and sociologists, such as Norman Cohn[214] and Guenther Lewy,[215] frequently point to the violent destructiveness engendered by such visions (ignoring, however, that violence is not inevitably a result), and therefore attempt to point out the great danger in tolerating, much less encouraging, such forms of antinomian religious expressions. It remains for historians following the lead of Christopher Hill to maintain a persistent reminder that such treasured values as full democracy, equality of women, economic justice and opportunity, self-determination, and freedom of religion and speech often find their most stalwart, consistent, and self-sacrificing proponents among these apocalyptic visionaries. In short, history itself witnesses that suggestions of passivity or withdrawal from society in biblical apocalyptic are hardly inevitable or unbiased conclusions, or even sociologically compelling. The dreamers of apocalyptic visions can be visionaries of a new order of equality, democracy, or world peace.

Visionary religion has always been dangerous and uncontrolled for any institutional status quo. Visionary religion draws deep from the hopes and passions of people, especially in dire and despairing conditions. Visionary religion speaks to the failure of established attitudes and traditions, and it opens the way to new possibilities. It accomplishes this by prying open the sealed doors of tradition and imagining possibilities beyond the realities dictated by world powers. Apocalyptic visions can lead to hope—and hopes have the potential of giving birth to *plans.* For Christians, to live with a constant sense of the advent of Christ is not an irresponsible disengagement from the world but a lifestyle *within* the world that is built on the vision of God's true kingship and dominion. It is to live as if the sentence on the beasts has already been carried out, despite the fact that their lives appear to be "prolonged for a season and a time."

---

212. C. Hill, *The English Bible and the Seventeenth-Century Revolution,* 76, 96.
213. F. Borchardt, *Doomsday Speculation as a Strategy of Persuasion: A Study of Apocalypticism as Rhetoric* (Atlanta: Mellon, 1987) 114, italics added.
214. N. Cohn, *The Pursuit of the Millennium* (New York: Oxford University Press, 1970).
215. G. Lewy, *Religion and Revolution* (New York: Oxford University Press, 1974).

DANIEL 8:1-27, THE RAM AND THE GOAT COMMENTARY

With chap. 8 the book of Daniel returns to the Hebrew language. With the change of language comes another set of observations that scholars have noted, such as the fact that from chap. 8 to chap. 12 we have visions, and not dreams. Some have suggested that chaps. 8–12 were added to the Aramaic original (chaps. 2–7) at a much later time. However this may be, it is important to note that chap. 8 has many parallels to chap. 7 as well as occasional references to chaps. 1–6. Porteous, for one, wonders whether one important difference is that chap. 7 was based on a genuine ecstatic vision, while chap. 8 (and the following chapters, for that matter) seems much more contrived and planned.[216] Goldingay, however, notes that there are considerably more scriptural allusions in chap. 8 than in chap. 7, and he suggests that the visionary style "adds mystery" to the discussion in chap. 8 and those following.[217] What is certainly clear is that the visions of chaps. 8–12 are much more transparent in their presentation of contemporary events, as will be clear in the commentary that follows on these chapters.

8:1-2, The Setting of Belshazzar's Reign and Daniel's Transportation to Susa. The editor is interested in relating this vision to the events during the reign of Belshazzar. He is a transitional figure, as seen from the fact that v. 2 moves to Susa, the capital of Persia, in the province of Elam, beside the River Ulai. Most commentators note a resemblance to the visions of transportation experienced by Ezekiel, and reckon that this is a vision of Daniel's being transported to the great city ("walled/fortified city") of the Persian Empire. Elam is modern Khuzistan, and the Ulai is a canal that is mentioned in extra-biblical sources. Except for the notion that Daniel is "carried" from the kingdom of the Babylonians to that of the Persians in his dream, there seems little significance to the specific location of the vision.

Furthermore, there may be significance to the note about Daniel's standing "by the river Ulai" (some commentators assume the Hebrew to actually read "the Ulai gate" here, but on analogies presented below, "river" seems best; "Ulai" [אוּלַי *'ûlāy*] is literally "perhaps"). It is interesting to note how often a visionary stands on a riverbank in the setting for a vision. Ezra gathers exiles "by the river Ahava" (Ezra 8:15, 21; called "Theras" in 1 Esdr 8:41); Ezekiel experiences his first vision "by the River Chebar" (Ezek 1:1), where he was with other exiles; and Pharaoh's dream takes place on the banks of the Nile (Gen 41:1). This is perhaps only to be attributed to the fact that riverbanks (or canals) are logical locations for settlements, or perhaps for geographical locations to be mentioned in a text, but the frequency of the use of such settings is worthy of note, particularly in the visionary section of Daniel (see chap. 12). Was there a diaspora tradition of gathering on a riverbank for certain ceremonies or services of penitence/remembrance? Or were canals a frequent setting because they were places of labor for the exiles? After all, canals in Mesopotamia—the agricultural lifeblood of the people—required massive human effort to maintain them so that they would not silt up and become blocked.[218] But such speculation ought not to go too far.

8:3-8, The Vision of the Ram and the Goat. The source of the images for this vision is debated among scholars. For example, art historians have noted that the Persians used the ram motif in architecture, as decorations on columns, for instance. In ancient astrological speculation (a form of wisdom that was of obvious interest to some of the Jewish apocalyptic writers as much as to the ancient Greeks, Persians, and Egyptians, etc.), the ram is the symbol of Aries, the sign under which the Persians were located, and Capricorn the goat is Syria (thus the Seleucid inheritors of their section of Alexander's empire). Collins, however, objects to this source for the

---

216. Porteous, *Daniel*, 119.
217. Goldingay, *Daniel*, 201-2.

218. Smith, *The Religion of the Landless*, 116-20.

images, noting that the events described in the vision refer to Alexander's empire *before* the battles of Issus in 333 BCE and Ipsus in 301 BCE, when the four generals took charge of the former united Hellenistic Empire were confirmed: Ptolemy (Egypt); Seleucus (Babylon/Syria); Lysimachus (Asia Minor); and Cassander (Macedonia-Greece).[219] In short, the ram must be Persia and the goat the Hellenistic Empire, united still under Alexander, who is the single "great horn" (v. 8). Whatever the source, a further curiosity is the move in this vision from wild beasts to apparently tamer beasts, even domestic livestock (goats certainly), which are depicted in battle.

The second horn of the ram is undoubtedly Cyrus, who defeated the Medes (the other horn). The ram struck in three directions, but most manuscripts omit the mention of east. Is this because the Persian Empire *was* the east as far as biblical writers were concerned? Was it because the Persians' eastern campaigns (into northern India) were of little interest to the biblical writers? Collins points out that east is included in two important early sources, Papyri 967 and a Dead Sea Scroll fragment,[220] and therefore should be reestablished in this passage to complete the balance of the "four corners" of the earth—a standard ancient manner of speaking of all the world.

It was stated that all beasts were powerless, beasts here representing nations, as noted in the Commentary on chap. 7. The interesting phrase that this verse uses for political and military power, that the ruler "does as he pleases," is a stock phrase found in both the Hebrew and the Aramaic sections of Daniel and is used to refer to rulers' having power to act of their will. Note its use in late biblical texts in reference to the emperors in Esth 1:8; 9:5; Dan 11:3, 16, 36; and Neh 9:24, 37. The phrase further seems to paint a picture of the arbitrary whim of political power from the perspective of the subordinated minorities and controlled populations.

The goat comes from the west with one "horn of vision" or "horn between its eyes" (v. 5). The goat symbolizes the Macedonian Greek juggernaut, with its great horn: Alexander the Great. The use of horns to symbolize rulers (see Commentary on chap. 7) is not uncommon outside the book of Daniel as well (Ps 132:17; Jer 48:25; Mic 4:13). The horn of a wild beast is its destructive power (and with these particular animals, the only real weapon). The fact that this goat moved without touching the ground, combined with references to these animals' having wings in chap. 7, serves to suggest the speed with which the Greek war machine moved.

It is interesting that Daniel would emphasize the "bitterness" of the battle—an Eastern diaspora perspective on battles that have passed into Western history as the great formative battles of the Greeks against the Persians. The Greek victories over the forces of the Eastern world in the ancient Near East would have permanent impact on the development of both Near Eastern and western European civilizations, and the classical Greek writers would provide symbols and themes of warfare for European nations that attempted to create empires in the nineteenth and twentieth centuries. Green notes with irony that the supposed "civilizing and missionary aspect" of the Greek conquests has been "greatly exaggerated, not least by modern historians anxious to find some moral justification for aggressive imperialism."[221] But there is no admiration for the bravery or *esprit de corps* of conquest in Hebrew Scriptures—no celebration of military culture, pride, and bravado—only the humble recognition that God, and not their own power, delivered them. Daniel's visions present the cold facts of empire: destruction and bitterness. The image of trampling the enemy is used throughout the Hebrew Bible as a powerful expression of overwhelming military conquest and defeat, almost suggesting the impunity of Cyrus (Isa 41:25; see also Mic 7:8, where a lion tramples its enemies, but note 2 Kgs 9:33 for the death of Jezebel; Isa 1:12 for the trampling of courts; and Ezek 34:17-22 for the images of goats and rams against the sheep of Israel). The preferred metaphorical self-image of the Jewish nation is the lamb—others are the beasts of prey or destruction.

No one can rescue the ram (v. 7), as no one could rescue anyone *from* the ram in v. 4. Great events are going on under the visionary

---

219. Collins, *Daniel*, 330.
220. Collins, *Daniel*, 329-30.
221. Green, "Greek Gifts?" 27.

eye of Daniel—or over the heads of the exiles, for whom sitting and watching was the only viable option. One thinks of ordinary people throughout the Third World, for whom warfare, politics, and government are matters of different-colored jets fighting overhead and land mines to watch out for while harvesting their crops.

The kingdom of Alexander is divided among his four generals after he is "broken" (v. 8). The use of the phrase "toward the four winds of heaven" probably suggests the helter-skelter notion of the pieces of the empire flying in different directions; but it may foreshadow another battle, keeping the imagery of 7:2, between the horns and the weapons of God. It is interesting that all the successor generals, then, are seen as antagonistic to God. This would have interesting implications for understanding Jewish attitudes to life under the Ptolemies even before the Seleucid nightmare began. All of this initial vision of the ram and goat is background to what follows, and the focus of interest is on Antiochus IV Epiphanes.

Earthly and Spiritual Battle with Antiochus IV Epiphanes. 8:9. Another horn/leader grows toward the south and the east and toward "the beautiful land." The Hebrew term (צבי *ṣĕbî*) can also be translated as "gazelle," standard iconography in modern Israel to represent the land. "Zvi" may refer to Zion and Jerusalem more specifically in Jer 3:19; Ezek 20:6, 15; Dan 11:16, 41; and *1 Enoch* 89:40.

8:10-11. In v. 10, the horn grows toward and does battle with "the host of heaven" or "the armies" of heaven. Here is an interesting association of the host/armies of heaven and stars, and this has resulted in yet another debate in modern scholarship on Daniel and the metaphorical imagery of the book. The belief that stars were actual beings is suggested in a variety of places in the Bible, usually associated with Canaanite/pagan belief (see 2 Kgs 23:5; Jer 19:13; Zeph 1:5). Isaiah 24:21 animates stars, and Isa 5:9-11 uses Canaanite images such as the battle between God and the sea. (For stars personified and doing battle, see Judg 5:20 and Pr Azar 1:41; see also Commentary on the Additions to Daniel.) The most commonly cited instance of the use of star imagery is Isaiah 14, an important discussion of God's warfare against Babylon, which includes the depiction of Babylon as a fallen star who attempts to raise his throne above the "stars of God." The importance here is the fact that celestial imagery is used for God's dealings with foreign nations. Goldingay notes that in 169 BCE, Antiochus had coins minted that pictured a star over his head.[222] Collins also points to the Canaanite myth of the morning star 'Attar doing battle against Baal[223] as a possible source for star imagery. The intention, clearly, is to focus on the battles as cosmic and not merely worldly.

Irrespective of the specific celestial images involved, the notion of spiritual warfare between the powers of the world and the hosts of heaven is implicit in this chapter and will carry on throughout Daniel's visions. Note that "trampling" (רמס *rāmas*) is one of the verbs used to describe conquest. The identity of "the prince of the host" who is challenged (v. 11) is certainly open to question. Porteous believes that it must be God.[224] The military associations of the term suggest an association with the angelic warrior Michael, the one like a son of man "coming with the clouds of heaven" (7:13 NRSV), who will be reintroduced as a prince in chaps. 11–12. In v. 11, however, the Temple offerings and the sanctuary are associated with this prince, creating problems for an easy identification with Michael. Thus most commentators suggest that the "prince of the host" in v. 11 can only refer to God. The "regular burnt offering" refers to the daily sacrifices discussed, and mandated, in the Mosaic laws (Exod 29:38-42; Numbers 28–29) and mentioned in Ezra 3:5; Neh 10:34; and Ezek 46:1-5.

It is important to remember that this interest in the temple cult must be seen in the context of the exile, in which priestly leadership became the dominant form of Jewish leadership, stepping into the vacuum left by the removal of the kingship. This interest is clearly seen in the development of the high priest figure in the visions of Zechariah—Joshua the

---

222. Goldingay, *Daniel*, 210.
223. Collins, *Daniel*, 332.
224. Porteous, *Daniel*, 125. Collins and Goldingay concur, the latter noting that this assigns too much authority to Michael, even though Gen 21:22 and 1 Sam 12:9 have a similar title for an army general. Lacocque, on the other hand, following his strong association of Daniel's vision with the Jerusalem Temple, believes that the specific term שר (*śar*) can also be used for priests in 1 Chr 24:5 or Ezra 8:24. The term is somewhat generic, however, and must be weighted according to the accompanying clarification. Its usual association is military, supporting a stronger association with Michael.

priest standing equal to the Davidic Zerubbabel—and Ezra the priest, who is intentionally contrasted with Nehemiah, the royal military leader.[225]

In short, spiritual warfare on earth is an attack on the ritual observances of the people, e.g., the offering and the temple sanctuary, which represent their unique life and identity in the absence of other, more secular symbols of royalty and administration. One is hard-pressed to suggest alternative realities among the Jewish people that are open to attack by foreign authorities other than the Temple and its observances. If Michael, as the angelic prince of the Israelite people, is being attacked on earth, what else can this battle involve but the Temple as the symbol of the people? Furthermore, in vv. 13-14, the trampling includes both the sanctuary and the "hosts," suggesting a possible identification with or close association between the priesthood of the sanctuary and the hosts of heaven.

8:12. This verse suggests the partial victory of Antiochus IV against the hosts of heaven and, by implication, against those earthly Jews who are associated spiritually with the hosts of heaven. This temporary setback in the spiritual battle is referred to elsewhere as well (7:25). It can hardly be otherwise, since the original hearers of these visions would have known that their present situation looked grim. The precise translation of this verse has vexed scholars for some time. Collins suggests the reading, "A host was given over together with the daily offering, in the course of transgression. It cast truth to the ground and it acted successfully."[226] The difficulties of a precise translation (and whether changes must be made in the Hebrew), however, do not make substantial changes in how this verse is understood.

8:13. The author now summarizes one of the main points of this entire chapter: "How long?" Porteous compares this agonized question to the initial chapter of Zechariah,[227] and Collins notes that this question is a regular feature of penitential literature in the Bible and even in ancient Near Eastern literature more generally.[228] The interesting concept in v. 13 is the "abomination that makes desolate" (NIV, "rebellion that causes desolation"; NRSV, "transgression that makes desolate"). Most scholars now accept the notion that this phrase in Hebrew is a play on the title "Baal Shamem—'Lord of Heaven'—who was identified with 'Olympian Zeus,'"[229] and thus is associated with an image that Antiochus IV is said to have erected within the Temple in Jerusalem, rebuilding the altar (and thus defiling it) in order to offer sacrifice to this god (see 1 Macc 4:38-39).

8:14. The answer to the question of how long is answered. That it is answered is perhaps more important than the answer. The *raison d'être* of apocalyptic literature is that it attempts to answer the agonized question, "How long?" and thus begins to offer comfort to those suffering under the heels of an oppressive and tyrannical regime (see Reflections). Despite this key element, the number of "evenings and mornings" left of their suffering is interesting. It is assumed that the 2,300 evenings and mornings refer to the daily sacrifices (twice a day) and thus would be 1,150 days. This is short of the three and a half years between 167 and 164 BCE, the time from the desecration of the Temple to its rededication, but Collins wonders whether it is shorter precisely because the vision comes after the desecration, and thus time had already begun to pass.[230] Goldingay, on the other hand, suggests that no specific length of time was intended, and perhaps we are to understand simply a "fixed, significant period."[231] This is closer to the perspective of this commentary, which points to the limitation to suffering that a number (any number) would imply.

Gabriel Appears to Daniel. 8:15-16. There is a break here as Daniel tries to understand what he has seen (note also the continued mention of the River Ulai as the location for this visionary experience). Whatever literary function these breaks perform (usually a change of scene or subject), they occur regularly in Daniel. Note the break between the actual events of Nebuchadnezzar's dream in chap. 2 and the interpretation, as well as the break in the vision in 7:15-16.

---

225. This is discussed in T. Eskenazi, *In a Time of Prose* (Atlanta: Scholars Press, 1988).
226. Collins, *Daniel*, 326.
227. Porteous, *Daniel*, 126.
228. Collins, *Daniel*, 334-35.
229. Goldingay, *Daniel*, 212.
230. Collins, *Daniel*, 336.
231. Goldingay, *Daniel*, 213.

With the break in v. 15, the scene shifts to a vision of "someone" with the "appearance of a man." This is another angelic figure who will introduce Daniel to Gabriel. Here we have the first occasion in the Bible in which an angelic figure is named; later, the reader will encounter Michael again, who was unnamed in the earlier material.

8:17. Daniel falls to the ground before the vision of Gabriel. Note that Daniel takes this extreme action only before the representatives of God. Daniel will say the obligatory "O king, live forever," but there is no mention that he ever bowed or was subservient "before the king" in earlier chapters. Daniel's actions might also be a physical reaction to the apparition itself, as if Daniel is simply overcome.

Daniel is told that his vision is for "the time of the end." This is an important theme in these visions. Apocalyptic derives its power from the fact that both the writer and the reader believe that they are, in fact, living in the end time. "The time of the end," for them, begins now. Apocalyptic writing, it must be remembered, remains a popular literature precisely because of the frequently recurring sense in history that "ours *must be* the last age."

Gabriel Begins to Interpret the Vision. 8:18. The impact of these experiences on Daniel is once again mentioned. The NIV renders the Hebrew more accurately as "deep sleep" (רדם *rādam*; the same term is used for the sleep imposed on Adam in Gen 2:21 before the divine surgery to make Eve), rather than the NRSV's "trance," providing us with interesting details about physiological effect of visionary experiences for the ancient writer. Such visions are clearly exhausting, and the visionary often requires assistance and strengthening by the angelic figure or the one to whom he is speaking.

Furthermore, the weakness of the people is an important theme, and the visionary experiences strengthen them in their struggle to maintain faith and identity in the face of defeat and subordination. Gabriel's response is to touch Daniel and raise him to his feet. Lacocque, interestingly, notes the importance of the theme of the healing touch of the heavenly one, or even of an authority figure (see Ezra 1:1, 5; Isa 6:7; Jer 1:9; Dan 9:21; 10:10, 16, 18; 4 Esdr 5:4; *1 Enoch*; Rev 1:17; it is used often in the Gospels as the touch of Jesus).[232]

8:19. The "period of wrath/indignation" is reminiscent of the notion of the "wrath of God" as judgment (Pss 38:3; 69:24; 102:10; Isa 10:5, 25; 26:20). This day of anger is also a day of judgment, and eventually salvation (Isa 30:27; Ezek 22:31). However, this period of wrath is equated with the "period of the time of the end." The idea that the end is a span of time rather than a single point at which all things end is emphasized by many scholars. Collins notes that the term often used for "end" (אחרי *'aḥărê*) was used by the writers of the Dead Sea Scroll materials to signify a span of years.[233] Goldingay, moreover, wants to detach the time of the end, the period of wrath, from the notion that it is the time of "God's punishment." The "wrath" here, in short, may be the furor of the foreign nations; thus the end would be the end of the tyranny of world empires.

232. Lacocque, *The Book of Daniel*, 171.
233. Collins, *Daniel*, 338.

❖ ❖ ❖ ❖

EXCURSUS: THE "PERIOD OF WRATH" AND MODERN THEOLOGY

Commentaries on the book of Daniel frequently lapse into decidedly modern theological issues when interpreting the reference "the period of wrath." The issue is clear: Moderns wish to avoid the simplistic idea that ancient Jews always believed that their suffering was punishment from God. Thus many wish to read this "period of wrath" as the tyranny of foreign nations against the Jews. Although the sins and cruelty of the foreign nations are clearly what is discussed in 8:23, there is strong biblical precedent for

Excursus: The "Period of Wrath" and Modern Theology

considering the exilic events as God's punishment and, therefore, for considering the suffering of the Jews in exile as a period of wrath. Indeed, that was at the root of the entire deuteronomic theology of exile, so a precedent for such thinking was clearly in the tradition. Deuteronomic theology involved the notion that "we brought this upon ourselves by rejecting God and God's prophets," rather than attributing power to the foreign gods and armies. There seems to be an element of this in Daniel's confession in chap. 9. The modern reader wishes to guard against the simplistic notion that horrible experiences are God's punishment—and even the biblical witness (especially in Deutero-Isaiah) pointed in more creative directions for interpreting the suffering of exile ("the refiner's fire," Jonah's message of exile as "preparation for our world mission," etc.). But in our caution to prevent a serious theological mistake of portraying God as an angry scorekeeper of sins, we must not overlook the fact that attributing the exile to God was at least one way for biblical writers to deny victory to foreign armies and gods. Early deuteronomic theologies of God's judgment did imply that it would be impious to resist those foreign rulers who carried out the judgment (e.g., Jeremiah 27–29).

One might see deuteronomic theology leading to a kind of fatalism—in other words, "Do not resist the conquerors, because that is your punishment." Such fatalism is totally foreign to Daniel. Even Jeremiah, after all, advised survival *and* resistance in his letter to exiles in Jeremiah 29, and Second Isaiah clearly amended deuteronomic theology by insisting that Jerusalem had "paid double" for its sins. The resistance shown in the Daniel tradition is clearly post-deuteronomic; yet it is informed by the deuteronomic tendency (seen especially in the editorial line of 1 Samuel 8) to lay particular blame on Israelite experiments with militant nationalism (what George Mendenhall called a return to Canaanite polity)[234] and kingship, so that new forms of social existence must be considered in the light of the previous failures. The political theology of Daniel, in short, learned from previous mistakes, while not necessarily denying that mistakes were made (see Commentary on Susanna 52).

Finally, it is surely a mistake to try to pretend—as moderns constantly try to do—that we live in a world in which mistakes do not have consequences, whether errors in personal choice, misguided national policies, or worldwide environmental negligence. Forgiveness, after all, does not always involve avoiding consequences.

234. See G. Mendenhall, *The Tenth Generation* (Baltimore: Johns Hopkins University Press, 1973).

8:20-22. The interpretation of Daniel's vision is significant in that political realities are now explicitly identified. Daniel's interpretations of dreams in chaps. 2 and 5 were somewhat vague apart from the specific identification of Nebuchadnezzar, but in the visions of chaps. 8–12, there is no doubt about the identity of those involved. The ram with two horns is the eastern empire, uniting the Medes and the Persians under Cyrus, and the goat is the king of Greece, Alexander the Great. The four horns are the kingdoms that follow, the four regions of the divided Alexandrian empire.

Antiochus IV Rises and Falls. 8:23. This verse equals in intensity any judgment made against the powers of the nations throughout the book of Daniel. Their careers are "transgressions reaching a full measure." Porteous notes that God recognizes the pagan nations' tendency to overstep their authority as God's tools.[235] But one can be much bolder and state that Daniel portrays this transgression to be the very nature of world empires, and not merely a tendency.

From the midst of these four kingdoms will arise one who is "skilled in intrigue." This is undoubtedly a reference to Antiochus IV, who created internal division in the Palestinian Jewish community by aligning himself

235. Porteous, *Daniel*, 128.

with certain factions of the people. This division is the reason why this figure is so often associated with intrigue and deceit. His attempts to propagandize the Jewish people by selectively choosing allies and rewarding them is an ancient form of a public relations campaign. One of the results of these policies was the breakup of the Jewish community into factions that remained active into the first century CE.

8:24. Antiochus will grow strong. The Hebrew inserts "but not with his power," which is omitted from English translations on the basis of Greek witnesses; it does not seem to add much here. In this verse, we see once again the notion that Antiochus IV will succeed for a time. The "powerful"/"mighty" that Antiochus destroys is typically taken to refer to the other claimants to the throne who are put out of the way by Antiochus IV.[236] But also in this verse, we have another reference to a group of people/angels that causes some controversy. In the Aramaic section, a group was called the "holy ones," and this is often taken to mean celestial or angelic beings. The phrase in Hebrew is literally "people of the holy ones" (עַם־קְדֹשִׁים 'am-qĕdōšîm), and suggests actual persons in league with the angelic forces. However, if angels are intended here, this would be another buildup to a confrontation with God, as noted in the vision itself.

8:25. The arrogance of this figure is also used often as a reference to Antiochus IV, and his arrogance builds to a desire to do battle with even the "Prince of princes." This is undoubtedly yet another reference to the angelic Michael, who is often referred to in this manner; but it certainly also could be a reference to God. The enigmatic expression "he shall be broken, and not by human hands" recalls God's action of finally destroying the world empires in Daniel 2 (the stone "not cut by human hand"). The image of the prince, then, seems to fit a battle against Michael, after which God intervenes, finally and thoroughly—from "offstage" as it were—breaking Antiochus IV without human hands. God is not often portrayed as taking an active part in Daniel's visions, but is a presiding, commanding presence whose will is carried out by secondary figures. The angelic warriors act, and stones and other things move, but not God.

This lack of human agency in the defeat of Antiochus IV is taken by Collins to be a further reference to the largely nonviolent character of Daniel. "It is apparent from this verse that Daniel does not base his hopes on the success of the armed rebellion of the Maccabees."[237]

8:26-27, The Conclusion and Sealing. Because this vision is for the "end times," Daniel is instructed to seal the vision—that is, to keep it to himself (or to his group?). This aspect of sealing and secrecy is typically understood to be a reference to the fact that this material supposedly remained secret from the time of Daniel (i.e., the end of the Babylonian Empire) until the time of Antiochus IV. We should not presume, however, that this sealing implies that the writers and the readers of this material were, in the first case, a secret sect.[238]

Once again, the impact of the vision on Daniel is repeated, this time mentioning the mental impact it makes on Daniel. He goes about the king's business, knowing that the king's power has already been taken away—the die is cast. Daniel's response to the apocalyptic assurance of the end is not to radically alter his responsibilities, but to know that God is ultimately in control.

---

236. Collins, *Daniel*, 340-41.

237. Collins, *Daniel*, 341. See the excursus on Daniel and nonviolence in chap. 11.

238. See Collins, *The Apocalyptic Vision of the Book of Daniel*, 210-18, who points to their very public responsibilities as teachers of wisdom in chaps. 10–12.

REFLECTIONS

Two major themes of Daniel 8 are worthy of reflection. The first is the use of metaphorical imagery to speak of political realities. The second is the notion of a limitation to the present reality.

Daniel 8:1-27 Reflections

1. Imagery and Political Realities. Rams and goats are spoken of in Daniel 8—animals that fight by knocking horned heads together. The names of rulers—although clearly alluded to—are not used. Instead, the reader is confronted with the simple reality of military-political entities. In today's conventions we use respectfully the names of generals and presidents as the chief actors of history, or we personify the enemy as one man, one woman, as if the destruction of warfare is aimed only at a single individual. But in the book of Daniel, the vision is concerned not with individuals but with the power realities—kingdoms and rulers who "do as they please." There is nothing to honor their imperial designs with respectability, and no cult of the hero. Tyrants and dictators portray themselves as benign paternal figures. Thus one will see an Iraqi dictator holding a child, a Soviet premier listening to the songs of young pioneers, a president playing with his dogs—all while their armies wreak havoc on the lives of other human beings around the world. The book of Daniel portrays world leaders in a different light: They are feuding animals. Berrigan writes: "There is no such thing as a purely earthbound war . . . war on earth is above all a spiritual reality. Whether in ancient Persia or in today's Persian Gulf, war is always and everywhere a demonic assault on God."[239]

The goat, not entirely coincidentally, is particularly ruthless. As this image of the Hellenists is often at odds with popular portrayals of the Greeks as one of the pillars of Western civilization, some comment on the goat is in order. Peter Green, in a short piece ironically entitled "Greek Gifts?" points out that Aristotle considered foreigners as "barbarians" hardly worthy of education. The Greek ideal was to cash in on conquests, not to spread civilization. Hellenistic treatment of Egyptians under the Ptolemies, for example, is recorded with frequent references to Egyptians who complain of mistreatment because of their race and nationality. Certainly, the Greeks influenced art and architecture wherever they went; but the peoples they conquered did not learn Greek culture in schools or by joining Greek societies. Indeed, Hellenism spread among two well-defined categories of persons: local aristocrats who were sent west to be educated, rather like the education of selected Indians in England during British imperial rule, and intelligent collaborators who comprised, at best, merely 2.5 percent of the ruling elite, compared to the otherwise imposing entirety of Greeks on foreign soil. These persons were hired as interpreters, tax collectors, accountants: "the prime motive in such cases was clearly, social and professional ambition."[240] It is interesting to note, then, that with either of these classes of people, one can hardly imagine a less compatible picture of "courtiers" than the ones presented in the early chapters of Daniel (but even here, recall, we are supposed to be reading about the visions of the courtier Daniel). Indeed, one wonders whether the Daniel tales were partly intended to satirize those Jews who served in the foreign militia, those who bowed to every statue and statute that was passed, no matter how compromising it may have been to Jewish faith and authenticity. In such a case, the Daniel stories were written about *ideal* Jewish courtiers in contrast to real ones.

2. How Long? Finally, there is the agonized question in chap. 8: "How long?" The second major theme of this chapter is that the time of wrath is limited and thus the people's suffering is limited as well. This is surely one of the most powerful appeals of apocalyptic literature and apocalyptic movements. Theologically, it is one of the most important messages of the book of Daniel for a modern world. It is the promise of the gospel that darkness will not last forever, that innocence will not be crushed forever, that justice will be had. Surely this is the most important function of "last judgment" scenes, such as the division of the sheep from the goats in Matthew 25 or most powerfully the Lazarus legend in Luke 16:19-31. Judgment scenes clearly are an important coexistent theme with reversal-of-fortune motifs in these materials.

---

239. D. Berrigan, "A Frightful Vision," *The Other Side* (September-October 1990) 37.
240. Green, "Greek Gifts?" 29.

DANIEL 9:1-27, TEXTUAL INTERPRETATION AND ANGELIC REVOLUTION

COMMENTARY

9:1, Chronological Setting. Daniel 9 is set in the first year of Darius, who is identified here as the son of Ahasuerus (usually taken to be Xerxes, who actually reigned after Darius). Clearly, we are again dealing with the book of Daniel's own idiosyncratic chronology, which has Darius "the Mede" following Belshazzar, who reigned during the time of Daniel's visions in chaps. 7–8. Whether important or not, this Darius is mentioned in a favorable light in a number of places in the book of Daniel.

9:2, Daniel and His Liberation Exegesis of "the Books." Daniel is engaged in study of "the books," here making reference to the prophet Jeremiah. It is impossible to say how early some of the writings that eventually became the Hebrew Bible (Old Testament) were used for study and reflection. It is interesting, however, that mention should be made of Jeremiah in this passage. As one of the prophets who made numerous references to the exile, Jeremiah's legacy was clearly of continued interest; witness the number of apocryphal texts that base themselves on some aspect of Jeremiah's, or his scribal associate Baruch's, life. What is clear from this reference in Daniel is the importance of Jeremiah's prophecies about the length of the exile. Jeremiah had predicted that the exile would last seventy years (Jer 25:11-12; 29:10-14). The dates we can be certain of are as follows: The initial surrender of King Jehoiachin and the fall and destruction of Jerusalem occurred in 597 BCE, and the massive deportation of Jewish residents by Nebuchadnezzar took place in 587/586 BCE. Cyrus the Persian conquered Babylon in 539 BCE, and Jewish groups began to return to Palestine, although under Persian control and auspices (see Ezra–Nehemiah, usually dated between 460 and 440 BCE). The Temple was probably rebuilt sometime between 520 and 515 BCE. No matter how you calculate it, Jeremiah was wrong, but his use of "seventy years" had become a tradition by Daniel's time. Diaspora Jews must have contemplated the meaning of such numbers, suggesting other interpretive possibilities. What, then, was the meaning of the "seventy years"? The book of Daniel extends the concept of exile by referring to seventy *weeks* of years—i.e., 490 years. Jeremiah's seventy years, however, was probably not intended to be a precise number in the first place, and may simply have meant an entire lifetime, so that Jeremiah was telling the exiles that *they*, undoubtedly, would never see Palestine again, even if their children would. But because the exile did not end, and a new David was not on the throne, and also because the foreign nations remained in power, later Jewish scholars, mystics, and seers returned to contemplating the possible meanings of Jeremiah's promised end of exile. And this is the question that Daniel is pondering. The significance of the letter in Jeremiah 29, with its appeal for nonviolence,[241] may also be important in the context of Daniel's call to nonviolent resistance to despotism.

Finally, it is important to note that a belief in the *continuous exile* is sociologically significant for the mind-set of the writers of the later sections of Daniel in the Hellenistic period. This is why texts like Jeremiah—which discuss exile and its end, after a necessary period of subordination to foreign power—were so important. The circumstances of subordination and suffering under Antiochus IV Epiphanes were considered part of the entire exile experience that had begun with the Babylonian conquest centuries before. In short, Daniel is engaging in a "liberation exegesis" of Jeremiah in the context of exile.

9:3-19, The Diaspora Prayer for Forgiveness and Deliverance. These verses include a standardized form of prayer or confession and request for deliverance, which can be compared to other texts with similar emphases and content. Before considering

---

241. I have elsewhere tried to argue that the letter to exiles in Jeremiah 29 was not simply a call to obey Babylon, but involved a strategy of resistance and survival as well. See D. Smith, "Jeremiah as Prophet of Nonviolence" *JSOT* 43 (1989) 95-107.

the meaning of this prayer, it is interesting to point out that there is considerable debate over whether this prayer was a late addition to the text. The debate focuses on the propriety of such a prayer in the context of the rest of the chapter.

Porteous and Lacocque note that v. 21 follows v. 2 quite comfortably, and vv. 3 and 20 look like "seams" written in to accommodate the addition of the prayer in vv. 4-19.[242] Lacocque even ventures to suggest that vv. 1-3 and 21-27 were written between 166 and 164 BCE, before the rededication of the Temple by Judas Maccabeus. Furthermore, as Goldingay and Collins note, the Hebrew of the prayer is much more regular and free of Aramaic influences.[243] Finally, many scholars have wondered why a prayer of confession would follow Daniel's seeking of illumination in the context of v. 2. Both Goldingay and Collins, however, while noting these arguments, go on to suggest good reasons why this prayer, even if very traditional and perhaps even pre-existing the book of Daniel in its present form, was added by the author of the rest of chap. 9. In addition the prayer uses vocabulary similar to the rest of chap. 9 (such as "poured out"/"poured" [נתך *nātak*] in vv. 11 and 27; the mention of Jerusalem only in these two places in the entire book of Daniel;

the use of "sin" [חטאת *ḥaṭṭā't*] in vv. 20, 24, and throughout the prayer).

The author of chap. 9 (and much of the later parts of Daniel) included the prayer at this point for good reasons, but not simply because it is a traditional prayer of lament and penitence (influenced by deuteronomistic theology) about the exile's being punishment for Israel's (and especially the kings') sins. The key to the inclusion of this prayer is precisely the relationship between the supposedly "different" parts of the chapter as a whole—that is, the relationship between the prayer and the appearance of the angelic figure Gabriel. In short, Gabriel responds to the prayer. Why would an angelic warrior respond to the prayer of a human being? The answer is in the nature of fasting as an essential aspect of communal prayers for deliverance. These prayers are part of an exilic tradition of calling God to spiritual warfare.

Prayers directed toward God, accompanied by fasting, were clearly a major element of diaspora life and passed into Scripture. Many of these prayers have similar themes, mention similar issues, and are accompanied by similar ritual acts—namely, fasting and often the wearing of sackcloth, traditional garb representing emotional distress.

What is important to note about these prayers for national forgiveness, usually prayed by an individual on behalf of the people as a whole, is that they are usually resorted to in times of great danger or distress.

242. Porteous, *Daniel*, 135; Lacocque, *The Book of Daniel*, 178.
243. Goldingay, *Daniel*, 236-37; Collins, *Daniel*, 347.

❖   ❖   ❖   ❖

EXCURSUS: ON FASTING, COMMUNAL PRAYER, AND HEAVENLY WARFARE

Among the theological developments that characterize post-exilic Israel, one notes a significant idealization of God's ability to deliver miraculously the community that trusts in God. Two aspects of this idealization are the role of communal fasting as a means of inviting God's intervention or protection and a highly stylized prayer of confession and salvation.

Fasting is often used in late biblical literature in combination with another term that is usually translated "to humble oneself" (להתענות *lĕhit'annôt*; see Dan 10:12). Although many instances of fasting in ancient Israelite practice are related to mourning for the dead or to the observance of acts of piety (Gen 50:10; 2 Sam 3:35 // 1 Chr 10:12; 2 Sam 1:12; Jdt 16:24), there is also some evidence of fasting at a time of

Excursus: On Fasting, Communal Prayer, and Heavenly Warfare

natural disaster (Jer 49:28-33; Joel 2:1-5).[244] Finally, fasting is associated with preparation for revelation. Moses ate no bread and drank no water before the theophany in Exod 34:28, and similarly it is implied that Elijah fasted for forty days and nights in 1 Kgs 19:8. The association of fasting with revelations and visions, such as that found in Daniel, whose fasting was rewarded with wisdom, is a recurrent theme in Jewish piety in the intertestamental and early common eras. Fasting as preparation for theophany may have become more explicit as contact with Hellenism became more pronounced; but in any case, passages like the following increased in frequency: "Therefore go away, and sanctify yourself for seven days, and do not eat bread and do not drink water and after this time come to this place and I shall reveal Myself to you" (*2 Bar* 20:5-6*a*; similar passages can be found in *2 Bar* 12:5; 21:1-3; *Apocalypse of Elijah* (1st–4th cent. CE) 1:21; the Greek Apocalypse of Ezra (2nd–9th cent. CE); Testament of Isaac (2nd cent. CE).

But why fast in some of these dangerous circumstances? Was fasting considered to be a special way of calling on God to take action? Both von Rad and Schwally, in their early and influential works on the concept of divine warfare, suggested that fasting was a part of the preparations for warfare in monarchical Israel. Von Rad stated that "the army stood . . . under strict sacral ordinances, they underwent a strict asceticism, the camp was to be ritually pure."[245] Schwally specifically mentioned fasting, and he compared Israelite military fasting to similar practices observed in the late nineteenth-century Native American ethnographic literature.[246] But there is only indirect support in other ancient Near Eastern texts for the practice of fasting before war.[247] Brongers, for example, denies that fasting was a preparatory rite for warfare, stating that "there is in the Old Testament not the slightest evidence of fasting before the battle."[248] Brongers may be correct with regard to pre-exilic texts. Even those texts that do associate fasting with military activity may be explained on other grounds, such as rites of penitence or mourning. In Judg 20:26, for example, a fast is part of the preparations of the sons of Israel before they face the recalcitrant tribe of Benjamin. Was this a case of mourning for the dead or a plea to God to help them? In 1 Samuel 7 there is a gathering at Mizpah to cry out to God, but was the fast an act of penitence or part of the preparations to face a Philistine threat? Not only are these cases ambiguous with regard to the question of military fasting, but virtually all commentators agree that these passages show post-exilic redactional activity as well, suggesting that the association of fasting may have been added later.[249]

But in post-exilic texts, as we have seen, fasting clearly becomes part of preparations for a crisis or even a military encounter. This is mentioned in 1 Macc 3:46, along with the wearing of sackcloth and other mourning practices, when the Maccabean forces gather at Mizpah. Note that the fasting comes after they have assembled for battle, thus the fast was part of the preparation (1 Macc 3:44; see also 2 Macc 13:12). This fasting rite in the Maccabean source was influenced by a uniquely post-exilic theology that allowed for a fast to call for God's miraculous assistance in warfare. No historical basis can be established for the practice of fasting before battles in the First Temple period. I suspect that it did not exist. I would argue that there was a unique post-exilic concept of calling on God to engage in spiritual warfare against the foreign enemy, either unilaterally, as in Daniel, or in assistance of human soldiers, as in Maccabees,

---

244. A. Malamat, "A New Record of Nebuchadnezzar's Palestinian Campaigns," *Israel Exploration Journal* 6 (1956) 246-56; W. Holladay, *Jeremiah* (Minneapolis: Fortress, 1989) 256.
245. G. Von Rad, *Der Heilige Krieg im alten Israel* (Zürich, 1951) 81.
246. F. Schwally, *Semitische Kriegsaltertümer* (Leipzig, 1901) 50-51. See also J. Blemensohn, "The Fast Among North American Indians," *American Anthropologist* 35 (1933) 451-69.
247. The evidence in Near Eastern materials does not appear to establish whether fasting was a part of preparations for war. This does not necessarily mean that it could not have been a uniquely Hebrew practice, but it raises doubts about the pre-exilic period. See S. M. Kang, *Divine War in the Old Testament and in the Ancient Near East* (Berlin: de Gruyter, 1989).
248. H. A. Brongers, "Fasting in Israel in Biblical and Post-Biblical Times," *Oudtestamentische Studien* 20 (1977), 7.
249. See B. Birch, *The Rise of the Israelite Monarchy* (Missoula, Mont.: Scholars Press, 1976) 64-70; J. Blenkinsopp, "Jonathan's Sacrilege 1 Sam 14, 1-16: A Study in Literary History," *CBQ* 26 (1964) 423-49.

Excursus: On Fasting, Communal Prayer, and Heavenly Warfare

and that fasting and/or wearing sackcloth and asking for forgiveness were seen as essential aspects of facing a crisis and calling on God to act on the community's behalf.

There is clear evidence of an increase of days for fasting in the post-exilic period, as mentioned in Zech 7:5 (NRSV): "When you fasted and lamented in the fifth month and in the seventh, for these seventy years, was it for me that you fasted?" Milgrom, for one, does not believe that there were any specific and regular fast days before the exile.[250] If he is correct, then such rites of fasting and prayers for deliverance were a diaspora innovation that became an established aspect of late Jewish piety, especially on those occasions when a great adversary or challenge was about to be faced.

A number of examples of such resorts to fasting can be cited, beginning with Ezra 8:21-23, 31 *b* (NRSV):

> Then I proclaimed a fast there, at the river Ahava, that we might deny ourselves before our God, to seek from him a safe journey for ourselves, our children, and all our possessions. For I was ashamed to ask the king for a band of soldiers and cavalry to protect us against the enemy on our way, since we had told the king that the hand of our God is gracious to all who seek him, but his power and his wrath are against all who forsake him. So we fasted and petitioned our God for this, and he listened to our entreaty . . . the hand of our God was upon us and he delivered us from the hand of the enemy and from ambushes along the way.

Jehoshaphat calls a communal fast to "come to seek help from the LORD" (2 Chr 20:4 NRSV), because the people felt powerless against this "great multitude." Although we are not told the content of the prayers, they are mentioned as an earnest part of the preparation.

Similarly, in the book of Esther all the main elements are present in chap. 4, where Esther prepares to face the Persian monarch on behalf of her people. Here, too, there is a tendency (1) to elaborate on Esther's and the Jews' pious preparations through (2) a gathering of "all" the Jews in reply to Esther's request and (3) prayers clearly rehearsing the power of God to deliver them: "You are LORD of all, and there is no one who can resist you, LORD" (Esth C, 4 NAB). Furthermore, there is the (4) emphasis on Esther's relative powerlessness in facing the king (she is convinced that she may die [Esth 4:16]) and (5) specific mention of the communal fast for Esther.

The association of a communal fast with a request for God to deliver those who cannot help themselves toward deliverance from enemies can also be seen in the Aramaic Papyri from Elephantine. Specifically, there is the letter requesting assistance to rebuild the Jewish religious center. In this letter, fasting and praying are associated with the punishment of the Egyptian enemies:

> And when this had been done [to us], we with our wives and our children were wearing sackcloth and fasting and praying to Yahweh the Lord of Heaven who let us gloat over that Vidranga. The [dogs] removed the fetter from his feet and all goods which he had acquired were lost. And all persons who sought evil for that Temple, all [of them] were killed and we gazed upon them.[251]

The emphasis is clearly on the powerlessness of the Jewish settlement to act for itself, on communal participation in the fast, and on the relationship between their fasting and the destruction of their enemies. In short, it is a further case of what we have already noted in biblical passages.

---

250. J. Milgrom, "Fasting," *Encyclopedia Judaica* (Jerusalem: Qetar 1971) 1191.
251. A. Cowley, *Aramaic Papyri of the Fifth Century B.C.* (Oxford: Clarendon, 1923) 112-14; see also B. Porten and A. Yardeni, *Textbook of Aramaic Documents from Ancient Egypt* (Jerusalem: Hebrew University Press, 1986) 71.

EXCURSUS: ON FASTING, COMMUNAL PRAYER, AND HEAVENLY WARFARE

Finally, fasting is enjoined in the *Testament of Joseph*. In this work, Joseph fasts continually to ask God to assist him in resisting the advances of Potiphar's wife, which clearly had little to do with penitence. In the summary of the work, fasting was recommended as a form of requesting God's assistance that was considered to be especially effective: "You see, my children, how great are the things that patience and prayer with fasting accomplish."[252]

The very phrase "to call on God" is frequently associated with prayers and fasting, and sometimes in the context of warfare or a response to a perceived crisis (see esp. 2 Chr 15:4: "in their distress they turned to Yahweh, God of Israel, and sought him, and he let them find him" [author's trans.]; note also Jer 29:13: "When you search for me, you will find me"; and Pss 40:16; 70:5). Calling on God is used in combination with fasting in the post-exilic period (see 1 Chr 16:11; 2 Chr 20:3-4; Dan 9:3; Jonah 3:5; cf. these references to 2 Chr 11:16, where many nations are seeking/calling God; see also Jer 50:4, "weeping as they seek the LORD their God" [NRSV]; Zech 8:21-22).

In sum, communal fasts to call on divine assistance are clearly an aspect of post-exilic theology. Communal fasting was an act of spiritual warfare that was either requested to assist with or to contrast with human military assistance. Since military action was impossible for a people dominated by foreign powers, the theology of God's assistance to the powerless is a notable development. The presence of such passages as the following one from Baruch suggests that the association of penitence (is fasting presumed here by the wearing of sackcloth?) as a prelude to calling on God's miraculous deliverance was maintained in the late Hellenistic period as well:

> I have taken off the robe of peace
>   and put on sackcloth for my supplication;
> I will cry to the Everlasting all my days.
>
> Take courage, my children, cry to God,
>   and he will deliver you from the power and hand of the enemy.
> (Bar 4:20-21 NRSV)

Such a practice finds its clear ideological context within other post-exilic and even late Hellenistic ideas that were expressed powerfully as late as in the book of Judith: "Your strength does not depend on numbers, nor your might on the powerful. But you are the God of the lowly, helper of the oppressed, upholder of the weak, protector of the forsaken, savior of those without hope" (Jdt 9:11 NRSV).[253]

But *how* is God expected to act on the Jewish community's behalf? Logically, either by miraculous intervention directly or by assisting and empowering a human militia. In the book of Daniel, human military action is rejected, but calling on the angelic hosts of heaven certainly was not. The politics of angelic assistance in circumstances of social or political subordination provides the key to understanding the rise of such concepts in post-exilic Israel. This interpretation of fasting is in contrast to tendencies to see fasting only in the context of asceticism, which is not a major element in exilic/post-exilic Hebrew tradition. It is critical to point out that in post-exilic texts fasting is always associated with a communal call on God to act when the odds seem overwhelming. Fasting was not merely a rite used to ask for forgiveness, but was an act of spiritual warfare that was presumed to have material results—to invite the direct intervention of God.[254]

---

252. "The Testament of Joseph," in J. H. Charlesworth, ed., *The Old Testament Pseudepigrapha*, 2 vols. (New York: Doubleday, 1983) 1:820-21.
253. Such a theology may well be behind such suggestive and controversial New Testament passages as Mark 9:29.
254. For further development of this theme, see "Hebrew Satyagraha: The Politics of Biblical Fasting in the Post-Exilic Period," *Food and Foodways* 5 (1993) 269-92.

As a result of this analysis, we can now turn to the prayer of confession and deliverance in Daniel 9 and compare it to three other prayers of this type, which do not necessarily include the aspect of fasting but do include the standard review of Israelite history that is typical of these confessional prayers. Not all confessional prayers were a communal fast, but the prayers are highly stylized whenever we find them (see 1 Kings 8; Ezra 9; Baruch 1–3). These prayers are separated by a considerable span of time (1 Kings 8 probably from the deuteronomic historian just before, or just after, the exilic events began [c. 600–595 BCE; Baruch, second century BCE; and Ezra, c. 450 BCE]), each exemplifying the maintenance of tradition.[255] The purpose of this comparison is to see the traditional elements in the prayer in Daniel within the context of post-exilic prayers of deliverance.

Obviously, there are a number of important themes in these exilic prayers of deliverance. The prayers convey a profound sense of the history of the relationship between God and God's people. As a part of this history, there is an acknowledgment that the human community has often failed to uphold its part of the relationship. Significantly, then, the affirmation of the law of God is implied in the acceptance of God's "righteous" anger and rejection of the people. It is for the sake of this law, the expression of God in human society, that the prayers plead for God's continued involvement with the Jewish community. Thus, although Jerusalem and national questions are not absent in these prayers, they are decidedly secondary to the overall affirmation of God's law—the ideology of ethical monotheism, despite human failing. It is also important to note that in the context of these prayers, the Mosaic covenant, which involves human responsibility, is pre-eminent over the Abrahamic and Davidic covenants, which consist of direct promises of God without human responsibility. Human failure does *not* lead to an assessment or renegotiation of God's law as unrealistic or antiquated. Rather, the prayer affirms the continued human aspiration to follow God's law and the relationship that this implies.

---

255. These texts can be compared to the Prayer of Azariah (see Commentary on Additions to Daniel) and 1QS 1.22–2.1.

9:20-23, The Angelic Hosts Respond to the Call. In response to the prayer, Daniel receives a visit from an angelic figure: Gabriel. What is interesting about this appearance is that it is not clear that Daniel is having a vision. Daniel has seen Gabriel before in a vision, and that is why Daniel now recognizes him. Is this ambiguity part of a reticence to distinguish between reality and visions? In any case, Gabriel is usually associated with messages and will later explain more to Daniel.

Gabriel declares that he has appeared in direct response to Daniel's prayers. Thus the story serves to verify the importance of prayer as an active engagement with powers relevant to the political and the spiritual condition of the Jewish people. Gabriel has come to explain the realities of power in the world. It is frequently noted that Gabriel says that he was "dispatched" at the beginning of Daniel's prayer, and not at the end. This is often taken to mean that Gabriel's explanations are *not* in answer to Daniel's prayer, but rather provide an answer to Daniel's situation. But surely this comment that Gabriel was sent after Daniel began praying is an emphasis on God's quick response to prayer, and not a comment on the irrelevance of the rest of the prayer (see Isa 65:24; cf. Matt 6:8).

9:24-27, Gabriel's Explanation of the "Seventy Weeks." It is interesting that Gabriel refers to "your" people and "your" city (rather than "the" holy city), which somewhat distances him from this matter. Perhaps this is to be attributed to the fact that Gabriel is not, according to vv. 11-12, the protector of Israel; that is the job of the one identified as Michael. Gabriel, then, is only the messenger.

The interpretation of the "seventy weeks" has, as can be imagined, been a conundrum of the book of Daniel. It appears to be a description of the total amount of time from the beginning of the exile to the end of political subjugation and the restoration of Jewish religious, if not also political, independence. "Seventy weeks" (of years, thus 490 years) refers to the time to put an end to sin, atone for iniquity, bring in righteousness, seal the prophet and his vision, and anoint a most holy place. God reaffirms the relationship with Israel. But what does this time refer to precisely? Scholars have often referred to the

Figure 1: A Selection of Exilic Prayers of Confession and Deliverance

(1) We have sinned, committed iniquity, wickedness, rebellion
    Ezra 9:6-7   1 Kings 8:47   Baruch 2:12   Daniel 9:5a, 9
(2) Turning from the commandments and from justice/ordinances*
    Ezra 9:10   1 Kings 8:58   Baruch 1:18   Daniel 9:5b, 10
(3) Not listening to "your servants the prophets"**
    Ezra 9:11   Baruch 1:21   Daniel 9:6, 10
(4) All Israel is guilty
    Ezra 9:7   1 Kings 8:46   Baruch 1:15   Daniel 9:7a, 11
(5) We are driven into foreign lands, as you threatened†
    Ezra 9:9   1 Kings 8:46   Baruch 2:1-2a   Daniel 9:7b, [12-13]
(6) Mention of Moses, the "servant of God"
    Ezra 9:11ff.   1 Kings 8:53   Baruch 2:20   Daniel 9:13
(7) God is correct in what God has done††
    Ezra 9:13   Baruch 1:15   Daniel 9:14

At this point, the prayers usually turn on the phrase "and now," and go from a review of Israel's confession of guilt to the request for deliverance:

(1) Remember that you brought us from Egypt
                1 Kings 8:51   Baruch 2:11   Daniel 9:15
(2) Please turn aside your righteous anger
    Ezra 9:15   Baruch 2:13   Daniel 9:16
(3) Preserve Jerusalem and the Temple (Holy Mountain)
    Ezra 9:9?   1 Kings 8:44b   Baruch 2:26   Daniel 9:16
(4) We are a disgrace amongst the neighbors (obviously not appropriate to Solomon's prayer)
    Ezra 9:7   Baruch 3:8   Daniel 9:16
(5) Listen, for your sake
    Ezra 9:14   1 Kings 8:28   Baruch 3:2   Daniel 9:17, 19
(6) Look on our situation (open eyes, ears, etc.)
                1 Kings 8:29a   Baruch 3:4-5   Daniel 9:18
(7) Forgive us
    Ezra 9:14   1 Kings 8:30   Daniel 9:19
(8) Act for *your name's sake,* and your people, and your city
    Ezra 9:14   1 Kings 8:29a   Baruch 2:15   Daniel 9:19

* See Deut 17:11, 17, 20.
** This is a particular theme in Jer 26:5; 29:19; 35:15; 44:4-5.
† See Jer 16:15; 23:3; 32:37.
†† God is "right" in *all* ways that God deals with Israel. See John Goldingay, *Daniel*, WBC 30 (Dallas: Word, 1988) 243.

fact that Jeremiah's prophecy was not only associated with 2 Chr 36:18-21 and Leviticus 25–26 so that "seventy weeks" takes on a sabbatical-year association, but also the fact that groups of 70 and 490 became a standard form of referring to periods of history in other apocalyptic works, pre-eminently in *1 Enoch* and *Jubilees*. Such a standardization, then, ought to warn against the idea that these numbers can be matched to actual events.

Some scholars suggest that the first "seven weeks" refers to the time from the destruction of the Temple (586 BCE), to the anointing of another high priest (presumably Joshua, from the book of Zechariah). The book of Daniel never mentions this precise date and is otherwise hardly known for its chronological exactitude. Whatever the beginning point is understood to be, the longer period of sixty-two weeks refers to the period of exile, which extends down to the time of specific interest to the writer of this passage—near the time of Antiochus IV Epiphanes (c. 165 BCE). This period ends with an "anointed one's" being cut off. Is this the murder of Onias III, the high priest who was deposed by Jason and then murdered by Jews in league with Antiochus IV's Hellenization campaigns?

The rest of v. 26 describes the activities of Antiochus, which seem to have cosmic significance ("flood," "war," "desolations"), reminding us of the descriptions of cataclysmic events in other apocalyptic works, especially the book of Revelation.

Verse 27 levels three accusations about the end events. First, Antiochus will make a covenant—presumably the covenant with apostate Jews, mentioned in 1 Macc 1:11. Second, Antiochus will attempt to change the sacrificial observances and rituals of the Temple, and third, in the place of the proper observances there will be an "abomination of desolation." This last element most likely refers to the erection of a pagan altar over the Jewish one, in order to make sacrifices to Zeus Olympus rather than the placing of a statue in the Temple.[256]

In apocalyptic literature, the final dispatch of evil powers is often portrayed as a brief, matter-of-fact end (as in Revelation). Accordingly, the end of the evil rule in Daniel's vision is brief and quick, without detail. This is perhaps for two reasons: It has not taken place as yet, and it is only a promised reality for the future.

256. See Josephus *Antiquities of the Jews* 12.5.4.

REFLECTIONS

Daniel 9 suggests two important theological notions: the important relationship of confession and action, and taking first steps.

1. Confession and Action. In Christian faith and practice there ought to be an integral connection between confession and action—whether that action be directed to mission, to social justice, to peacemaking, or to consciousness-raising. Confession involves the grave awareness that alone we are incapable of anything beyond self-interest and self-promotion. Action that is attempted apart from confession of weakness or failure is either unsuccessful or, even worse, successful by means of using, diminishing, or hurting others. Thus confession is prayer that prepares us not only to listen to God, but also to listen to each other (which is what George Fox called "answering that of God" in each person). Our confessions to others are acknowledgments that we need each other as well as our realization that we need God. The prayer of confession in Daniel 9 is typically communal in nature (note the first-person plural that dominates throughout).

Action, then, must arise from confession as much as from preparation. This is the reason why the Society of Friends (Quakers) insist that "business meetings" are actually meetings for worship, for the conduct of business, and that such monthly, quarterly, or yearly meetings begin with silent waiting on the Spirit of Christ, as does each Sunday morning worship. The ideal, when kept in mind, is to seek God's will in mutual discernment, and not merely a human consensus. The emphasis on Christ as "our Present Teacher" is the basis for our practice as well as for our faith; for a Quaker reader of Daniel 9, there is no difficulty with the fact that Daniel's prayer of confession and request for deliverance result in the receiving of instruction. The beginning of action is realization—not only the realization of what we cannot do on our own, but also the further realization of what is possible under the leading of God's Spirit. The angelic hosts have engaged the battle before us; we rise from silent listening to God and to each other in order to join the battle.

2. Taking First Steps in Discipleship. In Gabriel's reassuring words about the seventy weeks, Daniel learns that the present grim realities will indeed have their predetermined end. To be Christian in the modern world involves two seemingly contradictory notions, two "realities": The ruler of this world will often appear victorious, but the final battle has already been determined—and won. Evil (an entity often not clearly perceived) and its consequences of suffering (all too clearly perceived) will run its course and be struck down. We must not be paralyzed by the enormity of the opponent.

From the message of Daniel (and for Christians Revelation as well), the readers suffering under Hellenistic and then Roman oppression learn to trust that evil and suffering have a predetermined end. This is a powerful doctrine that obviously holds out hope in darkest hours. Despair visits us when the first reality overshadows the second. But we are called to be "adventists" in the radical sense of those who live under the ethics of expectation. Such an ethic will clearly express itself, as the Mennonite statement reads, "in active nonconformity to the world as it is." Nonconformity is the way we begin to take steps in the grim realities of world conflict, the growing population of poor and homeless people, and the distracting escapism of modern Western entertainment industries. We have a most unusual description of such an active nonconformity in the early Christian document the Epistle to Diognetus:

> The difference between Christians and the rest of mankind is not a matter of nationality, or language, or customs . . . they pass their lives in whatever township—Greek or foreign—each man's lot has determined; and conform to ordinary local usage in their clothing, diet, and other habits . . . nevertheless, the organization of their community does exhibit some features that are remarkable, and even surprising. For instance, though they are residents at home in their own countries, their behavior there is more like that of sojourners; they take their full part as citizens, but they also submit to anything and everything as if they were aliens. For them, any foreign country is a motherland, and any motherland is a foreign country . . . though destiny has placed them here in the flesh, they do not live after the flesh, their days are passed on the earth but their citizenship is above in the heavens . . . they show love to all men—and all men persecute them.[257]

To begin to wonder how we as Christians ought to express this nonconformity is the beginning of an ethic of expectation, a radical "adventism" as presumed by the writer of Daniel. How do we live with an expectation that is not yet fully realized? That is Daniel's question—and it is our own. It involves the courage to take first steps in faith. On this theme, an American Quaker legend lights the path. Joseph Hoag was a Vermont Quaker traveling in Knoxville, Tennessee, during Andrew Jackson's campaigns of the War of 1812, before the climactic Battle of New Orleans. Hoag, stopping for a rest at a local inn, had an interesting confrontation with one of Jackson's officers, who wanted to know why Quakers refused to fight. On hearing of Hoag's nonviolent principles, the officer said that, although he too would prefer to live in peace, he would be able to lay down his rifle only when everyone else laid down his armaments as well. Hoag's response has passed into Quaker folklore: "So, then, thou hast a mind to be one of the last men in the world to be good. I have a mind to be one of the first and set the rest an example."

257. Epistle to Diognetus sections 5-6.

DANIEL 10:1–12:13, THE FINAL VISION

COMMENTARY

Daniel 10–12 as a whole comprises the finale to the book, a single visionary experience, although amended by a secondary vision in chap. 12, which itself has a few additional amendments at the end. In fact, chap. 10 is actually a long introduction to the detailed vision of conflict that is elaborated in chap. 11 and part of chap. 12. This involves Daniel's preparations, his response to the visions, and the strengthening of the visionary by the heavenly messenger so that he can see and understand what he is about to experience. Lacocque outlines the vision simply and helpfully as prologue, 10:1–11:2a; revelation, 11:2b–12:4; and epilogue, 12:5-13.[258]

10:1. Chapter 10 begins in the third year of the reign of Cyrus. Once again, attempts to be precise about historical details defy us. But there are a number of particularly interesting aspects to this opening verse. First, Daniel's captive name, "Belteshazzar," is used here, despite the fact that the name was not used in the story of Darius in chap. 6, suggesting that, for the author of chaps. 7–12, the Persians do not necessarily have such a positive image, which will be confirmed. The "word," in any case, concerns "a great conflict/battle."

What is unusual about this introduction is the mention of a "word" coming to Daniel. This is the first occasion for a spoken message in place of a vision; yet as the chapter continues, it is clear that this message is not just an audio message. Is this a fragment of something else? We can only assume that "word" is to be taken as inclusive of the entire experience that follows. What is emphasized, however, is the auditory nature of the visionary experience.

10:2-6. Daniel is "mourning," which is clearly, and frequently, associated with fasting. (That mourning is associated with fasting as an aspect of diaspora faith and practice can be noted in Ezra 10:6; Neh 8:9; Esth 4:3; 9:22; for the significance of fasting, see Commentary on Daniel 9.) In this chapter, however, the mourning fast lasts an unusually long time. Physiological studies have proved that fasting or other forms of extreme dietary practices begin to take a physical and psychological toll within a few days. What is interesting about the time mentioned in these verses is that the time is the twenty-fourth day of the first month of the year; therefore, Daniel is mourning/fasting through Passover, the traditional Jewish celebration of release from captivity. Is this intended to express Daniel's lack of freedom by having him mourn during a time of celebration? If so, Daniel does not mention this significance, but the chronological note in v. 4 hardly allows this detail to pass unnoticed. Finally, we must note that the third year of Cyrus, according to v. 1, would place this event after the first mission of Jews back to Palestine under Sheshbezzar (see Ezra 1). This, too, is passed over by the author of Daniel.

Once again, the reference to Daniel's standing on the bank of the River Tigris (many scholars want to amend this to read "Euphrates") is an aspect of the fasting/mourning activity of Daniel. Daniel has a visionary experience (v. 5), similar at first glance to the image in Nebuchadnezzar's dream (chap. 2). The description of the person who appears to Daniel, however, is considerably different and resembles the descriptions of heavenly envoys in Ezek 9:2-3, 11; 10:2, 6-7:

(a) clothed in linen (Lev 6:10; 16:4—typically associated with priesthood, and thus probably to be understood as a sign of holiness, rather than implying a closer association with the Temple)
(b) belt of gold of Uphaz (Jer 10:9; should be Ophir? 1 Kgs 9:28)
(c) body like beryl (yellow jasper? One of the stones on high priest's breastplate: Exod 28:20; Ezek 28:13)
(d) face like a "vision of lightning" (lightning was in the arsenal of the storm god in the Semitic myth of the storm god vs. the sea god)
(e) eyes like torches of fire
(f) arms and legs like bronze
(g) sounds of words like the sounds of a crowd

As to the identity of the figure, the most obvious suggestion is that it is Gabriel, who will appear later in the vision. The main problem with this identification is that Daniel's reaction seems so different from the other times Gabriel appeared to him. But it is not so different from 8:15-18.[259]

It is instructive to compare this vision with Nebuchadnezzar's dream in chap. 2. First, Nebuchadnezzar saw in his dream a faceless statue, describing only the head. Daniel's vision notes not only the dress (because linen is associated with purity and the priesthood,

---

258. Lacocque, *The Book of Daniel*, 201.

259. Collins further suggests that Daniel 9 is a rough draft for the great vision and allows the identification of the figure as Daniel. See Collins, *Daniel*, 204.

the linen is thus of interest), but also the details of the face and the eyes; most important, Daniel's image speaks. In short, this image lives in a way that Nebuchadnezzar's vision of his kingdom does not. The latter was a lifeless idol.

10:7. Here we have an interesting admission that only Daniel saw these images.[260] We might expect, in a more fantastic description, the idea that many people saw this vision. This lends a certain credibility to those who argue that the basis for some elements of these reports may be actual experiences of Jewish visionaries.[261] What the people did share was a sense of presence and foreboding, which lends authenticity to the report about Daniel's experience, although why the author would choose this device, rather than simply having others see the vision, in order to authenticate the experience is suggestive. This fact alone tends to emphasize the importance of Daniel, whose stature has clearly grown more important in chaps. 7–12 (but see Commentary on 10:11).

The description of Daniel's "trembling" appears very similar to the kind of group religio/psychological experiences of modern charismatic movements (Pentecostal movements, Quakers, Russian Molokons) and Native American spiritual movements, like the Ghost Dance and the Maru cult of the Pomo people of central California.[262] This sign was clearly seen as evidence of a spiritual event, a sense of presence.

10:8-10. The impact of these experiences on Daniel is frequently described in chaps. 7–12. Not only does he seem exhausted and overcome emotionally and physically, but he also feels alone and is without strength. But three times he is lifted up and strengthened for the task of understanding what is to come (vv. 10, 16, 18). In this case, it is the roaring sound of the words that overcomes Daniel, but he is raised to his feet to receive the messenger.

---

260. Collins compares this detail with Acts 9:7, where only Paul sees the vision.

261. One of the most recent proponents of the idea that some apocalyptic reports may come from actual psychological phenomena is Michael Stone, "Apocalyptic: Vision or Hallucination?" *Milla wa-Milla* 14 (1974) 47-56.

262. Blenkinsopp suggests that such a group of ancient "trembler/quakers" can be found in Ezra 9:4; 10:3, 9; and Isaiah 2; 5. See Blenkinsopp, *Ezra–Nehemiah*, 178.

10:11. Daniel is called one who is "greatly beloved" (איש־חמדות *'îš-ḥămûdôt*), and surely these are intended to be comforting words. This phrase may well be the indication of why Daniel would become such a significant figure in Jewish religious folklore. He is no longer a mere Jew who can live and pray like all the others. Now he steps out from the crowd as having a special relationship with God.

10:12. This verse begins with a call to arms: "Fear not!" (cf. Deuteronomy 20, the laws of "Yahweh War"). Daniel has looked to God for strength, and receives the call to arms, and is honored for humbling himself before God. (For the significance of this act, see Excursus "On Fasting, Communal Prayer, and Heavenly Warfare.") God answers Daniel because of his "words" and his sincerity in seeking knowledge. Notice as well that Gabriel refers to the "first day that you set your mind to gain understanding." This is a theme of chap. 9, where Daniel's prayer begins to be answered even before he finishes praying (9:23).

10:13. This verse refers once again to the notion, apparently widespread in some circles of Jewish apocalyptic writing, that the various nations have spiritual counterparts, as Israel has the angel Michael (see Deut 29:26; 32:8-9; see also Ecclus 17:17; *Jub* 15:31-32). The sources of this notion have been debated by scholars, many of whom see its roots in the idea of a heavenly council of celestial beings, perhaps a Jewish attempt to deal with the complexity of gods among the various foreign powers. Such a reaction would seem natural in the Hellenistic period especially, when knowledge of many different peoples and their religious traditions was becoming common throughout the empire. Whatever the source of the idea, its function within Daniel is of particular interest—a heavenly version of the conflicts on earth between the foreign nations and the Jewish people. In this context, the specific mention of a conflict between Michael and Gabriel and the Persian Empire is further evidence that we must not rush to a positive evaluation of the Persian rulers. Keep in mind that the setting of this vision is within the reign of Cyrus, and although this is clearly a fictional account from the perspective of the second century BCE, the combination of this chronological note and the image of struggles with Persia need not be the result of hazy and inaccurate memories of "how good it was" under the Persians. The implication is clearly negative here.

The Persians were, of course, as capable of cruelty as was any other ancient empire, despite their somewhat undeserved reputation for enlightenment.[263] In addition to the discussion in the Introduction, one needs to recall that Cambyses killed over 2,000 people in the siege of Memphis. Darius's destruction of Miletus resulted in most of the males being murdered, and the women and children being led in chains to Susa.[264] Xerxes savagely crushed the Egyptian revolt, confiscating temple lands and increasing the tax burden and upkeep of garrisons, conditions that led to the revolt in the first place. When Xerxes died, both Egyptian and Babylonian sources claimed that his death was due to vengeance over injustices.[265] The biblical witness in Daniel, then, seems more in keeping with these reports than does the idea of Persian benevolence encountered in Ezra–Nehemiah (although even there Ezra mentions in his prayers that the Jews under the Persians are "slaves in our own land" [Neh 9:36]; cf. Ezra 9:8-9).

10:14-19. Gabriel explains to Daniel what is to happen "at the end of days." Throughout this work, various terms are used to describe the events at the end, but it is clear that the "end" is a series of events, rather than one single period of time. Gabriel's announcement of what Daniel is to see once again brings a reaction from Daniel—humility, weakness, and trembling. But the strengthening of the "beloved Daniel" continues, and he is able to carry on. The specific mention of Gabriel's touching his lips is a clear association with Isaiah 6, the call of Isaiah to be a prophet. These call narratives, like Isaiah 6 and Jeremiah 1 (cf. the call of Gideon in Judges 6) seem to be modeled on the call of Moses (Exodus 3) at the burning bush: the initial approach of God, the resistance of the one being called, the reassurance of God to the one called, and then the commission/message. The similarity of this pattern to Daniel's call in the vision is an interesting connection with the prophetic tradition, especially with calls like those of Isaiah and Ezekiel. Like Moses, Daniel protests that he cannot speak, and this brings the final touch from Gabriel that prepares Daniel for what he is about to see. When compared to other prophets, Daniel seems to need more reassurance than most, but this serves to heighten the drama of what he is about to witness. Finally, the relationship between Daniel and the heavenly messengers is also emphasized in this interaction.

The final verse of this call narrative once again repeats the admonition for Daniel not to fear, but to have strength and take courage. Daniel now announces that he is ready to listen. He is, in a sense, prepared for spiritual battle.

10:20–11:2a, The Angelic Battle with the Powers. The theme of struggle against the Persians is repeated in this short identification of who is involved in the actual events that Daniel and his readers perceive. Since the vision was announced in the time of Cyrus, it is logical that Gabriel begins by informing him that the battle against the "powers of the world" has already begun with the struggle against the Persian "prince," after which the battle will shift to a new power, the Greek "prince." The term "prince" (שר *śar*) is used to refer to the celestial beings set over the nations, as Michael is over Israel (here, however, Michael is joined in battle by Gabriel). Heidt, on the other hand, suggests that the term *śar* should be read as the slightly altered "demons" (the change involves a very slight difference in the Hebrew between שרים [*śārîm*] and שדים [*šēdîm*]), which would then relate to Paul's use in 1 Cor 10:20, quoting Deut 32:17 and Ps 106:37.[266]

Note how the Jewish writer of the final vision in chaps. 10–12 takes little comfort in the change of powers from Persian to Greek. There is no consideration here that one world power's policies are better than another's. This is the clear perspective of sufferers throughout history, who may hear the promises of the new regime to "love justice" and "liberate the people at long last"; but

---

263. Daniel L. Smith-Christopher, "Resistance in a 'Culture of Permission,'" in *Truth's Bright Embrace*, ed. F. S. A. Roberts (Newberg, Ore.: George Fox University Press, 1996) 15-38.
264. See Herodotus *The History* 6.22.
265. M. Dandamaev, *A Political History of the Achaemenid Empire* (Leiden: Brill, 1989) 75, 165, 182, 234.

266. W. G. Heidt, *Angelology of the Old Testament* (Washington, D.C.: Catholic University of America Press, 1949).

the Jewish writer knows that the reality is the struggle against the powers of the world. For the writer of Daniel, the rhetoric of the world powers is empty. The writer, then, is not among those who see an opportunity in this change of rulers. Hengel writes:

> Interest in Hellenistic civilization . . . remained predominantly limited to the well-to-do aristocracy of Jerusalem. Intensive economic exploitation and the social unconcernedness of the new masters and their imitators, who were concerned purely with economics, only served to exacerbate the situation of the lower strata of the population.[267]

Combined with the fact that even under the Seleucid rulers estimates are that merely 2.5 percent of the ruling aristocracy and royal appointments were non-Hellenist natives of the conquered lands,[268] we then begin to understand how the writer of Daniel sees world politics as a matter of spiritual warfare.

The "book of truth" is not the same, apparently, as the book of names of Dan 12:1. While the image of these various books is somewhat difficult to unravel, it is significant that we are dealing with the image of books at all; we are clearly in the realm of a literate writer and readership. The use of various books, however, recalls the kind of scribal work that a courtier might do within a foreign court. Like many scholars and students, Daniel is surrounded by, and even dreams about, books!

Finally, in 11:1, it is important to understand the referents. In the first year of Darius, Gabriel stood up to support Michael in his struggle, and was not on the side of Darius the ruler. The support is required, because in 10:21 it was emphasized that Michael stood alone in the battle while Gabriel was with Daniel to explain matters.

11:2b. This passage is quite explicit about the nations being referred to (Persia and Greece), but the names of the particular rulers remain a problem. The three additional kings mentioned are identified as Persian. As Darius is supposed to be Median, the most likely identifications of these Persian kings are Cyrus (560–530 BCE), Xerxes (486–465 BCE), and Artaxerxes (465–424 BCE), since these three are mentioned elsewhere in the Old Testament. Other suggestions have been made as well. If there is an emphasis on attacks on the Greeks, the most likely candidate for the final Persian ruler is Xerxes. But if Xerxes is in mind here, that would mean a long jump to the time of Alexander. Darius III Codomannus (336–330 BCE) was the final Persian ruler before Alexander the Great. It is difficult to count Darius I (522–486 BCE) among the Persian kings in this passage, when this reference in Daniel is usually taken to refer to the Median ruler just before Cyrus, rather than the historical Darius, who claimed the Persian throne after the death of Cambyses (530–522 BCE). What is clear from this passage, however, is the awareness that a succession of Persian kings ruled before the coming of Alexander. The final Persian ruler seems to stand for Persian rulers in general, gathering wealth that leads to megalomania and attacks on other kingdoms.

11:3. The warrior who arises is clearly Alexander the Great. His conquests allow him to do as he pleases, which is the expression of arrogant power that the book of Daniel has used previously.

11:4. This verse essentially repeats elements of the initial dream in chap. 8, which recalled the ram and the goat. Here, Alexander's sudden death in Babylon is recalled, and his empire is divided among his four generals. The use of the phrase "four winds of heaven" is probably not to be taken as a specific reference to the four generals who inherited Alexander's empire (after considerable jockeying for position in the years immediately following Alexander's death). Rather, it is a reference to the four geographical directions, a sense that the empire will be dramatically divided in different directions—a virtual explosion. The two generals that we are most interested in, once the dust has settled in the ancient Near East, are Seleucus, who reigned over much of the former Babylonian/Persian territories, and Ptolemy, who reigned over an expanded Egyptian territory that included Palestine.

11:5-39. These verses deal with the complex history in the relations between the Ptolemies and the Seleucids and the eventual

---

267. M. Hengel, *Judaism and Hellenism* (Philadelphia: Fortress, 1974) 56.
268. F. W. Walbank, *The Hellenistic World* (Cambridge, Mass.: Harvard University Press, 1981) 65.

rise to power of Antiochus IV Epiphanes, the Seleucid ruler who reigned over one of the most significant crises in Jewish life since the Babylonian exile. Scholars often comment that we have in these verses a strikingly accurate portrayal of the events between 301 and 175 BCE. A survey of these verses, therefore, will include historical comments, the likely referents of the enigmatic discussion of the kings of the north and of the south, who are, respectively, the Seleucids and the Ptolemies.

11:5. The king of the south, Ptolemy I Soter (323–283 BCE), reigned in Egypt. The former Alexanderian general Seleucus sought refuge under Ptolemy in his conflict with Antigonus. In 312 BCE, Ptolemy and Seleucus, as allies, soundly defeated Demetrius's son Antigonus at Gaza. After this, Seleucus then moved toward gaining control of the largest portion of Alexander's old regime, the eastern Persian sector, which Seleucus began to rule from Seleucia, near Babylon, in 305 BCE. Syria-Palestine, however, remained under the control of Ptolemy. Ironically, Palestine would become a bone of contention precisely as it had been in earlier centuries, and for precisely the same reason: its strategic location as the land bridge between the two great cultural centers of the ancient Near East, Egypt and Mesopotamia. The history of these two regimes in this period is fraught with complications and intrigue, and some patience is required to understand, even in a general way, the shifting tides in foreign policy. In 281 BCE, Seleucus acquired Asia Minor, and there were conflicts between Antiochus I and Ptolemy II in 280 and 274–271 BCE, and war between Antiochus II and Ptolemy II between 260 and 253 BCE.

11:6. The "alliance" mentioned in this verse is the marriage of Antiochus II Theos (261–246 BCE), a Seleucid, to Berenice, the daughter of Ptolemy II in 252 BCE. This was an attempt to stop the constant conflicts between the two regimes. Antiochus II, however, divorced his first wife, Laodice, in order to seal the political truce with Ptolemy through marriage to Berenice. Antiochus II and Laodice had already produced two sons, Seleucus and Antiochus. When Antiochus eventually left Berenice to reunite with Laodice, however, Laodice sought revenge by poisoning Antiochus II and having Berenice and her sons murdered. This paved the way for Seleucus II Callinicus (the son of Laodice) to assume the throne in Babylon.

11:7-8. The brother of the murdered Berenice became Ptolemy III Euergetes. He attacked the Seleucid realm (in reprisal of the murder of Berenice and her sons) and advanced as far as Babylon. His campaign succeeded in capturing many of the images of gods kept in Babylon, including some important Egyptian idols that were first taken by Cambyses, the Persian ruler, over 250 years earlier. What is notable here is the plunder of warfare, the taking of gods, idols, silver and gold (v. 8). We are once again reminded of the true motivation of military ideology despite all claims to patriotic fervor (or vengeance for the honor of Berenice)—namely, commerce.

11:9-13. Antiochus III the Great (223–187 BCE), one of the two sons of Seleucus II Callinicus, was able to recapture much of the western territories of his empire between 221 and 217 BCE, capturing Seleucia and eventually gaining control of the strategic ports of Tyre and Ptolemais. Verses 10-11 refer to the great battle of Raphia, which was part of Antiochus III's campaign to expand his territory. The battle took place in 217 BCE, and Greek sources tell us that Antiochus III brought 62,000 infantry, 6,000 cavalry, and 102 war elephants, matched against 70,000 infantry, 5,000 cavalry, and 73 elephants of Ptolemy IV. Even though Ptolemy IV was victorious, he settled for peace with Antiochus III (the reference to "being defeated" with regard to Antiochus III). This is undoubtedly the meaning of the reference to "return to his own land" (v. 9). At the same time, there may be a vague memory of a visit of Ptolemy IV to Jerusalem in the enigmatic work entitled 3 Maccabees, a pseudepigraphal work.

Ptolemy IV's army, interestingly, was composed now of a mix of Hellenistic soldiers and a large percentage of native Egyptians. These Egyptians were given a taste of power in this military campaign, and soon the Ptolemies were engaged in putting down revolutionary activity at home, as the Egyptians rose in rebellion in various locations. Despite his "exalted heart," then, Ptolemy would face the forces of Antiochus III again (v. 13).

The peace made between Ptolemy IV and Antiochus III after Antiochus's defeat at Raphia was not a sagacious move for the Egyptian monarch, and it gave time for Antiochus III to consolidate his regime. In 203 BCE, Ptolemy IV died, leaving a six-year-old son to assume power as Ptolemy V. Egypt was actually ruled by the regent Agathocles, who was ruthless and whose oppressive regency led to further revolts within the Egyptian populace. During this time (212–205 BCE), Antiochus was successful in the eastern regions of his empire, and soon he was able to create an alliance with Philip V of Macedonia, in order to attack Ptolemy once again.

11:14. The expressions "sons of the violent ones" of "your own people" appear in a very negative context in Ezek 7:22, referring to the violent sons of righteous people (the righteous are not held morally responsible for their children's actions), and in Jeremiah's reference to the "den of robbers," or "violent ones." Such allusions strongly imply a negative evaluation of those who are portrayed with this term. Was this an indication of Jewish involvement in the earlier insurrections against Ptolemy V? Most scholars consider it to be a reference to the rivalry between the Tobiad family (who sought the leadership of the Temple, the main position of authority in the Judean Jewish communities) and the family of Onias III, the high priest who clearly had Egyptian sympathies. These "lawless" people are identified either as the renegade Oniads who joined with the rival Tobiad faction,[269] or as a pro-Ptolemaic party who "fail/stumble" when General Scopas finally loses Jerusalem.[270]

General Scopas was a Ptolemaic military governor who retook Judea before finally losing it again to Antiochus III in 198 BCE. The "lawless" among the Jews may well have been inspired by a rival visionary faction, similar to the visionary circle responsible for, and responsive to, the visions of Daniel. But this other group (and their vision) is clearly rejected by the writer of Daniel. Many scholars suggest that this is another indication of the nonviolent ethos of Daniel, since the assumption is that the rival vision was acted upon violently and that it ultimately failed.

Perhaps this visionary faction was inspired by some attempt to revive a messianic speculation among the Egyptian Jewish community.

11:15-16. The "well-fortified city" (v. 15) is Sidon, where Scopas retreated after the fall of Jerusalem. At first, Antiochus III received a warm welcome from the Jewish residents of Jerusalem, to which he responded by promising tax relief and support for the temple treasury. It is possible that Jews assisted in the siege against Scopas at Sidon. The result of these events is that Antiochus III takes possession of Jerusalem and Judea, the "beautiful land" (v. 16).

11:17. Antiochus III's growing power led to a series of moves intended to further extend his influence into Egypt. He gave his daughter, Cleopatra (the first of this name), to be married to Ptolemy V. But if his intention was to use his daughter in a plot against the Egyptian regime, the plan failed badly, because Cleopatra was loyal to her new husband, and an alliance was created between Ptolemy V, Cleopatra, and Rome. Even though the opening years of his reign proved dismal, Ptolemy V proved an able monarch.

11:18-19. When Antiochus III moved west to Greece, "his face to the coastlands,"[271] he was defeated in 191 BCE by the Romans at the pass of Thermopylae, and again at Magnesia in Asia Minor in 190 BCE. As a result, Antiochis III was charged with massive tribute payments to Rome (15,000 talents of silver and all possessions west of Taurus) and was ordered to cease his interests in Egyptian land. Furthermore, one of his sons, Antiochus IV, was taken to Rome as a hostage against further advances. Antiochus III began to rob temples within his domain in order to raise the massive tribute payments, and it was while engaged in the robbery of a temple of Bel at Elymais (in a distant area of Elam) that he was assassinated in 187 BCE. Seleucus IV succeeded him, cursed with his father's massive tribute debts.

11:20. A tribute/tax collector, undoubtedly Heliodorus, arrived in Palestine in order to raise the necessary tribute funds. Seleucus IV, however, was killed in a plot involving Heliodorus. This reference to the tax collector in Jewish territories is a most interesting point, a memory of the kind of contact Jews

---

269. See Goldingay, *Daniel*.
270. See Josephus *Antiquities of the Jews* 12.3.

271. Collins, *Daniel*, 365.

had with the officials of the realm as opposed to the fictional contact of the courtier stories in Daniel 1–6. Such contact with officials like tax collectors represents the most likely historical reality for most of the Jewish people, who were, after all, merely sources of revenue rather than exalted workers in the emperor's palace.

11:21. This verse arrives at the focus of sustained attention in the great vision: the rise of Antiochus IV Epiphanes (175–163 BCE). The book of Daniel's emphasis on the nature of Antiochus IV is that he is deceitful and works in "quiet." Psalm 12 warns of deceit as false propaganda:

> They utter lies to each other
>   with flattering lips and a double heart
>   they speak.
> May the LORD cut off all flattering lips,
>   the tongue that makes great boasts.
> (Ps 12:2-3 NRSV)

This deceitfulness leads to the despoiling of the poor, according to Ps 12:5, "Because the poor are despoiled, because the needy groan, I will now rise up, says the LORD." Isaiah 30:9-11 equates deceit with faithlessness among the people:

> For they are a rebellious people,
>   faithless children,
> children who will not hear
>   the instruction of the LORD;
> who says to the seers, "Do not see";
>   and to the prophets, "Do not prophesy
>   to us what is right;
> speak to us smooth things,
>   prophesy illusions,
> leave the way, turn aside from the path,
>   let us hear no more about the Holy
>   One of Israel." (NRSV)

The rise to power of Antiochus IV is surrounded by intrigue. He is at least implicated in the death of Seleucus IV, but most certainly was responsible for the death of rivals to power, such as the son of Seleucus IV, who ruled for a time as co-regent with Antiochus IV.

11:22-23. Antiochus IV will be victorious in his battles for consolidation of power. But he will be deeply involved in lining up supporters from within the Jewish community as well. In the description of his destructive acts is a reference to the fall of a "prince of the covenant." This may be a reference to the same figure in 9:26, who is a (false?) leader from among the Jewish people. However, most scholars consider it to refer to the removal of Onias III as high priest. Antiochus IV is able to win the support of the new high priest, Jason, and of the Tobiad family, of whom Jason is a member. The Tobiads were descendants of Ammonites who married into power with the foreign regime; one of their descendants, Joseph, would become a well-known and influential tax collector in the Ptolemaic regime (221–198 BCE). Those in alliance with the Tobiads may well be the "small party" noted in v. 23, referring to an alliance with some of the Jewish people that created factions and dissensions.

11:24. In quiet, Antiochus comes into the land and lavishes on a "small party" plunder, spoil, and wealth. "Plunder" (בזה *bizzâ*) is found in many late sources (see 2 Chr 14:13; Ezra 9:7; Esth 9:10, 15-16). In its usage in this verse, the term refers to things taken from conquered peoples after a battle, usually in punishment for evil done by or to the Jewish nation. "Spoil" (שלל *šālāl*) is a term used in Josh 7:21 to refer to the goods taken by Achan, which caused so much grief for the early Jewish nation. "Wealth" does not necessarily have a military association, although it is used as such in Genesis 14. Ordinarily, it is used to refer to goods taken on journeys, as in Ezra 1:4, 6 and 8:21. The point here is that this wealth is the spoils of war, and it is given to the "small party" of Jews who align themselves with the Hellenizing portion of the leadership. Thus there appears to be strong condemnation of those who would accept these things, obtained through the wars of the deceitful ruler Antiochus IV.

11:25-27. The history of Antiochus's designs against Egypt is, once again, somewhat complex. When Ptolemy V died in 181 BCE, his young son became Ptolemy VI Philometor. Antiochus IV's sister, Cleopatra, was regent during the youth of Ptolemy Philometor. She died in 176 BCE, leaving the leadership in the hands of the ambitious and scheming courtiers Eulaeus and Lenaeus. They incited political unrest against Antiochus IV, prompting him to invade Egyptian territory. Those who plot against the northern ruler are these two who "eat of the royal food" (v. 26, author's trans.). The term translated "royal food" is a Persian loan word (the same term appears in Daniel 1 in reference to the food served to Daniel and the others).

Antiochus and Ptolemy attempt to make peace (v. 27). They "sit at one table and exchange lies," an eloquent evaluation by the writer of the sincerity of these peace negotiations—but also closely tied to the notion that these negotiations were intended, according to the writer, to avert what has already been determined by God. This treaty will fail.

11:28. The reference to the holy covenant may mean that Antiochus IV will continue his assault on the traditional Jewish parties of Palestine who are represented in the editor/writer of this material. It could also mean that he will not observe the "holy covenant"—e.g., treaty—formed in the previous verses. Most scholars, however, believe that a "holy covenant" must mean that Antiochus IV directed an assault on the Temple, as suggested in 1 Macc 1:20. This is the beginning, then, of the serious oppression of the Jews in Judea.

11:29-30. Antiochus invades Egypt once again. "Kittim" is taken to be a reference to Rome, to those forces who come from the western areas of the Mediterranean Sea. They are represented by the term "ships of Kittim" (although the Hebrew phrase ציים כתים [ṣiyyîm kittîm] could be read "beasts of Kittim," which may carry on some of the symbolism of chaps. 7–8; for ṣiyyîm as "beast," see Isa 13:21; 23:13; 34:14; Jer 50:39). Rome certainly did come to the aid of the co-regents Ptolemy Philometor and Ptolemy Euergetes, and demanded that Antiochus withdraw. Collins points to the humiliation of Antiochus, the "day of Eleusis," noted in a variety of classical sources.[272] The text suggests, however, that the result of this humiliation is that Antiochus unleashes considerable anger toward the Jewish people and their religion (cf. Ptolemy's rage toward the Jews in 3 Maccabees). There is a reference here to apostate Jews, "those who forsake" the covenant. This is to be noted also in Ezra 8, where God's wrath is against "those who forsake the covenant."

Persecutions and Divisions Among the Jews. 11:31. Here we have the clearest references to the events during the reign of Antiochus IV Epiphanes. Although there is some doubt as to who is really responsible for the attack on the Jewish cult in Jerusalem, the book of Daniel clearly lays the blame on the deceitful Antiochus, as well as those who went along with him.

Recent scholarship has emphasized that Antiochus's policies toward the Jews arose partly from his own imperial ambitions and were partly in support of Hellenizing elements within the Jewish population that called for modernization in the first place and the competition between Jason and Menelaus for the position of high priest, each offering money for the privilege. Certainly financial rewards were possible for those who entered more fully into the world economy created by Hellenistic conquests. It would certainly also be tempting for some Jews to abandon their religious scruples about treatment of the poor and advance toward the more luxurious and uncaring attitudes of the Greek elite.

The resulting policies, agreed on by the Jewish innovators and Antiochus's imperial support, include the occupation and profaning of the Temple, the abolishing of the burnt sacrifice, and the setting up of the "desolating abomination." It is very probable that one of Antiochus's actions was to garrison troops in Jerusalem, which necessitated the creation of a citadel to quarter the Greek troops.[273] It was placed near the temple mount. The Temple, then, would be transformed to serve the religious symbolism of the occupying troops. The Hebrew terms typically translated in English as "abomination that desolates" (השקוץ משומם haššiqqûṣ měšômēm) are often seen as a play on words with the name of the god to whom the new altar was dedicated: Baal Shamem. This god was honored throughout northern Syria and Phoenicia, and was typically seen as the equivalent of Zeus Olympios; both terms translate roughly as "God Most High." What actually was placed in the Temple is disputed. While it is tempting to insist that a statue or image of the god was set up on the altar in the Jerusalem Temple (especially noting the prominence of images in Daniel 2–3), it is likely that a new

---

272. Collins, *Daniel*, 384 and n. 134. For classical sources, see Polybius 29.27; Diodorus Siculus 31.2.

273. Smith, "Hellenization."

altar was built over the existing one, thus desecrating it, in order to be used for Baal Shamem.

11:32. This verse creates a clear distinction between the Jews who have become "friends" of the king and those who remain loyal to God. An important strategy of the Hellenistic rulers was to make allies of the most powerful members of conquered peoples by purchasing their loyalty. The ones who do remain loyal to God, interestingly, not only will stand firm, but also will "take action." Certainly these are the people with whom the writers and readers of Daniel identified, which will become more evident in the verse that follows.

11:33. The righteous are described in Hebrew as "the wise ones" (משׂכילים *maśkîlîm*) who will teach "the many" (רבים *rabbîm*).[274] The "action" taken by these wise ones is education; they are the leaders of the resistance, advising others to resist. The persecution of the wise ones includes death by "sword and flame" and "captivity and plunder." The sword represents policing power. The flame certainly recalls the form of capital punishment noted in Daniel 3, but it is also possibly a reference to the destruction of dwellings. Captivity is likely a reference to the current status of the Jewish population, or perhaps even to slavery, since prisons were not a significant institution at this time. Plunder most likely is the massive taxation that the Jewish people suffered under a succession of regimes.

11:34. This verse has incited a heated debate among commentators, since Collins had already focused attention on it in his early work on Daniel.[275] The meaning and implications of "little help" are pursued in the Excursus "Daniel and Nonviolence."

---

274. For this latter group, "the many," Collins reads "the common people," although this is interpretation as much as translation. See Collins, *Daniel*, 367.

275. Collins, *The Apocalyptic Visions of the Book of Daniel*.

❖ ❖ ❖ ❖

EXCURSUS: DANIEL AND NONVIOLENCE

The context for virtually all of the stories of Daniel 1–6 is that of nonviolent resistance to foreign political authority. The success of the Jewish courtiers in the foreign court comes from their spiritual strength and their courage, and not from their weaponry. Indeed, the defeat of Nebuchadnezzar by the "stone" that was formed by no human hand was a significant further indication of this spirit of resistance without arms (see Commentary on 2:39-45).

Many scholars believe that Dan 11:34 clearly reveals the writer of Daniel's attitude toward the violent Maccabean resistance, which was gaining ground at the same time as the events described in Daniel 7–12. The Maccabean resistance is described in Dan 11:34 as "little help." Despite some scholarly protest that little help is still at least *some* help (and is not necessarily a negative judgment), this "little help" is in the context of "those who join insincerely," and thus both groups are to be seen negatively. In other words, 11:34 compares the "little help" to another useless category: those who join the wise ones without full sincerity.

This passage is written, therefore, in the same spirit as other passages that display a contemptuous attitude toward the "violent ones" (see 11:14). These texts are further evidence of the nonviolent orientation of Daniel's visionary attitude to foreign power. The book of Daniel *does* call for resistance, but nonviolent resistance. Lebram agrees: "The principles of the pious man of the Apocalypse consist in the rejection of all violence, particularly of the implementation of the kingdom of God by force."[276]

---

276. J. Lebram, "The Piety of Apocalyptic," in D. Hellholm, *Apocalypticism in the Mediterranean World* (Tübingen: Mohr, 1983) 138.

Excursus: Daniel and Nonviolence

Goldingay, on the other hand, dismisses such a notion on the basis that most scholars assume this vision to be set *before* the Maccabean resistance was finally successful in liberating Jerusalem.[277] Presumably, then, the visionary behind Daniel would have abandoned such pacifistic notions when he saw how violence was so effective. Goldingay's assumption here that effectiveness was the measure of faithfulness can be criticized not only on political and philosophical grounds,[278] but also on textual grounds. Collins, for instance, cites other examples of the more nonviolent orientation in post-exilic, Hellenistic literature, such as the stories of Taxo in the *Testament of Moses*.[279] One can further cite the patient resistance of faith exemplified by Joseph in the Testament of the Twelve Patriarchs: "And if anyone wishes to do you harm, you should pray for him, along with doing good, and you will be rescued by the Lord from every evil."[280] Certainly, if Ginsberg was correct that the scriptural model for the "wise ones" in Daniel 11 was the suffering servant of Isa 52:13–53:12, there is even further support for this notion.[281] Ginsberg had argued that the very term "the wise," used in Daniel, is taken from Isa 52:13, "My servant will act wisely," and that the notion of the "wise" in Daniel who make many understand their cause, and cause many people to act righteously, was borrowed from the descriptions of the suffering servant in Second Isaiah. That at least some Hellenistic Jews were advocating a nonviolent approach is clear. Later Pharisaic aversion to killing is widely documented for the time of early rabbinic Judaism,[282] contemporary to the early nonviolence of Jesus and Christianity, particularly noted in the nonviolent teachings of Rabbi Yochanon Ben Zakkai.[283]

It could be argued that in the context of exile, *only* nonviolent resistance is possible. While this would suggest that Daniel's call to nonviolent resistance is not necessarily a principled rejection of all violence (a kind of ancient Hebrew pacifism), the book still insists at the very least that nonviolent resistance is effective and is based on spiritual values of allegiance to the sovereignty of God. Further, the book of Daniel never suggests that its recommended forms of resistance are only interim ethics until a time when Jews will once again be a world power. If anything, this interim period will end with the coming of the reign of God.

In the light of this, how to defeat one's enemies is a serious question in late post-exilic literature. Conquest was always an option—as in the Maccabean movement. But transformation (if not full conversion) was another option; Jonah provides an example, as does Isaiah 19 and particularly Isaiah 2 (nations' "learning the ways of God," and, therefore, not learning war anymore, which is accompanied by a universal destruction of weapons), and perhaps less certainly the story of Ruth. The message of Daniel 1–6, however, is certainly that enemies are conquered by transformation of character and behavior.

Confusion with anemic, liberal notions of pacifism is a serious exegetical block to appreciating fully the models of nonviolence in apocalyptic texts like Daniel 7–12, which presume the concept of spiritual warfare. The writers of these texts are not passive, nor are they averse to using militant language (the latter being a particular difficulty for modern interpreters). Modern Christian pacifists may be embarrassed by the militant language of Jesus and Paul (calling on "legions of angels," "bringing swords,"

---

277. Goldingay, *Daniel*, 303.
278. Goldingay's criticism of reading nonviolence in Daniel clearly involves the extra-textual assumptions that nonviolence is not an effective means of resistance, that violence is obviously the more effective means of achieving liberation, and that it is a very modern idea for some to try to "read back" into ancient sources. All points, it needs hardly be said, are at the very least debatable.
279. See also J. Licht, "Taxo, or the Apcalyptic Doctrine of Vengeance," *JJS* 12 (1961) 95-103.
280. Test. Joseph 18:2, in J. H. Charlesworth, ed., *Old Testament Pseudepigrapha* (Garden City, N.Y.: Doubleday, 1983) 823. See also Walter Harrelson, "Patient Love in the Testament of Joseph," *Perspectives in Religious Studies* 4 (1977) 4-13.
281. H. L. Ginsberg, "The Oldest Interpretation of the Suffering Servant," *VT* 3 (1953) 400-404. For Zerbe this is the most convincing argument in the otherwise highly skeptical review of the entire question of Daniel and nonviolence. G. Zerbe, "'Pacifism' and 'Passive Resistance' in Apocalyptic Writings: A Critical Evaluation," in J. H. Charlesworth and C. A. Evans, *The Pseudepigrapha and Early Biblical Interpretation* (Sheffield: JSOT, 1993) 65-95.
282. See L. Finkelstein, *The Pharisees* (Philadelphia: Jewish Publication Society, 1940) 286-91.
283. Emphasized most clearly in J. Neusner, *A Life of Rabban Yohanan Ben Zakkai* (Leiden: E. J. Brill, 1962), and *Development of a Legend: Studies in the Traditions Concerning Rabban Yohanan Ben Zakkai* (Leiden: E. J. Brill, 1970). See also S. Schwarzschild, "Shalom," *Confrontation* (1981) 166-76.

comparing faith to swords, armor, shields, etc.), but the use of such imagery indicates the writer's seriousness and the intensity of the resistance called for. Such imagery is also, inevitably, an ironic rejection of actual swords in favor of the more powerful spiritual ones. But "spiritual weapons" are to be wielded in a real world. The call to the "wise" in Daniel is clearly a call to a form of resistance that is not so removed from worldly realities that it does not engender material, political consequences, such as the reply of the enemies' "sword and flame . . . captivity and plunder" (Dan 11:33 NRSV).

Although Hellenistic texts may not have a fully developed condemnation of violent resistance similar to the later teachings of Jesus, it is clear that their calls for resistance apart from violence provide an important step in this direction. Lest we dismiss even the possibility that the writers of Daniel maintained a principled rejection of violence, we need to remind ourselves that other post-exilic writers were beginning to envision an era without warfare or domination of others, such as the post-exilic visions of Isa 2:2-4 and 19:22-25. See also *1 Enoch* 52:7-9, a work not otherwise noted for irenic tendencies, which also looks to an era when the breastplate will no longer be worn and iron, used to make weapons, will be taken away by God. We know from the study of visions that such hopes for the future cannot easily be dismissed, since the content of such utopian visions can reflect expressions of contemporary ethical beliefs.

Given all the theological/ethical possibilities raised by post-exilic discussions of foreigners, enemies, transformation, future peaceful disarmament, and resistance in foreign lands, to read Dan 11:34 as a further condemnation of the Maccabean "option" is hardly stretching historical credibility.[284]

---

[284]. See Daniel L. Smith-Christopher, "Between Ezra and Isaiah: Exclusion, Transformation, and Inclusion of the 'Foreigners' in Post-Exilic Biblical Theology," in M. Brett, ed., *Ethnicity and the Bible* (Leiden: E. J. Brill, 1996) 117-42.

11:35. For the wise, and for those who listen to them, martyrdom is a reality. The persecution of the wise makes them "refined," "purified," and cleansed ("to whiten"). This portrayal of the faithful is common in the exilic community.

Smelting and refining are often used in the literal sense of the production of metals, especially concerning the creation of idols (see Isa 40:19; 41:7; 46:6). But when used figuratively, these words can mean to "test" someone (see Ps 17:3); the figurative use of smelting as a test is explicit in Jer 6:29: "In vain the refining goes on, for the wicked are not removed" (see also Jer 9:6: "I will now refine and test them, for what else can I do with my sinful people?"). The trials of exile and conquest are often seen as God's testing of the people, as in Zech 13:9: "I will put this third into the fire, /refine them as one refines silver . . . and I will answer them. I will say, 'They are my people'" (NRSV); and Isa 48:10: "I have refined you . . . I have tested you in the furnace of adversity" (NRSV). The adversity of the "wise," therefore, is part of their particular selection by God.

The Impieties of the Greek Ruler. 11:36. In this section, we find some interesting comments about the religious attitudes of Antiochus IV. The king will act as he pleases, and this hubris includes the claim to near divinity. Associating themselves with cults of emperor worship was typical for Hellenistic rulers, so it was hardly unique of Antiochus IV. The title "Epiphanes" ("God manifest"), taken by Antiochus IV, may represent a perceived attitude on his part, and it would have been particularly offensive to the Jews. It is all the more offensive because of Antiochus's intrusion into the internal affairs of the Jewish religion—his intrigue in creating divisions within the Jewish community by buying and selling the high priesthood. The reference to the "God of gods" is an unusual reference to the Jewish God, but is the only possible implication in this verse. On the other hand, the "period of wrath" may refer to God's wrath;

it is used elsewhere in the book of Daniel to refer to the wrath of the foreign powers.

11:37. What is particularly interesting about this passage is the comment on Hellenistic religious practices by a Jewish observer. That Antiochus IV did not respect the gods of his ancestors is here apparently meant to be a criticism, indicating the level of sophistication of the writer of the visions. The writer lives in an obviously cosmopolitan world, in which the diversities of religious expressions hold some fascination for him. One can hardly imagine an earlier Jewish writer commenting on whether a particular practitioner of Canaanite ritual was "orthodox" or "heretical" in their Canaanite practice. Here, the implication points to impiety—even in Antiochus's own context and on his terms!

The expression "the one beloved by women" is probably a reference to a cult of Tammuz. Tammuz was an ancient Near Eastern deity particularly revered in a female cult (see Ezek 8:14, where Jewish women are implicated as having participated in this cult).

Antiochus's impieties toward his own traditional religious ways are paralleled, or perhaps pre-eminently represented, in his attacks on the God of gods as well as on the gods of his ancestors. This could be mistaken for monolatry—the worship of one god, without rejecting the idea that other gods may also exist—but the intention is to paint a picture of general impiety and disrespect.

11:38. The god that the visionary of Daniel 10–12 associates with Antiochus IV carries the interesting title "God of fortresses." The fortress refers, undoubtedly, to the citadel established in Jerusalem for the quartering of troops. It was associated with the abomination of desolation in the Temple. Collins has a particularly interesting discussion of this term, calling it "a derisive title, based on its association with the hated Akra, the garrison established by Antiochus in the City of David."[285] In other words, Antiochus associates religion with power based on the military, and he showers on this new form of religious expression the spoils of such power: gold and silver and precious stones. The passage implies a derision of the "loyalty" that money can buy from Antiochus's officials, who are rewarded handsomely. The writer paints a compelling picture of corruption at high levels because of economic gain. Walbank notes the spread of money after Alexander's campaigns in the east—and especially the fact that control of a city was the goal of this purchased loyalty.[286] Green points out that those natives who "went Greek" to seek acceptance were clearly motivated by "social and professional ambition."[287] The garrison is the prime symbol, then, of Antiochus's "reforms" and the ambitions of his Jewish compatriots. Hengel writes that the spirit of Greece was first encountered in the East not by the achievements of philosophy or art, but by its "perfected, superior technique of war."[288] A "god of the fortress" would be a bitter term for a false form of piety that is enforced by the sword rather than by conviction.

11:39. This verse further explicates the ambitious motivation of those who align themselves with power. Hengel points out that apostates were typically given the land dispossessed from the conquered peoples, who were seen as a threat to the state, and that these lands were often worked by semi-slaves (cf. 1 Macc 9:23ff.).[289] The worries of the exiles that they would lose their land (Ezek 11:14-18; 33:23-27) in the Babylonian exile suggests that this was a long-standing practice and a sensitive intra-communal issue throughout the period of foreign rule.

11:40-45, The End of Antiochus. Verse 40 begins the section that goes beyond prophecy that is based on known events. Here we are dealing with speculative material, most of which did not "come to pass," as here predicted. In v. 40, Antiochus IV is represented as overextending himself in a campaign against the south—Egypt. But there is no further record of Antiochus IV in Egypt; in fact, he died in the east during a campaign. In this new battle, great emphasis is placed on the amount of technology thrown into the fray—cavalry, chariots, and ships. Antiochus is described almost in the terms of a new Alexander—passing through nations "like a flood." The implication is that this is a time of building power. In v. 41, he brings his war machine into Judea once again, and many thousands of people are killed. A note on the

---

285. Collins, *Daniel*, 388.

286. Walbank, *The Hellenistic World*, 65 160-61.
287. Green, "Greek Gifts?" 29.
288. Hengel, *Judaism and Hellenism*, 12.
289. Hengel, *Judaism and Hellenism*, 12.

wide extent of the battle includes those who will be spared: the Edomites, the Moabites, and some from the Ammonites. Presumably, they are spared because these three archaic nations once again conspire with the aggressor against the Jewish people. In v. 42, Antiochus's reach extends even into Egypt. Note here that Egypt is named explicitly and that there are references to far-flung peoples of Libya and Ethiopia ("Cush"). The riches of war and command are emphasized: gold and silver and the apparent loyalty of nations. When he finally overextends himself (v. 44), he meets his end; typical of apocalyptic battles, it is brief, quick, and anti-climactic. He will die alone, despite having conquered so many nations. There is no one to help him—the ignoble end of a ravenous emperor. Alexander seems a fitting model here as well.

This section reads as a massive buildup that parallels in an interesting way the buildup in chap. 8, which resulted in attacks against the very stars of heaven. And then it is over. The buildup to a final end is a form familiar in the book of Revelation as well. In short, vv. 40-45 follow apocalyptic style, rather than historical events, toward a final crisis.

12:1-13, The Angels and the Nations at War. Chapter 12 consists of two main sections: A final note on the great vision of chaps. 10–12 (12:1-4) and an additional vision of the two figures on the riverbank, which seems to act as an epilogue to the book as a whole (12:5-13).

12:1. We are now reintroduced to Michael, whom the writer left in battle with the Persian and Greek forces (10:21–11:1). Michael is said to "arise," or perhaps to "stand" in the sense of standing before a judicial hearing, which seems warranted by the judgment that follows. Michael is called on because there is to be a time of great distress for the people as a whole, and Michael is meant to be a comforting presence. But most important, the time of great anguish is to be seen as the time of the deliverance of Israel. The obvious relevence of this idea to those who suffer stands without further comment.

Those who are "found written in the book" will survive. The concept of names written in a book for future judgment is a well-known biblical theme (see Ps 69:28; Isa 4:3; Mal 3:16-18) that is carried into the New Testament book of Revelation.

12:2. Historically and theologically, this verse is one of the most important in the entire book of Daniel because of its direct reference to resurrection. Many scholars have speculated that it is because of this reference that Daniel as a work was included in the Hebrew Bible canon by the rabbis in the first centuries of the common era, who affirmed the belief in resurrection as much as did Jesus of Nazareth. But at the same time, a sense of judgment and punishment is also evident here, giving rise to the notion of a final separation, or critical judgment, the good and the evil in the final days (cf. Matt 25:31-46, where the imagery of sheep and goats was clearly influenced by apocalyptic language).

Daniel's reference to resurrection is reminiscent of Isa 26:19: "O dwellers in the dust, awake and sing for joy!" (NRSV). It seems similar also to ideas about reanimation in Ezekiel 37. But it is further emphasized in Dan 12:2 that not all will rise in resurrection. Those who do will look forward to "everlasting life"—a notion that has passed into both rabbinic and Christian theological speculation. As many scholars have shown, this verse in Daniel is the only clear reference to the idea of resurrection and everlasting life (and punishment) throughout the Hebrew Bible. It is also found in roughly contemporary sections of *1 Enoch,* but like the idea of angels, is still a fluid notion that takes different forms in different contexts.[290]

12:3. This verse contains an affirmation of the wise, who were praised for their loyalty to God in 11:31-34, with an emphasis on the brightness of their glory. Light and images of light have served as the main symbol of righteousness throughout the book of Daniel, and this reward awaits those who are righteous. That the "righteous of the people" are equated with stars is once again a reference to a belief in stars as physical beings (see Commentary on 8:10-11).

12:4. The great vision concludes with an emphasis on Daniel's keeping secret what he has seen and understood. That secrecy must be maintained is emphasized because evil will increase (translating as "evil"

---

290. Matt 25:31-46 is a development along the lines pursued by Paul's interesting speculations about the nature of the resurrection body.

[הרעת *hārā'ōt*] rather than "knowledge" [הדעת *haddā'at*], two words that look very similar in the Hebrew text). Knowledge is power; thus knowledge of these events would be a comfort to those who seek to be strong in their faith and not "run back and forth." There is an emphasis as well on the avoidance of confusion, which is what is sought through knowledge provided by the wise.

The Epilogue to Daniel: The Two Figures on the Riverside. 12:5. This verse begins as an addition to the previous vision. Daniel is seeing something more, even after he has been asked to seal and keep secret what he has seen in v. 4. The location of this latter vision is clearly stated, once again, as taking place on a riverbank. The two figures stand on opposite banks of the river.

12:6. The first figure wants to know the same thing that Daniel (and, undoubtedly, the writer of this epilogue) wants to know—namely, the time when these things will come to pass. Note the reference again to linen, the garment of holiness as noted above in reference to the appearance of Gabriel (see Commentary on chap. 10). This one "clothed in linen" thus is a symbol of holiness, and may well represent the heavenly messenger, while the other is a figure like Daniel himself, or is Daniel himself, which is how the Greek version reads (note that it is Daniel who asks the follow-up question in v. 8). If this is a conversation between two angelic figures, then it suggests that these angels are concerned about the events that have been described. The giving of information associates Gabriel even more with this figure clothed in linen.

12:7. The answer given by the messenger angel (Gabriel?) is interesting: The end time will be "a time, and a time, and a half time," which is a repetition of 7:25. Both passages seem somewhat reminiscent of the words written on the wall for Belshazzar: "MENE, MENE, AND PARSIN" (but not including "TEKEL," which makes this comparison far from exact).

There is a reference to the "shattering of the power of the holy people," once again a collective reference to the entire period of suffering that has been seen in chaps. 10–12. On this, Collins suggests the reading "at the end of the power of the shatterer of the holy people."[291] Either version refers to the same reality, however: the end of the persecution by Antiochus IV.

12:8-9. The narrative returns to the first person, and now it is clearly Daniel who is speaking to the one clothed in linen. Daniel appears to request more information—a precise time (v. 8). It is interesting that the answer is not direct. Rather, Daniel is told to go his way (v. 9). In Hebrew, the two words for "closed" (סתמים *sětumîm*) and "sealed" (חתמים *ḥătumîm*) rhyme and are written very similarly, and the thought is a stock phrase about apocalyptic secrecy.

12:10. This verse refers to a difference between the righteous and the wicked, repeating elements from chap. 11. The wise "understand" and will know that they are to act as teachers of wisdom during the crisis period. Note that in Matt 24:37-44, Jesus' emphasis on the "final events" includes an "exhortation to watchfulness" precisely because the exact times are unknown. The warning that such events are close but not precisely known is an important technique in apocalyptic literature—with the accompanying emphasis on watchfulness and faithfulness.

12:11-13. One figure is given in v. 11, 1,290 days, as the time of the end. But then v. 12 has a second figure: 1,335 days. The significance of the two figures is impossible to determine. However, one thing is clear: This section was written by a later editor who continued to wonder when the vision of Daniel would actually be fulfilled. The message in vv. 11-12 is, then, essentially, "It may be at this time, but the faithful will remain strong even if the time continues." The final word in v. 13 is that Daniel should not worry, for his reward is certain in resurrection. The reader is to presume that his or her obedience to the advice of this book will result in a reward, not only for Daniel, but for the reader as well.

Most commentators read the end of chap. 12 as an indication of what happens to millennialist groups that risk making precise predictions about the coming of supernatural events. Certainly there have been many Christian and Jewish sects that have attempted such predictions. But it is interesting that many of these groups were not devastated when the designated time came and went—there

---

291. Collins, *Daniel*, 369.

are various theological ways that groups can explain away their error. Christianity as a whole had to deal with the delay of the return of Christ. But the summons to watchfulness in the light of this delay in Daniel is not a call to irresponsibility because of expectations of imminent changes. It is, rather, a call to faithfulness knowing that the end is predetermined, even if postponed.

The writer of the book of Daniel, it is true, tried to make precise predictions. But the very fact that we still have this work, and that it is still read with great reverence, is testimony not only to the elasticity of the numbers involved, but also to the fact that the sociology of the book, its attitude of apocalypticism, continues to speak to the condition of peoples in crisis. It is the accuracy of this aspect of the book, and not the numbers themselves, that offers the great comfort of the book of Daniel. Here, at last, is discussion of realities that are suffered by minorities or by people who are forcibly subordinated, discriminated against, or displaced.

REFLECTIONS

The great vision raises a host of important theological issues: resurrection, faith in persecution, the realism or lack of realism in apocalyptic thought. Any of these could be pursued to great benefit. However, the issue of the rise and prominence of angels in this vision, presaged by chaps. 7–9 and even hinted at in chaps. 1–6 (the fourth person in the furnace of Nebuchadnezzar, Daniel's salvation from the lions), may be a provocative entry into a discussion of other interesting issues for modern speculation, especially the subject of spiritual warfare.

Numerous scholarly studies reveal a lively interest in the subject of angels—in the Bible, in the intertestamental period, and in early Christianity. We need not rehearse the many insights provided by these studies on "angelology," most of which consist of amassing the evidence in biblical, Qumran, and non-canonical material.[292] Suffice it to say that there seems to be no coherent "doctrine" of angels such that we can see a detailed consistency in all the texts in which angels appear.

Although an "intermediary" figure is suggested as early as the "angel of the LORD" in Genesis 16 (cf. the angel of the Passover in Exodus), this appears to be an early form of a "presence of God" (note the interplay of references to an intermediary, and then to God, in Genesis 16, Hagar in the wilderness). Rowland, among others, sees a kind of evolution toward an increasingly personified figure—from Genesis 16 to Ezekiel, and thence to Daniel—until writers could speak of angels by name and rank in the late exilic period.[293]

What is perplexing is the question of why angels should become such a focus of attention. As the circumstances of the exilic life-style continue, there is an angelic population explosion in some of the Jewish writings. Just as significant, there is a complex bureaucracy of angels as well. The two most frequent metaphors are clearly court and military. Angels are messengers and courtiers, on the one hand, and military officers, on the other; they attend to matters of state in the kingdom of God, and they fight this kingdom's battles. Some angels are involved in a betrayal of the court and intrigue (the "fall" of some angels in *1 Enoch*). All of this strongly suggests that the guiding metaphor for angelic elaboration in Jewish Hellenistic (and perhaps late Persian) literature is precisely the realities of world empire, under whose boots the Jews lived. As the legions of Nebuchadnezzar, Cyrus, and Alexander marched across the ancient Near East, angelic legions marched from the Jewish apocalypticists' theological speculations. And just as legends about the emperor became more and more spectacular

---

292. Some recent studies include S. Olyan, *A Thousand Thousands Serve Him* (Tübingen: J. C. B. Mohr, 1993); Heidt, *Angelology of the Old Testament*; M. J. Davidson, *Angels at Qumran* (Sheffield: JSOT, 1992); C. Newsom, "Angels," *ABD*, 6 vols. (New York: Doubleday, 1992) 1:248-53; M. Mach, *Entwicklungsstaudien des jüdischen Engelglaubens in vorrabbinischer Zeit* (Tübingen: Mohr, 1992).
293. Christopher Rowland, *The Open Heavens* (London: SPCK, 1982) 78-123.

and removed from common experience, so also God somewhat retreats behind the layers of angelic bureaucracy. In Daniel, certainly, the angels are far more active than is the omniscient, omnipotent power represented as the Ancient of Days, about whom we have only impressive descriptions of power and thrones. This leads to a possible conclusion that God becomes the ultimate conquerer whose throne outshines and overpowers all the thrones of the earth, but about whom we know as little as we do about the emperor himself, to whom God is contrasted.

Stated in this way, we see an obvious reason why Daniel 1–6 is connected to Daniel 7–12. Emphasizing court tales vs. apocalyptic has overdrawn the contrast between the two halves of the book when, in fact, both halves deal with God's court vs. human courts. God as sovereign is an idea intended to challenge the idea of the emperor as sovereign. Daniel the visionary in chaps. 7–12 is also a courtier of the true king; the tales in chaps. 1–6 serve only to highlight the difference in loyalties between one who lives in one court, serving one king, while actually being obedient to the other king, his God.

This is not to deny that chaps. 7–12 certainly make the opposition to earthly rulers more obvious than do the stories in chaps. 1–6. The resistance in the first half of the book of Daniel stops short of actually pulling princes down from their thrones. One could argue that, in a profound sense, these rulers step down of their own accord, accepting a transformed basis for rulership and a new ethic of ruling in the light of their insights into the true sovereignty of God. But if the stories ended with a military conquest of the enemy, their effectiveness would have been seriously limited for those who knew that violent revolution was pointless. The power of the calls to resistance in Daniel is precisely the subversive call to resist *even under the present circumstances.*

If Daniel 1–6 is about previous loyalties, then the entire book of Daniel is a call to arms for spiritual warfare, or a training manual for serving in God's "court" while living in the human world. The weapons of war and the training for service both involve the same thing: knowledge of the truth. That is why the wise are warriors—their weapon is knowledge. In chaps. 7–12 (esp. chaps. 10–12), we see the offensive weapon of the faithful: truth (or "instruction," 11:35). Truth is a weapon far more powerful than a sword, which is why it is so often *called* a sword in both the Hebrew Bible and the New Testament (the prophets "slay with the sword": Job 5:15; Isa 49:2; Jer 25:16; Amos 4:10; "the sword, which is the word of God," Eph 6:17; Rev 1:16; 2:12).

Violence masquerades as action. Guns make people believe that they are doing something. But violence always covers truth, attempts to hide it or destroy it. Consider all the machinery of the former Soviet Union, dedicated to keeping words from its citizenry or the careful control of the news media by the United States during the Persian Gulf War. Further, in so many of the revolutionary struggles brought about by swords instead of truth, the swords are then soon turned on their own citizens when these revolutionaries are in power. Yet, all the millions spent on armaments cannot hide the truth forever. Dictators fear *knowledge* most of all.

"The wise will take action . . . and instruct the many." The beginning of action is knowledge. *The Pedagogy of the Oppressed,* by Paolo Freire, is the early classic of Latin American thought that fed directly into liberation theology's emphasis on conscientization.[294] Conscientization—education to make one conscious of the realities of one's social and spiritual condition—is the process of encouraging an emerging awareness of the mechanics of economic and social realities—in Daniel's case, spiritual realities. The importance of this basic truth should prevent anyone from the false criticism that Daniel advocates passive or resigned nonaction rather than a Maccabean, active engagement by means of violence. Daniel calls for war, but not warfare like that of the nations. To take Daniel seriously as a basis for contemporary theology, we must be prepared for a call to arms, for we are called to nothing less than spiritual warfare with

---

294. Paolo Freire, *The Pedagogy of the Oppressed* (New York: Herder & Herder, 1970).

material realities; what the early Quakers called "The Lamb's War" (borrowing the image from the other biblical apocalyptic work, Revelation). Daniel's final vision is a description of the powers of this world and the struggles of the "covenanted people" within the orbit of these powers.

"Speaking truth to power" is a recent Quaker ideal that is the equivalent of Daniel's imagery of Michael's taking up the sword of truth against the foreign powers. Speaking truth is not mere advocacy as opposed to action. Speaking truth *is* action because truth empowers, inspires, and guides. If God is our emperor and Christ is our victorious general, then no earthly power will command our total loyalty again. Truth, if taught, will not be defeated. The most revolutionary act under Antiochus IV, according to Daniel, was for one to *be* a Jew and to teach others to be a Jew. The most revolutionary act in the modern world is first of all to be a woman or a man of faith—to reject violence, to reject the abuse of the weak, and to embrace the gospel of life and teach it to others. The revolution of truth must arise from education and conviction by the truth, and never by coercion. Coercion always demands empty exercises in false discipline and obedience to idols, because both are necessary to the rule of the armed few. How can a democracy emerge from a militaristic, hierarchical, disciplined culture of unquestioned obedience to superiors? Truth rules by the power of the many. It is inherently democratic, because its power derives from the convictions of the masses, and not from the forced obedience of the masses. It is, in short, war by angelic power—a lamb's war. It is the way of Daniel the wise. It is a way of saying: "Michael has conquered—let us teach of his victory!"

THE ADDITIONS TO DANIEL
INTRODUCTION, COMMENTARY, AND REFLECTIONS
BY
DANIEL L. SMITH-CHRISTOPHER

THE ADDITIONS TO DANIEL

INTRODUCTION

THE GREEK TRANSLATION OF THE OLD TESTAMENT

The importance of the Greek translations of the Old Testament for biblical and textual research is hard to exaggerate. Indeed, Ernst Würthwein states that the Septuagint is so significant that "apart from it both Christendom and Western Culture would be inconceivable."[1] But how these Greek versions were produced is a controversial subject in scholarly debate.

According to the Letter of Aristeas, which scholars date from about the second century BCE into the first century CE, Ptolemy II Philadelphus commissioned the translation of the Jewish Scriptures to be a part of his great library at Alexandria. The text was miraculously translated by seventy-two elders in precisely seventy-two days, thus it was named "Septuagint." The translation was read and proved to be without error by the Jewish community itself. The story gives us the impression that there was one book that was considered "the" Greek version of the Old Testament. But scholarly views of the origin of the Septuagint suggest that the production was considerably more complex than a single event or version, and furthermore had much more to do with the need of Jews in the diaspora for a version of the Bible in their newly adopted language, Greek. The need for a Greek version of the Hebrew Bible sometime after Alexander's conquests of the ancient Near East, therefore, is a measure of cultural change and social transformation in the Jewish community.

Scholarly study of the Greek versions of Daniel focuses on two older Greek versions of the book of Daniel: the Old Greek or LXX version and the "Theodotion" version. Moore points out that in the story of Susanna, the differences between the LXX and the Theodotion versions are the greatest, while in the Song of the Three the differences are not very significant.[2] Bel and the Dragon occupies a middle position.

Although the entire Theodotion Old Testament is usually dated to the second century CE, the book of Daniel itself presents special problems. Since the Theodotion version of Daniel is cited in

---

1. E. Wurthwein, *The Text of the Old Testament,* trans. E. F. Rhoades (Grand Rapids: Eerdmans, 1979) 57.
2. C. A. Moore, *Daniel, Esther, and Jeremiah: The Additions,* AB 44 (Garden City, N.Y.: Doubleday, 1977) 16.

the New Testament, the book of Daniel that became a part of the later Theodotion version must itself be older. This Theodotion version of Daniel, however, became the accepted version for the Christian church, over the Old Greek version. In this commentary, I will use the Theodotion text and occasionally draw attention to differing readings in the LXX.

When these Greek translations were produced, many of the books of the Hebrew Bible were expanded with material that may or may not go back to a Hebrew or Aramaic original. Although, in the case of the additions to Daniel, many scholars argue that these stories do go back to Semitic originals, no evidence of a Semitic language version of these stories has been found as yet.

Writing as a Protestant scholar, I regard it a pity that Protestants generally have little exposure to the Greek additions to Daniel because of Luther's insistence on the Hebrew text as the acceptable canon of the Old Testament, as opposed to the traditional Christian use of the Greek canon of the Old Testament, which included these Deuterocanonical works. Apart from any theological issues of what constituted the canon (which is a doctrinal issue that quite properly has little bearing on scholarly and historical study of texts), these additions are fascinating indicators of concerns and issues in the Jewish community in the late Hellenistic period. A study of the additional Greek material about figures like Jeremiah, Daniel, Esther, and Joseph reveals further concerns with themes of intercultural contact, political occupation and exile, and the traditions of facing foreign power with faith in God's redeeming power. Such issues were on the minds of Jews in Hellenistic and Roman-occupied Near Eastern territories from the second century BCE into the common era. We will see in these additions to Daniel that many of the themes of the canonical book of Daniel—sovereignty, resistance, and idolatry, for example—are developed and expanded upon. This also means that a key to understanding these additions, as much as the canonical stories of Daniel, is the experience of disenfranchisement and loss of self-determination that exile, as well as political occupation in one's own homeland, involves.

(See the annotated bibliography for the Hebrew book of Daniel.)

OUTLINE OF THE ADDITIONS TO DANIEL

I. The Prayer of Azariah and the Song of the Three Jews, verses 1-68

    A. Verses 1-22, The Prayer of Azariah
    B. Verses 23-27, The Angelic Liberation from the Fire
    C. Verses 28-68, The Song of the Three Jews

II. Susanna, verses 1-64

III. Bel and the Dragon, verses 1-42

    A. Verses 1-22, The Story of Bel
    B. Verses 23-42, The Story of the Dragon

THE PRAYER OF AZARIAH AND THE SONG OF THE THREE JEWS

VERSES 1-68

OVERVIEW

Tradition assigns this addition to the name of one of Daniel's three companions, Azariah. But the other two, Hananiah and Mashael, are present in the second part of the text, the Psalm of Praise, because it is an extension of chap. 3, located between vv. 23-24 of the Hebrew/Aramaic text. Notably, their Jewish names rather than their Babylonian slave names are highlighted, further emphasizing that early tradition certainly did not miss the significance of the names, even if most modern commentators attach little importance to it.

Moore divides this section along the following lines: vv. 1-22, prayer; vv. 23-28, prose; vv. 29-34, ode; vv. 35-68, psalm.[3] However, Moore himself notes that not many scholars make a clear distinction between the ode and the psalm. There is little linguistic basis for such a differentiation. But the three general sections—prayer, prose, and psalm—are helpful divisions for a reading of this text.

3. Moore, *Daniel, Esther, and Jeremiah*, 41-43.

VERSES 1-22, THE PRAYER OF AZARIAH

COMMENTARY

Verses 1-2, Facing the Threat with Singing. The first section, the Prayer of Azariah (or The Three), is a prayer of confession and forgiveness, very much on the same model as Daniel 9. See the Commentary on Daniel 9 for extensive comparisons, but suffice it to say that here we find many of the same themes that were obviously typical of this form of penitential prayer of communal confession. What is significant here is the context of mortal danger that once again accompanies such prayers of confession. The obvious intention of such prayers was to call on the power of God's deliverance.

Part of the context is the importance of the danger itself. Twice, in vv. 1-2, it is emphasized that Azariah stood "in the midst of" the flames. It is not the case that there was no danger; they actually faced a true threat, and thus the earlier comments recorded in Daniel 3 that they would not bow down to Nebuchadnezzar's statue "even if God does *not* deliver them" ought to be fresh in mind.

The text records that the three "sang hymns" while in the furnace. The very term "hymn" comes from the Greek, and the call to sing to the Lord is often found in circumstances of great celebration (see Judg 16:24, where the Philistines sing to their gods; see also 1 Chr 16:9; 2 Chr 23:13; Jdt 15:13; 16:13). Such celebration is found elsewhere besides this instance in the fiery furnace. Note the striking similarity to Acts 16, where Paul and Silas sing hymns in prison (see below). The obvious theme is one of remembering God's liberating power, even in the midst of apparent defeat.

Verses 3-22, The Penitential Prayer in the Furnace. Although the Theodition text has only Azariah praying, in the

LXX tradition, all three men pray. This is a minor point, however, since it is clear that it is meant to be a communal prayer in any case. Moore finds this prayer "glaringly inappropriate"[4] because these three are praying a prayer of confession, even though they are being punished precisely for their obedience to God. However, as indicated in the Commentary on Daniel 9, this formulaic confession is appropriate as a preparation for calling on God's deliverance. Thus it is no more out of place than moderns who begin a prayer of request with a word of repentance and was clearly the set form in any case. Moore's criticism takes the setting of a story a bit too literally. The story is meant to teach—i.e., when in trouble, pray in this fashion.

Verses 3-8. Many of the phrases found in this confessional prayer are worthy of comment. For example, the phrase "God of *our* ancestors," found in vv. 3 and 29, is significant (note the late occurences of the first-person plural form in 1 Kings 8; Ezra 7:27; Dan 2:23; 1 Esdr 1:50; 4:60; Tob 8:5). The phrase is particularly significant in late biblical use. The second-person form "your ancestors" is more common in the deuteronomic materials. But the change to first person as the more typical form may not be an insignificant detail, given its prominent setting in prayers of confession, which emphasize the sins of "our" fathers as well. The speaker, then, is included in these prayers, and the reader/hearer of the story is equally drawn in. (Note also that Jerusalem is called the holy city of "our" ancestors in v. 5. Similarly, the phrase "ways of truth" [v. 4] is notable in Dan 4:37; 1 Esdr 4:40; Tob 3:2.)

Furthermore, the legal language of God as judge appears in the use of the expression "true judgments" in vv. 5 and 8. However, the term carries significant implications for God's assurance of social justice for the oppressed as well (cf. Zech 7:9-10: "Thus says the Lord of hosts: Render true judgments, show kindness and mercy to one another; do not oppress the widow, the orphan, the alien, or the poor; and do not devise evil in your hearts against one another"; Zech 8:16 adds, significantly, that true judgments "make peace").

The NRSV translation of v. 7 unfortunately misses an interesting progression in responding to the law. The first phrase contains the Greek term for "listening" (rendered in the NRSV as "obeyed"), which can be compared to Dan 7:28, where it is often translated "kept in mind." But if the term is read more as "heard," then we have the interesting progression:

Your commandments, we have not heard
>we have not considered
>we have not obeyed[5]

Verse 9. The circumstances of exile and political oppression come to mind powerfully in this verse. The suggestion is that the Jews face "enemies" and the "wicked," virtually embodied in a king who is called "unjust" and "the most wicked in the world." The same term for "wicked" (πονηρός *ponēros*) is used as a noun to refer to Satan in the New Testament (Matt 13:19). Forms of the same term occur in powerful pieces of sage advice in Sir: "Never trust your enemy, for like corrosion in copper, so is his *wickedness*" (12:10); "The knowledge of *wickedness* is not wisdom" (19:22); and, provocatively, "There is a cleverness that is *detestable*!" (19:23).

Verse 10. This verse laments the condition of "shame and reproach." Once again, the writer has used terms that often appear together in wisdom literature. Note Prov 19:26, which refers to "children who cause shame and bring reproach," and Sir 6:1, "a bad name incurs shame and reproach." The emphasis here, as is also found in some deuteronomic phrases, is on the public nature of Jewish life in a cosmopolitan world. They are very aware that their status as members of a defeated nation presents a challenge to the credibility of their faith claims. Clearly, the call to sing hymns in prison is either a bold belief that this prison does not represent ultimate realities, or it is a very public display of hopelessness that borders on insanity. Much of the post-exilic materials display a very keen awareness of the fact that for a people living under occupation, every aspect of life is circumspect, including the exercise of faith. The faith of occupied people is a faith

---

4. Moore, *Daniel, Esther, and Jeremiah*, 40, 60.

5. Moore, *Daniel, Esther, and Jeremiah*, 57, compares Deut 4:1; 5:1; 6:3; 7:12.

that is daily examined by the eyes and ears of their oppressors, and thus the fear of shame and reproach is quite real.[6] It is important to note the awareness of others' watching and controlling, which is an aspect of political occupation as well as other similar situations of what Erving Goffman called "institutions of total control":

Total institutions disrupt or defile precisely those actions that in civil society have the role of attesting to the actor and those in his presence that he has some command over his world—that he is a person with "adult" self-determination, autonomy, and freedom of action.[7]

Verse 11. This sense of being in the midst of foreigners who are watching is also clear in the deuteronomic phrase in v. 11: "for your name's sake." The danger is that the people's circumstances will be such that the covenant with God will appear to be annulled (v. 11*b*; cf. the deuteronomic fear of abrogating the covenant in Deut 31:16, 20; Judg 2:1; 1 Kgs 15:19; and in the prophetic literature in Isa 24:5; Jer 11:10; 14:21; Zech 11:10, 14).

Verses 12-14. The contingency of the covenant, alluded to in v. 11, is then compared to the unilateral promise to Abraham referred to in vv. 12-13. Note the reference to the "stars of heaven," clearly referring to God's promise to Abraham in Gen 15:5. Here we see the significance of the constant emphasis on "our ancestors," for they represent both the consistency of God's saving action in the past and the promise of God's saving presence in the future.

The reality of the present state of the people, however, is that they are *not* as numerous as the stars in the heavens or the sands on the shore. The threat is that they will diminish. Verse 14 refers to their being fewer than any other nation; the same worry is expressed in Bar 2:34, where the discussion is once again in the context of mentioning the promise to the patriarchs. The advice to encourage marriage and procreation was advised in the letter to the exiles in Jer 29:6, where Jeremiah commands: "Do not decrease!" Finally, note the importance of the hymn of praise in 1 Chr 16:19-22*a*, where the issue of being few in number is directly associated with the conditions of the post-exilic community:

When they were few in number,
 of little account, and strangers in the land,
wandering from nation to nation,
 from one kingdom to another people,
he allowed no one to oppress them;
 he rebuked kings on their account,
saying, "Do not touch my anointed ones."
(NRSV)

Verses 15-18. The list of offices that are missing among the people in v. 15 is an interesting reference to the lack of complete independence in post-exilic, occupied Palestine. The first two terms, "ruler" (ἄρχων *archōn*) and "prophet" (προφήτης *prophētēs*), are clear in the Greek, but the third term (ἡγούμενος *hēgoumenos*), translated simply as "leader" in the NRSV, is indeed an ambiguous word that often is used to translate quite different terms in Hebrew that delineate distinct and fairly specific levels of authority, whether political or military ("governor," "officer," etc.). But the generality of having no such leaders seems appropriate here—in essence a representation of not being master of one's own fate. Moore, however, protests that part of this is not accurate for a setting in the exile, since prophets like Ezekiel were active.[8] He argues, therefore, for a later historical setting for this writing, presumably when prophecy really was considered to have ended.[9]

That the Jews are not able to offer sacrifice is an interesting reference to the exilic period specifically, despite the fact that this work was clearly written during the time of the Second Temple (515 BCE?–70 CE). But the inability to offer sacrifice sets up an important mention of a "humble spirit and a contrite heart" (v. 16), which is deemed superior to temple sacrifice. Indeed, references to humbleness of spirit and contrition of heart are often seen in contexts of severe doubt about the efficacy of the sacrificial system:

---

6. Note the studies of Japanese Americans who were sent to concentration camps in the United States during World War II. See Daniel Smith, *The Religion of the Landless: The Sociology of the Babylonian Exile* (New York: Meyer-Stone, 1989) 71-73.
7. E. Goffman, *Asylums* (Aldine: Chicago, 1961) 43.

8. Moore, *Daniel, Esther, and Jeremiah*, 58.
9. This is, of course, a relative statement. Some Jewish groups, including Christianity and then second-century CE Christian sects, believed that prophecy never ceased.

For you have no delight in sacrifice;
   if I were to give a burnt offering, you would
      not be pleased.
The sacrifice acceptable to God is a broken spirit;
   a broken and contrite heart, O God, you will
      not despise. (Ps 51:16-17 NRSV)

I dwell in the high and holy place,
   and also with those who are contrite and
      humble in spirit,
to revive the spirit of the humble,
   and to revive the heart of the contrite.
(Isa 57:15 NRSV)

But this is the one to whom I will look,
   to the humble and contrite in spirit,
      who trembles at my word. (Isa 66:2 NRSV)

The final passage quoted, Isa 66:2, is perhaps most noted for its rejection of a narrow definition not only of the efficacy of sacrifice, but also of *who* is acceptable to God, and it suggests that foreigners will be added to the number of the people of God. Thus humble contrition becomes almost the very definition of faith.

Trust in contrition and humbleness is thus contrasted with outward expressions of religious observance. When it is said that no shame will come to those who trust in God (v. 17b), we are reminded of Ezra's faith in God when he rejected a military guard offered by the king, so as to avoid the shame of appearing faithless (Ezra 8:22).

Verses 19-22. In vv. 19-20, shame is contrasted with God's very public deliverance of the people. Once again, we are reminded of the public and, therefore, confessional and apologetic nature of shame and trust for Israelites under political occupation. The constant reference to mercy (ἐλέους *eleoys*; חסד *ḥesed*) is a reminder that God's mercy was often seen as God's liberating power against the overwhelming enemies of God's people.

Those who watch, assess, judge, and evaluate the occupied peoples (vv. 21-22) are referred to most powerfully in the final sentence, "Let them know . . ." with a reference to God's power to bring about the end of "their" power. (See Reflections at vv. 28-68.)

VERSES 23-27, THE ANGELIC LIBERATION FROM THE FIRE

COMMENTARY

Similar to Daniel 7–12, immediately following the penitential prayer an angelic messenger appears, representing God's assistance to humble servants. This passage takes its cue from an expansion of the Aramaic text in Daniel 3:22. Moore notes that many scholars have considered this prose section about angelic liberation to belong to the original Semitic version of Daniel 3, since there appears to be a gap between vv. 23 and 24 of that chapter.[10] Further, the prayer should be set before the deliverance. But note that in the Theodotion version of these events, the early death of the officers who threw the three into the fire is omitted, only to be mentioned here; therefore, no contradiction is evident. This prose section provides further details missing from the canonical version.

In typical fashion for Daniel, a list is provided to emphasize the way that the fire was made even hotter—so hot that it burned those who forced the Jews into the flames.[11] Thus vv. 23-25 serve as further clarification of the brief summary statement made in the Hebrew text.

Verses 26-27. The one who had the appearance of a "son of the gods" in the Aramaic text (Dan 3:25) and who caused Nebuchadnezzar such alarm is here explicitly identified as an angelic messenger of God. The agent of God's deliverance is the "angel of the Lord," or "messenger of the Lord" as

---

10. Moore, *Daniel, Esther, and Jeremiah*.

11. There is evidence that the historical Nebuchadnezzar used fire as a form of punishment and execution. See Moore, *Daniel, Esther, and Jeremiah*, 62; C. Kuhl, *Die drei Männer im Feure*, BZAW 55 (1940).

seen in such important passages as Genesis 16 (saving Hagar in the wilderness), Exod 3:2 (the presence in the burning bush in the call of Moses), Exod 14:19 (the protective presence of God with the people in the wilderness), and, in a more secular setting, in 2 Sam 2:5 (messengers sent by David). Thus, while this passage is typical of late post-exilic and apocalyptic literature in its detailed interest in angelic couriers of God's will, it is certainly also in line with much older textual representations of God's deliverance of the weak.

The text further explains exactly how the three Jews were spared by God. The heat of the flame was transformed by a "wind of dew" or "moist wind" that blew through the furnace. The term "dew" (δρόσος *drosos*) is used in a number of places throughout Scripture where it is related to God's saving grace. In the context of God's healing of rebellious Israel, Hos 14:5 has God saying, "I shall be like the dew to Israel." Micah 5:7 states that the remnant of Jacob "shall be like dew from the Lord." When God sows peace, the "skies shall give their dew" (Zech 8:12). Finally, and perhaps most powerfully, note Isa 26:19 (NRSV):

Your dead shall live, their corpses shall rise.
O dwellers in the dust, awake and sing for joy!
For your dew is a radiant dew,
and the earth will give birth to those long dead.

So it is not merely that a "dew" from heaven contrasts markedly with the flames, but that this dew is frequently associated with God's grace and power in comforting God's people (see also Sir 18:16; 43:22).[12] (See Reflections at vv. 28-68.)

---

12. See also the discussion of rain as justice in Moshe Weinfeld, *Social Justice in Ancient Israel and in the Ancient Near East* (Minneapolis: Fortress, 1995) 53.

VERSES 28-68, THE SONG OF THE THREE JEWS

COMMENTARY

In contrast to the first section, which singles out Azariah specifically and highlights his leadership of the three (in the Theodotion text), the psalm in vv. 30-65 emphasizes the equal participation of the three, who praise with "one voice." Significantly, the opening praise (v. 29) is to the God of "our" ancestors (see above).

These praises, which typically are accompanied by the refrain "praise to him and exalt him forever," are divided into rough subject areas in terms of their specific content:

vv. 30-34, blessings of God as Ruler/Enthroned
vv. 35-41, blessings from the "works of the Lord"[13]
vv. 42-51, blessings from astronomical/meteorological creations
vv. 52-59, blessings from the earth and geological creations
vv. 60-65, blessings from selected leaders (e.g., priests)

Verses 30-34, God Enthroned. The first set of blessings emphasizes God, God's Temple, and the glory of God's enthroned place over against those who rule in the world. This is in keeping with an important general emphasis in the Hebrew text of Daniel, where the oppressive rulers of the world are contrasted with the true and liberating rulership of God. It is the hope of the rule of God that gives hope to those who suffer from human rulers.

Verse 32 specifically mentions the "cherubim." Collins notes that the cherubim are hybrid winged creatures who often have been pictured as upholding or serving the throne of God, protecting God's holy garden (Genesis 3), or bearing God up in epiphanies (1 Chr 13:6).[14] Note that wind and cherubim

---

13. Moore suggests "Highest heavens," and then "Things *from* Heavens."

14. John J. Collins, *Daniel*, Hermeneia (Minneapolis: Fortress, 1993) 206.

are related in Ps 18:10; winds are often listed among the arsenal of God as divine warrior (clearly alluding to comparisons with Baal, the Canaanite storm god).

Verses 35-41, Works of the Lord. Included in this clearly differentiated list, interestingly, are heavens, angels, waters, and powers (cf. Psalm 148, where powers are seen in the context of the "host of heaven"), the sun/moon, and the stars of heaven. Indeed, as Collins notes, Psalm 148 is a very similar list of aspects of God's control over heavenly bodies, including angels.[15]

Verses 42-51, Astronomical Phenomena. It is not difficult to see in this list a reference to the ancient comparisons between the God of the Bible, Yahweh, and the ascendant god of the Canaanites, Baal. The Canaanite storm god and thus the "rider of the clouds," Baal ruled over meteorological phenomena such as this list represents, particularly those that begin and end the list, winds and lightning (cf. Psalm 29, which many scholars consider to be an ancient hymn to Baal, simply converted for Israelite use through changing the referent names of the god).

Verses 52-59, From the Earth and Geological Creations. This series emphasizes God as creator. It was often noted in Hebrew texts that God's qualifications to challenge the reality of idols is precisely God's authority as Creator of all creation, an authority that gives God power over the gods represented by idols of mere wood and stone (Isaiah 18–19 celebrates the creator: "The Lord . . . who formed the earth and made it." The recognition of the true God is then contrasted to the making of idols in Isaiah 20–22).[16]

Verses 60-65, Blessings from Leaders. What is notable by their absence from this list of the people of Israel is military or royal figures. Indeed, the series presents what Joel Weinberg calls the "Citizen-Temple-Community," an ethnopolitical enclave of occupied Palestine in which authority is vested in the Temple and temple personnel: people and priests.[17] Furthermore, once again the "humble in heart" are honored (Isa 57:15; 66:2; Sir 35:21; cf. Matt 11:29) among the people of God.

Verses 66-68, The Conclusion. In v. 66, the Jewish names of the prisoners of Babylonian imperialism are used, in contrast to their slave names. To be rescued from "Hades" is an interesting thematic association with the rescue from the fiery furnace—a comparison that can be seen in other texts as well. The chiastic form of v. 66b reads as follows:

A He delivered us
  B from the midst of the burning furnace
  B´ from the midst of the flame
A´ He delivered us

The deliverance is celebrated, as we would expect, in the context of God's delivering power, God's "steadfast love," translated often as "mercy"—a mercy that will "endure forever."

Mercy is often called for in the context of overwhelming fear of an enemy. Thus, given the context of the fiery furnace, to emphasize the themes of mercy, of God's creator authority over idolatry, and of God's rulership over the powers of this world is to place this material firmly in the context of political occupation and possibly a context of persecution. The very fact that this particular episode is the context for an extension of the tradition in Greek suggests that *persecution* is the preferred context for this hymn and that it remained an important context for later editors and readers in the Hellenistic period.

---

15. Collins, *Daniel*, 206; see also Moore, *Daniel, Esther, and Jeremiah*, 75.
16. J. Blenkinsopp has noted the increase in references to God as *creator* in the post-exilic period. See his *Ezra–Nehemiah*, OTL (London: SCM, 1988).
17. See J. Weinberg, *The Citizen Temple Community*, trans. D. Smith-Christopher (Sheffield: JSOT, 1992).

REFLECTIONS

This passage represents a significant development of the exilic theme and particularly the theme of persecution by foreigners. The theme of resistance, represented in Daniel 3 of the Hebrew text, is lengthened here. Thus the focus shifts from Nebuchadnezzar's mad megalomania to the successful resistance of the Jews. However, both themes must be held together for a full appreciation of what is accomplished by the editor, who skillfully placed this section into the earlier text. The presence of this tradition is ample proof of the significance of this theme of persecution and endurance for late (post 150 BCE?) occupied Palestine. The placement of a passage can often reveal what was on the redactor's mind in expanding the text.

God as Creator—that is, not God as a specific national deity, but the one God of all people—is celebrated as the one who controls ultimate authority over claims by human rulers to be universal rulers of the "four corners of the earth." Only God as Creator ultimately trumps the claims of rulership of Cyrus, Alexander, Nebuchadnezzar, or Tiglath-pileser III. God as Creator (and thus the emphasis on the God of "our" ancestors) becomes a universalist polemic for God's ultimate authority. This subversive theology of God's control contains great power in an age when empires extended throughout the known world. In short, naming the true God is a call to resist the false powers of the world.

For the Jews of occupied Palestine, as well as in the diaspora, resistance was fired by an appeal to the God not merely of a nation that once existed, but of all creation. Albert Memmi writes that the colonizer must always show strength as in "flashy symbols, the most striking demonstrations of the power of his country," which include "all military parades." Memmi says that it is a "deep necessity of colonial life; to impress the colonized is just as important as to reassure oneself."[18] But in the face of this, Memmi writes about the reinvestment of religion with new political meaning, particularly in Muslim countries:

> Now, the young intellectual who had broken with religions, internally at least, and ate during Ramadan, begins to fast with ostentation. He who considered the rites as inevitable family drudgery, reintroduces them into his social life, gives them a place in his conception of the world. To use them better, he reexplains the forgotten messages and adapts them to present-day needs. He then discovers that religion is not simply an attempt to communicate with the invisible, but also an extraordinary place of communion for the whole group. The colonized, his leaders and intellectuals, his traditionalists and liberals, all classes of society, can meet there, reinforce their bonds, verify and re-create their unity.[19]

Fanon writes that the native is "treated as an inferior but he is not convinced of his inferiority."[20] Memmi agrees: "In order for that legitimacy to be complete, it is not enough for the colonized to be a slave, he must also accept his role."[21] It is in the flame of religious resistance that we can see the beginnings of the fires of revolt. Just as Mary sang of the defeat of Roman occupation with the birth of the Messiah in the Gospel of Luke ("He has brought down the powerful from their thrones"), so also sang Paul and Silas, in the book of Acts, serenading their jailers with songs about the greatness of their liberator, who was once again about to send a "messenger" to liberate the chosen ones. Singing to the jailers, like singing in the flames of Nebuchadnezzar's furnace, represents a powerful refusal to be bowed by the power of the state, which is always preeminently represented in its power to do violence to those who disobey.

A similar theme occurs in the *Testament of Joseph* 8:5 (second century BCE). After Joseph resists the temptation to commit adultery, he is falsely accused and thrown into prison:

---

18. A. Memmi, *The Colonizer and the Colonized* (Boston: Beacon, 1965) 59.
19. Memmi, *The Colonizer and the Colonized*, 132-33.
20. F. Fanon, *The Wretched of the Earth* (New York: Grove, 1963) 53.
21. Memmi, *The Colonizer and the Colonized*, 89.

> When I was in fetters, the Egyptian woman was overtaken with grief. She came and heard the report how I gave thanks to the Lord and sang praise in the house of darkness, and how I rejoiced with cheerful voice, glorifying my God, because through her trumped up charge I was set free from this Egyptian woman.[22]

This example of ancient Jewish resistance raises an important question for Christians today: If the power of violence merely brings forth songs from the defiant, where then, is their power? The Jews of exile and occupation faced their more powerful conquerors with cries to God and songs of God's mastery over all creation. Would the cries of today's oppressed peoples in the slums of Cairo, the refugee camps of Lebanon and Jordan and Ethiopia, the poor sections of multiple cities sound any different to Babylonian, Persian, Greek, or Roman ears?

Christendom long ago sold itself to the modern nation-state and would not think of challenging the power and authority of that rule with radically alternative values or alternative ways of living. But Westerners can hardly believe that they still hear the defiant call, "God is great!" in the face of the West's overwhelming military might. Perhaps in reading about Hananiah, Mishael, Azariah, Joseph, and Paul and Silas, we should remember that there was once a faith that burned brightly in Christian hearts and souls as they confronted Roman power with a persistent faith that declared, "Jesus is Lord!"

---

22. *Testament of Joseph,* in 821, OTP, Charlesworth, Vol. 1; see also 495; E. Haenchen, *The Acts of the Apostles* (Philadelphia: Westminster, 1971); Conzelman also quotes Epictetus 2.6.26: "and then we shall be emulating Socrates when we are able to write paeans in prison" (*Acts of the Apostles*, H. Conzelman, Hermeneia [Philadelphia: Fortress, 1987] 132).

SUSANNA

VERSES 1-64

COMMENTARY

The story of Susanna stands in some of the Greek versions as the first of the Daniel stories, before the Hebrew Daniel 1, but after chap. 12 in others. The motivation to place the story before Daniel 1 was undoubtedly because Daniel is portrayed as a very young man (who is wise beyond his years) in this story.

There are significant differences between the style of the story of Susanna and the Hebrew/Aramaic stories in Daniel 1–6 (the non-miraculous form of deliverance, the internal Jewish matters, among others). Further, Susanna differs from the other two additional works included in the Greek canon of the book of Daniel mainly because of its focus on the subjects of women, sexual abuse, and internal corruption in the Jewish community.

It is often suggested that even though the story of Susanna is considered the most sophisticated and well-developed of the three additions to Daniel (the Song of the Three, for example, seems a hodgepodge of literary styles; Bel and the Dragon are clearly two separate stories), it was rejected by those rabbis who determined the canon because the court procedure was improper[23] and because the authority of elders is seriously questioned (especially in the LXX version). It can be argued, however, that there are important reasons why it is significant that Susanna appears in the Daniel collection. First, it presents a female model of courage in a community that needs all of its resources and in which all persons share the threat of political exile and occupation. Second, Susanna includes a significant criticism of internal communal corruption, similar to that found in Ezra and Nehemiah, where it is also directed against corrupt or corruptible leaders of the community. Furthermore, the story of Susanna gives us an interesting episode in the life of the young Daniel, the legendary hero.

Many theories have been suggested for the origin of the story. These include that it was a midrash on the evil prophets mentioned in Jeremiah 29; a late polemic between Pharisees and Sadducees on court procedure; and a folk tale that exhibits well-known themes in folklore, such as the wisdom of the elders overturned by a child.[24] No single view, however, has commanded wide agreement. While Susanna is a tale that has clear similarities with the themes of Daniel 1–6, there is nothing within the story that allows a clear date or even a sociopolitical context for the Jewish community that treasured and maintained this story as a part of its religious lore.

The story of Susanna affords us the opportunity to raise questions that have not previously arisen in the study of the book of Daniel—most important, the issue of women's rights and place in society. Indeed, besides Susanna there is only one other significant woman in the entire Daniel corpus: the queen mother, who makes her appearance in Daniel 5. There seems little evidence that Susanna was written with any aspect of the queen mother in mind as the "other woman" of the Daniel tradition. But was Susanna written with Daniel even in mind? Some scholars wonder whether Daniel originally had a role at all in an earlier form of the Susanna legend—perhaps references to him being added only when the story was made a part of the Daniel tradition at about the time of its translation into Greek (c. 100 BCE).

However, this account of life in the exilic community from a woman's perspective gives us the opportunity to consider a Jewish woman as doubly a symbol of resistance—both to the oppression of exile and to male domination within the Jewish community—and as a model of the kind of spiritual tenacity

---

23. This issue is pursued helpfully in Moore, *Daniel, Esther, and Jeremiah*, 87.

24. These and other suggestions are explained in more detail, with references to the technical literature, in the works of both Collins and Moore.

necessary for faithful resistance in circumstances of exile or occupation. It seems hard to deny that Susanna as a woman within Jewish society is meant to mirror the Jew in foreign society. She is called to resist oppression within that society as the Jews were generally called to resist oppression from outside. Her resistance, her ability to speak truth to power, is honored in this story, as well as the young Daniel's clever courtroom technique in defending her.

Mieke Bal has asserted that there is a "dominant reading" of biblical texts and interpretative strategies that is "a monolithically misogynist view of those biblical stories wherein female characters play a role, and a denial of the importance of women in the Bible as a whole."[25] Part of this dominant reading, according to Bal, is to dismiss certain aspects of texts and stories that seem to be "meaningless details," particularly where women are concerned. But attention to such details may have the effect of inverting previous perspectives. Such an analysis of the Susanna story, for example, has been provided by both Bal and Glancy, who focus important attention on Susanna as a woman whose actions are interpreted according to her "appearance" to the "male gaze."[26] Another way that one can become attuned to such details is through a survey of the literature on violence against women. This commentary will have occasion to relate the study of Susanna to feminist and other sociological studies of rape and violence against women.[27]

Glancy notes that Susanna is largely the passive victim and the crime that stands "behind" the story is violation of possessions and honor of men—in this case Joakim the husband. Brownmiller argues that male possession laws are the foundation for most modern rape laws in Western society in that rape "was first and foremost a violation of male rights of possession, based on male requirements of virginity, chastity, and consent to private access as the female bargain in the marriage contract."[28]

Similarly, then, Glancy notes the intriguing symmetry between Susanna, the "violated wife," and Joakim's privileged garden:

What is at stake in the story is not Susanna's physical well-being as she is threatened with rape and death but the honor of Joachim's household. When garden and wife are closed against intruders, Joachim's honor is secure. When the garden is open to intruders, or if the wife is open to a young lover, the entire household is ashamed, its honor lost.[29]

Glancy is surely correct in her insistence that modern readers often go along with the assumption of the story that the crime is attempted seduction rather than attempted rape—mainly because the modern reader is also beguiled by Susanna's reputed beauty. Seduction seems, from such a reading, "natural" or "normal." As Glancy puts it, the narrative of Susanna "relies on a code that represents femininity in terms of 'to-be-looked-at-ness.'"[30] Is it an overstatement to call what happens to Susanna rape? The elders, as we shall see, do not physically force themselves upon her. But the difficulty with calling their actions "seduction" is that this term does not adequately express the unequal power dynamics between Susanna and two respected (male) leaders of the community. While their confrontation may not have involved physical contact, in a real way it was overpowering to Susanna and would be referred to in modern terms as sexual harassment with important power dynamics involved. Brownmiller comments:

All rape is an exercise in power, but some rapists have an edge that is more than physical. They operate within an institutionalized setting that works to their advantage and in which a victim has little chance to redress her grievance.[31]

---

25. M. Bal, *Lethal Love: Feminist Literary Readings of Biblical Love Stories* (Bloomington: Indiana University Press, 1987) 2.

26. J. Glancy, "The Accused: Susanna and Her Readers," *JSOT* 58 (1993) 103-16.

27. For this study, I have consulted P. B. Bart and E. G. Moran, eds., *Violence Against Women* (London: Sage, 1993), esp. three essays therein: "Put Up and Shut Up: Workplace Sexual Assaults," Beth E. Schneider, 57-72; "'Riding the Bull at Gilley's': Convicted Rapists Describe the Rewards of Rape," Diana Scully and Joseph Marolla, 26-46; "The Imperishable Virginity of Saint Maria Goretti," Kathleen Young, 105-13. See also Susan Brownmiller, *Against Our Will: Men, Women, and Rape* (New York: Simon and Schuster, 1975); L. Baron and M. A. Straus, *Four Theories of Rape in American Society* (New Haven: Yale University Press, 1989); L. Ellis, *Theories of Rape: Inquiries into the Causes of Sexual Aggression* (New York: Hemisphere, 1989); and J. R. and H. Schwendinger, *Rape and Inequality* (London: Sage, 1983).

28. Brownmiller, *Against Our Will*, 377.
29. Glancy, "The Accused," 112.
30. Glancy, "The Accused," 112.
31. Brownmiller, *Against Our Will*, 256.

Given these dynamics, it is important to proceed with an assumption that we are dealing with what ought to be interpreted as attempted rape.

Glancy's analysis also alerts us to the significance of "seeing," "gazing," and "staring" in this story. The reader is invited to imagine the beauty of the bathing Susanna, for example, and thus to relate to the gaze of the hidden elders, who "burn with lust." Significantly, Daniel catches the deceit of the elders precisely on what they have done, and not on what they have seen. The focused attention of the criminal elders on Susanna is so intent on the attempted rape of her that they give no thought to anything else.

Finally, there is the curious reversal of roles for the figure of Daniel. Susanna is celebrated in this story as the persecuted Jew—persecuted by fellow Jews no less than by the Babylonians—and it is Daniel who assumes the role of the God-sent savior. Indeed, one would have to say that Daniel assumes the role of the angelic messenger—the God-sent salvation in virtually all the other Daniel stories. All of these details will be discussed at more length in the following analysis.

Verses 1-4, Introduction and Setting Among the Babylonian Exiles. The first character to whom the reader is introduced in this story is Joakim, the husband of Susanna.[32] He is among the exiles in Babylon, but is apparently rather well situated. The text describes him as rich, possessing a home with a fine garden. That Joakim is described as having married Susanna and built his fine home while in exile may well be a nod in the direction of Jeremiah's advice in his letter to exiles that they marry and build houses (and plant gardens) so that their numbers will not decrease while in exile (see Jeremiah 29).

We know from the book of Ezekiel (chaps. 14 and 20) that elders met in Ezekiel's home for important gatherings, much as the writer of Susanna reports the elders' meeting in the home of Joakim. While this detail may be dependent on sources such as Ezekiel, there is reason to believe that it was a significant memory of the sociological circumstances of the Babylonian exiles. This form of limited self-governance in exile is an important indicator that not only were the exiles able to maintain a familiar form of governance, but also that they settled in large enough groups to make this a viable social form.[33]

The Greek term used for Joakim's garden (παράδεισος *paradeisos*) is a Persian loan word from which we also get the English word *paradise* (see 2 Chr 33:20; Neh 2:8). There is another term that generally refers to a small garden (a vegetable garden? see Neh 3:16, 26). When this term is used together with the Greek term for a "paradise" (Eccl 2:5; Sir 24:30-31), it gives the reader the impression that the "paradise," in contrast to the smaller garden, is a large area kept in a somewhat natural state of beauty. Note that the Garden of Eden is called a "paradise."

It is significant that Susanna is described as being both beautiful and God-fearing. Is the reader meant to understand that these attributes go together or that they are traits that somehow balance each other? Is feminine beauty a potential danger in a male-oriented reading of these verses? It is not unusual for matriarchs of Israel to be described as beautiful (the descriptions of Sarah [Gen 12:14] and Rachel [Gen 29:17] use the same Greek terms; see also 1 Sam 25:3; 2 Sam 11:2; Ezek 16:13; Jdt 8:7). This very beauty, however, is taken almost inevitably as a foreshadowing of trouble (see Tob 3:14-15; 6:12). In her work on rape and violence against women, Susan Brownmiller notes the frequency with which rape cases are reported in the media with a comment about the "beauty" of the victim:

The murder of a beautiful young woman is no more regrettable, no greater tragedy, than the murder of a plain one, except in a culture that values beauty in women above other qualities. By putting greater store in the murder of a beauty, beauty acquires the seeds of its own destruction . . . thus the myth that rape is a crime of passion touched off by female beauty is given great credence, and women are influenced to believe that to be raped, and even murdered, is a testament to beauty.[34]

In contrast to, or in connection with, this beauty, Susanna "fears the Lord."

---

32. Glancy notes that it is significant that the male is introduced first, even though he is virtually absent from most of the story. See Glancy, "The Accused," 107.

33. For a full discussion of the import of this detail, see Smith, *The Religion of the Landless*.

34. Brownmiller, *Against Our Will*, 341.

The phrase used to describe Susanna as one who "feared the Lord" brings this text into an interesting relation with Sirach. The importance of "fear of the Lord" is repeated frequently in Sirach (Sir 1:13-14; 2:7-9; 6:16; 10:19-20; 21:6; 32:16; 34:14, 16), suggesting a possible relationship between the writer of Susanna and the wisdom tradition in late post-exilic Israel. Susanna, in short, practiced the way of the wise. Many readers, however, regard Sirach as blatantly misogynist (see Sir 25:16-26; 26:5-12; 42:9-14), so one must carefully note the contrasting positive view of a woman in Susanna. In short, one can make too much of wisdom connections (as has occurred frequently since such a suggestion was originally made by von Rad).[35] Furthermore, it is noted that Susanna's parents raised her in the knowledge of the law of Moses. This mention of the law of Moses is rather unique (and not present in the LXX version), but here in Susanna it serves as one piece of an important frame; the parents will be mentioned again in v. 62.

Verses 5-6, Introduction to the Corrupt Elders. Two elders are singled out and are introduced as being newly appointed judges. Verse 5 also features an unknown prophetic saying that is often related to Jer 23:14-15 and to the accusation against false elders in Jer 29:21-23.

The Greek term used here for "wickedness" (ἀνομία *anomia*) is used to translate a variety of Hebrew words that are rendered in English variously as "sin," "transgression," and "iniquity." Judgment is expressed against elders in Isa 3:14 and 9:15, and such leaders of the people were certainly vilified by Ezra (Ezra 10:14). The internal issues of wickedness suggest that Susanna was written in the Hellenistic era at a time when internal factions among the Jewish people began to tear apart the community and divide it into mutually antagonistic parties (a situation well established by the beginning of the New Testament era). It is this internal emphasis that gives Susanna its unique context in the rest of the book of Daniel.

Verses 7-12, The Lust of the Elders. Susanna takes daily walks in Joakim's garden—a detail that is essential to the development of the story. As she walks, she is seen by the two elders, who, seeing her, "desire" her (the term ἐπιθυμία [*epithymia*] is used for "covet" in Exod 20:17 LXX). The term *epithymia* runs throughout the story (vv. 8, 11, 14, 20, 56) and is a significant term that appears in wisdom tradition as well. According to Sirach, one is to "desire" wisdom and avoid the cheap lust of foolishness (Sir 16:1; 24:19). Consider also the wisdom context of the advice offered in 4 Maccabees:

Self-control, then, is dominance over the desires [*epithymia*]. Some desires are mental, others are physical, and reason obviously rules over both. (4 Macc 1:31-32 NRSV)

And why is it amazing that the desires of the mind for the enjoyment of beauty are rendered powerless? It is for this reason, certainly, that the temperate Joseph is praised, because by mental effort he overcame sexual desire. (4 Macc 2:1-2 NRSV)

Verse 9 contains an interesting interrelation of phrases and ideas. The elders do three things: (1) suppress their consciences; (2) turn away their eyes from heaven; and (3) forget their duty to administer justice. The term used in the first phrase, "suppressed" or "perverted," is common in wisdom literature (see Prov 6:14; 10:9; 11:20; Sir 19:25; 22:23). Perversion of judgment is also known in prophetic literature (see Isa 59:8; Mic 3:9; Hab 1:4).

The phrase "to look into heaven" is not common in the Bible, but similar ideas certainly occur. The book of Isaiah contains a call to vigilance for God's near deliverance (Isa 51:6) and describes Hezekiah as being weary from "looking into heaven" (Isa 38:14). Similarly Daniel "looked up" from fasting when he turned to God (Dan 10:5). Isaiah 33:15 suggests that people who survive God's judgment are those who "shut their eyes from looking on evil." Presumably, then, the phrase is a way to talk about trusting in God, and turning away from heaven is seen as the equivalent of the other two phrases in the verse. Moore notes, incidentally, that "heaven" could also be a replacement for "God" as is the case in the New Testament use of "kingdom of heaven" instead of

---

35. G. von Rad, *Wisdom in Israel* (Nashville: Abingdon, 1972).

"kingdom of God."[36] In general, the context reminds the reader of prophetic condemnation of the leaders of the Jewish community.

Verse 12 brilliantly establishes the importance of the "gaze," a dark sense of watching, in this story. The specific term used here is also used in Ps 37:12, where it is translated into English as: "The wicked plot against [or "watch for opportunities against"] the righteous, and gnash their teeth at them" (NRSV). Note that the wicked also "watched" Daniel to accuse him in Dan 6:12. In the story of Susanna, this gaze is intensified.

Verses 13-14, The Plot Is Set. When, in v. 13, the two elders discover each other heading back to look once again upon the beauty of Susanna, these false judges ply their trade on each other! They "examine" each other with the acumen of lawyers and discover the truth about themselves. They agree to keep each other's secret, and thus the second act of secrecy appears in the story (the first being the unnoticed watching of Susanna by these same elders, a watching that led to their taking their eyes off heaven). Throughout the story, secrecy is contrasted with openness, as the lustful gaze is contrasted with "seeing" in the sense of knowing the truth. The elders, however, now work in collusion. Brownmiller comments on modern cases:

When men rape in pairs or in gangs, the sheer physical advantage of their position is clear-cut and unquestionable. No simple conquest of man over woman, group rape is the conquest of Men over Women. It is within the phenomenon of group rape, stripped of the possibility of equal combat, that the male ideology of rape is most strongly evident. Numerical odds are proof of brutal intention. They are proof, too, of male bonding . . . and proof of a desire to humiliate the victim beyond the act of rape through the process of anonymous mass assault.[37]

Verses 15-27, The Main Events of the Story. The main events of the story must begin with the elders' secret entrance into the garden (a third act of secrecy). The writer does not specify when and how these men enter the garden, only that they are there when Susanna prepares to bathe. With the mention of Susanna's bath, the reader is reminded of David's walk on the roof of his palace and his lust for Bathsheba as he gazed on her bathing (2 Samuel 11). Like Susanna as well, Bathsheba is described as beautiful. Collins cites a number of other cases in Jewish tradition of men who are filled with desire when watching women bathe.[38] The LXX does not include the bath scene at all, however, but instead related that the elders desire her merely from watching her on her occasional walks in the garden.

Unlike David, whose position and power did not necessitate hiding, the elders watch Susanna in secret. Since the elders are in hiding, the maids who attend Susanna do not see them, and so the maids innocently shut the doors of the garden, leaving only the two elders and Susanna in the garden without further witnesses. At the moment the doors are shut, the elders become like David. They now have the power of the male over the female, of an elder over a young person, and of judges within the community.

In vv. 19-21, the elders speak as if Susanna can freely choose whether to comply with their desires—but she is not free. It is, rather, an act of coercion. Moore points out that the LXX is much stronger in the insistence of the elders and their initial approach to Susanna—suggesting rape.[39] If Susanna is unwilling to have sexual intercourse with each of them, then the judges will use their powerful weapon of false accusation—the word of a trusted official over a mere woman. False accusation by the powerful was the same weapon used against Daniel (Dan 6:25). It is worth pausing to reflect on the fact that false accusation is a threat *only* when there is an unequal distribution of power. Susanna's word is not equivalent to the word of the two male judges. Moreover, there are two of them to dispute Susanna's accusations—two is the required number of witnesses for a capital case (Deuteronomy 19).

In vv. 22-23, Susanna knows that she is threatened with being given over "into the hand" of her oppressor. Daniel, too, suffered the threat of being "in the hand" of his oppressor (Dan 3:15; cf. Deut 7:24; 32:39; 2 Kgs 18:29-30, 33-35; Jer 21:12; Dan 11:41; Mic 4:10).

---

36. Moore, *Daniel, Esther, and Jeremiah*, 96.
37. Brownmiller, *Against Our Will*, 187.
38. Collins, *Daniel*, 431.
39. Moore, *Daniel, Esther, and Jeremiah*, 97.

When faced with such overwhelming power over her, Susanna responds with the cry of the oppressed, "with a loud voice" (v. 24; see also vv. 42 and 60). Susanna thereby also fulfills Deut 22:24, which states that if a woman is threatened with rape within the city (that is, where she could be heard), she must call out; otherwise, she is suspected of complicity.[40] The same Greek term used here is used of the Jews crying out from the oppression of Pharaoh (Exod 2:23; 14:10 LXX), and it is the same "weapon" used by Hagar in the wilderness, when she cries out to God (Gen 21:16), who delivers her. Similarly, the Jews cry out for mercy from the king in 3 Macc 5:51. This is not to suggest, however, that this outcry is a special or unique term, but the recurrence of the theme is hardly coincidental. To call out with a loud voice occurs in other important contexts as well. In Num 20:16, the call of the people in slavery is answered by God's "sending an angel" (an obviously intriguing passage in the context of angelic deliverance in the Daniel tradition); and in Deut 26:7, the call is directed to the "God of our ancestors," a term noted in the Song of the Three (see also Jdt 4:9, 12; 5:12; Ezek 11:13, where Ezekiel pleads with God not to bring an end to the people).

But as Susanna cries out to God, the elders cry out to the other Jews. The elders make their accusation at this point in Theodotion, but in the LXX, they do not make their accusation public until the tribunal has been gathered. She has presented her fate to the only power that she now has: the delivering power of truth and, ultimately, of God. So Susanna joins Daniel and Mishael and Hananiah and Azariah, among many others, in becoming a model of piety and trustfulness in the context of exile and apparent defeat.

In response to Susanna's cries, the people in the house come to "see." But they do not see; they only know what the elders tell them. Curiously, it is not said that Susanna tries to tell another version of the events at this point in the story. She is calm before her accusers. The elders' version of the story is believed instantly; Susanna's youth and femininity (and beauty?) disqualify her immediately in the face of the older male judges. Even the servants are ashamed of her.

Verses 28-33, The Humiliation of the Oppressed. It is only at this point in the story that we hear of Susanna's children. When summoned to appear before the judges, Susanna comes with her parents, husband, and children. Although in the Theodotion text the husband is not mentioned specifically (Did he refuse to risk humiliation?), he is noted in the LXX version. Furthermore, as Collins points out, it is significant that they gather back at the house of Joakim—that is, the scene of the crime—so that they can all see the trees about which Daniel will soon question the "witnesses."[41] Why is the family included at this point? Is it because it is precisely the integrity of the family that is at issue here? In circumstances of exile and occupation and colonization, family takes on heightened importance. Memmi, for one, does not necessarily celebrate this fact, suggesting that the family becomes the only place where self-governing authority is still possible.[42] But we know that the familial structure was economically important too. Hence the tremendous importance given to the crisis of intermarriage in Ezra–Nehemiah.[43]

In the Septuagint version of the book of Susanna, she is stripped before her accusers. The intention of the translators was probably to convey that she was stripped naked, at least to the waist. (Being stripped for adultery is attested in Ezek 16:37-39; Hos 2:3, 10.) But there may be more going on here; Susanna has not even been adequately tried before this condemning act of stripping her is called for. The elders desire that Susanna be unveiled, so that they might "look" at her again. No reason is given for the order that Susanna be unveiled. Is her beauty supposed to be taken as further evidence against her by the court that has been called into session? Are we readers invited to be sympathetic to the elders' lust because of her reputed beauty? Why do they demand this humiliation of her? The Greek terms used here are correctly rendered in English as "feast the eyes" (NRSV). The same complex term is used in Ps 78:29 in reference to being satiated, filled. The Old

---

40. Collins, *Daniel*, 431.

41. Collins, *Daniel*, 431.
42. Memmi, *The Colonizer and the Colonized*, 98-99.
43. See Daniel Smith-Christopher, "The Mixed Marriage Crisis in Ezra 9–10 and Nehemiah 13: A Study of the Sociology of Post-Exilic Judean Community," in Eskenazi and Richards, eds., *Second Temple Studies 2* (Sheffield: JSOT, 1994) 243-65.

Greek adds the element of the elders' lust in looking at her. Thus Susanna is not merely overpowered; she is to be humiliated (note the discussion of the humiliation of the defeated in the Commentary on Daniel 5).

Verses 34-41, The Denunciation of Susanna. Verse 34 relates that the elders, rising to tell their stories, lay their hands on Susanna's head. Is this a way of identifying the guilt of the accused? In Lev 3:2, 8, 13 and 4:4, 11, 15, the officiating priest lays his hand on the sacrificial offering, an action intended to transfer punishment of guilt.[44] If this is true, then once again her guilt is presumed in their first act, before they even begin to tell their version of the events.

For the significance of "looking into heaven," see Commentary on v. 9. Here, Susanna's looking to heaven means trusting in the Lord. To trust in the Lord is an important post-exilic expression for faithfulness. God, according to Nebuchadnezzar, delivered servants who "trusted in him" (Dan 3:28) since no harm came to Daniel in the lions' den "because he had trusted in God" (Dan 6:23). Sirach teaches the reader to "consider the generations of old and see: has anyone trusted in the Lord and been disappointed?" (Sir 2:10 NRSV; see also 11:21; 32:24; see also the trust in God noted in 2 Macc 8:18; 3 Macc 2:4; 4 Macc 7:21). In the post-exilic context, trusting in the Lord is clearly a concept related to the power of God to deliver in circumstances of overwhelming threat. Once again, the writer uses terminology that equates Susanna's plight with the most serious of threats to Jews by foreigners in the book of Daniel and elsewhere.

The accusation brought against Susanna in vv. 36-41*a* is adultery. The elders, so they claim, saw her lying with a young man, who escaped when the elders presented themselves to the young couple in the course of sexual intimacy. The Greek terms used here make the sexual nature of this accusation clear (see Gen 19:5; 39:10; and Jdt 12:16). In the Theodotion version, the alleged young man was too strong for the elders to restrain him, while in the LXX the young man escapes in disguise. In the Theodotion version, the elders claim to be overpowered, but in reality it is Susanna who is overpowered by the elders' story. The judges are believed, and Susanna is convicted. The reader is invited to experience indignation at this injustice and to side with, if not identify with, the female against the authority of the male elders.

Verses 42-51, Susanna's Cry and Daniel's Arrival. Once again, Susanna is portrayed as the oppressed "crying out" to God. This is obviously an important theme in the story and, as the commentary has indicated, throughout the Bible—especially in the post-exilic period. But what is of further interest here is precisely what Susanna cries out. The phrase "O eternal God" is not widely attested in the Bible (Gen 21:33; Isa 26:4; 40:28), but it is found rather extensively in the book of Daniel (Dan 3:33 [v. 100 of The Song of the Three]; 4:31 [Theodotion]; 7:14, 27; 9:24; 12:2). It appears to be the case that this is yet another of the ways of referring to God ("the living God," "God of heaven," etc.) that became popular in the period of exile and occupation.

A second interesting phrase in this prayer is the reference to God as the "knower of secrets" or the "one who knows things hidden" (author's trans.). This aspect of God is of obvious importance in a story where evil and corruption have been associated with persons, ideas, and thoughts that are hidden. Truth will be a revelation in the sense that it will be released from its captivity at the hands of the powerful. Susanna knows their deceit, of course, and now finally protests her innocence (v. 43). Susanna, once again, is similar to Daniel (see Daniel 6).

Verse 44 is deceptively short, but politically powerful: "The Lord heard her cry." Compare the hearing of God in stories of two other women of Jewish history and lore: Hagar (Gen 21:12, 17) and Judith (Jdt 4:13; 8:17). In v. 45, God's action is to stir up trouble for human leaders once again—God's resistance to human oppression and incompetence. Daniel, now in the role usually expected of an angelic messenger, is "stirred" by the Spirit of God (see Judg 5:12; Isa 51:9, 17; 52:1; Dan 7:4; 11:25; 12:2; 2 Macc 13:4).

Daniel calls out, in prophetic tones, that he will not be a party to the shedding of innocent blood (cf. Jer 7:6 as a classic example of

---

44. Collins adds references to scapegoating in Lev 8:14, 18, 22; Exod 29:10, 15, 19, and especially Lev 24:14. See Collins, *Daniel*, 432.

this phrase in prophetic literature; it is used extensively as an image of killing the innocent, especially God's chosen messengers). Daniel describes the people as "fools." Jeremiah, too, condemned his listeners as fools (Jer 5:21), and the image of the fool runs through Sirach as the antithesis to the godly, the pious, and the wise: "The mind of fools is in their mouth/ but the mouth of the wise is in their mind" (Sir 21:26; see also Sir 4:27; 8:17; 16:23; 21:14).

Daniel calls on the judges to judge properly. The witnesses have not been thoroughly examined. This is necessary in Jewish law,[45] but is the reader to presume from the story that Daniel is reacting to the improper conduct of the trial or to some knowledge he possesses of the events that he has not yet revealed? Should the reader assume that Daniel was clever enough to sense something wrong about the elders' story or that such knowledge comes with being "stirred" by God? Whatever the reason for Daniel's coming to Susanna's defense, the other elders recognize in him a wisdom beyond his years.[46] Daniel is invited to come and to finally reveal what has been hidden from everyone but Susanna, the two corrupt judges, and Daniel himself.

Verses 52-59, The Examination of the Judges and the Truth Revealed. Daniel separates the two false judges, intending to examine each of them in turn. He requests that each judge be brought to him separately. What is interesting is that Daniel greets each of them with hostility. The first is called "an old relic of wicked days."[47] (Since the "day of adversity" is noted in Isa 50:9; 51:6; Jer 16:19; and Amos 6:3, one may wonder whether "the evil days" that are referred to here are the days leading up to the exile. After all, it was a central tenet of deuteronomistic theology that the exile was brought on by the sins of the people, and the leaders particularly.) Daniel delivers a searing condemnation of the generation of the exile in words similar to those of Jeremiah or Isaiah. In v. 53, Daniel lists the sins of leaders in a manner that is highly stylized in prophetic speech (see Isa 5:23; 29:21; Jer 7:6; 19:4; 22:3, 17) but is also noteworthy in wisdom literature (Prov 17:15; 24:24).

Verse 54 leaves no doubt that sexual impropriety/adultery is the accusation here (cf. the situation in Judith 12 that uses some of the same Greek terminology). Daniel's asking the elder about what kind of tree under which this alleged sin took place allows for a clever wordplay in Greek. The type of tree the elder names is called σχίνος (*schinos*; NAB and NRSV, "mastic"), and Daniel follows this up with a condemnation that calls for the false witness "to be cut in two," or σχίζω (*schizō*, v. 55). Moore, interestingly, suggests that we maintain the wordplay even in English and, therefore, supplies "clove tree" and "cleave" in the first instance, and "yew" and "hew" in the second instance.[48] It is also noteworthy that an angel appears as an agent of judgment in Daniel's condemnation of the lying elder.[49]

Verse 56 mirrors the preceding questioning, this time of the second elder. Once again, Daniel meets the false witness with hostility, and once again the specific vocabulary of abuse is noteworthy: Daniel calls him a "son of Canaan" (NAB and NRSV, "offspring of Canaan"). Both Ezra 9:1 and Neh 9:8 use "Canaanite" as a term of derision, referring to the peoples traditionally conquered by Joshua at the Israelites' entry into the land; by Ezra's time, the term had long since ceased to be an accurate description of an actual, contemporary cultural/religious group.[50] It is possible that Ezek 16:3 is intended to be a similar slur in the context of delivering a judgment. However, the use of "Canaan" as the name for the people who dwelled in Palestine before the Israelite settlement was common in the late Hellenistic literature (see Judith 5; Bar 3:22; 1 Macc 9:37). Its use here, strikingly, seems to be intended as an ethnic slur. Again, in this accusation, lust is given the blame for leading

---

45. See *m. 'Abot* 1.9, in which a similar case of examining witnesses is given in regard to the first-century CE rabbinic teacher Rabbi Yochanon ben Zakkai. There, however, the emphasis is on the rabbi's aversion to killing. Both the story about Susanna and the rabbinic case are similar to the illustration in the Gospel of John of the woman caught in adultery and Jesus' dismissal of the "witnesses" and those who would stone her. See J. Neusner, *A Life of Yohanan Ben Zakkai Ca. 1–80 CE* (Leiden: Brill, 1970); and *Development of a Legend: Studies on the Traditions Concerning Yohanan Ben Zakkai* (Leiden: Brill, 1970) 51-53.

46. Collins quotes just such a tradition. See Collins, *Daniel*, 433.

47. Moore translates this phrase as "aged in evil days" or "You who have grown old in wickedness," but I argue that "old relic *of* wicked days" makes more sense, especially in the light of Daniel's second appeal to history in the examination of the other elder.

48. Moore, *Daniel, Esther, and Jeremiah*, 106-7.

49. Collins, *Daniel*, 434, notes Isa 37:36 and Ezekiel 9 for the theme of the avenging angel.

50. See Daniel Smith, "Mixed Marriage," in *Second Temple Studies*, vol. 2 (Sheffield: JSOT, 1993) 60-65.

the judge into sin. The wisdom associations of this idea have already been noted (it plays a role in the beginning of the story, v. 14, and at the end, v. 56), but note also that "corruption" also turns up at the beginning and ending (vv. 9 and 56). There is a circular sense of "just rewards" in the story of Susanna; the lying, lustful elders are condemned for what they gave themselves up to in the beginning.

The contrast between the daughters of Israel and the daughters of Judah is quite interesting, although somewhat obscure. Are we to see in Daniel's statement a reference to the well-known northern propensity to mix with Canaanite religious ideas on a scale supposedly not tolerated in the southern kingdom before the exile? Collins doubts this, because Susanna herself is called an Israelite earlier, and he suggests that perhaps the later Samaritan split is what is referred to here.[51] This would be a post-exilic religious development in the Jewish community. The precise nature of the Samaritan split, however, is still quite controversial,[52] so this must remain an enigmatic reference in the story.

When questioned about the kind of tree under which they witnessed Susanna's "adultery" taking place, the second elder answers, "Under an evergreen oak" (v. 58). The reader is struck by the difference in the testimony of the elders and joins the surrounding community, as if sitting in a modern courtroom, when they all come to know the truth of the matter. The second elder, too, is condemned by Daniel to face the executing angel of God, who stands ready with sword in hand.

Verses 60-64, Reaction and Conclusion. The people cry out, but this time in jubilation. God is celebrated as the one who saves those who hope in God (see Pss 33:18; 42:5, 11; 69:6; Sir 34:13; 49:10; 2 Macc 2:18; 7:20; 9:20; 4 Macc 17:4). Verses 61-62 participate in the role-reversal that is typical of the Daniel stories—the guilty are condemned, and the innocent are vindicated.

Five verses seems a lot of text to dedicate to the happy ending of this story, but the passage serves to justify the conclusion that putting the world right and vindicating the innocent are extremely important aspects of the story. This is an idealistic ending—the restoration of the community under the law of Moses. And it is precisely these last five verses that represent the vision and the hope of the writer of the story of Susanna.

The LXX has a nice thought at the end:

On account of this, the youths are the beloved of Jacob, in their singlemindedness. Let us also watch out for capable young sons, for youths will be pious, and there will be in them a spirit of knowledge and understanding for ever and ever.[53]

Given Susanna's courage, obviously we should amend this quotation to read that we should watch out for capable sons and daughters! Collins suggests that this ending has the tendency to focus the story on youth vs. elders, rather than Theodotion's emphasis on the courage of Susanna. But we should note that the general themes of innocence, guilt, and truth are all seen as significant in the conclusion of the story. This should not distract the reader from the central elements of the story as a whole—that is, the oppression of the powerless by the powerful.

51. Collins, *Daniel*, 434.
52. See references to the Samaritan debate in Smith, *The Religion of the Landless*.
53. Collins, *Daniel*, 424.

REFLECTIONS

Germaine Greer has suggested two categories of rape: "grand rape" and "petit rape." The former is what we ordinarily associate with forcible rape. The latter, however, is a form of rape in which "the seducer in fact has some disproportionately unfair advantage over the woman. He need not threaten her, but it is his superior power which induces her to acquiesce against her will."[54] Clearly, the difference between seduction and rape is not so clear, especially in a case like that of Susanna.

54. Quoted by L. C. Curran, "Rape and Rape Victims in Metamorphoses," in *Women in the Ancient World*, J. Peradotto and J. P. Sullivan, eds. (Albany: SUNY Press, 1984) 263-86.

Only when one reads literature on rape does one begin to realize how complicit one becomes in Susanna's abuse by "understanding" (read: excusing) the near rape of her as just a symptom of the social circumstances of exile. Such a view diminishes Susanna's suffering and marginalizes her as a possession of her husband and as a temptress (only because she is beautiful). But it is only when we understand the story about rape, when we confront the sobering impact of using the term itself, that the story actually unfolds with all its power as a part of the Daniel corpus about resistance.

Susanna is approached by two men who try to exert their influence, power, and authority over her. The distribution of power and choice is clearly weighted in favor of these elders. She must either give herself to them or face death as a falsely accused adulteress. Susanna's courage, her turning to God in the face of overwhelming danger, is, therefore, the equivalent to Hananiah, Mishael, and Azariah standing before Nebuchadnezzar and refusing his command to bow down and pray to him.

The story of Susanna invites us to consider injustice within as well as outside of our religious life. Thus the context of exile is almost an ironic twist—as if to say to the reader, "The Babylonians aren't the *only* sources of injustice here." Finally, we must remember that the story is not only about the sin of the elders, but also about the corruptibility and foolishness of the entire exiled community. The elders are not the only fools identified by the young Daniel. The community in the story of Susanna is ready to judge her without a trial, and she is marched through a kangaroo court. The community, too, is showing signs of internal corruption and lack of fortitude. Daniel calls for solidarity as well as wisdom when he labels them fools for condemning "a daughter of Israel without examination and without learning the facts" (v. 48 NRSV). Note, further, the enigmatic saying "This is how you have been treating the daughters of Israel, and they were intimate with you through fear; but a daughter of Judah would not tolerate your wickedness" (v. 57 NRSV). It has been speculated that this verse refers to conditions before the exile, or perhaps to the Samaritan split (i.e., Samaritans = north/Israelites). In at least one significant passage, "daughters" is a metaphor for the people as a whole. In Ezekiel 23, the northern kingdom, called Oholah (Samaria), and the southern kingdom, called Oholibah (Jerusalem), are condemned for having committed "adultery" with Assyria, Babylonia, and Egypt. If Daniel intends a similar metaphor, then the "daughters" are the people as a whole, corrupted by the "foreigners," implied in his calling the corrupt elders "Canaanite" (v. 56). Susanna's treatment, then, is severely condemned by Daniel in terms that suggest that the elders' behavior is equivalent to idolatrous behavior of the people as a whole in previous eras.

It is clear that Susanna goes through all the steps of the otherwise oppressed *male* Jews in the Daniel tradition: confrontation with an overpowering threat, calling out to God, angelic/miraculous delivery, and punishment of the accusers. Reflection on this detail calls on us to face a most uncomfortable reality in the modern church: We can become so wrapped up in the faith and justice issues of the world that we fail to address the insidious presence of injustice within our own fellowship.

The continued second-class status of women within some churches, and particularly the continued refusal of some faith traditions to accept a woman's call to equal leadership in ministry, is simply an acceptance of the world's judgment of women, and it makes a mockery of the church's claim to seek justice and the full expression of the kingdom of God within our world.[55] Those who would continue such suppression and oppression, even in the church, ought to keep in mind that the story of Susanna emphasizes that "the Lord heard her cry"!

---

55. The world's judgment of women is only too clear. Between 1960 and 1987, the reported cases of rape in the United States increased 440%. See L. Baron and M. A. Straus, *Four Theories of Rape* (New York: Hemisphere, 1989).

BEL AND THE DRAGON

VERSES 1-42

OVERVIEW

This chapter consists of two stories that are only loosely related. There is considerable scholarly debate as to whether these stories originally belonged together or were artificially joined when they were made a part of the Daniel tradition.[56] Moore ingeniously suggests that just as the Susanna story represents Daniel as a precocious and wise youth, so also the stories of Bel and the Dragon—taking place during the Persian rule—represent the old and wise Daniel still true to his faith.[57] Certainly both stories deal with idolatry, although in one case the idol is fashioned by human hands and in the other case it is a living animal. Both parts obviously deal with the theme of idolatry in exile, already a major concern in Second Isaiah and in the Hebrew/Aramaic stories of Daniel 1–6. Finally, some scholars have suggested that Daniel brings these contests upon himself.[58] But let us not forget the ominous words of the king, which begin the episode of Bel and the Dragon: "Why do you not worship Bel?" (v. 4). From the lips of a man who can dispatch death in seconds, the implied threat is obvious. However, there is another clear difference between the stories of this chapter and Daniel 1–6, with which they otherwise have much in common. The Jewish courtier Daniel is much bolder now; he not only wisely advises the king, but also laughs at the king's mistakes. Indeed, one of the most important details of this story is precisely that Daniel has developed a dangerous sense of humor.

56. Moore, *Daniel, Esther, and Jeremiah,* 146-47.
57. Moore, *Daniel, Esther, and Jeremiah,* 9.
58. L. Wills, *The Jew in the Court of the Foreign King* (Minneapolis: Fortress, 1990) 134.

VERSES 1-22, THE STORY OF BEL

COMMENTARY

Verses 1-2, Introduction and Setting. In the LXX version of this story, Daniel is curiously identified as a priest, and there is an early mention of the prophet Habakkuk, who will play an important part in the second story about the "dragon." Moore wonders whether this mention of a priestly Daniel suggests that these stories were originally about another Daniel.[59] That is possible, but may simply be a detail that developed when these stories circulated separately.

The stories in Bel and the Dragon are identified with the Persian period in the Theodotion text, although the subjects are Babylonian ("Bel" is an epithet for "Marduk," the great national god of the Babylonians). It is possible that the chronological identification with the period of Cyrus is intended to establish Daniel as one of the trusted leaders of the empire ("friend of the king"), rather like Daniel's fame in Daniel 6. Once again, we see that the Greek stories that have become a part of the Daniel tradition take most of their clues from the sixth of the Aramaic/Hebrew stories, where the ruler is identified as Darius "the Mede" (who, nevertheless, is most likely modeled on the historical Darius, third

59. Moore, *Daniel, Esther, and Jeremiah,* 133.

ruler of the Persian Empire after Cyrus). What is curious, however, is that Cyrus is not mentioned by name throughout the rest of the story, creating suspicion that the opening lines were added later. In the story, the ruler is identified only as "the king" (in the LXX, Cyrus is not mentioned at all), and the reader may have questions about a story that has Cyrus worshiping a Babylonian idol.

In the writings of Herodotus, King Astyages (v. 1) dreams of his daughter giving "birth" to the destruction of his Median regime; in fact, Cyrus the Great is the grandson of Astyages, and he did defeat the Median Empire in his early moves toward the consolidation of power in the Persian Empire. This is the only mention of King Astyages in the Daniel tradition—clearly intended to make up for the mistake of placing Darius before Cyrus in Daniel 6.

Verses 3-4a, The Worship of the Idol. The idol Bel is introduced here. The idol is "fed" from the king's holdings every day and is honored each day by the king. Moore notes that the specific amounts fed to the idol are not so important as the intention to indicate "large amounts."[60] Furthermore, we know from Herodotus that a table, presumably for human food, was indeed present in certain Babylonian shrines.[61] Is it only a coincidence that once again the issue of food is at the heart of a Daniel story (cf. Daniel 1)?

It is written that the king traveled every day to "do honor" to the idol. Incidentally, we know that Cyrus claimed (in the Cyrus Cylinder) as part of his imperial propaganda for Babylonian consumption that he revered Marduk, and he further claimed that Marduk made his conquest of Babylon possible.[62] Since the identification of this king as "Cyrus" plays a rather insignificant role, however, little importance need be assigned to this coincidence. The term used for "doing honor," one of many used for acts of worship or reverence (typically translated as "doing reverence" or "homage" by kissing the hand or by prostration), is not only common in the Daniel stories (see Dan 3:5-7, 11-12, 14-15, 18, 27-28) but is also used of proper worship in the book of Psalms (Pss 22:27; 29:2; 45:12; 66:4; 72:11; 81:9) and in Isaiah (Isa 2:8, 20; 27:13; 37:38; 44:15, 17, 19; 45:14; 46:6; 49:7, 23; 66:23). Such acts, therefore, include the implication of recognizing a higher authority as well as a spiritual authority. The term runs through the story of Bel like a major theme.

Verses 4b-9, The King Establishes the Contest: Bel vs. Yahweh. The king's questioning of Daniel's refusal to honor Bel sets the stage for the coming challenge—and certainly implies a threat. Daniel must respond; it is not a matter of choice, as some commentators have suggested. This is similar to the opening sequences of the Hebrew/Aramaic Daniel traditions: Daniel does not stop praying to his God (Daniel 6), and Azariah, Mishael, and Hananiah do not bow to Nebuchadnezzar's statue (Daniel 3). The contrast between Bel and Yahweh sets the parameters for the challenge that follows, which is reminiscent of Elijah's challenge to the priests of Baal on Mt. Carmel.

Daniel contrasts the idol with the living God. The Greek term for "idol" (χειροποίητος *cheiropoiētos*) is an interesting, complex term composed of "made" (ποιέω *poieō*) and "hand" (χείρ *cheir*), thus "handmade god" (cf. Lev 26:1, 30, "carved image"; Judg 8:18; Isa 2:18; 10:11; 16:12; 19:1; 21:9; 31:7; 46:6; Wis 14:8). In contrast, the "living God" (cf. 3 Macc 6:28) is the God whom Daniel worships. "Living God" is also an interesting term, where one might have expected a more specific title that identifies this God with the Jews. At this point in Jewish tradition, however, the writer is asking his audience to take a somewhat more philosophical position. It is no longer a question of "your" god vs. "our" God, but the living God vs. mere idols; and thus Daniel's use of the phrase "living God" is not merely an alternative to the king's chosen object of reverence, but a direct challenge: the living God as opposed to your foolishness.

In v. 6, the king responds to Daniel's challenge instantly with a reasoned argument: If Bel does not live, how, then, does Daniel explain Bel's appetite? Daniel's reply entails what is perhaps the most shocking aspect of the entire Bel tradition, and a detail that dramatically sets this story apart from the rest of

---

60. Moore, *Daniel, Esther, and Jeremiah*, 134.
61. Herodotus *The History* 1:181.
62. *ANET*, 315-16.

the Daniel tradition, yet binds it inextricably to that tradition: Daniel *laughs.*

How is Daniel's laughter to be understood? Moore suggests that Daniel must have felt quite secure to mock the king in this way,[63] but there is much more to this laughter than mere security within the context of the story line. It is important to note that laughter in the Hebrew Bible is usually an act of derision and mockery (only a few exceptions to this can be noted, such as Gen 21:6; Eccl 2:2; 3:4). Abraham and Sarah laugh from incredulity bordering on irony (Gen 17:17; 18:12-13, 15). In Job, laughter is a sign of scorn or mockery, particularly as the result of reversal of fortune (Job 8:21; 17:6; 22:19; cf. Ps 80:6; Jer 20:8; 48:26, 39; Lam 1:7; 3:14; Ezek 23:32; Amos 7:9). The theme of laughter as reversal is clear, for example, in Ps 52:6-7:

The righteous will see, and fear,
  and will laugh at the evildoer, saying,
"See the one who would not take
  refuge in God,
but trusted in abundant riches,
  and sought refuge in wealth!" (NRSV)

In wisdom literature, laughter from mirth is discouraged (Eccl 7:4, 6; Sir 19:30; 27:13) as in Sir 21:20:

A fool raises his voice when he laughs,
  but the wise smile quietly. (NRSV)

As we approach the later Hellenistic period materials, the theme of laughter as scorn increases. Wisdom 5:3 speaks eloquently of the oppressors who once mocked the poor and righteous in laughter, while in Jdt 12:12, the Assyrian men fear that Judith will laugh at them if they do not sexually use her, and in 4 Macc 5:28, the martyr story of Eleazar has him saying to his persecutors, "You shall have no such occasion to laugh at me" (NRSV). Finally, social reversal is implicit in Jesus' dramatic remark in the Gospel of Luke: "Woe to you who are laughing now,/ for you will mourn and weep" (Luke 6:25*b* NRSV). When this is all taken into consideration, Daniel's laughter becomes an interesting advance in the entire corpus of Daniel stories. By the time of the writing of the story of Bel, the quiet confidence of Daniel, Hananiah, Azariah, and Mishael that God would deliver them had become the mocking laughter of the revolutionary reversal of fortune that is a central aspect of apocalyptic political doctrine.

Daniel warns the king not to be deceived. That the leaders of Israel deceived the Jews is a central aspect of the theology of Isaiah (e.g., Isa 3:12; 9:15) and Ezekiel (e.g., Ezek 8:17; 13:10), but openness to deception is considered a form of foolishness in the late wisdom tradition as well (e.g., Sir 3:24; 9:7-8; 15:12; 16:23). The idol is made of "clay and bronze," two materials that the reader of the book of Daniel is familiar with in association with handmade gods in Daniel 1–6, although one might have expected the more precious silver and gold at this point. His advising the king not to be deceived once again associates Daniel with wisdom.

In v. 8, the king's response is anger. The allusion to the anger of Nebuchadnezzar in Daniel 3 (see also Dan 9:16; 11:44) is the warning that a serious challenge is about to be set: If Bel is no god, then the priests will die; but if Bel is genuine, then Daniel will die for blasphemy. Collins notes the "cavalier introduction of the death penalty" in this story, but in any context of exile and occupation the threat of death is a constant reality.[64] Given this element, it seems strange that some scholars would continue to argue that these stories are "less negative" toward the king than are the stories of Daniel 1–6.[65]

Verses 10-17, The Contest Is Carried Out. Verse 10 clarifies that Daniel is alone, pitted against a large number of the priests of Bel. This adds drama to the story, of course, but sociologically it represents Daniel as a minority facing the majority Babylonian culture. Both aspects are important. (Note also the possible allusion to Elijah facing the priests of Baal in 1 Kings 18.) But the inclusion of the wives and children is a comment on the corruption of the entire pagan society. It is ambiguous, when the time arrives, whether the entire families are also punished when Bel is revealed to be false.

The priests invite the king to view the contest, indeed, to participate himself, by

---

63. Moore, *Daniel, Esther, and Jeremiah,* 136.

64. Collins, *Daniel,* 413.
65. Wills, *The Jew in the Court of the Foreign King,* 133-34.

overseeing the placement of the food in the idol's temple. The king is then invited to seal the door with his symbol of authority. (In the LXX, the priests as well as the king are invited to seal the opening.) We are reminded of another chamber that was sealed with the sign of the occupying ruler in Matt 27:66. The priests, then, invite the king to participate in their deception. This invitation further increases their risk, of course, but the priests are confident in the king's presence because of what they know is hidden—picking up a theme from the Susanna tradition of the hidden vs. the revealed. Daniel reveals truth; his opponents hide the truth.

After the king, then Daniel is invited to oversee the preparations. But Daniel takes one further precaution. Although the reader is not led to believe that Daniel knows about the secret entrance, he does know that the removal of the food must involve the priests' gaining access to it in some fashion. The spreading of ashes is meant, therefore, to detect *any* entrance into the chamber in the vicinity of the food. The Greek text clarifies that the priests of Bel did not observe Daniel's placing of the ashes on the floor; only the king witnessed this action, and thus the king is privy to Daniel's plan from the beginning.

The king rises early in the morning. The particular time reference may not necessarily be important, although rising early was a sign of intentionality, a measure of the importance of an act (cf. Moses with Pharaoh, Exod 8:20; 9:13). Sirach advises to seek wisdom "from early morning" (Sir 4:14; 6:36; and to seek God early, Sir 32:14; 39:5). The slow development of the story masterfully builds tension before the moment of revelation. It appears at first that Daniel is defeated. (Note that in the LXX Daniel challenges the priests to also verify that the seals have not been broken. The LXX at this point seems to enjoy heightening the extent of the irony.)

Verses 18-19, The Royal Fool and the Laughing Jew. Verses 18-19 must be read together. The king commits a foolish act by saying in a "loud voice": "You are great, O Bel, and in you there is no deceit at all!" He proclaims that his previous actions were correct before he even gives time to a full consideration of the facts. Now the king is portrayed as not only gullible, but foolish and hasty as well. The trap is set for Daniel to spring.

In response to the king's claim to power, to truth, and to religious wisdom, Daniel laughs and tells the king to look at the footprints in the ashes. In the LXX, Daniel laughs "heartily," increasing the level of mockery. The king is invited to "look [imperative] and know." The priests' faith is based on deception, but Daniel's faith is based on what is open and can be seen.

Verses 20-22, Daniel Reveals the Truth. When he realizes the truth about the priests' deception, once again he is enraged. He orders not only the priests but also their wives and children arrested. When the priests reveal the truth about their secret entrance, the king has them put to death. (One wonders whether they expected some form of clemency for this act of revelation.) In the LXX, however, Daniel reveals the hidden door—which presumes that he knew what was going to happen all along—and the king is taken to the houses of the priests, where the food is found. Although it is left somewhat vague whether the wives and children are also killed, it would not be totally unexpected, given their mention throughout the rest of the story. Once again, although moderns may be disturbed at this aspect of the punishment, it is not an unusual element of reversal in Hebrew lore. This detail also serves to magnify the megalomania of the king; his anger is so irrational that he will even kill children (cf. Dan 3:13; 8:6, 19; 9:16, 26). Perhaps we should view these events—fictional though they may be—with the same sadness of heart that, during the Passover seder, accompanies the spilling of drops of wine in remembrance of those Egyptians whose death was a part of liberation from Egyptian slavery.

Daniel, rather than participate in the killing of persons, destroys the idol and its house. This is an interesting contrast of Daniel's religious action and the king's murderous decree (note the number of executions in the book of Daniel: 2:13, 24; 3:23; 4:34; 6:34; 11:44). It is possible that Daniel's actions allude to Jer 51:44: "I will punish Bel in Babylon." (Bel is also mentioned in Isa 46:1 and in the apocryphal Letter of Jeremiah, which is largely concerned with idolatry as well.)

Many scholars have noted that the temple of Bel/Marduk was actually destroyed by the Persian ruler Xerxes I (486–465 BCE), and that occurrence must have been in the background of the events described in this story. One can hardly miss the significance of placing a Jew at the center of the destruction of the temple of Marduk—the very religious symbol of power for the conquering Babylonians.

VERSES 23-42, THE STORY OF THE DRAGON

COMMENTARY

Verses 23-42 bear an interesting relation to Daniel 6, as each places Daniel in the lions' den as punishment for his religious faith. However, the story of the dragon has some curious elements to it, not the least of which is the strange involvement of a prophet traditionally named Habakkuk.

Verse 23, The Setting and the "Dragon." The term used for "dragon" is a Greek term (δράκων *drakōn*) that translates the Hebrew for "serpent" (תנין *tannîn*), more specifically for "snake." In the Moses story, the connotation is clearly a snake (Exod 7:9-10, 12; Deut 32:33). But the term is also used to refer to the echoes of the ancient Canaanite belief about Yam (Job 7:12), the god of the sea, represented as a coiling serpent, and "Leviathan" (Job 9:13; 26:12; Pss 74:13-14; 104:26; 148:7; Isaiah 27; Amos 9:3). Many scholars have speculated about snake worship (zoolatry) as an aspect of Babylonian worship, but despite some interesting archaeological fragments, the case remains unconvincing. Since living snakes were certainly an aspect of Egyptian religious practice, some scholars have suggested that the origin of this story is in the Egyptian Jewish diaspora.[66]

Other scholars have suggested that the snake/dragon story is a midrash (a story that develops, or expands upon, an earlier short text) on Jer 51:34, 44:

King Nebuchadnezzar of Babylon has
    devoured me,
  he has crushed me;
he has made me an empty vessel,
    he has swallowed me like a monster;
he has filled his belly with my delicacies,
    he has spewed me out.
. . . .
I will punish Bel in Babylon,
    and make him disgorge what he has
      swallowed.
The nations shall no longer stream to him;
    the wall of Babylon has fallen. (NRSV)[67]

Ezekiel 29:3 LXX calls Pharaoh the "great dragon" (see also Ezek 32:2). Given this association of the "dragon" to the exile, one can see that, like Jeremiah and Ezekiel, the story of the dragon runs in close association with the tradition of Jonah in making references to the exilic experience. I would argue that there is a thematic connection between these texts, rather than interpreting the dragon story in the Daniel tradition as a specific development of the scriptural tradition of Jeremiah 51. If, for example, Jonah's "dragon" is an allegory of Babylon's "swallowing" of the Jewish community, then Daniel's destruction of the dragon is at least as compelling for its listeners as was his destruction of Bel and the sanctuary of Babylonian power.

Verses 24-26, The Challenge and the Contest. The king challenges Daniel—a clear reference to the story of Bel, which precedes this episode. The dragon, unlike the god Bel, however, is a living animal and not merely a handmade idol, lending credence to

---

66. Collins's discussion is helpful. See Collins, *Daniel*, 414.

67. The text from Jeremiah, incidentally, is also often seen as the basis for the Jonah story, particularly for those scholars who see in the Jonah story elements of an allegory of the exile. Many scholars dismiss the allegorical interpretation of Jonah as a reference to the Babylonian exile simply because the entire story cannot be matched up point by point with the experience of the exile. But this is wooden thinking. Certainly there is more to Jonah than merely an allegorical analogy of the exile, but that does not cancel its allegorical aspects.

the notion that this story is based on the keeping of sacred animals as symbols of deities.

Daniel's response to the king's challenge to him to worship the dragon is to focus not on the aspect of its being a living creature, but on who is actually sovereign, on who is "Lord," and—ultimately—on who is powerful. Thus Daniel presents a counterchallenge to the king. Daniel proposes to kill the dragon without using the weapons of worldly power—without "sword or club." Daniel will prove the truth without the world's tools, for it is inherently blasphemous to suggest that truth can be derived from weapons.

Verse 27, The Killing of the Serpent. The particular formula that Daniel mixes—that is, fat, hair, and pitch—does not appear to have particular significance. Although unpleasant even to the modern reader, this mixture hardly appears lethal. But perhaps that is just the point. Those commentators who have suggested that Daniel must have slipped something lethal into the mixture may well be missing a significant detail that Daniel succeeds precisely without lethal weapons. Some scholars have argued that the original Aramaic source for this story must have contained a reference to a wind that brought about the death of the dragon. The idea is that this wind is related to the story of Marduk's destruction of Tiamat in the Babylonian creation story in the *Enuma Elish*, where Marduk uses wind to burst the belly of the sea monster Tiamat. Others suggest that Daniel knew of the explosive nature of the mixture. Moore rehearses some of the traditional ways that this concoction has been amended to include lethal elements like nails, combs, and hatchets.[68] The result, in any case, is that when the serpent eats the cakes that Daniel makes from this mixture, the dragon bursts open. And with this Daniel demonstrates to the king that no true god could have been defeated so easily. This quick dispatch of the serpent becomes the opening sequence to the central theme of the story of the dragon: the Babylonians' attempt to avenge the destruction of Bel.

Verses 28-32, Daniel Thrown to the Lions. Verse 28 contains a startling concept. The Babylonians are angry because of Daniel's influence on the king, and to express their frustration they use a surprising phrase: "The king has become a Jew." By the time of the Hellenistic period, it is not inconceivable in Jewish thought that a foreigner might "become" a Jew—presumably referring to a convert. Collins objects that even this fact does not necessarily refer to conversion in the modern sense.[69] But can we even know what "conversion" meant in that period? A clear transformation of character and religious observance is suggested by the vocabulary of the passage. The degrees of transformation in the foreign king make an interesting study in the Daniel tradition, including the statements made by Nebuchadnezzar and Darius in Daniel 1–6.[70] The foreign monarchs often proclaim that they are impressed by the God of the Jews, and they even acknowledge this God's impressive achievements. But does this suggest conversion or transformation? I would argue that the oft-noted positive view of kings in Daniel 1–6 is only a positive view of transformed and humbled kings. Here in Bel and the Dragon, we have moved beyond simply a change of behavior in favor of the Jews. The reader must keep in mind that the story does not so much suggest that the king did, in fact, convert, but merely that the Babylonians accuse him of having done so. This accusatory context lends credence to reading this phrase as an actual conversion precisely because it would be considered so shocking.

Daniel, the Jewish exile, has revealed the religious foundation of the Babylonians to be based on fraud, so now the Babylonians seek to kill him. They force the king to hand Daniel over to them. Similar to Daniel's laughter in the story of Bel, the story of the dragon reveals some conceptual developments from the Hebrew/Aramaic Daniel stories. The Babylonian advisers do not even bother with a ruse to trick the king as they did in Daniel 3 and 6. Here, they resort to the only basis of their power in the first place: the threat of violence. They demand that either Daniel be handed over to them, or they will revolt against the king. Given what we know of the constant threat of revolt and rebellion in the Achaemenid and Hellenistic eras, such threats would have clear meaning.

---

68. Moore, *Daniel, Esther, and Jeremiah*, 142-44.

69. Collins, *Daniel*, Hermeneia, 415.

70. See Daniel L. Smith-Christopher, "Between Ezra and Israel: Exclusion, Transformation, and Inclusion of the 'Foreigner' in Post-Exilic Biblical Theology," in *Ethnicity and the Bible*, ed. M. Brett (Leiden: E. J. Brill, 1996).

The text suggests that Daniel was in the lions' den for six days, and then proceeds to exaggerate the danger by pointing out that the lions had not been fed their daily rations of two humans and two sheep. Surely this detail is intended to increase the horror of the threat to Daniel, so as to further magnify the miracle of his deliverance.

Verses 33-39, The Intervention of Habakkuk. The intervention of the prophet Habakkuk is one of the strangest aspects of all of the Daniel traditions. The writer tells us that Habakkuk, at home in Judea, had prepared bread and stew for the reapers when an angel appeared to tell him to take it instead to Daniel in Babylonia.[71] It is curious why Habakkuk should have been chosen. His time of prophecy was at the beginning of the Babylonian era—apparently prior to 598 BCE—and includes a message of doom for Jerusalem, facing the ravenous conquests of the Babylonians. However, there is a strong polemic against idolatry in Hab 2:18-19 that may well have recommended this prophet to the writer of this tale:

What use is an idol
  once its maker has shaped it—
  a cast image, a teacher of lies?
For its maker trusts in what has been made,
  though the product is only an
  idol that cannot speak!
Alas for you who say to the wood, "Wake up!"
  to silent stone, "Rouse yourself!"
  Can it teach?

See, it is gold and silver plated,
  and there is no breath in it at all. (NRSV)

There is a strong theme of punishment for the Babylonian conquerors in Habakkuk as well—although arguably not unique to the prophetic corpus.

An angel of God brings Habakkuk to Babylon and into the presence of Daniel. Habakkuk's feeding of Daniel (reminiscent of God's care for Elijah in his exile) is seen as God's answer to Daniel's prayer for aid, for Daniel responds with thanksgiving in terms that are familiar to the Daniel tradition: "You have remembered me, O God, and have not forsaken those who love you" (v. 38; cf. Ezra 8, where the fasting Jews are protected by God).

Verses 40-42, The Reversal. The king, like Darius in Daniel 6, comes to mourn Daniel. Darius was less certain of Daniel's death than is the king of the dragon story, but the result is similar. When the king learns that Daniel lives, he shouts "with a loud voice" (similar to the shouts earlier, "You are great, O Bel" [v. 18 NRSV]). What the king shouts is a statement of existence: There is no God but the God of Daniel. This is in keeping with the transformation (perhaps conversion) implied in the earlier accusation of the Babylonians (v. 28).

The story is complete with the expected reversal of fortune; those who sought to destroy Daniel are themselves destroyed. What is missing is any indication of a reward for Daniel—a curious omission, given its frequent mention in the other stories.

---

71. Collins points out other OT texts that report instances of spiritual "travel," especially comparing the reference here in v. 36 with the travels of Elijah, Elisha, and Ezekiel, who was also transported by an angel holding his hair (Ezek 8:3). See Collins, *Daniel*, 416.

REFLECTIONS

1. Stories like Bel and the Dragon presume the contact between cultures—the arguments over the validity of one religious belief over another. These are, therefore, diaspora issues as well as issues of political occupation, and part of their profundity is precisely the power of those who hold such false beliefs and the apparent lack of worldly power held by the Jews, who nevertheless prove the beliefs of the dominant power to be false. The suggestion is clear: If the oppressors' religious beliefs are false, then their power must be limited as well. Mockery is a powerful weapon for those living in the shadows. The laughing Daniel is an important symbol of resistance.[72]

---

72. See the role of humor in slave religion in A. Raboteau, *Slave Religion* (New York: Oxford University Press, 1978) 290-95.

2. The Babylonians in the stories of Bel and the Dragon are portrayed as idolatrous, and their persistence, their faith, is made "real" by superior force. The two go hand in hand, for the only way for idols to be portrayed to "live" is by force of arms. Thus Daniel overcomes them with wit and wisdom, and not with swords and clubs. Truth is hidden by violence, but it is revealed by the subversive teaching of the wise, and especially by the stories of clever Jews who are able to defeat the powerful with the weapon of cleverness and wisdom.

ABBREVIATIONS

BCE	before the Common Era
ca.	circa
CE	Common Era
cent.	century
cf.	compare
chap(s).	chapter(s)
d.	died
Dtr	Deuteronomistic historian
esp.	especially
fem.	feminine
HB	Hebrew Bible
l(l).	line(s)
lit.	literally
LXX	Septuagint
masc.	masculine
MS(S)	manuscript(s)
MT	Masoretic Text
n(n).	note(s)
neut.	neuter
NT	New Testament
OG	Old Greek
OL	Old Latin
OT	Old Testament
par(r).	parallel(s)
pl(s).	plate(s)
SP	Samaritan Pentateuch
v(v).	verse(s)
Vg	Vulgate
\\	between Scripture references indicates parallelism

Names of Pseudepigraphical and Early Patristic Books

Apoc. Abr.	*Apocalypse of Abraham*
2–3 Apoc. Bar.	Syriac, Greek *Apocalypse of Baruch*
Apoc. Mos.	*Apocalypse of Moses*

Ascen. Isa.	*Ascension of Isaiah*
As. Mos.	*Assumption of Moses*
Barn.	*Barnabas*
Bib. Ant.	Pseudo-Philo, *Biblical Antiquities*
1–2 Clem.	*1–2 Clement*
Did.	*Didache*
1–2–3 Enoch	Ethiopic, Slavonic, Hebrew *Enoch*
Ep. Arist.	*Epistle of Aristeas*
Gos. Pet.	*Gospel of Peter*
Herm. Sim.	Hermas, *Similitude(s)*
Ign. Eph.	Ignatius, *Letter to the Ephesians*
Ign. Magn.	Ignatius, *Letter to the Magnesians*
Ign. Phld.	Ignatius, *Letter to the Philadelphians*
Ign. Pol.	Ignatius, *Letter to Polycarp*
Ign. Rom.	Ignatius, *Letter to the Romans*
Ign. Smyrn.	Ignatius, *Letter to the Smyrnaeans*
Ign. Trall.	Ignatius, *Letter to the Trallians*
Jub.	*Jubilees*
POxy	B. P. Grenfell and A. S. Hunt (eds.), *Oxyrhynchus Papyri*
Pss. Sol.	*Psalms of Solomon*
Sib. Or.	*Sibylline Oracles*
T. Benj.	*Testament of Benjamin*
T. Dan	*Testament of Dan*
T. Iss.	*Testament of Issachar*
T. Job	*Testament of Job*
T. Jud.	*Testament of Judah*
T. Levi	*Testament of Levi*
T. Naph.	*Testament of Naphtali*
T. Reub.	*Testament of Reuben*
T. Sim.	*Testament of Simeon*

Names of Dead Sea Scrolls and Related Texts

CD	Cairo (Genizah text of the) Damascus Document
DSS	Dead Sea Scrolls
8HevXII gr	Greek scroll of the Minor Prophets from Nahal Hever
Q	Qumran
1Q, 2Q, etc.	numbered caves of Qumran, yielding written material; followed by abbreviation of biblical or apocryphal book
1Q28b	Rule of the Blessings (Appendix b to 1QS)
1QH	Thanksgiving Hymns (Qumran Cave 1)
1QM	War Scroll (Qumran Cave 1)
1QpHab	Pesher on Habakkuk (Qumran Cave 1)
1QpPs	Pesher on Psalms (Qumran Cave 1)
1QS	Rule of the Community (Qumran Cave 1)
1QSa	Rule of the Congregation (Appendix a to 1QS)
1QSb	Rule of the Blessings (Appendix b to 1QS)
4Q175	Testimonia text (Qumran Cave 4)
4Q246	Apocryphon of Daniel (Qumran Cave 4)
4Q298	Words of the Sage to the Sons of Dawn (Qumran Cave 4)
4Q385b	fragmentary remains of Pseudo-Jeremiah that implies that Jeremiah went into Babylonian exile. Also known as ApocJer^C or 4Q385 16. (Qumran Cave 4)

4Q389a	several scroll fragments now thought to contain portions of three pseudepigraphical works including Pseudo-Jeremiah. Also known as 4QApocJer[e]. (Qumran Cave 4)
4Q390	contains a schematized history of Israel's sin and divine punishment. Also known as psMos[e]. (Qumran Cave 4)
4Q394–399	Halakhic Letter (Qumran Cave 4)
4Q416	Instruction[b] (Qumran Cave 4)
4Q521	Messianic Apocalypse (Qumran Cave 4)
4Q550	Proto-Esther[a-f] (Qumran Cave 4)
4QFlor	Florilegium (or Eschatological Midrashim) (Qumran Cave 4)
4QMMT	Halakhic Letter (Qumran Cave 4)
4QpaleoDeutr	copy of Deuteronomy in paleo-Hebrew script (Qumran Cave 4)
4QpaleoExod	copy of Exodus in paleo-Hebrew script (Qumran Cave 4)
4QpNah	Pesher on Nahum (Qumran Cave 4)
4QpPs	Psalm Pesher A (Qumran Cave 4)
4QPrNab	Prayer of Nabonidus (Qumran Cave 4)
4QPs37	Psalm Scroll (Qumran Cave 4)
4QpsDan	Pseudo-Daniel (Qumran Cave 4)
4QSam	First copy of Samuel (Qumran Cave 4)
4QTestim	Testimonia text (Qumran Cave 4)
4QTob	Copy of Tobit (Qumran Cave 4)
11QMelch	Melchizedek text (Qumran Cave 11)
11QPs[a]	Psalms Scroll (Qumran Cave 11)
11QT	Temple Scroll (Qumran Cave 11)
11QtgJob	Targum of Job (Qumran Cave 11)

Targumic Material

Tg. Esth. I, II	First or Second Targum of Esther
Tg. Neb.	Targum of the Prophets
Tg. Neof.	Targum Neofiti

Orders and Tractates in Mishnaic and Related Literature

To distinguish the same-named tractates in the Mishnah, Tosefta, Babylonian Talmud, and Jerusalem Talmud, *m., t., b.,* or *y.* precedes the title of the tractate.

ʾAbot	ʾAbot
ʿArak.	ʿArakin
B. Bat.	Baba Batra
B. Meṣ.	Baba Meṣiʿa
B. Qam.	Baba Qamma
Ber.	Berakot
Dem.	Demai
Giṭ.	Giṭṭin
Ḥag.	Ḥagigah
Hor.	Horayot
Ḥul.	Ḥullin
Ket.	Ketubbot
Maʿaś.	Maʿaśerot
Meg.	Megilla
Menaḥ.	Menaḥot

Mid.	Middot
Moʻed Qaṭ.	Moʻed Qaṭan
Nazir	Nazir
Ned.	Nedarim
p. Šeqal.	pesachim Šeqalim
Pesaḥ.	Pesahim
Qidd.	Quddušin
Šabb.	Šabbat
Sanh.	Sanhedrin
Soṭah	Soṭah
Sukk.	Sukkah
Taʻan.	Taʻanit
Tamid	Tamid
Yad.	Yadayim
Yoma	Yoma (=Kippurim)

Other Rabbinic Works

ʼAbot R. Nat.	ʼAbot de Rabbi Nathan
Pesiq. R.	Pesiqta Rabbati
Rab.	Rabbah (following abbreviation of biblical book—e.g., Gen. Rab. = Genesis Rabbah)
Sipra	Sipra

Greek Manuscripts and Ancient Versions

<u>Papyrus Manuscripts</u>

𝔓¹	third-century Greek papyrus manuscript of the Gospels
𝔓²⁹	third- or fourth-century Greek papyrus manuscript
𝔓³³	sixth-century Greek papyrus manuscript of Acts
𝔓³⁷	third- or fourth-century Greek papyrus manuscript of the Gospels
𝔓³⁸	fourth-century Greek papyrus manuscript of Acts
𝔓⁴⁵	third-century Greek papyrus manuscript of the Gospels
𝔓⁴⁶	third-century Greek papyrus manuscript of the letters
𝔓⁴⁷	third-century Greek papyrus manuscript of Revelation
𝔓⁴⁸	third-century Greek papyrus manuscript of Acts
𝔓⁵²	second-century Greek papyrus manuscript of John 18:31-33, 37-38
𝔓⁵⁸	sixth-century Greek papyrus manuscript of Acts
𝔓⁶⁴	third-century Greek papyrus fragment of Matthew
𝔓⁶⁶	second- or third-century Greek papyrus manuscript of John (incomplete)
𝔓⁶⁷	third-century Greek papyrus fragment of Matthew
𝔓⁶⁹	third-century Greek papyrus manuscript of the Gospel of Luke
𝔓⁷⁵	third-century Greek papyrus manuscript of the Gospels

<u>Lettered Uncials</u>

א	Codex Sinaiticus, fourth-century manuscript of LXX, NT, Epistle of Barnabas, and Shepherd of Hermas
A	Codex Alexandrinus, fifth-century manuscript of LXX, NT, 1 and 2 Clement, and Psalms of Solomon
B	Codex Vaticanus, fourth-century manuscript of LXX and parts of the NT

Abbreviations

C	Codex Ephraemi, fifth-century manuscript of parts of LXX and NT
D	Codex Bezae, fifth-century bilingual (Greek and Latin) manuscript of the Gospels and Acts
G	ninth-century manuscript of the Gospels
K	ninth-century manuscript of the Gospels
L	eighth-century manuscript of the Gospels
W	Washington Codex, fifth-century manuscript of the Gospels
X	Codex Monacensis, ninth- or tenth-century manuscript of the Gospels
Z	sixth-century manuscript of Matthew
Θ	Koridethi Codex, ninth-century manuscript of the Gospels
Ψ	Athous Laurae Codex, eighth- or ninth-century manuscript of the Gospels (incomplete), Acts, the Catholic and Pauline Epistles, and Hebrews

Numbered Uncials
058	fourth-century fragment of Matthew 18
074	sixth-century fragment of Matthew
078	sixth-century fragment of Matthew, Luke, and John
0170	fifth- or sixth-century manuscript of Matthew
0181	fourth- or fifth-century partial manuscript of Luke 9:59–10:14

Numbered Minuscules
33	tenth-century manuscript of the Gospels
75	eleventh-century manuscript of the Gospels
565	ninth-century manuscript of the Gospels
700	eleventh-century manuscript of the Gospels
892	ninth-century manuscript of the Gospels

Names of Nag Hammadi Tractates
Ap. John	Apocryphon of John (also called the Secret Book of John)
Apoc. Adam	Apocalypse of Adam (also called the Revelation of Adam)
Ep. Pet.	Letter of Peter to Philip
Exeg. Soul	Exegesis on the Soul
Gos. Phil.	Gospel of Philip
Gos. Truth	Gospel of Truth

Ancient Versions
bo	the Bohairic (Memphitic) Coptic version
bo^{mss}	some manuscripts in the Bohairic tradition
d	the Latin text of Codex Bezae
e	Codex Palatinus, fifth-century Latin manuscript of the Gospels
$f\!f^2$	Old Latin manuscript, fifth-century translation of the Gospels
Ir^{lat}	the Latin translation of Irenaeus
latt	the whole Latin tradition (including the Vulgate)
mae	Middle Egyptian
sa	the Sahidic (Thebaic) Coptic version
sy	the Syriac version
sy^s	the Sinaitic Syriac version

Other Abbreviations

700*	the original reading of manuscript 700
ℵ*	the original reading of Codex Sinaiticus
ℵ¹	the first corrector of Codex Sinaiticus
ℵ²	the second corrector of Codex Sinaiticus
𝔐	the Majority text (the mass of later manuscripts)
C²	the corrected text of Codex Ephraemi
D*	the original reading of Codex Bezae
D²	the second corrector (c. fifth century) of Codex Bezae
f^1	Family 1: minuscule manuscripts belonging to the Lake Group (1, 118, 131, 209, 1582)
f^{13}	Family 13: minuscule manuscripts belonging to the Ferrar Group (13, 69, 124, 174, 230, 346, 543, 788, 826, 828, 983, 1689, 1709)
pc	a few other manuscripts

Commonly Used Periodicals, Reference Works, and Serials

AAR	American Academy of Religion
AASOR	Annual of the American Schools of Oriental Research
AB	Anchor Bible
ABD	*Anchor Bible Dictionary*
ABR	*Australian Biblical Review*
ABRL	Anchor Bible Reference Library
ACNT	Augsburg Commentaries on the New Testament
AcOr	*Acta Orientalia*
AfO	*Archiv für Orientforschung*
AfOB	Archiv für Orientforschung: Beiheft
AGJU	Arbeiten zur Geschichte des antiken Judentums und des Urchristentums
AJP	*American Journal of Philology*
AJSL	*American Journal of Semitic Languages and Literature*
AJT	*American Journal of Theology*
AnBib	Analecta Biblica
ANEP	J. B. Pritchard (ed.), *The Ancient Near East in Pictures Relating to the Old Testament*
ANET	J. B. Pritchard (ed.), *Ancient Near Eastern Texts Relating to the Old Testament*
ANF	Ante-Nicene Fathers
ANRW	*Aufstieg und Niedergang der römischen Welt*
ANTC	Abingdon New Testament Commentaries
ANTJ	Arbeiten zum Neuen Testament und Judentum
APOT	R. H. Charles (ed.), *The Apocrypha and Pseudepigrapha of the Old Testament*
ASNU	Acta Seminarii Neotestamentici Upsaliensis
ATANT	Abhandlungen zur Theologie des Alten und Neuen Testaments
ATD	Das Alte Testament Deutsch
ATDan	Acta Theologica Danica
Aug	*Augustinianum*
AusBR	*Australian Biblical Review*
BA	Biblical Archaeologist

BAGD	W. Bauer, W. F. Arndt, F. W. Gingrich, and F. W. Danker, *Greek-English Lexicon of the New Testament and Other Early Christian Literature*, 2nd ed. (Bauer-Arndt-Gingrich-Danker)
BAR	*Biblical Archaeology Review*
BASOR	*Bulletin of the American Schools of Oriental Research*
BBB	Bonner biblische Beiträge
BBET	Beiträge zur biblischen Exegese und Theologie
BBR	*Bulletin for Biblical Research*
BDAG	W. Bauer, W. F. Arndt, F. W. Gingrich, and F. W. Danker, *Greek-English Lexicon of the New Testament and Other Early Christian Literature*, 3rd ed. (Bauer-Danker-Arndt-Gingrich)
BDB	F. Brown, S. R. Driver, and C. A. Briggs, *A Hebrew and English Lexicon of the Old Testament*
BDF	F. Blass, A. Debrunner, and R. W. Funk, *A Greek Grammar of the New Testament and Other Early Christian Literature*
BEATAJ	Beiträge zur Erforschung des Alten Testaments und des antiken Judentum
BETL	Bibliotheca Ephemeridum Theologicarum Lovaniensium
BEvT	Beiträge zur evangelischen Theologie
BHS	*Biblia Hebraica Stuttgartensia*
BHT	Beiträge zur historischen Theologie
Bib	*Biblica*
BibInt	*Biblical Interpretation*
BibOr	Biblica et Orientalia
BJRL	*Bulletin of the John Rylands University Library of Manchester*
BJS	Brown Judaic Studies
BK	*Bibel und Kirche*
BKAT	Biblischer Kommentar, Altes Testament
BLS	Bible and Literature Series
BN	*Biblische Notizen*
BNTC	Black's New Testament Commentaries
BR	*Biblical Research*
BSac	*Bibliotheca Sacra*
BSOAS	*Bulletin of the School of Oriental and African Studies*
BT	*The Bible Translator*
BTB	*Biblical Theology Bulletin*
BVC	*Bible et vie chrétienne*
BWA(N)T	Beiträge zur Wissenschaft vom Alten (und Neuen) Testament
BZ	*Biblische Zeitschrift*
BZAW	Beihefte zur Zeitschrift für die alttestamentliche Wissenschaft
BZNW	Beihefte zur Zeitschrift für die neutestamentliche Wissenschaft
CAD	*The Assyrian Dictionary of the Oriental Institute of the University of Chicago*
CB	*Cultura Bíblica*
CBC	Cambridge Bible Commentary
CBOTS	Coniectanea Biblica: Old Testament Series
CBQ	*Catholic Biblical Quarterly*
CBQMS	Catholic Biblical Quarterly Monograph Series
ConBNT	Coniectanea Neotestamentica or Coniectanea Biblica: New Testament Series
ConBOT	Coniectanea Biblica: Old Testament Series
CP	*Classical Philology*
CRAI	Comptes rendus de l'Académie des inscriptions et belles-lettres

CRINT	Compendia Rerum Iudaicarum ad Novum Testamentum
CTM	*Concordia Theological Monthly*
DJD	Discoveries in the Judaean Desert
EB	Echter Bibel
EI	*Encyclopaedia of Islam*
EKKNT	Evangelisch-katholischer Kommentar zum Neuen Testament
Enc	*Encounter*
EncJud	C. Roth and G. Wigoder (eds.), *Encyclopedia Judaica*
EPRO	Etudes préliminaires aux religions orientales dans l'empire romain
ErIsr	*Eretz-Israel*
EstBib	*Estudios bíblicos*
ETL	*Ephemerides Theologicae Lovanienses*
ETS	Erfurter theologische Studien
EvQ	*Evangelical Quarterly*
EvT	*Evangelische Theologie*
ExAud	*Ex Auditu*
ExpTim	*Expository Times*
FAT	Forschungen zum Alten Testament
FB	Forschung zur Bibel
FBBS	Facet Books, Biblical Series
FFNT	Foundations and Facets: New Testament
FOTL	Forms of the Old Testament Literature
FRLANT	Forschungen zur Religion und Literatur des Alten und Neuen Testaments
FTS	Frankfurter Theologische Studien
GBS.OTS	Guides to Biblical Scholarship. Old Testament Series
GCS	Die griechischen christlichen Schriftsteller der ersten [drei] Jahrhunderte
GKC	Emil Kautzsch (ed.), *Gesenius' Hebrew Grammar*, trans. A. E. Cowley, 2nd ed.
GNS	*Good News Studies*
GTA	Göttinger theologischer Arbeiten
HALAT	*Hebräisches und aramäisches Lexikon zum Alten Testament*
HAR	*Hebrew Annual Review*
HAT	Handbuch zum Alten Testament
HBC	*Harper's Bible Commentary*
HBT	*Horizons in Biblical Theology*
HDB	*Hastings' Dictionary of the Bible*
HDR	Harvard Dissertations in Religion
HeyJ	Heythrop Journal
HNT	Handbuch zum Neuen Testament
HNTC	Harper's New Testament Commentaries
HR	*History of Religions*
HSM	Harvard Semitic Monographs
HSS	Harvard Semitic Studies
HTKNT	Herders Theologischer Kommentar zum Neuen Testament
HTR	*Harvard Theological Review*
HTS	Harvard Theological Studies
HUCA	*Hebrew Union College Annual*
IB	*Interpreter's Bible*
IBC	Interpretation: A Bible Commentary for Teaching and Preaching
IBS	*Irish Biblical Studies*
ICC	International Critical Commentary

IDB	*The Interpreter's Dictionary of the Bible*
IDBSup	supplementary volume to *The Interpreter's Dictionary of the Bible*
IEJ	*Israel Exploration Journal*
Int	*Interpretation*
IRT	Issues in Religion and Theology
ITC	International Theological Commentary
JAAR	*Journal of the American Academy of Religion*
JAL	Jewish Apocryphal Literature Series
JANESCU	*Journal of the Ancient Near Eastern Society of Columbia University*
JAOS	*Journal of the American Oriental Society*
JBL	*Journal of Biblical Literature*
JETS	*Journal of the Evangelical Theological Society*
JJS	*Journal of Jewish Studies*
JNES	*Journal of Near Eastern Studies*
JNSL	*Journal of Northwest Semitic Languages*
JPS	Jewish Publication Society
JQR	*Jewish Quarterly Review*
JR	*Journal of Religion*
JRH	*Journal of Religious History*
JSJ	*Journal for the Study of Judaism in the Persian, Hellenistic, and Roman Periods*
JSNT	*Journal for the Study of the New Testament*
JSNTSup	Journal for the Study of the New Testament Supplement Series
JSOT	*Journal for the Study of the Old Testament*
JSOTSup	Journal for the Study of the Old Testament Supplement Series
JSP	*Journal for the Study of the Pseudepigrapha*
JSS	*Journal of Semitic Studies*
JTC	*Journal for Theology and the Church*
JTS	*Journal of Theological Studies*
KAT	Kommentar zum Alten Testament
KB	L. Koehler and W. Baumgartner, *Lexicon in Veteris Testamenti libros*
KEK	Kritisch-exegetischer Kommentar über das Neue Testament (Meyer-Kommentar)
KPG	Knox Preaching Guides
LCL	Loeb Classical Library
LTQ	Lexington Theological Quarterly
MNTC	*Moffatt New Testament Commentary*
NCBC	New Century Bible Commentary
NHS	*Nag Hammadi Studies*
NIB	*The New Interpreter's Bible*
NIBC	*The New Interpreter's Bible Commentary*
NICNT	New International Commentary on the New Testament
NICOT	New International Commentary on the Old Testament
NIGTC	The New International Greek Testament Commentary
NJBC	*The New Jerome Biblical Commentary*
NovT	*Novum Testamentum*
NovTSup	Supplements to Novum Testamentum
NPNF	*Nicene and Post-Nicene Fathers*
NTC	New Testament in Context
NTG	New Testament Guides
NTS	*New Testament Studies*
NTT	*Norsk Teologisk Tidsskrift*

OBC	*The Oxford Bible Commentary*
OBO	Orbis Biblicus et Orientalis
OBT	Overtures to Biblical Theology
OIP	Oriental Institute Publications
Or	*Orientalia* (NS)
OTG	Old Testament Guides
OTL	Old Testament Library
OTM	Old Testament Message
OTP	*Old Testament Pseudepigrapha*
OTS	*Oudtestamentische Studiën*
PAAJR	*Proceedings of the American Academy of Jewish Research*
PEFQS	Palestine Exploration Fund Quarterly Statement
PEQ	*Palestine Exploration Quarterly*
PGM	K. Preisendanz (ed.), *Papyri Graecae Magicae*
PTMS	Pittsburgh Theological Monograph Series
QD	Quaestiones Disputatae
RANE	Records of the Ancient Near East
RB	*Revue biblique*
ResQ	*Restoration Quarterly*
RevExp	*Review and Expositor*
RevQ	*Revue de Qumran*
RSRel	*Recherches de science religieuse*
RTL	*Revue théologique de Louvain*
SAA	State Archives of Assyria
SB	H. L. Strack and P. Billerbeck, *Kommentar zum Neuen Testament aus Talmud und Midrasch,* 6 vols. 1922–61
SBAB	Stuttgarter biblische Aufsatzbände
SBB	Stuttgarter biblische Beiträge
SBL	Society of Biblical Literature
SBLDS	SBL Dissertation Series
SBLMS	SBL Monograph Series
SBLRBS	SBL Resources for Biblical Study
SBLSCS	SBL Septuagint and Cognate Studies
SBLSP	SBL Seminar Papers
SBLSS	SBL *Semeia* Studies
SBLSymS	SBL Symposium Series
SBLWAW	SBL Writings from the Ancient World
SBM	Stuttgarter biblische Monographien
SBS	Stuttgarter Bibelstudien
SBT	Studies in Biblical Theology
SEÅ	*Svensk exegetisk årsbok*
SJLA	Studies in Judaism in Late Antiquity
SJOT	*Scandinavian Journal of the Old Testament*
SJT	*Scottish Journal of Theology*
SKK	Stuttgarter kleiner Kommentar
SNTSMS	Society for New Testament Studies Monograph Series
SOTSMS	Society for Old Testament Studies Monograph Series
SP	Sacra Pagina
SR	*Studies in Religion/Sciences religieuses*
SSN	Studia Semitica Neerlandica
ST	*Studia Theologica*
SUNT	Studien zur Umwelt des Neuen Testaments
SVT	Supplements to Vetus Testamentum

SVTP	Studia in Veteris Testamenti Pseudepigraphica
SWBA	Social World of Biblical Antiquity
TB	Theologische Bücherei: Neudrucke und Berichte aus dem 20. Jahrhundert
TD	*Theology Digest*
TDNT	*Theological Dictionary of the New Testament*
TDOT	*Theological Dictionary of the Old Testament*
TextS	Texts and Studies
THKNT	Theologischer Handkommentar zum Neuen Testament
TLZ	*Theologische Literaturzeitung*
TOTC	Tyndale Old Testament Commentaries
TQ	*Theologische Quartalschrift*
TSK	*Theologische Studien und Kritiken*
TSSI	*Textbook of Syrian Semitic Inscriptions*
TToday	*Theology Today*
TynBul	*Tyndale Bulletin*
TZ	*Theologische Zeitschrift*
UBS	United Bible Societies
UBSGNT	*United Bible Societies Greek New Testament*
UF	*Ugarit-Forschungen*
USQR	*Union Seminary Quarterly Review*
UUÅ	Uppsala Universitetsårsskrift
VC	*Vigiliae Christianae*
VT	*Vetus Testamentum*
VTSup	Supplements to Vetus Testamentum
WA	M. Luther, *Kritische Gesamtausgabe* (= "Weimar" edition)
WBC	Word Biblical Commentary
WBT	Word Biblical Themes
WMANT	Wissenschaftliche Monographien zum Alten und Neuen Testament
WTJ	*Westminster Theological Journal*
WUNT	Wissenschaftliche Untersuchungen zum Neuen Testament
ZAH	*Zeitschrift für Althebräistik*
ZAW	*Zeitschrift für die alttestamentliche Wissenschaft*
ZNW	*Zeitschrift für die neutestamentliche Wissenschaft und die Kunde der älteren Kirche*
ZTK	*Zeitschrift für Theologie und Kirche*